# Legal Issues in Healthcare Fraud and Abuse:

## *Navigating the Uncertainties*

Fourth Edition

David E. Matyas, Esquire
Carrie Valiant, Esquire
Jason Eric Christ, Esquire
Anjali N.C. Downs, Esquire

Copyright 2012, 2009, 2008, 2007, 2006, 1997, 1994 by

**AMERICAN HEALTH LAWYERS ASSOCIATION**
1620 Eye Street, NW, 6th Floor
Washington, DC 20006-4010
Website: www.healthlawyers.org
E-mail: info@healthlawyers.org

All rights reserved.
No part of this publication may be reproduced, stored in a retrieval system, or transmitted, in any form, or by any means, electronic, mechanical, photocopying, recording, or otherwise, without the express, written permission of the publisher.

Printed in the United States of America
ISBN: 978-0-7698-5464-9
978-0-7698-5463-2 (Members)

*This publication is designed to provide accurate and authoritative information with respect to the subject matter covered. It is provided with the understanding that the publisher is not engaged in rendering legal or other professional services. If legal advice or other expert assistance is required, the services of a competent professional person should be sought.*
—from a declaration of the American Bar Association

# About the American Health Lawyers Association

Leading health law to excellence through education, information, and dialogue, the American Health Lawyers Association (Health Lawyers) is the nation's largest nonpartisan 501(c)(3) educational organization devoted to legal issues in the healthcare field. Health Lawyers provides resources to address the issues facing its active members who practice in law firms, government, in-house settings, and academia and who represent the entire spectrum of the health industry: physicians; hospitals and health systems; health maintenance organizations; health insurers; managed care companies; nursing facilities; home care providers; and consumers.

# RECENT TITLES FROM HEALTH LAWYERS

**The ACO Handbook: A Guide to Accountable Care Organizations, First Edition with CD-ROM**
© 2012, perfect bound

**Healthcare Finance: A Primer, Second Edition with CD-ROM**
© 2011, perfect bound

**AHLA's Guide to Healthcare Legal Forms, Agreements, and Policies, First Edition with November 2011 Supplement with CD-ROM**
© 2011, looseleaf

**Health Plans Contracting Handbook: A Guide for Payors and Providers, Sixth Edition with CD-ROM**
© 2011, perfect bound

**AHLA's Federal Healthcare Laws & Regulations, 2011-2012 Edition with CD-ROM**
© 2011, perfect bound

**The Medical & Healthcare Facility Lease: Legal and Business Handbook, First Edition with CD-ROM**
© 2011, perfect bound

**Data Breach Notification Laws: A Fifty State Survey, First Edition**
© 2011, perfect bound

**Fundamentals of Health Law, Fifth Edition with CD-ROM**
© 2011, perfect bound

**False Claims Act & The Healthcare Industry: Counseling & Litigation, Second Edition with 2011 Cumulative Supplement**
© 2011, perfect bound

**Healthcare Compliance Legal Issues Manual, Third Edition**
© 2011, perfect bound

**Healthcare Entity Bylaws and Related Documents: Navigating the Medical Staff/ Healthcare Entity Relationship, Third Edition**
© 2011, perfect bound

**The Law of Health Information Technology, First Edition**
© 2011, perfect bound

**Legal Issues in Healthcare Fraud and Abuse: Navigating the Uncertainties, 2010 Cumulative Supplement**
© 2010, perfect bound

**Physician Recruitment and Compensation Arrangements Practice Guide, Third Edition**
© 2010, perfect bound

**AHLA's Federal Healthcare Laws & Regulations, August 2010 Healthcare Reform Update to 2009-2010 Edition with CD-ROM**
© 2010, perfect bound

# About the Authors

David E. Matyas is a member of Epstein Becker & Green's Health Care and Life Sciences practice in the firm's Washington, D.C., office. Mr. Matyas represents and defends healthcare entities in connection with government audits and investigations; helps clients develop, implement and evaluate healthcare corporate compliance programs; counsels clients in planning and structuring transactions and business arrangements to minimize fraud and abuse and understand reimbursement implications in matters related to healthcare transactions; and advises clients on legal and regulatory matters in connection with investment documents, offering memoranda, filings with the SEC and other transactional documents. Mr. Matyas represents an array of healthcare providers including hospitals and health systems, pharmaceutical and medical device manufacturers, academic medical centers, retail and specialty pharmacies, ambulatory surgery centers, home health agencies, and physician organizations. He also advises investors and other financial institutions that invest in or support the healthcare industry. From 2005 to 2008, Mr. Matyas had been appointed by the Secretary of the Department of Health & Human Services to the Advisory Committee on Blood Safety & Availability, which provides advice on broad public health, ethical and legal issues related to the nation's supply of blood and blood products. From 2002 to 2008, Mr. Matyas served as a member of the Board of Directors for the American Health Lawyers Association. In 2005 and in 2010, Mr. Matyas was selected by the editors of *Nightingale's Healthcare News* as one of the "Outstanding Fraud & Compliance Lawyers." Mr. Matyas is also listed in the District of Columbia Healthcare category of *Chambers USA, The Best Lawyers in America, and in Washington, D.C., Super Lawyers* magazine.

Carrie Valiant is a member in Epstein Becker & Green's Health Care and Life Sciences Practice in the Washington, D.C., office where she co-chairs the firm's healthcare fraud group. Ms. Valiant has 25 years of experience concentrating in healthcare fraud and abuse and government healthcare program payment matters, including: defending clients undergoing civil and criminal investigation for healthcare fraud by the Department of Justice, the Department of Health and Human Services Office of the Inspector General, and other state and federal governmental authorities, including the negotiation of corporate integrity agreements; representing all segments of the healthcare industry in managing government healthcare program compliance risks, including the design and implementation of corporate compliance programs, preparation of OIG advisory opinion requests, and conducting internal investigations and voluntary self-disclosures. Ms. Valiant also advises clients on a variety of government healthcare program payment and certification matters, including substantial overpayment assessments, EMTALA complaints, and privacy and security breaches, including the preparation and negotiation of Corrective Action Plans. Ms. Valiant writes and lectures extensively on health law fraud topics and has been included on *Nightingale's Healthcare News'* 2004 and 2009 lists of Outstanding Healthcare Fraud and Compliance Lawyers and in the health law section of *The Best Lawyers in America*, 2006-2008, and has been ranked by *Chambers USA* as one of America's leading Healthcare lawyers. Ms. Valiant is also founder and President of the Healh Care Industry Access Initiative, a non-profit organization dedicated to promoting collaborative action across the healthcare industry to improve access to healthcare coverage and services.

Jason Eric Christ is an attorney in Epstein Becker & Green's Health Care and Life Sciences group who focuses his practice on representing clients in the healthcare industry in state and federal investigations and litigation pertaining to the healthcare fraud and abuse laws. Specifically he defends clients in civil and criminal matters involving various state and federal false claim laws, Stark Law, the Anti-kickback Statute, and the federal Health Care Fraud statute. On behalf of his clients, Mr. Christ responds to audits, subpoenas, Civil Investigative Demands and letter requests from fraud enforcement entities including government and government contractors and shepherds all phases of such investigations through final resolution. He also assists clients with complex electronic discovery involving electronic medical records and proprietary Health IT systems and counsel clients on document retention and data preservation practices. Additionally, Mr. Christ provides health regulatory counseling to a variety of entities including hospitals, urgent care centers, physician groups, pharmacies, manufacturers, suppliers, insurers, skilled nursing facilities, and medical professional staffing organizations. Mr. Christ received his law degree with honors from the University of Maryland School of Law. While in law school, he earned University of Maryland's concentration in healthcare law and served as managing editor of the Journal of Health Law & Policy. For his undergraduate degree, he attended the Pennsylvania State University and the American University in Cairo and received his B.A. with distinction. Mr. Christ writes, speaks and publishes on matters involving the healthcare fraud and abuse laws and electronic discovery and currently serves as a member of the adjunct faculty at the American University Washington College of Law's Health Law and Policy Institute. He is admitted to practice in the District of Columbia, Maryland and the U.S. District Court for the District of Columbia.

Anjali N.C. Downs is an attorney of Epstein Becker Green's Health Care and Life Sciences Practice in the firm's Washington, D.C., office. She practices in the firm's Health Care Fraud Practice Group, which focuses on federal and state fraud issues, including anti-kickback, self-referral, false claims, secondary payor issues, and false billings. Ms. Downs represents a variety of healthcare and life science organizations including health systems, pharmaceutical and medical device manufacturers, pharmacies, clinical laboratories, academic medical centers, physician group practices, dialysis providers, and medical transportation providers. Ms. Downs' experiences include conducting internal health regulatory investigations; assisting clients in preparing self disclosures; representing and defending healthcare entities undergoing government investigations, inquiries and audits; assisting clients in developing, implementing, and evaluating corporate compliance programs; and advising clients on physician contracting arrangements and a variety of healthcare joint ventures. Ms. Downs received her law degree, cum laude, from the Francis King Carey School of Law at the University of Maryland, and her Masters of Public Health in Community Heath Education and undergraduate degree in Psychology from the University of Maryland. While attending law school, Ms. Downs served as an Articles Editor for the Journal of Health Care Law and Policy. She is admitted to practice law in Maryland and the District of Columbia. Prior to law school, Ms. Downs was a member of the adjunct faculties of Georgetown University School of Nursing and Health Studies and Howard Community College in Columbia, Maryland.

# Dedications

**David E. Matyas**

Jaime, Daphne and Mackenzie—I cannot thank you enough for the love and support you provide to me on a daily basis. You have helped me not only be a better husband and father but also to be a better person.

**Carrie Valiant**

To my children, Ryan and Amanda Zellman—As toddlers, you played together on the floor while I wrote the first edition of this book at our dining room table. Now you are both wonderful young adults.

**Jason Eric Christ**

To my infinitely patient wife Heather—Thank you for indulging my well-intended but misguided belief that writing a book, doing a whole house renovation and having our first child wasn't taking on too much at the same time. We did it.

**Anjali N.C. Downs**

James, Mom and Dad—Thank you for making me feel I can do anything and supporting me while I do it.

# Table of Contents

About the Authors .................................................................................................................v
Dedications..........................................................................................................................ix
**Chapter 1 — The Fraud Enforcers: Who Are They and What Do They Do?**........................1
§ 1-1      Overview........................................................................................................1
§ 1-2      Department of Justice ....................................................................................3
      § 1-2(a)  United States Attorney's Offices
      § 1-2(b)  Criminal Division
      § 1-2(c)  Civil Division
      § 1-2(d)  The Federal Bureau of Investigation
§ 1-3      Department of Health and Human Services................................................6
      § 1-3(a)  Office of Inspector General
      § 1-3(b)  Centers for Medicare & Medicaid Services
      § 1-3(c)  Administration on Aging
      § 1-3(d)  Health Resources and Services Administration
      § 1-3(e)  Food & Drug Administration
      § 1-3(f)  Program Integrity Contractors
          § 1-3(f)(1)  Recovery Audit Contractors
          § 1-3(f)(2)  Zone Program Integrity Contractors
          § 1-3(f)(3)  Other Contractors
§ 1-4      Other Federal Agencies................................................................................14
§ 1-5      Multi-Agency Federal Initiatives ................................................................14
§ 1-6      Congress......................................................................................................15
§ 1-7      States............................................................................................................16
§ 1-8      Private Payors .............................................................................................17
§ 1-9      Private Citizens ...........................................................................................19
**Chapter 2 — Federal Anti-Kickback Laws** ..........................................................................21
§ 2-1      Overview......................................................................................................21
§ 2-2      Evolution of the Anti-Kickback Statute......................................................24
      § 2-2(a)  The Social Security Act of 1972
      § 2-2(b)  The Medicare-Medicaid Anti-Fraud and Abuse Amendments of 1977
      § 2-2(c)  Medicare and Medicaid Patient Program Protection Act of 1987
      § 2-2(d)  Health Insurance Portability and Accountability Act of 1996
      § 2-2(e)  Balanced Budget Act of 1997
      § 2-2(f)  Medicare Prescription Drug, Improvement, and Modernization Act of 2003
      § 2-2(g)  The Patient Protection and Affordable Care Act of 2010
§ 2-3      Safe Harbor Regulations ............................................................................30
      § 2-3(a)  History of the Various Safe Harbor Issuances
      § 2-3(b)  Investment Interest Safe Harbors
          § 2-3(b)(1)  Investment Interests in Large Entities
          § 2-3(b)(2)  Investment Interests in Small Entities

# Legal Issues in Healthcare Fraud and Abuse, Fourth Edition

§ 2-3(b)(3) Investment Interests in Entities in Medically Underserved Areas (MUAs)
§ 2-3(b)(4) Investments in Group Practices
§ 2-3(b)(5) Investments in Ambulatory Surgery Centers
§ 2-3(c) Space and Equipment Rental, and Personal Services and Management Contracts
§ 2-3(d) Sale of Practice
§ 2-3(e) Referral Services
§ 2-3(f) Warranties
§ 2-3(g) Statutory Exceptions with Analogous Safe Harbors
§ 2-3(g)(1) Employees
§ 2-3(g)(2) Discounts
§ 2-3(g)(3) Group Purchasing Organizations
§ 2-3(g)(4) Risk-Sharing Arrangements
§ 2-3(g)(5) Coinsurance and Deductible Waivers
§ 2-3(g)(6) Federally Qualified Health Centers
§ 2-3(g)(7) Electronic Prescribing
§ 2-3(h) Managed Care Safe Harbors
§ 2-3(i) Practitioner Recruitment
§ 2-3(j) Obstetrical Malpractice Insurance Subsidies
§ 2-3(k) Cooperative Hospital Services Organizations
§ 2-3(l) Referral Arrangements for Specialty Services
§ 2-3(m) Ambulance Replenishing
§ 2-3(n) Electronic Health Records and Community-Wide Information Systems
§ 2-3(o) Accountable Care Organizations and OIGs Waiver Authority

§ 2-4 Fraud Alerts and Special Advisory Bulletins .......................................................68
§ 2-4(a) Joint Ventures
§ 2-4(b) Routine Waivers of Coinsurance and Deductibles
§ 2-4(c) Hospital Incentives to Physicians
§ 2-4(d) Prescription Drug Marketing Practices
§ 2-4(e) Arrangements for the Provision of Clinical Laboratory Services
§ 2-4(f) Home Health Agencies
§ 2-4(g) Nursing Home Suppliers
§ 2-4(h) Nursing Home Arrangements with Hospices
§ 2-4(i) Rental of Space in Physician Offices by Persons or Entities to Which Physicians Refer
§ 2-4(j) Contractual Arrangements with Ambulance Companies
§ 2-4(k) Patient Assistance Programs for Medicare Part D Enrollees

§ 2-5 Additional Guidance and Advisory Opinions ....................................................83
§ 2-5(a) Early Guidance from CMS to Regional Offices and Fiscal Agents
§ 2-5(b) Advisory Opinions

§ 2-6 Case Law..............................................................................................................88
§ 2-6(a) Pre-Hanlester: The First Twenty Years of Case Law Under the Statute
§ 2-6(a)(1) *U.S. v. Greber*
§ 2-6(a)(2) *U.S. v. Kats*
§ 2-6(a)(3) *U.S. v. Bay State Ambulance*
§ 2-6(a)(4) *Other Pre-Hanlester* Cases
§ 2-6(b) Hanlester *Network v. Shalala*

§ 2-6(c) Significant Post-*Hanlester* Cases
  § 2-6(c)(1) The Anti-Kickback Statute's Intent Requirement
  § 2-6(c)(2) The Greber "One Purpose" Test
  § 2-6(c)(3) The Discount Safe Harbor

§ 2-7 Other Anti-Kickback Authority..........................................................................97
  § 2-7(a) Inducements to Beneficiaries
    § 2-7(a)(1) The Statute and Regulations
    § 2-7(a)(2) Special Advisory Bulletin
    § 2-7(a)(3) 2010 Modification to the CMP Provision
    § 2-7(a)(4) Comparison of the Anti-Kickback Statute and the CMP Concerning Inducements to Beneficiaries
  § 2-7(b) Anti-Kickback Statute Addressing Government Contractors
  § 2-7(c) TRICARE
  § 2-7(d) Federal "Sunshine Law"

§ 2-8 Major Issues in Anti-Kickback Interpretation and Enforcement ....................109
  § 2-8(a) Private Actions Under the Anti-Kickback Statute
  § 2-8(b) Integrated Delivery Systems: Physician Practice Acquisition and Divestiture
    § 2-8(b)(1) Practice Acquisitions
    § 2-8(b)(2) Practice Divestiture
  § 2-8(c) Regulation of Marketing Practices
  § 2-8(d) Professional Courtesy
  § 2-8(e) Carving Out Federal Healthcare Program Business and "Swapping" Issues
  § 2-8(f) Free Goods to Referral Sources
  § 2-8(g) Conflict-of-Interest Credentialing, Economic Credentialing, or Exclusive Credentialing
  § 2-8(h) Physician Recruitment and Relocation Arrangements
  § 2-8(i) Developments in Calculation of Damages for Anti-Kickback Cases
  § 2-8(j) Questioning Fair Market Value and "Bona Fide" Nature of Services Contracted For

**Chapter 3 — Federal Physician Self-Referral Prohibitions................................................131**

§ 3-1 Overview..................................................................................................131

§ 3-2 Legislative and Regulatory History .........................................................133

§ 3-3 The Statutory Prohibition and Definitions of Key Terms ........................138
  § 3-3(a) Scope of the Law
  § 3-3(b) Definitions of Key Terms
    § 3-3(b)(1) Referral
    § 3-3(b)(2) Designated Health Services
    § 3-3(b)(3) Ownership or Investment Interests
    § 3-3(b)(4) Compensation Arrangements
    § 3-3(b)(5) Fair Market Value
    § 3-3(b)(6) Physician
    § 3-3(b)(7) Immediate Family Member
    § 3-3(b)(8) Entity
  § 3-3(c) Special Rules on Compensation
    § 3-3(c)(1) Compensation Methodologies

### Legal Issues in Healthcare Fraud and Abuse, Fourth Edition

    § 3-3(c)(2) Physician's Compensation May Be Conditioned on Referrals to a Particular Provider
    § 3-3(c)(3) Modifying or Amending Agreements
  § 3-3(d) Stand in the Shoes

§ 3-4 Stark Law Exceptions ................................................................................ 154
  § 3-4(a) Ownership and Compensation Exceptions
    § 3-4(a)(1) Physician Services
    § 3-4(a)(2) In-Office Ancillary Services
    § 3-4(a)(3) Prepaid Plans
    § 3-4(a)(4) Academic Medical Centers
    § 3-4(a)(5) Implants in ASCs
    § 3-4(a)(6) Additional Regulatory Exceptions Applicable to both Ownership and Compensation Arrangements
  § 3-4(b) Ownership-Only Exceptions
    § 3-4(b)(1) Ownership in Publicly Traded Securities and Mutual Funds
    § 3-4(b)(2) Hospitals
    § 3-4(b)(3) Rural Providers
  § 3-4(c) Compensation Arrangement Exceptions
    § 3-4(c)(1) Rental of Office Space and Equipment
    § 3-4(c)(2) Bona Fide Employment Relationships
    § 3-4(c)(3) Personal Service Arrangements
    § 3-4(c)(4) Unrelated Payments
    § 3-4(c)(5) Physician Recruitment
    § 3-4(c)(6) Physician Retention
    § 3-4(c)(7) Isolated Financial Transactions
    § 3-4(c)(8) Certain Group-Practice Arrangements with a Hospital
    § 3-4(c)(9) Payments for Items and Services
    § 3-4(c)(10) Fair Market Value Exception
    § 3-4(c)(11) Non-Monetary Compensation
    § 3-4(c)(12) Medical-Staff Incidental Benefits
    § 3-4(c)(13) Managed Care Risk-Sharing Arrangements
    § 3-4(c)(14) Compliance Training
    § 3-4(c)(15) Exception for Indirect Compensation
    § 3-4(c)(16) Professional Courtesy
    § 3-4(c)(17) Charitable Donations Made by Physicians
    § 3-4(c)(18) Community-Wide Information System
    § 3-4(c)(19) Electronic Prescribing and Electronic Health Records
    § 3-4(c)(20) Stark Exceptions Relating to Anti-Kickback Statute Safe Harbors
    § 3-4(c)(21) Gainsharing
    § 3-4(c)(22) ACOs
  § 3-4(d) Reporting Requirements

§ 3-5 Definition of Group Practice ....................................................................... 191
  § 3-5(a) Single Legal Entity
  § 3-5(b) "Two or More" Physicians
  § 3-5(c) Full Range of Care
  § 3-5(d) Services Furnished by Group Practice Members

§ 3-5(e)  Distribution of Expenses and Income
§ 3-5(f)  Unified Business
§ 3-5(g)  Volume or Value of Referrals
§ 3-5(h)  Physician/Patient Encounters
§ 3-5(i)  Special Rule for Productivity Bonuses and Profit Shares

§ 3-6  Penalties and Enforcement ........................................................................200
§ 3-6(a)  Temporary Noncompliance
§ 3-6(b)  Alternative Method of Compliance with Signature Requirement
§ 3-6(c)  Period of Disallowance
§ 3-6(d)  Burden of Proof

§ 3-7  Advisory Opinions .....................................................................................204

§ 3-8  Self-Referral Disclosure Protocol .............................................................205

§ 3-9  Other Federal Self-Referral Restrictions .................................................208
§ 3-9(a)  Home Health Services Reimbursed by the Medicare Program
§ 3-9(b)  CHAMPUS/TRICARE and CHAMPVA
§ 3-9(c)  Disclosure Required of Certain Hospitals
         and Critical Access Hospitals
§ 3-9(d)  The Anti-Markup Rule

§ 3-10  Major Issues in Stark Law Interpretation ...............................................218
§ 3-10(a)  Relationship Between the Stark Law and the Anti-Kickback Statute
§ 3-10(b)  Knowledge Element for Indirect Financial Relationships
§ 3-10(c)  Joint Ventures Unrelated to the Provision of Designated
          Health Services
§ 3-10(d)  Hospital/Physician Arrangements Related to Designated
          Health Services
§ 3-10(e)  Corporate Affiliates

**Chapter 4 — False Claims: Civil and Criminal Enforcement ............................... 225**

§ 4-1  Overview .....................................................................................................225

§ 4-2  The Federal Civil False Claims Act ..........................................................226
§ 4-2(a)  Key FCA Considerations for Healthcare Entities
    § 4-2(a)(1)  Who Is a "Person"?
    § 4-2(a)(2)  What Is "Knowingly"?
    § 4-2(a)(2)(i)  Deliberate Ignorance
    § 4-2(a)(2)(ii)  Reckless Disregard
    § 4-2(a)(3)  What Is a "Claim"?
    § 4-2(a)(4)  What Is "Causing" a Claim to Be Submitted?
    § 4-2(a)(5)  What Is "False" or "Fraudulent"?
    § 4-2(a)(5)(i)  Retention of Overpayments and Reverse False Claims
    § 4-2(a)(6)  What Is "Material"?
§ 4-2(b)  Anti-Kickback Violations as False Claims
§ 4-2(c)  FCA Damages
§ 4-2(d)  Qui tam Relators
    § 4-2(d)(1)  How Is a Qui tam Action Initiated?
    § 4-2(d)(2)  What Happens if the Government Declines
              to Intervene?
    § 4-2(d)(3)  Who Can Be a Qui tam Relator?
    § 4-2(d)(3)(i)  Public Disclosure Bar

## Legal Issues in Healthcare Fraud and Abuse, Fourth Edition

§ 4-2(d)(3)(ii)  Original Source Rule
§ 4-2(d)(4)  Pleading Requirements for Qui tam Suits
§ 4-2(d)(5)  Retaliation
§ 4-2(e)  Statute of Limitations

§ 4-3  Other Civil Laws Pertaining to False Claims and Fraudulent Billing Activities ..................................................................................................252
§ 4-3(a)  Social Security Act
§ 4-3(b)  Program Fraud Civil Remedies Act

§ 4-4  Criminal Laws Pertaining to False Claims and Fraudulent Billing Activities .....................................................................................254
§ 4-4(a)  Social Security Act, Section 1128B
§ 4-4(b)  Mail and Wire Fraud
§ 4-4(c)  RICO Violations
§ 4-4(d)  Money Laundering
§ 4-4(e)  Healthcare Fraud
§ 4-4(f)  Making of False Statements
§ 4-4(g)  Theft or Embezzlement
§ 4-4(h)  Other Miscellaneous Crimes
§ 4-4(i)  Asset Freezes

§ 4-5  False Claims Theories Applicable to Multiple Segments of the Healthcare Industry................................................................265
§ 4-5(a)  Billing for Items or Services Not Actually Rendered
§ 4-5(b)  Providing Medically Unnecessary Services
§ 4-5(c)  Upcoding, DRG Creep, and Capitation Misclassification
§ 4-5(d)  Unbundling and Fragmentation
§ 4-5(e)  Filing False Cost Reports
§ 4-5(f)  Quality of Care
§ 4-5(g)  Waiver of Coinsurance and Deductibles
§ 4-5(h)  Express and Implied False Certification
§ 4-5(i)  Medicare Secondary Payor Issues
§ 4-5(j)  Recruitment of Homeless and Indigent Patients

§ 4-6  False Claims Enforcement Activities Specific to Particular Segments of the Healthcare Industry ............................................278
§ 4-6(a)  Hospitals
§ 4-6(a)(1)  Payments to Teaching Hospitals
§ 4-6(a)(2)  DRG Payment Window
§ 4-6(a)(3)  Outlier Payments
§ 4-6(a)(4)  Inpatient Admissions, Site of Service and One Days Stays
§ 4-6(b)  Investigational Devices
§ 4-6(c)  Nursing Homes/Long Term Care Facilities
§ 4-6(d)  Clinical Laboratories
§ 4-6(e)  Durable Medical Equipment and Home Medical Suppliers
§ 4-6(e)(1)  Provision of Medical Supplies to Nursing Homes
§ 4-6(e)(2)  Seat Lifts
§ 4-6(e)(3)  Telemarketing Schemes
§ 4-6(e)(4)  Certificates of Medical Necessity

§ 4-6(f)  Home Health Agencies
§ 4-6(g)  Medicare Contractors
§ 4-6(h)  Pharmacies and Pharmaceutical Manufacturers
§ 4-6(i)  Billing Companies, Consultants and Lawyers
§ 4-6(j)  Physicians
§ 4-6(k)  Dentists
§ 4-6(l)  Ambulance Companies
§ 4-6(m) Medical Device Companies
§ 4-6(n)  Medical Clinics and HIV Infusion Clinics

§ 4-7 False Claims Actions and Issues Under the Bankruptcy Code ..................................................................................308

**Chapter 5 — Administrative Sanctions Available to Federal Enforcers ......................... 311**

§ 5-1 Overview..................................................................................................311

§ 5-2 Exclusion From Medicare, Medicaid, and Other State Healthcare Programs.....................................................................................311
 § 5-2(a) Mandatory Exclusion
 § 5-2(b) Permissive Exclusion
 § 5-2(c) Persons Subject to Exclusion
 § 5-2(d) Notice
  § 5-2(d)(1) Notice of Intent to Exclude
  § 5-2(d)(2) Notice of Exclusion
  § 5-2(d)(3) Notice of Proposal to Exclude
 § 5-2(e) Effects of Exclusion
 § 5-2(f) Reinstatement of Excluded Individual or Entity

§ 5-3 Imposition of Civil Monetary Penalties.........................................................326
 § 5-3(a) Actions that May Result in the Imposition of CMPs
  § 5-3(a)(1) Submission of Improperly Filed Claims
  § 5-3(a)(2) Dealing with Excluded Individuals/Entities
  § 5-3(a)(3) Inducements to Beneficiaries
  § 5-3(a)(4) Payments to Induce Reduction or Limitation of Services (Gainsharing) and Other Cost Sharing Initiatives
  § 5-3(a)(5) Other Bases for CMPs
 § 5-3(b) Notice of Proposed Determination to Impose CMPs
 § 5-3(c) Amount of CMPs

§ 5-4 Suspension of Payments ............................................................................342
 § 5-4(a) Suspension of Payments to Medicare Providers
 § 5-4(b) Suspension of Payments to Medicaid Providers

§ 5-5 Hearing and Appeal Rights of Individuals and Entities Subject to Exclusion And Cmps ...................................................................................345
 § 5-5(a) The Rights of the Parties in a Hearing Before an ALJ
 § 5-5(b) Burden of Proof
 § 5-5(c) Evidentiary Standards in a Hearing Before an ALJ
 § 5-5(d) Scope of ALJ Authority in Exclusion Cases
 § 5-5(e) Appeal of the ALJ's Decision to the Departmental Appeals Board
 § 5-5(f) Judicial Review of the DHHS Secretary's Final Determination

## Legal Issues in Healthcare Fraud and Abuse, Fourth Edition

**Chapter 6 — State and Private Initiatives to Combat Fraud ............................................. 351**

§ 6-1  Overview .................................................................................................351

§ 6-2  State Self-Referral Laws .......................................................................353
 § 6-2(a)  Scope of the State Self-Referral Prohibitions
 § 6-2(b)  Exceptions to the Self-Referral Prohibitions
 § 6-2(c)  Advisory Opinions/Declaratory Statements
 § 6-2(d)  Penalties
 § 6-2(e)  Disclosure Laws

§ 6-3  State Anti-Kickback Proscriptions ......................................................360

§ 6-4  State Fee-Splitting Proscriptions .........................................................362

§ 6-5  State Commercial-Bribery and Racketeering Statutes .......................363

§ 6-6  State Statutes Regarding Deceptive Trade Practices
 and Consumer Protection .....................................................................364

§ 6-7  State False Claims Activities ................................................................366
 § 6-7(a)  State Law Governing Fraudulent Billing Practices
 § 6-7(b)  Waivers of Coinsurance and Deductible Amounts

§ 6-8  State Sunshine Acts Applicable to Pharmaceutical and Medical
 Device Manufacturers ...........................................................................368

§ 6-9  State Initiatives to Prevent and Detect Fraud .....................................369
 § 6-9(a)  Medicaid Fraud Control Units
 § 6-9(b)  Medicaid Program Integrity
 § 6-9(c)  Establishment of State Inspector Generals

§ 6-10  Trade Associations ...............................................................................373
 § 6-10(a)  American Medical Association
 § 6-10(b)  The American College of Radiology
 § 6-10(c)  American College of Physicians
 § 6-10(d)  Pharmaceutical and Research Manufacturers Association
 § 6-10(e)  Advanced Medical Technology Association

§ 6-11  Private-Payor Initiatives to Address Healthcare Fraud .....................381

**Chapter 7 — Compliance and Self-Reporting ................................................................... 385**

§ 7-1  Overview .................................................................................................385

§ 7-2  Why Have a Compliance Program? .....................................................386

§ 7-3  Federal Sentencing Guidelines .............................................................390

§ 7-4  The Sarbanes-Oxley Act Of 2002 .........................................................396

§ 7-5  Compliance Related Resources ............................................................398
 § 7-5(a)  Oig Compliance Program Guidances
 § 7-5(b)  Health Care Fraud Prevention and Enforcement Action Team (HEAT)
 § 7-5(c)  GAO Report
 § 7-5(d)  OIG/HCCA Roundtables
 § 7-5(e)  OIG/Health Lawyers Resources
 § 7-5(f)  CMS Guidance to Contractors
 § 7-5(g)  State Guidance

## Table of Contents

§ 7-6 Elements of an Effective Compliance Program ............................................. 412
    § 7-6(a) Establishment of Standards and Procedures
    § 7-6(b) Roles and Reporting Relationships of Personnel
        § 7-6(b)(1) Corporate Governance
        § 7-6(b)(2) The CCO and Other Personnel
        § 7-6(b)(3) Relationship Between the CCO and the General Counsel
    § 7-6(c) Background Checks
    § 7-6(d) Training
    § 7-6(e) Monitoring, Auditing, and Evaluating the Program
    § 7-6(f) Reporting System
    § 7-6(g) Disciplinary Action and Corrective Action
    § 7-6(h) Documentation

§ 7-7 Demonstrating Effectiveness: Conducting an Effectiveness Review ............. 427

§ 7-8 CIAs and Other Types of Compliance Agreements ........................................ 429

§ 7-9 Self-Reporting and Voluntary Disclosure ...................................................... 436
    § 7-9(a) OIG Voluntary Self Disclosure Protocol
    § 7-9(b) CMS Voluntary Self Referral Disclosure Protocol
    § 7-9(c) State Voluntary Self Disclosure Processes

### Chapter 8 — Fraud and Abuse Issues Affecting the Managed Care Industry ................. 447

§ 8-1 Overview .......................................................................................................... 447

§ 8-2 Managed Care and the Anti-Kickback Statute ............................................... 450
    § 8-2(a) The Managed Care Safe Harbors
        § 8-2(a)(1) Beneficiary Incentives
        § 8-2(a)(2) Price Reductions to Group Health Plans
        § 8-2(a)(3) Medicare SELECT
    § 8-2(b) Shared-Risk Statutory Exception
        § 8-2(b)(1) Price Reductions Offered to "Eligible Managed Care Organizations"
        § 8-2(b)(2) Safe-Harbor Protection for Contracts Involving "Substantial Financial Risk"
    § 8-2(c) Advisory Opinions

§ 8-3 Managed Care and the Physician Self-Referral Law ..................................... 467
    § 8-3(a) Prepaid Health Plans
    § 8-3(b) Personal-Service Arrangements
    § 8-3(c) Regulatory Exception for Risk-Sharing Arrangements

§ 8-4 Intermediate Sanctions Applicable to Mcos .................................................. 470

§ 8-5 Managed Care and the False Claims Act ....................................................... 473

§ 8-6 Federal Efforts to Address Fraud in Medicare Managed Care ...................... 474

§ 8-7 Managed-Care Fraud and State Medicaid Programs .................................... 477

§ 8-8 Examples of Potential Fraud Liability in the Managed Care Industry .......... 479
    § 8-8(a) Capitation Misclassification
    § 8-8(b) Defective Rate or Bid Submissions
    § 8-8(c) Marketing Schemes and Enrollment Practices
    § 8-8(d) Financial Relationships with Providers

## Legal Issues in Healthcare Fraud and Abuse, Fourth Edition

§ 8-8(e)  Failure to Provide Required Services, Misrepresenting Services to Qualify for Higher Payments, Underutilization, Quality of Care
§ 8-8(f)  Contracting/Bid Misrepresentations.
§ 8-8(g)  Cost Shifting.
§ 8-8(h)  Discount Skimming
§ 8-8(i)  Pharmacy Benefit Managers
§ 8-8(j)  Formulary Development and Implementation
§ 8-8(k)  Patient-Assistance Programs and the Medicare Part D Benefit
§ 8-8(l)  Medical Loss Ratios

### Chapter 9 — Representing Healthcare Organizations in Fraud and Abuse Matters....... 503

§ 9-1  Overview..................................................................................................503
§ 9-2  Categories and Types of Government Investigations ......................................503
    § 9-2(a)  Search Warrants
    § 9-2(b)  Grand Jury Investigations—Subjects, Targets and Witnesses
    § 9-2(c)  Civil Investigative Demands
    § 9-2(d)  Administrative Subpoenas
    § 9-2(e)  Search and Subpoena Authority of the OIG
        § 9-2(e)(1)  OIG Authority to Subpoena Documents and Witnesses
        § 9-2(e)(2)  Granting the OIG Immediate Access to Documents
    § 9-2(f)  Congressional Subpoenas
    § 9-2(f)  Undercover Operations
§ 9-3  Discovery in Healthcare Investigations in the Electronic Age ......................515
    § 9-3(a)  The Triggering Event
    § 9-3(b)  Litigation Hold
    § 9-3(c)  Considerations in Engaging a Litigation Support Vendor
    § 9-3(d)  Preservation and Collection
    § 9-3(e)  Culling—Limiting the Data Set
    § 9-3(f)  Document Review
    § 9-3(g)  Production
§ 9-4  Relationship Between Criminal and Civil Matters .........................................527
    § 9-4(a)  Double Jeopardy
    § 9-4(b)  Ex Post Facto Considerations
    § 9-4(c)  Considerations during Civil Settlements with the Federal Government
    § 9-4(d)  Criminal Settlement—The Use of Deferred Prosecution and Non-Prosecution Agreements
§ 9-5  Understanding the Privileges and Obligations Afforded to Lawyers and Their Clients...............................................................................................535
    § 9-5(a)  The Attorney/Client Communications Privilege
        § 9-5(a)(1)  Legal Advice
        § 9-5(a)(2)  The Attorney
        § 9-5(a)(3)  Communications

| | | |
|---|---|---|
| | § 9-5(a)(4) Confidentiality | |
| | § 9-5(a)(5) The Client | |
| | § 9-5(b) The Work-Product Doctrine | |
| | § 9-5(c) Waiver | |
| | § 9-5(d) Crime-Fraud Exception | |
| | § 9-5(e) Waiver as a Result of Voluntary Disclosure and the Selective-Waiver Doctrine | |
| | § 9-5(f) Allied-Lawyer Doctrine and Joint Defense Agreements | |
| | § 9-5(g) Hiring Outside Consultants | |
| | § 9-5(h) The Self-Critical Analysis Privilege | |
| | § 9-5(i) Lawyers' Ethical Obligations | |
| | § 9-5(i)(1) Duty of Confidentiality | |
| | § 9-5(i)(2) Duty to Disclose to Court | |
| | § 9-5(i)(3) Duty to Inquire | |
| | § 9-5(i)(4) Application of Rules to Government Attorneys | |
| § 9-6 | Fifth-Amendment Considerations | 561 |
| § 9-7 | Vicarious Liability and the Park Doctrine | 562 |
| § 9-8 | The Lawyer as Witness | 565 |
| § 9-9 | The Lawyer as Defendant | 566 |
| **Chapter 10 — The Future of Fraud and Abuse** | | **571** |
| § 10-1 | Federal Legislative Activities | 571 |
| § 10-2 | Federal Regulatory Initiatives | 572 |
| § 10-3 | Federal Enforcement Activities and Provider Self-Disclosure | 573 |
| § 10-4 | Litigation | 576 |
| § 10-5 | The Future and the Need for "Balance" | 578 |
| **Index** | | **581** |

# 1
# The Fraud Enforcers: Who Are They and What Do They Do?

## § 1-1 OVERVIEW

According to the Centers for Medicare and Medicaid (CMS) Office of Actuary, by 2020, healthcare will account for about 20% of all spending in the United States with government healthcare programs (predominantly Medicare and Medicaid) accounting for approximately one-half of all healthcare expenditures.[1] With the aging baby boomer population now becoming eligible for Medicare and with the expansion of the Medicaid program under the Health Reform legislation adopted in 2010, it is not surprising that states and the federal government have placed a high priority on curtailing unnecessary expenditures that result from fraud, waste and abuse.

The government's focus on healthcare fraud enforcement is not new. The government has a long history of pursuing healthcare entities and individuals in both civil and criminal matters, which, more often than not, traditionally originated through the actions of corporate insiders and whistleblowers. While government healthcare fraud and abuse investigations continue to involve matters brought by whistleblowers, the enforcement landscape has somewhat changed in the 21st Century as there are new players who use highly sophisticated tools, expertise and techniques to identify and investigate improper payments. Fraud, waste and abuse enforcement now involves complex computer driven data mining, government contractors who are paid contingencies to identify overpayments; contractors who identify potential fraud and refer cases to government attorneys; multi-agency strike forces that work in conjunction with federal, state and local governments; new laws that have created and strengthened the tools available to government attorneys and perhaps most significantly – a substantial budget to support these efforts.

---

[1] *See* National Health Expenditures Projections 2010-2020, Centers for Medicare and Medicaid Office of Actuary *available online at* http://www.cms.gov/NationalHealthExpendData/03_NationalHealthAccountsProjected.asp#num.

One need only contrast the $1.2 billion recovered by fraud enforcers for FY 2002 with the gargantuan $4.1 billion recovered for FY 2011 to see the effectiveness of these new fraud enforcement measures. Moreover, with increasing frequency, the government has succeeded in prosecuting individuals, obtaining prison sentences and fines under the criminal fraud statutes, and excluding individuals and companies from participation in federal healthcare programs. The near fourfold increase in recoveries, and increased use of criminal penalties and exclusion during the last decade is testament to the widely held belief that for healthcare entities, the risks are greater and the stakes are indeed higher.

This book was written to serve as a resource for lawyers, healthcare providers, compliance officers, consultants, investors and other stakeholders in the healthcare industry. It was designed not only to assist the reader in navigating the laws, legal theories, players and principles in the healthcare fraud enforcement environment but also to provide an understanding of the enforcement priorities, procedural issues and steps involved in the investigation and prosecution of healthcare fraud cases.

This introductory chapter provides the reader with an explanation of the key players in fighting healthcare fraud and their enforcement authority with chapters 2 through 5 addressing the types of activities and laws that are typically the subject of healthcare fraud investigations: the federal Anti-Kickback Statute (Chapter 2), the federal physician self-referral prohibitions (Chapter 3), the federal false claims prohibitions (Chapter 4), and other administrative sanctions that are available to the federal enforcers (Chapter 5). While chapters 2 through 5 focus on federal laws, Chapter 6 provides an overview of the state and private initiatives to fight healthcare fraud.

Chapters 7 and 8 address other significant issues affecting the healthcare industry in achieving compliance with the fraud and abuse laws. Chapter 7 addresses the topics of healthcare organizations adopting corporate compliance programs, the requirements that a healthcare organization must satisfy if it is subject to a Corporate Integrity Agreement, and the government's efforts to encourage (and in some cases require) healthcare providers to self-disclose possible violations and errors. Chapter 8 describes the intersection between the government's efforts to curb healthcare fraud and the managed care industry, which has begun to attract substantial attention over the last several years.

Chapter 9 provides an overview of many of the legal representation issues with which attorneys who practice in the subspecialty of healthcare fraud must be familiar.

Finally, Chapter 10 of this book provides the authors' outlook on the future of healthcare fraud in the 21st century, including areas of anticipated enforcement efforts, upcoming legislative activities and ongoing issues relating to healthcare fraud.

## § 1-2 DEPARTMENT OF JUSTICE

The Department of Justice (DOJ) is the federal executive agency tasked with enforcing the federal laws of the United States and administering justice. The DOJ is headquartered in Washington, D.C. and led by the Attorney General who oversees and directs the DOJ's overall activities, including all U.S. Attorney's Offices, the Criminal Division, and the Civil Division.

Today, the DOJ uses the False Claims Act (FCA) to recover billions of dollars per year in alleged healthcare fraud. In the years 2009–2010, the DOJ recovered more than $5 billion under the FCA. As Attorney General Eric Holder declared in 2010, "we have taken our fight against healthcare fraud to a new level."[2] The following year, Attorney General Holder addressed those gathered at the Healthcare Fraud Summit in Philadelphia and spoke about the progress that had been made by the DOJ in identifying and prosecuting fraud cases:

> Over the last two years – as a result of healthcare fraud actions we have pursued under the False Claims Act and the Food, Drug and Cosmetic Act—the Justice Department's Civil Division and our U.S. Attorneys' Offices have recovered nearly $8 billion in judgments, settlements, fines, restitutions, and forfeitures. Last year alone, we opened more than 900 civil investigations—and secured more than 700 criminal convictions against individuals involved in healthcare fraud schemes.[3]

It is clear that as the government continues to pay escalating healthcare delivery costs, it will increase its oversight of the providers and suppliers who seek reimbursement from government programs with the DOJ being one of the government's largest hammers.

### § 1-2(a) United States Attorney's Offices

Dispersed among each of the 93 federal districts in the United States is a United States Attorney's Office (USAO). Each office is led by a United States Attorney (USA), who, like the Attorney General, is appointed by the President and confirmed by the United States Senate. USAs supervise the

---

[2] Press Release, Office of Pub. Affairs, U.S. Dep't of Justice, *Departments of Justice and Health and Human Services Team Up to Crack Down on Healthcare Fraud* (Nov. 5, 2010), *available online at* http://www.justice.gov/opa/pr/2010/November/10-ag-1256.html.

[3] Eric Holder, Attorney General of the United States, Address at the Healthcare Fraud Summit in Philadelphia, Pa. (June 17, 2011), *transcript available online at* http://www.justice.gov/iso/opa/ag/speeches/2011/ag-speech-110617.html.

activities of their Assistant United States Attorneys (AUSAs), who are the nation's principal prosecutors of federal crimes, including healthcare fraud.

Because of the government's belief that there is a significant rise in healthcare fraud and the corresponding need to combat it, each USAO now designates a Criminal Healthcare Fraud Coordinator and Civil Healthcare Fraud Coordinator. These coordinators receive and review referrals from certain federal law enforcement agencies, such as the Department of Health and Human Services, Office of Inspector General, Office of Investigations and the Federal Bureau of Investigation (FBI), who themselves are tasked with investigating healthcare fraud and other related federal violations. Typically, if the referrals have merit and the USAO or the referring agency has sufficient resources, the referral will be accepted and the matter opened with the USAO—the ultimate goal being to collaborate to investigate and, if warranted, prosecute, civilly and/or criminally, the alleged, offending party(s).

Depending upon the complexity of the matter, a USAO will prosecute a case on its own, or it may seek assistance from attorneys with the DOJ's Criminal and Civil Divisions. Likewise, those Divisions may seek to initiate their own healthcare fraud investigation/prosecution in a federal district, and, in doing so, will request permission or assistance from the local USAO. Regardless of the scenario, there is no doubt that USAOs currently play a significant role in today's healthcare fraud enforcement.

In 1996, as part of the Health Insurance Portability and Accountability Act of 1996 (HIPAA),[4] Congress established a national Healthcare Fraud and Abuse Control Program (HCFAC), which was designed to coordinate federal, state and local law enforcement activities to thwart fraud and abuse in healthcare, including both public and private health plans. The HCFAC issues an annual report detailing the overall efforts of law enforcement, and, according to the FY 2011 Report, USAOs received 1,110 new healthcare fraud criminal matters involving 2,561 defendants and had 1,873 healthcare fraud criminal matters pending, involving 3,118 defendants. The 2011 FY Report further describes that during that year USAOs filed criminal charges in 489 healthcare fraud cases involving 1,430 defendants, and obtained 743 federal healthcare fraud related convictions. Also, as for civil matters, USAOs opened 977 new civil healthcare fraud investigations, and, at the conclusion of the year, had 1,069 pending civil healthcare fraud investigations.[5]

Without question, these numbers are staggering, especially when considered in the context of just one year's efforts. Indeed, in just 2011, the

---

[4] Health Insurance Portability and Accountability Act of 1996 (HIPAA), Pub. L. No. 104-191, tit. II § 201, 110 Stat. 1936 (1996).

[5] Healthcare Fraud and Abuse Control Program, The Department of Health and Human Services and the Department of Justice, Annual Report for Fiscal Year 2011, page 77 (Feb. 2012), *available online at* http://oig.hhs.gov/publications/docs/hcfac/hcfacreport2011.pdf.

federal government won or negotiated approximately $2.4 billion in healthcare fraud judgments and settlements, which does not even include related state Medicaid monies recovered as part of global, federal-state settlements.[6]

## § 1-2(b)  Criminal Division

The Criminal Division's Fraud Section initiates and coordinates complex healthcare fraud prosecutions, both on its own and in a supporting role with USAOs.[7] To that end, beginning in March 2007, the Fraud Section began working with the USAO for the Southern District of Florida and related federal-state law enforcement partners to create the first ever Medicare Fraud Strike Force (Strike Force) in Miami, Florida. Miami was chosen, in part, because a statistical analysis indicated astronomical Medicare billings in that area by hundreds of providers that could not be explained but for the existence of fraud.[8] The resulting product was the prosecution of hundreds of individuals and entities that never provided legitimate medical services, but instead existed solely to defraud Medicare and other Government healthcare programs.

Since its inception in 2007, the Strike Force has achieved unrivaled success, such that it was able to expand its efforts quickly into other cities – Los Angeles, Detroit, Houston, Brooklyn, Baton Rouge, Dallas and Tampa. In 2011 alone, Fraud Section attorneys in Strike Force cities opened or filed 44 new healthcare cases involving charges against 152 defendants. From these charges, 88 guilty pleas were secured and 11 jury trials litigated, producing 19 additional guilty verdicts.[9]

In addition to the Strike Force cases, the Criminal Division's Fraud Section attorneys conduct significant corporate investigations. These investigations span the United States and focus on the largest of healthcare providers, who, because of either a systemic corporate problem or just the actions of a few, have allegedly committed an atypically large amount of fraud over an extended period of time. Because of limited government resources, these corporate investigations have been few in number, but this may change in the near future because of two factors. First, HCFAC has achieved unparalleled financial success for a government program: the return-on-investment (ROI) for HCFAC, since 1997, is $5.1 returned to every $1.0 expended, and the average ROI over the last three years (2009–2011) has increased to $7.2.[10] Second, with an ever-growing number of sealed qui tam actions filed every

---

[6] *Id.* at 1.
[7] *Id.* at 81.
[8] Fact Sheet: Phase One Medicare Fraud Strike Force Miami-Dade County, Fla., page 1, *available online at* http://www.stopmedicarefraud.gov/heattaskforce/index.html.
[9] Healthcare Fraud and Abuse Control Program Annual Report for FY2011 at 81.
[10] *Id.* at 8.

year, the DOJ now has a significant number of referred cases from which they can choose to pursue based on strength of evidence and potential for ROI.

### § 1-2(c)  Civil Division

Just as with USAOs and the Criminal Division, the Civil Division plays an integral role in recovering money on behalf of defrauded federal healthcare programs, such as Medicare, Medicaid, and TRICARE. The Civil Division has either recovered or assisted in the recovery of over $1 billion almost every year for the last decade and $2.35 billion in 2011 alone.[11]

More often than not, the Civil Division will receive a referral in this area from a government contractor or as a whistleblower action having been filed under seal under the False Claims Act, qui tam action and then acting upon that referral, will coordinate with the applicable USAO and investigative agencies to pursue the matter. Although a large focus of the Civil Division during the beginning of the 21st century has focused on the pharmaceutical industry, the Civil Division pursues a wide array of cases that protect both the public fiscal and public health, and they litigate against a full spectrum of Medicare and Medicaid providers.

### § 1-2(d)  The Federal Bureau of Investigation

The FBI is the principal investigative agency of the DOJ. The FBI's authority extends beyond just Medicare and Medicaid fraud, to also address private insurance companies, businesses and individual victims of healthcare crimes. Over the years, the FBI's involvement in investigating healthcare fraud has increased in part because HIPAA specified mandatory funding to the FBI for healthcare fraud enforcement.[12] In fact, the FBI has created a separate Healthcare Fraud Unit within the Financial Crimes Section of the Criminal Investigative Division that concentrates on multi-district investigations of large healthcare corporations.

## § 1-3   DEPARTMENT OF HEALTH AND HUMAN SERVICES

### § 1-3(a)  Office of Inspector General

The mission of the Office of Inspector General (OIG) is to protect the integrity of Department of Health & Human Services (DHHS) programs as well as the health and welfare of program beneficiaries. DHHS OIG is

---

[11] *Id.* at 78.
[12] Health Insurance Portability and Accountability Act of 1996 (HIPAA), Pub. L. No. 104-191, tit. II § 201, 110 Stat. 1936, 1992 (1996).

## The Fraud Enforcers: Who Are They and What Do They Do?

the largest inspector general's office in the federal government, with more than 1,700 employees dedicated to combating fraud, waste and abuse and to improving the efficiency of DHHS programs.[13] The vast majority of OIG's resources are dedicated to the oversight of Medicare and Medicaid, but OIG's oversight also extends to programs under other DHHS institutions, including the Centers for Disease Control and Prevention (CDC), National Institutes of Health (NIH), and the Food and Drug Administration (FDA).

The Office of Inspector General consists of six components:

- **The Immediate Office of Inspector General (IO)**, which is directly responsible for the overall fulfillment of the OIG's mission and for promoting effective management and quality of the agency's processes and products;

- **The Office of Audit Services (OAS)**, which conducts independent audits of DHHS programs and/or DHHS grantees and contractors;

- **The Office of Evaluation and Inspections (OEI)**, which conducts national evaluations of DHHS programs from a broad, issue-based perspective;

- **The Office of Management and Policy (OMP)**, which provides mission and administrative support to the OIG;

- **The Office of Investigations (OI)**, which conducts criminal, civil and administrative investigations of fraud and misconduct related to DHHS programs, operations and beneficiaries; and

- **The Office of Counsel to the Inspector General (OCIG)**, which provides legal advocacy and counsel to the Inspector General and OIG's other components.

In addition to conducting investigations, studies and audits, the OIG also functions as an administrative agency providing the healthcare industry with guidance through the promulgation of regulations, Special Advisory Bulletins, Special Fraud Alerts, compliance program guidance, and Advisory Opinions.[14]

Although the OIG does not have the power to bring criminal prosecutions or civil enforcement actions, the OIG does have the ability to impose administrative sanctions, such as civil money penalties, against providers and suppliers who: knowingly submit false claims to the federal government; participate in unlawful patient referral or kickback schemes; fail to appropriately treat or

---

[13] *See* U.S. Department of Health and Human Services, Office of the Inspector General, *About Us*, available online at http://oig.DHHS.gov/about-oig/about-us/index.asp.

[14] *See* U.S. Department of Health and Human Services, Office of the Inspector General, *Advisory Opinions*, available online at: http://oig.DHHS.gov/compliance/advisory-opinions/index.asp.

refer patients at hospital emergency rooms; or engage in other fraudulent and abusive activities.

The OIG also has the power to impose exclusions from participation in all federal healthcare programs on healthcare providers and suppliers who have been convicted of healthcare fraud. Finally, the OIG monitors compliance with Corporate Integrity Agreements (CIAs). CIAs are typically offered by the OIG in exchange for their agreement to not impose monetary penalties or exclude the entity (or the officers, employees, directors or agents of the entity) under investigation. CIAs often require companies to establish and maintain a robust compliance program and take other specified auditing and monitoring steps to ensure that their future conduct is consistent with Medicare and Medicaid rules.

### § 1-3(b)  Centers for Medicare & Medicaid Services

The Centers for Medicare & Medicaid Services (CMS) is a federal agency within DHHS that administers and oversees the Medicare and Medicaid Programs and the Children's Health Insurance Program (CHIP). CMS partners with many state and federal law enforcement agencies as well as the contractors discussed in the next section to prevent and detect fraud and abuse. Within CMS, the Center for Program Integrity (CPI) promotes the integrity of federal healthcare programs through audits and policy reviews, identification and monitoring of program vulnerabilities, and support and assistance to states. CPI oversees those CMS interactions and collaborations with key stakeholders that relate to program integrity for the purposes of detecting, deterring, monitoring, and combating fraud and abuse.[15]

### § 1-3(c)  Administration on Aging

The Administration on Aging (AOA) is an agency of DHHS that, in part, seeks to educate older people and their caregivers about the benefits and services available to help them. Since 1997, AOA has worked with CMS, the OIG, DOJ, and Medicare contractors to train retired professionals to teach Medicare beneficiaries how to identify healthcare fraud, primarily in the bills they receive. As part of this effort, AOA creates Senior Medicare Patrol programs to recruit and train retired professionals to help older Americans better understand their Medicare billing statements, avoid unintended errors, and detect deliberate abuses. This outreach program has reached millions of beneficiaries through community education programs and the dissemination

---

[15] *See* U.S. Department of Health and Human Services, Centers for Medicare and Medicaid Services, Center for Program Integrity, *New Strategic Direction and Key Antifraud Activities* (Nov. 3, 2011), *available online at*: https://www.cms.gov/MedicaidIntegrityProgram/Downloads/cpiinitiatives.pdf.

### The Fraud Enforcers: Who Are They and What Do They Do?

of informational materials and tools. Since the program's inception in 1997, beneficiaries, families, and caregivers have filed hundred thousands of complaints that have been either resolved or referred for further investigation, which, as of 2011, has resulted in over $100 million in estimated savings.[16]

## § 1-3(d) Health Resources and Services Administration

As part of HIPAA, Congress authorized DHHS and DOJ to create the Healthcare Integrity and Protection Data Bank (HIPDB), which is a national healthcare fraud and abuse data collection program for the reporting and disclosure of certain final adverse action taken against healthcare providers, suppliers, practitioners.[17] This database is administered by the Health Resources Services Administration (HRSA), and health plans and federal and state governments are eligible to query the database and are required to report final adverse actions to the HIPDB.

The HIPDB collects information regarding licensure and certification actions, exclusions from participation in the federal healthcare programs, criminal convictions, civil judgments related to healthcare, and other adjudicated actions or decisions. However, excluded from the HIPDB reporting requirements are: (i) settlements in which no findings or admissions of liability have been made; (ii) administrative fines or citations, corrective action plans, and other personnel actions unless they are connected to the billing previsions or delivery of healthcare services and taken in conjunction with other licensure or certification actions, such as censure, reprimand, or probation; (iii) clinical privileging actions and similar paneling decisions made by health plans; (iv) "Removal Without Cause" actions taken by health plans, such as a health plan eliminating a physician for not maintaining a desirable target rate of patient visits; (v) initial overpayment determinations by federal or state government programs and their contractors and similar denial of claims decisions made by health plans; and (iv) non-disciplinary voluntary surrenders of a license or certification (such as when a practitioner moves out of state or is deceased).[18]

---

[16] *See* U.S. Department of Health and Human Services, Administration on Aging, *Senior Medicare Patrol (SMP)* (Nov. 7, 2011), *available online at*: http://www.aoa.gov/AoA_programs/Elder_Rights/SMP/index.aspx.

[17] Social Security Act § 1128(e); 42 U.S.C § 1320a-7e; 45 C.F.R Part 61. *See also* National Practitioner Data Bank, Healthcare Integrity and Protection Data Bank, *available online at* http://www.npdb-hipdb.com.

[18] 45 C.F.R. Part 61 (2012).

## § 1-3(e)  Food & Drug Administration

Although the Food & Drug Administration (FDA) has for many years addressed various types of fraud being perpetrated on the public, the FDA's profile in focusing on healthcare fraud was raised in 2010 when it received $1.7 million in HCFAC funding by DHHS for the FDA Pharmaceutical Fraud Pilot Program (PFPP). According to the FY2010 HCFAC report, the PFPP is "designed to detect, prosecute, and prevent pharmaceutical, biologic, and medical device fraud. The PFPP gathers information from sources inside and outside FDA and focuses on fraudulent marketing schemes, application fraud, clinical trial fraud, and flagrant manufacturing-related violations related to biologics, drugs, and medical devices." [19] In a short amount of time, the PFPP enhanced the healthcare fraud-related activities of FDA's Office of Criminal Investigations (OCI) and the OGC Food and Drug Division in order to further investigate criminal violations of the FDCA, the Prescription Drug Marketing Act, the Federal Anti-Tampering Act, and related federal statutes. As a result, in FY 2011, the FDA received twice the amount of funding (i.e., $3.4 million) for the PFPP. [20]

## § 1-3(f)  Program Integrity Contractors

The government has increasingly enlisted the assistance of government contractors to identify and combat fraud, abuse and waste. Specifically, CMS is authorized under the Social Security Act to enter into agreements with various entities to aid in a range of administrative and fraud prevention functions.[21] These entities, called Program Integrity Contractors, play an increasingly important role in the overall enforcement landscape. As of 2012, there are seven (7) types of Program Integrity Contractors:

- Recovery Audit Contractors
- Zone Program Integrity Contractors
- Medicare Administrative Contractors
- Comprehensive Error Rate Testing Contractors
- National Supplier Clearinghouse Contractors
- Coordination of Benefits Contractors
- Medicare Drug Integrity Contractors.

---

[19] The Department of Health and Human Services and The Department of Justice Healthcare Fraud and Abuse Control Program, *Annual Report for Fiscal Year 2010* 69 (Jan. 2011), *available online at*: http://oig.DHHS.gov/publications/docs/hcfac/hcfacreport2010.pdf.
[20] Healthcare Fraud and Abuse Control Program FY2011 at 73.
[21] Social Security Act §§1816(a) and 1842(a); 42 U.S.C. §§1395(h) and 1395(u).

## § 1-3(f)(1) Recovery Audit Contractors

After a successful multi-year demonstration project, Congress permanently established the Recovery Audit Contractor (RAC) program as part of the Tax Relief and Healthcare Act of 2006.[22] RACs are private entities that contract with CMS to identify improper payments in the form of either underpayments or overpayments. RACs typically employ some form of data mining or computer based methodology to identify providers to audit. Although initially RACs were only responsible for examining overpayments under Medicare Parts A and B, the 2010 Health Reform legislation extended RAC oversight to not only Medicare Parts C and D as well as state Medicaid programs.[23] RACS receive payments based on the amounts that they recovery for the program and in FY 2009 and FY 2010 ranged from 9% - 12.5% of amounts recovered.[24]

In October 2008, CMS announced the establishment of four permanent RACs:

- For Region A (New York, Rhode Island, Massachusetts, Vermont, New Hampshire, and Maine): Diversified Collection Services, Inc.
- For Region B (Minnesota, Michigan, Indiana): CGI Technologies and Solutions
- For Region C (Colorado, New Mexico, Florida, South Carolina): Connolly Consulting Associates Inc.
- For Region D (Arizona, Utah, Montana, Wyoming, North Dakota, and South Dakota): HealthDataInsights Inc.

In November 2008, two unsuccessful bidders filed bid protests with the Government Accountability Office (GAO), which then required CMS to issue an automatic stay until a determination was made by the GAO.[25] On February 4, 2009 the parties involved in the bid protest settled this matter with CMS whereby PRG-Schultz was added as a subcontractor for the RACs in Regions A, B, and D, and Viant was added as a subcontractor for Connolly Consulting Associates Inc in Region C.[26]

Although initially, RACs focused on DME, physician and outpatient claims, in 2010 RACs began reviewing complex coding issues, performing Diagnosis Related Group (DRG) validations and conducting medical

---

[22] Pub. L. No. 109-432, § 302(a), 120 Stat. 2922 (2006).
[23] *See* Patient Protection and Affordable Care Act, Pub. L. 111-148 §6411 (Mar. 23, 2010).
[24] *See Implementation of Recovery Auditing at the Center for Medicare & Medicaid Services: FY 2010 Report to Congress As Required by Section 6411 of Affordable Care Act* at p 5.
[25] *See* http://www.cms.gov/Research-Statistics-Data-and-Systems/Monitoring-Programs/recovery-audit-program/index.html?redirect=/RAC/03_RecentUpdates.asp.
[26] *See* http://www.cms.hhs.gov/RAC/.

necessity reviews.[27] As such a wide range of healthcare entities are subject to RAC auditing, including but not limited to: inpatient hospital; outpatient hospitals; physician/non-physician providers; home health; laboratory; ambulance; skilled nursing facilities; suppliers; inpatient rehabilitation facilities; critical access hospitals; long term care hospitals; ambulatory surgical center and others.[28]

RACs perform both automated and complex reviews. Automated reviews are billing reviews that identify errors that "on their face" are incorrect, such as billing for amputating the same appendage twice. Complex reviews are reviews of medical records to evaluate medical necessity, completeness of documentation and other assessments to determine whether the particular claim was properly reimbursed. CMS has imposed certain limitation on the number of records that a RAC can request.[29] For example, RACs can request to review "10% of average monthly Medicare paid claims per 45 days" for each National Provider Identifier (NPI), up to a maximum of 200.[30]

RACs are unquestionably becoming a major force in healthcare oversight. In FY 2010 RACs demanded $135.6 million in overpayments and corrected (not necessarily recovered) $92.3 million in both overpayments and underpayments. Contrast these 2010 amounts to the tremendous increase as RACS recaptured $797 million in FY 2011.[31] States are also in the process of creating their own Medicaid RAC program as required by Health Reform, demonstrating that RACs are both expanding and here to stay.[32]

While RACs are not fraud enforcement or fraud identification contractors, the discovery of an overpayment by a RAC auditor does not preclude the DHHS Secretary or the Attorney General from conducting an investigation and prosecuting an entity suspected of fraudulent behavior.

## § 1-3(f)(2)   Zone Program Integrity Contractors

Zone Program Integrity Contractors (ZPICs) were created as part of the Medicare Prescription Drug, Improvement and Modernization Act of 2003 (MMA).[33] In sum, ZPICs are responsible for analyzing data to identify

---

[27] *See Implementation of Recovery Auditing at the Center for Medicare & Medicaid Services: FY 2010 Report to Congress As Required by Section 6411 of Affordable Care Act* at p 5.
[28] *See* Recovery Audit Program Statement of Work (Sept. 1, 2011) *at* 8-9.
[29] *See* http://www.cms.hhs.gov/RAC/.
[30] *See* http://www.cms.hhs.gov/RAC/Downloads/RAC%20Medical%20Record%20Request%20Limits.pdf.
[31] Beryl H. Davis, Testimony before the Subcommittee on Government Organization, Efficiency, and Financial Management, Committee on Oversight and Government Reform, House of Representatives, (Feb 7, 2012).
[32] *See generally* http://www.cms.gov/medicaidracs/.
[33] *See* Medicare Prescription Drug, Improvement and Modernization Act of 2003 P.L. 108-173 (2003).

## The Fraud Enforcers: Who Are They and What Do They Do?

improper billing patterns, performing provider audits, investigating fraud leads, refering cases to the DHHS/OIG or DOJ for prosecution, and implementing administrative actions to recover improper payments (i.e., pre- and post-payment claims review, payment suspension, payment denial, or recoupment of overpayments). As such, ZPICs do not collect overpayments, but refer suspected overpayments to claims processors, such as MACs, fiscal intermediaries and carriers for collection.[34]

ZPICs perform more of an investigator role with the aim of routing out fraud and referring cases rather than RACs, which are more focused on finding and correcting amounts billed to Medicare in error. As such, since ZPICs do not recover overpayments themselves, they are not paid on a contingency fee basis like RACs.

There are 7 national ZPIC zones. CMS awarded ZPIC contracts to SafeGaurd Service, LLC for Zone 1; NCI, Inc. for Zone 2; Cahaba Safeguard Administrators, LLC for Zone 3; Health Integrity, LLC for Zone 4; NCI, Inc. for Zone 5; Cahaba Safeguard Administrators, LLC for Zone 6 and SafeGuard Services, LLC for Zone 7. Once ZPICs are fully operational they will be responsible for combating fraud and abuse throughout the Medicare program under Parts A and B (hospital, skilled nursing, home health, provider and durable medical equipment claims), Part C (Medicare Advantage health plans), Part D (prescription drug plans) and coordination of Medicare-Medicaid data matches (Medi-Medi).[35]

### § 1-3(f)(3)    Other Contractors

In addition to ZPICs and RACs, other private contractors fulfill more specific program integrity roles. Medicare Administrative Contractors (MACs), created by MMA, replaced fiscal intermediaries and carriers as the claims administration and processing entities that contract with CMS for the Medicare program. MACs, like their predecessors, perform a variety of program integrity functions such as routine auditing or providers, payment recovery, education and screening beneficiary allegations of fraud. MACs are the face of Medicare from a provider standpoint. By virtue of the fact that Medicare claims are processed, paid and rejected through MACs, they are on the front

---

[34] *See* Congressional Research Service 7-5700, RL34217, *Medicare Program Integrity: Activities to Protect Medicare from payment Errors, Fraud, and Abuse* (July 29, 2011) at p. 14.
[35] CMS, *CMS Enhances Program Integrity Efforts to Fight Fraud, Waste and Abuse in Medicare* (Oct. 6, 2008), *available online at* http://www.cms.hhs.gov/apps/media/press/release.asp?. *See also* DHHS OIG Report, Zone Program Integrity Contractors' Data Issues Hinder Effective Oversight (Nov. 2011). In this report the OIG performed an initial assessment of ZPICs and concluded that the newly formed entities should be overseen by CMS more closely and that CMS should provide ZPICs with better access to claims data to improve their ability to identify fraud and abuse, respond to requests for information and track overpayment collections.

lines of program integrity and oversight and work hand in hand with RACs, ZPICs and government agencies.

Other program integrity contractors include: Comprehensive Error Rate Testing Contractors (CERT – responsible for calculating improper payment rates);[36] National Supplier Clearinghouse Contractor (NSC – responsible for reviewing Medicare supplier enrollment applications for DME, prosthetics, orthotics, and supplies);[37] Coordination of Benefits Contractors (COB—responsible for identifying payment submitted to Medicare that should be the responsibility of another payor);[38] and Medicare Drug Integrity Contractors (MEDICs—responsible for oversight and identification of fraud for Medicare Part C and D).[39]

## § 1-4    OTHER FEDERAL AGENCIES

Although the key federal agencies concerned with healthcare fraud are the DOJ and DHHS, other federal agencies share the concern as they too are involved in the delivery of healthcare services. For example, healthcare programs are operated by the Department of Defense and the Department of Veterans Affairs and the Department of Labor has jurisdiction over self-insured employers offering health plans to their employees. Consequently, these agencies also have joined in instituting measures to investigate and prosecute healthcare fraud.

In addition, even though the United States Postal Service does not itself administer a federal or state healthcare program, it is involved in healthcare fraud investigations that include some component of fraud precipitated through use of the United States Mail System. Another federal agency that has taken an active role in attempting to educate consumers on healthcare fraud is the Federal Trade Commission (FTC).[40]

## § 1-5    MULTI-AGENCY FEDERAL INITIATIVES

Historically, there have been a number of federal initiatives to combat fraud, waste and abuse in specific geographic regions or specific activities. These collaborations took the form of multi-agency task forces or combined

---

[36] *See generally* http://www.cms.gov/cert/.
[37] *See generally* http://www.palmettogba.com/palmetto/providers.nsf/DocsCatHome/National%20Supplier%20Clearinghouse.
[38] *See generally* https://www.cms.gov/Medicare/Coordination-of-Benefits/COBGeneralInformation/index.html?redirect=/COBGeneralInformation/01_Overview.asp.
[39] ZPICs are expected to fully replace MEDICs sometime in the future.
[40] For example, in 2001, the FTC announced a comprehensive law enforcement effort to halt Internet scams based on the fraudulent marketing of healthcare products. Federal Trade Commission Press Release, *"Operation Cure All" Wages New Battle in Ongoing War Against Internet Health Fraud* (June 14, 2001), *available online at* http://www.ftc.gov/opa/2001/06/cureall.htm.

federal, state and local initiatives. More recently, in an effort to streamline collaboration among the various fraud enforcers, the Obama Administration has developed a new multi-agency initiative to address healthcare fraud. Specifically, in May 2009, Attorney General Eric Holder and DHHS Secretary Kathleen Sebelius announced the inception of the Healthcare Fraud Prevention and Enforcement Action Team (HEAT).[41] HEAT is comprised of federal law enforcement agents, prosecutors, attorneys, and auditors from both the DOJ and DHHS, in addition to state officials from the Medicaid Fraud Control Units. HEAT's mission includes:

- To gather resources across government to help prevent waste, fraud and abuse in the Medicare and Medicaid programs, and crack down on the fraud perpetrators who are abusing the system and costing us all billions of dollars.
- To reduce skyrocketing healthcare costs and improve the quality of care by ridding the system of perpetrators who are preying on Medicare and Medicaid beneficiaries.
- To highlight best practices by providers and public sector employees who are dedicated to ending waste, fraud and abuse in Medicare.
- To build upon existing partnerships between the Department of Justice and the Department of Health and Human Services such as our Medicare Fraud Strike Forces to reduce fraud and recover taxpayer dollars.[42]

The Medicare Strike Force team, discussed in §1-3 is one of HEAT's components. This multi-agency partnership composed of federal, state and local investigators was designed to combat Medicare fraud through use of community policing and data analysis. Thus far, the Medicare Strike Force has expanded its reach to Baton Rouge, Brooklyn, Detroit, Houston, Los Angeles, Miami-Dade, Tampa Bay, Dallas and Chicago.

## § 1-6  CONGRESS

Although Congress' role as lawmaker is familiar to most, its role as investigator is less frequently publicized, particularly in the healthcare area. Yet, Congress has broad investigatory powers to issue subpoenas, to compel the production of both documents and witnesses, to hold uncooperative witnesses in contempt and to grant immunity in exchange for testimony. Congressional staff can even take depositions without the presence of a Member of Congress.

---

[41] *See* http://www.stopmedicarefraud.gov/heattaskforce/index.html.
[42] *Id.*

Congressional hearings have focused a great deal of attention on healthcare fraud. This is particularly true in today's political climate in which healthcare has become a divisive battleground between the Republicans and Democrats in Congress. Moreover, since the passing of the Health Reform Law, constituents, lobbyist and stakeholders have increasingly pressured elected officials to support or oppose pieces of legislation affecting healthcare. Since the debate in Washington often focuses on how much a program costs and where costs can be cut, Medicare in particular, with estimated payments of $516 billion in 2010,[43] is squarely in the crosshairs of politicians who seek to cut expenses in response to the rising U.S. deficit. DHHS reported an estimate of almost $48 billion in Medicare improper payments in 2010. Given these numbers, Congress continues to aggressively monitor the healthcare industry.

Hearings have been held by Congressional committees with jurisdiction over healthcare issues, such as the House Commerce and Ways and Means Committee and the Senate Finance Committee. Additionally, other committees have initiated their own healthcare oversight activities. For example, the House Government Operations Committee's Subcommittee on Human Resources and Intergovernmental Relations has held hearings on healthcare fraud. Other committees that have held healthcare fraud hearings in recent years include: the Senate Judiciary Committee; the Senate Special Committee on Aging; the Senate Permanent Subcommittee on Investigations; the Oversight and Investigations Subcommittee of the House Commerce Committee; and the House Select Committee on Children, Youth and Families.

## § 1-7 STATES

States have increasingly become key government actors in healthcare oversight. Although the federal government's efforts to prosecute healthcare fraud have attracted the majority of the public's attention, states have also adopted laws and regulations regarding kickbacks, physician self-referrals, false claims, and fee-splitting. Commercial bribery statutes, which provide criminal penalties, state deceptive trade practices laws and consumer protection statutes are also used to enforce unlawful arrangements involving healthcare providers. (These state laws and initiatives are addressed in more detail in Chapter 6.)

As primary administrators of the Medicaid program, states are responsible for combating Medicaid fraud. In this regard, with the exception of North Dakota, all states and the District of Columbia have established Medic-

---

[43] GAO Report, Reported Medicare Estimates and Key Remediation Strategies (July 28, 2011), *available online at* http://gao.gov/products/GAO-11-842T.

### The Fraud Enforcers: Who Are They and What Do They Do?

aid Fraud Control Units (MFCUs).[44] MFCUs are usually part of the office of the State Attorney General and are certified annually by DHHS for meeting requirements concerning authority to prosecute fraud on a statewide basis or to refer cases to appropriate authorities for prosecution. States wishing to operate an MFCU can have most of the costs related to the establishment and operation of the MFCU reimbursed, at least in part, by the federal government.[45]

MFCUs are charged with the responsibility for investigating and prosecuting violations of all applicable state laws pertaining to fraud in the administration of the state's Medicaid program. In 1999, the jurisdiction of the MFCUs was expanded to allow state MFCUs, with federal approval, to investigate and prosecute fraud in federal healthcare programs if the matter is sufficiently related to Medicaid. This expansion also gave MFCUs the authority to investigate and prosecute complaints alleging abuse or neglect of patients not only in healthcare facilities receiving payments from the state Medicaid program, but also in non-Medicaid assisted living or "board and care" facilities.[46]

In carrying out these duties, if a MFCU discovers that overpayments have been made to a healthcare facility or other provider, then the MFCU is authorized to either attempt to collect such overpayment or refer the matter to an appropriate State agency for collection. Moreover, if the case is to be prosecuted, the MFCU will assist in preparing the prosecutor for trial.[47]

States, acting through their MFCUs, have greatly increased enforcement and recovery amounts. In fact, according to the OIG, in FY 2010, MFCUs were responsible for conducting 13,210 investigations and for recouping a staggering $1.8 billion in both civil and criminal matters.[48] Accordingly, MFCUs will likely continue to be a significant, if not more central player, in fraud enforcement.[49]

## § 1-8  PRIVATE PAYORS

Facing increasing pressure by employers to furnish coverage at a reasonable premium, third-party payors view healthcare fraud as a major cause of healthcare cost increases. As a result, they have initiated their own efforts to control healthcare fraud. For example, many private insurers have established their own fraud units that scrutinize the billing practices of providers

---

[44] *See* CMS State By State Fraud and Abuse Reporting Contact—Oct. 2011 *available online at* https://www.cms.gov/FraudAbuseforConsumers/.
[45] Social Security Act § 1903; 42 U.S.C. § 1396b.
[46] Ticket to Work and Work Incentives Improvement Act of 1999, Pub. L. No. 106-170, 113 Stat. 1860, 1913 (1999) § 407 (codified at 42 U.S.C. § 1396b(g)). *See also* http://www.namfcu.net/faq.
[47] 42 C.F.R. § 1007.11.
[48] *Id.*
[49] *See* DHHS-OIG MFCU Statistical Data for Fiscal Year 2010, *available online at* http://oig.hhs.gov.

submitting claims.[50] Providers viewed as defrauding the system—billing for services not rendered, medically unnecessary, or at inflated rates—may see their claims systematically denied. When the provider sues the insurer for wrongful claims denial, the insurer may file a healthcare fraud counterclaim based on RICO.[51]

Third-party payors also have joined forces with governmental authorities in combating healthcare fraud. In order to enhance the identification, prevention, detection, and prosecution of healthcare fraud in the private sector, in 1985, the National Healthcare Anti-Fraud Association (NHCAA) was formed as an association of private insurance carriers, Blue Cross and Blue Shield organizations, self-insured corporations, federal and state regulatory agencies, and law enforcement agencies.[52] Its mission is to increase awareness and improve the detection, investigation, prosecution and prevention of healthcare fraud. The NHCAA pursues it mission by: (1) maintaining a private/public partnership in combating healthcare fraud; (2) providing learning opportunities through The NHCAA Institute for Healthcare Fraud Prevention (an educational foundation that provides education and training to private- and public-sector healthcare anti-fraud personnel); (3) providing opportunities for private- and public-sector information-sharing; (4) serving as a national resource for healthcare anti-fraud information and professional assistance to government, industry and the media; and (5) recognizing and advancing professional specialization in the detection and investigation and/or prosecution of healthcare fraud through accreditation of healthcare anti-fraud professionals.[53]

Associations like the NHCAA are representative of the concerted effort to combat healthcare fraud on the private side, which has produced significant results. The Center for Policy Research, a component of America's Health Insurance Plans (a lobbying group for payors), released a report in 2011 estimating that enrollees in large plans (more than 5 million enrollees) saved $3.70 for every $.25 spent on fraud and abuse programs, enrollees in medium plans (1 to 5 million enrollees) saved $1.70 for every $.65 spent on fraud and abuse programs, and enrollees in small plans (fewer

---

[50] *See, e.g.*, Blue Cross and Blue Shield Association, *Healthcare Fraud, available online at*: http://www.bcbs.com/report-healthcare-fraud/ (indicating that BCBS has established a "National Anti-Fraud Department" to fight fraud); Aetna, *Excellence with Integrity, available online at*: http://www.aetna.com/about/compliance.html (indicating that Aetna has established a Special Investigations Unit to fight fraud).

[51] *See* discussion of these issues in Chapter 4, *infra*.

[52] National Healthcare Anti-Fraud Association, *Who we are, available online at:* http://www.nhcaa.org/eweb/DynamicPage.aspx?webcode=about_nhcaa&wpscode=WhoWeAre.

[53] *Id.*

## The Fraud Enforcers: Who Are They and What Do They Do?

than one million enrollees) saved $4.00 for every $1.30 spent on fraud and abuse programs.[54]

## § 1-9 PRIVATE CITIZENS

Private citizens also play an increasingly significant role in the detection and enforcement of healthcare fraud. Cases are referred to the government by private citizens (who are not otherwise government agents or contractors) in two broad fashions, via voluntary disclosure and by whistleblowers.

Often, companies discover billing mistakes or activities that run afoul of the fraud and abuse laws and choose to voluntarily disclose their findings to the government. There are certain benefits (and risks) offered by the government for voluntary disclosures. Accordingly, this form of self policing has become commonplace and the government routinely settles matters with entities that voluntarily disclose activities that violate the fraud and abuse laws. (See Chapter 7 for a discussion of voluntary disclosure.)

Traditionally, whistleblowers have always helped authorities by identifying fraud. For instance, patients receiving bills for un-rendered services would investigate why such bills were inaccurate, and disgruntled employees—or competitors—aware of fraudulent activity would report such activity to appropriate authorities. However, given the magnitude of settlements and judgments involving healthcare fraud, the number of private citizens who are willing to expose—and who are exposing—sources of healthcare fraud to the federal government increased dramatically over the past two decades. The reason for such a dramatic increase is simple: such individuals have something to gain as successful whistleblowers can receive between 15% and 30% of the monetary proceeds pursuant to the False Claims Act.[55] By way of example, in 2011, a large pharmaceutical company agreed to pay $2.3 billion to resolve criminal and civil liability arising from the illegal promotion of certain pharmaceutical products. The six whistleblowers involved with the case received more than $102 million from the federal share of the civil recovery.[56]

In addition to the general increase in the number of qui tam actions being brought under the FCA, the range of individuals bringing qui tam actions has also changed. Although at one time it was believed that whistleblowers were merely disgruntled employees wanting to "retaliate" against their former

---

[54] *See* America's Health Insurance Plans, Center for Policy and Research, *Research Brief: Insurers' Efforts to Prevent Healthcare Fraud* 2 (Jan. 2011), *available online at*: http://www.ahip.org/FraudPrevention2011/.

[55] *See* Chapter 4, *infra*, which addresses the federal False Claims Act and the whistleblower provision in greater detail.

[56] News Release, *Justice Department Announces Largest Healthcare Fraud Settlement in its History* (Sept. 2, 2009), *available online at*: http://www.DHHS.gov/news/press/2009pres/09/20090902a.html.

employer, this is no longer the case, as many recent whistleblower actions have been initiated by: (1) current employees who have sought internal resolution to their concerns about the company's "improper" activities but to no avail; (2) companies learning about the activities of a competitor; (3) vendors with which an organization contracts for the provision of services; (4) government contractors; and (5) patients being treated by healthcare organizations.

# 2
# Federal Anti-Kickback Laws

## § 2-1  OVERVIEW

There is probably no area of healthcare fraud that has drawn more controversy than the federal healthcare program anti-kickback statute (the Anti-Kickback Statute).[1] Interpretations of this proscription reach conduct far beyond the traditional, straightforward kickback or bribe, and now affect the healthcare community's conduct in a broad spectrum of ordinary business transactions. Arrangements among providers that must be considered in light of the Anti-Kickback Statute include such common arrangements as joint ventures, space and equipment leases, discounts on goods and services, physician recruitment incentives, management and personal services contracts, physician practice acquisition, and even employment arrangements. Anti-kickback violations can result in the imposition of significant criminal penalties and civil sanctions, including criminal fines, imprisonment, civil monetary penalties, exclusion from the various federal healthcare programs (e.g., the Medicare and Medicaid programs), and even liability under the federal False Claims Act (the FCA).

Multi-million-dollar settlement agreements between the government and entities accused of violating the federal healthcare program's Anti-Kickback Statute are commonplace. For example, National Medical Enterprises, Inc. (NME) (subsequently known as Tenet Healthcare Corp.) paid $379 million in criminal fines, civil damages, and penalties to settle allegations of, among other things, having made unlawful payments to induce doctors and other professionals either to refer Medicare and Medicaid patients to NME's psychiatric hospitals or to increase lengths of stay.

Another example was when TAP Pharmaceutical Products, Inc. agreed to pay $875 million to settle various allegations, including allegedly paying illegal remuneration to physicians and others to obtain orders to purchase TAP's prostate cancer drug, Lupron. Similarly, drug manufacturer Serono pleaded guilty to criminal charges and agreed to pay $704 million to settle charges that it had paid kickbacks to physicians in order to prescribe Serono's AIDS drug.[2]

In fact, in 2010, the Department of Justice (DOJ) recovered its largest settlement ever under the Anti-Kickback Statute for the conduct of a single

---

[1] Social Security Act § 1128B(b), 42 U.S.C. § 1320a-7b(b).
[2] *See Top 20 Cases Under the False Claims Act*, The False Claims Act Legal Center, *available online at* http://www.taf.org/top20.htm.

hospital when it entered into a settlement with The Health Alliance of Greater Cincinnati (Health Alliance) and the Christ Hospital for $108 million.[3] The settlement resolved allegations that Health Alliance and the Christ Hospital violated the federal False Claims Act (FCA) by billing the Medicare and Medicaid programs for cardiac services that were referred to The Christ Hospital in exchange for improper remuneration, including "free" time at The Christ Hospital's Heart Station.

While volumes have been written about the Anti-Kickback Statute, the statutory language is relatively brief:

(b)(1) Whoever knowingly and willfully solicits or receives any remuneration (including any kickback, bribe, or rebate) directly or indirectly, overtly or covertly, in cash or in kind—

(A) in return for referring an individual to a person for the furnishing or arranging for the furnishing of any item or service for which payment may be made in whole or in part under a Federal healthcare program, or

(B) in return for purchasing, leasing, ordering, or arranging for or recommending purchasing, leasing or ordering any good, facility, service, or item for which payment may be made in whole or in part under a Federal healthcare program,

shall be guilty of a felony and upon conviction thereof, shall be fined not more than $25,000 or imprisoned for not more than five years, or both.

(2) Whoever knowingly and willfully offers or pays any remuneration (including any kickback, bribe, or rebate) directly or indirectly, overtly or covertly, in cash or in kind to any person to induce such person —

(A) to refer an individual to a person for the furnishing or arranging for the furnishing of any item or service for which payment may be made in whole or in part under a Federal healthcare program, or

(B) to purchase, lease, order, or arrange for or recommend purchasing, leasing, or ordering any good, facility, service, or item for which payment may be made, in whole or in part under a Federal healthcare program,

shall be guilty of a felony and upon conviction thereof, shall be fined not more than $25,000 or imprisoned for not more than five years, or both.[4]

---

[3] Department of Justice, *Statement of Assistant Attorney General for the Civil Division Tony West Before the Senate Committee on the Judiciary*, (Jan. 26, 2011), *available online at* http://www.justice.gov/civil/opa/pr/testimony/2011/civ-testimony-110126.html.

[4] Social Security Act § 1128B(b), 42 U.S.C. § 1320a-7b(b).

## Federal Anti-Kickback Laws

The Health Reform Law amended the Anti-Kickback Statute by adding two new paragraphs to the law:

(g) In addition to the penalties provided for in this section or section 1128A, a claim that includes items or services resulting from a violation of this section constitutes a false or fraudulent claim for purposes of subchapter III of chapter 37 of title 31, United States Code.[5]

(h) With respect to violations of this section, a person need not have actual knowledge of this section or specific intent to commit a violation of this section.[6]

In addition to the above cited criminal penalties, violators are also subject to exclusion from the federal healthcare programs upon a determination by the Department of Health and Human Service (DHHS) Secretary (as delegated to the OIG) that a violation has occurred.[7] This allows the OIG to institute an action based on its own assessment that an anti-kickback violation has occurred, without waiting for a criminal conviction to trigger an exclusion. In addition, in 1997, Congress authorized the OIG to impose civil penalties in the form of treble damages plus $50,000 for each violation of the Anti-Kickback Statute.[8]

Several statutory exceptions are set forth in the Anti-Kickback Statute for the following:

- discounts which are properly disclosed and reflected in the costs claimed or charges made by the provider;
- payments by an employer to an employee for bona fide employment in the provision of covered items and services;
- amounts paid by providers to a group purchasing organization (GPO), where there is a written agreement between the providers and the GPO specifying the fee and the GPO discloses the amount of the administrative fee to providers purchasing from the GPO;
- waivers of coinsurance amounts in connection with certain federally qualified healthcare centers;
- activities protected by the safe harbor regulations (as will be described);
- certain risk-sharing arrangements;
- arrangements involving federally qualified health centers (FQHCs);
- waivers of cost-sharing under Medicare Part D; and

---

[5] The Health Reform Law, § 6402(f)(1), Social Security Act § 1128B(g); 42 U.S.C. 1320a-7b(g).
[6] The Health Reform Law, § 6402(f)(2); Social Security Act § 1128B(h); 42 U.S.C. 1320a-7b(h).
[7] Social Security Act § 1128(a)(7); 42 U.S.C. § 1320a-7(a)(7).
[8] Social Security Act § 1128B(b)(3); 42 U.S.C. § 1320a-7b(b)(3).

- discounts on certain drugs provided to beneficiaries under a Medicare coverage gap discount program.[9]

Those who engage in activities that fit within these exceptions are immune from prosecution under the Anti-Kickback Statute.

Despite the abundance of administrative interpretations, judicial decisions, and the promulgation of the safe harbor regulations, it is still unclear precisely which business arrangements the law prohibits and which business arrangements the law protects. Moreover, the reach of the Anti-Kickback Statute appears to be extending, rather than narrowing. As it is unlikely that this trend will reverse, the Anti-Kickback Statute promises to remain a central focus of healthcare activities for the foreseeable future.

## § 2-2  EVOLUTION OF THE ANTI-KICKBACK STATUTE

### § 2-2(a)  The Social Security Act of 1972

A statute proscribing kickbacks was first included in the Social Security Act (SSA) in 1972. Section 242(b) of the Social Security Amendments of 1972 added two new sections to the SSA - section 1877, applicable to the Medicare program, and section 1909, applicable to the Medicaid program.

At that time, the anti-kickback provision stated as follows:

(b) Whoever furnishes items or services to an individual for which payment is or may be made under this title and who solicits, offers, or receives any—

(1) kickback or bribe in connection with the furnishing of such items or services or the making or receipt of such payment, or

(2) rebate of any fee or charge for referring any such individual to another person for the furnishing of such items or services,

shall be guilty of a misdemeanor and upon conviction thereof shall be fined not more than $10,000 or imprisoned for not more than one year, or both.[10]

There was no requirement of intent (e.g., knowing and willful violation) in order to violate this provision, and violations were classified as misdemeanors. Although the illegal act had to be a "kickback," "bribe," or "rebate," these terms were not further defined in the statute; rather, courts were responsible for interpreting these terms. In one of the first prosecutions under this statute,

---

[9] Social Security Act § 1128B(b)(3); 42 U.S.C. § 1320a-7b(b)(3). Medicare Prescription Drug, Improvement, and Modernization Act of 2003 (MMA), Pub. L. 108-173, 117 Stat. 2066 codified at Social Security Act § 1860D-4(e)(6); 42 U.S.C. § 1395w-104(e)(6).

[10] Social Security Amendments of 1972, Pub. L. No. 92-603, 86 Stat. 1329 (1972).

*United States v. Porter*,[11] the federal government brought an action against a laboratory operator and group of physicians alleging that the laboratory's payment to the physicians for "handling fees" was a kickback in violation of this new law. In 1979, physicians were permitted to bill Medicare for a "handling fee" in addition to a laboratory fee to compensate physicians for time spent drawing blood samples. At that time, this "handling fee" was never more than six dollars. Rather than bill Medicare directly, however, the physicians billed the outside laboratory which paid the physicians up to $35 for each blood sample sent to the laboratory. The physicians claimed that the fees were for legitimate services and hence were "handling fees." The federal government claimed that the fees were "kickbacks" or "bribes."

Although the District Court in *Porter* convicted the two physicians and the laboratory operator, the Fifth Circuit Court of Appeals reversed the convictions. The Fifth Circuit acknowledged that because no provision of the statute or body of case law defined the words "kickback" or "bribe" the court "must assume that Congress used these words as they are commonly and ordinarily understood." According to the Fifth Circuit, the "handling fees" were not bribes because there was no element of corruption but rather a legitimate payment for services. The court also decided that the handling fees were not a kickback, since a kickback entails the secret return to an earlier possessor of part of a sum received. It was the lack of specificity in the law that led the court to its conclusion: "We are hard put to say with the degree of confidence required in a criminal conviction that these defendants were given clear warning by that statute that their conduct was prohibited by it, thus amounting to a criminal act."[12]

## § 2-2(b)   The Medicare-Medicaid Anti-Fraud and Abuse Amendments of 1977

As a result of *Porter* and other similar cases, as well as the federal government's inability to prosecute fraud and abuse situations under the statute, Congress enacted the Medicare-Medicaid Anti-Fraud and Abuse Amendments of 1977 (1977 Amendments). According to the Senate

---

[11] United States v. Porter, 591 F.2d 1048 (5th Cir. 1979).

[12] *Id.* at 1,054. In contrast to *Porter*, the court in *United States v. Hancock* upheld the conviction of two chiropractors for receiving "kickbacks" from a medical laboratory in which the chiropractors sent specimens for testing. The defendants relied upon the Fifth Circuit's holding in *Porter* to bolster their argument that these payments were not "kickbacks" because they were legitimate "handling fees" for actual services rendered. Nonetheless, the Seventh Circuit declined to follow the holding in *Porter* and held that the term "kickback" is to be interpreted more broadly to include "a percentage payment for granting assistance by one in a position to open up or control a source of income." *See* United States v. Hancock, 604 F.2d 999 (7th Cir. 1979).

Finance Committee report dated September 26, 1977, the existing language and penalties were insufficient to deter Medicare and Medicaid fraud.

> Recent hearings and reports, however, indicate that such penalties have not proved adequate deterrents against illegal practices by some individuals who provide services under Medicare and Medicaid. In addition, these misdemeanor penalties appear inconsistent with existing federal criminal code sanctions which make similar actions punishable as felonies. Also, it has been brought to the attention of the committee by U.S. Attorneys' offices which have utilized these Social Security Act sanctions in the prosecution of Medicare and Medicaid fraud cases that the existing language of these penalty statutes is unclear and needs clarification.[13]

The 1977 Amendments revised the anti-kickback provisions in an attempt to expand and provide greater specificity as to prohibited conduct. The 1977 Amendments broadened the statute to prohibit "any remuneration (including kickback, bribe, or rebate) directly or indirectly, overtly or covertly, in cash or in kind."[14] The 1977 Amendments also revised the statute to address not only those individuals and entities that solicit or receive remuneration in return for engaging in prohibited activity, but also those individuals and entities that offer or pay remuneration to induce a person to engage in such prohibited activity. Furthermore, the 1977 Amendments also elevated these fraudulent acts from misdemeanor status with a fine up to $10,000 and up to one year imprisonment, to felony status with a fine not to exceed $25,000 or imprisonment not more than five years. Another significant aspect of the 1977 Amendments was that they added two specific statutory exceptions for employees and certain discount arrangements.

In 1980, the 1977 Amendments were further modified to provide a requisite level of intent by adding the words "knowingly and willfully."[15]

## § 2-2(c)  Medicare and Medicaid Patient Program Protection Act of 1987

In the Medicare and Medicaid Patient and Program Protection Act of 1987, Congress not only gave the OIG civil sanction authority for kickback violations, but also mandated that the OIG promulgate regulations specifying permissible practices under the Anti-Kickback Statute.[16] The law's safe harbor

---

[13] S. Rep. No. 95-453, at 11 (1977).
[14] Medicare-Medicaid Anti-Fraud and Abuse Amendments of 1977, Pub. L. No. 95-142, 91 Stat. 1175 (1977).
[15] Omnibus Reconciliation Act of 1980, Pub. L. No. 96-499, 94 Stat. 2599 (1980).
[16] Medicare and Medicaid Patient and Program Protection Act of 1987, Pub. L. No. 100-93, 101 Stat. 682 (1987).

authority was Congress' response to the healthcare industry's request for some certainty in this uncertain area of the law. Prior to the 1987 law, the only route to obtaining protection from prosecution or other sanctions was through the adoption of express exceptions to the statute.

This provision provided that the DHHS, in consultation with the DOJ, was to publish proposed regulations not later than one year from the enactment of the law, and final regulations no later than two years from its enactment.

The statute stated that the regulations were to:

specify [ ] payment practices that shall not be treated as a criminal offense under section 1128B(b) of the Social Security Act and shall not serve as the basis for an exclusion under section 1128(b)(7) of such Act.[17]

The statute further specified that:

[A]ny practices specified in regulations pursuant to the preceding sentence shall be in addition to the practices described in subparagraphs (A) through (C) of section 1128B(b)(3) [the existing statutory exceptions].[18]

The legislative history directed DHHS to include in the regulations "any generic criteria that might apply to business arrangements generally."[19] (*See* discussion of these regulations at § 2-3, *infra*.)

## § 2-2(d) Health Insurance Portability and Accountability Act of 1996

In 1996, Congress passed the Health Insurance Portability and Accountability Act of 1996 (HIPAA), and although its main focus was to make health insurance coverage portable and continuous for workers, it also substantially increased the scope of fraud and abuse sanctions and established mechanisms for obtaining guidance from DHHS regarding the healthcare fraud and abuse laws, including the Anti-Kickback Statute.[20] HIPAA expanded the reach of the Anti-Kickback Statute beyond just the Medicare, Medicaid and other state healthcare programs to apply also to all "federal healthcare programs," with the exception of the federal employee health benefits program.[21] The term "federal healthcare program" also applies to all "State healthcare programs"

---

[17] *Id.*
[18] *Id.*
[19] H.R. REP. No. 100-85, pt. 2, at 27 (1987).
[20] Health Insurance Portability and Accountability Act of 1996, Pub. L. No. 104-191, 110 Stat. 1936 (1996) (HIPAA).
[21] Social Security Act § 1128B(f); 42 U.S.C. § 1320a-7b(f).

which include programs that receive funding under Title V (Maternal and Child Health Block Grants) and Title XX (Social Security Block Grants).[22]

HIPAA also created a new statutory exception for certain risk-sharing arrangements and required the DHHS to promulgate regulations implementing the risk-sharing exception through a negotiated rule making process which involved both the government and the managed care community.[23] (*See* discussion of the Interim Final Rule of the Shared-Risk Safe Harbors in § 2-3(g)(4), *infra*, as well as the discussion in Chapter 8.) Additionally, HIPAA created a mechanism by which the public could obtain advisory opinions from the DHHS to determine the applicability of certain laws, including the Anti-Kickback Statute, to particular factual situations.[24] (*See* discussion of the advisory opinion process in § 2-5, *infra*).

HIPAA also specifically created a new civil money penalty provision which prohibited individuals and entities from offering or transferring "remuneration" to Medicare and Medicaid beneficiaries in order to influence such beneficiaries to obtain healthcare items or services from a particular provider.[25] This provision, and the related regulations that were issued, are discussed in more detail in § 2-7(a), *infra*.

### § 2-2(e)  Balanced Budget Act of 1997

Contrary to common belief, prior to 1997, the government only had the ability to pursue criminal sanctions and civil sanctions through exclusion from the federal healthcare programs against an individual or entity for violating the Anti-Kickback Statute; the government could not impose civil monetary penalties. However, as part of the Balanced Budget Act of 1997 (BBA '97), Congress amended the civil money penalty (CMP) provisions to create a new statutory civil monetary penalty for violations of the Anti-Kickback Statute, in the amount of $50,000 for each violation, plus treble damages.[26] As cases brought under the Statute often allege numerous violations of the Anti-Kickback Statute, this CMP has proven to provide the government tremendous leverage in settlement negotiations.

### § 2-2(f)  Medicare Prescription Drug, Improvement, and Modernization Act of 2003

The Medicare Prescription Drug, Improvement and Modernization Act of 2003 (MMA) was enacted to provide for a voluntary program for prescription

---

[22] Social Security Act § 1128(g); 42 U.S.C. § 1320A-7(g).
[23] HIPAA, tit. II § 216, 110 Stat. 1936, 2007 (1996).
[24] *Id.* tit. II § 205, 110 Stat. 1936, 2001 (1996); 42 U.S.C. § 1320a-7d(b); 42 C.F.R. 1008 (1999).
[25] Social Security Act § 1128A(a)(5); 42 U.S.C. § 1320a-7a(a)(5).
[26] Balanced Budget Act of 1997, sec. 4304 (b)(2)(a); 42 U.S.C. § 1320a-7a(7).

drug coverage under the Medicare Program (Medicare Part D). In addition to the creation of a new drug benefit, MMA created statutory exceptions for arrangements involving FQHCs and for waivers of cost sharing under Medicare Part D. In addition, MMA required the DHHS Secretary to promulgate a safe harbor that embraces, with respect to healthcare entities, certain nonmonetary remuneration such as hardware, software, or information-technology devices used to provide electronic prescription-systems information.[27]

## § 2-2(g)  The Patient Protection and Affordable Care Act of 2010

The Patient Protection and Affordable Care Act (the Health Reform Law)[28] made two significant changes to the Anti-Kickback Statute. First, it ended the debate as to whether a violation of the Anti-Kickback Statute violates the FCA by providing that "a claim that includes items or services resulting from a violation of this [Anti-Kickback] section constitutes a false or fraudulent claim for purposes of the [False Claims Act]."[29] Therefore, if the government can show any kind of nexus between the amount of remuneration paid to a person and a referral, then by virtue of the Health Reform Law's "resulting from" provision, that anti-kickback violation taints subsequent claims for payment submitted to the government, rendering them all false claims under the FCA.

Second, section 6402 of the Health Reform Law explicitly states that "a person need not have actual knowledge of this [Anti-Kickback] section or specific intent to commit a violation of this section."[30] This means that a person can violate the Anti-Kickback Statute without the government having to prove specific intent to violate the statute. This also means that a person does not have to know about the Anti-Kickback Statute in order to violate it. As discussed in greater detail below, this modification to the Anti-Kickback Statute ended a longstanding debate regarding the intent requirement in the statute which followed the Ninth Circuit Court's 1995 opinion in *The Hanlester Network v. Shalala*.[31]

---

[27] Medicare Prescription Drug, Improvement and Modernization Act of 2003, Pub. L. No. 108-173, 117 Stat 2066, 2090 (2003).
[28] Patient Protection and Affordable Care Act (P.L. 111-148) § 6402(k), as amended by the Healthcare and Education Reconciliation Act of 2010 (Pub. L. 111-152) [hereinafter referred to as the "Health Reform Law"].
[29] The Health Reform Law, § 6402(f)(1); Social Security Act §1128B(g).
[30] The Health Reform Law, § 6402(f)(1); Social Security Act §1128B(h).
[31] Hanlester Network v. Shalala, 51 F.3d 1390 (9th Cir. 1995).

## § 2-3   SAFE HARBOR REGULATIONS

As described above, the Medicare and Medicaid Patient and Program Protection Act of 1987 authorized the OIG to promulgate "safe harbor" regulations to protect certain conduct from anti-kickback liability and to provide the industry with the types of activities that are permitted under the Statute.[32]

However, as a whole, the safe harbors still fall far short of creating a "bright line" test for anti-kickback violations that the OIG had promised. To a certain extent, this may be precisely the result intended by the OIG. Without clear guidelines, there may be a greater perception that an activity is not covered under the safe harbors and, therefore, will be considered fraudulent. This can create a "chilling effect" in that healthcare providers may fear that *any* practice not specifically permitted by the safe harbor regulations is prohibited, thereby subjecting providers to the prospect of civil and criminal penalties. Under these circumstances, many providers will refrain from engaging in any activity that remotely approaches violating the Anti-Kickback Statute, thereby making the statute "self-policing."

If a particular arrangement meets one of the applicable safe harbors, it is fully protected from both criminal and civil liabilities under the Anti-Kickback Statute.[33] On the other hand, the preamble to the first set of final safe harbor regulations makes clear that the safe harbors do not make any conduct illegal:

> This regulation does not expand the scope of activities that the statute prohibits. The statute itself describes the scope of illegal activities. The legality of a particular business arrangement must be determined by comparing the particular facts to the proscriptions of the statute.[34]

Similarly, failure to meet all of the requirements of a particular, applicable safe harbor does not make the conduct *per se* illegal. Rather, as the preamble to the final safe harbor regulations states regarding arrangements that do not fall squarely within a safe harbor:

> [An] arrangement may violate the statute in a less serious manner, although not be in compliance with a safe harbor provision. Here, there is no way to predict the degree of risk. Rather, the degree of risk depends on an evaluation of the many factors which are part of the decision-making process regarding case selection for investigation

---

[32] Medicare and Medicaid Patient and Program Protection Act of 1987, Pub. L. No. 100-93, 101 Stat. 682 (1987).

[33] 56 Fed. Reg. 35,954 (July 29, 1991). However, if an arrangement implicates two different safe harbors, (*e.g.*, an agreement between referral sources includes the provision of equipment through a lease arrangement and the provision of professional services as an employee), then both safe harbors must be satisfied in order to obtain full safe harbor protection.

[34] *Id.*

## Federal Anti-Kickback Laws

and prosecution. Certainly, in many (but not necessarily all) instances, prosecutorial discretion would be exercised not to pursue cases where the participants appear to have acted in a genuine good-faith attempt to comply with the terms of the safe harbor, but for reasons beyond their control are not in compliance with the terms of that safe harbor. In other instances, there may not even be an applicable safe harbor, but the arrangement may appear innocuous. But in other instances, we will want to take appropriate action.[35]

Unfortunately, the DHHS's pronouncements in this area were, at one time, somewhat ambiguous. In a December 1991 Program Memorandum, issued several months after the final safe harbor regulations, the OIG instructed the fiscal intermediaries to "ensure that all contracts between hospitals and hospital-based physicians *comply with* safe harbor provisions, and to notify the OIG of cases "that *may prove to be illegal within the meaning of the safe harbor provisions.*"[36] This Program Memorandum was later revised to modify the suggestion of "per se" illegality for arrangements not in conformity with the safe harbors. In a subsequent transmittal, DHHS acknowledged "confusion" over the prior issuance, and stated that "a hospital can have arrangements not covered in the safe harbor provisions that are not necessarily illegal."[37] However, the issuance still states that "to avoid all potential legal liability, contracts between hospitals and hospital-based physicians should comply with all the safe harbor regulations that may apply to the particular contract between the parties."[38]

Moreover, testimony in May 1992 by the OIG's Deputy Inspector General for Investigations suggested that the OIG might attempt to use lack of conformity with the safe harbor to prove criminal intent:

> The safe harbors regulations should also facilitate prosecution of the seriously abusive joint ventures because we are now able to show courts that those who choose to operate outside of the safe harbors can no longer claim that they are confused about how to operate a lawful joint venture.[39]

However, subsequent proposed safe harbor regulations clearly indicate that the OIG intends for compliance with the safe harbors to be *voluntary*.[40] The failure to comply with a safe harbor does not mean that an arrangement is illegal under the Anti-Kickback Statute. Rather, it simply means that the

---

[35] *Id.*
[36] CCH Medicare and Medicaid Guide ¶ 39,715, Program Memorandum, Transmittal No. A91-12 (Dec. 1991) (emphasis added).
[37] CCH Medicare and Medicaid Guide ¶ 13,915.44, Transmittal A-92-4 (Aug. 1992).
[38] *Id.*
[39] Hearing of the Subcommittee on Human Resources and Intergovernmental Relations, Committee on Government Operations (May 7, 1992) (statement of Larry D. Morey).
[40] 70 Fed. Reg. 38,081, 38,088 (July 1, 2005); 70 Fed. Reg. 59,015, 59,017 (Oct. 11, 2005).

legality of the arrangement must be evaluated on a case-by-case basis or by a facts and circumstances analysis. So long as the purpose of the arrangement is not to induce or reward the generation of federal healthcare program business, there would be no violation of the statute. Safe harbors do not require the restructuring of any arrangements, although parties may choose to restructure to take advantage of the safe harbor protection. However, parties unsure as to whether their existing or proposed arrangements fit within a safe harbor or whether they would be subject to OIG sanctions may apply for an advisory opinion.

### § 2-3(a)  History of the Various Safe Harbor Issuances

Set forth below is a listing of the various OIG safe harbor issuances:

- October 19, 1987—DHHS issued a Notice of Intent to Develop Regulations in the Federal Register. The notice asked the public to delineate generic "criteria" to be applied to particular types of business arrangements for safe harbor protection.[41]

- December 23, 1988—DHHS published a proposed regulation in the Federal Register,[42] but these regulations were withdrawn by DHHS days later "in order to consider this matter further."[43]

- January 23, 1989—DHHS again issued proposed regulations.[44] However, the new proposed regulations represented a significant tightening of the rule proposed the prior month. For example, in the December 23, 1988, Federal Register, the OIG included a proposed safe harbor that provided protection for waivers of inpatient deductible amounts; this safe harbor, however, was eliminated in the January 23, 1989, version.

- November 1989—A draft of the final safe harbor regulations was "leaked" to the healthcare industry.

- July 29, 1991—Almost four years after passage of the 1987 law, the OIG promulgated the first set of final safe harbor regulations.[45] These final safe harbor regulations covered the following eleven areas: (1) investment interests; (2) space rental; (3) equipment rental; (4) personal services and management contracts; (5) sale of practice; (6) referral services; (7) warranties; (8) discounts; (9) employees; (10) GPOs; and (11) waiver of beneficiary coinsurance and deductible amounts for

---

[41] 52 Fed. Reg. 38,794 (Oct. 19, 1987).
[42] 53 Fed. Reg. 51,856 (Dec. 23, 1988).
[43] 53 Fed. Reg. 52,448 (Dec. 28, 1988).
[44] 54 Fed. Reg. 3,088 (Jan. 23, 1989).
[45] 56 Fed. Reg. 35,932 (July 29, 1991).

## Federal Anti-Kickback Laws

Part A inpatient hospital services and certain federally qualified and federally funded health centers and healthcare facilities.

- November 5, 1992—The OIG published, in "interim final" form, safe harbors which addressed three specific areas related to managed care: (1) incentives offered to beneficiaries, such as the waiver or reduction of applicable coinsurance and deductible amounts, in order to encourage the use of the preferred provider network; (2) provider discounts to managed care plans; and (3) waivers of inpatient coinsurance and deductible amounts by Medicare SELECT PPOs.[46] Even though the regulation was published as an interim "final" rule, the public was permitted to submit post-publication comments, which the OIG acknowledged it would review in considering whether to revise the regulation.

- September 21, 1993—The OIG proposed several new safe harbor regulations, which addressed investment interests in rural areas, ambulatory surgical centers, and group practices. These new safe harbors also addressed specialty referral arrangements, cooperative hospital service organizations, recruitment practices, and the payment of obstetrical malpractice insurance subsidies paid to a practitioner in a rural area.[47]

- July 21, 1994—The OIG published proposed "clarifications" to the first set of final safe harbors that had been finalized in 1991.[48]

- January 25, 1996—The OIG revised the "interim final" managed care safe harbors and issued these managed care safe harbors in final form, effective upon publication.[49]

- November 19, 1999—The OIG issued several sets of regulations. First, the OIG finalized the proposed regulations that had been issued in 1993 and finalized the proposed clarifications from 1994. Second, the OIG issued an interim final rule, subject to public comments, setting forth two safe harbors for shared-risk arrangements.[50] This rule relates to the statutory exception for shared-risk arrangements that was added to the Anti-Kickback Statute as part of HIPAA.[51]

- December 4, 2001—The OIG published a final rule establishing a safe harbor for ambulance replenishing. This safe harbor protected arrangements involving hospitals or other receiving facilities that

---

[46] 57 Fed. Reg. 52,723 (Nov. 5, 1992).
[47] 58 Fed. Reg. 49,008 (Sept. 31, 1993).
[48] 59 Fed. Reg. 37,202 (July 21, 1994).
[49] 61 Fed. Reg. 2,122 (Jan. 25, 1996).
[50] 42 C.F.R. § 1001.952(t)-(u); *see also* 64 Fed. Reg. 63,504 (Nov. 19, 1999).
[51] 42 U.S.C. § 1320a-7b(b)(3)(F).

replenish drugs and medical supplies used by ambulance providers when transporting patients to the hospitals or receiving facilities.[52]

- September 25, 2002—The OIG published a proposed safe harbor that would expand the existing safe harbor for certain waivers of beneficiary coinsurance and deductible amounts to benefit Medicare SELECT policyholders.[53]
- July 1, 2005—The OIG published a proposed safe harbor in order to enable FQHCs to more easily provide medical care to underserved populations.[54]
- October 11, 2005—The OIG published a proposed safe harbor for certain arrangements involving the provision of electronic prescribing technology.[55]
- August 8, 2006—The OIG published a final rule establishing a safe harbors for certain electronic prescribing and electronic health records arrangements.[56] The electronic prescribing safe harbor protects arrangements whereby hospitals and certain other entities provide physicians (and certain other recipients under the safe harbor) with hardware, software, or information technology and training services necessary and used solely for electronic prescribing. The electronic health record safe harbor protects nonmonetary remuneration consisting of software or information technology and training services necessary and used predominately to create, maintain, transmit, or receive electronic health records if certain conditions are met. The transfer of such items must occur (and other conditions of the safe harbor must be met) on or before December 31, 2013.
- October 4, 2007—The OIG published the final rule relating to FQHC's.[57] The safe harbor protects the provisions of goods, items, services, donations or loans probived by a Donor to a FQHC, provided that certain conditions are met.

Annually, the OIG publishes a notice of solicitation requesting recommendations and proposals for developing new and modifying existing safe harbors.

---

[52] 66 Fed. Reg. 62,979 (Dec. 4, 2001).
[53] 67 Fed. Reg. 60,202 (Sept. 25, 2002).
[54] 70 Fed. Reg. 38,081 (July 1, 2005) (proposed safe harbors).
[55] 70 Fed. Reg. 59,015 (Oct. 11, 2005) (proposed safe harbors).
[56] 71 Fed. Reg. 45,110 (Aug. 8, 2006).
[57] 72 Fed. Reg. 56,632 (Oct. 4, 2007).

## Federal Anti-Kickback Laws

### § 2-3(b) Investment Interest Safe Harbors

The safe harbor for investment interests has drawn significant and sustained interest from the healthcare industry and there is a long history associated with the development of this safe harbor. The December 23, 1988, proposed safe harbor regulations aimed to protect small entities under two separate criteria.[58] First, the proposed regulation protected profit distributions in which a bona fide opportunity to invest was offered on an equal basis to those who could influence referrals and those who could not. Nothing required that the investors remain in a position to refer; the amount of the payment was proportional to the capital investment; and the capital was not related to the volume of referrals. Investments also were protected where the individual had a significant management role in the entity, if the investment was not related to the volume of referrals, and the payment was proportional to the capital contribution. However, as stated above, this regulation was withdrawn days after publication.[59]

The January 23, 1989, proposed regulations contained only a narrowly drafted safe harbor provision for return on investment from certain large, publicly held companies.[60] This proposed safe harbor required the entity to have $5 million in assets and a class of equity securities held of record by at least 500 persons. The previously considered safe harbor for investments in small entities was deleted; instead, comments were requested regarding extending safe harbor protection to smaller entities.

The final safe harbor for investment interests published in 1991 contained two separate sets of criteria: (1) investment interests in large, publicly held companies; and (2) investment interests held in smaller healthcare companies. In addition, in 1999, the OIG adopted a third set of criteria related to investment interests held in healthcare entities that are located in Medically Underserved Areas (MUAs), as well as investment interests held in ambulatory surgery centers (ASCs) and medical group practices.[61]

### § 2-3(b)(1)  Investment Interests in Large Entities

In order to qualify under the large entity safe harbor, a publicly traded company must have at least $50 million in undepreciated net tangible assets related to the furnishing of healthcare items or services. Moreover, equity securities must be registered with the Securities and Exchange Commission (SEC) and the investment interest must be obtained "on terms equally

---

[58] 53 Fed. Reg. 51,856 (Dec. 23, 1988).
[59] 53 Fed. Reg. 52,448 (Dec. 28, 1988).
[60] 54 Fed. Reg. 3,088 (Jan. 23, 1989).
[61] 42 C.F.R. 1001.952(a).

available to the public" through trading on a registered national securities exchange. Resulting from clarifications adopted by the OIG in 1999, language was added to this safe harbor in order to "clarify" that the investment interest (1) may not be subject to restrictions or limits on transferability that are not applicable to an investment held by members of the public and (2) must be obtained for the same price available to the general public.

For legal practitioners and their clients, the requirement that the investment interest must be obtained "on terms equally available to the public" through trading on a registered national securities exchange is perhaps the most frustrating of the standards, as it appears to preclude "roll-ups" of existing, provider-owned entities to meet the safe harbor. According to OIG staff:

> [I]f physicians buy shares in a closed deal before the shares go on sale to the public, that would not qualify. If they hold a special class of stock, a particular class of security that's only available to physician investors, that certainly is not qualifying. And also swapping limited partnership shares for publicly traded shares will not qualify. We think those don't meet the fundamental purposes behind this safe harbor to protect legitimately traded public securities. We're not saying all these deals . . . are necessarily bad, but we just will not give safe harbor protection.[62]

Additional requirements under this safe harbor include requirements that: neither the entity nor any investor (nor other individual acting on behalf of the entity or any investor in the entity) may make loans or loan guarantees to investors who may be in a position to refer business to the entity; dividends to investors must be in proportion to the amount of the investment and the entity may not market or furnish its services differently to passive investors than to non-investors.

## § 2-3(b)(2)    Investment Interests in Small Entities

To fit within the small entity safe harbor, each of the following eight standards must be satisfied.

> [*60/40 Investor Rule*] No more than forty percent (40%) of the value of the investment interests of each class of investments may be held in the previous fiscal year or previous twelve (12) month period by investors who are in a position to make or influence referrals to, furnish items or services to, or otherwise generate business for, the entity. [In 1999, the OIG added language to this requirement explaining that equivalent classes of equity investments may be combined.]

---

[62] Briefing by OIG on the Safe Harbor Regulations (Aug. 6, 1991).

## Federal Anti-Kickback Laws

[*Terms of Investment*] The terms on which an investment interest is offered to a passive investor,[63] who is in a position to make or influence referrals to, furnish items or services to, or otherwise generate business for the entity must be no different than the terms offered to other passive investors.

[*Investment Not Related to Referrals*] The terms on which an investment interest is offered to an investor who is in a position to make or influence referrals to, furnish items or services to, or otherwise generate business for the entity must not be related to the previous or expected volume of referrals, items, or services furnished, or amount of business otherwise generated, from that investor to the entity.

[*No Requirement to Generate Referrals*] There may not be any requirement that a passive investor make referrals to, be in a position to make or influence referrals to, furnish items or services to, or otherwise generate business for the entity as a condition for remaining as an investor.

[*Marketing Efforts*] The entity or any investor may not market or furnish the entity's items or services (or those of another entity as part of cross-referral agreement) to passive investors differently than to non-investors.

[*60/40 Revenue Rule*] No more than forty percent (40%) of the gross revenue of the entity in the previous fiscal year or previous twelve (12) month period may come from referrals or business otherwise generated from investors. In 1999, this requirement was changed to state that the only assets or revenues related to the furnishing of healthcare items or services may be counted for purposes of qualifying for these tests.

[*Prohibition on Loans*] Neither the entity nor any investor (nor other individual or entity acting on behalf of the entity or any investor in the entity) may loan funds to or guarantee a loan for an investor who is in a position to make or influence referrals to, furnish items

---

[63] According to 42 C.F.R. § 1001.952(a)(2)(viii), passive investors are defined in the final regulation as including limited partners, corporate shareholders, and holders of debt securities. Active investors are defined to include general partners who are responsible for the day-to-day management of the entity or those who agree in writing to undertake liability for the entity. The final safe harbor does not address whether members of a limited liability company (LLC) are passive investors, probably because this form of organization was not prevalent when the safe harbors were originally drafted. Presumably, the limited liability of LLC members would place them in the passive investor category as well. Nevertheless, limited partners and shareholders (and, presumably, LLC members) can qualify as active investors if they undertake entity liability, although this would defeat the purpose of the limited partnership and corporate forms of organization.

or services to, or otherwise generate business for the entity if the investor uses any part of such loan to obtain the investment interest.

[*Investment Return*] The amount of payment to an investor in return for the investment interest must be directly proportional to the amount of the capital investment of that investor.[64]

The most significant of these eight standards, and frequently the most difficult to meet, are the 60/40 Investor Rule and the 60/40 Revenue Rule. Under these rules, investors who are in a position to make or influence referrals to, furnish items or services to, or generate business for the entity comprise a "tainted pool" of investors and, as such, may account for only up to 40% of each class of the entity's investors and annual revenues. According to the preamble to the final safe harbor regulations, members of the "tainted pool" include not only physicians who refer patients to the entity, but also other potential referral sources, such as hospitals and other healthcare providers, as well as those who do business *in any manner* with the entity, including furnishing marketing or other services.[65] Thus, the "tainted pool" is not limited to only those investors who furnish Medicare- or Medicaid-covered items and services to the venture.

In the July 1994 proposed clarifications to the safe harbors, the OIG stated that an investor is tainted, with respect to the 60/40 Investor Rule, when the investor furnishes items or services to the joint venture, but that the OIG did not intend to have revenues that the joint venture derives from this investor also to be considered tainted for the 60/40 Revenue Rule. The OIG provides the following example:

> If a radiologist holds an investment interest in an imaging center and reads all of the films at the center, his or her reading of the film does not taint all the revenues from the referrals by non-investors. . . .
>
> We emphasize that if a radiologist-investor is reading the film and making referrals or otherwise generating business, then the revenues the joint venture derives from that activity would become tainted. For example, revenues would be tainted when a radiologist-investor takes part in a consultation with a non-investor internist, and during that consultation the radiologist recommends a procedure which is performed at the joint venture.[66]

In the 1999 final clarification, the OIG revisited this example in response to commenters' concerns, especially that the example seemed to imply that radiologist-investors seeking safe harbor protection would essentially be prohibited from practicing medicine because they would be precluded from

---

[64] 42 C.F.R. 1001.952(a).
[65] 56 Fed. Reg. 35,952, 35,964 (July 29, 1991).
[66] 59 Fed. Reg. 37,202, 37,205 (July 21, 1994).

## Federal Anti-Kickback Laws

recommending follow-up procedures. The OIG stated that they "continue to be persuaded that it is appropriate and consistent with our original intent that only healthcare related revenues be counted for purposes of the 60/40 revenue test." They did clarify, however, that:

> The occasional recommendation of additional testing by a radiologist to an attending physician with whom the radiologist has no financial arrangements and pursuant to a bona fide medical consultation is not prohibited under the anti-kickback statute. Accordingly, for purposes of the 60-40 revenue test, such consultative recommendations would not "taint" revenue derived from tests performed at the joint venture as a result of a subsequent referral of the patient by his or her attending physician for the recommended tests.[67]

In addition, the preamble to the final safe harbor regulations allows investors to "opt out" of the "tainted pool" by certifying in writing that they will not refer or otherwise generate business for, or furnish services to the entity, as follows:

> There are some very limited situations where, because of the special status or location of the investor, he or she does not fit within this category of investor doing business with the entity. For example, for the most part, retired physicians no longer make or influence referrals. In addition, typically a physician who resides and practices in a separate service area from the entity is similarly not "in a position to make or influence referrals." Or an investor could simply make an agreement barring him or her from actually making or influencing referrals to the entity. In all three examples, the determination whether an investor should be classified as doing business with the entity in which he or she has invested is a factual question. However, we will accept a written stipulation that for the life of the investment the investor will not make referrals to, furnish items or services for, or otherwise generate business for the entity. We emphasize that, because of the potential for abuse of this stipulation agreement, *the investor must be bound to this agreement for the life of the investment as long as he or she remains an investor.*[68]

This tactic, however, may not be useful where the primary goal of the venture is to provide the physician investors' patients with convenient access to needed healthcare services.

---

[67] 64 Fed. Reg. 63,518, 63,524 (Nov. 19, 1999).
[68] 56 Fed. Reg. 35,952, 35,964 (July 29, 1991) (emphasis added).

## § 2-3(b)(3) Investment Interests in Entities in Medically Underserved Areas (MUAs)

The safe harbor for investment interests in medically underserved areas (MUAs) was initially proposed by the OIG in 1993 as a safe harbor for investment interests in "rural" areas. The promulgated final rule expanded the scope to include MUAs, which by definition encompasses both rural and "urban" areas.[69]

Although many of the requirements for this safe harbor are similar to the small investment safe harbor (discussed earlier), there are several key areas that differ. This safe harbor eliminates the 60/40 Revenue Rule and changes the 60/40 Investor Rule to a 50/50 Investor Rule (*i.e.*, no more than 50% of the value of the investment interest of each class of investments may be held by investors who are in a position to make or influence referrals to, furnish items or services to, or otherwise generate business for the entity). In addition, the OIG has included a requirement that at least 75% of the business in the previous fiscal year or previous twelve-month period be derived from services furnished to persons in an MUA or who are members of a medically underserved population (MUP).

## § 2-3(b)(4) Investments in Group Practices

The OIG has adopted a safe harbor that protects returns on investments made to solo or group practitioners investing in their own practices as long as certain requirements are satisfied.[70] Cognizant of how most physician groups delegate much of the day-to-day management to one physician or a practice manager, the OIG deleted its proposal requiring that the group practice be composed of "active investors" and instead merely requires that the group practice be comprised of licensed professionals who practice as part of the group.

Additional requirements include that the physician's equity interest be held in the group practice itself and not a subdivision of the group, that the group satisfy the Stark Law's requirements for being a "group practice" and that revenues from ancillary services be derived from "in-office ancillary services" that meet the applicable definition under the Stark Law.[71] Moreover, the OIG has required that the group practice be organized "as a unified business with centralized decision-making, pooling of expenses and revenues, and a

---

[69] *See* 42 C.F.R. § 51c.102 ("Medically underserved population means the population of an urban or rural area designated by the Secretary as an area with a shortage of personal health services or a population group designated by the Secretary as having a shortage of such services.").
[70] 42 C.F.R. § 1001.952(p).
[71] *Id.*

## Federal Anti-Kickback Laws

compensation/profit distribution system that is not based on satellite offices operating substantially as if they were separate enterprises or profit centers."[72]

### § 2-3(b)(5)  Investments in Ambulatory Surgery Centers

In 1993, the OIG proposed adding a safe harbor protecting payments to surgeon-investors in ASCs who refer patients directly to the ASC and perform the surgery themselves on those patients.[73] In contrast to other investment interest safe harbors that limit investment by individuals in a position to refer, the proposed ASC safe harbor would have only protected entities whose investment interests were held entirely by such individuals.

However, in light of the tremendous volume of comments that the OIG received on this proposed safe harbor, the OIG had significantly revised the final rule by the time it was published in 1999. From the outset, the OIG created four different categories of ASC safe harbors: (1) surgeon-owned ASCs, (2) single-specialty ASCs, (3) multi-specialty ASCs (e.g., a mix of surgeons and specialists), and (4) hospital/physician-owned ASCs. In addition, not only can surgeons, physicians, and/or a hospital have an ownership interest in the entity, but certain other "non-tainted" investors can own an investment interest as long as they: (1) do not provide items or services to the ASC or its investors; (2) are not employed by the ASC or any investor; and (3) are not in a position to refer patients directly or indirectly to, or generate business for, the ASC or any of its investors.[74] Applicable to all four categories of ASCs are requirements that the ASC be Medicare certified, that the ASC's operating and recovery room space be dedicated exclusively to the ASC (i.e., if the ASC is located in a hospital, the ASC space must be dedicated exclusively to the ASC and not used by the hospital for the treatment of the hospital's inpatients or outpatients), and that all patients who are referred to the ASC by an investor must receive information about the investor's investment interest. In addition, all four categories include a requirement that all ancillary services be directly and integrally related to primary procedures performed at the ASC and that none may be separately billed to Medicare or other federal healthcare programs.[75]

With respect to the first three categories of ASC safe harbors (surgeon-owned ASCs, single-specialty ASCs and multi-specialty ASCs), each safe harbor requires that physician investors satisfy the "One-Third Practice Income Test," which requires that the physician investors derive at least one-third of their medical practice income for the previous twelve-month period from their own performance of procedures that require an ASC or hospital surgical

---

[72] 42 C.F.R. § 1001.952(p)(3)(ii).
[73] 58 Fed. Reg. 49,008 (Sept. 21, 1993).
[74] 42 C.F.R. § 1001.952(r).
[75] 64 Fed. Reg. 63,504, 63,535 (Nov. 19, 1999).

setting. Moreover, physician investors in the third category of ASC (i.e., a multi-specialty ASC) must satisfy another standard whereby at least one-third of the physicians' procedures that require an ASC or hospital surgical setting be performed at the ASC in which they are investing (the One-Third/One-Third Test).[76]

With respect to the fourth category (i.e., a hospital/physician ASC), the OIG has included a requirement that the hospital not be in a position to make or influence referrals directly or indirectly to the ASC or to any of its physician investors, which, from a practical perspective, may preclude many hospital/physician ASC joint ventures from qualifying for safe harbor protection.[77]

## § 2-3(c)   Space and Equipment Rental, and Personal Services and Management Contracts

The regulations create safe harbors for certain contracts for space rental, equipment rental, and personal services and management contracts.[78] These three separate safe harbors share common requirements.

Each safe harbor requires that a written agreement be executed. The agreement must be for a term of at least one year and must specify the aggregate payment amount as well as the premises, equipment or services covered. If the agreement does not contemplate full-time services, the agreement must also specify the schedule of intervals, their precise length, and the exact charge for such intervals. In addition, the payments must be based upon fair market value, and not vary on the volume or value of any Medicare- or state healthcare program-covered referrals or business generated between the parties. For purposes of space rental, fair market value means the value of the rental property for general commercial purposes. For purposes of equipment rental, fair market value means the value of the equipment when obtained from a manufacturer or professional distributor. However, the assessment of "fair market value" for space and equipment leases may not include additional value for location or convenience to sources of Medicare/state healthcare program business. An additional requirement for personal services and management

---

[76] 42 C.F.R. § 1001.952(r)(3); *see* OIG Advisory Op. No. 03-05.

[77] 42 C.F.R. § 1001.952(r)(4); *see* 64 Fed. Reg. 63,518, 63,538 (Nov. 19, 1999). *See also* OIG OIG Advisory Op. No. 01-17 (whether an ASC that is jointly owned by a hospital and five ophthalmologists violates the Anti-Kickback Statute). This arrangement met all of the requirements of the hospital-physician ASC safe harbor except one—as the hospital has a number of affiliation agreements with referring physicians, the hospital is in a position to make or influence referrals to the ASC. The OIG said it would not impose sanctions because the hospital had taken steps to limit its ability to direct or influence referrals to the ASC (*e.g.*, the hospital agreed not to take any actions to require or encourage affiliated physicians to refer patients to the ASC and the hospital would not track referrals made to the ASC) and found that these steps were satisfactory to reduce the likelihood that this arrangement would result in fraud.

[78] 42 C.F.R. §§ 1001.952(b)–(d).

## Federal Anti-Kickback Laws

contracts is that the services performed under the agreement must not involve the counseling or promotion of a business arrangement or other activity that violates any state or federal law.[79]

As part of the "clarifications" adopted by the OIG in 1999 and in order to "preclude schemes" involving the use of multiple overlapping contracts to circumvent the one year requirement, the OIG has added a requirement to all three safe harbors that the agreement cover all space, equipment or services for the term of the agreement.[80]

While these requirements appear sufficiently straightforward, it is far from simple to meet these safe harbors. Any agreements requiring percentage payments based on sales volume or any type of incentive compensation would be disqualified from safe harbor protection. Similarly, fee schedule payments, which by definition vary in the aggregate based on volume, would be outside the safe harbor. Even so-called "wear-and-tear" clauses in equipment leases, which provide for payments based on utilization in order to compensate equipment owners for the diminished value of heavily used equipment, are not protected.

Further, according to the OIG, "per-click" or "per use" fee arrangements between healthcare providers in a position to refer federal healthcare business may be prohibited under the Anti-Kickback Statute because payments under these arrangements are directly tied to the volume generated. Per-click arrangements commonly involve medical equipment leases that tie lease payments to the number of instances the equipment is used (or "clicked on"). Though per-click arrangements were once common for equipment such as gamma knives, lithotripters, MRI scanners and other types of equipment the OIG has been unequivocal in indicating that these arrangements will be subject to heightened scrutiny (in most instances these arrangements have been prohibited in a Stark context) because they are "inherently reflective of the volume or value of services ordered and provided."[81]

Despite this heightened scrutiny, on August 30, 2010, the OIG issued Advisory Opinion 10-14 addressing an arrangement whereby a hospital would compensate a sleep testing entity for providing sleep testing services on a per-click basis.[82] Under the arrangement, the sleep testing provider (the Requestor) contracted with a hospital (the Hospital) to provide the equipment, technology, supplies, and staff necessary to operate a sleep testing facility at

---

[79] In the July 1994 clarifications, the OIG proposed clarifying these safe harbors in order to prohibit parties from creating multiple overlapping agreements that purport to meet the safe harbors. 59 Fed. Reg. 37,205 (July 21, 1994).
[80] 42 C.F.R. §§ 1001.952(b)–(d).
[81] OIG Advisory Op. No. 10-14.
[82] Id. See also, OIG Advisory Op. No. 11-18. But see OIG OIG Advisory Op. No 10-23 (concluding that a similar Arrangement as that described in OIG Advisory Op. No. 10-14, does not pose a sufficiently low level of risk because of the marketing services that the Requestor would be providing).

the Hospital. Patients are referred to the Hospital's sleep testing facility by a physician. Under the arrangement, the Requestor was charging the Hospital a set per-test fee which was consistent with fair market value and not determined by taking in account the value or volume of referrals. While the arrangement could potentially generate prohibited remuneration under the Anti-Kickback Statute if the requisite intent was present, the OIG concluded that because there was an "acceptably low risk of improperly influencing or rewarding referrals," penalties would not be imposed absent a showing of such intent.

## § 2-3(d)   Sale of Practice

Although the "sale of practice" safe harbor originally only covered sales between practitioners, in 1999, the OIG expanded this safe harbor to also include the sale of a practice by a practitioner in an underserved area to a hospital.[83]

With respect to the sale of physician's practice to another practitioner, the sale must be completed within one year. The preamble to the final safe harbors makes clear that this does not mean that the payment period can only extend for a period of one year, but, rather, that the closing of the transaction must occur within one year of the first agreement (e.g., option, letter of intent) regarding the transaction.[84] In addition, the selling practitioner cannot remain in a position to generate business for the purchasing practitioner beyond the one-year period. Thus, the safe harbor would not protect any situation in which the physician who sells the practice is retained on its staff for any lengthy period of time following the practice purchase. While this does not necessarily mean all such transactions are illegal, it does mean that such transactions should be approached with caution, and the rationale for the transaction should be thoroughly documented.

With respect to payments made to a practitioner by a hospital or other entity to purchase the practitioner's practice, the safe harbor requires that: (1) the sale be completed within three years; (2) following the sale's completion, the practitioner not be in a position to make referrals to or generate business for the purchasing entity; (3) the practice be located in a Health Professional Shortage Area (HPSA) for the practitioner's specialty; and (4) the purchasing entity must, in good faith, engage in recruitment activities to find a new practitioner to take over the acquired practice.[85]

---

[83] 42 C.F.R. § 1001.952(e).
[84] 56 Fed. Reg. 35,952, 35,975 (July 29, 1991).
[85] 64 Fed. Reg. 63,518, 63,550 (Nov. 19, 1999).

## § 2-3(e)  Referral Services

The safe harbor regulations include a safe harbor for payments to "referral services." Under this safe harbor, a referral service may not exclude any person or entity that meets participation qualifications.[86] Although some providers feared that this requirement would mandate inclusion of all physicians in a particular geographic area, the final regulation makes clear that the referral service may qualify physicians according to its own criteria, so long as the criteria are applied equally to all participants and the referral service discloses to persons seeking referrals from the service how the group of its participants are selected, how individual participants are chosen, whether a fee is paid, the relationship between the participant and the service, and any restrictions that would exclude a participant.[87]

While it would appear that the referral service safe harbor would be relatively easy to meet, this is not always the case. The preamble states that the requisite disclosures must be made at the time the referral is made and not by follow-up letter.[88] Depending on the criteria the referral service has established for selecting participating physicians, this may prove difficult. For instance, if a referral service is comprised of the members of the active medical staff of a hospital, or members of a particular large group practice, then disclosure is straightforward. However, if the active staff or group alone does not provide full office coverage for the hospital's service area in all specialties, the hospital may wish to add certain members of the courtesy staff or others. Such additions would tend to make the requisite disclosure relatively unwieldy.

Additionally, the fees paid by the physician to the referral service may not exceed the actual cost for operating the service, and the fees may not be based on the volume or value of Medicare or state healthcare program business generated by the physician for the referral service. In fact, the OIG, in 1999, modified this safe harbor in order to state expressly that physicians cannot be charged varying membership fees based on referral patterns.[89] Finally, the referral service may not dictate to the physician how his services are to be furnished but may require that the physician not engage in discriminatory pricing.

Some in the healthcare industry have argued that the safe harbor permits a referral service run by a hospital to condition participation upon a certain number of inpatient admissions annually. However, caution should be exercised in this area. The safe harbor specifically states that physicians cannot be asked to pay a fee based on volume of Medicare or state healthcare program business

---

[86] 42 C.F.R. § 1001.952(f).
[87] *Id.*
[88] 56 Fed. Reg. 35,952, 35,976 (July 29, 1991).
[89] 64 Fed. Reg. 63,518, 63,526 (Nov. 19, 1999).

generated for the referral service. Rather, fee payments may be based only on the cost of operating the referral service. Moreover, according to the safe harbor preamble, the referral service safe harbor is relevant where the referral service does not charge a specific fee, but rather requires physicians to satisfy certain service obligations in order to participate in the referral service.[90] To the extent such obligations are related to requiring a particular volume of patient referrals, the referral service could be challenged as falling short of safe harbor protection.

### § 2-3(f)   Warranties

The safe harbors also protect payments or exchanges of value under certain manufacturer or supplier warranties. In order to qualify for safe harbor protection, both the buyer and the manufacturer or supplier must comply with specified reporting standards. The buyer must report in its cost report or claim for payment any price reduction or free item obtained as part of the warranty. The supplier or manufacturer must report such price reductions or free items on the buyer's invoice (or, if the amount is unknown, the existence of the warranty and the full documentation when known) and inform the buyer of its reporting obligations. The buyer also must furnish the invoice information to the Medicare or state healthcare program on request. Additionally, the warranty can only be for the item itself and cannot include payment to an individual or entity other than a beneficiary for any medical, surgical or hospital expenses incurred by a beneficiary. Finally, the safe harbor defines the term "warranty" under the Magnuson-Moss Warranty-Federal Trade Commission Improvement Act's definition of "written warranty" at 15 U.S.C. § 2301(6) governing the sale and warranty of consumer products, but the definition also includes one manufacturer's or supplier's agreement to replace another manufacturer's or supplier's defective item (which is covered by a "written warranty" as described above) on terms equal to the original written warranty.[91]

### § 2-3(g)   Statutory Exceptions with Analogous Safe Harbors

As previously stated, the Anti-Kickback Statute includes only a few statutory exceptions. However, over the years, the OIG has developed analogous safe harbors to these statutory exceptions.

---

[90] 56 Fed. Reg. 35,952, 35,975 (July 29, 1991).
[91] 42 C.F.R. § 1001.952(g). *But see* OIG OIG Advisory Op. No. 02-06, in which the OIG took the position that a reimbursement guarantee would not be protected by the warranty safe harbor because, according to the OIG, "the warranty must be related to product failure."

## Federal Anti-Kickback Laws

### § 2-3(g)(1)   Employees

As described earlier, the 1977 Amendments created a statutory exception for payments to employees. The employment exception extends to "any amount paid by an employer to an employee (who has a bona fide employment relationship with such employer) for employment in the provision of covered items or services."[92] The Senate Finance Committee reported that:

> The term would exclude any amount paid by an employer to an employee for employment in the provision of covered items and services if such employee has a bona fide employment relationship with the employer. The committee has specified that the employment relationship must be bona fide to insure that other arrangements involving the payment of a salary or related benefits will not be excluded from the definition of "any remuneration."[93]

When the 1977 Amendments were being considered on the floor of the United States House of Representatives, then-Representative Rostenkowski (D-IL), a member of the House Ways and Means Subcommittee on Health, stated as follows with regard to the employee exception:

> In broadening these criminal provisions, your committee sought to make clear that kickbacks are wrong no matter how a transaction might be constructed to obscure the true purpose of a payment. In exempting reimbursement by employers to employees "for employment in the provision of covered services," the committee intended to exempt only those payments that represented payments for legitimate employment. *For example, if a distributor of equipment or supplies pays a retailer on a commission basis for the use of his store to sell a product, such payment would represent a legitimate payment to a legitimate agent employed in a traditional manner to sell a product. That is a simple extension of the conventional chain of sale.* On the other hand, the payment by a laboratory of the salary of an employee of a physician or of a clinic as an inducement to the physician or the clinic to refer business to the laboratory uses the employment relationship simply as a guise to pay a kickback. We are in a complex area where right and wrong are often clouded with shades of gray. In such situations, the committee stresses the need to recognize that the substance rather than simply the form of a transaction should be controlling.[94]

---

[92] Social Security Act § 1128B(b)(3)(B); 42 U.S.C. § 1320a-7b(b)(3)(B).
[93] S. REP. No. 453, 95th Cong., 1st Sess. 12 (1977).
[94] 123 Cong. Rec. H30279 (daily ed. Sept. 22, 1977) (statement of Rep. Rostenkowski) (emphasis added).

However, in the final safe harbors, the protection provided for employment arrangements was narrowed based upon the definition of "employee" in the United States Internal Revenue Code.[95] The safe harbors provide that the term "employee" has the same meaning as it does for purposes of 26 U.S.C. § 3121(d)(2),[96] which adopts the "usual common law rules." The OIG states in the preamble that the term "employee" is defined not only by the Internal Revenue Code provision itself, "but also by the IRS's interpretation of that provision as codified in its regulations and other interpretive sources."[97] A common law employment relationship exists when:

> The person for whom services are performed has the right to control and direct the individual who performs the services, not only as the result to be accomplished by the work, but also as to the details and means by which that result is accomplished. That is, an employee is subject to the will and control of the employer not only as to what shall be done but how it shall be done.[98]

Thus, despite the significant legislative history described above suggesting that Congress intended a broader meaning for the term "employee," this position was rejected by the OIG:

> We continue to reject this approach because of the existence of widespread abusive practice by salespersons who are independent contractors and, therefore, who are not under appropriate supervision and control. . . .[99]

According to the OIG, "the employer-employee relationship is unlikely to be abusive, in part because the employer is generally fully liable for the actions of its employees and is therefore more motivated to supervise and control them." Moreover, according to the OIG, "Representative Rostenkowski's remarks do not reflect congressional intent in this case. His comments related to the House version of the employee exception that was rejected by the Conference Committee. Instead, Congress passed the Senate version, which expressly limited the exception to bona fide employment relationships."[100] Therefore, independent contractor arrangements fall outside safe harbor protection unless they otherwise meet the safe harbor for personal services and management contracts described at § 2-3(c), above.

Because the statute protects "employment in the provision of covered items or services," the OIG has suggested in speeches and certain correspondence that the employee exception "does not cover any and all payments to

---

[95] 56 Fed Reg. 35,987 (July 29, 1991).
[96] 42 C.F.R. § 1001.952(i).
[97] 56 Fed. Reg. 35,981 (July 29, 1991).
[98] 26 U.S.C. § 3121(d)(2).
[99] 56 Fed. Reg. 35,981 (July 29, 1991).
[100] Id.

## Federal Anti-Kickback Laws

employees. . . ."[101] Consequently, while there is no express fair market value limitation in the employee exception safe harbor, the OIG has indicated that payments in excess of the fair market value of the services furnished may suggest that the excess is for referrals, which are not a "covered item or service." These OIG positions continue to remain untested and contradict statements in the original safe harbor regulations as well as Congressional intent in adopting the employee exception.

### § 2-3(g)(2)    Discounts

The 1977 Amendments also added a statutory exception for discounts and other reductions in price which are properly disclosed and appropriately reflected in the costs or charges claimed by the provider. The statute permits "a discount or other reduction in price obtained by a provider of services or other entity under a federal healthcare program if the reduction in price is properly disclosed and appropriately reflected in the costs claimed or charges made by the provider or entity. . . ."[102]

In the Report of the Ways and Means Committee of the House of Representatives that accompanied the enactment of the 1977 Amendments, the committee generally described the discount exception as follows:

> [T]he bill would specifically exclude the practice of discounting or other reductions in price from the range of financial transactions to be considered illegal under [M]edicare and [M]edicaid, but only if such discounts are properly disclosed and reflected in the costs for which reimbursement could be claimed. The committee included this provision to ensure that the practice of discounting in the normal course of business transactions would not be deemed illegal. In fact, the committee would encourage providers to seek discounts as a good business practice which results in savings to [M]edicare and [M]edicaid program costs.[103]

In addition, when the 1977 Amendments were considered on the floor of the United States House of Representatives, Representative Rostenkowski stated in reference to a technical amendment, which was eventually adopted, that the purpose of the amendment was "to clarify that lawful discounts received by providers which are passed on under the program in the form of lower costs are to be encouraged."[104]

---

[101] Letter from D. McCarty Thornton, Associate General Counsel, OIG, to T.J. Sullivan, Technical Assistant, Office of the Associate Chief Counsel, IRS (Dec. 22, 1992), *available online at* http://oig.hhs.gov/fraud/docs/safeharborregulations/acquisition122292.htm.
[102] Social Security Act § 1128B(b)(3)(A); 42 U.S.C. § 1320a-7b(b)(3)(A).
[103] H.R. Rep. No. 393, 95th Cong., 1st Sess. pt. 1 (1977).
[104] 123 Cong. Rec. H30530 (daily ed. Sept. 23, 1977) (statement of Rep. Rostenkowski).

The OIG has adopted safe harbors related to the statutory exceptions as it has taken the position that its role is "to define innocuous arrangements that should not be prosecuted, including the statutory exceptions."[105] Despite the fact that discounts are protected by both a statutory exception and a safe harbor, very few discount arrangements were afforded any meaningful protection under the safe harbor provisions originally enacted in 1991. There has been much debate as to the relationship between the statutory exception and the safe harbors. In the preamble to the 1991 final safe harbors, the preamble to the 1994 proposed clarifications, and in the November 19, 1999, final rule, the OIG has taken the position that "the regulatory safe harbor protects all discounts or reductions in price protected by Congress in the statutory exception" and that the discount safe harbor "expands upon the statutory safe harbor by defining additional discounting practices not included in the statutory exception that are not abusive."[106] The first judicial decision to consider the relationship between the discount exception and the discount safe harbor is *United States v. Shaw*.[107]

In contrast to the statute, which only requires that the discount be "properly disclosed and appropriately reflected" in the entity's Medicare and Medicaid costs or charges, the safe harbor sets forth a restrictive definition of the term "discount," excluding such typical discount arrangements as discounts not applicable to Medicare or Medicaid and discounts given directly to beneficiaries (e.g., coinsurance waivers).[108] In addition, although the safe harbor originally excluded from the definition of "discount" the provision of discounted or free items or services in exchange for the purchase of different items or services, the OIG "clarified" this exclusion so as to allow this type of discount arrangement if the goods and services are reimbursed by the same federal healthcare program using the same methodology, such as a DRG payment, and where the discount is fully and accurately disclosed and reflected.[109] The OIG recognized that discounts offered on one good or service to induce the purchase of another good or service where there is no risk of cost shifting from one payment methodology to another or cost distortion should not pose a risk of program abuse. Indeed, such financial arrangements may allow the federal healthcare programs to recognize cost savings.

In addition to buyers and sellers, the OIG created in 1999 a new category of an "offeror," which is an individual or entity who is not a seller but who promotes the purchase of an item or service by a buyer at a reduced price (e.g., a manufacturer that sells to a wholesaler would be an "offeror").[110]

---

[105] 56 Fed. Reg. 35,952, 35,957 (July 29, 1991).
[106] 64 Fed. Reg. 63,518, 63,528 (Nov. 19, 1999).
[107] *See* United States v. Shaw, 106 F. Supp 2d 103 (D. Mass. 2000).
[108] 42 C.F.R. § 1001.952(h).
[109] 64 Fed. Reg. 63,518, 63,527 (Nov. 19, 1999).
[110] 64 Fed. Reg. 63,518, 63,528 (Nov. 19, 1999).

## Federal Anti-Kickback Laws

Similar to sellers, the ability of an offeror to qualify for safe harbor protection is dependent upon the offeror satisfying certain requirements that are based upon the type of purchaser. The OIG provides that nothing in the regulations precludes managed care organizations, wholesalers or group purchasing organizations from qualifying as "offeror."

In 1999, the OIG modified the proposed definition of a "rebate" to include any discount in which the methodology that will be used to calculate the rebate is fixed at the time of the sale of the good or service and disclosed to the buyer, but which is not received at the time of the sale of the good or service.[111] The OIG stated that it modified the definition of a rebate in order to extend safe harbor protection to charge-based buyers, such as pharmacies and outpatient clinics, for discounts made at the time of sale, as well as to buyers that are reimbursed based on federal program fee schedules. The OIG also eliminated the safe harbor requirement that charge-based buyers disclose the amount of discounts on claims submitted to the federal programs, which always was an awkward requirement for charge-based buyers.

The protection provided under the discount safe harbor is categorized based upon the type of party involved in the transaction (buyers, sellers, and offerors) with the safe harbor placing different requirements on the respective parties depending on the type of purchaser involved. The safe harbor provides protection to buyers that are Medicare and/or Medicaid risk contractors without imposing any reporting requirements. However, cost reporting entities not only must report the discount on the cost report but also must earn the discount within a single fiscal year and claim the benefit of the discount in that or the following fiscal year.[112] All other purchasers, such as Part B suppliers, can only take advantage of discounts made at the time of the original sale or the terms of the rebate must be fixed and disclosed in writing to the buyer at the time of the initial sale of the good or service.

With respect to sellers, the safe harbor provides protection for discounts given to cost reporting entities as long as the seller reports the discount on the purchaser's invoice and informs the buyer in a manner that is "reasonably calculated" to give notice to the buyer of its obligations to report such discount. In 1999, the OIG modified the safe harbor by deleting the requirement that a seller inform a buyer "in an effective manner" of the buyer's obligation to report the discount and replacing it with a requirement that the seller inform the buyer of its reporting obligations "in a manner that is reasonably calculated to give notice to the buyer."[113] However, the OIG declined to prescribe a specific form of notice and also declined to provide examples of seller impediments to the buyer's compliance with the reporting requirements.

---

[111] 64 Fed. Reg. 63,518, 63,527 (Nov. 19, 1999).
[112] 42 C.F.R. § 1001.952(h)(1).
[113] 64 Fed. Reg. 63,518, 63,528 (Nov. 19, 1999).

For cost reporting entities, the safe harbor also provides that if the value of the discount is unknown at the time of the sale, the seller can disclose the existence of the discount program on the invoice and furnish the additional documentation later. For all other type of entities, the seller's obligations are dependent upon whether the seller submits a claim or request for payment on behalf of the buyer or whether the buyer submits such claims on its own behalf.

### § 2-3(g)(3)   Group Purchasing Organizations

In 1986, following the pronouncements of the OIG and DOJ that they had no authority to protect GPO arrangements, Congress added a statutory exception authorizing payments to GPOs. The statute provides an exception for:

> (C) any amount paid by a vendor of goods or services to a person authorized to act as a purchasing agent for a group of individuals or entities who are furnishing services reimbursed under title XVIII or a State healthcare program if—
>
> (i) the person has a written contract with each such individual or entity, which specifies the amount to be paid the person, which amount may be a fixed amount or a fixed percentage of the value of the purchases made by each such individual or entity under the contract, and
>
> (ii) in the case of an entity that is a provider of services (as defined in section 1861(u)), the person discloses (in such form and manner as the Secretary requires) to the entity and, upon request, to the Secretary the amount received from each such vendor with respect to purchases made by or on behalf of the entity.[114]

However, within the final safe harbors, the OIG adopted a restrictive definition of GPOs, excluding GPOs that are wholly owned by a corporate entity that is part of the same corporate family as the entities for whom the GPOs are purchasing.[115] The safe harbor, like the statute, requires a written agreement between the GPO and those for whom the GPO is purchasing. The statute also requires that the agreement specify the amount the vendor pays the GPO irrespective of the amount, while the safe harbor permits the agreement to state that vendors will pay the GPO a fee of 3% or less of the purchase price of the vendor's goods. If the fee is more than 3%, the agreement must specify the amount, or if unknown, the maximum amount, of the GPO payment by each vendor. The GPO must disclose at least annually to "providers" (which includes hospitals, home health agencies, and others paid pursuant

---

[114] Social Security Act § 1128B(b)(3)(C); 42 U.S.C. § 1320a-7b(b)(3)(C).
[115] 42 C.F.R. § 1001.952(j)(2).

## Federal Anti-Kickback Laws

to Medicare Part A, but not Medicare Part B suppliers of services) and to the Medicare program on request, the amount received from each vendor for purchases made for the provider.[116]

Note that the statutory exception and the safe harbor protect only the payments that vendors may make to a GPO. However, the discounts obtained by the GPO's purchasers still must be analyzed separately under the provisions relating to discounts.

### § 2-3(g)(4)  Risk-Sharing Arrangements

As described earlier, HIPAA contained a statutory exception for certain risk-sharing arrangements.[117] The legislation sets forth an exception for "any remuneration between an organization and an individual or entity providing items or services" in a written agreement with a Medicare contracting managed care organization. Non-contracting managed care organizations are protected if the written agreement, through a risk-sharing arrangement, places the individual or entity at substantial financial risk for the cost or utilization of the services provided.

In addition, Congress authorized the development of safe harbors concerning risk-sharing arrangements through a negotiated rulemaking process. Under this new process, representatives of the federal agency and various interest groups were brought together to negotiate the text of the regulation. While generally a negotiated rulemaking committee produces a proposed rule, Congress provided that the committee's results, in this instance, were to be published as an interim final rule for public comment. Although the target date for publication was January 1997, it was not until January 1998 when the rulemaking committee issued a safe harbor proposal for shared-risk arrangements, which then did not get published in the *Federal Register* as an interim final rule until November 1999.[118]

In the interim final rule, the OIG set forth two safe harbors for shared risk arrangements. The first safe harbor protects price reductions that are offered to "Eligible Managed Care Organizations" (EMCOs), which are defined to include HMOs and CMPs with a risk or cost-based contract; Medicare+Choice organizations that receive a capitation payment; certain Medicaid managed care organizations, Programs for the All Inclusive Care for the Elderly, and federally qualified HMOs.[119] To qualify under the second safe harbor, the risk sharing arrangement must be part of a "Qualified Managed Care Plan" (QMCP), which is defined as a managed care entity that satisfies the requirements of the definition of a "health plan" located in the managed care safe

---

[116] 56 Fed. Reg. 35,987 (July 29, 1991).
[117] HIPAA, tit. II § 216, 110 Stat. 1936, 2007 (1996).
[118] 64 Fed. Reg. 63,504 (Nov. 19, 1999).
[119] 42 C.F.R. § 1001.952(t).

harbor related to beneficiary incentives.[120] Moreover, a QMCP must adopt processes and procedures to assure that the healthcare services are managed, (e.g., utilization review procedures, grievance procedure requirements). The safe harbor also requires either that no more than 10% of the QMCP's beneficiary population be Medicare beneficiaries (excluding those individuals where Medicare is secondary) or that no more than 50% are Medicare beneficiaries but only if the premium payments are made on a periodic basis and do not take into account various factors.

## § 2-3(g)(5)    Coinsurance and Deductible Waivers

The Anti-Kickback Statute provides two exceptions concerning coinsurance and deductible waivers. Section 1320a-7b(3)(D) pertains to a waiver of any coinsurance by a FQHC, while Section 1320a-7b(3)(G) was added as part of MMA for waivers or reductions by pharmacies of cost-sharing obligations imposed under Part D if certain conditions are met.

In addition, the OIG has created a safe harbor for waivers of coinsurance and deductible amounts pertaining to inpatient services furnished by hospitals and paid under the Prospective Payment System, and, as required by statute, to certain services furnished by FQHCs and similar healthcare facilities receiving Public Health Service and Title V grants.[121] The safe harbor does not apply to waivers with respect to physician and supplier services paid under Medicare Part B, nor does it apply to coinsurance and deductible waivers granted in the context of managed care arrangements.

Medicare Part B waivers have been the subject of an OIG Medicare Fraud Alert, which is described at § 2-4(b), below. On September 25, 2002, the OIG also issued a proposed rule that would expand the existing safe harbor for certain waivers of beneficiary coinsurance and deductible amounts relating to Medicare SELECT.[122] The expansion of the safe harbor would have protected waivers of coinsurance and deductible amounts under Part A or Part B for those beneficiaries covered by Medicare SELECT. Prior to this proposed rule the OIG only protected waivers of cost-sharing amounts for hospital inpatient services. The expansion of protection to cover all waivers of cost-sharing for Medicare services covered by Medicare SELECT would have had the effect of providing greater choice in coverage for beneficiaries while possibly lowering the price of supplemental insurance coverage under Medicare SELECT.[123] However, the OIG has never issued a final rule related to Medicare SELECT. Other waivers of coinsurance and deductible amounts

---

[120] 42 C.F.R. § 1001.952(u).
[121] 42 C.F.R. § 1001.952(k).
[122] 67 Fed. Reg. 60,202 (Sept. 25, 2002). Medicare SELECT is a Medicare supplemental insurance policy that requires beneficiaries to use a provider network to receive supplemental benefits.
[123] 67 Fed. Reg. 60,203 (Sept. 25, 2002).

## Federal Anti-Kickback Laws

in connection with managed care programs are the subject of a separate final safe harbor regulation.

### § 2-3(g)(6)  Federally Qualified Health Centers

MMA amended the Anti-Kickback Statute to create a new safe harbor for certain agreements involving FQHCs. On October 4, 2007, the OIG published a final rule establishing a safe harbor for certain health centers funded under Section 330 of the Public Health Service Act, which is a health center program designed to assist individuals living in medically underserved areas and populations with limited access to healthcare resources.[124] The safe harbor excludes remuneration between a health center and an individual or entity providing goods, items, services, donations, loans, or a combination of these to the health center pursuant to a contract, lease, grant, loan, or other agreement, provided that the agreement contributes to the health center's ability to maintain or increase its services to the medically underserved.[125] The remuneration must be "medical or clinical in nature or relate directly to patient services" such as billing services, administrative support services, technology support and the like. The proposed safe harbor clearly states that MMA does not protect remuneration from a health center to an individual or entity. This prohibition applies to individuals affiliated with the health center, including board members, physicians, or other healthcare professionals. In order for the remuneration to be protected the arrangement would have to be in writing, signed by the parties and cover all the goods, services, donations, and loans provided by the individual to the entity. The arrangement must contribute "meaningfully" to the health center's ability to treat medically underserved populations; therefore, an arrangement that only provides a minor benefit to a medically underserved population would not qualify for protection under this proposed safe harbor.[126]

### § 2-3(g)(7)  Electronic Prescribing

In August 2006, DHHS promulgated a final rule establishing an e-prescribing safe harbor,[127] and between 2005 and 2008 DHHS promulgated two additional rules, which taken together establish a comprehensive and uniform set of standards for e-prescribing under Medicare Part D.[128]

Safe harbor protection applies to e-prescribing hardware, software, and information technology and training services that are necessary and used

---

[124] 72 Fed. Reg. 56,632 (Oct. 4, 2007).
[125] 42 C.F.R. 1001.952(w).
[126] *Id.*
[127] 71 Fed. Reg. 45,110 (Aug. 8, 2006).
[128] 73 Fed. Reg. 18,918 (Apr. 7, 2008); 70 Fed. Reg. 67,568 (Nov. 7, 2005).

solely to receive and transmit electronic prescription information. Examples of protected products and services include electronic clinical support tools, tools that provide access to formulary information, and operating software required for hardware usage.[129] The final safe harbor applies if eight conditions are met. Among these conditions, the items and services may be provided: (a) in the case of a hospital, by the hospital to physicians who are members of its medical staff; (b) in the case of a group practice, by the group practice to prescribing healthcare professionals who are members of the group practice (including not only physicians, but other healthcare professionals who are authorized to prescribe by state licensing laws); and (c) in the case of a PDP sponsor or MA organization, by the sponsor or MA organization to pharmacists participating in the network of such sponsor or organization and to prescribing healthcare professionals.[130]

The safe harbor does not protect the donation of unnecessary technology or technology that is functionally equivalent to products and services already possessed by a recipient. If the OIG discovers that a donor had actual knowledge or acted in reckless disregard or deliberate ignorance of the fact that a recipient already possessed functionally equivalent technology, then neither party can receive safe harbor protection. However, the final safe harbor has abandoned language from the proposed safe harbor that would have required donors to certify that donated products and services are technically or functionally superior to those already possessed by the recipient. Instead, the OIG recommends that donors make "reasonable inquiries" (which should not usually require the use of technical experts) about a recipient's existing e-prescribing capabilities before donating.[131]

In addition to the "necessary" requirement, only technology used solely for e-prescribing purposes can receive safe harbor protection. For technology to serve an e-prescribing purpose, it must provide information or perform functions necessary to formulate, transmit, or receive a medically appropriate prescription for a patient. Technology that directly relates to e-prescribing, such as electronic clinical support software that identifies alternative drug therapies, drug-drug interactions, or payor formulary information, satisfies this requirement. Technology that bundles e-prescribing functions with unrelated functions, such as patient billing or scheduling, will not satisfy this requirement.[132]

Donated e-prescribing technology will not receive safe harbor protection unless it meets DHHS standards for e-prescribing systems.[133] These standards, established to ensure that e-prescribing technology is interoperable,

---

[129] 71 Fed. Reg. 45,116–45,117 (Aug. 8, 2006); 42 C.F.R. § 1001.952(x).
[130] 42 C.F.R. § 1001.952(x)(1).
[131] 71 Fed. Reg. at 45,123.
[132] *Id.* at 45,115.
[133] 42 C.F.R. § 1001.952(x)(2).

## Federal Anti-Kickback Laws

consist of rules relating to all aspects of e-prescribing, such as the electronic transmittal of information between providers and pharmacists, eligibility and benefits queries, formulary and benefit information, medication history, and network compatibility. Before being incorporated into law, DHHS tested many of these rules through pilot programs conducted at various provider and pharmacy settings throughout the country.[134]

The OIG also conditioned safe harbor protection on compliance with specific rules relating to the selection of donors and recipients. Recipients may not make the donation of e-prescribing technology a prerequisite for doing business with a donor, and neither the donor nor the recipient may directly or indirectly base selection on the volume or value of referrals or other business generated between the parties. The safe harbor permits selection based on the total number of prescriptions written by a recipient, but does not permit selection based on the value of prescriptions written by the recipient, or the volume or value of prescriptions written by a recipient that are reimbursable to any federal healthcare program.[135]

Also, parties seeking safe harbor protection must satisfy the following additional requirements: (1) where possible, recipients must have the ability to use donated e-prescribing technology on all patients without regard to payor status;[136] (2) arrangements between donors and recipients must be written and signed by the parties;[137] (3) the donor must not take any action to restrict the compatibility of donated e-prescribing technology with other e-prescribing or electronic health record systems;[138] and (4) such arrangements must identify with specificity the items or services being provided (but do not have to specify the value of the donated technology).[139] The final e-prescribing safe harbor abandoned language from the proposed safe harbor that would have limited the aggregate value of e-prescribing technology that a donor could provide to a qualifying recipient. As a result, in the final regulations, there is no cap on the value of services that a donor can provide or a recipient can receive.[140]

### § 2-3(h) Managed Care Safe Harbors

In November 1992, the OIG published a set of safe harbor regulations in "interim final" form, which protected certain limited managed care activities from the reach of the Anti-Kickback Statute.[141] Even though the

---

[134] 71 Fed. Reg. 45,115 (Aug. 8, 2006); Center for Medicare & Medicaid Services, http://www.cms.hhs.gov/eprescribing/ (last visited Aug. 11, 2011).
[135] 71 Fed. Reg. 45,118 (Aug. 8, 2006).
[136] 42 C.F.R. § 1001.952(x)(4).
[137] 42 C.F.R. § 1001.952(x)(7).
[138] 42 C.F.R. § 1001.952(x)(3).
[139] 71 Fed. Reg. 45,119 (Aug. 8, 2006); 42 C.F.R. § 1001.952(x)(7).
[140] 71 Fed. Reg. 45,118, 45,119 (Aug. 8, 2006).
[141] 57 Fed. Reg. 52,723 (Nov. 5, 1992).

regulation was published as a final rule, the public was permitted to submit post-publication comments, which the OIG acknowledged it would review in considering whether to revise the regulation. Subsequently, on January 25, 1996, the OIG issued these safe harbor regulations in "final" form, effective immediately upon publication.[142]

This set of final managed care safe-harbor regulations addresses three specific areas relevant to managed care activities: (i) incentives offered to beneficiaries, such as the waiver or reduction of applicable coinsurance and deductible amounts, in order to encourage the use of the preferred provider network; (ii) provider discounts to managed care plans; and (iii) waivers of inpatient coinsurance and deductible amounts by Medicare SELECT PPOs.[143]

The managed care safe harbors confirm that typical managed care arrangements, such as provider discounts and beneficiary incentives to use in-network providers, are indeed within the realm of anti-kickback scrutiny, and may place their participants—both managed care entities and their participating providers—at some legal risk of anti-kickback liability.

## § 2-3(i)  Practitioner Recruitment

In 1999, the OIG added a safe harbor for physician recruitment activities paid to physicians in order to induce physicians who have been practicing their specialty for less than one year to locate their primary practice to a HPSA for such physician's' specialty as long as the following nine requirements are satisfied.

- Written Agreement. The arrangement must be set out in writing, specify the recruitment benefits being provided, and specify the respective parties' obligations.
- 75% Revenue from New Patients. If a practitioner is leaving an established practice, at least 75% of the revenues of the new practice must be generated from new patients.
- Three Year Limitation. The period of the agreement cannot exceed three years and the terms of the agreement cannot be renegotiated during such three year period.
- No Requirement to Refer. There may not be any requirement that the physician make referrals to or otherwise generate business for the entity although the entity may require physician to maintain staff privileges.
- No Restrictions on Staff Privileges. The practitioner may not be restricted in where the practitioner may maintain staff privileges.

---

[142] 61 Fed. Reg. 2,122 (Jan. 25, 1996).
[143] 42 C.F.R. § 1001.952.

## Federal Anti-Kickback Laws

- Amount of Benefits. The amount of benefits provided to the physician may not vary in any manner based on the volume or volume of any expected referrals to or business generated for the entity.
- Agreement to Treat. The practitioner must agree to treat patients receiving Medicare benefits or assistance from a federal healthcare program in a nondiscriminatory manner.
- 75% of Revenues Generated from Underserved Area. At least 75% of the revenues of the new practice must be generated from patients residing in a HPSA, or a MUA or who are part of a MUP.
- Benefits Only Paid to Practitioner. Except for the practitioner who is being recruited, there may not be any payment or exchange of anything of value given to a person or entity in a position to make or influence referrals.[144]

On May 3, 2001, the OIG issued an advisory opinion pertaining to physician recruitment practices.[145] Based on the facts presented to the OIG, the OIG concluded that the arrangement would potentially generate prohibited remuneration if the necessary intent to induce referrals was present; however, the OIG would not impose administrative sanctions on the hospital in connection with the arrangement. A hospital, which is not designated as HPSA but operates in a medically underserved area, determined that they had a shortage of otolaryngologists and head and neck surgeons. The hospital sought to recruit a medical school graduate who agreed to relocate upon completion of a five-year residency program. Pursuant to the hospital's arrangement the hospital would loan the physician a certain sum of money during the five-year residency program and the physician's obligation to repay would begin upon completion of the residency. The physician would agree to repay the loan in three equal annual payments; however, the hospital would forgive the physician's obligation by one-third of his obligation for each year that he fulfilled his payment obligation.

The OIG concluded that according to the above arrangement the hospital would provide remuneration to a physician to relocate and practice within the hospital's service area. According to the Anti-Kickback Statute the physician is a potential referral source; therefore, the Anti-Kickback Statute is implicated. In addition, the hospital does not qualify as an HPSA and the arrangement is not limited to three years, two requirements of the safe harbor. Despite the fact that the arrangement falls short of multiple requirements of the safe harbor for physician recruitment, the OIG determined that they would not subject the hospital to administrative sanctions absent intent to induce

---

[144] 42 C.F.R. § 1001.952(n).
[145] OIG Advisory Op. No. 01-4.

referrals from the recruited physician.[146] The OIG notes that the hospital has a bona fide shortage of specialists to service a rural area and the potential recruit would not have a referral base upon relocation. In addition, the repayment period is limited to three years although the arrangement period is indeed eight years. The OIG also notes a variety of safeguards that the arrangement would contain, including the fact that the arrangement is not conditioned on the physician making referrals. Although the proposed arrangement did not conform to the strict parameters of the safe harbor, the OIG took a broad look at the factual circumstances surrounding the engagement with the physician. This advisory opinion indicated a willingness on the part of the OIG to expand the scope of the safe harbor by permitting arrangements that otherwise would not qualify for safe harbor protection.

### § 2-3(j)   Obstetrical Malpractice Insurance Subsidies

This safe harbor protects malpractice subsidies for obstetrical care paid by a hospital or other entity where such payment is for a practitioner (including a certified nurse-midwife) who engages in obstetrical practice as a routine part of the practitioner's medical practice in a primary care HPSA.[147] The payment of premiums must be made by the hospital or entity to the carrier and not directly to the physician.[148] The safe harbor prescribes numerous requirements in order to be eligible for subsidy. Included among the criteria for this safe harbor is a requirement that at least 75% of the practitioner's obstetrical patients, who are treated under the coverage policy, reside in a HPSA or MUA or be part of an MUP. In addition, for practitioners who are not full-time obstetricians or certified nurse-midwives, the safe harbor only protects payments related to obstetrical malpractice insurance.

### § 2-3(k)   Cooperative Hospital Services Organizations

This safe harbor protects most cooperative hospital service organizations (CHSOs) that qualify under Section 501(c)(3) of the Internal Revenue Code which operate by distributing earnings to members in accordance with the volume of services used by the member hospital.[149] The safe harbor requires that if the patron-hospital makes a payment to the CHSO, the payment must be for bona fide operating expenses of the CHSO. On the other hand, if the CHSO makes a payment to the patron-hospital, the payment must be for the purpose of paying a distribution of net earnings required to be made under Section 501(e)(2) of the Internal Revenue Code.

---

[146] *Id.*
[147] 42 C.F.R. § 1001.952(o).
[148] *Id.*
[149] 42 C.F.R. § 1001.952(q).

## § 2-3(l) Referral Arrangements for Specialty Services

This safe harbor excludes from the purview of the Anti-Kickback Statute any "exchange of value" among individuals or entities where one party "agrees to refer a patient to other party for the provision of a specialty services" in return for an agreement that the other party will "refer that patient back at a mutually agreed upon time or circumstance "as long as certain requirements are met.[150] In particular, the safe harbor requires that the timing and circumstances for the referral back to the originating physician or entity be "clinically appropriate," that the service for which the referral is made not be within the expertise of the referring individual or entity, and that the parties neither receive any payment from each other for the referral nor share or split a global fee in connection with the referred patient. Finally, unless the parties to the agreement belong to the same group practice, the only "exchange of value" is the remuneration the respective parties receive from third-party payor or the patient for the services furnished to the patient.

## § 2-3(m) Ambulance Replenishing

On December 4, 2001, the OIG adopted a final regulation establishing safe harbor protection for ambulance "restocking" or "replenishing" arrangements. This safe harbor protects certain arrangement involving hospitals or other receiving facilities that replenish drugs and medical supplies used by ambulance providers when transporting patients to the hospitals or receiving facilities. Essentially, this safe harbor provides protection for ambulance restocking such that a receiving facility can restock an ambulance provider with drugs or supplies without being penalized under the Anti-Kickback Statute.[151] This process enables an ambulance to leave the receiving facility with ample supplies in order to respond to the next emergency call. The final rule addresses three categories of restocking: general restocking, fair market value restocking and government-mandated restocking. Each category has specific requirements; however, in order to qualify for safe harbor protection certain threshold requirements must be met regardless of the category of restocking that is being provided. First, the ambulance provider and the hospital may not both bill for the same restocked drugs or supplies. Second, either the hospital or the ambulance provider must generate the necessary documentation for restocking. The party that does not generate the documentation must maintain a copy for at least five years. Third, it is impermissible to condition restocking on the volume or value of referrals. Finally, the receiving

---

[150] 42 C.F.R. § 1001.952(s).
[151] 66 Fed. Reg. 62,979 (Dec. 4, 2001).

facility and the ambulance provider must comply with all federal, state and local laws regulating ambulance services.[152]

In addition to the above requirements that must be met for all three categories of restocking, the safe harbor also provides specific conditions for each of the three categories of restocking. General restocking involves restocking of drugs and supplies for free as well as arrangements whereby the ambulance provider pays for the drugs or supplies. To qualify under the general restocking category, the receiving facility must restock medical supplies or drugs on an equal basis for ambulance providers and the restocking must be conducted publicly. Fair market value restocking involves arrangements where an ambulance provider pays the receiving facility fair market value for the drugs or supplies. Here, the restocking must be at fair market value and payment must be reasonable and made in advance of restocking. Finally, government-mandated restocking pertains to restocking of drugs and supplies pursuant to a State or local law. The safe harbor does not prescribe additional requirements in order to satisfy this category of restocking.

## § 2-3(n) Electronic Health Records and Community-Wide Information Systems

In an effort to promote interconnected, interoperable electronic health records (EHRs), the OIG finalized in August 2006 a safe harbor that protects the donation and receipt of the technology underlying EHR systems.[153] The EHR safe harbor protects technology necessary and used predominantly to create, maintain, and transmit or receive EHRs, including EHR computer software and related wireless internet services, clinical support tools, electronic messaging services, and helpdesk services.[154] However, the safe harbor does not protect hardware, hardware operating software, software primarily used for non-EHR purposes, or the provision of staff services to perform EHR related tasks such as the conversion of paper medical records into EHRs.[155] The safe harbor also does not protect the donation of unnecessary technology or technology that is functionally equivalent to products and services already

---

[152] *Id.*

[153] 71 Fed. Reg. 45,121 (Aug. 8, 2006). The final rule bore only a partial resemblance to the proposed rule. For example, the proposed rule called for separate "pre-interoperability" and "post-interoperability" safe harbors, whereas the final rule created a single safe harbor that will remain in effect after DHHS releases final interoperability standards. The final EHR safe harbor also provided more expansive safe harbor protections than the OIG had initially proposed. In addition, the OIG abandoned provisions from the proposed safe harbor that would have imposed a cap on the amount of technology or services that an entity can donate, and would have restricted safe harbor protection to technologies used "solely" for EHR purposes.

[154] *Id.* at 45,125; 42 C.F.R. § 1001.952(y).

[155] 71 Fed. Reg. 45,125 (Aug. 8, 2006).

## Federal Anti-Kickback Laws

possessed by a recipient.[156] If the OIG discovers that a donor had actual knowledge or acted in reckless disregard or deliberate ignorance of the fact that a recipient already possessed functionally equivalent technology, then neither party can receive safe harbor protection. Although donors do not have to certify that donated products and services are technically or functionally superior to those already possessed by the recipient, the OIG recommends that donors make "reasonable inquiries" (which should not usually require the use of technical experts) about a recipient's existing EHR capabilities before donating.[157] The OIG interprets the donation of software upgrades that enhance usability or technology that enhances the interoperability of donor and recipient systems as necessary and functionally superior.[158] In contrast to the safe-harbor for e-prescribing, which only covers technology used solely for e-prescribing, the EHR safe harbor covers multi-purpose technology as long as the technology is used predominately for EHR purposes and its other uses relate to patient care. For example, EHR technologies that have secondary functions associated with patient administration, scheduling, and billing can qualify for safe harbor protection.[159]

In order to qualify for safe harbor protection, arrangements for the donation and receipt of EHR technology must also comply with interoperability requirements, which the OIG describes as the ability of systems to communicate and exchange data accurately, effectively, securely, and consistently with different information technology systems without altering the meaning of the data.[160] The OIG's decision to create only one safe harbor, instead of separate pre- and post-interoperability safe harbors, reflects progress in the development of interoperability criteria for EHR systems that occurred between the publication of the proposed and final rules. By August 2006, informal criteria for certifying the interoperability of EHRs had become available. While DHHS has not yet incorporated these criteria into legally binding standards, the OIG "deems" all technology approved by certifying entities recognized by DHHS as interoperable, and reviews unapproved technology on a case by case basis.[161] When reviewing unapproved technology, the OIG considers whether the technology was as interoperable as was technologically feasible at the time it was donated. The OIG has specified, however, that the safe harbor does not cover technology that is only compatible with the products of specific vendors, or technology unique to a local community or a limited number of healthcare systems. Related to these interoperability requirements,

---

[156] *Id.* at 45,115, 45,123.
[157] *Id.* at 45,123.
[158] *Id.*
[159] *Id.* at 45,124; 42 C.F.R. § 1001.952(x); 42 C.F.R. § 1001.952(y).
[160] 71 Fed. Reg. 45,126 (Aug. 8, 2006); 42 C.F.R. § 1001.952(y)(2).
[161] 71 Fed. Reg. 45,121, 45,127 (Aug. 8, 2006); 42 C.F.R. § 1001.952(y)(2).

the OIG also requires that EHR systems be compatible with electronic prescribing systems.[162]

On January 7, 2011, the Office of the National Coordinator for Health Information Technology (ONC), an office within DHHS, released a final rule establishing a permanent certification program for the purpose of certifying health information technology.[163] As a result of this final rule, certifications issued by a certification body "authorized" by the ONC will constitute certification by a certifying entity recognized by DHHS. The final rule supersedes the Certification Guidance Document (CGD) guidance[164] that ONC had previously published.

The EHR safe harbor only applies to donors and recipients of EHR technology that meet the following eligibility criteria: entities that provide covered services and submit claims or payment requests to a Federal Healthcare Program are eligible donors, and entities that engage in the delivery of healthcare items and services are eligible recipients. Among eligible donors, the OIG has included health plans and clinical laboratories, but not pharmaceutical, medical device, and durable medical equipment manufacturers, or research entities.[165] The EHR safe harbor does not impose a cap on the value of items or services that can be donated or received, but it does require that each recipient contribute at least 15% of the value of the donation.[166]

The OIG also conditions safe harbor protection on compliance with specific rules relating to the selection of donors and recipients. Recipients may not make the donation of EHR technology a prerequisite for doing business with a donor, and donors may not select recipients or determine the value of a donation based on the volume or value of referrals or other business generated between the parties. The OIG identifies as examples of permissible criteria for selecting a recipient selections made in a "reasonable" and "verifiable" manner based on: (1) the total number of prescriptions written by a recipient; (2) the size of a recipient's medical practice; (3) the total number of hours a recipient practices medicine; (4) the recipient's overall use of automated technology for medical care; (5) whether the recipient is a member of the donor's medical staff; and (6) the level of uncompensated care provided by the recipient.[167]

Parties seeking safe harbor protection must satisfy the following additional requirements: (1) where possible, recipients must have the ability to use donated EHR technology on all patients without regard to payor status;[168]

---

[162] 71 Fed. Reg. 45,126–45,127 (Aug. 8, 2006); 42 C.F.R. § 1001.952(y)(10).
[163] 76 Fed. Reg. 1,262 (Jan. 7, 2011).
[164] 71 Fed. Reg. 44,296 (Aug. 4, 2006).
[165] 71 Fed. Reg. 45,127, 45,129 (Aug. 8, 2006); 42 C.F.R. § 1001.952(y)(1).
[166] 71 Fed. Reg. 45,132 (Aug. 8, 2006); 42 C.F.R. § 1001.952(y)(11).
[167] 71 Fed. Reg. 45,130 (Aug. 8, 2006); 42 C.F.R. § 1001.952(y)(5).
[168] 42 C.F.R. § 1001.952(y)(8).

## Federal Anti-Kickback Laws

(2) arrangements between donors and recipients must be written and signed by the parties;[169] and (3) such arrangements must identify with specificity the items or services being provided, the donor's costs of those items and services, and the recipients contribution.[170] Because the OIG expects EHRs to become widespread by 2013, it has indicated in the final rule that this EHR safe harbor will only remain in effect until December 31, 2013. In other words, to be eligible for this EHR safe harbor, the transfer of goods or services must take place before December 31, 2013. After that date, all arrangements involving the donation and receipt of EHR related items and services will be subject to a case-by-case analysis under the Anti-Kickback Statute.[171] In response to the OIG's 2010 annual solicitation, the OIG recieved proposals to modify the EHR safe harbor to remove the sunset provision and make it a permanent safe harbor. According to the OIG's Fall 2011 Semiannual Report to Congress, it is considering the suggestion. In addition, the OIG is also considering modifying the EHR safe harbor to remove laboratories as a protected donor.[172]

### § 2-3(o) Accountable Care Organizations and OIGs Waiver Authority

Section 3022 of the Health Reform Law requires CMS to establish a shared savings program "that promotes accountability for a patient population and coordinates items and services under parts A and B, and encourages investment in infrastructure and redesigned care processes for high quality and efficient service delivery."[173] The goal of the shared savings program is to improve beneficiary outcomes and increase value of care by: (1) promoting accountability for the care of Medicare FFS beneficiaries; (2) requiring coordinated care for all services provided under Medicare FFS; and (3) encouraging investment in infrastructure and redesigned care processes.[174] Providers, hospitals and suppliers may participate in the shared saving program by creating and participating in Accountable Care Organizations (ACOs).

On November 2, 2011, the OIG, in conjunction with CMS, issued an interim final rule with comment period establishing waivers of the Anti-Kickback Statute and certain other laws to particular arrangements involving

---

[169] 42 C.F.R. § 1001.952(y)(6).
[170] *Id.*
[171] 71 Fed. Reg. 45,133 (Aug. 8, 2006); 42 C.F.R. § 1001.952(y)(13).
[172] *Id.*
[173] The Health Reform Law, § 3022; Social Security Act § 1899.
[174] CMS, Medicare Shared Savings Program Overview Information, *available online at* https://www.cms.gov/sharedsavingsprogram/.

ACOs under the Medicare shared savings program.[175] While not technically a safe harbor, the interim final rule establishes five waivers of application of the Stark law, the federal Anti-Kickback Statute, and the Civil Monetary Penalty (CMP) provisions related to gainsharing and beneficiary inducements. In summary, the Secretary will waive application of these laws to ACOs formed in connection with the Shared Savings Program.

There are five different waivers address several different circumstances:

- an "ACO pre-participation" waiver of the Stark Law, the federal Anti-Kickback Statute and the Gainsharing CMP that applies to ACO-related start-up arrangements in anticipation of participating in the Shared Savings Program, subject to certain limitations, including limits on the duration of the waiver and the types of parties covered;
- an "ACO participation" waiver of the Stark Law, the federal Anti-Kickback Statute, and the Gainsharing CMP that applies broadly to ACO-related arrangements during the term of the ACo's participation agreement under the Shared Savings Program and for a specified time thereafter;
- a "shared savings distributions" waiver of the Stark Law, the federal Anti-Kickback Statute, and Gainsharing CMP that applies to distributions and uses of shared savings payments earned under the Shared Savings Program;
- a "compliance with the Physician Self-Referral Law" waiver of the Gainsharing CMP and the Anti-Kickback Statute that applies to ACO arrangements that implicate the Stark Law and meet an existing exception; and
- a "patient incentive" waiver of the Beneficiary Inducements CMP and the federal Anti-Kickback Statute for medically related incentives offered by ACOs under the Shared Savings Program to beneficiaries to encourage preventative care and compliance with treatment regimens.

The interim final rule sets forth certain conditions that must be met in order for the Stark law, Anti-Kickback Statute and CMP laws to be waived. With respect to start-up arrangements:

1. the arrangement must be undertaken by a party or parties acting with the good faith intent to develop the ACO that will participate in the shared savings program starting in a particular year (target year) and to submit a completed application to participate in the shared savings program for that year;

---

[175] 76 Fed. Reg. 67,992 (Nov. 2, 2011). Significantly, the interim final rule merely appears in the *Federal Register* and has not been codified anywhere in the Code of Federal Regulations.

2. the parties developing the ACO must be taking diligent steps to develop an ACO that would be eligible for a participation agreement that would become effective during the target year, including taking diligent steps to meet the requirements of 42 C.F.R. 1006 and 425.108 concerning ACO governance, leadership and management;
3. the ACO's governing body has made and duly authorized a *bona fide* determination that the arrangement is reasonably related to the purposes of the shared savings program;
4. the arrangement, its authorization by the governing body and the diligent steps to develop the ACO are documented (the final rule sets forth particular criteria concerning the documentation);
5. the description of the arrangement is publicly disclosed at a time and in a place and manner established by the Secretary (the public disclosure need not include the financial or economic terms of the arrangement); and
6. if an ACO does not submit an application for a participation agreement by the last available due date for the target year, the ACO must submit a statement on or before the last available application due date for the target year, describing the reasons it was unable to submit an application.

Most of these factors are consistent for the other waivers, except that instead of the arrangement needing to be undertaken in the target year, the ACO must have entered into a participation agreement and remain in good standing. For the ACO participation waiver, factors 2 through 5, listed above, are the same, except that the ACO must be meeting the governance, leadership and management requirements. For the shared savings distribution waiver, in addition to having entered into a participation agreement and remain in good standing, the following conditions must also be met:

- the shared savings are earned by the ACO pursuant to the shared savings program;
- the shared savings are earned by the ACO during the term of its participation agreement, even if the actual distribution or use of the shared savings occurs after the expiration of that agreement;
- the shared savings are (a) distributed to or among ACO participants, its ACO providers/suppliers, or individuals and entities that were ACO participants or providers/suppliers during the year in which the shared savings were earned by the ACO and (b) used for activities that are reasonably related to the purposes of the shared savings program; and
- with respect to the Gainsharing CMP waivers, payments of shared savings distributions made directly or indirectly from a hospital to a

physician are not made knowingly to induce the physician to reduce or limit *medically necessary* items or services.

To be in compliance with the physician self-referral law waiver, the financial relationship must be reasonably related to the purpose of the shared savings program and the financial relationship must comply with a Stark law exception. Finally, the waiver for patient incentives requires the following conditions be met:

- there is a reasonable connection between the items or services and the medical care of the beneficiary;
- the items of services are in-kind; and
- the items or services are for preventative care or services or advance one or more delineated clinical goals.

For arrangements that meet any of the waivers, the waiver period begins on the start date of the participation agreement and ends on the earlier of the expiration of the term of the participation agreement, including any renewals, or the date on which the participation agreement has been terminated. However, a beneficiary may keep items received before expiration or termination and may continue to receive the remainder of any service initiated prior to expiration or termination.

According to the interim final rule, an arrangement need only fit in one waiver to be protected; "parties seeking to ensure that an arrangement is covered by a waiver for a particular law may look to any waiver that applies to that law."[176] As opposed to the issuance of most final rules in which the text of the actual rule is codified in the Code of Federal Regulations, CMS and OIG propose (and requested comments on this approach) that because the waivers cover multiple legal authorities and to ensure that the waivers, if modified, remain consistent over time and across relevant laws, they will include the waiver text in the *Federal Register* and make the waiver text available on both the CMS and OIG website.

In addition, the CMS' Centers for Medicare and Medicaid Innovation has the authority to promulgate similar waivers for other demonstration programs and initiatives.

## § 2-4     FRAUD ALERTS AND SPECIAL ADVISORY BULLETINS

The OIG's interpretations of the Anti-Kickback Statute are a robust resource for practitioners. Though agency interpretations and guidance documents do not bind courts or even the enforcement agency in a precedential sense, these documents have traditionally been valued by practitioners because

---

[176] *Id.* at 67,994.

## Federal Anti-Kickback Laws

they represent the OIG's thinking with regards to particular activity. Whereas the safe harbors describe conduct that is explicitly permissible, the OIG has published various issuances in the past several years which describe conduct that the OIG views as impermissible under the Anti-Kickback Statute. In the past, the OIG issued "fraud alerts" as a method for identifying fraudulent and abusive practices within the healthcare industry. Although initially the majority of the OIG's fraud alerts were disseminated internally within the government, the OIG began issuing "Special Fraud Alerts" and "Special Advisory Bulletins," which are distributed directly to members of the healthcare provider community and are posted on the OIG's Internet website.[177]

### § 2-4(a)    Joint Ventures

The topic of the first Special Fraud Alert was joint-venture arrangements, which identified a "proliferation" of business arrangements between individuals in a position to refer business and those providing services for which Medicare and Medicaid pay. More specifically, the Special Fraud Alert addressed certain joint-venture arrangements characterized by the OIG as "shells."[178] The Special Fraud Alert stated the OIG's belief that certain joint ventures may be created not for the proper purpose of raising investment capital legitimately to start a new business, but rather for the improper purpose of locking up a stream of patient referrals from provider investors and compensating them for such referrals. The OIG specifically refers to durable medical equipment (DME) and clinical laboratory joint ventures. With respect to shell DME joint ventures, the OIG considers joint ventures that are formed between existing DME suppliers and providers, in which the joint venture owns very little of the DME or other capital equipment, as being suspect. In addition, the OIG suspects DME joint ventures in which one of the ongoing entities is responsible for all day-to-day operations of the joint venture, such as delivery of the DME and billing.

---

[177] Although most of the Special Fraud Alerts have addressed potential kickback arrangements, the OIG has issued several other Special Fraud Alerts which address other fraud and abuse provisions. For example, during the Summer of 1996, the OIG released a Special Fraud Alert concerning the provision of services in nursing facilities and focusing mostly on activities that the OIG considers as possibly violating the Medicare/Medicaid false claims provisions. *See* 61 Fed. Reg. 30,623 (June 17, 1996). Another example is the Special Fraud Alert the OIG issued in 1999 concerning physician liability for certifications made to Medicare. This Special Fraud Alert states the OIG's position that physicians are legally responsible for reviewing and completing certifications of medical necessity in connection with durable medical equipment and home healthcare services. The OIG cautions physicians that they may be subject to substantial criminal, administrative, and civil penalties if they sign such certifications with reckless disregard as to the truth of the information submitted. *See* 64 Fed. Reg. 1,813 (Jan. 12, 1999).

[178] Five OIG Special Fraud Alerts, including one discussing joint-venture arrangements, were published in the *Federal Register* on Dec. 19, 1994, and are *available online at* http://oig.hhs.gov/fraud/docs/alertsandbulletins/121994.html.

Similarly, with respect to clinical laboratory joint ventures, the OIG considers suspect joint ventures formed between existing laboratories and providers where the existing laboratory serves as "manager." Very little testing is conducted on the premises of the joint venture laboratory even though it is Medicare certified. Instead, the reference laboratory does the bulk of the testing at its central processing laboratory. Regardless of the actual location of testing, the local "shell" laboratory bills Medicare directly for these tests.[179]

This Special Fraud Alert identifies several features which the OIG will use to identify suspect joint ventures. The questionable features of a suspect joint venture manifest themselves in one or more of the following three areas: (1) the manner in which investors are selected and retained; (2) the nature of the business structure of the joint venture; and (3) the financing and profit distributions. Characteristics of the venture's financing and profit distributions may suggest a suspect structure, for example, if the amount of capital invested by the physicians is disproportionately small and the return on investment is disproportionately large when compared to a typical investment in a new business enterprise. In addition, where physician investors are permitted to "borrow" the amount of the investment from the entity and pay it back from profit distributions, thus eliminating the need to contribute cash to the partnership, the venture may be suspect. Further, where investors are paid extraordinary return on the investment in comparison with the risk involved, such as over 50% to 100% per year, the venture may be suspect. The identity of a joint venture's investors may also raise concerns if it appears that they were chosen because they are in a position to make referrals. For example, physicians expected to be high referrers may be offered a greater investment opportunity. Similarly, investors may be encouraged to divest if they do not sustain an acceptable level of referrals or if they cease to practice in the service area.

With the proliferation of joint ventures, the OIG clarified its position with respect to suspect arrangements under the safe harbor in a April 2003 Special Advisory Bulletin. The bulletin focuses on contractual arrangements where an original provider expands its business into a related healthcare business through a venture with an existing provider of a related service.[180] For example, a physician group (original provider) establishes a new company to provide home dialysis supplies to their patients. The new company established by the original provider contracts with an existing supplier of home dialysis supplies to operate the new company and provide all goods and services to that company.[181] Here, the original provider of home dialysis supplies is partnering with an existing provider of related services in order to service

---

[179] In fact, the OIG challenged a clinical laboratory joint venture arrangement in Inspector General v. Hanlester Network. *See* discussion below.

[180] 68 Fed. Reg. 23,148 (Apr. 30, 2003).

[181] *Id.*

## Federal Anti-Kickback Laws

the original provider's existing patients. In this instance, the existing provider is likely a competitor of the original provider since they operate in a related line of business. Through a contractual joint venture arrangement the existing provider manages the new line of business and may also supply inventory, billing services and employees to further the joint venture.

Generally the OIG expressed concern over this type of joint venture arrangement for a number of reasons, including the fact that the original provider is expanding into a related line of business, which is dependent upon referrals from the original provider. The expansion, that is essentially controlled by the existing provider, receives referrals from the original provider and is compensated based on the volume of business generated by the original provider. The original provider typically does not contribute capital to the joint venture, rather it contracts out all of the operations to the existing provider including the provision of human resources and inventory. However, the original provider shares in the economic benefit of the new business and is given the opportunity to bill insurers and patients for business that the existing provider (a competitor) would ordinarily be billing had the joint venture not been formed.

The bulletin notes that these contractual arrangements may not be protected by a safe harbor and thus may violate the Anti-Kickback Statute. The OIG states that these arrangements would not qualify for protection under the discount safe harbor because that safe harbor does not apply to "prices offered by a seller to a buyer in connection with a common enterprise."[182] A protected price reduction must be based on an arms length transaction and the OIG previously stated that joint venture arrangements "are not arms length transactions."[183] Therefore, since the original owner is given an opportunity to generate profit from an arrangement with an existing provider that is otherwise a competitor, the Anti-Kickback Statute may be implicated and no safe harbor protection afforded.

In October 2006, the OIG responded to a request for guidance on how the Anti-Kickback Statute applied to physician ownership and investment in medical device companies. In its response, the OIG stated that the principles set forth in both its 1989 Special Fraud Alert on Joint Ventures and subsequent guidance documents relating to joint ventures apply with full force to physician investments in the medical device industry, as well as all health industry sectors.[184] The OIG advised physicians and medical device companies to closely scrutinize these types of investments under the fraud

---

[182] *Id.*
[183] *See* 56 Fed. Reg. 35,977 (July 29, 1991).
[184] Letter from Vicki Robinson, Chief, Industry Guidance Branch, Department of Health and Human Services Office of Inspector General, to the Advanced Medical Technology Association (Oct. 6, 2006), *available online at* http://oig.hhs.gov/fraud/docs/alertsandbulletins/GuidanceMedicalDevice%20(2).pdf.

and abuse laws, expressing concerns about the growing number of physician investments in medical companies and the potential for these types of investments to induce kickbacks and other abusive practices. The OIG also noted that each investment arrangement will be evaluated on a case-by-case basis, and that the characteristics described as unlawful in fraud alerts and other guidance are not exhaustive. The OIG also stated that the amount of revenue generated by a physician investor, both directly and indirectly, is a relevant factor in examining the legality of an investment arrangement under the Anti-Kickback Statute.

Over the years, the OIG has issued a number of Advisory Opinions related to the formation of joint ventures. For example, Advisory Opinion 09-17 addresses the formation of a joint venture among a hospital and three ambulance companies to provide transportation services in a county that includes some medically underserved areas.[185] The Requestor was an ambulance company with four owners (Owners) that was operating in a specific county. The arrangement involved a newly formed joint venture company that was capitalized and owned in equal shares by four non-profit entities (Owners), including a hospital (Hospital-Owner) and three ambulance providers. The newly formed entity (Ambulance Company) was operated by one of the three owner ambulance providers (Manager-Owner) through a management contract (the "Management Agreement") which at times may have referred "overflow" business to the Ambulance Company. Ultimately, the OIG determined that the arrangement did not satisfy the small entity investment safe harbor. Instead, the OIG focused on three favorable features of the joint venture (1) the Owners' return on investment through the equity joint venture; (2) the Transport Agreement; and (3) the Management Agreement to conclude that despite the arrangement was "highly susceptible to fraud and abuse," the OIG would not impose sanctions. Interestingly, while in the past the OIG has looked favorably on municipal-owned arrangements that serve a public need, this opinion signals that a privately owned arrangement may also receive favorable consideration from the OIG if a community need is met.

## § 2-4(b)   Routine Waivers of Coinsurance and Deductibles

In May 1991, the OIG issued a Special Fraud Alert regarding routine waivers of coinsurance and deductible amounts under Medicare Part B. According to the Special Fraud Alert, "[w]hen providers, practitioners or suppliers forgive financial obligations for reasons other than genuine financial hardship of the particular patient, they may be unlawfully inducing that patient to purchase items or services from them" in violation of the Anti-Kickback

---

[185] OIG Advisory Op. No. 09-17.

## Federal Anti-Kickback Laws

Statute.[186] While waivers may appear to help Medicare beneficiaries, the Special Fraud Alert takes the position that coinsurance makes patients "better healthcare consumers" who "select items and services because they are medically needed, rather than simply because they are free." The Special Fraud Alert does except copayment forgiveness in consideration of a particular patient's financial hardship, but only when "used occasionally to address the special financial needs of a particular patient." Routine use of financial hardship forms, with no "good faith attempt to determine the beneficiary's actual financial condition," however, is impermissible.

The Special Fraud Alert enumerates certain "suspect marketing practices" that may indicate unlawful waiver activities, including advertisements stating "No Out-of-Pocket Expense" or "Medicare (or Insurance) Accepted as Payment in Full" or granting "discounts" to Medicare beneficiaries; higher charges to Medicare beneficiaries to offset the cost of the waiver; failure to collect coinsurance for a specific group of patients, such as patients from a particular hospital, to induce referrals; and sham insurance programs, charging nominal "premiums" unrelated to actuarial risk and programs, covering coinsurance only for services furnished by the entity offering the insurance.

The OIG issued guidance on February 2, 2004, clarifying that hospitals can offer discounts to uninsured and underinsured patients without violating the Anti-Kickback Statute. The OIG reiterated that the Anti-Kickback Statute does not prohibit discounts to uninsured patients so long as the discount is not be linked to the generation of business payable by a federal healthcare program. Moreover, the OIG guidance indicated a greater concern for the proffering of discounts to underinsured patients, when the discount is linked to business payable by the Medicare program. The OIG also clarified that there is no OIG rule or regulation requiring a hospital to engage in collection practices prior to being reimbursed for discounts granted to uninsured patients. The OIG stated that collection efforts were established by CMS and relate to bad debt rules; however, these requirements do not apply to OIG enforcement of the Anti-Kickback Statute. In addition, according to the CMS Frequently Asked Questions regarding charges for the uninsured, discounts to the underinsured may create liability under the civil monetary penalties that prohibit inducements offered to Medicare or Medicaid beneficiaries.[187]

In the same guidance issued by the OIG on February 2, 2004, the issue of reducing or waiving cost-sharing amounts for Medicare Beneficiaries was addressed. Cost-sharing is a mechanism to help control over-utilization of medical services, such that with cost-sharing in place a patient will not be enticed to accept services that are not necessary or overpriced. Accordingly,

---

[186] OIG Special Fraud Alert, *Routine Waiver Coinsurance and Deductibles Under Medicare Part B*, 59 Fed. Reg. 65,374 (Dec. 14, 1994).
[187] *See* CMS, Questions on Charges for the Uninsured, *available online at* hhtp://www.cms.gov/AcuteInpatientPPS/downloads/FAQ_Uninsured.pdf.

beneficiaries pay a discrete portion of their care, while the other portion is covered by the Medicare or Medicaid program. The OIG discussed the parameters of cost-sharing waivers to Medicare and Medicaid beneficiaries in the guidance issued in 2004. Generally, it is impermissible to waive fees associated with cost-sharing for a Medicare or Medicaid beneficiary, when the waiving party knows or should know that the waiver is likely to influence the selection of a certain provider or supplier.[188] This is an impermissible inducement and it is prohibited by the Anti-Kickback Statute. However, the prohibition against inducements to Medicare and Medicaid beneficiaries does not apply to the uninsured.[189]

The OIG guidance elaborates on two exceptions to the aforementioned general rule. Medicare coinsurance or deductibles may be waived if the beneficiary is experiencing financial hardship. First, Medicare cost-sharing amounts may be waived if: (1) the waiver is not offered as part of any advertisement or solicitation; (2) the party offering the waiver does not routinely waive coinsurance or deductible amounts; and (3) the party waives the coinsurance and deductible amount after determining in good faith that the individual is in financial need or reasonable collection efforts have failed.[190] A hospital is able to set its own criteria for determining financial need; however, the rubric should include objective criteria such as cost of living, income and family size of the beneficiary.[191] Second, hospitals may waive fees associated with Medicare cost-sharing for inpatient hospital services if the elements of the safe harbor are met.[192]

Another area of interest for the OIG relates to the waiver of copayments and deductibles by ambulance providers. On July 20, 2001, the OIG issued three advisory opinions which address a similar factual scenario.[193] In all three opinions, a local government was interested in alleviating the copayment costs owed to independent ambulance providers or suppliers by the local residents. There is a special rule for providers and suppliers that are owned

---

[188] 42 U.S.C. § 1320a-7a(a)(5).
[189] OIG Guidance, *Hospital Discounts Offered to Patients Who Cannot Afford to Pay Their Hospital Bills*, Feb. 2, 2004.
[190] *See* OIG Guidance (Feb. 2, 2004); 42 U.S.C. § 1320a-7a(i)(6)(A).
[191] OIG Guidance, *Hospital Discounts Offered to Patients Who Cannot Afford to Pay Their Hospital Bills*, Feb. 2, 2004.
[192] *See* 42 CFR § 1001.952(k). A hospital may waive coinsurance and deductible amounts for inpatient hospital services if: (1) the hospital does not later claim the amount reduced or waived as a bad debt; (2) the hospital offers to reduce or waive the coinsurance or deductible amounts without regard to the reason for admission, length of stay, or diagnostic related group filing; (3) the hospital's offer to reduce or waive the coinsurance or deductible amounts is not made as part of a price reduction agreement between the hospital and a third-party payer.
[193] *See* OIG Advisory Op. No. 01-10, 01-11, 01-12.

## Federal Anti-Kickback Laws

and operated by a state or subdivision of a state.[194] CMS has stated that this provision would apply to a state or municipal ambulance company that is a Medicare Part B supplier; therefore, a state or a subdivision of the state is not required to collect copayments or deductibles from residents and would not incur sanctions from the OIG if the waiver is implemented for residents of the state or subdivision.

The major difference between the three opinions is that one, OIG Advisory Opinion 01-12, poses a situation in which the city government was requiring an ambulance company that the city contracted with for ambulance services to waive any out-of-pocket Medicare copayments for city residents. The OIG concluded that this practice would constitute grounds for sanctions since the city was forcing the independent ambulance provider to waive the copayments and deductibles.[195] The city can assume the copayment obligation owed to the ambulance provider, but they are prohibited from mandating that the provider waive the owed copayment. The other two, OIG Advisory Opinions 01-10 and 01-11, involve a local government offering to waive copayments and deductibles for their residents pursuant to the *CMS Carrier Manual* provision permitting local and state governments to forgo collection of out-of-pocket expenses. The OIG confirmed that this CMS provision only applies to situations where the government is the ambulance supplier and not to contracts with outside ambulance suppliers where the government requires the ambulance supplier to waive out-of-pocket copayments or deductibles. With these three advisory opinions, the OIG clarified their position with respect to the waiver of out-of-pocket expenses for governmental units.

The issue of patients' copayment responsibilities also was addressed by the OIG in its November 2005 Special Advisory Bulletin related to Patient Assistance Programs (*see* § 2-4(k), *infra*).

### § 2-4(c)  Hospital Incentives to Physicians

In May 1992, the OIG released a Special Fraud Alert addressing financial incentives offered by hospitals and other healthcare facilities to recruit and retain physicians.[196] The list of suspect activities ranges from those activities long considered to be flagrant violations of the statute (*i.e.*, payments to physicians for each patient admitted to a hospital) to physician "perks," which were considered by many to be acceptable financial incentives (*i.e.*, payment for continuing education courses and travel to conferences, as well as training

---

[194] *See* CMS Carrier Manual § 2309.4 (stating that "a facility which reduces or waives its charges for patients unable to pay, or charges patients only to the extent of their Medicare and other health insurance coverage, is not viewed as furnishing free services and may therefore receive program payment.").
[195] *See* OIG Advisory Op. No. 01-12.
[196] OIG Special Fraud Alert, *Hospital Incentives to Physicians,* 59 Fed. Reg. 65,375 (Dec. 19, 1994).

for physician office staff in medical coding). Other suspect arrangements listed in the Special Fraud Alert include:

- free or significantly discounted office space or equipment;
- free or significantly discounted billing services;
- income guarantees;
- low-interest loans; and
- inappropriately low-cost physician coverage in hospital group insurance plans.

The Special Fraud Alert does not distinguish among the enumerated activities as to which the OIG considers more egregious than others. Also left unclear under the Special Fraud Alert is the relevance of the existing safe harbor and statutory exception relating to employees. Presumably, incentives offered to bona fide physician employees should be immune from prosecution or the imposition of civil sanctions. The Special Fraud Alert's broad-brush treatment of physician recruitment activities is especially significant in light of the OIG's intention to protect only rural physician recruitment activities under the proposed safe harbor.

Many of the "incentives" identified in the Special Fraud Alert benefit not only the physician, but also the offering hospital. For instance, physician training in CPT coding procedures may enable hospitals to bill Medicare properly for patients who receive outpatient services at the hospital. Similarly, payment to physicians for continuing medical education ensures that physicians on the medical staff maintain appropriate skills, and thus may be a significant risk management tool for hospitals.

The OIG has revisited the issue of hospital incentives to physicians through gainsharing mechanisms. Gainsharing refers to an arrangement between a hospital and a physician where the hospital gives a physician "a percentage share of any reduction in the hospital's costs for patient care attributable in part to the physician's efforts."[197] The hospital is creating an incentive for a physician to increase the cost savings of the hospital by providing the physician a share of the savings that is attributable to Medicare and Medicaid. Pursuant to section 1128A(b)(1) of the SSA, a hospital is prohibited from directly or indirectly inducing a physician to reduce services to Medicare or Medicaid beneficiaries.[198] On February 3, 2005, however, the OIG released an advisory opinion approving a gainsharing arrangement between a hospital and a group of heart surgeons. This may suggest that the OIG is more narrowly interpreting the prohibition on physician incentives provided

---

[197] *See Gainsharing Arrangements and CMPs for Hospital Payments to Physicians to Reduce or Limit Services to Beneficiaries, OIG Special Advisory Bulletin* (July 1999).
[198] *See* § 1128A(b)(1) of Social Security Act.

## Federal Anti-Kickback Laws

by hospitals in the form of gainsharing. (For a more detailed discussion of gainsharing, see Chapter 5.)

### § 2-4(d)  Prescription Drug Marketing Practices

In August 1994, the OIG published a Special Fraud Alert entitled "Prescription Drug Marketing Schemes" in which the OIG expresses a concern that drug companies have increased their marketing activities to go beyond "traditional advertising and educational contacts" and are now offering physicians, suppliers and patients "valuable, non-medical benefits in exchange for selecting specific prescription drug brands."[199]

Within this Special Fraud Alert, the OIG identifies three specific examples of activities which violate the Anti-Kickback Statute. The first case was a "product conversion" program whereby a drug company offered a cash award to pharmacies each time the pharmacy/pharmacist successfully persuaded a physician to use that drug company's product instead of a competitor's product. The second case concerned a "frequent flier" campaign in which a drug company arranged to give free airline frequent flier mileage to physicians each time a physician completed a questionnaire for a new patient placed on the drug company's product. The third case identified by the OIG pertains to a theoretical "research program" in which physicians received remuneration from a drug manufacturer under the guise of research when, in reality, the physicians were required only to perform minimal tasks.[200]

### § 2-4(e)  Arrangements for the Provision of Clinical Laboratory Services

In October 1994, the OIG issued a Special Fraud Alert identifying arrangements pertaining to clinical laboratory services it believes implicate the Anti-Kickback Statute.[201] First, while recognizing the legitimate role phlebotomists may perform in physicians' offices (e.g., collection of specimens from patients for testing by the laboratory), the OIG expresses a concern with laboratories that offer phlebotomy services that are unrelated to traditional laboratory functions. These activities can generally be considered to be tasks that would ordinarily be the responsibility of the physician's office staff, for example, taking of vital signs or nursing functions.

---

[199] OIG Special Fraud Alert, *Prescription Drug Marketing Practices,* 59 Fed. Reg. 65,376 (Dec. 19, 1994).
[200] *See* OIG Advisory Op. No. 98-2 (whether certain discounted pricing arrangements on generic pharmaceuticals pose a risk of fraud and abuse); OIG Advisory Op. No. 00-10 (whether the promotion of an expensive new drug to certain beneficiaries constitutes prohibited remuneration to beneficiaries).
[201] OIG Special Fraud Alert, *Arrangements for the Provision of Clinical Laboratory Services,* 59 Fed. Reg. 65,377 (Dec. 19, 1994).

Second, the OIG indicates in this Special Fraud Alert that it will focus on the practice of laboratories providing services to End Stage Renal Dialysis facilities at low rates for tests included in the composite rate for which the laboratory bills the facility directly, when the facility agrees to refer all or most of its non-composite rate business to the laboratory.

Third, the OIG voices concern with laboratories that agree to perform managed care work free of charge in order to induce non-managed care business. Particularly, the OIG is scrutinizing arrangements under which a laboratory offers to write off charges for the physician's managed care work.

## § 2-4(f)   Home Health Agencies

In June 1995, the OIG issued a Special Fraud Alert which identifies several factors which the OIG believes contribute to the home health services industry being particularly susceptible to fraud and abuse.[202] These factors include the following: (1) Medicare covers an unlimited number of home health agency visits per patient; (2) beneficiaries are not responsible for most copayments related to home health services; (3) beneficiaries do not receive any explanations of benefits regarding the home health services they receive; and (4) there is limited direct medical supervision of the health services provided by non-medical personnel. Consequently, the OIG describes several types of fraudulent conduct which the OIG believes violate the Anti-Kickback Statute.

The OIG notes its disapproval of the following practices by home health agencies:

1. paying a fee to a physician for each plan of care certified by the physician on behalf of the home health agency;
2. disguising referral fees as salaries for services never rendered (or in excess of fair market value for the services rendered);
3. providing hospitals with discharge planners, home care coordinators, or home care liaisons in order to induce referrals;
4. providing free service to retirement homes or adult congregate living facilities in return for home health referrals; and
5. subcontracting with retirement home or adult congregate living facilities for the provision of home health services in order to induce the facility to make referrals to the home health agency.

In addition, the Special Fraud Alert identifies several sales tactics and marketing activities that can constitute illegal kickbacks as well a result in the submission of false claims. The OIG explains that it "has learned of high pressure sales tactics employed by some agencies in the home health community

---

[202] 60 Fed. Reg. 40,847 (Aug. 10, 1995).

### Federal Anti-Kickback Laws

to maximize their patient population and their profits. These agencies target healthy beneficiaries on the street or in their homes and offer non-covered services, such as grocery shopping or housekeeping, in exchange for Medicare identification numbers." The Special Fraud Alert states that physicians have reported that home health agencies have attempted to pressure physicians into ordering unnecessary personal care services by telling the physician that the patient has requested these services and that if the physician does not order them, then the patient "will find another physician if their demands are not met."

### § 2-4(g) Nursing Home Suppliers

In August 1995, the OIG issued a Special Fraud Alert regarding fraud and abuse in the provision of medical supplies to nursing facilities.[203] In this Special Fraud Alert, the OIG describes certain medical suppliers which it believes are fraudulently obtaining money from the Medicare and Medicaid programs when furnishing medical supplies to nursing homes and their residents.

Although the OIG focuses primarily on potentially fraudulent billing activities, the OIG also describes certain nursing home supplier activities that are specific violations of the Anti-Kickback Statute. The OIG considers suppliers providing non-covered medical products, such as disposable underpads or adult diapers, for free as part of incontinence care kits an inappropriate "inducement" to the nursing home to obtain the opportunity to receive Medicare reimbursement.

### § 2-4(h) Nursing Home Arrangements with Hospices

In March 1998, the OIG issued a Special Fraud Alert regarding fraud and abuse in nursing home arrangements with hospices. In this Special Fraud Alert, the OIG stated that the relationship between hospices and nursing homes is particularly vulnerable to fraud and abuse because nursing home patients are particularly desirable from a hospice's financial standpoint and that a hospice's access to nursing home patients is dependent upon the nursing home operator.

In particular, this Special Fraud Alert highlights several practices suggesting the presence of kickbacks, including:

- a hospice offering free goods or goods at below fair market value to induce a nursing home to refer patients to the hospice;
- a hospice paying "room and board" payments to the nursing home in amounts in excess of what the nursing home would have received directly form Medicaid had the patient not been enrolled in hospice;

---

[203] *Id.* at 40,849.

- a hospice paying amounts to the nursing home for "additional" services that Medicaid considers to be included in its room and board payment to the hospice;
- a hospice referring its patients to a nursing home to induce the nursing home to refer its patients to the hospice; and
- a hospice providing staff at its expense to the nursing home to perform duties that otherwise would be performed by the nursing home.

### § 2-4(i) Rental of Space in Physician Offices by Persons or Entities to Which Physicians Refer

On February 23, 2000, the OIG issued a Special Fraud Alert concerning the rental of space in physician offices by persons or entities to which the physicians refer. The OIG is concerned that such arrangements are often disguised kickbacks to physician landlords designed primarily to induce referrals. The OIG sets forth three factors which they consider in determining the suspect nature of rental arrangements

The first factor is the appropriateness of the rental agreement. This is a threshold question which essentially asks whether space that is now being rented is space that has been traditionally provided for free or nominal costs. The best example of this nominal space offering is consignment closets for durable medical equipment and supplies.

The second factor is the rental amounts themselves. With regard to rental payments, the rates should be at fair market value, be fixed in advance, and not take into account the volume or value of referrals between the parties.

The third and final factor involves time and space considerations. This inquiry determines whether the rental amount is based upon the actual time and space needs of the supplier renting the space. For example, an ultrasound provider using the rented space four hours per week, but paying rent as if he will use the space for ten hours per week raises the possible inference that he is paying additional rent to induce referrals from the physician-landlord.

### § 2-4(j) Contractual Arrangements with Ambulance Companies

In addition to the Special Fraud Alerts, which are distributed directly to members of the healthcare provider community, the OIG issues "Medicare Fraud Alerts," which are generally disseminated internally within the government and address topics of more narrow interest to particular provider types. One example of these Medicare Fraud Alerts that addresses the Anti-Kickback Statute includes a 1991 Medicare Fraud Alert regarding municipalities soliciting contracts with private ambulance companies to

## Federal Anti-Kickback Laws

furnish services to residents.[204] The Medicare Fraud Alert addressed certain contractual arrangements requiring the ambulance company to pay the municipality a set fee per patient referred or demanding from the ambulance company "a flat monetary amount to secure the exclusive right to handle all emergency calls for ambulance services." According to the Medicare Fraud Alert, the ambulance company offering the highest monetary amount may be granted the contracts. The Medicare Fraud Alert concluded that, in such circumstances, both the municipality and the ambulance company may be in violation of the Anti-Kickback Statute.

On March 24, 2003, the OIG issued a final compliance program guidance to assist ambulance suppliers in establishing and maintaining existing compliance programs.[205] The guidance lists a variety of fraudulent activity that the OIG has pursued as a violation of the Anti-Kickback Statute. The list includes activities such as the improper transport of individuals with other acceptable means of transportation; medically unnecessary trips, trips claimed but not rendered, and upcoding from basic life support to advanced life support services. The guidance makes recommendations to ambulance suppliers that are interested in reducing the incidence of fraudulent or abusive activity. The guidance suggests minimum requirements for a compliance program as well as mechanisms by which an ambulance supplier can identify and respond to risks regarding the Anti-Kickback Statute.[206]

### § 2-4(k) Patient Assistance Programs for Medicare Part D Enrollees

Many pharmaceutical manufacturers sponsor patient assistance programs (PAPs), which assist patients (usually those with chronic illnesses) whose outpatient prescription drugs are not covered (either in whole or in part) by an insurance program. With the evolution of the new Medicare Part D benefit, which includes various patient co-payments responsibilities, the OIG issued a Special Advisory Bulletin in November 2005 that addresses the application of the Anti-Kickback Statute when pharmaceutical manufacturers offer assistance to financially needy Medicare beneficiaries who enroll in Part D by subsidizing their cost-sharing obligations.[207] Although the OIG concluded that pharmaceutical manufacturer PAPs that subsidize Part D cost-sharing amounts present heightened risks under the Anti-Kickback Statute, the bulletin

---

[204] OIG, Medicare Fraud Alert No. 91-27 (1991).
[205] 68 Fed. Reg. 14,245 (Mar. 24, 2003) (Notice).
[206] *Id.* The guidance suggests that an ambulance supplier should have a compliance program with certain basic elements including a compliance officer, educational and training programs, and internal monitoring and reviews. In addition, the OIG recommends that an ambulance supplier evaluate the internal and external risk factors that may possibly affect their business.
[207] 70 Fed. Reg. 70,623, 70,624 (Nov. 22, 2005).

identifies methods of providing assistance that mitigate or vitiate the potential for fraud and abuse, as well as potentially abusive PAP structures.

First, the OIG provided a list of important points concerning PAPs and Medicare Part D.

- PAPs need not disenroll all Medicare beneficiaries from their existing PAPs to be compliant with fraud and abuse laws.
- Occasional, inadvertent cost-sharing subsidies provided by pharmaceutical manufacturers should not be problematic under the Anti-Kickback Statute.
- Nothing in the Special Advisory Bulletin impacts programs that assist uninsured patients.
- The Special Advisory Bulletin does not prevent pharmacies from waiving cost-sharing amounts owed by a Medicare beneficiary on the basis of good-faith individualized assessment of the patient's financial need, so long as the waiver is neither advertised nor routine nor actually compensated by a third party.

Most significantly, the OIG made it clear that in the circumstances described in the bulletin, cost-sharing subsidies provided by bona fide, independent charities unaffiliated with pharmaceutical manufacturers should not raise anti-kickback concerns, even if the charities receive manufacturer contributions. The independent charity PAP must not function as a conduit for payments by the pharmaceutical manufacturer to patients and must not impermissibly influence beneficiaries' drug choices. Conversely, if a manufacturer of a drug covered under Part D were to subsidize cost-sharing amounts, either directly or indirectly through a PAP, incurred by Part D beneficiaries for the drug, the Anti-Kickback Statute would be implicated and the subsidies prohibited, because the manufacturer would be giving something of value to beneficiaries to use its product.[208]

Following the publication of this Special Advisory Bulletin, a number of pharmaceutical manufacturers and patient advocacy groups argued that the OIG's position was limiting the ability to provide necessary assistance to individuals in need. As a result, the DHHS Secretary issued a letter to the President of the Pharmaceutical Research and Manufacturers Association (PhRMA) stating that "lawful opportunities exist to provide drug assistance

---

[208] In addition, CMS has issued guidance that states' PAPs may elect to provide free drugs to financially needy Medicare Part D enrollees outside the Part D benefit. *See CMS Frequently Asked Questions, available online at* http://questions.cms.hhs.gov/cgi-bin/cmshhs.cfg/php/enduser/std_adp;php?p_faqid=6153 (regarding PAPs providing assistance with Part D drug costs to Part D enrollees outside of the Part D benefit and without counting towards "true out of pocket" [TrOOP] expenditure).

**Federal Anti-Kickback Laws**

to Medicare beneficiaries" and that DHHS will work with PhRMA "to create opportunities for the Medicare drug benefit and PAPs to work in tandem."[209]

## § 2-5 ADDITIONAL GUIDANCE AND ADVISORY OPINIONS

Although it was not until 1996 that the OIG was authorized by Congress to issue advisory opinions (as will be discussed), in the early years following the enactment of the 1977 Amendments, the Health Care Financing Administration, (now referred to as CMS),[210] and OIG regularly furnished advice and guidance regarding anti-kickback interpretation not only to the Regional Offices and the fiscal agents but also to members of the public. Although the DOJ later requested that CMS and the OIG cease such activities, these early pronouncements are instructive regarding the government's initial interpretations of prohibited conduct.

### § 2-5(a) Early Guidance from CMS to Regional Offices and Fiscal Agents

Following the passage of the 1977 Amendments, CMS issued three Intermediary Letters that described specific types of conduct which CMS considered suspect under the Anti-Kickback Statute. These letters were based upon DHHS authority to avoid unnecessary utilization and abuse.

The first Intermediary Letter addressed kickbacks between end stage renal disease (ESRD) suppliers and dialysis facilities.[211] The letter was precipitated by a change in Medicare payment policy for home dialysis services which allowed Medicare beneficiaries the option of either obtaining all services, supplies, and equipment through the dialysis facility, paid on the basis of a composite rate, or obtaining the necessary equipment and supplies, directly from ESRD suppliers, paid on reasonable charge basis. Beneficiaries were required to make an election as to their preferred option. The letter stated as follows:

> It has come to our attention that some suppliers may be offering a rebate to dialysis facilities in return for the facility encouraging the patients they supervise to continue or to begin to deal directly with suppliers. Depending on the nature of the offer and the nature of the encouragement, these or similar arrangements may be in violation of [the Anti-Kickback Statute]....[212]

---

[209] February 9, 2006, letter from DHHS Secretary Leavitt to Billy Tauzin, President and CEO of PhRMA, *available online at* http://oig.hhs.gov/fraud/docs/alertsandbulletins/2006/TauzinPAP.pdf.
[210] For the sake of consistency and ease of understanding, references to this agency will be provided as CMS in this title, rather than alternating between CMS and HCFA based on chronology.
[211] CCH MEDICARE AND MEDICAID GUIDE ¶ 33,083, Part A/B I.L. No. 83-13/83-7 (Sept. 1983).
[212] *Id.*

DHHS issued a second Intermediary Letter which addressed the issue of offering "free goods."[213] This Intermediary Letter addressed rebates, kickbacks and/or "free goods" offered by manufacturers in return for the purchase of pacemakers and intraocular lenses as potential violations of the Anti-Kickback Statute. Examples of possible violations cited in the second Intermediary Letter included the following:

(A) Some pacemaker manufacturers offer pacemaker monitoring equipment to hospitals and physicians at no charge, to induce the purchase, or the recommendation for purchase, of their pacemakers rather than competing models.

(B) Some manufacturers of intraocular lenses and related products are furnishing additional products or other gifts to ophthalmologists at no charge in exchange for ordering their products.[214]

The second letter concluded by urging the Medicare carriers[215] to report such activity to the OIG for investigation and advising them to notify pacemaker and intraocular lens suppliers regarding this potential violation.

The third Intermediary Letter addressed certain payments to respiratory therapists.[216] At issue was an arrangement whereby DME suppliers paid respiratory therapists for services performed in delivering, setting up and maintaining equipment. Suppliers and therapists argued that such arrangements were legal as bona fide employer/employee relationships, and that the arrangement was legal so long as payments were only made for services actually rendered and not made in return for referrals. CMS disputed these arguments, stating that:

[t]he statute . . . proscribes payment or receipt of any remuneration that is intended to induce a referral. The opportunity to generate a fee is itself a form of remuneration. The offer or receipt of such fee opportunities is illegal if intended to induce a patient referral. Thus, a supplier who induces patient referrals by offering therapists fee generating opportunities is offering illegal remuneration, even if the therapist is paid no more than his or her usual fee.

Thus, CMS concluded by stating that:

payments to a therapist for services performed for a DME supplier (delivering, setting up, and maintaining equipment; instructing patients in the use of the equipment, etc.) which are intended to induce the referral of patients to the supplier will be viewed by

---

[213] CCH MEDICARE AND MEDICARE GUIDE ¶ 33,553, Part A/B I.L. No. 83-19/83-11 (Dec. 1983).
[214] *Id.*
[215] Part B of the Medicare program is largely administered by the "Medicare carriers" which are insurers that contract with CMS to make coverage determinations, pay claims, investigate utilization patterns, and provide administrative hearings for certain appeals on behalf of the government.
[216] CCH MEDICARE AND MEDICARE GUIDE ¶ 34,127, Part B I.L. No. 84-9 (Sept. 1984).

CMS as an illegal remuneration under the statute and investigated accordingly.[217]

CMS instructed its Medicare carriers to review carefully any arrangements to make preliminary determinations as to "whether payments made to the therapist for any services performed include compensation for the referral of patients to the supplier," and enumerated the various factors to be considered in making such determinations, including "whether the therapist provides services to the DME supplier only for those patients which he refers, whether the supplier uses therapists to install and service equipment for patients not referred by therapists, whether there are unusual geographic or medical reasons for using therapists in certain cases, and how similar equipment is installed and maintained by other suppliers in the area." Arrangements falling under such criteria were to be referred to the OIG regional office for "further investigation and possible prosecution as a violation of the illegal remuneration statute."[218]

In April 1985, however, CMS modified this third Intermediary Letter by deleting the broad language regarding fee generating opportunities and stating that the language quoted above "unduly prejudiced the legality of certain referral arrangements which cannot be determined without consideration of ... relevant factors and practice patterns."[219]

## § 2-5(b) Advisory Opinions

In the late 1970s and early 1980s, CMS and the OIG frequently issued letters to members of the public in response to individual inquiries on the application of the statute. However, the DOJ acted to prevent DHHS from continuing to issue advisory opinions, taking the position that only the federal courts have the authority to interpret criminal statutes, and only the DOJ has prosecutorial authority and discretion. Then in 1996, over considerable objections from the DOJ and OIG, Congress adopted a mechanism by which the public can now obtain advisory opinions on whether an existing or proposed arrangement violates certain statutes, including the Anti-Kickback Statute.[220] As part of HIPAA, Congress directed the DHHS Secretary to issue advisory opinions concerning whether an existing or proposed arrangement constitutes prohibited remuneration within the meaning of the Anti-Kickback Statute, satisfies the statutory exceptions to the statute, and/or meets a safe harbor.

---

[217] *Id.*
[218] *Id.*
[219] CCH MEDICARE AND MEDICARE GUIDE ¶ 35,544, Program Memorandum (Carriers) B-85-2 (Apr. 1985).
[220] Social Security Act § 1128d; 42 U.S.C. § 1320a-7d. Although the 1996 legislation only established the OIG Advisory Opinion process as a 3 ½-year demonstration project, Congress reauthorized this process. *See also* 42 C.F.R. § 1008; 63 Fed. Reg. 38,324 (July 16, 1998).

However, DHHS is prohibited by the statute from issuing advisory opinions on whether amounts under an arrangement reflect the fair market value for any goods, services, or property.

The advisory opinion process is limited to particular arrangements for particular parties and, although parties can request an advisory opinion for a proposed arrangement, the parties must attest that they have a "good faith" intention to enter into the arrangement if they receive a positive advisory opinion from the OIG.

Although the OIG's advisory opinions are made public,[221] they are legally binding only as to DHHS and the individual parties requesting the opinions. Therefore, an advisory opinion cannot be relied upon or introduced into evidence by a person or entity that was not the requestor to prove that the person or entity did not violate the law. On the other hand, the failure of a party to seek an advisory opinion "may not be introduced into evidence to prove that the party intended to violate" the law.[222] Parties requesting advisory opinions are assessed a "reasonable fee" which equals the costs incurred by the Secretary of DHHS in responding to the request (e.g., salaries and benefits payable to attorneys, outside experts, and any other individuals who have worked on the request, as well as administrative and supervisory support for such persons).

Once the parties submit a request for an advisory opinion to the OIG, the OIG has ten working days to formally accept the request, inform the requestor that more information is necessary or decline to accept the request. Once accepted, there is a sixty-day period in which the OIG is to issue the opinion, provided, however, that this sixty-day period is tolled under certain circumstances including situations when requests for additional information are made, there is a need for an expert opinion or advice, or the OIG has not received the full amount of payment due for the expenses associated with producing the advisory opinion. In addition, at any time prior to the OIG's issuance of the advisory opinion, the requestors have the right to withdraw their request.[223]

Not surprisingly, there are few advisory opinions in which the OIG states that the arrangement does not implicate the Anti-Kickback Statute in the first instance. Moreover, there are very few advisory opinions that have been issued in which the OIG has stated that an arrangement would violate the Anti-Kickback Statute as the parties to the advisory opinion request may rescind their request upon learning the OIG's conclusion but prior to its actual issuance. Consequently, the majority of opinions issued under the Anti-Kickback

---

[221] *See* http://www.dhhs.gov/progorg/oig/advopn. In addition to being posted on the OIG's website, OIG Advisory Opinions are available in hard-copy form at the headquarter offices of the OIG. Generally, documents submitted and utilized in rendering an OIG Advisory Opinion are protected from disclosure under the Freedom of Information Act. *See* 5 U.S.C. § 552.

[222] 42 C.F.R. § 1008.53.

[223] 42 C.F.R. 1008.40.

## Federal Anti-Kickback Laws

Statute conclude that although the proposed or existing arrangement does, in fact, implicate the Anti-Kickback Statute, based upon the facts, the OIG will not impose sanctions against the parties. Although the rationale for why the OIG reached this conclusion is somewhat different in each opinion, the OIG generally has focused on the following four factors in determining whether it will impose sanctions on an arrangement that does implicate the Anti-Kickback Statute:

- increased risk of overutilization;
- increased program costs;[224]
- patient freedom of choice; and
- unfair competition. [225]

In July 2008, DHHS issued a final rule amending its policies relating to the collection and payment by individuals requesting an Advisory Opinion.[226] Under the July 2008 Rule, parties no longer are required to deposit $250 to the U.S. Treasury upon requesting an OIG Advisory Opinion. According to the OIG, this policy change eliminates the resource demands that arise when a party rescinds its request for an advisory opinion and seeks to recoup its initial deposit. The July 2008 rule also sets forth that parties can no longer pay the U.S. Treasury by way of check or money order but instead must pay for these charges directly through wire or electronic funds transfer.

In recent years, the OIG has been active in issuing advisory opinions – the OIG issued 17 Advisory Opinions in 2009, 26 in 2010, and 22 in 2011, on a wide variety of issues.

---

[224] There is a difference of opinion over whether the Anti-Kickback Statute is aimed only at arrangements that result in overutilization and increased costs to the government. In a 1979 Medicare Program Regional Letter, DHHS stated that in deciding whether any particular conduct is proscribed, it would examine whether the activity or practice in question "contributes significantly to the cost of the Medicare and Medicaid programs." *Medicare Program Regional Letter*, Trans. No. 79-29 (Nov. 1979). *See also* S. REP. NO. 92-1230, 92d Cong., 2d Sess. at 208 (1972); H. R. REP. No. 95-393, 95th Cong., 1st Sess., pt. 1 at 48 (1977). *But see* United States v. Ruttenberg, 625 F.2d 173, 177 (7th Cir. 1980); United States v. Bay State Ambulance and Hosp. Rental, Inc., 874 F.2d 20, 32 (1st Cir. 1989).

[225] *See, e.g.*, OIG Advisory Op. No. 98-13 ("In assessing the potential risk of fraud or abuse under the Anti-Kickback Statute, our concerns are principally fourfold: increased risk of overutilization, increased program costs, patient freedom of choice, and unfair competition."); *see also* OIG Advisory Op. No. 98-3; OIG Advisory Op. No. 98-7; OIG Advisory Op. No. 05-12 ("Like any kickback scheme, such arrangements can lead to overutilization of services, increased costs for Federal healthcare programs, corruption of professional judgment, and unfair competition.").

[226] 73 Fed. Reg. 40,982 (July 17, 2008); 42 C.F.R. § 1008.31(b); 42 C.F.R. § 1008.36(b); 42 C.F.R. § 1008.43(d).

## § 2-6 CASE LAW

### § 2-6(a) Pre-Hanlester: The First Twenty Years of Case Law Under the Statute

During the years following the 1977 Amendments, the OIG repeatedly expressed frustration at its inability to convince the DOJ to aggressively prosecute healthcare fraud cases focusing on kickback allegations. Nonetheless, U.S. Attorneys prosecuted a few cases that, on appeal, resulted in several courts broadly construing the scope of the Anti-Kickback Statute. To date, these cases still continue to be cited by both the government and the private bar.

#### § 2-6(a)(1) U.S. v. Greber

*United States v. Greber*[227] is the landmark case on the scope of the Anti-Kickback Statute in which the Third Circuit Court of Appeals adopted the "one purpose" test. Dr. Greber, an osteopathic physician board certified in cardiology, was President of Cardio-Med, Inc., an organization which provided diagnostic services for cardiac patients. When Cardio-Med performed a test at the request of a referring physician, Cardio-Med also forwarded a portion of the Medicare reimbursement it received to the referring physician. This fee was purportedly for "interpretations" by the referring physicians. However, evidence was introduced that physicians received these interpretation fees even though Dr. Greber evaluated the tests. In addition, the amount paid to the physicians was more than Medicare allowed for such services. Hence, Dr. Greber was convicted of, among other things, tendering kickbacks in violation of the Medicare fraud and abuse statute. He appealed his conviction, but the appellate court held that "if *one purpose* of the payment was to induce future referrals, the Medicare statute has been violated."[228]

After the *Greber* case, the issue confronting the healthcare industry was whether the broad "one purpose" test was applicable merely to the egregious facts presented, or whether the test would be generally applicable to all kickback cases.

---

[227] United States v. Greber, 760 F.2d 68 (3d Cir.), *cert. denied*, 474 U.S. 988 (1985).
[228] *Id.* at 69 (emphasis added).

## § 2-6(a)(2)  U.S. v. Kats

In *United States v. Kats*,[229] a physician owned a 25% interest in Community Clinic, which collected blood and urine specimens and forwarded the specimens to Tech-Lab. Tech-Lab billed Community Clinic, which in turn billed the Medi-Cal and Medicare programs. According to the court's description of the facts, 50% of the laboratory payments were "kicked back" to Community Clinic. The Ninth Circuit Court of Appeals followed the *Greber* holding, and upheld a jury instruction allowing conviction unless the payment was "wholly and not incidentally attributable to the delivery of goods and services." The Ninth Circuit stated that it is not a defense that there are other purposes behind the payment as long as one of the material purposes is to induce referrals.

## § 2-6(a)(3)  U.S. v. Bay State Ambulance

*United States v. Bay State Ambulance and Hospital Rental, Inc.*[230] concerned the award of a hospital ambulance contract. Allegedly, the ambulance company made illegal payments to a hospital official, who sat on the bid committee, consisting of a management consulting contract, loans and other consideration, including automobiles and cash. The court cited with approval *Greber's* holding that any amount of inducement is illegal under the Anti-Kickback Statute but stopped short of explicitly adopting the Third Circuit's broad "one purpose" test. The district court had instructed the jury that the *primary purpose*, as opposed to an incidental or minor purpose, of the payments must be improper in order to obtain a conviction under the Anti-Kickback Statute, and thus the less favorable *Greber* standard was not directly challenged on appeal. The court in *Bay State Ambulance* also noted that the government was not required to prove that payments received were not reasonable for the work performed because "the gravamen of Medicare fraud is inducement. Giving a person an opportunity to earn money may well be an inducement to that person to channel potential Medicare payments towards a particular recipient."[231]

An argument advanced by the defendants in *Bay State Ambulance* was that the then-proposed safe harbor regulations did not prohibit payment for actual work done. The defendants admitted that the proposed safe harbors would not govern their actions, due to the fact that the law was different at the time. However, they urged the court to consider the safe harbors in order to determine whether "reasonable payments for actual services can ever be

---

[229] United States v. Kats, 871 F.2d 105 (9th Cir. 1989).
[230] United States v. Bay State Ambulance and Hosp. Rental, Inc., 874 F.2d 20, 32 (1st Cir. 1989).
[231] *Id.* at 29.

illegal."[232] The court disagreed. First, the court explained that the judiciary is cautious of allowing subsequent congressional comments on the intent of prior legislation to control. Second, the court explained that the safe harbors do not exclude all payments for actual work done, but instead only protect a "small subset of transactions" in which the defendants would not fall.

### § 2-6(a)(4)  Other Pre-*Hanlester* Cases

Other cases also have interpreted the scope of the Anti-Kickback Statute. Courts examining payment arrangements have demonstrated a willingness to examine the substance, and not merely the form, of payment arrangements in order to determine whether the parties are engaging in proscribed activities. Typically, as in the *Greber* and *Bay State Ambulance* cases, suppliers attempt to characterize their payments to healthcare providers or practitioners as some sort of fee for services rendered. For instance, in *United States v. Lipkis*,[233] the Ninth Circuit Court of Appeals considered a laboratory referral arrangement in which the laboratory agreed to make certain payments to a medical practice. In return for the payment, the medical practice's management company was to provide the laboratory with certain services, including collecting specimens, spinning down blood, supplying forms and stickers, and providing insurance. In upholding the conviction for Medicare fraud of the president of the medical practice's management company, the court observed that "[t]he fair market value of these services was substantially less than the compensation [the management company] received from [the laboratory], and there is no question that [the laboratory] was paying for the referrals as well as the described services."[234]

Similarly, suppliers attempted to characterize their payments to physicians and others as "handling fees"[235] or as fees for consulting services.[236] Courts considering these claims typically looked beyond what the parties stated was the reason for the payments and instead considered whether the payments were, in actuality, being made to induce patient referrals. Consequently, the mere fact that an agreement does not expressly provide for payments for referrals, but, rather, calls for payments for certain services, may not be sufficient to remove the arrangement from the scope of the anti-kickback provision.

---

[232] *Id.* at 31.
[233] United States v. Lipkis, 770 F.2d 1447 (9th Cir. 1985).
[234] *Id.* at 1,449.
[235] *See* United States v. Hancock, 604 F.2d 999 (7th Cir.), *cert. denied*, 444 U.S. 991 (1979); *see also* United States v. Porter, 591 F.2d 1048 (5th Cir. 1979).
[236] *See* United States v. Ruttenberg, 625 F.2d 173 (7th Cir. 1980); *see also* United States v. Tapert, 625 F.2d 111 (6th Cir.), *cert. denied*, 449 U.S. 952 (1980).

## § 2-6(b)   Hanlester Network v. Shalala

In 1995, the United States Court of Appeals for the Ninth Circuit issued its decision in *The Hanlester Network v. Shalala* finding that the government had not proven that the defendants had acted with the requisite intent ("knowingly and willfully") in order to have received remuneration in return for referrals.[237] The court in *The Hanlester Network* case considered the circumstances under which a return on investment from participation in a joint venture will constitute a violation of the Anti-Kickback Statute, and the Ninth Circuit determined that certain participants in the joint venture should not be excluded under the Anti-Kickback Statute.

This case involved a network of three clinical laboratories that had been established as physician joint ventures by the Hanlester Network of Santa Ana, CA. The joint ventures established by the Hanlester Network were organized as limited partnerships with over one hundred physicians participating as investors. The investment arrangement basically consisted of physicians as limited partners who owned between three and seven shares at $500 per share. Although there was no express requirement that physician investors refer to the laboratory, physician investors were required to sell back their shares if they retired, lost their medical license, or relocated outside the laboratory's service area. In addition, each joint venture laboratory was operated under a management agreement with SmithKline Beecham Clinical Laboratories (SBCL). The management agreement provided the payment to SBCL of either $15,000 per month or 76% of the revenues generated by the joint-venture laboratory, whichever was greater.

In December 1989, the OIG issued notices of proposed program exclusion to five individuals and five entities involved in the joint ventures. The notices of proposed exclusion against the Hanlester Network participants detailed the OIG's case, which appeared to implicate many of the risk factors detailed in the OIG's Special Fraud Alert on Joint Ventures (see discussion of the OIG's Special Fraud Alert on Joint Ventures below), including that the physicians received a return on investment in excess of $1,500 per physician and that the labs also allegedly "removed physician investors or encouraged physician investors to withdraw as limited partners" if they in fact did not meet referral expectations. The OIG also alleged that SBCL bore the entire financial risk of operations and received approximately 80% of the net cash receipts of the joint venture lab as payment.

Simultaneously, the OIG announced the settlement of charges against SBCL for $1.5 million. The settlement agreement set forth the government's position that SBCL "violated the statute as a result of the manner in which SBCL was compensated in its contractual role as laboratory manager and

---

[237] The Hanlester Network v. Shalala, 51 F.3d 1390 (9th Cir. 1995).

SBCL's knowledge of, or in some instances participation in, activities of Hanlester and these physician-owned laboratories and that the amount of compensation each party received under some of the many agreements was disproportionate to the relative responsibilities and business risks borne by the parties.

The Ninth Circuit reversed the program exclusions against several appellants, apparently based on the particular facts of the case. The court held that the term "inducement" contained in the Anti-Kickback Statute means something more than encourage, but something less than an agreement.[238] In particular, the court held that " 'to induce' connotes an intent to exercise influence over reason and judgment in an effort to cause a desired action and is on its face a stronger term than merely 'to encourage' or 'to influence.' "[239] The Ninth Circuit found that "the fact that a large number of referrals resulted in the potential for a high return on investment, or that the practical effect of low referral rates was failure for the labs, is insufficient to prove that appellants offered or paid remuneration to induce referrals" in violation of the Anti-Kickback Statute.[240] The Ninth Circuit noted that limited partners were paid dividends based on their ownership share, and not the volume of their referrals, and payments were made to limited partners whether or not they referred business to the joint venture.

The Ninth Circuit, however, held that the Hanlester Network's marketing director had made certain verbal representations to prospective investors that were violations of the Anti-Kickback Statute. These representations, the Ninth Circuit found, rose to the level of an impermissible "inducement" under the Anti-Kickback Statute, and that the Hanlester Network and the joint venture laboratories' organizational entities could be held vicariously liable under the Anti-Kickback Statute for the marketing director's actions, regardless of the fact the marketing director acted in a manner contrary to the organizations' stated policies.

In addition, the Ninth Circuit held that vicarious liability in the context of a criminal statute could not be extended to the individual partners in the Hanlester and joint venture organizational entities, and further, that the individual partners did not act with the requisite intent in order to constitute an independent violation of the Anti-Kickback Statute. Citing then-recent Supreme Court precedent in the case of *Ratzlaf v. United*

---

[238] Inspector Gen. v. Hanlester Network, Departmental Appeals Board, Appellate Division, Dec. No. 1275 (Sept. 18, 1991), *available online at* http://www.hhs.gov/dab/decisions/index.html.
[239] *Id.*
[240] *Id.* at 1,399.

## Federal Anti-Kickback Laws

*States*,[241] the Ninth Circuit held that a party may violate the federal fraud and abuse laws "knowingly and willfully" only if he or she (i) *knows* that the Anti-Kickback Statute prohibits offering or paying remuneration to induce referrals and (ii) engages in the prohibited conduct with the specific intent to disobey the law. While the marketing director's conduct was sufficiently egregious to infer the requisite intent to violate the law, the Ninth Circuit found that the other partners displayed no such conduct, nor did they approve of her representations.[242]

The Ninth Circuit then examined whether the appellants violated the Anti-Kickback Statute in light of the government's argument that the joint venture was a "sham" that merely enabled appellants to receive remuneration from SBCL in return for referrals. The court examined the laboratory services agreement between the Hanlester Network and SBCL, whereby SBCL received either $15,000 per month or 76% of the joint venture laboratories' net revenues. While the court acknowledged that this structure enabled appellants to receive "substantial economic benefit" from their relationships with SBCL, the Ninth Circuit determined that "[t]he management services agreement between SBCL and appellants reflects a relatively common practice in the clinical laboratory field. There is no evidence that appellants intended to conceal payments from SBCL to physicians in return for referrals." The Ninth Circuit also found that no payments were made by SBCL to the appellants. Rather, payments flowed from the joint ventures to SBCL. Consequently, the Ninth Circuit found that the government had not proven that the appellants acted with the requisite intent ("knowingly and willfully") in order to have received remuneration in return for referrals.

### § 2-6(c) Significant Post-Hanlester Cases

### § 2-6(c)(1) The Anti-Kickback Statute's Intent Requirement

Prior to the enactment of the Health Reform Law, there was much controversy and differing court opinions in that a number of courts rejected the Ninth Circuit's opinion in *The Hanlester Network*. For example, The United States District Court for the Southern District of Ohio in *United States v. Neufeld* declined to follow the Ninth Circuit's adoption of the Supreme

---

[241] Ratzlaf v. U.S., 114 S. Ct. 655, 657 (1994). The Supreme Court in *Ratzlaf* interpreted the term "willfulness" in the context of § 5322 and its related code sections. The Court held that willfulness requires both knowledge of the reporting requirement, and specific intent to commit the crime. The *Ratzlaf* case involved the attempt to circumvent the requirement that financial institutions report cash transactions in excess of $10,000. The Court noted that currency restructuring is not "inevitably nefarious." As such, the Court held that he had to be aware of the illegality of the type of structuring in which he engaged.

[242] Hanlester Network v. Shalala, 51 F.3d 1400 (9th Cir. 1995).

Court's definition of the term "willful" as formulated in *Ratzlaf*.[243] The District Court distinguished the Supreme Court's interpretation of the term "willful" in the *Ratzlaf* case by noting that in *Ratzlaf*, the Supreme Court was addressing the term in the context of the federal anti-structuring statute,[244] which is different from the Anti-Kickback Statute. The District Court states that *Ratzlaf* does not "lend support to the definition of 'willful' in the [anti-kickback] statute as requiring a knowledge of illegality," and that the *Ratzlaf* analysis "is neither useful nor applicable to the question of the scienter standard for the [anti-kickback] statute." The District Court based this conclusion on both the statutory language of the Anti-Structuring and Anti-Kickback Statutes and on the underlying nature of the offenses being prohibited by these statutes. The District Court in *Neufeld* also ruled that the determination as to whether the compensation was in exchange for the referral of patients is a factual determination that should be decided by the jury.

The Eighth Circuit addressed the definition of "knowingly and willfully" in *United States v. Jain*.[245] Dr. Jain and his corporation were convicted for receiving payments from a hospital for referring patients. The defendant's primary contention on appeal was that the district court's jury instructions did not apply a correct definition of the term "willfully." The defendant argued that the "willfully" standard enunciated in *Hanlester* should apply in this case; the government argued that "willfully" only requires that the defendant intend to commit the act that constituted the Anti-Kickback violation. The Eighth Circuit affirmed the District Court's application of a middle ground and upheld an instruction that stated that the word "willfully" means "unjustifiably and wrongfully known to be such by the defendant" However, the court did not adopt the *Ratzlaf* standard, which required the government to prove that the defendant knew that his actions violated a specific statute.

However, as addressed above, the Health Reform Law ended the *Hanlester* debate by providing that "a person need not have actual knowledge of this [Anti-Kickback] section or specific intent to commit a violation of this section" in order to be found guilty of violating the Anti-Kickback Statute.[246]

## § 2-6(c)(2)  The Greber "One Purpose" Test

In *United States v. McClatchey*, the Tenth Circuit adopted the "one purpose" rule from *Greber* when applying the Anti-Kickback Statute.[247] Dennis

---

[243] United States v. Neufeld, 908 F. Supp. 491 (S.D. Ohio 1995).
[244] The anti-structuring statute includes certain federal financial reporting requirements for monetary instruments transactions. *See* 31 U.S.C. §§ 5322, 5324.
[245] United States v. Jain, 93 F.3d 436 (8th Cir. 1996).
[246] The Health Reform Law, § 6402(f)(2); Social Security Act § 1128B(h); 42 U.S.C. 1320a-7b(h).
[247] United States v. McClatchey, 217 F.3d 823 (10th Cir. 2000).

## Federal Anti-Kickback Laws

McClatchey was a hospital executive at Baptist Medical Center (BMC) in Kansas City, KS. He was involved in several contractual arrangements with two physicians, Drs. Robert and Ronald LaHue, on behalf of BMC. The LaHues provided physician services to numerous Medicare patients in nursing facilities through their organization, Blue Valley Medical Group, and controlled a large number of potential referrals for hospital services. BMC paid each of the LaHues $75,000 per year for medical director and consulting services. In 1998, however, the government charged Mr. McClatchey, the LaHues, and others with violations of the Anti-Kickback Statute, alleging that the payments greatly exceeded the value of any services provided by the two doctors and that they were intended to induce the doctors to refer patients to BMC. The jury convicted Mr. McClatchey and three other defendants of conspiring to violate the Anti-Kickback Statute, but the trial court ruled that there was insufficient evidence from which a reasonable jury could have concluded that they had a specific intent to violate the statute.[248]

The Tenth Circuit reversed and reinstated the jury's guilty verdict and implicitly rejected the "primary purpose" test advanced by the defense in favor of the "one purpose" rule (which provides that the Anti-Kickback Statute may be violated where one purpose of the payment in question is to induce referrals, regardless of the existence of other legitimate purposes for the payment).[249] However, the court specifically stated that there must be an offer or payment of remuneration to induce and that defendants could not be convicted "merely because they hoped or expected or believed that referrals may ensue from remuneration that was designed wholly for other purposes.[250] The Tenth Circuit revisited *McClatchey's* application of the "one purpose" rule in *United States v. LaHue*[251] and held that it was bound by the decision in *McClatchey* to follow the rule. The court also rejected the LaHues' argument that the statute was vague, something not addressed in the *McClatchey* opinion. It concluded that the statute clearly applied to the conduct of the doctors, and that they therefore could not argue that the statute was vague on its face or as applied to them. The Court also found that the statute articulated a clear enough standard that it did not impermissibly encourage arbitrary or discriminatory enforcement.

Then again in 2011, the Seventh Circuit Court of Appeals joined other Circuits in adopting the "one purpose" test in *United States v. Borrasi*[252]. Dr. Borrasi owned a corporate group of healthcare providers, Integrated

---

[248] United States v. Anderson, 85 F. Supp.2d 1047, 1065–68 (D. Kan. 1999), *rev'd sub nom.* United States v. McClatchey, 217 F.3d 823 (10th Cir. 2000).
[249] United States v. McClatchey, 217 F.3d 835 (10th Cir. 2000).
[250] *Id.* at 834.
[251] United States v. LaHue, 261 F.3d 993 (10th Cir. 2001), superseding earlier decision at 254 F.3d 900 (10th Cir. 2001).
[252] United States v. Borrasi, 639 F.3d 774 (7th Cir. 2011).

Health Centers, S.C. (Integrated) and apparently Dr. Borrasi and several officers of an inpatient psychiatric hospital allegedly conspired to pay a sum kickbacks and bribes to Dr. Borrasi and others working at Integrated in exchange for referring Medicare patients to Rock Creek. Allegedly, to conceal these kickbacks, Dr. Borrasi and other Integrated employees were placed on Rock Creek's payroll, were awarded false titles and fabricated job descriptions, and were asked to submit false time sheets. After a December 2006 indictment against Dr. Borrasi for violating the Anti-Kickback Statute, Dr. Borrasi then proceeded to trial where the jury returned a guilty verdict. On appeal, Dr. Borrasi contended, among other things, that his actions fell within the employee safe harbor. However, the Seventh Circuit held, in adopting the "one purpose" test, that even if some of Rock Creek's payments were compensation for Borrasi's professional services, because "at least part of the payments to Borrasi was 'intended to induce' him to refer patients to Rock Creek," the Anti-Kickback Statute was violated.[253]

### § 2-6(c)(3) The Discount Exception and Safe Harbor

The U.S. District Court for the District of Massachusetts addressed the "discount exception" to the Anti-Kickback Statute in *United States v. Shaw*.[254] In this case, the government alleged that Dr. Shaw, an executive of a healthcare company that provided products and services to patients suffering from ESRD, conspired to pay remuneration to independent dialysis clinics for the purpose of inducing such clinics to use the company's products and services for non-routine and medically unnecessary tests that were reimbursed by Medicare. According to the government, the inducements for referring orders for the company's services took the form of rebates and special pricing, grants, entertainment and hunting trips, and write-offs of bad debts for blood laboratory tests of indigent and HMO patients.

Dr. Shaw contended that the rebates and special pricing, seventy of the seventy-eight alleged illegal instances of remuneration, were covered by the discount exception to the Anti-Kickback Statute and were, therefore, not illegal. He argued that the company attempted in good faith to report price reductions, that communications to buyers constituted adequate disclosure, and that the price reductions were a form of a "discount or other reduction in price" allowed by the exception and not a "rebate" as in the prohibited "remuneration." Although the court denied Dr. Shaw's motion to dismiss on the ground that the indictment contained all the elements of the charged offense of conspiring to pay illegal kickbacks, and that the government did not have to state that the conduct failed to meet the discount exception, the

---

[253] Quoting *Greber*, 760 F.2d at 72.
[254] United States v. Shaw, 106 F. Supp.2d 103 (D. Mass. 2000).

## Federal Anti-Kickback Laws

opinion contains an extensive discussion of the exception and the interplay between the discount exception to the Anti-Kickback Statute and the discount safe harbor. The court stated it would interpret the exception in light of those discounting arrangements that qualified under the safe harbor. However, the court recognized that the exception has "independent status" from the safe harbor regulations and would not control how a court interprets and applies the discount exception. Further, the safe harbor's definition of "discount" is not controlling for purposes of determining the application of the exception. Therefore, even though earlier versions of the safe harbors did not protect rebates to charge-based buyers, they do not preclude reliance on the discount exception in the context of a rebate arrangement.

Second, the court stated that the question of whether the conduct qualified for the discount exception was a factual issue for the jury. According to the court, the issue for the jury is "whether the reason for offering or accepting the 'discount or other reduction in price' was to induce referrals of or be reimbursed for federal healthcare program business." Finally, the court noted that an essential component of the discount exception was that the federal or state health programs share in and benefit from reduced costs.

## § 2-7 OTHER ANTI-KICKBACK AUTHORITY

### § 2-7(a) Inducements to Beneficiaries

The Anti-Kickback Statute is a broad criminal statute applicable not only to financial arrangements by and between healthcare providers in a position to refer patients to one another, but also to a host of other financial arrangements, including inducements that may be given to beneficiaries in order to encourage them to order or purchase services from a particular provider or supplier.[255] In fact, in the 1991 final safe harbors, the OIG addressed that the provision of free goods to Medicare beneficiaries or Medicaid recipients may be subject to scrutiny:

> We decline to protect the offer of free gifts to beneficiaries within this safe harbor provision, as we have declined to protect this practice within the safe harbor provision governing discounts. The statute clearly contemplates that illicit remuneration may involve payments "in cash or in kind." The practice of offering free gifts may well induce beneficiaries to purchase additional or unnecessary items or services. Such inducements could easily become excessive, and there is no distinct financial or other cut-off point below which we could be sure that gifts remained non-abusive. Because we understand that

---

[255] 42 U.S.C. § 1320a-7b.

such inducements are an area of significant abuse, we believe that protection of this practice would be unwarranted.[256]

Nevertheless, despite the breadth of the Anti-Kickback Statute and its ability to apply to inducements to beneficiaries, in 2996 as part of HIPAA, Congress added a new CMP provision prohibiting individuals and entities from offering or transferring "remuneration" to Medicare and Medicaid beneficiaries in order to influence such beneficiaries to obtain healthcare items or services from a particular provider.

### § 2-7(a)(1)  The Statute and Regulations

The CMP Statute addressing inducements to beneficiaries prohibits a person from:

> offer[ing] to or transfer[ing] remuneration to any individual eligible for benefits under [Medicare or Medicaid] that such person knows or should know is likely to influence such individual to order or receive from a particular provider, practitioner, or supplier any item or service for which payment may be made, in whole or in part, under [Medicare or Medicaid].[257]

The CMP Statute defines remuneration as including the waiver of coinsurance and deductibles and transfers of items or services for free or for other than fair market value. However, there are limited exceptions provided in the statute. For instance, coinsurance waivers that are based on financial need and meet other requirements are protected. Additionally, in light of the potential application of this provision to managed care arrangements, the statute excepts from the scope of illegal remuneration differentials in coinsurance and deductible amounts that are part of a benefit plan design (e.g., as part of a PPO or similar managed care product) and that are disclosed and meet other standards defined by DHHS. There also is an exception for incentives given to individuals to promote the delivery of preventive care as determined by DHHS in regulations.

In the Spring of 2000, the OIG issued two separate sets of regulations addressing the CMP provision. First, the OIG issued a final rule, effective

---

[256] 56 Fed. Reg. 35,952, 35,963 (July, 29 1991).
[257] Social Security Act § 1128A(a)(5); 42 U.S.C. § 1320a-7a(a)(5) (as modified by HIPAA, tit. II § 216, 110 Stat. 1936, 2007 (1996)). Although this CMP was added in 1996, as part of HIPAA § 231(h) Pub. L. 104-191, Congress made modifications to this provision in 1997 and 1998 (BBA '97 § 4331(e) and § 4523(c) Pub. L. 105-33 and the Omnibus Consolidated and Emergency Supplemental Appropriations Act of Fiscal Year 1999 § 5201 Pub. L. 105-277). In addition to adding the CMP for inducements to beneficiaries, HIPAA included other modifications and additions to the OIG's CMP authority including, but not limited to, the OIG's authority to impose penalties against excluded individuals retaining ownership or control of an entity, upcoding and claims for medically unnecessary services, and false certification of eligibility for home health services.

## Federal Anti-Kickback Laws

immediately, that addressed the various changes that were made to the OIG's CMP authority as a result of HIPAA, including the CMP for inducements to beneficiaries.[258] Second, the OIG issued a notice of proposed rulemaking providing a safe harbor specific to this CMP for independent renal-dialysis facilities that pay premiums for Medicare Part B or Medigap for financially needy beneficiaries with ESRD.[259] Not surprisingly, in the final CMP regulation, it was the preventive care exclusion from the definition of remuneration that received the greatest attention. In the final regulations, the OIG has defined the term preventive care as any service that is a prenatal service or a post-natal well-baby visit or is a specific clinical service described in the U.S. Preventive Services Task Force's *Guide to Clinical Preventive Care Services*.

With respect to the scope of permissible incentives, the OIG provides examples such as healthcare items or services (e.g., blood sugar screenings, cholesterol tests, medic alert jewelry) and non-healthcare items or services (e.g., gift certificates, t-shirts, infant car seats, Thanksgiving turkeys). In addition, the OIG states that permissible incentives can include price reductions to promote the delivery of preventive care in the form of (1) waiving all or part of a copayment and (2) offering care as a free community service and forgoing billing Medicare and Medicaid as well as the beneficiaries. The OIG also limits the provision of these incentives by requiring that there be a reasonable relationship of the incentive to the value of the preventive care services and that the incentives may not include cash or cash equivalents.

### § 2-7(a)(2)  Special Advisory Bulletin

In August 2002, the OIG issued a Special Advisory Bulletin providing bright-line guidance for the healthcare industry to determine whether practices comply with the statutory prohibition on offering gifts or inducements to federal healthcare beneficiaries.[260] The OIG clarified that it will apply the prohibition on inducements to beneficiaries according to four principles.

1. The OIG has interpreted the prohibition to permit Medicare or Medicaid providers to offer beneficiaries inexpensive gifts (other than cash or cash equivalents) or services without violating the statute. For enforcement purposes, inexpensive gifts or services are those that have a retail value of no more than $10 individually, and no more than $50 in the aggregate annually per patient.

---

[258] 65 Fed. Reg. 24,400 (Apr. 26, 2000).
[259] 65 Fed. Reg. 25,460 (May 4, 2000). Subsequently, the OIG withdrew the notice of proposed rulemaking on Dec. 9, 2002. *See* 67 Fed. Reg. 72,896 (Dec. 9, 2002).
[260] OIG Special Advisory Bulletin, *Offering Gifts and Other Inducements to Beneficiaries*, (Aug. 2002).

2. Providers may offer beneficiaries more expensive items or services that fit within one of the five statutory exceptions: waivers of cost-sharing amounts based on financial need; properly disclosed copayment differentials in health plans; incentives to promote the delivery of certain preventive care services; any practice permitted under the federal Anti-Kickback Statute pursuant to 42 CFR 1001.952; or waivers of hospital outpatient copayments in excess of the minimum copayment amounts.

3. The OIG is considering several additional regulatory exceptions. The OIG may solicit public comments on additional exceptions for complimentary local transportation and for free goods in connection with participation in certain clinical studies.

4. The OIG will continue to entertain requests for advisory opinions related to the prohibition on inducements to beneficiaries. However... given the difficulty in drawing principled distinctions between categories of beneficiaries or types of inducements, favorable opinions... are expected to be, limited to situations involving conduct that is very close to an existing statutory or regulatory exception.

### § 2-7(a)(3)  2010 Modification to the CMP Provision

In 2010, as part of the Health Reform Law, Congress further limited the scope of the CMP by amending the statute such that illegal remuneration does not include "remuneration which promotes access to care and poses a low risk of harm to patients and Federal healthcare programs...."[261]

On January 3, 2011, the OIG issued Advisory Opinion 11-01, applying this "access to care" exception to a proposed arrangement by a network of tax-exempt pediatric children's hospitals (collectively, "Hospitals").[262] The program involved waiving insurance co-payments for child patients and providing free lodging and transportation for those children and their families. The Hospitals were still billing the federal programs, but not charging patients for co-payments. Because the Hospitals' patients were primarily Medicaid patients, the CMP law and its beneficiary inducement provisions were implicated. In analyzing the arrangement, the OIG bifurcated the analysis and discussed the Hospitals' waiver of co-payments (insurance-only billing) on one hand and the lodging and transportation issue on the other. Regarding waiving co-payments, the OIG justified its decision not to impose sanctions in part by acknowledging the historical aspect of how the Hospitals have never charged patients, their families, or third party payors for services. The OIG further bolstered this conclusion in stating that "history is joined with certain

---

[261] The Health Reform Law, § 6402; Social Security Act § 1128A(i)(6)(F); 42 U.S.C. 1320a-7a(i)(6)(F).
[262] OIG Advisory Op. No. 11-01.

## Federal Anti-Kickback Laws

aspects of the [Hospitals'] operations and relationships with physicians that, taken together, reduce the risk that the Insurance-Only Billing Policy would result in overutilization or unnecessary services." Regarding free lodging and transportation, the OIG acknowledged that that arrangement would fit within the contours of the "access to care" exception and would also pose a low risk of harm to federal healthcare programs. In addition, the OIG has provided further guidance concerning the routine waiver of coinsurance and deductibles in several advisory opinions.[263]

### § 2-7(a)(4)  Comparison of the Anti-Kickback Statute and the CMP Concerning Inducements to Beneficiaries

Although both the Anti-Kickback Statute and the CMP Statute address inducements to beneficiaries, there are a number of differences between the statutes. First, the penalties imposed upon violators of these statutes differ. While a violation of both statutes can result in the imposition of CMPs and exclusion from participation in the federal healthcare programs, the Anti-Kickback Statute is a criminal statute in which violators are subject to a criminal fine and/or imprisonment.

Second, historically these statutes had differing "mens rea" requirements. Prior to the passage of the Health Reform Law, the Anti-Kickback Statutes prohibited a person or entity from "knowingly and willfully" engaging in the various activities proscribed under the statute. In contrast, the CMP Statute prohibition on inducements to beneficiaries provides that the intent requirement is merely that a person either "knows" or "should know" that the remuneration furnished to the beneficiaries would likely influence their choice of supplier or provider. However, since the passage of the Health Reform Law, a person need not have actual knowledge of the Anti-Kickback Statute or specific intent to commit a violation of the Anti-Kickback Statute in order to violate the Statute.[264] Thus, the intent requirements between the Anti-Kickback Statute and the CMP Statute have become more consistent.

Third, the definition of the term remuneration under the CMP Statute excludes financial arrangements that satisfy a statutory exception to the

---

[263] *See* OIG Advisory Op. No. 97-4; OIG Advisory Op. No. 98-5 (whether a healthcare plan's method of coordinating insurance benefits, which effectively requires a nursing home to forgo certain Medicare cost-sharing amounts constitutes grounds for criminal, civil monetary, or exclusion penalties); OIG Advisory Op. No. 98-6 (whether waiving coinsurance obligations for participants in a clinical study sponsored by CMS will constitute grounds for criminal or civil monetary penalties); OIG Advisory Op. No. 99-6 (whether not billing pediatric oncology patients for coinsurance and deductible amounts constitutes grounds for imposition of criminal, civil monetary, or exclusion penalties); OIG Advisory Op. No. 99-1 (whether an arrangement for the provision of back-up emergency ambulance services that involves waivers of copayments and deductible amounts constitutes prohibited remuneration within the meaning of the Anti-Kickback Statute).

[264] The Health Reform Law, § 6402(f)(2); Social Security Act § 1128B(h); 42 U.S.C. 1320a-b7(h).

Anti-Kickback Statute and/or qualifies under one of the safe harbor regulations. However, the converse is *not* true; conduct that meets the requirements of an exception to the CMP for inducements to beneficiaries is not expressly protected from prosecution under the Anti-Kickback Statute. Accordingly, providers must structure arrangements that include the offering of inducements to beneficiaries in light of both the CMP Statute and the Anti-Kickback Statute.

This section offers a more-detailed discussion of the Anti-Kickback Statute and the CMP Statute as they relate to inducements to Medicare and Medicaid beneficiaries.

## § 2-7(b) Anti-Kickback Statute Addressing Government Contractors

Criminal and civil sanctions also are provided in another federal anti-kickback law applicable to government contractors.[265] Despite this similarity, there are differences between the healthcare Anti-Kickback Statute and the Public Contracts Anti-Kickback Act (PCAKA). The PCAKA specifically defines "kickback" as it relates to government contracts.[266] Here, the definition of kickback is modified to include the provision of anything of value "for the purpose of improperly obtaining or rewarding favorable treatment."[267] This clause can be interpreted to cover providing kickbacks in exchange for obtaining placement on a bidders list without meeting the requisite requirements or obtaining an unwarranted waiver of bidding or contracting deadlines. In 2005, the Court of Federal Claims decided *Morse Diesel International, Inc. v. United States*, which expanded the scope of this statutory element.[268] Violations of the PCAKA are punishable by fines as well as up to ten years imprisonment, and, unlike the Anti-Kickback Statute, the government may recover civil penalties of twice the amount of each kickback and up to $10,000 for each occurrence of prohibited conduct. In addition, the government also has

---

[265] 41 U.S.C. § 51 *et seq*. The Public Contracts Anti-Kickback Act prohibits a person from (1) providing, attempting to provide or offering to provide a kickback; (2) soliciting, accepting, or attempting to accept any kickback; or (3) including the price of prohibited kickback in the contract price in either a prime government contract or a subcontract to the prime.

[266] 41 U.S.C. § 52. A kickback is defined as any money, fee, commission, credit, gift, gratuity, thing of value, or compensation of any kind which is provided directly or indirectly, to any prime contractor, prime contractor employee, subcontractor, or subcontractor employee for the purpose of improperly obtaining or rewarding favorable treatment in connection with a prime contractor in connection with a subcontract relating to a prime contract.

[267] *Id.*

[268] *See* Morse Diesel International, Inc., d/b/a AMEC Construction Management, Inc. v. United States, 66 Fed.Cl. 788 (2005). This non-healthcare related anti-kickback case held that a fee commission splitting arrangement that was designed to "cement" a business relationship implicated the Public Contracts Anti-Kickback Act such that this arrangement was for the purpose of improperly obtaining or rewarding favorable treatment. The court stated the arrangement was a "gratuity designed to induce favorable treatment and line the brokers' pockets down the road."

## Federal Anti-Kickback Laws

the right to offset the amount of the kickback against moneys owed to the contractor. According to *United States v. Purdy*,[269] specific intent to procure government-related business and specific knowledge of government involvement are not required elements for a violation of the statute. Unlike the Anti-Kickback Statute, the PCAKA does not contain safe harbors; however, in order to implicate the PCAKA, the alleged kickback must be in connection with a government prime contract or subcontract under a government prime contract. Therefore, absent a government contract, the statute does not apply.[270]

The United States attempted to use this federal statute as a separate count in a Medicare/Medicaid fraud case in *United States v. Kensington Hospital*.[271] The United States District Court for the Eastern District of Pennsylvania dismissed the count relating to the Anti-Kickback Statute. The court ruled that, with respect to the Medicaid claims, the physician's relationship with the state Medicaid plan did not involve a "prime contract," as Medicaid is a grant program rather than a contractual action. According to the statute a prime contract "means a contract or contractual action entered into by the United States for the purpose of obtaining supplies, materials, equipment, or services of any kind."[272] With respect to the Medicare program, the court ruled that the Anti-Kickback Statute did not apply because the defendants were not subject to any "subcontractor" relationship.

Nevertheless, in *United States v. Warning*,[273] the same court held that defendants could be held liable under the Anti-Kickback Statute in connection with the submission of Medicare claims. In *Warning*, the defendants argued that the charges of violation of the Anti-Kickback Statute should be dismissed for the same reason the Medicaid claims were dismissed in *Kensington* (i.e., the claims did not involve a "prime contract"). However, the court in *Warning* ruled that in contrast to the Medicaid program which is a grant program lacking contractual action, Medicare pays benefits to medical providers pursuant to direct contractual arrangements, which qualify as a "prime contract" under the Anti-Kickback Statute.[274]

In September, 2004 the Eastern District of Pennsylvania decided a case involving alleged violations of the FCA and the PCAKA.[275] In *Merck-Medco Managed Care, L.L.C.*, the anti-kickback claim arose from a pharmacy ben-

---

[269] United States v. Purdy, 144 F.3d 241 (2d Cir. 1998).
[270] *See* United States v. Metzinger, No. Civ. A. 94-7520, 1995 U.S. Dist. LEXIS 6074 (E.D. Pa. Apr. 28, 2995).
[271] United States v. Kensington Hosp., 760 F. Supp. 1120 (E.D. Pa. 1991). *See also* United States v. Kensington Hosp., 1992 U.S. Dist. LEXIS 11150 (E.D. Pa. July 28, 1992); United States v. Kensington Hosp., 1993 U.S. Dist. LEXIS 383 (E.D. Pa. Jan. 14, 1993).
[272] 41 U.S.C. § 52(4).
[273] United States v. Warning, et al., 1994 WL 396432 (E.D. Pa. 1994).
[274] *Id.*
[275] United States v. Merck-Medco Managed Care, L.L.C. and Medco Health Solutions, Inc. *et al.*, 336 F. Supp. 2d 430 (2004).

efit manager's alleged payment to the health plan in exchange for favorable treatment and the solicitation and acceptance of kickbacks from drug companies to change patients' prescription drugs.[276] The government alleged that Medco "kicked back a payment of $87.4 million to a health plan that had entered into an agreement with the Medicare program to provide managed care services."[277] Citing *Kensington*, Medco claimed that the PCAKA did not extend to contracts involving Medicare; however, the court disagreed. The court stated that here Medco, a subcontractor, issued kickbacks to a primary contractor in exchange for favorable treatment and this activity was contemplated by the PCAKA and by *Kensington*.[278] In dicta, the court called the government's allegations "thin" and "suspects that, without more, the Government will be unable to save its case on this count from summary judgment."[279] However, because the court was obligated to apply a favorable inference to the plaintiff's case, the defendant's motion to dismiss was ultimately denied as to the anti-kickback claim. The anti-kickback count appears to be pending in the United States District Court, Eastern District of Pennsylvania.

## § 2-7(c) TRICARE

TRICARE, formerly known as the Civilian Health and Medical Program of the Uniformed Service (CHAMPUS), is a regionally managed healthcare program for active duty and retired military members of the uniformed services, their families, and survivors. The program is administered by the Assistant Secretary of Defense for Health Affairs and is governed by Title 32 C.F.R. Section 199. These regulations authorize administrative remedies for fraud and abuse and include a prohibition on "[a]rrangements by providers with employees, independent contractors, suppliers, or others which appear to be designed primarily to overcharge TRICARE through various means (such as commissions, fee-splitting, and kickbacks) used to divert or conceal improper or unnecessary costs or profits."[280] Although TRICARE officials are neither presently interpreting this language as applicable to a provider's return on investment in a healthcare venture nor otherwise using the safe harbor regulations as a standard, this is clearly an area to watch in the future.

---

[276] *Id.* at 448.
[277] *Id.*
[278] *Id.* at 449.
[279] *Id.* at 450.
[280] 32 C.F.R. 199(c)(12) (July 1, 2005).

## § 2-7(d)   Federal "Sunshine Law"

Section 6002 of the Health Reform Law includes provisions from the Physician Payment Sunshine Act (Sunshine Act).[281] The Sunshine Act was introduced originally in 2007 by Senators Chuck Grassley (R-IA) and Herb Kohl (D-WI), and then re-introduced in 2009. Although the Sunshine Act does not prohibit any specific financial relationships, it requires "applicable manufacturers" including all drug, device, biological or medical supply manufacturers to submit electronic "Transparency Reports" disclosing certain payments or transfers of value to "covered recipients" (physicians and teaching hospitals[282]).[283] Further, the Sunshine Act requires all applicable manufacturers and applicable Group Purchasing Organizations (GPOs) to report information related to any "ownership or investment interests" annually.

Under Section 6002, the effective date for manufacturers and GPOs to begin recording transfers of value for the first report was January 1, 2012, and the first report was scheduled to be due to the Secretary by March 31, 2013, which includes all data from the 2012 calendar year. However, in a proposed rule issued by CMS on December 19, 2011 (the "Sunshine Proposed Rule"), CMS states that the final rule will not be published in time for applicable manufacturers and applicable GPOs to begin collecting the required information on January 1, 2012.[284] Therefore, CMS stated that they "will not require applicable manufacturers and applicable GPOs to begin collecting the required information until after the publication of the final rule. . ." In addition, CMS also sought comments on whether 90 days would be sufficient after the final rule is published for applicable manufacturers and GPOs to begin collection data and on the feasibility of making the first annual report on March 31, 2013. Further, the Sunshine Proposed Rule limits the definition of a covered drug or biological to those that, by law, require a prescription to dispense and limits the definition of a covered device or medical supply to that that, by law, require premarket approval by, or premarket notification to, the FDA.

Under the Sunshine Proposed Rule, "applicable manufacturers" must report:

1.  applicable manufacturer or applicable GPO name;

---

[281] The Health Reform Law, § 6002; Social Security Act, § 1128G; 42 U.S.C. 1320a-7h.

[282] CMS proposes defining a teaching hospital as an institution that receives payments for indirect medical education or direct graduate medical education during the most recent year for which information is available.

[283] An applicable manufacturer is subject to the reporting requirements if its product is sold or distributed in the United States, regardless of where the product is manufactured, or where the entity is located or incorporated, and includes the entity that holds the approval, licensure or clearance for the product, even if the entity contracts out the actual manufacturing. In addition, an entity under "common ownership" with, and that "provides assistance or support" to, an applicable manufacturer is also subject to the reporting requirements.

[284] 76 Fed. Reg. 78,742 (Dec. 19, 2011).

2. the covered recipient's name;
3. the covered recipient's business address, specialty (physician only), and National Provider Identifiers (NPI) number (if applicable);
4. the date of the payment or other transfer of value;
5. a description of the form of payment or other transfer of value (e.g., cash or cash equivalent, in-kind items or services, and stock, stock option or any other ownership intrest, dividend, profit or other return on investment);
6. a description of the nature of payment (e.g., charitable contributions, food and beverages, direct compensation and other);
7. name of the associated covered drug, device, biological, or medical supply, as applicable;
8. name of entity that received the payment or other transfer of value, if not provided to the covered recipient directly;
9. whether the payment or other transfer of value was provided to a physician holding ownership or investment interest in the applicable manufacturer; and
10. whether the payment or other transfer of value should be granted a delay in publication because it was made pursuant to a product research agreement, development agreement or clinical investigation.

Specific items that would need to be reported include: (1) consulting fees; (2) compensation for services other than consulting; (3) honoraria; (4) gifts; (5) entertainment; (6) food; (7) travel (including the specific destination); (8) education; (9) research; (10) charitable contributions; (11) royalties or licenses; (12) current or prospective ownership or investment interests; (13) compensation for serving as faculty or a speaker for a continuing medical education program; (14) grants; and (15) "any other nature of the payment or other transfer of value as defined by the Secretary."

Manufacturers and GPOs are also required to report physician ownership interests in private companies. Under the Sunshine Proposed Rule, CMS proposes that an applicable manufacturer or GPO must report:

- applicable manufacturer or applicable GPO name;
- the name of the ownership or investment physician;
- the specialty, business address and NPI number of the ownership or investment physician;
- whether the ownership or investment interest is held by the physician, or an immediate family member of the physician;
- the dollar amount invested; and

## Federal Anti-Kickback Laws

- the value and terms of each ownership or investment interest.

In addition, CMS proposes that an applicable GPO must report any payments or other transfers of value provided to the physician owner or investor, including the following: (1) amount of payment or other transfer of value in U.S. dollars; (2) the date of payment or other transfer of value; (3) the form of payment or other transfer of value; (4) the nature of payment or other transfer of value; and (5) the name of the associated covered drug, device, biological, or medical supply, as applicable.

CMS proposes that a "payment or transfer of value" includes all payments and transfers of value unless otherwise excluded. The Sunshine Proposed Rule provides the following additional guidance on excluded payments and transfers of value: (1) transfers of value made indirectly to a covered recipient through a third party, where the manufacturer is unaware of the recipient's identity; (2) items less than $10, provided the aggregate amount provided by the manufacturer to a covered recipient does not exceed $100 during the calendar year; (3) free product samples intended for patient use; (4) educational materials that directly benefit patients or intended for patient use; (5) transfers of value when the covered recipient is a patient and not acting in his/her professional capacity; (6) discounts and rebates; (7) loans of covered devices for a short-term tiral period, not to exceed 90 days, to permit evaluation of the covered device by the covered recipient; (8) items or services provided under a contractual warranty, including the replace of a covered device, where the terms of the warrant are set forth in the purchase or lease agreement for the covered device; (9) dividends or other profit distributions from, or ownership or investments interests in, a publicly traded security or mutual fund; (10) in the case of an applicable manufacturer who offers a self-insured plan, payments for the provision of healthcare to employees under the plan; (11) in the case of a covered recipient who is a licensed non-medical professional, a transfer of anything of value to the covered recipient if the transfer is payment solely for the non-medical professional services of the licensed non-medical professional; (12) in the case of a covered recipient who is a physician, a transfer of anything of value to the covered recipient if the transfer is payment solely for the services of the covered recipient with respect to a civil or criminal action or an administrative proceeding; and (13) in-kind items provided for charity care.

Penalties for failing to report include the imposition of a CMP. The Sunshine Proposed Rule includes several facts that may be used to determine the amount of a CMP, including the: (i) length of time the manufacturer or GPO fails to report; (ii) length of time the manufacturer or GPO knew of the payment or transfer of value or ownership or investment interest; (iii) amount of the payment or transfer of value or ownership or investment interest that the manufacturer or GPO failed to report; (iv) level of culpability; (v) nature and amount of information reported in error; and (v) degree of diligence exercised in correcting information reported in error. In addition, CMS proposes that the Secretary of DHHS, CMS, OIG or their designees may audit, evaluate or inspect applicable manufacturers and GPOs regarding their compliance with timely, accurate and complete submissions.

Prior to the enactment of the Sunshine Act provisions, a number of pharmaceutical companies including Merck, Pfizer, AstraZeneca, Johnson & Johnson, and Eli Lilly explicitly supported the premise of these requirements and had voluntarily begun disclosing these types of payments.[285]

Further, hospitals and medical schools have also been proactive in beginning to disclose financial relationships regulated by the Sunshine Act. For example, in December 2008, the Cleveland Clinic announced that it would begin to disclose on its website all of its doctors' business relationships. Specifically, the website will list the companies with which the doctor has a financial stake and will include information on equity, royalties, fiduciary positions, and consulting arrangements that pay at least $5,000 per year.[286] Other healthcare providers that have announced similar plans include Stanford University School of Medicine and Partners HealthCare.[287]

States have also enacted legislation in advance of the Sunshine Act's effective date. For example, in August 2008, Massachusetts Governor Deval Patrick (D) signed a bill into law calling for state regulators to devise rules "no less restrictive" than Pharmaceutical Research and Manufacturers of America's and the Advanced Medical Technology Association's industry codes. The law also requires that companies disclose gifts to healthcare providers of at least $50 to the Department of Public Health. The state will then

---

[285] *See, e.g.*, Merck, *Transparency at Merck: Advancing the Dialogue Toward a Healthier Future*, available online at http://www.merck.com/corporate-responsibility/business-ethics-transparency/ethics-financial-support-third-parties/home.html (last visited Aug. 16, 2011); Eli Lilly and Company, *Lilly Set to Become First Pharmaceutical Research Company to Disclose Physician Payments* (Sept. 24, 2008), *available online at* http://www.prnewswire.com/cgi-bin/micro_stories.pl?ACCT=916306&TICK=LLY&STORY=/www/story/09-24-2008/0004891376&EDATE=Sep+24,+2008; NEW YORK TIMES, *Drug Maker to Report Fees to Doctors* (Sept. 25, 2008), *available* online at http://www.nytimes.com/2008/09/25/health/policy/25drug.html; Pfizer, *Pfizer Posts Details About Interactions With U.S. Physicians, Other Healthcare Professionals And Clinical Research Partners* (March 31, 2010), *available online at* http://www.pfizer.com/files/news/press_releases/2010/hcp_payment_033110.pdf; Johnson & Johnson, *Johnson & Johnson Announces Support For Kohl-Grassley Physician Payments Sunshine Act of 2009* (May 7, 2009), *available* online at http://www.jnk.com/connect/news/all/20090507_130000.

[286] Cleveland Clinic, *Cleveland Clinic Discloses Doctors' Industry Ties* (Dec. 2, 2008), *available* online at http://www.nytimes.com/2008/12/03/business/03clinic.html?ref=clevelandclinic.

[287] *See, e.g.*, Stanford School of Medicine, *Stanford Medical School to Provide Online Disclosure of Faculty's Consulting Activities* (Apr. 1, 2009), *available online at* http://med.stanford.edu/news_releases/2009/april/disclosure.html; Partners HealthCare, *Partners HealthCare to Implement New Industry Interaction Recommendations* (Apr. 10, 2009), *available online at* http://www.partners.org/documents/CommissionPressRelease_PartnersHealthCare2009.pdf.

### Federal Anti-Kickback Laws

publish all disclosures on a website. Failure to disclose will result in a fine not to exceed $5,000 for each violation.[288] The Massachusetts law differs from the proposed federal Sunshine Act in that the Massachusetts law covers not only physicians, but pharmacists, hospitals, nursing homes, and health benefit plan administrators. Furthermore, the Massachusetts plan bans gifts altogether rather than just requiring disclosure.[289]

However, any state law requiring manufacturers to disclose or report the same type of information required to be reported under the Sunshine Act will be preempted. The Sunshine Act will not preempt any state statute or regulation that requires the disclosure or reporting of information that is:

- not of the type required to be disclosed or reported under the Sunshine Act;
- an exclusion under the Sunshine Act (except when the state statute pertains to the exclusion for items valued at under $10); or
- provided for other reasons (e.g., public health surveillance, pursuant to a government investigation or administrative proceeding).

## § 2-8   MAJOR ISSUES IN ANTI-KICKBACK INTERPRETATION AND ENFORCEMENT

### § 2-8(a)   Private Actions Under the Anti-Kickback Statute

Historically, the Anti-Kickback Statute does not afford an explicit private right of action to bring suit against a competitor. For example, in *West Allis Memorial Hospital, Inc. v. Bowen*,[290] a hospital attempted to enjoin a competitor from waiving coinsurance and deductible amounts or in the alternative declare such programs as nonviolative of the Anti-Kickback Statute. The court held that the hospital did not have standing to bring suit under the Anti-Kickback Statute:

> [W]e find that neither the structure of [the Anti-Kickback Statute] nor its legislative history suggests that Congress intended to provide a private remedy to Medicare providers . . . which may be injured as a result of a competitors noncompliance with the provisions of that statute. . . . The legislative history of [the Anti-Kickback Statute] further supports the conclusion that it is the Government,

---

[288] *See* Mass. Gen. Law 111N; 105 CMR 970.000.
[289] Additional information on some of these state initiatives can be found in Chapter 6.
[290] West Allis Memorial Hosp., Inc. v. Bowen, 852 F.2d 251 (7th Cir. 1988).

and not private parties, which is charged with the enforcement of the Medicare program. . . .[291]

More recent enforcement efforts by private litigants, however, have been more successful, largely because plaintiffs are not seeking a direct federal cause of action, but rather are using the Anti-Kickback Statute creatively to state a cause of action under a separate statutory authority. For example, even before Congress amended the law in 2010 as part of the Health Reform Law, plaintiffs, with mixed success, were using the FCA as a vehicle for enforcing the Anti-Kickback Statute. For example, in *United States ex rel. Roy v. Anthony*,[292] the U.S. District Court for the Southern District of Ohio denied the defendant's motion to dismiss and held that a qui tam plaintiff may bring a private cause of action against a party under the FCA when the party's activity allegedly violated the Anti-Kickback Statute. Although the court stated that "[t]his vague assertion creates a tenuous connection between the Fraud & Abuse Statute and the False Claims Act, . . . the connection is sufficient to overcome the burden of a 12(b)(6) motion. Under the facts alleged, the Plaintiff could produce evidence that would show that the kickbacks allegedly paid to the defendant physicians somehow tainted the claims for Medicare. Additionally, the Plaintiff may establish that the claims for Medicare payments were constructively false or fraudulent."[293] However, as stated above, in light of the modification to the Anti-Kickback Statute in 2010, there is no longer a question that an action can be brought under the FCA for violation of of the Anti-Kickback Statute.

In addition, private litigants also have challenged the validity of certain contracts on the basis of a violation of the Anti-Kickback Statute. For example, in *Vana v. Vista Hospital Systems, Inc.* a hospital sought to void long-term rental contracts held by the doctors and evict the physicians from two office building that the hospital owned. The hospital claimed that the contracts violated both the federal and state Anti-Kickback Statutes since the hospital administration offered the doctors low rent to induce patient referrals even though the physicians were not fully aware of this intent. The court agreed with the hospital and found that the leases were invalid.[294] In another example, a federal district court refused to allow a marketing company to proceed with a breach of con-

---

[291] *Id.* at 255; *See also* State Medical and Oxygen Supply, Inc. v. American Medical Oxygen Co., 750 P.2d 1085 (Mont. Sup. Ct. 1988).

[292] United States *ex. rel.* Roy v. Anthony, 914 F. Supp. 1504 (S.D. Ohio 1994).

[293] *Id.* at 1,506–07.

[294] Vana v. Vista Hosp. Sys., Inc., 1993 WL 597402 (Cal. Super. Ct. 1993). *See also* Nursing Home Consultants, Inc. v. Quantum Health Servs., 926 F. Supp. 835 (Ark. Cir. Ct. 1996); Medical Dev. Network Inc. v. Professional Respiratory Care/Home Medical Equip. Servs. Inc., 673 So. 2d 565 (Fla. Dist. Ct. App. 1996); Modern Medical Labs. Inc. v. Smith-Kline Beecham Clinical Labs. Inc., (N.D. Ill., Aug. 16, 1994).

## Federal Anti-Kickback Laws

tract suit against a durable medical equipment supplier based upon the defense that the contract allegedly violated the Anti-Kickback Statute.[295]

Another case that exemplifies how a plaintiff may attempt to bring a private action claim under the Anti-Kickback Statute is *Zichichi v. Jefferson Ambulatory Surgery Center, LLC*.[296] In this case, the plaintiff, Dr. Zichichi, was a founding member and initial investor in Ambulatory Surgery Center, LLC (ASC, LLC) and after the plaintiff was injured in a car accident and was no longer able to perform surgery, the remaining members of ASC, LLC, voted to terminate Dr. Zichichi's membership and ownership rights. Plaintiff brought suit alleging ASC, LLC's breach of contract, breach of fiduciary duty, fraud, conspiracy, conversion, defamation, and that ASC, LLC's actions were in violation of the safe harbor provisions of the Anti-Kickback Statute. The court held that the plaintiff's only viable claims were those of breach of contract and that the plaintiff's allegations that the arrangement violated the Anti-Kickback Statute were without merit because no private right of action exists under the Anti-Kickback Statute.[297]

### § 2-8(b)  Integrated Delivery Systems: Physician Practice Acquisition and Divestiture

While the early 1990s were defined by hospital systems buying up physician practices, and the late 1990s and the first years of the twenty-first century were defined by those same hospitals divesting practices that they were competing to purchase just a few years earlier, as a result of the Health Reform Law, there has been a resurgence of physician practice acquisition.

Both physician practice acquisitions and physician practice divestitures by hospitals can raise anti-kickback issues. The issue is whether the payment for or sale by the hospital of the physician's practice is really an inducement to the physician to refer patients to the hospital.

### § 2-8(b)(1)  Practice Acquisitions

In the early to mid-1990s, while solo and small-group physicians found it difficult to cope with regulatory requirements imposed on physician practices, large multi-specialty groups and hospitals wanted to "integrate" with more physicians/physician groups in order to sell a more comprehensive package of healthcare services to third-party payors and employers.

---

[295] Nursing Home Consultants, Inc., v. Quantum Health Servs., Inc., 926 F. Supp. 835 (E.D. Ark. 1996).
[296] Zichichi v. Jefferson Ambulatory Surgery Center, LLC, et al., 2007 U.S. Dist. Lexis 82798 (E.D. La. 2007).
[297] *Id.* at US Dist. Lexis 82798, 21.

Consequently, a number of questions arose concerning both the fraud and abuse and tax-exempt implications with hospital systems acquiring physician practices. In December 1992, the Associate General Counsel for the OIG responded to an informal inquiry from the Internal Revenue Service (IRS) regarding hospital purchases of physician practices.[298] The IRS presented the OIG with a scenario in which a physician practice would be acquired either by a hospital or another entity that also would acquire one or more hospitals (and potentially other healthcare providers as well). The physicians from those practices would continue to treat patients and be affiliated (through an employment relationship or otherwise) with the hospital or other entity which acquired their practices. The practice acquisition could arise through a number of different methods or arrangements and the ensuing relationships or affiliations would vary. The end result in each case, however, would be the common ownership or control of both the hospital and the physician practice by a single entity.

The OIG responded that such acquisitions may violate the Anti-Kickback Statute because they "merely [are] sophisticated disguises to share the profits of business at a hospital with referring physicians in order to induce the physicians to steer referrals to the hospital."

The OIG focused on two aspects of physician practice acquisition which may result in violations of the Anti-Kickback Statute: (1) the total amount paid for the physician practice and the nature and type of items for which the physician receives payment; and (2) the amount and manner in which the physician is subsequently compensated for providing services to patients. For these payments, the letter states "it is necessary to consider the amounts paid . . . to determine whether they reasonably reflect the fair market value . . . " The letter states that when attempting to assess "fair market value," traditional or common methods of economic valuation do not comport with the proscriptions of the Anti-Kickback Statute. Indeed, the letter states that "[m]erely because [a] buyer may be willing to pay a particular price is not sufficient to render the price paid fair market value." Rather, the fact that a buyer may benefit from referrals from the seller is important to the anti-kickback analysis.

The letter further states that items ordinarily included in determining fair market value may have to be excluded from consideration in order to comply with DHHS's strict interpretation of the anti-kickback provisions. Six specific items were enumerated as raising questions about whether payment was being made for the value of a referral stream:

1. payment for goodwill;
2. payment for value of an ongoing business unit;

---

[298] Letter from D. McCarty Thornton, Associate General Counsel, OIG, to T.J. Sullivan, Technical Assistant, Office of the Associate Chief Counsel, IRS (Dec. 22, 1992), *available online at* http://oig.hhs.gov/fraud/docs/safeharborregulations/acquisition122292.htm.

## Federal Anti-Kickback Laws

3. payment for covenants not to compete;
4. payment for exclusive dealing agreements;
5. payment for patient lists; or
6. payment for patient records.[299]

The letter also suggests that a very revealing inquiry would be to compare the financial welfare of the involved physicians before and after the acquisition. Presumably, improved economic condition for the physicians would indicate that they may have impermissibly benefited from the acquisition. Also, the OIG would review referrals before and after the acquisition for patterns which evidence increased "loyalty" to the hospital purchaser.

Following publicity regarding this letter, many in the healthcare industry wondered whether a hospital could ever pay a physician more for her practice than the fair market value of the hard assets of the practice—i.e., real estate, furnishings, and equipment. Such an interpretation would mean that a hospital would be required to pay far less for a physician's practice than another physician. It also would fail to recognize any value at all for the practice as an ongoing business with a continuing location, telephone number, trained employees, and consistent cash flow.

In this regard, it is important to note that the OIG letter did not treat goodwill and other payments described above as absolutely prohibited. Rather, such payments are treated as "raising an issue" under the Anti-Kickback Statute. Indeed, in a subsequent letter from the OIG to the AHA, the OIG emphasized that the earlier letter did not indicate that payments for intangible assets by a hospital to a physician are necessarily illegal per se.[300] The OIG's letter to the AHA also addressed the issue of acquisition of physician practices by both physicians and hospitals. The OIG's letter to the AHA described two different acquisitions—one in which a physician's practice is purchased by another physician, and the other in which a physician's practice is purchased by a hospital. In both scenarios, the valuation process is the same. After reaching agreement on the price of the practice, the parties then value the remainder of the practice and assign a value for the expectation of future patronage by patients to the practice being acquired. Thus, the total price of the practice includes an amount for the tangible assets as well as for the intangible assets.

According to the OIG's letter to the AHA, the physician-to-physician practice purchase is "far less problematic" than the physician to hospital practice purchase. Although both situations could implicate the Anti-Kickback Statute, the hospital purchaser will be in a position to benefit from referrals to

---

[299] *Id.*
[300] Letter from D. McCarty Thornton, Associate General Counsel, OIG, to John E. Steiner Jr., Assistant General Counsel, American Hospital Association (Nov. 2, 1993), *available online at* http://oig.hhs.gov/fraud/docs/safeharborregulations/acquisition110293.htm.

the practice, and thus, the OIG believes that it is always questionable whether a portion of that amount paid for the practice by the hospital is for future referrals. The OIG emphasized in this AHA letter that it is the intent of the parties that is relevant to determine the applicability of the Anti-Kickback Statute. Thus, "the fact that a hospital purchases a physician practice for the same amount that another physician might pay does not insulate the hospital from liability under the [anti-kickback] statute." The OIG's AHA letter further states that offering the *same* price that another physician would offer could be motivated by a desire to pay for future referrals.

This exchange of letters underscores the importance of obtaining an assessment of fair market value in any practice purchase transaction. While the OIG has not issued any guidelines regarding appraisals of practice value, considerable literature exists in this area relating to tax-exempt organizations, which must meet standards prohibiting "private inurement." As private inurement analysis is similar to anti-kickback analysis, both involving an assessment of whether the remuneration paid is commensurate with the fair market value of what was purchased, the IRS guidelines should be equally relevant for anti-kickback purposes.[301]

In order to determine the quality of an appraisal, the IRS has developed certain guidelines, which require that an appraisal be conducted by an independent appraiser.[302] Moreover, the IRS favors appraisals which include certain components:

- an executive summary;
- a discussion of the nature of the business and the history of the enterprise from its inception;
- the economic outlook in general and the condition and outlook of the specific industry in particular;
- the book value of the stock, if any, or other hard assets, and the financial condition of the business, including at least two years of balance sheets and enumerated financial ratios;
- the earning capacity of the company, supported by five years of profit-and-loss statements;

---

[301] *See* Charles F. Kaiser and Amy Henchey, *Valuation of Medical Practice*, 1995 (FY 1996) EXEMPT ORGANIZATION CONTINUING PROFESSIONAL EDUCATION TECHNICAL INSTRUCTION PROGRAM TEXTBOOK (1996 CPE Text); Charles F. Kaiser et al., *Integrated Delivery Systems and Joint Venture Dissolutions Update*, 1994 (FY 1995) EXEMPT ORGANIZATION CONTINUING PROFESSIONAL EDUCATION TECHNICAL INSTRUCTION PROGRAM TEXTBOOK (1995 CPE Text); Charles F. Kaiser and John F. Reilly, *Integrated Delivery Systems*, 1993 (FY 1994) EXEMPT ORGANIZATION CONTINUING PROFESSIONAL EDUCATION TECHNICAL INSTRUCTION PROGRAM TEXTBOOK (1994 CPE Text).

[302] Charles F. Kaiser and John F. Reilly, *Integrated Delivery Systems*, 1993 (FY 1994) EXEMPT ORGANIZATION CONTINUING PROFESSIONAL EDUCATION TECHNICAL INSTRUCTION PROGRAM TEXTBOOK, at 212, 235.

## Federal Anti-Kickback Laws

- the dividend-paying capacity of the company (if a corporation);
- the estimated value of goodwill and/or other intangibles;
- descriptions of the stock or assets to be sold; and
- comparable taxable companies and the market price of their respective stocks.[303]

### § 2-8(b)(2)   Practice Divestiture

As mentioned, many hospitals that purchased physician practices in the early 1990s decided to divest themselves of these practices in the late 1990s and early 2000s, as the practices, generally, were unprofitable. When a hospital is trying to divest itself of an unprofitable physician practice, it may be tempted to enter into a quick deal to rid itself as quickly as possible of a hemorrhaging business line. As these divestitures often involve the original selling physician or practice group reacquiring the practice assets, however, physician practice divestitures are likely to result in heightened scrutiny from both IRS and healthcare regulators. For example, if a hospital sells a physician practice for less than it paid, it could be accused of having overpaid for the practice in the first place.

Although the OIG has not issued any formal guidance regarding the issues involved in physician practice divestiture, the OIG has informally stated that the sale of these practices could, in fact, implicate the federal fraud and abuse laws. The key issue is whether the arrangement constitutes a fair market value arrangement, the same issue that should have been the focus during the acquisition of the practice. As mentioned earlier, the various elements of the proposed disengagement arrangement would need to be identified, such as tangibles such as office space and equipment as well as the intangibles, such as patient charts and the value of the practice's name, and, where necessary, should be the subject of a valuation by an outside, independent appraisal firm. For example, if the physicians will be reacquiring practice assets from the hospital, these assets should be independently appraised to support their reacquisition purchase price. Valuations of goodwill or accounts receivable sold to the physicians should also be valued in accordance with independent valuations. Finally, the parties may be able to value and assign a purchase price or consideration to other elements of the divestiture, such as the early termination of the physicians' employment agreements, the physicians' execution of releases in favor of the hospital, and the physicians' willingness to assume any long-term lease obligations of the hospital that relate to the physicians' practice sites.

---

[303] *Id.*

## § 2-8(c)   Regulation of Marketing Practices

For the marketing and sales personnel of a healthcare provider, understanding what the government permits in marketing one's items and services is often complex and confusing. Moreover, marketing activities constitute not only "remuneration" given to a healthcare provider but, as described above, also applies to improper remuneration given to Medicare beneficiaries and Medicaid recipients.

For example, the government has alleged that the sales and marketing personnel of healthcare providers have offered, for example, cash gifts, airline tickets, free lodging at a resort, opera tickets, gift certificates (including gift certificates for dinner, car washes, dry-cleaning, shoe shines, and oil changes), sporting event tickets, computers, fax machines, VCRs, medical textbooks, and dinners at five-star restaurants all in an effort to induce the healthcare provider to refer patients to them for items or services that will be paid for by the Medicare and Medicaid programs.

Although the OIG has not issued one particular document that the public can look to in order to identify potential marketing anti-kickback concerns, it has done so through a number of issuances. For example, as explained above, the OIG has issued a Special Fraud Alert dealing with prescription drug marketing practices, regarding the OIG's concern that pharmaceutical manufacturers are offering physicians, suppliers and patients improper benefits in exchange for selecting specific prescription drug brands. In that same Special Fraud Alert, the OIG outlines the factors it looks at when considering if a payment or gift may be improper under the Anti-Kickback Statute. The OIG provides that a payment or gift may be improper if it is:

- made to a person in a position to generate business for the paying party;
- related to the volume of business generated; and
- more than nominal in value and/or exceeds fair market value of any legitimate service rendered to the payor, or is unrelated to any service at all other than the referral of patients.[304]

In addition, in the preamble to the original safe harbors, the OIG recognizes the legitimacy of marketing federal healthcare program business, yet also identifies factors that the OIG looks at when determining whether marketing activities have violated the anti-kickback prohibition:

> We, of course, recognize that many of these advertising and marketing activities do not warrant prosecution in part because (1) they are passive in nature, i.e., the activities do not involved direct contact

---

[304] *Prescription Drug Marketing Scheme Special Fraud Alert,* Aug. 1994.

with program beneficiaries, or (2) the individual or entity involved in these promotions is not involved in the delivery of healthcare. Such individuals or entities are not in a position of public trust in the same manner as physicians or other healthcare professionals who recommend or order products or services for their patients. Thus, we agree that many advertising and marketing activities warrant safe harbor protection under the personal services and management contracts safe harbor.[305]

The OIG continues by saying that it has been their experience that promoters and consultants often "become involved in marketing activities that encourage healthcare providers and others to violate the statute." The OIG cites as examples the development of impermissible joint venture arrangements and the routine waiver of coinsurance and deductibles. Thus, the OIG added to the personal services and management safe harbor the provision that the service is not protected if it involves the counseling or promotion of an illegal activity.

The OIG's pronouncements and focus on improper marketing to physicians and providers underscores the importance that healthcare providers institute policies focusing on training their marketing and sales force on the "dos and don'ts" of the provision of gifts, meals, and entertainment to their customers. These policies should outline the principles and procedures necessary to make sure their sales and marketing programs do not run afoul of the Anti-Kickback Statute. For example, the policies should address that provider's definition of "nominal value" as well as the importance that gifts and entertainment occur only on an occasional basis and always benefit patient care.

The OIG has also spoken regarding the issue of telemarketing by durable medical equipment suppliers by issuing a Special Fraud Alert.[306] In that Special Fraud Alert, the OIG references the fact that Section 1834(a)(17) of the SSA prohibits suppliers of durable medical equipment from making unsolicited telephone calls to Medicare beneficiaries regarding the furnishing of a covered item, except in three specific situations: (1) the beneficiary has given written permission to the supplier to make contact by telephone; (2) the contact is regarding a covered item the supplier has already furnished the beneficiary; and (3) the supplier has furnished at least one covered item to the beneficiary during the preceding fifteen months. The fraud alert clarifies that the use of independent marking firms to make unsolicited telephone calls is also prohibited stating "[s]uppliers cannot do indirectly that which they are prohibited from doing directly."[307] Moreover, a durable medical equipment

---

[305] 56 Fed. Reg. 35,974 (July 29, 1991).
[306] 68 Fed. Reg. 10,254 (Mar. 4, 2003).
[307] *Id.* at 10,255.

supplier must verify that third parties that the supplier contracts with are not participating in the prohibited activity.

## § 2-8(d)  Professional Courtesy

The term "professional courtesy" is used to describe the practice by a physician of waiving all, or part of, his fee for services provided to the physician's office staff, other physicians and their families. Over time, the term has also encompassed the waiver of coinsurance obligations or other out of pocket expenses for physicians and their families. Professional courtesy enjoys a long historical tradition in the healthcare field. In fact, when the AMA first issued its code of medical ethics, it made the reciprocal treatment of physicians and their families an obligation that medical professionals owed to each other.[308] This was the standard until 1957 when the code was revised and the practice became more a matter of etiquette then ethics.[309] The AMA encourages physicians today to use their best judgment when offering professional courtesy. Physicians are cautioned that waiving patient copayments may be especially problematic.

In general, the OIG looks at two factors when determining whether a professional courtesy arrangement runs afoul of the fraud and abuse laws (i) how the recipients of the professional courtesy are selected; and (ii) how the professional courtesy is extended.[310] If recipients are selected in a manner that directly or indirectly takes into account their ability to affect past or future referrals, the Anti-Kickback Statute may be implicated. If the professional courtesy is extended through a waiver of copayment obligation other statutes may be implicated, including the prohibition on inducements to beneficiaries.[311]

As was discussed, in May 1991, the OIG issued a Special Fraud Alert focusing on routine waivers of coinsurance and deductible amounts under Medicare Part B. According to the Special Fraud Alert, "when providers, practitioners, or suppliers forgive financial obligations for reasons other than the genuine financial hardship of the particular patient, they may be unlawfully inducing that patient to purchase items of services from them[,]" in violation of the Anti-Kickback Statute.[312] This consideration, amplified by the September 2000 compliance program guidance, shows the suspect nature of the forgiveness of copayments. Professional courtesy involves forgiveness of financial obligations based upon the special relationships between physicians and others in the healthcare industry and is not based on genuine financial hardship.

---

[308] *Rethinking Professional Courtesy,* AMERICAN MEDICAL NEWS, (Mar. 8, 1999).
[309] *Id.*
[310] OIG, *Compliance Program Guidance for Individual and Small Group Physician Practices* (Sept. 2000).
[311] Social Security Act § 1128A(a)(5); 42 U.S.C. 1320a-7a(a)(5)).
[312] *See* 59 Fed. Reg. 65,372, 65,375 (Dec. 19, 1994).

Therefore, such practices could potentially conflict with the language of the program guidance and the Special Fraud Alert.

## § 2-8(e)  Carving Out Federal Healthcare Program Business and "Swapping" Issues

Recognizing the significant liability associated with violating the Anti-Kickback Statute, many in the healthcare industry have attempted to shield themselves from liability when entering into arrangements by "carving out," or excluding, patients who participate in a federal healthcare program from the purview of the arrangement. For example, a medical supplier might agree to furnish a physician with medical supplies and pay the physician a rebate at the end of the year based upon the volume of supplies the physician orders. The parties may then attempt to protect themselves from any liability under the Anti-Kickback Statute by providing that the rebate will not apply to any supplies ordered for federal healthcare program patients (e.g., Medicare, Medicaid).

Several problems arise in attempting to carve out this patient population. First, it is difficult from an administrative standpoint to implement a successful carve-out as patients may receive benefits under these healthcare programs in a less obvious manner (e.g., Medicare may be the secondary payor for a working aged, disabled, or ESRD patient with group health coverage).

Second, there is still an issue as to whether the remuneration as to the private-pay patients may be an indirect "inducement" as to the federal healthcare program patients. For example, in the context of clinical laboratory services in which Medicare generally will only reimburse the laboratory that furnished the service and not the physician who ordered the test (unless the physician's laboratory performs the test), clinical laboratories have typically offered physicians discounts on their private business. As physicians generally will use one laboratory for all of their patients' needs, discounts on private business generally can be expected to result in the referral of the physician's Medicare laboratory work, as well to the laboratory giving the discount. The issue is whether laboratory discounts on a physician's private laboratory business can be considered an impermissible "inducement" as to the physician's Medicare laboratory referrals in violation of the Anti-Kickback Statute. The government has termed these types of arrangements as "swapping" arrangements.

Third, even if the parties successfully carve out federal healthcare program patients (and therefore may avoid liability under the Anti-Kickback Statute), the parties still may have liability exposure under state anti-kickback laws which generally are implicated regardless of payor.

There has been no case law which has addressed a party's success in avoiding liability under the Anti-Kickback Statute by carving out patients who participate in these programs, and the pronouncements by the government on this issue are scarce. However, the one area in which the OIG has proscribed the practice of "carving out" federal programs is in the context of the discount safe harbor which excludes from the definition of discount, "a reduction in price applicable to one payor but not to Medicare or a State healthcare program."[313] The basis for the exclusion of these price reductions is found in the preamble:

> For example, we are aware of cases where laboratories offer a discount to physicians who then bill the patient, but do not offer the same discount to the Medicare program. In some of these cases, the discount offered to the physician is explicitly conditioned on the physician's referral of all of his or her laboratory business. Such a "discount" does not benefit Medicare, and is therefore inconsistent with the statutory intent for discounts to be reported to the programs with costs and charges reduced appropriately to reflect the discounts.[314]

The OIG has issued a number of Advisory Opinions reaffirming skepticism with arrangements seeking to carve out federal healthcare program beneficiaries and payments as a means of circumventing the Anti-Kickback Statute. For example, in Advisory Opinion 11-11, the OIG reviewed two proposals from a supplier (the Requestor) that furnishes medical supplies, equipment and related services to skilled nursing facilities (SNFs). The related services included the emergency delivery of medical supplies and equipment, inventory control, visits by customer service representatives, customized resident-specific packaging and simple returns of products for credit. Based on the facts provided, when the Requestor furnished medical supplies and equipment that were covered by Medicare Part B, the Requestor billed the Medicare program directly. When the supplies and services were not covered, the Requestor billed the SNF directly. Generally, the Requestor charged the SNF a markup to cover the costs of the related services and the Requestor's overhead and profit.

Under the facts of Advisory Opinion 11-11, the SNF issued a request for proposals soliciting bids to be an exclusive supplier of covered items and related services to the SNF. The Requestor submitted bids in response to the request. According to the OIG's analysis, the arrangements proposed in the request could potentially generate prohibited remuneration under the AKS and the OIG could potentially impose sanctions. With regard to one of the proposals, the OIG focused on the fact that the Requestor would charge the SNF an amount that would be below the Requestor's costs for non-covered

---

[313] 42 C.F.R. § 1001.952(h)(3).
[314] 56 Fed. Reg. 35,977 (July 29, 1991).

items or services. According to the OIG, these facts suggest a nexus between the below cost payment rates and the referrals of other federal healthcare program business because (1) the SNF is in a position to direct or refer business to the Requestor; (2) the provision of both covered and non-covered services suggests a link between the two; and (3) both parties have motives for agreeing to the arrangement (*i.e.*, the SNF minimizes out-of-pockets expenses and the Requestor secures business as an exclusive supplier of covered items). In further discussing the improper nexus, the OIG looked for indicia that the rate was not commercially reasonable and stressed that prices offered to SNFs below the suppliers total costs of providing the items and services gives rise to an inference that the arrangement may be a "swapping" arrangement. The OIG stated,

> [b]ased on the facts presented here, we are unable to exclude the possibility that the Requestor may be offering improper discounts to the SNF for the Non-covered Items and related services with the intent to induce referrals of more lucrative Federal business. Nor are we able to exclude the possibility that the SNF may be soliciting improper discounts on business for which it bears risk in exchange for referrals of business for which it bears no risk.[315]

## § 2-8(f)   Free Goods to Referral Sources

A practice which the safe harbor regulations decline to protect is the practice of offering "free goods" to potential referral sources, except in extremely limited circumstances (i.e., credits on purchases of like items) as described earlier. Although DHHS recognized in the July 1991 safe harbors that many of these arrangements are cost effective, DHHS also stated that these arrangements have a potential for "enormous" abuse. One example in the preamble to the 1991 safe harbor concerns the practice of giving away free computers:

> In some cases the computer can only be used as part of a particular service that is being provided, for example, printing out the results of laboratory tests. In this situation, it appears that the computer has no independent value apart from the service that is being provided and that the purpose of the free computer is not to induce an act prohibited by the statute. Rather, the computer is part of a package of services provided at a price that can be accurately reported to the programs. In contrast, sometimes the computer that is given away is a regular personal computer, which the physician is free to use for a variety of purposes in addition to receiving test results. In that situation the

---

[315] OIG Advisory Opinion No. 11-11 (emphasis added).

computer has a definite value to the physician, and, depending on the circumstances, may well constitute an illegal inducement.[316]

Even early anti-kickback case law recognized the potential illegality of "free goods" arrangements. In *United States v. Perlstein*,[317] a nursing home administrator's conviction was upheld under the Anti-Kickback Statute for accepting approximately $416 per month in free alcoholic beverages in exchange for the opportunity to provide pharmaceutical items to the nursing home patients. Prior to the beverage arrangement, the nursing home administrator had demanded cash payments based on a percentage of Medicaid payments. Only when the cash payment arrangement failed did the administrator demand the beverage arrangement. Moreover, when one drug supplier refused to participate in the scheme, the administrator refused to allow that supplier to continue supplying the nursing home. The court therefore concluded that the drug suppliers were "not selected to service these Medicaid recipients for any reason other than a willingness to make payments to Perlstein."[318]

In most of these cases, however, the government was able to prove that the "free goods" were furnished for no purpose other than to induce the purchase or recommendation of a particular supplier of Medicare/Medicaid-covered items or services. Thus, to the extent the free goods offered to provide a benefit not only to the referral source, but also to the offeror, the result may differ. Of course, the benefit must meet some business objective other than capturing a referral source.

In addition to these cases, in 1994, the OIG identified in the Special Fraud Alert for the clinical laboratory industry that it is focusing on various "free goods" arrangements as being particularly troublesome: (1) free pick-up and disposal of biohazardous waste products unrelated to the laboratory's collection of specimens; (2) provision of free computers and fax machines, unless the equipment is integral to, and exclusively used for, the laboratory's work; and (3) provision of free laboratory testing for physicians, their families and their employees.

This issue arose again in 1998, when the OIG was asked to issue an Advisory Opinion as to whether a pharmacy could offer pharmacist services to a hospital for free. A mail-order pharmacy was contemplating placing a licensed pharmacist in hospitals interested in the pharmacy's services. The pharmacist would be employed by the mail order pharmacy and would work with hospital employees by performing all the billing and collections for pharmacy

---

[316] 56 Fed. Reg. 35,978 (July 29, 1991).

[317] United States v. Perlstein, 632 F.2d 661 (6th Cir. 1980), *cert. denied,* Perlstein v. United States, 449 U.S. 1084 (1981).

[318] *Id.* at 663. *See also* United States v. Bay State Ambulance and Hosp. Rental, Inc., 874 F.2d 20, 32 (1st Cir. 1989) (the offer of "free goods" in the context of cars and cash being offered in return for the award of an ambulance contract); United States v. Levin, 973 F.2d 463 (6th Cir. 1992).

## Federal Anti-Kickback Laws

services, preparing pharmaceutical care plans, overseeing patient compliance with pharmaceutical are plans, securing patient's insurance coverage for pharmaceuticals, and processing prescriptions through the pharmacy's distribution center. Relying in part on the arrangements for the provision of clinical laboratory services fraud alert, the OIG stated that the proposed arrangement creates too much of an incentive for influencing patient referrals and is therefore suspect under the anti-kickback law.[319]

A frequent question is whether nominal gifts, such as turkeys at Christmas and the like, could possibly violate the Anti-Kickback Statute. In one of the Department Appeals Board (DAB) decisions in *Inspector General v. Hanlester Network* case, the DAB stated that "de minimis or very remote forms of remuneration, such as drug samples or recruitment lunches, may not be subject to prosecution. . . ."[320] Nevertheless, the safe harbor regulations do not recognize the concept of "de minimis" payments:

> We do not believe the Medicare and Medicaid programs would be properly serviced if we assured protection in all instances of "substantial compliance," "technical violations," or "de minimis" payments. Unfortunately, these are vague concepts, subject to differing interpretations. In this regulation, we have attempted to provide bright lines, to the extent possible, for safe harbors in order to provide clarity and predictability as to what conduct is immune from government action. Our endorsement of the concepts mentioned above would only serve to blur these lines and produce litigation as to what "substantial," "technical" and "de minimis" really mean. The OIG therefore declines to adopt these concepts.[321]

In addition, both the Pharmaceutical Research and Manufacturers of America (PhRMA) and Advanced Medical Technology Association (AdvaMed) have included limitations on the provisions of gifts in their Codes related to interactions with healthcare providers. (See discussion of these Codes in Chapter 6.)

### § 2-8(g) Conflict-of-Interest Credentialing, Economic Credentialing, or Exclusive Credentialing

In the past, a healthcare facility's determination on whether to grant privileges to a physician was based largely on quality considerations. Over the years, however, economic considerations have become part of certain facilities' credentialing processes. For example, some healthcare facilities have

---

[319] *See* OIG Advisory Op. No. 98-16.
[320] Inspector Gen. v. Hanlester Network, Departmental Appeals Board, Appellate Division, Dec. No. 1275 (Sept. 18, 1991), *available online at* http://www.hhs.gov/dab/decisions/index.html.
[321] 56 Fed. Reg. 35,954 (July 29, 1991).

required physicians to take a "loyalty oath" in order to ensure that physicians will refer their patients to that facility. Other healthcare facilities have refused to grant staff privileges to physicians who own, have financial interests in, or have leadership positions with competing healthcare entities. These practices are commonly referred to as "conflict-of-interest credentialing," "economic credentialing," or "exclusive credentialing."

Some courts have upheld decisions by hospital boards denying medical-staff privileges on the basis of economic credentialing. For example, in 1992, a Florida physician was denied clinical privileges in large part because of his contractual responsibilities as program chairman and developer of a competing program at a nearby community hospital. The court held that the defendant hospital was within its rights to deny the physician medical privileges on the basis of economic reasons.[322] In 2006, however, the affirmed a preliminary injunction stopping a hospital's use of an economic credentialing policy in which the hospital refused to grant or renew hospital privileges to several cardiologists with ownership interests in competing facilities.[323] Conversely, in 2011, an Arkansas District Court refused to force the reinstatement of a doctor who claimed that he had been terminated because of his refusal to compromise patient care for the economic benefit of his employer, a rehabilitation center. The court stated, "[a]lthough preservation of the physician-patient relationship is a profoundly important public interest, public policy also favors [the rehabilitation center's] ability to enforce legitimate rules and policies."[324]

One argument against healthcare facilities' use of economic credentialing is that this practice violates the Anti-Kickback Statute. For a number of years, the American Medical Association communicated with the OIG and requested guidance on whether hospitals violate the Anti-Kickback Statute when the hospitals refuse to grant privileges to physicians who own or have other financial interests in competing healthcare entities, hold leadership positions with competing healthcare entities, refer to competing healthcare entities, or fail to admit some specified percentage of their patients to the hospital. As a result, on December 9, 2002, the OIG issued a request for public comments regarding this issue.[325] The OIG sought responses to a number of credentialing-related questions.

1. Do hospital privileges represent some form of "remuneration"?
2. What are the implications of a hospital's denial of privileges to a physician who competes with the hospital?

---

[322] Rosenblum v. Tallahassee Mem'l Reg'l Med'l Ctr., Inc., Case No. 91-589 (Fla. Cir. Ct. 1992).
[323] Baptist Health v. Murphy, 226 S.W. 3d 800 (Ark. 2006) *remanded to* Murphy v. Health, 2010 Ark. 326 (Ark. 2010) (granting permanent injunction); *aff'd,* Baptist Health v. Murphy, 2010 Ark. 458 (Ark. 2010), *rehearing denied* (Nov. 11, 2010).
[324] Roudachevski v. All-American Care Centers, Inc., 2011 U.S. Dist. LEXIS 38317 (E.D. Ark. Mar. 31, 2011).
[325] 67 Fed. Reg. 72,894 (Dec. 9, 2002).

## Federal Anti-Kickback Laws

3. Should the exercise of discretion by the hospital affect the analysis under the Anti-Kickback Statute?
4. Can privileges ever be conditioned on referrals, other than minimums necessary for clinical proficiency?
5. What is the effect of credentialing restrictions that apply only to members of a group practice?

Although the OIG has yet to issue either a Special Fraud Alert or any regulations regarding this issue, in the OIG's 2005 Supplemental Compliance Program Guidance for Hospitals, it again addressed this issue by stating that certain of these credentialing practices may implicate the Anti-Kickback Statute. The OIG provided that

> conditioning privileges on a particular number of referrals or requiring the performance of a particular number of procedures, beyond volumes necessary to ensure clinical proficiency, potentially raise substantial risks under the statute. On the other hand, a credentialing policy that *categorically* refuses privileges to physicians with significant conflicts of interest would not appear to implicate the statute in most situations.[326]

Consequently, the OIG states that a determination whether a particular credentialing practice violates the Anti-Kickback Statute depends "on the specific facts and circumstances, including the intent of the parties."[327]

### § 2-8(h)   Physician Recruitment and Relocation Arrangements

The first reported federal court case to address physician recruitment activities by hospitals under the Anti-Kickback Statute is *Polk County v. Peters*, which did not arise from a governmental enforcement action, but rather from the hospital's attempt to obtain repayment of amounts advanced to the physician through an income guarantee.[328] The recruitment arrangement at issue provided the physician with an income guarantee for twelve months, an amount for moving expenses, an amount to pay for the physician's first year's malpractice insurance premiums, office space in the hospital at no cost for three months, and then a stipend for rental and utilities for six months commencing with the physician's occupancy. Under the arrangement, the hospital's obligation to advance the money under the income guarantee was specifically conditioned on the physician's agreement: (1) to practice medicine in the community on a full-time basis for at least 12 months; (2) to use best

---

[326] 70 Fed. Reg. 4,858, 4,869 (Jan. 31, 2005) (emphasis in original).
[327] *Id.*
[328] Polk County v. Peters, 800 F.Supp. 1451 (E.D. Tex. 1992).

efforts to develop his practice in the community; and (3) to "utilize Hospital for his patients who require hospitalization, unless, in Physician's professional judgment, the use of another medical facility is necessary or desirable in order to provide proper and appropriate treatment and care to such patient (or to comply with the desires of a patient or the patient's family)."[329]

According to the facts of the case, when the physician failed to utilize the hospital as the physician's "primary hospital," the hospital terminated the arrangement and requested that the physician make arrangements to repay the money advanced. In holding the contract unenforceable, the court reviewed the Anti-Kickback Statute, relevant case law, as well as the administrative interpretation in the May 1992 OIG Special Fraud Alert on Hospital Incentives to Physicians, and concluded that the contract was "well within the purview of" violating the Anti-Kickback Statute:

> While the hospital may well have been motivated to a greater or lesser degree by a legitimate desire to make better medical services available in the community, there can be no doubt that the benefits extended to Defendant were, in part, an inducement for him to refer patients to the hospital. The Court must, therefore, find that the Agreement made on the basis of this action violates [the Anti-Kickback Statute.][330]

Over the years, there have been a number of other investigations and cases regarding hospitals' physician recruitment and relocation practices. For example, in 2003, a federal grand jury in San Diego, California returned indictments against Tenet HealthSystem Hospitals, Inc., Alvarado Hospital Medical Center (one of Tenet's hospitals), the hospital's CEO and the hospital's director of business development, alleging that the hospital entered into over 100 relocation arrangements with physicians and specialists and paid over $10 million to fund the physician relocation agreements.[331]

At the same time, the OIG has provided hospitals with some guidance over the years concerning some recruitment arrangements that while implicating the Anti-Kickback Statute might not otherwise be found to violate the statute. For example, in a 2003 letter (i.e., not in the form of an Advisory Opinion but instead as an informal letter from the OIG's General Counsel), the OIG responded to a hospital's request for guidance concerning a proposal to provide temporary malpractice insurance assistance to the hospital's medical staffs in several states in order to "to forestall disruption in the provision of

---

[329] *Id.*
[330] *Id.* at 1,456.
[331] *See* Criminal Indictment in the case of United States of America v. Weinbaum, Tenet Health System and Alvarado Hospital Medical Center, Case Number 03CR1587L filed in US District Court for the Southern District of California. This indictment case can be found at: http://news.findlaw.com/wsj/docs/tenet/ustenet71703sind.pdf.

### Federal Anti-Kickback Laws

medical services in these states."[332] Although the OIG had historically considered hospitals paying malpractice insurance premiums on behalf of medical staffs to be a potential violation, the OIG pointed out that not only did the potential arrangement possibly fall within one of two safe harbors, the OIG stated that the proposed arrangement contained a number of safeguards: the premium assistance would be for a fixed period of time and would only be provided in states experiencing malpractice insurance access or affordability problems; only current active medical staff members would be eligible except in cases where employees were new to the area or had been in practice less than one year; premium assistance was not based on volume or value of services; and physicians were going to be required to continue to contribute to premium costs in an amount equal to their current contributions.

## § 2-8(i) Developments in Calculation of Damages for Anti-Kickback Cases

An interesting development is the way in which courts are assessing damages in cases with Anti-Kickback violations. Generally speaking there are two primary ways in which damages are calculated in Anti-Kickback cases. First, up until around 2003, courts generally calculated damages in Anti-Kickback cases by examining the government's actual net loss—that is, the additional amount the government had to pay by virtue of the illegal kickbacks, as compared to what would have been paid had all the claims been valid. The rationale being that because the defendant provided valuable services to the government through patient care, it would be unjust to force disgorgement of the government payments that were not attributable to illegal kickbacks. For example, in *United States v. Vaghela*, the Eleventh Circuit reversed the district court for clear error in calculating the defendant's restitution as the total amount billed to Medicare during the period of illegal referrals, $50,420, as opposed to the amount received by the defendant in exchange for referrals, $23,400.[333] Further, in *United States v. Westinghouse Savannah River*, involving a qui tam action against a government contractor, the court states that "[T]he district court properly required the plaintiff to prove damages by showing how much more the government paid . . . to perform the subcontract than it would have paid another firm absent the false . . . certification."[334]

More recently, however, courts have taken a different approach in calculating damages, namely that a defendant violating the Anti-Kickback Statute

---

[332] A copy of the IG's letter is *available online at* http://oig.hhs.gov/fraud/docs/alertsandbulletins/MalpracticeProgram.pdf.
[333] United States v. Vaghela, 169 F.3d 729, 736 (11th Cir. 1999).
[334] United States *ex rel.* Harrison v. Westinghouse Savannah River Co., 352 F. 3d 908, 923 (4th Cir. 2003).

is liable for the entire amount paid by the government, without taking into account the value of the services provided during the kickback scheme. The rationale being that government reimbursement is a essentially a subsidy with conditions attached; when those conditions are not satisfied—such as because an individual is engaging in illegal kickbacks—the individual is then entitled to nothing and must repay all amounts received from the federal government. For example, in *United States v. Rogan* the court stated that "The government offers a subsidy (from the patients' perspective, a form of insurance), with conditions. When the conditions are not satisfied, nothing is due. Thus the entire amount . . . received on these 1,812 claims must be paid back."[335]

## § 2-8(j) Questioning Fair Market Value and "Bona Fide" Nature of Services Contracted For

In recent years, the government and the courts have started to chip away at the Anti-Kickback statutory exceptions, safe harbors and defenses by scrutinizing the extent to which agreements are consistent with fair market value and whether the parties are actually contracting for "bona fide" services.

As discussed above, the 7th Circuit decision in *United States v. Borrasi* seemingly limits the scope of the employee safe harbor by suggesting that if the employment compensation is not for "bona fide" employee services, then anti-kickback liability may attach.[336]

In addition to challenging the *bona fide* nature of the services provided under an arrangement, the government and courts have also started to question whether an arrangement was, in fact, fair market value, even when there was an independent third party valuation performed. Historically, if a party could demonstrate that an arrangement was consistent with fair market value it would support the legitimacy of the arrangement. However, in the case of *United States ex rel. Singh v. Bradford Regional Medical Center*, the court determined that despite there being an independent third party valuation, the arrangement was not fair market value and was based on the volume and value of the referrals.

*Bradford* involves an arrangement between Bradford Regional Medical Center (BRMC) and a physician group, V&S Medical Associates (V&S).[337] V&S was a significant source of referrals to BRMC for both inpatient admis-

---

[335] United States v. Rogan, 517 F.3d 449, 453 (7th Cir. 2008).
[336] United States v. Borrasi, 639 F.3d 774, 781 (7th Cir. 2011). *See also* Bloomberg BNA, Health Law Resource Center, *Settlements Reached in Three More Cases of Alleged Kickbacks of Cardiac Referrals* (Sept. 23, 2009) (where government alleged that cardiologists were paid part-time employment contracts at full-time cardiology faculty member rates in order to increase patient volume and that the cardiologists provided minimal or no services in exchange for the compensation).
[337] United States, *ex rel.*, Singh v. Bradford Regional Medical Center, 752 F. Supp. 2d 602 (2010).

## Federal Anti-Kickback Laws

sions and outpatient procedures, including diagnostic tests performed on a nuclear imaging camera located at BRMC. In 2001, V&S entered into a 63-month lease with General Electronic (GE) for a nuclear camera. Concerned about losing a significant referral stream, BRMC threatened to revoke the physician's medical staff privileges, alleging that V&S violated BRMC's Policy on Physicians with Competing Financial Interests (the "Policy"). The Policy provided that a physician who had a financial relationship with a competing healthcare entity (that might have significant impact upon BRMC) would be ineligible for hospital privileges. Ultimately, BRMC and V&S negotiated an arrangement whereby BRMC subleased the GE camera from V&S, and the V&S physicians agreed to not compete with BRMC to provide nuclear imaging services during the period of the sublease. The terms of the sublease included a pass-through of the monthly amounts due by V&S under the GE lease, plus an additional $23,655 per month for "all other rights" including the covenant not to compete.

Despite the sublease calling for the relocation of the GE camera, the camera remained in V&S's offices. The GE camera was used for a period of months and then remained unused for the remainder of the sublease because V&S entered into a different lease to acquire a new camera, for which BRMC reimbursed V&S. The new camera was located at BRMC, however, BRMC and V&S did not enter into a written agreement for this new camera.

Prior to entering into the arrangement, BRMC acquired an independent third party valuation of the sublease. The report determined that the amounts to be paid pursuant to the sublease were reasonable. To conduct the valuation, the consultant compared the revenues BRMC expected to generate with the sublease in place to the revenues that BRMC expected to generate without the sublease in place. The projections were based on the expectation that V&S would refer business to BRMC if the sublease was in place. Although the parties ultimately entered into the arrangement, the terms of the arrangement were not documented in a formal written contract (although they were evidenced by other writings). Although the court ultimately did not find a violation of the Anti-Kickback Statute because it could not determine whether the parties acted with the requisite intent, the court evaluated the fair market value assessment that was provided by the independent third party and determined that the arrangement was not consistent with fair market value and did take into account the volume and the value of the referrals.

The *Bradford* decision demonstrates that just having a fair market valuation may not be enough and that the valuation may not consider the value or volume of anticipated referrals.

Another significant case is *United State ex rel. Kosenske v. Carlisle HMA, Inc.*, in which the court refused to find that the arrangement was fair market value simply because of the negotiation process between the parties.[338] In *Kosenske*, an anesthesiology practice engaged in negotiations with a hospital that ultimately resulted in an exclusive Anesthesiology Services Agreement and addressed the provision of services in a pain clinic. Although the District Court determined that the arrangement at the pain clinic was fair market value, the Third Circuit concluded that "there was no arm's length negotiations that could vouch for the fair match of services and compensation" and went on to state, "a negotiated agreement between interested parties does not "by definition" reflect fair market value."[339]

---

[338] 554 F.3d 88 (3rd Cir. 2009).
[339] *Id.* at 97.

# 3
# Federal Physician Self-Referral Prohibitions

## § 3-1  OVERVIEW

Born out of frustration in the 1980s with a lack of enforcement of the federal healthcare program anti-kickback statute (Anti-Kickback Statute) (discussed in Chapter 2), Congress began to adopt restrictions on physicians' ability to refer to entities with which they have a financial relationship. In 1980, Congress adopted a provision that limited the ability of a physician to certify or recertify a plan of care for a Medicare patient to receive services from a home health agency in/with which the physician has a significant ownership interest or significant financial or contractual relationship.[1] In 1988, Congress adopted a provision in the Medicare Catastrophic Coverage Act of 1988 prohibiting a physician from referring patients to entities furnishing infusion therapy services in which the physician had an investment interest or other financial relationship.[2] In 1989, Congress repealed the Medicare Catastrophic Coverage Act of 1988, but as part of the 1989 Omnibus Reconciliation Act of 1989, Congress adopted a physician self-referral proscription applicable to entities providing Medicare-covered clinical laboratory services, which became effective January 1, 1992.[3] This law often is referred to as the "Stark Law" after Pete Stark (D-CA), the Congressman who introduced and strongly supported the statute. In 1993, Congress expanded the Stark Law beyond clinical laboratory services to a host of "designated health services" and expanded the scope of the Stark Law provisions to include services under the Medicaid Program.[4]

Contemporaneous with the adoption of self-referral laws in 1989 and 1993, a series of studies was published analyzing financial arrangements between physicians and healthcare entities, which gave critical support to the efforts to adopt the self-referral legislation. One study conducted by

---

[1] Social Security Act § 1814(a); 42 U.S.C. § 1395f(a); *see also* 42 C.F.R. § 424.22.
[2] Medicare Catastrophic Coverage Act of 1988 Pub. L. No. 100-360, 102 Stat. 683 (1988); Medicare Catastrophic Coverage Repeal Act of 1989 Pub. L. No. 101-234, 103 Stat. 1979 (1989).
[3] Omnibus Reconciliation Act of 1989, Pub. L. No. 101-239, 103 Stat. 2106 (1989).
[4] Omnibus Budget Reconciliation Act of 1993 (OBRA '93), Pub. L. No. 103-66, 107 Stat. 312 (1993). The 1989 version of the Stark Law is referred to as "Stark I." The expansion of the Stark Law in 1993 is generally referred to as "Stark II."

the Office of Inspector General (OIG) addressed the OIG's examination of physician-owned healthcare entities and the effect of such financial relationships on utilization of healthcare services.[5] This study examined trends in physician ownership as well as referral practices in three areas: clinical laboratories; physiological testing laboratories; and durable medical equipment (DME) suppliers. The OIG study found that 12% of physicians who participated in the Medicare program had ownership or investment interests in healthcare businesses to which they made referrals. Those investments covered a wide range of services, including diagnostic imaging centers, laboratories, health maintenance organizations (HMOs), ambulatory surgical centers (ASCs), home health agencies (HHAs), radiation therapy centers, hospitals, and DME suppliers.

Although the 1989 OIG study did not find widespread abuse throughout all segments of the healthcare industry, the OIG recommended that the Centers for Medicare & Medicaid Services (CMS),[6] then known as the Healthcare Financing Administration, pursue legislative and regulatory changes to require entities billing Medicare to disclose the names of physician-owners and physician-investors, and to require all Part B claims to contain the name and provider number of the referring physician.

Also in 1989, the Florida legislature authorized a similar study examining the joint-venture ownership or compensation arrangements between persons providing healthcare.[7] The results of this study indicated that physician ownership of healthcare businesses providing diagnostic testing and other ancillary services was quite common in Florida, and that a large percentage of patients were referred to a physician-owned facility by the physician-investor.[8] Further, the General Accounting Office (GAO) published a study in 1993 that found that Florida doctors who own diagnostic imaging centers referred patients for imaging services "significantly" more often than non-owners.[9]

---

[5] Office of Inspector General Report to Congress, No. OA-12-88-01410, CCH MEDICARE AND MEDICAID GUIDE ¶ 37,838 (May 1989).

[6] As part of the efforts by Department of Health and Human Services (DHHS) Secretary Tommy G. Thompson to revamp the Healthcare Financing Administration (the agency which administers the Medicare and Medicaid programs), it was renamed the Centers for Medicare & Medicaid Services on (June 14, 2001).

[7] See FLA. STAT. CH. 89-354 (1989).

[8] See Jean M. Mitchell and Elton Scott, *New Evidence of the Prevalence and Scope of Physician Joint Ventures*, 269 JAMA 80 (1992). Based upon the result of this study, in 1992, the Florida legislature enacted a physician self-referral prohibition, which will be described in more detail in Chapter 9. FLA. STAT. ANN. § 455.236 (1993).

[9] Gen. Acct. Off. Rep. No. T-HRD-93-14, *Medicare: Physicians Who Invest In Imaging Centers Refer More Patients for More Costly Services* (Apr. 20, 1993). *See also* Jean M. Mitchell and Elton Scott, *Physician Ownership of Physical Therapy Services: Effects on Charges, Utilization, Profits and Service Characteristics*, 268 JAMA 2055 (1992); Jean M. Mitchell and Jonathan H. Sunshine, *Consequences of Physicians' Ownership of Healthcare Facilities—Joint Ventures in Radiation Therapy*, 327 NEW ENG. J. MED. 1497 (1992).

## Federal Physician Self-Referral Prohibitions

Studies of the impact of physicians having financial relationships with entities to which they refer patients continue in the 21st century. Jean Mitchell, an economist and Professor at the Georgetown Public Policy Institute, who was the principal researcher for the Florida studies conducted in the 1990s, continues to examine physician self-referral arrangements. In 2010, Dr. Mitchell was awarded a $1.45 million dollar grant from the National Institute on Aging for a project entitled "Financial Incentives, Treatment of Medicare Beneficiaries with Spine Problems and Changes in their Health," which is a three-year study evaluating physician ownership of specialty hospitals and ambulatory surgery centers and whether there is any impact on patient care. Dr. Mitchell is also the lead researcher for a project evaluating the effect of physician ownership on use of anatomic pathology services for prostate, bladder and GI biopsies and a project evaluating the consequences on care when urologists have an ownership interest in a center that utilizes intensity modulated radiation therapy (IMRT) versus other alternative cancer treatments.[10]

This chapter describes the Stark Law and regulations, including the definitions of the principal terms and phrases that control the scope of the law, the various exceptions that exempt particular financial relationships, the penalties for violating the law, and the reporting requirements under the law. This chapter also addresses a number of major issues in Stark Law enforcement, such as the interrelationship between the Stark Law and the Anti-Kickback Statute.

## § 3-2  LEGISLATIVE AND REGULATORY HISTORY

In 1989, Congress adopted the first version of the Stark Law, which was applicable to entities providing Medicare-covered clinical laboratory services, and which became effective January 1, 1992 (commonly referral to as Stark I).[11] Unlike the Anti-Kickback Statute (which currently is applicable to all federal healthcare programs other than federal employee health benefit plans), Stark I applied only to Medicare services. Moreover, although early drafts of the proposed 1989 legislation envisioned a very broad prohibition (which would have been applicable to virtually all types of physician-owned entities), the legislation enacted in 1989 only contained such a prohibition with respect to physician-owned clinical laboratories.

Stark I became effective prior to the adoption of any regulations and CMS took the position that the statute was self-implementing.[12] In fact, *proposed* regulations addressing Stark I were not published until March 11, 1992

---

[10] Jean M. Mitchell, Biographical Statement as a member of the faculty of Georgetown University, which can be found at: http://explore.georgetown.edu/people/mitchejm/ (last viewed Mar. 10, 2012).
[11] Omnibus Reconciliation Act of 1989, Pub. L. No. 101-239, 103 Stat. 2106 (1989).
[12] Letter from Kathleen A. Buto, Director, Bureau of Policy Development, Healthcare Financing Administration, to Clifford E. Barnes, Epstein Becker & Green, P.C., Washington, D.C. (Mar. 30, 1993) (on file with authors).

(three months after the statute became effective), and these proposed regulations proved merely to be a recitation of the statute itself.[13] Although the statute gave CMS the authority to adopt further exceptions to the self-referral prohibition, and despite industry demands that further exceptions be adopted, CMS declined to expand the list of statutory exceptions in the proposed rule.

In August 1993, the Stark Law was broadened as a part of the Omnibus Budget Reconciliation Act of 1993 (OBRA '93) (commonly referred to as Stark II).[14] Even though the prohibition was not broadened to all payors (which many had expected), it was extended to apply to the provision of Medicaid services and to apply to a host of "designated health services," which include:[15]

- physical therapy services;
- occupational therapy services;
- radiology, including magnetic resonance imaging, computerized axial tomography scans, and ultrasound services;[16]
- radiation therapy services and supplies;
- DME and supplies;
- parenteral and enteral nutrients, equipment, and supplies;
- prosthetics, orthotics, and prosthetic devices;
- home health services and supplies;
- outpatient prescription drugs; and
- inpatient and outpatient hospital services.

Stark II became effective January 1, 2005. In August 1995, eight months after Stark II became effective, CMS published final regulations interpreting Stark I (Stark I Final Regulations).[17] CMS issued the Stark I Final Regulations with a 60-day comment period. In the preamble, CMS stated that, although Stark I applied only to clinical laboratory services, this rule "will affect how we review referrals involving any of the designated health services."[18] CMS further stated in the preamble, "[u]ntil we publish a rule covering the designated

---

[13] 57 Fed. Reg. 8,588 (proposed Mar. 11, 1992).
[14] OBRA '93, Pub. L. No. 103-66, 107 Stat. 312 (1993).
[15] Although OBRA '93 expanded the self-referral law to apply to designated health services, the list of designated health services was slightly modified in 1994. *See* Social Security Amendments of 1994, Public L. No. 103-432, 108 Stat. 4398 (1994).
[16] The statutory provision listing radiology as a designated health service was originally enacted to include radiology "or other diagnostic services." This original provision raised serious concern as to whether a physician's professional diagnostic services (e.g., surgical biopsy and diagnostic cardiac catheterization) were included within the scope of prohibited referrals. The statute was amended to its present form as part of the Social Security Act Amendments of 1994.
[17] 60 Fed. Reg. 41,914 (Aug. 14, 1995).
[18] *Id.* at 41,916.

## Federal Physician Self-Referral Prohibitions

health services, we intend to rely on our language and interpretations in this final rule when reviewing referrals for the designated health services in appropriate cases."[19]

It was not until January 1998 (three years after the statutory effective date of Stark II) that CMS published proposed Stark II regulations applicable to all designated health services (Proposed Stark II Regulations).[20] Publication of the Proposed Stark II Regulations resulted in thousands of comments being submitted to CMS by members of the public who generally took exception to the manner in which CMS proposed to interpret the Stark Law. On this same date, CMS also published, as an interim final rule with a comment period, regulations setting forth the process for private parties to obtain "advisory opinions" regarding arrangements subject to the Stark Law.[21]

The healthcare community waited several more years for the publication of the final Stark II regulations. On January 4, 2001, almost three years to the day after the Proposed Stark II Regulations were issued, CMS published "Phase I" of the final Stark II regulations (Phase I Stark II Final Regulations), which implemented only certain portions of the Stark Law:

(1) the Stark Law's prohibition;

(2) exceptions to the law that apply to both ownership and compensation arrangements;

(3) the definitions of key terms included in the Stark statute; and

(4) certain new regulatory exceptions.[22]

In a departure from usual government policy, CMS provided that most of the provisions in the Phase I Stark II Final Regulations would not take effect for a full year (until January 2, 2002) to give the healthcare community sufficient lead time to accomplish any necessary restructuring of existing financial relationships for compliance purposes, as well as to give CMS time to fix any unintended "glitches" included in the Phase I Stark II Final Regulations.[23] Moreover, CMS issued the Phase I Stark II Final Regulations with a 90-day comment period, and later granted a 60-day extension.

CMS noted that the Phase I Stark II Final Regulations differed substantially from the proposed rules due to the extensive number of comments

---

[19] *Id.*
[20] 63 Fed. Reg. 1,659 (Jan. 9, 1998).
[21] 63 Fed. Reg. 1,646 (Jan. 9, 1998).
[22] 66 Fed. Reg. 856 (Jan. 1, 2001) (codified at 42 C.F.R. Parts 411 & 424).
[23] The one exception to the January 4, 2002, effective date for the final regulations was a provision related to a physician's ability to certify and re-certify a patient's need for home health services if the physician has a substantial financial interest in the home health agency, which became effective April 6, 2001. *See* 66 Fed. Reg. 8,771 (Feb. 2, 2001).

received after issuing the proposed rules. CMS outlined the four main concerns expressed in the comments after the proposed regulations:

(1) the proposed rule intruded into the organization and delivery of medical care within physicians' offices;

(2) the proposed rule was contrary to CMS's longstanding policies on coverage and other areas;

(3) the proposed rule was unclear in many ways, and requires "bright line" rules, given the potential for serious consequences for violation; and

(4) some aspects of the proposed rule were administratively impractical or would be prohibited due to the high cost of monitoring compliance.[24]

In response to these concerns, CMS stated that it wanted to be cautious in interpreting the reach of the Stark Law for fear of prohibiting physician arrangements that potentially are beneficial. Instead, in the Phase I Stark II Final Regulations, CMS attempted to focus on the main abuse for which the Stark Law was aimed to deter: physician financial relationships that result in overutilization of services. Stating that it has been "mindful of the criticism that the ... proposed rule inappropriately micro-managed physician practices," CMS sought to establish "bright line" rules for physicians and healthcare entities as a means of ensuring compliance while minimizing administrative costs."[25] Furthermore, in accordance with the Stark Law statutory language and intent, CMS stated it tried to "interpret the prohibitions narrowly and the exceptions broadly."[26]

Although CMS stated in the preamble to the Phase I Stark II Final Regulations that Phase II would be published "shortly," it was not for another three years (March 2004) that CMS published Phase II as an interim final rule with comment period (Phase II Stark II Final Regulations).[27] As a result of the comment period and the fact that CMS did not address the issue of general application of the Stark Law to traditional fee-for-service Medicaid, CMS acknowledged it would be issuing Phase III sometime in the future.

In the meantime, Congress made certain modifications to the Stark Law as part of both the Medicare Prescription, Drug, Improvement and Modernization Act of 2003 (MMA) and the Deficit Reduction Act of 2005 (DRA). In MMA, Congress created a temporary moratorium (through June 2005) on physician ownership in specialty hospitals, even those located in rural areas. The statute defined the phrase "specialty hospital" as one engaged primarily or exclusively in the care and treatment of: "(i) patients with a cardiac

---

[24] 66 Fed. Reg. 860 (2001).
[25] Id.
[26] Id.
[27] 69 Fed. Reg. 16,054 (Mar. 26, 2004).

## Federal Physician Self-Referral Prohibitions

condition[;] (ii) patients with an orthopedic condition[;] (iii) patients receiving a surgical procedure[; and] (iv) any other specialized category of services that the Secretary designates . . .."[28] Exempt from the moratorium were specialty hospitals that were either in existence or already under development on November 18, 2003, as long as they did not increase the number of physician-investors, or substantially alter the number of beds or types of services offered. Despite efforts to extend the moratorium beyond June 2005, Congress was unable to maintain the existence of the MMA-established moratorium; instead, the DRA required the Secretary of the Department of Health and Human Services (DHHS) to submit interim and final reports on the development of a strategic plan concerning aspects of physician investment in specialty hospitals, and that, until the sooner of the final report being released or eight months after enactment of the DRA, DHHS was to continue the suspension of enrolling new specialty hospitals.[29]

MMA also included a provision within the new prescription-drug benefit that required DHHS to create an exception to the Stark Law to protect certain arrangements involving the provision of non-monetary remuneration that is necessary to receive and transmit electronic prescription-drug information.[30] As a result, in October 2006, CMS finalized two exceptions for compensation arrangements involving certain electronic prescribing and electronic health records arrangements.[31]

Then, in September 2007, CMS issued the long-awaited Phase III Stark II Final Regulations (Phase III Stark II Final Regulations), which included a number of significant changes to CMS's interpretation of the Stark Law, and these changes are discussed throughout this chapter.[32]

While traditionally CMS issues stand-alone Stark regulations, in 2007 CMS began including extensive changes to the Stark regulations in other regulatory issuances such as the Medicare Physician Fee Schedule (MPFS), the Hospital Outpatient Prospective Payment System (HOPPS) or the Hospital Inpatient Prospective Payment Systems (IPPS).[33]

---

[28] Medicare Prescription Drug, Improvement, and Modernization Act of 2003, Pub. L. No. 108-173 (MMA), § 507, codified at 42 U.S.C. § 1395nn(h)(7).
[29] Deficit Reduction Act of 2005, Pub. L. No. 109-171 (DRA), § 5006.
[30] 42 U.S.C. § 1395w-104(e)(6). Similarly, Congress mandated that a similar safe harbor be created under the Anti-Kickback Statute (as discussed in greater detail in Chapter 2).
[31] 42 C.F.R. § 411.357(v) and (w).
[32] 72 Fed. Reg. 51,012 (Sept. 5, 2007). Phase III Stark II Final Regulations became effective Dec. 4, 2007.
[33] *See, e.g.*, 72 Fed. Reg. 47,130 (Aug. 22, 2007); 72 Fed. Reg. 66,222 (Nov. 27, 2007);. *See also* the Proposed FY 2008 IPPS rule at 72 Fed. Reg. 24,680 (May 3, 2007); 73 Fed. Reg. 48,434 (Aug. 19, 2008); 73 Fed. Reg. 69,726 (Nov. 19, 2008); 74 Fed. Reg. 61,738 (Nov. 25, 2009); 75 Fed. Reg. 73,170 (Nov. 29, 2010); 76 Fed. Reg. 74,122, (Nov. 30, 2011).

With the passage of the Patient Protection and Affordable Care Act, as modified by the Health Care and Education Reconciliation Act of 2010 (Health Reform Law),[34] Congress again placed significant limitations on physicians' ownership interest in hospitals located both in urban and rural areas. Specifically, the Health Reform Law limits the ability of a hospital to have physician owners unless the ownership interest was obtained by the physicians prior to December 31, 2010, and that the hospital had a provider agreement in place as of that date. The Health Reform Law further precludes a physician owned hospital that is grandfathered into the exception from expanding the number of licensed beds, operating or procedure rooms beyond the number that existed as of the date the hospital is licensed following enactment of the law. PPACA establishes that a facility can seek a waiver from the expansion limitation if the hospital is, among other things, in a county that has percentage increase in population over the last 5 years that is 150% of the population growth in the state or is a hospital that constitutes a "High Medicaid Facility."[35] (These issues are addressed in greater detail below.)

As part of the Health Reform Law, Congress also established a self-disclosure protocol related to Stark violations (referred to as the self-referral disclosure protocol or SRDP)[36] and Congress modified the Stark Law to include a requirement that in order for a physician to fall within the in-office ancillary services exception for the provision MRI, CT, PET (and any other designated health services identified by the Secretary), the physician must inform the individual in writing at the time of the referral that the individual may obtain the services from another healthcare provider and provide the patient with a written list of suppliers who furnish services in the area in which such patient resides.[37]

## § 3-3 THE STATUTORY PROHIBITION AND DEFINITIONS OF KEY TERMS

### § 3-3(a) Scope of the Law

The Stark Law prohibits a physician (or an immediate family member of such physician) who has a "financial relationship" with an entity from referring patients to the entity for "designated health services" covered by the Medicare program, unless an exception is available. In the event a proscribed

---

[34] *See* Patient Protection and Affordable Care Act of 2010, Pub. L. No. 111-148, as amended by Health Care Education Affordability Reconciliation Act of 2010, Pub. L. No. 111-152.
[35] 42 U.S.C. § 1395nn(i).
[36] *See* Patient Protection and Affordable Care Act of 2010, Pub. L. No. 111-148 § 6409.
[37] 42 U.S.C. § 1395nn(b)(2).

referral is made (and no exception is available), the entity performing the services is prohibited from submitting a claim for the services to the Medicare program or billing any individual, third-party payor or other entity for the services. The term "financial relationship" is defined in the Stark Law to include both compensation arrangements and investment and ownership interests.

It was not until the expansion of the Stark Law under OBRA '93 that Congress extended certain aspects of the Medicare prohibition on physician referrals to the Medicaid program.[38] The Medicaid program, which is jointly administered and funded by the federal government and the several states, provides medical assistance to individuals who meet certain income and resource requirements. The share contributed by the federal government to each state for medical expenditures under its Medicaid program is called "federal financial participation" (FFP).[39] To be eligible to receive FFP, each state must operate its Medicaid program in accordance with certain federal laws and regulations, and a state plan must be approved by CMS.[40] As a result of changes made to the Social Security Act (SSA) in 1993, the Medicaid statute now bars FFP to states where designated health services are furnished to an individual based on a physician referral that would result in a denial of payment for the services under the Medicare program if Medicare covered the services to the same extent, and under the same terms and conditions, as the service is covered under the state Medicaid plan.[41] Although the issue of how the Stark Law is to be interpreted under the Medicaid program was expected to be addressed in the Phase III Stark II Final Stark Regulations, CMS has still not addressed this issue.

## § 3-3(b)  Definitions of Key Terms

### § 3-3(b)(1)  Referral

In the case of an item or service for which payment may be made under Part B of Medicare, the term "referral" is defined in the Stark Law as the request by a physician for the item or service, including the request by a physician for a consultation with another physician, and any test or procedure ordered by (or to be performed by) that other physician (or someone under her supervision).[42] The regulations further provide that a designated health service is not personally performed or provided by the referring physician if it is performed or provided by any other person, including employees of

---

[38] *See* Social Security Act § 1903; 42 U.S.C. § 1396.
[39] Social Security Act § 1902(a); 42 U.S.C. § 1396a(a).
[40] Social Security Act § 1902(a)(13); 42 U.S.C. § 1396a(a)(13).
[41] Social Security Act § 1903(s); 42 U.S.C. § 1396b(s).
[42] Social Security Act § 1877(h)(5)(A); 42 U.S.C. § 1395nn(h)(5)(A).

the referring physician, independent contractors, and members of a physician group practice.[43]

The request or establishment of a plan of care by a physician that includes the provision of a designated health service constitutes a referral.[44] Thus, the physician need not actually refer the patient to an entity, or recommend that the patient obtain services from an entity, in order to trigger the statutory referral prohibition; instead, the physician need only order the service and the patient ultimately receive the service from an entity with which the physician has a financial relationship. Moreover, CMS has stated that any time a physician orders anything, it is "pursuant to a plan of care" on the physician's part, even if not officially called that.[45] As a result of the Stark Law's broad definition of the term "referral," the ordering of designated health services within a group practice, as well as patient referrals for designated health services within a managed care network, constitute "referrals," even though certain exceptions may apply (as will be discussed).

In contrast to the position stated by CMS in the proposed Stark II regulations, the final regulations make it clear that referrals for designated health services that the referring physician personally performs are not considered "referrals" to which the Stark Law prohibition applies.[46] In addition, under the Stark Law, certain referral relationships are deemed not to constitute a referral if the services are furnished by (or under the supervision of) a specialist pursuant to a consultation. The Stark Law excludes from the term "referral" (1) a request by a pathologist for clinical diagnostic laboratory tests and pathological examination services; (2) a request by a radiologist for diagnostic radiology services; and (3) a request by a radiation oncologist for radiation therapy, if such services are furnished by or under the supervision of the pathologist, radiologist, or radiation oncologist.[47]

### § 3-3(b)(2)   Designated Health Services

The Stark Law applies to a host of designated health services. Because the statute does not provide any definitions for these designated health services, CMS had proposed to define each of the designated health services based upon the coverage rules of the Medicare Part B program. However, recognizing the confusion that this raised, CMS defined certain designated health services (e.g., clinical laboratory services, physical therapy, radiology and certain other imaging services, and radiation therapy services) in the final regulations by publishing specific lists of the Current Procedural Terminology (CPT) and

---

[43] 42 C.F.R. § 411.351.
[44] Social Security Act § 1877(h)(5)(B); 42 U.S.C. § 1395nn(h)(5)(B).
[45] 60 Fed. Reg. 41,914, 41,967 (Aug. 14, 1995).
[46] 42 C.F.R. § 411.351.
[47] Social Security Act § 1877(h)(5)(C); 42 U.S.C. § 1395nn(h)(5)(C).

## Federal Physician Self-Referral Prohibitions

CMS Common Procedure Coding System (HCPCS) codes that physicians and providers most commonly associate with a given service. For these designated health services, CMS published in an attachment to Phase I of the final regulations specific lists of CPT and HCPCS codes that define the entire scope of these designated health services and are "controlling."

CMS, however, has not used the CPT and HCPCS codes to define the remaining designated health services (i.e., DME and supplies, prosthetics, orthotics, prosthetic devices and supplies, home health services, outpatient prescription drugs, and inpatient and outpatient hospital services) because it believes that the existing definitions for these designated health services create "sufficiently clear 'bright line' rules."[48]

Excluded from this definition are services that are part of a composite rate, unless the listed designated health services are themselves payable through a composite rate. In the Stark I Final Regulations, CMS promulgated a general exception applicable to ownership and compensation arrangements alike for services furnished in an ASC, an end-stage renal disease (ESRD) facility, or a hospice if payment for those services is included in the ASC rate, the ESRD composite rate, or as part of the per diem hospice charge.[49] According to CMS, "referrals for laboratory tests that are performed in an ASC and included in the ASC rate should be excepted because there is no incentive to overutilize these services."[50] In the final regulations, CMS provided protection for the provision of those types of services that otherwise might qualify as a designated health service if they are provided as part of a bundled or comprehensive payment rate. This includes services that are part of an ASC or a skilled nursing facility (SNF) payment rate group.[51]

Initially, CMS did not include within the list of designated health services (and in particular the definition of radiology services) those CPT codes applicable to nuclear medicine or positron emission tomography scans but in 2006, the list of designated health services was expanded to include these services.[52]

---

[48] 66 Fed. Reg. 923 (2001). CMS also posts the list, titled "List of CPT/HCPCS Codes Used to Describe Certain Designated Health Services Under the Physician Referral Provisions (Section 1877 of Social Security Act)," on the Internet, *available online at* http://www.cms.gov. CMS updates the list annually in an addendum to the annual final physician-fee schedule rule, which is generally published in late October or early November. CMS has stated its intention to publish a "comprehensive" list each year that will be more than "a listing of changes to prior year's table." If CMS makes any changes to the list, it will publish a revised list and responds to any public comments.

[49] 42 C.F.R. § 411.355(d).

[50] 60 Fed. Reg. 41,970 (1995).

[51] 66 Fed. Reg. 923 (2001).

[52] *See* list of codes that became effective Jan. 1, 2006, *available online at* http://www.cms.hhs.gov/mlnproducts/downloads/011006finalcodelist.zip.

With respect to the application of the Stark Law to medical device and pharmaceutical manufacturers, CMS stated in 2001 that manufacturers should not be considered entities that furnish DHS. "We agree that, in most cases, drug manufacturers are not entities that furnish DHS to patients for purposes of [the Stark Law], and therefore, the ordering, dispensing, or prescribing of drugs would not constitute a referral to the manufacturer of the drugs."[53] Then, in the FY 2009 IPPS Proposed Rule, CMS asked for public comment on whether the Stark Law should apply to physician-owned implant and medical device companies.[54] When the FY 2009 IPPS Final Rule was published, CMS did not adopt any modifications that would expand the scope of the Stark law to apply to implant and medical device companies but has potentially left this issue open for future issuances.[55]

### § 3-3(b)(3) Ownership or Investment Interests

Under the Stark Law, ownership or investment interests can arise "through debt, equity or other means," and include "an interest in an entity that holds an ownership or investment interest in any entity providing the designated health service."[56] Thus, physician ownership or investment in a parent organization that owns a facility furnishing designated health services also falls under the self-referral proscription, with the result that the physician is prohibited from referring to the subsidiary facility (and the facility is prohibited from submitting a claim for payment) unless an exception is met.

The final regulations exclude several items from the definition of what constitutes an "ownership or investment interest," including an interest in a retirement plan,[57] stock options, convertible securities, unsecured loans subordinated to a credit facility, and an "under arrangements" contract with a hospital.[58] It is important to note that, while many of these exempted financial relationships are not ownership interests, CMS has stated that they otherwise may constitute compensation arrangements. This means that, to the extent a physician acquires a stock option from a designated health services provider (e.g., a hospital), such a financial relationship will not be able to rely upon an

---

[53] 66 Fed. Reg. at 872 (Jan. 4, 2001).
[54] 73 Fed. Reg. at 23,694–23,695.
[55] 73 Fed. Reg. at 48,690.
[56] Social Security Act § 1877(a)(2); 42 U.S.C. § 1395nn(a)(2).
[57] In the CY 2008 MPFS Proposed Rule, CMS expressed its concern that physicians may have been using retirement plans to purchase or invest in other entities (i.e., entities other than the one that sponsors the retirement plan) and to which they refer patients. 72 Fed. Reg. at 38,183. Therefore, in the FY 2009 IPPS Final Rule, CMS finalized its proposal to exclude from the scope of covered "ownership and investment interests" an interest in "an entity that arises from a retirement plan offered by that entity to a physician (or family member of a physician) through the physician's (or immediate family members') employment with that entity." 42 C.F.R. § 411.354(b)(3)(i).
[58] 42 C.F.R. § 411.354(b)(3).

## Federal Physician Self-Referral Prohibitions

ownership-only exception (e.g., the exception for an ownership interest in a hospital); instead, the relationship will need to qualify for another exception applicable to compensation arrangements, which may or may not be available.

An indirect-ownership interest is an unbroken chain of ownership interests between the referring physician, other persons or entities, and the entity providing the designated health service. For example, the referring physician has an ownership interest in a "holding company," and the holding company has an ownership interest in the entity providing the designated health service. A provider of designated health services only has an indirect ownership relationship if it has "actual knowledge" or acts in "reckless disregard or deliberate ignorance" that an indirect financial relationship exists with the referring physician.[59]

### § 3-3(b)(4)  Compensation Arrangements

Compensation arrangements under the Stark Law are defined to include "any arrangement involving any remuneration, direct or indirect, between a physician . . . and an entity."[60] The term "remuneration" includes "any payment or other benefit made directly or indirectly, overtly or covertly, in cash or in kind" with certain specific exceptions. The Stark Law expressly excludes from the definition of the term "remuneration":

(1) the forgiveness of amounts owed for inaccurate tests or procedures mistakenly performed tests or procedures, or the correction of minor billing errors;

(2) the provision of items, devices, or supplies that are used solely to (a) collect, transport, process, or store specimens for the entity providing the item, device, or supply or (b) order or communicate the results of tests or procedures for such entity;

(3) a payment by an insurer or a self-insured plan to a physician to satisfy a claim, submitted on a fee for service basis, for the furnishing of health services by that physician to an individual who is covered by a policy with the insurer or by the self-insured plan, if

    (i) the health services are not furnished, and the payment is not made, pursuant to a contract or other arrangement between the insurer or the plan and the physician;

    (ii) the payment is made to the physician on behalf of the covered individual and would otherwise be made directly to such individual; and

    (iii) the amount of the payment is set in advance, does not exceed fair market value (FMV), and is not determined in a manner that

---

[59] 42 C.F.R. § 411.354(b)(5).
[60] 42 C.F.R. § 411.354(c).

takes into account directly or indirectly the volume or value of any referrals, and

(iv) the payment meets such other requirements as may be imposed by regulation.[61]

To identify indirect-compensation arrangements, CMS has adopted what it characterizes as a "simple" test based upon three elements.[62] First, there must be "an unbroken chain" of persons or entities that have financial relationships between them. CMS takes the position that an excepted financial relationship still constitutes a link in a chain that establishes an indirect-compensation arrangement, and does not specify any other circumstances that might break the chain.[63]

The second element of an indirect-compensation arrangement is that the aggregate compensation received by the referring physician from the entity with which she has a direct financial relationship must vary with, or otherwise reflect, the volume or value of referrals or other business generated between the physician and designated health services entity.[64] Under the third element, a designated health services provider must have "actual knowledge" or have acted in "reckless disregard" that the aggregate compensation paid to the physician otherwise satisfies the second criterion.[65] As will be discussed, if there is a reason to suspect a financial relationship exists, then a duty is established to make an inquiry into the nature of the relationship. Once the indirect-compensation arrangement has been identified, the question becomes whether it meets the new exception for indirect-compensation arrangements discussed in greater detail in this chapter.

A component of the definition for an indirect-compensation arrangement is a "knowledge" element. For an indirect-compensation arrangement, the designated health services entity must have "actual knowledge" or "acts in reckless disregard or deliberate ignorance" that the referring physician "receives aggregate compensation that varies with, or otherwise reflects, the volume or value of referrals."[66] CMS has stated that this requirement does not impose an "affirmative duty" on designated health services providers to inquire or investigate whether an indirect financial relationship exists.[67] By the same

---

[61] Social Security Act § 1877(h)(1)(C); 42 U.S.C. § 1395nn(h)(1)(C).
[62] 66 Fed. Reg. 865 (2001).
[63] For example, in a situation where a physician who has an ownership interest in a hospital (where the interest qualified for the exception for ownership in a hospital), which in turn has a contractual relationship with a clinical laboratory for services for which the physician refers, the physician would, in fact, have an indirect compensation arrangement with the clinical laboratory. See 66 Fed. Reg. 865–66 (2001).
[64] Id. at 866.
[65] Id. at 866.
[66] 42 C.F.R. § 411.354(c)(2)(iii).
[67] 66 Fed. Reg. 865 (2001).

## Federal Physician Self-Referral Prohibitions

token, however, CMS has stated that providers "in possession of facts that would lead a reasonable person to suspect the existence of an indirect financial relationship [must] take reasonable steps to determine whether such a financial relationship exists" and whether an exception is met.[68] CMS applies this knowledge standard only to the designated health services provider that receives a tainted physician referral—but not to the physician who makes the referral.

### § 3-3(b)(5)   Fair Market Value

The concept of FMV is relevant to many of the Stark Law exceptions, and has been the source of substantial confusion in the healthcare community. In the final regulations, CMS provided additional definitional guidance for what constitutes FMV in relationships between healthcare providers, and addresses documenting FMV. FMV means the value in arm's-length transactions, consistent with "general market value."[69] In other words, FMV constitutes the price that an asset would bring as the result of bona fide bargaining between, or the compensation in a service agreement negotiated by, well-informed buyers and sellers who are not in a position to generate business for each other. As a result, the general benchmark for FMV is the price at which bona fide sales have been consummated for assets of like type, quality, and quantity in the particular market at the time of the transaction, or the compensation included in bona fide service agreements with comparable terms at the time of the agreement.

In this regard, CMS has stated that, when FMV is included in an exception that also includes the "volume or value" standard, the parties may be precluded from relying on comparables that involve entities and physicians in a position to refer and generate business.[70] In establishing "fairness" in such situations, CMS places the burden with the parties to the particular arrangement.[71]

With regard to the use of independent valuation consultants to determine FMV, CMS has provided that there is no requirement to use such outside sources if other "appropriate" valuation methods are available.[72] Nonetheless, CMS has stated that, although internally generated surveys can be used to determine FMV in certain circumstances such surveys do not have "strong evidentiary value" due to their susceptibility to manipulation and absence of independent verification.[73]

---

[68] *Id.*
[69] 42 C.F.R. § 411.351.
[70] 66 Fed. Reg. 944 (2001).
[71] *Id.*
[72] *Id.* at 945.
[73] *Id.*

For space leases and equipment rentals, FMV means the value for commercial purposes, not taking into account its "intended use" or its proximity to referral sources.[74] CMS has made clear that this "intended use" limitation still allows development upgrades and maintenance that customize premises for healthcare usages to be factored into FMV, and allows rental payments that reflect the FMV of the area in which the property is located (e.g., medical property in a medical community).[75] "Intended use" is taken into account only where the lessee pays inflated amounts to enhance her medical practice; that is, the lessee pays additional amounts greater than that paid by other medical practitioners in the same building.[76]

In the Phase II Stark II Final Regulations, CMS provided guidance in connection with hourly payments for a physician's personal services by using one of two possible methodologies: (1) an hourly payment that is less than or equal to the average hourly rate for emergency room physician services in the relevant physician market; or (2) an hourly rate based upon the 50th-percentile national compensation level for physicians with the same specialty by benchmarking against various publicly available surveys.[77] However, in the Phase III Stark II Final Stark Regulations, CMS removed the "safe harbors" under which physician compensation for personal services would be deemed FMV because several of the designated surveys were no longer published or not readily available and the antitrust laws limited the feasibility of obtaining rates paid for emergency room physicians at competitor hospitals. In its place, the Phase III preamble declared "[r]eference to multiple, objective, independently published salary surveys remains a prudent practice" for evaluating FMV. Removal of the safe harbor may cause one to believe independent valuation would be the next best alternative, however this is not so CMS however, reiterated its stance from Phase II that a "good faith reliance on an independent valuation (such as an appraisal) may be relevant to a party's intent, [but] it does not establish the ultimate issue of the accuracy of the valuation figure itself. . . ."[78]

The preamble to the Phase III Stark II Final Regulations also addressed hourly compensation of physicians for both clinical and administrative work. CMS took the stance that a FMV hourly rate may be used to compensate physicians for both administrative and clinical work, provided that "the rate paid for clinical work is fair market value for the clinical work performed and the rate paid for administrative work is fair market value for the administrative work performed." CMS's position is that the FMV for administrative services may differ from the FMV for clinical services (which ignores the fact that

---

[74] 42 C.F.R. § 411.351.
[75] 66 Fed. Reg. 945 (2001).
[76] *Id.* An example is where physical therapists pay inflated rent to be in the same building occupied by orthopedists.
[77] 69 Fed. Reg. at 16,107.
[78] 72 Fed. Reg. at 51,015.

a physician may not be inclined to take on administrative work at a hospital's request for less than the hourly "opportunity cost" of clinical practice). Finally, Phase III clarified that a FMV hourly rate may be used to determine annual salary, so long as the multiplier accurately reflects the number of hours "actually worked" by the physician.

In 2009, in *U.S. ex rel. Kosenske v. Carlisle HMA, Inc.*, the Third Circuit Court of Appeals reversed a district court ruling thereby allowing the FCA action to proceed with one of the issues in the case being whether an arrangement reflected FMV.[79] The Third Circuit, in focusing on Stark's underlying statutory scheme, stated:

> Finally, it is clear that there were no arm's length negotiations that could vouch for the fair match of service and compensation that the whole statutory scheme is designed to assure. . . . First, as a factual matter, negotiations in 1992 could not possibly reflect the fair market value of the consideration given and received more than six years later under materially different circumstances. Second, as a legal matter, a negotiated agreement between interested parties does not "by definition" reflect fair market value. To the contrary, the Stark Act is predicated on the recognition that, where one party is in a position to generate business for the other, negotiated agreements between such parties are often designed to disguise the payment of non-fair-market-value compensation.[80]

Another significant case addressing the importance of fair market value, is the decision by the United States District Court for the Western District of Pennsylvania in *U.S. ex rel. Singh v. Bradford Regional Medical Center*.[81] At issue in Bradford was a hospital's lease of a nuclear camera from a physician group. Physicians competing with the physician group at issue filed a qui tam suit under the False Claims Act's whistleblower provisions, alleging that the lease arrangement did not satisfy a Stark Law exception and therefore the hospital's claims for services provided to patients referred by the physicians at issue violated the Stark Law. Although the government declined to intervene in this case and the dismissed many of the claims in the case, the court ruled that the nuclear camera lease arrangement implicated the Stark Law even though the parties had obtained a written valuation report from a third party, the court ruled that the arrangement did not qualify as a FMV deal.[82]

---

[79] *See* U.S. *ex rel.* Kosenske v. Carlisle HMA, Inc., 554 F.3d 88 (3rd Cir. 2009).
[80] *Id.* at 97.
[81] United States *ex rel.* Singh v. Bradford Regional Medical Center, 2010 U.S. Dist. LEXIS 119355 (W.D. Pa. Nov. 10, 2010)
[82] *See also*, U.S. *ex rel.* Drakeford v. Tuomey, 2010 WL 4000188, slip copy (D.S.C. 2010) in which it was alleged that agreements between Tuomey Healthcare System in Sumter, South Carolina and various physicians violated the Stark Law with one of the central issues in the case being whether the physicians' compensation exceeded fair market value.

## § 3-3(b)(6)  Physician

CMS has defined a "physician" to mean a doctor of medicine or osteopathy, a doctor of dental surgery or dental medicine, a doctor of podiatric medicine, a doctor of optometry, or a chiropractor, as defined in the SSA.[83] Thus, the scope of the Stark Law extends beyond medical doctors.

## § 3-3(b)(7)  Immediate Family Member

Although the Stark Law does not define the term "immediate family member," regulations implementing the law define this term as including a husband or wife; natural or adoptive parent, child, or sibling; stepparent, stepchild, stepbrother, or stepsister; father-in-law, mother-in-law, son-in-law, daughter-in-law, brother-in-law, or sister-in-law; grandparent or grandchild; and spouse of a grandparent or grandchild.[84]

## § 3-3(b)(8)  Entity

Although in the Phase I Stark II Final Regulations, CMS adopted the definition of the term "entity" as "the person or entity to which CMS makes payment for the DHS,"[85] in 2007, as part of the CY 2008 MPFS Proposed Rule, CMS proposed to revise the definition of the term "entity" to include not only the person or entity that bills for the DHS but also any person or entity that "performs" the DHS as well as any person or entity that "presented a claim or caused a claim to be presented" to Medicare for the DHS.[86]

CMS did not finalize its proposal in the CY 2008 MPFS Final Rule, but CMS adopted a modified definition in the FY 2009 IPPS Final Rule so as to include any person or entity that "has performed services that are billed as DHS."[87] By changing the definition of "entity" to include persons and entities that "perform" DHS, CMS specifically stated in the preamble to the regulations that it intended to include within the scope of the Stark Law those physician groups and other organizations that provide inpatient and/or outpatient services to a hospital "under arrangements."[88] Consequently, any physician who maintains a financial relationship with the "under arrangement" organization/DHS entity can only make DHS referrals to the organization if that

---

[83] 42 C.F.R. § 411.351. See also Social Security Act § 1861(r); 42 U.S.C. § 1395x(r).
[84] 42 C.F.R. § 411.351.
[85] 42 C.F.R. § 411.351; see 66 Fed. Reg. at 943.
[86] 72 Fed. Reg. at 38,224.
[87] 42 C.F.R. § 411.351; see 73 Fed. Reg. at 48,721. However, in the FY 2009 IPPS Final Rule, CMS did not adopt the concept of including within the definition of "entity" those who present or cause a claim to be submitted to Medicare.
[88] 73 Fed. Reg. at 48,721.

financial relationship meets a Stark Law exception. While it may be possible to structure a physician's *compensation* arrangement with such an "under arrangement" organization to satisfy a compensation arrangement exception, only under very limited circumstances will a physician be able to maintain an *ownership* or investment interest in an "under arrangement" organization after October 1, 2009.[89]

In the FY 2009 IPPS Final Rule, CMS specifically addresses two sets of services that, in many instances, are provided to hospitals by physician organizations under arrangements: lithotripsy services and cardiac catheterization services. With respect to lithotripsy and as a result of the District of Columbia District Court decision in 2002 finding that lithotripsy is not a DHS, CMS stated in the FY 2009 IPPS Final Rule that that lithotripsy services will not be subject to these principles.[90]

With respect to cardiac catheterization services, CMS states that the final rule does not prohibit physicians from furnishing services, in part because "[w]here a group practice or other physician organization provides the service and bills for it, the service is not DHS and the physician self-referral statute will not apply."[91] Yet, this statement ignores the practical reality of cardiac catheterization practices as Medicare billing rules provide that cardiac catheterization services generally must be billed by a hospital.[92] As a result of this position, a group of physicians and physician-owned entities that provide cardiac catheterization services (Cath Labs) across Colorado brought a lawsuit to overturn CMS's position.[93] To stop the definitional change prior to its October 1, 2009, effective date, plaintiffs sought a declaration that the expanded definition "'is contrary to clear congressional intent, based on an impermissible construction of the Stark Law, arbitrary and capricious, and exceeds the agency's authority,' in contravention of the Administrative Procedure Act . . . ."[94] The district judge's interpretation of the definitional change recognized that "absent an applicable exception, the Stark Law will prohibit the individual physician Plaintiffs from making referrals to their own Cath Labs." However, the court never reached a decision on the merits. The court ultimately dismissed the case for lack of subject matter jurisdiction, reasoning in its Memorandum Opinion that even though the Cath Labs were not entitled to DHHS administrative review because they do not bill or receive payments from Medicare, their contracting hospitals could bring such a challenge.

---

[89] Specifically, the only remaining ownership exception available would be the rural provider exception (*see* Section 3-4(b)(3) for a description of the rural provider exception).
[90] 73 Fed. Reg. at 48,730; *see also* Lithotripsy Society v. Thompson, 215 F. Supp. 2d 23 (D.C. 2002).
[91] 73 Fed. Reg. at 48,729–48,730.
[92] *See* Medicare Provider Reimbursement Manual, Part I, Ch. 21, § 2118.1.
[93] Colorado Heart Institute v. Johnson, 609 F. Supp. 2d 30 (D.D.C. 2009).
[94] *Id.* at 34.

## § 3-3(c)  Special Rules on Compensation

CMS has adopted several "special" rules on compensation methodologies and requirements. Although these rules might appear to contradict other guidance provided by other regulatory agencies (e.g., the OIG), they in fact are permitted under the Stark Law.

### § 3-3(c)(1)  Compensation Methodologies

In the Phase I Stark II regulations, CMS began to take the position that compensation will be considered to be "set in advance" if the aggregate compensation, which can include per-use and/or per-service methodologies, as well as specific formulas (as long as the formula is set out in writing and in sufficient detail so that it can be objectively verified).[95] CMS also requires that the "formula may not be changed or modified during the course of the agreement in any manner that reflects the volume or value of referrals or other business generated by the physician."[96]

CMS also has provided that unit-based compensation (including time-based or per-unit compensation) will be deemed not to take into account "the volume or value of referrals" if the per-unit or per-click based compensation is FMV at the inception of the arrangement, and does not vary during the course of the arrangement in any manner that takes into account referrals of designated health services.[97]

Finally, for those exceptions that provide that the compensation cannot be based on "other business generated between the parties," CMS has taken the position that compensation methodologies based on per-unit and per-time measurements are permitted, as long as the compensation is FMV for items and services actually provided, and does not vary during the course of the compensation arrangement in any way that takes into account referrals.[98]

However, in the CY 2008 MPFS Proposed Rule, CMS proposed to modify the special rules on compensation in such a way that a percentage based formula could only be used for paying for personally performed physician services. In addition, CMS proposed to exclude per-click based payments to a physician lessor for services rendered by an entity lessee to patients who are referred to the entity by the physician lessor. CMS commented that these situations are inherently susceptible to abuse because the physician has an incentive to profit from referring a higher volume of patients to the lessee.[99]

---

[95] 42 C.F.R. § 411.354(d)(1).
[96] Id.
[97] 42 C.F.R. § 411.354(d)(2).
[98] 42 C.F.R. § 411.354(d)(3).
[99] 72 Fed. Reg. at 38,184.

While these proposals were not addressed in the CY 2008 MPFS Final Rule, CMS adopted a number of changes to the ability of entities to use percentage and per click arrangements when the FY 2009 IPPS Final Rule was issued. Specifically, instead of modifying the "special rules on compensation" and the definition of "set in advance," CMS revised several exceptions (i.e., the office space and equipment lease exceptions, as well as the fair market value and indirect compensation arrangements exceptions) to address the use of percentage-based compensation formulae and per-click arrangement. Therefore, effective October 1, 2009, these exceptions prohibit compensation arrangements that use a formula based on either: a percentage of the revenue raised, earned, billed, collected, or otherwise attributable to the services performed or business generated in the office space or by the use of the equipment; or per-unit of services rental charges, to the extent that such charges reflect services provided to patients referred between the parties.[100]

### § 3-3(c)(2)  Physician's Compensation May Be Conditioned on Referrals to a Particular Provider

CMS expressly provides that compensation paid to a physician from a bona fide employer, or under a managed care or other contract, may be conditioned on the physician's referring patients to a particular provider, practitioner, or supplier.[101] These types of "mandated referral" requirements are permissible as long as:

(1) the arrangement is in writing;

(2) the compensation is set in advance and is consistent with FMV;

(3) the arrangement complies with an ownership or compensation exception;

(4) the referral requirement does not apply if a patient expresses a different choice of provider, the patient's insurance decides the provider, or if the referral is not in the best medical interest of the patient, as determined by the physician; and

(5) the required referrals relate solely to the physician's services covered by the scope of the employment or the contract, and the referral requirement is reasonably necessary to effectuate the legitimate business purposes of the compensation relationship.

Notwithstanding the ability of an employer to condition the employee to refer patients to a particular provider or entity, the employment exception

---

[100] 42 C.F.R. §§ 357(a)(5), 357(b)(4), 357(l)(3); and 357(p)(1); *see also* 73 Fed. Reg. at 48,709–48,721.
[101] 42 C.F.R. § 411.354(d)(4).

(as will be discussed) does not otherwise permit the employee's compensation to vary based upon the volume or value of referrals (unless part of a productivity bonus that satisfies various requirements).

### § 3-3(c)(3)  Modifying or Amending Agreements

The preamble to the Phase III Stark II Final Rule suggested that in order to satisfy the requirement that compensation be "set in advance" the parties who wished to change the compensation under a contract during the contract term must terminate that contract and enter into a new agreement to reflect the changed compensation.[102] However, in the FY 2009 IPPS Final Rule, CMS reversed its position and stated that it will allow parties to amend the compensation terms of an agreement. Although CMS did not adopt any modifications to the actual language in the regulations, in the preamble, CMS states that it will allow modifications to be made as long as the following criteria are met: (1) all of the requirements of an applicable exception must be satisfied; (2) the amended rental charges or other compensation (or the formula for the amended rental charges or other compensation) must be determined before the amendment is implemented and the formula is sufficiently detailed so that it can be verified objectively; (3) the formula for the amended rental charges must not take into account the volume or value of referrals or other business generated by the referring physician; and (4) the amended rental charges or compensation (or the formula for the new rental charges or compensation) must remain in place for at least one year from the date of the amendment.[103]

### § 3-3(d)  Stand in the Shoes

The Phase III Stark II Final Regulations adopted the first "stand in the shoes" concept that was designed to treat compensation arrangements between DHS entities and group practices as if the arrangements are also with the referring physicians.[104] As adopted in the Phase III Stark II Final Regulations, a physician is to "stand in the shoes" of his/her "physician organization" and is deemed to have the same compensation arrangement—with the same parties and on the same terms—as the physician organization.[105] The effect of this interpretation of the Stark Law and the application of the stand in the shoes was twofold. First, it rendered some arrangements that would have con-

---

[102] 72 Fed. Reg. at 51,044.
[103] 73 Fed. Reg. at 48,697.
[104] 42 C.F.R. § 354(c)(3); *see also* 72 Fed. Reg. at 51,028.
[105] A "physician organization" means a physician (including a professional corporation of which the physician is sole owner), a physician practice, or a group practice that complies with the regulatory requirements for group practices. A "physician practice" as used in this definition is not defined. 42 C.F.R. § 411.351.

## Federal Physician Self-Referral Prohibitions

stituted indirect compensation arrangements to now be direct compensation arrangements that must meet a direct compensation exception. Second, arrangements that did not implicate Stark at all under the prior regulations may now be implicated. Some distinctions between the indirect exception and other potentially relevant direct exceptions is that "indirect" compensation is not subject to the requirement that it be set forth in writing and signed by both parties, or be set in advance for one year, giving parties substantial latitude in establishing and amending their arrangements to meet immediate business needs, so long as those modifications are not based on the volume or value of referrals.

As a result of numerous comments from the healthcare community, CMS explained in the FY 2009 IPPS Proposed Rule that it was revisiting the "stand in the shoes" policy and that it was looking to achieve the goal of "simplifying the analysis of many financial arrangements" while reducing program abuse. To this end, in the FY 2009 IPPS Proposed Rule, CMS proposed two new alternatives to addressing these concerns (1) a "multi-faceted approach" to analyzing stand in the shoes arrangements; or (2) the development of a new exception for "mission support" payments, leaving the current stand in the shoes rules intact.[106]

When CMS issued the FY 2009 IPPS Final Rule, it revised the "physician stand in the shoes" provisions to apply only if "the only intervening entity between the physician and the entity furnishing DHS is his or her physician organization and the physician has an ownership or investment interest in the physician organization."[107] Moreover, CMS adopted a provision in the regulations that physicians with only a "titular ownership interests (that is, physicians without the ability or right to receive the financial benefits of ownership or investment)" are not required to undergo the "stand in the shoes" analysis.[108]

A significant question that arose after the issuance of the initial stand in the shoes policy was whether the analysis applied to arrangements involving physicians who are part of an academic medical center. However, in the FY 2009 IPPS Final Regulations, CMS specifically included language in the regulations that provides that the stand in the shoes provisions do not apply to arrangements that satisfy the requirements of the AMC exception.[109]

In the FY 2009 IPPS Proposed Rule, CMS also proposed that a DHS entity would be deemed to "stand in the shoes" of an organization in which it has a 100% ownership interest and would be deemed to have the same compensation arrangements with the same parties and on the same terms as does

---

[106] 73 Fed. Reg at 23,686.
[107] 42 C.F.R. § 354(c)(3); *see also* 73 Fed. Reg. at 48,693–48,699.
[108] 42 C.F.R. § 354(c)(3); *see also* 73 Fed. Reg. at 48,693–48,699.
[109] 42 C.F.R. § 354(c)(3)(ii)(B); *see also* 73 Fed. Reg. at 48,698.

the organization that it owns.[110] Nevertheless, this proposal was not included in the FY 2009 IPPS Final Rule.[111]

As part of the CY 2010 MPFS Final Rule, CMS made two "clarifications" to the stand in the shoes principles. First, CMS clarified that it did not intend that all physicians in a physician organization be required to execute an agreement entered into by the group. In addition, CMS clarified that the relevant referrals and other business generated between the physician organization and the entity furnishing DHSs are the referrals of all physicians in the physician organization, not simply referrals made by each physician who stands in shoes of the physician organization.[112]

## § 3-4 STARK LAW EXCEPTIONS

The Stark Law contains certain exceptions: some apply to both ownership and compensation arrangements, some apply only to ownership arrangements, and some apply only to compensation arrangements. It is only necessary, however, that a financial relationship satisfies the criteria of *one* exception in order to permit patient referrals. Thus, the availability of an exception should permit referrals even if a financial relationship does not meet the criteria of another exception, even if that other exception appears more specific to the parties' relationship.[113]

### § 3-4(a) Ownership and Compensation Exceptions

### § 3-4(a)(1) Physician Services

An exception is provided for physician services provided personally by or under the personal supervision of another physician in the same group practice as the referring physician.[114] CMS has interpreted the level of supervision required under this exception to correspond with its interpretation associated with the in-office ancillary services exception, which is the level of supervision required under the payment and coverage rules applicable to the particular service at issue.[115] CMS stated in the preamble to the Stark II final regulations that this exception was not expanded to include non-physician practitioners. CMS noted, however, that the in-office ancillary services exception

---

[110] 73 Fed. Reg. at 23,689.
[111] 73 Fed. Reg. at 48,669.
[112] 74 Fed. Reg. at 61,932–93.
[113] For example, if a referral is permitted under the in-office ancillary services exception, then the relationship between the physician and the group practice need not also meet the employee exception.
[114] 66 Fed. Reg. 879 (2001).
[115] *Id.*

## Federal Physician Self-Referral Prohibitions

will cover most referral designated health services provided by non-physician practitioners in a group setting.[116]

### § 3-4(a)(2)  In-Office Ancillary Services

In the preamble to the Phase III Stark II Final Regulations, CMS characterized the in-office ancillary services exception as "one of the most important exceptions" to the physician self-referral rule.[117] In general, the in-office ancillary services exception allows a physician or a group practice to order and provide DHS (other than most DME) in the office, provided the DHS is "truly ancillary" to the medical services furnished by the group.[118] Congress's main objective in adopting this exception included "permitting the provision of in-office ancillary services for the convenience of patients during their patient visits" and "permitting the provision of in-office ancillary services in a dedicated building used for these services."[119] CMS has interpreted these goals as not intending to protect part-time rentals of ancillary services. CMS further states that the exception should not "turn on the nuances of architectural design."[120]

The exception generally does not protect the furnishing of DME (with certain exceptions), such as external ambulatory infusion pumps, or parenteral and enteral nutrients (PEN) and relevant equipment and supplies (e.g., infusion pumps used for such PEN).[121] However, the final regulations expanded the ability of physicians to furnish DME in their offices.[122] CMS set out certain DME permitted to be furnished in-office to include canes, crutches, walkers and folding manual wheelchairs, and blood glucose monitors (which are required by patients for purposes of ambulating, and which the patient uses in order to depart from the physician's office).[123]

In order to qualify for the in-office ancillary services exception, the referring physician (or another physician who is a member of the same

---

[116] *Id.* at 880.
[117] 72 Fed. Reg. at 51,032.
[118] *Id.*
[119] 66 Fed. Reg. 888 (2001).
[120] *Id.*
[121] 42 C.F.R. § 411.355(b).
[122] CMS's interpretation of the statute's prohibition against physicians furnishing DME in their offices was a highly controversial area in the Proposed Stark II Regulations. Critics noted that, under the old interpretation, an orthopedist could set a patient's leg in a cast, yet could not furnish the patient crutches to leave the office. The Proposed Stark II Regulations changed this slightly by allowing crutches to be furnished in-office, provided that the physician did not "profit" from such an arrangement. In addition to expanding the ability of physicians to furnish DME in their offices, the final regulations eliminated the restriction on the physician's ability to profit from the arrangement.
[123] 42 C.F.R. § 411.355(b)(4)(i). A blood glucose monitor may be furnished only by a physician or employee of a physician or group practice that also furnishes outpatient diabetes self-management training to the patient.

group practice) must personally furnish the services. If other individuals (e.g., technicians) perform the services, those individuals must be directly supervised by the referring physician or another physician in the group practice in order for those services to qualify.

To be exempt, in-office ancillary services also must be furnished either (i) in a "centralized" building used by the group practice for the provision of some or all of the group's clinical laboratory services, or for the centralized provision of the group's designated health services (other than clinical laboratory services); or (ii) in the "same building" in which:

- the referring physician or group practice has an office that is normally open to their patients at least thirty-five hours per week, and the referring physician or group members regularly practices medicine and furnishes physician services to patients in that office at least thirty hours per week;

- the patient usually receives physician services from the referring physician or a member of the group practice, the group practice has an office that is normally open to patients at least eight hours per week, and the referring physician regularly practices medicine and furnishes physician services to patients in that office at least six hours per week; or

- the referring physician must be present and order the designated health service in connection with a patient visit during the time the office is open or the referring physician or a group practice member is present while the designated health service is furnished during the time the office is open, the referring physician or group practice has an office that is normally open eight hours per week, and the referring physician or group member regularly practices medicine and furnishes physician services to patients at least six hours per week in that office (including "some" services that are unrelated to designated health services).[124]

The regulations define the term "same building" as a structure with, or combination of structures that share, a single street address as assigned by the U.S. Postal Service, excluding all exterior spaces (e.g., lawns, courtyards, driveways, parking lots) and interior parking garages.[125] Separate physician office suites within the same medical office building could fall within the "same building" requirement if the street address for all of the suites were the

---

[124] 42 C.F.R. § 411.355(b)(2).
[125] 42 C.F.R. § 411.351. In the case of a referring physician whose principal medical practice consists of treating patients in their private homes, the "same building" requirements of the in-office ancillary services exception will be met if the referring physician provides the designated health services contemporaneously with a physician service that is not a designated health service provided by the referring physician to the patient in the patient's private home.

## Federal Physician Self-Referral Prohibitions

same, although the suite numbers could be different or located on different floors. CMS has noted that neither a statutory requirement nor legislative history exists for "one single centralized location for a group to provide designated health services."[126] Thus, there is no requirement that a centralized building service all of the group's offices or provide the group's entire designated health services.

A "centralized building" means

> all or part of a building, including . . . a mobile vehicle, van, or trailer that is owned or leased on a full-time basis (that is, 24 hours per day, 7 days per week, for a term of not less than 6 months) by a group practice and is used exclusively by the group practice.[127]

Space shared by more than one group practice, by a group practice and more than one solo practitioner, or by a group practice and another provider (e.g., a diagnostic imaging facility) is not considered to be a centralized building.[128] It is important to note that individual physicians can share space for ancillary services in a building, yet group practices cannot share space in a centralized location, especially as there is no statutory requirement for exclusive use of space for the performance of ancillary services. Group practices are not precluded by the sharing limitation from providing services to other providers (e.g., purchased diagnostic tests) in the group practice's centralized building, and group practice also may have more than one centralized building.

Certain billing requirements must be met in order to qualify for this exception. The designated health services must be billed by one of the following:

(i) the physician performing or supervising the service;

(ii) the group practice in which that physician is a member;

(iii) the group practice if the supervising physician is a "physician in the group";

(iv) an entity that is owned by the referring or supervising physician or her group practice; or

(v) an independent third-party billing company.[129]

The Stark II Final Regulations expressly state that a group practice may have, and bill under, more than one Medicare billing number, subject to any applicable Medicare program restrictions. This allows group practices that have been established through acquisition of previously operating medical

---

[126] 66 Fed. Reg. 892 (2001).
[127] 42 C.F.R. § 411.351.
[128] *Id.*
[129] 42 C.F.R. § 411.355(b)(3).

practices, and/or that wish to retain different group billing numbers, to differentiate among sites or services.

For purposes of this in-office ancillary services exception, a designated health service is "furnished" in the location where the service is actually performed for a patient, or where an item is dispensed to a patient in a manner that is sufficient to meet the applicable Medicare payment and coverage rules.[130] Unlike the proposed Stark II regulations (which would have required that the patient use the item in the physician's office in order for it to be considered "furnished" in the office), this change allows in-office dispensing of drugs and other items for home use.

Although in the Phase III preamble, CMS stated that the Stark Law does not "supersede" Medicare payment and billing rules and policies—including rules on reassignment, supervisor, or purchased diagnostic tests—several inconsistencies exist between the Medicare payment and billing rules and the Stark regulations. For example, following enactment of the MMA, CMS permitted independent contractor physicians to reassign his or her Medicare claim to an entity, regardless of whether the services were performed on the entity's premises.[131] However, in the Phase III preamble CMS noted that an independent contractor physician must provide his or her services inside the group practice's facilities.[132]

Significantly, the Phase III Stark II Final Regulations foreshadowed future limitations on the scope of the in-office ancillary services exception. CMS warned that it is "considering" whether certain types of arrangements—such as those involving in-office pathology labs and sophisticated imaging equipment—should continue to be eligible for protection under the in-office ancillary services exception.[133] Removing these categories of services from protection would be a significant adverse development for physician groups. Also, given the specific statutory delineation of permissible services rendered under the exception (e.g., not DME other than infusion pumps, and not parenteral and enteral equipment, services and supplies), this proposed prohibition may be outside CMS's authority. As discussed below, in the CY 2008 MPFS Final Rule, CMS limited pathology labs in other ways, such as prohibiting the "markup" of certain services.[134]

It is still unclear what amount of physician services will satisfy the in-office ancillary services requirement that "some" physician services furnished in the "same building" be unrelated to the furnishing of DHS. In the Phase III preamble, although it declined to provide a quantitative measure, CMS

---

[130] 42 C.F.R. § 411.355(b)(5).
[131] *See, e.g.,* 42 C.F.R. § 424.74.
[132] 72 Fed. Reg. at 51,034.
[133] *Id.*
[134] 72 Fed. Reg. at 66,401.

## Federal Physician Self-Referral Prohibitions

provided some guidance as to what qualifies as "some."[135] Without providing a bright line test, CMS noted the "critical factor" is whether the premises are used for the "regular provision of the group practice's physician services, even if on a part-time basis."[136] Although it appears that CMS will analyze each case individually, it will consider certain factors, including "the nature of the group's overall practice (for example the specialties of the group's physicians) and the referring physician's full range of practice."[137] Moreover, claims based on "sham arrangements," such as a satellite office that seemingly satisfies the same building requirements, will be denied. CMS has noted that the part-time rental of office space in a free-standing imaging facility "purportedly to provide physician services" unrelated to DHS constitutes a sham if few or no such services were "actually contemplated or provided."

CMS has characterized "part-time, shared, off-site" facilities as being readily subject to abuse,[138] and has voiced its concerns with so-called "pod labs."[139] Initially, CMS addressed this "potential" for abuse in the Phase I Final Rule, which redefined "centralized building," requiring a group practice to own or lease space on an "exclusive and full-time basis."[140] The CY 2007 MPFS Proposed Rule also included additional requirements to meet the centralized building test.[141] While those proposals were never adopted, CMS has continued to caution that "as with facilities in the same building, off-site arrangements must fully comply with the in-office ancillary service exception in operation, not only on paper."[142] However, rather than change the definition of "centralized building," CMS has expanded the anti-markup provisions at 42 C.F.R. § 414.50 to make it financially impractical for certain arrangements to exist.[143]

---

[135] 72 Fed. Reg. at 51,032–51,033.
[136] *Id.* at 51,033.
[137] *Id.*
[138] 72 Fed. Reg. at 51,033.
[139] *Id.*; 71 Fed. Reg. 48,982, 49,056–49,057 (Aug. 22, 2006). "Pod labs" include arrangements under which physicians order anatomic pathology services from off-site laboratories which they share with several other physician groups. Usually these pod labs are located away from the group's office and consequently, they do not qualify as in the "office of the billing physician" under the Anti-Markup Rule. In Phase III, CMS explained that "condominium" arrangements are "particularly vulnerable to non-compliance," and "staff and operations at the off-site facilities should be closely monitored." Additionally, in the proposed 2007 MPFS, CMS explained that "the arrangements [it] seek[s] to address through [its] proposed change to the definition of centralized building primarily involves independent contractor physicians."
[140] 66 Fed. Reg. 856, 952–953 (Jan. 4, 2001).
[141] 71 Fed. Reg. 49,056–49,057. The proposal included modifying the centralized building definition to require a minimum square footage of 350 feet, that the space permanently contain the equipment necessary to perform substantially all of the DHS performed in that space.
[142] 72 Fed. Reg. at 51,033.
[143] *See, e.g.,* 72 Fed. Reg. at 66,401; 73 Fed. Reg. at 69,799–69,817.

## § 3-4(a)(3)   Prepaid Plans

An exemption also has been established for services furnished to enrollees of certain health plans. Qualifying health plans include health plans with Medicare risk or cost contracts pursuant to SSA § 1876, carrier-dealing prepayment organizations under SSA § 1833(a)(1)(A), organizations that receive payments on a prepaid basis under certain demonstration projects, and federally qualified HMOs. The exception, however, does not extend to state-licensed HMOs, preferred provider organizations, Medicaid-contracting HMOs, or non-licensed managed care plans. Moreover, the preamble to the Stark I regulations makes clear that this exception does not apply to *all* services furnished by one of the enumerated prepaid plans, but only to plan *enrollees*. Consequently, services furnished to "walk-in" patients or to relatives of enrollees would not qualify for the prepaid plan exemption.[144]

The prepaid-plan exception is primarily useful in the context of payor/provider integration activities. The availability of the prepaid-plan exception means that qualifying health plans may be physician-owned and also furnish designated health services directly as a line of business or in a subsidiary organization. Qualifying health plans also may contract with physician-owned providers for furnishing services to Medicare and Medicaid enrollees. Significantly, only those enumerated managed care organizations (MCOs) with formal government relationships can both own designated health services and be physician owned. This produces the "backwards" result that MCOs whose focus is Medicare have the most flexibility regarding physician ownership of designated-health services entities, while those MCOs having the least Medicare nexus (e.g., commercial plans with only an incidental Medicare connection stemming from few Medicare eligibles in employer group health plans) have the least flexibility.

These issues are addressed in greater detail in Chapter 8.

## § 3-4(a)(4)   Academic Medical Centers

CMS has adopted an exception for compensation paid to a bona fide employee of a component of an academic medical center (AMC). A "component" of an AMC is defined to include an affiliated medical school, faculty practice plan, hospital, teaching facility, institution of higher education, departmental professional corporation, or a nonprofit support organization who primary purpose is supporting the teaching mission of the AMC.[145] This exception requires that the arrangement be among components of an "academic medical center" which must consist of each of the following:

---

[144] 60 Fed. Reg. 41,951 (1995).
[145] 42 C.F.R. § 411.355(e).

- either an accredited medical school (or university where appropriate) or an "accredited academic hospital";
- one or more faculty practice plans affiliated with the medical school, the affiliated hospital(s), or the accredited academic hospital; and
- one or more "qualified affiliated hospital(s)" in which a majority of the physicians on the medical staff at the affiliated hospital(s) are (a) faculty members of the affiliated medical school or (b) of one or more of the educational programs at the accredited academic hospital, and a majority of all hospital admissions are made by physicians who are "faculty members." [146]

In order to qualify for this exception, it is necessary that the arrangement be with a "physician" who:

- is a bona fide employee of a "component" of the AMC;
- employed by the "component" on a full-time or on a substantial part-time basis;
- licensed to practice medicine in the state;
- has a bona fide faculty appointment at an affiliated medical school (or with one or more of the educational programs at an accredited academic hospital); and
- provides "substantial" academic or clinical services, (or a combination of such services).[147]

The following are other requirements that AMCs must satisfy.

- All monetary transfers between components (defined as an affiliated medical school, faculty practice plan, hospital, teaching facility, institution of higher education, or departmental professional corporation) of the AMC must directly or indirectly support the missions of teaching, indigent care, research, or community services.
- There must be a written agreement between the components of the AMC that has been approved by the governing body of each component.
- All money paid to a referring physician for research must be used solely to support bona fide research.
- The physician's compensation arrangement must not violate the Anti-Kickback Statute.

---

[146] 42 C.F.R. § 411.355(e)(2).

[147] For purposes of this exception, the term "substantial" will be deemed to meet this requirement if the physician spends at least 20% of her professional time or eight hours per week providing academic and/or clinical services. However, a physician that does not satisfy these requirements will not automatically be considered to not provide substantial services. 42 C.F.R. § 411.355(e)(1)(D).

This exception also requires that the compensation paid by all medical-center components to the referring physician be set in advance; does not exceed FMV; is not determined in a manner that takes into account the volume or value of any referrals or other business generated by the physician; and does not violate the Anti-Kickback Statute or any federal or state law or regulation governing billing or claims submission.

Significantly, the preamble to the Phase III Stark II Final Regulations included a major clarification concerning faculty physician compensation. Under the Phase III Stark II Final Regulations, faculty practice plans can be structured as group practices. This allows the faculty practice plans to take advantage of the physician services exception, the special rules regarding compensation of physicians in a group practice, and the in office ancillary services exception. The in office ancillary services exception however, would only protect referrals within the faculty practice plan, not those to other components of the AMC.[148] In addition to the above exceptions, the indirect compensation exception is also "potentially applicable." The AMC exception is designed to "supplement—not supplant" other exceptions, therefore to the extent a hospital or other entity cannot take advantage of the AMC exception, the compensation arrangements with physicians can still be structured to meet another exception.

One of the minor clarifications contained in Phase III pertained to situations in which a physician received compensation from multiple components of the AMC. In such a situation the compensation amount from each component must be set out in advance using a qualified methodology, and must not take into account the volume or value of referrals or other business generated by the physician with the AMC. At the same time however, the compensation from each component need not meet the fair market value test, but rather the physician's aggregate compensation from all the components must be fair market value.

Although the Phase III Stark II Final Regulations left unanswered the question of whether a component of an AMC could be a "physician organization" for purposes of the "stand in the shoes" provisions, in the FY 2009 IPPS Final Rule, CMS specifically included language in the regulations that states that the stand in the shoes provisions do not apply to arrangements that satisfy the requirements of the AMC exception.[149]

In 2008, the Western District of Kentucky reviewed the applicability of the AMC exception.[150] *United States ex rel. Villafane v. Solinger* involved alleged Stark Law violations being bootstrapped into a FCA qui tam action. After the government declined intervention, the defendants moved for summary judgment on the basis that the Stark law was not violated because the arrangements fit within the AMC exception. Due to the lack of a "jurisprudential consensus about

---

[148] 72 Fed. Reg. at 51,023.
[149] 42 C.F.R. § 354(c)(3)(ii)(B); *see also* 73 Fed. Reg. at 48,698.
[150] United States *ex rel.* Villafane v. Solinger, 543 F. Supp. 2d 678, 687 (W.D. Ky. 2008).

## Federal Physician Self-Referral Prohibitions

the meaning or applicability of the AMC's many elements," the judge instead, "looked to the history and evolution of the exception for its primary guidance."[151]

The two main issues in *Villafane* were whether the defendant physicians provided substantial academic or clinical services to the AMC and whether the total compensation received by the physician defendant's from the AMC was at fair market value. The regulations for the AMC exception do provide a "safe harbor" for meeting the substantial academic or clinical services requirement, however the defendants' could not meet the "safe harbor" requirements. This was not dispositive because "a physician who fails to meet this safe harbor 'is not precluded from qualifying' under this requirement."[152] The court concluded that while the defendants did not fall within the safe harbor and failed to use a time keeping system that was of high quality or accuracy, they met the "substantial" requirement because "Defendants' annual work assignments and performance reviews, as well as curricula vitae indicate they were tasked with and completed substantial academic and clinical services."[153] The judge further determined that the defendants complied with the regulations regarding calculating fair market value by "presenting a 'comparison . . . [to] aggregate compensation paid to physicians practicing in similar academic settings located in similar environments . . . demonstrating that their compensation is comparable to similarly situated academics.'"[154]

### § 3-4(a)(5)  Implants in ASCs

CMS has adopted an exception for all prosthetic devices—including intraocular lenses used as part of cataract surgery—that are implanted in a Medicare-certified ASC but that may not otherwise be included in the bundled ASC payment rate.[155] CMS created this exception, in part, in order to prevent procedures currently performed in ASCs to be shifted to what CMS considers more-costly hospital-outpatient settings. This exception, however, is limited to only a narrow field of devices and applies only in certain settings.

### § 3-4(a)(6)  Additional Regulatory Exceptions Applicable to both Ownership and Compensation Arrangements

CMS has promulgated a number of additional exceptions for both ownership and compensation arrangements concerning the provision of the following items: eyeglasses or contact lenses that are prescribed after cataract surgery; EPO and other dialysis drugs provided by or in ESRD facilities;

---

[151] *Id.*
[152] *Id.* at 688.
[153] *Id.* at 689–690.
[154] *Id.* at 692.
[155] 42 C.F.R. § 411.355(f).

preventive screening tests, immunizations, and vaccines; and intra-family rural referrals.[156]

## § 3-4(b)  Ownership-Only Exceptions

### § 3-4(b)(1)  Ownership in Publicly Traded Securities and Mutual Funds

The Stark Law includes a specific exemption for ownership of publicly traded securities and mutual funds. The exemption applies to ownership of investment securities (e.g., shares or bonds, debentures, notes, or other debt instruments) purchased on terms generally available to the public. The securities must be listed on the New York Stock Exchange; the American Stock Exchange; any regional exchange in which quotations are published on a daily basis; or foreign securities listed on a recognized foreign, national, or regional exchange in which quotations are published on a daily basis. Alternatively, the securities could be traded under an automated interdealer quotation system operated by the National Association of Securities Dealers.[157]

In order to qualify for the exemption, the corporation must have total stockholder equity exceeding $75 million at the end of the corporation's most recent fiscal year or must have an average of $75 million for the previous three fiscal years.[158] Ownership of shares in a regulated investment company under the Internal Revenue Code (IRC) also is exempt if, at the end of the company's most recent fiscal year or on average for its most recent three fiscal years, the company had total assets exceeding $75 million, which applies to investments in mutual funds.

It is noteworthy that this dollar amount is different from the $50 million required for safe harbor protection from the Anti-Kickback Statute, and is reduced from the earlier $100 million threshold found in Stark I. However, the calculation of the amount is now based on stockholder equity, instead of total assets as in the pre-OBRA '93 test. Consequently, entities are prevented from borrowing funds to meet the monetary threshold. In addition, this recalculation of the amount is different from the "net tangible" assets, which can be counted toward safe-harbor protection as described in Chapter 2.

CMS originally had included in the Proposed Stark I Regulations a requirement that the qualifying assets be obtained in the ordinary course of business, and not for the primary purpose of qualifying for the exception. This requirement was eliminated from the Final Stark I Regulations. CMS also declined to allow use of a consolidated balance sheet by a group of affiliated

---

[156] 42 C.F.R. §§ 411.355(g)–(i).
[157] Social Security Act § 1877(c); 42 U.S.C. § 1395nn(c).
[158] Social Security Act § 1877(c); 42 U.S.C. § 1395nn(c).

## Federal Physician Self-Referral Prohibitions

corporations to meet the monetary threshold.[159] Rather, only the assets of the corporation in which the physician owns stock are counted toward meeting the asset test.[160]

Originally, the Stark Law required that the investment security be purchased on terms generally available to the public. As a result of OBRA '93, the criterion has been relaxed to permit ownership of investment securities "which *may* be purchased on terms generally available to the public." This apparent relaxation of the standard is important to confirm the legality of many transactions that occurred to divest physicians of ownership interests in designated health service providers, as well as to permit transactions on an ongoing basis with respect to currently exempted investment interests.

### § 3-4(b)(2)  Hospitals

When Stark II was adopted, Congress included both an exception from the ownership proscription those designated health services provided by hospitals located in Puerto Rico, as well as designated health services furnished by hospitals outside of Puerto Rico where the referring physician has an ownership interest in the hospital itself (and not in a subdivision or component of the hospital), and the referring physician is authorized to perform services at the hospital.[161]

As described earlier, as part of MMA, Congress adopted a temporary moratorium on physician ownership in specialty hospitals, defined as those hospitals engaged primarily or exclusively in the care and treatment of: "(i) patients with a cardiac condition[;] (ii) patients with an orthopedic condition[;] (iii) patients receiving a surgical procedure[; and] (iv) any other specialized category of services that the Secretary designates . . . ."[162] Although the moratorium was not extended beyond June 2005, a different moratorium was established in 2006 as part of the DRA, whereby Congress mandated that DHHS continue to suspend enrolling new specialty hospitals into the Medicare program until the earlier of (1) DHHS submitting its final report on the development of a strategic plan concerning physician ownership in specialty hospital or (2) eight months after enactment of the DRA (i.e., September 2006).[163]

As part of the Health Reform Law, Congress has placed significant limitations on physicians' ownership interest in hospitals located both in urban and rural areas. Now, the Stark Law provides that a hospital cannot be owned by physicians unless the ownership interest was obtained by the physi-

---

[159] 60 Fed. Reg. 41,952 (1995).
[160] *Id.*
[161] Social Security Act §§ 1877(d)(1) and (d)(3); 42 U.S.C. §§ 1395nn(d)(1) and (d)(3); 42 C.F.R. § 411.356(c)(3)(I).
[162] 42 U.S.C. § 1395nn(h)(7).
[163] DRA § 5006.

cians prior to enactment of Health Reform and that the hospital had a provider agreement in place as of December 31, 2010.[164] Those hospitals that qualify for this grandfather provision are significantly limited in expanding the number of licensed beds, operating or procedure rooms beyond the number that existed as of the date the hospital is licensed following enactment of the law. Health Reform establishes that a facility can seek a waiver from the expansion limitation in two separate sets of circumstances: (1) a hospital, that among other things, is in a county that has percentage increase in population over the last five years that is 150% of the population growth in the state; or (2) a hospital that constitutes a "High Medicaid Facility," which is not the sole hospital in a county and, for the three most recent years, has a larger percentage of Medicaid inpatient admissions than any other hospital in the county. Health Reform establishes that the Secretary is to promulgate regulations by January 2012 that set forth the process by which a hospital can apply for one of these exceptions. CMS issued these regulations as part of the CY 2012 Medicare Hospital Outpatient Prospective Payment System regulations.[165]

As part of these limitations, Congress imposed additional requirements in order to ensure that the physicians' ownership interests are "bona fide". For example, the terms upon which a physician is offered an ownership interest in the hospital can be no different than the terms upon which a non-physician would be offered the same interest. Congress also provided that, not only is the hospital prohibited from loaning money to a physician, but the hospital cannot guarantee a loan that a physician might obtain from a third party. Congress also enacted a number of disclosure requirements that the hospital and physician owners must make to patients concerning the existence of the ownership interest. The Health Reform legislation requires the hospital to disclose to patients if the hospital does not have a physician on-site 24/7. Congress adopted the specialty hospital moratorium in 2003 when a number of incidents occurred at specialty hospitals allegedly because there was not adequate physician coverage. Although CMS adopted regulations a few years prior that require certain of these items to be disclosed by hospitals to patients[166], Congress apparently saw a need to codify these requirements into the Social Security Act.[167]

The Health Reform Law also included a provision requiring the Secretary to collect information regarding physician ownership in hospitals. Although the Stark Law already included a provision providing the Secretary with the authority to request information regarding physician ownership and compensation arrangements that healthcare entities may have with physicians, as discussed above, CMS has not been able to finalize a process by which it intended to collect this information.

---

[164] 42 U.S.C. § 1395nn(i).
[165] 76 Fed. Reg. 74,122, 74,157 (Nov. 30, 2011).
[166] 42 C.F.R. § 489.20(u)–(v).
[167] 42 U.S.C. § 1395nn(i); 42 C.F.R. § 411.362.

## Federal Physician Self-Referral Prohibitions

### § 3-4(b)(3)    Rural Providers

Currently, the Stark Law exempts designated health services furnished by physician-owned entities located in a rural area, but as stated above, the limitations on physician ownership in hospitals also applies to those hospitals that are located in rural areas.

The regulation defines the term "rural area" as an area that is not an urban area under 42 C.F.R. § 412.62(f)(1)(ii). The exception applies only if substantially all of the designated health services furnished by the entity are furnished to individuals residing in the rural area. The standard adopted in the regulations is that at least 75% of the entity's services must be furnished to individuals who reside in the rural area.[168]

The rural exception applies only to physician *ownership interests*. Rural entities furnishing designated health services do not enjoy similar protection for their compensation arrangements with physicians.

### § 3-4(c)    Compensation Arrangement Exceptions

### § 3-4(c)(1)    Rental of Office Space and Equipment

The exceptions for the rental of office space and equipment protects arrangements are substantially similar and require that the lease be set out in writing, signed by the parties, specify the premises or equipment, and be for a term of at least one year.[169] CMS has provided in the regulations that a holdover month-to-month rental for an agreement that already satisfied the one year requirement will be permitted provided the holdover rental is on the same terms and conditions and for a period of less than 6 months. CMS confirmed in the Phase III Stark II Final Regulations that lessors can charge a holdover rental premium provided that the amount of the premium was set in advance in the lease agreement (or in any subsequent renewal) at the time of its execution and the rental rate (including the premium) remains consistent with fair market value and does not take into account the volume or value of referrals or other business generated between the parties.[170]

The exceptions also require that the space and equipment rented or leased must not exceed that which is "reasonable and necessary" for legitimate business purposes and CMS has indicated that office-sharing arrangements require the lessee to have exclusive use of the space for the time it will be used. In the Phase III Stark II Final Regulations, CMS clarified that these

---

[168] 42 C.F.R. § 411.356(c)(1).
[169] Social Security Act § 1877(e)(1)(A)-(B); 42 U.S.C. § 1395nn(e)(1)(A)-(B); *see also* 42 C.F.R. § 411.357(a)-(b).
[170] 42 C.F.R. §§ 411.357(a)(7) and (b)(6).

established blocks of time, for which the lessee will have exclusive use, should be incorporated into the lease agreements.[171]

The rental charges over the term of the lease must be set in advance, consistent with FMV, commercially reasonable even if no referrals are made between the parties and not be determined in a manner that takes into account the volume or value of any referrals or other business generated between the parties. Unlike the Anti-Kickback Statute's safe-harbors criteria for office space and equipment leases, the Stark Law does not require that the *aggregate* payment over the term of the lease be specified in advance. Consequently, under the Stark Law, there may be flexibility to establish equipment lease rates based on a fee schedule, or a space rental arrangement with a formula for imposing common area maintenance charges. However, as stated above, in connection with acceptable compensation methodologies, effective October 1, 2009, percentage and per-click compensation methodologies will no longer be permitted under the space and equipment rental exceptions.[172]

As significant element of compliance with these exceptions is the definition of FMV, which is defined for Stark purposes as:

> the value in arm[']s length transactions, consistent with general market value, and, with respect to rentals or leases, the value of rental property for general commercial purposes (not taking into account its intended use) and, in the case of a lease of space, not adjusted to reflect the additional value the prospective lessor or lessee would attribute to the proximity or convenience to the lessor where the lessor is a potential source of patient referrals to the lessee.[173]

With respect to leases, an important issue in determining FMV is whether the costs of capital improvements should be allocated over the useful life of the improvements or be passed on in their entirety to the physician lessee who requested the improvements. While CMS stated that this determination is case specific, CMS also declared that the costs of improvements that are unlikely to be chargeable to a subsequent tenant should be allocated to the lessee for whose unique benefit they are made. At the same time, improvements that the lessor reasonably expects would be chargeable to subsequent lessees may be allocated over their expected useful life.

Specific to office leases, CMS has provided that the lessee may make payments for the use of common areas if the payments do not exceed the lessee's pro rata share of expenses for such common space, based on the ratio of space used exclusively by the lessee to the total amount of space (other than common areas) occupied by all persons using the common areas. In the Phase III Stark II Final Regulations, CMS defined common areas as including

---

[171] 72 Fed. Reg. at 51,045.
[172] 42 C.F.R. §§ 357(a)(5), 357(b)(4); *see also* 73 Fed. Reg. at 48,709–48,721.
[173] Social Security Act § 1877(h)(3); 42 U.S.C. § 1395nn(h)(3). *See also* 42 C.F.R. § 411.351.

## Federal Physician Self-Referral Prohibitions

foyers, central waiting rooms, break rooms, vending areas, etc., to the extent that the areas are, in fact, used by the sublessee (e.g., a sublessee cannot pay rent for a break room that it will never use). CMS stated that common areas that contain certain limited equipment may be shared—for example, hallways used to weigh patients or draw fluid samples. The permissible equipment in shared common areas is limited to the type that is "not usually separately leased" (for example, scales). CMS noted that non-exclusive arrangements, other than for common space (as described above), do not satisfy the requirements of the lease exceptions.[174]

### § 3-4(c)(2) Bona Fide Employment Relationships

The exemption for bona fide employment relationships was added by OBRA '93. This exemption protects arrangements between employers and physicians or their immediate family members who have a bona fide employment relationship with the employer for the provision of services if the employment is for identifiable services, the amount of payment is consistent with FMV, and is not determined in a manner that takes into account (directly or indirectly) the volume or value of any referrals by the referring physician. The payment provided pursuant to the employment agreement must be commercially reasonable even if no referrals were made to the employer.[175]

The requirement that payment made to employees not be determined based on the volume or value of referrals does *not* prohibit payments in the form of productivity bonuses based on services *performed personally* by the employee (or immediate family member of the employee). It is important to note that this bonus flexibility is limited to personally performed services and, thus, is not as broad as the bonus flexibility included in the group-practice definition, which permits bonus compensation to include profit sharing or be indirectly based on revenues from "incident to" services. It also is important to note that the employee exception is not sufficient to protect physician members of a group practice who also are owners of the group practice; the employment exception only protects the compensation arrangements, not the ownership relationships. For such physicians, it would be necessary to meet the in-office ancillary services exception (and the group-practice definition), which applies to *both* ownership and compensation arrangements.

---

[174] 72 Fed. Reg. at 51,045.
[175] Social Security Act § 1877(e)(2); 42 U.S.C. § 1395nn(e)(2); 42 C.F.R. 411.357(c).

## § 3-4(c)(3)    Personal Service Arrangements

The exemption for personal service arrangements protects compensation arrangements between a physician and an entity where the physician is an independent contractor and not an employee of the entity. In order to qualify for the exemption, a written agreement must contain the following elements:[176]

- the agreement must be signed by the parties;
- the agreement must specify the services covered by the arrangement;
- The arrangement must cover all of the services to be provided by the physician to the entity;
- the term of the agreement must be for one year or more;[177]
- The aggregate services contracted for must not exceed those that are reasonable and necessary for the legitimate business purposes of the arrangement;
- the compensation to be paid over the term of the agreement must be set in advance, not exceed FMV, and not be determined in a manner that takes into account the volume or value of any referrals or other business generated between the parties; and
- the services to be performed under the arrangement must not involve the counseling or promotion of a business arrangement or other activity that violates any state or federal law.

The personal services exception requires that personal service arrangements cover "all" of the services to be furnished by the physician. This requirement is met if all separate arrangements between the entity and the physician (and any physician family members) incorporate each other by reference, or if they cross-reference a master list of contracts that is maintained and updated centrally and is available for CMS's review. In the preamble to the Phase III Stark II Final Regulations, CMS explained that the exception permits—but does not require—the use of a master list. CMS warned that arrangements with family members of a physician also must be included on the master list.[178]

This exemption largely mirrors the safe harbor for personal services and management contracts under the Anti-Kickback Statute. Unlike that safe harbor, however, the standard for compensation under the Stark Law exception

---

[176] Social Security Act § 1877(e)(3); 42 U.S.C. § 1395nn(e)(3); 42 C.F.R. § 411.357(d).

[177] The Phase III Stark II Final Regulations modified the personal services arrangements exception to allow a "holdover personal services arrangement" for up to six months following expiration of an agreement of at least one year that met the exception requirements. The personal service holdover was modeled after the lease holdover and thus must be on the same terms and conditions as the immediately preceding agreement.

[178] 72 Fed. Reg. at 51,046.

### Federal Physician Self-Referral Prohibitions

does not require that *aggregate* compensation payable to the physician be specified in advance. Significantly, the personal-services exception does not contemplate the payment of any bonus or incentive compensation. In order to attain the flexibility to pay bonus compensation, the exceptions for employment or in-office ancillary services must be consulted.

The Stark Law exception for personal service arrangements also includes specific language applicable to provider contracts between physicians and managed care plans.[179] Generally, the personal-service exception requires that compensation cannot vary based on the volume or value of referrals. However, withholds or bonuses paid to physicians participating in managed care plans may indeed be based on referrals (or, more accurately, the lack thereof), and the prepaid plan exception described earlier covers only a small subset of the universe of managed care plans. Therefore, an "exception within an exception" was necessary to ensure that provider contracts under managed care would not be considered a compensation arrangement triggering the self-referral ban for any designated health services furnished directly by the managed care plan. These issues are discussed in greater detail in Chapter 8.

In 2007, the District Court for the Western District of Louisiana undertook the task of interpreting the personal services exception.[180] In *United States ex rel. Roberts v. Aging Care Home Health, Inc.*, the government alleged Aging Care, a home health agency, violated the Stark Law by compensating physicians in exchange for referrals. Aging Care relied on the personal services exception but this defense failed because many of the contracts were not for a term of one year or more, "the actual services performed were not specified in the agreement, not reasonably necessary, and exceeded fair market value."[181]

### § 3-4(c)(4)   Unrelated Payments

The statute exempts payments provided by a hospital to a physician if such payments do not relate to the provision of designated health services.[182] The Stark regulations also provide that, in order to be "unrelated," the remuneration must be wholly unrelated to the furnishing of designated health services, and must not in any way take into account the volume or value of a physician's referrals.[183]

---

[179] Social Security Act § 1877(e)(3)(B); 42 U.S.C. § 1395nn(e)(3)(B).
[180] *See* United States *ex rel.* Roberts v. Aging Care Home Health, Inc., 474 F. Supp. 2d 810 (W.D. La. 2007).
[181] *Id.* at 819.
[182] Social Security Act § 1877(e)(4); 42 U.S.C. § 1395nn(e)(4).
[183] 42 C.F.R. § 411.357(g).

## § 3-4(c)(5)  Physician Recruitment

The physician-recruitment exemption protects payments made by a hospital to a physician to induce the physician to relocate to the geographic area served by the hospital and to become a medical staff member. In order to qualify for this exemption, (1) the physician cannot be required to refer patients to the hospital, (2) the amount of the payment cannot be determined in a manner that takes into account (directly or indirectly) the volume or value of any referrals by the referring physician, and (3) the arrangement must meet other requirements that *may* be imposed by regulation to protect against program or patient abuse.[184]

CMS regulations provide that a hospital can make payments to an existing group in order to assist the group in recruiting the physician as long as the remuneration is passed directly through to, and remain with, the recruited physician, except for actual recruitment expenses. In the case of an income guarantee, the costs allocated by the physician or group practice to the recruited physician may not exceed the actual additional incremental costs attributable to the recruited physician.[185] CMS provides that a group can either allocate the actual additional incremental costs attributable to the recruited physicians or allocate aggregate overhead and other expenses, not to exceed 20% of aggregate costs, where the recruited physician is replacing a deceased, retiring or relocating physician in an underserved area. A physician who merely "co-locates" with a physician practice, for example, by leasing office space from the group, is not eligible under the exception.[186]

The regulations also provide that the physician practice may not "impose on the recruited physician practice restrictions that unreasonably restrict the recruited physician's ability to practice medicine in the geographic areas served by the hospital."[187] In the Phase III Stark II Final Regulations, CMS stated its intent was only to prohibit such restrictions that would have a "substantial effect" on the recruited physician's ability to remain and practice medicine in the hospital's geographic service area after leaving the physician practice. CMS noted that following restrictions are not considered to have a substantial effect on the recruited physician's ability to remain in the hospital's geographic service area:

- Restrictions on moonlighting.
- Prohibitions on soliciting patients and/or employees of the practice.
- Requirement that the recruited physician is to treat Medicaid and indigent patients.

---

[184] Social Security Act § 1877(e)(5); 42 U.S.C. § 1395nn(e)(5).
[185] 42 C.F.R. § 411.357(e)(1).
[186] 72 Fed. Reg. at 51,053.
[187] 42 C.F.R. § 411.357(e)(4)(vi).

- Requirement that the recruited physician not use confidential or proprietary information of the practice.
- Requirement that the recruited physician repay losses of his/her practice that are absorbed by the physician practice in excess of any hospital recruitment payments.
- Requirement that the recruited physician pay a predetermined amount of reasonable damages, that is liquidated damages, if the physician leaves the physician practice and remains in the community. CMS remarks however, that it may consider a significant or unreasonable payment of this type to have a substantial effect on the physician's ability to remain in the area. CMS also states that any practice restrictions or conditions that do not comply with applicable state and local law run a significant risk of being considered unreasonable.[188]

In order to qualify under the recruitment exception, the recruited physician must (1) relocate her medical practice to the geographic area served by the hospital (the area composed of the lowest number of contiguous ZIP Codes from which the hospital draws at least 75% of its inpatients) as evidenced by the physician moving her medical practice at least 25 miles; or (2) derive 75% of her revenues from professional services furnished to patients not seen previously by the physician during the prior three years.[189]

CMS clarified that for all physicians subject to the relocation requirement, the physician must relocate his/her practice from an area outside the geographic service area to a location inside the geographic service area and either move his/her medical practice at least 25 miles or have a new medical practice that derives at least 75% of its revenues from professional services furnished to patients, including hospital inpatients, not seen or treated by the physician at his/her prior medical practice site during the preceding three years measured on an annual basis, whether calendar or fiscal. In the preamble, CMS re-affirmed its position that physicians already on a hospital's medical staff, even courtesy privileges, are not eligible for recruitment assistance under the exception.[190] However, the regulations provide that residents and physicians who have been in practice one year or less are exempt from the "relocation" requirement and CMS stated in the preamble to the Phase III Stark II Final Regulations that a "residency" includes all training, including post-residency fellowships.[191] Also exempt now are physicians who for two immediately prior years were employed full-time by a federal or state bureau of prisons, the Department of Defense, Department of Veterans Affairs or facilities of the Indian Health Service, provided that such physician did not

---

[188] 72 Fed. Reg. at 51,053–51,054.
[189] 42 C.F.R. § 411.357(e)(2)(i).
[190] 72 Fed. Reg. at 51,048.
[191] *Id.* at 51,051.

maintain a separate private practice in addition to such full-time employment. Also exempt are physicians for whom CMS has issued an advisory opinion finding that such physician did not have an established medical practice comprised of a significant number of patients who are or could become patients of the recruiting hospital.[192]

A significant aspect of this exception is determining the "geographic area served by the hospital" and the regulations provide that the geographic area served by a hospital is deemed to be the area comprised of all of the contiguous zip codes from which the hospital's inpatients are drawn when the hospital draws fewer than 75% of its inpatients from contiguous zones. Nevertheless, hospitals located in rural areas are permitted to determine the geographic area that they serve using an alternative test that encompasses the lowest number of contiguous (or in some cases non-contiguous) zip codes from which the hospital draws 90% of its inpatients. Special provisions allow hospitals in rural areas to recruit physicians to areas outside of the hospital's geographic service if CMS determines through its advisory opinion process that the area has a demonstrated need for a recruited physician.[193]

In the preamble to the Phase III Stark II Final Regulations, CMS commented on several scenarios pertaining to the determination of geographic service area. The first question discussed how a hospital should determine its geographic service area if the contiguous zip codes proximate to the hospital account for only 69% of its inpatients, but due to the hospital's national reputation the remainder of its inpatients are drawn from distant, noncontiguous zip codes. CMS responded that, although it does not expect many hospitals to be in this situation, such a hospital under the Phase II definition of "geographic area serviced by the hospital" would be prohibited from relying on the recruitment exception. The problem is that the hospital would fail to satisfy either the original "at least [75%] of inpatients" drawn from contiguous zip codes (applicable for all hospitals) or the "at least [90%] of inpatients" test now available for rural hospitals. For this reason, CMS in Phase III modified the regulations to allow the hospital to include all of the contiguous zip codes from which inpatients are drawn when it draws fewer than 75% (or 90% for rural hospitals) from those contiguous zip codes. In the end, the hospital in the scenario would qualify for the recruitment exception under the Phase III Stark II Final Regulations.[194]

Another scenario involved a hospital with a zip code "hole" in the contiguous service area, resembling a donut. CMS explained that if the "hole" zip code is surrounded by contiguous zip codes and no people live in the "hole" zip code, for example, the "hole" zip code is assigned to a large office building

---

[192] 42 C.F.R. § 411.357(e)(3).
[193] 42 C.F.R. § 411.357(e)(2)(iii).
[194] 72 Fed. Reg. at 51,050.

## Federal Physician Self-Referral Prohibitions

or commercial district, then the hospital may recruit a physician to establish a practice in the "hole."[195] CMS stated that if multiple configurations containing the same number of zip codes permit the hospital to meet the applicable percent of inpatient test, (75% for all hospitals or 90% for rural hospitals), then the hospital is free to use any of the configurations.[196] CMS stated that a hospital may use any configuration that satisfies the lowest number of zip/codes for the applicable percent of inpatients test on the date it enters into the recruitment arrangements, meaning the date on which all parties have signed the written agreement. CMS acknowledged that this may result in different geographic service areas for different arrangements.

CMS has stated that the "volume or value" condition prohibits the amount of assistance payable to a physician or group practice from taking into account in any manner the volume or value of past or anticipated referrals to the hospital. CMS said, for example, the unconditional payment of actual moving expenses would not take into account the volume or value of referrals. CMS also confirmed that hospitals may impose "reasonable credentialing restrictions" on physicians when they compete with the recruiting hospital, but such restrictions may not take into account the volume or value of referrals.[197]

Furthermore, in the Phase III Stark II Final Regulations, CMS stated that nothing in the regulations precludes a hospital from requiring a physician practice to repay any monies advanced to the group on behalf of the recruited physician if the physician does not fulfill his/her community services requirement. However, CMS warned, if requiring the physician practice to make such repayment is used to "shield" the recruited physician from any real liability for failure to fulfill his/her service obligation, the parties would be "at significant risk of noncompliance" with the fraud and abuse laws.[198]

### § 3-4(c)(6)  Physician Retention

In the Phase II Stark II Final regulations, CMS added an exception for retention payments made *directly* to a physician if the payment is to retain the physician's medical practice in the geographic area served by the hospital that is either a health professional shortage area (HPSA) or is an area with a demonstrated need for the physician as determined through a Stark advisory opinion. This exception also requires that the physician have a bona fide firm, written recruitment offer from an unrelated hospital that specifies the remuneration being offered, and requires the physician to move his or her practice at least 25 miles *and* outside of the geographic area served by the hospital. Moreover, the retention payment is limited to the *lower of* (i) the amount obtained

---

[195] *Id.*
[196] *Id.*
[197] 72 Fed. Reg. at 51,049.
[198] *Id.* at 51,051.

by subtracting the physician's current income from the income the physician would receive from comparable services in the bona fide recruitment offer or (ii) the reasonable costs the hospital would expend in recruiting a new physician.[199]

## § 3-4(c)(7)    Isolated Financial Transactions

This exception protects isolated transactions (e.g., a one-time sale of property or practice) where the amount of the payment is consistent with FMV and does not take into account, directly or indirectly, the volume or value of any referrals between the parties. In addition, the remuneration provided must be commercially reasonable even if no referrals were made.[200] The Stark regulations further require that "there can be no additional transactions between the parties for six months after the isolated transaction" unless it meets one of the other exceptions.[201] For example, following an "isolated transaction," a physician can be employed by the other party so long as the employment arrangement meets the requirements of the employment exception.

The preamble to the Phase III Stark II Final Regulations clarified certain issues relating to the use of a promissory note to secure installment payments in an isolated transaction and the applicability of the exception in the context of post-closing adjustments and actions to collect on a breach of warranty. Specifically, CMS clarified that while a promissory note is one means of securing the payment of installment payments in a transaction, the promissory note does not need to be immediately negotiable in order to satisfy the requirement. Moreover, CMS stated that the use of a promissory note that may, for example, only be subject to collection upon a failure to make payment of the required installment payments, is permitted.[202] CMS also clarified that any post-closing adjustment occurring after the expiration of the six-month period from the date of the purchase or sale transaction would be treated as a separate, additional transaction. Therefore it would need to satisfy the requirements of another exception.[203]

---

[199] 42 C.F.R. § 411.357(t).
[200] Social Security Act § 1877(e)(6); 42 U.S.C. § 1395nn(e)(6).
[201] 42 C.F.R. § 411.357(f).
[202] 72 Fed. Reg. at 51,055.
[203] It is important to note, however, that notwithstanding such limitation on the length of the post-closing adjustment period, CMS does not view claims based upon the breach of representations or warranties in a transaction to constitute post-closing adjustments or separate transactions from the original transaction. Therefore, they may occur at any time without jeopardizing the applicability of this exception to a transaction.

## § 3-4(c)(8)  Certain Group-Practice Arrangements with a Hospital

The Stark Law contains an exception for designated health services furnished "under arrangements" to a hospital by a group practice. This exception addresses an issue that arose because a number of hospitals rely on large group practices to provide certain designated health services (e.g., laboratory and radiology services) for patients of the hospital. Medicare allows the furnishing of services "under arrangements," but requires the *hospital* to bill Medicare for the services furnished. The self-referral ban's "in-office ancillary services" exception, however, requires the *group practice* to bill for the services. Thus, a separate exception was necessary.

The exception is essentially a "grandfather" of certain existing relationships, and applies if:

(1) the arrangement began before December 19, 1989, and the arrangement has continued in effect without interruption since that date;

(2) substantially all of the designated health services furnished to patients of the hospital are furnished by the group under the arrangement;

(3) the compensation paid over the term of the agreement is consistent with FMV, the compensation per unit of services is fixed in advance, and is not determined in a manner that takes into account the volume or value of any referrals or other business generated between the parties;

(4) the compensation is provided pursuant to a written agreement that specifies the services to be furnished and the compensation to be paid, and that would be commercially reasonable even if no referrals were made to the entity; and

(5) with respect to inpatient services, the services must be furnished pursuant to the provision of inpatient hospital services under SSA § 1861(b)(3).[204]

## § 3-4(c)(9)  Payments for Items and Services

This exception protects payments made by a physician to a laboratory in exchange for the provision of clinical laboratory services. This exception is broad, and does not require that any other standards be met. This exception also protects payments made by a physician to an entity as compensation for items or services (other than clinical laboratory services) if the items or services are furnished at a price that is consistent with FMV.[205]

---

[204] Social Security Act § 1877(e)(7); 42 U.S.C. § 1395nn(e)(7); 42 C.F.R. § 411.357(h).
[205] Social Security Act § 1877(e)(8); 42 U.S.C. § 1395nn(e)(8); 42 C.F.R. § 411.357(i).

### § 3-4(c)(10)   Fair Market Value Exception

CMS has added an exception that largely mirrors the existing compensation-arrangement exceptions, but provides more flexibility when an agreement does not otherwise meet certain requirements under other exceptions (e.g., the agreement is not for the term of a year). The most significant issue raised by the FMV exception may be the requirement that such arrangements not violate the Anti-Kickback Statute. Thus, the question becomes the extent to which the parties are comfortable operating outside of a safe harbor or specific advisory opinion.

In the FY 2009 IPPS Final Rule, CMS modified the fair market value exception such that after October 1, 2009, percentage and per-click compensation methodologies will no longer be permitted under this exception.[206]

### § 3-4(c)(11)   Non-Monetary Compensation

In the proposed regulations to Stark II, CMS set out a new exception titled "De Minimis Compensation," which permitted non-cash items or services to be provided to a physician or her family member that did not exceed $50 per gift and an aggregate of $300 per year.[207] In the proposed version, this exception would apply only if the entity providing the compensation makes it available to all "similarly situated" individuals, regardless of whether they referred patients to the entity.

In the final regulations, CMS changed the name of this exception to "Non-Monetary Compensation" to eliminate any "unintentional implication" that the $300 limit is inconsequential in producing referrals and also provided that the $300 amount will be adjusted by any increases in the Consumer Price Index.[208] For the calendar year beginning January 1, 2012, the compensation limit under this exception was increased to $373 per year.[209] In addition, CMS eliminated the $50 per-gift limit in the final regulations.

In the Phase III Stark II Final Regulations, CMS also addressed circumstances in which an entity inadvertently exceeds the yearly amount and that the Stark Law will not be implicated if: the value of the non-monetary compensation is no more than 50% of the limits, and the physician returns the excess value by the later of the end of the year in which it was paid or 180 days following the date the excess compensation was received. The regulation

---

[206] 42 C.F.R. § 357(l); *see also* 73 Fed. Reg. at 48,709–48,721.

[207] 63 Fed. Reg. 1,699 (1998). Notably, CMS has stated explicitly in connection with this exception that (because drug manufacturers typically do not fall within the purview of the Stark Law) as a general rule, the Stark Law does not prohibit free drugs, free training, or gifts provided to physicians by drug manufacturers. *See* 66 Fed. Reg. 920 (2001).

[208] 42 C.F.R. § 411.357(k)(1)-(2).

[209] *See* http://www.cms.hhs.gov/PhysicianSelfReferral/50_CPI-U_Updates.asp#TopOfPage.

### Federal Physician Self-Referral Prohibitions

also provide that this exception for inadvertently exceeding the yearly amount can only be used by an entity once every 3 years with respect to the same physician.[210]

### § 3-4(c)(12)  Medical-Staff Incidental Benefits

In the final regulations, CMS created an exception that permits hospital to furnish to its medical staffs certain incidental *benefits* of low value, such as parking, meals, or free computer/Internet access.[211] In order to qualify for this exception, the benefits must:
- be offered to all members of the medical staff, without regard to the volume or value of their referrals or other business generated;
- only be offered when the medical-staff members are making rounds or performing duties that benefit the hospital or its patients;
- be used only on the hospital's campus;
- be reasonably related to the furnishing of medical services at the hospital;
- be consistent with industry practice norms;
- be of low value (i.e., less than $25); and
- not violate the Anti-Kickback Statute.[212]

While the exception for medical-staff incidental benefits permits those benefits that are less than $25, this amount is to be adjusted each year based upon the Consumer Price Index-Urban All Item (CPI-U) for the 12-month period ending the preceding September 30.[213] For the calendar year beginning January 1, 2012, the value of any medical staff incidental benefits furnished under this exception must be less than $31 per occurrence.[214]

### § 3-4(c)(13)  Managed Care Risk-Sharing Arrangements

In response to the unintended effect of Stark on commercial health plans, CMS created a compensation exception for remuneration pursuant to a "risk-sharing arrangement" (including, but not limited to, withholds, bonuses, and risk pools) between a MCO and a physician for the provision of items or services to enrollees of the health plan.[215] This exception was intended to supplement the personal-services exception, which would only permit managed care

---

[210] 42 C.F.R. § 411.357(k)(3).
[211] 42 C.F.R. § 411.357(m).
[212] 42 C.F.R. § 411.357(m)(1-8).
[213] 42 C.F.R. § 411.357(m).
[214] *See* http://www.cms.hhs.gov/PhysicianSelfReferral/10_CPI-U_Updates.asp#TopOfPage.
[215] 42 C.F.R. § 411.357(n).

incentive compensation that met CMS' Physician Incentive Plan (PIP) rules for Medicare managed care plans. As Medicare PIP rules substantially restrict the amount of financial risk that can be passed along to physicians, commercial plans with a relatively small number of Medicare beneficiaries would have had to alter substantially their risk-sharing plans with physicians in order to allow the physicians in their managed care networks to refer patients in network for designated health services. CMS has stated that it will "monitor" this exception, and may revisit the issue in the future it if perceives ongoing abuse from this exception.[216]

## § 3-4(c)(14)   Compliance Training

Because CMS views compliance training programs as "beneficial," CMS adopted in the Stark final regulations an exception for compliance training provided by a healthcare entity to physicians who practice in the entity's community.[217] Compliance training is broadly defined to include training that address general compliance areas (e.g., establishment of policies and procedures, training of staff, internal monitoring, and reporting) and more-specific training topics (e.g., billing, coding, reasonable and necessary services, documentation, and unlawful referral arrangements).[218]

## § 3-4(c)(15)   Exception for Indirect Compensation

As set forth above, CMS has defined an indirect compensation arrangement as one in which there are three elements.[219] First, there must be "an unbroken chain" of persons or entities that have financial relationships between them. Second, the aggregate compensation received by the referring physician from the entity with which she has a direct financial relationship must vary with, or otherwise reflect, the volume or value of referrals or other business generated between the physician and designated health services entity.[220] Third, a designated health services provider must have "actual knowledge" or have acted in "reckless disregard" that the aggregate compensation paid to the physician otherwise satisfies the second criterion.[221]

By the same token, CMS created an exception for indirect-compensation arrangements that satisfy the following three requirements:

(i) the compensation received by the physician from the person or entity with which the referring physician has the direct financial relationship

---

[216] 66 Fed. Reg. 913 (2001).
[217] 42 C.F.R. § 411.357(o).
[218] *Id.*
[219] 66 Fed. Reg. 865 (2001).
[220] *Id.* at 866.
[221] *Id.* at 866.

## Federal Physician Self-Referral Prohibitions

is "fair market value" for services and items actually provided, "not taking into account" the volume or value of referrals for the entity furnishing designated health services;

(ii) the compensation arrangement between the physician and the entity with which the physician has the direct financial relationship is set out in writing, is signed by the parties, and specifies the services covered (except for bona fide employment arrangements, which need not be in writing but must be for identifiable services and commercially reasonable even if no referrals are made to the employer); and

(iii) the arrangement does not violate the Anti-Kickback Statute or any laws or regulations governing billing or claims submission.[222]

### § 3-4(c)(16)   Professional Courtesy

In recognition that providing free or discounted professional courtesy to physicians and their families, CMS adopted an exception permitting professional courtesy if the following requirements are met:

- the professional courtesy is offered to all physicians on the entity's bona fide medical staff, or in the entity's local community, without regard to volume or value of referrals or other business generated between the parties;
- the healthcare items and services provided are of a type routinely provided by the entity;
- the professional courtesy policy is set out in writing and approved in advance by the entity's governing body;
- the professional courtesy is not offered to a physician (or immediate family member) who is a federal healthcare program beneficiary, unless there is a good-faith showing of financial need;
- if the professional courtesy involves any whole or partial reduction of any coinsurance obligation (for example, a waiver of co-pays), the reduction or waiver is disclosed to the insurer in writing; and
- the arrangement does not violate the Anti-Kickback Statute or any federal or state laws and regulations covering billing or claims submission.[223]

---

[222] 42 C.F.R. § 411.357(p).
[223] 42 C.F.R. § 411.357(s).

### § 3-4(c)(17) Charitable Donations Made by Physicians

CMS has created an exception for donations by physicians to an organization exempt from federal income tax under the IRC (or to an exempt supporting organization, e.g., a hospital foundation).[224]

### § 3-4(c)(18) Community-Wide Information System

Subject to certain conditions, a Stark exception addresses the provision of information technology (including hardware and software) and services to community physicians to enable them to participate in a community-wide health information system designed to enhance the overall health of the community.[225] This exception requires that the items or services be principally used by the physician as part of the community-wide health-information system, that these items and services be provided to the physician in a manner that does not take into account the physician's volume or value of referrals, and that the health-information system (including both hardware and software) must be "community-wide" (i.e., it is available to all providers, practitioners, and residents of the community who desire to participate).

### § 3-4(c)(19) Electronic Prescribing and Electronic Health Records

In 2006, CMS created two exceptions for compensation arrangements involving certain electronic prescribing and electronic health records arrangements.[226] The first of these exceptions applies to the provision of items or services that are necessary and used solely to receive and transmit electronic prescription information. This exception requires compliance with criteria similar to those listed under the Anti-Kickback safe harbor that protects the same arrangements.

The second exception established the conditions under which entities furnishing DHS may donate to physicians interoperable electronic health records software, information technology and training services. In order to qualify for protection under this exception, the relevant items or services must be necessary and used predominantly to create, maintain, transmit or receive the electronic health records of the donor's or physician's patients. Additionally, this exception requires compliance with criteria similar to those listed

---

[224] 42 C.F.R. § 411.357(j).
[225] 42 C.F.R. § 411.357(u).
[226] 42 C.F.R. § 411.357(v) & (w).

## Federal Physician Self-Referral Prohibitions

in the electronic prescribing exception, as well as requiring cost sharing and selection of physician recipients of donated technology.

These exceptions essentially mirror the safe harbors that the OIG contemporaneously developed and issued on the same day in the *Federal Register* (*see* Chapter 2).[227]

### § 3-4(c)(20) Stark Exceptions Relating to Anti-Kickback Statute Safe Harbors

CMS created two exceptions to the Stark Law for certain arrangements that satisfy all of the requirements under two safe harbors under the Anti-Kickback Statute: an exception for referral-service arrangements and one for obstetrical-malpractice insurance.[228]

In the 2009 IPPS Final Rule, CMS amended the exception for obstetrical malpractice insurance subsidies by adding an alternate methodology for meeting the exception's requirements. Although the exception only had provided protection if the arrangement complies with the applicable federal Anti-Kickback Statute safe harbor, CMS extended protection to payments from hospitals, federally qualified health centers, and rural health clinics that are used to pay for "some or all of the costs of malpractice insurance premiums" for a physician who regularly engages in obstetrical practice as a routine part of a medical practice, if all of the following conditions are met: (1) the physician's medical practice is located in a rural area, a primary care Health Professional Shortage Area (HPSA) or an area with demonstrated need for the physician's obstetrical services as determined by the Secretary in an advisory opinion issues in accordance with Social Security Act Section 1877(g)(6); or (2) at least 75% of the physician's obstetrical patients reside in a medically underserved area (MUA) or are members of a medically underserved population (MUP).[229]

### § 3-4(c)(21) Gainsharing

In the FY 2009 IPPS Proposed Rule, CMS requested comments on whether it should create a new exception regarding "gainsharing" arrangements.[230] CMS suggested that it was searching for a set of gainsharing principles that would permit physicians and hospitals to align their incentives to improve the quality of care and reduce costs without risking patient or

---

[227] *See* 71 Fed. Reg. 45,125 (Aug. 8, 2006); 42 C.F.R. § 1001.952(x) and (y).
[228] 42 C.F.R. §§ 411.357(q) and (r).
[229] 42 C.F.R. § 411.357(r).
[230] 73 Fed. Reg. at 23,692.

program abuse. Less than three months later, CMS proposed actual regulatory language regarding an exception targeting "incentive payments" and "shared savings programs" in the CY 2009 Proposed MPFS.[231]

In the CY 2009 MPFS Proposed Rule, CMS proposed extending the exception beyond traditional gainsharing programs to protect both incentive payment programs and shared savings programs.[232] CMS defined incentive payment programs as provider or payer based "quality improvement and reimbursement methodology aimed at moving towards payments that create stronger financial support for patient focused, high value care."[233] Whereas a shared savings program is a cost savings or waste reduction program that "seeks to align physician economic incentives with those of hospitals."[234] Because some programs include components of both shared savings and incentive payment programs, CMS proposed one exception to cover both in an effort to ease administration and assist compliance efforts.[235]

While the goals of shared savings programs and incentive payment programs are aligned with CMS policies and objectives, CMS expressed concern about the implementation of these programs. Among its concerns is the possibility that these programs may compromise patient quality to reduce costs or that they will be used to disguise payments for referrals.[236] To ensure that incentive plans are non-abusive and properly structured, the proposed exception included three criteria—transparency, quality controls, and safeguards against payments for referrals.[237] The proposed regulations can be divided into four categories, including those regulating the structure and parameters of the program; those regulating the participants; those regulating payments; and those that are common to most exceptions.

In order to satisfy the proposed exception, the goal of the gainsharing program must be either to reduce costs or to promote quality. If the program's goal relates to costs, CMS would require that the program not adversely affect or diminish the quality of care. CMS is attempting to establish a bright line rule regarding what quality patient measures may be used in programs seeking to increase patient quality, by mandating that the "patient quality measure be listed in CMS's Specifications Manual for National Hospital Quality Measures."[238] Additionally, performance is to be measured by an objective methodology that is verifiable and supported by credible medical evidence.[239] To accomplish this, programs must be reviewed prior to commencement

---

[231] 73 Fed. Reg. at 38,548.
[232] Id.
[233] Id. at 38,549.
[234] Id.
[235] Id. at 38,552.
[236] Id. at 38,548, 38,550.
[237] Id. at 38,552.
[238] Id. at 38,553.
[239] Id.

## Federal Physician Self-Referral Prohibitions

and at annual intervals, which must be completed and documented by an independent entity.[240] The measurement would be made by comparing the outcomes against a pre-determined baseline. If at any time the review indicates a decrease in patient quality of care, immediate corrective action must be taken. CMS would also require the hospital provide "written disclosure to patients affected by the program."[241]

The proposed regulation places several requirements on who may participate in the programs. The CY 2009 MPFS Proposed Rule limits the programs to only those offered by hospitals but may in the future extend it to other DHS entities.[242] Physician participation is limited to those physicians currently on the hospital's staff at the commencement of the program. If the hospital limits participation to physicians from a specific department the hospital must allow all physicians in that department to participate. Physicians who participate in a program must do so in pools of at least five members and these pools must be formed at the commencement of the program.[243] "[P]hysicians are barred from participating . . . in the design or implementation of any . . . program that involves items, supplies or devices in which the physician has a financial interest."[244] At the same time, the regulations restrict a hospital's ability to limit physician access to items, supplies, or devices.[245]

The proposed regulations also include parameters relating to payment. The proposal limits the remuneration to cash or cash equivalent. The remuneration must be paid either directly to the physician or a qualified physician organization and must be distributed per capita.[246] The remuneration may not be "based in whole or in part on a reduction in the length of stay."[247] Additionally, the amount "paid to a participating physician . . . may not include any amount that takes into account the provision a greater volume of Federal healthcare patient procedures or services than the volume provided . . . immediately preceding the commencement of the program."[248] The payments must also not include "financial rewards for already implemented changes."[249]

As with many of the Stark Law exceptions, the agreement with the physicians must be in writing and signed by the parties. The compensation must be set in advance, not vary of the term of the agreement, nor take into account the volume or value of referrals or other business generated between the parties. Additionally, the agreement must be for at least one year but no longer

---

[240] *Id.* at 38,553–38,554.
[241] *Id.* at 38,557.
[242] *Id.* at 38,552–38,553.
[243] *Id.* at 38,554.
[244] *Id.* at 38,555.
[245] *Id.*
[246] *Id.* at 38,553.
[247] *Id.* at 38,552.
[248] *Id.* at 38,555.
[249] *Id.*

than three years.²⁵⁰ Finally, the agreement may not violate the Anti-Kickback Statute or any other federal or state law or regulation relating to billing or claims processing.²⁵¹

After reviewing the comments received regarding the Proposed Rule, CMS decided not to issue a final rule regarding the gainsharing exception in the CY 2009 MPFS Final Rule.²⁵² CMS indicated that they had not received "sufficient information or agreement among commentators," and thus they reopened the comment period for 90 days.²⁵³ In so doing, CMS "hope[s] to acquire information that will better inform the development of an exception that is sufficiently flexible to encourage the development and implementation of beneficial, nonabusive incentive payment and shared savings programs that foster high quality, cost-effective care for our beneficiaries."²⁵⁴ The time frame for issuing a final rule on the Stark gainsharing exception remains uncertain, but an eventual regulation in the near future seems likely. Pointedly, CMS expressed clear disagreement with commenters' suggestions that "we must or should delay the issuance of a final exception until the completion of the gainsharing demonstrations authorized by section 1866C of the Act and section 5007 of the DRA."²⁵⁵

## § 3-4(c)(22)  ACOs

As set forth in Chapter 2, Section 3022 of the Health Reform Law requires CMS to establish a shared savings program "that promotes account ability for a patient population and coordinates items and services under parts A and B, and encourages investment in infrastructure and redesigned care processes for high quality and efficient service delivery."²⁵⁶ As providers, hospitals and suppliers may participate in the shared saving program by creating and participating in Accountable Care Organizations (ACOs), the issue arises the extent to which the Stark Law (as well as other laws such as the Anti-Kickback Statute and the Civil Money Penalties (CMPs) will apply to ACO financial relationships.

On November 2, 2011, CMS, in conjunction with OIG, issued an interim final rule with comment period establishing waivers of the Stark Law, Anti-Kickback Statute and certain other laws to particular arrangements involving ACOs under the Medicare shared savings program.²⁵⁷ The interim final rule

---

[250] *Id.* at 38,557.
[251] *Id.*
[252] *See* 73 Fed. Reg. 69,793–69,798.
[253] *Id.* at 69,794.
[254] *Id.* at 69,798.
[255] *Id.*
[256] The Health Reform Law, § 3022; Social Security Act § 1899.
[257] 76 Fed. Reg. 67,992 (Nov. 2, 2011). Significantly, the interim final rule merely appears in the *Federal Register* and has not been codified anywhere in the Code of Federal Regulations.

## Federal Physician Self-Referral Prohibitions

establishes five waivers of application of these laws, four of which apply to the Stark Law:

- an "ACO pre-participation" waiver of the Stark Law, the federal Anti-Kickback Statute and the Gainsharing CMP that applies to ACO-related start-up arrangements in anticipation of participating in the Shared Savings Program, subject to certain limitations, including limits on the duration of the waiver and the types of parties covered;
- an "ACO participation" waiver of the Stark Law, the federal Anti-Kickback Statute, and the Gainsharing CMP that applies broadly to ACO-related arrangements during the term of the ACo's participation agreement under the Shared Savings Program and for a specified time thereafter;
- a "shared savings distributions" waiver of the Stark Law, the federal Anti-Kickback Statute, and Gainsharing CMP that applies to distributions and uses of shared savings payments earned under the Shared Savings Program;
- a "compliance with the Physician Self-Referral Law" waiver of the Gainsharing CMP and the Anti-Kickback Statute that applies to ACO arrangements that implicate the Stark Law and meet an existing exception.

For the pre-participation waiver, the following conditions must be met:

1. the arrangement must be undertaken by a party or parties acting with the good faith intent to develop the ACO that will participate in the shared savings program starting in a particular year (target year) and to submit a completed application to participate in the shared savings program for that year;
2. the parties developing the ACO must be taking diligent steps to develop an ACO that would be eligible for a participation agreement that would become effective during the target year, including taking diligent steps to meet the requirements of 42 C.F.R. 1006 and 425.108 concerning ACO governance, leadership and management;
3. the ACO's governing body has made and duly authorized a *bona fide* determination that the arrangement is reasonably related to the purposes of the shared savings program;
4. the arrangement, its authorization by the governing body and the diligent steps to develop the ACO are documented (the final rule sets forth particular criteria concerning the documentation);
5. the description of the arrangement is publicly disclosed at a time and in a place and manner established by the Secretary (the public

disclosure need not include the financial or economic terms of the arrangement); and

6. if an ACO does not submit an application for a participation agreement by the last available due date for the target year, the ACO must submit a statement on or before the last available application due date for the target year, describing the reasons it was unable to submit an application.

For the ACO participation waiver, factors 2-5, listed above, are the same, except that the ACO must be meeting the governance, leadership and management requirements.

For the shared savings distribution waiver, in addition to having entered into a participation agreement and remain in good standing, the following conditions must also be met:

- the shared savings are earned by the ACO pursuant to the shared savings program;
- the shared savings are earned by the ACO during the term of its participation agreement, even if the actual distribution or use of the shared savings occurs after the expiration of that agreement;
- the shared savings are (a) distributed to or among ACO participants, its ACO providers/suppliers, or individuals and entities that were ACO participants or providers/suppliers during the year in which the shared savings were earned by the ACO and (b) used for activities that are reasonably related to the purposes of the shared savings program; and
- with respect to the Gainsharing CMP waivers, payments of shared savings distributions made directly or indirectly from a hospital to a physician are not made knowingly to induce the physician to reduce or limit *medically necessary* items or services.

To be in compliance with the physician self-referral law waiver, the financial relationship must be reasonably related to the purpose of the shared savings program and the financial relationship must comply with a Stark law exception.

For arrangements that meet any of the waivers, the waiver period begins on the start date of the participation agreement and ends on the earlier of the expiration of the term of the participation agreement, including any renewals, or the date on which the participation agreement has been terminated. According to the interim final rule, an arrangement need only fit in one waiver to be protected; "parties seeking to ensure that an arrangement is covered by a waiver for a particular law may look to any waiver that applies to that law."[258]

---

[258] 76 Fed. Reg. at 67,994.

As opposed to the issuance of most final rules in which the text of the actual rule is codified in the Code of Federal Regulations, CMS and OIG propose (and requested comments on this approach) that because the waivers cover multiple legal authorities and to ensure that the waivers, if modified, remain consistent over time and across relevant laws, they will include the waiver text in the *Federal Register* and make the waiver text available on both the CMS and OIG website.

## § 3-4(d)   Reporting Requirements

The Stark Law requires that any entity that provides items or services for which payment may be made under Medicare must submit to CMS certain information about such entity's financial relationship with physicians under time periods prescribed by the entity's Medicare carrier.[259] In the Phase II Stark II Final Regulations, however CMS waived all reporting requirements for designated health service entities providing less than twenty Part A and B services during a calendar year. Moreover, CMS decided not to require regular submission of information of other providers, but instead only require information to be submitted upon request by CMS.[260] An entity must retain (and, if requested, disclose on 30 days' notice) records concerning the nature of its financial relationships with physicians. Consequently, even though the regulation does not require a provider to maintain records of its financial relationships with physicians, simply creating or assembling the records upon receipt of a request could prove difficult if a systematic process to preserve and organize this information has not already been put into place.

As part of the DRA, Congress required the Secretary of the Department of Health and Human Services to develop a strategic and implementing plan to address certain issues relating to physician-owned specialty hospitals.[261] In preparing its report, CMS sent a voluntary survey to 130 specialty hospitals and 220 competitor hospitals that sought information regarding, among other things, the hospitals' ownership and investment relationships and their compensation arrangements with physicians. Then, in August 2008, CMS issued its Final Report to Congress and that it would require all hospitals to provide information on a periodic basis concerning the investment interests and compensation arrangements with physicians.[262]

In 2007, CMS began its initiative to implement a survey to investigate the investment/ownership and compensation arrangements between physicians and hospitals to determine whether they are in compliance with the Stark

---

[259] Social Security Act § 1877(f); 42 U.S.C. § 1395nn(f); 42 C.F.R. § 411.361.
[260] 42 C.F.R. § 411.361.
[261] Deficit Reduction Act of 2005, Pub. L. No. 109-171, § 5006.
[262] A copy of the CMS Final Report to Congress can be found *at* http://www.cms.hhs.gov/PhysicianSelfReferral/06a_DRA_Reports.asp#TopOfPage.

Law and implementing regulations. This survey—entitled the "Disclosure of Financial Relationships Report" (DFRR)—was designed to be a mandatory survey for 500 hospitals selected by CMS. The extensive worksheet contains 8 worksheets and covers direct and indirect physician investment and ownership in hospital, payments to the hospital by physician ownerships, a listing of each rental, personal service and recruitment arrangement between a hospital and physicians, and a series of questions targeting information on other types of compensation arrangements, including non-monetary compensation or medical staff incidental benefits that exceeded published limits and charitable donations by a physician to a hospital. The survey is to be completed, certified by a hospital officer and submitted to CMS within 60 days. Technically, the hospital could face penalties of $10,000 per day for late responses under civil monetary penalty provisions.[263] However, according to the preamble to the proposed regulation, CMS is unlikely to invoke this authority and likely will work with the entities to comply with the reporting requirements, even granting extensions for 'good cause" shown.[264]

Under the Paperwork Reduction Act, CMS was required to obtain clearance from the Office of Management and Budget (OMB) prior to sending out the survey. Although the DFRR was under review by OMB for several months, on April 10, 2008, OMB reported that CMS had withdrawn its request for clearance of the DFRR survey.[265] Just a few weeks later, on April 30, 2008, CMS re-introduced the DFRR as part of the FY 2009 IPPS Proposed Rule, and CMS solicited comments on the following areas of the DFRR:

- whether the collection efforts should be recurring, and, if so, on what basis (annually, etc.);
- whether CMS is collecting too much or not enough information, and whether they are collecting the correct (or incorrect) type of information;
- the amount of time it will take hospitals to complete the DFRR and the costs associated with completing the DFRR;
- whether CMS should direct the DFRR to all hospitals and whether they should stagger the collection so that only a certain number of hospitals are surveyed each year; and
- whether hospitals, once having completed the DFRR, should send in yearly updates and report only changed information.[266]

In the original DFRR that CMS submitted to OMB, CMS estimated that it would take a hospital five hours to complete. CMS then increased this estimate

---
[263] 42 C.F.R. § 411.361(f).
[264] 73 Fed. Reg. at 23,697.
[265] See http://www.reginfo.gov/public/do/PRAViewICR?ref_nbr=200710-0938-003.
[266] 73 Fed. Reg. at 23,695–23,698.

in the FY 2009 IPPS Proposed Rule to 31 hours and that it would cost hospitals $1,550 to complete (based on a $50 per hour rate for an accountant). When CMS issued the FY 2009 IPPS Final Rule, CMS again revised its estimate of the number of hours it would take to complete the DFRR from 31 hours to 100 hours and "that many hospitals may choose to involve accounting staff and attorneys for legal review. Therefore, the costs per hospital, associated with completing the DFFR has increased from $1,550 to $4,080."[267] Nevertheless, pursuant to the requirements of the Paperwork Reduction Act, CMS stated in the FY 2009 IPPS Final Rule that it was sending changes to the DFRR to OMB for its review and approval and that a separate Federal Register notice would be published, which would "set forth a public comment period of 30 days from the date of display."[268]

CMS published that Federal Register notice on December 19, 2008, indicating that the OMB would be accepting comments on the DFRR until January 20, 2009.[269] In the brief notice, CMS explained that "[t]he DFRR collection instrument will be used by CMS to (1) identify arrangements that potentially may not be in compliance with the physician self-referral statute and implementing regulations; and (2) to identify examples and areas of non-compliance that may assist us in any future rulemaking concerning the reporting requirements and other physician self-referral provisions."[270] The results of the notice and comment period have not yet been published.

Although, as set forth above, the Stark Law already included a provision providing the Secretary with the authority to request information regarding physician ownership and compensation arrangements that healthcare entities may have with physicians, Congress included in the Health Law Reform Law a provision that the Secretary "shall collect physician ownership and investment information" for all hospitals that have physician owners pursuant to the grandfather provision.[271]

## § 3-5 DEFINITION OF GROUP PRACTICE

Despite the misnomer used widely in the healthcare industry that there is a "group practice exception," the group-practice requirements are not themselves an exception to the Stark Law. Instead, the group-practice requirements provide merely a definitional prerequisite for compliance with relevant exceptions, such as the exceptions for physicians' services and in-office ancillary services.

Both structural and operational requirements apply for qualifying as a group practice. These requirements are important, because group practices have greater flexibility in paying physicians incentive-based compensation

---

[267] *Id.* at 48,741.
[268] *Id.* at 48,745.
[269] Comment Request, 73 Fed. Reg. 77,701 (Dec. 19, 2008).
[270] *Id.* at 77,702.
[271] 42 U.S.C. § 1395nn(i)(4)

under the Stark Law than do other physician organizations that fall short of group practice qualification. Phase I of the Stark II Final Regulations provides the following nine conditions that must be met to satisfy the definition of "group practice."[272]

### § 3-5(a)   Single Legal Entity

A group practice must be structured as a "single legal entity" that is formed "primarily" for the purpose of being a physician group practice in any organizational form recognized by the state in which the group practice achieves its legal status.[273] The single legal entity comprising the group practice may be organized by any party or parties, including, but not limited to, physicians, healthcare facilities, or other persons or entities (including, but not limited to, physicians individually incorporated as professional corporations).[274] Hospital-owned medical groups can qualify as group practices under the Stark Law, provided the hospital-owned group meets the remaining requirements of the group practice definition. Although separate entities are required in those states that prohibit the corporate practice of medicine, hospitals should be permitted to operate group practices directly in states where such structures are allowed. The practical effect of this new "separate entity" element of the final regulations is that a hospital will be restricted in the incentive compensation that it can offer to its directly employed physicians, unless it creates a new corporate "box" for its employed physicians simply for Stark Law compliance purposes.

Several other important caveats exist to this structural requirement for group practices. The single legal entity comprising the group practice may not be organized or owned (in whole or in part) by another medical practice that is an operating physician practice, regardless of whether the other medical practice qualifies as a group practice.[275] Also, the single-legal-entity requirement does not include informal affiliations of physicians formed substantially to share profits from referrals, nor does it include separate group practices under common ownership or control through a physician practice-management company, hospital, health system, or other entity or organization. CMS has not been willing to extend protection to more loosely affiliated groups or conglomerations of groups that it feels are not practicing as "true" groups.

---

[272] 42 C.F.R. § 411.352.
[273] 42 C.F.R. § 411.352(a). The following are examples of recognized legal forms for group practices: partnership, professional corporation, limited liability company, foundation, nonprofit corporation, faculty practice plan, or similar association.
[274] *Id.*
[275] *Id.*

## § 3-5(b)  "Two or More" Physicians

The group-practice definition requires that at least two physicians are "members of the group," whether as employees or direct or indirect owners.[276] This definition is a change from the proposed regulations' implicit restriction against groups consisting of one physician-owner and one physician employee. Independent contractors to a group, however, will not qualify under this standard. Consequently, the final regulations do not recognize groups having one physician-owner and multiple physician contractors.

## § 3-5(c)  Full Range of Care

Each physician who is a "member of the group" must furnish "substantially the full range of patient care services that the physician routinely furnishes, including medical care, consultation, diagnosis, and treatment, through the joint use of shared office space, facilities, equipment, and personnel."[277] This requirement suggests that each member of a group practice must provide services using space, facilities, and equipment that are leased or owned by the group, and with staff provided by the group. The extent to which "joint use" by the physicians is actually required is not entirely clear, however. This is a significant issue for multi-state, geographically diverse group practices, where all the physicians practicing at a particular site may jointly use space, equipment, and personnel, but may not use these resources of other group sites.

## § 3-5(d)  Services Furnished by Group Practice Members

Substantially all of the patient-care services of the physicians who are "members of the group" must be furnished through the group and billed under a billing number assigned to the group, and the amounts received must be treated as receipts from the group.[278] To properly analyze this requirement, several key terms must be discussed in further detail.

An ongoing source of Stark Law controversy has been the definition of a "member of the group"—in particular, whether independent contractors qualify as members of the group. It is important to identify who fits into the definition of a member of the group for purposes of "counting" for the various "substantially all" tests in the group practice definition. This calculation also had been important for purposes of the ability of the group to

---

[276] 42 C.F.R. § 411.352(b).
[277] 42 C.F.R. § 411.352(c).
[278] 42 C.F.R. § 411.352(d).

pay incentive compensation to independent contractors beyond personally performed services.[279]

While the proposed Stark II regulations did not include independent contractors as members of the group, in the final regulations, "member of the group" means a direct or indirect physician-owner of a group practice (including a physician whose interest is held by her individual professional corporation or by another entity), a physician-employee of the group practice (including a physician employed by her individual professional corporation that has an equity interest in the group practice), a *locum tenens* physician (as defined), or an on-call physician while the physician is providing on-call services for members of the group practice.[280] A physician is a member of the group during the time she furnishes "patient care services" to the group. The final regulations state that an independent contractor or a leased employee is not a member of the group.[281]

Nevertheless, the phrase "physician in a group practice" means a member of the group practice, as well as an independent-contractor physician during the time the independent contractor is furnishing patient care services (as defined in the final regulations) to the group practice under a contractual arrangement with the group practice to provide services to the group practice's patients in the group practice's facilities.[282] The contract must contain the same restrictions on compensation that apply to members of the group practice under the "volume or value" requirement, or the contract must fit within the Stark Law personal-services exception. Further, the independent contractor's arrangement with the group practice must comply with the Medicare program's reassignment rules. However, CMS, in the Phase III Stark II Final Regulations, revised the definition of "physician in the group practice" to "clarify" that an independent contractor must furnish patient care services pursuant to a contract made directly with the group practice in order for the physician to qualify as a "physician in the group practice." Previously, physicians with contractual arrangements could qualify as "physicians in the group" but not necessarily as "members" of the group, but the Stark regulations did not precisely dictate how the contractual arrangement should be structured, leaving open the possibility for contracting though another entity. However, in Phase III Stark II Final Regulations, CMS made an explicit requirement that independent contractors have a direct contractual arrangement with the group.

---

[279] In the final regulations, CMS recognized that the statutory language permits in-office ancillary services to be supervised by "physicians in the group," not merely by group "members," and allows independent contractors to be paid incentive compensation the same as group members, thus eliminating at least some significance of the member definition.

[280] 42 C.F.R. § 411.351.

[281] "*Locum tenens* physician" means a physician who substitutes (i.e., "stands in the shoes") in exigent circumstances for a regular physician who is a member of the group in accordance with applicable Medicare reassignment rules and regulations, including section 3060.7 of the *Medicare Carriers Manual*.

[282] 42 C.F.R. § 411.351.

## Federal Physician Self-Referral Prohibitions

CMS specifically said, in the preamble, that the definition of "physician in the group practice" does not extend to contractors between the group practice and another entity, such as a staffing company.[283]

The phrase "patient care services" means any tasks performed by a physician in the group practice that (1) address the medical needs of specific patients or patients in general, regardless of whether they involve direct patient encounters; or (2) generally benefit a particular practice. Patient-care services can include the services of physicians who do not directly treat patients, such as time spent by a physician consulting with other physicians or reviewing laboratory tests, as well as time spent training staff members, arranging for equipment, or performing administrative or management tasks.[284]

The "substantially all" test has been defined as at least 75% of the total patient-care services of the group practice members.[285] For purposes of compliance with the 75% test, the final regulations make clear that "patient care services" must be measured by one of the following: (i) the total time each member spends on patient-care services documented by any reasonable means, including (but not limited to) time cards, appointment schedules, or personal diaries (e.g., if a physician practices 40 hours a week and spends 30 hours on patient-care services for a group practice, the physician has spent 75% of her time providing patient-care services for the group); or (ii) any alternative measure that is reasonable, fixed in advance of the performance of the services being measured, uniformly applied over time, verifiable, and documented.[286]

The following examples are provided to illustrate how the 75% test is calculated an aggregate basis, taking into account that independent contractors need not be counted for purposes of complying with the "substantially all" test.

> Example 1: A group practice consists of three physician partners, five full-time physician employees, two part-time physician employees, and a contractor physician who spends one morning a week at the group practice to deliver specialty services. The two partners and the full-time employees practice only through the group. The two part-time employees devote 50% of their time to the group, and the contractor physician spends 10% of her time with the group.
>
> 8 physicians at 100%   =   700%
>
> 2 physicians at 50%   =   100%
>
> 800% divided by 10 = 80%

---

[283] 72 Fed. Reg. at 51,018.
[284] 42 C.F.R. § 411.351.
[285] 42 C.F.R. § 411.352(d).
[286] *Id.*

Example 2: In another group practice, three physician-partners spend 100% of their patient care hours through the group. Five part-time physician employees spend 70% each, and two other part-time physician employees spend 25% of their time at the group practice. A contractor physician devotes 10%.

$$3 \text{ physicians at } 100\% = 200\%$$
$$5 \text{ physicians at } 70\% = 350\%$$
$$2 \text{ physicians at } 25\% = 50\%$$
$$600\% \text{ divided by } 10 = 60\%$$

Note that in both situations, the time spent by the contractor physician is not added for purposes of satisfying the 75% test.

Using 75% as the threshold, the first group practice described would qualify under the 75% test, but the second group practice would not. Of course, a group that meets the 75% test also must comply with remaining requirements of the "group practice" definition, in addition to one of the exceptions discussed earlier, in order to protect the group physicians' referrals within the group.

Two caveats to this "75% test" exist: (a) the data used to calculate compliance with this "substantially all test" and related supportive documentation must be made available to the DHHS Secretary upon request; and (b) the "substantially all" test does not apply to any group practice that is located solely in a HPSA.[287] Further, for a group practice located outside of a HPSA, any time spent by a group-practice member providing services in a HPSA should not be used to calculate whether the group practice has met the "substantially all test," regardless of whether the member's time in the HPSA is spent in a group practice, clinic, or office setting. These provisions regarding submission of data to the government, and special rules for time spent in HPSAs, are new requirements not previously found in the proposed Stark II regulations.

The final regulations address the operational issue of how a group would address the 75% test during its formative stage. The final regulations state that, during a group's "start-up" phase (defined as the first twelve months from the date of the initial formation of the group practice), the group practice must make a reasonable, good-faith effort to ensure that it complies with this requirement as soon as practicable, but no later than twelve months from the date of the initial formation of the group practice. This provision, however,

---

[287] 42 C.F.R. §§ 411.352(d)(ii)(3), (4).

does not apply when an existing group practice admits a new member, or when an existing group practice reorganizes.[288]

### § 3-5(e)  Distribution of Expenses and Income

All overhead expenses and income from the practice must be distributed according to methods that are determined before payment is received for these services.[289] The final regulations make clear that this provision does not prevent a group practice from adjusting its compensation methodology prospectively, subject to restrictions on the distribution of revenue from designated health services discussed in the section (regarding the special rule for productivity bonuses and profit shares). This requirement is not limited specifically to profit shares or productivity bonuses paid to "members" of the group.

### § 3-5(f)  Unified Business

Although not a requirement in the statute, CMS has adopted a requirement in the final regulations that the group practice be a "unified business." In order to satisfy this condition, the physician practice must have a centralized decision-making body that maintains effective control over the group's assets and liabilities (including, but not limited to, budgets, compensation, and salaries); consolidated billing, accounting, and financial reporting; and centralized utilization review.[290] This element could have implications for the operations of groups that were formed through the acquisition or merger of several previously independent medical groups that joined together, but desired to maintain a certain degree of independence at their various practice sites despite their corporate integration.[291]

### § 3-5(g)  Volume or Value of Referrals

This condition, which comes from the statute, prohibits any physician who is a member of a group practice directly or indirectly from receiving compensation based on the volume or value of referrals by the physician, except as specifically authorized under the special rule for productivity bonuses and profit shares.[292] Although this requirement does not apply expressly

---

[288] 42 C.F.R. § 411.352(d)(ii)(5).
[289] 42 C.F.R. § 411.352(e).
[290] 42 C.F.R. § 411.352(f)(l).
[291] Note that the final regulations provide that (notwithstanding the "unified business" requirements) location and specialty-based compensation practices are permitted with respect to revenues derived from services that are not designated health services, and may be permitted with respect to revenues derived from designated health services, but only as shall be described with regard to productivity bonuses and profit shares.
[292] 42 C.F.R. § 411.352(g).

to physicians who fall outside the definition of "members of the group" (e.g., independent contractors), compensation to a group's independent contractors is still important when independent-contractor physicians supervise ancillary services, and when groups bill for designated health services provided by independent contractors. In such circumstances, the group's arrangement with an independent contractor is required to satisfy the group-practice "volume or value" requirement or otherwise comply with the more narrow Stark Law personal-services exception.

### § 3-5(h)   Physician/Patient Encounters

Members of the group must personally conduct no less than 75% of the physician/patient encounters of the group practice.[293] This requirement comes from the statute, and was set forth in the proposed Stark II regulations, except to the extent that the final regulations provides a more detailed definition of who qualifies as a "member of the group," as discussed earlier. Independent contractors can supervise in-office ancillary services and be paid incentive compensation, but cannot be counted for the "substantially all" tests. This is the only standard where a group having a large number of independent contractors could be affected detrimentally, because independent contractors are not "members of the group." The end result is that a group practice can have as many independent contractors as it wishes, so long as physician "members of the group" conduct at least 75% of the group's physician/patient encounters.

### § 3-5(i)   Special Rule for Productivity Bonuses and Profit Shares

The Stark regulations provide that a physician in a group practice may be paid a share of "overall profits" of the group, or a "productivity" bonus based on services that she has personally performed (including services "incident to" those personally performed services), provided that the share or bonus is not determined in any manner that is directly related to the volume or value of referrals of designated health services by the physician.[294]

Under these rules, "overall profits" means the group's entire profits derived from designated health services payable by Medicare or Medicaid, or the profits derived from designated health services payable by Medicare or Medicaid of any component of the group practice that consists of at least five physicians.[295] The sharing of profits from a subset of physicians practicing within a larger group (i.e., "pooling" arrangements) should be allowable, so

---

[293] 42 C.F.R. § 411.352(h).
[294] 42 C.F.R. § 411.352(i).
[295] 42 C.F.R. § 411.352(i)(2).

long as the subset is comprised of five or more physicians, the distribution is not based directly on any physician's referrals or orders for designated health services within the group, and the remaining requirements of the group practice rules are met.

The regulations set forth specific examples of profit-distribution methodologies that will not be deemed to relate directly to the volume or value of referrals (and, therefore, will not constitute violations the Stark Law), including:

- dividing profits per capita;
- distributing revenues derived from designated health services based on the distribution of the group practice's revenues attributed to services that are not designated health services payable by any federal healthcare program or private payor;
- where revenues derived from designated health services constitute less than 5% of the group practice's total revenues, allocating a portion of those revenues to each physician in the group practice that constitutes 5% or less of her total compensation from the group; or
- dividing overall profits in a reasonable and verifiable manner that is not directly related to the volume or value of the physician's referrals of designated health services.[296]

In addition to profit distributions, a productivity bonus for personally performed services also may be paid within a group practice, provided such productivity bonus does not relate directly to the volume or value of a physician's referrals for designated health services within the group. Such productivity bonuses can include services "incident to" a physician's personally performed services.[297] Productivity-bonus arrangements that meet the one of following conditions will be deemed not to relate directly to the volume or value of referrals of designated health services:

(i) bonus is based on the physician's total patient encounters or relative value units (RVUs);[298]

(ii) bonus is based on the allocation of the physician's compensation attributable to services that are not designated health services payable by any federal healthcare program or private payor;

(iii) revenues derived from designated health services are less than 5% of the group practice's total revenues, and the allocated portion of those

---

[296] 42 C.F.R. §§ 411.352(i)(2)(i)–(iv).

[297] "Incident to" services means those services that meet the Medicare requirements for incident to services as set forth in Social Security Act § 1861(s)(2)(A) and Section 2050 of the *Medicare Carriers Manual*.

[298] The methodology for establishing RVUs is set forth in 42 C.F.R. § 414.22, which are the rules for how CMS determines physician RVUs for general Part B Medicare payment purposes.

revenues to each physician in the group practice constitutes 5% or less of her total compensation from the group practice; or

(iv) bonus is calculated in a reasonable and verifiable manner that is not directly related to the volume or value of the physician's referrals of designated health services.[299]

One of the most confusing, yet recurring, questions is whether physicians may receive compensation based on services billed as "incident to" physicians' professional services or other services supervised by physicians. This issue arises because, for the purposes of the in-office ancillary services exception, the Stark statute allows a group practice to pay productivity bonuses to its physicians based on "services personally performed or services incident to such personally performed services," so long as the bonus is not based directly on volume or value of referrals.[300] In contrast, physicians compensated under the employment, personal services, or AMC exceptions may be compensated for personally performed services, but not "incident to" services as they are now defined by CMS.

Over time, CMS has modified its position as to whether group practice physicians may be paid based on incident to services but at the present time, the answer depends, in part, on what types of supervised services are involved and which Stark Law exception applies. A "referral" for DHS excludes services personally performed by a physician, but includes services performed by a physician's employees or any other person, such as an independent contractor or another member of the physician's group practice.[301] In the Phase III Stark II Final Regulations, CMS defined "incident to" services by explicit cross reference to the relevant sections of CMS's Medicare Benefit Policy Manual. However, CMS also made clear that services covered by Medicare under a separate benefit category, such as diagnostic x-ray tests, diagnostic laboratory tests and other diagnostic tests, do not qualify as "incident to" services under Medicare coverage and payment rules and, therefore, also do not qualify under the Stark Law.[302]

## § 3-6 PENALTIES AND ENFORCEMENT

The Stark Law provides significant civil (but not criminal) sanctions for violations including denial of payment; refunds of amounts collected in violation; a civil money penalty (CMP) of up to $15,000 for each bill or claim for a service a person knows (or should know) is for a service for which payment may not be made; the imposition of up to three times the amounts for each item or service

---

[299] 42 C.F.R. §§ 411.352(i)(3)(i)–(iv).
[300] *See* 42 U.S.C. § 1395nn(h)(4)(A).
[301] 42 C.F.R. § 411.351; *see also* 72 Fed. Reg. at 51,019.
[302] 42 C.F.R. § 411.351; *see also* 72 Fed. Reg. at 51,023–24.

wrongfully claimed; potential exclusion; and a CMP of up to $100,000 for each arrangement or scheme that the physician or entity knows (or should know) has a principal purpose of assuring referrals that, if directly made, would be in violation of the proscription.[303] The statute does not define the term "circumvention scheme," but does mention "cross-referral arrangements" as one example of a prohibited scheme. Although the statute prohibits the making of referrals in violation of its proscription, the penalties set forth in the Stark Law focus mostly on the presentation of claims for services provided in violation of the law.

To date, there have been few government initiated investigations of providers for having engaged in violations of the Stark Law. Instead the majority of such investigations have been initiated by whistleblowers who have bootstrapped an allegation of violating the Stark Law to a claim under the Federal False Claims Act. The issue of bootstrapping violations of the Stark Law into false claim actions in addressed in greater detail in Chapter 4.

### § 3-6(a)  Temporary Noncompliance

In the Phase II Stark II Regulations, CMS provided an exception to when the government will impose penalties if an arrangement involves "temporary noncompliance." CMS provides that a violation has not occurred if an arrangement met an exception for at least 180 consecutive calendar days preceding the date when the agreement was no longer in compliance; the financial relationship fell out of compliance for reasons beyond the control of the entity and the matter was resolved within 90 days; and the arrangement does not violate the Anti-Kickback Statute.[304]

However, CMS made clear in the preamble to the Phase III Stark II Final Regulations preamble that arrangements that were never in compliance cannot satisfy the temporary non-compliance exception. In this regard, CMS explained that the temporary non-compliance provisions will not protect a hospital that has an immediate need for ER coverage but has not executed a formal written contract with a physician.[305] In addition, CMS provides a laundry list of documentation that entities should maintain for financial relationships that fall out of compliance. This list includes the following:

- the terms of the arrangement;
- whether and how an arrangement fell out of compliance with a particular exception;
- the reasons for the arrangement falling out of compliance;

---

[303] Social Security Act § 1877(g); 42 U.S.C. § 1395nn(g); 42 C.F.R. §§ 411.353(b)–(d); 42 C.F.R. §§ 1003.102 – 1003.105.
[304] 42 C.F.R. § 411.353(f).
[305] 72 Fed. Reg. at 51,025.

- steps taken to bring the arrangement into compliance;
- relevant dates; and
- other similar information.

However, because this list of supporting documentation is found in the preamble, not the regulations, the question remains whether parties that fail to create and maintain this exact list of materials will be deemed out of compliance with the rules regarding temporary non-compliance.

## § 3-6(b) Alternative Method of Compliance with Signature Requirement

In the FY 2009 IPPS Final Rule, CMS adopted a provision that allows an entity under certain circumstances to submit a claim for a DHS if the compensation arrangement between the entity and a referring physician fully complied with an applicable exception except with regard to the signature requirement. More specifically, if the failure to comply with the signature requirement was "inadvertent" and the parties obtain the required signature(s) within 90 consecutive calendar days immediately following the date on which the compensation arrangement became noncompliant, the arrangement qualifies for the exception, without regard to whether any referrals occur or compensation is paid within the 90 day period. If the failure to comply was "not inadvertent," the parties must obtain the required signature(s) within 30 consecutive calendar days following the date on which the compensation arrangement became noncompliant to enjoy the protection of the exception.[306] In both circumstances, the compensation arrangement otherwise must have complied with all criteria of the applicable exception. CMS in the preamble gives as an example an arrangement where the exception requires that the arrangement not violate the federal Anti-Kickback Statute. In that example, the alternative method for compliance with the signature requirement of the Stark exception would not be available to the parties unless this requirement for anti-kickback compliance was satisfied.[307]

An entity may use the provision for alternative method for compliance with signatures only once every three years with respect to the same referring physician. CMS specifically declines to extend relief to failures to satisfy other prescribed procedural or "form" criteria of an exception such as the amount of compensation or the description of the services.

---

[306] 42 C.F.R. § 353(g); *see also* 73 Fed. Reg. at 48,705–48,709.
[307] 73 Fed. Reg. at 48,706.

## § 3-6(c) Period of Disallowance

In the CY 2008 MPFS Proposed Rule, CMS solicited public comments addressing how it might set forth in the regulations what the period of disallowance would be for financial relationships that implicate, but fail to satisfy the requirement of one or more of the various exceptions.[308] As a response to public comments, in the FY 2009 IPPS Final Rule, CMS finalized the period of disallowance rules, which set forth the period of disallowance in situations where a problematic financial relationship is brought into compliance. More specifically, CMS adopts in the regulations that the period of disallowance begins at the time the financial relationship fails to satisfy the requirements of an applicable exception and ends not later than:

- where the non-compliance is unrelated to compensation, the date the financial relationship satisfies all of the requirements of an applicable exception;
- where the non-compliance is due to the payment of excess compensation, the date on which all excess compensation is returned, by the party that paid it and the financial relationship satisfies all other requirements of an applicable exception; or
- where the non-compliance is due to the payment of compensation that is of an amount insufficient to satisfy the requirements of an applicable exception, the date on which all additional required compensation is paid, by the party that owes it, to the party to which it is owed and the financial relationship satisfies all of the other requirements of an applicable exception.[309]

In the preamble to the regulations, CMS states that the regulation "only prescribes the outside period of disallowance for certain situations" and that the regulations "does not prevent parties from arguing that the period of disallowance ended earlier then the prescribed outside period, on the theory that the financial relationship ended at an earlier time."[310]

## § 3-6(d) Burden of Proof

In the CY 2008 MPFS Proposed Rule, CMS proposed to add a provision in the regulations addressing the burden of proof in disputes concerning whether a DHS payment should be denied in connection with prohibited referrals. Although this issue was not included in the CY 2008 MPFS Final Rule, CMS adopted this provision in the FY 2009 IPPS Final Rule stating that

---

[308] 72 Fed. Reg. at 38,183.
[309] 42 C.F.R. § 411.353 (c)(1); see 73 Fed. Reg. at 48,700.
[310] 73 Fed. Reg. at 48,700.

the burden of proof (otherwise known as the burden of persuasion) is on the claimant throughout the course of the appellate proceeding (and at each level of appeal), whereas the burden of production is initially on the claimant but may shift to us or our contractor during the course of the proceeding.[311]

CMS explains in the preamble that because government funds are at issue, "it is appropriate to place the burden on providers and suppliers to show that they are entitled to payments from the public fisc, and not on the government to show that the provider or supplier is not entitled to such payment."[312]

## § 3-7 ADVISORY OPINIONS

Until the passage of the Balanced Budget Act of 1997, neither the OIG nor CMS were authorized to issue advisory opinions under the Stark Law. However, the Stark Law now requires the issuance of written advisory opinions concerning whether a referral relating to designated health services is prohibited under the Stark Law.[313]

On January 9, 1998, CMS promulgated a "Final Rule with Comment Period," which not only sets forth the framework for how a private party can obtain an advisory opinion from CMS, but also incorporates certain limitations that have been placed on the OIG with respect to the substance of advisory opinions under the Anti-Kickback Statute and other fraud and abuse provisions. CMS has stated that, in advisory opinions regarding the Stark Law, it will not assess FMV for any goods, services, or property, nor will the agency determine whether an individual is a bona fide employee within the meaning of the IRC.[314] Moreover, CMS has verified that each advisory opinion issued will only be binding on the DHHS Secretary and the party/parties who requested the opinion.

In contrast to the plethora of advisory opinions that have been issued by the OIG under the Anti-Kickback Statute and other fraud and abuse provisions, relatively few advisory opinions have been issued by CMS addressing the Stark Law.[315] However, from 2004 to 2005, CMS issued more than a dozen advisory opinions on the specific issue of whether a particular specialty hospital qualified for the exception to the specialty-hospital moratorium if it either was in existence or already "under development" on November 18, 2003.[316] Therefore, in order to determine whether a hospital was, in fact, "under development," Congress provided that a specialty hospital could apply to CMS

---

[311] 42 C.F.R. § 411.353(c)(2); see 73 Fed. Reg. at 48,738.
[312] 73 Fed. Reg. at 48,738.
[313] 42 U.S.C. § 1395nn(6).
[314] 42 C.F.R. § 411.370 et. seq.
[315] CMS advisory opinions are *available online at* http://www.cms.gov/Medicare/Fraud-and-Abuse/PhysicianSelfReferral/advisory_opinions.html.
[316] Social Security Act § 1877(h)(7)(B); 42 U.S.C. § 1395nn(h)(7)(B).

## Federal Physician Self-Referral Prohibitions

for a determination by applying for guidance through the advisory-opinion process.[317]

In fact, the first advisory opinion since completion of Phase III Stark II Final Rulemaking was posted on October 3, 2007 (CMS-AO-2007-01). It considered an issue created by a Phase II change in the physician recruitment rules, opining that the repayment terms in a recruitment arrangement between a hospital and a physician could not be amended without violating the Stark Law.[318] The proposed amendment involved the elimination of an excess receipts provision. CMS concluded that removal of the excess receipts provision may provide for additional compensation. Since the physician has already relocated, this additional compensation would not be "for the purpose of inducing relocation and may directly or indirectly reflect the volume or value of the recruited physician's actual or potential referrals."[319]

Two additional advisory opinions were released in 2008. The first, released in May 2008, addressed a hospital group's ability to provide a software interface to physician practice groups for the purpose of allowing physician practice groups to order and communicate the results of tests or procedures furnished by the hospital group.[320] CMS blessed this arrangement with the caveat that the interface: (1) only be used to order and communicate test results furnished by the hospital group; (2) not be modified to perform additional functions; and (3) not be able to be sold by the physician practices.[321]

The second advisory opinion of 2008, released in June, addressed the rural provider exception. CMS approved of a physician owned DHS's ability to bill Medicare for services rendered on patients referred by the physician owners. CMS concluded that the arrangement satisfied the rural provider ownership and investment exception because the all of the DHS are furnished outside of an MSA and more than 75% of the DHS is furnished to individuals residing outside of an MSA.[322]

## § 3-8  SELF-REFERRAL DISCLOSURE PROTOCOL

Traditionally, entities that discovered a Stark violation refunded monies to their Medicare contractor or, if more certainty was desired, they historically could self-disclose to the OIG. However, in a March 24, 2009, Open Letter,

---

[317] *See* CMS One Time Notifications, *available online at* http://www.cms.hhs.gov/transmittals/downloads/R62OTN.pdf and http://www.cms.hhs.gov/transmittals/downloads/R79OTN.pdf.
[318] CMS Advisory Opinion No. 2007-01, *available online at* http://www.cms.gov/Medicare/Fraud-and-Abuse/PhysicianSelfReferral/Downloads/CMS-AO-2007-01.pdf.
[319] *Id.* at 5.
[320] CMS Advisory Opinion No. 2008-01, *available online at* http://www.cms.gov/Medicare/Fraud-and-Abuse/PhysicianSelfReferral/Downloads/CMS-AO-2008-01.pdf.
[321] *Id.* at 3.
[322] CMS Advisory Opinion No. 2008-02, *available online at* http://www.cms.gov/Medicare/Fraud-and-Abuse/PhysicianSelfReferral/Downloads/CMS-AO-2008-02.pdf.

the OIG closed that door by announcing that it would no longer accept Stark self-disclosures that do not involve a violation of the Anti-Kickback Statute.[323] However, as part of the Health Reform Law, Congress required CMS to create a vehicle through which healthcare providers and suppliers can disclose actual or potential violations of the Stark Law.[324] In September 2010, CMS issued the CMS Voluntary Self-Referral Disclosure Protocol (SRDP), which was then revised in May 2011.[325]

Like the OIG's Provider Self-Disclosure Protocol, the SRDP is open to "all healthcare providers of services and suppliers, whether individuals or entities, and is not limited to any particular industry, medical specialty, or type of service." CMS states that the SRDP is intended to facilitate matters that "in the disclosing party's reasonable assessment, are actual or potential violations [of the Stark Law]."[326] Accordingly, a party must have reasonable certainty that a violation has occurred and cannot use the process to seek an advisory opinion from CMS on the legality of conduct under the Stark Law.

Interestingly, the SRDP can be used even if the entity is being audited or investigated. However, CMS states that "the disclosure must be made in good faith. . . . [a] disclosing party that attempts to circumvent an ongoing inquiry . . . will be removed from the SRDP." Although unclear, presumably, this means that if the underlying investigation is not related to the particular Stark violation being self-disclosed, the protocol can be used. But if it is related, the entity potentially could be rejected from the SRDP.

Another provision in the Health Reform Law sets forth that a person has engaged in a false claim under the Federal Civil False Claims Act if such person does not report and return overpayments on the later of either 60 days from discovery or the date on any corresponding cost report, if applicable. However, this timing requirement for returning overpayments is suspended upon entry into the SRDP to give the parties time to achieve resolution.

As the SRDP is explicitly intended to be used for actual or potential Stark violations, CMS is the appropriate agency to address Stark self-disclosures. However, violations that include potential liabilities under other federal statutes or laws are not appropriate for the SRDP. By way of example, CMS states "conduct that raises liability risks under the physician self-referral statute may also raise liability risks under the . . . anti-kickback statute and should be disclosed through the OIG's Self-Disclosure SRDP." Although CMS goes on to state that it will coordinate self-disclosures with the OIG and Department of Justice (DOJ), CMS also warns that "the disclosing party's initial decision

---

[323] *See* An Open Letter to Healthcare Providers, March 24, 2009, *available online at* http://oig.hhs.gov/fraud/docs/openletters/OpenLetter3-24-09.pdf.
[324] *See* Patient Protection and Affordable Care Act of 2010, Pub. L. No. 111-148, § 6409.
[325] *See* CMS Voluntary Self-Referral Disclosure Protocol *available online at* http://www.cms.gov/PhysicianSelfReferral/Downloads/6409_SRDP_Protocol.pdf
[326] *Id.*

## Federal Physician Self-Referral Prohibitions

of where to refer a matter involving non-compliance. . . should be made carefully."

According to the SRDP, the submission to CMS should include the following:

- identifying information on the entity including: name, address, national provider identification numbers (NPIs), CMS Certification Number(s) (CCN), and tax identification number(s) and if appropriate a diagram of ownership and control relationships;

- a description the matter being disclosed, including the type of financial relationship(s), the parties involved, the time periods of the non-compliance, the dates or a range of dates whereby the conduct was cured, and type of claims at issue and a description of why the conduct occurred and "the individuals believed to be implicated";

- a "complete legal analysis" of the application of why the entity believed it violated the physician self-referral law and any physician self-referral exception that applies to the conduct and/or that the disclosing party attempted to use. In addition, CMS states that "the submission should include a description of the potential causes of the incident or practice (e.g., intentional conduct, lack of internal controls, circumvention of corporate procedures or Government regulations)";

- a description of the circumstances under which the disclosed matter was discovered and the remedial measures taken since discovery;

- a statement regarding past similar conduct and other criminal, civil or regulatory actions;

- a description of the existence and adequacy of a pre-existing compliance program including remedial efforts to prevent a recurrence of the incident and efforts to restructure the non-compliant relationship;

- a description of appropriate notices, if applicable, provided to other Government agencies, (e.g., Securities and Exchange Commission and Internal Revenue Service) in connection with the disclosed matter;

- disclosure of knowledge of other pending inquiries by Government agencies or contractors;

- a financial analysis that demonstrates that a full examination of the disclosed conduct has occurred, which should (1) set forth the total amount, by year, that is actually or potentially owed; (2) describe the methodology used to set forth the amount that is actually or potentially due and owing; and (3) a summary of auditing activity undertaken and a summary of the documents relied upon;

- a certification from the entities CEO, CFO or authorized representative that the disclosure contains truthful information and is based on a good faith effort to bring the matter to CMS' attention for the purpose of resolving any potential liabilities.

Although the filing required under the SRDP is similar, it is not identical to the requirements for filing under the OIG's Provider Self-Disclosure Protocol and, in fact, is arguably more complicated. Specifically, under the OIG's Voluntary Self-Disclosure Protocol, the OIG allows the disclosing party to conduct its internal review *after* the initial disclosure of the matter, and the OIG promises to generally agree for a reasonable time period to forego its investigation of the matter if the disclosing party agrees to conduct its internal review in accordance with the OIG's internal investigation guidelines and self-assessment guidelines (for estimated financial impact of the violation) that are included in the Provider Self-Disclosure Protocol. This allows entities to apply for entry into the Protocol on a timely basis while permitting additional time for a comprehensive investigation and quantification to be performed and submitted to the OIG.

Unlike the OIG's self-disclosure process, the SRDP requires the disclosing party to conduct a "complete legal analysis" of the application of why the entity believed it violated the Stark Law and any exception that applies to the conduct and/or that the disclosing party attempted to use and a description of the potential causes of the incident or practice (e.g., intentional conduct, lack of internal controls, circumvention of corporate procedures or Government regulations).

## § 3-9    OTHER FEDERAL SELF-REFERRAL RESTRICTIONS

### § 3-9(a)   Home Health Services Reimbursed by the Medicare Program

Even before the Stark Law was enacted, the SSA limited a physician's ability to certify or recertify a plan of care for a patient receiving services from a HHA to the extent the physician had an ownership interest in or a substantial financial interest with the HHA.[327] CMS promulgated regulations regarding this limitation and defined the phrase "significant ownership interest" as ownership of 5% or more in the capital, stock, or profits of the HHA, or having an interest in 5% or more in any mortgage, deed of trust, note, or secured obligation of the HHA.[328] Moreover, the phrase "significant financial or contractual relationship" is defined by the regulations as

---

[327] Social Security Act § 1814(a); 42 U.S.C. § 1395F(a).
[328] 42 C.F.R. § 424.22.

## Federal Physician Self-Referral Prohibitions

any compensation as an officer or director of the HHA; or has direct or indirect business transactions with the [HHA] that, in any fiscal year, amount to more than $25,000 or 5 percent of the agency's total operating expenses, whichever is less. Business transactions means contracts, agreements, purchase orders, or leases to obtain services, supplies, equipment, space and salaried employment.[329]

In December 1995 and February 1996, Thomas Hoyer, Director of CMS's Office of Chronic Care and Insurance Policy, responded to two separate requests for clarification of these regulations in the context of hospital-owned HHAs. Mr. Hoyer stated in one of these letters that

> [i]f a home health agency is owned by a hospital and that hospital purchases a physician practice and those physicians are then compensated in excess of the indicted thresholds to certify and recertify plans of care, the home health agency is in violation of the provisions located at 42 C.F.R. 424.22. . . . In addition, . . . payment of compensation to a physician by a home health agency's parent organization or related organization where the home health agency is based, would very likely be considered to be paid by the home health agency.[330]

Following Mr. Hoyer's response to these requests for clarification, one of the individuals who requested CMS to provide clarification then made a request to the OIG for a statement of the OIG's views. In response, D. McCarty Thornton, Chief Counsel to the Inspector General, expressed the OIG's concern with physician self-referral, but explained that "CMS has the responsibility for enforcement of [42 C.F.R. § 424.22]." Nevertheless, Mr. Thornton sets forth in this letter that the OIG has jurisdiction to bring an action to the extent a provider knowingly submits claims in violation of this regulation:

> Certainly if a provider knowingly submits claims in violation of 42 CFR 424.22, the provider is potentially liable under the Civil False Claims Act, 31 U.S.C. 3729, including the qui tam provisions of that Act. Those who present such claims are at risk of a qui tam suit filed by competitors or by a suit filed initially by the Department of Justice. In addition, if a provider submits such claims and they know or should know of the impropriety of the claims, they are potentially

---

[329] *Id.*

[330] Letters from Thomas E. Hoyer, Director, Office of Chronic Care and Insurance Policy, Healthcare Financing Administration, to: (1) James C. Pyles, Esq., Powers, Pyles, Sutter & Verville PC, Washington, DC (Dec. 15, 1995); and (2) William T. Cuppelt, CPA, Doak, Cuppelt & Poling, Charleston, WV (Feb. 22, 1996) (on file with authors).

liable under the Civil Monetary Penalty law, 42 U.S.C. 1320a-7a, and are subject to enforcement action by the OIG.[331]

The HHA self-referral restriction has been enforced. For example, a physician settled allegations that the physician violated, among other statutory and regulatory provisions, the HHA self-referral restrictions. The action was initially filed by a qui tam relator, and the DOJ chose to intervene in the case. Among other allegations, the DOJ alleged that the physician submitted false claims to the United States based upon statutory and regulatory violations, including the HHA self-referral restrictions.[332] Specific to the HHA self-referral restrictions, the DOJ alleged that the physician had a significant ownership interest in a HHA in which the physician referred patients.

In the final Stark II regulations, CMS took the position that the congressionally mandated Stark Law superseded the HHA self-referral regulations under the SSA. In the preamble to the final Stark II rule, CMS stated that "the home health agency (HHA) rule and its exceptions have been superceded by section 1877 of the Act."[333] However, CMS has not completely repealed the HHA self-referral rule. The new rule provides that:

> [t]he need for home health services to be provided by an HHA may not be certified or recertified, and a plan of treatment may not be established and reviewed, by any physician who has a financial relationship, as defined in § 411.351 of this chapter, with that HHA, unless the physician's relationship meets one of the exceptions in section 1877 of the Act, which sets forth general exceptions to the referral prohibition related to both ownership/investment and compensation; exceptions to the referral prohibition related to ownership or investment interests; and exceptions to the referral prohibition related to compensation arrangements.[334]

Therefore, the HHA self-referral rule is still in effect, although the definitions and exceptions are cross-referenced to the Stark Law. For example, a physician can no longer rely on the 5% ownership exception of the HHA self-referral rule, and the physician must meet a relevant ownership or compensation exception under the Stark law.

---

[331] Letter from D. McCarty Thornton, Chief Counsel to the Inspector General, Inspector General Division, Department of Health and Human Services to James C. Pyles, Esq., Powers, Pyles, Sutter & Verville, PC, Washington, DC (June 18, 1996) (on file with authors).

[332] *See*, e.g., *Referral to wife's HHAs cost a Texas Physician more than $1.7 million*, HOME HEALTH LINE (Mar. 24, 2000); United States *ex rel.* Ben Sewell v. Caroline Haggard et. al., Civil Action No. SA-94-CA-109-OG. The settlement agreement is on file with the authors.

[333] 66 Fed. Reg. 856, 936 (2001).

[334] 42 C.F.R. § 424.22(d).

## § 3-9(b)  CHAMPUS/TRICARE AND CHAMPVA

The Civilian Health and Medical Program of the Uniformed Services (CHAMPUS) adopted a regulation, based on a statutory provision included in the Defense Appropriations Act, excluding from coverage inpatient mental-health services furnished to a patient who is referred by a physician or other healthcare professional with authority to admit with an "economic interest" in the facility.[335] A waiver of this coverage exclusion can be obtained in the same manner as obtaining pre-admission authorization and by disclosing the economic interest.[336]

Initially, the regulation did not define the term "economic interest." One reason given for not doing so was as follows:

[A]s evidenced by the recent rules of the DHHS Inspector General establishing "safe harbors" from anti-kickback laws, any serious effort to sort out various forms of economic relationships and interest inevitably would become extremely complicated. Further, based on some of the reactions to the safe harbor regulation, even very elaborate definitions and distinctions leave substantial gray areas.[337]

In March of 1999, however, the Secretary of Defense issued a definition, which provides that an "economic interest" is:

(1) Any right, title, or share in the income, remuneration, payment, or profit of a CHAMPUS-authorized provider, or of an individual or entity eligible to be a CHAMPUS-authorized provider, resulting, directly or indirectly, from a referral relationship; or any direct or indirect ownership, right, title, or share, including a mortgage, deed of trust, note, or other obligation secured (in whole or in part) by one entity for another entity in a referral or accreditation relationship, which is equal to or exceeds 5% of the total property and assets of the other entity.

(2) A referral relationship exists when a CHAMPUS beneficiary is sent, directed, assigned or influenced to use a specific CHAMPUS-authorized provider, or a specific individual or entity eligible to be a CHAMPUS-authorized provider.

(3) An accreditation relationship exists when a CHAMPUS-authorized accreditation organization evaluates for accreditation an entity that is an applicant for, or recipient of CHAMPUS-authorized provider status.[338]

---

[335] 32 C.F.R. § 199.4(g)(73).
[336] *Id.*
[337] 56 Fed. Reg. 52,193 (Oct. 18, 1991).
[338] 32 C.F.R. § 199.2; *see also* 64 Fed. Reg. 11,765, 11,768–69 (Mar. 10, 1999).

Aside from providing a definition, the 1999 changes broadened the scope of the self-referral CHAMPUS provisions by including within CHAMPUS participation agreements a requirement to refer CHAMPUS beneficiaries only to providers with which the referring provider does not have an economic interest.[339] Moreover, the participation-agreement requirement does not explicitly provide for a waiver of the economic interest.[340]

In addition to the CHAMPUS/TRICARE self-referral provisions, the Civilian Health and Medical Program of the Department of Veterans Affairs (CHAMPVA) provides a self-referral prohibition. Specifically excluded from coverage are "services that are provided to a beneficiary who is referred to a provider of such services by a provider who has an economic interest in the facility to which the patient is referred, unless a waiver is granted."[341] Unlike the CHAMPUS regulations, the CHAMPVA regulations (Title 38 of the Code of Federal Regulations) do not explicitly define an "economic interest."[342]

### § 3-9(c) Disclosure Required of Certain Hospitals and Critical Access Hospitals

In the FY 2008 IPPS Final Rule, CMS revised the regulations governing Medicare provider agreements so as to require a hospital (including a critical access hospital) to disclose to all patients whether it is physician-owned and, if so, the names of its physician owners.[343]

In the FY 2009 IPPS Final Rule, CMS further clarified that it intended for this provision to mirror the Stark Law and apply not only to physicians but also immediate family members of physicians. In addition, in the FY 2009 IPPS Final Rule, CMS added a requirement that a physician owned hospital must require all physicians who are members of the hospital's medical staff to agree (as a condition of medical staff membership) to disclose in writing to all patients whom they refer any ownership or investment interest in the hospital held by the physician (or an immediate family member of such physician) and that such disclosure occurs at the time of referral.[344]

### § 3-9(d) The Anti-Markup Rule

Section 1842(n) of the Social Security Act places certain limitations on the ability of a physician to mark-up the charges in connection with a physician's bill for the technical component of diagnostic tests (described in

---

[339] 32 C.F.R. § 199.6(a)(13)(xi); *see also* 64 Fed. Reg. 11,765, 11,770 (1999).
[340] 32 C.F.R. § 199.6(a)(13)(xi); *see also* 64 Fed. Reg. 11,765, 11,770 (1999).
[341] 38 C.F.R. § 17.272.
[342] *See* 38 C.F.R. § 17.30 *et seq.*
[343] 42 C.F.R. § 489.20(u).
[344] 42 C.F.R. § 489.20(u)(2); *see* 73 Fed. Reg. 48,686.

## Federal Physician Self-Referral Prohibitions

Section 1861(s)(3)) (referred to as the Anti-Markup Rule).[345] Specifically, the Anti-Markup Rule provides that if the billing physician or a physician with whom the billing physician shares a practice did not perform or supervise the diagnostic test, the proper Medicare payment is "the actual acquisition costs (net of any discounts) or, if lower, the supplier's reasonable charge."[346] Medicare rules also have restricted, by imposing certain supervision requirements, who may bill for the professional component of diagnostic tests.[347]

In the CY 2007 MPFS Proposed Rule, CMS noted its "concern" about the existence of certain arrangements that are not within the intended purpose of the physician self-referral rules and which allow physician group practices to bill for services furnished by a contractor physician in a "centralized building."[348] Specifically, CMS was concerned that allowing group practices or other suppliers to realize a profit from the purchase or contract for diagnostic tests may lead to overutilization and higher costs to the Medicare program.[349]

In the CY 2008 MPFS Proposed Rule, CMS published revisions to the Anti-Markup Rule, by limiting the payment for the technical component (TC) or professional component (PC) of a diagnostic test that is either purchased from an "outside supplier" or performed at a site other than the "office of the billing physician or other supplier" to the lowest of either: (1) the performing supplier's net charge to the billing physician or other supplier; (2) the billing physician or other supplier's actual charge; or (3) the fee schedule amount for the test if the performing supplier had billed directly.[350] Additionally, CMS redefined "entity" to exclude a physician's practice when it bills Medicare for the PC of a diagnostic test in accordance with § 414.50.[351]

Under these rules, "net charge" is calculated without considering "the cost of equipment or space leased to the performing supplier by or through the billing physician or other supplier."[352] Thus, the group practice's overhead charges may not be considered in the amount billed to CMS. In the CY 2008 MPFS Final Rule, CMS defined "outside supplier" as "someone who is not an employee of the billing physician or other supplier and who does not furnish the test or interpretation to the billing physician or other supplier

---

[345] 42 U.S.C. § 1395u(n)(1)(A).
[346] *Id.* CMS regulations implementing section 1842(n) of the Social Security Act appear at §§ 414.50 and 402.1(c)(15).
[347] 71 Fed. Reg. at 49,054.
[348] 72 Fed. Reg. at 38,179; 71 Fed. Reg. at 49,054.
[349] 71 Fed. Reg. at 49,054.
[350] *Id.*
[351] *Id.* at 66,400. The definition of "entity" is found at found at § 411.351. Previously, CMS defined entity to exclude a physician's practice only when it billed for the TC of a diagnostic test. The new definition includes both the TC and PC billed in accordance with § 414.50.
[352] *Id.* at 66,401.

under a reassignment that meets the requirements of § 424.80."[353] The office of the billing physician or other supplier was defined as the "medical office space where the physician or other supplier regularly furnishes patient care," or for a physician organization, it is "space in which the physician organization provides substantially the full range of patient care services" it generally provides.[354] Significantly, this definition does not include space that meets the definition of "centralized building"[355] for the purposes of the physician services and in-office ancillary services exceptions.[356] Thus, to avoid application of the new rule, the TC and PC services cannot be provided in an office used solely for diagnostic testing they must be performed in the same office were the group practice regularly provides physician services.

On January 3, 2008, CMS issued a final order delaying the applicability of the Anti-Markup Rule until January 1, 2009, except as to: (1) the technical component of a purchased diagnostic test; and (2) any anatomic pathology services furnished in space utilized by a physician group practice as a "centralized building" for the purposes of complying with the physician self-referral rules that does not qualify as the "same building" under § 411.355(b)(2)(i).[357] CMS did not delay the applicability of the Anti-Markup Rule to anatomic pathology diagnostic testing arrangements because those arrangements "precipitated [its] proposal for revision of the anti-markup provisions and remain [its] core concern."[358] Some commenters have claimed that no appreciable risk of overutilization exists as to anatomic pathology testing because of its invasive nature.[359] CMS explained that it was "skeptical" that the risk was lower for those tests than other types of diagnostic tests, and since "Congress made no exception for biopsies or other minimally invasive tests" it would not provide for such an exception to accord with Congressional intent.[360]

With respect to services that were still subject to the Anti-Markup Rule, a group of physicians challenged the Anti-Markup Rule and the Final Order, which delayed its application as to certain arrangements.[361] The DC Circuit held that all plaintiffs lacked standing to challenge the Final Order. The court noted that although the language of the Anti-Markup Rule and the Final Order

---

[353] *Id.* at 66,402. In the 2008 Proposed MPFS, CMS had contemplated a specific anti-markup provision applicable to part-time employees who reassign their claims. However, most commenters were opposed to this particular proposal, and in the Final Rule CMS noted that "part-time employees are treated no differently than full-time employees or contractors who reassign benefits." *Id.* at 66,308.
[354] 72 Fed. Reg. at 66,401.
[355] 42 C.F.R. § 411.351.
[356] 72 Fed. Reg. at 66,308.
[357] 73 Fed. Reg. at 404 (Jan. 3, 2008).
[358] *Id.* at 405.
[359] 72 Fed. Reg. at 66,313.
[360] *Id.*
[361] Atlantic Urological Assoc. v. Leavitt, No. 08-141 (RMC), 2008 WL 1931441, at *2 (D.D.C. May 5, 2008).

is not identical, the effect on the plaintiffs is the same: "they cannot mark up the technical or professional components of pathology tests performed in their own laboratories if the labs are not in the 'same building' as their practices."[362] Accordingly, the plaintiffs lacked standing because their claim was "not likely to be redressed by a favorable decision"—they could not show that, by invalidating the Final Order, the court would effectively eliminate the effect of the earlier regulation, the Anti-Markup Rule.[363] As a result of *Atlantic Urological Assoc.*, the Anti-Markup Rule became effective in 2008 for the TC of diagnostic tests and for the TC and PC of anatomic pathology diagnostic testing services.

Then, in the CY 2009 MPFS Proposed Rule, CMS proposed two alternatives for revising the Anti-Markup Rule.[364] Under the first proposal, the Anti-Markup Rule would apply when the PC or TC of a diagnostic test is either: (1) purchased from an outside supplier or (2) "performed or supervised by a physician who does not share a practice with the billing physician or physician organization (as defined at § 411.351)."[365] Physicians who are employed by or contract with a single physician or physician organization would be considered to "share a practice" with that physician or organization. However, under the proposal, a physician who is an employee of or independent contractor with more than one billing physician or organization would not "share a practice" with those entities.[366] CMS explains that physicians who provide his or her efforts for a single organization has a "sufficient nexus" with that practice such that the Anti-Markup Rule should not apply.[367] CMS noted that this proposal is a simpler and more "bright-line" approach to capture potentially abusive arrangements while preserving the viability of non-abusive relationships that involve diagnostic testing facilities but might not have satisfied the "in the office of the billing physician or other supplier" as defined in the 2008 MPFS.[368]

CMS's second proposal maintained much of the current regulatory text from the final 2008 MPFS "to determine whether a physician 'shares a practice'" with the billing physician or supplier.[369] Although CMS claimed it was

---

[362] *Id.* at *7.
[363] *Id.*
[364] 73 Fed. Reg. 38,502, 38,545 (July 7, 2008).
[365] *Id.*
[366] *Id.* CMS further noted that it would not consider a physician who provides services at a free clinic or who moonlights in a hospital emergency department or as a hospitalist to be "sharing a practice" such that the Anti-Markup Rule would apply to the services he or she provides for his or her physician organization. *Id.* at 38,546.
[367] *Id.*
[368] CMS provides an example of these non-abusive relationships: "a centralized laboratory staffed with full-time employees that is used by a physician practice with multiple office locations, sometimes referred to as a 'hub and spoke' arrangement." 73 Fed. Reg. at 38,546.
[369] *Id.*

"re-proposing to apply the anti-markup provision to [the] TCs and PCs of non-purchased tests that are performed outside the 'office of the billing physician or other supplier,'" it proposed several changes (or "clarifications") to that rule, including (1) that the "office of the billing physician or other supplier" includes space within the "same building" in which the billing physician or supplier "regularly furnishes" patient care; (2) the anti-markup provision applies if the TC is either conducted or supervised outside the office of the billing physician or supplier; (3) if the TC is supervised by a physician located in the office of the billing physician or supplier, the TC is not purchased from an "outside supplier"; (4) only the "performing supplier" with respect to the TC is the supervising physician and for the PC, the "performing supplier" is the physician who performed the PC; (5) a new exception for diagnostic tests order by a physician in a physician organization that does not have any owners who have the right to receive profit distributions; and (6) CMS solicited comments on defining "net charge" and whether CMS should delay implementation of the Anti-Markup Rule further, beyond the current January 1, 2009 date.[370]

In the CY 2009 MPFS Final Rule, CMS finalized the application of the anti-markup rule to instances where a physician or other supplier bills for the PC or TC of a diagnostic test performed or interpreted by a physician who does not share a practice with the billing physician or other supplier.[371] In the final rule, CMS deleted the "purchased tests and interpretations from an outside supplier" language as a separate basis for imposing the anti-markup limitation.[372] Upon review of the comments, CMS "concluded that employing the concept of a purchased TC or PC as a separate basis for imposing an anti-markup payment limitation is unnecessary, redundant, and potentially confusing . . . As finalized, the anti-markup payment limitation will apply to TCs and PCs that meet neither the requirements of Alternative 1 nor Alternative 2, without regard to whether the TC or PC was purchased from an outside supplier."[373]

CMS did incorporate in the final rule, however, both of the alternate proposals described above for determining whether the performing physician "shares a practice" with the billing physician or other supplier, subject to some modifications. Importantly, the anti-markup rule can be avoided by meeting either Alternative 1 (the "substantially all" test) or, on a case-by-case basis, Alternative 2's "site-of-service" approach.[374] First, arrangements should be analyzed under Alternative 1.[375] In the final rule, CMS

---

[370] *Id.*
[371] 42 C.F.R. § 414.50; 73 Fed. Reg. at 69,799.
[372] 73 Fed. Reg. at 69,813.
[373] *Id.*
[374] *See* 42 C.F.R. § 414.50; 73 Fed. Reg. at 69,800.
[375] 73 Fed. Reg. at 69,800.

modified the proposed "bright line" first alternative, by explaining that a performing physician is deemed to "share a practice" with the billing physician when he or she performs "substantially all" of his or her professional services for the billing physician.[376] "Substantially all" means that the performing physician must provide at least 75% of his or her professional services to the billing physician or other supplier.[377] Unlike the proposed first alternative, the final Alternative 1 recognizes the comments and concerns raised about part-time physicians and locum tenens situations; accordingly, a performing physician can meet the "substantially all" test "even if the physician works for one or more billing physician groups or other healthcare entities."[378]

If a performing physician does not meet the "substantially all" test, the billing physician or other supplier may avoid the anti-markup rule by satisfying the "site of service" test. Alternative 2 retains many of the features from the proposed rule, basically requiring that the diagnostic test be performed in the "same building" (as defined in the Stark rules at § 411.351) in which the ordering physician or other ordering supplier regularly furnishes patient care.[379] Minor modifications from the proposed rule include:

- a physician or other supplier may have more than one "office of the billing physician or other supplier," and the "office of the billing physician or other supplier" is defined as space in which the ordering physician or other ordering supplier regularly furnishes care (and with respect to physician organizations, is the space in which the ordering physician performs substantially the full range of patient care services that the ordering physician provides generally);

- with respect to the TC, it is now required that the physician supervising the TC must be an owner, employee, or independent contractor of the billing physician or other supplier;

- with respect to the PC, the physician performing the PC must be an employee or independent contractor of the billing physician or other supplier.[380]

The revised final anti-markup rule took effect on January 1, 2009.

---

[376] *See* 42 C.F.R. § 414.50; 73 Fed. Reg. at 69,800.
[377] *See* 42 C.F.R. § 414.50; 73 Fed. Reg. at 69,800.
[378] 73 Fed. Reg. at 69,800–69,801.
[379] 73 Fed. Reg. at 69,801.
[380] *Id.*

## § 3-10 MAJOR ISSUES IN STARK LAW INTERPRETATION

### § 3-10(a) Relationship Between the Stark Law and the Anti-Kickback Statute

Substantial confusion often exists over the distinction between the Stark Law and the Anti-Kickback Statute, as well as how and when to apply each of these laws. One of the most significant differences between these laws is that under the Stark Law, if a physician has a financial relationship with an entity to which the physician refers Medicare or Medicaid patients for designated health services, then this financial relationship *must* fall within an exception. Failure to meet a Stark Law exception means the referral is strictly prohibited. In contrast, the safe harbors and exceptions under the Anti-Kickback Statute are *optional* exceptions that can be used by providers to avoid anti-kickback liability. As discussed in Chapter 2, the safe harbors were written to delineate those financial arrangements that will not be viewed as violative of the Anti-Kickback Statute. Consequently, safe harbor conformity is purely voluntary, and failure to conform to one of the safe harbor provisions does not mean that the financial arrangement is illegal.

This dichotomy can create confusion as to what rules to follow when analyzing physician financial arrangements. However, if a financial relationship is not permitted under the Stark Law for purposes of making referrals, it is irrelevant whether the arrangement fits within a safe harbor to the Anti-Kickback Statute. For example, a joint venture may qualify for safe-harbor protection if it meets the requirements of the small-entity investment safe harbor. Depending upon the nature of the joint venture, however, there may not be an exception under the self-referral ban that would permit physician-investors to refer patients to the joint venture. In fact, until the recent implementation of the advisory opinion process under the Anti-Kickback Statute, providers had to operate with uncertainty as to whether the government would view conduct as violating the Anti-Kickback Statute or satisfying a safe harbor. Now, providers rightfully may choose whether to qualify for a safe harbor, seek an advisory opinion, or otherwise proceed with an arrangement under a business judgment of risk under a "facts and circumstances" analysis. Additionally, arrangements may fall outside of the safe harbors that the OIG would not "bless" with a favorable advisory opinion because the facts are not yet sufficiently developed (e.g., newly operational joint ventures) or for other reasons.

On the other hand, even if an arrangement is permitted under the self-referral ban, the arrangement still must be examined under the Anti-Kickback Statute to determine whether the arrangement qualifies for safe-harbor protection, or whether it potentially implicates the Anti-Kickback Statute. For example, an arrangement may fit within the personal-services exception of

## Federal Physician Self-Referral Prohibitions

the self-referral ban, but may not meet the safe-harbor criteria for personal-services contracts unless the aggregate compensation is set in advance. Of course, because the Anti-Kickback Statute is intent-based, an arrangement's qualification for a self-referral exception might, in the appropriate circumstances, provide an argument regarding the parties' lack of intent to violate the Anti-Kickback Statute.

Much of the distinction between the Anti-Kickback Statute and the Stark Law has been blurred in several important ways in the final regulations. First, although the Stark Law is not an intent-based statute, the final regulations included a "knowledge" element in some definitions and exceptions, which makes "state of mind" part of Stark Law analysis.

Second, a large number of the Stark Law exceptions now include a requirement that the arrangement not otherwise "violate" the Anti-Kickback Statute, thus complicating Stark Law analysis, especially in areas that the OIG has identified as suspect practices.

Third, inconsistencies exist between what CMS has permitted in certain Stark Law exceptions and what the OIG previously identified as being a "suspect practice." For instance, CMS has created a new Stark Law exception for hospitals offering physicians compliance training. Nevertheless, the OIG previously issued the *Special Fraud Alert on Hospital Incentives to Physicians*, in which the OIG identified CPT coding training as being a suspect practice under the Anti-Kickback Statute. Therefore, given that CMS published the final regulations and is responsible for interpreting the Stark Law, and that the OIG is responsible for interpreting the Anti-Kickback Statute, it is unclear what effect, if any, this new exception will have on the Special Fraud Alert.

### § 3-10(b) Knowledge Element for Indirect Financial Relationships

As stated, included in the final regulations are new definitions for both indirect-compensation arrangements and indirect-ownership and investment interests. A component of each of these new definitions is a "knowledge" element. A designated health services provider only has an indirect-ownership relationship if it has "actual knowledge" or acts in "reckless disregard or deliberate ignorance" that an indirect financial relationship exists with the referring physician.[381] For an indirect-compensation arrangement, the designated health services entity must have "actual knowledge" or "acts in reckless disregard or deliberate ignorance" that the referring physician "receives aggregate compensation that varies with, or otherwise reflects, the volume or value of referrals."[382]

---

[381] 42 C.F.R. § 411.354(b)(5).
[382] 42 C.F.R. § 411.354(c)(2)(iii).

CMS explains its position in the preamble to the final regulations that the public should consider this new "knowledge" requirement to be a positive revision, as it "more fairly balances the burden of compliance against the risk of abuse."[383] In fact, CMS states that this requirement does not impose any "affirmative duty" on designated health services providers to inquire or investigate whether an indirect financial relationship exists.[384] By the same token, however, CMS states that providers "in possession of facts that would lead a reasonable person to suspect the existence of an indirect financial relationship [must] take reasonable steps to determine whether such a financial relationship exists" and whether an exception is met.[385] Moreover, CMS applies this knowledge standard only to the designated health services provider that receives a tainted physician referral—but not to the physician who makes the referral.

## § 3-10(c) Joint Ventures Unrelated to the Provision of Designated Health Services

Another matter of controversy under the Stark Law has been whether parties to a joint venture would be deemed to have a financial relationship with one another for Stark Law purposes. In the final Stark I regulations, CMS confirms that joint ventures between physicians and hospitals that are unrelated to the provision of clinical laboratory services (or designated health services under Stark II), such as a physician hospital organization or a management services organization, should not implicate the Stark Law, and therefore should not prohibit the physicians from referring patients to the hospitals. The preamble to the Stark I regulations states that

> [i]n the case of a joint venture held with a hospital, if the physician has no ownership or investment interest in the hospital, a prohibition based on ownership would not apply at all. That is, even though a physician may own a venture with a hospital, as separate partners, that does not mean that the physician actually owns any part of the hospital.[386]

In the preamble to the final Stark II regulations, however, CMS "revisited the issue of common ownership" and determined that such relationships should be analyzed in the same manner as all other types of indirect financial relationships. This new and surprising interpretation of the Stark Law has substantial Stark Law implications, as a multitude of financial relationships

---

[383] 66 Fed. Reg. 865 (2001).
[384] *Id.*
[385] *Id.*
[386] 60 Fed. Reg. 41,956 (1995) (emphasis in original).

that never before were previously considered to even remotely implicate the Stark Law now will need to be reviewed.

Another issue is that, to the extent that co-ownership arrangements should be analyzed as creating indirect ownership/investment relationships between the co-owners, no broad exception exists for all indirect-ownership and investment interests. Rather, only an indirect-compensation exception has been established to date, and that exception has standards that are irrelevant to ownership interests (e.g., the agreement must be signed by the parties and specify the services). For example, if a hospital and certain physicians co-own an office building, then CMS appears to take the position that this co-ownership creates an indirect financial relationship between the hospital and physicians that, in the absence of an exception, will preclude the physicians from referring patients to the hospital. Yet there is no exception for ownership in an office building, because no one ever conceived that such an exception would be needed to protect a situation that should not implicate the Stark Law in the first instance. In some cases, the "ownership of a hospital" exception may be available to protect the indirect-ownership interests that may be deemed to occur in this scenario, but this analysis probably would not solve the problem where a hospital's sister subsidiary (e.g., MSO) is the co-ownership participant with the physician, such that an indirect arrangement between the physician and the hospital is deemed to exist. Moreover, other designated health service providers may not have any exception to rely upon.

### § 3-10(d) Hospital/Physician Arrangements Related to Designated Health Services

As a result of not only the Stark Law but also a number of other health regulatory issues (e.g., state certificate-of-need requirements, licensure, limitations on the ability of certain types of providers to bill for services in particular practice settings), one common structure for certain "designated health services" arrangements between hospitals and physicians is for there to be an entity that will provide a host of items and services to the hospital under either a "management services joint venture" or pursuant to an "under arrangements" relationship.

Under these arrangements, physicians, either with or without participation by a hospital, will establish an entity (e.g., a limited liability company) for the purpose of providing various items and administrative, leasing, and/or management services (e.g., property leasing, equipment leasing, information systems, billing services, non-clinical personnel, as well as overall management of the delivery of the particular healthcare service in question) for which the hospital will bill third-party payors as a being furnished as a provider-based service. The range of services provided by the entity may vary.

The hospital will then compensate the entity for the fair market value of the services provided.

One such type of arrangement that received significant attention and publicity concerned urologists owning an entity that would lease a lithotripter to a hospital, for which the hospital would pay the entity on a per-patient or per-use basis for use of the lithotripter. Although lithotripsy is not listed among the various designated health services, CMS took the position that, when provided in a hospital setting, lithotripsy became a designated health service as being a "hospital inpatient or outpatient service." The American Lithotripsy Society and the Urology Society of America were successful in their lawsuit against CMS, as the District Court held that Congress did not intend for lithotripsy to be included as a designated health service and, therefore, CMS's interpretation was beyond the scope of the statute and the Administrative Procedures Act.[387] Nevertheless, the issue remained that these urologists owned an entity that, in turn, had a compensation arrangement with the hospital. This same analysis applies to other arrangements for medical services (e.g., cardiac catheterization, ambulatory surgery) when a hospital contracts with a physician-owned entity (either in total or in part), and those physicians refer patients to the hospital, irrespective of whether the items and services that are subject to the arrangement are themselves "designated health services."

However, as described above, as part of the FY 2009 IPPS Final Rule, effective October 1, 2009, CMS revised the definition of the term "entity" so as to include any person or entity that "has performed services that are billed as DHS."[388] By changing the definition of "entity" to include persons and entities that "perform" DHS, CMS specifically stated in the preamble to the regulations that it intended to include within the scope of the Stark Law those physician groups and other organizations that provide inpatient and/or outpatient services to a hospital "under arrangements."[389] As a result of this modification, the only ownership exception for services billed "under arrangement" would be the narrow rural provider exception. However, a group of urologists filed suit challenging the regulation

## § 3-10(e) Corporate Affiliates

Another important issue under the Stark Law is whether a physician who has a financial relationship with one entity in a corporate family, which does not furnish clinical laboratory or other designated health services, would be precluded from referring patients to other entities within the same corporate family. Although it is clear from the statute that any ownership

---

[387] *American Lithotripsy Society and Urology Society of America v. Tommy G. Thompson*, 215 F. Supp. 2d 23 (2002).
[388] 42 C.F.R. § 411.351; *see* 73 Fed. Reg. at 48,721.
[389] 73 Fed. Reg. at 48,721.

## Federal Physician Self-Referral Prohibitions

interest in a parent organization is attributed to the subsidiary organization, other intra-corporate family relationships were not entirely clear under the statutory language. One particular issue was whether a physician with a financial relationship in a subsidiary entity would be precluded from referring patients to that entity's sister subsidiary that furnishes designated health services.

CMS has confirmed in both the final Stark I regulations and the final Stark II regulations, however, that the physician's financial relationship with a subsidiary would not, in itself, trigger the Stark Law:

> Subsidiary entities that are related via a common parent may or may not have any ownership interest in each other. If a physician has an ownership interest in a subsidiary that, in turn has an ownership interest in a brother laboratory, the physician could be regarded as having an indirect ownership interest in the laboratory. *However, this would not be the case if the brother/sister corporations have no ownership relationship.*[390]

Also at issue has been whether a physician's ownership interest in a subsidiary company necessarily means that the physician has an ownership interest in the parent organization that may furnish designated health services. CMS makes clear in the final regulations:

> [I]f the physician has an ownership interest in the subsidiary without owning any portion of the parent laboratory, the physician will not be considered to have an ownership interest in the laboratory. The physician would have an ownership interest in the laboratory only if the non-laboratory subsidiary had an ownership interest (for example, through stock or debt instruments) in the parent laboratory.[391]

---

[390] 60 Fed. Reg. at 41,945.
[391] *Id.*

# 4
# False Claims: Civil and Criminal Enforcement

## § 4-1 OVERVIEW

The scope of enforcement actions against fraudulent billing has broadened considerably in recent years. Historically, only federal law enforcement agencies pursued healthcare fraud in the Medicare and Medicaid programs. These enforcement actions typically focused on false claims (e.g., billing for services not rendered and similarly blatant fraudulent billing practices), and they almost exclusively targeted healthcare providers in connection with their billing under the federal Medicare or state Medicaid programs.

In recent decades, however, not only are private parties commencing actions for healthcare fraud on behalf of the government, but recent enforcement actions have focused on more-subtle billing issues, such as routine waivers of coinsurance and deductible amounts, bootstrapping violations of the Anti-Kickback Statute or self-referral law as being a false claim, failure to create and maintain paperwork and billing for services the government alleges were not medically necessary. Largely as a result of private actions and new data mining tools, investigations are being commenced in which Medicare payment policy is not necessarily clear, but fraud is nonetheless alleged. In addition, many of these actions have involved not only federal and state payment programs but also private healthcare third-party payors.

One thing is clear: individuals and entities who conduct business in the healthcare arena—whether provider, supplier, physician, payor, or claims administrator—will be held to a high standard with respect to knowledge and adherence to the rules of the game.

This chapter provides an overview of the federal statutory authorities for pursuing criminal and civil actions against providers for submitting false claims and engaging in other fraudulent billing activities, and provides examples of how these statutes have been applied to a wide array of conduct.[1]

---

[1] This chapter provides an overview of the False Claims Act, civil money penalty law, and exclusion provisions as they have been applied in the healthcare context. However, this chapter should not be regarded as a comprehensive review of these laws, or a comprehensive inventory of the various activities that can implicate these laws. An additional resource to which the reader may refer is an American Health Lawyers Association publication authored by Robert Salcido, Esquire: FALSE CLAIMS ACT & THE HEALTHCARE INDUSTRY: COUNSELING AND LITIGATION (2nd ed. 2011).

## § 4-2 THE FEDERAL CIVIL FALSE CLAIMS ACT

In an effort to address widespread fraud among government contractors during the Civil War, Congress enacted the Federal Civil False Claims Act (FCA) in 1863. Currently, the FCA is one of the primary vehicles through which the government combats fraud, waste, and abuse against itself. Accordingly, it is also the primary tool used to enforce healthcare fraud.

The FCA imposes liability on anyone who:

(A) knowingly presents, or causes to be presented, a false or fraudulent claim for payment or approval;

(B) knowingly makes, uses, or causes to be made or used, a false record or statement material to a false or fraudulent claim;

(C) conspires to commit a violation of subparagraph (A), (B), (D), (E), (F), or (G);

(D) has possession, custody, or control of property or money used, or to be used, by the Government and knowingly delivers, or causes to be delivered, less than all of that money or property;

(E) is authorized to make or deliver a document certifying receipt of property used, or to be used, by the Government and, intending to defraud the Government, makes or delivers the receipt without completely knowing that the information on the receipt is true;

(F) knowingly buys, or receives as a pledge of an obligation or debt, public property from an officer or employee of the Government, or a member of the Armed Forces, who lawfully may not sell or pledge property; or

(G) knowingly makes, uses, or causes to be made or used, a false record or statement material to an obligation to pay or transmit money or property to the Government, or knowingly conceals or knowingly and improperly avoids or decreases an obligation to pay or transmit money or property to the Government.[2]

A person found to have violated this statute is liable for a civil penalty for each claim of not less than $5,500 and not more than $11,000, plus three times the amount of damages sustained by the federal government (i.e., treble damages).[3] Enforcement of the FCA is strengthened by its powerful qui

---

[2] 31 U.S.C. § 3729(a)(1).

[3] *Id.* Although the statute provides that a civil penalty can be imposed of not less than $5,000 and not more than $11,000 per violation, in 1999 these amounts were increased by a Department of Justice rule implementing the Debt Collection Improvement Act of 1996, which permits periodic adjustment of penalties imposed under federal law to account for inflation. 64 Fed. Reg. 47,099 (Aug. 30, 1999).

## False Claims: Civil and Criminal Enforcement

tam provisions, which permits private whistleblowers to sue on behalf of the government and retain fifteen to 30% of the proceeds of the suit.[4]

Under the FCA, liability may be imposed upon an individual or entity based upon a finding of a "preponderance of the evidence," versus the criminal burden of proof of "beyond a reasonable doubt" that a defendant "knowingly" violated the statute. The FCA defines the terms "knowing" and "knowingly" to mean that a person: "(1) has actual knowledge of the information; (2) acts in deliberate ignorance of the truth or falsity of the information; or (3) acts in reckless disregard of the truth or falsity of the information;" and provides that "no proof of specific intent to defraud is required."[5]

Under the FCA, civil actions must be brought within six years after the date of the violation or within three years after the date when material facts are known or should have been known by the government, but in no event more than 10 years after the date on which the violation was committed.[6]

As a practical matter, few healthcare organizations litigate violations of the FCA. Many healthcare organizations believe they are not in a position to contest an FCA action by engaging in protracted litigation for a variety of reasons including, but not limited to: the actual cost of litigation; the fact that the government can exclude the entity from participation in the Medicare and Medicaid programs pending the court's determination; and, for publicly traded companies or companies entering into a corporate transaction (e.g., a merger or obtaining third-party financing), the "black cloud" that an FCA case can bring to the organization. Significantly, a corporation's cooperation and voluntary disclosure are among the factors considered by DOJ in prosecuting FCA cases and, therefore, it is often in a corporation's best interest not to litigate for this reason.[7]

There have been a number of recent amendments that have expanded the scope of the government's ability to prosecute false claims. In 2009, Congress enacted the Fraud Enforcement and Recovery Act of 2009 (FERA).[8] Although the primary purpose of FERA was to address fraudulent activity associated with the financial industry,[9] FERA expanded the application of

---

[4] 31 U.S.C. § 3730(d).
[5] 31 U.S.C. § 3729(b).
[6] 31 U.S.C. § 3731(b).
[7] Memorandum from Larry D. Thompson, Deputy Attorney General of the United States, to Heads of Department Components & United States Attorneys, Principles of Federal Prosecution of Business Organizations (Jan. 20, 2003), *available online at* http://www.justice.gov/dag/cftf/corporate_guidelines.htm.
[8] PUB. L. NO. 111-21, § 4, 123 Stat. 1617, 1621-25 (codified as amended at 31 U.S.C. §§ 3729-3733 (2009)).
[9] *See* S. REP. NO. 111-10, at 3-4 (2009) ("This bipartisan legislation will reinvigorate our Nation's capacity to investigate and prosecute the kinds of financial frauds that have so severely undermined our financial markets and hurt so many hard working people in these difficult economic times.... The [FCA] must be corrected and clarified in order to protect from fraud the Federal assistance and relief funds expended in response to our current economic crisis.").

the False Claims Act (FCA), which has significantly impacted the healthcare industry. For example, FERA amended the liability provisions of the FCA by broadening the scope of FCA violations as well as the types of claims that can constitute a FCA violation. These amendments that were specifically intended to override and reverse the Supreme Court's decision in *Allison Engine Co. v. U.S. ex rel. Sanders*[10] and the decision of the United States Court of Appeals for the D.C. Circuit in *U.S. ex rel. Totten v. Bombardier Corp.*[11] FERA also expanded the reverse false claims provision of the FCA by covering acts in which a person "has possession, custody, or control of property or money used, or to be used, by the Government and *knowingly delivers or causes to be delivered, less than all of that money or property*" as well as "*knowingly conceals or knowingly and improperly avoids or decreases an obligation to pay or transmit money or property to the government.*"[12] Congress also added a definition of the term "obligation" as being "an established duty, whether or not fixed arising from an express or implied contractual, grantor-grantee, licensor-licensee, relationship, from a fee-based or similar relationship, from statute or regulation, or from the retention of any overpayment."[13]

In addition to the changes to the FCA by FERA, in March of 2010, the Patient Protection and Affordable Care Act and the Healthcare and Education Reconciliation Act (collectively "the Health Reform Law")[14] became law, which had a significant impact on the scope and reach of the FCA. The Health Reform Law amended several false claims provisions contained within the FCA, as well as other statutes. These amendments include limiting the public disclosure bar,[15] subjecting payments made through the state-based Exchanges to the FCA,[16] imposing a time limit of 60 days for overpayment retention,[17] and explicitly providing that a claim submitted to the government in violation of the Anti-Kickback Statute is a false claim, subject to FCA liability.[18] These concepts are more fully discussed below.

---

[10] 553 U.S. 662, 128 S. Ct. 2123 (2008) (holding that liability may only be imposed under section 3729(a)(2) of the FCA when the Government can prove that "a defendant intended that the government itself pay the claim.").

[11] 380 F.3d 488 (D.C. Cir. 2004), *cert denied*, 544 U.S. 1032 (2005) (holding that FCA liability under 3729(a)(1) requires the presentment of a false or fraudulent claim for payment directly to the government).

[12] 31 U.S.C. § 3729(a)(1)(D) and (G) (2009) (emphasis added).

[13] 31 U.S.C. § 3729(b)(3).

[14] Patient Protection and Affordable Care Act, Pub. L. No. 111-148 & 111-158. 124 Stat. 119 (2010) and Healthcare and Education Reconciliation Act 111-152. 124 Stat. 1029 (2010).

[15] Patient Protection and Affordable Care Act § 10104(j)(2); 31 U.S.C. § 3730(e)(4)(A).

[16] Patient Protection and Affordable Care Act § 10104(j)(2)§ 1313(a)(6).

[17] Patient Protection and Affordable Care Act § 10104(j)(2) § 6402(d)(2).

[18] Patient Protection and Affordable Care Act § 6402(g); 42 U.S.C. § 1320(a)-7b(g)).

**False Claims: Civil and Criminal Enforcement**

## § 4-2(a) Key FCA Considerations for Healthcare Entities

Assessing potential liability under the FCA involves areas of interpretation unique to healthcare entities that should be considered whenever allegations of healthcare fraud arise. The proceeding sections define key concepts and terms relevant to the FCA.

### § 4-2(a)(1) Who Is a "Person"?

While the FCA prohibits a "person" from presenting (or causing to be presented) a false claim to the government, the FCA does not define who (or what) constitutes a "person." Therefore, a number of courts have considered whether or not certain healthcare entities may be considered a "person" for purposes of the FCA prohibition. In the past, some courts held that the term "person" encompasses states, municipalities, corporations, and others, thereby leaving state and municipal operated healthcare providers vulnerable to FCA actions.[19] In 2000, however, the Supreme Court held that in suits initiated by private persons, the FCA does not impose liability upon a state or a state agency.[20] The Court's decision was based primarily on the presumption that, at least in circumstances in which a private plaintiff brings suit, the term "person" does not include sovereign entities, as the monetary damages under the statute are punitive in nature and, therefore, inconsistent with the presumption against imposing punitive damages against a governmental entity.[21] Nevertheless, in 2003, the Supreme Court held in *Cook County v. United States ex rel. Chandler*,[22] that a local government, such as a county, is a potentially liable "person" subject to a qui tam action brought under the FCA by a private party.

### § 4-2(a)(2) What Is "Knowingly"?

Prior to the 1986 amendments, courts were split as to the scienter requirement under the FCA. Some courts construed the FCA as requiring proof of specific intent, noting that the statute is derived from a criminal statute or

---

[19] *See, e.g,* United States v. Regents of University of Minnesota, 154 F.3d 870 (8th Cir. 1998); United States *ex rel.* Long v. SCS Bus. & Tech. Inst., 999 F. Supp. 78 (D.D.C. 1998). An additional question presented to the Court (but left unresolved) was whether the qui tam provisions of the False Claims Act are unconstitutional as an improper delegation of Executive Branch powers to a private citizen.

[20] Vermont Agency of Natural Resources v. United States *ex rel.* Stevens, 120 S.Ct. 1828 (2000). The Supreme Court also addressed the question of whether relators who bring suit under the qui tam provisions of the False Claims Act have standing based upon injury to the government. This portion of the decision is discussed in the section that addresses qui tam actions.

[21] *Id.* at 1,869.

[22] Cook County v. United States *ex rel.* Chandler, 538 U.S. 119 (2003).

emphasizing the penal nature of the statute. Other courts found no specific intent was required, noting the civil and remedial nature of the statute. In 1986, Congress amended the FCA to provide that no proof of specific intent to defraud is required in order to show a violation of the statute. As part of the debate surrounding these amendments, the legislative history of the statute provides as follows:

> [a]ttempts to reach what has become the "ostrich" type situation where an individual has "buried his head in the sand" and failed to make simple inquiries which would alert him that false claims are being submitted. While the Committee intends that at least some inquiry be made, the inquiry need only be "reasonable and prudent under the circumstances," which clearly recognizes a limited duty to inquire as opposed to a burdensome obligation.[23]

According to the 1986 amendments, sufficient intent is present when a defendant knows the information submitted to be false or acts in deliberate ignorance of, or reckless disregard for, the truth or falsity. Consequently, courts generally are in agreement that liability under the FCA cannot be imposed when a person merely acts "negligently."[24] However, greater discussion has occurred over further defining the meaning of "deliberate ignorance" and "reckless disregard."[25] Although the legislative history stated above requires a reasonable inquiry under the circumstances, some courts have concluded that the FCA requires a duty of reasonable inquiry into the truth of the claim the "person" is presenting for payment.[26]

---

[23] S. Rep. No. 99-345, U.S.S.C.A.N., 5266, 5285-5286.

[24] *See, e.g.*, Minnesota Ass'n of Nurse Anesthetists v. Allina Health Sys. Corp., 276 F.3d 1032, 1053 (8th Cir. 2002) ("it is important to remember that the standard for liability is knowing, not negligent, presentation of a false claim"); United States *ex rel.* Phillips v. Pediatric Servs. of Am., Inc., 142 F. Supp. 2d 717 (W.D.N.C. 2001) (holding that defendants' imperfectly completed certificates of medical necessity for home oxygen therapy were not false claims, but merely "the types of mistakes commonly encountered in the course of business"); United States *ex rel.* Mathews v. HealthSouth Corp., 140 F. Supp. 2d 706 (W.D. La. 2001) (dismissing relator's claims, holding that at worst, relator alleged that defendant negligently failed to monitor its compliance with applicable Medicare regulations); United States *ex rel.* Swafford v. Borgess Medical Center, 98 F. Supp. 2d 822 (W.D. Mich. 2000) (where defendants showed concern about proper interpretation of regulations "and investigated the question of what procedures were required to submit a proper claim for reimbursement," plaintiff failed to prove defendants acted with reckless disregard or deliberate ignorance); *see also* Luckey v. Baxter Healthcare Corp., 2 F. Supp. 2d 1034 (N.D. Ill. 1998), *aff'd* 183 F.3d 730 (7th Cir. 1999); Hindo v. University of Health Sciences/The Chicago Med. Sch., 65 F.3d 608 (7th Cir. 1995); United States *ex rel.* Hochman v. Nackman, 145 F.3d 1069 (9th Cir. 1998).

[25] *See, e.g.,* United States v. Krizek, 111 F.3d 934 (D.C. Cir. 1997), *on remand at* 7 F. Supp. 2d 56 (D.D.C. 1998), and *remanded by* 192 F.3d 1024 (D.C. Cir. 1999).

[26] *See* United States v. Lorenzo, 768 F. Supp. 1127 (E.D. Pa 1991); United States v. Entin, 750 F. Supp. 512 (S.D. Fla. 1990).

### False Claims: Civil and Criminal Enforcement

### § 4-2(a)(2)(i)   Deliberate Ignorance

The concept of deliberate ignorance, also described as willful blindness, has been written into the FCA through case law. Individuals and entities should not expect to avail themselves of a defense predicated on pure ignorance arising from a lack of knowledge of a rule, regulation or other authority. In *United States v. Lorenzo* a provider confronted numerous facts that should have alerted him that his Medicare claim forms were false. In *Lorenzo*, a dentist claimed he relied upon information learned at a seminar and from a carrier representative when he billed Medicare for oral cancer examinations provided to nursing home residents. The court found that applicable statutes and regulations made it clear that the dentist could not bill for the services and that he received and ignored information that should have put him on notice that his claims were improper. First, several employee dentists and the medical director of a group of nursing homes challenged his right to bill Medicare for the services. Second, one carrier had routinely denied the claims that he had submitted.[27]

Similarly, in *United States v. Cabrera-Diaz*, a district court concluded that an anesthesiologist and his billing secretary were liable under the FCA because an audit conducted by the fiscal agent demonstrated most of their sampled claims "had been overstated, falsely reported, unsupported or undocumented."[28] The court concluded that after the audit the parties had either actual knowledge of the falsity of their claims or hid behind a "shield of self-imposed ignorance."[29]

In a 2010 case, the Ninth Circuit upheld a jury verdict against a physician for submitting over 3,500 false claims to Medicare.[30] In this case, the court found substantial evidence supporting the jury verdict because the defendant physician should have known the Medicare billing regulations sufficiently well to inform his practices.[31] The court stated that "Medicare providers have a duty to familiarize themselves with billing requirements."[32] The jury relied on circumstantial evidence, including the fact that Medicare sent materials to the defendant explaining the requirements for billing consultations and the correct usage of codes for various procedures. Therefore, the court held that the defendant acted either with actual knowledge or in deliberate ignorance or with reckless disregard of the falsity of the claims that were submitted.[33]

Conversely, many courts have not imposed FCA liability when a person received mixed signals concerning whether or not Medicare payment

---

[27] United States v. Lorenzo, 768 F. Supp. 1127 (E.D. Pa 1991).
[28] United States v. Cabrera-Diaz, 106 F. Supp. 2d 234, 238 (D.P.R. 2000).
[29] *Id.*
[30] U.S. v Chen, 402 Fed. Appx. 185 (9th Cir. 2010).
[31] *Id.* at 187.
[32] *Id.*
[33] *Id.* at 188.

should be made. For example, in *Covington v. Sisters of the Third Order of St. Dominic*,[34] the court refused to grant summary judgment to the relators, even though they had presented evidence that hospital personnel knew they were receiving overpayments from its fiscal intermediary. The court's ruling was based on the fact that the hospital had undertaken some steps, however insufficient they were, to determine whether an overpayment existed and to notify the intermediary of the error. Similarly, courts have refused to impose FCA liability when a provider had some basis to believe it was entitled to receive payment[35] and where a defendant made limited inquiries of government personnel to learn of the government's interpretation of the rules governing payment.[36] Also, at least one circuit has held that a person does not act in deliberate ignorance merely by failing to ask the government for its opinion or seeking advice from counsel when the defendant has no basis to suspect wrongdoing and the practice is standard in the industry.[37]

### § 4-2(a)(2)(ii)   Reckless Disregard

Sometimes providers will not receive signals that claims are unjustified but will exhibit indifference as to the truthfulness of the claims. This "reckless disregard" to the truth can lead to liability under the FCA.[38] In *United States v. Krizek*, a district court found that a psychiatrist had submitted claims recklessly when his billing staff used rough approximations and submitted claims without supervision.[39] These rough approximations led to occasions in which the psychiatrist's office billed for more than 20 hours of patient visits in a twenty-four hour period. In this case, the defendant argued that although he may have acted "negligently" in delegating billing responsibilities to others, he had not violated the FCA. The court, however, imposed liability by stating that the psychiatrist's failure to "supervis[e] [his] agents in their submission of claims on his behalf" constituted "reckless disregard as to the truth or falsity of the submissions."[40]

Also, in *United States v. Mackby*, the Ninth Circuit held a non-physician owner of a physical therapy clinic liable under the FCA for using the provider identification number of a physician that did not work at the clinic.[41] Although

---

[34] Covington v. Sisters of the Third Order of St. Dominic, 61 F.3d 909 (unpublished), 1995 U.S. App. LEXIS 20370 (9th Cir. July 13, 1995).
[35] United States v. Am. Enters., Inc., MEDICARE & MEDICAID GUIDE (CCH) § 44,580 (N.D. Ga. April 23, 1996).
[36] United States *ex rel.* Swafford v. Borgess Med. Ctr., 98 F. Supp. 2d 822 (W.D. Mich. 2000).
[37] United States *ex rel.* Quirk v. Madonna Towers, Inc., 278 F.3d 765 (8th Cir. 2002).
[38] *See Chen*, 402 Fed. Appx. 185.
[39] United States v. Krizek, 859 F. Supp. 5 (D.D.C. 1994), *aff'd in part, rev'd in part*, 111 F.2d 934 (D.C. Cir. 1997).
[40] *Id.*
[41] United States v. Mackby, 261 F.3d 821 (9th Cir. 2001), 339 F.3d 1013 (9th Cir. 2003), *writ of cert. denied* 541 U.S. 936 (2004).

## False Claims: Civil and Criminal Enforcement

the defendant claimed he had twice requested that his office manager contact Medicare and have the clinic's billing number changed, the court concluded that given his managerial role in the clinic and the percentage of Medicare beneficiaries who received services there, his failure to ensure compliance was reckless disregard for the truth or falsity of the claims.

### § 4-2(a)(3)  What Is a "Claim"?

Section 3729(b)(2) of the FCA defines a "claim" as:

any request or demand, whether under a contract or otherwise, for money or property and whether or not the United States has title to the money or property, that is presented to an officer, employee, or agent of the United States; or is made to a contractor, grantee, or other recipient, if the money or property is to be spent or used on the Government's behalf or to advance a Government program or interest, and if the United States Government provides or has provided any portion of the money or property requested or demanded; or will reimburse such contractor, grantee, or other recipient for any portion of the money or property which is requested or demanded; and does not include requests or demands for money or property that the Government has paid to an individual as compensation for Federal employment or as an income subsidy with no restrictions on that individual's use of the money or property.[42]

Based on the language of the FCA and case law interpreting the application of the FCA, the definition of "claim" also extends to instances in which the government pays open-ended grants to states, to reports and statements submitted to the government to reduce one's obligation to make payment to the government, and to claims submitted by downstream government contractors.

Even though Medicare claims are submitted to Medicare Administrative Contractors (MACs) that contract with CMS to process Medicare claims, rather than being submitted directly to the federal government, the term "claim" under the FCA applies. Therefore, the FCA has been uniformly held to apply to false federal healthcare program claims.[43]

In *United States v. Krizek*, the U.S. Court of Appeals for the District of Columbia Circuit rejected the prosecution's argument that each item or service reported by a single CPT code on a HCFA (now CMS) 1500 Form constituted a separate claim for purposes of computing penalties under the

---

[42] 31 U.S.C. § 3729(b)(2).
[43] *See* United States v. Cabrera-Diaz, 106 F. Supp. 2d 234 (D.P.R. 2000).

FCA. Instead, the court held that each HCFA 1500 Form was a "claim" because it represented a single request or demand for payment.[44]

In 2008, the Supreme Court of the United States rendered a unanimous decision in *Allison Engine Co. v. United States ex rel. Sanders* strictly construing the language of the FCA by holding that mere proof that a false or fraudulent claim was paid using government funds is not sufficient to establish liability under the FCA.[45] Instead, the Court held that the government or a relator must show that a defendant intended for the government to pay the claim, or that the government actually paid the specific claim at issue itself. Because healthcare claims are often paid by government contractors or in the case of Medicare Part C and D programs entities who receive funds from the government, who are not officers or employees of the United States he *Allison Engine* case had significant ramifications for the government's ability to prosecute under the FCA. The Allison Engine holding was, however, short lived.

As described above, Congress expressly overruled Allison Engine when it passed FERA. Congress stated that it intended "to clarify and correct [the Court's] erroneous interpretations of the law," which was "contrary to Congress's original intent in passing the [FCA] ...."[46] The legislation eliminated the judicially established requirement that the government need be the intended or actual payer of the specific claim. The amendments expressly provide that "any request or demand ... for money or property" is a claim independent of "whether or not the United States has title to the money or property" if the request or demand is "presented to an officer, employee, or agent of the United States."[47] Congress further expanded the definition of a claim to requests or demands made to non-Federal entities such as "a contractor, grantee, or other recipient, *if the money or property is to be spent or used on the Government's behalf or to advance a Government program or interest*," so long as Federal funds are involved.[48] Significantly, the current FCA does not just attach to claims made directly to the government, it attaches to claims made to downstream entities who are contractors or agents of the government.

### § 4-2(a)(4)   What Is "Causing" a Claim to Be Submitted?

The FCA prohibition extends not only to the submission of a claim to the federal government, but also, more broadly, to those who "cause" a claim to

---

[44] United States v. Krizek, 859 F. Supp. 5 (D.D.C. 1994), *aff'd in part, rev'd in part*, 111 F.3d 934 (D.C. Cir. 1997). *See also* Cantrell v. New York Univ., 326 F. Supp. 2d 468 (S.D.N.Y. 2004).
[45] Allison Engine Co. v. United States *ex rel.* Sanders, No. 07-214, 2008 U.S. LEXIS 4704, (S. Ct. June 9, 2008).
[46] S. Rep. No. 111-10, at 10.
[47] 31 U.S.C. § 3729(b)(2)(A) (emphasis added).
[48] *Id.*

## False Claims: Civil and Criminal Enforcement

be submitted. This type of liability occurs when the person responsible for the falsity is not the one who submits the claim, but instead directs others (who may or may not know of the falsity) to submit the claim on their behalf. For some time, these types of claims arose mostly out of the employer/employee or principal/agent context, where the guilty parties used their authority to direct others to submit false claims.[49] However, this type of liability also applies to individuals and entities offering billing advice to healthcare providers.[50] In these cases, the billing consultants and advisors do not submit the claims to the government, but their clients rely on their advice when submitting their own claims. Although billing consultants and advisors do provide legitimate advice on how to comply with the numerous complex rules surrounding federal healthcare program reimbursement, there are a few cases in which they have provided advice to fraudulently inflate their clients' reimbursement from the government. These fraudulent activities led to a Special Advisory Bulletin on the Practices of Billing Consultants released by the OIG in 2001.[51]

### § 4-2(a)(5)    What Is "False" or "Fraudulent"?

The FCA imposes liability if a claim is either "false" or "fraudulent." Determining whether a claim is false is considerably less complicated than determining whether a claim is fraudulent. For example, a claim can be entirely accurate, and therefore not false, but still be submitted fraudulently.

In the healthcare industry, a claim may be considered "false" if any of the items or services claimed on the billing form were not provided as claimed. In other words, each answer included by a supplier on claims to federal healthcare programs can potentially give rise to a false claim if the services were not rendered exactly as claimed (e.g., the date of service or the CPT code is incorrect). Similarly, Congress imposed a requirement that the services provided under Medicare Parts A and B are "reasonable and necessary for the diagnosis or treatment of illness or injury or to improve the functioning of a malformed body member."[52] If those services are unnecessary, the claim is potentially false.

---

[49] *See, e.g.*, United States v. Kensington Hosp., 760 F. Supp. 1120 (E.D. Pa. 1991) (involving physicians who were suspended from participating in the Medicaid program who caused a hospital to submit improper bills on their behalf); United States v. Mackby, 261 F.3d 821 (9th Cir. 2001) (involving an owner of a physical therapy clinic who instructed his staff to use his father's physician identification number on bills to federal healthcare programs).

[50] *See, e.g.,* United States v. Metzinger, No. 94-7520 (E.D. Pa. Sept. 17, 1996); United States *ex rel.* Schilling v. KPMG Peat Marwick, No. 98-901-CIV-T-17F (M.D. Fla. 1998), *settlement filed* (Oct. 23, 2001); United States v. Ernst & Young LLP, No. 04-cv-00041 (E.D. Pa *settlement announced* July 20, 2004).

[51] OIG Special Advisory Bulletin, Practices of Billing Consultants, *available online at* http://www.oig.hhs.gov/fraud/docs/alertsandbulletins/consultants.pdf. For further discussion, *see* § 4-6(i); "Billing Companies and Third-Party Consultants."

[52] 42 U.S.C. § 1395y(a)(1)(A).

Hospital administrators and chief financial officers also open themselves up to FCA liability when they sign cost reports certifying that, to the best of their knowledge and belief, the reports are "true, correct, complete and prepared from the books and records of the provider in accordance with applicable instructions, except as noted" and that they are "familiar with the laws and regulations regarding the provision of healthcare services, and that the services identified in [the] cost report were provided in compliance with such laws and regulations."[53] Accordingly incorrect information on costs reports can be considered "false" under the FCA.

Sometimes, the government contends that a claim is *fraudulent* even though the services were provided as claimed and the certification is accurate. For example, FCA liability potentially can exist when a provider receives an inflated payment that the provider knows is incorrect yet still uses the funds, and when a person submits false information to the government to get a government contract or obtain grant funds. [54] In some cases, the government or qui tam relator has sought to extend FCA liability to apply to each claim an entity submits when that entity has violated some other unrelated regulation. For further discussion, *see* § 4-4(f), *infra*, where if a claim is deemed fraudulent, the government also can pursue criminal charges in addition to civil sanctions under the FCA.

## § 4-2(a)(5)(i)  Retention of Overpayments and Reverse False Claims

The FCA has historically contained a "reverse false claims" provision that addresses false statements made by an individual or entity who already has received funds or material from the government in order to avoid or decrease a liability owed to the government.[55] Prior to FERA, in order to assert this type of claim, it must be found that the liability to the government consisted of a current, specific, legal obligation to pay the government that existed at the time that the false record or statement was made, and that the false record or statement must be material to the attempt to conceal, avoid, or decrease an obligation to the United States.[56]

---

[53] *See* 42 C.F.R. § 413.24(f)(4)(iv) (2005).
[54] *See* Covington v. Sisters of the Third Order of St. Dominic, 1995 U.S. App. LEXIS 20370 (9th Cir. 1995); United States v. American Health Enters., Inc., 1996 U.S. Dist. LEXIS 7894 (D. Ga. 1996).
[55] 31 U.S.C. § 3729(a)(7).
[56] *See e.g.*, United States v. TDC Management Corp., 24 F.3d 292, 298 (D.C. Cir. 1994); United States v. Q Int'l Courier, Inc., 131 F.3d 770 (8th Cir. 1997); United States *ex rel.* Lamers v. City of Green Bay, 998 F. Supp. 971 (E.D. Wis. 1998), *aff'd* 168 F.3d 1013 (7th Cir. 1999); United States *ex rel.* A+ Homecare, Inc. v. Medshares Management Group, et al., No. 97-01059 (6th Cir. 2005) (slip op. at 11-13).

## False Claims: Civil and Criminal Enforcement

With the enactment of FERA, the scope of liability under the reverse false claims provision was increased.[57] The major impact of FERA on the scope of reverse false claims was to subject the mere failure to refund an overpayment to the government to FCA liability; that is, there is no longer a requirement for the submission of a false statement or report for an overpayment to fall under the FCA. To accomplish this, Congress amended the FCA liability provision to include "knowingly and improperly avoids or decreases an obligation to pay or transmit money or property to the Government."[58] The FCA amendment provisions define "obligation" as a duty arising from a contract, grant, or license as well as from a "fee-based or similar relationship... statute or regulation, or ... the retention of any overpayment."[59] Significantly Health Reform amended the Social Security Act and now requires that an overpayment be reported or returned by the later of 60 days after the date the overpayment was identified or the date any corresponding cost report is due to avoid penalties.[60] The new limited time frame for which entities have to return overpayments is a very significant development. Routine audits that generate claims billed in error now must be returned within 60 days or potentially convert to false claims under the meaning in the FCA.

Health Reform defines an "overpayment" as "any fund that a person receives or retains under title XVII or XIX to which the person, after applicable reconciliation, is not entitled..."[61] More recently, in CMS' proposed rule regarding overpayments, CMS provided examples of what constitutes an overpayment: Medicare payments for non-covered services; Medicare payments in excess of the allowable amount for an identified covered service; errors and non-reimbursable expenditures in cost reports; duplicate payments; and receipt of Medicare payment when another payor had the primary responsibility for payment.[62] Significantly, CMS also proposed that overpayments must be report and returned if a person (to include a company) identifies overpayments with 10 years of the date it was received consistent with the 10 year outer limit of the FCA.[63]

### § 4-2(a)(6)   What Is "Material"?

The 2009 amendments to the FCA (i.e., FERA) codify a judicially established element of materiality with respect to the claim. Specifically, Congress

---

[57] Fraud Enforcement and Recovery Act of 2009 (FERA), Pub. L. No. 111-21 § 4(a), 123 Stat. 1617.
[58] *Id. See also* 31 U.S.C. § 3729(a)(1)(G).
[59] *Id. See also* 31 U.S.C. § 3729(b)(3).
[60] *See* 42 U.S.C. § 1320a-7k(d) *as amended by* the Patient Protection and Affordable Care Act § 10104(j)(2).
[61] Patient Protection and Affordable Care Act § 6402.
[62] 77 Fed. Reg. 9,179 (Feb. 16, 2012).
[63] 77 Fed. Reg. 9,179, 9,184 (Feb. 16, 2012).

added the term "material" to a number of sections in the FCA. For example, the statute now prohibits "knowingly mak[ing], us[ing], or caus[ing] to be made or used, a false record or statement *material* to a false or fraudulent claim" and ""knowingly mak[ing], us[ing], or caus[ing] to be made or used, a false record or statement *material* to an obligation to pay or transmit money or property to the Government...."[64] The FCA defines the term "material" when it results in "a natural tendency to influence, or be capable of influencing, the payment or receipt of money or property."[65] Thus, this element does not require that the Government was actually influenced by the false or fraudulent claim. Instead, this broad definition merely requires a *tendency* to influence payment, thereby requiring additional interpretation and analysis to determine whether the materiality element has been established.

## § 4-2(b)  Anti-Kickback Violations as False Claims

As described more fully in Chapter 2, the Anti-Kickback Statute does not itself provide for a private right of action. However, the Health Reform Law added a new subsection 1320a-7b(g) that clarifies that any claim that includes items of services listed in violation of section 1320a-7b shall be considered to be a false or fraudulent claim under 31 U.S.C. § 3729-33.[66] As a consequence, anti-kickback claims are now claims under the FCA, which does include a private right of action by qui tam relators. Prior to the Health Reform Law, for almost two decades, the government and qui tam relators attempted to "bootstrap" anti-kickback claims to the FCA to obtain civil penalties. This bootstrapping rested upon the theory that, when a provider submitted a claim to a federal healthcare program, the claim included an implicit certification that the provider was in compliance with the Medicare Act, which required compliance with other laws, including the Anti-Kickback Statute.

For instance, in *Roy v. Anthony*,[67] a former employee of several physicians in the Midwest brought a whistleblower suit for false claims against the physicians alleging that they referred to diagnostic centers in violation of the Anti-Kickback Statute. The defendants settled the case in March 1995 for more than $1.5 million after a federal district court judge permitted the suit to go forward, ruling that the plaintiff could prove that the charged Medicare claims in question were false because they were submitted in violation of the applicable federal anti-kickback and physician self-referral laws.

In *Pogue v. American Healthcorp*, a federal district court judge originally dismissed a qui tam action and ruled that Medicare claims are not necessarily false even if they are submitted in violation of the anti-kickback

---

[64] 31 U.S.C. § 3729(a)(1)(B) and (G) (emphasis added).
[65] *Id.* § 3729(b)(4).
[66] Social Security Act § 1128B(g); 42 U.S.C. § 1320a-7b(g).
[67] *See* United States *ex rel.* Roy v. Anthony, No. C-1-93-0559 (S.D. Ohio 1994).

## False Claims: Civil and Criminal Enforcement

and self-referral statutes. The court later reversed its earlier ruling and held that the plaintiff may bring a claim under the FCA, but must show that the defendants engaged in fraudulent conduct with the purpose of inducing payment from the government.[68] In a similar case, *United States ex rel. Pogue v. Diabetes Treatment Centers of America, Inc.*, the defendant was accused of providing illegal kickbacks to physicians in return for patient referrals in violation of both the Stark Law and the Anti-Kickback Statute. Moreover, even though the claims to Medicare were for medically necessary services, the relator claimed that liability under the FCA was a result of an "implied certification" in that the claims were presumed to comply with all statutes, rules, and regulations governing the Medicare program when the claims were submitted. The district court agreed with the theory, and rejected the defendant's motion to dismiss.[69]

Not all courts, however, allowed a kickback allegation to be bootstrapped into a FCA violation. For example, the Fifth Circuit in 1997 in *United States ex rel. Thompson v. Columbia/HCA Healthcare* held that claims for services rendered in violation of a statute do not necessarily constitute false claims within the meaning of the FCA.[70]

Howe ver, with the modification to the Social Security Act as part of the Health Reform Law, there is no longer a question that a violation of the Anti-Kickback Statute is, in fact, actionable under the FCA.

### § 4-2(c)  FCA Damages

As stated above, a person or entity who violates the FCA is liable for a civil penalty of not less than $5,500 (and not more than $11,000), plus three

---

[68] United States *ex rel.* Pogue v. American Healthcorp., Inc., 1995 WL 626514 (M.D. Tenn. Sept. 14, 1995); United States *ex rel.* Pogue v. American Healthcorp., Inc., 914 F. Supp. 1507 (1996).
[69] United States *ex rel.* Pogue v. Diabetes Treatment Centers of America, Inc., 238 F. Supp. 2d 258 (D.D.C. 2002). *See also* United States *ex rel.* Franklin v. Parke-Davis, 2003 U.S. Dist. LEXIS 15754 (Massachusetts District Court agreed with the government's argument that Parke-Davis's alleged violation of the Medicaid anti-kickback provision caused false claims); United States *ex rel.* Augustine v. Century Health Servs., Inc., 289 F.3d 409 (6th Cir. 2002) (court held liability under the FCA can attach if an entity violates its continuing duty to comply with the regulations on which payment is conditioned).
[70] United States *ex rel.* Thompson v. Columbia/HCA Healthcare, 125 F.3d 899 (5th Cir. 1997) holding that claims for services rendered in violation of a statute do not necessarily constitute false claims within the meaning of the FCA. According to the court, however, false certifications of statutory or regulatory compliance are violations of the FCA *only* when such certifications are a prerequisite for obtaining a government benefit.; *See also* United States v. Rogan, 459 F. Supp. 2d 692, 707–709 (N.D. Ill. 2006) holding that violations of the Anti-Kickback Statute were material to claim submission and therefore actionable under the FCA; United States *ex rel.* Kosenske v. Carlisle HMA, Inc., No. 07-4616, slip op. (3d Cir. Jan. 21, 2009) holding that "[f]alsely certifying compliance with the Stark or Anti-Kickback Acts in connection with a claim submitted to a federally funded insurance program is actionable under the FCA."

times the amount of damages that the government sustains.[71] These substantial penalties explain why the FCA is used so often by the government in prosecuting healthcare fraud cases. A majority of courts have ruled that proof of damages is not essential in establishing FCA liability. However, courts require the prosecution to prove that the submission of a claim or statement is capable of causing harm to the federal government.[72]

As a practical matter, the amount of damages the government sustains is usually the difference between the amount it paid on the claim and the amount it would have paid had the claim not been false. However, there are some areas where calculating damages presents more of a problem. For example, damages associated with defective or nonconforming goods should be "the difference between the market value of the [products the government] received and retained and the market value that the [products] would have had if they had been of the specified quality."[73] Amounts can also be calculated using the "benefit of the bargain" rule or the "out of pocket" rule of damages.[74] Similarly, in cases where the FCA claim is related to a violation of the Anti-Kickback Statute or other regulation, the government has presented a variety of theories of damages.[75] In practice, most healthcare related fraud or false claim cases are resolved by settlement. Consequently, court awarded FCA damages are somewhat rare. During settlement discussions, the government often determines the amount of injury and demands a multiple of two to three times the actual damages. The particular multiple demanded often depends of a number of factors such as the considerations in the Thompson memo, the length and scope of the wrongdoing, corrective action, litigation risk to the government, and whether the false claim resulted from merely reckless as opposed to intentional behavior.

### § 4-2(d)  Qui tam Relators

One of the most significant features of the FCA is the qui tam or whistleblower provisions of the statute. The FCA authorizes qui tam actions to be brought on behalf of the federal government by a private party having direct knowledge of the fraud.[76] These provisions have had an enormous impact on healthcare investigations and settlements. According to the Department of Justice, as of 2010, the United States has obtained more than $27 billion

---

[71] 31 U.S.C. § 3729.
[72] *See* United States v. McNinch, 356 U.S. 595 (1958).
[73] United States v. Bornstein, 423 U.S. 303, 316 n.13 (1976).
[74] *See* United States v. Ben Grunstein & Sons Co., 137 F. Supp. 197 (D.N.J. 1956).
[75] For a more detailed discussion of calculating damages, *see* Robert Salcido, Esquire: FALSE CLAIMS ACT & THE HEALTHCARE INDUSTRY: COUNSELING AND LITIGATION (2nd ed., AHLA 2011).
[76] 31 U.S.C. § 3730(b)(1). The term "qui tam" is from the latin phrase: "Qui tam pro domino rege quam pro se ipso," which means: "Who sues on behalf of the King as well as for Himself."

## False Claims: Civil and Criminal Enforcement

since the FCA was strengthened in 1986. Of the $3 billion obtained in 2010, $2.3 billion was associated with qui tam suits.[77]

Qui tam plaintiffs are permitted to recover a portion of the amounts recovered in qui tam suit. The qui tam portion of the recovery is dependent upon whether the government has intervened in the action. If the government has intervened, the qui tam plaintiff may recover from 15% up to 25% of the proceeds of the action or settlement, depending on the extent to which the qui tam plaintiff "substantially contributed" to the prosecution.[78] However, this potential recovery is limited to a maximum of 10% if the action is based primarily on disclosures of specific information relating to allegations or transactions in a criminal, civil, or administrative hearing; in a congressional, administrative, or General Accounting Office (GAO) report, hearing, audit, or investigation; or from the news media.[79] In addition, qui tam plaintiffs are entitled to recover reasonable attorneys' fees and costs. If the government does not intervene, the qui tam plaintiff can recover between 25% and 30% of the proceeds of the action or settlement, plus reasonable expenses, attorney's fees, and costs.[80] In either case, the actual recovery is decided by the court in which the action is held and may be the subject of further litigation.[81]

### § 4-2(d)(1)　　How Is a Qui tam Action Initiated?

In a qui tam action, a private party commences the action in federal court by filing the complaint and relevant documentation "under seal" and serving these documents on the DOJ only. Initially, the defendant is not served. The DOJ, by statute, then has at least sixty days to evaluate whether to pursue the action.[82] If good cause can be shown, the government may obtain an extension of time beyond the 60-day period.[83] This may result in a qui tam complaint pending for an extended period of time before the defendant is even aware of the action. During this time period, the government will conduct its own investigation of the fraud alleged in the complaint. The complaint may then remain under seal for another extended period of time while the defendant is apprised of the existence of the case and limited facts to facilitate settlement discussions. During this "seal" period, defendants may be

---

[77] DOJ Press Release, *"Justice Department Recovers $3 Billion in Fraud and False Claims in Fiscal Year 2010"* (Nov. 22, 2005), *available online at* http://www.justice.gov/opa/pr/2010/November/10-civ-1335.html.
[78] 31 U.S.C. § 3730(d)(1).
[79] *Id.*
[80] 31 U.S.C. § 3730(d)(2).
[81] *See* United States *ex rel.* Pedicone v. Mazak Corp., 807 F. Supp. 1350 (S.D. Ohio 1992), *overruled by* United States *ex rel.* Smith v. Lampers, 69 Fed. Appx. 719 (6th Cir. 2003).
[82] 31 U.S.C. § 3730(b)(2).
[83] 31 U.S.C. § 3730(b)(3).

served with formal investigative subpoenas or may be subject to less formal governmental inquiries.

If the government elects to pursue the action (i.e., intervene), the government has the primary responsibility for prosecuting the action and has "wide latitude to assume the conduct of the litigation."[84] Subject to court hearing, the government may dismiss or settle the action, even over the objections of the qui tam plaintiff. The courts also may impose other limitations on qui tam plaintiffs, including number of witnesses, length of testimony, and cross-examination. If the government elects not to pursue the action, it is up to the qui tam plaintiff to pursue the action.[85]

### § 4-2(d)(2)  What Happens if the Government Declines to Intervene?

Critics have argued that when the government declines intervention in the action the qui tam provisions of the FCA violate Article II and the "Take Care" Clause of Article II. Pursuant to Article II of the United States Constitution, the Executive must take care that the laws will be faithfully executed. By granting private citizens with the authority to enforce violations of the FCA, critics maintain that the qui tam provisions violate separation of powers and the Take Care Clause. Such challenges to the qui tam provisions of the FCA were unsuccessful for some time.

In 1999, a panel of the Fifth Circuit affirmed the holding of the Southern District of Texas that the qui tam provisions of the FCA were unconstitutional in those instances in which the government declines intervention.[86] The decision was significant in that it represented the first time that a Circuit Court of Appeals held that a purely relator-driven FCA case was unconstitutional. The decision itself, however, was immediately vacated by the full Fifth Circuit's *sua sponte* grant of rehearing before the court en banc.

The United States Supreme Court in *United States ex rel. Stevens v. Vermont Agency of Natural Resources*[87] did little to clarify the issues surrounding qui tam relators and the Take Care Clause. However, it did review whether a private person has standing to sue under Article III of the United States Constitution to litigate claims of fraud upon the government.[88]

---

[84] United States v. *ex rel.* Stillwell v. Hughes Helicopters, Inc., 714 F. Supp. 1084, 1090 (C.D. Cal. 1989).
[85] 31 U.S.C. § 3730(c).
[86] Riley v. St. Luke's Episcopal Hospital, 196 F.3d 514 (5th Cir. 1999), *rev'd*, 252 F.3d 749 (5th Cir. 2001).
[87] United States *ex rel.* Stevens v. Vermont Agency of Natural Resources, 529 U.S. 765 (2000).
[88] *Id.* According to the *Stevens* Court, a plaintiff must satisfy three requirements in order to establish Article III standing:

> First, he must demonstrate "injury in fact"—a harm that is both "concrete" and "actual or imminent, not conjectural or hypothetical. Second, he must establish

## False Claims: Civil and Criminal Enforcement

Ultimately, the Supreme Court held that private relators do have such standing as the government has partially assigned its rights under the statute to relators. Therefore, the injury to the government is sufficient to confer standing upon the relator. In a footnote to the *Stevens* opinion, Justice Scalia stated that the court was not expressing a view on constitutional challenges based upon the Take Care Clause of Article II.[89]

In *United States ex rel. Eisenstein v. City of New York*, the United States Supreme Court held that while the Federal government may have knowledge of and minimally participate in every FCA lawsuit, the United States is not a "party" to such an action where it fails to intervene.[90] The relators, employees of the City of New York, brought a qui tam action against the City alleging that a fee imposed on non-resident workers withheld tax revenue from the Federal government in violation of the FCA. The Government declined to intervene and the district court subsequently granted the motion to dismiss. The relators filed a notice of appeal fifty-four days later. The Court of Appeals for the Second Circuit dismissed on the grounds that the relators untimely filed. The relators argued on appeal that, although statutory requirements provide for filing within 30 days, this period is extended to 60 days where the Government is a party.[91]

The relators claimed that the Government was a party because 1) it was a real party in interest with the right to share in any damage award; 2) the FCA requires that the action is brought in the name of the Government;[92] and 3) the Government has certain rights during the proceeding. The Supreme Court unanimously affirmed, concluding that the United States is not a party unless it exercises its right to intervene and "[t]o hold otherwise would render the intervention provisions of the FCA superfluous...."[93] The Court looked to the express discretion on the part of the Government to choose to intervene to support its holding. The Court noted that, although the Government may have an interest in the qui tam action and such an action is brought in the name of the Government, neither this interest nor the naming requirement automatically establishes the Government as a party. Finally, the Court noted

---

causation—a "fairly ... trace[able]" connection between the alleged injury in fact and the alleged conduct of the defendant. And third, he must demonstrate redressability—a "substantial likelihood" that the requested relief will remedy the alleged injury in fact. These requirements together constitute the "irreducible constitutional minimum" of standing which is an "essential and unchanging part" of Article III's case-or-controversy requirement, *ibid.*, and a key factor in dividing the power of government between the courts and the two political branches. (internal citations omitted)

[89] Vermont Agency of Natural Resources v. United States *ex rel.* Stevens, 120 S.Ct. 1865 (2000).
[90] United States *ex rel.* Eisenstein v. City of New York, No. 08-660, slip op. at 3 (U.S. June 8, 2009)
[91] *Id.* at 2; *see also* FED. R. APP. P. 4(a)(1)(A)-(B); 28 U.S.C. §§ 2107(a)-(b).
[92] *See* 31 U.S.C. § 3730(b)(1) ("The [qui tam] action shall be brought in the name of the Government.").
[93] *Eisenstein*, No. 08-660, *slip op. at 5*.

that the rights of the Government during a qui tam action in which it declines to intervene are limited and, thus, are not sufficient to elevate the status of the Government to that of a party.

### § 4-2(d)(3)   Who Can Be a Qui tam Relator?

Healthcare organizations that become the targets of qui tam lawsuits often express frustration that the qui tam relator was the cause (or, worse still, the beneficiary) of the alleged fraud. Indeed, the framers of the FCA recognized that wrongdoers might be rewarded under the act, acknowledging the qui tam provisions are based upon the idea of "setting a rogue to catch a rogue."[94] While perpetrators of the fraud may be awarded a lesser recovery for their qui tam efforts, the government still can pursue and obtain recoveries in such cases.

Still, qui tam plaintiffs must satisfy certain elements in order to maintain actions under the FCA. For example, in order to prevent "parasitic" litigation by individuals who learn of fraud through secondary sources, the FCA deprives the courts of jurisdiction over qui tam actions unless the plaintiff is the "original source." This means that a qui tam relator's lawsuit is barred if it is "based upon the public disclosure of allegations or transactions" from various previous proceedings.[95] Publicly disclosed information includes allegations or transactions in criminal, civil, and administrative hearings, as well as those contained "in a congressional, administrative, or [GAO] report, hearing, audit, or investigation, or from the news media."[96]

A highly controversial issue is whether government employees are barred from initiating a qui tam action; however, several court decisions have held that a government employee is not per se barred from serving as a relator.[97] Another controversial debate has been whether compliance officers should have the ability to bring a FCA case against a provider. The underlying theme in this area has been whether compliance officers, by nature of their position, are bound by a professional obligation not to bring such cases. Some have argued that allowing a compliance officer to bring such suits would create a chilling

---

[94] Mortgages, Inc. v. United States Dist. Court, 934 F.2d 209, 213 (9th Cir. 1991), *quoting* Cong. Globe, 37th Cong. 3d Sess. 955-56 (1863) (remarks of Sen. Howard).
[95] 31 U.S.C. § 3730(e)(4)(A).
[96] *Id.*
[97] *See, e.g., United States ex rel.* LeBlanc v. Raytheon Co., Inc., 913 F.2d 17 (1st Cir. 1990) (while a government employee is not barred from bringing a qui tam suit on behalf of the government, a government employee whose job is to uncover fraud cannot qualify as a qui tam relator under the "original source" exception); United States *ex rel.* Fine v. MK-Ferguson Co., 861 F. Supp. 1544 (D.N.M 1994) (DOE Inspector General employees are not barred from being qui tam relators); United States v. CAC-Ramsay, Inc., 744 F. Supp. 1158 (S.D. Fla. 1990) (DHHS Inspector General employee is not barred from bringing qui tam lawsuit); United States *ex rel.* Fine v. Chevron, U.S.A., Inc., 72 F.3d 740 (9th Cir. 1995), *cert. denied*, 116 S. Ct. 1877 (1996) (former DOE Inspector General is barred from being a qui tam relator because he is not "original source" of information).

## False Claims: Civil and Criminal Enforcement

effect on compliance within the company as individuals would be less willing to disclose potential issues within the company. Conversely, some have argued that, unlike in-house counsel, compliance officers do not have a privileged relationship with their employers. While acknowledging that a compliance officer should first try to resolve the issue internally, some argue that the failure of the company to adequately address the issue obligates the compliance officer to report these issues to the government or risk becoming a target themselves.[98]

With respect to lawyers and law firms serving as relators, the Third Circuit has held that a law firm that finds alleged fraud in the course of civil discovery proceedings in an unrelated litigation is *not* an "original source."[99] Rather, the relator must possess "substantive information about the particular fraud, rather than merely background information that enables a putative relator to understand the significance of a publicly disclosed transaction allegation."[100] The court stated that since the information obtained by the law firm came from an employee of the insurance company in the original litigation, the law firm did not have "direct knowledge" of the fraudulent practice and, therefore, could not be an original source under the FCA.[101] In addition, the Ninth Circuit has ruled that a former federal government employee who learns of fraud in the course of his employment, and who is required by the terms of his or her employment to disclose the fraud, is not acting "voluntarily" within the meaning of the Act, and therefore, cannot qualify as an "original source."[102]

### § 4-2(d)(3)(i)    Public Disclosure Bar

Originally, the FCA barred civil actions for false claims *based upon* the public disclosure of allegations or transactions in a criminal, civil, or administrative hearing, in a congressional, administrative, or Government Accounting Office report, hearing, audit, or investigation, or from the news media, unless the action is brought by the Attorney General or the person bringing the action is an original source of the information."[103]

---

[98] *See* United States *ex rel.* Gober v. Univ. of Ala. At Birmingham, No. 01-cv-00977-VEH, (N.D. Ala. *settlement agreement filed* Apr. 14, 2005) (where one of two qui tam relators was a former research compliance officer and alleged that the facility unlawfully billed federal healthcare programs for services that were also billed to sponsors of research trials).

[99] United States *ex rel.* Stinson, Lyons, Gerlin & Bustamante, P.A. v. Prudential, 944 F.2d 1149 (3d Cir. 1991); *see* United States *ex rel.* Kreindler & Kreindler v. United Technologies Corp., 985 F.2d 1148 (2d Cir. 1993) (attorney barred as qui tam relator because information regarding fraud was publicly available in the record of previous litigation, and attorney, as counsel in that prior litigation, was not original source of information regarding fraud); United States *ex rel.* Doe v. John Doe Corp., 960 F.2d 318 (2d Cir. 1992) (attorney barred form bringing qui tam lawsuit even though he was an original source of the information regarding fraud because information was publicly disclosed).

[100] *Stinson*, at 1160.

[101] *Id.*

[102] United States *ex rel..* Fine v. Chevron, U.S.A., Inc., 72 F.3d 740 (9th Cir. 1995).

[103] 31 U.S.C. § 3730(e)(4)(A).

One of the issues surrounding the scope of the public disclosure bar had been whether it includes public disclosures only from federal sources or if it also includes state and/or local sources. This was the central question on appeal in *Graham Cnty. Soil & Water Conservation Dist. v. U.S. ex rel. Wilson*, which was decided by the U.S. Supreme Court in 2010.[104] The Supreme Court decided that there was nothing in the statute that suggested a limitation to only federal and held that state and local sources were encompassed by the public disclosure bar.[105] However, as the Court acknowledged, the Health Reform Law (discussed below) effectively rendered their decision moot in *Graham* by explicitly restricting the bar to disclosures made in federal sources or the news media.[106]

Another issue concerning public disclosure concerned how the prior filing of a similar action can serve as a bar to the subsequent filing. For example, in *United States ex rel. Poteet v. Lenke*, a Federal district court held that the relator was barred from bringing a second qui tam suit alleging nearly identical claims of kickbacks to physicians by a medical device company.[107] The relator, a former manager of travel services for the defendant medical device company, initially brought suit in the Western District of Tennessee against the company and numerous physicians alleging improper kickbacks in the form of recreational activities and excessive travel arrangements in exchange for use of the company's products. The initial suit was dismissed under the FCA's public disclosure rule because a separate suit, claiming substantially identical allegations, had been filed previously in a separate jurisdiction. The relator subsequently brought suit in the District of Massachusetts narrowing the allegations to the promotion of off-label use of the company's products. The Court dismissed the suit because the significant similarity between the suits satisfied the "based upon" requirement.

However, the Health Reform Law narrowed this limitation by restricting it to disclosures made in federal sources or the news media. Moreover, the amended law procedurally modified the public disclosure rule by removing it as a jurisdictional question for the court and instead made it an affirmative defense. Although unclear, this will increases the burden on defendants hoping to avail themselves of this defense. Significantly, the Health Reform Law amended the public disclosure bar by removing *"based upon"* language and replaced it with a new standard, i.e., *"substantially the same allegation."* As amended, the public disclose rule now reads:

> (4)(A) The court shall dismiss an action or claim under this section, unless opposed by the Government, if *substantially the same*

---

[104] 130 S.Ct. 1396 (2010).
[105] *Graham*, 130 S.Ct. at 1400.
[106] *Graham*, 130 S.Ct. at 1400 n.1. *See also* ACA § 10104(j)(2).
[107] 604 F.Supp. 2d 313 (2009)

## False Claims: Civil and Criminal Enforcement

*allegations* or transactions as alleged in the action or claim were publicly disclosed—

(i) in a Federal criminal, civil, or administrative hearing in which the Government or its agent is a party;

(ii) in a congressional, Government Accountability Office, or other Federal report, hearing, audit, or investigation; or

(iii) from the news media,

unless. . .the person bringing the action is an original source of the information.

Another issue that has arisen is what constitutes the first public disclosure. In *United States ex rel. Meyer v. Horizon Health Corp.*, the Ninth Circuit held that the relators' allegations were barred under the public disclosure rule of the FCA and that the withdrawal of the original source prohibited the remaining relators from satisfying the "original source" exception (addressed *infra* at 4-2(d)(3)(ii)).[108] The suit originated from allegations of improper admissions of patients to a psychiatric facility with the knowledge that the patients could not benefit from treatment. The relators, who were psychiatric nurses and a facility program director, filed the qui tam suit subsequent to the program director's independent wrongful termination suit. After a series of dismissals and re-filing of amended complaints, the program director withdrew and the district court dismissed based on the determination that, 1) the wrongful termination suit constituted a public disclosure, and 2) the remaining relators were not original sources. The remaining relators argued that their disclosure to a Medicare investigator prior to the wrongful termination suit was the first public disclosure. The Court held that such a disclosure was not public because disclosure to a government employee does not constitute a public disclosure "until it is actually disclosed to the public." Furthermore, the Court held that such a disclosure does not fall within the three categories of public disclosure enumerated in the statute.[109]

Finally, the question arise in 2011 whether a federal agency's response to a Freedom of Information Act (FOIA) request was a public disclosure for purposes of the FCA.[110] The Supreme Court held that, given the broad language of the public disclosure bar, FOIA responses were within the meaning of "reports," and therefore triggered the public disclosure bar.[111]

---

[108] 565 F.3d 1195 (2009).
[109] *Id.* at 1,202.
[110] Schindler Elevator Corp. v. U.S. *ex rel.* Kirk, the Supreme Court 131 S. Ct. 1885 (2011).
[111] *Id.* at 1,889.

### § 4-2(d)(3)(ii)   Original Source Rule

The defense to the public disclosure bar is the original source rule. Civil actions by qui tam relators are barred by statute unless the relator is an "original source" of the information that gave rise to the FCA claim.[112] Under the FCA, an "original source" is one who has "direct and independent knowledge of the information on which the allegations are based and has voluntarily provided the information to the Government...."[113] Thus, former employees frequently initiate qui tam actions[114] as well as competitors or beneficiaries (i.e., patients),[115] as they can often satisfy the "original source" standard,

However, interpretation of the "provided the information" (prior to public disclosure) provision has been inconsistent and led to a three-way split among Circuit Courts of Appeals. The First and Fourth Circuits had held that the qui tam relator is only required to provide information to the government prior to filing the qui tam action.[116] The Second and Ninth Circuits had held that the relator must be the source, directly or indirectly, to the entity that made the public disclosure of the suit's allegations; therefore, to overcome the public disclosure bar, there must be some relationship between the relator's disclosure and the public disclosure.[117] Finally, the Sixth and D.C. Circuits had taken a middle path, holding that the relator must provide the information to the government prior to the public disclosure "but not requiring the relator to be the cause of the public disclosure."[118]

As a result, Congress modified the original source rule as part of the Health Reform Law. Congress elected to keep the original source intact, but changed the prior language, which required "direct and independent" knowledge to "knowledge that is independent of and materially adds to the publicly disclosed allegations." In amended form it reads:

> (B) For purposes of this paragraph, "original source" means an individual who either (i) prior to a public disclosure under subsection (e)(4)(a), has voluntarily disclosed to the Government the information on which allegations or transactions in a claim are based, or (2) who has knowledge that is independent of and materially adds to the publicly disclosed allegations or transactions, and who has

---

[112] 31 U.S.C. § 3730(e)(4)(A).
[113] 31 U.S.C. § 3730(e)(4)(B).
[114] *See, e.g.*, United States *ex rel.* Theresa Burr v. Blue Cross and Blue Shield of Florida, Inc., No. 91-134-Civ.-J-16 (M.D. Fla. 1995).
[115] *See* discussion of the *National Health Laboratories* case in NATIONAL INTELLIGENCE REP., (March 12, 1993), at 1. *See also* Cooper v. Blue Cross and Blue Shield of Florida, Inc., 19 F.3d 562 (11th Cir. 1994).
[116] U.S. *ex rel.* Duxbury v. Ortho Biotech Prods., 579 F.3d 13, 22, 28 (1st Cir. 2009).
[117] *Id.* at 22.
[118] *Id.*

## False Claims: Civil and Criminal Enforcement

voluntarily provided the information to the Government before filing an action under this section.

### § 4-2(d)(4)   Pleading Requirements for Qui tam Suits

According to the standard set by Federal Rule of Civil Procedure 9(b), complaints for FCA suits must be pled with particularity. While courts generally agree that Rule 9(b) applies to FCA claims, there is a split among Circuits regarding the extent to which specific incidences of false claims must be alleged in the pleading. The First, Fifth, and Seventh Circuits have held that the Rule 9(b) standard can be met for FCA claims without alleging specific false claims.[119] In *Lusby*, the court held that allegations regarding a contractual obligation with the government, intent to defraud the government, and evidence that the contractual obligations were not met were sufficient under the Rule 9(b) standard, even though no allegation of time and place of actual payment by the government was made in the complaint.[120] Thus, no allegation of "presentment," even though an element of a FCA offense, was required to save the complaint from a Rule 12(b)(6) dismissal.

In contrast, the Sixth, Eighth, Tenth, and Eleventh Circuits adhere to the position that specific false claims must be alleged in a FCA complaint.[121] The court in *Hopper* stated, "[a] False Claims Act complaint satisfies *Rule 9(b)* if it sets forth facts as to time, place, and substance of the defendant's alleged fraud, specifically the details of the defendants [sic] allegedly fraudulent acts, when they occurred, and who engaged in them."[122]

The U.S. Supreme Court has denied certiorari in both *Hopper* & *Duxbury*, therefore the Circuit split remains.[123]

### § 4-2(d)(5)   Retaliation

Prior to the FERA amendments to the FCA, only employees (and to limited extent family members) were protected against retaliation by a provision entitling them to relief for unlawful discharge or discrimination related to the employee's lawful conduct in furtherance of a cause of action under the FCA statute. Therefore, once an employee filed a qui tam action, the

---

[119] *See Duxbury*, 579 F.3d 13; U.S. *ex rel.* Grubbs v. Kanneganti, 565 F.3d 180 (5th Cir. 2009); U.S. *ex rel.* Lusby v. Rolls-Royce Corp., 570 F.3d 849 (7th Cir. 2009).

[120] *Lusby*, 570 F.3d at 854.

[121] *See* Hopper v. Solvay Pharm., Inc., 588 F.3d 1318 (11th Cir. 2009); U.S. *ex rel.* Bledsoe v. Cmty. Health Sys., Inc., 501 F.3d 493 (6th Cir. 2007); U.S. *ex rel.* Joshi v. St. Luke's Hosp., Inc., 441 F.3d 552 (8th Cir. 2006); U.S. *ex rel.* Sikkenga v. Regence Bluecross Blueshield of Utah, 472 F.3d 702 (10th Cir. 2006).

[122] *Hopper,* 588 F.3d at 1324 (internal citations omitted).

[123] U.S. *ex rel.* Hopper v. Solvay Pharm., Inc., 2010 U.S. LEXIS 5167 (U.S., 2010) (*cert. denied*); Ortho Biotech Prods., L.P. v. U.S. *ex rel.* Duxbury, 130 S. Ct. 3454 (U.S., 2010) (*cert. denied*).

employee enjoyed protection under the statute from retaliatory conduct by their employer. FERA expanded the protections for relators by broadening the retaliation provisions to apply not only to employees but also to contractors and agents.[124]

In addition to FERA, in 2010 the Dodd-Frank Act,[125] a financial sector reform bill passed in the wake of the 2008-2009 financial crisis, was designed to expand the scope of actions that can be brought by whistleblowers and increase the protection available to these individuals from acts of retaliation. Dodd Frank expanded protection of qui tam relators under the FCA to include "associated" discrimination and established that the statute of limitations for retaliation claims under 3730(h) is 3 years, thereby voiding the Supreme Court's holding in *Graham County Soil & Water Conservation Dist. v. U.S. ex rel. Wilson*, 545 U.S. 409 (2005) which tied the statute of limitations of 3730 (h) to state law. After the recent changes in Dodd-Frank and Fera the current Section 3730(h)(1) reads:

> Any employee, contractor, or agent shall be entitled to all relief necessary to make that employee, contractor, or agent whole, if that employee, contractor, or agent is discharged, demoted, suspended, threatened, harassed, or in any other manner discriminated against in the terms and conditions of employment because of lawful acts done by the employee, contractor, or agent on behalf of the employee, contractor, or agent or associated others in furtherance of other efforts to stop 1 or more violations of this subchapter.[126]

Qui tam relators are not immune from liability when they file FCA claims in bad faith. In *United States ex rel. Scott v. Metropolitan Health Corp.*, a Federal judge ruled that a whistleblower had to pay $1.6 million in attorneys' fees accrued by a hospital as a result of her false retaliation claims.[127] The suit began as a qui tam action under the FCA, which resulted in the relator's receipt of 18% of the structured settlement. The suit continued after its initial settlement because the relator filed a $10 million claim against the organization alleging that she had been fired in retaliation of the qui tam actions. The court found that the relator had submitted her retaliation claims knowing they were illegitimate, as she had falsely altered corporate minutes and committed other misconduct while employed and the company had suspended her as a result of her conduct. Consequently, the court found that Scott acted in bad faith by filing the retaliation suit, as she knew or should have known that her falsification of corporate minutes was the actual cause of her termination.

---

[124] 31 U.S.C. § 3730(h)(1).
[125] The Dodd-Frank Wall Street Reform and Consumer Protection Act Pub.L. 111-203 (2010).
[126] 31 U.S.C. 3730(h)(1).
[127] United States *ex rel.* Scott v. Metropolitan Health Corp., 375 F.Supp.2d 626 (W.D. Mich. 2005).

# False Claims: Civil and Criminal Enforcement

## § 4-2(e) Statute of Limitations

According to the statutory provisions of the current FCA, civil actions must be brought within six years after the date of the violation or within three years after the date when material facts are known or should have been known by the government, but in no event more than ten years after the date on which the violation was committed.[128] For example, qui tam suits filed by former employees may be time-barred under the FCA.[129] In *United States ex rel. Lowman v. Hilton Head Health Sys., L.P.*, a former employee filed a qui tam motion eight years after he started working, alleging that defendants fraudulently obtained Medicare reimbursements by billing for services without medical necessity and by misrepresenting the level of services provided.[130] The court dismissed the suit as time-barred because the employee learned of the alleged malfeasance shortly after he began working at the facility on March 10, 1997, but he did not file suit until September 1, 2005, which was not within six years of the alleged violations or three years after he knew the relevant facts.[131]

The Second Circuit in *United States v. Baylor Univ. Med. Ctr.* determined the Government's FCA claims were time-barred because Fed. R. Civ. P. 15(c)(2) did not allow the Government's complaints-in-intervention to relate back to a relator's qui tam complaint.[132] As part of FERA, Congress amended the FCA to provide that "any such Government pleading shall relate back to the filing date of the complaint of the person who originally brought the action, to the extent that the claim ... arises out of the conduct, transactions, or occurrences" established in the qui tam complaint.[133] Therefore, independent of whether or not the Government's complaint includes new claims, the Government filing relates back to the original filing date of the qui tam action so long as there is some relationship to the original complaint. As stated by the D.C. Circuit, the amended statute allows the government to keep a complaint under seal (beyond 60 days with a showing of good cause) and also relate back to the relator's complaint for an indefinite period time.[134] This provision offers significant latitude with respect to what type of new claim the Government may file and allows the Government to perform lengthy investigations that may extend beyond the statute of limitations.

---

[128] 31 U.S.C. § 3731(b).
[129] *Id.* § 3731(b).
[130] United States *ex rel.* Lowman v. Hilton Head Health Sys., L.P., 487 F. Supp. 2d 682, 683 (D.S.C. 2007).
[131] *Id.* at 697.
[132] United States v. Baylor Univ. Med. Ctr., 469 F.3d 263, 268 (2d Cir. 2006).
[133] § 3731(c); *See also* U.S. *ex rel.* Miller v. Bill Harbert Int'l Constr., Inc., 608 F.3d 871 (D.C. Cir. 2010) (qui tam complaint timely filed but gov't held the complaint under seal for several years).
[134] *Miller*, 608 F.3d at 879-80.

## § 4-3 OTHER CIVIL LAWS PERTAINING TO FALSE CLAIMS AND FRAUDULENT BILLING ACTIVITIES

### § 4-3(a) Social Security Act

Section 1128A of the Social Security Act (SSA) provides authority for the imposition of civil money penalties (CMPs) for certain activities involving federal healthcare programs. This statutory provision specifically provides for the imposition of CMPs against any person that knowingly presents or causes to be presented a claim that is improperly filed. While the FCA is the DOJ's primary healthcare fraud enforcement mechanism, the CMP law is the OIG's primary tool for assessing and recovering false claims. Among its provisions, the penalty applies to a claim that:

- is for a medical item or service that the person knows or should know was not provided as claimed, which includes claims for an item or service that is based on a code that the person knows or should know will result in a greater payment than applicable;[135]
- is for a medical or other item or service and the person knows or should know the claim is false or fraudulent;
- is for a medical or other item or service during a period of time in which the person making the claim was excluded from the program to which the claim was made;
- is presented for a physician's service by a person who knows or should know that the individual who provided that services was not a licensed physician, was licensed as a physician but such license was obtained through misrepresentation, or misrepresented that the physician was certified in a medical specialty;
- is for a pattern of medical or other items or services that a person knows or should know are not medically necessary;
- in violation of the reassignment provisions or other conditions of participation of the federal healthcare programs;[136] or
- is known to be an overpayment and is not reported and returned within a set period of time.[137]

---

[135] *See, e.g.,* United States v. Abington Memorial Hospital, No. 03-2412 (E.D. Pa. *settlement* May 24, 2005) (hospital settled with government for $4.2 million for overbilling Medicare by unbundling and/or duplicating charges for blood chemistry tests and certain urinalysis services, upcoding hematology services, double billing for platelet counts and hematology profiles, and unbundling two hematology procedure codes).

[136] Social Security Act § 1128A(a); 42 U.S.C. § 1320a-7a(a); *see also* 42 C.F.R. § 1003.102.

[137] Social Security Act § 1128A(a)(10).

### False Claims: Civil and Criminal Enforcement

Furthermore, the statute prohibits a person from knowingly giving a person information that she knows or has reason to know is false or misleading with respect to coverage of inpatient hospital services under the Medicare program or that could reasonably be expected to influence the decision when to discharge a patient from the hospital.

Although the CMP under this statute previously was $2,000, it is now provides for penalties of $10,000 for each improper item or service; $15,000 for each individual with respect to whom false or misleading information was given; $50,000 for each false record or statement made to support a claim; $50,000 for ordering a service during a time in which the provider or supplier was excluded from the federal healthcare program; and, other penalties including a $15,000 daily penalty for failure to report and refund a claim known to be improper. Additionally, such actions are subject to an assessment of up to three times the amount claimed for each such item or service.[138] The statute of limitations for imposing CMPs is six years after the date the claim was presented.[139] For purposes of CMPs, a principal is liable for any penalties and assessments brought against an agent who is acting within the scope of the principal/agent relationship.[140]

Similar to the FCA, as described, a person is subject to this provision when the person "knowingly" presents such a claim. Therefore, the level of intent required to prove that a person has violated this provision has been heightened. Moreover, Congress heightened the intent required for violation of this statute by providing a definition of "should know" as "acting in deliberate ignorance of the truth or falsity of the information" or "in reckless disregard of the truth or falsity of the information"; and no proof of specific intent to defraud is required

### § 4-3(b)   Program Fraud Civil Remedies Act

The Program Fraud Civil Remedies Act of 1986 provides that any person who makes, presents or submits a claim that the person "knows or has reason to know" is false, fictitious, or fraudulent is subject to CMPs of up to $5,000 per false claim or statement and up to twice the amount claimed in lieu of damages.[141] This statute goes beyond the FCA and the CMPs of the SSA to provide for penalties and assessments against those who make false statements.[142]

Under this statute, the Office of Inspector General (OIG) has authority to investigate allegations of liability, and then is required to report its findings

---

[138] *Id.*
[139] Social Security Act § 1128A(c)(1); 42 U.S.C. § 1320a-7a(c)(1).
[140] Social Security Act § 1128A(l); 42 U.S.C. § 1320a-7a(l).
[141] 31 U.S.C. § 3801 *et seq.*
[142] 31 U.S.C. § 3802(a)(2).

and conclusions to the "reviewing official" at the Department of Health and Human Services (DHHS). If adequate evidence exists that a violation has occurred, written notice is sent to the Attorney General who is responsible for either approving or disapproving the referral of these allegations to the "presiding officer." If a reviewing officer refers allegations of liability to a presiding officer, the reviewing officer then provides notice to the person alleged to have violated this statute. Persons so notified may request a hearing regarding these allegations.[143] The statute provides that such hearing must be commenced within six years after the date on which the false claim or statement is made.[144]

## § 4-4 CRIMINAL LAWS PERTAINING TO FALSE CLAIMS AND FRAUDULENT BILLING ACTIVITIES

### § 4-4(a) Social Security Act, Section 1128B

Section 1128B(a) of the Social Security Act, 42 U.S.C. § 1320a-7b(a), sets forth criminal penalties for engaging in certain activities involving a federal healthcare program. The statute sets forth that it is a felony to knowingly and willfully make or cause to be made any false statement of a material fact in any application for any payment, or for use in determining rights to such payment, under a federal healthcare program.[145] The language of the provision is far broader than merely billing for services not rendered. Rather, a claim containing *any false statement of a material fact* is actionable under this provision.

The statute also sets forth other specific activities that constitute the submission of false statements or representations. For example, it includes concealing information from the government, specifically, information of an event affecting the initial or continued right to a payment under a federal healthcare program.[146] It also prohibits a person from applying to receive federal payment for the use and benefit of another and knowingly and willfully converting such payment to another use; presenting (or causing to be presented) a claim for physician services knowing that the person who furnished

---

[143] 31 U.S.C. § 3803.
[144] 31 U.S.C. § 3808(a).
[145] Social Security Act §§ 1128B(a)(1)–(2); 42 U.S.C. §§ 1320a-7b(a)(1)–(2).
[146] Social Security Act § 1128B(a)(3); 42 U.S.C. § 1320a-7b(a)(3). Concealment of a felony is also a separate offense under the U.S. Criminal Code. It is unlawful to "hav[e] knowledge of the actual commission of a felony cognizable by a court of the United States," and to "conceal [ ] and [ ] not as soon as possible make known the same to some judge or other person in civil or military authority under the United States." 18 U.S.C. § 4.

## False Claims: Civil and Criminal Enforcement

the services is not a licensed physician; and disposing of assets in order for an individual to become eligible for medical assistance.[147]

For convictions under this provision, the administrator of the relevant federal healthcare program has the option to suspend the eligibility of that individual for up to one year as deemed appropriate.

It is also unlawful under the Social Security Act § 1128B(c) for a person to knowingly and willfully make, cause to be made, induce, or seek to induce, any false statement or representation of a material fact as to the conditions or operation of any institution, facility, or entity: (i) in order to qualify for certification or recertification as any entity for which certification is required, including a hospital, skilled nursing facility, home health agency (HHA), health maintenance organization, or competitive medical plan; or (ii) in response to required disclosure of information under § 1124A of the SSA.[148]

With respect to Medicaid-covered services, the Social Security Act § 1128B(d) prohibits knowingly and willfully charging money or other consideration in excess of the rates established by the state for services furnished under the state's Medicaid plan. The statute also prohibits charging, soliciting, accepting, or receiving any gift, money, donation, or other consideration in addition to amounts required to be paid under the state's Medicaid plan as a precondition of admitting a patient to, or as a requirement for a patient's continued stay in a hospital, nursing facility, or intermediate-care facility for the mentally disabled.[149]

Each violation of the provisions related to the furnishing of items or services for which payment is made under a federal healthcare program is a felony punishable by a fine of up to $25,000 and/or up to five years' imprisonment. With respect to violations by all other persons, such violations are misdemeanors and are punishable by a fine of up to $10,000 and/or up to one year of imprisonment.[150]

---

[147] Social Security Act § 1128B(a)(4)-(6); 42 U.S.C. §§ 1320a-7b(a)(4)–(6) (as amended by Health Insurance Portability and Accountability Act of 1996, Pub. L. No. 104-191, tit. II § 217, 110 Stat. 1936, 2009 (1996)).

[148] Social Security Act § 1128B(c); 42 U.S.C. § 1320a-7b(c).

[149] Social Security Act § 1128B(d); 42 U.S.C. § 1320a-7b(d). The issue of supplementation may arise in various contexts. For instance, "duration of stay" agreements may be sought from a patient by a nursing facility. These agreements provide that a resident and/or the resident's family guarantee payments at private rates for a period of time as a condition of admission to a facility. However, if a "duration of stay" agreement is entered into by a resident who subsequently becomes certified by Medicaid, the courts have generally, but not always, found such payments to be proscribed "supplementation." *See* Rosen v. Board of Medical Examiners of State of Iowa, 539 N.W.2d 345 (Iowa 1995); Dunlap Care Center v. Iowa Dept. of Social Services, 353 N.W.2d 389 (Iowa 1984); Glengariff Corp. v. Snook, 122 Misc. 2d 784, 471 N.Y.S.2d 973 (N.Y. Sup. Ct. 1984). *But see* Resident v. Noot, 305 N.W.2d 311 (Minn. 1981).

[150] Social Security Act §§ 1128B(a), (c); 42 U.S.C. §§ 1320a-7b(a), (c).

## § 4-4(b)   Mail and Wire Fraud

The U.S. Criminal Code prohibits the use of the mails for the purpose of executing any scheme or artifice to defraud or for obtaining money or property by means of false or fraudulent representations.[151] In addition, persons are prohibited from transmitting any communication by means of wire, radio, or television for the purpose of executing any scheme or artifice to defraud, or for obtaining money or property, by means of false or fraudulent representations.[152] Violation of these provisions is a felony punishable by a fine of up to $1,000 and/or up to five years' imprisonment for each violation.

Healthcare providers may be prosecuted under the mail-fraud statute for submitting claims for services never rendered, filing claims for services billed at inflated rates, waiving co-payments, and billing for services that were not medically necessary.[153] Note, however, that the fraudulent conduct need not itself constitute a separate violation of federal law in order to constitute a "scheme or artifice to defraud." Thus, private insurance fraud may be actionable as mail fraud.

One reason that Medicare claims frequently are prosecuted under mail fraud is that the statute allows a district court to grant an injunction or restraining order to stop the fraud and seize the defendant's assets.[154] For example, in *United States v. American Therapeutic Corporation,* charges were brought against affiliated healthcare providers for filing false Medicare claims and committing mail fraud. Pursuant to the mail fraud statute, the district court granted a preliminary injunction freezing all of the defendants' assets up to

---

[151] 18 U.S.C. § 1341.

[152] 18 U.S.C. § 1343.

[153] *See* United States v. Imo, No. 4:09-cr-00426 (S.D. Tex May 27, 2011) (jury convicted owner and manager of physical therapy clinic of 14 counts of healthcare fraud and three counts of mail fraud in a $45 million scheme to bill Medicare and Medicaid for services never performed); United States v. Martinez, No. 4:04-cr-00430-DCN (N.D. Ohio Jan. 12, 2006) (jury convicted doctor of drug distribution, mail fraud, wire fraud, and healthcare fraud, for an illegal scheme that yielded him more than $12 million); United States v. Hames, No. 3-01-CR-323-P (N.D. Tex. *sentencing* Dec. 15, 2004) (nursing home owners convicted of conspiring to commit healthcare fraud, mail fraud, and making false statements in connection with a scheme to defraud Medicare); United States v. Nichols, 977 F.2d 583 (6th Cir. 1992) (dentist convicted of mail fraud for submitting claims for services never rendered, for filing claims for services billed at inflated rates, and for waiving co-payments); United States v. Campbell, 845 F.2d 1374 (6th Cir. 1988) (court upheld the conviction of an ophthalmologist who was found guilty of mail fraud for billing Medicare for treatments that he either did not perform or were not medically necessary); United States v. Siddigi, 959 F.2d 1167 (2d Cir. 1992) (oncologist mailed claims for chemotherapy injections that he neither supervised nor performed himself); United States v. Talbott, 590 F.2d 192 (6th Cir. 1978) (dentists billed Ohio Medicaid for dental examinations, services and treatments that were either medically unnecessary or performed unprofessionally).

[154] 18 U.S.C. § 1345.

## False Claims: Civil and Criminal Enforcement

the value of the alleged healthcare fraud, in this case almost $85 million.[155] The Sixth Circuit has clarified that the statute authorizes preliminary injunction order to freeze not only property obtained through federal healthcare offenses, but also property of *equivalent value*.[156] Mail and wire fraud violations may also trigger the applicability of RICO and money-laundering penalties, as described in the next subsection.

### § 4-4(c)   RICO Violations

The Racketeer Influenced and Corrupt Organizations Act (RICO), enacted as part of the Organized Crime Control Act of 1970, has been applied both by the federal government and private parties in contexts far beyond organized crime. The federal criminal RICO statute prohibits a person from receiving any income, directly or indirectly, from a pattern of racketeering activity, defined as committing a predicate act (e.g., mail or wire fraud) at least twice within 10 years.[157] The elements of a criminal RICO violation, which the government must prove beyond a reasonable doubt, are:

- The existence of an enterprise, which is defined as "any individual, partnership, corporation, association or other legal entity, and any union or group of individuals associated in fact although not a legal entity;"[158]
- that the enterprise affected interstate commerce;
- that the defendant was employed by or associated with the enterprise;
- that the defendant participated, either directly or indirectly, in the conduct of the affairs of the enterprise; and
- that the defendant committed a predicate act at least twice within 10 years.[159]

A RICO violation is a felony punishable by a fine of up to $25,000 and/or up to 20 years' imprisonment.[160]

Note that RICO, like the mail-fraud statute, does not require that the underlying fraudulent scheme itself be a violation of federal law. Thus, private insurance fraud also may be actionable under RICO.

RICO also provides for a private right of action for persons injured in their business or property.[161] Successful private litigants can be awarded treble

---

[155] United States v. Am. Therapeutic Corp., 10-23765-CIV, 2011 WL 2746302 (S.D. Fla. Jan. 28, 2011).
[156] U.S. v. DBB, Inc., 180 F.3d 1277 (11th Cir. 1999).
[157] 18 U.S.C. § 1961, *et seq.*
[158] 18 U.S.C. § 1961(4).
[159] United States v. Kopituk, 690 F.2d 1289 (11th Cir. 1982).
[160] 18 U.S.C. § 1963.
[161] 18 U.S.C. § 1964(c).

(i.e., triple) damages and the cost of the suit, including attorney's fees.[162] It is important to note that the defendant need not be convicted of any predicate act; the plaintiff only is required to show that the defendant engaged in conduct that would amount to a predicate offense.

Increasingly, RICO is considered a "very broad statute" and is interpreted in an expansive manner by the Supreme Court.[163] Already established as a powerful federal remedy in healthcare fraud claims, a 1999 ruling by the U.S. Supreme Court created new remedies for individuals. The Court ruled that a class of 84,000 Nevada plaintiffs, who claim they overpaid millions in medical copayments in the late 1980s, could sue the managed care company Humana Inc. under RICO.[164] Industry leaders viewed the ruling as one opening up a "lucrative cause of action for civil plaintiffs."[165]

The burden on industry may not be what was originally feared as federal courts have not been reluctant to narrow claims under this cause of action. The U.S. District Court for the Southern District of Florida dismissed a complaint filed by a class various healthcare providers that accused 20 Blue Cross Blue Shield plans of engaging in a conspiracy to defraud them of payments to which they were entitled.[166] The court found that the plaintiffs failed to sufficiently plead a conspiracy in counts alleging RICO. The court held that the new pleading standards for conspiracy announced in *Bell Atlantic Corp. v. Twombly* applied to RICO cases. The court also held that the plaintiffs failed to sufficiently allege fraud, which requires they set forth the "who, what, when, where, and how" of the fraud. The plaintiffs failed to identify any specific instance where a false representation was made by any defendant to any plaintiff, it said.

Claims brought by doctors alleging Keystone Health Plan Central Inc. and affiliated entities violated Pennsylvania's prompt-payment law and federal fraud and racketeering statutes was allowed to proceed, but only after the U.S. District Court for the Eastern District of Pennsylvania dismissed RICO claims.[167] Although the court found the Pennsylvania Quality Health Care Accountability and Protection Act allowed the plaintiffs to pursue a private right to enforce prompt-pay claims, it found no right to enforce the insurer's duty of good faith and fair dealing under state law.

Additionally, courts will not always certify a class to bring a private RICO suit if there is too much variance among the proposed plaintiffs and the defendant's different activities. One court said that if it certified a class, it

---

[162] *Id.*
[163] *Supreme Court Approves Use of RICO in Nevada Health Fraud Claim Against Humana*, BNA HEALTHCARE DAILY REP. 2 (Jan. 21, 1999).
[164] Humana Inc. v. Forsyth, No. 97-303 (U.S. Jan. 20, 1999).
[165] *Supreme Court Approves Use of RICO in Nevada Health Fraud Claim Against Humana*, BNA HEALTHCARE DAILY REP. 2 (Jan. 21, 1999).
[166] Solomon v. Blue Cross & Blue Shield Assoc., No. 03-22935-CIV (S.D. Fla. May 23, 2008).
[167] Grider v. Keystone Health Plan Central Inc., No. 2001-CV-05641 (E.D. Pa. Sept. 18, 2003).

## False Claims: Civil and Criminal Enforcement

would "be guilty of creating a litigation management nightmare by certifying an action in which thousands and potentially millions of mini-trials would inevitably need to."[168]

### § 4-4(d) Money Laundering

The U.S. Criminal Code prohibits knowingly engaging or attempting to engage in a "monetary transaction in criminally derived property" if the value is greater than $10,000 and derived from "specified unlawful activity," including mail and wire fraud, as well as theft or bribery in programs involving federal funds, as well as "any act or activity constituting an offense involving a Federal healthcare offense."[169]

Although the statute provides criminal and civil penalties, it is most frequently used for its civil forfeiture and broad civil penalty provisions. Civil penalties (the greater of $10,000 or the value of the transaction) may be imposed against anyone who conducts a violative transaction, whether or not the person benefits from it. Consequently, this provision could be used to penalize attorneys who assist clients in secreting or moving funds.

Forfeiture can be applied to any property involved in a transaction in violation of the statute, as well as any property traceable to such property. Thus, if both "dirty" and "clean" funds are used to purchase property, the entire property can be subject to forfeiture. Additionally, forfeiture can occur without first obtaining a conviction. Indeed, it can occur without notice to the affected individual, based upon the government's ex parte application, supported by affidavit, to a district judge.

In *United State v. Valdez*, the government sought the forfeiture of more than $1.7 million in cash, the defendant's residences, and five vehicles, as well as a monetary judgment of $41.8 million from a Texas psychiatrist found guilty of one count of conspiracy to commit healthcare fraud, six counts of healthcare fraud, six counts of making false statements related to healthcare matters, and three counts of money laundering.[170]

In *United States v. Guerra*, a Florida woman was convicted of taking part in a scheme that paid kickbacks to patient recruiters and to patients so they could obtain Medicare beneficiaries' names and identification numbers to bill Medicare for medical equipment and prescription drugs.[171] She was sentenced to a total term of 70 months' imprisonment and issued a preliminary order of forfeiture to specify that Guerra would forfeit a monetary sum of more than $7.6 million. The court further specified that, if the ordered forfeiture amount was later found to be incorrect, a maximum fine of $1.3 million would be

---

[168] Agostino v. Quest Diagnostics Inc., No. 04-4362 (D.N.J. Feb. 11, 2009).
[169] 18 U.S.C. §§ 1956–57.
[170] United States v. Valdez, No. 3:10-cr-01632 (W.D. Tex. July 1, 2011).
[171] United States v. Guerra, No. 1:05-cr-20144-PCH-1 (11th Cir. Aug. 18, 2010).

imposed. The government also used the money laundering forfeiture provisions in *United States v. Meier*,[172] which concerned false ambulance claims, the proceeds of which were withdrawn from a bank account to buy a boat, which the government seized by using the forfeiture provisions. In another money-laundering case, a podiatrist was charged with defrauding four government plans and two private health insurance plans for certain surgical procedures that were either never performed or were not medically necessary.[173] In its indictment of the podiatrist, the federal government utilized the money-laundering provision and accused the podiatrist with having used part of the proceeds from these third-party payors to make improvements to his personal property. In addition to seeking forfeiture of the podiatrist's bank accounts, including a joint bank account, the government sought forfeiture of property that had at one time been held by the podiatrist but later had been transferred to the podiatrist's wife.

### § 4-4(e) Healthcare Fraud

The U.S. Criminal Code includes a general prohibition against committing any scheme to defraud a federal healthcare program or making any false or fraudulent representations. The statute provides that it is a crime to knowingly and willfully execute,[174] or attempt to execute, a scheme or artifice:

to defraud any healthcare benefit program; or

to obtain, by means of false or fraudulent pretenses, representations, or promises, any of the money or property owned by, or under the custody or control of, any *healthcare benefit program*.[175]

The Health Reform Law also clarified the intent requirement in Section 10606(b), which now states:

"With respect to violation of [1347], a person need not have actual knowledge of this section or specific intent to commit a violation of this section."[176]

---

[172] United States v. Brian Meier, Criminal No. 91-00235 (E.D. Pa. 1991).
[173] United States v. Clayman, No. CR2 9621 (S.D. Ohio (filed Feb. 28, 1996)).
[174] For the purposes of this section, a person need not have actual knowledge of this prohibition or specific intent to commit a violation. 18 USC § 1347(b). Also, a "deliberate ignorance" instruction was upheld when, despite her professed lack of knowledge of the conspiracy, a defendant had actual knowledge of the scheme, managed the provider's office, and was responsible for submitting fraudulent claims for the provider. U.S. v. Hayes, 574 f3d 460 (8th Cir. 2009).
[175] 18 U.S.C. § 1347 (emphasis added) (as added by Health Insurance Portability and Accountability Act of 1996, Pub. L. No. 104-191, tit. II § 242, 110 Stat. 1936, 2016 (1996) and amended by the Patient Protection and Affordable Care Act of 2010, Pub. L. 111-148 § 10606(b). *See, e.g.,* United States v. Murphy, No. 4:02-CR-011-Y (N.D. Tex. convicted May 23, 2003) (physician convicted of submitting over $1 million in fraudulent medical claims); United States v. Barbera, No. 02 Cr. 1268 (S.D.N.Y June 2, 2004) (urologist who "hired" a member of "the mob" and then helped him to obtain union health plan benefits convicted of healthcare fraud).
[176] 18 U.S.C. § 1347(b)

## False Claims: Civil and Criminal Enforcement

Moreover Health Reform also extended the definition of what constitutes a federal healthcare offense[177] to include violations of the Anti-Kickback Statute, the Employee Retirement Income Security Act or 1974 (ERISA) and the Federal Food, Drug and Cosmetic Act.

Violation of this statute can result in a fine and/or imprisonment for not more than ten years. If the violation results in serious "bodily injury,"[178] however, such person shall be fined and/or imprisoned for not more than twenty years. Finally, if the violation results in death, such person shall be fined and/or imprisoned for any term of years or for life.

Congress prescribed this criminal provision to apply not only to federal- and state-funded health programs but also to "healthcare benefit program," defined as "any public *or private* plan or contract, affecting commerce, under which any medical benefit, item or service is provided to any individual, and includes any individual or entity who is providing a medical benefit, item, or service for which payment may be made under the plan or contract."[179] This means that authority exists for the federal government to charge providers with using false pretenses to obtain reimbursements or other funds from private health plans.

Similar to mail fraud and money laundering, individuals convicted of a healthcare offense are subject to a court ordering forfeiture of the person's property "derived, directly or indirectly, from gross proceeds traceable to the commission of the offense."[180]

Cases concerning fraud offenses typically center on parties who defrauded public payors, or public payors in conjunction with private payors. For example, in *United States v. Edwards*, the United States District Court for the Northern District of Texas ordered a former medical clinic executive to serve a 30-month prison term and pay over $370,000 in restitution for filing fraudulently coded claims and diagnosis codes to Medicare, Medicaid, and private insurance companies in order to receive higher payments than those authorized by the payors, in violation of 18 U.S.C. § 1347.[181] In this case, it was alleged that the executive directed employees under her supervision to submit claims that were "upcoded" with higher level physician encounters, additional diagnoses and laboratory tests, and/or additional symptoms that were not approved by the clinician. In *United States v. Davis*, a psychologist was found to have violated 18 U.S.C. § 1347 when he used college students to do the "lion's share of his work while still billing Medicaid as if he had performed the tests himself."[182]

---

[177] *See* 18 U.S.C. 24(a).
[178] For a definition of the phrase "bodily injury," *see* 18 U.S.C. § 1365.
[179] 18 U.S.C. § 24(b) (emphasis added) (as added by Health Insurance Portability and Accountability Act of 1996 (HIPAA), Pub. L. No. 104-191, tit. II § 241, 110 Stat. 1936, 2016 (1996)).
[180] 18 U.S.C. § 982(a)(6) (as added by HIPAA, tit. II § 249, 110 Stat. 1936, 2020 (1996)).
[181] *See, e.g.*, United States v. Edwards, No. 5:07-cr-00076 (N.D. Tex. Mar. 14, 2008).
[182] United States v. Davis, 471 F.3d 783, 785 (7th Cir. 2006).

In 2011, A Brooklyn Neurologist pled guilty to healthcare fraud in connection with a scheme involving double billing, upcoding, and billing for services not provided including instances in which he billed for services when he was out of the country.[183] In another matter, two defendants pled guilty healthcare fraud and money laundering in a Detroit based Rehabilitation Clinic fraud scheme. The defendants admitted to billing for "exotic and expensive medications that were medically unnecessary and were never provided," and paying patients to come to the clinic and receive medication likely to generate the "greatest reimbursements from Medicare."[184]

### § 4-4(f)   Making of False Statements

HIPAA added to the U.S. Criminal Code a specific prohibition that a person can be subject to a fine and/or imprisonment of up to five years when such person, in any matter involving a healthcare program:

> knowingly and willfully (1) falsifies, conceals, or covers up by any trick, scheme, or device a material fact; or (2) makes any materially false, fictitious, or fraudulent statements or representations, or makes or uses any materially false writing or document knowing the same to contain any materially false, fictitious, or fraudulent statement or entry.[185]

Violation of this statute can result in a fine and/or imprisonment of not more than five years.

### § 4-4(g)   Theft or Embezzlement

HIPAA added a theft or embezzlement provision specifically applicable to healthcare:

> Whoever knowingly and willfully embezzles, steals or otherwise without authority converts to use of any person other than the

---

[183] See DOJ Press Release *Brooklyn Neurologist Pleads Guilty in Healthcare Fraud Scheme* available online at http://www.justice.gov/opa/pr/2011/July/11-crm-886.html.

[184] See DOJ Press Release *Former "Most Wanted" Healthcare Fraud Fugitives Plead Guilty to $9.1 Million Detroit Medicare Fraud Scheme*, available online at http://www.stopfraud.gov/opa/pr/2011/August/11-crm-1081.html.

[185] 18 U.S.C. § 1035 (as added by HIPAA, tit. II § 244, 110 Stat. 1936, 2017 (1996)); *see, e.g.,* U.S. v. Ary-Berry, 2011 WL 1758738 (5th Cir. May 6, 2011) (massage therapist falsely wrote down the provider number for physical therapist and durable medical equipment provider to allow her to bill for broader range of services); United States v. Moon, No. 2:05-CR-3 (M.D. Tenn. Dec. 12, 2005) (oncologist convicted of lying to a federal agent concerning her overcharging public and private health plans for medication); United States v. Fletcher Allen Healthcare Inc., Civil No. 2:03-CV-270 (D. Vt. Oct. 6, 2003) (Vermont's largest hospital, Fletcher Allen Healthcare, settled with government and agreed to pay a $1 million fine for allegedly misleading regulators over the cost of a hospital expansion project).

## False Claims: Civil and Criminal Enforcement

rightful owner, or intentionally misapplies any of the moneys, funds, securities, premiums, credits, property or other assets of a healthcare benefit program, shall be fined ... or imprisoned not more than 10 years or both; but if the value of such property does not exceed the sum of $100 the defendant shall be fined ... or imprisoned not more than one year or both.[186]

Similarly, 18 U.S.C. § 666 prohibits agents or employees of an organization or of a state or local government agency from embezzling, stealing, or converting $5,000 or more if the organization or agency receives "benefits in excess of $10,000 under a federal assistance program" in any one-year period. Receipt of Medicare funds by a provider, even though paid through an intermediary, constitutes the receipt of benefits under a federal assistance program.[187] For example, if an employee of a hospital that receives more than $10,000 a year from the Medicare program embezzles $5,000 from the hospital, that employee could be prosecuted under this statute.

### § 4-4(h)  Other Miscellaneous Crimes

A number of miscellaneous statutes also exist in the federal government's arsenal of criminal penalties. The first is 18 U.S.C. § 286, which subjects anyone involved in a conspiracy to defraud the federal government to obtain the payment of a false claim to a fine, imprisonment of up to ten years, or both.[188] In *United States v. Gupta*, a private healthcare consultant and several home healthcare agencies were convicted for Medicare fraud and conspiracy under 18 U.S.C. § 286.[189] Medicare reimburses home healthcare agencies for its consulting contracts as long as the consultant is not related to the agency by ownership or control, pursuant to 42 C.F.R. § 413.17.[190] The healthcare provider is treated as dealing with itself in related party contracts not negotiated at arm's length.[191] A knowing and intentional violation of related party regulations was found to support a finding of criminal intent under 18 U.S.C. § 286.[192] In this case, the record showed extensive criminal activity, as it involved seven

---

[186] 18 U.S.C. § 669 (as added by Health Insurance Portability and Accountability Act of 1996, Pub. L. No. 104-191, tit. II § 243, 110 Stat. 1936, 2017 (1996)).

[187] *See* United States v. Fischer, 168 F.3d 1273 (11th Cir. 1999) (upholding conviction of president of company for fraud and bribery for paying kickback to CFO of a hospital authority, which received more than $10 million annually in Medicare payments, to secure loan from hospital for his company), *aff'd*, 529 U.S. 667 (2000); United States v. Edgar, 304 F.3d 1320 (11th Cir. 2002) (holding Section 666 is not unconstitutional, and upholding the conviction of two former hospital executives).

[188] 18 U.S.C. § 286.

[189] United States v. Gupta, 463 F.3d 1182, 1186 (11th Cir. 2006).

[190] *Id.* at 1,187.

[191] *Id.*

[192] *Id.* at 1,193.

corporations, numerous straw owners, Medicare reimbursements of over $15 million, and repeated failure to disclose related party status over a seven-year period.[193] The court found the evidence sufficient to prove that the consultant concealed his relationship with the agencies in order to submit inflated cost reports and receive Medicare reimbursement for consultation services the costs of which were not bargained for at arm's length, in violation of 18 U.S.C. § 286.[194]

Second, 18 U.S.C. § 287 creates penalties of fines and up to five years imprisonment for knowingly presenting a fraudulent, false, or fictitious claim to any federal agency or official.[195] In *United States v. Alexander*, the Eleventh Circuit upheld an internist's conviction on appeal, finding that there was sufficient evidence of a conspiracy to make false Medicare claims under 18 U.S.C. § 287.[196] The Department of Health and Human Services (DHHS) began investigations in the case, subsequent to a tip received from a whistleblower, that Delellis Promotions, Inc. (DPI), and its owner, Christine Delellis, were engaged in Medicare fraud.[197] The investigations revealed that DPI and Delellis submitted fraudulent requests for reimbursement and paid illegal monetary kickbacks for Medicare patient referrals.[198] Alexander was implicated when DHHS recorded a conversation where Delellis told an undercover government investigator that she could have Alexander sign the Certificate of Medical Necessity (CMN) for a mechanical wheelchair that Medicare initially refused to reimburse in exchange for "a couple of bucks," and DPI subsequently submitted an electronic CMN for reimbursement for the wheelchair, identifying Alexander as the referring physician.[199] Though the court addressed several claims on appeal, the evidence that Alexander signed the CMN without treating the patient was sufficient to support her conviction.[200]

Finally, an even broader conspiracy statute, 18 U.S.C. § 371, exists to penalize two or more persons who conspire and act in any offense or fraud against the federal government or its agencies.[201]

### § 4-4(i)   Asset Freezes

The fraud injunction statute, 18 U.S.C. § 1345, allows the government to enjoin fraudulent conduct and to preserve assets during the pendency of the

---

[193] *Id.* at 1,198 (citing United States v. Holland, 22 F.3d 1040, 1046 (11th Cir. 1994) ("factors relevant to the extensiveness determination…")).
[194] *Gupta*, 463 F.3d 1182 at 1195.
[195] 18 U.S.C. § 287.
[196] United States v. Alexander, 237 Fed. Appx. 399, 399 (11th Cir. 2007).
[197] *Id.* at 401–402.
[198] *Id.* at 402.
[199] *Id.* at 403.
[200] *Id.* at 409.
[201] 18 U.S.C. § 371.

### False Claims: Civil and Criminal Enforcement

government's investigation (i.e., *before* indictment). As a result of HIPAA, the statute was broadened to apply so as to prevent the dissipation or alienation of assets obtained as a result of the commission of a federal healthcare fraud offense.[202]

Generally, section 1345 allows for two types of injunctions. The first is "[a]n injunction against violation of the mail fraud, wire fraud, banking laws, or the commission of a federal healthcare offense."[203] The second is "[a]n order enjoining alienation of any property obtained as a result of such violations and for a restraining order to prohibit any person from withdrawing, transferring, removing, dissipating, or disposing of any such property *or property of equivalent value....*"[204]

## § 4-5 FALSE CLAIMS THEORIES APPLICABLE TO MULTIPLE SEGMENTS OF THE HEALTHCARE INDUSTRY

### § 4-5(a) Billing for Items or Services Not Actually Rendered

The most obvious form of provider conduct constituting the submission of a false claim is when a provider submits a claim for services that were never rendered. For example, in the Special Fraud Alert entitled "Fraud and Abuse in the Provision of Services in Nursing Facilities," the OIG provides the example of a physician who billed $350,000 for having performed comprehensive physical examinations of nursing facility residents, even though the physician never saw a single resident.[205] The practice of submitting claims for items or services not actually rendered applies to more than just the nursing-home industry. In fact, an abundance of case law exists that exemplifies a full array of different types of healthcare providers who have been convicted for submitting claims to a federal or state healthcare program for services they did not perform.[206]

In addition, the OIG, in its various compliance guidance issuances for the healthcare industry, warns against billing for items or services not rendered.

---

[202] United States v. DBB, Inc., 180 F.3d 1277 (11th Cir. 1999). The issue on appeal was whether the statute authorized a federal court to grant injunctions freezing property of equivalent value whether or not it is traceable to the alleged federal healthcare fraud. The court held that subsection (a)(2)(B) of the statute provides broad relief where the property obtained is not easily identifiable.

[203] 18 U.S.C. § 1345(a).

[204] 18 U.S.C. § 1345(b) (emphasis added).

[205] *See* 61 Fed. Reg. 30,623 (June 17, 1996).

[206] *See, e.g.*, United States v. Varoz, 740 F.2d 772 (10th Cir. 1984); United States v. Gordon, 548 F.2d 743 (8th Cir. 1977); United States v. Skodnek, 933 F. Supp. 1108 (D. Mass. 1996); United States v. Sherman, 160 F.3d 967 (3d Cir. 1998); *see also* Office of Inspector General, Department of Health and Human Services, Semiannual Rep. (Oct. 1, 1995–Mar. 31, 1996); GAO Rep., HRD-92-69, *Fraud and Abuse in the Health Insurance System* (1992) (example provided of a man and his sons billing for almost 400,00 phantom visits from 1980 to 1987).

*Billing for services not actually rendered involves submitting a claim that represents that the provider performed a service all or part of which was simply not performed. This form of billing fraud occurs in many healthcare entities, including hospitals and nursing homes, and represents a significant part of the OIG's investigative caseload.*[207]

In 2009, the DOJ settled FCA claims against a Kansas cardiologist and his medical group that, for a period of approximately five years, billed Medicare twice for the same services as well as for services not provided.[208] In addition, claims were submitted without the proper supporting documentation. The case was settled for approximately $1.3 million.

## § 4-5(b) Providing Medically Unnecessary Services

Enforcement authorities have taken the position that a claim submitted for medically unnecessary services is a false claim. Services provided under Medicare Parts A and B must be "reasonable and necessary for the diagnosis or treatment of illness or injury or to improve the functioning of a malformed body member." [209] Consequently, government enforcers allege that any medically unnecessary service, which is billed with this certification, is a false claim.[210]

A less obvious example of billing for medically unnecessary services has been seen in the context of the clinical laboratory industry in which several laboratories have entered into settlements with the government related to the laboratories' billing practices. As will be described in greater detail *infra*, the government argued in the *National Health Laboratories* case that the laboratory's practice of marketing additional tests as part of a standard panel and then billing third-party payors and patients for these additional tests perpetrated a practice of billing for unnecessary tests, and hence violated the FCA.

Another method of billing for medically unnecessary services is referred to as "hard coding," which is the practice of creating methodologies whether through data programming or systematic policy that cause unnecessary services or services unsubstantiated by the patient's condition, diagnosis or treatment to be billed or reimbursed. With the more recent adoption of electronic medical records and coding and billing information technologies, the concept of "hard coding" or coding by default will likely be a driving element in false claims actions in the digital age. In 2004, Gambro Healthcare settled with the government and agreed to pay $350 million for defrauding Medicare

---

[207] *See e.g.*, 65 Fed. Reg. 59,434 (Oct. 5, 2000); 65 Fed. Reg. 14,295 (Mar. 16, 2000).
[208] Press Release, Department of Justice, *Kansas Cardiologist to Pay U.S. $1.3 Million to Settle False Claims Act Allegations* (Mar. 3, 2009), *available online at* http://www.justice.gov/opa/pr/2009/March/09-civ-184.html.
[209] 42 U.S.C. § 1395y(a)(1)(A).
[210] *See, e.g.*, United States v. Campbell, 845 F.2d 1374 (6th Cir. 1988).

## False Claims: Civil and Criminal Enforcement

and Medicaid. Among other elements, the settlement resolved allegations that Gambro Healthcare obtained payments from Medicare for medications and services that were not medically necessary through "hard coding."[211]

The most significant obstacle the government faces in bringing charges against certain providers (e.g., physicians) for allegedly providing medically unnecessary services is the general deference offered to members of the medical community. In Social Security disability cases, there is a principle that DHHS is to give controlling weight to the medical opinion of an applicant's treating physician; this principle is referred to as the "treating physician rule."[212] Although there have only been a few cases addressing the applicability of the "treating physician rule" in the context of issues related to Medicare reimbursement,[213] defendants can attempt to assert that this principle should also apply in the context of false claims cases.

### § 4-5(c)  Upcoding, DRG Creep, and Capitation Misclassification

Upcoding is the term for the practice of billing Medicare or Medicaid using a billing code providing a higher payment rate than the billing code intended to be used for the item or service furnished to the patient. For example, in *United States v. Larm*,[214] a physician and his wife, who was also his office manager, were convicted for submitting false claims to the state Medicaid program for not having used the most appropriate billing code. The treatment in question was a routine allergy shot that was administered by Dr. Larm's nurse and not by him personally. When submitting his bills, Dr. Larm used a billing code for a "[b]rief examination, evaluation and/or treatment, same or new illness." However, the jury agreed with the prosecution that Dr. Larm should have used a billing code for "[m]inimal service: injections, minimal dressing, etc. not necessarily requiring the presence of a physician."[215] On appeal, the Larms argued that the treatment provided did, in fact, fit within the billing code they provided. However, the Ninth Circuit held that the "snug fit between [the minimal service billing code] and the service

---

[211] United States v. Gambro Healthcare U.S. Inc., No. 4:01-CV-00553-DDN (E.D. Mo. *settlement* Dec. 2, 2004); United States v. Gambro Supply Corp., case number unavailable (E.D. Mo. plea entered Dec. 1, 2004).

[212] *See* 20 C.F.R. § 404.1527.

[213] *See, e.g.*, State of New York v. Secretary of DHHS, 924 F.2d 431 (2d Cir. 1991); Klementowski v. Secretary, Dep't of DHHS, 801 F. Supp. 1022 (W.D.N.Y. 1992); United States v. Prabhu, 442 F. Supp. 2d 1008, 1032 (D. Nev. 2006); *see also* United States *ex rel.* Hockett v. Columbia/HCA, 498 F. Supp. 2d 25, 65, n. 29 (D.D.C. 2007).

[214] United States v. Larm, 824 F.2d 780 (9th Cir. 1987), *cert. denied,* Larm v. United States, 484 U.S. 1078 (1988).

[215] *Id.* at 783.

actually rendered forecloses any argument that [brief examination code] was the correct code."[216]

This case is particularly significant because code descriptions may overlap and Medicare carriers typically decline to assist physicians and suppliers to determine the appropriate codes under which to bill for their services. In this case, however, the prosecutors proved criminal intent by introducing evidence that the Medicare carrier previously warned the Larms that the office-visit billing code required the presence of a physician. The Ninth Circuit, therefore, held that sufficient evidence was presented at trial for the jury to find that the Larms knew that the improper billing code was being used, and therefore had violated the statute.[217]

As part of HIPAA, Congress added to the existing list of specific activities subject to CMPs: engaging in a

> pattern or practice of presenting ... a claim for an item or service that is based on a code that the person knows or should know will result in a greater payment to the person than the code the person knows or should know is applicable to the item or service actually provided.[218]

Similar to upcoding, Diagnosis-Related Group (DRG) "creep" is the practice of billing Medicare or Medicaid with a DRG code that provides a higher payment rate than the DRG intended to be used for the item or service furnished to the patient. For example, Sacred Heart Hospital in California entered into a civil settlement with the DOJ for $3.25 million relating to allegations that the hospital switched primary and secondary diagnoses in order to obtain higher reimbursement.

In the 1990s, a significant set of investigations regarding this practice concerned the nationwide investigation of hospitals' coding practices related to pneumonia, in which most hospital cases are grouped into one of four DRGs, one of which results in significantly higher reimbursement than the other DRGs. The government issued subpoenas to numerous hospitals whose occurrence of the higher-reimbursed DRG was considered high. As a result, the OIG investigated more than 100 hospitals and entered into settlements with several hospital hospitals resulting in settlements of more than $20 million.[219]

In 2006, Pediatrix Medical Group (which provides neonatal intensive care in 32 states and Puerto Rico), settled FCA charges and agreed to pay over $25 million to settle allegations that Pediatrix submitted claims using

---

[216] *Id.*
[217] *Id.*
[218] Social Security Act § 1128A(a)(1); 42 U.S.C. § 1320a-7a(a)(1) (as amended by HIPAA, tit. II § 231, 110 Stat. 1936, 2014 (1996)).
[219] OIG SEMI-ANNUAL REP., p. 11 (Apr. 1, 2000, to Sept. 30, 2000).

## False Claims: Civil and Criminal Enforcement

codes for critically ill infants when as many as one-third were not critically ill at admission. [220]

Another example involved an ambulance service that allegedly upcoded basic life support services as advanced life support services.[221] Accordingly, the levels of service for the transports were not billed at the correct level.

In the managed care industry, potential false claims liability also can occur in the context of "capitation misclassification," which can result in capitation rates that are higher than intended for the relevant enrollees. This issue is discussed in greater detail in Chapter 5.

### § 4-5(d)   Unbundling and Fragmentation

Unbundling is the practice through which providers submit bills piecemeal, rather than for the procedure or product as a whole. One example of how providers have utilized unbundling to obtain higher reimbursement is set forth in a 1992 GAO report which describes how a group of Massachusetts anesthesiologists billed Medicare for the insertion of intravenous lines and catheters that had already been reimbursed as part of the overall anesthesia service.[222]

Fragmentation is the practice of billing separately, or "fragmenting" claims, for services where a global billing code is provided, but would result in a lower payment rate. A September 1992 study by the OIG addressed the fragmentation of surgical claims and found that physicians frequently billed for biopsies and/or explorations separately when they were performed as part of another surgical procedure.[223] Other "fragmented" billing practices addressed in the study include billing for duplicate codes where the surgical procedure involved the removal of multiple cysts, lesions, and the like, and billing for mutually exclusive procedures (e.g., removal of gallbladder and connection of gallbladder to the intestine).[224]

For example, in the late 1990s, the OIG, DOJ, and multiple states established "Project Bad Bundle," a national project aimed at identifying hospitals that unbundled blood-chemistry tests when using automated equipment and then billed for each analysis separately, or billed for an automated test in

---

[220] Press Release, U.S. Attorney's Office for the District of Colorado, *Pediatrix Agrees to Pay Over $25 Million to Settle Claim of False Billings* (Sept. 21, 2006).

[221] Department of Justice, Healthcare Fraud and Abuse Control Program, Annual Report for Fiscal Year 2010 (January 2011).

[222] *See* GAO Rep. HRD-92-69, *Fraud and Abuse in the Health Insurance System*, reported in CCH Medicare & Medicaid Guide ¶ 40,198 (May 7, 1992); *see also* Senate Investigative Staff Rep., *Fraud and Abuse in the Healthcare System*, reported in CCH Medicare & Medicaid Guide ¶ 42,515 (July 7, 1994).

[223] OIG. Rep., No. OEI-12-88-00901, *Fragmented Physician Claims*, reported in CCH Medicare and Medicaid Guide ¶ 40,739 (Sept. 1, 1992).

[224] *Id.*

addition to several of the analyses separately. As part of this project, hospital outpatient laboratories were targeted, using an ongoing computer-based audit of claims submitted for outpatient laboratory services. A letter from the United States Attorney's Office was sent to each hospital identifying the scope of the abusive practice at that facility and its potential exposure under the FCA. In many jurisdictions, the hospitals were invited to participate in a self-audit program, the results of which were separately verified. In recognition of their participation in this self-audit process, the hospitals generally received the benefit of double (rather than triple) damages for settlement purposes.[225]

## § 4-5(e)  Filing False Cost Reports

Another common form of healthcare fraud concerns healthcare facilities (e.g., nursing homes, hospitals, and HHAs) that include false and/or fraudulent information on cost reports submitted to healthcare programs such as Medicare and Medicaid.

Despite the complexities surrounding the manner with which providers are to complete cost reports, providers are held accountable for their inaccuracies. For example, in *Godwin v. Visiting Nurse Association Home Health Services*, a former bookkeeper brought a qui tam action claiming that the defendant had created false invoices in order to obtain reimbursement under the cost report for services that were otherwise not reimbursable.[226] Fraud cases also have been brought against providers who have failed to disclose on their cost reports that a supplier was a "related party."[227]

In a Special Fraud Alert released by the OIG concerning fraud in the home health industry, the OIG noted that it had reviewed cost reports of several HHAs that included inappropriate costs for extravagant travel, luxury cars, entertainment, lobbying, gifts, and other personal expenses unrelated to patient care.[228]

A number of qui tam actions have been brought against hospitals (and even against an accounting firm) for false cost reports for which the preparation of reserve cost reports has served as the evidence for such allegedly false cost reports.[229] In these cases, the government alleges that the provider

---

[225] OIG Semi-Annual Rep. p 9 (Apr. 1, 1997 to Sept. 30, 1997), *available online at* http://oig.hhs.gov/reading/semiannual/1997/97fsemi.pdf.

[226] Godwin v. Visiting Nurse Association Home Health Services, 831 F. Supp. 449 (E.D. Pa. 1993).

[227] *See, e.g.*, United States v. Calhoun, 97 F.3d 518 (11th Cir. 1996); United States v. Alemany Rivera, 781 F.2d 229 (1st Cir. 1985), *cert. denied* 475 U.S. 1086 (1986); United States v. Oakwood Downriver Medical Center, 687 F. Supp. 302 (E.D. Mich. 1988). For a description of the "related party" rule, *see* 42 C.F.R. § 413.17.

[228] 60 Fed. Reg. 40,847 (Aug. 10, 1995). This fraud alert is discussed in greater detail in § 4-6(f), *infra*.

[229] *See e.g.*, United States *ex rel.* Alderson v. Columbia/HCA Healthcare Corp., et al. (No. 97-2035-CIV-T-23E); United States *ex rel.* Alderson v. Quorum Health Resources, et al. (No. 99-413-CIV-T-23B);

## False Claims: Civil and Criminal Enforcement

includes unallowable costs on cost reports, but that secret or reserve cost reports are maintained in the event the government seeks payment of these unallowable costs. Thus, the government argues that these reserve cost reports and the information contained therein demonstrates that the provider knew, when it submitted the cost reports, that non-allowable or inflated claims for reimbursement were included on the cost report.

A few examples of settlements in the area of improprieties in the submission of cost reports include the following:

- Beth Israel Medical Center settled civil charges for allegedly filing false cost reports and agreed to pay almost $73 million. The government alleged that Beth Israel included costs for non-reimbursable items that it spent to support physicians in their private clinical practices, included the costs of employees' housing and parking, increased the share of overhead expenses related to methadone clinics, all which should have been caputed under non-reimbursable cost centers;[230]

- Quorum Health Group, Inc., an owner and operator of acute care hospitals and local and regional healthcare systems nationwide, and a provider of contract management services for nonprofit hospitals, agreed to pay $77.5 million to settle a 1993 qui tam lawsuit that alleged Quorum submitted false cost reports. The government alleged that reserve cost reports that Quorum maintained evidenced the false costs included on the cost reports; and

- Beverly Enterprises of California, a subsidiary of Beverly Enterprises, Inc., pled guilty to criminal mail fraud and making false statements to Medicare. As part of the civil settlement, Beverly paid $170 million to settle allegations that Beverly, from 1992 to 1998, improperly charged Medicare for the salaries of nurses caring for non-Medicare patients.

### § 4-5(f)   Quality of Care

Related to the statutory provision against reverse false claims, a number of FCA cases have arisen based upon the theory of poor quality of care. Recently, the FCA increasingly has been used to enforce certain quality of care standards beyond the traditional state-survey process.[231] The FCA is

---

United States *ex rel.* Schilling v. KPMG Peat Marwick, LLP (No. 98-901-CIV-T-17F). *See* § 4-6(i), *infra*, for discussion of billing company/consultant issues.

[230] Press Release, U.S. Attorney for the Southern District of New York, *Beth Israel Medical Center Agrees to Pay More Than $70 Million to Settle Charges that it Defrauded Medicare* (Nov. 30, 2005).

[231] Although the theory is applicable to other industries as well, the use of the FCA to enforce quality of care standards has predominantly been in the nursing-home context. Indeed, some

implicated by quality of care issues ranging from worthless services claims, where the quality of care is so substandard that the services completely lack value to the patient and hence any payment made to providers of such services is a false claim under the statute, to claims where care is provided that does not meet standards of quality of care. [232] Traditionally, quality of care issues that arose in the nursing-home context were addressed through personal injury and negligence actions. As part of the Omnibus Reconciliation Act of 1997, Congress passed the Nursing Home Recovery Act. The act places upon each state the responsibility for certifying nursing facilities' compliance with quality-related requirements regarding provision of services, residents' rights, and administration and ownership of nursing facilities. These standards are enforced through state surveys, and through the issuance of deficiency statements and corrective actions.

It is often the case that the DOJ becomes aware of potential FCA cases involving quality of care through the state surveyor's reports during an annual investigation for nursing-facility compliance with Medicare/Medicaid conditions of participation or a reported complaint against the facility.

When DOJ settles a case that alleges quality of care claims, the OIG may require a corporate integrity agreement that includes a requirement for the use of an independent quality monitor.[233] In this situation, "[t]he quality monitor not only will address the specific issues underlying the allegations, but also will look at the entity's delivery of care and evaluate the provider's ability to prevent, detect, and respond to patient care problems."[234] As of this writing, according to the OIG Quality of Care website, approximately 20 healthcare institutions have CIAs that require independent quality monitors.[235]

A number of cases illustrate the application of this theory. In *US ex rel. Aranda v. Community Psychiatric Center of Oklahoma*, the court rejected the defendant's Rule 12(b)(6) motion.[236] The court agreed that a quality of care claim was properly alleged based on the fact that failure to meet quality of care standards could result in exclusion from federal healthcare programs and also because federal requirements for Medicaid program require states to provide services consistent with quality of care standards.[237]

---

prosecutors have expressed an intent to use the theories developed in the nursing home cases discussed in this section to hospitals.

[232] *See, e.g.,* Mikes v. Straus, 274 F.3d 687 (2nd Cir. 2001); U.S. *ex rel.*, Insoon Lee v. SmithKline Beecham, Inc. 245 F.3d 1048 (2001, 9th Cir); U.S. *ex rel.* Aranda v. Community Psychiatric Center of Oklahoma 945 F. Supp. 1485 (1996 W.D. Okla.).

[233] Office of Inspector General, Department of Health and Human Services, Quality of Care Corporate Integrity Agreements http://oig.hhs.gov/compliance/corporate-integrity-agreements/quality-of-care.asp (last visited July 5, 2011).

[234] *Id.*

[235] *Id.*

[236] 945 F. Supp. 1485, 1489 (1996 W.D. Okla.).

[237] *Id.* at 1,488.

## False Claims: Civil and Criminal Enforcement

In February 1996, the U.S. Attorney's Office for the Eastern District of Pennsylvania entered into a $600,000 settlement agreement with the owner and manager of a nursing home in the first FCA case that specifically addressed the quality of certain services provided to a healthcare facility's patients.[238] The government alleged that the continued billing to the Medicare and Medicaid programs for inadequate nutritional services and wound care constituted false claims to the federal government. Under the terms of the settlement, the nursing home not only paid a substantial fine, but also agreed to implement a nutrition-monitoring and quality-assurance program and report to the federal government on all nutritionally compromised or at-risk residents for at least one year.

With the success of the 1996 case, the United States Attorney's Office in Philadelphia, PA, sued another three nursing homes in 1998.[239] The government alleged that the nursing homes violated the FCA by submitting claims for care provided to nursing home residents who had suffered various injuries as a result of "nutritional, wound care and nursing services that were not adequately rendered."[240] The parties ultimately settled the case for $500,000, which settlement required the implementation of a compliance plan that addressed the nutritional and wound care needs of all residents.[241]

In *U.S. ex rel., Insoon Lee v. SmithKline Beecham, Inc.*, although the Ninth Circuit upheld the dismissal of the plaintiff's complaint based on failure to meet Rule 9(b) standards, the court stated that allegations of worthless services could constitute a claim under the FCA.[242] In this case, a qui tam action was brought by a lab supervisor with over 20 years of experience working for the company. He observed occasions when control samples fell outside the required range and the company would falsify results of the control tests, report the results of patient tests, and bill the government for those tests even though the results were inherently unreliable.[243] In this case, the court allowed the complaint to be amended because the court reasoned that when a "party to a government contract knowingly or with deliberate ignorance charged the government for worthless services, then there would be fraud on the government that may be pursued under the FCA."[244]

---

[238] United States v. GMS Management-Tucker, Inc., No. 96-1271 (E.D. Pa. Feb. 21, 1996).

[239] United States v. Chester Care Center, et al., Case No. 98-CV-139 (E.D. Pa. 1998), 1998 U.S. Dist. LEXIS 4836 (E.D. Pa. Feb. 2, 1998).

[240] United States. v. Chester Care Center, 98-CV-139 (E.D. Pa. 1998), complaint at 15.

[241] In yet another use of this theory of liability, the United States Attorney in Missouri brought a false claims action against NHC Healthcare Center, a nursing home, arguing that the nursing home "had such woefully low staff numbers at its facility that it could not possibly have rendered all the care that it billed the Medicare and Medicaid programs." United States v NHC Healthcare Corp., No. 00-3128-CV-S-B-D (W.D. Mo. filed Apr. 12, 2000).

[242] 245 F.3d 1048, 1052-53 (2001, 9th Cir).

[243] *Id.* at 1,050.

[244] *Id.* at 1,053.

More recently, in *U.S. ex rel. Landers v. Baptist Memorial Healthcare Corp*, the relator a former employee, alleged that Baptist used scrub nurses rather than RNs to perform patient assessments during surgery and failed to have sufficient staff to meet patient needs in violation of applicable standards of case. The case against Baptist rested on a false certification theory, which argued that because of Baptists inadequate staffing, they falsely certified compliance with Medicare Conditions of Participation (COP) rules. The court dismissed the case holding that the "Conditions of Participation are equality of care standards directed towards an entities ability to participate in the Medicare program rather than a prerequisite to a particular payment."[245] Similarly, in *U.S. ex rel. Conner v. Salina Regional Health Center*, the Tenth Circuit considered whether inadequate staffing, failure to maintain medical records and sanitation that could violate Medicare's Conditions of Participation constituted false claims. The Tenth Circuit held that violations of the COPs are most properly enforced through administrative mechanisms such as removal from the Medicare program and would not otherwise lead the government to make a payment that it would not have otherwise have made. Accordingly, it upheld the lower court's dismissal.[246]

## § 4-5(g)  Waiver of Coinsurance and Deductibles

DHHS has stated that certain instances of Medicare Part B coinsurance and deductible waivers may be a misstatement of the actual charge for the service, and thus constitute a false claim. In a Special Fraud Alert issued in 1991, the OIG asserted as follows:

> A provider, practitioner, or supplier who routinely waives Medicare co-payments or deductibles is misstating its actual charge. For example, if a supplier claims that its charge for a piece of equipment is $100, but routinely waives the co-payment, the actual charge is $80. Medicare should be paying 80 percent of $80 (or $64), rather than 80 percent of $100 (or $80). As a result of the supplier's misrepresentation, the Medicare program is paying $16 more than it should for this item.[247]

Waiving coinsurance, copayments, and deductibles may also be actionable under federal law as constituting mail fraud. In a Sixth Circuit decision, the court upheld the defendant's conviction for mail fraud based, in part, upon the fact that "the defendants schemed to obtain money by waiving co-payment …" for privately insured patients.[248]

---

[245] U.S. *ex rel.* Landers v. Baptist Memorial Healthcare Corp. 25 F. Supp. 2d 972 (W.D. Tenn. 2007).
[246] U.S. *ex rel.* Conner v. Salina Regional Health Center 543 F.3d 1211 (10th Cir. 2008).
[247] 59 Fed. Reg. 65,372, 65,374 *et seq.* (Dec. 19, 1994).
[248] United States v. Nichols, 977 F.2d 583 (6th Cir. 1992).

## False Claims: Civil and Criminal Enforcement

Nor does this analysis differ substantially in a managed care context. Although the final managed care safe harbors protect Part A inpatient coinsurance and deductible waivers offered in connection with a Medicare SELECT plan from anti-kickback liability, the preamble to the regulations makes clear that other waivers, particularly waivers under Part B, still are not protected.[249] Again, according to the OIG in the preamble to the managed care safe harbors:

> [R]outine waivers of coinsurance and deductibles are an area of significant abuse in the Medicare program. Such waivers result in the submission of false claims to the Medicare program because providers misstate their charges or claims submitted to the program.[250]

Thus, even in the managed care context, the waiver of certain coinsurance and deductible amounts may result in allegations of false claim submissions.

### § 4-5(h)   Express and Implied False Certification

The aforementioned theories of liability under the FCA fall into the category of factually false claims. That is, the FCA violation stems from receiving payment for services that were not actually rendered or goods that were not provided. However, there may be FCA liability even though payment was received for services or goods actually provided but where some condition of payment was not met.

The seminal case describing this area of law is *Mikes v. Straus*.[251] In *Mikes*, the plaintiff, a board-certified pulmonologist, initiated a qui tam action against her employer alleging they submitted false claims for spirometry services.[252] Although the spirometry services were actually provided to patients and the request for payment reflected the level of services provided, the plaintiff alleged that the claims were false because "the defendants' failure to calibrate the spirometers rendered the results so unreliable as to be 'false' under the [FCA]."[253] Plaintiff's argument was that professional guidelines promulgated by the American Thoracic Society required daily calibration of spirometers to ensure accurate test results.[254] Thus, the claim was not factually false certification, where a claim for payment "involves an incorrect description of goods or services provided or a request for reimbursement for goods or services never provided."[255] Rather, the claim rested on a theory of legally

---

[249] 61 Fed. Reg. 2,122 (Jan. 25, 1996).
[250] 61 Fed. Reg. 2,122, 2,129 (Jan, 25, 1996).
[251] 274 F.3d 687 (2nd Cir. 2001) (the gov't declined to intervene in this case, however the plaintiff proceeded on her own).
[252] *Id.* at 693.
[253] *Id.* at 693, 694–95.
[254] *Id.* at 694.
[255] *Id.* at 697.

false certification where liability for a false claim "is predicated upon a false representation of compliance with a federal statute or regulation or prescribed contractual term."[256]

There were two theories of false certification upon which the plaintiff based her claims in *Mikes*. The first theory is "express false certification," which is a claim for payment that falsely certifies regulatory, statutory, or contractual compliance when such compliance is a prerequisite to receiving payment.[257] In *Mikes*, the defendants submitted Medicare claim forms that contained required certifications that claims were for services that were *medically indicated and necessary*; furthermore, the form stipulated that no Medicare benefits would be paid without the form being submitted.[258] In this case, the court decided that the claims did not survive summary judgment under this theory because "'medical necessity' does not impart a qualitative element mandating a particular standard of medical care." Rather, the court reasoned, medical necessity relates to the level of service provided, not the quality.[259]

The second theory under which the plaintiff in *Mikes* proceeded was a theory of "implied false certification." The court adapted this theory to the healthcare context and decided that "implied false certification is appropriately applied only when the underlying statute or regulation upon which the plaintiff relies *expressly* states the provider must comply in order to be paid."[260] Under this theory, liability may only be found when "a defendant submits a claim for reimbursement while knowing… that payment expressly is precluded because of some noncompliance by the defendant."[261] As above, the court found the plaintiff's claims without merit under this theory.[262]

Today, the implied certification theory has been accepted as a viable theory under which a qui tam plaintiff can proceed. Since *Mikes*, which was decided by the Second Circuit Court of Appeals, implied certification was upheld in that Circuit in *Kirk*.[263] The theory has also been adopted by the Ninth Circuit.[264] A recent unpublished opinion from the Fourth Circuit suggests that a theory of implied certification, if adequately pleaded, could proceed.[265] Although many of these cases do not survive a Rule 12(b)(6)

---

[256] *Id.* at 696.
[257] *Id.* at 698.
[258] *Id.*
[259] *Id.*
[260] *Id.* at 700.
[261] *Id.*
[262] *Id.* at 701.
[263] *See* U.S. *ex rel.* Kirk v. Schindler Elevator Corp., 601 F.3d 94 (2nd Cir. 2010).
[264] *See* Ebeid *ex rel.* U.S. v. Lungwitz, 616 F.3d 993 (9th Cir. 2010) (Implied false certification occurs when an entity has previously undertaken to expressly comply with a law, rule, or regulation, and that obligation is implicated by submitting a claim for payment even though a certification of compliance is not required in the process of submitting the claim.).
[265] U.S. *ex rel.* Godfrey v. KBR, Inc., 360 Fed. Appx. 407 (4th Cir. 2010).

## False Claims: Civil and Criminal Enforcement

motion because of the heightened pleading standard, the Tenth Circuit Court of Appeals recently reversed a district court's dismissal of a FCA case and allowed a case to proceed based on an implied certification theory.[266] In *Lemmon*, the plaintiff premised her FCA claim on observed violations of statutory and contractual obligations that led to the submission of false claims, which were paid by the government.[267] The complaint plead specific instances of such conduct, documented by the plaintiff, including the specific violative conduct, the dates on which the alleged violations occurred, how the plaintiff either observed or participated in the violative conduct, and how the defendant knew that the conduct violated their obligations.[268]

### § 4-5(i)  Medicare Secondary Payor Issues

The concept of the Medicare program as a secondary payor in certain circumstances has been in existence since the inception of the Medicare program. Initially, the Medicare program was secondary only to workers' compensation programs. During the 1980s, Congress enacted a series of laws to cut Medicare costs by making employer group health plans the primary payors of healthcare expenses for certain employees and their spouses who qualify for Medicare coverage. Although the precise scope of the secondary payor application has varied somewhat over the years, generally Medicare may be secondary payor for working-aged employees and their spouses, as well as disabled employees and employees (and their dependents) who have end-stage renal disease.[269]

In order to recover an improper payment, Medicare is authorized to bring an action against any entity that is primarily responsible for payment or against any entity that has received payment.[270] The MSP program is also enforceable through the creation of a private cause of action for damages. The successful plaintiff is entitled to collect double the amount otherwise provided in the "case of a primary plan which fails to provide primary payment (or appropriate reimbursement) …"[271] As discussed, MSP obligations also have been the subject of a series of private qui tam lawsuits under the FCA.

### § 4-5(j)  Recruitment of Homeless and Indigent Patients

Perhaps the most odious of healthcare fraud activities centers around recruiting homeless beneficiaries to engage in fraudulent claims schemes.

---

[266] U.S. *ex rel* Lemmon v. Envirocare of Utah, Inc., 614 F.3d 1163 (10th Cir. 2010).
[267] *Id.* at 1,169.
[268] *Id.*
[269] Social Security Act § 1862(b); 42 U.S.C. § 1395y(b).
[270] Social Security Act § 1862(b)(2)(B)(ii); 42 U.S.C. § 1395y(b)(2)(ii)(iii).
[271] Social Security Act § 1862(b)(3)(A); 42 U.S.C. § 1395y(b)(3).

Often these unfortunate individuals provide their beneficiary numbers to schemers who then manufacture claims for services not provider or worse, these homeless individuals actually receive unnecessary medical care.

In April 2010, a Tustin, California hospital executive pled guilty to paying kickbacks for homeless patients recruited from Los Angeles' "Skid Row" area. He admitted to paying "marketers" who recruited the transient Medicare and Medi-Cal beneficiaries and transported them to the hospital for inpatient stays. The kickbacks were concealed by a consulting contract between the hospital and the "marketing" homeless center. Medicare and Medi-Cal were billed for medically unnecessary services for these beneficiaries.[272]

The previous year, several executives of the City of Angels Medical Center entered into a $10 million consent judgment to resolve allegations they paid kickbacks to recruiters who paid homeless Medicare and Medi-Cal beneficiaries to be admitted to the hospital where medically unnecessary services were performed and billed.[273]

## § 4-6  FALSE CLAIMS ENFORCEMENT ACTIVITIES SPECIFIC TO PARTICULAR SEGMENTS OF THE HEALTHCARE INDUSTRY

The following sections highlight some FCA theories applicable to particular industries and/or highlight recent issues relating to such industries. The discussion is not intended to be an exhaustive discussion of these industries and the corresponding FCA issues related to such industries. Rather, its intent is to provide a sense of the types of issues particular to specific industries.

### § 4-6(a)  Hospitals

### § 4-6(a)(1)  Payments to Teaching Hospitals

Under Part A of the Medicare program, the federal government subsidizes teaching hospitals for the cost of medical education by paying the costs for residents, interns, and fellows, as well as the salaries for the hospitals' clinical faculty who perform training for these individuals. Medicare Part B pays for physician services provided by clinical faculty in a teaching hospital, as long as certain criteria are met, including a requirement that "the physician renders sufficient personal and identifiable physicians' services to the patient to exercise full, personal control over the management of the portion of the case for which the payment is sought."[274]

---

[272] OIG, Healthcare Fraud and Abuse Control Program, Annual Report for 2010, p. 24.
[273] OIG, Healthcare Fraud and Abuse Control Program, Annual Report for 2009, p. 20.
[274] Social Security Act § 1842(b)(7)(A); 42 U.S.C. § 1395(u)(b)(7).

## False Claims: Civil and Criminal Enforcement

Under this requirement, the issue is to what extent the teaching physician must be involved in furnishing services to the patient to bill Medicare Part B for services where residents and interns also are involved in the patient's care. In that regard, in 1969, HCFA issued Intermediary Letter 372 to clarify what level of involvement and supervision was necessary to qualify as an attending physician for Medicare billing purposes. The policy requires that a single attending physician should personally examine the beneficiary within a reasonable time after admission, confirm the diagnosis and course of treatment, and be continuously involved in the care of the beneficiary throughout the patient's stay.

Due to an increase in improper billing, in June 1996, the OIG announced an investigation that sought to impose FCA liability upon hospitals that did not bill for the services of interns and residents in accordance with the requirements of Intermediary Letter 372. The investigation covered the periods from 1990 to 1995.

The University of Pennsylvania Health System (UPHS) agreed in December 1995 to pay $30 million to settle federal government allegations that UPHS, among other things, submitted false claims to Medicare by billing the program for physician services actually provided by interns and residents without adequate supervision of the attending physicians. The billing was done by a University of Pennsylvania physician group called Clinical Practices.[275]

Interestingly, only after the announcement of the UPHS settlement, CMS issued a final rule with an effective date of July 1, 1996, specifying the coverage criteria for the services of clinical faculty where interns and residents are involved in the furnishing of care.[276] This rule provides that, in order for clinical faculty to bill Medicare for services provided by residents and interns, the clinical faculty must be physically present with the resident during either the "key portion" or "all critical portions" of the medical services provided.

In 1998, several organizations representing teaching hospitals and their physicians sought a declaratory judgment that would invalidate the bases of the Inspector General's audits of teaching hospitals.[277] The court dismissed the case, finding a lack of subject matter jurisdiction because, under the Administrative Procedure Act, there had been no final agency action and the plaintiffs had an adequate legal remedy. According to the court, a final agency

---

[275] *See Settlement Agreement between the U.S. and the University of Pennsylvania Health System* (Dec. 12, 1995). Other settlements have included settlements with the University of Pittsburgh for $17 million; the Georgetown University Medical Center for $5.2 million; Yale University School of Medicine for $1.2 million; and Mercy Health System of Southeastern Pennsylvania for $1.2 million. According to the Office of Inspector General's Semi-Annual Report through September 2000, seven institutions had entered into settlements with the federal government that resolved potential FCA liability, which have resulted in the over $76 million in settlement amounts.

[276] 42 C.F.R. § 415.172.

[277] Association of Am. Med. Colleges, et al. v. United States, CV-98-1734 (C.D. Cal. 1998).

action does not occur until the government seeks to enforce the results of an audit, and an adequate legal remedy is available because the plaintiffs can obtain judicial review by defending a possible audit prosecution under the FCA.[278] On appeal, the Ninth Circuit Court of Appeals upheld the dismissal by the district court.[279]

## § 4-6(a)(2)    DRG Payment Window

Under Medicare law, DRG payment includes all of a hospital's "operating costs of inpatient hospital services," which has been defined as incorporating all operating costs and ancillary services operating costs, including all services provided to a patient by a hospital that participates in the prospective payment system (or an entity wholly owned or operating by the hospital) during the three days immediately preceding the date of the patient's admission to the hospital. This rule commonly has been referred to as the "DRG Payment Window" rule.[280]

Pursuant to the so-called "DRG 72-Hour Window Project," which began in late 1994 in Pennsylvania, the OIG and the DOJ currently are investigating thousands of hospitals nationwide for allegedly submitting improper claims to Medicare for outpatient services in violation of the DRG Payment Window rule. In the OIG's April 1, 2000, to September 30, 2000, *Semi-Annual Report*, the OIG noted that settlements with more than 2,799 hospitals have been reached, resulting in settlement amounts in excess of $73 million.[281]

## § 4-6(a)(3)    Outlier Payments

The Medicare program may make outlier payments to hospitals for inpatient services that exceed the average cost of typical care.[282] To obtain an outlier payment from Medicare, the hospital must make a request by submitting a standard claim form that omits certain coding information. Medicare then determines the reimbursement rate based on the actual cost incurred and the ratio of the cost of the services and the charge to the patient of most recent outlier claim (the cost-to-charge ratio). This determination typically requires at least two to three years to settle, creating the potential for an artificially inflated cost-to-charge ratio that results in over-payment for the most recent claims. Hospitals can take advantage of the outlier system by "turbocharging" or rapidly inflating its charges while maintaining or reducing its cost, thereby

---

[278] *Id.*
[279] Association of Am. Med. Colleges v. United States, 217 F.3d 770 (9th Cir. 2000).
[280] 42 C.F.R. § 412.2(c)(5).
[281] OIG SEMI-ANNUAL REP., p. 9 (Apr. 1, 2000, to Sept. 30, 2000).
[282] 42 U.S.C. § 1395ww(d)(5)(A)(ii).

## False Claims: Civil and Criminal Enforcement

obtaining outlier payments in excess of the amount to which the hospital is entitled. [283]

The improper filing of outlier payments has resulted in several settlement agreements between the federal government and various members of the healthcare industry. In June 2006, Tenet Healthcare Corp. agreed to settle outlier payment claims brought by the Department of Justice for more than $900 million plus interest.[284] The Government alleged that, between 1995 and 2003, Tenet "artificially and purposefully inflated the charges billed for inpatient and outpatient care substantially in excess of any increase in the [associated] costs."[285] The resulting outlier payments were purportedly improper and inflated because the calculations were based on inappropriate state-wide cost-to-charge ratios. The Government further alleged that Tenet filled outlier payments for services that were not provided to the patients. In 2007, the Department of Justice agreed to settle allegations of improper outlier payments against two Hospitals in New Jersey. In separate agreements, Raritan Bay Medical Center and Warren Hospital agreed to each pay $7.5 million. The hospitals allegedly submitted inflated outlier payments that, "when adjusted to costs pursuant to the outlier Statute and regulations, [the] charges no longer reasonably reflected or approximated Warren's actual costs."[286]

In *United States ex rel. Monahan v. Robert Wood Johnson University Hospital at Hamilton*, a federal district court held that turbocharging may constitute a violation of the FCA where the hospital "intentionally filed claim statements based on charges that were unrelated to costs ... and did not disclose to the Government that it had drastically increased its charges, which might lead to payments that were at odds with the clear intent and purpose of the outlier program."[287] The relators brought a qui tam suit, in which the federal government intervened, against the defendant hospital to recover outlier

---

[283] In 2003, the Centers for Medicare and Medicaid Services published a final rule that modified the procedure for obtaining outlier payments such that the cost-to-charge ratio may be determined based on either the most recent settled cost report or statewide average cost-to-charge ratio when an accurate value is indeterminable or the value falls outside reasonable parameters. *See* Change in Methodology for Determining Payment for Extraordinarily High-Cost Cases (Cost Outliers) Under the Acute Care Hospital Inpatient Prospective Payment System, 68 Fed. Reg. 34,494 (June 9, 2003) (codified at 42 C.F.R. §§ 412.84(h)-(i)).

[284] Civil Settlement Agreement (Redacted) between U.S. and Tenet Healthcare Corp. § III(1) (June 28, 2006), *available online at* http://op.bna.com/hl.nsf/id/sfak-6r8rxg/$File/FinalRedactedTenetAgreement.pdf.

[285] *Id.* § II(E)(1).

[286] Civil Settlement Agreement between U.S. and Warren Hospital § II(D) (Dec. 5, 2007), *available online at* http://op.bna.com/hl.nsf/id/bbrk-79ru7q/$File/warrensettlement.pdf; Civil Settlement Agreement between U.S. and Raritan Bay Medical Center § II(D) (Feb. 13, 2007), *available online at* http://op.bna.com/hl.nsf/id/jthn-6zbqyz/$File/Raritan%20Bay%20Medical%20Center%20Settlement%20Agreement.pdf.

[287] United States *ex rel*. Monahan v. Robert Wood Johnson University Hospital at Hamilton, No. 02-5702, 2009 U.S. Dist. LEXIS 38898, at *24 (D. N.J. May 7, 2009).

payments obtained from 1998 to 2001 as a result of an alleged intentional manipulation of the charge structure designed to inflate inpatient treatment costs. The defendant allegedly obtained "millions of dollars ... in outlier payments for cases that either were not extraordinarily costly or were much less costly than [presented.]"[288] The defendant argued that the charge structure was designed in accordance with the applicable regulations and, thus, the resulting claims were not violations of the FCA. Denying the defendant's motion to dismiss, the Court concluded that the allegations of false claims for outlier payments was sufficient to state a violation of the FCA since "[t]he claims, as submitted, were not reasonably related to the [d]efendant's costs."[289]

### § 4-6(a)(4) Inpatient Admissions, Site of Service and One Days Stays

Recently, the government began investigating what it perceives as over utilization of hospital inpatient admissions. In these investigations, the government often argues that patients should have more appropriately been deemed outpatient or be placed in observation status, which typically, although not always, reimburses at a lower level than an impatient admission. Of particular concern to the government are "one day stays," (patients who are admitted and discharged in less than a 24-hour period), and "same day stays" (patients who are admitted and discharged in the same calendar day).

In July 2010, several hospital systems in the Philadelphia area paid the government $7.9 million to settle FCA allegations that they improperly billed Medicare for one day inpatient hospital stays that should have been appropriately classified as outpatient or observational visits. Admitting patients who did not meet the Medicare/Medicaid criteria for inpatient admission resulted in payment for the hospitals at a higher rate than outpatient visits.[290] After reviewing 170 admissions in 2010, it was determined that 30% of the admissions at a critical access hospital in Minnesota were unnecessary. This resulted in overpayments of $1 million over six years.[291]

In 2009, six Indiana and Alabama hospitals paid $8 million to FCA allegations that they overcharged Medicare from 2002 to 2008 by performing kyphoplasty, a minimally-invasive procedure, on an inpatient basis. The procedure can be performed safely on an outpatient basis despite the encouragements by the procedure device manufacturer that hospitals perform it on an inpatient basis.[292] The same charges were brought against Yale New

---

[288] *Id.* at *4.
[289] *Id.* at *26.
[290] OIG, Healthcare Fraud and Abuse Control Program, Annual Report for 2010, p. 23.
[291] *Id.*
[292] OIG, Healthcare Fraud and Abuse Control Program, Annual Report for 2009, p. 21.

### False Claims: Civil and Criminal Enforcement

Haven Hospital for unnecessarily performing Gamma Knife procedures on an inpatient basis. The Hospital paid $885,953 to resolve the allegations.[293]

In 2010, nine hospitals settled FCA claims for providing spinal procedures on an inpatient basis when they should have been performed on an outpatient basis.[294] Overall, these hospitals settled claims for more than $9.4 million.[295]

### § 4-6(b)  Investigational Devices

Pursuant to a 1996 final rule promulgated by CMS, Medicare provides coverage to medical devices and related services that: (1) have an approved FDA investigational device exemption (IDE) and are used in accordance with an FDA-approved protocol; and (2) are of the same type as a device for which a manufacturer has received FDA clearance or approval for marketing (i.e., a new generation of a legally marketed device), described in the rule as "nonexperimental/investigational."[296] Medicare, however, will not cover first-of-a-kind or substantially different devices (described in the rule as "experimental/investigational").

Prior to the promulgation of this rule, however, CMS's policy did not allow coverage for such devices. In 1986, Medicare issued an insert to the *Medicare Carriers Manual* that set forth CMS's policy that Medicare would not pay for treatment involving any medical device that had not been approved by the Food and Drug Administration (FDA).

Notwithstanding these inserts, CMS permitted local contractors to pay for these services using devices that were generally accepted by the medical community or, if the device was "rarely used, novel or relatively unknown," the contractor could pay for it if there was authoritative evidence of safety and effectiveness. Thus, local contractors regularly reimbursed hospitals for services that involved investigational devices. Moreover, despite the issuance of the 1986 manual inserts, CMS's contractors continue to pay for services involving investigational devices.

In the summer of 1994, the Seattle, Washington, office of the OIG issued subpoenas to more than 125 hospitals across the country requesting years' worth of billing information related primarily to procedures performed on Medicare and Medicaid beneficiaries. It was later revealed that the

---

[293] *Id.* at 22.
[294] Press Release, Department of Justice, *Nine Hospitals in Seven States to Pay U.S. More Than $9.4 Million to Resolve False Claims Act Allegations Related to Kyphoplasty* (May 17, 2010).
[295] *Id.*
[296] 60 Fed. Reg. 48,422 (1995). In February 1996, the FDA announced the availability of an interagency agreement between FDA and CMS which will describe procedures by which FDA will assist CMS in identifying nonexperimental/investigation devices and that are potentially covered by Medicare under the September 1995 final rule. 61 Fed. Reg. 7,011 (Feb. 23, 1996).

government investigation was spurred in part by a qui tam lawsuit in which the relator alleged that these hospitals had defrauded Medicare and other federal healthcare programs by submitting claims and receiving payments for hospital services provided to patients who elected to participate in clinical trials involving nearly sixty different investigational cardiac devices that had not been approved for marketing by the FDA.[297]

In response to the subpoenas, some of the hospitals filed suit against DHHS, challenging the government's policy of non-coverage and non-payment on the grounds of failure to follow proper rulemaking procedures, or, in the alternative, to issue national coverage determinations for each device. In April 1996, the District Court for the Central District of California ruled in favor of the plaintiffs, and held that CMS's policies regarding payments for investigational devices were void for failure to comply with the rulemaking requirements of the Administrative Procedures Act.[298]

On appeal, the government sought to uphold the validity of the manual insert. The government also argued that the plaintiff's action was barred by the statute of limitations.[299] The court held that, because the District Court was silent on that issue, it was unclear whether the DHHS Secretary's defense was rejected, waived, or overlooked, and accordingly remanded the case back to the District Court, which held that the statute of limitations had expired.[300]

Ultimately, the government entered into settlement agreements with all of the hospital-defendants except for forty hospitals who became defendants in ongoing litigation,[301] and those hospitals that were voluntarily dismissed from the original Washington litigation. In 2004, the United States District Court for the District of Connecticut ruled on three motions to dismiss filed on behalf of the forty hospital-defendants. Two of the motions were denied and a third (whether the actions are barred by the relevant statutes of limitations) was denied in part and granted in part as to all common-law causes of action relating to Medicare claims filed prior to March 31, 1988, and as to all common-law causes of action for fraud relating to Medicare claims paid by the government prior to March 31, 1991.[302]

Perhaps more significant than the ability of the government to move forward with FCA cases against these hospitals is that the OIG investigational activities involved an area in which Medicare coverage policy at the

---

[297] The government investigation prompted a February 1996 congressional hearing in the U.S. Senate on this issue, which included the appearance of a witness cloaked in a black hood—the then-anonymous qui tam relator. It is now known that the relator was a former sales representative and clinical-support person for cardiovascular device manufacturers.

[298] Cedars-Sinai Medical Center v. Shalala, 939 F. Supp. 1457 (C.D. Cal. 1996).

[299] Cedars-Sinai Medical Center v. Shalala, 125 F.3d 765 (9th Cir. 1997).

[300] Cedars-Sinai Medical Center v. Shalala, No. CV-95-02902-JGD (C.D. Cal. May 27, 1998), *upheld on appeal,* Cedars Sinai Medical Center v. Shalala, 177 F.3d 1126, 1130 (9th Cir. 1999).

[301] *In re* Cardiac Devices Qui Tam Litigation, All Cases, 221 F.R.D. 318 (Conn. Cir. Ct. 2004).

[302] *Id.*

## False Claims: Civil and Criminal Enforcement

time was ambiguous. Medicare historically has paid for services involving "investigational" devices used during an otherwise covered procedure, but has not covered procedures solely for the purpose of implanting an investigational device.

Another example is a settlement entered into in 2007 as a result of the Department of Justice alleging that Arizona Heart Hospital, Arizona Heart Institute, and AHI Cardiovascular Surgeons, Ltd. Submitted claims for services to Medicare beneficiaries involving the implantation of endoluminal graft devices for treatment of thorasic and abdominal aortic aneurysms. The issue was that the devices had not received final marketing approval from the FDA and were therefore implanted either without investigational device exemption (IDE) or outside of an approved IDE protocol. Arizona Heart Hospital settled by agreeing to pay $5.8 million (and submit to a corporate integrity agreement with OIG) and the physician group agreed to pay $900,000.[303]

### § 4-6(c)  Nursing Homes/Long Term Care Facilities

In June 1996, the OIG released a Special Fraud Alert identifying activities in the provision of services in nursing facilities that the OIG believes violate the Medicare/Medicaid false claims provisions. This Special Fraud Alert acknowledges that nursing facilities are particularly susceptible to fraud and abuse because they represent convenient resident "pools," making it lucrative for unscrupulous persons to carry out fraudulent schemes.[304]

This Special Fraud Alert specifically identifies several activities that the OIG considers as possibly violating the Medicare/Medicaid false claims provisions. First, the Special Fraud Alert provides several examples of healthcare providers in nursing facilities submitting claims for services that were not rendered, or were not provided as claimed. For example, the OIG identified a psychotherapist who worked at various nursing facilities and manipulated Medicare billing codes charging for three hours of therapy when, in fact, the he spent only a few minutes with each resident.

In this Special Fraud Alert, the OIG also provides examples of ways in which providers have falsified claims in order to circumvent coverage limitations. For example, as Medicare only covers limited types of procedures performed by podiatrists (e.g., Medicare only covers toenail removal and not toenail clippings), the OIG investigators found podiatrists improperly billing for toenail removals when the services were actually toenail clippings. The OIG became "suspicious" of a certain provider who billed for eleven toenail removals for one specific patient.

---

[303] Settlement Agreement between United States and Arizona Heart Hospital (Nov. 5, 2007) *available online at* http://op.bna.com/hl.nsf/r?Open=jthn-78nsks.
[304] 61 Fed. Reg. 30,623 (June 17, 1996).

Finally, the Special Fraud Alert identifies the following certain activities that generally may be characteristic of fraudulent or abusive activities;

- "Gang visits" by one or more medical professionals, where large numbers of residents are seen in a single day. The practitioner may be providing medically unnecessary services, or the level of service provided may not be of a sufficient duration or scope consistent with the service billed to Medicare or Medicaid;
- Frequent and recurring "routine visits" by the same medical professional. Seeing residents too often may indicate that the provider is billing for services that are not medically necessary;
- Unusually active presence in nursing facilities by healthcare practitioners who are given or request unlimited access to resident medical records. These individuals may be collecting information used in the submission of false claims; and
- Questionable documentation for medical necessity of professional services. Practitioners who are billing inappropriately may also enter, or fail to enter, important information on medical charts.[305]

Nursing homes and long term care facilities have also been subject to FCA repercussions for failure to care for patients in a proper way. For example, in *United States ex rel. Toomey v. Maxwell Manor Nursing Facility*,[306] a nursing home's patients were, among other things, routinely abused, neglected, mistreated, sexually assaulted, and overmedicated. The qui tam suit alleged that the facility billed Medicaid for inadequate services and inappropriate care. The parties settled for $1.6 million. Also, in January 2010, five nursing homes operated by Cathedral Rock plead guilty to FCA allegations that they maintained staffing that was inadequate for proper nursing or wound care; that residents often did not receive prescribed medications, records were falsified, and claims were submitted for services that were not provided.[307]

In October 2009, SCCI Hospitals of America, Inc. paid $830,166 to settle liability under the FCA. The long term acute-care hospital admission chain allegedly (1) admitted patients who did not meet admission criteria, (2) held and treated patients who no longer needed hospitalization, (3) had referring physicians modify orders to get around medical necessity requirements,

---

[305] *Id.*; *see also* United States v. St. Luke's Subacute Hospital and Nursing Centre Inc., No. 02-0044 MHP (N.D. Cal. *sentencing* Apr. 15, 2004) (CEO of nursing home sentenced to six and a half years in prison for directing employees to create false nursing schedules in an attempt to document inflated nursing costs prior to a Medicare audit).

[306] United States *ex rel*. Toomey v. Maxwell Manor Nursing Facility, No. 00C1102 (N.D. Ill. *settlement* Nov. 22, 2004).

[307] HHS/DOJ, Healthcare Fraud and Abuse Control Program, Annual Report for Fiscal Year 2010, 30.

## False Claims: Civil and Criminal Enforcement

(4) discharged patients who were not well enough for discharge, and (5) upcoded DRG classifications.[308]

### § 4-6(d)   Clinical Laboratories

Allegations of false claims in the laboratory area have focused on whether laboratory physician order forms cause the physician to order (and thus the laboratory to perform and bill) for higher-priced groups of tests intended to make a specific diagnosis instead of performing and billing separately for only those laboratory tests that are medically necessary. Medicare audits of laboratories frequently focus on this issue, and settlements have occurred. The OIG also has focused on this issue in several studies.

One case addressing this issue concerns the $111.4 million settlement entered into by National Health Laboratories (NHL) with the DOJ. NHL marketed its automated blood chemistry panel, known as SMAC, with two additional tests—HDL cholesterol and serum ferritin. In marketing the panel, NHL made statements indicating that the additional tests were provided at nominal or no extra charge. In fact, physicians were billed this nominal charge for these additional tests (or nothing if the doctors objected), while insurers, patients, and federal and state health insurance programs were charged the full, higher amount.

The government argued that by marketing these additional tests as part of the SMAC and misleading individuals as to the charge of these tests, a large number of tests were unnecessarily performed. Therefore, the government claimed NHL violated the FCA for having billed for tests it knew were not reasonable or medically necessary.

As part of its settlement, NHL pled guilty to two felony counts of submitting false claims to CHAMPUS, paid $1 million on these two criminal counts, paid $100 million to settle Medicare fraud charges, and paid $10.4 million to a coalition of state Medicaid programs. In addition, NHL president and Chief Executive Officer Robert Draper pled guilty to two counts of submitting false claims to CHAMPUS and California's Medi-Cal program. Draper was sentenced to three months in federal prison, two months of community confinement, three years' probation, a five-year ban from work involving healthcare billing to state or federal health insurance programs, and a $500,000 fine.

Since the NHL settlement, the federal government has been able to enter into a number of other significant settlements with clinical laboratories addressing substantially similar issues. For example, MetPath, Inc., agreed in September 1993 to pay $35 million to settle federal allegations that its blood-test billing practices resulted in overcharges to the Medicare program. MetPath also settled a state investigation of the same practices, as did NHL.

---

[308] HHS/DOJ, Healthcare Fraud and Abuse Control Program, Annual Report for Fiscal Year 2010, 24

Additionally, in May 1995, Corning Clinical Laboratories (formerly MetPath) agreed to pay $8.6 million to settle a qui tam suit in which it was alleged that MetPath billed the Medicare program for tests it never performed.

Other laboratory settlements also have focused on medical necessity issues. In March 1995, Allied Clinical Laboratories agreed to pay $4.9 million to settle a qui tam suit alleging the company fraudulently billed the Medicare program for non-reimbursable tests by inserting false diagnosis codes into electronic billings.[309] Similarly, Corning Bioran agreed in February 1996 to pay the federal government $6.8 million to settle allegations that it fraudulently billed Medicare for unnecessary laboratory tests.

## § 4-6(e)  Durable Medical Equipment and Home Medical Suppliers

The OIG has focused generally on fraudulent activities conducted by suppliers of durable medical equipment (DME) and other home medical supplies. In May 1995, for instance, a U.S. District Court entered a consent judgment of $21 million with lifetime exclusion against an operator of a DME company for allegedly filing claims with Medicare for delivering medical equipment that did not comply with program requirements, and that contained false certifications of medical necessity.[310]

In August of 2008, Rotect Healthcare Inc. agreed to settle allegations that it submitted false claims to Medicare. Even though the government never intervened in the case, Rotect agreed to pay $2 million to the federal government, $1.4 million to a whistleblower for expenses and attorney's fees and costs in addition to her share from the settlement. Rotect entered into a three-year corporate integrity agreement with OIG.[311]

### § 4-6(e)(1)  Provision of Medical Supplies to Nursing Homes

In August 1995, the Inspector General issued a Special Fraud Alert that concerned the provision of medical supplies to nursing facilities.[312] According to this Special Fraud Alert, nursing facilities and their residents have become "common targets" for fraudulent schemes involving medical supplies, both with and without the involvement of the facilities' management and staff.

---

[309] United States *ex rel*. Ramona Wagner v. Allied Clinical Laboratories, No. C-1-94-092, 1995 WL 254405 (S.D. Ohio filed Mar. 20, 1995).
[310] *See* United States v. Mickman, No. 89-7826 (E.D. Pa. May 15, 1994).
[311] United States *ex rel*. Bell-Messier v. Rotech Healthcare Inc., E.D. Tex., No. 5:04CV0075, *settlement announced* (Aug. 26, 2008).
[312] 60 Fed. Reg. 40,847, 40,849 *et seq.* (Aug. 10, 1995). *See* Chapter 2 of this title for a description of the anti-kickback aspects of this Special Fraud Alert.

## False Claims: Civil and Criminal Enforcement

Fraudulent billing schemes related to the provision of medical supplies to nursing homes uncovered by the OIG included the following:

- Submission of claims to Medicare Part B, by suppliers, for general medical supplies (e.g., tape, adhesive remover, skin creams and syringes) that were misrepresented as medically necessary for certain beneficiaries, and that instead should have been provided by the nursing homes and reflected in their Medicare cost reports. The OIG stated that one supplier billed Part B for an "oral/nasal hygiene program," which consisted of supplies such as saline solution, latex gloves, and cotton swabs that were not only not medically necessary, but also not used for the care of the beneficiaries identified in the Part B claims;

- Submission of claims to Medicare Part B, by suppliers, for "female external urinary devices" when no such devices were delivered. The OIG stated that one supplier delivered only adult diapers, and that another delivered only incontinence care products, but both billed Part B for "female external urinary devices"; and

- Submission of claims to Medicare Part B, by suppliers, for general medical supplies. The OIG stated that one supplier billed Part B for supplies that were appropriately claimed by the nursing facility on its Medicare cost report as expenses related to patient care. In the OIG's view, this resulted in the supplier misrepresenting its entitlement to payment, as well as the eligibility and coverage status of certain beneficiaries.

Subsequent to the Special Fraud Alert, the GAO released a report that cited suppliers' ability to bill Medicare directly for supplies to nursing home residents as a key reason why the residents are an "attractive target" for fraudulent schemes.[313]

Significant convictions and indictments have been obtained by the federal government since the OIG issued the Special Fraud Alert addressing the provision of medical supplies to nursing homes. For example, in 1996, a federal court sentenced a California nursing home owner to 11 years in prison, fined him $300,000, and ordered him to pay $3.2 million to Medicare for, *inter alia*, fraudulently billing Medicare for Medical supplies, such as catheters, that were never ordered or supplied to patients. One week earlier, in an Operation Restore Trust undertaking, a grand jury in the Eastern District of Michigan indicted four individuals on racketeering, conspiracy, and mail-fraud charges

---

[313] *See* GAO REP., No. HEHS-96-18, *Fraud and Abuse: Providers Target Medicare Patients in Nursing Facilities* (Jan. 24, 1996).

for allegedly defrauding the Medicare program of more than $25 million.[314] The indictment charges, *inter alia*, that the defendants were involved in a conspiracy to fraudulently obtain Medicare reimbursement for items such as incontinence kits for nursing home residents.

In what began as a qui tam action, a whistleblower alleged that long term care nursing chain Harborside Healthcare created HHC Nutrition Services, a phony DME provider through which McKesson Corp. provided kickbacks to Harborside in return for Harborside purchasing its DME from McKesson. As part of the eventual federal settlement in 2009, the Boston-based Harborside also agreed to pay the government $1.4 million and forego $498,000 in claims that had not yet been billed to Medicare.[315]

More recently, in *United States ex rel. Jamison v. McKesson Corp.*, McKesson succeeded in obtaining a dismissal of an FCA case brought by a qui tam relator concerning allegations of improper joint venture arraignments between it and nursing home. The Fifth Circuit affirmed the lower court's dismissal under the public disclosure bar holding that the relator's allegations were no more than descriptions of generic practices in the nursing home/supplier industry.[316]

### § 4-6(e)(2)    Seat Lifts

A Medicare Fraud Alert addressed several false billing schemes related to repairs made to seat lift chairs.[317] This fraud alert identifies several improper activities conducted by DME suppliers such as billing for more repair hours than actually provided, for repairs when parts were merely mailed to beneficiaries who live in a different state from the supplier (and thus the beneficiaries made the repairs themselves), and for repairs of chairs still under warranty. Medicare carriers are encouraged to scrutinize claims for repairs when the beneficiary is physically located outside the state in which the supplier is conducting business and to periodically review claims in order to determine whether a warranty is in effect.

### § 4-6(e)(3)    Telemarketing Schemes

One type of fraud in the DME industry that has been the subject of widespread publicity is based on telemarketing schemes. Such schemes

---

[314] United States v. Quisinberry, Weiss, Jackson & Saul, Crim. No. [unavailable] (E.D.Mich. Jan. 11, 1996).
[315] United States *ex rel.* Jamison v. Harborside Healthcare, N.D. Miss., number not available, *settlement announced* (Oct. 8, 2009).
[316] United States *ex rel.* Jamison v. McKesson Corp., No. 10-60376, 2011 U.S. App. (5th Cir. Aug. 5, 2011).
[317] Medicare Fraud Alert No. 94-03, CCH MEDICARE & MEDICAID GUIDE ¶ 13921.30.

## False Claims: Civil and Criminal Enforcement

are generally described as "boiler room" operations in which patients are contacted and offered "free" equipment (usually based on a waiver of coinsurance and deductible amounts). The supplier obtains any requisite certification of medical necessity by asking the patient for the identity of his physician, and contacting the physician with a completed certificate of medical necessity requiring only the physician's signature. To obtain the signature, the physician may be told that the supplier's staff discussed the patient with the physician's staff. Certificates may include false diagnostic information in order to justify furnishing the beneficiary with a full range of equipment

OIG has expressed concern over DME suppliers contacting Medicare beneficiaries based solely on a treating physician's prescribing durable medical equipment for the beneficiary. OIG has clarified that DME suppliers may contact a beneficiary when (1) the beneficiary has previously given written consent to be contacted by telephone, (2) the contact is regarding a covered item that that the beneficiary has already received from the supplier, or (3) the supplier has furnished at least one covered item to the beneficiary in the preceding 15 months.[318]

On October 2, 1998, the president of a DME company pled guilty to two counts of mail fraud. The DME company billed the TRICARE program and private insurance companies for DME that was never provided to Medicare beneficiaries or for DME other than what customers actually received.[319] The president of the company had obtained a list of persons with handicapped license plates from a state motor vehicle office, and directed employees to use telemarketing techniques to sell scooters and adjustable beds, while offering free DME with no copayment obligation to people with physical handicaps. The DME company billed insurance companies for more-sophisticated and more-expensive equipment, such as motorized wheelchairs and hospital beds, than actually provided.

### § 4-6(e)(4)  Certificates of Medical Necessity

For many DME items, the DME supplier must receive a certificate of medical necessity (CMN), which evidences the proof of medical necessity for the particular item of DME. The supplier must maintain these CMNs in their records before claims for payment may be made to the Medicare program. Actions against DME suppliers under the FCA often allege falsification or alteration of these CMNs, and take many forms. Examples of such falsification include adding information to a CMN, completing portions of the CMN by a supplier that a doctor must complete, or whiting out and replacing

---

[318] OIG Special Fraud Alert on Telemarketing by Durable Medical Equipment Suppliers, (Jan. 14, 2010).
[319] *See* DOJ Healthcare Fraud Rep. (1998), *available online at* http://www.usdoj.gov/dag/pubdoc/health98.htm.

information on already-completed CMNs. Notwithstanding the accuracy of the information that a supplier might place on a CMN, if the supplier inappropriately added information to the CMN, then such conduct is still actionable under the FCA.[320]

One of the items of DME for which Medicare provides coverage is home oxygen therapy, which accounts for one of the largest portions of Medicare payments of DME. According to a 1999 OIG study, 23% of the oxygen CMNs reviewed in the study was defective.[321] In its report, the OIG estimated that Medicare paid $263 million in 1996 for home oxygen-therapy claims that were supported by defective CMNs.[322]

In addition, whether a Medicare beneficiary even qualifies for home oxygen therapy depends on the results of an arterial blood gas or pulse oximetry test. The Medicare program prohibits a DME supplier from performing such a test in order to qualify a Medicare beneficiary for home oxygen therapy. Rather, a physician or some other independent source must perform the test.

## § 4-6(f)   Home Health Agencies

A Special Fraud Alert, released by the OIG in June 1995 as an Operation Restore Trust federal initiative, addressed fraud in the home health industry.[323] Citing a five-fold increase in Medicare payments for home health, the OIG stated that home healthcare is an area that is "particularly vulnerable to abuse." (A description of Operation Restore Trust is contained in Chapters 1 and 8.)

With respect to false claims, the OIG indicated that the following three activities are under scrutiny in the area of home health: (1) claims for visits that were never made or were made to ineligible beneficiaries; (2) fraudulent agency cost-report claims; and (3) high-pressure sales tactics. See Chapter 2 for a discussion of the OIG's kickback concerns in the home health industry.

According to the Special Fraud Alert, the OIG had uncovered instances in which HHAs have submitted claims to Medicare for visits that were not made or were not authorized by a physician, as well as for visits that were to beneficiaries who were not homebound or who did not require a qualifying service. The OIG stated that it believed beneficiaries' names have been forged on visit logs and physician signatures on plans of care. More important, the OIG asserted that HHAs are liable for all claims for services provided by subcontractors, and that both agencies and physicians are responsible for ensuring the medical necessity of claims submitted to the Medicare program.

---

[320] *See, e.g.,* United States v. Wolk, No, 93-5773 (E.D. Pa. Memorandum and Order Jan 17, 1995).
[321] Office of Evaluation and Inspections, Office of Inspector General, *Usage and Documentation of Home Oxygen Therapy*, No. OEI-03-96-00090 (Aug. 1999).
[322] *Id.*
[323] 60 Fed. Reg. 40,847 *et seq.* (Aug. 10, 1995).

## False Claims: Civil and Criminal Enforcement

With respect to sales tactics by HHAs, the OIG stated that it had learned of high-pressure tactics used by some agencies to maximize their patient populations and profits, which could result in false claims liability. According to the Special Fraud Alert, these agencies offered beneficiaries non-covered services (e.g., grocery shopping or housekeeping) in exchange for their Medicare identification numbers. The OIG also indicated that physicians had reported that some agencies were pressuring them to order unnecessary services by claiming that their patients wanted these services and would find another physician if these patients' demands were not met.

Shortly after the issuance of the Special Fraud Alert, a federal grand jury indicted ABC Home Health Services, Inc. (later known as First American Healthcare of Georgia, Inc.), the largest privately held home healthcare provider in the U.S., for conspiracy to defraud the Medicare program of more than $14 million.[324] The indictment alleged, *inter alia*, that ABC fraudulently billed Medicare by claiming personal expenses (e.g., airplane trips to Cozumel, Mexico, and maid services) on its cost reports. In February 1996, a jury convicted ABC's owner, Robert J. "Jack" Mills, on numerous counts of Medicare fraud, including committing mail fraud and submitting false claims.[325]

In July 1998, Olsten Corporation settled certain civil matters with the United States for approximately $40.9 million, in addition to criminal penalties associated with the investigation. The civil settlement settled allegations that Olsten and Columbia/HCA submitted or caused to be submitted false claims in the form of inflated management fees that allegedly included acquisition costs of HHAs. The government alleged that Olsten sold certain of its HHAs to Columbia at less than fair market value, in exchange for an excessive management fee paid by Columbia/HCA to Olsten to manage the HHAs. The civil settlement also resolved allegations that Olsten filed fraudulent cost reports that sought Medicare payment for non-reimbursable costs including personal expenses of corporate executives.

In connection with the settlement, Kimberly Home Healthcare, Inc., a subsidiary, entered a criminal plea agreement in three districts and paid more than $10 million in criminal fines. Kimberly pled guilty to three separate felony charges (conspiracy, mail fraud, and anti-kickback violations) in the Middle and Southern Districts of Florida and the Northern District of Georgia, and paid $10.08 million in criminal fines.

In December of 2009, three New York home health agencies settled for $24 million allegations that they submitted false claims to Medicare and Medicaid programs. New York Medicaid covers only services provided by home health aides with valid certificates of training. It was alleged that the agencies

---

[324] *See* BNA's HEALTH LAW REP., Aug. 31, 1995, p. 1321-1322; Apr. 6, 1995, p. 523; *see also* GAO REP., No. OSI-95-17, *Allegations Against ABC Home Healthcare* (July 1995).
[325] *See* United States v. Mills, No. CR-295-42 (S.D. Ga. Feb. 4, 1996).

billed for services after they provided the aides with falsified certificates or knew that the aides were using falsified certificates.[326]

## § 4-6(g)  Medicare Contractors

In *United States ex. rel. McCoy v. California Medical Review, Inc.*, two employees brought a qui tam action against a peer review organization alleging that the PRO falsely certified performance of contractually required reviews of hospital discharges that were never performed. This case was subsequently settled in early 1992 for $16 million to be paid to the federal government, plus an additional $335,000 in attorney's fees and costs.[327]

Healthcare plans and other contractors are vulnerable to fraud allegations in their capacity as claims administrators for the Medicare program. For instance, Blue Cross and Blue Shield of Michigan agreed in January 1995 to pay $27.6 million to settle a qui tam lawsuit in which the federal government intervened. The lawsuit alleged that the company defrauded the government by performing inadequate audits of certain hospitals' Medicare cost reports to determine which costs the Medicare program should pay. Also alleged in the suit was that the company corrected audits that HCFA had asked to review, which resulted in Medicare improperly paying for claims based on these corrected audits.[328]

The DOJ also intervened in a qui tam action under the FCA against Florida Blue Cross. The government alleged in its amended complaint that Florida Blue Cross, in its capacity as Medicare carrier for the state, mishandled Medicare claims and failed to process claims in accordance with Medicare requirements.[329] In addition, Blue Cross and Blue Shield of Massachusetts agreed in September 1994 to pay the federal government $2.75 million to settle a qui tam lawsuit alleging that it falsely reported the efficiency of its performance in administering Medicare claims.[330]

Private insurers also have been subject to Medicare fraud allegations in substantially unsuccessful qui tam lawsuits alleging that the insurers failed to meet their obligations to perform MSP determinations, thereby resulting in inappropriate primary Medicare coverage for certain Medicare beneficiaries. In a series of qui tam lawsuits, a law firm brought suit

---

[326] HHS/DOJ, Healthcare Fraud and Abuse Control Program, Annual Report for Fiscal Year 2010, 33.

[327] United States ex. rel. McCoy v. California Medical Review, Inc., 723 F. Supp 1363 (N.D. Cal. 1989).

[328] United States *ex rel.* Flynn v. Blue Cross and Blue Shield of Michigan, No. 93-1794 (C.D. Md. settled Jan. 18, 1995).

[329] United States *ex rel.* Theresa Burr v. Blue Cross and Blue Shield of Florida, Inc., No. 91-134-Civ.-J-16 (M.D. Fla. 1995).

[330] *See* United States v. Blue Cross and Blue Shield of Massachusetts, No. 93-11321 WD (C.D. Mass. filed June 16, 1993).

## False Claims: Civil and Criminal Enforcement

under the FCA against five insurers based upon information obtained in the course of conducting discovery in an unrelated legal action arising out of an automobile accident. Through the discovery process, the law firm obtained documents, which indicated that several insurance companies may have failed to process and pay as primary payor the medical expense claims of certain working-aged individuals for whom Medicare is the secondary payor.[331]

Anthem Health Plans, one of Connecticut's largest Medicare contractors, agreed to pay the federal government over $74 million to settle allegations that Blue Cross and Blue Shield of Connecticut (which Anthem purchased in 1997) falsified cost reports from 1989 to 1991. The allegations brought against Blue Cross and Blue Shield of Connecticut were in connection with its role as a Medicare fiscal intermediary.[332] The government alleged that Blue Cross and Blue Shield of Connecticut altered its books and falsified cost reports so that they would pass government performance standards as a fiscal intermediary. Although the government stated that the problem initially may have begun as innocent accounting mistakes, the government argued that Anthem employees tried to cover up those mistakes by falsifying records and sending out more overpayments to hospitals in Connecticut to which the hospitals were not entitled. According to the government, Blue Cross and Blue Shield of Connecticut paid more than $32 million to Connecticut hospitals that the hospitals did not deserve, half of it to cover up previous overpayments.

In 2008, a Medicare Part A fiscal intermediary agreed to a settlement of $2.1 million of charges of violating the False Claims Act by providing excessive outlier payments to hospitals. It was alleged that BlueCross BlueShield of Tennessee (BCBS-T), doing business as Riverbend Government Benefit Administrators, the primary Medicare Part A fiscal intermediary for New Jersey, failed to adjust the cost-to-charge ratios for the New Jersey hospitals in a timely fashion. This failure resulted in excessive outlier payments by Medicare to the hospitals.[333]

---

[331] *See* United States *ex rel.* Stinson, Lyons, Gerlin & Bustamante, P.A. v. Prudential, 944 F.2d 1149 (3d Cir. 1991); United States *ex rel.* Stinson, Lyons, Gerlin & Bustamante, P.A. v. Pan Am. Life Ins. Co., No. 90-411, 1992 U.S. Dist. LEXIS 7990 (E.D. La. May 28, 1992); United States *ex rel.* Stinson, Lyons, Gerlin & Bustamante, P.A. v. Pilot Life Ins. Co. No. C-90 29-G, 1991 U.S. Dist. LEXIS 14483 (M.D.N.C. June 6, 1991); United States *ex rel.* Stinson, Lyons, Gerlin & Bustamante, P.A. v. Blue Cross & Blue Shield of Georgia, Inc., 755 F. Supp. 1040 (S.D. Ga. 1990); United States *ex rel.* Stinson, Lyons, Gerlin & Bustamante, P.A. v. Provident Life & Accident Ins. Co., 721 F. Supp. 1247 (S.D. Fla. 1989).

[332] A fiscal intermediary is an insurance company or data processing company that contracts with CMS to process Medicare or Medicaid claims on behalf of the federal government.

[333] *See* Settlement Agreement Between the United States and Blue Cross and Blue Shield of Tennessee, (Aug. 5, 2008) *available online at http://op.bna.com/hl.nsf/r?Open=jthn-7hes7w*.

## § 4-6(h)  Pharmacies and Pharmaceutical Manufacturers

Although pharmacy fraud may involve many of the same types of fraudulent activities that are actionable in other segments of the healthcare industry, pharmacy fraud also has some of its own unique fraud issues. For instance, in the summer of 1992 the FBI concluded an undercover investigation entitled "Operation Goldpill." The investigation not only uncovered evidence of fraudulent billing practices, but also uncovered a "drug diversion" scheme that involved collusion among patients, physicians, and pharmacies, resulting in unnecessary Medicaid billings for doctor visits and prescribed drugs.[334] The government also has focused on pharmacy practices of switching patients to more expensive drugs than the generic version that had been prescribed by the patients' physician. For example, in 2008, CVS Caremark Corp. agreed to pay $36.7 million to resolve claims that, between 2000 and 2006, it improperly switched patients from a tablet version of a generic drug to a more expensive capsule version to increase Medicaid reimbursement while providing no additional medical benefit to beneficiaries.[335] The states alleged that Caremark encouraged doctors to switch patients to different brand name prescriptions, while falsely claiming that switching medications would save the consumers money and concealing the fact that rebates acquired through the switching process would not be passed along to health plans and patients. Other retail pharmacies have also entered into similar settlements concerning the same practices.[336]

Apart from issues relating to pharmacies, recent enforcement activity has focused on pharmaceutical manufacturers themselves, particularly with respect to their pricing practices. For example, in 1997, the DOJ commenced an investigation to examine the practices of pharmaceutical pricing practices. The genesis of the investigation was a 1995 qui tam lawsuit filed by a Florida-based pharmacy. The relator alleged that more than twenty drug manufacturers misrepresented the price used to benchmark Medicare and Medicaid

---

[334] FBI Press Release, *"Operation Goldpill" Targets Healthcare Crime* (June 30, 1992). More specifically, physicians would recruit patients eligible for Medicaid and then write prescriptions for these patients, despite the fact that these patients were not ill. The patient then would have the prescription filled by a pharmacist also involved in the scheme. The patient would sell the prescription drugs to a "non-con" man (a term used for criminals who trade in non-narcotic prescription medication), who in turn would sell the drugs to the public or pharmacies. Meanwhile, the Medicaid program would be billed for the unwarranted office visit and the prescription drugs. Additionally, pharmacies committed various fraudulent billing practices, including dispensing generic drugs while billing for higher priced brand names, billing both Medicaid and insurance carriers for a drug or dispensing fee, and billing for prescriptions never written or filled.

[335] DOJ Press Release, *CVS Caremark Corp. to Pay $36.7 Million to U.S., 23 States, & D.C. to Settle Medicaid Prescription Drug Fraud Allegations* (Mar. 18, 2008), *available online at* http://www.usdoj.gov/opa/pr/2008/March/08_crt_214.html;. United States et al., *ex rel.* Bernard Lisitza v. CVS Caremark Corp., No. 1:03-cv-00742 (N.D. Il. 2003).

[336] *Id.*

## False Claims: Civil and Criminal Enforcement

reimbursement for such drugs, while concurrently selling these drugs to physicians at a discount.

The genesis of much of this enforcement activity centered around that fact that, historically, Medicare reimbursed providers for Part B drugs based on 95% of the drugs' average wholesale price (AWP). This formula has been subjected to significant public scrutiny in recent years, due to a generally acknowledged truism that AWP is neither "average," "wholesale," nor a "price." Under an AWP reimbursement system, providers sometimes can acquire drugs at prices below AWP, yet be reimbursed at 95% of AWP. The AWP-based reimbursement has been the subject of both litigation and government fraud settlements with pharmaceutical manufacturers who allegedly manipulated their products' AWPs and/or marketed the "spread" between the acquisition cost of the product and the reimbursement.

As a result, a number of pharmaceutical manufacturers have entered into settlements with the government based upon their drug pricing. For example, in 2001, Bayer Corporation settled allegations with the government that Bayer caused physicians and other providers to submit false claims to the Medicaid program by falsely inflating its reported drug prices to the Medicaid program. The $14 million settlement reached with the federal government and forty-five states resolved allegations that Bayer falsely inflated the drug prices used by the government to set Medicaid reimbursement rates for such drugs. That same year, TAP Pharmaceuticals was involved in a massive criminal fine and civil settlement. TAP pleaded guilty to conspiring to violate the Prescription Drug Marketing Act, and was fined $290 million. It settled its federal FCA liabilities by paying $560 million for fraudulent claims it filed with the Medicare and Medicaid programs and $25.5 million for state civil liabilities. The false claims were a result of fraudulent pricing schemes, sales and marketing misconduct, and failure to provide TAP's best price. The government alleged in its complaint that, during the 1990s, TAP reported to the Medicare program an AWP "significantly higher" that the average sales price it offered its prostate-cancer drug Lupron to physicians and other customers.[337]

Another set of investigations of (and subsequent settlements by) pharmaceutical manufacturers concerns the government's theory that improper marketing and promotion of drugs can result in liability under the FCA. For example, in 2004, Pfizer, a division of the Warner-Lambert Company, paid $430 million in fines in order to resolve allegations that, by marketing the drug Neurontin for off-label uses not approved by the FDA and by other conduct, Warner-Lambert caused the submission of false and/or fraudulent claims to Medicaid.[338] In December 2010, Dey, Inc., agreed to a $280 million

---

[337] DOJ Press Release, *TAP Pharmaceutical Products Inc. and Seven Others Charged with Healthcare Crimes; Company Agrees to Pay $875 Million to Settle Charges* (Oct. 3, 2001), *available online at* http://www.usdoj.gov/opa/pr/2001/October/513civ.htm.
[338] *See* OIG SEMIANNUAL REP. (Apr. 1 through Sept. 30, 2004).

settlement of charges that Dey caused false and fraudulent claims to be submitted resulting in higher amounts received by the company than if truthful prices had been reported. The difference in the cost was used by Dey to market and promote its products.[339]

## § 4-6(i)  Billing Companies, Consultants and Lawyers

Due to the complex nature of reimbursement regulations, billing companies and consulting firms frequently provide physicians and other Medicare suppliers with advice concerning proper billing for their services. However, billing companies and consultants face potential FCA exposure if their advice causes their clients to submit false claims to the federal healthcare programs. (*See* § 4-2(a)(4), *supra*.)

In addition to scrutinizing the services provided by billing companies to healthcare providers, the government has extended its focus to consultants who provide healthcare reimbursement advice. In January of 1997, the OIG advised its agents and prosecutors to look out for providers who use consultants (sometimes referred to as "optimization consultants") to maximize their Medicare reimbursement. The "Medicare Alert" instructed OIG enforcement personnel to investigate providers using such consultants and advised agents to enlist Medicare fiscal intermediaries to scrutinize the arrangements. This alert was in response to *United States v. Metzinger Associates*.[340]

Metzinger Associates provided billing services to hospitals and was accused of engaging in a "CPT-4 Maximization" scheme that involved using improper coding methods (e.g., upcoding, unbundling, and rebundling) to gain increased Medicare reimbursement. The scheme affected more than 200 hospitals in 17 states, and led to the government's claim against two Metzinger executives and 11 participating hospitals. The two Metzinger executives entered into a settlement with the government that excluded them from Medicare and Medicaid for three years, and subjected them to $60,000 in fines. Also included in the settlement was an agreement by the executives to provide 250 hours of consulting time to help with fraud cases.

Similarly, in December 2000, the government and qui tam relator John Schilling alleged that KPMG Peat Marwick knowingly made false, exaggerated, and ineligible claims for payment on behalf of five hospitals. Additionally, KPMG allegedly prepared "reserve" cost reports that estimated the effect a government audit would have on the hospitals' reimbursements if the audit determined that the claimed costs were not allowable. According to the complaint, KPMG's FCA liability derived from the "duty to report known errors

---

[339] U.S. *ex rel.* Ven-A-Care of the Florida Keys Inc. v. Dey Laboratories, D. Mass., No. 05-11084-PBS.

[340] United States v. Metzinger, No. 94-7520 (E.D. Pa. Sept. 17, 1996), *final settlement* (Apr. 21, 1997).

## False Claims: Civil and Criminal Enforcement

that result in unwarranted federal payments."[341] Although KPMG was only paid $200,000 for the services it provided to the hospitals, it entered into a $9 million settlement agreement with the government, adamantly denying any wrongdoing.

In 2004, the United States filed a complaint against Ernst & Young LLP seeking to recover more than $900,000 in laboratory payments improperly submitted to Medicare by the firm's client hospitals. The hospitals retained Ernst & Young to provide healthcare consulting services concerning accurately assigning codes to the services they performed for reimbursement from Medicare and insurance companies. However, the advice led to improper claims, and Ernst & Young settled with the government by agreeing to pay $1.5 million and adamantly denied wrongdoing. Ironically, five of the hospital clients retained Ernst & Young for an outpatient laboratory review related to the investigation of the *Metzinger* case mentioned earlier.[342]

Not only are traditional consultants and billing companies increasingly becoming the subject of FCA actions, but attorneys also are now at risk of potential FCA liability. In *United States v. Anderson*, the government indicted two healthcare attorneys in connection with consulting contracts between a hospital and physicians that were drafted by these attorneys.[343] Ultimately, the District Court acquitted both attorneys and found that the attorneys "did not prepare sham agreements to paper over a fraud but, rather, tried their best to prepare agreements that would reflect what they intended to be legal transactions ...."[344] The significance of the case stems from the government's willingness to make an attorney's legal advice actionable under the FCA in an attempt to look beneath the surface of potential sham arrangements.

More recently, the former general counsel for Tenet, Christi Sulzbach was accused of making false certifications to the government. Specifically, the government contended that declarations made as part of Tenet's corporate integrity agreement were in fact false. This case was resolved in favor for the defendant, nevertheless attorney are not immune from prosecution and should exercise care in making any statement to the government. (See Chapter 9 for further discussion of this case.)[345]

---

[341] United States *ex rel.* Schilling v. KPMG, Complaint at 1–2. Interestingly, the GAO criticized HCFA in a report, noting that HCFA continued to use auditing services by KPMG and extended its contract with the accounting firm in 1998 and 1999, despite the fact that HCFA officials were aware of the allegations against KPMG. *See* GAO Rep., *HCFA Extended its Contract with Accounting Firm Implicated in Major Fraud* (GAO-01-136R) (Oct. 31, 2000).

[342] United States v. Ernst & Young LLP, No. 04-cv-00041 (E.D. Pa. *settlement announced* July 20, 2004).

[343] United States v. Anderson, No. 98-20030 (D. Kan 1999).

[344] *Id.*

[345] *See discussion of* U.S. v. Sulzbach, Case No. 07-61329 Civ Marra. S.D.F.L., in chapter 9 section 9-7.

The OIG has issued several advisory opinions relating to arrangements between billing companies/consultants and healthcare providers. Often the issue that the OIG finds troubling is percentage-compensation arrangements where the consultant/billing company's fee is based upon a certain percentage of revenue derived from a federal healthcare program.

For example, in a 1998 advisory opinion, the OIG examined a contractual arrangement for distribution and billing services between a billing/consulting company and a manufacturer of orthopedic products to determine whether the arrangement constitutes grounds for sanction under the Anti-Kickback Statute.[346] Pursuant to the arrangement, the manufacturer would consign certain products to the billing/consulting company who, in turn, would consign them to physicians. Because the goods are provided on a consignment basis, the goods would remain the property of the manufacturer until sold to a patient. Under the proposed arrangement, the billing/consulting company would market and service the manufacturer's customer accounts. In addition, the billing/consulting company would bill for these products under its own supplier number and forward reimbursements to the manufacturer, less the consulting fee, which ranged from 20 to 25% of collected revenue. Although percentage-compensation arrangements are not per se prohibited, the OIG found the proposed arrangement problematic for a variety of reasons. For example, the OIG found that the billing/consulting company would have opportunities to unduly influence referral sources and patients, as the arrangement calls for active marketing by the consultant/billing company directly to Medicare patients.

On March 9, 2000, the OIG issued another advisory opinion relating to billing companies. In the advisory opinion, the OIG examined a consulting company that would enter into contracts with hospitals to audit hospital bills for undercharges and overcharges to private insurers paying on a charge basis. The OIG concluded that the arrangement would not subject either party to sanctions for violations of the Anti-Kickback Statute.[347] Hospitals would compensate the consulting company by paying the company a percentage of the amount that the hospitals recover through the consulting company's work. Critical to the OIG's conclusion, however, was the fact that the consulting company was not auditing bills reimbursed by the federal or state healthcare programs.

A whistleblower lawsuit charged that a St. Louis pain management clinic submitted claims to Medicare and Medicaid for spinal decompression services using a DRX-9000 machine, a nonsurgical treatment for back pain. The submitted claims falsely state, however, that patients received direct one-on-one therapy from a physical therapist. The clinic did not actually employ any

---

[346] OIG Advisory Op. No. 98-1 (Mar. 19, 1998).
[347] OIG Advisory Op No. 00-1 (Mar. 16, 2000).

## False Claims: Civil and Criminal Enforcement

physical therapists. Claims also falsely used physical therapy codes to obtain payment for use of the DRX-9000 machine, which is not an actual covered service. The government also charged the billing company whose main operations were the conduct of billing operations for the pain clinic. As part of a settlement with the government, the billing company UPC agreed to exclusion from participation in federal healthcare programs for five years.[348]

### § 4-6(j)  Physicians

As with the other industries, physicians risk FCA liability under the traditional theories of FCA cases such as upcoding, billing for items or services not rendered, and the like. An additional area of potential liability for physicians under the FCA derives from the treating physician's role for determining the medical necessity for a particular item or service reimbursable under the Medicare program. Because Medicare pays for only those items or services that are "medically necessary," the Medicare program largely relies on the judgment of the treating physician. Medicare requires physicians to certify to the medical necessity for many items and services through prescriptions, orders, or (in certain specific circumstances) CMNs. These documentation requirements verify that the physician has reviewed the patient's condition, and has determined that services or supplies are medically necessary.

Two areas where such certification plays a key role are home health services and DME. In response to concern for whether physicians adequately assess Medicare beneficiaries' needs for these services, the OIG issued a Special Fraud Alert to increase awareness of the significance of CMNs.[349] In the Special Fraud Alert, the OIG listed examples of such inappropriate certifications that the OIG had discovered during the course of its investigations, including the following.

- A physician knowingly signs a number of forms provided by a HHA that falsely represent that skilled nursing services are medically necessary in order to qualify the patient for home health services.

- A physician certifies that a patient is confined to the home and qualifies for home health services, even though the patient tells the physician that her only restrictions are due to arthritis in her hands, and she has no restrictions on her routine activities, such as grocery shopping.

- At the prompting of a DME supplier, a physician signs a stack of blank CMNs for transcutaneous electrical nerve stimulator (TENS) units.

---

[348] United States *ex rel.*. Richards v. Naushad, E.D. Mo., No. 4:08-CV-00066, (*settlement announced* Mar. 9, 2010).

[349] OIG Special Fraud Alert, *Physician Liability For Certifications In The Provision of Medical Equipment and Supplies and Home Health Services* (January 1999), *available online at* http://oig.hhs.gov/fraud/docs/alertsandbulletins/dme.htm.

The CMNs are completed later with false information in support of fraudulent claims for the equipment. The false information purports to show that the physician ordered and certified to the medical necessity for the TENS units for which the supplier has submitted claims.

- A physician signs CMNs for respiratory medical equipment falsely representing that the equipment was medically necessary.
- A physician signs CMNs for wheelchairs and hospital beds without seeing the patients, then falsifies medical charts to indicate that the physician treated them.
- A physician accepts anywhere from $50 to $400 from a DME supplier for each prescription she signs for oxygen concentrators and nebulizers.

In 2005, a physician was found guilty on four counts that he caused false and fraudulent claims to be submitted to Medicare for evaluations that he never performed or personally supervised, and sixteen counts of signing bogus CMNs for Medicare beneficiaries who received motorized wheelchairs but did not qualify for the DME. The physician billed Medicare in excess of $4 million and was paid $1.4 million, which led to a sentence of five years in prison and a $250,000 fine.[350]

In June 2011, a Las Vegas oncologist agreed to settle allegations that he submitted false claims to federal healthcare programs by agreeing to pay $5.7 million, plus interest. The federal government alleged that between 2007 and 2009, the physician submitted false claims for intensity modulated radiation therapy, a treatment intended for those types of cancer where extreme precision is required to spare surrounding organs or healthy tissue. The false claims consisted of double-billing Medicare, TRICARE, and the FEHBP for several procedures affiliated with radiation treatment plans; billing for certain high reimbursement radiation oncology services when a different, less expensive service should have been billed; and billing for medically unnecessary radiation oncology services.[351]

## § 4-6(k)  Dentists

Increased investigations by state MFCUs have led to several settlements and convictions of dentists who have attempted to defraud the Medicaid program. For example, New York began an enforcement sweep against

---

[350] United States v. Mauskar, No. H-03-0368 (S.D. Tex. *conviction* Nov. 17, 2005).

[351] Press Release, Department of Justice, *Las Vegas Physician to Pay U.S. $5.7 Million to Resolve False Claims Act Allegations Related to Radiation Oncology Services and Other Procedures* (June 30, 2011) *available online at* http://www.justice.gov/opa/pr/2011/June/11-civ-866.html.

## False Claims: Civil and Criminal Enforcement

dentists in 2001 that has resulted in more than 30 convictions, with more than $4 million paid in restitution.

Similarly, the state of Florida charged 10 dentists and nine other individuals on racketeering, fraud, and other felony counts for their participation in separate schemes that billed Medicaid for approximately $10 million.[352] It was alleged that those involved were treating children who were recruited and driven to south Florida clinics.[353] Schemes of this type usually involve the practice of paying drivers to entice children with cash and/or food to accompany them to the facility. In a press release from the Florida Attorney General's office, Robert Butterworth stated that "[i]t is unlawful for any medical practitioner, program, clinic, or other type of Medicaid provider to solicit individuals to become patients of that facility or doctor."[354]

The government investigated and alleged that FORBA Holdings LLC, which provides business management and administrative services to 69 dental clinics, pressured them to generate revenues leading to unnecessary root canals, crowns and tooth extractions. The government saw the allegations as an example of exploiting children at a time when Medicaid funds are already low. OIG said there was additional evidence that unlicensed and uncertified staff were performing procedures. FORBA agreed to enter into a five-year corporate integrity agreement with OIG and pay $24 million.[355]

### § 4-6(l)   Ambulance Companies

Medicare reimburses for ambulance services with a fee schedule in which providers are reimbursed on a pre-established fee for each service. Medicare only reimburses for ambulance services that are medically necessary, meaning another form of transportation would be counter indicated based on the patient's condition at the time of transport. In addition, the ambulance, equipment, and personnel must meet Medicare requirements, which at times include a signed certification from a physician or authorized individual. Ambulance fraud settlements have traditionally centered on allegations of: (1) improper relationships with referral sources; (2) falsifying paperwork; (3) upcoding level of service; and (4) billing for medically unnecessary transports, the latter being especially true with respect to the transportation of patients to and from dialysis facilities.

---

[352] *State Charges 19 in Dental Clinic Probe of Child Solicitation Medicaid Schemes*, HEALTHCARE DAILY, Vol. 5, No. 238 (Dec. 11, 2000).
[353] *Id.*
[354] *Id.*
[355] United States *ex rel.* McDaniel v. FORBA Holdings LLC, D. Md., No. 8:07-cv-0-3416-AW, *unsealed* (Jan. 20, 2010): *see also* Settlement Agreement Between United States and FORBA Holdings, LLC (Jan. 15, 2010) *available online at* http://op.bna.com/hl.nsf/r?Open=jthn-7zvsxv.

In a report released in January 2006, the OIG stated that 25% of ambulance transports in 2002 did not meet Medicare's program requirements, resulting in an estimated $402 million of improper payments.[356] Previous OIG studies indicated that Medicare's ambulance transport benefit was vulnerable to abuse. A 1994 report found that 70% of dialysis-related transport claims were paid in error, while results from a 1998 survey showed that two-thirds of claims did not meet program requirements. [357]

Settlements that highlight the potential abuse regarding ambulance services and reimbursement for such services include the following:

- a $200,000 settlement to resolve allegations that the ambulance company inflated mileage to increase Medicare reimbursement;
- a $120,000 settlement to resolve allegations that an ambulance company sought reimbursement for advanced life-support services (for which Medicare reimburses at a greater rate) when only basic life-support services were provided;
- the conviction of a co-owner and operator of an ambulance company sentencing him to nine years in federal prison and ordering him to pay more than $2.4 million in restitution to Medicare;[358]
- the conviction of the CEO and an employee of a Mobile, AL, ambulance company for defrauding Medicare out of approximately $650,000 over a three-year period beginning in 1992, by billing for ambulance services where many of the beneficiaries walked to an ambulance and rode in the front seat; and
- the $1.6 million settlement between the government and an ambulance company concerning medically unnecessary transport of dialysis patients over the course of four years.[359]

Based on the OIG's review of ambulance claims in 2002, it suggested that CMS "implement program integrity activities designed to reduce improper payments" for ambulance services with the highest risk for error (e.g., dialysis

---

[356] OIG REP., *Medicare Payments for Ambulance Transports* (OEI-05-02-00590) (Jan. 2006).
[357] *See* OIG REP., *Medical Necessity of Medicare Ambulance Services* (OEI-09-95-00412) (Dec. 29, 1998).
[358] United States v. Shpirt, CR 02-485A (C.D. Cal. *sentencing* Sept. 2, 2005). Evidence at trial showed defendant regularly submitted claims to Medicare that stated patients were bedridden when they were not, and that patients were being transported for dialysis treatments when they were actually transported for treatments for which Medicare would not pay.
[359] Arrangements between ambulance companies and other healthcare providers has been the subject of a number of OIG advisory opinions, especially given the potential for prohibited referrals between the ambulance company and the healthcare provider. For example, on (January 27, 1999), the OIG issued an advisory opinion that the provision of backup ambulance transportation services as a community services free of charge to Medicare beneficiaries would not risk sanctions under the Anti-Kickback Statute.

## False Claims: Civil and Criminal Enforcement

transports and non-emergency cases).[360] These program-integrity activities should include the following:

- instructing Medicare contractors to implement prepayment edits that would more closely scrutinize nonemergency and dialysis-related ambulance-transport claims;
- instructing Medicare contractors to obtain documentation from ambulance suppliers and at least one third-party provider associated with the transport when conducting postpayment medical reviews; and
- directing contractors to educate third-party providers on when it is appropriate to use an ambulance for nonemergency transports.[361]

After being convicted of overbilling the Medicare program in 2004, the owner of an ambulance company and his wife agreed to settle a civil lawsuit over the fraud for $6 million. It was alleged that between 1998 and 2002, Greybor Medical Transportation Inc. and its owners regularly submitted claims to Medicare for ambulance transport of "bed-confined" beneficiaries who were not in fact confined. The government alleged that some of the patients actually sat in the front seat of the ambulance. This would violate the policy that Medicare pay only for non-emergency ambulance transportation if it is the only option available and the patient is bed-confined. The government also charged that the Greybor ambulances sometimes transported multiple patients simultaneously but submitted claims claiming they were being transported separately, resulting in higher reimbursements rates. The owner was sentenced to 108 months in federal prison and agreed to relinquish his claim to an additional $1 million in suspended payments held by Medicare. The government filed the civil case in 2003 after the owners were indicted on the criminal charges.[362]

More recently, in a qui tam action brought in New York, Metropolitan Ambulance & First Aid Corp. paid $2.8 million to the government to resolve allegations that it forged and falsified paperwork justifying medical necessity for ambulance trips.[363] In June of 2011, the City of Dallas agreed to pay $2.4 million to settle allegations that it upcoded 911 claims to a higher level of service than what was medically necessary or actually provided. Accordingly to the government, Dallas submitted claims that falsely represented that Advanced Life Support (ALS) service were appropriate and furnished when in fact the patients either did not require ALS service or ALS service was not rendered.[364]

---

[360] OIG Rep., *Medicare Payments for Ambulance Transports* 5 (OEI-05-02-00590) (Jan. 2006).
[361] *Id.*
[362] United States v. Greybor Medical, C.D. Cal., No. CV 03-01770-CAS-SH (*filed* Mar. 12, 2003).
[363] *See* Department of Justice Press Release, *New York Companies Pay U.S. $2.85 Million to Resolve Claims for Fraudulent Medicare Appeals at* http://www.justice.gov/opa/pr/2010/June/10-civ-662.html
[364] *See* Department of Justice Press Release, *City of Dallas to Pay $2.47 Million to Resolve Allegations That it Caused Improper Medicare and Medicaid Ambulance Claims at* http://www.justice.gov/usao/txn/PressRel11/dallas_ambulance_settle_pr.html

## § 4-6(m)  Medical Device Companies

The FCA has also become a mechanism that the government has used in connection with the medical device industry. For example, in *United States ex rel. Westfall v. Axiom Worldwide, Inc.*, two former sales employees of a medical device company brought a qui tam suit alleging the use of false and fraudulent representations regarding the medical devices to knowingly induce the physicians to submit false or fraudulent claims to Medicare.[365] The relators alleged that the defendants established a scheme to promote the submission of claims reimbursable at a rate of $156 per patient rather than the actual rate of $15 or less. The defendants argued that (1) the court did not have jurisdiction because the information upon which the claim was based had been previously disclosed publicly, and (2) the relators were not original sources of the information. The Court found that the defendants had disclosed details of the allegations an investigative report to a trade journal prior to the filing of the suit and that such a disclosure constituted a public disclosure. The Court noted that, although the report did not specifically identify the defendants' fraudulent activities, the report adequately "detailed account[s] of how physicians submit illegal claims to Medicare in connection with the [medical device]."[366] The Court concluded, however, that the relators had direct and independent knowledge of the false or fraudulent conduct three years prior to the public disclosure, qualifying as original sources and establishing jurisdiction. The Court ultimately dismissed without prejudice the narrow issue of whether the relator adequately pleaded the FCA claim.

In 2007, the Department of Justice announced that five medical device companies responsible for 95% of the hip and knee replacement market had agreed to settle allegations that the companies independently established arrangements with surgeons as a means to financially induce the use of their respective products.[367] The Government alleged that the companies employed "various forms of financial arrangements," including "fee-for-service contracts, fixed fee contracts, and product development contracts," to improperly promote the use of their products and to increase market share.[368] Furthermore,

---

[365] United States *ex rel.* Westfall v. Axiom Worldwide, Inc., No. 8:06-cv-571-T-33TBM, 2009 U.S. Dist. LEXIS 27646, at *6 (M.D. Fla. Mar. 20, 2009).

[366] *Id.* at *18.

[367] Press Release, U.S. Dep't of Justice, *Five Companies in Hip and Knee Replacement Industry Avoid Prosecution by Agreeing to Compliance Rules and Monitoring* (Sept. 27, 2007), *available online at* http://www.usdoj.gov/usao/nj/press/files/pdffiles/hips0927.rel.pdf.

[368] Civil Settlement Agreement between U.S. and Biomet, Inc. § II(C) (Sept. 27, 2007), *available online at* http://www.usdoj.gov/usao/nj/press/files/pdffiles/BiometCivilSettlement.pdf; Civil Settlement Agreement between U.S. and DePuy Orthopaedics, Inc. § II(C) (Sept. 27, 2007), *available online at* http://www.usdoj.gov/usao/nj/press/files/pdffiles/DePuyCivilSettlement.pdf; Civil Settlement Agreement between U.S. and Smith & Nephew, Inc. § II(C) (Sept. 27, 2007), *available online at* http://www.usdoj.gov/usao/nj/press/files/pdffiles/SmithNephewCivilSettlement.

## False Claims: Civil and Criminal Enforcement

these arrangements allegedly caused the filing of false and fraudulent claims to Medicare for improper replacement procedures. Four of the companies, Biomet, Inc., DePuy Orthopaedics, Inc., Smith & Nephew, Inc., and Zimmer, Inc., each agreed to pay between $26 and $170 million and entered into an 18-month deferred prosecution agreement in order to avoid criminal prosecution.[369] As a reward for being the first company to voluntarily cooperate with the Government, Stryker Orthopedics, Inc., entered into a non-prosecution agreement.

In 2008, two major medical device companies entered into settlement agreements with the federal government. Bayer HealthCare LLC signed a settlement agreement regarding allegations of violations of the federal Anti-Kickback Statute.[370] More specifically, Bayer purportedly paid direct-to-consumer suppliers and distributors of diabetic supplies nearly $2.5 million to convert Medicare beneficiaries from competitor products to Bayer products.[371] As part of the settlement, Bayer agreed to pay $97.5 million and to enter into a corporate integrity agreement with the Office of the Inspector General for the Department of Health and Human Services. Medtronic Spine LLC (formerly Kyphon, Inc.) agreed to settle allegations of improper inducement of healthcare providers to inappropriately perform kyphoplasty procedures and to submit false and fraudulent claims to Medicare.[372] Although Medtronic did not admit wrongdoing, the agreement required the company to pay $75 million plus interest and to enter into a corporate integrity agreement with the DHHS OIG.

In 2009, the Department of Justice announced a settlement agreement with NeuroMetrix, Inc., in which the company admitted to allegations of violations of the federal Anti-Kickback Statute and of causing physicians to improperly bill Medicare for nerve conduction studies at a higher rate than was actually performed.[373] The Government further alleged that, in order to induce purchasers of the company's medical device to recommend the use of the device to others, NeuroMetrix supplied the recommending physicians

---

pdf; Civil Settlement Agreement between U.S. and Zimmer, Inc. § II(C) (Sept. 27, 2007), *available online at* http://www.usdoj.gov/usao/nj/press/files/pdffiles/ZimmerCivilSettlement.pdf.

[369] *E.g., id.* § III(2).

[370] Press Release, U.S. Dep't of Justice, *Bayer Healthcare to Pay U.S. $97.5 Million to Settle Allegations of Paying Kickbacks to Diabetic Suppliers* (Nov. 25, 2008), *available online at* http://www.usdoj.gov/opa/pr/2008/November/08-civ-1050.html.

[371] *See* Civil Settlement Agreement between U.S. and Bayer HealthCare LLC § II(C) (Nov. 25, 2008), *available online at* http://op.bna.com/hl.nsf/id/sfak-7lqser/$File/Bayer%20Settlement.pdf

[372] Press Release, U.S. Dep't of Justice, *Medtronic Spine, Formerly Kyphon Inc., to Pay U.S. $75 Million to Resolve Allegations of Defrauding Medicare* (May 22, 2008), *available online at* http://www.usdoj.gov/opa/pr/2008/May/08-civ-455.html; Civil Settlement Agreement between U.S. and Zimmer, Inc. § II(E) (n.d.), *available online at* http://op.bna.com/hl.nsf/id/jthn-7evn7z/$File/Medtronic%20Inc.%20Settlement%20Agreement.pdf.

[373] Press Release, U.S. Dep't of Justice, *NeuroMetrix Agrees to Deferred Prosecution for Illegal Kickbacks Paid to Physicians* (Feb. 9, 2009), *available online at* http://www.usdoj.gov/usao/ma/Press%20Office%20-%20Press%20Release%20Files/Feb2009/NeurometrixPR.html.

with free disposable biosensors that are required for use with the device. The company agreed to pay a criminal penalty of $1.2 million and nearly $2.5 million in civil penalties and damages.

In October 2009, an employee of an infusion clinic participated in a conspiracy in which Medicare beneficiaries were recruited and paid cash in exchange for allowing their Medicare numbers to be billed at numerous Miami-area clinics for infusion therapy services that were never actually provided.[374]

### § 4-6(n)  Medical Clinics and HIV Infusion Clinics

A Miami-area HIV infusion clinic operated a $4.8 million scheme to defraud Medicare by submitting claims for injection and infusion that were medically unnecessary and often never provided.[375] Beneficiaries were induced to provide their Medicare numbers and signatures, which were then used to submit the fraudulent claims. The founder of the clinic was sentenced to 120 months in prison; the owner/operator to 70 months. Two other co-conspirators were sentenced to 84 months and 33 months.

Two other Miami-area HIV infusion clinics employed an individual who falsely claimed to be a physician's assistant. The PA examined patients, prepared treatment plans, and prepared false medical paperwork for the clinics that purportedly provided infusion treatments to Medicare beneficiaries.[376] $12 million in false claims were submitted to Medicare when the patients were, in fact, receiving mere vitamin infusions. The PA was sentenced to 108 months imprisonment.

## § 4-7  FALSE CLAIMS ACTIONS AND ISSUES UNDER THE BANKRUPTCY CODE

Upon filing a petition for bankruptcy, § 362 of the Bankruptcy Code entitles a debtor to an automatic stay from adverse creditor action.[377] However, the courts have found that the Government can proceed with its FCA claim against a defendant up to the point of entry of judgment under the police and regulatory powers exception to the automatic stay, pursuant to 11 U.S.C.S. § 362(b)(4).[378] In *United States ex rel. Fullington v. Parkway Hosp., Inc.*, the United States elected to intervene in a qui tam FCA claim while the defendant hospital was in the midst of a Chapter 11 bankruptcy proceeding. The hospital

---

[374] HHS/DOJ, Healthcare Fraud and Abuse Control Program, Annual Report for Fiscal Year 2010, 29.
[375] HHS/DOJ, Healthcare Fraud and Abuse Control Program, Annual Report for Fiscal Year 2010, 11.
[376] HHS/DOJ, Healthcare Fraud and Abuse Control Program, Annual Report for Fiscal Year 2010, 12.
[377] 11 U.S.C. § 362.
[378] United States *ex rel.* Fullington v. Parkway Hosp., Inc., 351 B.R. 280, 281 (D.N.Y. 2006).

contended that the automatic stay arising under 11 U.S.C.S. § 362 served to stay the action. The court determined that the pecuniary advantage test was the appropriate standard to apply regarding the § 362(b)(4) exception and when applying the test, the court found that the fact that the government was seeking monetary damages for past fraud did not prevent the application of the § 362(b)(4) exception, as the action served the important public policy interest of deterring fraud upon the government.[379]

---

[379] *Id.* at 288.

# 5
# Administrative Sanctions Available to Federal Enforcers

## § 5-1　OVERVIEW

Although the original Medicare and Medicaid fraud and abuse statutes only provided for the imposition of criminal penalties, over the years, Congress amended the laws to grant the Secretary of the Department of Health and Human Services (DHHS) the authority to exclude persons or entities from future participation in the federal and state healthcare programs and to impose additional administrative sanctions. The DHHS Secretary has delegated this authority to the Office of the Inspector General (OIG), which also has the authority to impose civil money penalties (CMPs) on persons or entities that engage in prohibited conduct.

This chapter reviews the Social Security Act's (SSA's) provisions related to exclusion and the imposition of CMPs and assessments, and provides a general description of hearing and appeal rights of those individuals and entities subject to these proceedings.

## § 5-2　EXCLUSION FROM MEDICARE, MEDICAID, AND OTHER STATE HEALTHCARE PROGRAMS

The SSA provides for both mandatory and permissive exclusion for a wide range of financial misconduct and quality concerns. According to the OIG, the OIG's exclusion authorities are intended to protect the federal healthcare programs and beneficiaries from "untrustworthy healthcare providers, i.e., individuals and entities whose behavior has demonstrated that they pose a risk to program beneficiaries or to the integrity of these programs."[1] Some violations are subject to mandatory automatic exclusion from the Medicare, Medicaid, and other state healthcare programs, without any discretion on the part of the OIG. In contrast, other violations are subject to permissive exclusion, in which the OIG can exercise discretion in deciding whether to impose exclusion.

---

[1] 67 Fed. Reg. 11,928 (Mar. 18, 2002).

## § 5-2(a) Mandatory Exclusion

Mandatory exclusion from the Medicare, Medicaid, and other state healthcare programs is imposed when an individual or entity has been convicted of a criminal offense related to:

- the delivery of service under the Medicare program or any state healthcare program;
- neglect or abuse of patients in connection with the delivery of a healthcare item or service;
- the delivery of a healthcare item or service or with respect to any act or omission in a healthcare program operated in whole or in part by a federal, state, or local government of a criminal offense relating to fraud, theft, embezzlement, breach of fiduciary responsibility, or other financial misconduct; or
- a felony for the unlawful distribution, prescription, or dispensing of a controlled substance.[2]

For purposes of exclusion from the Medicare and Medicaid programs, an individual is considered to have been convicted of a criminal offense when judgment of conviction has been entered against the individual or entity, "regardless of whether [t]here is a post-trial motion or an appeal pending or [whether] [t]he judgment of conviction or other record relating to the criminal conduct has been expunged or otherwise removed."[3] For example, in *Matter of Jeanne Hebert*, the mandatory five-year exclusion of a director of nursing was upheld even though the state court had expunged a misdemeanor conviction. Although the petitioner had complied with the terms of her probation, the DHHS Department Appeals Board (DAB) held that "post-pleading erasures of convictions [are] included within the statutory definition of conviction."[4]

---

[2] SSA §§ 1128(a)(1)–(4); 42 U.S.C. §§ 1320a-7(a) (1)–(4); 42 C.F.R. §§ 1001.101(a)–(d). In addition to the provisions in the "Mandatory Exclusion" SSA § 1128(a) related to an individual or entity convicted of a criminal offense, CMS and OIG are required to exclude from participation from the Medicare program any supplier of durable medical equipment and supplies or prosthetic devices, orthotics, and prosthetics that knowingly contacts Medicare beneficiaries by telephone regarding the furnishing of such items and supplies and whose conduct establishes a pattern of such contacts. *See* SSA §§ 1834(a)(17)(c), (h)(3); 42 U.S.C. §§ 1395m(a)(17)(c), (h)(3); 42 C.F.R. § 402.2(e)(2). In addition, the DHHS Secretary is required to exclude any individual who fails to enter an agreement to repay Health Education Assistance Loans or who breaches any provision of such agreement until all past due obligations are repaid. *See* SSA § 1892(a)(3); 42 U.S.C. § 1395ccc(a)(3).

[3] SSA § 1128(i)(1); 42 U.S.C. § 1320a-7(i)(1); 42 C.F.R. § 1001.2(d).

[4] Jeanne Hebert v. The Inspector General, No. C-92-012, Decision No. CR195 (D.A.B. May 11, 1992). *See, e.g.*, Robert Tschinkel v. The Inspector General, No. C-05-01, Decision No. CR1323 (D.A.B. June 29, 2005); Myrna Baptisa v. The Inspector General, No. C-11-380, Decision No. CR2410 (D.A.B. Aug. 8, 2011).

## Administrative Sanctions Available to Federal Enforcers

The definition of the term "conviction" also includes a plea of nolo contendere, as well as entry into "participation in a first offender, deferred adjudication, or other arrangement or program where judgment of conviction has been withheld."[5] For example, the DAB upheld the mandatory five-year exclusion of a physician even though the state court had expunged the criminal conviction upon the physician's completion of a deferral program.[6] In explaining why federal, not state law, applies, the DAB stated, "[t]he goals of criminal law generally involve punishment and rehabilitation of the offender, possibly deterrence of future misconduct by the same or other persons, and various public policy goals. Exclusions imposed by the [Inspector General], by contrast, are civil sanctions, designed to protect the beneficiaries of healthcare programs and the federal fisc, and are thus remedial in nature rather than primarily punitive or deterrent."

Therefore, depending upon the nature of the charge, nolo contendere pleas may disqualify a party from participating in the Medicare program for a minimum exclusion period.[7] Consequently, what may be considered a favorable settlement on the state level could create exposure to mandatory exclusion from the Medicare and Medicaid programs on the federal level.

In addition, a conviction cannot be collaterally attacked (i.e., relitigated) during an exclusion proceeding. Therefore, the mere fact of the conviction triggers the mandatory exclusion, regardless of whether the conviction was warranted. For instance, in *Travers v. Sullivan*,[8] an appellate court affirmed a federal district court holding that due process was not denied by refusing the plaintiff's request to relitigate a state court conviction in the context of a Medicaid exclusion action. The Court of Appeals held that no evidentiary hearing was required before the DHHS Secretary imposed a mandatory sanction and, therefore, the district court did not abuse its discretion in entering a protective order barring all discovery.

Generally, when an individual is subject to mandatory exclusion, the minimum exclusion period is five years.[9] However, the Balanced Budget Act of 1997 added a "three strikes and you're out" provision: If an individual or entity has been convicted on or after August 5, 1997, and if that conviction was preceded by one conviction that may have resulted in exclusion, then

---

[5] SSA §§ 1128(i)(3)–(4); 42 U.S.C. §§ 1320a-7(i)(3)–(4); 42 C.F.R. § 1001.2(d).
[6] Henry Gupton v. The Inspector General, No. A-07-6, Decision No. 2058 (D.A.B. Jan. 8, 2008), *aff'd* Gupton v. Leavitt, 575 F. Supp. 2d 874 (E.D. Tenn. 2008); *see also* Glenda Gale Feuge v. Inspector General, No. C-11-209, Decision No. CR2381 (D.A.B. June 6, 2011).
[7] *See, e.g.*, Carrie Marshall v. The Inspector General, No. C-10-889, Decision No. CR2274 (D.A.B. Oct. 22, 2010); Karen McDermott Minister v. The Inspector General, No. C-09-652, Decision No. CR2031 (Nov. 24, 2009); Myers v. Secretary of DHHS, 893 F.2d 840 (6th Cir. 1990); Carlos Zamora v. Inspector General, 89-100, Decision No. 1104 (D.A.B. Sept. 25, 1989).
[8] Travers v. Sullivan, 801 F. Supp. 394 (E.D. Wash. 1992), *aff'd*, 20 F.3d 993 (Wash. 1994). *See, e.g.*, Anderson v. Thompson, 311 F. Supp. 2d 1121 (D. Kan. 2004); Friedman v. Sebelius, 755 F.Supp. 2d 98 (D.D.C. 2010).
[9] SSA § 1128(c)(3)(B); 42 U.S.C. § 1320a-7(c)(3)(B); 42 C.F.R. § 1001.102(a).

the exclusion period must not be less than 10 years; further, if the individual or entity had been convicted of two or more offenses for which an exclusion may be effected, then the individual or entity is to be permanently excluded.[10]

In determining the length of such exclusion, the OIG may consider both aggravating and mitigating circumstances, and it is within the OIG's discretion to determine the extent to which it will consider any or all of the aggravating and mitigating circumstances that may be present.[11] Aggravating circumstances may include, for instance, the extent of the government's financial loss as a result of the acts resulting in the conviction (or other similar acts). The monetary threshold for an aggravating circumstance is an actual or intended financial loss to the government of $5,000.[12] Moreover, the OIG can consider the total amount of the government's financial loss, including "amounts resulting from similar acts not adjudicated" and "regardless of whether full or partial restitution has been made."[13] Where the government's financial loss results from an overpayment by any federal healthcare program of an intentionally improper billing, the threshold for an aggravating factor is only $1,500.[14]

Other non-financial aggravating circumstances include whether the act was committed over a period of a year or more, and whether the sentence imposed by the court for the act included incarceration.[15] Additionally, the OIG may consider records of prior crimes, civil actions, and sanctions, as well as convictions or adverse actions taken by federal, state, or local government agencies or boards based on similar circumstances.[16] Other aggravating factors include whether the acts that resulted in exclusion adversely affected beneficiaries or patients. For example, a relevant aggravating factor is whether acts resulting in convictions or similar acts had a significant adverse physical or mental effect on one or more program beneficiaries.[17] In convictions that involved patient abuse or neglect, it is relevant whether the individual's or entity's actions were premeditated, were part of a continuing pattern of behavior, or consisted of nonconsensual sexual acts.[18]

---

[10] SSA § 1128(c)(3)(G); 42 U.S.C. § 1320a-7(c)(3)(G); 42 C.F.R. § 1001.102(d).
[11] 42 C.F.R. § 1001.102(b)-(c).
[12] 42 C.F.R. § 1001.102(b)(2)(i).
[13] 42 C.F.R. § 1001.102(b)(1).
[14] 42 C.F.R. § 1001.102(b)(3)(i).
[15] 42 C.F.R. §§ 1001.102(b)(2), (5).
[16] 42 C.F.R. §§ 1001.102(b)(6), 102(b)(8), 102(b)(9).
[17] 42 C.F.R. § 1001.102(b)(3).
[18] 42 C.F.R. § 1001.102(b)(4). *See, e.g.,* Lazaro v. The Inspector General, No. C-98-276, Decision No. CR603 (D.A.B. June 22, 1999), in which the petitioner physician was excluded from participation in Medicare, Medicaid, and other state healthcare programs for a 20-year period for submitting more than twenty false claims daily to the Medi-Cal program. There, the ALJ determined that three aggravating factors existed: Dr. Lazaro's acts resulted in a loss to the Medi-Cal program grossly in excess of $1,500; as a result of Dr. Lazaro's conviction, he was incarcerated for 13 months; and Dr. Lazaro had a prior administrative-sanction record of a medical-license suspension and exclusion from Medi-Cal.

### Administrative Sanctions Available to Federal Enforcers

If aggravating factors justify an exclusion longer than five years, then the OIG may also consider several specific mitigating factors, as a basis for reducing the period of exclusion to no less than five years. The only mitigating factors that may be considered are:

- whether the criminal proceeding records demonstrate that the individual had a mental, emotional, or physical condition before or during the commission of the offense that reduced the individual's culpability;
- whether the individual or entity to be excluded cooperated with federal or state officials, but only if such cooperation resulted in others being convicted, excluded, or subject to CMPs, or the investigation of additional cases or reports being issued by the appropriate law enforcement agency identifying program vulnerabilities or weaknesses; and
- whether the individual or entity to be excluded was convicted of three or fewer misdemeanors, and the government's total financial loss resulting from the acts leading to the conviction and similar acts is less than $1,500.[19]

States may request a waiver of exclusions for program-related crimes (but not for crimes related to patient abuse) on behalf of individuals and entities that are the sole community physician or sole source of essential specialized services in the community.[20] Historically, the administrator of a federal healthcare program could also request a waiver of exclusions if it was determined that the exclusion would impose a hardship on individuals entitled to benefits under Medicare Part A or B. The Patient Protection and Affordable Care Act (the Health Reform Law) removed the requirement that the hardship be only on individuals entitled to Part A or B benefits and expanded the scope of this waiver to include any exclusion that the administrator of a federal healthcare program determines would impose a hardship on *any* beneficiary.[21] However, state waivers apply only to the programs under which the waiver request is made. Interestingly, if a state program waiver is rescinded, any existing Medicare derivative waiver of the exclusion will also be automatically rescinded. The decision regarding such waiver is not subject to administrative or judicial review.

### § 5-2(b) Permissive Exclusion

The preamble to the regulations pertaining to the OIG's exclusionary authority states that the basis for permissive exclusions (i.e., at the discretion

---

[19] 42 C.F.R. §§ 1001.102(c)(1)–(3).
[20] SSA § 1128(c)(3)(B); 42 U.S.C. § 1320a-7(c)(3)(B); 42 C.F.R. § 1001.1801.
[21] Patient Protection and Affordable Care Act (P.L. 111-148) § 6402(k), as amended by the Health Care and Education Reconciliation Act of 2010 (Pub. L. 111-152) [hereinafter referred to as the Health Reform Law].

of the Secretary of DHHS) falls within two basic categories: (1) derivative exclusions, whereby an individual or entity is excluded based on the action previously taken by a court, licensing board, or other agency; and (2) non-derivative exclusion, whereby there has not been a determination by a court of law, but merely an administrative finding of misconduct (e.g., poor quality of care).[22] The statute enumerates certain activities that may cause an individual or entity to be excluded.[23]

1. Conviction for a misdemeanor crime relating to fraud, theft, embezzlement, breach of fiduciary duty, or other financial misconduct relating to the general delivery of healthcare, with respect to any act or omission in a healthcare program or participation in a federal, state, or local government.[24]

2. Conviction connected to the interference or obstruction of a criminal investigation or audit[25] relating to:

    a. fraud, theft, embezzlement, breach of fiduciary duty, or other financial misconduct relating to the general delivery of healthcare, with respect to any act or omission in a healthcare program or participation in a federal, state, or local government;

    b. Medicare or Medicaid fraud, patient abuse, or fraud relating to the general delivery of healthcare or participation in a federal, state, or local government;

    c. felony conviction related to healthcare fraud or controlled substances; or

    d. the use of funds received from any federal healthcare program.[26]

3. Misdemeanor conviction for the unlawful manufacture, distribution, prescription, or dispensing of a controlled substance.[27]

4. Revocation or suspension of a license to provide healthcare based upon professional competence, professional performance, or financial integrity; or the surrender of a license during pending

---

[22] 67 Fed. Reg. 11,928 (Mar. 18, 2002).
[23] In addition to those items listed in SSA § 1128(b), additional circumstances are set forth in the SSA and corresponding regulations that can result in an individual or entity being excluded from participation in the federal and state healthcare programs.
[24] SSA § 1128(b)(1); 42 U.S.C. § 1320a-7(b)(1). *See* 42 C.F.R. § 1001.201.
[25] The Health Reform Law amended this language to include convictions relating to obstruction of audits.
[26] SSA § 1128(b)(2); 42 U.S.C. § 1320a-7(b)(2). *See* 42 C.F.R. § 1001.301. Section 6408(c)(2) of the Health Reform Law broadened the scope of this exclusion to include convictions relating to the use of funds received from any federal healthcare program.
[27] SSA § 1128(b)(3); 42 U.S.C. § 1320a-7(b)(3). *See* 42 C.F.R. § 1001.401.

## Administrative Sanctions Available to Federal Enforcers

disciplinary proceedings concerning professional competence, professional performance, or financial integrity.[28]

5. Exclusion from providing services under any other federal or state healthcare program.[29]

6. Submission of claims in excess of the entity's normal charge; provision of healthcare that is substantially in excess of the patient's needs or that fails to meet professional recognized standards of care; or failure of a medical plan to provide services required by law or contract that adversely affect Medicare beneficiaries or Medicaid recipients.[30]

7. Violation of SSA §§ 1128A (CMPs), 1128B (criminal penalties including violation of the Anti-Kickback Statute), or 1129 (CMPs related to benefits for the aged, blind, and disabled).[31]

8. Control of entities by persons who have been convicted of various program-related abuses, had CMPs imposed upon them, or have been excluded from Medicaid or other state health programs.[32]

9. Failure to provide required information concerning ownership or control interests as required by law.[33]

10. Failure to disclose requested information regarding ownership and significant business transactions of subcontractors and suppliers.[34]

11. Failure to supply payment information.[35]

12. Failure to grant "immediate access" upon "reasonable request" to a facility, of records or documents by the DHHS Secretary, a state Medicaid agency, the OIG, or others.[36]

13. Failure to take corrective action regarding abuses of the prospective payment system.[37]

14. Default on health education loans or scholarship obligations.[38]

---

[28] SSA § 1128(b)(4); 42 U.S.C. § 1320a-7(b)(4). *See* 42 C.F.R. § 1001.501.
[29] SSA § 1128(b)(5); 42 U.S.C. § 1320a-7(b)(5). *See* 42 C.F.R. § 1001.601.
[30] SSA § 1128(b)(6); 42 U.S.C. § 1320a-7(b)(6). *See* 42 C.F.R. §§ 1001.701–1001.801; see also SSA § 1156(b); 42 U.S.C. § 1320c-5(b).
[31] SSA § 1128(b)(7); 42 U.S.C. § 1320a-7(b)(7). *See* 42 C.F.R. § 1001.901.
[32] SSA § 1128(b)(8); 42 U.S.C. § 1320a-7(b)(8). *See* 42 C.F.R. § 1001.1001.
[33] SSA § 1128(b)(9); 42 U.S.C. § 1320a-7(b)(9). *See* 42 C.F.R. § 1001.1101.
[34] SSA § 1128(b)(10); 42 U.S.C. § 1320a-7(b)(10). *See* 42 C.F.R. § 1001.1101.
[35] SSA § 1128(b)(11); 42 U.S.C. § 1320a-7(b)(11). *See* 42 C.F.R. § 1001.1201. Historically, the basis for this exclusion only applied to individuals or entities furnishing items or services payable under Medicare or a state healthcare program. The Health Reform Law expanded the scope of this section to also apply to individuals or entities who order, refer for furnishing, or certify the need for items and services payable under Medicare or a state healthcare program.
[36] SSA § 1128(b)(12); 42 U.S.C. § 1320a-7(b)(12). *See* 42 C.F.R. § 1001.1301.
[37] SSA § 1128(b)(13); 42 U.S.C. § 1320a-7(b)(13). *See* 42 C.F.R. § 1001.1401.
[38] SSA § 1128(b)(14); 42 U.S.C. § 1320a-7(b)(14). *See* 42 C.F.R. § 1001.1501.

15. Either having a direct or indirect ownership or control interest in a sanctioned entity in which the person knows, or should know, of the action constituting the basis for the conviction or exclusion, or being an officer or managing employee of such an entity.[39]

16. Making false statements or misrepresenting material facts.[40]

For persons excluded under elements 1–3, the statute requires a three-year exclusion unless the DHHS Secretary determines, in accordance with regulations, that a shorter or longer period should be imposed due to mitigating or aggravating circumstances. With respect to items 4 and 5, the law requires the period of exclusion to be not less than the period during which the individual's or entity's license to provide healthcare is revoked, suspended, or surrendered, or the individual or entity is excluded or suspended from participation in a federal healthcare program. Regarding item 6, the law requires that the exclusion not be for a period less than one year. Finally, the period of exclusion for item 12 must be equal to the sum of the period in which an individual denied immediate access to a facility, plus an additional period set by the DHHS Secretary that is not to exceed 90 days.[41] For the remaining items and activities, the regulations set forth different periods of exclusion.

The OIG has published a set of non-binding criteria that it will use in assessing whether to impose a permissive exclusion under Section 1128(b)(7) of the Social Security Act, which gives the OIG the authority to exclude individuals or entities that have committed fraud, kickbacks, or another prohibited activities described in Sections 1128A, 1128B, and 1129. These criteria, which are divided into four general categories, act as a guide in the OIG's assessment, rather than presenting sole factors in determining if permissive exclusion is appropriate.[42] First, the OIG will consider the circumstances of the misconduct and the seriousness of the offense. In analyzing this question, the OIG will consider such questions as whether a criminal sanction was imposed and its length, whether the misconduct represents a continuous pattern of wrongdoing and whether the defendant's misconduct was active or passive. Second, the OIG considers the defendant's response to allegations of unlawful conduct. Here, the OIG looks at whether the response was credible and appropriate, whether the defendant was cooperative, and whether the defendant takes steps to mitigate the questionable conduct. The third category for the OIG is the likelihood that the same offense or some similar

---

[39] SSA § 1128(b)(15); 42 U.S.C. § 1320a-7(b)(15). *See* 42 C.F.R. § 1001.1051.

[40] SSA § 1128(b)(16); 42 U.S.C. § 1320a-7(b)(16). The Health Reform Law amended the SSA's language on permissive exclusions to cover this additional activity, which includes "knowingly mak[ing] or caus[ing] to be made any false statement, omission, or misrepresentation of a material fact in any application, agreement, bid, or contract to participate or enroll as a provider of services or supplier under a Federal healthcare program."

[41] SSA § 1128(c)(3); 42 U.S.C. § 1320a-7(c)(3). *See* 42 C.F.R. §§ 1001.201–1701.

[42] 62 Fed. Reg. 67,392 (Dec. 24, 1997).

abuse will occur in the future. In making this determination, the OIG looks at the uniqueness of the circumstance; the defendant's prior and subsequent conduct; and whether the defendant made efforts to contact the OIG, the Healthcare Financing Administration (HCFA, now the Centers for Medicare & Medicaid Services [CMS]), or any of its contractors to determine if its conduct complied with the law. Finally, the fourth category the OIG considers is the defendant's financial responsibility, or the extent to which the defendant was threatened by bankruptcy. Specifically, the OIG looks to whether, if allowed to continue program participation, the defendant will be able to operate without a significant threat to its ability to provide healthcare items or services. [43] Consequently, as previously described, the OIG has set forth, in the various regulations describing the circumstances in which it excludes a person or entity, a number of factors that may be considered to be aggravating (as a basis for lengthening the period of exclusion) or mitigating (as a basis for decreasing the length of exclusion).[44]

## § 5-2(c) Persons Subject to Exclusion

One significant issue considered in the OIG's final regulations was whether the OIG's exclusion authority against those who "furnish" covered items and services should extend beyond individuals and entities who submit claims to the federal healthcare programs to include those who do not receive program payments directly. When the OIG published the final regulations in 1992, it chose not to provide for that extension:

> Because the effect of exclusion is denial of payment for items or services furnished by an excluded individual or entity, it would be difficult to administer exclusions against entities that the Secretary does not directly reimburse. Thus, for the present time, to the extent that manufacturers, suppliers and distributors do not receive payment directly from the Medicare and state healthcare programs for the items they supply, these regulations will not affect them.[45]

In 1998, however, the OIG modified the definition of the term "furnished" so as to include "items and services manufactured, distributed or otherwise provided by individuals or entities that do not directly submit claims . . . ."[46] The regulations make clear that this does not limit the authority of the OIG to exclude entities managed or controlled by excluded individuals.[47] Also,

---

[43] *Id.* at 67,393–67,394.
[44] *See* 42 C.F.R. §§ 1001.201-1701.
[45] 57 Fed. Reg. 3,300 (Jan. 29, 1992).
[46] 42 C.F.R § 1000.10; 63 Fed. Reg. 46,676, 46,678 (Sept. 2, 1998).
[47] 42 C.F.R. § 1001.1001.

although the OIG may not subject certain entities to exclusion under the regulations, criminal penalties against such entities still may be sought.

In 2010, the OIG published guidance outlining criteria that it will use in determining whether to impose an exclusion under Section 1128(b)(15) of the Social Security Act.[48] Section 1128(b)(15) gives the OIG the authority to exclude an individual owner, officer or managing employee of a sanctioned entity. The guidance document clarifies the basis for exclusions based on whether the individual is (1) an owner, or (2) an officer or managing employee. The burden of proof is higher for excluding owners, and a presumption of exclusion is created if sufficient evidence exists that the owner knew or should have known of the conduct. If significant factors disfavor exclusion, then the presumption may be overcome. In contrast, there is no knowledge requirement with regards to officers and managing employees, giving the OIG authority to exclude any officer or managing employee merely because of their position within the sanctioned entity. However, when there is evidence that an officer or managing employee knew or should have known of the conduct, there is a presumption in favor of exclusion.

The guidance document outlines several factors that the OIG will consider in deciding whether to exclude an officer or managing employee of a sanctioned entity in the absence of evidence that the person either knew or should have known of the misconduct. First, the OIG will consider the circumstances of the misconduct and the seriousness of the offense. Analysis of this factor includes (1) consideration of the nature and scope of the misconduct for which the entity was sanctioned (or any other relevant misconduct), (2) the nature of the criminal sanction imposed against the entity or individuals, (3) whether there was evidence that the misconduct resulted in actual or potential harm to beneficiaries or other individuals or financial harm to any federal healthcare program or any other entity, and (4) whether the misconduct was an isolated event or part of a pattern of wrongdoing. Second, the OIG considers the individual's role in the sanctioned entity. This analysis includes considering (1) the individual's current position and other positions that the individual has held throughout his or her tenure, and (2) the relation of the individual's position to the underlying conduct, including whether the misconduct occurred within the individual's chain of command. Third, the OIG considers the individual's actions in response to the misconduct. Here, the OIG looks at (1) whether the individual took steps to stop the misconduct or mitigate its effects, including whether the individual might have taken such steps because he or she had reason to know of an investigation, and (2) whether the individual disclosed the misconduct to the appropriate federal

---

[48] Guidance for Implementing Permissive Exclusion Authority Under Section 1128(b)(15) of the SSA, *available online at* http://www.oig.hhs.gov/fraud/exclusions/files/permissive_excl_under_1128b15_10192010.pdf (last accessed Sept. 11, 2011).

or state authorities, including whether he or she cooperated with investigators and prosecutors. Lastly, the OIG will consider information about the entity including (1) whether the sanctioned entity or a related entity has any previous convictions or findings of liability and what the underlying conduct was for such an action, and (2) the size and corporate structure of the entity.[49]

The OIG's permissive authority with regards to owners, officers, and managing employees of sanctioned entities has been the subject of much attention in recent years. In an effort to increase accountability of drug company executives, in 2011, the OIG considered the exclusion of Howard Solomon, Chief Executive Officer of Forest Laboratories.[50] Although a subsidiary to Forest Laboratories, Forest Pharmaceuticals, pled guilty to two misdemeanors in 2010 involving distribution and promotion of its drugs, Solomon himself was not named in the criminal action. Although the OIG ultimately discontinued its efforts to exclude Solomon after protest from the company and business groups, the case demonstrates the OIG's willingness to investigate and sanction executives who were not directly involved in healthcare fraud.

There have also been efforts to strengthen the OIG's statutory authority to exclude individuals controlling a sanctioned entity. On February 11, 2011, Congressman Wally Herger introduced the "Strengthening Medicare Anti-Fraud Measures Act of 2011," which would broaden the scope of Section 1128(b)(15) of the Social Security Act to include entities affiliated with sanctioned entities.[51] Specifically, the proposed bill amends Section 1128(b)(15) enabling the OIG to exclude (1) an individual with an ownership or control interest in a sanctioned entity or an affiliated entity of a sanctioned entity and who knows or should know of the conduct forming the basis for the conviction or exclusion, (2) an officer or managing employee of a sanctioned entity or an affiliated entity of a sanctioned entity, and (3) any affiliated entity of a sanctioned entity. The bill does not require a current relationship with the sanctioned entity as long as there was a relationship at the time of the conduct that formed the basis of the sanction. The bill was referred to the House Subcommittee on Health on February 18, 2011. A similar attempt to expand the OIG's permissive authority in 2010 was passed in the House of Representatives, but did not get past the Senate.[52]

The Health Reform Law also included a provision that would have given states similarly broad authority to exclude individuals and entities from participation in Medicaid.[53] Section 6502 of the Health Reform Law amended the Social Security Act to require states to exclude any individual or entity that

---

[49] *Id.*
[50] Alicia Mundy, *U.S. Drops Effort to Oust Forest Labs CEO*, WALL ST. J., (Aug. 6, 2011), *available online at* http://online.wsj.com/article/SB10001424053111903885604576490631294926432.html.
[51] H.R. 675, 112th Cong. (1st Sess. 2011).
[52] H.R. 6130, 111th Cong. (2nd Sess. 2010).
[53] The Health Reform Law, § 6502.

owns, controls, or manages an entity that is affiliated with an individual or entity that has been suspended or excluded from participation. However, the Medicare and Medicaid Extenders Act of 2010 repealed Section 6502.[54] Nevertheless, the recent congressional action regarding the exclusion of owners and manager demonstrates an increased emphasis on accountability with upper management and owners.

## § 5-2(d)  Notice

### § 5-2(d)(1)  Notice of Intent to Exclude

An individual or entity that the OIG intends to exclude must be given reasonable notice of the exclusion.[55] If the OIG proposes to impose a mandatory or permissive exclusion for a period exceeding five years, it must first send written notice of its intent to exclude, the basis for the exclusion, and the potential effect of exclusion. If the OIG also is proposing that a provider agreement be terminated, the notice must so state. However, providing a notice of intent to exclude is not required for exclusions resulting from failure to grant immediate access, violations of the prospective payment system (PPS), or defaults of health education loan or scholarship obligations.[56]

The individual or entity has 30 days from the receipt of the notice (deemed to be five days after the date on the notice) to submit documentary evidence and written argument concerning whether the exclusion is warranted and any related issues. Oral argument also may be requested in writing if the exclusion is for the furnishing of excessive, medically unnecessary, or substandard services, or for failure of a health maintenance organization (HMO) or competitive medical plan to furnish medically necessary services.[57]

### § 5-2(d)(2)  Notice of Exclusion

If the OIG determines that exclusion is warranted after the individual or entity responds to the notice of intent to exclude, then a written notice of this decision must be sent to the individual or entity. The written notice must include the basis for the exclusion, the length of the exclusion, and (if applicable) the factors considered in setting the length of the exclusion. The written notice must also state the effect of the exclusion, the earliest date the OIG will consider reinstating the applicable requirements and procedures, and the individual's or entity's appeal rights. Generally, such exclusions are effective

---

[54] H.R. 4994, 111th Cong. (2nd Sess. 2010).
[55] SSA § 1128(c); 42 U.S.C. § 1320a-7(f).
[56] 42 C.F.R. § 1001.2001.
[57] 42 C.F.R. § 1001.2001(b).

twenty days from the date of the notice. However, the OIG may amend the notice letter if additional information is revealed that justifies imposing a new exclusion period on the individual or entity.[58] Amendment of the notice letter can be done no later than 15 days prior to the final exhibit exchanges held before a hearing conducted before an Administrative Law Judge (ALJ).[59]

### § 5-2(d)(3)   Notice of Proposal to Exclude

The written notice is not effective until sixty days after the date of the notice for exclusions resulting from (1) making false or improper claims; (2) fraud and kickbacks; (3) violating the limitations on physician charges; or (4) billing for services of an assistant at surgery during a cataract operation.[60] This is because these types of exclusions warrant a hearing prior to the exclusion. Therefore, the individual has an opportunity to postpone the effective date of the exclusion by filing a written request for a hearing. The request must set forth the following:

1. the specific issues or statements in the notice with which the individual or entity disagrees;
2. the basis for the disagreement;
3. the defenses on which reliance is intended;
4. any reasons why the proposed length of exclusion should be modified; and
5. reasons why the health or safety of individuals does not warrant exclusion prior to the hearing.[61]

If the individual or entity does not request a hearing, then a notice of exclusion is sent. If a hearing is requested, then the exclusion does not become effective until an ALJ upholds the decision to exclude, except in the circumstance in which the OIG determines that the health or safety of individuals warrants exclusion prior to the hearing. The parties determination review rights will be examined in detail in § 5-4.

### § 5-2(e)   Effects of Exclusion

When an individual or entity is excluded, items and services furnished by the excluded individual or entity will not be reimbursed under a federal healthcare program.[62] Regulations provide that the CMS will not pay claims

---

[58] 42 C.F.R. § 1001.2002.
[59] *Id.*; 42 C.F.R. § 1005.8.
[60] 42 C.F.R. § 1001.2003.
[61] *Id.*
[62] 42 C.F.R. § 1001.1901(b).

submitted by an excluded provider for dates of service that are 15 days or more after the date notice was sent.[63] Moreover, no payment will be made for any item or service furnished, at the medical direction of, or prescribed by, a physician or other authorized individual who is excluded when the person furnishing such item or service knew or had reason to know of the exclusion.[64] Excluded individuals or entities also may not take assignment of claims on or after the effective date of the exclusion.[65]

In 1999, the OIG issued a Special Advisory Bulletin entitled "The Effect of Exclusion from Participation in Federal Healthcare Programs," which further describes that no federal healthcare program payment may be made for any items or services furnished by an excluded individual or entity or directed or prescribed by an excluded physician:

> This payment ban applies to all methods of Federal program reimbursement, whether payment results from itemized claims, cost reports, fee schedules or a prospective payment system (PPS). . . . The prohibition against Federal program payment for items or services furnished by excluded individuals or entities also extends to payment for administrative and management services not directly related to patient care, but that are a necessary component of providing items and services to Federal program beneficiaries. This prohibition continues to apply to an individual even if he or she changes from one healthcare profession to another while excluded. In addition, no Federal program payment may be made to cover an excluded individual's salary, expenses or fringe benefits, regardless of whether they provide direct patient care.[66]

In 2010, the OIG published a notice informing the public of the OIG's intent to update the 1999 Special Advisory Bulletin on the Effect of Exclusion from Participation in Federal Healthcare Programs.[67] The OIG sought public comments to assist in supplementing the guidance in the Special Advisory Bulletin, with comments due on January 11, 2011. In the notice, the OIG noted its awareness that exclusion has a significant impact on not only those that are excluded, but also on entities that have employed or contracted with excluded persons and have consequently faced liability for overpayments and civil monetary penalties. To date, the 1999 Special Advisory Bulletin has not been formally updated.

---

[63] 42 C.F.R. § 1001.1901(c)(2).
[64] 42 C.F.R. § 1001.1901(b)(1).
[65] 42 C.F.R. § 1001.1901(b)(2).
[66] *See* OIG Special Advisory Bulletin, *The Effect of Exclusion from Participation in Federal Healthcare Programs* (September 1999), *available online at* http://oig.hhs.gov/fraud/docs/alertsandbulletins/effected.htm.
[67] 75 Fed. Reg. 69,452 (Nov. 12, 2010).

## Administrative Sanctions Available to Federal Enforcers

Exceptions exist in which the federal healthcare programs may make payment to an excluded entity. These exceptions include (1) inpatient institutional services furnished to a patient admitted to the institution before the date of exclusion; (2) home health and hospice care provided under a plan of care that was established before the effective date of the exclusion; and (3) healthcare items ordered by a practitioner, provider, or a supplier from an excluded manufacturer before the exclusion became effective and that are delivered within 30 days of the effective date of the exclusion.[68] These exceptions to exclusion apply unless the DHHS Secretary determines that the health and safety of individuals receiving treatment warrants an exclusion taking effect earlier.[69]

Excluded individuals or entities that submit claims for items or services provided during the exclusion period can be subject to CMP liability under SSA § 1128A, and to criminal liability under SSA § 1128B.[70] Additionally, submitting claims or causing claims to be submitted may result in an individual or covered entity being denied reinstatement to a program.[71] Exclusion is effective as to all federal healthcare programs, as well as all other executive branch procurement and non-procurement programs and activities.[72] The OIG directs each state agency administering or supervising a state healthcare program to exclude the individual or entity for the same time period.[73] State healthcare programs may provide for periods of exclusion in excess of those provided for by the OIG.[74]

The exclusion does not directly affect an individual or entity's state licensure. However, state-licensure authorities are notified of the facts and circumstances of exclusions, and are requested to take appropriate action and keep the OIG apprised of any action taken. This notification takes place even before the exclusion becomes final.[75]

### § 5-2(f)   Reinstatement of Excluded Individual or Entity

At the end of the exclusion period, the excluded individual or entity is not automatically reinstated into the Medicare program when the individual or entity obtains a program provider number or its equivalent.[76] Rather, after the exclusion period has ended, the excluded individual or entity must request reinstatement. In order to qualify for reinstatement, the OIG must

---

[68] 42 C.F.R. § 1001.1901(c)(3).
[69] SSA § 1128(c)(2)(B); 42 U.S.C. § 1320a-7(c)(2)(B); 42 C.F.R. § 1001.1901(c)(3).
[70] 42 C.F.R. § 1001.1901(b)(3).
[71] Id.
[72] 42 C.F.R. § 1001.1901(a), as amended by 60 Fed. Reg. 32,916 (June 26, 1995).
[73] SSA § 1128(d); 42 U.S.C. § 1320a-7(d).
[74] SSA § 1128(d)(3)(B)(ii); 42 U.S.C. § 1320a-7(d)(3)(B)(ii).
[75] SSA § 1128(e); 42 U.S.C. § 1320a-7(e).
[76] 42 C.F.R. § 1001.3001(a)(1).

have reasonable assurances that the actions that caused the exclusion have not recurred and will not recur. Additionally, the OIG considers whether all fines and debts have been paid, and whether CMS has determined that the individual complies with or will comply with the applicable conditions of participation or supplier conditions for coverage under the statutes and regulations. As part of their review of OIG action, ALJs may not require the OIG to reinstate excluded individuals and entities.[77] Decisions on the part of the OIG to deny reinstatement are not subject to administrative or judicial review.[78] Reinstatement becomes effective after OIG grants the request and issues the required notice; the notice will provide the effective date of reinstatement.[79]

## § 5-3  IMPOSITION OF CIVIL MONETARY PENALTIES

In 1981, Congress enacted SSA § 1128A, which authorizes the OIG to impose CMPs for certain activities, and describes the procedures relevant to the OIG's CMP authority. There is a six-year statute of limitations within which the Secretary of DHHS may initiate a proceeding. The statute of limitations begins to run from the date a claim was presented, a request for payment was made, or other occurrence took place.[80]

### § 5-3(a)  Actions that May Result in the Imposition of CMPs

#### § 5-3(a)(1)  Submission of Improperly Filed Claims

As described in greater detail in Chapter 4, Congress authorizes the imposition of CMPs against any person that knowingly presents or causes to be presented a claim that is improperly filed. This authority applies to a host of improper actions such as the submission of claims for:

- an item or service that is based on a code that the person knows or should know will result in a greater payment than applicable;
- a medical or other item or service where the person knows or should know the claim is false or fraudulent;
- reimbursement for physicians' services by a person who knows or should know that the individual who furnished the service was not licensed as a physician, obtained her license through a misrepresentation of material fact, or falsely represented to the patient at the time the service was furnished that the physician was certified in a medical specialty by a medical specialty board;

---

[77] 42 U.S.C. § 1320a-7(g); 42 C.F.R. § 1001.3002.
[78] 42 C.F.R. § 1001.3004(c).
[79] 42 C.F.R. § 1001.3002(d).
[80] SSA § 1128A(c); 42 U.S.C. § 1320a-7a(c).

### Administrative Sanctions Available to Federal Enforcers

- medical or other items or services furnished during a period of exclusion from the federal healthcare program under which the claim was made; or
- other items or services that a person knows or should know are not medically necessary.[81]

A claim is considered to be "improper" if the DHHS Secretary determines that the person submitting it knew or should have known it was false or fraudulent. The OIG defines "should have known" as those who act in "deliberate ignorance" or with "reckless disregard" of the verity of information specified on the claims they submit.[82]

## § 5-3(a)(2)  Dealing with Excluded Individuals/Entities

In addition to imposing penalties on providers who submit claims during a period of time in which they were excluded from participation in federal and state healthcare programs, the Health Insurance Portability and Accountability Act of 1996 (HIPAA) added a CMP for persons who either retain a direct or indirect ownership or control interest in an entity that is participating in a program, or are officers or managing employees of such entity.[83] Moreover, the statute prohibits a provider from arranging or contracting with an individual or entity that the person knows or should know is excluded from participation in federal and state healthcare programs.[84] Additionally, the Health Reform Law amended the Social Security Act to require that state Medicaid programs terminate a provider or supplier whose participation has been terminated.[85]

According to a 1999 OIG Special Advisory Bulletin, providers and contracting entities have an affirmative duty to check on individuals' and entities' program-exclusion status prior to entering into employment and contractual relationships by checking the OIG's List of Excluded Individuals/Entities (LEIE)[86] and the General Services Administration's Excluded Parties List System (EPLS).[87] To hold a provider liable, the SSA requires that the provider submitting the claim or an item or service provided by an excluded individual

---

[81] *See* SSA § 1128A(a); 42 U.S.C. § 1320a-7a(a); 42 C.F.R. § 1003.102.
[82] 42 C.F.R. § 1003.101.
[83] SSA §§ 1128A(a)(1)(D), (a)(4), and (a)(6); 42 U.S.C. §§ 1320a-7a(a)(4), (a)(4), and (a)(6); 42 C.F.R. § 1003.102.
[84] SSA § 1128A(a)(1); 42 U.S.C. § 1320a-7a(a)(1).
[85] The Health Reform Law, § 6501.
[86] *Available online at* http://oig.hhs.gov/exclusions/index.asp.
[87] *Available online at* https://www.epls.gov/. 64 Fed. Reg. 52,791 (Sept. 30, 1999); Department of Health and Human Services Special Advisory Bulletin, *The Effect of Exclusion From Participation in Federal Healthcare Programs* (Sept. 1999).

or entity knew or should have known that the person was excluded.[88] A failure to consider program-exclusion status can lead to CMP liability for providers and contracting entities. This restriction applies even if the excluded individual changes healthcare professions while excluded.

## § 5-3(a)(3)   Inducements to Beneficiaries

Certain financial incentives to beneficiaries may also subject participants to the imposition of CMPs. A person may not offer or transfer any remuneration to a government healthcare program beneficiary that the person knows or should know is likely to influence such individual to order or receive any items or services payable under the government healthcare program from a particular provider, practitioner, or supplier.[89] Given the breadth of the OIG's authority under Section 1128A(a)(5), throughout the years the OIG has issued guidance to inform the healthcare industry about permissible practices. For example, in August 2002, the OIG issued a Special Advisory Bulletin, "Offering Gifts and Other Inducements to Beneficiaries" to provide "bright-line guidance that will protect the Medicare and Medicaid programs, encourage compliance, and level the playing field among providers."[90] In this Special Advisory Bulletin, the OIG stated that remuneration did not include the non-routine, unadvertised waivers of copayments or deductible amounts based on individual financial need or the exhaustion of reasonable collection efforts. The Special Advisory Bulletin also exempted incentives of nominal value. The OIG further defined "nominal value" as those items worth no more than $10 per item, and with an annual aggregate value of $50 for all items furnished.[91] The OIG's stance on nominal value is not limited to incentives offered in connection to preventive care.[92]

In 2004, the OIG issued additional guidance that excluded waivers of deductible amounts and coinsurance from the definition of remuneration if three criteria were met: (1) the waiver is not offered as part of an advertisement or solicitation; (2) the person or entity involved does not routinely waive coinsurance and deductible amounts; and (3) the person or entity involved make a good-faith effort to determine that the individual benefited by the waiver demonstrated financial need, or the person or entity failed to collect these

---

[88] 42 C.F.R. § 1003.102(a)(2).
[89] SSA § 1128A(a)(5); 42 U.S.C. § 1320a-7a(a)(5); 42 C.F.R. § 1003.102(b)(13).
[90] OIG Special Advisory Bulletin, *Offering Gifts and Other Inducements To Beneficiaries* (Aug. 30, 2002).
[91] 65 Fed. Reg. 24,411 (2000); *see also* OIG Special Advisory Bulletin, *Offering Gifts and Other Inducements To Beneficiaries* (Aug. 30, 2002); OIG Advisory Op. No. 02-14 (Oct. 7, 2002).
[92] Although the OIG issued a request for public comments on situations in which free transportation can be provided to beneficiaries, no final guidance has been issued by the OIG on this practice.

### Administrative Sanctions Available to Federal Enforcers

amounts after attempting reasonable collection efforts.[93] However, paying the premiums for a beneficiary's Medicare Part B or supplemental insurance is not protected by this exception.[94] Because "financial need" varies depending upon the circumstances, the OIG recommends that in determining "financial need" providers are to make a case-by-case determination in accordance with a reasonable set of income guidelines that apply uniformly in all cases.[95] Also, the OIG stated that "under the fraud and abuse laws, the 'financial need' criterion is not limited to 'indigence,' but can include any reasonable measures of financial hardship."[96]

In 2010, the Health Reform Law[97] amended the definition of "remuneration" in the SSA to codify the OIG's guidance and to exclude several new items. Now, remuneration does not include:

- Remuneration that promotes access to care and poses a low risk of harm to patients and federal healthcare programs;
- The offer or transfer of items or services for free or less than fair market value if:
  a. the items or services consist of coupons, rebates, or other rewards from a retailer;
  b. the items or services are offered or transferred on equal terms, to the general public, regardless of health insurance status; and
  c. the offer or transfer is not tied to the provision of other items or services reimbursed by the program under Medicare or a state healthcare program;
- The offer or transfer of items or services for free or less than fair market value if:
  a. the items or services are not offered as part of any advertisement or solicitation;
  b. the items or services are not connected to the provision of other services reimbursed by the program under Medicare or a state healthcare program;
  c. there is a reasonable connection between the items or services and the individual's medical care; and

---

[93] OIG, *Hospital Discounts Offered to Patients Who Cannot Afford to Pay their Hospital Bills* (Feb. 2, 2004), *available online at* http://oig.hhs.gov/fraud/docs/alertsandbulletins/2004/fa021904hospitaldiscounts.pdf.
[94] OIG Special Advisory Bulletin, *Offering Gifts and Other Inducements To Beneficiaries* (Aug. 30, 2002).
[95] 65 Fed. Reg. 24,404 (2000).
[96] Office of Inspector General Guidance, *Hospital Discounts Offered To Patients Who Cannot Afford To Pay Their Hospital Bills* (Feb. 19, 2004).
[97] The Health Reform Law, § 6402(d)(2)(B).

d. the person offering or transferring the items provides them after making a good faith determination that the individual is in financial need.

- The waiver by a Prescription Drug Plan sponsor under Medicare Part D or an MA organization offering an MA-PD plan under Medicare Part C of any copayment for the first fill of a covered Part D generic drug for individuals enrolled in such a plan. [98]

Also excluded from the regulations' definition of remuneration are the "differentials in coinsurance and deductible amounts as part of a benefit plan design (as long as the differentials have been disclosed in writing to all beneficiaries, third party payers and providers), to whom claims are presented."[99] The OIG clarified, however, that plan designs that effectively waive federal healthcare program coinsurance obligations might implicate other federal laws, including the Anti-Kickback Statute.[100] This exclusion is particularly important for providers furnishing services to beneficiaries who have fee-for-service Medicare as the primary payor and an employer benefit plan as the secondary payor. Thus, in the preamble of the final regulation, the OIG stated that it currently is developing a safe harbor for waivers of coinsurance, subject to fee schedules, that would protect employer plans. Additionally, the regulations clarify that CMPs do not apply to managed care organizations that provide inducements to individuals to entice them to enroll in a particular health plan. However, a CMP may be imposed where inducements are offered by a managed care plan to an enrollee to induce them to use a specific provider, practitioner, or supplier.

Also excluded from remuneration are incentives that promote preventive care.[101] The OIG permits the use of incentives waiving all or part of a co-payment; offering care as a free community service; and choosing not to bill the beneficiary, Medicare, and Medicaid for services.[102] This leniency on the part of the OIG is subject to two limitations with respect to scope. First, incentives may not be disproportionately large such that they appear to be offered for the purpose of inducing beneficiaries to obtain services beyond preventative care. Second, incentives cannot be comprised of cash or cash equivalents.[103]

---

[98] *Id.*
[99] 42 C.F.R. § 1003.101.
[100] OIG Special Advisory Bulletin, *Offering Gifts and Other Inducements To Beneficiaries* (Aug. 30, 2002); *see also* OIG Advisory Op. No. 03-10 (May 15, 2003).
[101] SSA § 1128A(i)(6)(D).
[102] *But see* OIG Advisory Op. No. 01-14 (Sept. 4, 2001).
[103] 42 U.S.C. § 1003.101.

## Administrative Sanctions Available to Federal Enforcers

### § 5-3(a)(4)   Payments to Induce Reduction or Limitation of Services (Gainsharing) and Other Cost Sharing Initiatives

In the early 1980s, Medicare payments to hospitals were generally based on a PPS, which reimburses hospitals according to the classification of the patient admission by the hospital into the appropriate Diagnosis Related Group (DRG), regardless of the patient's length of stay. As a result of the implementation of PPS, certain hospitals adopted physician incentive plans that gave physicians financial incentives to control the length of stay of Medicare beneficiaries (a practice commonly referred to as "gainsharing" or "shared savings"). Generally speaking, gainsharing refers to any arrangement whereby a hospital pays a physician a share of the savings in the hospital's costs related to patient care attributable, at least in part, to the physician's efforts.

In 1986, the GAO issued a report in which it made a number of recommendations with respect to hospital physician incentive plans.[104] In the same year, Congress provided the DHHS Secretary with authority to impose CMPs on hospitals that "knowingly make[ ] a payment, directly or indirectly, to a physician as an inducement to reduce or limit services provided with respect to individuals" who are entitled to Medicare or Medicaid benefits, and who are under the direct care of the physician.[105] Penalties are $2,000 for each individual with respect to whom such payment is made, an amount that also may be imposed in the same manner upon the physician who accepted the payment.[106]

In December of 1994, the OIG issued a proposed rule to implement this authority:[107]

> [t]he precise structure and application of a physician incentive plan will ultimately determine whether CMPs would be assessed against a hospital or a physician under this provision . . . [I]t is impossible and impractical for the OIG to specifically indicate in regulations which specific criteria may make up an acceptable hospital physician incentive plan.[108]

In the preamble to the proposed rule, the OIG lists the following recommendations made by the GAO in its report on physician incentive payments by hospitals.

---

[104] GAO Rep. No. HRD-86-103, *Medicare: Physician Incentive Payments by Hospitals Could Lead to Abuse* (July 1986).
[105] SSA § 1128A(b); 42 U.S.C. § 1320a-7a(b).
[106] SSA § 1128A(b); 42 U.S.C. § 1320a-7a(b).
[107] 59 Fed. Reg. 61,571 (Dec. 1, 1994) (to be codified at 42 C.F.R. pt. 1003).
[108] *Id.* at 61,573.

- Such plan payments should be based on the cost performance of a group of physicians, rather than by individual physicians.
- Payments should be based on performance over a relatively long period of time (e.g., over a one-year period, as opposed to a single month or quarter).
- Incentive payments should not be based on the hospital's profits resulting from treating any individual patient.
- Any physician payment system of this type by a hospital should include a strong program of utilization review and quality of care review.[109]

On July 8, 1999, the OIG issued a Special Advisory Bulletin regarding hospital gainsharing. In the accompanying press release, June Gibbs Brown, the then-Inspector General of DHSS stated,

[i]n recent months, the Office of Inspector General has received several requests for advisory opinions about the legality of hospital-physician gainsharing arrangements. "After consulting with experts inside and outside the federal government and reviewing the legislative history of the prohibition on hospital payments to physicians to reduce or limit care, we have determined that gainsharing arrangements raise significant issues that cannot be resolved through the advisory opinion process. Without adequate safeguards, gainsharing could pose a risk of abuse, could adversely affect patient care and could be manipulated to reward physicians for patient referrals."[110]

The advisory bulletin reiterated the breadth of the prohibition against gainsharing, and stressed that such breadth was intentional. In addition, the OIG explained that it considered extensively whether it would be appropriate to protect individual gainsharing arrangements from OIG administrative sanctions through the issuance of favorable advisory opinions. The OIG concluded, however, that gainsharing arrangements all contain "common elements that preclude our issuance of any favorable opinion."[111] The OIG stated that, given the high risk of abuse that might arise with gainsharing arrangements, "the OIG believes that immunizing such arrangements from sanction would be imprudent and inappropriate."[112]

In April 2000, the OIG issued an advisory opinion that addressed a non-profit hospital's proposed cost-savings program to determine whether the

---

[109] 59 Fed. Reg. 61,572 (Dec. 1, 1994) (to be codified at 42 C.F.R. pt. 1003).

[110] OIG Press Release, *Inspector General Issues Special Advisory Bulletin on Hospital-Physician "Gainsharing"* (July 8, 1999).

[111] OIG Special Advisory Bulletin, *Gainsharing Arrangements and CMPs for Hospital Payments to Physicians to Reduce or Limit Services to Beneficiaries* (July 8, 1999).

[112] *Id.*

arrangement was an impermissible gainsharing arrangement.[113] According to the OIG, the question raised by the request was whether the arrangement would constitute grounds for sanctions under the CMP for financial incentives to reduce or limit items or services, found in SSA § 1128A(b)(1).[114]

Pursuant to the proposed cost-savings program, the nonphysician employees would be permitted to submit written cost-savings suggestions to the human resource department of the hospital. If the hospital determines that a suggestion has merit and is feasible, it will pay the employee a percentage of the cost savings generated by the suggestion. The hospital would pay the nonphysician employees a percent of the quantifiable and measurable cost savings that are derived from the proposal during the first year that the suggestion is implemented. For cost-savings suggestions that cannot be measured or quantified, the hospital will estimate its savings and pay the employee an amount based upon a predetermined sliding scale, subject to a maximum reward.

The hospital certified that, pursuant to its cost-savings plan:

- no payments will be made directly or indirectly to physicians under the proposed arrangement;
- the proposed arrangement will not reward or implement suggestions that would reduce or limit healthcare services provided to its patients, or that would impair the quality of care delivered to its patients;
- the proposed arrangement will not reward suggestions that identify specific vendors, directly or indirectly; and
- the proposed arrangement will not reward or implement suggestions that shift costs to any federal healthcare program.

Based upon the specific circumstances presented, the OIG concluded that the arrangement would not violate the SSA.[115] The decision was based on the fact that SSA § 1128A(b)(1) only applies to arrangements between hospitals and physicians. Therefore, the OIG concluded that, "[s]ince physicians are prohibited from participating, directly or indirectly, in the Proposed Arrangement, the Proposed Arrangement does not implicate section 1128A(b)(1) of the [SSA]."[116]

Although the OIG concluded that the arrangement could potentially implicate the CMP provisions of the SSA for the reduction or limitation of

---

[113] OIG Advisory Op. No. 00-02.
[114] The advisory opinion also addressed whether the arrangement implicated the Anti-Kickback Statute. According to the Office of Inspector General, the arrangement could potentially generate prohibited remuneration under the Anti-Kickback Statute if the requisite intent to induce referrals were present. However, the Office of Inspector General stated that it would not subject the hospital to sanctions arising under the Anti-Kickback Statute pursuant to §§ 1128(b)(7) or 1128A(a)(7) of the act in connection with the establishment of the proposed arrangement itself; provided, however, that its conclusion does not apply to specific payments made by the hospital for specific suggestions.
[115] *Id.*
[116] *Id.*

direct patient-care services (as well as the Anti-Kickback Statute), the OIG said it would not seek sanctions against the parties. According to the OIG, the proposed arrangements contain sufficient safeguards to protect against the concerns over the CMP provisions and the Anti-Kickback Statute. For example, the OIG found that safeguards to protect against the inappropriate reduction of services included the following:

- objective historical data is used to establish a "floor," beneath which no savings would accrue to the physician group;
- physicians will be terminated from the arrangement if there are significant changes from historical measures of a patient's case severity, and if agents and payors evidence a steering of more costly patients to other hospitals; and
- the aggregate payment to the physician group will not exceed 50% of the cost savings.

In 2005, Lewis Morris, chief counsel to the OIG, testified before Congress that "absent a change in law, it is not currently possible for gainsharing arrangements to be structured without implicating the fraud and abuse laws."[117] Generally, the OIG has indicated through various advisory opinions that arrangements targeted at overall savings implicate the CMP statute. However, some limited arrangements may be permissible on a case-by-case basis. The OIG is generally concerned with the arrangements being used to disguise improper remunerations, as well as patient care being compromised.[118]

The OIG has issued additional gainsharing advisory opinions that confirm that on a case-by-case basis, some arrangements may be permissible.[119] Generally speaking, the OIG has identified specific safeguards that must be present in order for the OIG to determine that a particular arrangement is acceptable. These safeguards include:

- The transparency of the arrangement, including the transparency of the incentives for specific actions and procedures, and whether it will allow for public scrutiny and individual physician accountability.
- Credible support that the arrangement will not adversely affect patient care and a process for periodic review to ensure that clinical care has not been adversely impacted.

---

[117] Testimony of Lewis Morris, Chief Counsel to the Inspector General, U.S. Department of Health and Human Services, House Committee on Ways and Means Subcommittee on Health, Hearing (Oct. 7, 2005).

[118] OIG Advisory Op. Nos. 05-01 (Feb. 3, 2005), 05-02 to 05-04 (Feb. 17, 2005), 05-05 to 05-06 (Feb. 25, 2005).

[119] *See, e.g.*, OIG Advisory Op. Nos. 05-02 to 05-03 (Feb. 17, 2005), 05-06 (Feb. 25, 2005), 06-22 (Nov. 16, 2006), 07-21 to 07-22 (Jan. 14, 2008), 08-09 (Aug. 7, 2008), 08-15 (Oct. 14, 2008), 08-21 (Dec. 8, 2008), 09-06 (June 30, 2009).

## Administrative Sanctions Available to Federal Enforcers

- The payments under the proposed arrangement are based on all procedures regardless of the patient's insurance coverage and they are subject to a cap on payments for federal healthcare program procedures. The procedures performed under the proposed arrangement are not disproportionately performed on federal healthcare program beneficiaries and cost savings are based on the actual out-of-pocket acquisition costs, not on accounting convention.

- There is protection against inappropriate reductions in services by establishing baseline thresholds, beyond which no savings will inure to the physicians, based on objective historical and clinical measures. The baseline thresholds are reasonably related to the Hospital's (or comparable hospitals') practice and patient populations and are action specific and not based on isolated patient outcome.

- There is no restriction on the availability of devices.

- The Hospital and physician will provide written disclosures of their involvement in the arrangement to patients whose care may be affected by the proposed arrangement and will provide patients an opportunity to review the cost savings recommendations prior to admission to the hospital.

- The financial incentives are reasonably limited in duration and amount.

- Profits are distributed to members on a per capita basis, mitigating any incentive for an individual provider to generate disproportionate cost savings.

In addition to enumerating the safeguards that must be present in order to approve the proposed arrangement, the OIG has also enumerated certain features of gainsharing plans that "heighten the risk that payments will lead to inappropriate reductions or limitations of services."[120] These include:

- There is no demonstrable direct connection between individual actions and any reduction in the hospital's out-of-pocket costs.

- The individual actions that would give rise to the savings are not specifically identified.

- There are insufficient safeguards protecting against the risk that other unidentified actions may actually account for "savings."

- There is questionable validity and statistical significance in the quality of care indicators.

---

[120] *See, e.g.*, OIG Advisory Op. Nos. 05-02 to 05-03 (Feb. 17, 2005).

- There is no independent verification of cost savings, quality of care indicators, or other critical aspects of the arrangement.[121]

On January 11, 2001, the OIG analyzed another gainsharing arrangement between a cardiac surgeon group and a hospital.[122] Pursuant to the arrangement, the physician group would receive a percentage of the hospital's cost savings that arise from the group's implementation of certain cost-reduction measures.

The passage of the Health Reform Law has revived the discussion on gainsharing through the incorporation of accountable care organizations (ACOs), the extension of the Gainsharing Demonstration and bundled payment initiatives. All of these innovations seek to coordinate care by aligning the financial incentives of healthcare providers. Arguably, these shared savings models are exactly the type of gainsharing activity that the OIG has historically sought to prohibit.

ACOs consist of groups of providers and suppliers that will qualify for receiving Medicare payments for shared savings by meeting certain criteria, including quality performance standards. Section 3022 of the Health Reform Law establishes the Medicare Shared Savings Program (Shared Savings Program). Under the Shared Savings Program, if providers and suppliers meet certain criteria working together as an ACO, they will be eligible for shared savings payments.[123] In addition, ACOs may also be eligible to receive additional Medicare payments for shared savings. To encourage the formation of ACOs, on March 31, 2011, CMS and the OIG jointly issued a notice with comment period outlining proposals for waivers of certain federal laws, including the CMP law.[124]

In addition to creating ACOs, the Health Reform Law also extends through September 30, 2011 (for those projects in operation as of October 1, 2008), the Medicare Hospital Gainsharing Demonstration (Gainsharing Demonstration) project created by the Deficit Reduction Act of 2005, and extends certain reporting dates until March 31, 2013.[125] The purpose of the Gainsharing Demonstration is to evaluate if gainsharing aligns incentives between hospitals and physicians in order to improve the quality and efficiency of care, and to improve hospital operational and financial performance. However, the current Gainsharing Demonstration projects incorporate the existing fraud and abuse restrictions thus requiring the applicants to structure their arrangements accordingly and to seek necessary protections through other vehicles (e.g., advisory opinion process, safe harbors, etc.).

---

[121] OIG Advisory Op. Nos. 05-02 to 05-03 (Feb. 17, 2005).
[122] OIG Advisory Op. No. 01-01 (Jan. 11, 2001).
[123] The Health Reform Law, § 3022.
[124] 76 Fed. Reg. 19,655 (published Apr. 7, 2011).
[125] Deficit Reduction Act of 2005 (Pub. L. No. 109-171), Section 5007(d)(3).

## Administrative Sanctions Available to Federal Enforcers

Finally, on August 23, 2011, the CMS Innovation Center announced the Bundled Payments for Care Improvement initiative (Bundled Payments initiative) to encourage healthcare providers to better coordinate patient care.[126] The Bundled Payments initiative aligns the financial incentives for hospitals, physicians and non-physician practitioners through the use of a single negotiated payment for all services provided during an episode of care. However, unlike ACOs, there has been no official request to waive the fraud and abuse laws for the for the Bundled Payments initiative. Participating healthcare entities will propose a target price for an episode of care. The Bundled Payments initiative is based on four broadly defined models of care, three that are retrospective bundled payment arrangements and one that is prospective. Under the retrospective arrangements, the healthcare entity will be paid for services under a negotiated discount to the fee-for-service payment system. At the conclusion of the episode of care, the total payments will be compared to the target price. If total payments are below the target price than the healthcare entity may share the savings with the providers. If the total payments exceed the target price the healthcare entity will be required to pay CMS the difference. Under the prospective payment arrangement, the healthcare entity will be paid based upon a dingle prospective bundled payment for the episode of care. With the emphasis on shared savings programs, presumably, the OIG will begin to evaluate its stance on gainsharing.

### § 5-3(a)(5)   Other Bases for CMPs

The CMP statute also provides that the following are bases for the imposition of CMPs:

- violation of an assignment agreement, a participant agreement, or certain other agreements not to charge;[127]
- giving information that one knows or should have known is false or misleading that could reasonably be expected to influence the decision when to discharge such person or another individual from the hospital;[128]

---

[126] Center for Medicare & Medicaid Innovation, Bundled Payments for Care Improvement, *available online at* http://innovations.cms.gov/areas-of-focus/patient-care-models/bundled-payments-for-care-improvement.html. The Bundled Payments initiative is separate from the Medicare National Pilot Program on Payment Bundling, established under Section 3023 of the Health Reform Law.

[127] SSA § 1128A(a)(2); 42 U.S.C. § 1320a-7a(a)(2). *See also* SSA 1833(l), 1842(b)(18); 42 U.S.C. §§ 1395l(l), 1395u(b)(18); 42 C.F.R. §§ 402.1, 1003.105(a)(i) (referring to 1003.102(b)(1)); SSA § 1833(h)(5)(D); 42 U.S.C. § 1395l(h)(5)(D); 42 C.F.R. §§402.1(c)(1), (d)(1), (e)(i). On (March 31, 2004), the OIG issued an alert that focused on physicians charging extra for services covered by Medicare. *See* http://oig.hhs.gov/fraud/docs/alertsandbulletins/2004/FA033104AssignViolationI.pdf.

[128] SSA § 1128A(a)(3); 42 U.S.C. § 1320a-7a(a)(3). 42 C.F.R. § 1003.102(b)(4).

- violations of the Anti-Kickback Statute;[129]
- a physician falsely certifying that a patient satisfies the requirements for home health services;[130]
- ordering or prescribing an item or service during a period of exclusion where the person knows or should know that a claim for such an item or service will be made under a federal healthcare program;[131]
- knowingly making, using, or causing to be made or used, a false record or statement material to a fraudulent claim for payment for items and services furnished under a federal healthcare program;[132]
- knowingly making or causing to be made any false statement, omission, or misrepresentation of a material fact in any application, bid, or contract to participate or enroll as a provider of services or a supplier under a federal healthcare program;[133]
- failing to grant timely access, upon request, to the Inspector General of DHHS, for purposes of audits, investigations, evaluations, or other statutory functions;[134] and
- knowing about an overpayment and not reporting and returning the overpayment.[135]

Similar to the discussion related to permissive exclusion, and in addition to those items listed in SSA § 1128A, additional provisions throughout the SSA (and corresponding regulations) may result in the imposition of CMPs

## § 5-3(b)  Notice of Proposed Determination to Impose CMPs

An individual or entity may not be subject to CMPs until the individual or entity has been given written notice.[136] This notice must include the following:

1. reference to the statutory basis for the penalty, assessment, or exclusion;

---

[129] *See* Chapter 2. *See also* SSA § 1128A(a)(7); 42 U.S.C. § 1320a-7a(a)(7); 42 C.F.R. § 1003.102(b)(11).

[130] SSA § 1128A(b)(3); 42 U.S.C. § 1320a-7a(b)(3). 42 C.F.R. § 1003.102(b)(14).

[131] SSA § 1128A(a)(8); 42 U.S.C. § 1320a-7a(a)(8). The Health Reform Law amended the SSA to add this as a basis for imposition of a CMP.

[132] SSA § 1128A(a)(8); 42 U.S.C. § 1320a-7a(a)(8). The Health Reform Law amended the SSA to add this as a basis for imposition of a CMP.

[133] SSA § 1128A(a)(9); 42 U.S.C. § 1320a-7a(a)(9). The Health Reform Law amended the SSA to add this as a basis for imposition of a CMP.

[134] SSA § 1128A(a)(9); 42 U.S.C. § 1320a-7a(a)(9). The Health Reform Law amended the SSA to add this as a basis for imposition of a CMP.

[135] SSA § 1128A(a)(10); 42 U.S.C. § 1320a-7a(a)(10). The Health Reform Law amended the SSA to add this as a basis for imposition of a CMP.

[136] SSA § 1128A(c)(2); 42 U.S.C. § 1320a-7a(c)(2).

### Administrative Sanctions Available to Federal Enforcers

2. a description of the claims, requests for payment, or incidents with respect to which the sanctions are imposed (except that actions based on statistical sampling must merely describe the sample and sampling technique utilized by the OIG);
3. the reason the claims are subject to the sanction;
4. the amount of the proposed penalty and assessment, and the period of the proposed exclusion;
5. any circumstances that were considered when determining the amount of the penalty or assessment and the period of the exclusion;[137]
6. instructions for responding to the notice, including a specific statement informing the respondent of her right to a hearing, and of the fact that failure to request a hearing within sixty days permits the imposition of the proposed penalty, assessment, and/or exclusion without the right to appeal; and
7. in certain cases, that the imposition of exclusion may result in termination of the provider's agreement in accordance with SSA § 1855(b)(2)(C).[138]

Any person subject to sanction by the OIG has the right to appeal; however, the assessment becomes final if an appeal is not requested within the time permitted.[139]

## § 5-3(c) Amount of CMPs

The amount of a given CMP that may be imposed by the OIG varies depending on the amount authorized for the particular violation.[140] Amounts may include a fixed penalty for each item or service claimed, plus an additional assessment of a multiple of the amount claimed for the item or service. For example, the OIG may impose a penalty of not more than $10,000 for each item or service that was not provided as claimed, plus an assessment of not more than three times the amount claimed for each item or service that was the basis for the penalty in lieu of the damages sustained by the United States or a state agency due to such a claim.[141] In addition, the OIG may impose a penalty of not more than $15,000 for each person for whom a determination was made that false or misleading information was given, and $50,000 for each act committed in violation of the Anti-Kickback Statute, plus three times the amount of remuneration offered, paid, solicited, or received in violation of

---

[137] 65 Fed. Reg. 24,418 (Apr. 26, 2000).
[138] 42 C.F.R. § 1003.109.
[139] *Id.*
[140] *See* 42 C.F.R. §§ 402.105, 1003.103.
[141] SSA § 1128A(a); 42 U.S.C. § 1320a-7a(a).

the Anti-Kickback Statute.[142] When determining the amount of remuneration offered, paid, solicited, or received, the OIG need not look at actual losses (e.g., whether the losses were recovered).[143]

The Federal Civil Monetary Penalty Inflation Adjustment Act of 1990, as amended by the Debt Collection Improvement Act of 1996, requires federal agencies to adjust certain CMPs for inflation every four years. Although SSA violations are exempt from such inflation adjustment, inflation adjustment applies to CMPs assessed under the Healthcare Quality Improvement Act of 1986[144] and the Program Fraud Civil Remedies Act of 1986.[145]

The OIG takes into account various factors in determining the actual amount of the penalties and assessments imposed, depending upon the type of violation. Factors include the nature and circumstances of the claim, as well as the degree of culpability, history of prior offenses, financial condition of the person submitting the claim, completeness and timeliness of the refund, and the amount of remuneration offered or transferred.[146] The regulations set forth specific aggravating and mitigating circumstances that may affect the amount of the CMP.

For instance, with respect to the nature and circumstances of the claim, mitigating circumstances are limited to circumstances in which the violations were of the same type and occurred within a short period of time, there were few such violations, *and* the total amount claimed or requested was less than $1,000. Aggravating circumstances extend to circumstances in which there are violations of several types occurring over a lengthy period of time; many (or a pattern of) such violations; substantial amounts are claimed; or the false or misleading information resulted in harm to a patient, a premature discharge, or the necessity of additional services.[147] In one case, the court justified a penalty of seventy times the amount collected from Medicare due to aggravating circumstances.[148]

Similarly, with respect to the degree of culpability, the only recognized mitigating circumstance is if the violation was a result of an unintentional or unrecognized error in the claims-submission process, and corrective steps were taken promptly after the error was discovered. It is an aggravating circumstance if there is knowledge that: the item or service was not provided as claimed, or that the claim was false or fraudulent; the item or service was furnished during a period the respondent had been excluded from participation such that

---

[142] *Id.*
[143] Chapman v. U.S. Dep't of Health and Human Servs., 821 F.2d 523 (10th Cir. 1987).
[144] Healthcare Quality Improvement Act of 1986, Pub. L. No. 99-660, tit. IV, 100 Stat. 3784 (1986).
[145] Program Fraud Civil Remedies Act of 1986, Pub. L. No. 99-509, tit VI, sub. tit. B, 100 Stat. 1934–1948 (1986).
[146] 42 C.F.R. § 1003.106.
[147] 42 C.F.R. § 1003.106(b)(1).
[148] Mayers v. U.S. Dep't of Health & Human Servs., 806 F.2d 995 (11th Cir. 1986).

## Administrative Sanctions Available to Federal Enforcers

no payment could be made; the information could reasonably be expected to influence the decision of when to discharge a patient from the hospital; or that remuneration would influence a beneficiary to order or receive an item or service reimbursable under Medicare or a state healthcare program.[149]

Unless extraordinary mitigating circumstances exist, the regulations direct that the aggregate amount of the penalty and assessment should never be less than double the approximate amount of damages and costs sustained by the government (including the costs attributable to the investigation, prosecution, and administrative review of the case).[150] According to the preamble to the 1992 regulations, the OIG converted its former "guidelines" into "binding rules, except to the extent that their application in a particular case could result in an amount that exceeds constitutional limitation."[151] Therefore, ALJs are authorized to reduce the amount of a CMP "only to the point where the amount was constitutionally impermissible."[152]

The OIG encourages provider cooperation in combating healthcare fraud, and such cooperation will be considered when negotiating the terms of a settlement.[153] In 1998, the OIG published a provider self-disclosure protocol, which outlines specific steps that providers may take to investigate and resolve fraud matters.[154] The self-disclosure protocol is open to all healthcare providers, regardless of industry, medical specialty, type of service, or whether the provider is an individual or entity.[155] Over the years, the OIG has also issued several open letters to healthcare providers that serve as additional guidance for providers who wish to self-disclose.[156] In its 2009 letter, the OIG imposed a $50,000 minimum settlement amount for submissions. In the letter, the OIG also announced that due to resource constraints and a desire to focus on kickbacks, the OIG would no longer accept disclosures of matters that only involve liability under the physician self-referral law. However, individuals and entities may still self-disclose matters that involve liability under the physician self-referral law if it also involves liability under the Anti-Kickback Statute. For example, in 2011, after self-disclosing to the OIG, Pacifica Hos-

---

[149] 42 C.F.R. § 1003.106(b)(2).
[150] 42 C.F.R. § 1003.106(c).
[151] 57 Fed. Reg. 3,323 (1992).
[152] *Id.*
[153] OIG, *An Open Letter to Healthcare Providers* (Apr. 24, 2006), *available online at* http://oig.hhs.gov/fraud/docs/openletters/Open%20Letter%20to%20Providers%202006.pdf.
[154] 63 Fed. Reg. 58,399 (Oct. 30, 1998).
[155] *Id.* at 58,400.
[156] *See, e.g.,* OIG, *An Open Letter to Healthcare Providers* (Apr. 15, 2008), *available online at* http://oig.hhs.gov/fraud/docs/openletters/OpenLetter4-15-08.pdf; *An Open Letter to Healthcare Providers* (Mar. 24, 2009), *available online at* http://oig.hhs.gov/fraud/docs/openletters/OpenLetter3-24-09.pdf.

pital of the Valley agreed to pay $764,250 for allegedly violating CMP law with regards to physician self-referrals and kickbacks.[157]

## § 5-4 SUSPENSION OF PAYMENTS

The Health Reform law enumerates separate standards for Medicare and Medicaid payment suspension. Section 6402(h) grants the Secretary the authority to suspend payments to a provider or supplier, "pending an investigation of a credible allegation of fraud against the provider of services or supplier, unless the Secretary determines there is good cause not to suspend such payments."[158] On February 2, 2011, CMS issued a Final Rule[159] implementing section 6402(h) of the Health Reform Law, which grants the Secretary the authority to suspend Medicare and Medicaid payments pending investigation of "credible allegations of fraud," unless the Secretary determines that there is good cause not to suspend such payments.[160]

### § 5-4(a) Suspension of Payments to Medicare Providers

In the Final Rule, CMS defines "credible allegation of fraud" as "an allegation of fraud from any source, including but not limited to the following: (1) Fraud hotline complaints. (2) Claims data mining. (3) Patterns identified through provider audits, civil false claims cases, and law enforcement investigations." Allegations are considered to be credible when they have "indicia of reliability."[161] However, in the Final Rule, CMS indicates that States should have the flexibility to determine what "credible allegations of fraud" is and the term "indicia of reliability" is not defined by the Health Reform Law nor by the Final Rule. Although the Health Reform Law requires CMS to consult with OIG, CMS notes, in the Final Rule, that it retains the ultimate authority whether to impose payment suspension upon a provider or supplier. Not only has Congress entrusted CMS to establish the parameters for payment suspension, it also grants CMS the authority to decide when to forgo suspension for good cause. CMS enumerates four circumstances under which CMS may find good causes exists to not suspend or continue to suspend payments:

- OIG or other law enforcement agency has specifically requested that a payment suspension not be imposed because such a payment suspension may compromise or jeopardize an investigation;

---

[157] OIG, Selected Provider Self-disclosure Protocol Settlements, http://oig.hhs.gov/fraud/enforcement/cmp/self_disclosure.asp (last visited Aug. 12, 2011).
[158] The Health Reform Law, § 6402(h); codified at 42 C.F.R. § 405.371.
[159] 76 Fed. Reg. 5,862 (Feb. 2, 2011).
[160] The Health Reform Law, § 6402(h); codified at 42 C.F.R. §§ 405.371(b), § 455.23.
[161] 76 Fed. Reg. at 5,961; codified at 42 C.F.R. § 405.370(a).

## Administrative Sanctions Available to Federal Enforcers

- it is determined that beneficiary access to items or services would be so jeopardized by a payment suspension in whole or part as to cause a danger to life or health;
- it is determined that other available remedies implemented by CMS or a Medicare Contractor can more effectively or quickly protect Medicare funds than would implement a payment suspension; or
- CMS determines that a payment suspension or a continuation of a payment suspension is not in the best interests of the Medicare program.[162]

The Final Rule imposes limits on the length of time payment may be suspended upon a "credible allegation of fraud." A suspension will not continue if it has been in effect for 18 months and there has not been a "resolution of the investigation."[163] However, a suspension may extend beyond 18 months if the case has been referred to the OIG and administrative action is pending or being considered, or where the DOJ submits a written request to CMS for continuation of suspension explaining how criminal and/or civil action may be affected if an extension is not granted.

The Final Rule also requires CMS to conduct an evaluation every 180 days to determine whether there is good cause not to continue a suspension. As part of this evaluation, CMS must request a certification from OIG or other law enforcement agency as to whether that agency intends to continue to investigate the matter.

### § 5-4(b) Suspension of Payments to Medicaid Providers

The Health Reform Law and the Final Rule mandate suspension of Medicaid payments where an investigation of a "credible allegation of fraud" exists. The Health Reform Law amended section 1903 of the Social Security Act to provide that States shall not receive the federal financial participation in cases where they fail to suspend Medicaid payments during any period when there is pending an investigation of a "credible allegation of fraud," as determined by the State, unless the State determines that there is good cause not to suspend such payments.[164] Prior to the issuance of the Final Rule, the threshold level of evidence necessary to suspend payments was a "receipt of reliable evidence." The Final Rule lowers this threshold by requiring only a "credible allegation."

The Final Rule sets forth the same definition of "credible allegation of fraud" used for the Medicare program but adds that the allegation must be

---

[162] 76 Fed. Reg. at 5,961; codified at 42 C.F.R. § 405.371(b).
[163] A "resolution of an investigation" will occur "when legal action is terminated by settlement, judgment, or dismissal, or when the case is closed or dropped because of insufficient evidence to support the allegations of fraud." *Id.*
[164] The Health Reform Law, § 6402(h); codified at 42 C.F.R. § 405.371(2).

"verified by the State."[165] Allegations are considered to be credible "when they have indicia of reliability and the State Medicaid agency has reviewed all allegations, facts, and evidence carefully and acts judiciously on a case-by-case basis."

The Final Rule clarifies that an investigation need not originate in or with a law enforcement agency in order to satisfy the requirement for a "pending investigation" rather State Medicaid agency investigations are sufficient to trigger a payment suspension to protect Medicaid funds.[166] However, for each instance of payment suspension, the State must make a formal, written suspected fraud referral to its MFCU or an appropriate law enforcement agency.[167]

The Final Rule establishes several "good cause" exceptions by which States may decide to not suspend payments or continue a payment suspension previously imposed. Some of these exceptions are substantially similar to those available to CMS for the Medicare program. The good cause exceptions unique to the Medicaid program are:

- the State determines that suspension should be removed based upon the submission of written evidence by the subject of the payment suspension;
- Medicaid recipient's access to items or services would be jeopardized by a payment suspension because either the provider is the sole community physician or the sole source of essential specialized services in a community, or the provider serves a large number of recipients within an HRSA-designated medically underserved area; or
- law enforcement declines to certify that a matter continues to be under investigation.[168]

Additionally, a State may find good cause exists to only partially suspend payments where an investigation is solely and definitively centered on only a specific type of claim, or arises form only a specific business unit or provider.

A state may suspend Medicaid payments without first notifying a provider. However, the State must notify the provider within five days of taking such action. Further, law enforcement officials, may request, in writing, a delay in notification of up to 30 days, renewal up to two times for a total of 90 days.[169] The duration of the suspension of payment is similar to the durations established for the Medicare program; suspension of payment will not continue after either the agency or prosecuting authorities determine that

---

[165] 76 Fed. Reg. at 5,966; codified at 42 C.F.R. § 455.2.
[166] 76 Fed. Reg. at 5,932; codified at 42 C.F.R. § 455.2.
[167] *Id.* at 5,933; codified at 42 C.F.R. § 455.23(d).
[168] *Id.* at 5,966; codified at 42 C.F.R. § 455.23(e).
[169] *Id.* at 5,932; codified at 42 C.F.R. § 455.23(b).

## Administrative Sanctions Available to Federal Enforcers

there is insufficient evidence of fraud by the provider or legal proceedings related to the provider's alleged fraud are completed.[170]

## § 5-5 HEARING AND APPEAL RIGHTS OF INDIVIDUALS AND ENTITIES SUBJECT TO EXCLUSION AND CMPs

### § 5-5(a) The Rights of the Parties in a Hearing Before an ALJ

Any individual or entity that is excluded from participation under Section 1128 of the SSA is "entitled to reasonable notice and opportunity for a hearing thereon by the Secretary to the same extent as is provided in [SSA] Section 205(b)."[171] SSA § 205(b) states the procedures to be followed by the Secretary of DHHS in issuing decisions affecting the rights of those applying for benefits under the SSA, and that the DHHS Secretary must make findings of fact and issue a decision. The decision of the DHHS Secretary, if unfavorable to the individual, must contain a statement of the case setting forth a discussion of the evidence, the DHHS Secretary's determination, and the reason(s) upon which it is based. The individual or entity has sixty days after receiving notice of the DHHS Secretary's decision to request a hearing on the decision. Upon such request, the DHHS Secretary must conduct a post-decision hearing at which the individual may present evidence. The DHHS Secretary must then affirm, modify, or reverse the findings of fact and decision.[172]

In almost all exclusions pursuant to Section 1128 of the SSA, a party excluded from program participation is not entitled to an administrative hearing until *after* the exclusion has gone into effect. The OIG supports the position that a pre-exclusion hearing is not required by due process. Thus, exclusion decisions generally are not reviewed until after all post-exclusion administrative remedies have been exhausted.[173]

However, parties excluded under SSA § 1128(b)(7) for violations of the Medicare criminal provisions including kickbacks (SSA § 1128B), or the CMP provisions (SSA § 1128A) are expressly granted the right to a hearing before their exclusion goes into effect.[174] The DHHS Secretary may override this right to a pre-exclusion hearing by making a finding that the health and safety of beneficiaries warrants the exclusion taking effect immediately.

---

[170] *Id.* at 5,940; codified at 42 C.F.R. § 455.23(c).
[171] SSA § 1128(f); 42 U.S.C. § 1320a-7(f).
[172] SSA § 205(b); 42 U.S.C. § 405(b).
[173] Shalala v. Illinois Council on Long Term Care, 529 U.S. 1 (2000).
[174] SSA § 1128(f); 42 U.S.C. § 1320a-7(f).

Thus, an excluded individual or entity may not be subject to CMPs until there is an opportunity for a hearing before an ALJ.[175] Under the OIG regulations, all parties have the following rights:

- to be accompanied, represented, and advised by an attorney;
- to participate in ALJ conferences;
- to conduct discovery, as permitted;
- to agree to stipulations of fact or law;
- to present relevant evidence;
- to present and cross-examine witnesses;
- to present oral argument, as permitted by the ALJ; and
- to submit written briefs, proposed findings of facts, and conclusions of law.[176]

In addition, the Civil Monetary Penalties Act expressly states that the DHHS Secretary may not issue a determination to exclude a person from participation under the programs until that person has been given written notice and an opportunity for the DHHS Secretary's determination to be made on the record.[177] Discovery includes requesting the production of relevant documents in the possession of the OIG. The ALJ may grant a motion for a protective order or deny a motion for an order compelling discovery if the ALJ determines that the discovery sought is irrelevant, is unduly burdensome, will unduly delay the proceeding, or seeks privileged information.[178] Changes in the discovery process were designed to deter discovery abuses, streamline the process, and avoid protracted litigation. Furthermore, an ALJ is authorized to issue a subpoena requiring an individual to attend a hearing, and to provide documentary evidence at or prior to a hearing.[179]

## § 5-5(b)  Burden of Proof

The burden of proof in ALJ hearings varies depending on the type of case. The party subject to exclusion bears the burden of proof (with respect to affirmative defenses and any mitigating circumstances) in exclusion cases for furnishing excessive, unnecessary, or substandard services; for submitting false or improper claims; or for committing fraud, kickbacks, or other prohibited activities.[180] The OIG bears the burden of going forward and the burden

---

[175] SSA § 1128A(c)(2); 42 U.S.C. § 1320a-7a(c)(2).
[176] 42 C.F.R. § 1005.3.
[177] SSA § 1128A(c)(2); 42 U.S.C. § 1320a-7a(c)(2).
[178] 42 C.F.R. § 1005.7.
[179] 42 C.F.R. § 1005.9(b).
[180] 42 C.F.R. § 1005.15(b).

## Administrative Sanctions Available to Federal Enforcers

of persuasion with respect to all other issues. In all other exclusion cases, the ALJ may allocate the burden of proof as the ALJ deems appropriate.

In this regard, it is significant to note that the regulations provide that the OIG "[w]ill not exclude any individual or entity if that individual or entity *can prove* that the remuneration that is the subject of the exclusion is exempted from serving as the basis for an exclusion."[181] Thus, it is the responsibility of the entity being excluded to prove that it meets a safe harbor by introducing relevant documentation. This portion of the regulation is expected to be subject to challenge over the next several years, as some attorneys believe that this standard inappropriately shifts the burden of proof to the excluded party. As with CMP cases, the burden of persuasion is judged by a preponderance of the evidence.[182]

With respect to CMP cases, the party subject to the penalty bears the burden of proof with respect to affirmative defenses and any mitigating circumstances. However, the OIG bears the burden of proof with respect to all other issues.[183]

### § 5-5(c)  Evidentiary Standards in a Hearing Before an ALJ

The ALJ determines the admissibility of evidence and, although not bound by the Federal Rules of Evidence, may apply the Federal Rules of Evidence where appropriate. However, the ALJ must exclude irrelevant or immaterial evidence, as well as evidence privileged under federal law.[184] The ALJ also must rule as inadmissible evidence concerning offers of compromise or settlement made in the action, to the extent provided in Rule 408 of the Federal Rules of Evidence.[185] The ALJ also may exclude relevant evidence "if its probative value is substantially outweighed by the danger of unfair prejudice, confusion of the issues, or by considerations of undue delay or needless presentation of cumulative evidence."[186] Evidence of crimes, wrongs, or acts other than those at issue is admissible in order to demonstrate motive, opportunity, intent, knowledge, preparation, identity, lack of mistake, or exis-

---

[181] 42 C.F.R. § 1001.951(a)(2)(ii) (emphasis added).

[182] 42 C.F.R. § 1001.2007(c).

[183] 42 C.F.R. § 1005.15(b). The burden of proof encompasses both the burden of going forward and the burden of persuasion. The burden of going forward requires a party to produce sufficient evidence on an issue in order to escape a directed verdict. The burden of persuasion becomes relevant only when the burden of going forward has been satisfied. Once a party sustains their burden of going forward and all the evidence has been introduced, the burden of persuasion requires the party to prove their case by a "preponderance of the evidence." *See* John William Strong et al. eds., McCormick on Evidence § 336 (4th ed. 1992); *see also* Inspector General v. Anesthesiologists Affiliated, [1990 Transfer Binder] Medicare & Medicaid Guide (CCH) 38,554 (DAB Feb. 5, 1990).

[184] 42 C.F.R. §§ 1005.17(a)–(c), (e).

[185] 42 C.F.R. § 1005.17(f).

[186] 42 C.F.R. § 1005.17(d).

tence of a scheme, regardless of whether they occurred during the statute of limitations period or whether they were referenced in the OIG's notice of exclusion.[187] The ALJ is authorized to affirm, increase, or reduce the penalties, assessment, or exclusion proposed or imposed by the OIG or to reverse the imposition of the exclusion.[188]

The evidentiary standards applied in an exclusion hearing before an ALJ are the same as in CMP cases. Importantly, however, in exclusion cases in which the period of exclusion began prior to the hearing, the period of exclusion will be deemed to have commenced on the date that exclusion originally went into effect.[189]

### § 5-5(d)   Scope of ALJ Authority in Exclusion Cases

As described, the ALJ is authorized to affirm, increase, or reduce the penalties, assessments, or exclusion proposed or imposed by the OIG,[190] or reverse the imposition of an exclusion. However, the ALJ has no authority to set a period of exclusion at zero, or to reduce a period of exclusion to zero.[191] The ALJ does not have authority to review the OIG's discretionary exclusion under SSA § 1128(b), nor to determine the exclusion's scope or effect.[192] In any case where the ALJ finds that an act described in the statutory provisions for permissive exclusion was committed, some period of exclusion must be imposed.[193] According to the preamble of the OIG civil sanction regulation,

> when the ALJ finds a violation, he or she must remedy it with some period of exclusion . . . [I]n every case where the Inspector General has exercised his or her discretion to impose an exclusion, and where the ALJ concurs that violation did occur, some period of exclusion is necessary to remedy the violation. Although circumstances such as the absence of proof of harm to beneficiaries or the programs may mitigate the length of exclusion, they do not eliminate the need for some remedial period of exclusion.[194]

Once exclusion under SSA § 1128 has been upheld by an ALJ, however, the exclusion becomes effective immediately, regardless of the availability of further administrative or judicial review. Where an ALJ imposes a period of exclusion and where the party was excluded prior to the ALJ decision, the period of exclusion relates back to the date the exclusion originally became effective.

---

[187] 42 C.F.R. § 1005.17(g).
[188] 42 C.F.R. § 1005.20(b).
[189] *Id.*
[190] 42 C.F.R. § 1005.20(b).
[191] 42 C.F.R. § 1005.4(c)(6).
[192] 42 C.F.R. § 1005.4(c)(5).
[193] 42 C.F.R. § 1005.4(c)(6).
[194] 57 Fed. Reg. 3,325 (1992).

## § 5-5(e) Appeal of the ALJ's Decision to the Departmental Appeals Board

The ALJ's decision is final and binding on all parties 30 days after the ALJ serves notice on the parties with a copy of the decision, unless the initial decision is appealed to the Departmental Appeals Board (DAB), or an extension of time to file the appeal is granted by the DAB.[195]

Consideration by the DAB is discretionary, and there is no right to appear personally before the DAB or to appeal ALJ interlocutory rulings to the DAB.[196] The DAB may affirm, increase, reduce, reverse, or remand any penalty, assessment, or exclusion determined by the ALJ. The DAB's standard of review for "disputed issues of fact" is whether the initial decision is supported by substantial evidence on the whole record, and the standard for "disputed issues of law" is whether the initial decision was erroneous.[197]

Unless remanded to the ALJ, the DAB's decision is final and binding 60 days after the parties are served with the decision.[198] Any petition for judicial review must be filed within that time period. With respect to CMPs, the filing of a DAB appeal automatically stays the effective date of the ALJ's decision.[199] Further stays following the DAB's decision pending judicial review must be requested from the ALJ, who must rule on such requests within 10 days of receipt. Additionally, such stays require the posting of a bond or other adequate security.[200]

## § 5-5(f) Judicial Review of the DHHS Secretary's Final Determination

A final determination by the Secretary of DHHS to impose a penalty, assessment, or exclusion under the Civil Monetary Penalties Act becomes final at the expiration of the 60-day period for appeal given to the excluded individual.[201] Any person receiving an adverse determination from the Secretary of DHHS may appeal that determination to the United States Court of Appeals for the circuit where the person resides or where the claim was presented by filing a written petition requesting that the DHHS Secretary's determination be modified or set aside.[202]

---

[195] Note that certain types of exclusion actions are excepted. 42 C.F.R. § 1005.20(d).
[196] 42 C.F.R. §§ 1005.21(d), (g).
[197] 42 C.F.R. §§ 1005.21(h).
[198] 42 C.F.R. § 1005.21(j).
[199] 42 C.F.R. § 1005.22(a).
[200] 42 C.F.R. § 1005.22(b).
[201] SSA § 1128A(g); 42 U.S.C. § 1320a-7a(g).
[202] SSA § 1128A(e); 42 U.S.C. § 1320a-7a(e).

An excluded party has the right to judicial review of the DHHS Secretary's final determination regarding exclusion, and may commence a civil action within sixty days after notice of the DHHS Secretary's decision is mailed (or within such other time as the DHHS Secretary allows).[203]

In contrast to an appeal of a determination under Section 1128A for CMPs, a decision to exclude under Section 1128 may be appealed to the United States District Court for the district where the party resides or has a principal place of business, or in the United States District Court for the District of Columbia. The Medicare and Medicaid Patient and Program Protection Act of 1987 provides that where an action for both CMPs and an exclusion is based on the same conduct and is tried in the same administrative action, judicial review of both actions will lie exclusively in the United States Court of Appeals.[204]

---

[203] SSA § 1128(f); 42 U.S.C. § 1320a-7(f).
[204] SSA § 1128A(e); 42 U.S.C. § 1320a-7a(e).

# 6
# State and Private Initiatives to Combat Fraud

## § 6-1　OVERVIEW

Until recently, the majority of the public's attention has focused largely on the federal government's efforts to prosecute healthcare fraud. However, most states—along with trade associations, private organizations, and private industry payors—have proposed and implemented their own initiatives to stop fraudulent and abusive activity in the healthcare industry, and after the turn of the century, state activities to address healthcare fraud significantly increased.

States have enacted laws, joined organizations, and implemented programs to specifically address these issues. Furthermore, trade associations have developed guidelines for their industries; private organizations have disseminated information to educate the industry and the public; and private payors have developed their own investigatory units to detect and deter healthcare fraud and abuse. These activities complement the work of the federal government in this area, and have begun to demonstrate success in preventing fraud and abuse.

Some states have enacted laws that prohibit self-referral—that is, the referral of patients for healthcare services by a physician or other healthcare professional to healthcare facilities in which the healthcare professional has an investment or other financial relationship. Several of these state laws are similar to the federal self-referral law, applicable to physician referrals for clinical laboratory services and other "designated health services."[1] Other states have attempted to combat the perceived conflict of interest in self-referrals by requiring physicians and other healthcare professionals to disclose their financial interests in a healthcare facility, prior to referring those patients to that facility.

In addition to self-referral statutes, many states have enacted laws that prohibit certain financial arrangements between healthcare providers that constitute illegal remuneration in return for the referral of patients (e.g., kickbacks or bribes). Unlike the Anti-Kickback Statute, which currently applies to illegal remuneration paid in connection with services covered by most federal

---

[1] *See* discussion in Chapter 3, *supra*.

and state healthcare programs, many of these state anti-kickback laws apply to private third-party payors as well. States also may have laws prohibiting fee splitting among healthcare professionals in return for patient referrals, which may be interpreted similarly to the state anti-kickback proscriptions. Commercial-bribery statutes (which provide criminal penalties), state deceptive trade practices laws, and consumer protection statutes also may apply to prohibit certain payment arrangements involving healthcare providers.

Another way states have attempted to control healthcare fraud is to focus on the fraudulent billing practices engaged in by some healthcare providers. Some states have adopted legislation prohibiting providers from waiving a patient's copayments or deductible amounts. Case law in other states suggests that such practices may constitute fraud. In addition to freestanding anti-fraud statutes, many states have enacted insurance fraud legislation, which can be used to combat fraudulent billing practices related to non-government healthcare payors (e.g., private insurance companies). Several state false claim statutes also have been enacted, and some of these statutes contain specific qui tam provisions. Alternatively, some states have enacted freestanding qui tam statutes.

Additionally, states have established agencies and implemented programs to combat fraud and abuse. Most states have established Medicaid Fraud Control Units (MFCUs) to coordinate statewide efforts to uncover and prosecute fraud in the Medicaid context.[2] States also have established healthcare fraud task forces to identify major areas of abuse in healthcare delivery, and develop ways to eradicate such abuses. These task forces comprise not only individuals from state agencies, but also individuals from federal agencies, private medical organizations, and private insurers. As part of Medicaid program integrity activities, some states have formulated automated fraud and abuse detection processes that search for patterns of practice that may indicate fraud, thus reducing the time necessary to detect it.

In partnership with the states, the federal government also has initiated several collaborative efforts between government agencies to combat healthcare fraud and abuse. For example, the Office of Inspector General (OIG) of the Department of Health and Human Services (DHHS) has partnered with state auditors to assist the states in reviewing their Medicaid programs. The Centers for Medicare & Medicaid Services (CMS) also has organized a Medicaid Fraud and Abuse Control Technical Assistance Group (TAG) to facilitate states' communication with one another regarding Medicaid program integrity issues.

Private insurers have implemented measures to control healthcare fraud, such as challenging providers' waivers of coinsurance and creating policies to "self-police" provider activities. Often, federal investigations

---

[2] *See* 42 U.S.C. § 1396a(a)(61); 42 C.F.R. Part 1007.

## State and Private Initiatives to Combat Fraud

of providers and the subsequent settlements with the federal government precipitate private industry measures. For example, once a settlement is finalized with the federal government, a private insurer might bring its own action against the provider, typically based upon the findings of the federal investigation.

Trade associations, such as the American Medical Association (AMA), have created policies that also address these issues. Other trade organizations have joined the AMA in its attempt to combat healthcare fraud. For example, the Advanced Medical Technology Association (formerly known as the Health Industry Manufacturers Association), the American College of Radiology, the American Urological Association, and the Pharmaceutical and Research Manufacturers of America have established guidelines and policies to eliminate inappropriate activities of industry members with respect to healthcare practitioners.

Additionally, organizations exist that combine private industry payors, trade associations, private organizations, and federal and state officials to address issues relating to fraud and abuse. The National Healthcare Anti-Fraud Association (NHCAA) is a prime example of this type of organization. The NHCAA has created systems and techniques to combat fraud in the private sector. Private nonprofit organizations also exist to address the fraud and abuse problem in the healthcare industry. Taxpayers Against Fraud (TAF) is one such organization that focuses specifically on the federal False Claims Act (FCA) and proactively exercising qui tam provisions.

This chapter provides an overview of these various state and private efforts to address healthcare fraud and abuse.[3]

## § 6-2  STATE SELF-REFERRAL LAWS

As discussed in Chapter 3, the federal government has attempted in various ways to limit or prohibit physicians from referring patients to a healthcare facility with which the physician has a financial relationship. Consequently, state lawmakers also have directed their attention to these financial relationships and the impact on the healthcare delivery system. While the majority of states have adopted some form of a self-referral prohibition, states have been far from uniform in their approach. Additionally, because the federal self-referral legislation does not preempt state self-referral laws, states may prohibit activities that are permissible under federal law. A state-by-state analysis of self-referral proscriptions is therefore necessary with respect to

---

[3] This chapter provides an overview of state healthcare fraud statutes through the use of examples, and *should not* be regarded as a comprehensive 50-state survey on these state laws. For a more-detailed state survey, *see* the 50-state survey prepared by the American Health Lawyers Association's Fraud and Abuse Practice Group.

any potential arrangements involving financial relationships with healthcare providers.

## § 6-2(a) Scope of the State Self-Referral Prohibitions

State self-referral laws are important because they often reach referrals that the federal self-referral law does not otherwise address. Set forth below is a brief summary of how some of these state laws differ from the scope of the federal law.

While a number of state self-referral laws are similar to the federal self-referral statute in that they apply only to physicians' self-referrals (e.g., Tennessee),[4] most states have broader statutes that apply to other health professionals. For example, the Maryland self-referral law applies to any "person who is licensed, certified or otherwise authorized . . . to provide healthcare services [under Maryland law] in the ordinary course of business or practice of a profession."[5] New Hampshire's statute extends to all "healthcare practitioners," defined under the statute as "any person licensed or registered as a healthcare provider."[6]

As discussed in Chapter 3, the federal self-referral prohibition is limited to certain "designated health services." While a couple states have enacted self-referral laws that mirror the list of designated health services under federal law, most state legislatures have enacted laws that apply to an array of differing healthcare services. For example, the Georgia self-referral statute extends to "clinical laboratory services, physical therapy services, rehabilitation services, diagnostic imaging services, pharmaceutical services, durable medical equipment, home infusion therapy services (including related pharmaceuticals and equipment), home health services, and outpatient surgical services."[7] The California self-referral statute includes "laboratory, diagnostic nuclear medicine, radiation oncology, physical therapy, physical rehabilitation, psychometric testing, home infusion therapy, or diagnostic imaging goods or services."[8] In fact, some states have enacted quasi-blanket bans on self-referral activities. For instance, Maine's statute covers referrals for "diagnosis, treatment, or rehabilitative services."[9] South Carolina's statute prohibits referrals for "designated health services," which includes "any healthcare procedure, service, or item provided by a healthcare provider."[10]

---

[4] TENN. CODE. ANN. § 63-6-601-§ 63-6-608.
[5] MD. CODE ANN., HEALTH OCC. § 1-301(h).
[6] N.H. REV. STAT. ANN. § 125:25-a.
[7] GA. CODE ANN. § 43-1B-3(2).
[8] CAL. BUS. & PROF. CODE § 650.01(a).
[9] ME. REV. STAT. ANN. tit. 22, § 2084(5).
[10] S.C. CODE ANN. §§ 44-113-30(A), 44-113-20(4).

Similar to the federal self-referral law, most state self-referral laws also prohibit healthcare providers from making referrals to facilities where immediate family members have a financial relationship with an entity to which the healthcare provider refers patients. However, the definition of "immediate family members" varies somewhat among the states. In Maryland, the prohibition is extended to the provider's spouse, child, child's spouse, parents and parents-in-law, and siblings and sibling's spouses.[11] South Carolina's law extends the lineage even further to include the provider's grandchildren and their spouses.[12] The Virginia self-referral statute broadens the definition of "immediate family member" to include stepchildren, stepchildren's spouses, and stepparents.[13]

## § 6-2(b) Exceptions to the Self-Referral Prohibitions

Virtually all state self-referral statutes contain exceptions to the prohibitions. The applicable exceptions allow a physician to refer patients to an entity with which the physician maintains some kind of financial relationship. Therefore, the exceptions establish that certain referrals are allowed in spite of the state's self-referral prohibition. Although the range of these exceptions varies widely among the states, there are certain core exceptions that appear in almost every state statute, such as those that shall be described for publicly traded stock and for rural areas. Other common state-law exceptions essentially mirror those enumerated in the federal self-referral prohibition or the language of the safe-harbor provisions promulgated under the Anti-Kickback Statute.

One common exception includes physician ownership of publicly traded stock in a healthcare facility. For example, Florida's exception provides that a physician-investor in an entity that is not a "designated health service" may refer patients to the entity so long as the investment interest is held in publicly traded, registered securities and the assets of the entity exceed $50 million.[14] California's exception is similar, and its minimum corporate-asset value is set at $75 million.[15] The exception in the Illinois statute sets the minimum asset value at $30 million,[16] while Maryland's statutory exception has no assigned minimum value.[17]

Another common exception is ownership of, or investment interest in, an entity located in a rural area. The scope of this exception varies among

---

[11] MD. CODE ANN., HEALTH OCC. § 1-301(j).
[12] S.C. CODE ANN. § 44-113-20(9).
[13] VA. CODE ANN. § 54.1-2410.
[14] FLA. STAT. ANN. § 456.053(5)(b)(1).
[15] CAL. BUS. & PROF. CODE § 650.02(b)(3).
[16] 225 ILL. COMP. STAT. § 47/20(c)(2).
[17] MD. CODE ANN., HEALTH OCC. § 1-301(b)(2).

the states. Florida exempts referrals from physicians who have an investment interest in an entity that "is the sole provider of designated health services in a rural area."[18] Under New York law, a referral is exempt if the provider's healthcare facility is located in a rural area and either the referring physician or the patient also is located in that rural area.[19] The geographic proximity of certain healthcare providers to other providers is the factor that allows the application of some state exceptions to self-referral prohibitions. For example, California law provides a referral exception for healthcare providers whose "regular practice is located where there is no alternative provider of the service within either 25 miles or 40 minutes traveling time, via the shortest route on a paved road."[20] In addition, the California statute provides that when the exception is claimed, the referring licensee must disclose the financial interest to the "patient, or the patient's parents or legal guardian in writing."

A group-practice exception is now commonly incorporated into state self-referral statutes. As a general rule, states define "group practice" as it is defined under the federal self-referral law. A group practice generally exists if members provide all services through that group, if bills are submitted in the group's name, and if methods of dividing expenses and income are determined prior to the formulation of the group practice.[21] The group-practice exception in the Nevada statute also requires that practitioners have "joint use of shared offices, facilities, equipment and personnel located at any site of the group practice."[22]

In an affiliated approach, similar to one federal exemption, many state self-referral laws permit the provision of "ancillary services" in the physician's own office or the office of the physician's group practice.[23] The New York statute incorporates the standard elements of the group-practice exemption into its statutory definition of "in-office ancillary services" to essentially combine the group practice and in-office ancillary office exceptions.[24] Maryland's statute has a similar exception,[25] yet "ancillary services" does not include magnetic resonance imaging (MRI), radiation-therapy services, or computerized tomography (CT) scans.[26] In Ohio, the self-referral statute provides an exemption for in-office ancillary services only if the third-party

---

[18] FLA. STAT. ANN. § 456.053(3)(k)(1) (defining "rural area" as a "county with a population density of no greater than 100 persons per square mile").
[19] N.Y. PUB. HEALTH LAW § 238-a(4).
[20] CAL. BUS. & PROF. CODE § 650.02(a).
[21] *See, e.g.*, FLA. STAT. ANN. § 456.053(3)(h); ME. REV. STAT. ANN. tit. 22 § 2084(3); MD. CODE ANN., HEALTH OCC. § 1-301(f); CAL. BUS. & PROF. CODE § 650.01(b)(6).
[22] NEV. REV. STAT. § 439B.425(5)(a)(1).
[23] CONN. GEN. STAT. § 20-7a(c).
[24] N.Y. PUB. HEALTH LAW § 238-a(2).
[25] MD. CODE ANN., HEALTH OCC. § 1-302(d)(4).
[26] MD. CODE ANN., HEALTH OCC. § 1-301(k)(2).

## State and Private Initiatives to Combat Fraud

payor is aware of the investment or other financial interest, and had previously agreed in writing to pay for the health service.[27]

Many states also provide exceptions for personal-services contracts, space and equipment leases, and employment agreements similar to those provided in the federal self-referral statute. For example, the California self-referral statute provides an exception for a space or equipment lease between a healthcare provider and the recipient of the referral if: the lease is in writing; it has commercially reasonable terms; it has a fixed periodic rent payment; it is for a term of one year or more; and either party's referral of any person or the volume of services each party provides does not affect the lease payments.[28] Maryland's statute provides an exception for compensation arrangements relating to a bona fide employment relationship,[29] while New York's law exempts physician-recruitment arrangements involving a certain geographic location.[30] Several state statutes incorporate additional compensation exceptions. New York's statute exempts "remuneration for medical director services in hospices or non-profit blood centers."[31] New Jersey's law excludes several compensation arrangements from the statutory definition of "financial interest," effectively exempting the arrangement from the self-referral prohibition. "Straight salaries," "annual retainers," and arrangements with healthcare facilities that "provide services to the medically indigent" are some examples of permissible arrangements.[32] California's statute is similar,[33] and it has an additional exception relating to referrals to a facility "owned or operated by a university," so long as the referring provider is "compensated or employed by" that university.[34]

### § 6-2(c)  Advisory Opinions/Declaratory Statements

Various states have enacted statutory provisions that allow individuals to obtain guidance from the state with respect to that state's self-referral law. For example, the Virginia Practitioner Self-Referral Act requires the Board of Health Professions to "establish standards, procedures, and criteria for determining compliance with, exceptions to, and violations of the Practitioner Self-Referral Act," as well as "establish standards, procedures, and criteria for advising practitioners and entities of the statute's applicability to activities

---

[27] Ohio Rev. Code. Ann. § 4731.67(C)–(D).
[28] *See* Cal. Bus. & Prof. Code § 650.02(b)(2). *See also*, Md. Code Ann., Health Occ. § 1-301(c)(2 (v); Ohio Rev. Code Ann. § 4731.68(C).
[29] Md. Code Ann., Health Occ. § 1-301(c)(2)(ii).
[30] N.Y. Pub. Health Law § 238-a(b)(iv).
[31] N.Y. Pub. Health Law § 238-a(5)(b)(3).
[32] N.J. Admin. Code § 13:35-6.17(a)(2).
[33] Cal. Bus. & Prof. Code § 650.01(b)(2).
[34] Cal. Bus. & Prof. Code § 650.02(e).

and investments."[35] The Georgia Patient Self-Referral Act directs the state professional licensing boards to encourage licensed healthcare providers to use the "declaratory statement procedure" in order to prospectively determine the applicability of the statute, as it applies to such providers.[36] Florida's self-referral statute provides that the state professional licensing boards should encourage licensee use of the declaratory-statement procedure to determine the applicability of the self-referral law to that licensee.[37]

## § 6-2(d)  Penalties

The penalties for violating the state self-referral laws vary by state. Many states have incorporated the self-referral prohibition into their professional-licensing statutes. At a minimum, a violation would result in professional discipline such as denial, suspension, or revocation of a professional license. In some states, however, these laws are found in the state's insurance code, and hence provide for civil penalties well beyond licensure implications. Even when the professional licensure statutes include the self-referral law, some states have added civil penalties applicable to the health professional.

For example, in addition to disciplinary action against a physician, violators of the Florida self-referral law are subject to civil penalties similar to the federal self-referral proscription—$15,000 for each claim submitted to a third-party payor in violation of the statute, and up to $100,000 for each cross-referral scheme.[38] Minnesota's law provides for a myriad of penalties for non-disclosure of a financial interest; these penalties range from formal reprimand to revocation of the referring physician's license.[39] In Minnesota, the physician who refers in violation of the prohibition might also be ordered to provide "unremunerated professional services."

Under the Tennessee statute, civil penalties up to $5,000 can be imposed for each unlawful referral.[40] In Connecticut, a self-referral violation can result in a civil money penalty up to $10,000.[41] Ohio's statute provides for up to $5,000 for the first violation, and up to $20,000 for each subsequent violation and the board of medicine is able to limit, revoke, or suspend licensure, "upon a second or subsequent violation."[42]

---

[35] VA. CODE ANN. §§ 54.1-2412(B)(2)-(3).
[36] GA. CODE ANN. § 43-1B-4(2).
[37] FLA. STAT. ANN. § 456.053(5)(b)(4).
[38] FLA. STAT. ANN. § 456.053(5)(b)(4)(e)-(f).
[39] MINN. STAT. §§ 147.141, 147.091(p).
[40] TENN. CODE. ANN. § 63-6-607.
[41] CONN. GEN. STAT. §§ 20-7a, 19a-17(6).
[42] OHIO REV. CODE ANN. §§ 4731.225 and 4731.22.

## State and Private Initiatives to Combat Fraud

### § 6-2(e) Disclosure Laws

Some states do not prohibit physician self-referral, but physicians and other healthcare providers are required to disclose their financial interests to those patients they refer to healthcare facilities in which they have an investment interest. For example, Kansas, Louisiana, Oklahoma, Hawaii, Utah, and Arizona do not currently prohibit physicians or other healthcare practitioners from referring patients to entities in which the practitioner has a financial interest. These states do require, however, that physicians disclose their financial interest to their patients, prior to referring them to such entity.[43] Some states that have enacted self-referral bans require disclosure of interests exempted from, or not implicated by, the self-referral ban.

Particular state disclosure requirements are diverse and vary widely. South Dakota's statute merely requires disclosure of the "general nature" of the financial interest, but does not specify the method of disclosure.[44] Most states require written disclosure,[45] while some others allow posting of the disclosure as an alternative.[46] In Connecticut, disclosure is permitted in verbal or posted form.[47] Hawaii's statute calls for the retention of the disclosure documentation for a certain time period,[48] while Maryland's statute mandates that the disclosure is documented in the referred patient's medical chart.[49] Other state statutes are quite specific as to the information that must be disclosed. For example, some states require a written disclosure form that lists the facilities in which the physician has a financial interest, informs the patient that she has the choice of whether to use the services of that facility, and that other such facilities are available to the patient. South Carolina's self-referral law includes such requirements, as well as a requirement that the patient is informed of "a schedule of typical fees for items or services usually provided by the entity or, if impracticable because of the nature of the treatment, a written estimate specific to the patient."[50] Maryland's law also is specific; unless the referral is made by telephone, written notice of disclosure is required

---

[43] *See, e.g.*, KAN. STAT. ANN. § 65-2837(29); LA. REV. STAT. ANN. § 37:1744(B); OKLA. STAT. ANN. tit. 59, § 725.4; HAW. REV. STAT. § 431:10C-308.7(c); UTAH CODE ANN. § 58-67-801; ARIZ. REV. STAT. ANN. § 32-1401(25)(ff).

[44] S.D. CODIFIED LAWS § 36-2-19.

[45] *See, e.g.,* MD. CODE ANN., HEALTH OCC. § 1-303(b)(1); HAW. REV. STAT. § 431:10C-308.7(d) (2005); N.H. REV. STAT. § 125:25-b (2005).

[46] CAL. BUS. & PROF. CODE § 650.01(f).

[47] CONN. GEN. STAT. § 20-7a(c).

[48] HAW. REV. STAT. § 431:10C-308.7(d) (statute requires two-year retention of disclosure form).

[49] MD. CODE ANN., HEALTH OCC. § 1-303(b)(2).

[50] S.C. CODE ANN. § 44-113-40 (additional requirement that the names and addresses of at least two alternative sources be made available to patient).

for each patient, in addition to a notice "posted in the form of a sign, in the physician's office."[51]

In Florida, the self-referral statute mandates that both the referring and referred-to providers must disclose to the patient. The referring provider must disclose the financial interest involved and information on "at least" two alternative sources of service.[52] The provider, who was referred to, must disclose the same information, along with a schedule of fees or a "patient-specific fee estimate."

The majority of state disclosure statutes require that disclosure is provided to the patient; some states, however, also require disclosure to third-party payors.[53] Massachusetts requires referring "practitioners" to disclose their financial interests in certain entities to the applicable state licensing board.[54] In contrast, the New York statute mandates that the facility providing covered healthcare services disclose the names of the practitioners who have a financial interest in them.[55]

## § 6-3   STATE ANTI-KICKBACK PROSCRIPTIONS

In an affiliated approach to combating healthcare fraud and abuse, most states have enacted statutes prohibiting certain financial arrangements between healthcare practitioners that constitute illegal remuneration in return for patient referrals.

The majority of states have adopted freestanding anti-kickback proscriptions similar to the Anti-Kickback Statute. Nevertheless, these state laws (which prohibit the payment of kickbacks and other remuneration for patient referrals) vary widely in scope, specificity, and potential penalties. For example, some state anti-kickback statutes incorporate the federal provisions by reference.[56]

State penalties for anti-kickback violations encompass a broad range, generally including civil fines, in addition to a possible criminal conviction. For example, the Rhode Island statute provides for a fine of not more than $1,000 and a potential prison sentence of up to one year.[57] A violation of Alabama's anti-kickback law carries a potential felony conviction, with

---

[51] *See* MD. CODE ANN., HEALTH OCC. § 1-303(b).
[52] FLA. STAT. ANN. § 456.052(1)-(2).
[53] *See* ME. REV. STAT. ANN. tit. 22, § 2085(2)(D)(8) (investment interest must be disclosed, upon request of third-party payor); *See also* 225 ILL. COMP. STAT. § 47/20 (b)(8).
[54] MASS. GEN. LAWS ch. 112, § 12AA.
[55] *See* N.Y. PUB. HEALTH LAW § 238-c.
[56] *See* KY. REV. STAT. ANN. § 216.2950 (the statute reads, in pertinent part, that "any conduct or activity by any provider which violates the provisions of 42 U.S.C. § 1395nn or 42 U.S.C. § 1320A-7B(b) . . . shall be deemed to violate the provisions of this section.").
[57] R.I. GEN. LAWS § 5-48.1-3.

## State and Private Initiatives to Combat Fraud

fines up to $10,000.[58] In California, an anti-kickback violation is punishable upon a first conviction by one year of imprisonment and a civil fine of up to $50,000.[59] Although the penalty provisions of the referenced statutes are relatively straightforward, the penalty provisions of some state anti-kickback laws are reasonably complex.[60]

Even in those states where freestanding anti-kickback statutes are not enacted, professional licensure laws may interpret anti-kickbacks or similar practices as unprofessional conduct, thereby subjecting the licensee to disciplinary action.[61] For example, although Virginia does not have a freestanding statute, its physician and hospital-licensure statutes both contain anti-kickback prohibitions. The Virginia Professions and Occupations Code prohibits the solicitation or receipt of remuneration in exchange for referrals to a hospital or healthcare facility.[62] Additionally, a hospital in Virginia is prohibited from "knowingly and willfully" offering or paying remuneration directly or indirectly to induce a physician to refer patients to the hospital.[63]

Florida's physician licensure law provides that the following acts shall constitute grounds for which disciplinary action may be taken:

> Paying or receiving any commission, bonus, kickback, or rebate, or engaging in any split-fee arrangement in any form whatsoever with a physician, organization, agency, or person, either directly or indirectly, for patients referred to providers of healthcare goods and services, including, but not limited to, hospitals, nursing homes, clinical laboratories, ambulatory surgical centers, or pharmacies. The provisions of this paragraph shall not be construed to prevent a physician from receiving a fee for professional consultation services.[64]

Some state anti-kickback statutes apply to a myriad of referrals for healthcare goods and services while others merely apply to goods and services that are reimbursable only under state health programs. For example, Alabama's anti-kickback statute only prohibits kickbacks for Medicaid services.[65]

California has an anti-rebate statute in the California Business and Professions Code that prohibits any licensed healthcare professional from

---

[58] ALA. CODE § 22-1-11 (felony conviction can result in prison sentence of up to five years).
[59] CAL. BUS. & PROF. CODE § 650.
[60] ARIZ. REV. STAT. ANN. § 13-3713 (A) (provides for "(1) class 3 felony if consideration had value of $1,000 or more, (2) class 4 felony if consideration had value between $100 and $1,000, and (3) class 6 felony if consideration had value of $100 or less.").
[61] *See, e.g.*, ALASKA STAT. § 08.71.170 (relating to opticians); VT. STAT. ANN. tit. 26, § 1354 (2005); Neb. Rev. Stat. § 71-148.
[62] VA. CODE ANN. § 54.1-2962.1.
[63] VA. CODE ANN. § 32.1-135.2.
[64] FLA. STAT. ANN. § 458.331(1)(i).
[65] ALA. CODE § 22-1-11(b).

offering, delivering, receiving, or accepting any "rebate, refund, commission, preference, patronage dividend, discount or other consideration" for the referral of patients.[66] The California law, however, includes exceptions for service, equipment and space, and rental arrangements in which payment is based on a percentage of gross revenues. New York's anti-kickback statute provides that no provider shall, "solicit, receive, accept or agree to receive or accept any payment or other consideration in any form from another person . . . or to purchase, lease or order any good facility, service or item for which payment is made under title eleven of article five of this chapter."[67]

It is important to note that, as with self-referrals, the federal and state governments have concurrent jurisdiction over conduct prohibited by the anti-kickback laws. Therefore, violations could result in prosecution by the states, the federal government, or both.

## § 6-4  STATE FEE-SPLITTING PROSCRIPTIONS

Many states have enacted fee-splitting statutes that may also operate to preclude kickbacks or other illegal-remuneration arrangements. Fee-splitting generally occurs when a physician or other healthcare provider refers a patient to another healthcare provider and subsequently collects a portion of the fee paid by the patient for the referred services. Several states that prohibit fee-splitting allow physicians who practice in a group setting to share or pool fees.[68] Other states allow the sharing of fees, so long as the practice is disclosed. For example, Kentucky's fee-splitting prohibition permits two licensed physicians to divide fees, so long as the patient is aware of the division and the division is proportionate to the services rendered.[69]

Some states may take a broader view of the fee-splitting proscription, and prohibit healthcare providers from paying fees to anyone—regardless of whether that person is a source of patient referrals—based on the fees associated with patient services. For example, Illinois law precludes physicians from "dividing with anyone, other than physicians with whom the licensee practices in a partnership, professional association, limited liability company, or medical or professional corporation any fee, commission, rebate or other form of compensation for any professional services not actually and personally rendered."[70] This provision has been interpreted as prohibiting an agreement between a physician and a marketing firm, where the compensation arrangement provided that the marketing firm would receive a fee of 10% of all billings the physician collected in connection with the referrals received by

---

[66] *See* CAL. BUS. & PROF. CODE § 650.
[67] N.Y. SOC. SERV. LAW § 366-d.
[68] MINN. STAT. § 147.091(p).
[69] KY. REV. STAT. ANN. § 311.595(19).
[70] 225 ILL. COMP. STAT. § 60/22(A)(14).

### State and Private Initiatives to Combat Fraud

the marketing company.[71] An Illinois Court of Appeals held that the contract violated public policy because payment to the marketing company might not represent a portion of each patient's billing.

Several states have adopted narrow fee-splitting prohibitions, applicable only to certain providers,[72] while others have broader fee-splitting laws. For example, New York considers doctors and other healthcare professionals to commit professional misconduct if they split fees for professional services rendered. Subject to certain exceptions, New York's law applies to arrangements between healthcare professionals and unlicensed persons or entities.[73]

## § 6-5 STATE COMMERCIAL-BRIBERY AND RACKETEERING STATUTES

Several states have enacted commercial-bribery statutes that could also be construed to prohibit kickbacks and similar illegal remuneration.[74] For instance, New Jersey's commercial-bribery statute states that a person commits a crime if "he solicits, accepts or agrees to accept any benefit as consideration for knowingly violating or agreeing to violate a duty of fidelity to which he is subject as . . . a physician."[75] Similarly, Texas law provides that

> a person who is a fiduciary commits an offense if, without the consent of his beneficiary, he intentionally or knowingly solicits, accepts, or agrees to accept any benefit from another person on agreement or understanding that the benefit will influence the conduct of the fiduciary in relation to the affairs of his beneficiary.[76]

A "fiduciary" is defined in this Texas statute to include a physician.

Interpretation of state racketeering statutes also may include prohibition of kickbacks and similar illegal remuneration and may provide for a private cause of action. For example, New Mexico's Racketeering Act defines the term "racketeering" as including any act involving illegal kickbacks. The New Mexico statute further provides that any person whose "person, business or property" is injured by a "pattern" of racketeering may file a civil

---

[71] E&B Mktg., Inc. v. Ryan, 568 N.E.2d 339 (Ill. App. Ct. 1991).
[72] Mich. Comp. Laws Ann. § 750.428 (applicable only to "physicians and surgeons").
[73] See N.Y. Educ. Law § 6509-a. See also N.Y. Educ. Law § 6530(18)-(19) (prohibition on fee-splitting extends to "any arrangement or agreement whereby the amount received in payment for furnishing space, facilities, equipment or personnel services used by a licensee constitutes a percentage of, or is otherwise dependent upon, the income or receipts of the licensee from such practice").
[74] See, e.g., Colo. Rev. Stat. § 18-5-401; Haw. Rev. Stat. § 708-880; Kan. Stat. Ann. § 21-4405; Mo. Rev. Stat. § 570.150.
[75] N.J. Stat. Ann. § 2C:21-10.
[76] Tex. Penal Code Ann. § 32.43.

action.⁷⁷ Therefore, while the state may only enforce some of the statutes discussed, these statutes may provide an independent basis for a private individual to challenge an arrangement involving kickbacks or similar illegal remuneration.

## § 6-6 STATE STATUTES REGARDING DECEPTIVE TRADE PRACTICES AND CONSUMER PROTECTION

Many states have enacted statutes targeting unfair trade practices, and have enacted consumer protection laws. These measures may be sufficiently broad to encompass arrangements involving undisclosed financial relationships between healthcare providers, including self-referrals, kickbacks, and similar forms of remuneration.⁷⁸ For example, the Illinois legislature has enacted a statute, specific to healthcare, prohibiting unfair and deceptive marketing practices.⁷⁹ Moreover, Illinois' Consumer Fraud and Deceptive Business Practices Act has been used in the healthcare context.⁸⁰

Many states' unfair trade practices statutes and consumer protection laws provide that litigants may receive substantial monetary damage awards. For example, the Montana Unfair Trade Practices and Consumer Protection Act states that it is an "unfair trade practice" to make a "secret payment or allowance of rebates refunds, commissions, or unearned discounts . . . to the injury of competitor."⁸¹ A private plaintiff who is harmed by a violation of this statute is entitled to receive three times the amount of actual damages sustained.

These types of statutes may be especially significant in states that have not yet enacted statutes prohibiting self-referrals or kickbacks. For example, an amendment to the Arkansas Deceptive Trade Practices Act makes the " . . . concealment, suppression, or omission of material facts in connection with the provision of services" an unlawful trade practice, and subjects violators to both civil and criminal penalties.⁸² Thus, even though Arkansas has not adopted a self-referral prohibition, it is possible that a physician's referral of a patient to a healthcare entity, in which the provider has a financial interest or relationship, is a material fact that must be disclosed to the patient.

In fact, states' consumer protection laws have been the basis for several government investigations and settlements. For example, a settlement agreement between Miles, Inc., a pharmaceutical manufacturer, and several state

---

⁷⁷ N.M. STAT. ANN. §§ 30-42-3(11), 30-42-6(B).
⁷⁸ MINN. STAT. ANN. § 325F.69.
⁷⁹ 305 ILL. COMP. STAT. § 5/8A-16 (2005).
⁸⁰ *See* 815 ILL. COMP. STAT. §§ 505/2, 505/10a(a). Johnston v. Anchor Org. for Health Maintenance, 621 N.E. 2d 137 (Ill. App. 1993).
⁸¹ MONT. CODE ANN. § 30-14-222.
⁸² ARK. CODE ANN. § 4-88-108(2).

## State and Private Initiatives to Combat Fraud

attorneys general demonstrates that state consumer protection laws may be used to challenge certain financial relationships between healthcare providers.[83] It was alleged that the manufacturer engaged in unfair and deceptive trade practices and consumer fraud by offering and paying pharmacies a certain sum of money for each prescription they filled for a new product of the manufacturer without disclosing to consumers and physicians the fact of the payment. Allegedly, the manufacturer offered and paid these sums to solicit or arrange the switch from a competitor's product to the manufacturer's new product. Pursuant to the settlement agreement, the manufacturer agreed to discontinue offering compensation or paying pharmacies or pharmacists to dispense any drug that Miles, Inc., manufactured or sold.[84]

Similarly, Merck, a pharmaceutical manufacturer, and Medco Containment Services, Inc., a prescription-benefits manager and mail-service pharmacy, have settled with several state attorneys general for allegedly having violated state consumer protection laws.[85] The allegation concerned a pharmacy "switch" program in which Medco pharmacists telephoned physicians to discuss changes in prescriptions without disclosing Medco's affiliation with Merck or without accurately disclosing the purpose of the call. Additionally, it was alleged that such statutes may have been violated because Medco did not disclose to plan members its programs for telephoning physicians, which resulted in a potential change in their prescriptions. By the terms of the settlement agreement, which included the payment of $115,000 from the companies to each of the states involved,[86] Merck and Medco assured the states that their conduct in providing prescription-drug benefit management would comply with state consumer protection laws, including clear and conspicuous disclosures about their programs. This settlement suggests that the state attorneys general involved in this litigation may have been of the opinion that Merck's ownership of Medco so tainted Medco's advice to its clients and physicians that failure to disclose the relationship amounted to a deceptive practice.

---

[83] In the Matter of Miles, Inc., No. C7-94-3189 (D. Minn. Apr. 4, 1994).

[84] The states that were parties to this settlement agreement include Arizona, Connecticut, Illinois, Massachusetts, Minnesota, Missouri, New Mexico, New York, North Carolina, Texas, and Wisconsin.

[85] In the Matter of Merck & Co., Inc. & Medco Containment Servs., Inc., No. C-6-95-10614 (D. Minn. Oct. 25, 1995).

[86] The states that were parties to this settlement agreement include Arizona, California, Connecticut, Florida, Illinois, Iowa, Maryland, Massachusetts, Minnesota, Missouri, New Mexico, New York, North Carolina, Pennsylvania, Texas, Vermont, and Wisconsin.

## § 6-7 STATE FALSE CLAIMS ACTIVITIES

### § 6-7(a) State Law Governing Fraudulent Billing Practices

States also have enacted statutes that prohibit persons from filing false claims with private insurers. For example, in Pennsylvania, a person who knowingly presents to an insurer or self-insured "any statement forming a part of, or in support of, a claim that contains any false, incomplete or misleading information concerning any fact or thing material to the claim" commits insurance fraud.[87] Illinois law provides for a conviction of "aggravated fraud," if a person "makes or causes to be made" three or more false claims to an insurance company.[88] Delaware passed legislation creating the crime of "Healthcare Fraud," which prohibits the knowing or reckless submission of fraudulent healthcare claims to "any healthcare benefit program."[89]

With the adoption of the Deficit Reduction Act of 2005 (DRA), the states were provided with a significant incentive to revisit the issue of either adopting a new statute or revising any existing state false claims provisions. The DRA added a provision to the federal Medicaid statute that provides for an increase of ten percent in a state's share of any amounts recovered as part of an action brought under the state's false claims act. In order to qualify for this increase, however, the state's false claims act must meet certain criteria, namely that the state statute includes provisions that are similar to the FCA.[90] In 2006, the OIG published a notice in the *Federal Register* that sets forth the OIG's guidelines for reviewing state false claims acts.[91]

As of 2012, 15 states (California, Georgia, Hawaii, Illinois, Indiana, Iowa, Massachusetts, Michigan, Nevada, New York, Rhode Island, Tennessee, Texas, Virginia, and Wisconsin) have had their false claims laws approved by the OIG, thereby allowing those states to recover a higher percentage of monetary settlements and judgments in actions brought under their state false claims acts. Of the state false claims laws that have not been approved by OIG (Colorado, Connecticut, Delaware, Florida, Louisiana, Montana, New Hampshire, New Jersey, New Mexico, North Carolina, and Oklahoma), the OIG found that the states' qui tam provisions insufficiently mirrored the FCA, explaining that the state law provisions were not as effective as the FCA in rewarding qui tam actions.[92]

---

[87] 18 PA. CONS. STAT. § 4117(A)(2) (2005).
[88] 720 ILL. COMP. STAT. § 5/46-2.
[89] DEL. CODE ANN. tit. 11, § 913A.
[90] Deficit Reduction Act of 2005, Pub. L. No. 109-171, § 6031.
[91] 71 Fed. Reg. 48,552 (Aug. 21, 2006).
[92] *See* State False Claims Act Reviews on the OIG website at: http://oisg.hhs.gov/fraud/falseclaimsact.asp.

### State and Private Initiatives to Combat Fraud

However, since this provision was adopted in 2005, the FCA has been amended by the Fraud Enforcement and Recovery Act of 2009, the Patient Protection and Affordable Care Act of 2010 (the "Health Reform Law") and the Dodd-Frank Wall Street Reform and Consumer Protection Act. As a result of these amendments the OIG has stated that it will analyze compliance using the FCA as amended but will provide a two-year grace period, (generally ending on March 31, 2013), during which state acts that were previously approved by OIG will continue to be deemed compliant pending state act amendment and resubmission to OIG.[93]

## § 6-7(b)  Waivers of Coinsurance and Deductible Amounts

The issue of whether providers routinely may waive coinsurance and deductible amounts, and whether such practices are considered "false claims," may vary by state as well as by the terms of the individual insurance policy. State law may contain an express proscription of coinsurance and deductible waivers applicable to particular healthcare providers. For example, the Colorado physician-licensure law expressly prohibits waivers of coinsurance and deductible amounts.[94] Similarly, the Florida Department of Insurance regulations state that waiver of coinsurance and deductible amounts constitute the act of presenting a "false claim" to the insurer unless the existence of the waiver arrangement is disclosed to the payor in the manner specified by law.[95] Under this Florida regulation, as applied to healthcare providers, a waiver does not forgive or write off any unpaid deductible amount after attempting reasonable collection efforts.

State case law and attorney general opinions also may address the legal implications of coinsurance and deductible waivers. Some cases have determined that coinsurance and deductible waivers may constitute fraud.[96] However, some states have a more liberal view of coinsurance waivers.[97]

---

[93] *Id.*
[94] COLO. REV. STAT. § 18-13-119.
[95] FLA. ADMIN. CODE ANN. § 69B-153.003.
[96] *See* Feiler v. New Jersey Dental Assocs., 489 A.2d 1161 (N.J. Super. Ct. App. Div.), *cert. denied*, 491 A.2d 673 (N.J. 1984). *See also* 1983 Ga. Att'y Gen. Op. 53 (finding a dentist may be subject to disciplinary action by the Georgia Board of Dentistry for the waiver of a patient's copayment).
[97] *See* 64 Cal. Att'y Gen. Op. 782 (Oct. 16, 1981) (finding a dentist's waiver of a patient's copayment does not violate California's laws against misrepresentation and fraud).

## § 6-8 STATE SUNSHINE ACTS APPLICABLE TO PHARMACEUTICAL AND MEDICAL DEVICE MANUFACTURERS

In addition to the federal efforts (addressed in Chapter 3) to limit the relationships between healthcare providers and pharmaceutical and medical device manufactures, a number of states have adopted "sunshine" laws to limit the kinds of gifts and contributions that drug and device manufacturers can make to providers and require that certain permissible contributions be disclosed.[98]

For example, Massachusetts has adopted regulations regulating provider-industry relations that were designed to "ensure that the relationship between pharmaceutical or medical device manufacturers and healthcare practitioners do not interfere with the independent judgment of healthcare practitioners."[99] To do so, the law requires that manufacturers adopt and implement a marketing code of conduct detailing a compliance program to implement and monitor the requirements of the code.[100] The regulations define a healthcare practitioner as "a person [or a partnership or corporation of such persons] who prescribes prescription drugs . . . and is licensed to provide healthcare" and their agents, employees, officers, or contractors.[101] The law limits manufacturers' ability to provide meals to practitioners, requiring that meals only be provided as part of an informational presentation, in the practitioner's office or hospital, to the practitioner, and not other guests or spouses. The law also expressly prohibits manufacturers from providing healthcare practitioners with: (i) funds for assistance with educational conferences, continuing medical education, and professional events, (including lodging, travel, and other personal expenses); (ii) entertainment or recreational items; (iii) payments of any kind to induce the use of the manufacturers' products; and (iv) any other payment or remuneration prohibited by federal and Massachusetts law.[102] Additionally, manufacturers must submit an annual report to the Massachusetts Department of Public Health disclosing the nature, purpose, and value of any "fee, payment, subsidy, or other economic value of at least $50" to a healthcare practitioner in connection with sales and marketing.[103]

Vermont has had a sunshine law in effect since 2002, and like the Massachusetts law, the Vermont law requires annual reports from manufacturers

---

[98] To date, California, Connecticut, the District of Columbia, Minnesota, Nevada, Vermont, and West Virginia have adopted some form of compliance or manufacturer disclosure laws.
[99] 105 CMR 970.001.
[100] 105 CMR 970.005(1).
[101] 105 CMR 970.004.
[102] 105 CMR 970.006–008.
[103] 105 CMR 970.009.

on any allowable gifts given to providers, with few exceptions.[104] When originally enacted, the Vermont law did not require manufacturers to disclose information that the company claimed is a trade secret. This exception to disclosure allowed manufactures to keep much of their activities and information private. For example, in 2008, of the 78 manufacturers that disclosed payments, 37 requested that some or all of their data be listed as trade secrets.[105] However, in 2009, Vermont amended this law by making it much stricter and more comprehensive by no longer including a carve-out for trade secrets.[106]

## § 6-9  STATE INITIATIVES TO PREVENT AND DETECT FRAUD

### § 6-9(a)  Medicaid Fraud Control Units

Since the 1970s, federal law has provided financial assistance to states to establish a Medicaid Fraud Control Unit, which is charged with investigating and prosecuting Medicaid provider fraud, abuse of patients in Medicaid residential facilities, and fraud in program administration.[107] MFCUs usually exist in the office of the state attorney general, and an MFCU will receive referrals to investigate fraud and abuse from the state's Medicaid agency, as well as referrals from private industry, concerned citizens, and whistleblowers. Although originally the MFCU program was voluntary, federal law now requires each state to have a MFCU unless the state can demonstrate to the satisfaction of the DHHS Secretary that it has a minimum amount of Medicaid fraud and Medicaid beneficiaries will be protected from abuse and neglect. To date, only North Dakota has been granted a waiver to not have a MFCU.[108]

Each MFCU receives a federal grant, annually, from the OIG (currently 75% of the MFCUs costs) and is required to operate on an interdisciplinary model and must employ investigators, auditors, and attorneys.[109] The OIG has developed a set of performance standards that were originally published in 1994 which is part of the certification process to assess whether a MFCU

---

[104] 18 V.S.A. § 4632.
[105] WILLIAM H. SORREL, VERMONT ATTORNEY GENERAL, PHARMACEUTICAL MARKETING DISCLOSURE JULY 1, 2008 –JUNE 30, 2008 10 (Apr. 2009), *available online at* http://www.atg.state.vt.us/display.php?smod=151.
[106] *See* 18 V.S.A. § 4632(a)(5).
[107] *See* 42 U.S.C. § 1396b(q)(2); 42 C.F.R. Part 1007.
[108] *See* National Association of Medicaid Fraud Control Units' website at: http://www.namfcu.net/about-us/about-mfcu. The territories, while they receive Medicaid funds, do not have MFCUs.
[109] In fiscal year (FY) 2010, the combined Federal and State grant expenditures for the State Medicaid Fraud Control Units (MFCU) totaled $205.5 million, of which Federal funds represented $153.8 million. The 50 MFCUs employed 1,827 individuals. *See* http://oig.hhs.gov/fraud/medicaid-fraud-control-units-mfcu/expenditures_statistics/fy2010.asp.

is operating effectively. In 2011, the OIG proposed a number of revisions to these standards.[110]

The National Association of Medicaid Fraud Control Units (NAMFCU) plays a large role in investigating fraud and abuse that impacts multiple states at the same time. Furthermore, the NAMFCU provides a nationwide forum to share information about Medicaid fraud control, as well as builds interstate partnerships regarding law enforcement and federal issues affecting the MFCUs. The NAMFCU attempts to improve the quality of the investigations and prosecutions through education and training programs that provide technical assistance to its members, and to inform the public about MFCUs. [111]

Collectively, in FY 2010, the MFCUs reported conducting 13,210 investigations, of which 9,710 were related to Medicaid fraud and 3,500 were related to patient abuse and neglect, including patient funds cases. Investigations resulted in 1,603 individuals' being indicted or criminally charged: 1,048 for fraud and 555 for patient abuse and neglect. In total, 1,329 convictions were reported in FY 2010, of which 839 were related to Medicaid fraud and 490 were related to patient abuse and neglect. In FY 2010, states reported $1.8 billion in recoveries for both civil and criminal cases handled by the 50 MFCUs and the total number of civil judgments and settlements for the fiscal year was 1,077.[112]

## § 6-9(b)  Medicaid Program Integrity

Most state Medicaid programs conduct Medicaid program integrity activities to deter fraud and abuse, and specifically to protect the accuracy of payments issued to providers. State program integrity activities consist of measures to issue correct payments and reclaim inappropriate payments. These measures may include controlling the enrollment of high-risk providers, employing advanced technology to make use of relevant data, and benefiting from legislation that encourages certain monitoring activities or expands legal authority. CMS aids the states in the technical implementation of program integrity, and conducts assessments of these activities.

As part of Medicaid program integrity, many states control enrollment to exclude those providers who present a high risk for fraud and abuse. Although each state approaches controlling enrollment differently, many typically focus on those providers that are not state-licensed or those who have aberrant billing practices, as well as providers previously excluded from a Medicaid program for different causes. Furthermore, enrollment procedures

---

[110] See 76 Fed. Reg. 62,074 (Oct. 6, 2011).
[111] See National Association of Medicaid Fraud Control Units' website at: http://www.namfcu.net/about-us/about-mfcu.
[112] See http://oig.hhs.gov/fraud/medicaid-fraud-control-units-mfcu/expenditures_statistics/fy2010.asp.

## State and Private Initiatives to Combat Fraud

for providers identified as high-risk are usually more stringent, and include on-site inspections of facilities, criminal background checks, requisite surety bonds, and time-limited enrollment.

In 2005, as part of DRA, Congress established the Medicaid Integrity Program (MIP), which significantly expanded CMS's efforts and "dramatically increased" resources available to combat fraud, waste and abuse in Medicaid.[113] In addition to identifying overpayments made to providers involving federal Medicaid funds, the Medicaid Integrity Group (MIG) (which is within CMS's the Center for Program Integrity) reviews the activities of providers, audits claims, and conducts provider education. While MIG utilizes contractors to carry out many of its review and audit activities, the DRA specifically mandated an increase of 100 full-time agency staff dedicated to assisting states in their MIP activities.[114] As part of this program, CMS has promulgated the Comprehensive Medicaid Integrity Plan (CMIP). The most recent plan addresses not only CMS's planned activities for FY 2009, but also the next four (4) fiscal years (i.e., through 2013).[115]

In 2010, as part of the Health Reform Law, Congress established the requirement that all states and territories establish a Medicaid Recovery Audit Contractor (RAC). Program, although states may seek exceptions from implementing the entire Medicaid RAC program or any of the requirements of the RAC program.[116] In October 2010, CMS issued a State Medicaid Director Letter to provide initial guidance on the implementation of these RAC programs. Each state and territory was required to submit a State Plan Amendment to CMS, in order to establish a state Medicaid RAC program subject to the exceptions and requirements provided by the Secretary.[117]

CMS published a Notice of Proposed Rule Making in November 2010 and subsequently issued a final rule implementing the Medicaid RAC program in September 2011.[118] The originally proposed implementation date of April 1, 2011, was delayed in order to give states sufficient time to develop their RAC programs. Although Medicaid RAC program requirements are generally consistent with the Medicare RAC program, states have been given flexibility in the design of their RAC programs in a number of areas. For example, each state is required to set its own limits on the number and frequency of records to be reviewed by the RACs, as well as the types of claims that will be excluded from review. Each state will establish its own audit areas, but the

---

[113] Pub. L. No. 109-171, § 6034, 120 Stat. 74, 74-79 (to be codified at 42 U.S.C. § 1396u-6).

[114] Pub. L. No. 109-171, § 6034(c) and (e)(3), 120 Stat. 74, 76 (to be codified at 42 U.S.C. § 1396u-6).

[115] *See* https://www.cms.gov/DeficitReductionAct/Downloads/CMIP2009-2013.pdf.

[116] Pub. L. 111-148 (2010), as amended by the Healthcare and Education Reconciliation Act of 2010, Pub. L. 111-152 (2010).

[117] *See* CMS, State Medicaid Director Letter Re: Recovery Audit Contractors (RACs) for Medicaid (Oct. 1, 2010), *available online at* https://www.cms.gov/smdl/downloads/SMD10021.pdf.

[118] *See* 75 Fed. Reg. 69,037 (Nov. 10, 2010); 76 Fed. Reg. 57,808 (Sept. 16, 2011).

states are not required to provide advanced notice of those issues to providers. Each state will also establish its own appeals process and its own educational outreach programs for providers. Further, CMS has encouraged, but is not requiring, alignment with the Medicare RAC program in a number of areas, including medical necessity reviews, extrapolation of audit findings, external validation of the accuracy of RAC findings, and types of claims audited.[119]

## § 6-9(c)  Establishment of State Inspector Generals

New York, a state leader in increasing its attention to addressing Medicaid fraud, created an agency specifically to work closely with the New York Attorney General's Medicaid Fraud and Control Unit and to work to strengthen partnerships with federal and local law enforcement agencies. In 2006, the New York State Office of the Medicaid Inspector General (NY-OMIG) was created as an independent office in the Department of Health to specifically coordinate fraud, waste and abuse activities in the Medicaid program.[120] In addition to establishing an office to combat Medicaid fraud, New York entered into a Federal-State Health Reform Partnership (F-SHRP) with the United States Department of Health and Human Services in which New York is to receive $1.5 billion over five years ($300 million annually) in grant funds and a waiver from the federal government to restructure its long-term care delivery services in exchange for increasing its fraud and abuse recovery efforts. Under the F-SHRP agreement, New York is required to meet aggressive fraud and abuse recovery targets,[121] including the recovery of $1.6 billion in fraud and abuse payments by 2011.[122]

For FY 2010, the NY-OMIG reported that it was responsible for, among other things:

- referring 110 cases to the New York State Attorney General for potential criminal prosecution;
- collaborating with the State Attorney General's Medicaid Fraud Control Unit and other state and federal agencies on the Medicare Fraud Strike Force led by the United States Department of Justice;
- referring almost 2,000 cases to local agencies for further action;

---

[119] 76 Fed. Reg. 57,817 (Sept. 16, 2011).
[120] The Office was created in New York Executive Order No. 140.1 (Feb. 2, 2006).
[121] Press Release, *Governor Pataki Announces 1.5 Billion Dollar Healthcare Reform Initiative* (Oct. 3, 2006), *available online at* http://www.omig.state.ny.us/data/content/view/77/41/.
[122] 2008–2009 Budget Hearing Presentation: Joint Budget Hearing before the S. Fin. Comm. and the Assembly Ways & Means Comm., 2008 Leg., 3–4 (NY 2008) (statement of James G. Sheehan, New York Medicaid Inspector General).

## State and Private Initiatives to Combat Fraud

- avoiding costs of $1.9 billion through various initiatives, including the restricted recipient program, pre-payment reviews and use of card swipe terminals at points of service;

- recovering approximately $454 million in improper Medicaid payments as a result of NY-OMIG's program integrity activities; and

- excluding and/or terminating participation with over 900 providers.[123]

At the same time, the NY-OMIG has focused on compliance to prevent improper payments on a going forward basis. For example, the NY-OMIG promulgated regulations requiring New York Medicaid providers to adopt corporate compliance programs.[124] Additionally, the NY-OMIG Office is working with the state health commissioner to develop protocols to facilitate provider self-disclosure and collections of overpayments.[125]

Other states have also taken initiatives to strengthen fraud and abuse initiatives. For example, in 2003, the Texas Legislature created an Office of Inspector General (TX-OIG) to strengthen fraud and abuse enforcement and recovery efforts in the Texas health and human services programs. The TX-OIG reviews, audits, and investigates fraud, abuse, and waste involving state and federal funds; recommends policies to enhance the protection and detection of fraud, waste, and abuse; and provides education, technical assistance, and training to providers and contractors to prevent fraud, abuse and waste.[126] According to the information prepared by the TX-OIG, since the program's inception through the first quarter of 2012, it has been responsible for recovering and ensuring that the state avoided the payment of improper costs of more than $6 billion.[127]

## § 6-10 TRADE ASSOCIATIONS

A number of trade associations have established guidelines and policies to eliminate inappropriate activities of industry members. Organizations have developed ethical guidelines concerning conflicts of interest that address issues such as healthcare practitioners who simultaneously have investments in healthcare entities and make referrals to those healthcare entities. In addition, a number of trade associations have addressed the ethical implications of their members accepting and/or giving benefits that may be offered in an

---

[123] *See* 2010 New York OMIG Annual Report at http://www.omig.ny.gov/data/images/stories/annual_report/annual_report_2010.pdf.
[124] N.Y Code, Title 18, Part 521.
[125] N.Y. Pub. Health Law § 32(18).
[126] *Id.*
[127] *See* http://oig.hhsc.state.tx.us/Reports/Summary%20of%20Cost%20Recovery%20and%20Cost%20Avoidance%20FY04%20thru%201Qtr%20FY12.pdf.

attempt to influence health professionals' ordering patterns. Manufacturers of drugs and devices typically have physician-marketing programs, which include gifts of merchandise and travel. Manufacturers may structure such gifts as educational programs to acquaint the physician with the benefits of the new product, or the gifts may be designed to assist the physician with her practice. Gifts may range from minimal value (e.g., textbooks and meals) to substantial value (e.g., fax machines, computer systems, or conferences at vacation resorts).

In addition to the guidelines and recommendations that will be described in this section, other trade organizations have addressed these issues, including the American College of Surgeons, American College of Emergency Physicians, the American Urological Association, and the American Association of Electrodiagnostic Medicine.

### § 6-10(a) American Medical Association

The AMA has been active in providing its members with guidance on the propriety of financial arrangements with entities to which the physicians may refer patients. In 1986, the AMA's Council on Ethical and Judicial Affairs (AMA Council) published a report on conflicts of interest in the practice of medicine.[128] At that time, the AMA Council viewed conflicts of interest as inherent in the practice of medicine. Similarly, the issue of referring patients to outside facilities in which physicians have an investment interest did not significantly differ in principle from other conflicts presented generally by fee-for-service medicine. With all of these arrangements, the AMA Council's primary guidance reminds physicians that the profession of medicine is unique, and that physicians are expected to place patient interests before their own.

In 1991, the AMA Council issued a subsequent report recommending more restrictive guidelines for physician referral to healthcare facilities in which the physician has an ownership interest.[129] In this report, the AMA Council noted that, since the issuance of its initial reports and opinions, several studies were performed that analyzed the issue of physician self-referral. The AMA Council concluded from these studies, as well as from its own analysis, that it was necessary to strengthen its opinion on self-referral.

Consistent with this position, the AMA Council offered two recommendations to its members. The first recommendation provided that, "in general, physicians should not refer patients to a healthcare facility outside their office practice *at which they do not directly provide care or services* when they have

---

[128] AMA Council, *Conflicts of Interest,* Rep. No. A(I-86) (1986).
[129] AMA Council, *Conflicts of Interest: Physician Ownership of Medical Facilities,* Rep. No. C(I-91) (1991), *available online at* http://www.ama-assn.org/ama1/pub/upload/mm/369/ceja_ci91.pdf.

## State and Private Initiatives to Combat Fraud

an investment interest in the facility."[130] The AMA Council was clear that the ethical guidelines do not prohibit an investment interest in a healthcare facility, such as a hospital or ambulatory surgical facility where the physician directly provides care and services. The AMA Council continually made this recommendation in ethical updates, and has further clarified that a physician must have "personal involvement" with the provision of care in a facility in which the physician has an ownership or other financial interest.[131] In addition, the AMA Council approved of self-referral to a shared clinical lab, so long as the facility is a "true extension of the physician's practice" and the transaction complies with the ethical guidelines.[132]

The AMA Council's second recommendation allowed a physician to refer patients to an entity in which the physician maintains an ownership interest "if there is a demonstrated need in the community for the facility and alternative financing is not available."[133] According to the AMA Council's clarification of this recommendation, "demonstrated need" exists "when there is no facility of reasonable quality in the community or when use of existing facilities is onerous for patients." Under such circumstances, and to the extent that several other requirements are satisfied, the AMA Council took the position that the investment should be justified by the facility having the potential for substantial improvement over the existing facilities.[134]

The second recommendation also addressed those physicians who already have an interest in a healthcare entity. The AMA Council recommended that physicians re-evaluate their activities and comply with the guidelines in its 1991 report to the fullest extent possible. "If compliance with the need and alternative investor criteria is not practical, it is essential that the identification of reasonably available alternative treatment facilities be provided."

In 2009, the AMA's Council issues Opinion E-8.0321 entitled Physicians' Self-Referrals which codified into the Code of Medical Ethics the AMA's policy on these issues.[135]

The AMA Council also developed a number of guidelines concerning physicians receiving gifts from pharmaceutical and medical-device

---

[130] *Id.* at 4.
[131] AMA Council, *Conflicts of Interest: Health Facility Ownership by a Physician,* Op. No. E-8.032 (2004). "Personal involvement" does not mandate that the physician must be present at every patient visit to the referred-to facility. According to the Council, "personal involvement" equates to the physician's participation in the patient's care "on site for a significant percentage of visits and a significant portion of the time during which services are rendered."
[132] *Id.*
[133] AMA Council, *Conflicts of Interest: Physician Ownership of Medical Facilities,* Rep. No. C(I-91) (1991), *available online at* http://www.ama-assn.org/ama1/pub/upload/mm/369/ceja_ci91.pdf.
[134] *Id.*
[135] *See* http://www.ama-assn.org/ama/pub/physician-resources/medical-ethics/code-medical-ethics/opinion80321.page?.

manufacturers, which eventually were codified into the AMA Code of Medical Ethics. In general, these guidelines stated that physicians may accept gifts from these types of companies when the gifts primarily provide a benefit to patients, are not of substantial value, serve a genuine educational function, and are not in the form of cash.[136]

The first guideline provided, in part, that "any gifts accepted by physicians individually should primarily entail a benefit to patients and not be of substantial value." Thus, gifts of diagnostic equipment are permissible because of the primary benefit to the patient; such gifts, however, must not have substantial value on the open market. Similarly, gifts such as textbooks, modest meals with a speaker, or other gifts are permissible if a genuine educational function is served and the physician receives only modest value in the general range of $100. With these measures in mind, the AMA Council's guidelines regarding when a pharmaceutical or other company may invite physicians to a dinner with a scheduled speaker include that:

- the dinner should be a modest meal, similar to what physicians routinely might have while dining at their expense; and
- when educational meetings occur in conjunction with a dinner, the educational component must have independent value.

The second guideline provides that individual gifts of minimal value (e.g., pens and note pads) are permissible if related to the physician's work. The third guideline involves conferences and meetings, and recommends that physicians should disclose any financial support or conflict of interest as appropriate.

The fourth guideline provides that industry subsidies of continuing medical education (CME) conferences are permissible, but only when funneled through the conference's sponsor and not directly paid to the physicians. The interpretations note that whether a subsidy comes from the company's educational division (as opposed to the sales division) is irrelevant. As further clarification, this guideline strongly recommends against a physician "directly accepting checks or certificates which would be used to offset" conference registration fees.

The fifth guideline provides that physicians should not accept any subsidy, either direct or indirect, to defray the travel, lodging, or other personal expenses associated with attending conferences or meetings. Physicians also should refuse subsidies for compensation of their time. Payment of reasonable expenses for such items may be acceptable, however, only when meetings

---

[136] AMA Council, *Gifts to Physicians from Industry,* 265 JAMA 501 (1991). *See also* AMA Council, *Guidelines on Gifts to Physicians from Industry: An Update,* 47 FOOD DRUG COSM. L.J. 445 (1992); *see also* AMA Council, *Gifts to Physicians from Industry,* Op. No. 8.061, which can be found at http://www.ama-assn.org/ama/pub/physician-resources/medical-ethics/code-medical-ethics/opinion8061.page?.

## State and Private Initiatives to Combat Fraud

serve a "genuine research purpose." For example, physicians may accept such expenses when they attend a meeting to review and comment on a product, or to serve with a group of clinical investigators or a focus group, but only when such meetings serve a "genuine research purpose." In order to ascertain a "genuine research purpose," the physician should consider (1) whether a valid study protocol exists, (2) whether there has been recruitment of physicians with appropriate qualifications or expertise, and (3) whether there has been recruitment of an appropriate number of physicians.

Bona fide faculty (as opposed to mere attendees) may accept reasonable travel and lodging expenses at educational meetings. An industry may subsidize a social event at a conference only to the extent that the value of the event to the physician is modest, the event facilitates discussion among attendees, and the educational part of the conference occupies a substantial majority of the time. For instance, the guidelines do not permit a company to rent an expensive entertainment complex for an evening during a medical conference and invite the attendees, because this does not constitute modest hospitality.

Generally, if physicians are providing genuine services, they can receive reasonable compensation for time and travel expenses. The guidelines provide, however, that implementation of "token advisory or consulting arrangements" cannot justify any form of compensation.

The sixth guideline provides that subsidies are appropriate to enable students, residents, and fellows to attend "carefully selected" educational conferences where the academic or training institution selects the students who attend, but only when the academic departments or the conference sponsor distribute the funds, and no funds are distributed directly from the company to the attendees. The intent of this guideline is to ensure that financial difficulties do not prevent residents, students, or fellows from attending any major educational conferences. However, the sixth guideline was not intended to allow for reimbursement of travel expenses for such things as conferences designed specifically for residents, students, or fellows. Therefore, subsidies may be used for reasonable lodging and travel expenses for students, residents, and fellows to attend the "major educational, scientific or policymaking meetings of national, regional or specialty medical associations."

Finally, the seventh guideline provides that no gift should be accepted if there are strings attached. For example, "physicians should not accept gifts if they are given in relation to the physician's prescribing practices." In addition, if a company underwrites a medical conference or lecture other than its own, the organizers of the conference or lecture maintain sole responsibility for and control of the "content, faculty, educational methods and materials" of the conference or lecture.

Similar to these positions, the AMA Council established model guidelines involving real or perceived conflicts of interest in clinical research. These guidelines include that:

- clinical investigators should disclose any material ties to companies whose products they are investigating, including financial ties, and
- any published research should enclose an explanatory statement that discloses conflicts of interest or potential conflicts of interest.[137]

Although the AMA Council's "recommendations" and guidelines are not legally binding on AMA members, the existence of these recommendations carries significant weight in the medical community. Moreover, many state legislatures have modeled their physician-licensure statutes to incorporate the AMA Council's guidelines. For example, in Ohio, the physician-licensure law requires that physicians adhere to the ethical standards of professional organizations such as the AMA.[138] Thus, the AMA Council's guidelines regarding physician self-referral could be viewed as mandatory in Ohio. Nevertheless, as AMA Council guidelines generally are not framed in mandatory language (i.e., "should not" rather than "cannot"), it is not clear whether the self-referral guidelines are specifically binding on physicians.

### § 6-10(b) The American College of Radiology

The American College of Radiology (ACR) adopted a statement of policy regarding self-referral by radiologists and radiation oncologists in 1992. This policy provides in part:

> The practice of referring patients to healthcare facilities in which they [radiologists and oncologists] have a financial interest is not in the best interest of patients. This practice of self-referral may also serve as an improper economic incentive for the provision of unnecessary treatment or services. Even the appearance of such conflicts or incentives can compromise professional integrity . . .
> The American College of Radiology believes that radiologists and radiation oncologists should make efforts to restructure the ownership interests in existing imaging or radiation therapy facilities because self-referral may improperly influence the professional judgments of those physicians referring patients to such facilities.[139]

---

[137] AMA Council, *Conflicts of Interest: Biomedical Research,* Op. No. 8.031 at http://www.ama-assn.org/ama/pub/physician-resources/medical-ethics/code-medical-ethics/opinion8031.page?.

[138] OHIO REV. CODE ANN. § 4731.22(18)(a).

[139] Am. Coll. of Radiology, Substitute Resolution No. 24, Radiologists, *Radiation Oncologists and Self-Referral* (Sept. 16, 1992). *See also* Am. Coll. of Radiology, *Code of Ethics: Bylaws, Article XII* (2004).

### State and Private Initiatives to Combat Fraud

This position has not been included within the ACR's Code of Ethics.[140]

## § 6-10(c) American College of Physicians

The American College of Physicians (ACP) adopted the following guidelines on physicians' receipt of gifts.

- Gifts, hospitality, or subsidies offered to physicians by the pharmaceutical industry ought not to be accepted if acceptance might influence or appear to others to influence the objectivity of clinical judgment. A useful criterion in determining acceptable activities and relationships is: Would you be willing to have these arrangements generally known?

- Independent institutional and organizational CME providers that accept industry-supported programs should develop and enforce explicit policies to maintain complete control of program content.

- Professional societies should develop and promulgate guidelines that discourage excessive industry-sponsored gifts, amenities, and hospitality to physicians at meetings.

- Physicians who participate in practice-based trials of pharmaceuticals should conduct their activities in accord with basic precepts of accepted scientific methodology.[141]

In an effort to further clarify its position on gifts to physicians, the ACP endorsed an AMA task-force policy statement in its March 2001 Board of Regents meeting. The AMA statement holds that physicians should be aware that "accepting gifts that do not comply with ethical guidelines may give the appearance of undue influence and jeopardize the physician-patient relationship."[142] Moreover, the ACP's Ethics Manual reiterates the organization's position, and recommends that physicians, when posed with a gift situation, ask themselves, "What would the public or my patients think of this arrangement?"[143]

---

[140] *See* http://www.acr.org/SecondaryMainMenuCategories/mbr_chapter/FeaturedCategories/volunteer_svcs/Volunteer-Services_1/Commission-and-Committees/Standing-Committees/ethics/code_of_ethics.aspx.
[141] *Annals of Internal Medicine*, vol. 112 no. 8, 624–26 (Apr. 15, 1990); *Annals of Internal Medicine*, vol. 117 no. 11, 947, 952 (Dec. 1, 1992).
[142] *Regents Debate Gifts to Physicians, Migraines*, ACP-ASIM OBSERVER (May 2001), *available online at* http://www.acponline.org/journals/news/may01/collegebriefs.htm#gifts.
[143] Am. Coll. of Physicians, *Ethics Manual, available online at* http://www.acponline.org/ethics/ethics_man.htm.

## § 6-10(d) Pharmaceutical and Research Manufacturers Association

As a part of its Code on Interactions with Healthcare Professionals, the Pharmaceutical and Research Manufacturers of America (PhRMA) included many of the AMA Council's Guidelines on Gifts to Physicians from Industry in 2002.[144] The PhRMA Code of Interactions with Healthcare Professionals also includes an endorsement of the position statements of the ACP with respect to relationships between physicians and the pharmaceutical industry.

In 2008, the Pharmaceutical Research and Manufacturers of America (PhRMA) released a revised Code on Interactions with Healthcare Professionals. Effective January 2009, the voluntary Code updates the previous version of the PhRMA Code by revising certain existing provisions and adding several new provisions to the Code.[145] For example, a new provision in the Code expressly prohibits companies from providing entertainment or recreational activities to healthcare professionals. The provision applies irrespective of the value of the activity, whether the healthcare professional is providing bona fide services to the company, or whether the activity is secondary to an educational purpose. In addition, the Code will now include a new section specifically addressing relationships with managed care formulary committees. A company may engage as a speaker or consultant a healthcare professional that also serves as a member of a committee that sets formularies or develops clinical practice guidelines. The Code suggests that the company require the healthcare professional to disclose this relationship to the committee for a period of at least two years after the termination of the arrangement and to follow procedures established by the committee.

## § 6-10(e) Advanced Medical Technology Association

The Advanced Medical Technology Association (AdvaMed, formerly known as the Health Industry Manufacturers Association), adopted a Code of Ethics in 1993 as part of its mission "to encourage ethical business practices and socially responsive industry conduct."[146] AdvaMed updated its Code of Ethics in January 2004, and changed the name to "The Code of Ethics for Interactions with Healthcare Professionals." Then, in 2009, AdvaMed further revised its "Code of Ethics on Interactions with Healthcare Professionals"

---

[144] Pharmaceutical & Research Mfrs. Ass'n, *Code of Interactions with Healthcare Professionals* (Apr. 2002), *available online at* http://www.phrma.org/publications/policy//2004-01-19.391.pdf.
[145] The Code is *available online at* http://www.phrma.org/files/PhRMA%20Marketing%20Code%202008.pdf.
[146] Health Indus. Mfrs. Ass'n, *Code of Ethics* (1993).

## State and Private Initiatives to Combat Fraud

to broaden a number of the requirements in a manner similar to PhRMA. Specifically, the revised Code:

- contains a new section which provides that AdvaMed may list for pubic view on its website the companies that certify their adoption of the Code;
- adopts an explicit prohibition on providing entertainment, recreation, or gifts of any type to healthcare professionals;
- provides guidelines which allow companies to enter into royalty arrangements with healthcare providers in exchange for substantial contributions that improve medical technologies; addresses evaluation and demonstration projects under which companies my provide no-charge products to physicians and patients for educational purposes; and
- revises and clarifies the current sections on reimbursement, consulting agreements, company-conducted training and education for healthcare professionals, and research and educational grants.[147]

## § 6-11 PRIVATE-PAYOR INITIATIVES TO ADDRESS HEALTHCARE FRAUD

Private payors also recognize the increased need to combat healthcare fraud, and many have responded with private industry investigatory activities. As a result, providers must remain aware of the possibility of a state or federal government investigation, as well as acknowledge the investigatory capabilities of private payors. Third-party payors, who face increasing pressure from employers to furnish coverage at a reasonable premium, view healthcare fraud as a major cause of healthcare-cost increases. Moreover, as private health insurance payors are increasingly entering into partnerships with the government through Medicare Advantage, Medicare Part D, and Medicaid managed care, for example, compliance with (and oversight of providers' compliance with) fraud and abuse laws is becoming more important for private payors.[148] The government is expecting increased referrals from its contractors,[149] and has begun to ratchet up fraud and abuse requirements for the private sector. For example, the Centers for Medicare and Medicaid Services (CMS) has issued

---

[147] Advanced Med. Tech. Ass'n, *Code of Ethics for Interactions with Healthcare Professionals* (Jul. 2009), *available online at* http://www.advamed.org/NR/rdonlyres/61D30455-F7E9-4081-B219-12D6CE347585/0/AdvaMedCodeofEthicsRevisedandRestatedEffective20090701.pdf.

[148] Steven E. Skwara, *Increased Government Oversight of Managed Care Plan—Are You Ready?* 11 COMPLIANCE TODAY 55, (March 2009).

[149] *Id.* at 55 (citing BNA, *Prosecutors Look Beyond False Claims Act to Fight Healthcare Fraud*, Healthcare Daily Report, vol. 13, No. 66 (Apr. 7, 2008)).

specific requirements for private plans operating under the Medicare Part D program and has issued fraud and abuse requirements for Medicare Advantage plans. As government funds to the private sector continue to increase and as private payors play a larger role in administering government healthcare programs, it is likely that the private sectors' responsibility for combating fraud and abuse will increase as well.

As a result, many private insurers have established their own fraud units, which scrutinize the billing practices of providers submitting claims.[150] Providers viewed as defrauding the system—billing for services not rendered, medically unnecessary, or at inflated rates—may see their claims systematically denied. Many private payors have created internal policies to allow certain departments to take initiative to detect and deter fraud and abuse. Most maintain their own internal mechanisms to combat fraud called Special Investigations Units (SIUs). SIUs typically lead the healthcare fraud and abuse programs of private payors, and consist of teams of investigators who maintain working relationships with the Federal Bureau of Investigation (FBI), DHHS, the OIG, and other federal and state enforcement agencies. SIUs receive referrals to investigate suspicious activity from claims processors and analysts, government agencies, other healthcare companies, and private associations such as the NHCAA (described below). These units also create and distribute materials to educate consumers and the public about healthcare fraud. As a result, private payors are more likely to invest better resources in SIUs, such as highly advanced technology. In fact, the Blue Cross and Blue Shield Association (BCBSA) touts that its National Anti-Fraud Department works in conjunction with each of the Blue Cross and Blue Shield affiliated plans and that collectively they have 600 employees conducting anti-fraud efforts for these plans.[151]

In addition to private payors' major fraud detection and enforcement initiatives, private payors are also focusing on fraud prevention. For example, Humana has launched a nationwide campaign to educate physicians and providers on how they can prevent fraud, waste, and abuse.[152] Through its Principles of Business Ethics Compliance and Fraud Prevention Guide, Humana educates its providers on different kinds of fraud, abuse and waste including statutory fraud and abuse violations, contracting with the government, conflicts of interest, and gifts from the insurance industry and drug and device

---

[150] For example, Aetna established a *Special Investigations Unit to "detect, deter, and ultimately end fraud."* See Fighting Healthcare Fraud, *available online at* http://www.aetna.com/about/compliance.html.

[151] http://www.bcbs.com/report-healthcare-fraud/anti-fraud/what-the-blues-are-doing.html.

[152] Humana, Fraud, Waste & Abuse, *available online at* http://www.humana.com/about/fraud/.

## State and Private Initiatives to Combat Fraud

manufacturers. The Guide also instructs doctors on how to prevent, detect, and report fraud.[153]

Third-party payors have joined forces with governmental authorities in other ways to combat healthcare fraud. The NHCAA was formed in 1985 to enhance the identification, prevention, detection, and prosecution of healthcare fraud in the private and public sectors.[154] The NHCAA is an association of private insurance carriers, Blue Cross and Blue Shield organizations, self-insured corporations, and federal and state regulatory and law enforcement agencies. The goals of the organization include promoting information-sharing among members (with appropriate legal safeguards); engaging in public education on healthcare fraud issues; training members and non-members through national and regional conferences, seminars, and workshops; and serving in an advisory capacity to industry, regulatory, and legislative bodies.[155]

The federal government also has pledged to share information with private payors, promising in 1998 to "make its best effort" to provide general information concerning healthcare fraud to private insurers.[156] This pledge stems from a Health Insurance Portability and Accountability Act of 1996 (HIPAA) mandate, requiring the DOJ and DHHS to coordinate their efforts to fight healthcare fraud in both public and private health plans. As such, the DOJ issued a Statement of Principals for the sharing of information between DOJ and private plans. As such, the DOJ has stated that it will designate Information Exchange Coordinators to coordinate any such exchanges of information and that DOJ "expects that private health plans likewise will designate Information Exchange Coordinators and will inform [DOJ] as soon as possible. [157]

Private nonprofit organizations also have participated in combating healthcare fraud and abuse. The National Council Against Health Fraud (NCAHF) is a nonprofit, voluntary organization that focuses upon "health fraud, misinformation, and quackery."[158] Formed in 1984, the organization's membership includes health professionals, educators, researchers, attorneys, and concerned citizens. The NCAHF primarily investigates and evaluates claims about health products and services, while simultaneously educating consumers, professionals, legislators, and others about health fraud.

---

[153] Humana, Principles of Business Ethics Compliance and Fraud Prevention Guide (Jan. 2009), *available online at* http://apps.humana.com/marketing/documents.asp?file=1112774.

[154] Nat'l Healthcare Anti-Fraud Ass'n (NHCAA), *NHCAA Fact Sheet* (2005), *available online at* http://www.nhcaa.org/content/Files/NEW%5FN05010%5FFact%20Sheet07%5F05.pdf.

[155] NHCAA, *About NHCAA, available online at* http://www.nhcaa.org/about_nhcaa/.

[156] *DOJ Releases Guidelines for Sharing Health Fraud Information With Insurers*, BNA HEALTHCARE DAILY REP. (Oct. 28, 1998).

[157] http://www.justice.gov/ag/readingroom/hcarefraud2.htm.

[158] Nat'l Council Against Health Fraud, *NCAHF Mission Statement available online at* http://www.ncahf.org/about/mission.html.

Another organization, Taxpayers Against Fraud (TAF), is the only non-profit public-interest organization that focuses solely on combating fraud against the federal government "through the promotion and use of the federal False Claims Act and its qui tam provisions."[159] Most qui tam actions now involve Medicare fraud and fraud against other federally funded healthcare programs. TAF collaborates closely with plaintiffs and their attorneys who are in the process of litigating qui tam claims, in addition to educating the public on qui tam issues, maintaining a library of FCA information, writing reports, and responding to queries from government officials and the general public.

---

[159] Taxpayers Against Fraud, *About TAF,* available onlinje at http://www.taf.org/abouttaf.htm.

# 7
# Compliance and Self-Reporting

## § 7-1　OVERVIEW

Over the last 20 years, the focus of healthcare companies on fostering an environment of compliance has evolved from having a few informal elements of a compliance program to now implementing comprehensive formalized programs. Much of the contemporary view of compliance programs is found in Chapter Eight of the Federal Sentencing Guidelines (Sentencing Guidelines) released in 1991 by the U.S. Sentencing Commission (Sentencing Commission). The Sentencing Guidelines set forth sentencing policies and practices for "organizations" found guilty of engaging in a federal felony or a Class A misdemeanor.[1] The Sentencing Guidelines adopt the principle that, if an organization can exhibit that it has implemented an "effective compliance and ethics program," then the entity's culpability score will be lessened, thereby reducing potential fines and penalties.[2] Over the next 20 years, healthcare compliance programs were shaped through the enactment of various laws and the issuance of governmental guidance. In the eyes of the government, compliance programs not only serve as a means to reduce fraud and waste, they also highlight the importance of corporate responsibility and help to maintain public support for federal funding to the healthcare industry.

In 2010, with the enactment of the Patient Protection and Affordable Care Act (the "Health Reform Law"),[3] the trend toward mandatory compliance programs was solidified even further. Section 6401(a) of the Health Reform Law grants the DHHS the authority to require providers and suppliers to establish a compliance program as a condition of enrollment in the Medicare, Medicaid, and CHIP programs.[4] The legislation calls for the Secretary to act in consultation with the OIG to establish core elements for inclusion in all provider compliance programs.[5] Although Congress left it to DHHS to decide which segments of the healthcare industry should be required to have a compliance program, Congress specifically

---

[1] U.S. SENTENCING GUIDELINES MANUAL § 8 (2001).
[2] U.S. SENTENCING GUIDELINES MANUAL § 8C2.5f (2001).
[3] The Patient Protection and Affordable Care Act (Pub. L. 111-148), as amended by the Healthcare and Education Reconciliation Act of 2010 (Pub. L. 111-152) (hereinafter the "Health Reform Law").
[4] The Health Reform Law, §6401(a)(7)(A).
[5] *Id.* at §6401(a)(7)(B).

required that all nursing and skilled nursing facilities adopt compliance and ethics programs based on more specific regulations.[6] On February 2, 2011, CMS issued final regulations regarding certain requirements under sections 6102 and 6401. CMS has not settled upon guidelines regarding mandatory compliance programs for all enrollees. In Spring 2011, CMS issued a notice of proposed rulemaking in the Unified Agenda entitled "Compliance Program For Providers and Suppliers" (Proposed Rule).[7] The Proposed Rule will "establish the core elements of a compliance program for Medicare, Medicaid and SCHIP providers and suppliers" and require a compliance program as a condition of enrollment.[8]

For Medicare Advantage (Part C) and Part D plans, CMS has issued a Final Rule that became effective January 1, 2011, requiring implementation of a compliance program.[9]

Although having a compliance program is not yet legally mandated for all providers and suppliers, in reality every healthcare organization should implement one as a means of preventing fraud and mitigating criminal and civil penalties assessed by the government for improper action.

This chapter begins with a brief description of why it is necessary for healthcare organizations to implement compliance programs. Next, following a brief summary of the Sentencing Guidelines and the Sarbanes-Oxley Act of 2002, this chapter examines various Office of Inspector General (OIG) guidances that address how to demonstrate that an organization's corporate compliance program is, in fact, effective. This chapter will also describe the compliance obligations healthcare entities must agree to when executing a corporate integrity agreement (CIA) with the OIG as part of a settlement agreement. Finally, this chapter describes the government's efforts to encourage healthcare providers to self-report potential violations of law.

## § 7-2   WHY HAVE A COMPLIANCE PROGRAM?

In addition to the prospect of reducing criminal fines and penalties, healthcare organizations have recognized a number of additional benefits to adopting a compliance program. A corporate compliance program can:

---

[6] Nursing and skilled nursing facilities are also subject to the compliance program mandates set forth in Section 6401(a) The Health Reform Law (Sec. 6102 Accountability Requirements for Skilled Nursing Facilities and Nursing Facilities). "A nursing facility (NF) or SNF shall have in operation a compliance and ethics program that is effective in preventing and detecting criminal, civil, and administrative violations and in promoting quality of care, consistent with regulations developed by the Secretary, working jointly with the DHHS OIG." CMS Final Rule. 5941. (E)(1).
[7] Office of Information and Regulatory Affairs, Office of Management and Budget, Compliance Program for Providers and Suppliers (CMS-6307-P), *available online at* http://www.reginfo.gov/public/do/eAgendaViewRule?pubId=201104&RIN=0938-AQ58.
[8] As of (December 30, 2011), the Proposed Rule was undergoing review with the Office of Management and Budget. There was no date identified for publication.
[9] 75 Fed. Reg. 19,678 (Apr. 15, 2010); codified at 42 C.F.R. §§ 422.503(b)(4)(vi), 423.504(b)(4)(vi).

- demonstrate to employees and the community-at-large that the entity is committed to honesty and acting responsibly;
- encourage employees to report potential problems;
- create a process by which the organization can identify and prevent criminal and unethical conduct; and
- reduce the entity's exposure to civil damages and administrative remedies, such as exclusion from participation in federal and state healthcare programs.

Another benefit of proactively adopting a corporate compliance program is that voluntarily establishing a program may be less burdensome than implementing a program required by the government through a CIA as part of settling a fraud and abuse investigation. It is hoped that, if an organization can demonstrate that it has adopted a compliance program that the government views as "effective," then the organization will not be required to execute a CIA—or, at a minimum, that the CIA's requirements will not be as intrusive and onerous.

Finally, an organization that has adopted a corporate compliance program may be able to better protect its board of directors from personal liability, as illustrated by the shareholder lawsuit filed following the settlement in the mid-1990s of Caremark International. After Caremark pleaded guilty to making illegal payments to physicians and entered into a settlement agreement with the federal and state governments for $250 million, Caremark's shareholders filed a derivative suit against its directors, accusing them of breaching their fiduciary duties by failing to monitor the company's employees and failing to institute corrective measures, which might have prevented the unlawful conduct that exposed the company to substantial fines.[10] The Delaware state court stated that the Sentencing Guidelines "offer powerful incentives for corporations today to have in place compliance programs to detect violations of law, promptly to report violations to appropriate public officials when discovered, and to take prompt, voluntary remedial efforts."[11] The judge acknowledged that directors of healthcare corporations without an effective compliance program meeting all of the requirements of the Sentencing Guidelines could be held personally liable for the resultant losses. Here, because Caremark had adopted a compliance program, the court held that the members of the Board of Directors had satisfied their duties.

In 2006, 10 years after the Delaware state court rendered the *Caremark* decision, the Delaware Supreme Court reviewed the *Caremark* standard and further explained what is necessary to prove director "oversight" liability.

---

[10] *In re* Caremark International Inc. Derivative Litigation, 698 A.2d 959 (Del.Ch. 1996).
[11] *Id.* at 969.

In *Stone v. Ritter*,[12] the shareholders brought a derivative action against the directors of the organization alleging a breach of duty in failing to implement any statutorily required monitoring, reporting or information controls that would have enabled them to learn of corporate wrongdoing.[13] In affirming the Court of Chancery's decision, the Delaware Supreme Court discussed the duty to act in good faith and, quoting the *Caremark* Court, noted that the "duty to act in good faith to be informed cannot be thought to require directors to possess detailed information about all aspects of the operation of the enterprise."[14] In order to demonstrate director oversight liability, the court held, the directors must have either failed to implement some sort of reporting system or internal controls or failed to monitor or oversee those operations. However, as an external consultant's report showed and similar to *Caremark*, the organization had a reasonable reporting system in place. The court stated, "Although there ultimately may have been failures by employees to report deficiencies to the Board, there is no basis for an oversight claim seeking to hold the directors personally liable for such failures by the employees. With the benefit of hindsight, the plaintiffs' complaint seeks to equate a bad outcome with bad faith."[15] Nevertheless, the decisions in *Caremark* and *Stone* illustrate why healthcare entities should adopt compliance programs and why officers and directors should be interested in their effectiveness.[16]

In addition to these court decisions, in the late 2000s, the OIG began incorporating certain Board Member obligations into CIAs. For example, on January 14, 2009, Eli Lilly and Company (Eli Lilly) entered into a CIA with the OIG.[17] This CIA required Eli Lilly to establish a Committee of the Board of Directors (Committee) of at least three members, to be responsible for the review and oversight of matters related to compliance with federal healthcare program requirements, FDA requirements, and the obligations of the CIA. Under the CIA, the Chief Compliance Officer was required to make at least four reports a year to the Committee regarding the compliance program. The CIA required that at a minimum the Committee would be responsible for:

- meeting quarterly to review and oversee Eli Lilly's compliance program;
- arranging for the performance of a review on the effectiveness of Eli Lilly's compliance program for each Reporting Period; and

---

[12] Stone v. Ritter, 911 A.2d 362 (Del. 2006).
[13] *Id.* at 364.
[14] *Id.* at 368 (quoting *In re* Caremark, *supra*).
[15] *Id.* at 373.
[16] *See* McCall v. Scott, 239 F.3d 808 (6th Cir. 2001) (holding the *Caremark* standard does not require a director to have intentionally acted to harm the corporation); *see also In re* Abbott Laboratories Derivative Shareholders Litigation, 293 F.3d 378 (7th Cir. 2002).
[17] CIA between the OIG and Eli Lilly and Company (Jan. 2009), *available online at* http://oig.hhs.gov/fraud/cia/agreements/eli_lilly_and_company_01142009.pdf.

## Compliance and Self-Reporting

- adopting a resolution, for each Reporting Period, summarizing the Committee's review and oversight of Eli Lilly's compliance with federal healthcare program requirements, FDA requirements, and the obligations of the CIA.

The OIG continues to include similar obligations for Board of Directors within CIAs.[18]

In addition, the OIG now requires more from the Board of Directors in connection with oversight on quality of care issues. For example, in the CIA between Cathedral Rock and the OIG, the board was required to: "(i) review the adequacy of Cathedral Rock's system of internal controls, quality assurance monitoring, and resident care; (ii) ensure that Cathedral Rock's response to state, federal, internal, and external reports of quality of care issues is complete, thorough, and resolves the issue(s) identified; and (c) ensure that Cathedral Rock adopts and implements policies and procedures that are designed to ensure that each individual cared for by Cathedral Rock receives the highest practicable physical, mental, and psychosocial level of care attainable."[19]

Liability for corporate compliance oversight does not solely lie with directors and managers. In 2008, the duties articulated in the *Caremark* and *Stone* decisions were extended to non-director officers of a corporation, including General Counsel. In *Miller v. McDonald*, the plaintiff brought an action against various officers and directors of the company alleging breach of fiduciary duty, corporate waste, fraud and fraudulent transfer.[20] The allegations specified that the defendants allowed or took part in routine waste of the company's limited resources for their own personal and unnecessary expenses and failed to implement a system of adequate internal controls, which would have allowed for the reporting of any accounting issues or other anomalies.[21] Among the defendants was the organization's Vice President of Operations and In-House General Counsel. In terms of the breach of fiduciary duty, the plaintiff's claim against the General Counsel rested on the allegation that he breached his duty of care by failing to implement an adequate monitoring system to protect the company from harm or corporate wrongdoing.[22] The court, however, noting that under Delaware and Florida law *both* officers and directors owed fiduciary duties to a corporation,

---

[18] *See* Corporate Integrity Agreement between the OIG and American Medical Response, Inc. (May 2011), *available online at* http://oig.hhs.gov/fraud/cia/agreements/american_medical_response_inc_05202011.pdf; Corporate Integrity Agreement between the OIG and Hill-Rom, Inc. (Sept. 2011), *available online at* http://oig.hhs.gov/fraud/cia/agreements/Hill_Rom_CIA_09232011.pdf.

[19] Corporate Integrity Agreement between the OIG and Cathedral Rock Corporation, Cathedral Rock Management LP, Cathedral Rock Investments, Inc., Cathedral Rock Management I, Inc. and C. Kent Harrington (Jan. 2010), *available online at* http://oig.hhs.gov/fraud/cia/agreements/cathedral_rock_01062010.pdf.

[20] Miller v. McDonald (*In re* World Health Alternatives, Inc.), 385 B.R. 576, 580 (Bankr. D. Del. 2008).

[21] *Id.* at 583–585.

[22] *Id.* at 590.

found that the plaintiff appropriately asserted that as in-house counsel and the only lawyer in top management, he had a "duty to know or should have known of these corporate wrong doings and reported such breaches of fiduciary duties by the management."[23]

## § 7-3  FEDERAL SENTENCING GUIDELINES

As previously discussed, the foundation of compliance programs, as we know them today, is based on Chapter Eight of the Sentencing Guidelines released in 1991 by the Sentencing Commission. As part of the Sentencing Reform Act,[24] the Sentencing Commission was tasked with the responsibility of developing standards for and eliminating the disparity in how defendants are sentenced. This responsibility included establishing guidelines for how federal judges are to sentence "organizations" that are convicted of federal crimes.[25] Over time, the Sentencing Guidelines have been amended to reflect the results of a multi-year review of the Sentencing Guidelines by the Sentencing Commission, recommendations from the Sentencing Commission's "Ad Hoc Advisory Group on the Organizational Sentencing Guidelines,"[26] and the requirements of the Sarbanes-Oxley Act (SOA),[27] as will be discussed in greater detail. The Health Reform Law also amended the Sentencing Guidelines by requiring the Sentencing Commission to include that "the aggregate dollar amount of fraudulent bills submitted to the Government healthcare program shall constitute prima facie evidence of the amount of the intended loss by the defendant."[28] As such, due to the nature of the amount of moneys

---

[23] *Id.*

[24] 18 U.S.C. §§ 3551–3626, 28 U.S.C. §§ 991–998.

[25] The term "organization" is defined to include "corporations, partnerships, associations, joint stock companies, unions, trusts, pension funds, unincorporated organizations, governments and political subdivisions thereof, and non-profit organizations." U.S. SENTENCING GUIDELINES MANUAL § 8A1.1, cmt. n.1 (2005).

[26] After having been tasked with reviewing the effectiveness of the organizational guidelines and soliciting suggestions for their improvement, the Ad Hoc Advisory Group on the Organizational Sentencing Guidelines delivered a report to the Sentencing Commission, *available online at* http://www.ussc.gov.

[27] "Pursuant to section 994 of title 28, United States Code, and in accordance with this section, the United States Sentencing Commission shall review and amend, as appropriate, the Federal Sentencing Guidelines and related policy statements to ensure that. . .(6) the guidelines that apply to organizations in United States Sentencing Guidelines, chapter Eight, are sufficient to deter and punish organizational criminal misconduct." Sarbanes-Oxley Act of 2002, tit. VIII § 805, Pub. L. No. 107-204, 116 Stat. 745 (codified as amended in scattered sections of 15 U.S.C.).

[28] The Health Reform Law, § 10606(a)(2). The 2011 Sentencing Guidelines state, "In a case in which the defendant is convicted of a Federal healthcare offense involving a Government healthcare program, the aggregate dollar amount of fraudulent bills submitted to the Government healthcare program shall constitute prima facie evidence of the amount of the intended loss, i.e., *is evidence sufficient to establish the amount of the intended loss, if not rebutted.* U.S. SENTENCING GUIDELINES MANUAL § 2B1.1 Application Note No. 3(F) (2011).

## Compliance and Self-Reporting

a healthcare provider may have obtained as a result of a billing mistake, it is possible that the penalty imposed under the Sentencing Guidelines will be greatly increased. The Health Reform Law also required the Sentencing Commission to increase the offense level for various healthcare crimes based upon certain dollar thresholds.[29]

If an organization is found to have violated federal law, then the organization can reduce the criminal fines and penalties imposed upon it to the extent it has adopted an effective compliance and ethics program.[30] The existence of an effective corporate compliance and ethics program can reduce an organization's "Culpability Score" used in calculating the appropriate fine. In April 2011, the Sentencing Commission issued *Chapter Eight Fine Primer: Determining the Appropriate Fine Under the Organizational Guidelines* (Primer) to assist the sentencing court in calculating the appropriate fine pursuant to Chapter Eight.[31] The Primer presents another important resource for organizations in establishing and maintaining their compliance programs.

By way of example, an organization can reduce its potential fine range for a criminal conviction, by as much as 95% in some cases, when it can show that it has in place an effective compliance and ethics program and that the violation was just a deviation from the organization's otherwise compliant nature. Generally, the reduced score is contingent upon prompt reporting to the government and the lack of involvement of high-level personnel in the illegal conduct. However, the 2010 amendments to the Sentencing Guidelines included criteria that would enable an organization to receive a reduced score even if high-level personnel were involved. These criteria include:

- the individual or individuals with operational responsibility for the compliance and ethics program have direct reporting obligations to the governing authority or an appropriate subgroup thereof;
- the compliance and ethics program detected the offense before discovery outside the organization or before such discovery was reasonably likely;
- the organization promptly reported the offense to the appropriate governmental authorities; and
- no individual with operational responsibility for the compliance and ethics program participate in, condoned, or was willfully ignorant of the offense.[32]

---

[29] *Id.*
[30] U.S. SENTENCING GUIDELINES MANUAL § 8C2.5(f) (2011).
[31] U.S. Sentencing Commission, Office of the General Counsel, *Chapter Eight Fine Primer: Determining the Appropriate Fine Under the Organizational Guidelines* (April 2011), *available online at*, http://www.ussc.gov/Legal/Primers/Primer_Organizational_Fines.pdf.
[32] U.S. SENTENCING GUIDELINES MANUAL § 8C2.5(f)(C) (2010).

The constitutionality of the Sentencing Guidelines has been examined by the Supreme Court, which has resulted in the Sentencing Guidelines no longer being viewed as mandatory but instead being "advisory" at the sentencing phase of trial.[33]

The Sentencing Guidelines' compliance program criteria are also relevant to the Department of Justice (DOJ) in the decision of whether to charge an organization with a crime. In 2003, then-Deputy Attorney General Larry D. Thompson issued a memorandum entitled "Principles of Federal Prosecution of Business Organizations," which advises federal prosecutors to examine nine criteria when deciding whether to charge a business entity. One of those criteria directs prosecutors to decide "[w]hether the corporation has a compliance program in place that is adequately designed to prevent wrongdoing by employees and is enforced by management."[34] The DOJ has looked to the Sentencing Guidelines' standard of "effective" as authoritative criteria for compliance programs.

In 2006, then-Deputy Attorney General Paul McNulty issued a memorandum entitled "Principles of Federal Prosecution of Business Organizations." This memorandum replaced the guidance issued by both the Thompson Memorandum and the McCallum Memorandum.[35] As with the Thompson Memorandum, the McNulty Memorandum listed nine criteria that prosecutors must consider including whether or not the company has a compliance program. However, unlike the Thompson memorandum, the McNulty memorandum makes it clear that prosecutors must consider the existence and adequacy of a corporation's *pre-existing* compliance program. However, these factors, according to the memorandum, are not dispositive, and prosecutors are generally granted "wide latitude in determining when, whom, how and even whether to prosecute for

---

[33] In *Blakely v. Washington*, the Supreme Court, addressing a state's sentencing guidelines, suggested that the Sixth Amendment requires that every fact that increases a defendant's effective maximum sentence must be found by a jury beyond a reasonable doubt or admitted by the defendant. This decisions cast significant doubt on the constitutionality of the federal sentencing system. After *Blakely*, the Supreme Court addressed the issue of the Sentencing Guidelines in the consolidated cases of *United States v. Booker* and *United States v. Fanfan*, in which a divided Supreme Court issued two distinct majority opinions. The Sentencing Guidelines now are viewed as an intricate set of suggestions whereby federal judges must continue to consult the guidelines at sentencing, but are no longer obliged to sentence within the ranges prescribed therein.

[34] Memorandum from Larry D. Thompson, Deputy Attorney General, U.S. Department of Justice, to Heads of Department Components, United States Attorneys, *Principles of Federal Prosecution of Business Organizations* (Jan. 20, 2003) [hereinafter Thompson Memorandum], reprinted in UNITED STATES ATTORNEYS' MANUAL, Title 9, CRIMINAL RESOURCE MANUAL, § § 161–62, *available online at* http://www.usdoj.gov/dag/cftf/corporate_guidelines.htm.

[35] Memorandum from Paul J. McNulty, Deputy Attorney General, U.S. Department of Justice, to Heads of Department Components, United States Attorneys, *Principles of Federal Prosecution of Business Organizations* (Dec. 12, 2006) [hereinafter McNulty Memorandum], reprinted in UNITED STATES ATTORNEYS' MANUAL, Title 9, CRIMINAL RESOURCE MANUAL, § 162, *available online at* http://www.justice.gov/dag/speeches/2006/mcnulty_memo.pdf. The McCallum Memorandum directed the department heads of the U.S. Attorneys offices to develop a written waiver of the attorney client privilege or work product doctrine review process.

## Compliance and Self-Reporting

violations of federal criminal law."[36] The memorandum warned that merely having a compliance program may not be enough; certainly, crimes or problems that occur even when there is a corporate compliance program in effect may be signs that enforcement of those programs is lacking and/or that they were not implemented in an effective way. The absence of an effective compliance and ethics program may give a court reason to place an organization on probation. If so, an organization could be required to implement a compliance and ethics program under court supervision as a condition of the probationary term.[37] In fact, during fiscal year 2010, approximately 70% of culpable organizations received one month or more of probation and of those 28% were ordered to establish compliance programs.[38] Of the 149 organizations sentenced under Chapter Eight guidelines during fiscal year 2010, for which data are available, fine guidelines were applied in 60 cases. Of these 60 cases, 100% did not have a compliance program in place at the time of the committed offense and 100% did not have any prior criminal or administrative violations.[39]

In addition, the federal government has included the requirement that a healthcare entity either establish a corporate compliance program as a condition to avoiding criminal prosecution or continue to demonstrate its good faith and commitment to full compliance with federal healthcare laws. For example, in December 2005, as part of a settlement to avoid criminal prosecution for healthcare fraud, the University of Medicine and Dentistry of New Jersey (UMDNJ) not only agreed to reimburse the federal and state government $4.9 million, but also agreed, as part of a Deferred Prosecution Agreement (DPA), to commit itself to "achieving exemplary corporate citizenship, to best practices of effective corporate governance, and the highest principles of integrity and professionalism . . . ."[40] As part of the terms of the DPA, UMDNJ agreed to various requirements related to the development of its compliance program, including (1) establishing a Chief Compliance Officer (CCO) who reports to the UMDNJ president and board of trustees; (2) establishing a hotline and email address for employees and others to notify of any concerns about unlawful conduct or other wrongdoing; and

---

[36] McNulty Memorandum.
[37] U.S. SENTENCING GUIDELINES MANUAL § 8D1.4 (2005).
[38] U.S. Sentencing Comm'n, FY2010 Annual Report, *available online at* http://www.ussc.gov/Data_and_Statistics/Annual_Reports_and_Sourcebooks/2010/ar10toc.htm and U.S. Sentencing Comm'n 2010 Sourcebook of Federal Sentencing Statistics, Table 54-Chapter Eight Organizational Sentencing Components, USSCFY06, *available online at* http://www.ussc.gov/Data_and_Statistics/Annual_Reports_and_Sourcebooks/2010/SBTOC10.htm.
[39] *Id.*
[40] DOJ, US Attorney's Office, District of New Jersey, press release, *"UMDNJ Accepts Federal Monitor of Operations; Healthcare Fraud Prosecution Deferred,"* (December 29, 2005), *available online at* http://www.usdoj.gov/usao/nj/publicaffairs/NJ_Press/files/umdnj1229_r.htm (related documents *available online at* http://www.usdoj.gov/usao/nj/publicaffairs/NJ_Press/files/2005linkspage.htm).

(3) developing training and education programs recommended by a federal monitor assigned to ensure that the terms of the DPA have been satisfied.[41]

Similarly, in 2011, as part of a settlement to avoid criminal prosecution, Maxim Healthcare Services, Inc. (Maxim), entered into a 24-month DPA and committed to enhancing, supporting and maintaining its existing training and education programs related to federal healthcare laws compliance. In conjunction with the training and education programs, the CEO and Board of Directors are required to communicate their review and endorsement of the training programs. In addition, Maxim agreed to maintain a confidential hotline and e-mail address for employees and others to notify Maxim of any concerns about unlawful conduct, other wrongdoing, or evidence that Maxim's practices do not conform with the requirements of the DPA.[42]

In order to have an effective compliance program, the Sentencing Guidelines state that an organization shall "[(]1) exercise due diligence to prevent and detect criminal conduct; and [(]2) otherwise promote an organizational culture that encourages ethical conduct and a commitment to compliance with the law."[43] However, the Sentencing Guidelines make clear that the program is not *per se* ineffective if there is a failure to prevent or detect the instant offense.[44]

The Sentencing Guidelines provide the following requirements to prove that an organization has adopted a program that promotes "an organizational culture that encourages ethical conduct and a commitment to compliance with the law."

(1) The organization shall establish standards and procedures to prevent and deter criminal conduct.

(2) (A) The organization's governing authority shall be knowledgeable about the content and operation of the compliance and ethics program and shall exercise reasonable oversight with respect to the implementation and effectiveness of the compliance and ethics program.

(B) High-level personnel of the organization shall ensure that the organization has an effective compliance and ethics program, as described in the Sentencing Manual. Specific individual(s) within high-level personnel shall be assigned overall responsibility for the compliance and ethics program.

(C) Specific individual(s) within the organization shall be delegated day-to-day operational responsibility for the compliance and ethics program. Individual(s) with operational responsibility shall

---

[41] *Id.*
[42] Deferred Prosecution Agreement between Maxim Healthcare Services, Inc. and the United States Attorney's Office for the District of New Jersey (Sept. 12, 2011). *See, e.g.*, Deferred Prosecution Agreement between Wellcare Health Plans, Inc., and the United States Attorney's Office for the Middle District of Florida and the Florida Attorney General's Office (May 5, 2009).
[43] U.S. SENTENCING GUIDELINES MANUAL § 8B2.1(a) (2011).
[44] *Id.*

## Compliance and Self-Reporting

report periodically to high-level personnel and, as appropriate, to the governing authority, or an appropriate subgroup of the governing authority, on the effectiveness of the compliance and ethics program. To carry out such operational responsibility, such individual(s) shall be given adequate resources, appropriate authority, and direct access to the governing authority or an appropriate subgroup of the governing authority.

(3) The organization shall use reasonable efforts not to include within the substantial authority personnel of the organization any individual whom the organization knew, or should have known through the exercise of due diligence, has engaged in illegal activities or other conduct inconsistent with an effective compliance and ethics program.

(4) (A) The organization shall take reasonable steps to communicate periodically and in a practical manner its standards and procedures, and other aspects of the compliance and ethics program, to the individuals referred to in subdivision (B) by conducting effective training programs and otherwise disseminating information appropriate to such individuals' respective roles and responsibilities.

(B) The individuals referred to in subdivision (A) are the members of the governing authority, high-level personnel, substantial authority personnel, the organization's employees, and, as appropriate, the organization's agents.

(5) The organization shall take reasonable steps—

(A) to ensure that the organization's compliance and ethics program is followed, including monitoring and auditing to detect criminal conduct;

(B) to evaluate periodically the effectiveness of the organization's compliance and ethics program; and

(C) to have and publicize a system, which may include mechanisms that allow for anonymity or confidentiality, whereby the organization's employees and agents may report or seek guidance regarding potential or actual criminal conduct without fear of retaliation.

(6) The organization's compliance and ethics program shall be promoted and enforced consistently throughout the organization through

(A) appropriate incentives to perform in accordance with the compliance and ethics program; and

(B) appropriate disciplinary measures for engaging in criminal conduct and for failing to take reasonable steps to prevent or detect criminal conduct.

(7) After criminal conduct has been detected, the organization shall take reasonable steps to respond appropriately to the criminal conduct and to prevent further similar criminal conduct, including making any necessary modifications to the organization's compliance and ethics program.[45]

The Sentencing Guidelines require that an organization's governing authority must not only be familiar with the content and operation of the organization's compliance and ethics program, but must also reasonably oversee the program's implementation and effectiveness. Someone in the organization's high-level personnel must be assigned "overall responsibility" for the program. Although the individual assigned day-to-day operational responsibility for the program does not necessarily have to be a high-level person, that individual should provide reports to the governing authority at least annually.[46]

The Sentencing Guidelines do not require effective compliance and ethics programs to look the same among all organizations. The goal should be to create a program that, from the government's perspective, shows that an organization took reasonable steps to meet the requirements of the Sentencing Guidelines. The applicable industry practice or the standards called for by any applicable governmental regulation will be a factor. Similarly, an organization's size will influence the formality and scope of the actions it should take to meet the requirements of the Sentencing Guidelines, including the necessary features of the organization's standards and procedures. Although small organizations must demonstrate the same degree of commitment to ethical conduct and compliance as larger organizations, they may do so with less formality and fewer resources. Also, an organization should keep in mind that the recurrence of similar misconduct will be considered when determining whether the organization took reasonable steps to meet the requirements of the Sentencing Guidelines.[47]

## § 7-4 THE SARBANES-OXLEY ACT OF 2002

After corporate scandals made headlines early in the 21st century, the SOA was enacted to assist in preventing and detecting corporate fraud and misconduct. The SOA requires that publicly traded companies adhere to significant governance standards that broaden a governing body's role in overseeing

---

[45] U.S. Sentencing Guidelines Manual § 8B2.1(b) (2011). The 2011 Sentencing Guidelines include an application note regarding § 8B.21(b)(7). The note clarifies that subsection (b)(7) has two aspects. First, the organization must appropriately respond to the conduct by taking "reasonable" steps to remedy the harm—including compensating any victims, self-reporting and cooperating with authorities. Second, the organization must take action to avert the potential for such criminal conduct to reoccur by employing the steps set forth in subsections (b)(5) and (c), which may include the "use of an outside professional advisor to ensure adequate assessment and implementation of any modifications."

[46] U.S. Sentencing Guidelines Manual § 8B2.1 Application Notes No. 3 (2011).

[47] U.S. Sentencing Guidelines Manual § 8B2.1 cmt. n.2 (2005).

## Compliance and Self-Reporting

financial transactions and auditing procedures. Among the requirements of SOA is that the principal executive officer and the principal financial officer of all publicly traded organizations must certify to the accuracy of the company's annual and quarterly reports to the Securities and Exchange Commission (SEC). The SOA requires that these officers have established, maintained, and reviewed the organization's systems of internal controls so as to "ensure that material information relating to the issuer and its consolidated subsidiaries is made known to such officers by others within those entities, particularly during the period in which the periodic reports are being prepared."[48]

Moreover, Section 404 of SOA requires an organization's management to present an internal control report in the organization's annual report, containing both (1) a statement of the responsibility of management for establishing and maintaining an adequate internal control structure and procedures for financial reporting; and (2) an assessment, as of the end of the most recent fiscal year, of the effectiveness of the company's internal control structure and procedures for financial reporting. Also, in the regulations adopted under Section 406 of SOA, companies must disclose whether they have adopted a code of conduct for senior officers and, if not, why.[49] At a minimum, the code of conduct is to promote:

- honest and ethical conduct, including the ethical handling of actual or apparent conflicts of interest between personal and professional relationships;
- full, fair, accurate, timely, and understandable disclosure in reports and documents that a registrant files with or submits to the SEC, and in other public communications made by the company;
- compliance with applicable laws, rules, and regulations;
- prompt internal reporting to an appropriate person or persons; and
- accountability for adherence to the code.[50]

Compliance with these aspects of the SOA has been achieved by many organizations under their compliance programs structured using the Sentencing Guidelines.

Although SOA technically only applies to publicly traded organizations, privately held organizations as well as nonprofit organizations have identified the importance of complying with SOA. Indeed, some states' attorneys general have already proposed that elements of the SOA be applied to nonprofit organizations.

---

[48] Sarbanes-Oxley Act of 2002 § 302, 15 U.S.C. § 7241.
[49] Sarbanes-Oxley Act of 2002 § 406, 15 U.S.C. § 7264; *see also* 68 Fed Reg. 5,109 (Jan. 31, 2003); Am. Health Lawyers Ass'n (Health Lawyers), Sarbanes-Oxley Act Task Force Members Briefing, *A New Day for Healthcare Organizations: Sarbanes-Oxley Certification Requirements, Compliance and Exposures*, (Jan. 2004) (on file with authors).
[50] 68 Fed Reg. 5,109 (Jan. 31, 2003).

## § 7-5 COMPLIANCE-RELATED RESOURCES

Over the years, a number of compliance-related resources have been developed to assist providers in developing and implementing compliance programs. These resources include compliance program guidances, Healthcare Fraud Prevention and Enforcement Action Team (HEAT) guidances and other resources.

### § 7-5(a) OIG COMPLIANCE PROGRAM GUIDANCES

In the keynote address at the 2011 annual Healthcare Compliance Association (HCCA) Compliance Institute, Daniel Levinson, Inspector General of DHHS, discussed the five major building blocks of the "compliance pyramid."[51] The 2011 compliance pyramid highlights those elements that the OIG believes are important to "maintain an ethical and healthy organization."

**2011 Compliance Pyramid**

|  | Maintain an Ethical and Healthy Organization |  |
|---|---|---|
| Understand Consequences of Noncompliance | | Prepare for New Challenges |
| Establish an Effective Compliance Program | | Utilize Available Resources |

While the Sentencing Guidelines provide an overall structure for an organization's assessment of compliance program effectiveness, the OIG has promulgated more-specific voluntary "industry compliance guidances" that provide specific criteria for "effectively" meeting the requirements of the Sentencing Guidelines, as well as examples of what the OIG expects an

---

[51] Daniel Levinson, Inspector General, Office of the Inspector General, Department of Health and Human Services, Keynote Address at the Healthcare Compliance Association, Compliance Institute (Apr. 2011).

## Compliance and Self-Reporting

"effective" compliance program to include. From 1997 to 2008, the OIG released 12 compliance program guidances and supplemental guidances.[52]

The OIG's first venture into assisting healthcare providers and organizations in this area occurred in February 1997, with the OIG's "Model Compliance Plan for Clinical Laboratories."[53] By February 1998, when the OIG promulgated its issuance for the hospital industry, significant changes could be seen in the OIG's approach. The OIG no longer referred to this type of compliance issuance as a "model" compliance program, but instead referred to the hospital issuance and subsequent issuances as compliance "guidances." Although this modification may seem like a mere change in semantics, it reflects the OIG's recognition that no one document either can, or should, act as a "model" for an entire portion of the healthcare industry. To this end, the OIG stated in the "Compliance Guidance for Hospitals" that "each program must be tailored to fit the needs and resources of an individual hospital, depending upon its particular corporate structure, mission, and employee composition."[54]

This approach is echoed in later OIG compliance issuances. In fact, in contrast to most of the compliance program guidances that encourage healthcare providers to adopt fairly elaborate programs, the OIG's "Compliance Program Guidance for Individual and Small Group Physician Practices" recognizes that it may be impractical for physician practices to fully implement all seven elements of a traditional, full-scale program. To this end, the OIG stated that it "recogniz[es] the financial and staffing resource constraints faced by physician practices."[55] Therefore, the final guidance stresses flexibility in the manner by which a practice implements voluntary compliance measures.

The OIG also changed its approach toward the type of information contained in the issuances. For example, in the "Model Compliance Plan for Clinical Laboratories," the OIG addressed very specific billing issues,

---

[52] The OIG has developed and issued compliance program guidance directed at the following segments of the healthcare industry: clinical laboratories; hospitals; home health agencies; third-party medical billing companies; durable medical equipment, prosthetics, orthotics, and supply companies; Medicare+Choice organizations offering coordinated care plans; hospices; nursing facilities; individual and small group physician practices; ambulance sup1dsa W pliers; and pharmaceutical manufacturers. On (November 29, 2005), the OIG issued a draft compliance program guidance for recipients of Public Health Service research awards. This guidance contained an eighth element to the guidance structure, entitled "Establishing Roles and Responsibilities and Assigning Oversight Responsibility." On (November 30, 2008), the OIG issues supplemental compliance guidance for nursing facilities. This guidance contained new discussions of compliance recommendations and an expanded section on risk areas. Copies of these guidances are *available online at* http://oig.hhs.gov/compliance/compliance-guidance/index.asp.

[53] The OIG amended and republished the laboratory compliance issuance in August 1998 "to reflect HCFA policy changes and to be consistent with the OIG's Compliance Program Guidance for Hospitals." 63 Fed. Reg. 45,076 (Aug. 24, 1998). The revised laboratory issuance was titled "Compliance Program Guidance for Clinical Laboratories."

[54] 63 Fed. Reg. 8,987, 8,988 (Feb. 23, 1998).

[55] 65 Fed. Reg. 59,434 (Oct. 5, 2000).

including, in part, advising the selection of particular test and diagnosis codes, the design of a laboratory's requisition form, and annual notifications that the OIG believes laboratories should send to physicians. Some of these issues that quickly became obsolete when CMS changed its Medicare billing policies to prevent this from happening in future guidances. However, the OIG's "Compliance Program Guidance for Hospitals" and later OIG compliance guidances (including the revised laboratory issuance) included more broad level discussions of certain billing and operational issues that should be addressed as part of an effective compliance program. These later compliance guidances are somewhat less specific with respect to the actual state of the law, and instead they contain greater emphasis on the importance of the compliance program infrastructure.

All of the compliance guidances issued by the OIG follow the same basic structural format. Each begins with an introduction that describes the benefits of a compliance program and discusses the application of the OIG guidance. The next section deals with elements of a compliance program and focuses on what policies and procedures an organization should include, such as designation of a compliance officer and compliance committee, effective training and education programs, open lines of communication, enforcement of the compliance program, auditing and monitoring, responding to detected offenses, and developing corrective action plans. These later guidances describe, in detail, the compliance officer's job, the goals and functions of an organization's compliance committee, and various methods by which an organization can train employees on compliance-related issues.

Within the section regarding compliance program elements in the discussion of written policies and procedures, the OIG lists areas of special concern—risk areas that healthcare organizations should emphasize when writing policies and procedures and conducting training. Those general topics of concern include joint ventures; unbundling and upcoding; anti-kickback and self-referral concerns; and billing for items or services that are medically unnecessary, not provided, and/or unordered. The OIG does not provide the industry with guidance on the particular policy that it believes should be adopted. Rather, the OIG only identifies the topics that it believes should be addressed in the compliance program's policies and procedures.

In 2005, the OIG released the "Supplemental Compliance Program Guidance for Hospitals." While the 1998 "Compliance Program Guidance for Hospitals" provided guidance on establishing sound internal controls, the supplement discussed the important roles of corporate leadership and self-assessment of compliance programs. This supplement, along with the 2004 amendments to the Sentencing Guidelines, places more responsibility on an organization's corporate leadership.

Similarly, in September 2008, the OIG issued a supplemental compliance program guidance for nursing facilities, which is similar to the supplemental guidance issued for hospitals in 2005. Specifically, the OIG states that this supplemental guidance was in response to "developments in the nursing facility industry, including significant changes in the way nursing facilities deliver, and receive reimbursement for, healthcare services, evolving business practices, and changes in the Federal enforcement environment."[56]

Although an organization is not required to meet every element set forth in the industry compliance guidances in order to establish an "effective" compliance program, the organization should be familiar with the applicable industry guidance and the elements contained in that guidance. Organizations should pay attention to those areas in which its compliance program differs from the OIG guidance, and should be prepared to articulate why those differences do not undermine the effectiveness of the organization's compliance program. For example, the industry compliance guidances generally discourage organizations from appointing their general counsel as the CCO, because of a concern that a conflict will arise between the duties required for the person's role as counsel and the duties required for the role as a compliance officer. Some organizations, however, believe that the general counsel is the most suitable professional to fill the role of CCO.[57] In performing an assessment of the organization's compliance program, the organization will need to recognize that it has deviated from the OIG's recommendations, demonstrate why the compliance program is "effective" even with this deviation, and demonstrate the procedures adopted to address the OIG's concerns, (e.g., procedures to diffuse the potential conflict of duties).[58]

Simply implementing the OIG's compliance guidance as though it were an actual "compliance program" will not result in an organization having adopted an "effective" corporate compliance program. Rather, the ultimate challenge is for organizations to develop compliance programs to include mechanisms that address the Sentencing Guidelines and the OIG's compliance program guidances in such a manner that they create a culture of compliance, weaving compliance into the "fabric" of the organization's operations. This suggests a dynamic program with frequent review and revision that takes into account the development of an organization.

---

[56] 73 Fed. Reg. 56,832, 56,834 (Sept. 30, 2008).
[57] *See* U.S. Dep't of Health & Human Servs. (DHHS) & Health Lawyers, AN INTEGRATED APPROACH TO CORPORATE COMPLIANCE: A RESOURCE FOR HEALTHCARE ORGANIZATION BOARDS OF DIRECTORS (2004), *available online at* http://www.oig.hhs.gov/fraud/docs/complianceguidance/Tab%204E%20 Appendx-Final.pdf.
[58] *See* §§ 7-5(c) and 7-6(b)(3), *infra*, for discussions of the relationship between an organization's general counsel and its compliance officer.

## § 7-5(b)  Healthcare Fraud Prevention and Enforcement Action Team (HEAT)

In May 2009, the DOJ and DHHS announced the creation of the Healthcare Fraud Prevention and Enforcement Action Team (HEAT) to fight Medicare fraud. The mission of HEAT is (1) to gather resources across the government to help prevent waste, fraud and abuse; (2) to reduce healthcare costs and improve quality of care; (3) to highlight best practices by providers and public sector employees; and (4) to build upon existing partnerships between DOJ and DHHS to reduce fraud and recover taxpayer dollars.[59]

In 2011, the OIG launched a provider compliance training initiative as an outgrowth of the HEAT's efforts. In Spring 2011, the OIG and other government entities provided in-person trainings in Houston, Tampa, Kansas City, Baton Rouge, Denver and Washington, D.C., that focused on Medicare and Medicaid fraud and the importance of implementing an effective compliance program. Video tapes of the training programs are available on the OIG's website. In addition to the training programs, the OIG is also issuing eleven free videos and podcasts covering major healthcare fraud and abuse laws, the basics of healthcare compliance programs and what to do if compliance issues arise.[60]

## § 7-5(c)  GAO Report

In 1999, the General Accounting Office (GAO) published a report, entitled *Early Evidence of Compliance Program Effectiveness Is Inconclusive*, that found that the principal measure of a compliance program's effectiveness is the program's ability to prevent improper Medicare payments.[61] The report found, however, that measuring and quantifying this effectiveness is very difficult, due to the lack of comprehensive baseline data in this area, as well as the number of variables. Instead, the GAO looked at indirect indicators to assess the effectiveness of the compliance programs reviewed, such as:

- refunds of provider-identified overpayments;
- self-disclosure of potential misconduct;
- the frequency of disciplinary measures taken against noncompliant employees; and

---

[59] Stop Medicaid Fraud, HEAT Task Force, *available online at* http://www.stopmedicarefraud.gov/heattaskforce/index.html.

[60] To date, the OIG had released videos and audio podcasts on the following issues: Physician Self-Referral Law, False Claims act, Federal Anti-Kickback Statute, Exclusion Authorities & Effects of Exclusion, and an Introduction by Daniel Levinson, the Inspector General.

[61] U.S. General Accounting Office, REPORT TO CONGRESSIONAL REQUESTERS, MEDICARE: EVIDENCE OF COMPLIANCE PROGRAM EFFECTIVENESS IS INCONCLUSIVE, GAO/HEHS-99-59 (Apr. 1999), *available online at* http://www.gao.gov/archive/1999/he99059.pdf.

- increased employee awareness of proper billing rules and other compliance policies and procedures (including awareness of reporting mechanisms and training programs).

The GAO concluded that evidence of compliance program effectiveness was lacking because of its inability to demonstrate a causal relationship between compliance programs and the decline of Medicare overpayments.[62] Nevertheless, the categories identified in the report as being indirect indicia of compliance program effectiveness supplement the guidance included in the Sentencing Guidelines and OIG compliance guidances. Indeed, the GAO report suggests that, to demonstrate compliance program effectiveness, providers should look for, and be ready to quantify, actions emblematic of a compliant organization in the categories described earlier.

### § 7-5(d)   OIG/HCCA Roundtables

In 1999, the OIG, along with the HCCA, conducted a roundtable discussion on compliance program effectiveness. This roundtable resulted in the creation of a report, entitled *Building a Partnership for Effective Compliance*, that addressed the issue of assessing and demonstrating compliance program effectiveness.[63] Although many similarities exist between the elements that the GAO relied upon in its report and those that the OIG developed during the roundtables, the elements included in the roundtable reports are far more extensive than those identified in the GAO report.

Unlike the GAO report, the participants in the first roundtable focused on a compliance program's audit requirements as one method in assessing compliance program effectiveness. The participants recommended three types of audits: baseline, or initial, audits; proactive audits based upon an organization's identification of certain risk areas; and audits to quantify the breadth and depth of a suspected or identified problem.[64]

In addition to actual auditing, participants suggested that organizations maintain certain documentation. For example, the participants suggested maintaining documentation of:

- audit results;
- logs of hotline calls and their resolution;
- corrective action plans;
- due diligence efforts regarding business transactions;

---

[62] *Id.* at 20.
[63] DHHS OIG & Healthcare Compliance Association (HCCA), Building a Partnership for Effective Compliance, *available online at* http://www.oig.hhs.gov/fraud/docs/complianceguidance/roundtable.htm.
[64] *Id.*

- records of disciplinary action;
- documentation of modification and distribution of policies and procedures;
- records of employee training programs (including the number of training hours, the courses offered, and identity of the attendees); and
- a record of disclosures and refunds made to federal healthcare programs.[65]

The OIG participants identified factors that the OIG should review in order to determine whether a provider has an effective compliance program. The OIG stated that it would look beyond a provider's policies and procedures, as well as the program's "paper" representations, to assess how the compliance program performs during a provider's day-to-day operations. For example, rather than looking only at the number of training sessions conducted, the government also would review whether employees retained the information provided during the training session. Government participants also stated that they would look for evidence of management's commitment and good-faith efforts to implement a compliance program, as evidenced through management's funding and support of the program and the background of the CCO.

Following the initial roundtable, the OIG and HCCA have conducted three additional government/industry forums related to compliance.[66] The second roundtable, held on July 24, 2000, was an opportunity for physicians to discuss the role of compliance in their practices, to inform the OIG of issues surrounding the implementation and maintenance of compliance programs, and to comment on the OIG's then-proposed compliance program guidance for physician practices. The third roundtable discussion, held in July 2001, presented an opportunity for healthcare providers operating under a CIA to inform the OIG of the issues surrounding the implementation and maintenance of compliance programs. The meeting also offered the OIG the opportunity to present its CIA policy objectives, and receive providers' insights on ways to accomplish those objectives.

---

[65] *Id.*
[66] OIG & HCCA, BUILDING A PARTNERSHIP FOR EFFECTIVE COMPLIANCE, A REPORT ON THE HCCA-OIG PHYSICIAN'S ROUNDTABLE (July 24, 2000) (a roundtable for physicians to discuss the role of compliance in their practices), *available online at* www.oig.hhs.gov/fraud/docs/complianceguidance/roundtable0700.pdf; OIG & HCCA, BUILDING A PARTNERSHIP FOR EFFECTIVE COMPLIANCE, THE THIRD GOVERNMENT-INDUSTRY ROUNDTABLE (July 30, 2001) (a roundtable discussion on Corporate Integrity Agreements), *available online at* http://www.oig.hhs.gov/fraud/docs/complianceguidance/Roundtable0901.pdf; OIG & HCCA, CONTINUING A PARTNERSHIP FOR EFFECTIVE COMPLIANCE, A SUMMARY OF THE GOVERNMENT-INDUSTRY ROUNDTABLE ON THE ROLE OF GOVERANCE IN COMPLIANCE PROGRAMS (June 16, 2004) (a roundtable discussion of the role of governance in compliance programs), *available online at* http://www.oig.hhs.gov/fraud/docs/complianceguidance/ComplianceRoundtable112204.pdf.

## Compliance and Self-Reporting

On June 16, 2004, the fourth roundtable was held to discuss the role of governance in compliance programs. The objective of the meeting was to share perspectives on the methods that healthcare organizations and their boards of directors use to oversee their compliance programs. The roundtable included discussion on structures and processes for reporting to a board, methods for boards to ensure compliance program effectiveness, how to organize and assemble an effective board, and legal issues.

In addition to the roundtables on compliance, the OIG and HCCA have conducted two roundtables focused on quality of care issues. The first quality of care roundtable held on December 5, 2007, provided an opportunity for the long term care industry to share experiences regarding board of director's oversight of quality of care.[67] The second quality of care roundtable focused on how a hospital's board of directors can use performance based tools to promote quality of care.[68]

### § 7-5(e)   OIG/Health Lawyers Resources

Since 2003, in collaboration with the American Health Lawyers Association (Health Lawyers), the OIG has published three educational resources entitled *Corporate Responsibility and Corporate Compliance: A Resource for Healthcare Boards of Directors* (*Corporate Responsibility*);[69] *An Integrated Approach to Corporate Compliance: A Resource for Healthcare Organization Boards of Directors* (*Integrated Approach*);[70] and *Corporate Responsibility and Healthcare Quality: A Resource for Healthcare Board of Directors* (*Healthcare Quality*).[71] The first resource provides information to help corporate directors establish, and affirmatively demonstrate, that they have followed a reasonable compliance-oversight process. The second

---

[67] OIG & HCCA, DRIVING FOR QUALITY IN LONG-TERM CARE: A BOARD OF DIRECTORS DASHBOARD GOVERNMENT-INDUSTRY ROUNDTABLE (December 5, 2007), *available online at* http://www.oig.hhs.gov/fraud/docs/complianceguidance/Roundtable013007.pdf.

[68] OIG & HCCA, DRIVING FOR QUALITY IN ACUTE CARE: A BOARD OF DIRECTORS DASHBOARD GOVERNMENT-INDUSTRY ROUNDTABLE (Nov. 10, 2008), *available online at* http://www.oig.hhs.gov/fraud/docs/complianceguidance/RoundtableAcuteCare.pdf.

[69] DHHS & Health Lawyers, CORPORATE RESPONSIBILITY AND CORPORATE COMPLIANCE: A RESOURCE FOR HEALTH CARE BOARDS OF DIRECTORS (2004), *available online at* http://www.oig.hhs.gov/fraud/docs/complianceguidance/Tab%204E%20Appendx-Final.pdf [hereinafter DHHS/Health Lawyers, CORPORATE RESPONSIBILITY].

[70] DHHS & Health Lawyers, AN INTEGRATED APPROACH TO CORPORATE COMPLIANCE: A RESOURCE FOR HEALTH CARE ORGANIZATION BOARDS OF DIRECTORS (2004), *available online at* http://www.oig.hhs.gov/fraud/docs/complianceguidance/Tab%204E%20Appendx-Final.pdf [hereinafter DHHS/Health Lawyers, INTEGRATED APPROACH].

[71] DHHS & Health Lawyers, CORPORATE RESPONSIBILITY AND HEALTHCARE QUALITY, A RESOURCE FOR HEALTH CARE BOARDS OF DIRECTORS, *available online at* http://www.oig.hhs.gov/fraud/docs/complianceguidance/CorporateResponsibilityFinal%209-4-07.pdf [hereinafter DHHS/Health Lawyers, HEALTH CARE QUALITY].

resource addresses the roles of the in-house corporate general counsel and an organization's CCO in supporting the compliance-oversight function of healthcare organization's governing boards. The third resource highlights the importance of proper oversight with regard to quality of care.

In *Corporate Responsibility*, two categories of questions are suggested for healthcare directors to ask about an organization's compliance program efforts to demonstrate that they are overseeing the program. The first category includes the following "structural questions" to assist in understanding the scope of the program.

- How is the compliance program structured, and who are the key employees responsible for its implementation and operation? How is the board structured to oversee compliance issues?
- How does the organization's compliance reporting system work? How frequently does the board receive reports about compliance issues?
- What are the goals of the organization's compliance program? What are the inherent limitations in the compliance program? How does the organization address these limitations?
- Does the compliance program address the significant risks of the organization? How were those risks determined, and how are new compliance risks identified and incorporated into the program?
- What will be the level of resources necessary to implement the compliance program as envisioned by the board? How has management determined the adequacy of the resources dedicated to implementing and sustaining the compliance program?

The second category of questions was designed to assist the directors in overseeing the operations of the compliance program, and is therefore called "operational questions."

- How has the code of conduct or its equivalent been incorporated into corporate policies across the organization? How can the organization demonstrate that the code is understood and accepted across the organization? Has management taken affirmative steps to publicize the importance of the code to all of its employees?
- Has the organization implemented policies and procedures that address compliance risk areas, and established internal controls to counter those vulnerabilities?
- Does the CCO have sufficient authority to implement the compliance program? Has management provided the CCO with the autonomy and sufficient resources necessary to perform assessments and respond appropriately to misconduct?

## Compliance and Self-Reporting

- What is the scope of compliance-related education and training across the organization? Has the effectiveness of such training been assessed? What policies/measures have been developed to enforce training requirements and to provide remedial training as warranted?
- How is the board kept apprised of significant regulatory and industry developments affecting the organization's risk? How is the compliance program structured to address such risks?
- How are "at risk" operations assessed from a compliance perspective? Is conformance with the organization's compliance program periodically evaluated? Does the organization periodically evaluate the effectiveness of the compliance program?
- What processes are in place to ensure that appropriate remedial measures are taken in response to identified weaknesses?
- What is the process by which the organization evaluates and responds to suspected compliance violations? How are reporting systems (e.g., the compliance hotline) monitored to verify appropriate resolution of reported matters?
- Does the organization have policies that address the appropriate protection of whistleblowers and those accused of misconduct?
- What is the process by which the organization evaluates and responds to suspected compliance violations? What policies address the protection of employees and the preservation of relevant documents and information?
- What guidelines have been established for reporting compliance violations to the board?
- What policies govern the reporting to government authorities of probable violations of law?

In *Integrated Approach*, the OIG and Health Lawyers addressed the roles of the in-house corporate general counsel and an organization's CCO in supporting the compliance oversight function of healthcare organizations' governing boards. The publication concludes that

> [u]ltimately it is important that a Board receives a sufficient flow of information to effectively conduct its compliance oversight. Establishing and coordinating the roles and responsibilities of the General Counsel and the Chief Compliance Officer within healthcare organizations to best serve the organization and best assist the Board in its compliance oversight function is essential.[72]

---

[72] DHHS/Health Lawyers, INTEGRATED APPROACH *at 9*.

The OIG and Health Lawyers designed a list of questions that boards should ask related to this issue.

- To what extent is the general counsel utilized by the board to provide relevant advice regarding compliance matters?
- Where and how is the general counsel involved in each of the fundamental elements of the compliance program?
- How does the general counsel receive notice of, and provide input on, the organization's response to identified or suspected compliance failures?
- What are the roles of the organization's CCO and general counsel in operating the corporate compliance program? Who has responsibility for reporting to the board on compliance matters?
- How is the board notified when disagreements arise among management, the CCO, and/or the general counsel relating to the organizational response to specific compliance matters?
- Does the board understand how the organization utilizes the attorney/client and work-product privileges when responding to third-party requests for information?
- Are processes in place to enable the general counsel to bring issues of legal compliance to the appropriate authorities within the organization?

*Healthcare Quality* aims to assist healthcare directors in carrying out their oversight role. The publication states, "[g]iven that directors have an obligation to assure that the organization has an 'effective' compliance program in place to detect and deter legal violations, they may fairly be regarded as having a concomitant duty to make reasonable inquiry regarding the emerging legal and compliance issues associated with quality of care initiatives, and to direct executive leadership to address those issues."[73] The oversight obligation being imposed upon board members stems from their fiduciary duty to the organization and the fact that financial relationships themselves may influence or impact quality of care issues.[74] In attempting to guide directors, suggested questions were provided that attempt to evaluate the quality and safety measures employed by the organization. The suggested questions are as follows:[75]

- What are the goals of the organization's quality improvement program? What metrics and benchmarks are used to measure progress

---

[73] DHHS/Health Lawyers, Health Care Quality at 4.
[74] *Id.*
[75] *Id.* at 9–11.

towards each of these performance goals? How is each goal specifically linked to management accountability?

- How does the organization measure and improve the quality of patient/resident care? Who are the key management and clinical leaders responsible for these quality and safety programs?

- How are the organization's quality assessment and improvement processes integrated into overall corporate policies and operations? Are clinical quality standards supported by operational policies? How does management implement and enforce these policies? What internal controls exist to monitor and report on quality metrics?

- Does the board have a formal orientation and continuing education process that helps members appreciate external quality and patient safety requirements? Does the board include members with expertise in patient safety and quality improvement issues?

- What information is essential to the board's ability to understand and evaluate the organization's quality assessment and performance improvement programs? Once these performance metrics and benchmarks are established, how frequently does the board receive reports about the quality improvement efforts?

- How are the organization's quality assessment and improvement processes coordinated with its corporate compliance program? How are quality of care and patient safety issues addressed in the organization's risk assessment and corrective action plans?

- What processes are in place to promote the reporting of quality concerns and medical errors and to protect those who ask questions and report problems? What guidelines exist for reporting quality and patient safety concerns to the board?

- Are human and other resources adequate to support patient safety and clinical quality? How are proposed changes in resource allocation evaluated from the perspective of clinical quality and patient care? Are systems in place to provide adequate resources to account for differences in patient acuity and care needs?

- Do the organization's competency assessment and training, credentialing, and peer review process adequately recognize the necessary focus on clinical quality and patient safety issues?

- How are "adverse patient events" and other medical errors identified, analyzed, reported, and incorporated into the organization's performance improvement activities? How do management and the board address quality deficiencies without unnecessarily increasing the organization's liability exposure?

## § 7-5(f) CMS Guidance to Contractors

In 2005, CMS recognized the importance that its fee-for-services contractors (which CMS defined as including Medicare Part A fiscal intermediaries, Medicare Part B carriers, and durable medical equipment regional carriers [DMERC]) adopt compliance programs as well. In developing this document, entitled "Compliance Program Guidance for Medicare Fee-For-Service Contractors," CMS explained that it relied upon a number of sources for information on compliance programs, such as on-site reviews of existing compliance programs implemented by Medicare fee-for-service contractors conducted by CMS compliance teams, the Sentencing Guidelines, the various OIG guidances, and contemporary literature in the field of compliance. CMS recognized that

> a compliance program is not a panacea guaranteed to eliminate the risk that fraud, waste, abuse or inefficiency will occur. Nevertheless, CMS believes that the establishment of an effective compliance program will protect the Medicare Trust Fund by significantly reducing the risk of unlawful or improper conduct, and will likely lead to other programmatic efficiencies.[76]

In addition to this more general compliance guidance, the Medicare Learning Network, maintained by CMS, provides Medicare-Fee-For-Service providers with information and guidance on how to avoid common billing errors and other improper activities identified through various CMS claims review programs.[77] For example, in 2011 CMS released publications on the documentation needed to support a claim submitted for chiropractic services, power mobility devices, positive airway pressure (PAP) devices, oxygen therapy supplies and E& M services. In conjunction with this, in October 2010, CMS began releasing a quarterly compliance newsletter, "Medicare Quarterly Provider Compliance Newsletter" to emphasize the top billing and other compliance issues of each quarter.

## § 7-5(g) State Guidance

Given the new requirements in section 6401(a) of the Health Reform Law, State Medicaid programs will have to determine how they will adapt their current standards to correspond. Prior to the enactment of the Health Reform Law, New York State was the only state to have adopted legisla-

---

[76] CMS, COMPLIANCE PROGRAM GUIDANCE FOR MEDICARE FEE-FOR-SERVICE CONTRACTORS (2005), *available online at* https://www.cms.gov/MedicareContractingReform/12_ComplianceProgramGuidance.asp.

[77] CMS, Provider Compliance, Medicare Learning Network, *available online at* https://www.cms.gov/MLNProducts/.

## Compliance and Self-Reporting

tion mandating compliance plans and programs for federal healthcare program enrollees.[78] Specifically, effective July 1, 2009, the New York Office of Medicaid Inspector General (NY-OMIG) adopted regulations requiring that healthcare providers licensed in New York that receive, or expect to receive, at least $500,000 per year from the New York Medicaid program implement an "effective" compliance program that meets certain required elements. Providers must certify annually that they have a compliance program with these elements in place.

The New York requirements set out that the compliance program should be applicable to: (1) billings; (2) payments; (3) medical necessity and quality of care; (4) governance; (5) mandatory reporting; (6) credentialing; and (7) "other risk areas that are or should with due diligence be identified by the provider."[79] At a minimum, compliance programs must have the following elements:

- Policies and Procedures: There must be written policies and procedures that describe the "compliance expectation as embodied in a code of conduct or code of ethics, implement the operation of the compliance program, provide guidance to employees and others on dealing with potential compliance issues, identify how to communicate compliance issues to appropriate compliance personnel, and describe how potential compliance problems are investigated and resolved."[80]

- Compliance Officer: The provider must designate an employee who shall be responsible for the day-to-day operation of the compliance program (the compliance officer). The compliance officer should report directly to the CEO or other senior administrator designated by the CEO and should periodically report directly to the governing body on the activities of the compliance program.

- Compliance Training: The provider must provide initial and periodic training and education regarding compliance requirements and expectations to appropriate employees, including executives and members of the governing body.

- Confidential Compliance Reporting: The compliance officer must be accessible to all employees, including executives and governing

---

[78] Chapter 442 of the Laws of 2006, which established the Office of the Medicaid Inspector General (NY-OMIG), also created a new Social Services Law § 363-d, which mandates that Medicaid providers adopt and implement compliance programs. *See also*, N.Y. COMP. CODES R. & REGS. tit. 18, § 521.1.

[79] N.Y. COMP. CODES R. & REGS. tit. 18, § 521.3.

[80] NY-OMIG, Mandatory Provider Compliance Programs, Frequently Asked Questions, *available online at* http://www.omig.ny.gov/data/content/view/261/53.

body members and there must be a procedure for anonymous, confidential reporting of compliance issues and questions.

- Employee Discipline: The NY-OMIG regulations require that the disciplinary policies "encourage good faith participation in the compliance program. . .[and] articulate expectations for reporting compliance issues and assist in the resolution and outline sanctions for: (i) failing to report suspected problems; (ii) participating in non-compliant behavior; or (iii) encouraging, directing, facilitating or permitting either actively or passively non-compliant behavior."[81]

- Internal and External Audit of Risk Areas: There must be a mechanism for the routine identification of compliance risk areas, including but not limited to internal audits and as appropriate external audit, and for evaluation of potential or actual non-compliance.

- Reports to the NY-OMIG: There must be a process for identifying, responding to, and reporting compliance issues to the Department of Health or the NY-OMIG, and a mechanism for refunding overpayments.[82]

- Non-intimidation and Non-retaliation: The provider must have a policy of non-intimidation and non-retaliation for good faith participation of employees and agents in the compliance program.

## § 7-6 ELEMENTS OF AN EFFECTIVE COMPLIANCE PROGRAM

Charged by the Health Reform Law to ensure enrolled providers and suppliers establish legitimate and operational compliance programs, CMS published a Proposed Rule on September 23, 2010,[83] and solicited public comment in order to establish threshold compliance program requirements. On February 2, 2011, the Final Rule pertaining to sections 6102 and 6401(a) was published in the Federal Register.[84] However, CMS has not settled upon guidelines regarding mandatory compliance programs for all enrollees. Instead, the agency extended its rulemaking period in regards to section 6401(a) allowing for additional public comment and "regulatory negotiation." As previously mentioned, CMS has issued a Proposed Rule regarding the elements of an

---

[81] N.Y. COMP. CODES R. & REGS. tit. 18, § 521.3.
[82] The NY-OMIG also has a process for reporting self-disclosures. This will be discussed in § 7-9.
[83] Medicare, Medicaid, and Children's Health Insurance Programs; Additional Screening Requirements, Application Fees, Temporary Enrollment Moratoria, Payment Suspensions and Compliance Plans for Providers and Suppliers, 75 Fed. Reg. 58,204 (Sept. 23, 2010).
[84] 76 Fed. Reg. 5,862 (Feb. 2, 2011).

## Compliance and Self-Reporting

effective compliance programs, which is currently undergoing review with the Office of Management and Budget.

Although CMS has not yet issued a specific proposal as to the mandatory core elements for a compliance program for all providers and suppliers, CMS specifically solicited comments regarding the use of the seven elements of an effective compliance program, set forth in Chapter Eight of the Sentencing Guidelines, as the core required elements of provider compliance plans. Further, CMS has outlined practical principles derived from the core elements in order to support preliminary development of a compliance program. In addition, the specific requirements for Medicare Advantage and Part D plans shed light on the elements that CMS deems important from a compliance perspective.[85] With this knowledge, providers establishing new or enhancing existing programs can begin to identify ways to ensure these elements are incorporated so as to conform to the forthcoming rule from CMS.

Despite the delay in issuing the requirements for all providers, in the February 2, 2011, Final Rule, CMS did release the specific compliance elements required for nursing facilities (NFs) and skilled nursing facilities (SNFs) as required under Section 6102 of the Health Reform Law. In addition, CMS made clear that NFs and SNFs are subject to both compliance requirements under sections 6102 and 6401(a). By March 23, 2013, three years from the enactment of the Health Reform Law, all NF and SNFs must have a compliance program in place that is "effective in preventing and detecting criminal, civil, and administrative violations."[86] Larger NFs will be required to adopt "more formal" programs and three years from promulgating the Final Rule, the Secretary will be charged with completing a comprehensive evaluation of the compliance programs of enrolled nursing care providers. Under the new mandate, NF and SNF compliance programs must include eight requirements.

The adoption of mandatory compliance programs should not be taken lightly by current and prospective enrollees. Sections 6102 and 6401(a) represent the evolution of healthcare compliance and the final requirements by CMS will be a progression from previous federal guidance. Although CMS has not issue yet finalized the specific elements that must be incorporated into a corporate compliance program, the various government issuances described in this chapter provide guidance on the elements that the government considers relevant. According to the Sentencing Guidelines, a "compliance and ethics program shall be reasonably designed, implemented, and enforced so that the program is generally effective in preventing and detecting criminal

---

[85] 75 Fed. Reg. 19,678 (Apr. 15, 2010) codified at 42 C.F.R. §§ 422.503(b)(4)(vi), 423.504(b)(4)(vi).
[86] The Health Reform Law, §6102 (b)(1).

conduct."[87] The Sentencing Guidelines provide the structure, and the other guidances and publications described provide suggestions to implement this structure.

## § 7-6(a)   Establishment of Standards and Procedures

At the heart of an organization's compliance program are its standards and procedures. Not only does the first element of the Sentencing Guidelines provide that a compliance program must establish standards and procedures to "prevent and detect criminal conduct," but four of the remaining six elements provide guidance on the content, form, and enforcement of the organization's standards and procedures. Consequently, it is not surprising that all of the OIG's Compliance Program Guidances stress the importance that "every compliance program should require the development and distribution of written compliance policies, standards, and practices that identify specific areas of risk and vulnerability" to the particular provider.[88]

There is no established format for these standards and procedures. In fact, organizations that adopt "off the shelf" policies may find that they are inapplicable to their organizations' operations, and/or conflict with other policies adopted and maintained in other manuals. Therefore, organizations must tailor their standards and procedures to their specific operations. Despite this, many organizations have adopted the same general format for their compliance program's policies and procedures. Organizations typically adopt a code of conduct that sets forth the organization's general commitment to compliance and the broad standards that apply to all employees.[89] For example, the code of conduct may include the healthcare entity's mission statement, a description of the organization's commitment to providing quality healthcare, an explanation of the ethical tenets by which the organization expects its employees and agents to abide, and a brief statement of each of the various major laws with which the organization seeks compliance.

The code of conduct then will be supplemented by specific policies related to the implementation of the compliance program. For example, the organization may establish specific policies and procedures on the duties and responsibilities of the COO, the documentation that must be maintained by the compliance department, the manner with which the organization is to conduct background checks, and how the organization will respond to potential violations of its policies and procedures.

---

[87] U.S. Sentencing Guidelines Manual § 8B2.1(b) (2011).

[88] *See, e.g.,* Compliance Program Guidance for Hospices, 64 Fed. Reg. 54,034 (Oct. 29, 1999).

[89] Although some organizations refer to this document as a "Code of Conduct," others may refer to it as the organization's "Standards of Conduct," "Code of Business Ethics," or some similar term of art. Regardless of its title, they all generally address the same types of issues.

## Compliance and Self-Reporting

The code of conduct also is typically supplemented with standards and procedures relevant to the provider's business and that address the "risks and vulnerabilities" applicable to that particular type of healthcare provider.

An organization's standards and procedures should not be voluminous and unwieldy, but instead should be organized and maintained in a manner that is easy for employees to access and understand. No compliance program manual can answer all questions concerning substantive legal, operational, and billing issues. To the extent an organization has other manuals and/or policies or procedures, it is not necessary that the compliance program's standards and procedures replicate what is otherwise included in another policy; instead, the compliance program can merely cross-reference the policies and procedures contained in those other manuals. Also, to the extent complicated laws with nuanced solutions are involved, the compliance policies and procedures can delineate a process for resolving matters that arise, instead of setting out the actual resolution. In addition, the policies and procedures should set forth reasonable and attainable requirements, instead of setting lofty requirements that are impossible to meet.

Another significant issue is that an organization must ensure that the standards and procedures are written at the appropriate reading levels, and are comprehensible to the intended audience. To this end, organizations that have employees whose primary language is not English should consider translating the applicable sections of the organization's standards and procedures into the employees' primary language(s).

Although certain aspects of an organization's compliance program should be distributed to all employees and agents (e.g., via the code of conduct), it is not necessary that every employee obtain a manual with each and every compliance program policy. Some organizations, therefore, develop specialized compliance program binders for different categories of employees within the organization. For example, nursing staff will receive a "nursing staff" compliance manual with all general compliance program policies as well as specific policies related to providing nursing services, while the members of the billing department receive a "billing staff" manual with both the general policies and specific policies related to billing, coding, and documentation. Some organizations have decided to eliminate printed manuals and post their organization's compliance program policies and procedures on the organization's Internet and/or intranet website(s), coupled with educating their employees on the applicable policies and procedures (*see* § 7-6(d), *infra*).

Finally, these compliance program policies and procedures should be reviewed on a periodic basis (e.g., annually), and updated to reflect changes in law and policy.

## § 7-6(b)    Roles and Reporting Relationships of Personnel

### § 7-6(b)(1)    Corporate Governance

The role of an organization's governing body stems from the basic principle of a fiduciary's duty of care. State statutes that create the duty of care, and the courts that interpret them, apply the duty almost the same with respect to for-profit and nonprofit organizations. In most states, the duty of care involves determining whether a director acted in good faith, with the level of care that an ordinarily prudent person would exercise in similar circumstances, and in a manner that the director reasonably believes is in the best interest of the corporation.

Many states also apply the "business judgment rule" to determine whether a director's duty of care has been met with respect to corporate decisions. This rule essentially provides that a director will not be held liable for a decision made in good faith and where the director is disinterested, reasonably informed under the circumstances, and rationally believes the decision to be in the best interest of the corporation. With respect to the duty of care, a director's obligations arise in two contexts: decision-making functions and oversight functions. Obligations with respect to corporate compliance are within the oversight function. A director's failure to reasonably oversee the implementation and management of a compliance and ethics program may put an organization at risk and in some cases expose individual directors to personal liability.[90]

Advancing the principle established by *In re Caremark*, that all executives are responsible for overseeing compliance programs to detect and address fraud and abuse;[91] both executives and boards of directors are being held subject to increased liability for individual and organizational misconduct. One way of reducing the potential for organizational misconduct is the requirement for executives to ensure a compliance program is in place. Executive accountability for the implementation of compliance programs is codified in the Sentencing Guidelines.[92] The charge given executives and boards of directors, however, does not end with the adoption and maintenance of a compliance program. An organization's leadership has ultimate responsibility for compliance oversight and, as previously described, can be held both collectively and individually liable for their actions and that of the organization.

---

[90] *See In re* Caremark International Inc. Derivative Litigation, 698 A.2d 959 (Del.Ch. 1996).
[91] *Id.*
[92] "High-level personnel" are to ensure that an effective compliance program is implemented and certain individuals are to be assigned responsibility for overseeing the program. U.S. Sentencing Guidelines Manual § 8B2.1(b) (2011).

## Compliance and Self-Reporting

The current Sentencing Guidelines provide that individuals charged with managing an organizational compliance program should have: 1) adequate resources to effectively carry out oversight responsibility; and a 2) protocol for establishing clear lines of communication with "substantial authority personnel"[93] through periodic updates about emerging program compliance issues.[94] These guidelines represent an expectation that executives endow their compliance programs with proper assets and remain aware and responsive to program happenings.

The most critical element in meeting the governing body's duty of care is the "process [it] follows in establishing that it had access to sufficient information and that it has asked appropriate questions."[95] Directors and senior management can improve their understanding of the content and operation of the compliance and ethics program by periodically considering certain topics. In *Corporate Responsibility*, the OIG and Health Lawyers laid out a series of questions that corporate-governance personnel can answer to gain this understanding. Based on these questions and considerations, the actions the governing body of a healthcare corporation might take are discussed in this section.

The responsibility of directors and senior management is to provide oversight, and not to manage the day-to-day affairs of an organization. Therefore, a healthcare organization should designate a Chief Compliance Officer (CCO) and delegate appropriate authority to that person to oversee the implementation and maintenance of the compliance program. The OIG and CMS take the position that the CCO should have direct access to the organization's board of directors and/or to senior management, particularly to make reports concerning actual or potential cases of noncompliance. This may be somewhat impractical, however, given the limited number of people who have access to the members of the governing body and given the time constraints placed on board meetings. Therefore, some organizations have established a subcommittee of the board of directors that is responsible for overseeing the compliance program (similar to boards that have subcommittees responsible for executive-compensation and audit functions). This "Compliance Committee" is appointed by the board of directors to assist the board in overseeing the management of the compliance program and the appropriate implementation

---

[93] "Substantial authority personnel" refers to "individuals who within the scope of their authority exercise a substantial measure of discretion in acting on behalf of an organization. The term includes high-level personnel of the organization, individual who exercise substantial supervisory authority . . ., and any other individuals who, although not a part of an organization's management, nevertheless exercise substantial discretion when acting within the scope of their authority . . . Whether an individual falls within this category must be determined on a case-by-case basis." U.S. SENTENCING GUIDELINES MANUAL § 3E1.1 (Nov. 2010), *available online at* http://www.ussc.gov/Guidelines/2010_guidelines/Manual.htm.

[94] USSG §8B2.1(b)(2)(C).

[95] DHHS/Health Lawyers, CORPORATE RESPONSIBILITY.

of processes related to the compliance program, including communication of policies and procedures, training, monitoring, and enforcement.

The Compliance Committee of the board of directors should be comprised of three or more directors, a majority of whom should not be executive directors and who are free from any relationship that would interfere with the exercise of their independent judgment. The members of the committee should be appointed by the board on recommendation of a nominating committee. The Compliance Committee of the board should meet regularly at least four times per year, prepare and/or approve an agenda before each meeting, and prepare written minutes for each meeting. The committee should meet privately, separately, and regularly with management and advisors of the organization (including in-house counsel, outside counsel, the director of compliance, and independent consultants) to discuss any matters that the committee or others believe should be discussed. The committee should have the authority, at the expense of the organization, to retain outside counsel and independent consultants within the committee's discretion. The Compliance Committee should have many responsibilities, such as:

- confirming that the organization has adopted and implemented policies and procedures that are expected to encourage the organization's employees and agents to act in compliance with applicable laws, regulations, and medical/health standards;
- receiving reports from the director of compliance concerning or related to the operation of the compliance program, such as issues related to training and education, hotline reports/disclosures of wrongdoing, potential or existing government investigations or litigation, internal and external audits, and compliance risk assessment;
- receiving a comprehensive report from the director of compliance on an annual basis with an assessment and update of the compliance program; and
- reporting and recommending to the board any actions to assist the organization in being fully compliant, and ensuring that the organization has the sufficient resources to undertake those actions.

Most important, it is the governing body's responsibility to make sure that each element listed in this section is in place to ensure an effective compliance and ethics program. Additionally, there should be evidence that the board or senior management actively supports the compliance program's efforts. Without this support, employees inevitably will not take the program seriously. To demonstrate this support, organizations could have one or more senior executives write a letter or provide the "introduction" to the code of conduct to demonstrate the management team's support. However, recognizing that "actions speak louder than words," members of the governing body should attend compliance training sessions and compliance committee meetings, and ensure that the organization has allocated the necessary financial resources to developing and implementing the compliance program.

## § 7-6(b)(2)   The CCO and Other Personnel

A healthcare organization must appoint a high-level person to serve as the CCO, who is directly responsible for the day-to-day operation and monitoring of the compliance program. The CCO must report to the organization's governing authority on the status of the program at least annually. The CCO should oversee and monitor the development and implementation of the organization's compliance policies, as well as the achievement and maintenance of compliance standards, including audits, training, and the investigation and response to employee compliance complaints/reports. The CCO also should establish methods to reduce the organization's vulnerability to fraud, waste, and abuse.

Although not specifically mentioned in the Sentencing Guidelines, many organizations create a compliance committee (different and separate from the board-level committee described earlier) that is designed to assist and advise the CCO and support the compliance program's efforts. This committee should consist of individuals with experience in the various functional areas of the healthcare organization, and who have institutional history and an appreciation for the organization. To this end, this committee generally will consist of individuals with varying responsibilities within the organization (e.g., operations, finance, audit, legal, human resources, and clinical management), as well as managers from key operating units within the organization. Ideally, a well-functioning committee should meet regularly and have an agenda. In addition, employees should feel comfortable with bringing matters to the attention of the committee, and should feel that the committee has the power to address or resolve the issues brought to their attention.

Similarly, many large healthcare organizations (especially those with multiple locations) often will appoint local compliance officers (also referred to as compliance liaisons and compliance coordinators) who are responsible for ensuring that local operations fulfill their compliance obligations. These local compliance personnel should not only provide the CCO with valuable input on the compliance program's operations, but also facilitate and support the program's efforts by training employees and agents at that location, conducting applicable audits, and/or serving as a local resource for that facility's managers and employees. Compliance departments of large organizations also may have additional personnel (e.g., an assistant compliance officer) who manage the implementation of the training schedules, distribute the code of conduct, and maintain all applicable documentation. Some organizations also have realized the benefit of having subject-matter experts within the compliance department who are experts in high-risk areas (e.g., laboratory, physician coding, and documentation) take primary responsibility for training individuals on these issues and conducting audits when necessary.

### § 7-6(b)(3)  Relationship Between the CCO and the General Counsel

The person or persons in charge of a compliance program must have adequate authority to make reports to the governing body of a healthcare organization. The OIG does not suggest a proposed reporting structure; nevertheless, in order to ensure that appropriate "checks and balances" exist, it has expressed its reservations with having a CCO report to either the general counsel or the chief financial officer (CFO). Similarly, the OIG and CMS believe that the functions of the CCO and the general counsel should be kept separate. However, the American Bar Association's Task Force on Corporate Responsibility (ABA Task Force) has recommended that the general counsel should have "primary responsibility for assuring the implementation of an effective legal compliance system under the oversight of the board of directors."[96] Although healthcare organizations should be cognizant of the government's views towards these individuals' involvement in the compliance program, organizations may need to determine whether the OIG's advice is practical for their organization, or whether the organization can include legal counsel or the CFO within the framework of the compliance program, yet still provide for the appropriate checks and balances.

The relationship between a CCO's obligations and a general counsel's duty presents a potential conflict of interest. The general counsel is ethically obligated to vigorously represent, defend, and protect the confidences of the organization it represents, especially when fraud or misconduct may have occurred. In contrast, a person in charge of an organization's compliance program must report and correct alleged fraud or other misconduct, and sometimes must advise the government of noncompliance. In *Integrated Approach*, the results of a survey conducted by Health Lawyers show that a variety of structures exist among healthcare organizations with regard to the relationship between these two roles. The publication provides assistance to an organization's governing body in evaluating the organization's approach to the reporting structure of its own compliance program.[97] Given the conflicting approaches of the OIG and the ABA Task Force, *Integrated Approach* provides

---

[96] James H. Cheek III et al., REPORT OF THE AMERICAN BAR ASSOCATION, TASK FORCE ON CORPORATE RESPONSIBILITY (2003), *available online at* http://www.americanbar.org/content/dam/aba/migrated/leadership/2003/journal/119c.authcheckdam.pdf.

[97] DHHS/Health Lawyers, INTEGRATED APPROACH.

## Compliance and Self-Reporting

three acceptable compliance models. The first model, preferred by OIG and CMS, involves a total separation of the general counsel and CCO functions. The second model combines the general counsel and the CCO into one person or entity. A third model separates the functions of the general counsel from those of the CCO, but has the CCO report directly to the general counsel.

No matter which structure a healthcare organization chooses, it is imperative that the governing body overseeing the compliance program understands how the organization is addressing the roles of the general counsel and the CCO, and ensures that a structure is in place to provide the governing body with the appropriate information and assessments of the compliance program.

### § 7-6(c)   Background Checks

The Sentencing Guidelines require that an organization use due care not to delegate substantial discretionary authority to an individual who the organization knew, or should have known through the exercise of due diligence, had a propensity to engage in illegal activities. This requirement means that healthcare organizations need to conduct background checks on existing employees and new employees alike—especially when the employee works in an area that the organization has identified as being vulnerable.

While some organizations generally check an applicant's background for supervisor/managerial level positions, many are reluctant to perform such checks on lower-level employees. However, the background of a lower-level employee working in an area where vulnerabilities may exist (e.g., a billing clerk) can be equally as important as that of a supervisor or manager. At a minimum, the organization should check references for such individuals, and determine whether new hires or existing employees have been excluded from participation in the federal healthcare programs. The OIG website contains the "List of Excluded Individuals/Entities," a database that provides a list of parties excluded from participation in federal healthcare programs.[98] The "Online Searchable Database" form of the list enables healthcare organizations to enter the name of an individual or business, and determine whether an exclusion currently is in effect. Similarly, the General Services Administration maintains the "List of Parties Excluded from Federal Procurement and Nonprocurement Programs," which identifies those parties excluded from receiving federal contracts or certain subcontracts, as well as those excluded from receiving certain types of federal financial and nonfinancial assistance and benefits.[99]

---

[98] OIG, *List of Excluded Individuals/Entities, available online at* http://www.oig.hhs.gov/fraud/exclusions/listofexcluded.html.

[99] Gen'l Servs. Admin., *List of Parties Excluded from Federal Procurement and Nonprocurement Programs, available online at* http://www.epls.gov/.

## § 7-6(d)  Training

The Sentencing Guidelines require a healthcare organization to adequately train its directors, officers, high-level personnel, substantial authority personnel, employees, and agents on the organization's standards and procedures. This requirement frequently is resisted as an unwarranted drain on company resources and as a diversion of company personnel from business operational concerns. As most healthcare organizations are substantially regulated, however, many already have a training-program structure that can be supplemented by the corporate compliance issues.

Nevertheless, organizations need to tailor their training to particular employees. The Sentencing Guidelines require that an organization provide training to *all* employees in a manner that the employee can understand. Therefore, the training provided to a billing clerk as opposed to the training provided to a non-decision-making employee (e.g., receptionists, janitors, and cafeteria workers) will be very different. Organizations need to develop training programs geared specifically to non-decision-making employees so that these employees also are conversant in the essential elements of the organization's compliance program. The organization should set as a training goal that, at the completion of all initial training, *any* employee of the organization that is approached can provide essential information regarding the compliance program (e.g., the names of the compliance officers, reporting mechanisms, and elements of the organization's code of conduct). Organizations also need to develop specific training programs for managers and supervisors, so that these employees are trained to answer questions and respond to situations regarding the compliance program.

With the different types of technology that are available, organizations can use different formats for efficiently and effectively conducting compliance program training sessions: in-person seminars, compliance training videos, computer-based instructional programs, and/or Internet/intranet websites. Regardless of the format chosen, an organization must ensure that participants are attentive and understand the principles addressed during the training sessions. Therefore, following training sessions, many organizations require participants to take a comprehension test. Those individuals who do not receive an acceptable score either must attend another training session or receive additional one-on-one training. In addition to these traditional forms of training, some organizations use periodic newsletters and emails to update employees on compliance-related issues, which can be useful tools in reminding employees that they need to be cognizant of compliance issues.

## § 7-6(e)  Monitoring, Auditing, and Evaluating the Program

The Sentencing Guidelines require that organizations take reasonable steps to ensure that the compliance and ethics program is being followed. This includes monitoring and auditing to detect criminal conduct. Organizations should develop an audit schedule that methodically touches upon the organization's areas of vulnerability. This audit schedule should include both operational issues (e.g., proper billing) and compliance issues (e.g., training documentation). The audit team should benchmark audit results and perform a review of an issue more than once at specific intervals for determining whether improvement is occurring. Static performance or a decline in results would suggest that the compliance program is not entirely "effective," whereas improvement would be indicative of "effectiveness."

In addition to auditing substantive and operational issues, an organization should audit its compliance program periodically to determine whether the program is accomplishing its goals. (*See* § 7-7, *infra*.)

## § 7-6(f)  Reporting System

Although the Sentencing Guidelines provide that an organization is to adopt a reporting system so that employees can report potential misconduct, they do not dictate the type of reporting system that should be utilized. Although the majority of healthcare organizations use a "hotline" (either operated internally or subcontracted out to an outside "hotline" operator) to receive calls from individuals wishing to report a compliance issue, some organizations use other formats to create open lines of communication (e.g., use of emails, drop boxes/post office boxes, or dedicated messaging services).

Although the government has stated its preference for anonymous reporting (presumably as it is a safeguard against retribution), the use of anonymous reporting can increase the risk of bad-faith reporting by disgruntled personnel, and may make a thorough investigation of the complaint difficult. Thus, if an organization adopts an anonymous reporting mechanism, then the organization should develop a tracking system that assigns every complainant a tracking number. The complainant can use this tracking number to call the hotline after a specified time period and provide any additional information needed for the CCO to complete the investigation.

Regardless of the type of formal reporting system used as part of the compliance program, organizations should take steps not to disrupt the informal reporting mechanisms that may have existed within the organization before the implementation of the compliance program. Use of informal mechanisms already in place (assuming they are effective and with which employees feel comfortable), along with the adoption of more-formalized mechanisms, should serve to increase the likelihood of reports.

In order to increase the potential use of the compliance program's reporting mechanisms, the organization should undertake efforts to publicize its existence. Posters, letters, wallet cards, and newsletter articles are appropriate methods for notifying employees of the existence and purpose of the reporting system. In addition, it is necessary that an entity communicate to employees that information provided through the reporting system (including the name of the parties making the report) will be treated confidentially, and that individuals who make "good faith" reports will not be subject to any retaliatory actions. Nevertheless, organizations must make it clear to employees that the organization's non-retribution policy does not mean that employees will automatically avoid the consequences of their own wrongdoing simply by reporting the wrongdoing.

### § 7-6(g)   Disciplinary Action and Corrective Action

When instances of noncompliant behavior occur, healthcare entities must respond swiftly and seriously. Employees who, upon investigation, are found to have violated the organization's compliance program policies, or any law, rule, or regulation under which the entity operates, should be subject to immediate discipline up to and including termination. As most organizations' human resource departments have adopted a progressive disciplinary process, discipline for inappropriate behavior associated with violation of the compliance program should follow similar processes.

Although many organizations focus their disciplinary procedures upon low- and mid-level employees, the government expects that disciplinary measures also be taken against high-level personnel who do not adhere to or who violate the compliance program. In fact, the OIG Compliance Program Guidances suggest that organizations include adherence to the compliance program as a job requirement for supervisors and managers. Therefore, organizations need to pay particular attention to ensuring that disciplinary measures apply to and are enforced against all personnel.

Because transgressions of employees in different positions may differ, an organization may not necessarily be able to punish employees with varying levels of responsibility in the same manner. However, the organization should strive to ensure that higher- and lower-level employees alike are subject to punishment commensurate with their transgressions. In addition, through training, all personnel should be made aware of the existence of such disciplinary measures.

At a minimum, the disciplinary component of a corporate compliance program should contain the following elements:

1. a requirement that employees report suspected wrongdoing;

## Compliance and Self-Reporting

2. the imposition of disciplinary measures for employees who fail to report;
3. the imposition of disciplinary measures against supervisors/managers when appropriate;
4. flexibility to address specific issues that arise; and
5. consistent enforcement throughout all levels of the organization.

Upon receipt of reports or reasonable indications of suspected noncompliance, it is imperative that an organization immediately investigate the allegations to determine whether a violation has, in fact, occurred. Although each internal investigation may be different, it is advisable that CCOs develop a general methodology by which an investigation will be conducted. For example, some CCOs use a multi-step approach similar to the following in conducting internal investigations of possible compliance infractions.

Step 1: **Select the Members of the Investigative Team.** Depending upon the type of possible infraction, the CCO will need to determine what personnel possess the requisite skill sets to examine the particular issue(s) at hand. The CCO must decide whether the organization has sufficient internal resources to conduct the investigation, or whether external resources are also needed. As part of this process, it will also be necessary to determine the role of legal counsel and whether any aspects of the investigation are otherwise confidential under particular privileges (see discussion in Chapter 9).

Step 2: **Research the Issue.** Before conducting an investigation of the particular facts surrounding the issue, the CCO and the members of the investigative team should have a full understanding of the relevant laws, regulations, and government issuances.

Step 3: **Develop an Investigation Strategy.** The investigative team must develop a strategy for reviewing and examining the particular facts surrounding the possible infraction. This will require members of the investigation team to review documents and possibly interview "witnesses."

Step 4: **Prepare Findings.** At the conclusion of the investigation, the information should be organized in a manner so as to enable the organization to determine whether an infraction did, in fact, occur. Although there may be certain risks in preparing a formal written report (e.g., disclosure to unintended parties, misinterpretation of certain findings), it is necessary to advise senior management and/or the governing body on the results of the investigation and the subsequent steps that will need to be taken.

Step 5: **Determine the Nature of Communications with the Government.** If the investigation team confirms that there was an infraction, some type of corrective action will be required. The OIG states in various Compliance Program Guidances that it considers overpayment returns and self-disclosures to be evidence of an effective compliance program. (*See* § 7-9, *infra*.)

## § 7-6(h)  Documentation

Documentation is a key factor in determining a compliance program's effectiveness. An organization must be able to demonstrate the actions it has taken throughout the development and implementation process to evaluate the reasonableness of the decisions made in establishing and maintaining the program. Therefore, organizations should establish guidelines to assist in creating a written record of the organization's compliance activities.

One method that many compliance officers use is to maintain one or more log books. Some compliance officers maintain a log of all communications received through any of the organization's compliance-reporting systems (e.g., calls through the hotline, anonymous letters, calls directly to the compliance officer). Each entry included in the log book will receive a tracking number, a summary of the nature of the potential compliance issue, the course of action(s) taken to investigate and respond to the matter, and a summary of how and when the issue was resolved (and/or the appropriate corrective action that was taken). Another log book might include a list of all compliance-related documents that the compliance officer is aware of but that are not maintained in the compliance department. Examples include background-check verification forms (which might be maintained in employees' personnel files), results of billing audits (which might be maintained in the audit department), and billing policies and procedures (which might be maintained in the billing and/or business office).

In addition, many large healthcare organizations have their local compliance officers/liaisons forward monthly compliance reports to the CCO. This enables the compliance officer to receive written communications on the compliance efforts at the local level.

Compliance officers also should maintain documentation that sets forth the history of the compliance program's development, descriptions of the duties and responsibilities of all individuals directly responsible for the compliance program's activities, publications regarding the compliance program, materials promoting the use of the reporting system, and government contracts.

The compliance department may generate or receive documents that are of a confidential nature. These documents should be protected from general disclosure or distribution. Some documents may be of a confidential nature as the result of a communication with legal counsel. Therefore, compliance officers should consult with legal counsel to determine which documents should be maintained as confidential, and develop procedures by which such documents are appropriately marked and secured.

## § 7-7 DEMONSTRATING EFFECTIVENESS: CONDUCTING AN EFFECTIVENESS REVIEW

Developing a compliance program is only half the challenge for healthcare organizations; the remaining challenge is to demonstrate that the program is, in fact, effective. Although organizations may be required to conduct an effectiveness review as part of its obligations under a CIA, organizations not otherwise subject to a CIA also recognize the benefit to voluntarily conducting an assessment of how the compliance program is functioning. Section 8B2.1(c) of the Sentencing Guidelines provides that an organization must periodically assess the risk of occurrence of criminal conduct. Commentary to the section explains that the assessment should consider (1) the nature and seriousness of such criminal conduct, (2) the likelihood that certain criminal conduct may occur because of the nature of the organization's business, and (3) the prior history of the organization, which may indicate types of criminal conduct that the organization should take action to prevent and detect.

A major difference between a CIA-imposed effectiveness review and one performed voluntarily by an organization may be who conducts the review. Although CIAs generally require that an independent review organization (IRO) conduct the effectiveness review, organizations that are voluntarily performing this review may delegate some or all of the review tasks to internal employees in order to be most cost-effective. Although such delegation is possible (and indeed useful), organizations probably should not delegate the review to a compliance officer, members of the compliance committee, or anyone integrally involved with the compliance program, because their personal involvement in the compliance program may have a chilling effect on the review. If performed internally, however, the organization may wish to use legal counsel as the coordinator, in order to ensure that any issues discovered during the review process are protected from disclosure to third parties under the attorney/client privilege and/or the work-product doctrine.

To adequately assess the effectiveness of an organization's compliance program, the reviewer should strive to obtain access to documents beyond policies and procedures. If possible, the reviewer should request access to interview a limited number of employees or, at a minimum, the compliance officer.

Although no assessment of an organization's compliance program is complete without an audit of billing/financial processes, organizations may wish to perform this part of the review independently from its annual billing/financial audit to ensure that compliance issues are not overshadowed by billing/financial concerns. Instead, organizations may wish to coordinate the effectiveness review and the billing/financial audit so that the results of the billing/financial audit may be utilized during the effectiveness review. Such bifurcation will aid in determining the impact of the compliance program in billing/financial areas. It will also help to identify specific areas where random claims could be reviewed, which can help determine if the compliance program policies are effective in ensuring accurate billing.

As part of the effectiveness review, the organization may wish to employ benchmarking techniques to assess whether any trends exist that may demonstrate that the organization is noncompliant. Organizations can use their first effectiveness review as the basis for this benchmarking, because this review will serve as a "snapshot" of the organization's operation before the implementation of a compliance program. For example, if an organization identifies a problem or disgruntlement in a department during the effectiveness review in the first year, then the organization can compare performance in that department during the next annual review. Alternatively, if the review identifies weak training material in the prior year, the organization can compare training material in the subsequent year to gauge improvement.

In addition, organizations can benchmark from one effectiveness review to the next the number of hotline calls received, disciplinary measures imposed, or amounts refunded. This will help assess whether the compliance program is becoming more or less effective, or to pinpoint areas that need improvement. In order to perform such benchmarking and gauge improvement, the organization will need to retain documentation from prior reviews, and review the same topics in subsequent years.

After the assessment is complete, the reviewer will have access to a wide variety of information covering all aspects of the organization's compliance program. This assessment is likely to demonstrate neither an exceptionally effective nor a completely ineffective compliance program. Rather, the effectiveness review is likely to demonstrate that the compliance program has elements of both. In order to develop corrective action plans, the organization must take care in identifying weak areas, which should be reviewed again to track improvement as part of the organization's benchmarking activities.

## § 7-8 CIAS AND OTHER TYPES OF COMPLIANCE AGREEMENTS

Even though a provider may deny that it has committed any wrongdoing in connection with a healthcare fraud investigation, the provider may agree to enter into a settlement agreement with the government in order to avoid lengthy and uncertain litigation arising out of such investigations by the federal government. As part of the settlement agreement, the OIG often will agree not to seek to exclude the healthcare provider from participation in the federal healthcare programs (under its permissive exclusion rights, which are discussed in greater detail in Chapter 5), so long as the provider agrees to a number of obligations concerning the establishment and maintenance of a compliance program.

Originally, these compliance obligations were included as a section of a global settlement agreement among the healthcare provider, DOJ, and the OIG. Currently, however, the settlement-negotiation process is bifurcated, whereby the healthcare provider enters into two separate agreements: (1) a settlement agreement with DOJ; and (2) a CIA with the OIG. Although such agreements with the OIG are generally referred to as CIAs, historically some organizations have entered into similar agreements with the OIG referred to by a different name. For example, National Home Medical (known also as K & L Home Health Center) entered into a "Pharmacy Integrity Requirements Agreement" with the government. Similarly, a number of academic medical centers (e.g., University of Texas Health Science Center and University Medical Associates [Medical University of South Carolina]) have entered into "Institutional Compliance Agreements," while individual practitioners have entered into "Integrity Agreements." In addition, a number of entities had self-reported compliance issues and thereafter entered into agreements referred to as "Corporate Compliance Agreements." Although there are some nuances between these different types of agreements, all will be referred to as CIAs in this discussion.

Historically, when a healthcare provider would enter into a settlement agreement with the government, the OIG would sometimes agree to a Certification of Compliance Agreement (CCA) instead of a CIA.[100] A CCA is considerably less expensive and less onerous than a CIA. For example, none

---

[100] The following elements make a provider a possible candidate for a CCA: (1) Whether the organization self-disclosed the alleged misconduct; (2) Whether the organization engaged in conduct with large monetary damage to the federal healthcare programs; (3) Whether the case involved successor liability; (4) How long ago the misconduct occurred; (5) Whether the misconduct could reoccur; (6) Whether the provider is still participating in federal programs or in the line of business that gave rise to the fraudulent conduct; and (7) What existing compliance program the provider has. With No IRO, 'Certification of Compliance Agreement' Beats CIA in Fraud Settlement, REPORT ON MEDICARE COMPLIANCE, (Oct. 24, 2005).

of the CCAs negotiated by OIG required the use of an IRO, which is often the most expensive element of a CIA. However, the government has now discontinued the use of CCAs.

The number of CIAs that the government has entered into with healthcare organizations has increased dramatically in the last decade. While the government had entered into fewer than five CIAs in 1994, in the beginning of 2012 the OIG currently has approximately 330 CIAs currently listed on its website.[101] Although a number of these CIAs have been with hospital providers, the OIG also has entered into CIAs with a wide variety of other types of suppliers and providers, including (in part) individual practitioners (e.g., physicians, nurses, chiropractors), ambulance providers, durable medical equipment manufacturers and suppliers, nursing facilities, clinical laboratories, pharmacies, and pharmaceutical manufacturers. Over the years, the scope and sophistication of CIAs have evolved. For example, as previously stated, in recent years the OIG has begun incorporating more Board of Director responsibilities into CIAs.

As stated, CIAs outline certain obligations that the healthcare provider agrees to undergo in order to establish an effective compliance program. CIAs typically address the seven core elements of an effective compliance program, which track the Sentencing Guidelines. For example, the more comprehensive CIAs require that the organization:

- hire a compliance officer/appoint a compliance committee;
- implement Board of Director compliance obligations including meeting quarterly to oversee the compliance program, ensuring that the entity implements policies and procedures and adopting a signed resolution for each Reporting Period;
- develop written standards and policies;
- implement a comprehensive employee training program (CIAs are now also requiring Board of Directors training);
- review claims submitted to federal healthcare programs;
- establish a confidential disclosure program; and
- restrict employment of ineligible persons.[102]

CIAs also include a number of notification and reporting requirements, such as notification to the OIG of any ongoing investigations or legal proceedings conducted or brought by a governmental entity. When an entity subject to a CIA discovers that an overpayment may have occurred, it may be required to make certain notifications to payors and complete specific forms

---

[101] http://oig.hhs.gov/compliance/corporate-integrity-agreements/cia-documents.asp.
[102] Copies of various CIAs are *available online at* http://oig.hhs.gov/compliance/corporate-integrity-agreements/index.asp.

## Compliance and Self-Reporting

for submission to Medicare Carriers and/or Intermediaries. CIAs also require that if the entity determines that it has engaged in a "Reportable Event" then it must disclose the "Reportable Event" to the OIG within certain timeframes (i.e., within 30 days).[103]

Providers also are required to submit to the OIG an initial "Implementation Report" and then subsequent "Annual Reports" concerning the status of and findings regarding the entity's compliance activities. All such reports submitted to the OIG must include a certification by the organization's compliance officer that the organization is in compliance with all of the CIA's requirements, and that the information in the report being submitted is "accurate and truthful." Consequently, as this certification is being made by compliance officers "under penalty of perjury," it is extremely important that, from the inception of the CIA, the compliance officers develop procedures to ensure that they are confident that all of the CIA's requirements have been satisfied. Therefore, as CIAs generally require that all "Covered Persons" (which includes not only the healthcare entity's employees, but also its contractors/agents and [for hospitals] members of the hospital's medical staff) receive training, it will be necessary that the compliance officers have a process by which they can attest that all such covered persons have, in fact, received training.

In addition to these provisions (which, for the most part, are relatively standard in every CIA), a number of other provisions are included in CIAs that may be more controversial and, therefore, the subject of more-extensive negotiations between the OIG and the provider or the provider's counsel. One issue that may be negotiated is the length of the CIA. When the compliance program/integrity provisions were initially included as part of the global settlement agreements among the healthcare providers, DOJ, and OIG, the compliance obligations generally were effective for three years. Currently, the OIG generally requires that a CIA be effective for a minimum of five years, with some large providers (e.g., Fresenius Medical Care Holdings and HCA—The HealthCare Company) agreeing to terms of eight to ten years. However, in a 2000 "Open Letter to Healthcare Providers," Inspector General June Gibbs Brown explained that the OIG would give more deference when negotiating a CIA to a provider who self-discloses misconduct, and might not even require a CIA as part of the resolution of the matter.[104]

---

[103] Historically, instead of using the term "Reportable Event," the OIG had used in CIAs the term "Material Deficiency." The terms "Material Deficiency" and "Reportable Event" generally are defined in the CIAs as being a "substantial overpayment" or a "matter that a reasonable person would consider a probable violation of criminal, civil, the employment of or contracting with a Covered Person who is an Ineligible Person [(as defined by the CIA)]; or the filing of a bankruptcy petition."

[104] June Gibbs Brown, *An Open Letter to Healthcare Providers,* (March 9, 2000), *available online at* http://oig.hhs.gov/compliance/open-letters/index.asp.

Another issue that may be negotiated concerns the audits that the provider will be required to perform under the CIA. At first, CIAs required that providers conduct internal audits of certain issues that were specifically related to the conduct that gave rise to the investigation (e.g., if a provider was found to have improperly billed for certain types of procedures, then the CIA would require that the entity conduct audits of those types of procedures). In contrast, current CIAs require healthcare providers to perform broader audits than just an audit of the particular issue that gave rise to the investigation. For example, a hospital that may be settling an investigation of a particular Diagnosis-Related Group pairing (e.g., pneumonia) may be required to undergo coding audits not only of its pneumonia patients, but also the rest of its inpatients. In light of the resources required to perform these audits (regardless of whether these audits are conducted internally or by an IRO), however, providers generally try to negotiate a CIA that has a narrower scope of issues and claims that are subject to the audit requirements. Claims review also may be required for cases that do not involve errors in claims submission at all, such as certain report inaccuracies or cases involving physician financial relationships.

Generally, the OIG takes the position that the party subject to the CIA should not perform its own audits, but instead should contract with an IRO (e.g., an accounting, consulting, or auditing firm) to conduct a detailed review of the entity's Medicare and Medicaid billings, as well as with the entity's compliance with the CIA.[105] If the healthcare provider can demonstrate to the OIG that it has the internal capabilities to conduct an objective audit, however, then it may be possible that the OIG will agree that the entity can perform its own internal audit, but that an IRO will need to validate the healthcare provider's audit results. In some cases, the OIG will allow a provider to perform such reviews after an IRO has performed such reviews for one or two years.

When an IRO is in fact required, the OIG stresses that the IRO should be objective and independent. The passage of the SOA, coupled with an increased focus on issues relating to auditor independence, led the OIG to review its prior guidance regarding the factors that should be considered when assessing an IRO's independence. The OIG issued additional guidance in its "Frequently Asked Questions Related to IRO Independence"[106] in 2004 in response to inquiries. Following that, in 2010, the OIG issued a document entitled, "OIG Guidance on IRO Independence and Objectivity" (IRO

---

[105] To assist IROs in performing these duties, the American Institute of Certified Public Accountants developed Statement of Position 99-1 (May 21, 1999), entitled "Guidance to Practitioners in Conducting and Reporting on Agreed-Upon Procedures Engagement to Assist Management in Evaluating the Effectiveness of its Corporate Compliance Program."

[106] DHHS Office of the Inspector General, FREQUENTLY ASKED QUESTIONS RELATED TO IRO INDEPENDENCE.

## Compliance and Self-Reporting

Guidance).[107] The OIG has adopted the standards for auditor independence and objectivity set forth in *Government Auditing Standards (2007 Revision)* (referred to as the *Yellow Book*) issued by the Government Accountability Office (GAO).

Under these standards, CIA reviews are considered performance audits. Therefore, IROs are subject to the independence standards set forth in the *Yellow Book* that relate to performance audits. The standards also provide that IROs involved in CIA-related services would be subject to "specific standards that apply when an audit organization agrees to perform nonaudit services for the same client. . . . The standards require the IRO to evaluate whether providing the services creates an independence impairment either in fact or appearance with respect to the entity for which the IRO is performing a CIA review."[108] Following the OIG's adoption of these standards, two overarching principles must be considered when assessing the independence of an IRO:

1. audit organizations must not perform management functions or make management decisions; and

2. audit organizations should not audit their own work, nor should they provide nonaudit services in situations where the nonaudit services are significant and/or material to the subject matter of the audits.

The IRO Guidance provides that objectivity includes, "being independent in fact and appearance when providing audit and attestation engagements, maintaining an attitude of impartiality, having intellectual honesty, and being free from conflicts of interest."[109] With respect to independence, the IRO Guidance identifies that in all matters relating to the audit work the IRO:

- must be free from personal, external, and organizational impairments to independence, and must avoid the appears of such impairments of independence;

- must maintain independence to remain impartial and to be viewed as impartial by the OIG; and

- avoid situations that would call the IRO's impartiality into question

Finally, the IRO Guidance sets forth specific examples of nonaudit services furnished by an IRO to an entity under a CIA that likely would and likely would not "present an impairment to the IRO's independence and objectivity."

It should be noted that even if individuals or groups within an IRO organization responsible for performing the CIA-related services are separate

---

[107] DHHS Office of the Inspector General, OIG GUIDANCE ON IRO INDEPENDENCE AND OBJECTIVITY [hereinafter, IRO Guidance] *available online at* http://oig.hhs.gov/fraud/cia/docs/OIG_guidance_on_IRO_independence_2010.pdf.

[108] *Id.* (citing Government Auditing Standards, paragraphs 3.20-3.30).

[109] *Id.*

from individuals or groups from the same IRO conducting the CIA reviews, it does not eliminate or reduce the independence concerns.[110] Ultimately, an IRO must provide a certification that the IRO has evaluated its professional independence and objectivity with respect to the review and concluded that it is indeed independent and objective.

In addition, a number of CIAs include an obligation that an IRO be engaged to perform an "arrangements review." An IRO engaged to perform an arrangements review generally is responsible for conducting an assessment of the process by which an organization has established procedures to review and approve financial relationships with referral sources, and for ensuring that the requisite mechanisms for tracking and monitoring compliance have been adopted.[111]

If the OIG enters into a "quality-of-care" CIA to resolve allegations of fraud that impact the quality of patient care, the OIG requires that the provider retain an independent quality monitor (Monitor). According to the OIG website, "[t]he quality monitor not only will address the specific issues underlying the allegations, but also will look at the entity's deliver of care and evaluate the provider's ability to prevent, detect, and respond to patient care problems."[112] Unlike IRO's, the OIG selects the Monitor with consultation with the entity and the OIG has the sole discretion to remove the Monitor.

In general, the Monitor will be responsible for assessing the effectiveness, reliability, and thoroughness of the following:

- The entity's quality control systems, including, but not limited to (i) whether the systems in place to promote quality of care and to respond to quality of care issues are operating in a timely and effective manner, (ii) whether the communication system is effective, allowing for accurate information, decisions, and results of decisions to be transmitted to the proper individuals in a timely fashion, and (iii) whether the training programs are effective, thorough, and competency-based.

- The entity's response to quality of care issues including (i) the ability to identify the problem, (ii) the ability to determine the scope of the problem, including, but not limited to, whether the problem is isolated or systematic, (iii) the ability to create a corrective action plan

---

[110] *See* GAO YELLOW BOOK, Subchapter 3.17.

[111] *See e.g.*, Integrity Agreement between the OIG and Tenet Healthcare Corporation (Sept. 2006), *available online at* http://oig.hhs.gov/fraud/cia/agreements/TenetCIAFinal.pdf. Historically, in some instances a CIA would require the entity to engage a legal IRO. The scope of work for a legal IRO was to "identify current arrangements that could pose a risk of violating the Anti-Kickback Statute and/or the Stark Law and to develop and implement appropriate corrective actions when those risks have been identified." Integrity Agreement between the OIG and Leonard Ginsburg (Aug. 2004).

[112] OIG, Quality of Care Corporate Integrity Agreements, *available online at* http://oig.hhs.gov/compliance/corporate-integrity-agreements/quality-of-care.asp.

## Compliance and Self-Reporting

to respond to the problem, (iv) the ability to execute the corrective action plan, and (v) the ability to evaluate whether the assessment, corrective action plan, and execution of that plan was effective, reliable, and thorough;

- the entity's development and implementation of corrective action plans and the timeliness of such actions;
- the entity's proactive steps to ensure that each resident receives care in accordance with treatment standards and federal, state and local rules and regulations; and
- the entity's compliance with staffing requirements.

The obligations of having a Monitor are onerous on the entity because the Monitor must have immediate access to the entity, at any time and without prior notice, including access to the entity's patients. In addition, the Monitor should have immediate access to: (1) the CMS quality indicators; (2) internal or external surveys or reports; (3) Disclosure Program disclosures; (4) resident satisfaction surveys; (5) staffing data in the format requested by the Monitor, including reports detailing when a certain amount of the staff are hired on a temporary basis; (6) reports of abuse, neglect, or an incident that required hospitalization or emergency room treatment; (7) reports of any falls; (8) reports of any incident involving a resident that prompts an internal investigation; (9) resident records; (10) documents in the possession or control of any quality assurance committee, peer review committee, medical review committee, or other such committee; and (11) any other data in the form the Monitor determines relevant to fulfilling the duties required under the CIA. In addition, the entity must provide the Monitor with a monthly report of occurrences related to death or injury of patients, fires, storm damage, flooding or major equipment failures that may pose a threat to patients, strikes or other work actions that could affect patients, and any other incidents that could impact patient care or involves or causes actual harm to a resident.[113]

With respect to healthcare providers that complete Medicare cost reports, Medicare generally recognizes that the costs associated with the operations of an organization's voluntarily adopted corporate compliance program are allowable costs. Therefore, these entities may include these expenses on their cost reports for which they will receive reimbursement. When an entity is subject to a CIA, however, the costs associated with an organization's efforts to comply with the CIA generally are not recognized as "allowable costs" and, therefore, are not reimbursable.[114]

---

[113] *Id.*

[114] However, to the extent a healthcare provider can demonstrate that certain aspects and costs of their entity's corporate compliance program were incurred prior to the effective date of the CIA, it may be able to negotiate that a certain portion of the costs of maintaining the compliance program and ensuring compliance with the CIAs requirements should, in fact, continue to be recognized as allowable.

One of the OIG's priorities is to ensure that entities conform to their CIA obligations.[115] To this end, it is not surprising that CIAs include significant penalties if a provider is found to have not satisfied its CIA obligations. CIAs include stipulated penalties (between a few hundred dollars to a few thousand dollars) for each day the entity has failed to perform specific tasks (e.g., not maintaining a compliance officer, failing to meet the annual report deadlines, not retaining an IRO). In addition, CIAs provide that an entity will be subject to exclusion for failing to satisfy the general requirements and obligations of the CIA (e.g., failing to report a material deficiency or failing to retain an IRO). Although CIAs generally provide that entities found to have committed a material breach of their CIA obligations will receive a notice to this effect and be given an opportunity to cure, the OIG also tries to include provisions in the CIAs limiting the ability of the healthcare entity to be able to seek judicial review of such a determination.

On December 7, 2005, the OIG for the first time formally proposed to exclude a facility from participating in government healthcare programs for failing to meet the terms of a CIA. In a written statement to South Shore Hospital and Medical Center in Miami, FL, OIG Chief Counsel Lewis Morris stated that the hospital had failed to submit timely, complete, and accurate implementation reports and annual reports; failed to implement all the IRO requirements of the CIA; and failed to notify the OIG of its acquisition by new owners. The statement also noted that the hospital has "a long history of non-compliance."[116] Ultimately, South Shore Hospital and Medical Center was excluded from federal healthcare program participation in March 2006.[117]

## § 7-9  SELF-REPORTING AND VOLUNTARY DISCLOSURE

For many years, healthcare providers have self-disclosed certain matters to a government agency and/or a government contractor (e.g., a Medicare Carrier or Fiscal Intermediary). In fact, the federal False Claims Act authorizes healthcare providers to report possible violations to the government, with the incentive that civil damages can be reduced from treble to double[118] In addition to

---

[115] See OIG, *FY 2001 Work Plan* 41. In addition, failure to conform to the requirements of a CIA may become an action under the federal False Claims Act (discussed in Chapter 4). *See, e.g.*, United States of America *ex rel.* McCarthy v. Straub Clinic and Hospital, 140 F.Supp. 2d 1062 (D. Haw. 2001).

[116] OIG Press Release, *OIG Proposes to Exclude Miami Hospital from Participation in Federal Healthcare Programs* (Dec. 7, 2005), *available online at* http://oig.hhs.gov/publications/docs/press/2005/120705release.pdf.

[117] *See OIG Excludes Miami Hospital from Participation in Federal Healthcare Programs* (Mar. 10, 2006), *available online at* http://www.oig.hhs.gov/publications/docs/press/2006/South%20Beach%20final.pdf.

[118] 31 U.S.C. § 3729(a).

reducing civil damages, as administered by the DOJ, the voluntary-disclosure provisions of the statute provide numerous incentives to self-disclose. For example, a self-disclosing healthcare provider can reasonably expect that a prosecutor will not pursue a criminal action against that provider when there is full cooperation, appropriate action with personnel, and appropriate steps to prevent future occurrences. Similarly, it is highly unlikely that the government will take adverse administrative action (specifically, exclusion from federal healthcare programs) when a provider self-discloses. Also, under the voluntary disclosure program, the government usually does not issue subpoenas, and the disclosing party can conduct its own investigation.

## § 7-9(a)　OIG Voluntary Self-Disclosure Protocol

The OIG has attempted to further encourage healthcare providers to self-report improprieties directly to the OIG. In fact, the OIG has stated that the best evidence that a provider's compliance program is operating effectively is when the provider "identifies problematic conduct, takes appropriate steps to remedy the conduct and prevent it from recurring, and makes a full and timely disclosure of the misconduct to appropriate authorities."[119] Therefore, in the OIG Compliance Program Guidances for various industries, the OIG provides that evidence of an effective compliance program requires prompt reporting to the applicable government agency.

In 1995, under the auspices of Operation Restore Trust, the OIG and DOJ developed the pilot Voluntary Disclosure Program by which healthcare providers in five states (Texas, New York, Florida, California, and Illinois) operating in four healthcare industries (home health, hospice, durable medical equipment, and nursing home) could voluntarily disclose instances of potential fraud and abuse that may have given rise to corporate liability.[120] Although the pilot Voluntary Disclosure Program ended in 1997 with very limited participation by healthcare providers, it provided the OIG with "valuable insight into the variables influencing the decision to make a disclosure to the Government," and influenced the development of the Provider Self-Disclosure Protocol (Protocol), which was unveiled by the OIG in 1998.[121]

In contrast to the pilot Voluntary Disclosure Program, the Protocol is open to all types of healthcare providers, and does not include the limitations that had been part of the pilot program. For example, the Protocol does not

---

[119] OIG, *An Open Letter to Healthcare Providers* (Nov. 20, 2001), *available online at* http://www.oig.hhs.gov/compliance/open-letters/index.asp.
[120] *OIG Fact Sheet: Operation Restore Trust Accomplishments* (May 20, 1997), *available online at* http://oig.hhs.gov/oas/reports/region4/49602121.pdf.
[121] *See* 63 Fed. Reg. 58,399 (Oct. 30, 1998).

include limitations on who may participate in the self-disclosure process in that corporate entities and individual providers alike can participate, as well as providers and suppliers who may already be subject to a government inquiry. The Protocol also does not include specific timeframes upon which a disclosure must be made.[122]

The Protocol describes the standards and type of information the OIG expects to be included. First, the healthcare provider must submit "basic information" to the OIG, such as the name, address, and provider/supplier number. This initial disclosure also should include a description of the matter by specifying the type of claim or conduct at issue, naming the individuals and/or entities involved, indicating whether the disclosing party has knowledge that the matter is currently under investigation, and explaining why the disclosing party believes that a violation of federal law has occurred. The submission also must include a certification by the disclosing party (or, in the case of an entity, a representative of the healthcare entity) that to the best of that individual's knowledge, the information contained in the submission is truthful and was made in a good-faith effort to assist the OIG in its inquiry.[123]

As part of the disclosure process, the disclosing party will need to conduct an internal investigation and submit a report based on the results of the investigation. However, the internal review may occur after the initial disclosure of the matter and the OIG will generally agree, for a reasonable time, "to forego an investigation of the matter if the provider agrees that it will conduct the review in accordance with [the Protocol]."[124] The two principal sections of the disclosing party's report are to address (1) the "nature and extent" of the matter and (2) the process by which the matter was discovered and responded to by the disclosing party. As part of the report, the disclosing party must estimate the monetary impact of the disclosed matter, and must either review all of the claims affected during the relevant time period or prepare a statistically valid sample of the claims that can be projected to all of the claims affected.[125] The Protocol contains detailed guidance relating to developing the self-assessment workplan, including sampling requirements relating to sample elements, sample size, confidence levels, random numbering, and the like.

---

[122] Although the Protocol does not include specific timeframes upon which the provider is to disclose, other OIG documents provide specific timeframes for making such disclosures. The OIG sets forth in various of the Corporate Compliance Guidances to particular industries that the entity should report "credible evidence of misconduct . . . within a reasonable period, but not more than 60 days after determining that there is credible evidence of a violation." *See, e.g.*, OIG Supplemental Compliance Program Guidance for Hospitals, 70 Fed. Reg. 4,858, 4,876 (Jan. 21, 2005).

[123] 63 Fed. Reg. at 58,403.

[124] *Id.* at 58,401.

[125] The determination of whether to conduct a complete 100% claims review or a sample is based on the following: the implicated population size, the variance of characteristics to be reviewed, the cost of the self-assessment, available resources, and the estimated duration of the review. *Id.* at 58,402.

## Compliance and Self-Reporting

After receiving the disclosure submission, the OIG will begin to verify the information included in the submission, with the extent of the OIG's verification process being "depend[ent], in large part, upon the quality and thoroughness of the internal investigative and self-assessment reports."[126] Any new information discovered during this process may be treated as a new matter apart from the protocol and disclosure made. During this process, the OIG will not accept any payments pertaining to the disclosed matter, and the disclosing party should not attempt to refund any payments to any of the government's contractors without the OIG's prior consent.

No matter how cooperative and honest a party is throughout the disclosure process, however, the OIG does not guarantee that the provider will be protected against civil or criminal liability. Therefore, there are a number of risks to self-reporting these types of matters. For example, as a result of the internal investigation, an employee may learn about the matter and become a qui tam relator. Moreover, a less than full disclosure based on inadequate facts may be worse than no disclosure at all, thus impairing the healthcare provider's credibility and increasing the likelihood of suspicion.

In addition, a risk exists that all materials developed as part of the disclosing party's internal investigation and government disclosure may no longer be privileged documents. Although the OIG states that it is "prepared to discuss with provider's counsel ways to gain access to the underlying information without the need to waive the protections provided by an appropriately asserted claim of privilege,"[127] the DOJ has not been as understanding. The DOJ has instructed its prosecutors that one of the considerations to weigh when evaluating whether an organization has "cooperated" with the government is "the completeness of [the organization's] disclosure, including, if necessary, a waiver of the attorney-client and work product protections."[128] Although the DOJ maintains that it does not *require* a waiver of the attorney/client privilege to prove cooperation, more prosecutors are demanding waivers. (*See* § 9-4, *infra*.)

Even when counsel to a healthcare provider believes that the risks to disclosure outweigh the benefits, another factor comes into play. Section 307 of the SOA places affirmative reporting responsibilities on a corporation's attorney. In certain circumstances, the SOA requires counsel to report material failures of legal compliance to the highest levels of corporate authority, and permits disclosure to third parties to prevent substantial injury to the corporation or investors. The SOA converts counsel into a reporting instrument where counsel has traditionally been deployed to carry on privileged and work-product investigations to determine how to advise the healthcare organization.

---

[126] *Id.* at 58,403.
[127] *Id.*
[128] Thompson Memorandum.

Nevertheless, there are a number of benefits to voluntarily reporting these matters to the OIG. Based on the government's history of handling self-disclosure cases, it is unlikely that the government will institute a criminal proceeding against the self-disclosing party. As discussed, however, even if the criminal action is pursued, the Sentencing Guidelines provide relief from substantial fines to those who voluntarily disclose. Voluntary disclosure allows the healthcare provider to control the time, place, and manner of disclosure (including being able to control public exposure), thus minimizing the cost and disruption of a formal investigation. Although there is always a risk that an employee could bring a qui tam action as a result of the internal investigation, it is also possible that by voluntarily disclosing the matter to the government, the disclosing party may preempt an employee from initiating a qui tam action. Another benefit is that the healthcare provider may gain credibility with the government at an early stage; to this end, the government has acknowledged that it will attempt to provide the disclosing party with affirmative "credit" by reducing fines and penalties and possibly avoiding exclusion from the Medicare and/or Medicaid programs by cooperating with the government. Finally, as stated, to the extent the healthcare provider can demonstrate that it has established an effective corporate compliance program, it may be able to avoid the imposition of a CIA. For the previous six month reporting period ending September 30, 2011, the OIG reported that self-disclosure cases resulted in $8.4 million in DHHS receivables.[129]

In April 2006, Inspector General Daniel Levinson issued an open letter to healthcare providers, in which he encouraged the use of the Protocol to resolve potential CMP liability under the Stark Law and Anti-Kickback Statute.[130] The open letter states that the OIG is

> seeking to increase awareness in the hospital and physician communities of a way to resolve conduct that may result in liability under the OIG's CMP authorities for physician self-referral and anti-kickback violations. This new initiative supplements the [Protocol] by providing guidance on how these types of disclosures will be resolved. The initiative incorporates the SDP process, whereby OIG confers with the Department of Justice (DOJ) to ensure that it is aware of each disclosure and has an opportunity to opine before OIG accepts a provider into the Protocol and is presented with the results of OIG's review of the [Protocol] matter before it is resolved under OIG's CMP authorities.[131]

---

[129] OIG, Semiannual Report, (2011), *available online at* http://oig.hhs.gov/reports-and-publications/archives/semiannual/2011/fall/HHS-OIG-SAR-Fall2011.pdf.

[130] OIG, Open Letter to Healthcare Providers (Apr. 24, 2006), *available online at* http://oig.hhs.gov/compliance/open-letters/index.asp.

[131] *Id.*

## Compliance and Self-Reporting

The open letter, however, limits its applicability to only CMPs, as the OIG notes that it is not in a position to bind either CMS or DOJ. Moreover, the OIG states that a provider's participation in the Protocol will be contingent on "full cooperation and complete disclosure of the facts and circumstances surrounding the violation."

On April 15, 2008, Inspector General Daniel Levinson wrote an open letter to healthcare providers in order to clarify certain OIG policies in an effort to increase the efficiency of the self-disclosure protocol (SDP).[132] In order to improve the self-disclosure process, the 2008 Open Letter provided that along with the basic information requested in the SDP, the initial submission must contain a complete description of the conduct being disclosed, a description of the provider's internal investigation or a commitment regarding when it will be completed, an estimate of the damages to the Federal healthcare programs along with the methodology used in reaching that estimate and a statement of the laws that have been potentially violated.

As stated in the previous Open Letter, the 2008 Open Letter sets forth that providers will be removed from participation in the SDP *unless* they disclose in good faith *potential fraud* (not merely overpayment) and respond in a timely fashion to any requests from the OIG. The 2008 Open Letter further provides that a ". . . provider's submission of a complete and informative disclosure, quick response to OIG's requests for further information, and performance of an accurate audit are indications that the provider has adopted effective compliance measures."[133] The OIG also explained that when negotiating the resolution of applicable administrative monetary and permissive exclusion authorities in exchange for the appropriate monetary payment, a CIA may not be required.[134]

Although the 2008 Open Letter sets forth how the OIG has "streamlined" its internal process for dealing with cases such as these in an attempt to encourage cooperative self-disclosure, there are some limitations of the SDP. For example, the requirement that the investigation and damage assessment be done within three months may prove difficult to accomplish.

However, in 2009, Inspector General Daniel Levinson wrote an open letter to healthcare providers that specified that OIG will no longer accept self-disclosure of matters that only involve liability under the physician self-referral law, which is commonly referred to as the Stark law. As explained in the letter, OIG has committed to a refined aim of focusing their resources on kickbacks intended to induce or reward physician referrals. The letter notes that, while the OIG is narrowing the scope of the SDP, they "urge providers not to draw any inferences about the Government's approach to enforcement

---

[132] OIG, *An Open Letter to Healthcare Providers* (Apr. 15, 2008), *available online at* http://oig.hhs.gov/compliance/open-letters/index.asp.
[133] *Id.*
[134] *Id.*

of the physician self-referral law."[135] Although the OIG announced in 2009 that it would no longer accept disclosures related solely to Stark law violations, it was not until the passage of the Health Reform Law that DHHS was required to develop a self-disclosure protocol for matters related solely to the Stark law (*see* § 7-9(b)).

In addition to the OIG's Protocol, in 2008, the Department of Defense issued a final rule on the Contractor Business Ethics Compliance Program and its disclosure requirements. As the Federal Acquisition Regulation (FAR) applies to all government contractors and subcontractors, it will affect the healthcare industry and create additional self-disclosure requirements for many healthcare entities including pharmaceutical and device companies and insurance companies involved in federal sales. Specifically, the FAR requires that, effective December 12, 2008, government contractors must implement a new mandatory disclosure requirement.[136] This disclosure requirement is triggered whenever the entity has "credible evidence" of: (i) "significant overpayment" from the government; (ii) certain criminal violations involving fraud; or (iii) a violation of the False Claims Act.[137] In the preamble to the final rule, the Civilian Acquisition Council and the Defense Acquisition Council noted that the "credible evidence" standard allows contractors to "take some time for preliminary examination of the evidence to determine its credibility before deciding to disclose to the Government."[138]

## § 7-9(b)  CMS Voluntary Self-Referral Disclosure Protocol

Section 6409 of the Health Reform Law requires that the Secretary of DHHS, in cooperation with the OIG, establish a Medicare self-referral disclosure protocol (SRDP) that sets forth a process by which a provider or supplier may self-disclose potential or actual violations of the Stark Law.[139] Under Section 6409, the amounts owed may be reduced based on:

- the nature and extent of the improper or illegal practice.
- the timeliness of such self-disclosure.
- the cooperation in providing additional information related to the disclosure.

---

[135] http://oig.hhs.gov/fraud/docs/openletters/OpenLetter3-24-09.pdf.
[136] Federal Acquisition Regulation, 73 Fed. Reg. 67,064 (Nov. 12, 2008) (codified at 48 CFR pt. 2, 3, 9, 42 & 52).
[137] 73 Fed. Reg. 67,064, 67,090 (Nov. 12, 2008); codified at 48 CFR 3.1002.
[138] 73 Fed. Reg. 67,064, 67,073 (Nov. 12, 2008)
[139] The Health Reform Law, § 6409; 42 U.S.C. 1395nn.

## Compliance and Self-Reporting

- such other factors that the Secretary considers appropriate.[140] CMS has included in the SRDP the following additional factors that CMS may consider in reducing the amounts owed: (1) the litigation risk associated with the matter disclosed and (2) the financial position of the disclosing party.[141]

Similar to the OIG Protocol, the SRDP requires a written submission describing the actual or potential violations of law. The written submission must contain two main components and be accompanied by a certification signed by the Chief Executive Officer, Chief Financial Officer, or other authorized representative, attesting to the veracity of the information contained in the disclosure and that the disclosure is based on a good faith effort to bring the matter to CMS' attention for the purpose of resolving the disclosed potential liabilities. The two main components of the disclosure are the description of the actual or potential violation and the financial analysis.

Notably, under the description of the actual or potential violation, in addition to the provider or supplier's basic information, the provider or supplier must include a description of the matter being disclosed, including the types of financial relationships and the specific period of non-compliance. The written submission must identify the type of designated health services that are at issue and the type of transaction or conduct that gave rise the actual or potential violation. In addition, CMS requires that the written submission include the names of the entities and individuals involved. The SRDP also requires a complete legal analysis, including a detailed discussion of any applicable Stark Law exceptions and a description of pre-existing compliance programs and efforts taken to prevent the conduct from reoccurring. As opposed to the OIG Protocol, the conduct or non-compliance must be rectified before submitting a disclosure to CMS.

As part of the initial disclosure under the SRDP the disclosing party must conduct a financial analysis. According to the SRDP, the financial analysis should:

- set forth the total amount, itemized by year, that is actually or potentially due and owing based upon the applicable "look back" period (i.e., the period of non-compliance).
- describe the methodology used to determine the amount owing. If estimates were used, the written submission should include an explanation for how estimates were calculated.
- set forth the total amount of remuneration a physician received based upon the applicable "look back" period.

---

[140] *Id.*
[141] CMS Voluntary Self-Referral Disclosure Protocol, OMB Control Number: 0938-1106, *available online at* https://www.cms.gov/PhysicianSelfReferral/Downloads/6409_SRDP_Protocol.pdf.

- provide a summary of any auditing activity undertaken and a summary of documents the disclosing part has relied upon.

The written submission must be submitted electronically and in writing to CMS. Once the disclosing provider or supplier submits the disclosure electronically, CMS will immediately send an acknowledgment email. This acknowledgment email will confirm that the obligation under section 6402 of the Health Reform Law to return any potential overpayment within 60 days will be suspended until a settlement is entered, the provider or supplier withdraws from the SRDP, or CMS removes the provider or supplier from the SRDP.[142]

Upon receiving the written submission, CMS will begin its verification process. The SRDP states

[t]o facilitate CMS' verification and validation process, CMS must have access to all financial statements, notes, disclosures, and other supporting documents without the assertion of privileges or limitations on the information produced. In the normal course of verification, CMS will not request production of written communications subject to the attorney-client privilege. However, there may be documents or materials, which CMS believes are critical to resolving the disclosure that may be covered by the work product doctrine CMS is prepared to discuss with disclosing party's counsel ways to gain access to the underlying information without waiver of protections provided by an appropriately asserted claim of privilege.[143]

As of the end of 2011, CMS has issued three settlements under the SRDP. On February 10, 2011, CMS entered into a settlement with a general acute care hospital located in Massachusetts. According to the CMS SRDP Settlement website, the hospital disclosed through the SRDP that it had violated the Stark Law by "(1) failing to satisfy the requirements of the personal services arrangements exception for arrangements with certain hospital department chiefs and the medical staff for leadership services, and (2) failing to satisfy the requirements of the personal services arrangements exception for arrangements with certain physician groups for on-site overnight coverage for patients at the hospital."[144] CMS settled the disclosed violations for $579,000.00. On September 10, 2011, CMS entered into a settlement under the SRDP for $60,000 to resolve violations with a physician group practice. The practice disclosed that it had violated the Stark law by prescribing and supplying a certain type of DME that did not meet the in-office ancillary

---

[142] *Id.*
[143] *Id.*
[144] https://www.cms.gov/PhysicianSelfReferral/DPS/itemdetail.asp?filterType=none&filterByDID=-99&sortByDID=1&sortOrder=ascending&itemID=CMS1249488&intNumPerPage=10.

## Compliance and Self-Reporting

exception.[145] On November 11, 2011, CMS entered into its second settlement under the SRDP for the amount of $130,000.00. This settlement resolves violations disclosed by a critical access hospital in Mississippi. Under the SRDP, the hospital had disclosed that it failed to satisfy the requirements under the personal services exception for arrangements with certain hospital and emergency room physicians.[146]

### § 7-9(c)    State Voluntary Self-Disclosure Processes

In addition to the OIG and CMS self-disclosure protocols, some states are now developing their own provider self-ing guidelines. For example, the New York OMIG requires that overpayments be self-disclosed.[147] In a 2010 Compliance Alert, NY-OMIG identifies the potential benefits of self-disclosure as being:

- forgiveness or reduction of interest payments (for up to two years);
- extended repayment terms;
- waiver of penalties and/or sanctions;
- timely resolution of the overpayment; and
- recognition of the effectiveness of the provider's compliance and an increased chance that the NY-OMIG will not implement a CIA.[148]

The NY-OMIG requires specific information be included in a self-disclosure and requires that at a minimum the provider include in an initial disclosure, in addition to basic information: (1) the basis for the initial disclosure, including how it was discovered; (2) the time period covered and an assessment of the financial impact; (3) the Medicaid program rules potentially implicated; and (4) any corrective action taken to address the problem. According to NY-OMIG, ultimately the provider should be prepared to present a summary of the identified cause of the issue, a detailed list of claims and the names of individuals involved.[149]

---

[145] https://www.cms.gov/Medicare/Fraud-and-Abuse/PhysicianSelfReferral/SelfReferral-Disclosure-Protocol-Settlements-Items/091011-Settlement.html.

[146] https://www.cms.gov/PhysicianSelfReferral/DPS/itemdetail.asp?filterType=none&filterByDID=-99&sortByDID=1&sortOrder=ascending&itemID=CMS1254832&intNumPerPage=10.

[147] *See also* Texas Office of Inspector General, Provider Self-Reporting Guidelines, *available online at* https://oig.hhsc.state.tx.us/providerselfreporting/self_reporting.aspx.

[148] http://www.omig.ny.gov/data/images/stories/compliance_alerts/compliance_alert_2010-03_12-01-10.pdf. The NY-OMIG website contains a list of CIAs that have been entered into with NY-OMIG. See http://www.omig.ny.gov/data/content/view/171/248/.

[149] http://www.omig.ny.gov/data/images/stories/self_disclosure/omig_provider_self_disclosure_guidance.pdf.

# 8
# Fraud and Abuse Issues Affecting the Managed Care Industry

## § 8-1  OVERVIEW

In response to rising healthcare costs, the managed care industry has experienced tremendous growth since its inception in the mid-1970s. In 1988, the percentage of Americans receiving health insurance through their employers and who were enrolled in some type of managed care organization (MCO) was 27%; by 2010, the percentage of Americans covered under a MCO had increased to 99%.[1] The term MCO is used in this chapter to refer to all types of MCOs, which include health maintenance organizations (HMOs), preferred provider organizations (PPOs), and point-of-service plans (POSs).

Some of this enrollment growth can be attributed to initiatives by federal and state governments to promote managed care to the Medicare and Medicaid populations. For example, in 1982, as part of the Tax Equity and Fiscal Responsibility Act, Congress established the first iteration of Medicare managed care by establishing a process by which Medicare would contract with so-called "risk contractors" and "cost contractors" to provide Medicare-covered services to Medicare beneficiaries under various payment arrangements.[2] Later, as part of the Balanced Budget Act of 1997 (BBA 97), Congress established Part C of the Medicare program in an attempt to provide Medicare beneficiaries with more choices in the types of managed care products in which they could enroll.[3] (At the time, these MCOs contracting with Medicare under Part C were referred to as "Medicare+Choice" organizations.) In order to further promote Medicare enrollment in MCOs, the Medicare Prescription

---

[1] Kaiser Family Foundation, 2010 Employer Benefits Survey, Table 5.1, *available online at* http://ehbs.kff.org/.
[2] Tax Equity and Fiscal Responsibility Act of 1982, Pub. L. No. 97-248, 96 Stat. 324 (*codified as amended at* 42 U.S.C. § 1395mm). As to risk contractors, this legislation limited health-plan eligibility to federally qualified HMOs and competitive medical plans (which generally referred to risk-bearing organizations that are not federally qualified and for which a state license usually is required).
[3] Balanced Budget Act of 1997, Pub. Law No. 105-33, 111 Stat. 329 (*codified as amended at* 42 U.S.C. § 1395w-21 *et seq.*).

Drug Improvement and Modernization Act of 2003 (MMA) expanded the MCO options and increased the payment rates to Medicare+Choice organizations (which were renamed Medicare Advantage plans). The MMA also established Part D of the Medicare program to provide Medicare beneficiaries with the opportunity to enroll in prescription drug plans (PDPs).[4]

On the Medicaid side, states are increasingly seeking federal waivers to furnish Medicaid benefits through MCOs in an attempt to manage costs. The number of Medicaid recipients receiving Medicaid services through Managed Care Entities (MCEs), as they are known in the Medicaid program, has grown substantially in recent years. As of June 2009, 36 million Medicaid beneficiaries, or 72%, were enrolled in Managed Care.[5] Indeed, Medicare and Medicaid managed care is expected to continue to grow as a proportion of federal healthcare program expenditures as baby boomers, who are accustomed to receiving healthcare benefits through MCOs, reach the age of Medicare eligibility and as states seek ways to manage the costs associated with the population newly eligible for expanded Medicaid benefits under health reform.

Although managed care establishes disincentives for healthcare providers to participate in traditional forms of healthcare fraud (i.e., the structure of managed care discourages ordering and billing for medically unnecessary services), the increased role of managed care in the federal healthcare programs has not necessarily resulted in a decrease in fraud committed by healthcare contractors. Instead, the shift from traditional fee-for-service provision of healthcare to managed care has changed the scope of activities in which contractors can engage, as well as the theories under which fraud actions may be brought.

Nevertheless, fighting healthcare fraud in the managed care industry can be more challenging as the theories underlying these actions are both subtle and complicated. As James Sheehan, then an Assistant United States Attorney in Philadelphia, PA, and later head of New York's Office of the Medicaid Inspector General (NY-OMIG) described the complexity of detecting fraud and abuse in managed care:

> Investigating fraud in the managed care setting is more difficult than in the fee-for-service setting because fraudulent activity in the managed care environment is extremely subtle. . . . In the managed care setting, fraud comes in a variety of different, more subtle forms including; denying appropriate care; providing inadequate treatment; establishing barriers to treatment such as inconvenient locations and

---

[4] Medicare Prescription Drug Improvement and Modernization Act of 2003, Pub. Law No. 108-173, 117 Stat. 2066 (*codified as amended at* 42 U.S.C. § 1395w-101 *et seq.*). In this chapter, the term PDP is used to refer to all Medicare plan sponsors that provide a prescription drug benefit (i.e., both stand-alone prescription drug plans and Medicare Advantage plans that offer Part D benefits).

[5] CMS, Medicaid Managed Care Enrollment as of (June 30, 2009), http://www.cms.gov.

## Fraud and Abuse Issues Affecting the Managed Care Industry

appointment hours, long waiting times, and specialist unavailability; inflating reporting of numbers of patients treated and treatment costs in order to increase future per-patient fixed fees; threatening or inducing utilization review agents to reduce utilization; paying fiduciaries to reduce utilization; selecting and retaining certain less qualified providers; and falsifying quality of care and treatment-outcome data.[6]

Law enforcement officials concede that tracking managed care fraud can be more difficult than in the fee-for-service industry. Managed care plans generally do not submit claims for reimbursement; therefore, as one observer noted, "there isn't much of a paper trail, meaning investigators must rely heavily on whistleblowers from inside the health plans."[7] Moreover, most MCOs view their top priority as similar to the government's in combating provider fraud and abuse within their health plans. Thus, managed care fraud is typically thought to be fraud by providers *against* MCOs, and not fraud *by* MCOs against the government. Toward that end, MCOs have expended resources in creating internal Fraud Units, and working with the government to reduce provider fraud. Not surprisingly, a December 2011 OIG report on Medicaid Managed Care Fraud[8], which sought, in part, to determine what major concerns MCEs and States have regarding fraud and abuse in Medicaid managed care, found that the major concern related to services billed by providers but not rendered.

As a result, the government has developed cooperative initiatives among various agencies in order to better understand and address fraud within the managed care industry. For example, as far back as the 1990s, the Department of Justice (DOJ) organized the Managed Care Fraud Working Group, which coordinates the managed care enforcement activities of DOJ, the Federal Bureau of Investigations (FBI), the Department of Health and Human Services (DHHS), and the National Association of Attorneys General.[9]

This chapter addresses not only the underlying laws that specifically address fraud and abuse in the managed care industry, but also the developing legal theories upon which government enforcers and private parties are bringing legal actions against Medicare and Medicaid MCOs.

---

[6] James G. Sheehan, *Quality and Necessity: Investigation and Prosecution of HMOs and Providers Care for Denial of Service, in* HEALTHCARE FRAUD (Am. Bar Ass'n & Nat'l Ass'n of Medicaid Fraud Control Units, 1998) (on file with authors).

[7] Laurie McGinley, *U.S. Takes Aim at HMO Fraud in Medicare and Medicaid*, WALL ST. J., (Oct. 19, 1998), at A28.

[8] Medicaid Managed Care: Fraud and Abuse Concerns Remain Despite Safeguards, OEI-01-09-00550, (Dec. 2011).

[9] *See* DEP'T OF JUSTICE, CRIMINAL RESOURCE MANUAL: 978 GUIDELINES FOR IMPLEMENTATION OF THE HEALTHCARE FRAUD AND ABUSE CONTROL PROGRAM, 2 (last updated Apr. 1998), *available online at*. http://www.justice.gov/usao/eousa/foia_reading_room/usam/title9/crm00978.htm.

## § 8-2  MANAGED CARE AND THE ANTI-KICKBACK STATUTE

As set forth in greater detail in Chapter 2, the Anti-Kickback Statute provides criminal penalties for individuals and entities that knowingly and willfully offer, pay, solicit or receive remuneration "in return for purchasing, leasing, ordering, or *arranging for or recommending* purchasing, leasing or ordering any good, facility, service, or item for which payment may be made in whole or in part under a Federal healthcare program. . . ."[10]

Contrary to the conventional view that the Anti-Kickback Statute is aimed exclusively at overutilization and does not apply to managed care arrangements, the plain language of the statute is sufficiently broad to extend to managed care arrangements. Moreover, nothing in the language of the Anti-Kickback Statute excludes its application to managed care. Although the essence of managed care is to establish financial incentives that encourage medically appropriate and cost-effective utilization of healthcare services at both the beneficiary and provider levels, those incentives may still be susceptible to illegal kickbacks. Kickbacks are most recognizable in the fee-for-service system; nevertheless, the overarching purpose of the Anti-Kickback Statute (beyond combating overutilization) is to remove the corrupting influence of financial considerations from the medical decision-making process.

The Anti-Kickback Statute proscribes illegal remuneration with respect to services that a federal healthcare program covers "in whole or in part." Consequently, even in the cases of health plans that do not market directly to the Medicare population, employer-group health plans inevitably include individuals who are eligible for Medicare coverage by virtue of being working aged or disabled, or having end-stage renal disease (ESRD). Similarly, retirees may have primary Medicare coverage, yet remain on the employer-group health plan to retain "gap" coverage. Furthermore, employer-group health plans cannot simply "carve-out" such federal healthcare program enrollees from the incentives offered to avoid the reach of Anti-Kickback Statute. Employer-group health plans are required under Medicare to offer "the same benefit" plan to all enrollees, regardless of their eligibility for participation in the Medicare program.[11] Therefore, even if a managed care plan does not have products *specifically* tailored and marketed to the Medicare or Medicaid population, the Anti-Kickback Statute potentially still could be implicated.

---

[10] 42 U.S.C. § 1320a-7b(b) (emphasis added).
[11] Social Security Act § 1862(b)(1)(A); 42 U.S.C. § 1395y(b)(1)(A).

# Fraud and Abuse Issues Affecting the Managed Care Industry

## § 8-2(a) The Managed Care Safe Harbors

In November 1992, the OIG published a set of safe-harbor regulations that protected certain limited managed care activities from the reach of the Anti-Kickback Statute.[12] Although the regulation was published as an "interim final" rule, the public was permitted to submit post-publication comments. In January 1996, the OIG issued a revised version of these safe harbors in "final" form.[13]

The managed care safe-harbor regulations address three specific areas relevant to managed care activities: (i) incentives offered to beneficiaries, such as the waiver or reduction of applicable coinsurance and deductible amounts to encourage the use of the preferred provider network; (ii) provider discounts to MCOs; and (iii) waivers of inpatient coinsurance and deductible amounts by Medicare SELECT PPOs.[14]

The managed care safe harbors confirm that typical managed care arrangements (e.g., provider discounts and beneficiary incentives to use in-network providers) fall within the realm of anti-kickback scrutiny, and may place their participants—managed care entities and their participating providers alike—at some legal risk of anti-kickback liability. In fact, the OIG makes clear in the preamble of the final safe harbors that managed care activities implicate the Anti-Kickback Statute, despite the fact that MCOs are not "providers" who make "referrals." According to the OIG, the Anti-Kickback Statute "covers recommendations on which providers to use, and would include the preferred or approved provider lists of HMOs and PPOs, especially where such providers have agreed to discount their fees in return for such designations."[15] Nevertheless, the final managed care safe-harbor preamble states definitively that "the safe harbors do not create affirmative obligations on individuals or entities since compliance with these safe harbors is purely voluntary."[16]

For purposes of qualifying for both the beneficiary-incentive and price-reduction safe harbors, the managed care entity must meet the safe-harbor definition of the term "health plan." The final safe harbors define "health plan" as a managed care entity that has a formal relationship with the Medicare or Medicaid program, or has its premium structure regulated by a state insurance or enabling statute governing HMOs or PPOs. The final safe harbor expanded the definition to include Employee Retirement Income Security Act (ERISA) plans and other self-funded or self-insured employer or union

---

[12] 57 Fed. Reg. 52,723 (Nov. 5, 1992).
[13] 61 Fed. Reg. 2,122 (Jan. 25, 1996). These final regulations were effective upon publication.
[14] 42 C.F.R. §§ 1001.952(k)–(m) (2011).
[15] 61 Fed. Reg. 2,124 (1996).
[16] *Id.* This was a decided shift in tone from the OIG's proposed safe-harbor clarification issuance that had immediately preceded this release, which appeared to require discounts to meet the discount safe harbor.

plans that contract directly with healthcare providers or insurance companies, as well as entities (e.g., PPOs) that act as intermediaries between contract healthcare providers and employers, union welfare funds, or insurance companies. Moreover, the OIG broadened the definition of a health plan so that an entity that furnishes or arranges for the furnishing of items and services to enrollees in exchange for a "fee" as well as for a "premium" can meet the definition of a "health plan."[17]

Despite this expanded definition, health plans still must meet other safe-harbor criteria to qualify for that protection. As will be described, the safe-harbor criteria differentiate substantially between Medicare- and Medicaid-contracting health plans and all other health plans, placing far fewer requirements on the contracting health plans. As a result, health plans have greater protection from anti-kickback liability for their Medicare and Medicaid products than for their commercial products that may only incidentally cover Medicare and Medicaid eligibles. Nevertheless, one former OIG Chief Counsel stated that if a plan has minimal Medicare and Medicaid business, then the risk of enforcement under the Anti-Kickback Statute may be minimal:

> [T]hose of you who have plans with only small or incidental Medicare or Medicaid business really should not lose sleep over the fact that you're not in a safe harbor, because one of the main determinants of OIG interest is amount of Medicare and Medicaid business. So if you have no direct contact with the programs, but you have some enrollees who are say in an employer plan with Medicare primary or secondary, and only a few of those, I wouldn't worry about it too much.[18]

### § 8-2(a)(1)    Beneficiary Incentives

MCOs frequently rely on coinsurance differentials and other financial incentives to encourage beneficiaries to use their preferred provider network. Unlike HMOs (which can rely on their capacity to "lock in" their enrollees to use network providers), PPOs and POSs typically allow patients the flexibility to choose out-of-network providers, but reduce all or a portion of patients' coinsurance obligations to encourage patients to use cost-effective network providers. MCOs also may use other beneficiary incentives, such as furnishing additional coverage or reducing premium amounts.

The safe harbor for health plans that offer beneficiary incentives (e.g., differentials in coinsurance and deductible amounts) applies only to

---

[17] 42 C.F.R. § 1001.952(l)(2) (2011).
[18] D. McCarty Thornton, Chief Counsel to the Inspector General, Address to the Group Health Association of America (June 14, 1993) (on file with authors).

Medicare- and Medicaid-contracting health plans. Thus, the safe harbor provides no protection for commercial managed care plans that furnish coverage to Medicare eligibles in an employer-group health plan and use beneficiary incentives to encourage provider-network use. Specifically, in the "interim final" regulation, the OIG protected coinsurance differentials only for those health plans that have a formal contractual relationship with the Centers for Medicare & Medicaid Services (CMS) or a state healthcare program. Nevertheless, the OIG requested public comment on whether safe-harbor protection for beneficiary incentives should be afforded to health plans without formal Medicare and Medicaid contracts. The preamble to the "interim final" regulation stated:

> An example of some of the incentives we are not protecting is an agreement between a PPO and a contract healthcare provider whereby that provider agrees not to charge the health plan or enrollee all or part of the coinsurance and deductible amounts. When the contract provider bills the program directly (and not the health plan) and agrees to waive all coinsurance and deductibles, the agreement typically is characterized as an agreement to 'accept Medicare payment as payment in full.' Although such waiver programs may be offered in conjunction with a package of healthcare benefits and thus have some features similar to the other waiver programs we are protecting in this safe harbor provision, we are not convinced that the Medicare and Medicaid programs are properly protected against overutilization. As discussed above, when a health plan under contract with [CMS] or a State healthcare program waives cost-sharing amounts, utilization and costs are controlled or monitored. This is not necessarily the case with HMOs and PPOs or their providers that bill the Medicare and Medicaid programs on a fee-for-service basis.[19]

The OIG's final safe harbor similarly declined to extend protection beyond contracting health plans. Instead, the OIG continued to voice concern that fee-for-service payment "makes these situations subject to the same potential abuses and risks as exist with incentives offered by non-managed care plans or providers. . . ."[20] The preamble to the final regulations states:

> [W]here managed care providers agree to accept Medicare payment as payment in full, the burden of the reduced cost sharing incentives offered to beneficiaries comes at the expense of the Medicare program, because the program will end up paying 100 percent of the provider's fee . . . . In the case of contract plans, the reimbursement formulae take into account the cost sharing obligations of beneficiaries that the

---

[19] 57 Fed. Reg. 52,726 (1992).
[20] 61 Fed. Reg. at 2,130 (1996).

Medicare or Medicaid programs may require, so there is no problem with illegal waivers of coinsurance or deductibles.[21]

Thus, the OIG apparently equated managed care coinsurance differentials designed to encourage beneficiary use of the cost-efficient provider network with a provider's waiver of coinsurance, and will only permit such waivers by Medicare- or Medicaid-contracting health plans and (as will be described) for certain providers in connection with Medicare SELECT plans.

## § 8-2(a)(2)    Price Reductions to Group Health Plans

These safe harbors also protect price reductions that providers offer to MCOs under certain circumstances. Unlike the beneficiary-incentive safe harbor (which applies only to Medicare- and Medicaid-contracting health plans), the price-reduction safe harbor enables non-contracting health plans to qualify for safe-harbor protection, albeit based on different criteria.

Every health plan must have a contract between the provider and the health plan, and it must be for the sole purpose of furnishing covered items and services to health-plan enrollees. Thus, contracts for utilization-review or enrollment-screening services would not qualify for safe-harbor protection unless they otherwise meet the previously established safe harbors for employment or personal-services contracts.[22]

In addition, the health plan must meet certain standards, depending on the health plan's relationship with the Medicare and Medicaid programs. The first category of safe-harbor criteria applies to risk-based health plans with formal program contracts. This category imposes the fewest criteria to qualify for safe-harbor protection: Risk contractors merely may not claim payment for items and services furnished in accordance with the agreement (except as approved by the federal or state program), nor may they otherwise shift the burden of the agreement to the extent that increased payments are claimed from Medicare or a state healthcare program.[23]

The second category of safe-harbor protection applies to cost-based health plans with formal program contracts. In addition to the risk-contractor standards, cost-based health-plan contractors also must ensure that:

1. the provider agreement is for at least one year;
2. the provider agreement specifies in advance the covered items and services to be furnished to the enrollees, as well as the methodology for computing the provider's payment; and

---

[21] *Id.*
[22] 42 C.F.R. § 1001.952(m) (2011).
[23] 42 C.F.R. § 1001.952(m)(1)(i) (2011).

## Fraud and Abuse Issues Affecting the Managed Care Industry

3. the health plan reports (on the applicable cost report or other claim form filed with the government) the amount paid to the provider for the covered items and services furnished to enrollees.[24]

A third category of safe-harbor protection is offered for non-contracting health plans that do not pay providers on an at-risk capitated basis. To qualify for safe-harbor protection, these health plans are required to enter into a provider agreement for a term of at least one year. The agreement must specify:

- the covered services;
- which party is to file claims;
- the provider's schedule of fees (which must remain in effect throughout the term of the agreement unless the federal or state program authorizes a payment update); and
- that the party submitting the claim must not claim or request payment for amounts in excess of the fee schedule.

If the provider or health plan files cost reports with Medicare or a state healthcare program, then each party to the agreement must fully and accurately report the fee schedule amounts charged under the agreement and, upon request, report to Medicare or a state healthcare program the terms of the agreement and the amounts paid in accordance with the agreement. Finally, the non-submitting party must not claim program payment or otherwise shift the burden of the agreement such that increased payments are claimed from Medicare or a state healthcare program.[25]

A fourth category of safe-harbor protection was added in the January 1996 final regulation for capitated payments that health plans may make to providers. Its criteria are similar to those applicable to the safe harbor for non-risk providers of non-contracting health plans in that it also requires an agreement for not less than a year, and must specify in advance the covered services and fees that must remain in effect throughout the agreement (although the fee may be expressed in a per-month or other basis, and also must specify copayments). Further, both the provider and health plan must, upon request, report the terms of the agreement and the amounts paid to Medicare and state healthcare programs in accordance with the agreement. Finally, the contract healthcare provider must not claim payment from Medicare, a state healthcare program, or (except for copayment amounts) an enrollee; moreover the health plan must not pay the provider for covered services in excess of the amounts specified in the agreement.[26]

In expanding safe-harbor protection to cover capitated arrangements, the OIG recognized that the amount a provider accepts under a capitated

---

[24] 42 C.F.R. § 1001.952(m)(1)(ii) (2011).
[25] 42 C.F.R. § 1001.952(m)(1)(iii) (2011).
[26] 42 C.F.R. § 1001.952(m)(1)(iv)(E) (2011).

arrangement in exchange for a certain flow of patients may implicate the Anti-Kickback Statute. However, because capitation does not provide an incentive for overutilization, the OIG concluded that safe-harbor protection is warranted.[27] At the same time, the OIG declined to provide specific safe-harbor protection to withholds or risk-incentive pools, or to other types of incentive programs offered by health plans that do not contract with Medicare or Medicaid. The OIG voiced concern that "there are no uniform standards or definitions applicable to each of these different types of mechanisms." According to the OIG:

> [B]ecause these types of payment mechanisms offer additional remuneration to providers that is related to the volume or value of services provided, their use is particularly vulnerable to abuse. They can be used to manipulate provider payment levels and can be used to inappropriately affect the flow of Medicare and Medicaid reimbursable business.[28]

Moreover, the OIG believes that, in some cases, providers subject to a withhold may be submitting false claims to the Medicare and Medicaid programs. The OIG asserts:

> If the provider does not ultimately receive the withheld amount or does not have a reasonable expectation of receiving it, and includes the full amount of the potential fee on the claim form, he or she has misrepresented the amount of his or her fee and stands to be overpaid by the Medicare or Medicaid programs.[29]

Thus, where managed care providers have little likelihood of actually receiving withheld payments and claim their full fee to Medicare or Medicaid, the OIG states that "net effect is the same as an express waiver of coinsurance."[30]

In the final safe-harbor regulation, the OIG also declined to revise the criteria for fee-for-service discounts to health plans. The regulations continue to state that claims to the Medicare program may not be in excess of the provider's fee schedule in order to qualify for safe-harbor protection. Thus, the OIG effectively precluded safe-harbor protection for broker-model PPOs that operate by negotiating discounts with providers and then marking up the fees to the purchaser to defray the PPOs' costs. Further, the OIG declined to protect PPO fees paid by contracting providers based on a percentage of billed charges or revenues to cover the PPOs' marketing services to third-party payors.

---

[27] 61 Fed. Reg. 2,131 (1996).
[28] *Id.* at 2,132.
[29] *Id.*
[30] *Id.*

## Fraud and Abuse Issues Affecting the Managed Care Industry

The OIG stated that "blanket" protection for these types of PPO financial arrangements is not warranted, because arrangements that set fees based on the volume or value of services provided to patients are subject to abuse. Nevertheless, the OIG stated in the preamble that, "by not protecting such payment mechanisms under the safe harbor, we do not prohibit them."[31] Thus, a PPO's intermediary arrangement would need to qualify under a separate safe harbor in order to attain absolute protection from anti-kickback liability. Indeed, the OIG describes several options that PPOs may use to cover administrative or marketing costs that would not implicate the Anti-Kickback Statute. For instance, PPOs may include such costs in the "premiums" (presumably, the fees) charged to insurers or employers where the PPOs administer health plans for such entities, or enter into separate contracts with providers for management services that meet the safe harbor for personal services and management contracts. Presumably, other existing safe harbors also may be relevant. Financial arrangements between PPOs and payors that do not meet any safe harbor will continue to be evaluated on a case-by-case basis.

The managed care safe harbor for price reduction also places considerable oversight obligations on MCOs to ensure that contracting providers meet the safe-harbor standards where safe-harbor protection is sought. To meet the safe harbor, participating-provider contracts must specify whether the provider or health plan will submit Medicare claims, and claims must be submitted in accordance with those contractual provisions. Additionally, Medicare claims cannot be submitted in excess of the provider's fee-schedule amount.

MCOs had objected to being deprived of safe-harbor protection based on the conduct of contracting providers, which the MCO cannot reasonably ensure. They requested safe-harbor protection for the health plan that is similar to that granted to sellers in the discount safe harbor, where the provider does not satisfy the safe-harbor criteria despite instructions from the health plan. According to the OIG, however, it is appropriate to condition safe-harbor protection for the health plan on provider compliance:

> Managed care health plans have an ongoing relationship with contract healthcare providers that includes monitoring and utilization review of the services provided to plan enrollees. This relationship is different from the usual relationship between buyers and sellers. Because of this special, ongoing relationship, health plans have a greater ability to monitor and ensure compliance with the requirements of the safe harbor regarding the submission of claims to the Medicare or Medicaid programs. Unless plans are held accountable in some way for the propriety of claims submitted to the programs, they will have no interest in ensuring the accuracy of those claims.[32]

---

[31] *Id.*
[32] *Id.* at 2,134.

Although the OIG states that it expects health plans to report any such contract-related violations to the Medicare or Medicaid programs, it provides no assurance to the reporting health plan of immunity from prosecution. According to the OIG, it merely would "consider the actions taken by the health plan in deciding whether any action was warranted under the [Anti-Kickback Statute]."[33]

### § 8-2(a)(3)   Medicare SELECT

The final managed care safe harbors permit certain hospital coinsurance waivers in connection with the Medicare SELECT policies. Medicare SELECT policies are Medigap policies that restrict full payment of benefits to services furnished by a network of preferred providers. Medigap policies provide private insurance designed to supplement Medicare coverage by paying for costs that Medicare does not cover, such as coinsurance or deductibles. Medicare SELECT policies originally were permitted in only 15 states on a demonstration basis, but legislative authority extended the program to all 50 states.

In the 1992 "interim final" managed care safe-harbor regulations, the OIG amended the then-existing safe harbor that permits hospital waivers of inpatient coinsurance and deductible amounts in order to permit such waivers in the context of Medicare SELECT policies. The safe-harbor amendment was necessary only because the original coinsurance waiver safe harbor issued in July 1991 for inpatient hospital services restricted the safe harbor's application to activities not involving managed care, and the very narrow focus of the beneficiary-incentive safe harbor included in the original regulation would not cover Medicare SELECT products that do not have formal program contracts.

Despite a number of comments requesting expansion of this safe harbor to managed care plans beyond the Medicare SELECT program and to healthcare services beyond inpatient hospital services. Nevertheless, the OIG declined to extend safe-harbor protection for the waiver of Part A inpatient hospital-deductible and coinsurance amounts beyond the Medicare SELECT program. The OIG stated that Medicare SELECT plans are distinguishable in many ways from other Medigap plans and preferred provider arrangements. According to the OIG, Medicare SELECT plans currently are subject to greater standards and oversight than other PPOs, and they are subject to civil monetary penalties (CMPs) for failure to meet certain requirements.[34]

Moreover, the OIG voiced substantial concern that inpatient coinsurance waivers made as part of a hospital's agreement with a MCO may be abusive

---

[33] *Id.*
[34] *Id.* at 2,127.

## Fraud and Abuse Issues Affecting the Managed Care Industry

and anticompetitive. In support of its position, the OIG cited the capacity of managed care to "direct the flow of large numbers of admissions to specific hospitals by designating them as preferred or exclusive providers in return for an agreement to waive coinsurance and deductibles," as well as the fact that the hospital's waiver results in the health plan having "no financial liability" where the Medicare program is the primary payor, which may make the health plan "less concerned" about guarding against the overutilization or inappropriate utilization of services.[35]

In addition, under the safe harbor, Medicare SELECT PPO products are not granted safe-harbor protection for coinsurance waivers or reductions that affect services other than inpatient hospital services. Such services would include hospital outpatient services, ambulatory surgical center (ASC) services, physician services, and ancillary healthcare services. This omission is significant, given managed care's emphasis on preventive and other noninpatient services. In the final managed care safe harbors, the OIG continued to deny safe-harbor protection for coinsurance waivers in the context of outpatient services covered under Medicare Part B:

> [R]outine waivers of coinsurance and deductibles are an area of significant abuse in the Medicare program. Such waivers result in the submission of false claims to the Medicare program because providers misstate their charges on claims submitted to the program . . . We also believe that the routine waiver of coinsurance and deductibles may result in over utilization or inappropriate utilization of services.[36]

In 2002, however, the OIG issued a proposed rule to expand the safe harbor for waivers of coinsurance and deductibles under the Medicare SELECT program for beneficiaries under Medicare Part A or B programs, thus expanding the protection already granted to Medicare SELECT policyholders.[37] The proposed rule would allow expanded protection for waivers involving Part B cost-sharing initiatives.

The OIG provided several rationales for this proposed expansion of the safe harbor. The results of a Medicare SELECT demonstration indicated that the absence of a safe harbor for waivers of Part B cost-sharing amounts was a serious obstacle to expanding the Medicare SELECT networks beyond hospitals.[38] The OIG also cited Congress's action to make the Medicare SELECT program permanent as another reason for this expansion, as it granted a greater selection of Medicare supplemental-insurance coverage plans to Medicare beneficiaries. The OIG further stated that the increase

---

[35] *Id.* at 2,128.
[36] *Id.* at 2,129.
[37] 67 Fed. Reg. 60,202 (Sept. 25, 2002).
[38] *Id.* at 60,203.

in prospective-payment methodologies and consumer preference for flexible managed care arrangements as reasons for the expansion of the safe harbor.

## § 8-2(b)  Shared-Risk Statutory Exception

In light of the narrowness of the managed care safe harbors, Congress legislated as part of the Health Insurance Portability and Accountability Act of 1996 (HIPAA) an exception to the Anti-Kickback Statute for certain risk-sharing arrangements. This "shared risk exception" excludes from the Anti-Kickback Statute:

> any remuneration between an organization and an individual or entity providing items or services, or a combination thereof, pursuant to a written agreement between the organization and the individual or entity if the organization is an eligible organization under Section 1876 or if the written agreement, through a risk-sharing arrangement, places the individual or entity at substantial financial risk for the cost or utilization of the items or services, or a combination thereof, which the individual or entity is obligated to provide.[39]

In addition to creating this statutory exception, Congress authorized the OIG to issue regulations through a negotiated rulemaking process under the Negotiated Rulemaking Act,[40] and to follow the standards for formation and use of the advisory committees pursuant to the Federal Advisory Committee Act.[41] Although the intention was to create a rule in an expedited process, the ultimate promulgation of this rule ironically took a longer period than normal, as it was not until more than seven months of negotiations that the Negotiated Rulemaking Committee (NR Committee) unanimously approved an outline of two safe harbors, which are referred to in the industry as "Prong I" and "Prong II."

The NR Committee agreed that Prong I of the safe harbor should afford protection from the Anti-Kickback Statute for most Medicare HMOs. Consequently, this prong discusses price reductions offered to "covered entities." In this context (which is different from the term's use under the privacy and

---

[39] Social Security Act § 1128B(b); 42 U.S.C. § 1320a-7b(b) (2000) (as modified by the Health Insurance Portability and Accountability Act of 1996, Pub. L. No. 104-191, tit. II § 216, 110 Stat. 1936, 2007 (1996)).

[40] *See* Negotiating Rulemaking Act of 1990, 5 U.S.C. §§ 561–69 (2000). Generally, the Negotiated Rulemaking Act of 1990 provides the framework for a federal agency to organize a committee comprised of government officials and members from the affected industry, and applies when a reasonable likelihood exists that such a committee can be convened with a balanced representation of persons who can adequately represent the identified interest, and are willing to negotiate in good faith and in an expedited manner to reach a consensus. Although a negotiated rulemaking committee typically produces a proposed rule, Congress provided that the NR Committee's results in this instance were to be published as an "interim final" rule for public comment.

[41] 5 U.S.C. app. § 2 (2000).

security elements of HIPAA), the term "covered entities" is defined to include most Medicare MCOs, Medicaid capitated arrangements, and the Department of Defense's healthcare program known as TRICARE. After months of negotiations, the government finally obliged the private-sector members' request to include protection for financial arrangements with "downstream providers." Downstream providers are those entities that are under contract with covered entities holding direct contracts with the government to provide the services that the plan is obligated to offer. The limitation, however, is that no downstream protection is provided for federally qualified health centers that receive supplemental payments, nor does it protect cost-based or federally qualified HMOs.

In addition, certain types of risk arrangements are not protected by Prong I. For example, one party to a contract cannot provide or receive remuneration in return for, or to induce the other party to provide or accept, business for which payment can be made by a federal healthcare program on a fee-for service or cost basis other than that business covered by the contract. Additionally, an arrangement is not protected if, for example, an individual or cost entity increases the number of claims submitted, or increases the charges or costs for services in order to subsidize the costs of less-profitable lines of business.[42]

Unlike the broad scope of Prong I, Prong II of the NR Committee's proposal is very narrow. It only covers managed care risk-sharing arrangements in which a federal program pays on a fee-for-service basis, as well as Medicaid section 1115 waivers that do not fit within Prong I. This safe harbor applies to arrangements in which Medicare is the primary payor on a fee-for-service basis for retirees in an employer-sponsored plan. Under Prong II: (i) no more than 10% of an MCO's enrollees can be Medicare beneficiaries where a federal healthcare program is the primary payor; or (ii) at least 50% of an MCO's enrollees are non-Medicare beneficiaries where a federal program is not primary *and* the payments for premiums under the risk-sharing arrangement must be received on a periodic basis that does not take into account the dates services are provided, the frequency of services or the extent, or kind of services provided.

Following the development of these prongs, the NR Committee recommended, through the OIG, that the Secretary of DHHS adopt the NR Committee's proposal as an "interim final" rule. Although it was estimated that the OIG's office would produce an interim final rule within three months of the NR Committee's proposal, it was not until November 19, 1999, that the OIG published the shared-risk safe harbors in the *Federal Register* as an interim final rule.[43]

---

[42] *See* Negotiated Rulemaking Comm. for the Shared-Risk Exception, *Minutes* (Jan. 21–22, 1998) (last modified Sept. 3, 1998) (on file with authors).

[43] 64 Fed. Reg. 63,504 (Nov. 19, 1999); 64 Fed. Reg. 71,317 (Dec. 21, 1999) (correction amendment).

### § 8-2(b)(1)   Price Reductions Offered to "Eligible Managed Care Organizations"

The first shared-risk safe harbor protects price reductions that are offered by anyone (e.g., a participating provider or suppliers) to "eligible managed care organizations" (EMCOs). EMCOs are defined to include HMOs and competitive medical plans with a risk or cost-based contract, any Medicare Part C plans (i.e., Medicare Advantage plans) that receive a capitation payment, certain Medicaid MCOs, Programs for the All Inclusive Care for the Elderly (PACE), and federally qualified HMOs.[44]

This safe harbor is divided into two categories of requirements that must be satisfied in order to receive safe-harbor protection. The first category establishes standards for arrangements between EMCOs and any individual or entity that contracts directly with the EMCO to provide or arrange for items or services. Such direct contractors are referred to as "first tier" contractors.[45] In order to receive protection under this safe harbor, the arrangement between the EMCO and the first-tier contractor must include the following elements:

1. the EMCO and the first-tier contractor must have an agreement that is set out in writing;
2. it must be executed by both parties;
3. it is for a term of at least one year;
4. it must specify the items and services covered under the agreement; and
5. it must specify that the first-tier contractor cannot claim payment in any form from a federal healthcare program for items or services covered under the agreement, except for

    (i) HMOs and competitive medical plans that have cost-based contracts,

    (ii) federally qualified HMOs without a CMS contract, and

    (iii) federally qualified health centers that claim supplemental payments from a federal healthcare program.[46]

Additionally, this safe harbor prohibits the EMCO and the first-tier contractor from negotiating financial terms to the arrangement that "swap" business. Neither party may give or receive remuneration in return for, or to induce, the provision or acceptance of fee-for-service business reimbursed by

---

[44] 42 C.F.R. § 1001.952 (2011).
[45] 42 C.F.R. § 1001.952(t)(1)(i) (2011).
[46] Id.

## Fraud and Abuse Issues Affecting the Managed Care Industry

a federal healthcare program for the managed care business. This is known as the "no swapping" provision of the risk-sharing safe harbor.

The second category of this safe harbor addresses financial arrangements between first-tier contractors and downstream contractors or between successive tiers of downstream contractors. The requirements of this second category are mostly similar to the first category. The parties must have an agreement that is:

- set out in writing;
- executed by both parties;
- effective for a term of at least one year;
- outlines the items and services covered under the agreement; and
- specifies that the first-tier contractor cannot claim payment in any form from a federal healthcare program for items or services covered under the agreement.

Additionally, an anti-swapping prohibition applies.[47]

The major difference between the two categories is that downstream contractors only qualify for the broad safe-harbor protection if the underlying agreement between the first-tier contractor and the EMCO does not involve an HMO or competitive medical plan with a cost-based contract, a federally qualified HMO without a risk-based CMS contract, or a federally qualified health center receiving supplemental payments. Therefore, only downstream contractors of risk-based, CMS-contracting EMCOs will qualify for the broad protection of this safe harbor. Other downstream contractors seeking safe-harbor protection for risk-sharing arrangements would need to qualify under the safe harbor discussed in the next subsection.

### § 8-2(b)(2) Safe-Harbor Protection for Contracts Involving "Substantial Financial Risk"

The second shared-risk safe harbor protects "contractual relationships between managed care entities and their contractors and subcontractors where the contractors and subcontractors are at "substantial financial risk" for the cost or utilization of items or services they provide or order for federal healthcare program beneficiaries."[48]

To qualify for protection under this shared risk safe harbor, the risk sharing arrangement must be part of a "qualified managed care plan" (QMCP). This key term is defined as a managed care entity that satisfies the requirements of the definition of a "health plan" that the OIG adopted in 1996 as

---

[47] 42 C.F.R. § 1001.952(t)(1)(ii) (2011).
[48] 64 Fed. Reg. 63,514 (Nov. 19, 1999).

part of the managed care safe harbor related to incentives that managed care plans offer to beneficiaries (discussed in § 8-2(a)(1)). In addition, this safe harbor requires that a QMCP adopt processes and procedures to ensure that the healthcare services are managed. Such processes and procedures would include, for example, procedures addressing utilization review, quality assurance, grievance and hearings, non-discrimination, and member hold-harmless measures.[49]

Additionally, to satisfy the definition of a QMCP: (1) no more than 10% of the entity's beneficiary population may be Medicare beneficiaries, excluding those individuals where Medicare is the secondary payor; or (2) no more than 50% of the entity's beneficiary population are Medicare beneficiaries. The second provision also requires that the premium payments are made on a periodic basis; that these payments do not take into account the dates of services provided, the frequency of services, or the extent or kind of services provided; and that the periodic payments for the non-federal healthcare program beneficiaries do not take into account the number of federal healthcare program fee-for-service beneficiaries that are covered by the arrangement, or the amount of services generated by such beneficiaries.[50]

Similar to the safe harbor for price reductions offered to EMCOs, this safe harbor provides protection for two categories of entities: first-tier contractors and downstream contractors. For safe-harbor protection, both categories must satisfy the criterion that the applicable party (i.e., the first-tier contractor or the downstream contractor) must be at substantial financial risk for the cost or utilization of services that the party is obligated to provide. The regulations specify four payment methodologies that may qualify as placing a contractor at "substantial financial risk": periodic fixed payments per patient; percentages of premiums; diagnosis-related groups (DRGs); and bonus and withhold arrangements.

With respect to the last payment methodology, the OIG has required that the target payment for individuals and non-institutional providers who are first-tier contractors must be at least 20% greater than the minimum payment. The target payment for an institutional provider who is a downstream contractor (e.g., a hospital or nursing home), however, must be at least 10% greater than the minimum payment. Further, the bonus or withhold amount must be in direct proportion to the ratio of the contractor's actual utilization to its target utilization.[51]

Alternatively, for contractors that are physicians, the OIG adopts the definition of "substantial financial risk" that CMS has created related to payments by HMOs to physicians under a physician incentive plan (PIP). Under the PIP

---

[49] *Id.*
[50] 42 C.F.R. § 1001.952(u) (2011).
[51] 64 Fed. Reg. 63,514 (Nov. 19, 1999).

## Fraud and Abuse Issues Affecting the Managed Care Industry

regulations,[52] substantial financial risk generally is determined by calculating whether an incentive plan involves risk for services based on the use or cost of referral services beyond a risk threshold, which the rule generally sets at 25%. To the extent a PIP involves substantial financial risk, the affected organization must ensure that several requirements are satisfied, including a requirement that stop-loss protection has been obtained for the relevant physician or physician groups, that enrollee surveys be conducted, and that information be disclosed to CMS and beneficiaries, upon request.

In addition to the "substantial financial risk" requirement, arrangements between QMCPs and first-tier contractors must satisfy additional standards. The parties must have a written agreement that:

- is executed by both parties;
- has a term of at least one year;
- itemizes the items and services covered under the agreement;
- requires the first-tier contractor to participate in a quality-assurance program; and
- specifies a methodology for determining payment (including the intervals at which payments will be made and the formula for calculating incentives and penalties, if any) that is commercially reasonable and consistent with fair market value (FMV).

Such payment methodology must be negotiated in an arm's-length transaction. The anti-swapping prohibition discussed earlier also applies.[53]

Further, the QMCP (or, in the case of a self-funded employer plan that contracts with a QMCP to provide administrative services, the self-funded employer plan) must submit the claims for covered items or services directly to the government program in accordance with a valid reassignment agreement. The safe harbor, however, includes an exception for inpatient hospital services, other than psychiatric services, if the hospital is reimbursed by a federal healthcare program under a DRG methodology.[54]

Similarly, arrangements between first-tier contractors and downstream contractors, or between multiple downstream contractors, must satisfy the following additional standards. Payments by QMCPs to first-tier contractors and downstream contractors for providing or arranging for items or services that are reimbursed by a federal healthcare program must be identical to the payment arrangements between the parties for items or services provided to non-federal healthcare beneficiaries who have similar health status to the federal beneficiaries. Such payments, however, may be adjusted where the adjustments are related to utilization patterns, or to actual costs incurred by

---

[52] 42 C.F.R. § 422.208(a) (2011).
[53] 42 C.F.R. § 1001.952(u)(1)(i)(A) (2011).
[54] *Id.*

providing items or services to the relevant population. The anti-swapping prohibition discussed earlier also applies.[55]

## § 8-2(c)  Advisory Opinions

As described in greater detail in § 2-5(b), the OIG offers a mechanism for obtaining advisory opinions regarding whether specific conduct or an arrangement violates certain fraud and abuse laws. The first OIG advisory opinion pertaining specifically to the managed care industry was issued in 1998. In this request, the OIG was asked whether an arrangement in which an independent physician association (IPA) would acquire a minority equity interest in an MCO would constitute grounds for the imposition of sanctions under the Anti-Kickback Statute.[56]

The business transaction in this advisory opinion involved an IPA purchasing an equity interest of less than 15% in an MCO. As consideration, the IPA would assign a certain percentage of the IPA's physician-service agreements to the MCO. This percentage would not exceed FMV based on an arm's-length transaction, and would not be based on the volume or value of referrals or business otherwise generated between the parties. The IPA would receive a separate class of non-voting stock, and would have the right to elect not less than one member to the board. The IPA would receive distribution of profits in direct proportion to the FMV of the investment. Additionally, the IPA would offer an "Incentive Stock Plan" to its shareholder-physicians if the physician agrees to assume a certain level of financial risk and agrees to certain other criteria, including the execution of a physician-services agreement with the MCO for a term of five years. The IPA also would enter into three ancillary personal-service agreements with the MCO, each for ten years (a network service agreement, a medical management program agreement, and an administrative services agreement). Additionally, the physicians and shareholder hospitals would be compensated for services rendered to MCO enrollees.

After analyzing the various components to the business transaction, the OIG concluded that the proposed arrangement would not be subject to sanctions arising under the Anti-Kickback Statute, provided that all compensation in connection with the proposed arrangement was paid at FMV. Accordingly, the OIG opined that the arrangement posed "no more than a minimal risk of fraud and abuse," and would not likely increase costs to the federal healthcare programs.[57]

---

[55] 64 Fed. Reg. 63,514 (Nov. 19, 1999).
[56] Dep't of Health & Human Servs. (DHHS), OIG, Adv. Op. No. 98-19 (Dec. 14, 1998), *available online at* http://oig.hhs.gov/fraud/docs/advisoryopinions/1998/ao98_19.htm.
[57] *Id.*

## Fraud and Abuse Issues Affecting the Managed Care Industry

In 2003, the OIG examined another managed care arrangement in which a national MCO offering multiple healthcare products (including Medigap policies) proposed to contract with various PPOs to include the MCO's Medigap policyholders in the PPO's hospital networks.[58] As part of the arrangement, the MCO would receive a discount on inpatient (i.e., Medicare Part A) deductibles incurred by its policyholders at PPO-network hospitals, but pay an administrative-services fee to the PPO each time the MCO and its policyholders received the discount from the network hospitals. To encourage use of the PPO-network hospitals, the MCO proposed offering policyholders who used a network hospital for an inpatient stay a "credit" that would apply for their next renewal premium.

The OIG considered the fact that the safe harbor for waivers of inpatient deductibles excludes such waivers when they are part of an agreement with an insurer, and that the safe harbor protecting reduced premium amounts offered by health plans only applies if the reduction is offered to *all* enrollees. Nevertheless, the OIG concluded that, even though the arrangement did not qualify for safe-harbor protection, the arrangement presented a low risk of fraud and abuse. In fact, the OIG determined that the proposed arrangement had the potential to lower costs both for Medigap policyholders choosing network hospitals and other policyholders, because the MCO stated that the discount it received would be reported to state insurance regulators, and thereby would be included in the information used for setting state premium rates for all insurers.

Additional advisory opinions that have been issued by the OIG specific to Medicare Part D and the appropriateness of patient-assistance programs are described in § 8-8(h).

## § 8-3 MANAGED CARE AND THE PHYSICIAN SELF-REFERRAL LAW

As described in greater detail in Chapter 3, the federal physician self-referral law, commonly referred to as the Stark Law, prohibits physicians from ordering "designated health services" for Medicare (and, to some extent, Medicaid) patients from entities with which the physician (or an immediate family member) has a "financial relationship."[59] The Stark Law may apply to MCO arrangements in several ways. For example, the Stark Law potentially is implicated if a physician has a participating-physician agreement with an MCO that "furnishes" designated health services. In addition, the Stark Law

---

[58] DHHS OIG Adv. Op. No. 03-10 (May 8, 2003), *available online at* http://oig.hhs.gov/fraud/docs/advisoryopinions/2003/ao03_10.htm. *See also*, Advisory Opinions 08-13, 10-01, 10-02, 10-03, 10-21, 11-09, and 11-19.

[59] Social Security Act § 1877(a)(1); 42 U.S.C. § 1395nn(a)(1) (2000).

could present an issue for physician-owned managed care plans. Although the application of the Stark Law to the managed care industry has not appeared to be high on the list of the government's enforcement priorities, because the Stark Law is a strict liability statute, one *must* satisfy one of the promulgated exceptions to the statute so as to not be found to have violated the law.

## § 8-3(a)  Prepaid Health Plans

The Stark Law includes an exception applicable to ownership and compensation arrangements alike for services furnished to enrollees of certain health plans. The statute specifically excepts services furnished through the following particular types of MCOs:

- a Medicare cost contractor or risk contractor;
- a healthcare prepayment plan;
- an entity receiving payments on a prepaid basis under a demonstration project;
- a federally qualified HMO; or
- a Medicare Advantage plan.[60]

In the Stark II Phase II final regulations issued in 2004 (discussed in § 3-2), CMS extended the purview of this exception to include Medicaid managed care plans analogous to the Medicare plans previously provided for in the exception.[61]

Nevertheless, the prepaid health-plan exception does not extend to all managed care entities (e.g., PPOs or non-licensed managed care plans). Consequently, non-qualifying health plans must choose between physician ownership and owning designated health services (i.e., physician-owned MCOs, non-Medicare-contracting MCOs, non-federally qualified HMOs, or PPOs must contract with outside designated health service providers to furnish designated health services to Medicare and Medicaid patients). Similarly, non-qualifying health plans that own and directly furnish designated health services must be sure that their compensation relationships with physicians (e.g., provider contracts, medical director contracts) meet one of the Stark Law's compensation exceptions in order to enable network-contracting physicians to refer patients for any designated health services that the health plan owns and furnishes directly.

Moreover, CMS has taken the position that the prepaid health-plan exception only applies to enrollees in the line of business that is protected, and does *not* apply to financial arrangements for the services of enrollees in any other

---

[60] Social Security Act § 1877(b)(3); 42 U.S.C. § 1395nn(b)(3).
[61] 69 Fed. Reg. 16,054 (Mar. 26, 2004), *codified at* 42 C.F.R. §§ 411.355(c)(6)–(9).

## Fraud and Abuse Issues Affecting the Managed Care Industry

plan or line of business furnished by the MCO, or to which the MCO provides administrative services.[62]

The prepaid health-plan exception is useful primarily in the context of payor/provider integration activities. The availability of the prepaid health-plan exception means that qualifying health plans may be physician-owned and also furnish designated health services directly as a line of business or in a subsidiary organization. Qualifying health plans also may contract with physician-owned entities furnishing or providing designated health services to Medicare and Medicaid enrollees.

In the final regulations, CMS narrowed its proposed interpretation regarding when an MCO is deemed to be "furnishing" a designated health service. In the proposed regulation, CMS took the position that an MCO "furnished" designated health services whenever it arranged for DHS through contracts with providers and billed Medicare or Medicaid for the designated health services. In the final regulations, however, CMS took the position that an MCO "furnishes" designated health services only when it owns the designated health service entity, or employs the provider who furnishes the designated health services.[63] As such, most MCOs will not be viewed as furnishing designated health services merely through their contractual arrangements with providers.

### § 8-3(b)  Personal-Service Arrangements

Another significant exception related to managed care arrangements is the compensation exception for personal-service arrangements. In addition to the various requirements of this exception (discussed in § 3-4(c)(3)), the exception provides that the compensation must be "set in advance, does not exceed FMV, and is not determined in a manner that takes into account the volume or value of any referrals or other business generated between the parties, except for certain [PIP]s."[64] The exception provides that PIPs may take into account directly or indirectly the volume or value of referrals or other business generated between the parties (through a withhold, capitation, bonus, or otherwise) so long as the following apply:

- no specific payment is made directly or indirectly under the plan to a physician or physician group as an inducement to reduce or limit medically necessary services to a specific individual enrolled;

---

[62] 66 Fed. Reg. 913 (Jan. 4, 2001).
[63] *Id.* at 914.
[64] Social Security Act § 1877(e)(3); 42 U.S.C. § 1395nn(e)(3) 2011); *see also* 42 C.F.R. § 411.357(d)(1).

- health plans that place physicians at "substantial financial risk" must comply with any the regulations applicable to PIPs (described at § 8-2(b)(1)); and
- the plan must provide the DHHS Secretary with access to descriptive information regarding the plan, and permit the DHHS Secretary to determine whether the plan is in compliance with the requirements.[65]

In the proposed Stark regulations, CMS only protected PIP payments made directly by the MCO. In the final regulations, however, CMS modified this exception to apply to payments made by downstream subcontractors as well.[66]

### § 8-3(c) Regulatory Exception for Risk-Sharing Arrangements

In response to the unintended effect of the Stark Law on commercial MCOs described in § 8-3(a), CMS created an exception in the Stark regulations for a bona fide "risk-sharing arrangement" between an MCO or an IPA and a physician for the provision of items or services to enrollees of the health plan, even when such an arrangement does not fall within existing statutory exceptions (e.g., the prepaid health-plan exception).[67] In its preamble to the Stark II Phase II Final Regulations, CMS explained that this exception was meant to protect all risk-sharing compensation (e.g., withholds, bonuses, and risk pools) to a physician by any entity that is downstream of any type of health plan.[68]

Therefore, this exception also serves to supplement the personal-services exception, which would only permit managed care incentive compensation that met CMS's rules for PIPs applicable to Medicare managed care plans. Medicare rules for PIPs substantially restrict the amount of financial risk that can be passed along to physicians. As a result, if this exception had not been created, commercial plans with a relatively small number of Medicare beneficiaries would have had to substantially alter their risk-sharing plans with physicians in order to allow the physicians in their managed care networks to refer patients for designated health services to be provided within the network.

## § 8-4 INTERMEDIATE SANCTIONS APPLICABLE TO MCOS

The DHHS Secretary is authorized to impose sanctions against MCOs with contracts to provide services to Medicare beneficiaries (i.e., MCOs

---

[65] 42 C.F.R. § 411.357(d)(2) (2011).
[66] 69 Fed. Reg. 16,054 (Mar. 26, 2004), *codified at* 42 C.F.R. §§ 411.355(c)(6)–(9).
[67] 42 C.F.R. § 411.357(n) (2011).
[68] 69 Fed. Reg. 16,067 (Mar. 26, 2004).

### Fraud and Abuse Issues Affecting the Managed Care Industry

under Medicare Part C as well as those with contracts under Social Security Act § 1876). MCOs can be subject to intermediate sanctions for engaging in the following activities:[69]

- failing substantially to provide medically necessary items and services that resulted in an adverse effect, or has a substantial likelihood of adversely affecting, an individual;
- imposing premiums in excess of permitted premiums;
- expelling or refusing to re-enroll a beneficiary in violation of law;
- denying or discouraging enrollment of individuals whose medical condition or history indicates a need for substantial medical services in the future;
- misrepresenting or falsifying information furnished to the Medicare program or to other individuals or entities;
- failing to ensure prompt payment of claims for services and supplies furnished to enrollees;
- employing or contracting for the provision of healthcare, utilization review, medical social work, or administrative services with individuals or entities that have been excluded from program participation;
- operating a PIP that may directly or indirectly have the effect of reducing or limiting services provided to enrollees;
- interfering with healthcare professionals' advice to enrollees;
- failing to comply the requirements that an MCO enforce the limit on balance billing under a private fee-for-service plan;
- enrolling an individual in a plan without their prior consent or that of their designee;
- transferring an enrollee to a new plan without their consent solely for the purpose of obtaining a commission; or
- failing to comply with the marketing restriction of section 1851.[70]

---

[69] With respect to those provisions of the Social Security Act that apply to HMOs and competitive medical plans that continue to contract with Medicare as a "cost contractor," *see* Social Security Act § 1876(i)(6); 42 U.S.C. § 1395mm(i)(6); 42 C.F.R. §§ 417.500 (2011).
With respect to those provisions of the Social Security Act that apply to Medicare Advantage plans, *see* Social Security Act § 1857(g); 42 U.S.C. § 1395w-27(g); 42 C.F.R. § 422.750 *et seq.* (2011).
*See also* CTRS. FOR MEDICARE & MEDICAID SERVS. (CMS), MEDICARE MANAGED CARE MANUAL: CH. 15 INTERMEDIATE SANCTIONS, *available online at* http://www.cms.hhs.gov/manuals/downloads/mc86c15.pdf.
[70] The Patient Protection and Affordable Care Act added the last three grounds for imposing CMPs on any Medicare or Medicaid MCO or PDP. Patient Protection and Affordable Care Act (P.L. 111-148) § 6408(b), as amended by the Healthcare and Education Reconciliation Act of 2010 (Pub. L. 111-152) [hereinafter referred to as the "Health Reform Law"].

In addition to (or in lieu of) other remedies available, violations of these provisions generally may result in the imposition of a CMP (e.g., $25,000) for each offense, and some violations may result in the imposition of a flat $100,000 penalty in addition to a per-offense penalty. The penalty is $50,000 for misrepresenting or falsifying information furnished to the Medicare program or other individuals or entities.[71]

These prohibitions apply to the MCO and anyone it employs or contracts with.

The DHHS Secretary also is authorized to impose other sanctions, such as suspending the MCO's ability to enroll Medicare beneficiaries, suspending payment, or requiring the entity to suspend all marketing activities. Areas that have been cited in enrollment suspensions include involuntary disenrollments and improper oversight of sales agents.

CMS regulations also provide that an MCO's contract with the Medicare program can be terminated (and CMPs imposed) for the following actions:[72]

- failing to substantially carry out the terms of its contract;
- carrying out its contract in a manner that is inconsistent with its effective and efficient implementation;
- failing to meet the contracting-organization requirements;
- committing or participating in fraudulent or abusive activities affecting the Medicare program, including submission of fraudulent data;
- experiencing financial difficulties so severe that its ability to make necessary health services available is impaired to the point of posing an imminent and serious risk to the health of its enrollees, or otherwise fails to make services available to the extent that such a risk to health exists;
- failing to comply with the requirements relating to grievances and appeals;
- failing to provide CMS with valid data as required;
- failing to implement an acceptable quality-improvement program;
- failing to comply with the service-access requirements; and
- failing to comply with Medicare's marketing requirements for MCOs.

The process by which CMS can impose these sanctions against an MCO is initiated by CMS sending a written notice to the MCO stating the nature and basis of the proposed sanction.[73] The notified MCO has fifteen days to

---

[71] The Health Reform Law, § 6408(a).
[72] 42 C.F.R. §§ 422.510(a) (20111), 417.494. *See also* CMS, MEDICARE MANAGED CARE MANUAL: CH. 15 INTERMEDIATE SANCTIONS.
[73] 42 C.F.R. §§ 422.756, 417.500 (2011). *See also* CMS, MEDICARE MANAGED CARE MANUAL: CH. 15 INTERMEDIATE SANCTIONS.

## Fraud and Abuse Issues Affecting the Managed Care Industry

respond to CMS, but absent circumstances in which a threat exists to the health and safety of enrollees, the MCO may provide the MCO with an additional fifteen-day extension. If the MCO submits a response, then a CMS official not involved in the initial determination conducts an informal reconsideration that includes a review of the evidence, and will produce a written decision that affirms or rescinds the initial determination. If the CMS official affirms the initial determination, then the sanction is effective on the date specified in the notice of CMS's reconsidered determination, except for offenses in which CMS determines there is a serious threat to enrollees' health and safety, in which case the sanction can be effective prior to issuance of CMS's reconsidered determination.

If the MCO chooses not to seek reconsideration of the decision after the requisite response time, then it is required to submit a Corrective Action Plan (CAP) to CMS that describes the measures that the plan will take to correct the problems, including a timetable for completion. The CAP outlines how the MCO will correct the violation(s) and avoid such issues in the future, as well as ensure that the plan will comply with federal regulations. Sanctions against the MCO remain in effect until CMS determines that the violations are corrected and that the CAP is satisfactory.

## § 8-5  MANAGED CARE AND THE FALSE CLAIMS ACT

Although false claims allegations primarily have been made in the context of fee-for-service providers, MCOs are vulnerable to charges of violating the federal civil false claims act (FCA, discussed in greater detail in Chapter 4).

For MCOs, FCA-related alleged conduct generally involves activities that increase costs to the Medicare program through an MCO's misreporting of information and data, or the adoption of policies and procedures (including physician-compensation and coverage-decision policies) that potentially harm Medicare enrollees. For example, in connection with allegations of having reported inaccurate information to the Medicare program related to enrollees and their eligibility, Humana paid a $14.5 million penalty in 2000.[74] More recently, in 2011, CareSource, CareSource Management Group Co. and CareSource USA Holding Co. agreed to pay the United States and the state of Ohio $26 million to resolve allegations that CareSource entities submitted false data and received reimbursement for services it did not provide.[75]

Additional activities and theories upon which MCOs can face liability under the FCA are discussed in greater detail in § 8-8.

---

[74] *See Humana Pays $14.5 Million to Settle Charge of Giving Inaccurate Medicare Information*, BNA HEALTHCARE DAILY (June 7, 2000).
[75] *See* Dep't of Justice (DOJ) Press Release, *Ohio-Based Managed Care Plan Contractor CareSource & Entities to Pay $26 Million to Resolve False Claims Allegations* (Feb. 1, 2011), *available online at* http://www.justice.gov/opa/pr/2011/February/11-civ-138.html.

## § 8-6 FEDERAL EFFORTS TO ADDRESS FRAUD IN MEDICARE MANAGED CARE

To ensure proper payments to MCOs and to PDPs, CMS has stated that it has developed methods to determine the accuracy of such payments, as well as concentrated attention on the payment areas that are most vulnerable to fraud and abuse. These include:

- devising a "robust set of measures" to review payments for inaccuracies;
- creating standards to discover outliers in payments and to detect trends;
- identifying risks associated with data in the payment system;
- scrutinizing error rates and risk-adjustment factors; and
- supervising plans on a consistent basis. [76]

One way in which the government anticipates deterring fraud involving its managed care contractors is by *requiring* MCOs and PDPs to adopt compliance programs. In this area, CMS treats MCOs and PDPs differently than entities operating in other segments of the healthcare industry, in which the adoption of a corporate compliance program is voluntary (unless otherwise subject to a Corporate Integrity Agreement, discussed in greater detail at § 7-8). As a condition to contracting, CMS requires MCOs and PDPs to have a corporate compliance program that includes:

- written policies, procedures, and standards of conduct that articulate the organization's commitment to comply with all applicable federal and state standards;
- the designation of a compliance officer and a compliance committee that will be accountable to senior management;
- effective training and education between the compliance officer and organization employees;
- effective lines of communication between the compliance officer and the organization's employees;
- enforcement of standards through well-publicized disciplinary guidelines;
- procedures for internal monitoring and auditing; and

---

[76] CMS, *Medicare Strengthens Oversight in Payment for Medicare Advantage and Prescription Drug Plans*, ¶ 3 (Nov. 10, 2005), *available online at* http://new.cms.hhs.gov/apps/media/press/release.asp?Counter=1728.

# Fraud and Abuse Issues Affecting the Managed Care Industry

- procedures for ensuring prompt responses to detected offenses, and for the development of corrective-action initiatives.[77]

The OIG has issued voluntary compliance program guidance to MCOs operating under Medicare Part C, which should prove useful for assisting PDPs.[78] The OIG guidance not only addresses the various elements for inclusion in an MCO's compliance program (e.g., the development of policies and procedures, appointment of a compliance officer), but also provides guidance on the substantive areas that the compliance program should focus. These include the process by which Medicare beneficiaries elect to participate in the MCO, quality-assessment and performance-improvement efforts, claims processing, marketing activities, data collection, and submission processes.

In connection with PDPs, CMS has developed Chapter 9 of the *Prescription Drug Benefit Manual*, entitled "Part D Program to Control Fraud, Waste and Abuse," which consolidates the various compliance plan requirements for PDPs. As PDPs enter into contracts with third parties to perform functions that otherwise are the responsibility of the PDP, the PDPs maintain ultimate responsibility for fulfilling the terms and conditions set out in the contract with CMS.[79] In this document, CMS identifies various activities that can constitute fraud, waste, and abuse for each of the different "players" responsible for furnishing services under the Part D benefit (e.g., with PBMs and pharmacies). CMS highlighted the following partial list of activities specific to PDPs (many of which will be discussed in greater detail in § 8-8):

- failing to provide medically necessary services;
- violating the Medicare marketing guidelines, or other federal or state laws, rules, and regulations regarding improper enrollment of beneficiaries;
- inappropriately overestimating or underestimating the bid to manipulate risk corridors and/or payments, including miscalculations of administrative-ratio costs within the bids;
- providing coverage for "non-covered Part D drugs," as listed in the PDP's approved formularies;
- billing multiple payors (except for purposes of coordination of benefit transactions);

---

[77] 42 C.F.R. §§ 422.503(b)(vi) (2011), 422.504(b)(iv)(2011).
[78] 64 Fed. Reg. 61,893, 61,894 (Nov. 15, 1999).
[79] 42 C.F.R. 423.505(b) (2011). *See* CMS, Prescription Drug Benefit Manual Ch.9, *Part D Program to Control Fraud, Waste and Abuse, available online at* http://www.cms.hhs.gov/PrescriptionDrugCovContra/Downloads/PDBManual_Chapter9_FWA.pdf.

- incorrectly calculating the true out-of-pocket cost (TrOOP);[80]
- submitting inaccurate or incomplete data (e.g., prescription drug event data or Part D plan quarterly data) to CMS;
- manipulating catastrophic coverage to increase payment by CMS;
- failing to disclose or misrepresenting rebates, discounts, or price concessions;
- engaging in "bait and switch" pricing, in which a beneficiary is led to believe that a drug will cost one price, but at the point of sale the beneficiary is charged a higher amount; and
- providing false or misleading information regarding the number of its members who have applied for and qualify for the low-income subsidy in order to receive unwarranted low-income subsidies.

Also specific to its efforts at controlling fraud and abuse within Part D, CMS has contracted with private organizations that serve as "Medicare Drug Integrity Contractors" (MEDICs). MEDICS are responsible for identifying and investigating potential Part D fraud and abuse, developing potential Part D fraud or abuse cases for referral to law enforcement agencies, acting as a liaison to law enforcement, and serving as an auditor of PDP and subcontractor Part D operations.[81]

The Health Reform Law requires the expansion of the Medicare Recovery Audit Contractor (RAC) program to the Medicare Part C and Part D programs. The role of RACs is to (1) ensure that Medicare MCOs and PDPs have an anti-fraud plan in place that is reviewed regularly, (2) examine reinsurance claims to determine if PDPs incurred reinsurance costs above allowable levels; and (3) compare PDP estimates of enrollment of high-cost beneficiaries with actual enrollments.[82]

CMS acknowledged in a 2010 Solicitation for Comments that the payment structure in the Medicare Part C and Part D programs is different than in the Medicare FFS program.[83] CMS, therefore, identified several questions to which it wanted comments from industry, such as: what methods will the RACs use to identify underpayments and overpayments; could MCOs and PDPs plans use RACs within their own plans to identify overpayments; to what extent successful overpayment recoupment models already exist among

---

[80] Under the Medicare Part D program, coverage is provided up to a certain level, followed by a gap in that coverage until a beneficiary satisfies certain levels of expenditure, called "True Out of Pocket" costs (TrOOP). Once these costs are incurred by the beneficiaries, Part D resumes coverage and also provides additional catastrophic-coverage benefits. Any attempt by an MCO to manipulate or falsify the TrOOP calculations to deny Part D coverage to beneficiaries by keeping them in the uncovered gap could constitute fraud.
[81] CMS, Prescription Drug Benefit Manual Ch.9.
[82] The Health Reform Law, § 6411(b)(5).
[83] 75 Fed. Reg. 81,278 (Dec. 27, 2010).

## Fraud and Abuse Issues Affecting the Managed Care Industry

private plans that may be applicable to plans that contract with Medicare; and many others. Based on comments received on these questions in early 2011, further CMS rulemaking on RAC expansion is likely.

### § 8-7 MANAGED-CARE FRAUD AND STATE MEDICAID PROGRAMS

Similar to the growth of Medicare managed care, state Medicaid programs have increased the role of MCOs in arranging for the delivery of health services to the states' Medicaid populations. CMS estimated that, in 1991, 2.7 million Medicaid beneficiaries were enrolled in some form of managed care; by 2009, this number had grown to 36 million—accounting for approximately 70% of all Medicaid recipients across the nation in 2009.[84]

Until Congress enacted BBA 97, in order for a state to operate its Medicaid program under a managed care model, the state would have needed to obtain either an "1115 waiver" or "1915(b) waiver" from the DHHS Secretary.[85] BBA 97 provided that a state could require Medicaid recipients to enroll into a managed care program by incorporating managed care permanently into the state plan.[86]

As a condition for receiving federal financial-participation payments, a state must ensure that the MCOs with which it contracts comply with various requirements related to program integrity. Medicaid laws provide that a state must ensure that the MCOs with which it contracts prohibit the MCOs from having a relationship with individuals or entities that have been debarred, suspended, or otherwise excluded from participation in procurement activities under the Federal Acquisition Regulation or other government provisions.[87]

---

[84] https://www.cms.gov/medicaiddatasourcesgeninfo/04_mdmancrenrllrep.asp.

[85] An "1115 waiver" allows the DHHS Secretary to authorize a state to implement a time-limited experimental, pilot, or demonstration project in order to cover new services, offer different service packages, and/or test reimbursement methods. Social Security Act § 1115(a); 42 U.S.C. § 1315(a) (2000). As such, many state 1115 waivers have required Medicaid recipients to enroll in managed care plans in an effort to reduce costs and enable states to cover additional people.

Under a "1915(b) waiver," a state may request, in part, to cover specific populations in managed care programs, but are generally more narrowly focused and are confined to specific federal Medicaid requirements. Social Security Act § 1915(b); 42 U.S.C. § 1395n(b) (2000).

[86] Balanced Budget Act of 1997, Pub. L. 105-33, title IV, § 4701, *codified at* Social Security Act § 1932; 42 U.S.C. § 1396u-2 (2000).

[87] Social Security Act § 1932(d)(1) 42 U.S.C. § 1396u-2(d)(1); *see also* 42 C.F.R. § 438.610. If a state finds that a managed-care entity is not in compliance with these requirements, the state is required to notify the DHHS Secretary of such noncompliance, and may only continue an existing agreement with the entity if directed by the DHHS Secretary (in consultation with the OIG).

Federal Medicaid laws also prohibit MCOs from engaging in similar activities that can result in a Medicare MCO being sanctioned as described in § 8-4, *supra*. These activities include the following:

- failing substantially to provide medically necessary items and services that are required (under law or under contract) to be provided;
- imposing premiums on individuals enrolled under this subsection in excess of the premiums permitted by law; or
- improperly discriminating among individuals, including expulsion or refusal to re-enroll an individual or engaging in any practice that would reasonably be expected to have the effect of denying or discouraging enrollment.[88]

Federal and state officials recognized that the shift towards managed care required a change in the strategies to address and control fraud within the state Medicaid programs.[89] Although states are required to institute a fraud-detection program (as discussed in greater detail in § 6-8(a)), many states found it difficult to initiate formal managed care fraud and abuse programs.

In 1999, the OIG examined detection and referral processes, provisions, and data in ten states operating under a managed care model. As a result of this study, the OIG recommended that it coordinate with CMS to accomplish the following:

- establish guidelines for states and MCOs to follow in developing and carrying out proactive detection and referral activities for fraud and abuse;
- ensure that states monitor MCOs' fraud and abuse programs for compliance with CMS/OIG guidelines; and
- continue to develop, sponsor, and emphasize detection and referral training for states and Medicaid MCOs.[90]

As part of its National Medicaid Fraud and Abuse Initiative to achieve these goals, CMS developed a document, entitled "Guidelines for Addressing Fraud and Abuse in Medicaid Managed Care," which identifies the roles of Medicaid MCOs and federal and state entities in preventing, detecting, and curing fraud and abuse in a Medicaid managed care program.[91] These

---

[88] Social Security Act §§ 1903(m), 1932(d)(2); 42 U.S.C. §§ 1396b(m), 1396u-2(d)(2); *see also* 42 C.F.R. §§ 438.610, 438.70. In addition to other remedies available under law, the DHHS Secretary can impose CMPs against the MCO, as well as deny payment to the state for medical assistance furnished under the contract.

[89] Steven Wiggs, *Fraud Control in Medicaid Managed Care: Mission Impossible*, NAAG HEALTHCARE FRAUD REP. (Oct./Nov. 1996).

[90] DHHS OIG, MEDICAID MANAGED CARE FRAUD AND ABUSE REPORT 3 (June 1999), *available online at* http://oig.hhs.gov/oei/reports/oei-07-96-00250.pdf.

[91] CMS, *Guidelines for Addressing Medicaid Fraud and Abuse* (October 2000), *available online at* http://www.cms.hhs.gov/FraudAbuseforProfs/02_MedicaidGuidance.asp&num;TopOfPage.

### Fraud and Abuse Issues Affecting the Managed Care Industry

guidelines stress the importance of Medicaid MCOs adopting a comprehensive corporate compliance program. In May of 2002, CMS's Medicaid Alliance for Program Safeguards issued a follow-up set of guidelines to Medicaid MCOs and prepaid health plans describing ways in which they can construct an effective compliance program.[92] Later that same year, when CMS adopted the final regulations for Medicaid managed care, it included a requirement that all Medicaid MCOs must have adopted a corporate compliance program "designed to safeguard against fraud and abuse." [93]

## § 8-8 EXAMPLES OF POTENTIAL FRAUD LIABILITY IN THE MANAGED CARE INDUSTRY

### § 8-8(a) Capitation Misclassification

Capitation refers to a type of managed care payment mechanism whereby a provider is paid a certain amount, usually on a monthly basis, for each member to whom the provider potentially may provide healthcare services. In return for this set reimbursement, the provider generally agrees to provide all the healthcare services that these members require (regardless of the level or expense of services needed) that fall within the scope of their practice and/or contract.

Consequently, one area of potential false claims liability for MCOs is "capitation misclassification," in which the MCO receives capitation rates that are higher than intended for the relevant enrollees. For example, CMS determines, based on various factors, the capitation rate it will pay for Medicare beneficiaries who enroll in managed care plans in certain geographic areas. CMS also will increase the capitation rate to MCOs with beneficiaries who are "institutionalized."[94] Thus, if a Medicare beneficiary is incorrectly classified by the MCO as being "institutionalized," then the MCO may receive an unwarranted supplemental capitation payment for that beneficiary.

In 1998, DHHS and the OIG reported that Kaiser Foundation Health (Kaiser) rceived overpayments of more than $200,000 for 315 Medicare beneficiaries incorrectly classified as institutionalized. Institutionalized-status requirements specify that a beneficiary must be a resident of a qualifying facility for a minimum of thirty consecutive days immediately prior to the first day of the current reporting month. The OIG found that overpayments were made due to the fact that more than 250 beneficiaries had

---

[92] CMS, *Guidelines for Constructing a Compliance Program for Medicaid Managed Care Organizations and PrePaid Health Plans* (May 2002), *available online at* http://www.cms.hhs.gov/FraudAbuseforProfs/02_MedicaidGuidance.asp&num;TopOfPage.

[93] 67 Fed. Reg. 40,989 (June 14, 2002), *codified at* 42 C.F.R. § 438.608.

[94] CMS, MEDICAID MANAGED CARE MANUAL: CH. 8 - PAYMENTS TO MEDICARE ADVANTAGE ORGANIZATIONS (Nov. 2007), *available online at* https://www.cms.gov/manuals/downloads/mc86c08.pdf

been admitted or discharged during the thirty-day residency requirement. The OIG recommended that Kaiser should continue to strengthen internal-control procedures, refund the overpayments, and review the status of other beneficiaries in order to identify and refund any additional overpayments.[95] Since the mid-1990s, the OIG has stated continuously in its annual Work Plan that it will examine CMS payments of capitation rates.[96]

This issue has been a continuing theme in managed care fraud settlements. In 2000, United Healthcare of Illinois, Inc., paid $2.9 million to settle allegations that it violated the FCA and defrauded Medicare by obtaining excessive per-capita advance payments for beneficiaries who were institutionalized.[97] In 2010, the owners of America's Health Choice Medical Plans Inc., a Medicare Advantage plan, and their affiliated primary care provider paid $22.6 million to resolve allegations that they falsely increased the severity of beneficiary diagnoses to obtain higher Medicare payments.[98]

### § 8-8(b) Defective Rate or Bid Submissions

Similar to fee-for-service providers, who can be accused of fraud in connection with any misstatements in the healthcare provider's enrollment application or its submission of claims for payments, all information that MCOs must submit to the government in connection with obtaining or maintaining the managed care contract may also provide a potential basis for a false claim action. Examples of this procurement fraud may include representations regarding the provider network, provider credentials, or financial solvency.

For instance, in the context of the Federal Employee Health Benefits Program, PacifiCare Health Systems agreed in 2002 to pay $87 million to settle allegations that it and its predecessor companies violated the FCA with respect to the submission of inflated claims for insurance payments based on rates that were not developed in accordance with regulations promulgated by the Office of Personnel Management and rating instructions.

Rate development also is important in the Medicare context as a potential basis for fraud allegations. When determining the rates that MCOs received from the Medicare program, MCOs previously would submit an adjusted community rate (ACR) proposal, which was the premium that

---

[95] DHHS OIG, REVIEW OF MEDICARE PAYMENTS FOR BENEFICIARIES WITH INSTITUTIONAL STATUS: KAISER FOUNDATION HEALTH PLAN (Oct. 2002), *available online at* http://oig.hhs.gov/oas/reports/region5/50100094.pdf.
[96] *See, e.g.,* DHHS OIG, WORK PLAN: FY 2006 18 (2006), *available online at* http://oig.hhs.gov/publications/docs/workplan/2006/workplanFY2006.pdf.
[97] *See Chicago-Based HMO to Pay $2.9 Million, Enter CIA to Address Medicare Misbillings,* BNA HEALTHCARE DAILY (Nov. 27, 2000).
[98] DOJ Press Release, *available online at* http://www.justice.gov/opa/pr/2010/November/10-civ-1351.html.

## Fraud and Abuse Issues Affecting the Managed Care Industry

the MCO would charge its non-Medicare enrollees for Medicare covered services, adjusted for the Medicare members' greater use of services. In the late 1990s, however, the OIG completed several reviews of administrative costs included in ACR proposals, and found several instances in which MCOs included inappropriate costs. These instances involved wrongfully including such items as:

- lobbying costs and entertainment costs;
- net cost allocations related to distributing plan costs among various lines of business;
- unresolved advertising, printing, and other expenses due to insufficient documentation; and
- unresolved costs of a related organization that were related to the plan.[99]

In 1998, as part of the roll-out of the Medicare+Choice plans, CMS adopted modifications in the ACR filing requirements. In order to "ensure the accuracy of the ACRs," CMS stated more specifically the nature of the administrative services that should be included and excluded from the calculations.[100]

As a result of the MMA in 2003, CMS now requires participating MCOs to submit information about monthly aggregate-bid amounts.[101] The monthly aggregate-bid amount for coverage of a Medicare Advantage-eligible beneficiary with a nationally average risk profile represents the Medicare Advantage organization's estimate of the revenue required to provide coverage under three factors.[102] Each bid is for a uniform benefit package for the service area, and contains all estimated revenue required by the plan (including administrative costs and return on investment). The bid is based on plan assumptions about the amount of revenue required from enrollee cost-sharing.[103] The regulations state that "as a condition for receiving a monthly payment. . .the [Medicare Advantage] organization agrees that [it]. . .must certify (based on best knowledge, information, and belief) that the information in its bid submission is accurate, complete, and truthful and fully conforms to the requirements in § 422.254."[104] MCOs that do not

---

[99] See DHHS OIG SEMI-ANNUAL REPORT OCTOBER 2001–MARCH 2002 22, *available online at* http://oig.hhs.gov/reading/semiannual/2002/Spring%20SemiAnnual%202002.pdf.

[100] *Compare* 63 Fed. Reg. 34,968, 35,010 (June 26, 1998), *codified at* 42 C.F.R. § 422.310 *with* 42 C.F.R. § 417.594.

[101] 42 C.F.R. § 422.254(a) 2011).

[102] 42 C.F.R. § 422.252 (2011). These three factors are: 1) "the unadjusted MA statutory non-drug monthly bid amount for coverage of original Medicare benefits, 2) the amount for basic prescription drug benefits under Part D (if any), and 3) the amount of provision for supplemental healthcare benefits (if any)." *Id.*

[103] 42 C.F.R. § 422.254(b) (2011).

[104] 42 C.F.R. § 422.504(l) (2011).

properly certify bid submissions may be subject to intermediate sanctions as described in § 8-5, *supra*.

With respect to PDPs, the CMS *Prescription Drug Benefit Manual* identifies improper bid submissions as an example of an area that will be targeted for investigation. PDPs that inappropriately overestimate or underestimate its bid in order to manipulate risk corridors and payments (including miscalculations of administrative-ratio costs within the bid) will be exposed to liability for claims of waste, fraud, and abuse.[105]

In order to protect against improper bid submissions, Congress has required that CMS audit one-third of the bid submissions by MCOs and PDPs.[106]

## § 8-8(c) Marketing Schemes and Enrollment Practices

An area of heightened scrutiny has involved the marketing practices of Medicare and Medicaid MCOs. For example, CMS regulates the manner with which MCOs inform eligible individuals about the organization to protect potential beneficiaries from deceptive or high pressure marketing. In 2008, CMS issued regulations that address marketing practices by managed care organizations and that codify a number of the issues addressed in the *Medicare Marketing Guidelines*, described below, such as:

- door-to-door solicitation or other unsolicited direct contact;
- in-home marketing appointments on topics and products not previously approved by the beneficiary prior to the meeting;
- cross-selling non-healthcare related products to a potential enrollee; or
- offering gifts or payments, including meals of any sort (excluding those of nominal value[107] such as pens or pill boxes). [108]

With respect to in-home marketing appointments, the rule limits the scope of sales discussions by requiring advanced approval. Thus, other health-related products can only be sold during a separate appointment, which must follow at least 48 hours after the initial meeting. In response to the proposed

---

[105] CMS, Prescription Drug Benefit Manual Ch.9.
[106] Social Security Act §§ 1857(d)(1), 1860D-12(b)(3)(c); 42 U.S.C. §§ 1395w-27(d)(1), 1395w-112(b)(3)(c).
[107] CMS, Medicare Marketing Guidelines for Medicare Advantage (MA), Medicare Advantage Prescription Drug Plans (MA-PD), Prescription Drug Plans (PDP) and 1876 Cost Plans (*Medicare Marketing Guidelines*) *at* 14, *available online at* https://www.cms.gov/ManagedCareMarketing/03_FinalPartCMarketingGuidelines.asp (defining "nominal value" to include "an individual item worth $15 or less, or aggregate items throughout the year worth $50 or less, where prices are based on the retail purchase price of the item.").
[108] 73 Fed. Reg. 54,208 (Sept. 18, 2008).

## Fraud and Abuse Issues Affecting the Managed Care Industry

rule, the Medicare Payment Advisory Commission (MedPAC) commented that this pre-approval process may be too limiting and cumbersome on beneficiaries who may realize during the course of a sales presentation, that he or she is interested in another type of product.[109] Consequently, MedPAC recommended that the scope of all in-home presentations be made broad enough to encompass all possible products offered by the insurer, agent, or broker. Nonetheless, CMS declined to change its proposal in the final rule.

Additionally, the regulations prohibit sales activities in a variety of other specific settings. In this context, sales activities include discussing plan specific information (such as premiums, cost-sharing, or benefits) and collecting and distributing applications, but not advertising activities such as sponsoring educational events.[110] For example, CMS prohibits sales activities at health education fairs as well as in settings primarily devoted to healthcare delivery. However, under the final rule, sales activities are permitted in common areas of healthcare settings, such as in hospital cafeterias.

The regulations also address CMS approval of marketing materials. CMS previously employed a "file and use" approval system based on past records and the nature and content of the marketing materials.[111] The regulations do away with the former "file and use" policy and instead approve marketing materials if they either use model language without substantive modification, or materials that are identified by CMS as not containing substantive content warranting CMS review.[112] The policy aims to level the playing field for contractors, reduce redundancies and focus CMS attention and resources on materials containing substantive content.

CMS's *Medicare Marketing Guidelines* prohibit additional marketing activities not addressed in the regulation, including using marketing techniques that mislead or confuse beneficiaries, and using marketing methods that discriminate among potential Medicare enrollees based on their income or health status.[113]

The *Medicare Marketing Guidelines* describe in further detail CMS's expectations regarding appropriate marketing to Medicare beneficiaries. For instance, it is prohibited as misleading and/or confusing to claim that the MCO is endorsed or recommended by CMS, but an MCO can use the term "Medicare-approved."[114] The *Medicare Marketing Guidelines* also provide specific guidance on font size, the use of testimonials, and particular language

---

[109] Letter from Glenn M. Hackbarth, Chairman, Medicare Payment Advisory Commission (MedPAC) to Kerry Weems, Acting Administrator, Centers for Medicare & Medicaid Services, (July 14, 2008) (on file with author).
[110] CMS, MEDICARE MARKETING GUIDELINES at 90-91.
[111] 73 Fed. Reg. 28,581 (May 16, 2008).
[112] *Id.* at 28,582.
[113] CMS, MEDICARE MARKETING GUIDELINES.
[114] *Id.* at 21.

that describe benefit and plan information.[115] Additionally, the *2012 Medicare Marketing Guidelines Update* includes a provision that all marketing material include a prominent disclaimer informing the public that "other plans may be available in the service area."[116]

With respect to enrollment discrimination, MCOs are required to refrain from marketing only to healthy beneficiaries (a practice known as "cherry-picking") while avoiding beneficiaries with a high risk for costly or prolonged treatment needs (a practice known as "lemon-dropping").

For example, in 2008, Amerigroup settled with the Department of Justice for $225 million for allegedly systematically avoiding enrolling certain patient groups in its Illinois Medicaid MCO.[117] The case settled following a trial by jury that resulted in a judgment of over $334 million, which was under appeal at the time of settlement. The case involved allegations that Amerigroup refused to enroll pregnant women, discouraged prospective enrollees who needed specialized medical care from enrolling, and retroactively disenrolled prematurely born infants. According to one of the government's press releases, Amerigroup was paid, in part, to help low income pregnant women who had inadequate prenatal care to find care.[118] The theory was that Amerigroup engaged in fraudulent inducement when it misrepresented in its contract with Illinois Medicaid that it would not discriminate based on need for healthcare services when it had no intention of doing so, that the enrollment forms submitted included implied certifications of compliance with the non-discrimination provision, and that the capitation rates paid to the MCO were based on the promise not to discriminate, such that the MCO received inflated capitation payments, all in violation of the federal and state FCA. The jury found for the plaintiffs in the amount of $48 million in government damages, based on testimony demonstrating the difference between the medical loss ratios (MLRs) of Amerigroup and other Medicaid MCOs, which automatically triggered $144 million in treble damages The jury also found over 18,000 false claims, based on the number of enrollment forms that contained at least one female between the ages of 17 and 44 for the relevant time period, which, at $10,500 each ($5,500 minimum federal FCA penalty plus $5,000 Illinois Whistleblower Reward and Protection Act), triggered FCA penalties of over $190 million. When Amerigroup's motion for judgment as a matter of law or new trial was denied, the case was ultimately settled.

---

[115] *See generally* CMS, MEDICARE MARKETING GUIDELINES.

[116] *Id.* at 21.

[117] U.S. Department of Justice Press Release, (Aug. 14, 2008), *Amerigroup to End Appeal and Pay $225 Million to United States and Illinois to Settle Pregnancy Discrimination Case*, available online at http://www.justice.gov/usao/iln/pr/chicago/2008/pr0814_01.pdf.

[118] U.S. Department of Justice Press Release, (Mar. 13, 2007), *U.S. Judge Raises Total Damages to More than $334 Million against Amerigroup HMO in Pregnancy Discrimination Case*, available online at http://www.justice.gov/usao/iln/pr/chicago/2007/pr0313_01.pdf.

## Fraud and Abuse Issues Affecting the Managed Care Industry

The *Medicare Marketing Guidelines* specifically state that an MCO may not discriminate based on race, ethnicity, religion, gender, sexual orientation, *health status*, or *geographic location* within the service area.[119] The *2012 Medicare Marketing Guidelines Update* added that plans may not discriminate based on national origin, mental or physical disability, claims experience, medical history, genetic information, or evidence or insurability.[120] Additionally, the 2012 update established additional protections for persons requiring interpretation to ensure that relevant enrollment and plan information is readily available. The new guidelines require plan sponsors' call centers to have interpreter services and require all marketing materials to be available in any language that is the primary language of more than 5% of a plan sponsor's plan benefit package service area.[121] Basic enrollment information must also be available to individuals with disabilities (such as hearing and visual deficiencies) and plan must have TTY numbers available for potential enrollees' use.[122]

The *2012 Medicare Marketing Guidelines Update* placed new focus on marketing from third-parties.[123] If a third-party is not affiliated or contracted by the plan sponsor, CMS does not review any of the marketing materials from that third-party. Plan sponsors that provide marketing material by third-party entities are responsible for the marketing content. The plan sponsor must ensure that these materials have the appropriate disclaimers stating that "Medicare has neither reviewed or endorsed this information" and "this is not a complete listing of plans available in your service area." CMS is concerned that third-parties are "representing themselves as an objective or unbiased source of information."[124]

CMS also discourages, but does not prohibit, the use of physicians as marketing agents. Its concern is that physicians may not be in the best position to provide beneficiaries with complete information on HMO risk enrollment, and that beneficiaries could be confused as to whether the physician is giving advice based on the patient's best medical interest. Moreover, the physician's knowledge of the beneficiary's health status may lead to enrollment discrimination.[125]

In order to inform Medicare beneficiaries of the various limitations to which CMS subjects Medicare MCOs, CMS and the OIG in October 1996 promulgated a Medicare Beneficiary Advisory Bulletin entitled "What

---

[119] *Id.* at 22 (emphasis added).
[120] *Id.* at 22.
[121] *Id.* at 23-24, 49 and 112.
[122] *Id.* at 22-23, 35 and 55.
[123] *Id.* at 51-52.
[124] CMS Memorandum, *Reminder to Plan Regarding Third Party Marketing Activities and Educational Events* (Sept. 28, 2010), *available online at* http://www.cms.gov/ManagedCareMarketing/Downloads/broker_websites_20092810.pdf.
[125] CMS, MEDICARE MARKETING GUIDELINES at 107-108.

Medicare Beneficiaries Need to Know About Health Maintenance Organizations (HMO) Arrangements: Know Your Rights." [126] This document described to Medicare beneficiaries their enrollment rights (including the manner with which the MCO markets itself to Medicare beneficiaries), their disenrollment rights, their rights to receive medical services, and how a Medicare beneficiary can voice any complaints. Moreover, the Medicare Beneficiary Advisory Bulletin described other problematic marketing activities. For instance, because pre-enrollment health screening and questions about an enrollee's health and physical status are generally prohibited, the bulletin cautions beneficiaries to be wary of MCOs that ask for information regarding the number of physicians or frequency of physician visits, frequency of hospitalization, or frequency of exercise. Beneficiaries also are cautioned to be alert for improper screenings when HMOs offer free physical exams before enrollment, or free screenings or diagnostic tests at health fairs or marketing presentations. The bulletin also advised beneficiaries to be wary if HMO representatives discourage the beneficiary from enrolling because of more limited accessibility to specialists or delays in obtaining services. Of course, as HMOs also are required to give Medicare beneficiaries full information regarding the limitations of HMO risk enrollment (including that the beneficiary cannot continue to use non-HMO-contracting physicians and hospitals), it is not clear where the line is drawn between required objective information and improper enrollment screening.[127]

In Chapter 9 of the *Prescription Drug Benefit Manual*, CMS lists a number of potential examples of activities that PBMs might engage in that should be targeted for investigation, including the following:[128]

- receiving payments to switch a beneficiary from one drug to another, to influence the prescriber to switch the patient to a different drug, or to place a product on a formulary;
- making formulary decisions in which cost takes precedence over clinical efficacy and appropriateness;
- ensuring that the Pharmaceutical and Therapeutic Committee is properly staffed with the appropriate professional backgrounds, and that these individuals are free of any conflicts of interest;
- intentionally providing (or arranging for a pharmacy to provide) less than the prescribed quantity of a medication without informing the patient or making arrangements to provide the balance, yet billing for the fully prescribed amount; and

---

[126] DHHS OIG Medicare Beneficiary Advisory Bulletin, *What Medicare Beneficiaries Need to Know About Health Maintenance Organizations (HMO) Arrangements: Know Your Rights* (Oct. 1996), *available online at* http://oig.hhs.gov/fraud/docs/alertsandbulletins/adbulhmo.pdf.
[127] *Id.*
[128] CMS, Prescription Drug Benefit Manual Ch.9.

## Fraud and Abuse Issues Affecting the Managed Care Industry

- failing to offer negotiated prices and passing along discounts to beneficiaries.

Despite the lengthy *Medicare Marketing Guidelines,* the OIG remains concerned about beneficiaries' vulnerabilities to the sales and marketing practices of Medicare Advantage Plans. The OIG published a report in March of 2010 detailing weaknesses in enforcement of the *Medicare Marketing Guidelines*.[129] OIG's main concern is that "aggressive, deceptive and fraudulent marketing practices could result in Medicare beneficiaries enrolling in plans that do not meet their healthcare needs." In the report, OIG examined MA plan sponsors' compensation of sales agents, including analyzing over 13,000 sales agent marketing complaints reported to CMS during both the 2008 and 2009 enrollment periods. In its investigation, OIG found that plan sponsors who contracted with independent sales agents had compensation arrangements that led to inappropriate financial incentives and that many plan sponsors did not take steps to ensure that their sales agents met CMS's qualification regulations. In response to this investigation, the OIG enumerated what it found to be the most concerning issues including: 1) "providing misleading information about plan benefits, 2) enrolling Medicare beneficiaries without their consent, and 3) engaging in aggressive sales tactics." To alleviate these concerns the OIG made several recommendations to CMS including:

- "Audit plan sponsors and include an assessment of the vulnerabilities identified,
- Issue additional regulations concerning FMO payments,
- Issue regulations requiring plan sponsors to contact all new enrollees to ensure that they understand the rules, and
- Issue guidelines clarifying that plan sponsors should terminate unlicensed sales agents immediately upon discovery."

Despite the OIG's lengthy report on issues involving marketing practices, CMS did not agree with a majority of the OIG's recommendations, including the last three enumerated above.

The Health Reform Law has also put the marketing practice of Medicare plans in the spotlight, in an effort to decrease the costs to federal health programs and reduce the incidence of fraud. Section 6408 of the Health Reform Law established enhanced penalties for Medicare plans.[130] While the Secretary already had the authority to impose sanctions and CMPs on Medicare plans, this new provision increases the types of violations subject to sanctions and penalties. The new penalties began to apply to prohibited acts occurring

---

[129] Office of the Inspector General, *Beneficiaries Remain Vulnerable to Sales Agent's Marketing of Medicare Advantage Plans* (March 2010), *available online at* http://oig.hhs.gov/oei/reports/oei-05-09-00070.pdf.
[130] The Health Reform Law, § 6408.

on or after January 1, 2010. The provision provides sanctions and CMPs for "plans that enroll individuals in a MA or Part D plan without their consent (except Part D dual eligibles), transfer an individual from one plan to another for the purpose of earning a commission, fail to comply with marketing requirements, or employ or contract with an individual or entity that violates the terms of the contract." When a plan misrepresents or falsifies information furnished to the Secretary or to an individual, the new provision also provides for an additional assessment equal to the amount claimed by the plan on the false information.

## § 8-8(d)   Financial Relationships with Providers

Several fraud theories can arise related to an MCO's practices in paying providers. For example, MCOs might face liability under the FCA for allegedly failing to pay providers and process healthcare claims in a timely and otherwise appropriate manner. In this regard, in 2005, AmeriChoice of Pennsylvania settled with the federal government for $1.6 million to resolve allegations regarding improper claims processing and coverage determinations occurring nearly a decade earlier.[131] Specifically, the settled allegations involved a failure to process and pay claims in a timely fashion, or at all, as well as a failure to cover home health services to qualified beneficiaries. As part of the settlement the MCO was restricted from processing claims in a manner that automatically (1) "downcodes" evaluation and management services or changes codes to those reflecting a reduced intensity, or (2) "bundles" certain services together to bill for only one service. However, the ability of the MCO to downcode based on a review of supporting documentation was preserved. Interestingly, this is the mirror image of behavior usually ascribed to fee-for-service providers (e.g., downcoding vs. upcoding, bundling vs. unbundling; described in §§ 4-5(c), 4-5(d) above), and the government views it as similarly actionable under the FCA.

Overpayment recoveries from providers also may trigger false claims liability. In October 2006, Keystone Mercy Health Plan paid $5 million to settle with the United States allegations in connection with its Pennsylvania Medicaid managed care operations that it kept certain Coordination of Benefits (COB) overpayments it recovered from providers instead of turning them over to the Pennsylvania Department of Public Welfare (DPW).[132] The government alleged that the DPW contract gave DPW the exclusive right

---

[131] Philadelphia Business Journal, *Americhoice to pay $1.6 million to Resolve Claims Allegations* (June 30, 2005), *available online at* http://www.bizjournals.com/philadelphia/stories/2005/06/27/daily39.html.

[132] Press Release, U.S. Attorney's Office, *Eastern District Pennsylvania, Keystone Mercy Health Plan to Pay Government $5 Million to Resolve Civil Liabilities under the False Claims Act*, *available online at* http://www.justice.gov/usao/pae/News/Pr/2006/oct/Keystonepress.html.

## Fraud and Abuse Issues Affecting the Managed Care Industry

to the recoveries it made after expiration of certain time limits, despite the MCO's arguments that the provision applied to recoveries from third parties, such as other insurance companies, and not to recoveries from providers.[133]

Failure to pay providers was a major theme in the Tower Health case in California.[134] Tower Health contracted with a public HMO to furnish provider network services to Medi-Cal recipients, but reportedly its owners siphoned off funds to affiliated companies instead of paying network providers, and submitted false financials to the HMO that it was solvent. Tower's owners were charged criminally.

Another significant set of issues that may raise potential fraud liability involves the financial incentives that MCOs create in their relationships with providers that may result in the reduction of enrollee access to medically necessary services. In its "Comprehensive Plan for Program Integrity," CMS recognized that "managed care brings a shift of fraud and abuse incentives from those found with a traditional fee-for-service healthcare delivery program. While concerns under fee-for-service focus on over-utilization of services, under managed care, incentives are in the provision of inadequate amounts of services."[135] Consequently, the Managed Care Fraud Working Group (described in § 8-1, *supra*) has focused much of its attention on underutilization in managed care, specifically the extent to which underutilization may be deemed to be fraudulent activity.

In connection with MCOs that operate PIPs, federal regulations prohibit MCOs from making specific payment to physicians as an inducement to reduce or limit medically necessary services with respect to a specific individual.[136] If the MCO places physicians at "substantial financial risk" for services not furnished by the physicians, then the MCO must provide adequate stop-loss protection, and conduct periodic surveys of previous and current enrollees to determine enrollee access to and satisfaction with the MCO's services. Finally, MCOs must furnish descriptive information to the Medicare program to permit a determination of whether the plan is in compliance with these requirements.

Although federal courts generally have addressed the appropriateness of MCO's financial incentive arrangements with providers, most of these cases have concerned violation of an MCO's fiduciary duty under ERISA.[137]

---

[133] *Id.*, Settlement Agreement, p.2

[134] *See* California Office of the Attorney General Press Release, *Attorney General Lockyer Announces Indictment of Tower Health Executives in Medi-Cal Fraud Case* (July 20, 2005), *available online at* http://oag.ca.gov/news/press_release?id=1198.

[135] CMS, COMPREHENSIVE PLAN FOR PROGRAM INTEGRITY, Pub. No. HCFA-02142, U.S. Gov't Printing Office, Washington, DC, Feb. 1999.

[136] *See* 42 CFR § 417.479.

[137] Herdrich v. Pegram, 154 F.3d 362, (7th Cir. 1998), *reh'g en banc denied*, 170 F.3d 683 (7th Cir. 1999), 530 U.S. 211 (2000); Shea v. Esensten, 107 F.3d 625 (8th Cir. 1997), *cert. denied*, 531 U.S. 871 (2000).

Nevertheless, physician-incentive arrangements and the denial or failure to provide medically necessary care have received attention under state fraud theories. For example, in 1998, the Texas Attorney General filed a lawsuit against several MCOs pursuant to Texas law that prohibited MCOs from giving improper financial incentives to doctors to limit patient care.[138] The attorney general alleged that the MCOs illegally compensated physicians who limited medical care to members, and penalized those who did not limit care. The allegations stated that the HMOs placed physicians in a conflict-of-interest situation, where physicians risked losing compensation from the HMO if they provided medically necessary care, yet stood to gain financially if they limited care. The lawsuit sought injunctive relief and civil penalties up to $10,000 for each violation.[139]

Aetna, one MCO involved with the litigation, reached a settlement agreement in 2000 with the attorney general.[140] Under the terms of the agreement, Aetna agreed to give more enrollees access to the state's independent-review process; to create an ombudsman position to assist enrollees with complaints and problems; to end financial incentives to physicians that create disincentives for care; to clearly define medical necessity and deliver medically necessary care; and to help those enrollees with chronic illnesses by providing better care and access to specialists and experimental treatment.[141]

In 1998, a class-action lawsuit also was filed in Texas by an MCO's primary-care physicians, alleging that the negative-incentive provisions of the HMO's payor contract acted to improperly limit medically necessary care and constituted a violation of Texas state law. At issue was Harris Methodist's policy of giving pooled groups of physicians either bonuses for coming in under budget or, in the case of pharmacy expenditures, imposing financial penalties for going over budget. Physicians who overspent their pharmacy budget were responsible for 35% of the deficit, but they could keep 49% of any pharmacy budget surplus. The eventual $3.4 million settlement in this case was the first penalty imposed under a state law that prohibits HMOs from using financial incentives that reward physicians for limiting medically necessary care. Under the terms of the settlement, the HMO paid $2.6 million to physicians who exceeded prescription-drug budgets and $725,000 to physicians who lost bonuses when they did not meet targets for expenditures on prescriptions, specialists, and hospital care.[142]

---

[138] Richard A. Oppel Jr., *Physicians Find Fault With Aetna U.S. Healthcare Settlement in Texas*, N. Y. TIMES, (Apr. 21, 2000).
[139] Milt Freudenheim, *Aetna Settles Texas Suit Over Doctors' Cost Rules*, N.Y. TIMES, (Apr. 12, 2000).
[140] Texas Att'y Gen. & Aetna U.S. Healthcare, Inc., Settlement Agreement (2000), *available online at* http://www.oag.state.tx.us/notice/avc_fin1.pdf.
[141] *Id.*
[142] *Texas HMO Agrees to Pay Back $3.4M to Physicians*, MANAGED CARE MAGAZINE (Sept. 1998); *Harris Methodist pays docs $3.4 million, eliminates physician risk contacts*, MANAGED CARE OUTLOOK (Aug. 28, 1998).

## Fraud and Abuse Issues Affecting the Managed Care Industry

Beyond cases involving the failure to provide medically necessary care, other managed care practices can lead to potential liability under the quality of care theory. For example, MCOs have been accused of engaging in fraud for not devoting sufficient resources to ensure that its providers have the requisite credentials. In 2003, the United States Attorney's Office for the Eastern District of Pennsylvania entered into a joint agreement with the largest HMO in the Philadelphia area. The agreement was designed to ensure that the HMO's enrollees received healthcare services only from qualified healthcare providers. The case grew out of the revelation that a subcontractor retained to provide mental-health services for the HMO hired a person who had falsely claimed to be a psychiatrist.[143] As a result, a number of HMO enrollees received inadequate treatment from the doctor, including taking prescription medications. This benchmark agreement set forth a model credentialing plan for MCOs to ensure that the providers have all the required qualifications and licenses. The credentialing plan provided for comprehensive credential checks at the time of hiring, as well as subsequent audits to ensure that the providers maintained the required licenses. The plan covered all the HMO's providers, as well as all the providers employed by its subcontractors for mental health, dental care, chiropractic care, nursing homes, and ASCs.

### § 8-8(e)  Failure to Provide Required Services, Misrepresenting Services to Qualify for Higher Payments, Underutilization, Quality of Care

While typically managed care services are furnished indirectly through participating providers and are a function of medical necessity, sometimes MCOs are contractually required to furnish certain services directly, such as case management and disease management services, and their failure to do so, and related misrepresentations, can serve as the basis for FCA enforcement.

For instance, in February 2011, the Ohio-based Medicaid managed care contractor CareSource agreed to pay $26 million to the U.S. and the state of Ohio to resolve allegations of FCA violations. Specifically, it was alleged that CareSource failed to provide required screening, assessment and case management for adults and children with special healthcare needs. Reportedly, CareSource submitted false data to the state of Ohio so that it appeared that it

---

[143] *HMO, U.S. Attorney form credential policy for healthcare workers*, PHILADELPHIA BUS. J., (Feb. 13, 2003).

was providing the required services[144] and so that it could retain the incentive portion of capitation payments.[145]

Similarly, in the same month, APS Healthcare Midwest agreed to pay $13 million to the state of Georgia and the US to settle allegations that it submitted claims for disease and case management services that it never provided to Georgia Medicaid beneficiaries.[146]

Quality measurement and reporting also is an area susceptible to FCA settlements. In January 2011, AmeriHealth Mercy Health Plan, a Third Party Administrator for Kentucky's Medicaid Managed Care Plan, agreed to pay over $2 million to the Kentucky Medicaid program for falsely reporting its Health Effectiveness Data and Information Set (HEDIS) score for the Cervical Cancer Screening (CSS) measure to the Department of Medicaid Services in 2009 in order to obtain more than $600,000 in bonus money.[147] Specifically, the health plan excluded members as having a full hysterectomy where there was no medical evidence of a full hysterectomy, and counted members as having received a Pap smear where there was no medical evidence of a Pap smear.

Utilization management activities also may serve as the basis for FCA settlements. In 2006, IntraCorp settled with the United States and six states for $3.15 million to resolve allegations relating to failing to provide adequate written utilization review criteria, training and quality assurance programs and controls.[148] Despite the settlement, in the context of relator's challenge to the reasonableness of the settlement amount[149], the District Court found that, while there were obvious operational deficiencies, the record did not support anything more than negligence as to those deficiencies such that the government and relator would have significant difficulty in establishing liability under the FCA. Allegations regarding non-compliance with URAC

---

[144] DOJ Press Release, *Ohio-Based Managed Care Plan Contractor CareSource & Entities to Pay $26 Million to Resolve False Claims Allegations*, available online at: http://www.justice.gov/opa/pr/2011/February/11-civ-138.html.

[145] CareSource Settlement Agreement, p. 2.

[146] Attorney General of Georgia Press Release, *APS Healthcare Pays $13 million to Settle Investigation into False Medicaid Claims*, available online at http://law.ga.gov/00/press/detail/0,2668,87670814_87670929_168474870,00.html.

[147] *See* Kentucky Office of the Attorney General Press Release, *AmeriHealth Mercy to Pay $2 Million for Submitting False Report* (Jan. 26, 2011), available online at http://migration.kentucky.gov/Newsroom/ag/amerihealthmercy.htm.

[148] *See District Court Approves Settlement of Alleged Utilization Review Deficiencies*, BNA HEALTHCARE DAILY (Apr. 13, 2006) (stating under the settlement $1.65 million was to be divided amongst the six participating states and the relator was to receive $3.15 million).

[149] U.S. *ex rel.* Nudelman v International Rehabilitation Associates d/b/a Intracorp, Civ. Action No. 00-1837 (E.D. Pa. Apr. 4, 2006), *available online at* http://www.paed.uscourts.gov/documents/opinions/06D0439P.pdf; *see also* U.S.*ex rel.* Nudelman v. International Rehabilitation Associates d/b/a Intracorp, Civ. Action No. 00-1837 (E.D. Pa. Oct. 30, 2006), *available online at* http://www.paed.uscourts.gov/documents/opinions/06D1342P.pdf.

## Fraud and Abuse Issues Affecting the Managed Care Industry

accreditation standards, as well as alleged misrepresentation to URAC as to the manner in which utilization review was conducted for the purpose of obtaining accreditation, were found to be insufficient for FCA purposes, since accreditation, or certification of URAC compliance, was not a specific requirement or pre-condition to payment, nor were the services so flawed as to be completely worthless.

Allegations that Health Insurance Plan of Greater New York (HIP) falsified data to obtain accreditation also was found to be insufficient for FCA purposes in *U.S. ex rel Sterling v. Health Insurance Plan of Greater New York*.[150] In this case, a HIP supervisor was alleged to have altered data submitted to the National Committee for Quality Assurance (NCQA) for purposes of accreditation regarding the percentage of children diagnosed with Pharyngitis who were tested for strep throat. The court dismissed the case, finding that there was no intent that the government rely on the false data to NCQA as a condition of payment, but, rather, only the intent to obtain accreditation. Thus, there was not a sufficient connection between the alleged fraud and the government's payment. Moreover, presenting medical data to NCQA is not equivalent to presenting a claim to the government in violation of the FCA.

### § 8-8(f)  Contracting/Bid Misrepresentations.

Representations made to CMS in connection with the contracting process also may serve as the basis for FCA enforcement. In 2007, America's Health Choice, Inc. (AHC), Florida, agreed to pay to the OIG $100,000 in civil monetary penalties for misrepresenting information to DHHS.[151] The allegations involved submitting documents on at least three occasions that misrepresented the academic credentials of a health plan employee and submitting at least seven notices to the Center for Healthcare Dispute Resolution (CHDR) with the dates of submission falsified to appear in compliance with CHDR's request for claims data.

### § 8-8(g)  Cost Shifting.

As health plans participating in the Medicare and Medicaid programs typically have private product lines as well, there is a potential for improper cost (and beneficiary) shifting among these plans. In February 2011, Blue Cross Blue Shield of Illinois settled with the DOJ for $25 million to resolve

---

[150] United States *ex rel.* Sterling v. Health Ins. Plan of Greater New York, Inc., No. 06CV1141, 2008 U.S. Dist. LEXIS 76874 (S.D.N.Y. Sept. 30, 2008).

[151] *See* OIG, Enforcement Actions-Managed Care on 11-07-2007, *available online at* http://oig.hhs.gov/fraud/enforcement/cmp/managed_care.asp; *see also* DHHS and OIG, *Healthcare Fraud and Abuse Control Program Annual Report for FY 2008*, (Sept. 2009) at 25, *available online at* http://oig.hhs.gov/publications/docs/hcfac/hcfacreport2008.pdf.

allegations that it advised enrollees in its private health plan that children were not covered for private duty nursing, and referring these enrollees to the state Medicaid plan.[152] According to the allegations, the MCO terminated certain service coverage for medically-fragile, technologically dependent children to shift their care to a state/federal funded Medicaid program. This practice was allegedly based on stringent internal coverage criteria that were not disclosed to beneficiaries in plan policy materials.

### § 8-8(h)   Discount Skimming

Several MCOs have been required to settle allegations of fraud for failing to pass on discounts that the MCOs have negotiated with providers. For example, in the state of Washington, an owner of a PPO was convicted and sentenced to imprisonment, while he and the PPO paid approximately $2.5 million to settle a FCA case for failing to pass discounts along to a federal healthcare program.[153] In another case, Blue Cross and Blue Shield of Massachusetts agreed to pay nearly $10 million to settle two lawsuits that alleged that it negotiated secret discounts from hospitals and failed to disclose them to subscribers in violation of statutory, contractual, and common-law obligations.[154]

### § 8-8(i)   Pharmacy Benefit Managers

Many MCOs contract with a pharmacy benefit manager (PBM) to manage the MCO's drug benefit. Although PBMs initially streamlined the claims process and the distribution system, PBMs currently provide a mechanism for MCOs to reduce costs through the ability to negotiate significant volume discounts. In addition, some PBMs apply managed care principles to the distribution of prescription drugs by accepting a capitated fee from the MCO to provide prescription drugs to enrollees. This arrangement creates the same managed care incentives to control utilization of prescription drugs. As such, it presents the same fraud and abuse challenges (e.g., quality of care, underutilization, and denial of access to prescription drug benefits to increase MCO and PBM profits).

PBMs with pharmacy components may contract with pharmaceutical manufacturers for the purchase of drugs from the manufacturers and the

---

[152] DOJ Press Release, *BlueCross BlueShield of Illinois to Pay $25 Million to Settle Civil Medicaid Fraud Claims*, available online at http://www.justice.gov/usao/iln/pr/chicago/2011/pr0224_01.pdf.
[153] *See* DOJ, Healthcare Fraud Report 1995 and 1996, Selected Cases, *available online at* http://www.usdoj.gov/opa/health/hcf2.htm.
[154] *Blue Cross Blue Shield Pays $10 Million To Settle Negotiated Discount Case,* BNA HEALTHCARE DAILY (July 13, 1998); *see also Iowa Blues Announce Settlement Plan In Copay, Discount Disclosure Disputes,* BNA HEALTHCARE DAILY (Jan. 2, 1997).

## Fraud and Abuse Issues Affecting the Managed Care Industry

provision of data to the manufacturer, which also may create various potential fraud issues. In September 2005, AdvancePCS, a major PBM wholly owned by Caremark Rx, Inc., agreed to settle a case for $137.5 million in which the government alleged that the PBM solicited and received kickbacks from various drug manufacturers in return for featuring their drugs on the MCOs' formularies. The government alleged that AdvancePCS received payments from pharmaceutical manufacturers in the form of excessive administrative fees, as well as overpriced products and services agreements, as an improper reward for favorable treatment for the manufacturer's drugs on the formularies provided to the PBM's customer plans. The government claimed that in certain instances, as a result of these payments, the PBM promoted and switched beneficiaries to comparable drugs that were more expensive than the drugs initially prescribed by the enrollee's physician.[155] The government further alleged that AdvancePCS paid kickbacks to potential customers, such as MCOs, that contracted with federally funded healthcare plans to provide their prescription-drug services. The government alleged that these hidden financial relationships on both ends of the prescription-drug market constituted illegal kickbacks under the FCA.

Two years later, in 2008, Caremark, which acquired AdvancePCS, settled with 28 states for AdvancePCS drug switching practices.[156] The states alleged deceptive business practices, in that doctors were encouraged to switch patients to different brand-name prescription drugs with representations that the patients and/or health plans would save money, but doctors were not adequately informed of the effect the switch would have on costs to patients and health plans. The client health plans also were not informed that rebates that accrued in the drug switching process would be retained by the PBM and not passed through to the health plan. The settlement required substantial changes in how the PBM conducts business, including prohibiting drug switches with greater patient or net cost, or where the patient was switched from a similar drug in the last two years, as well as disclosure requirements regarding the effects on patient copayments, material differences in side effects or efficacy, the financial incentives to the PBM, that patients may decline drug switches, inform prescribers when materials are funded by pharmaceutical manufacturers. The PBM also was required to monitor the effects of drug switches on the health of patients, refrain from making unsubstantiated claims of savings for drug switches to patients or prescribers, reimburse patients for out-of-pocket expenses for drug switch-related healthcare costs and notify patients that

---

[155] DOJ Press Release, *Justice Department Recovers $1.4 Billion in Fraud & False Claims in Fiscal Year 2005; More Than $15 Billion Since 1986*, available online at http://www.justice.gov/opa/pr/2005/November/05_civ_595.html

[156] *See, e.g,*. http://www.oag.state.tx.us/oagnews/release.php?id=2372.

reimbursement is available, and obtain express, verifiable authorization from the prescriber for all drug switches.[157]

In 2006, Medco Health Solutions (Medco) agreed to pay $155 million plus interest to settle allegations that it submitted false claims and solicited kickbacks from pharmaceutical manufacturers to favor their drugs, and paid kickbacks to health plans to obtain business.[158] The specific allegations included both allegations related to Medco's pharmacy operations and those related to its benefit management operations. Managed care-related allegations, which the government characterized as improper kickbacks to the extent they were not passed through, shared, or disclosed, included promoting a formulary that favored expensive drugs; making improper payments to health plans to induce the plans to select or retain Medco as their PBM, such as implementation allowances, contract allowances, data fees, credits, up-front payments, cash and services; soliciting and receiving improper payments from pharmaceutical manufacturers to provide favorable consideration for their products in formulary placement and drug switches, such as providing rebates, discounts, patient conversion payments, market share movement payments, market share incentives, data fees, commissions, mail service purchase discounts, administrative or management fees, educational grants, outcomes research studies, clinical consulting services, nominally-priced products, disease management program payments, and strategic alliances.

Pharmaceutical manufacturers also have entered into settlements related to their relationships with PBMs. In April 2007, Pfizer settled on behalf of its acquired subsidiary, Pharmacia and Upjohn Company, Inc. in connection with a PBM bidding transaction.[159] Specifically, Pharmacia solicited bids from PBMs to be selected as vendor for Pharmacia's "Bridge Program" to provide distribution, patient assistance and insurance reimbursement for its human growth hormone product, Genotropin. Pharmacia allegedly rated the bids according to criteria including cost, quality and responsiveness and selected and notified of the award one bidding PBM whose bid was $12 million less expensive, over a three year period, than the nearest competitor's bid and who was recommended for selection by Pharmacia employees.[160] When Pharmacia learned of an opportunity to improve the formulary positioning and/

---

[157] Illinois Attorney General Press Release, *Madigan, 28 Attorneys General Reach Settlement with Caremark for Drug Switching Practices*, available online at http://illinoisattorneygeneral.gov/pressroom/2008_02/20080214.html.

[158] DOJ Press Release, *Medco to Pay U.S. $155 Million to Settle False Claims Act Cases*, available online at http://www.justice.gov/opa/pr/2006/October/06_civ_722.html.

[159] *See Pfizer Units Agree to Pay $34.7 Million to Resolve Drug Promotion Allegations*, BNA HEALTHCARE DAILY (April 3, 2007); *see also Pfizer Unit Sentenced to Pay $19.7 Million After Admitting it Offered Kickback to PBM*, BNA HEALTHCARE DAILY (Apr. 27, 2007).

[160] *See* Criminal Information, *United States v. Pharmacia & Upjohn Co.*, 1:07-CR-10099-RGS (D. Mass. Apr. 2, 2007); *see also* Government's Sentencing Memorandum, United States v. Pharmacia & Upjohn Co., 1:07-CR-10099-RGS (D. Mass. Apr. 24, 2007).

# Fraud and Abuse Issues Affecting the Managed Care Industry

or formulary ancillary relationships of Pharmacia's drug products at a competing PBM, Pharmacia retracted the award to the first PBM and awarded the Bridge Program contract to the competing PBM. Significantly, Pharmacia had prepared a financial analysis showing the anticipated financial benefits of millions of dollars resulting from the anticipated improvement in formulary positioning and formulary ancillary benefits. Pharmacia paid $20 million in criminal fines and pled guilty to one count of violating the anti-kickback statute for offering excess payments on the Bridge Program contract to induce the purchase of Pharmacia's pharmaceutical products.

In Chapter 9 of the *Prescription Drug Benefit Manual*, CMS lists a number of potential examples of activities that PBMs might engage in that should be targeted for investigation, including the following:[161]

- receiving payments to switch a beneficiary from one drug to another, to influence the prescriber to switch the patient to a different drug, or to place a product on a formulary;
- making formulary decisions in which cost takes precedence over clinical efficacy and appropriateness;
- intentionally providing (or arranging for a pharmacy to provide) less than the prescribed quantity of a medication without informing the patient or making arrangements to provide the balance, yet billing for the fully prescribed amount; and
- failing to offer negotiated prices and passing along discounts to beneficiaries.

## § 8-8(j) Formulary Development and Implementation

Although PDPs are not required to have a formulary or designated list of prescription drugs, a formulary is an essential cost-management tool for PDPs. As required by the MMA, the United States Pharmacopoeia (USP) has developed a list of Part D formulary categories and classes. Consequently (and similar to improper conduct between pharmaceutical manufacturers and PBMs), the government has concentrated on improper financial relationships between the pharmaceutical manufacturers and the MCOs.

In a 2004 case similar to the AdvancePCS investigation (described at § 8-8(i)), but in the context of a pharmaceutical manufacturer and an MCO (instead of a PBM), the government alleged that a pharmaceutical manufacturer provided rebates and other payments to an MCO in exchange for keeping the manufacturer's drug on the MCO's approved formulary. Under federal law, the manufacturer was required to give its best and lowest price to Medicaid. However, when the MCO requested a price reduction to keep the

---

[161] CMS, Prescription Drug Benefit Manual Ch.9.

cost in line with the leading competitor's drug, the manufacturer responded with a $10 million "price reduction package" of payments and benefits to the insurer, including an annual "data fee" of 2% of the annual gross sales of the manufacturer's drugs to the insurer.[162] The government also alleged that the manufacturer offered the insurer other benefits, including an interest-free loan in the form of "prepaid rebates" and $3 million worth of deeply discounted tablets. According to the government, these payments served to secure a place for the manufacturer's product on the MCO's approved drug list, but did not result in any price reduction to Medicaid. The manufacturer settled these allegations for $345.5 million, and pled guilty to a criminal charge that it overbilled Medicaid for its popular allergy medicine.

Similarly, in a case against TAP Pharmaceutical Products, Inc. (TAP), the relator and later the government alleged that the company had offered "educational grants" usable for any purpose to an HMO in return for including TAP's drug on the HMO's formulary.[163]

## § 8-8(k)  Patient-Assistance Programs and the Medicare Part D Benefit

For years, pharmaceutical manufacturers, patient-advocacy groups, and charitable organizations have sponsored patient assistance programs (PAPs) to provide financial assistance to patients who do not have insurance coverage for outpatient prescription drugs. Although Part D offers Medicare beneficiaries coverage for outpatient prescription drugs, Medicare beneficiaries who enroll in Part D have cost-sharing obligations that some beneficiaries may not be able to afford, yet do not qualify for the low-income subsidy. Consequently, the issue arises regarding whether PAPs constitute improper remuneration to the provider of the service (e.g., a physician, clinic, or pharmacy) under the Anti-Kickback Statute, or improper inducement to the Medicare beneficiary under either the Anti-Kickback Statute or the CMP statute related to the provision of inducements to beneficiaries (*see* § 2-7(a)).

---

[162] *See* DOJ Press Release, *Schering-Plough to Pay $345 Million to Resolve Criminal and Civil Liabilities for Illegal Marketing of Claritin* (July 30, 2004), *available online at* http://www.usdoj.gov/opa/pr/2004/July/04_civ_523.htm.

[163] United States *ex rel.* Gerstein v. TAP Holdings, Inc., Civ. No. 98-10547 (D. Mass.) (settlement filed Oct. 2001); DOJ Press Release, *TAP Pharmaceutical Products, Inc. and Seven Others Charged With Healthcare Crimes; Company Agrees to Pay $875 Million to Settle Charges* (Oct. 3, 2001), *available online at* http://www.usdoj.gov/opa/pr/2001/October/513civ.htm.

## Fraud and Abuse Issues Affecting the Managed Care Industry

The agency has addressed these arrangements in a series of OIG Advisory Opinions.[164] In each scenario, the OIG concluded that, even though the proposed arrangements could potentially result in prohibited remuneration under the anti-kickback statute, it would not impose sanctions because the arrangements would maintain safeguards sufficient to ensure minimal risk.

In November of 2005, the OIG published a Special Advisory Bulletin entitled "Patient Assistance Programs for Medicare Part D Enrollees."[165] This bulletin focuses on arrangements that involve pharmaceutical manufacturers that subsidize (either directly or indirectly) cost-sharing amounts, but not subsidies of Part D premiums or PAPs established by MCOs to subsidize cost-sharing requirements. Although the OIG states in the bulletin that it is "mindful of the importance of ensuring that financially needy beneficiaries who enroll in Part D receive medically necessary drugs and OIG supports efforts of charitable organization and others to assist," the OIG also states that "we conclude that pharmaceutical manufacturer PAPs that subsidize Part D cost-sharing amounts present heightened risks under the [A]nti-[K]ickback [S]tatute."[166] In addressing these PAPs, the OIG organized its discussion by types of PAPs, including single-manufacturer-sponsored PAPs, independent-charity PAPs, coalition-model PAPs, and bulk replacement models.

Following publication of this Special Advisory Bulletin, a number of pharmaceutical manufacturers announced their intention to discontinue their PAPs, which then resulted in a number of patient-advocacy groups and public officials asking DHHS to resolve questions about the future permissibility of PAPs. In January of 2006, CMS issued a statement on its "perspective" on PAPs, stating in part that "lawful avenues exist for pharmaceutical companies and others to help Part D beneficiaries with their drug costs."[167] The following month, DHHS Secretary Michael O. Leavitt issued a letter to the Pharmaceutical Research and Manufacturers of America stating that "PAPs can continue to assist Part D enrollees through a properly structured program that operates entirely outside the Part D benefit. Under this approach, the beneficiary does not use his or her Part D

---

[164] *See, e.g.*, OIG Adv. Op. No. 06-19 (Nov. 2006) *available online at* http://oig.hhs.gov/fraud/docs/advisoryopinions/2006/AdvOpn06-19E.pdf; OIG Adv. Op. No. 07-04 (Apr. 2007), *available online at* http://oig.hhs.gov/fraud/docs/advisoryopinions/2007/AdvOpn07-04.pdf; OIG Adv. Op. No. 08-01 (Feb. 2008), OIG Adv. Op. No. 10-06 (May 2010), *available online at* http://oig.hhs.gov/fraud/docs/advisoryopinions/2010/AdvOpn10-06.pdf; OIG Adv. Op. No. 10-12 (Aug. 2010), *available online at* http://oig.hhs.gov/fraud/docs/advisoryopinions/2010/AdvOpn10-12.pdf.

[165] OIG Special Advisory Bulletin, *Patient Assistance Programs for Medicare Part D Enrollees*, 70 Fed. Reg. 70,623 (Nov. 22, 2005).

[166] *Id.*

[167] CMS, *CMS Perspective on Pharmaceutical Company Patient Assistance Programs*, (Jan. 26, 2006), *available online at* http://oig.hhs.gov/fraud/docs/alertsandbulletins/2006/CMSPAP.pdf.

benefit to obtain the drug and the cost of the drug is not applied toward the enrollee's [TrOOP]."[168]

In the months following publication of the Special Advisory Bulletin, the OIG issued two favorable advisory opinions related to PAPs under the Part D benefit.[169] In OIG Advisory Opinion 06-03, the OIG concluded that, although a PAP that provides free outpatient prescription drugs to financially needy Medicare Part D enrollees outside of the Part D benefit could potentially generate prohibited remuneration under the Anti-Kickback Statute, the OIG would not impose administrative sanctions.[170] Although it reaffirmed its concern that PAPs that subsidize the cost-sharing amounts for manufacturer's drugs payable under Part D raise fraud and abuse risks, the OIG found that sufficient safeguards were in place in the particular arrangement to ensure that the PAPs operated entirely outside of the Part D benefit and, therefore, posed little risk. The OIG found persuasive that, under the program, the PAP notified the patients' Part D plans that free drugs were being provided in order to ensure that no payment was made for the drugs, and that no part of the drugs' value was counted toward a patient's TrOOP. In addition, the determination regarding whether the patient qualified for financial assistance was unrelated to the patient's choice of Part D plan, the benefit design, or where the patient is on the plan's benefit spectrum.

In OIG Advisory Opinion 06-08, the agency addressed an arrangement in which a free clinic would distribute prescription drugs at no charge to financially needy patients, including Medicare beneficiaries enrolled in Part D.[171] These drugs were being provided through several PAPs sponsored by pharmaceutical manufacturers. The OIG concluded that, even though

---

[168] (Feb. 9, 2006), letter from DHHS Secretary Michael O. Leavitt to The Honorable Billy Tauzin, President and CEO of the Pharmaceutical Research and Manufacturers of America, *available online at* http://oig.hhs.gov/fraud/docs/alertsandbulletins/2006/TauzinPAP.pdf.

[169] In addition to the OIG Advisory Opinions related to Medicare Part D, the OIG has also issued a number of Advisory Opinions related to non-Medicare Part D PAPs (i.e., items covered under Part B). *See, e.g.,* OIG Adv. Op. No. 02-13 (Oct. 2002); OIG Adv. Op. No. 03-03 (Feb. 2003); OIG Adv. Op. No. 04-05 (June 2004); OIG Adv. Op. No. 04-15 (Oct. 2004). OIG Advisory Opinions are *available online at* http://oig.hhs.gov/fraud/advisoryopinions/opinions.html.

[170] OIG Adv. Op. No. 06-03 (Apr. 2006), *available online at* http://oig.hhs.gov/fraud/docs/advisoryopinions/2006/AdvOpn06-03F.pdf. This Advisory Opinion addresses two similar PAPs operated by a manufacturer and marketer of prescription drugs. The programs collectively include Medicare Part D enrollees and provide medications for cancer and hepatitis, as well as other outpatient drugs. To be eligible under either PAP, a patient must (a) use one or more of the PAP's covered drugs; (b) have an income below 325% or 250% of the federal poverty level (depending on the PAP); and (c) in the case of Part D enrollees, have already spent at least 3% of the beneficiary's household income on outpatient prescription drugs during that coverage year. Once a Part D enrollee qualifies for assistance, the assistance would continue for the remainder of the year, even if the patient's use of the drug was periodic, and neither Medicare nor any Part D plan or enrollee would be charged for the provision of the drugs to such enrollee.

[171] OIG Adv. Op. No. 06-08 (June 2006), *available online at* http://oig.hhs.gov/fraud/docs/advisoryopinions/2006/06-08.pdf.

## Fraud and Abuse Issues Affecting the Managed Care Industry

donations from the PAPs would enable the clinic to conserve its limited resources, it would not impose sanctions because the arrangement posed minimal risk. Furthermore, because the benefit being conferred on the free clinic was actually conferred on the public (by enabling the clinic to increase the availability of healthcare for this underserved patient population), the OIG concluded that it would not impose sanctions on the arrangement. The OIG also concluded that the clinic did not generate referrals for any PAP sponsors payable by a federal healthcare program, due to the fact that the physicians at the clinic were volunteers who did not receive compensation from the clinic for their services and the clinic received no reimbursement for any drugs it dispensed. The OIG also concluded that, by dispensing drugs to Medicare beneficiaries, the free clinic did not offer an improper inducement to the Medicare beneficiary, because the clinic did not seek reimbursement from any federal healthcare program. In more recent opinions regarding PAP arrangements issued by the OIG, the agency has put forth the same legal analysis and conclusion concerning varying entities and service arrangements for financially needy patients.[172]

### § 8-8(l)   Medical Loss Ratios

The new minimum MLR rules in the Health Reform Law require that after January 1, 2011, insurers spend at least 85% of large group premium revenue and 80% of small group and individual policy premium revenue on medical care and healthcare quality improvement activities.[173] As MCOs and regulators implement this rule and develop more questions about how different MCO activities will be classified, it creates new ground for traditional fraud activities or may lead to new liabilities.

The previous fraud prosecution of WellCare and certain of its executives for activities at the state level provide some indication of likely federal level issues that will arise under the MLR rules. In 2002, Florida enacted a law requiring Medicaid MCOs to direct 80% of the Medicaid premium paid for behavioral health services upon the actual provision of those services.[174] If the MCO expended less than 80% of the premium, the difference was required to be returned to the state Medicaid agency. In May 2009, the United States filed charges against WellCare Health Plans, Inc. and several of its former executives for conspiracy to commit Medicaid fraud, false statements, and other charges alleging that WellCare submitted fraudulently inflated behavioral

---

[172] *See, e.g.*, OIG Adv. Op. No. 09-04 (May 2009), *available online at* http://oig.hhs.gov/fraud/docs/advisoryopinions/2009/AdvOpn09-04.pdf; OIG Adv. Op. No. 10-12 (Aug. 2010), *available online at* http://oig.hhs.gov/fraud/docs/advisoryopinions/2010/AdvOpn10-12.pdf.
[173] 76, Fed. Reg. 29,964 (May 23, 2011).
[174] DOJ Press Release, *Five Former Executives Indicted on Helath Care Fraud Charges*, *available online at* http://www.fbi.gov/tampa/press-releases/2011/ta030211a.htm.

health expenditure information to the Florida Medicaid and Healthy Kids programs. The fraudulent information allegedly was contained in Behavioral Healthcare Worksheets for the Medicaid program and in annual required filings under the Healthy Kids program, and primarily involved establishment of a wholly owned entity, Harmony Behavioral Health, Inc. (Harmony) to which money was transferred and reported as expenditures on medical services. Pursuant to a deferred prosecution agreement, WellCare was required to pay $40 million in restitution, forfeiture of another $40 million to the United States, and to cooperate in the criminal investigation against former executives.[175] A former employee of the MCO admitted his involvement in a scheme to submit inflated medical expenditure information in the company's annual certification to the state Medicaid agency in order to reduce the payback obligations for behavioral healthcare services.

The plan also paid $137.5 million in civil penalties to resolve a qui tam investigation brought by the Plan's former financial analyst. Allegations of false claims involved payments to providers through one account for expenses incurred by another account, "swapping across years"—that is, paying inflated amounts to providers in the current year with the intention to recapture payments in later years; claiming inflated reinsurance premiums paid to a wholly owned subsidiary; and overstating the number of enrollees.

In March 2011, a Tampa Florida grand jury returned an indictment charging five other former WellCare executives with conspiracy to commit Medicaid fraud, false statements, and other related charges.[176] The indictment alleges not only that false worksheets and encounter date were submitted, but also points to the use of inconsistent methodologies across the various reporting periods as part of the conspiracy as well as failing or untruthfully responding to questions from Florida's Agency for Healthcare Administration (AHCA) when AHCA independently calculated the MLRs and found a wide variance.[177] The indictment also describes documents reflecting different payback calculations for calendar year 2005 identifying a range of potential refunds from $0 to over $11 million depending solely upon the per patient per month inpatient rate selected. The indictment also describes agreements executed in late 2006 between WellCare and Harmony, but effective as of January 2006, reflecting the selected inpatient rate on which the Harmony payment would be based. The indictment also includes counts relating to false statements made to federal agents that the expenditures on the Behavioral Healthcare Worksheets and the costs associated with the behavioral healthcare encounter data submissions to AHCA were not inflated.

---

[175] *Id.*
[176] See *Former WellCare Execs Charged in Scheme Over Ineligible Medicaid Contract Expenses,* BNA HEALTHCARE DAILY (Mar. 7, 2011).
[177] See Indictment, United States v. Farha, M.D. Fla., No. 8:11-CR-115-T-30 MAP, *available online at* http://op.bna.com/hl.nsf/r?Open=bbrk-8elkyx.

# 9
# Representing Healthcare Organizations in Fraud and Abuse Matters

## § 9-1 OVERVIEW

Representing clients in the ever-changing and complex field of health law presents unique challenges. Nowhere is that challenge more acute than the balancing act healthcare attorneys perform when advising clients about potential exposure to federal and state fraud and abuse laws. Healthcare attorneys who advise clients on fraud and abuse issues are often faced with difficult considerations, such as how to preserve the attorney/client privilege and work-product doctrine; how to advise clients on structuring a transaction after learning that one of the parties to the transaction may have acted with "bad intent" in contravention of the Anti-Kickback Statute; how to advise a client on whether to voluntarily disclose conduct to the government that falls into regulatory gray areas; or how a client should respond to a request for documents or demand for an interview with a federal investigatory agency.

This chapter provides an overview of important considerations when advising and counseling health entities in healthcare fraud and abuse matters, including understanding: the forms of government fraud and abuse investigations; electronic discovery and response to document requests and subpoenas; how to protect the attorney/client relationship while maintaining ethical obligations; and how interact with the government in healthcare fraud and abuse related matters. In addition, this chapter discusses how lawyers can be drawn into government investigations in non-traditional ways, for example, as a witness to—or even a defendant of—a government investigation.

## § 9-2 CATEGORIES AND TYPES OF GOVERNMENT INVESTIGATIONS

Entities often have difficulty distinguishing whether a particular request from the government or private entity is in fact an "investigation" or a routine request done in the normal course of business. Consequently, it is critical that attorneys who represent healthcare entities be able to distinguish between benign interactions with government entities and those interactions that demonstrate the commencement of an investigation. In the case of an executed search warrant, a grand jury summons, or receipt of a subpoena or civil demand, there is certainty that the government has launched an investigation. However, not all government overtures that precede an investigation are obvious.

There is not one particular government agency charged with investigating and prosecuting healthcare fraud and abuse. As discussed in Chapter 1, there are numerous federal, state and private entities who conduct audits and investigations on behalf of governmental payers and programs. For example, the Office of Inspector General (OIG), the Federal Bureau of Investigation (FBI) and the Department of Justice (DOJ) hold the authority to appear at one's place of work or home to question or obtain documents from healthcare providers and their employees. federal and state agencies and Congress often utilize subpoenas and other formal letters or request documents or access to individuals. The OIG occasionally exerts its additional power to "immediately access" providers' records and the FBI, at times, will execute search warrants in connection with more egregious healthcare fraud activities. Consequently, the government actors who enforce fraud and abuse are as diverse as the methods they employ to gather evidence.

The improper handling of government requests for information or subpoenas can result in serious consequences, including charges of obstruction of justice, or putting the company or individual at risk by revealing documents that could lead to exposure to unrelated liability. Accordingly, healthcare providers should proactively educate their employees on how to respond should the government make any such overture. Attorneys must also be able to counsel clients on the particular meaning of such a government overture. This section gives an overview of the types of healthcare fraud and abuse investigations and the forms in which they manifest.

## § 9-2(a)  Search Warrants

With permission from the court, the government can execute a search warrant or "raid" of a healthcare entity. Although not as common as a subpoena, search warrants are nonetheless used by fraud investigators to secure evidence of healthcare fraud. Unsurprisingly, they are the most disruptive and serious of government overtures. A search warrant is an investigative tool that enables federal law enforcement officers to search and seize healthcare fraud evidence, including evidence of the commission of a criminal offense, contraband, or the fruits of a crime and property used to commit a criminal offense.[1] A search warrant is a likely sign that criminal charges against the subject of

---

[1] Fed. R. Crim. P. 41.

## Representing Healthcare Organizations in Fraud and Abuse Matters

the warrant will ensue. It may also be a sign that the government has concerns about spoliation or destruction of evidence. This concern is particularly acute in the digital age, where evidence can be easily overwritten or destroyed. Unlike subpoenas and investigational demands, search warrants can only be issued upon court authorization and, under the Fourth Amendment, only upon a showing of probable cause. Moreover, search warrants must describe, with particularity, the place to be searched and the persons or things to be seized.

Healthcare organization personnel should be educated to contact counsel immediately upon being served with a search warrant. In such situations, counsel should attempt to minimize the harm of the search. Officers taking property under a search warrant are required to furnish a copy of the search warrant and a receipt for property taken, including a written inventory of the property.[2] Thus, as a preliminary matter, the search warrant should be reviewed and copied. In addition, even though federal agents have the right under a search warrant to seize property, and cannot be stopped from doing so, in most cases affirmative consent to the government's search or seizure of the property need not be given. By withholding consent to the search, the right to object to the seizure of privileged materials after the fact will be preserved. Agents may seize privileged materials, although the *U.S. Attorney's Manual* states that a search warrant should not be used to obtain privileged documents.[3] If counsel determines that the search or seizure involves documents protected by the attorney/client privilege, then counsel can alert the agents to the privileged nature of the documents, and take steps to ensure that the privileged documents are sealed and not reviewed until a determination has been made by an independent judicial officer that they are not privileged.

Similarly, statements furnished to government agents should be limited to the location of materials listed on the search warrant. A search warrant is not an order to compel testimony, especially from company personnel during work hours. Accordingly, employees can be instructed that they may remain silent and not answer questions posed by the agents. During the execution of the warrant, employees and counsel should not attempt to block or interfere with the government agents. After the agents leave, each employee at the location where the property was seized should be interviewed to determine whether employees made any statements to the agents during the search, and to confirm what documents were seized.

---

[2] FED. R. CRIM. P. 41(f)(2).
[3] Department of Justice, U.S. ATTORNEYS MANUAL § 9-19.220.

## § 9-2(b) Grand Jury Investigations—Subjects, Targets and Witnesses

The involvement of a grand jury in a healthcare fraud matter means that the matter is being probed as criminal, as opposed to civil, matter. In the past, grand juries were typically reserved for the most egregious fraud cases; however, increasingly they are used as a criminal probe in parallel criminal and civil investigations. Federal grand juries are convened by the courts, and consist of between sixteen and twenty-three individuals.[4] As grand jury proceedings are conducted in secrecy, the only individuals that may be present when the grand jury is in session are the attorneys for the government, the witness under examination, interpreters (when needed), and recording or transcribing personnel. Although a witness's legal counsel may not be present during grand jury testimony, counsel still may play an important role.

The attorney can contact the federal prosecutor to determine if the witness is a target, subject, or witness in a criminal investigation.[5] A target is a person who the prosecutor or grand jury believes may be linked to the commission of a crime. A subject is an individual who is "within the scope of the grand jury's investigation," meaning that the government is investigating the "subject," but for whom no determination has yet been made.[6] A subject may become a target, a fact witness or neither. A fact witness is neither a subject nor a target and may appear before a grand jury merely to provide testimony.

The designations of subject, target or witness have important meanings to healthcare attorneys. Knowing whether an individual is a target, subject or mere fact witness is crucial for the witness to determining whether the individual should assert the Fifth Amendment privilege against self-incrimination. If the individual who is summoned by the grand jury is being represented by counsel for the company under investigation, this information is critical to determining whether a potential conflict exists and whether the individual should have separate counsel. And while knowing these designations is important, counsel should also recognize that they may change during the course of an investigation. The government typically clarifies its position and

---

[4] FED. R. CRIM. P. 6(a)(1).

[5] The Department of Justice's *United States Attorneys' Manual* defines a "target" of an investigation as

> a person as to whom the prosecutor or the grand jury has substantial evidence linking him or her to the commission of a crime and who, in the judgment of the prosecutor, is a putative defendant. An officer or employee of an organization which is a target is not automatically considered a target even if such officer's or employee's conduct contributed to the commission of the crime by the target organization. The same lack of automatic target status holds true for organizations which employ, or employed, an officer or employee who is a target...

[6] Department of Justice, U.S. ATTORNEYS MANUAL § 9-11.151.

shifts its focus as it gathers evidence. Hence, witnesses or subjects sometimes become targets. Accordingly, counsel should seek clarification from the government as to the disposition of key individuals in a given case as the matter progresses.. In some instances the DOJ will also notify subjects or targets of their status prior to a grand jury appearance.[7]

Federal grand juries have subpoena power, but only when investigating a violation of federal criminal law. Therefore, a grand jury subpoena cannot be issued when only a civil investigation is being conducted. There are two types of grand jury subpoenas: a subpoena for documents only (*subpoena duces tecum*) and a subpoena for testimony (*subpoena ad testificandum*). Grand jury subpoenas are drafted by the prosecutor directing the investigation on behalf of the grand jury.[8] Grand jury subpoenas for documents can be broad. The Federal Rules of Criminal Procedure 17(c)(2) allows a subpoena to be quashed or modified if "compliance [with the subpoena] would be unreasonable or oppressive."[9] To determine reasonableness, courts often consider whether the materials requested are relevant and described with reasonable particularity, as well as whether the scope of materials requested covers a reasonable temporal scope.[10] Another factor taken into consideration is whether the request for production of documents is "unduly burdensome." As healthcare entities are increasingly forced to preserve and produce large quantities of electronic information in response to federal investigations, it seems likely that there will be increasing challenges to subpoenas for which strict compliance is too expensive or onerous.

Although disclosure of information presented to the grand jury outside the grand jury is generally prohibited, disclosure may be permitted when made to government personnel (such as investigators) in order to assist the government attorneys in their criminal enforcement duties, to government attorneys for use in the performance of the attorneys' duties, and when so directed by a court in connection with judicial proceedings.[11] Nonetheless,

---

[7] *See* Department of Justice, U.S. ATTORNEYS MANUAL § 9-11.151 stating "It is the policy of the Department of Justice to advise a grand jury witness of his or her rights if such witness is a "target" or "subject" of a grand jury investigation." This is effectuated by the issuance of a target letter—a sample of which is *available online at* http://www.justice.gov/usao/eousa/foia_reading_room/usam/title9/crm00160.htm. *See also* U.S. ATTORNEYS MANUAL § 9-11.153 Notification of Targets—in which prosecutors are "encouraged to notify such person a reasonable time before seeking an indictment."
[8] *See* FED. R. CRIM. P. 6.
[9] F.R.Cr. P. 17(c)(2).
[10] *In re* Grand Jury Matters, 751 F.2d 13, 18 (1st Cir. 1984).
[11] FED. R. CRIM. P. 6(d)—(e). Although this suggests that disclosure of grand jury proceedings to a government attorney may be permitted in the context of civil proceedings, the Supreme Court has held that grand jury materials can only be used by government attorneys in the matters to which those materials pertain, unless the government petitions the court and satisfies the standard of a "particularized showing of need." United States v. Sells Engineering, Inc., 463 U.S. 418 (1983); Ill. v. Abbott & Assocs., 460 U.S. 557 (U.S. 1983); United States v. John Doe, Inc. I, 481 U.S. 102 (U.S. 1987) (reviewing a concrete application of the "particularized need" standard to a request for disclosure to Government attorneys); *see also* United States v. Rogan, 2005 U.S. Dist. LEXIS 26034 (D. Ill. 2005).

many federal prosecutors will obtain a court order prior to disclosing the contents of subpoenaed documents to a government civil attorney. As to grand jury subpoenas for testimony, federal prosecutors have the power to not only issue these subpoenas, but in some cases can immunize and compel witness testimony before a grand jury.

## § 9-2(c) Civil Investigative Demands

Civil Investigative Demands (CIDs) require an entity to produce documentary materials, answer interrogatories, and provide oral testimony relevant to a false claims investigation. Although CIDs may be issued only *before* the government files an action, CIDs may be issued after a qui tam suit has been filed by a relator, but before the government has intervened in the action.[12]

Originally, CIDs could only be issued by the Attorney General. However, in 2009, as part of the Fraud Enforcement and Recovery Act of 2009 (FERA),[13] Congress authorized the delegation of the Attorney General's authority to issue civil investigative demands. United States Attorney General Eric Holder delegated his authority, in January 2010, to the Assistant Attorney General for the Civil Division. In March 2010, the Assistant Attorney General for the Civil Division further broadened this power to various U.S. Attorneys throughout the United States, making it even easier for CIDs to be issued.[14]

Now that procedural barriers to issuing CID have been removed, CIDs have become a common tool of federal investigators. The prosecutorial advantage of a CID is that unlike subpoena, a CID recipient can be compelled to answer interrogatories—that is, provide written answers to questions not just furnish documentary information that already exists.

In order to issue a CID, the Attorney General, or designee, must only have "reason to believe that any person may be in possession, custody, or control of documentary material or information relevant to a false claims law investigation."[15] At a minimum, the CID must "state the nature of the conduct constituting the alleged violation of the false claims law which is under investigation, and the applicable provision of law alleged to be violated."[16] Furthermore,

---

[12] Avco Corp. v. United States Dep't of Justice, 884 F.2d 621(D.C. Cir. 1989); *see also* United States v. Witmer, 835 F.Supp. 208 (M.D. Pa. 1993), *aff'd without op.*, 30 F.3d 1489 (3rd Cir. 1994).
[13] Pub. L. No. 111-21, § 4, 123 Stat. 1617, 1621-25 (codified as amended at 31 U.S.C. § 3733(a)(1) (2009)).
[14] Redelegation of Authority to Assistant Attorney General, Civil Division, to Branch Directors, Heads of Offices and United States Attorneys in the Civil Division Cases. 75 Fed. Reg. 14,070 (Mar. 24, 2010).
[15] 31 U.S.C. § 3733(a)(1).
[16] 31 U.S.C. § 3733(a)(2)(A).

## Representing Healthcare Organizations in Fraud and Abuse Matters

the Attorney General must appoint a "false claims law investigator" to serve as custodian of the discovery material obtained pursuant to a CID.[17]

Prior to the 2009 Amendments, only the designated false claims law investigator, authorized employees of the DOJ, members of Congress, or members of a government agency who needed the discovered information in furtherance of their statutory duties could access the information obtained through the CID. Currently, the Attorney General or designee holds the authority to also share information obtained through the CID with the qui tam relator if "the Attorney General or designee determines it is necessary as part of any false claims act investigation."[18] FERA also removed the substantial need and application requirements for disclosure of information to other agencies and established an "official use" policy that authorizes "any use that is consistent with the law, and the regulations and policies of the Department of Justice. . . ."[19]

The Attorney General can petition to enforce a CID in any U.S. District Court in which the person receiving the CID resides, is found, or transacts business, and any person receiving a CID can petition to modify or set aside the demand.[20] The petition for modification or set-aside must be served upon the false claims law investigator identified in the demand, and must be filed within twenty days after the date of service of the CID or at any time before the return date specified in the demand, whichever date is earlier, or within any longer period of time prescribed in writing by the false claims law investigator identified in the demand. The petition to set aside or to modify the discovery demand may be based on a failure by the government to comply with the provisions of 31 U.S.C. § 3733 or upon "any constitutional or other legal right or privilege of the petitioner."[21]

### § 9-2(d) Administrative Subpoenas

The Health Insurance Portability and Accountability Act of 1996 (HIPAA) added, in part, 18 U.S.C. § 3486, which empowers the Attorney General (or the Attorney General's designee) to issue administrative subpoenas to obtain records for investigations relating to federal criminal healthcare fraud offenses.[22] This provision empowers the DOJ to issue administrative subpoenas to obtain records that are not subject to the constraints applicable to

---

[17] 31 U.S.C. § 3733(i)(1).
[18] 31 U.S.C. § 3733(a)(1).
[19] 31 U.S.C. § 3733(l)(8).
[20] 31 U.S.C. § 3733(j).
[21] 31. U.S.C. § 3733(j)(3).
[22] 18 U.S.C. § 3486, *amended by* Pub.L. No. 105-277 (Oct. 21, 1998) *and* Pub. L. No. 105-314 (Oct. 30, 1998). Originally, administrative subpoenas were called "Authorized Investigative Demands," or AIDs.

grand jury matters set forth in Rule 6 of the Federal Rules of Criminal Procedure. Administrative subpoenas allow information obtained in a criminal investigation in response to the subpoena to be shared with the Civil Division of the DOJ. This is helpful in pursuing healthcare fraud violations as it enables potential contemporaneous investigations of both civil and criminal matters. The scope of an administrative subpoena issued under 18 U.S.C § 3486 must be "reasonably relevant" to the investigation at issue.[23] The statute requires the subpoena to "describe the objects required to be produced and prescribe a return date within a reasonable period of time. . ." and prevents production of records from any place more than 500 miles distant from where the subpoena is served.[24] The administrative subpoena provision also provides for judicial enforcement through contempt actions and immunizes persons complying in good faith with such demands from civil liability for disclosure of information.[25]

Because administrative subpoenas are not subject to the constraints of grand jury subpoenas, and because the information acquired from these demands is also suited for civil and administrative actions, there has been an increase in the use of these instruments in government investigations. Due to this increase, a number of challenges to administrative subpoenas have been made, producing a growing body of law governing this investigative tool. Most importantly, courts have addressed the enforceability of administrative subpoenas. *In re Subpoena Duces Tecum (United States v. Bailey)*,[26] the Fourth Circuit held that district court orders enforcing administrative subpoenas are immediately appealable.[27] The court also held that the fact that the subject of an administrative subpoena (i.e., the recipient of the subpoena) complies with the subpoena does not render an appeal moot.[28] Therefore, counsel for a healthcare organization in receipt of an administrative subpoena may have the option of challenging it in the court of appeals either before or after compliance.

In this regard, there is no requirement that an administrative subpoena be supported by probable cause.[29] Nevertheless, it is difficult to challenge merely on the basis that it is "overly burdensome."[30] Moreover, the government may

---

[23] 18 U.S.C. § 3486(a)(1)(B)(i)-(ii); *see also In re* Administrative Subpoena John Doe, 253 F.3d 256 (6th Cir. 2001).

[24] 18 U.S.C. at § 3486 (a)(2)-(3).

[25] *See* Department of Justice, U.S. ATTORNEYS MANUAL § 9-44.200.

[26] *In re* Subpoena Duces Tecum (United States v. Bailey), 228 F.3d 341 (4th Cir. 2000).

[27] Ordinarily, a person served with a subpoena may not appeal the denial of a motion to quash that subpoena without first resisting and being held in contempt. This rule was developed in the context of grand jury subpoenas. However, the court in this case reasoned that a district court order enforcing an administrative subpoena should be considered "final" for purposes of 28 U.S.C. § 1291, because administrative subpoenas are distinguishable from grand jury subpoenas in that "there is no ongoing judicial proceeding that would be delayed by an appeal." *Id.* at 345–46.

[28] *Id.*

[29] *See* Department of Justice, U.S. ATTORNEYS MANUAL § 9-44.200.

[30] *See In re* Administrative Subpoena (Smith v. United States), 289 F.3d 843 (6th Cir. 2001).

resort to a grand jury subpoena if an administrative subpoena is challenged on appeal. The Fourth Circuit has held that to be reasonable, an administrative subpoena does not have to be supported by probable cause, but must be: (1) authorized for a legitimate government purpose; (2) limited in scope to reasonably relate to and further its purpose; (3) sufficiently specific so that a lack of specificity does not render compliance unreasonably burdensome; and (4) not overly broad for the purposes of the inquiry as to be oppressive.[31]

The Sixth Circuit added that an administrative subpoena is properly enforced if: (1) it satisfies the terms of its authorizing statute; (2) the documents requested are relevant to the DOJ investigation; (3) the information sought is not already in the DOJ's possession; and, (4) enforcing the subpoena will not constitute an abuse of the court's process.[32]

Irrespective of standard or type of subpoena, there are benefits of engaging in negotiations with the government regarding the scope of a particular request rather than, for example, immediately challenging a subpoena in court. The government places a value on cooperation that should not be ignored.[33] Moreover, the government can remedy many defects in scope or service simply by issuing another subpoena.

## § 9-2(e)   Search and Subpoena Authority of the OIG

### § 9-2(e)(1)   OIG Authority to Subpoena Documents and Witnesses

In connection with investigational inquiries into potential wrongdoing, the OIG has broad authority to subpoena witnesses and documents.[34] This authority extends to both civil and criminal investigations.[35] Thus, the OIG may conduct criminal investigations pursuant to its subpoena power without affording any of the procedural protection available in criminal investigations by a grand jury.

To the recipient, an OIG subpoena may appear overly broad. Although recipients can attempt to narrow the scope and otherwise obtain clarification of an overly broad OIG subpoena, such attempts may not be successful. In any case, challenges to OIG subpoenas should be approached in light of the OIG's power to obtain immediate access to review documents (as will be discussed).

---

[31] U.S. v. Bailey, *supra* note 16, at 349.
[32] *In re* Administrative Subpoena (Doe v. United States), 253 F.3d 256, 265 (6th Cir. 2001) (citing United States v. Markwood, 48 F.3d 969, 980 (6th Cir. 1995)).
[33] *See* Department of Justice, U.S. ATTORNEYS MANUAL § 9-27.600–630 discussing cooperation as grounds for non-prosecution agreement.
[34] *See* Social Security Act § 205(d), 42 U.S.C. § 405(d); Social Security Act § 1128A(j), 42 U.S.C. § 1320a-7a(j); 5 U.S.C. app. § 6(a)(4); 42 C.F.R. § 1006.1 (2005).
[35] United States v. Medic House, Inc., 736 F. Supp. 1531 (W.D. Mo. 1989).

When the OIG addresses subpoenas to an entity, the entity can designate one or more individuals to testify on its behalf.[36] Testimony at investigational inquiries is taken under oath or affirmation. Such testimony is non-public, and attendance of non-witnesses is within the discretion of the OIG. However, witnesses may be accompanied, represented, and advised by an attorney, and the OIG staff may attend and ask questions.

### § 9-2(e)(2)  Granting the OIG Immediate Access to Documents

The Social Security Act (SSA) authorizes program exclusion for any individual or entity that "fails to grant immediate access, upon reasonable request" to the DHHS Secretary (or an agent of the DHHS Secretary), the Inspector General, a state survey agency, or state Medicaid Fraud Control Unit (MFCU).[37]

OIG regulations interpret "failure to grant immediate access" to include failing to produce, making available for inspection, and copying all requested records within 24 hours of such request or providing a compelling reason why the documents cannot be produced within 24 hours. In addition, if the OIG reasonably believes that requested documents are about to be altered or destroyed, then the regulations define "immediate access" as "at the time the request is made."[38]

A "reasonable request" for immediate access must be made in writing and be signed by a designated representative of the OIG.[39] The request must include "a statement of authority for the request;" the entity's or individual's rights; the definition of "reasonable request" and "immediate access"; and the penalties that would be imposed for failure to comply (including the effective date, length, scope, and effect of any potential exclusion) and the earliest date that a request for reinstatement would be considered.[40] Additionally, for a request to be "reasonable," there must be *information to suggest* that the individual or entity has violated statutory or regulatory requirements" under a federal healthcare program.[41] Individuals and entities failing to grant immediate access may be subject to program exclusion during the period in which the immediate access was not granted, as well as a potential additional period of time as a penalty.[42]

---

[36] 42 C.F.R. § 1006.2(e).
[37] Social Security Act § 1128(b)(12); 42 U.S.C. § 1320a-7(b)(12); *see also* 42 C.F.R. § 1001.1301. Each state Medicaid Fraud Control Unit possesses identical immediate access authority to that of the OIG.
[38] 42 C.F.R. § 1001.1301(a)(3).
[39] 42 C.F.R. § 1001.1301(a)(3)(ii).
[40] 42 C.F.R. §§ 1001.1301(a)(2), (a)(3).
[41] *Id.* (emphasis added).
[42] 42 C.F.R. §§ 1001.1301(b), (c).

**Representing Healthcare Organizations in Fraud and Abuse Matters**

## § 9-2(f)  Congressional Subpoenas

Congress, through a Committee or subcommittee, also holds broad authority to compel entities to produce documents and testimony for investigational purposes through Congressional subpoenas.[43] Historically, Congress used this power sparingly. However, recently, in an effort to mitigate healthcare fraud and abuse, an increasing number of entities have been called upon to produce documents or appear in person, particularly targeting pharmaceutical companies and their executives.[44] Healthcare delivery and payment have also become highly politicized. It seems likely that Congress will increase its own investigations accordingly.

Congressional subpoenas are rarely challenged judicially since they fall under the protection of the Speech and Debate Clause of the Constitution,[45] which provides an "absolute bar to judicial interference," so long as Congress is acting with legitimate legislative purpose.[46] The Supreme Court in the *Eastland* case stated that they would refrain from questioning the motive of subpoenas as long as it related to possible legislative actions, even if there is "no predictable end result."[47] If an entity refuses to cooperate with Congress, it can be issued a citation for contempt.[48] The Constitution affords private citizens some protection through the Fifth Amendment privilege against self-incrimination. However, Congress may still compel testimony by granting the individual partial or full immunity.[49]

Of particular importance, documents that are protected from disclosure under the attorney-client privilege or the work product doctrine are typically not exempt from disclosure to Congress. While there is no official rule or legislation that states that privileges of any kind do not apply, Congress has nonetheless historically refused to acknowledge the affect of the attorney-client privilege. This creates a difficult scenario for attorneys and their clients. Often an attorney will need to consult ethics rules to determine his or her obligations. For example, in the District of Columbia, "the lawyer has a professional responsibility to seek to quash or limit the subpoena. . .to protect confidential documents and client secrets. If, thereafter, the Congressional subcommittee

---

[43] House Rule III(e)(1). *See also* Senate Rule XXVI(1).
[44] By way of example, in September 2010, Johnson & Johnson CEO William Weldon testified in front of Congress regarding questionable circumstances that led to a recall of non-prescription cold and pain medications made by Johnson & Johnson's McNeil Consumer Healthcare unit. Additionally, Congress has also targeted the FDA. In 2008, the House Energy and Commerce Oversight and Investigations Subcommittee subpoenaed FDA criminal investigators and documents regarding their approval of the Sanofi-Aventis antibiotic, Ketek.
[45] U.S. Constitution, Art. 1, Sec. 6, clause 1.
[46] Eastland v. U.S. Servicemen's Fund, 421 U.S. 491, 516 (1975).
[47] *Id*, at 509.
[48] Louis Fisher, Congressional Investigations: Subpoenas and Contempt Power 7 (2003).
[49] Wilkonson v. U.S., 365 U.S. 399, 409 (1961).

overrules these objections, orders production of the document and threatens to hold the lawyer in contempt absent compliance with the subpoena, then, in the absence of a judicial order forbidding the production, the lawyer is permitted. . . to produce the documents."[50] Some courts have held that production of privileged materials to Congress waives the privilege (even if they are required to be produced by Congressional subpoena).[51] This means that attorneys and their counsel need to respond carefully to Congressional subpoenas and exercise due caution if producing privileged materials. Such materials may not only constitute a waiver, but Congressional investigations also are not subject to investigative secrecy as are other government investigations.[52] As such, materials produced to Congress should have no expectation of privacy, and may even be made available by Congress via the internet.[53]

## § 9-2(g)   Undercover Operations

Law enforcement agencies (e.g., the FBI) may, from time to time, target certain geographic areas for healthcare fraud "undercover" operations aimed at detecting unscrupulous providers. Such undercover operations may involve, for example, federal agents posing in the role of a potential referral source to determine if a vendor of healthcare services and/or supplies offers illegal inducements. Such "undercover" operations can be expected to increase with the growth of the government's financial resources dedicated to healthcare fraud. In fact, a review of the facts described in early anti-kickback case law demonstrates that a number of those enforcement actions emanated from "undercover" operations.[54]

The FBI and other agencies have used a variety of undercover techniques to gather information on fraudulent practices. For example, in *United States v. Akpan*,[55] the FBI used an FBI Special Agent and a Houston, Texas, police officer to pose as patients of two doctors suspected of billing for services not rendered. The two agents convinced the doctors that they had been involved

---

[50] *See* DC Rule Prof Conduct 1.6(d)(2)(A) and Opinion 288 Compliant with Subpoena from Congressional Subcommittee to Produce Lawyer's Files Containing Client Confidences of Secrets," *available online at* http://www.dcbar.org/for_lawyers/ethics/legal_ethics/opinions/opinion288.cfm.
[51] *See generally* United States v. Phillip Morris, 212 F.R.D. 421 (D.D.C. 2002). *See also* American College of Trial Lawyers White Paper, *The Attorney-Client Privilege in Congressional Investigations* (2010).
[52] *See, e.g.*, the investigation exception (b)7 under the Freedom of Information Act (FOIA) 5 U.S.C. § 552; the "seal" provisions of the False Claims Act, and grand jury secrecy under the Fed R. Civ. Pro 6(e).
[53] Commonwealth v. Phillip Morris, 1998 WL 1248003 (Mass. Super. July 30, 1998).
[54] *See, e.g.*, United States v. Duz-Mor Diagnostic Lab., Inc., 650 F.2d 223 (9th Cir. 1981) (FBI agent posing as representative of a group of investors planning to purchase nursing homes); United States v. Universal Trade & Indus., Inc., 695 F.2d 1151 (9th Cir. 1983) (medical clinic administrator working in concert with the FBI).
[55] United States v. Akpan, 407 F.3d 360 (5th Cir. 2005).

## Representing Healthcare Organizations in Fraud and Abuse Matters

in an automobile accident and needed to be treated for injuries resulting from that accident. By billing for physical therapy treatments that the two agents never received, the doctors provided evidence that eventually lead to a twenty-two-count indictment against the two. In 2000, the FBI utilized an informant to pose as a Russian criminal interested in the process of staging automobile accidents to uncover a scheme by a medical clinic to defraud insurance companies by submitting fraudulent claims of medical injuries. The undercover operation led to the indictment of ten individuals.[56] More recently, undercover agents also posed as patients and presented to medical clinics under common ownership in Washington. According to the indictment, the defendant owners billed for higher levels of service than what was provided; and for services not provided.[57] Clearly healthcare entities that believe that they are too small to be on the radar of healthcare fraud enforcers should think again.

Healthcare entities should also not believe that they are too big to be subject to a sting operation. One of the most aggressive undercover operations in healthcare fraud history was "Operation Headwaters," which involved the FBI, OIG, and the United States Postal Service. federal agents created a bogus entity known as "Southern Medical Distributors" (SMD), which acted as a distributor of medical supplies. Various manufacturers and distributors approached SMD, offering inducements to undercover personnel to purchase enteral products. The operation's probe of the enteral industry led to eleven criminal convictions, including three by corporate subsidiaries of major healthcare organizations, and recovered over $670 million for the benefit of the United States and the Medicare and Medicaid programs.[58]

## § 9-3 DISCOVERY IN HEALTHCARE INVESTIGATIONS IN THE ELECTRONIC AGE

Healthcare investigations typically involve some degree of discovery. The government uses its various subpoena and document request powers to compel healthcare entities and their counsel to produce information relevant

---

[56] United States v. Birkin, 366 F.3d 95 (2d Cir. 2004).
[57] *See* South Sound Doctor, Accused of Healthcare Fraud, (U.S. Attorney for the Western District of Washington Oct. 5, 2008), *available online at* http://www.justice.gov/usao/waw/press/2009/oct/johnson.html.
[58] *See* News Release, Office of the United States Attorney, Southern District of Illinois, *Subsidiary of Novartis Pleads Guilty to Nine Felony Audit Obstruction Charges and Is Sentenced With $4.5 Million Fine*, (Feb. 11, 2005), *available online at* http://www.usdoj.gov/usao/ils/newsreleases/05%20February/02.11.05Novartis%20plea%20pr.pdf; *see also* United States v. Carroll, 320 F. Supp. 2d 748 (S.D. Ill. 2004); *see also* Abbott Firm Guilty Plea to Obstruction, Chicago Tribune, July 24, 2003 *available online at* http://articles.chicagotribune.com/2003-07-24/business/0307240284_1_cg-nutritionals-sting-operation-marketing-practices.

to the investigation. Electronically stored information (ESI) can complicate compliance with such a request.

As technology continues to improve, entities increasingly prefer to retain records digitally. The use of electronic mail, messaging and other electronic communications media to conduct business in the healthcare industry is commonplace. These types of communications are often memorialized or preserved on servers, hard drives and other media yet they lack the discretion reserved for more formal methods of communication. They are also routinely requested by prosecutors and government attorneys to be produced in response to a subpoena.

Furthermore, the Health Information Technology for Economic and Clinical Health (HITECH) Act of 2009[59] and the Patient Protection and Affordable Health Care Act of 2010[60] explicitly encourage the adoption and use of electronic health records (EHR). The HITECH act offers financial incentives, through funding and grants, for healthcare providers to implement and support the use of electronic health records.[61] Additionally, as of 2015, the Center for Medicare & Medicaid Services plans to reduce Medicare payments by 1% to entities not using EHRs "meaningfully,"[62] creating an inevitable rise in electronically stored information. EHRs are often proprietary applications that are designed to be secure and limit access to individuals who have the need to view records. Thus, they are among the most difficult type of ESI to produce since there is no standard format and often lack a litigation friendly built-in data export tool.[63] Because of the unique private and often proprietary nature of EHRs and the government's interest in investigating healthcare fraud through the subpoena process, healthcare investigations are often heavily laden with difficult electronic discovery.

Recent amendments to the Federal Rules of Civil Procedure regarding electronic discovery explicitly differentiate electronically stored information from other document type requests.[64] However, authorities that govern federal and state investigations remain silent on electronic discovery and limited case law exists to guide decision making.

As a result, electronic discovery has emerged to be among the most vexing, onerous and the least understood emerging areas of law.

The government routinely subpoenas Medicare claims related data including bills, coding summaries and medical records. Within the past decade, the government has also increasingly subpoenaed internal company documents

---

[59] Pub.L. 111-5, 123 Stat. 226.
[60] Pub.L. 111-148, 124 Stat. 119, to be codified at 42 U.S.C. § 300jj-51.
[61] 42 U.S.C. §§ 300jj-11 to -19, -31 to -38.
[62] 42 U.S.C. § 1395w-4(a)(7).
[63] *See* Christ, J.; Huddock, R; *Electronic Health Records Pose Several Challenges*, Nat. Law J. (Dec 14, 2009).
[64] F.R.C.P. 26(a) (added "electronically stored information" as its own category).

## Representing Healthcare Organizations in Fraud and Abuse Matters

including e-mail, electronic memoranda, spreadsheets, presentations, videos, and at times, whole databases maintained by the company under investigation. The government makes such requests with two aims: (1) gather information related to whether a particular claim should or should not have been paid; and (2) to determine whether the company, or individuals in the company, acted in violation of the law. Moreover, the government regularly changes or clarifies its focus in the middle of an investigation and requests different ESI.

Failure to exercise sound judgment and due caution throughout discovery can have very serious consequences for not just healthcare entities, but also the attorneys who represent them. The next section set out, in 6 phases, the electronic discovery process in healthcare investigations: (1) triggering events; (2) litigation holds; (3) possible vendor engagements; (4) preservation and collection; (5) searching and culling; (5) document review; and, (6) production.

### § 9-3(a) The Triggering Event

The obligation to preserve relevant information, including ESI, commences with a so-called "triggering event." Fed. R. Civ. Proc. 37(f) protects parties from sanctions if data is lost or destroyed as a "result of the routine, good faith operation of an electronic information system." However, once a triggering event has occurred, parties must act to preserve relevant information. A triggering event can be as definitive as a court order, subpoena or other discovery request, or as ambiguous as one or more events that put the entity or individual on notice that should anticipate litigation. This duty to preserve "arise[s] not only during litigation but also extends to that period before the litigation when a party reasonably should know that the evidence may be relevant to anticipated litigation."[65] Case law has not yet sufficiently established the universe of what is and what is not a triggering event that may suggest "anticipated" action.[66] The more difficult question arises when an entity receives some overture from a possible litigant or the government that falls short of an obvious indication that an investigation or litigation is imminent.

---

[65] Silvestri v. General Motors, 271 F.3d 583, 591 (4th Cir. 2001).
[66] Some general guidelines have been decided where the defendant "should have known" to place a litigation hold on their ESI. *See* Zubulake v. Warburg, 220 F.R.D. 212 (S.D.N.Y. 2003) (Duty to preserve evidence arose when an employee filed a complaint with an administrative agency; may have arisen earlier depending on the conversations employee had with supervisors and subsequent actions taken); PML North America v. Hartford Underwriters Insurance, Co., 2006 U.S. Dist. Lexis 94456 (E.D. Mich. 2006) (Duty to preserve documents arose when defendant received a letter from plaintiff threatening litigation); and *In re* NTL, Inc. Securities Litigation; Golden Partners, et al. v. Blumenthal, et al., 2007 U.S. Dist. LEXIS 6198 (S.D.N.Y. 2007) (Duty to preserve documents arose with the internal circulation of a "Document Hold" memorandum).

In the health industry, entities receive routine government audit requests from government payors in the normal course of business. Absent unusual circumstances, these are generally not considered triggering events that necessitate preservation beyond that which is requested by the government auditors. But, what if a more specialized or focused audit is requested? What if government agents appear onsite and request access to information but do not issue a subpoena or written document request? Are these triggering events? The answer depends heavily on specific facts and circumstances. Counsel often has the difficult job of assessing whether circumstances have arisen that suggest anticipated litigation.[67] This is especially true of government investigations where the government is unwilling or unable to share information with the company under investigation or where a complaint is filed by a qui tam relator under seal.

The Sedona Conference Work Group consisting of lawyers, consultants, academics and jurists and has produced a series of documents setting forth best practice guidelines for addressing electronic discovery issues. The Sedona Guidelines suggest that for potential triggering events, "[a] recommended practice is for the legal department to have a separate checklist of circumstances by which it considers whether a preservation obligations has been triggered and, if so, what steps need to be taken to identify the scope of the obligation and what has to been [*sic*] to meet the obligation."[68]

## § 9 3(b)  Litigation Hold

Once an entity has determined that a triggering event has occurred, a litigation hold, also called a "hold notice," or "document destruction suspension notice," should be drafted and circulated. A litigation hold serves to put individuals who create, maintain or are otherwise in the custody of relevant information on notice that they should suspend destruction of a

---

[67] The oft cited Judge Scheindlin, S.D.N.Y. offers some guidance, "How does one conclude that litigation is reasonably anticipated? Obviously courts will answer this question with hindsight if they are asked to impose a sanction because a party failed to take steps to preserve data. Some of the questions a court might ask would include: Did an organization create a process for evaluating the threat of litigation? Was a response team created to assess the threat and report to a responsible decision-maker? Did the decision-maker evaluate the threat in light of prior experience with similar facts and circumstances? In evaluating the credibility of the threat, other questions might be asked: Was the threat made by a known or unknown person or entity? Did the threat arise from a regulatory action or criminal proceedings? Did the threat arise from a respected attorney sending a notice to preserve? Did the threat arise from an event such as a plane crash or plant explosion? Did responsible media coverage alert the company of similar actions involving similar products or issues? Judge Shira A. Sheindlin: The Ten most FAQ's in the Post (December 1, 2006) World of E-Discovery (Nov. 29, 2006).

[68] The Sedona Guidelines: Best Practice Guidelines & Commentary for Managing Information & Records in the Electronic Age, *available online at* http://www.thesedonaconference.org/publications_html?grp=wgs110 at p. 43.

## Representing Healthcare Organizations in Fraud and Abuse Matters

defined list of document or information.[69] The litigation hold is the first step in the preservation process and should be implemented as soon as practical after the triggering event. The litigation hold has two purposes. First, it puts individuals on notice that they should maintain, and not alter or destroy relevant information, regardless of form (whether electronic or physical); and, second, it suspends automatic destruction policies that might inadvertently delete, alter or remove relevant ESI.[70] Since most entities have routine destruction policies that can auto delete items like e-mail, server backup tapes subject to tape rotation or electronic medical records subject to purge after a period of years, the litigation hold must reach the correct personnel in the entity's information technology department who are responsible for the storage and disposition of the data.[71] Failure to timely impose a litigation hold and preserve data can result in monetary sanctions and adverse jury inferences regarding the information destroyed.[72] It can also jeopardize trust with the court and the opposing party, which in fraud cases, is typically the government.

Government investigational demands for document production can be broad. Civil investigative demands and administrative subpoenas are required to describe the documents to be produced and to provide a "reasonable period of time" to assemble and review the material prior to production.[73] Administrative subpoenas add an explicit requirement of relevancy for document production requests.[74] Essentially, the scope of a litigation hold should include documents that are relevant or reasonably related to the circumstances that gave rise to the triggering event. Deciding what is and what is not relevant to a subpoena is among the most challenging exercises an attorney must undertake. Often the government is unwilling or unable to speak in detail about exactly what conduct it is investigating. Nonetheless, many attorneys find it beneficial to make an overture to the government early in the preservation process of an investigation to clarify or narrow the scope of what may appear to be a very broad subpoena, as well as to negotiate time extensions and rolling production of

---

[69] *See id.* at p. 43-44.
[70] *See generally Id.* at p. 42-50.
[71] *See* Sedona Guidelines, *at* p. 44 noting, "An effective litigation response team may often include persons in the organization responsible for oversight and administration of the information and records management policy, representatives from the legal department (preferably with some litigation experience), representatives of the IT department, other senior level managers or executives as may be appropriate to the matter or case, as well as sufficient staff to implement the response."
[72] *See* United States v. Phillip Morris, 27 F. Supp. 2d 21 (D.D.C. 2004) ($2.7M fine against company based on failure of 11 executives to save e-mail in contravention of existing litigation hold; each executive was then fined $250,000); Mosaid Technologies v. Samsung Electrics Co., 348 F. Supp.2d 332 (D.N.J. 2005) (jury permitted to infer that e-mails not produced were unfavorable because of failure to institute litigation hold).
[73] 31 U.S.C. § 3733(a)(2)(B)(i-ii); 18 U.S.C. § 3486(a)(2).
[74] 18 U.S.C. § 3486(a)(1)(B)(i).

responsive materials. Subpoena return dates generally do not take into account the considerable time period necessary to accomplish a forensically sound preservation and collection of potentially responsive materials, much less review and ready for production the various materials collected. Doing so assists both parties in defining the scope of the investigation and therefore the scope of preservation. In particularly nebulous investigations, it may be advantageous to distribute a copy of the hold notice to the government. In doing so, if items are not preserved that later are revealed as relevant to the investigation, the government at a minimum was on notice that they were not subject to the hold.

## § 9-3(c)  Considerations in Engaging a Litigation Support Vendor

Once the entity has undertaken its initial preservation steps, due to the complex nature of electronic discovery, entities often engage external litigation support vendors who are capable of collecting relevant ESI consistent with industry standards. Since it is commonly understood that preservation of relevant documents extends to the document's metadata, most law firms and their clients elect to retain third party professionals who are capable of preserving and handling said data in a forensically sound manner. Although somewhat circular in definition, metadata is data whose function is to provide information about one or more aspects of data. Metadata usually "include[s] the author [or authors] of the document, the dates and authors of modifications of the document, when and by whom a document was reviewed, and when the document was last accessed" and by whom.[75] In practical terms, metadata can provide file information such as time, location, authorships, last access or saved point, size, where stored on a network, and other background information about a particular electronic record.

Litigation support vendors can be used to assist with preservation, collect responsive data and assimilate data into a usable format, allowing attorneys to review and produce it to the requesting party. This is especially important in fraud investigations where in some instances spoliation can lead to sanctions or charges of obstruction of justice.

Vendor selection must be approached cautiously. Vendors range from self-employed individuals who specialize in one particular area to major firms that handle every aspect of the electronic discovery process. One must take into consideration the reputation and integrity of the firms considered, as well as the services they offer to meet an entity's needs.[76] Cost of course

---

[75] *In re* Telxon Corp. Sec. Litig., No. 5:98CV2876, 2004 WL 3192729, *at* *16 (N.D. Ohio July 16, 2004).

[76] *See generally*, The Sedona Conference, Best Practices for the Selection of Electronic Discovery Vendors: Navigating the Vendor Proposal Process. (July 2005).

## Representing Healthcare Organizations in Fraud and Abuse Matters

is another very significant issue. Depending on the scope of a discovery request, at times vendor fees can eclipse attorney fees. It is incumbent on the attorney to maintain and control vendor fees and establish clear supervision to preserve the attorney client privilege and work product privilege with respect to the vendor's services.

At a minimum, a vendor should set forth a preservation and collection plan with deadlines, specific events, a list of individuals within the company with whom the vendor will need assistance (typically IT employees), and the costs associated with its services. Vendors should also be equipped and qualified to assist with government negotiations on the scope of preservation and production of documentation and serve as a witness to the collection process if need be. Moreover, during litigation, an e-discovery vendor should be able to establish feasible deadlines for document production. This is particularly important given the fact that entities can be held in contempt for failing to comply with deadlines.[77]

Retaining and supervising e-discovery vendors should be approached carefully. In 2011, a client sued its law firm for malpractice after the law firm inadvertently produced 3,900 privileged documents to the government and subsequently to a third party. The law firm employed an e-discovery vendor as well as numerous contract employees to assimilate and review the client's ESI for relevant and privileged information and allegedly failed to guard against inadvertent disclosure.[78] In 2008, Electronic Evidence Discovery, Inc. (EED) settled with Sullivan & Cromwell to resolve a fee dispute over discovery services. Sullivan claimed that EED consistently missed deadlines and made a number of errors causing the firm to, in turn, miss deadlines and harm its position with government attorneys. Although the terms of the settlement were confidential, the amount in dispute exceeded $700,000.[79]

### § 9-3(d) Preservation and Collection

In order to make materials available efficiently to the opposing party and guard against spoliation, relevant materials are often collected, copied or removed from their respective locations. This process is called preservation and collection. The term forensic data preservation refers to the use of techniques and guidelines that preserve the integrity of data consistent with

---

[77] *In re* Fannie Mae Securities Litigation, 2009 U.S. App. LEXIS 9 (D.C. Cir. Jan. 6, 2009). (The Office of Federal Housing Enterprise Oversight appealed an order holding it in contempt for failing to comply with a discovery deadline to which it had agreed, reemphasizing the fact that attorneys need to be aware of the scope and breadth of what they are agreeing to and whether the time frame is feasible.)

[78] J-M Mfg. Co. v. McDermott, Will & Emery, LLP, No. BC462832 (Cal. Sup. Ct., County of Los Angeles 2011).

[79] Sullivan & Cromwell Settles E-Discovery Dispute Law 360 *available online at* http://www.law360.com/articles/44146/sullivan-cromwell-settles-e-discovery-dispute.

acceptable industry standards.[80] Depending on the particulars of a case or investigation, whether data has been forensically preserved and collected can be of paramount importance. This is particularly true in criminal matters, matters involved fraud or data theft or matters involving a government entity.

As a threshold matter, the universe of potentially responsive or relevant material should be defined. Citing *Silvestri v. GM*, 271 F. 3d 583 (4th Cir. 2001), the Sedona Guidelines state, "The duty to preserve applies to any and all relevant documents, tangible things, or electronic information in the possession, custody, or control of the party no matter where located."[81] Absent an agreement or court order, parties are not generally responsible for failing to preserve materials for which they did not reasonably believe would be sought in litigation.[82] Although not specifically required during government investigations, if the parties are litigating a fraud case, Fed.R.Civ.P 26(f) requires the parties to "confer as soon as practicable. . .[and] discuss any issues about preserving discoverable information; and develop a proposed discovery plan." The discovery plan typically results from negotiations and lists the custodians from whom relevant materials will be sought, the methodology for extracting and the data, the sources of the materials (or data) and agreements as to format and timing of production. During this conference, parties typically discuss sources that, although potentially relevant, are nonetheless not reasonably accessible under Fed.R.Civ.P 26(b)(2)(C) discussed below.

Relevant information resides in many locations and in many forms. Paper-based files are the easiest to preserve, provided that individuals who are the custodians of the files (which may include third party offsite storage vendors) are informed of their preservation duties. Electronically based materials present an entirely different challenge. Relevant data can reside in a multitude of locations including but not limited to: desktop and laptop hard

---

[80] The Sedona Conference Glossary: E-Discovery & Digital Information management 3rd at p.23 define forensics as: "The scientific examination and analysis of data held on, or retrieved from, ESI in such a way that the information can be used as evidence in a court of law. It may include the secure collection of computer data; the examination of suspect data to determine details such as origin and content; the presentation of computer based information to courts of law; and the application of a country's laws to computer practice. Forensics may involve recreating "deleted" or missing files from hard drives, validating dates and logged in authors/editors of documents, and certifying key elements of documents and/or hardware for legal purposes."

[81] The Sedona Conference Commentary On: Preservation, Management and Identification of Sources of Information that are Not Reasonably Accessible, (July 2008) at p.4.

[82] *See* Healthcare Advocates v. Harding et. al., 497 F. Supp. 2d 627, 640-41 (E.D. Pa 2007) (finding that no duty to preserve arose when temporary files subject to deletion were not reasonably anticipated to be discoverable to litigation). *See also* Petcou v. Robinson Worldwide, Inc., 2008 WL 542684 (N.D. Ga 2006) in an employment discrimination case denying plaintiffs request for sanctions when defendant failed to suspend deletion of company e-mail because defendant had insufficient notice to preserve e-mail and "It did not appear that Defendant acted in bad faith in following its established policy for retention and destruction of emails." *Id.* at 2.

## Representing Healthcare Organizations in Fraud and Abuse Matters

drives, removable media such as flash storage devices, CDs and DVDs, smart phones, cameras, voicemail, fax and photocopy machines with memory, company servers, backup tapes and third party electronic storage or disaster recover vendors. There is no one size fits all solution. Each company has its own IT infrastructure, and in particular health entities often use proprietary databases and customized software for coding and billing platforms, which in most cases contain materials, such as electronic medical records that are highly relevant to fraud and abuse investigations. As such, a preservation plan must take into account the production needs of the matter and the particulars of the client's IT infrastructure.

In some instances preservation obligations extend to both the file and the background information about the file, that is, the metadata. It has increasingly become more commonplace in litigation to produce, the "native" version of documents, meaning the original form, with its metadata. Whether, and what types, of metadata should be preserved or produced is typically dealt with during Fed.R.Civ.P 26(f) conferences. However, in the absence of such conference, as is the case in most healthcare fraud and abuse investigations, in matters that are criminal or could become criminal, metadata should not be ignored.

### § 9-3(e)  Culling–Limiting the Data Set

Retrieval of documents that are responsive, relevant, privileged and/or related to particular events, issues or people can be challenging when attempting to sift through voluminous electronically stored data. Manual searches for pertinent documents can be overwhelmingly impractical, demanding the need for sophisticated, computer-operated searches using key terms. Parties typically agree to the creation of and implementation of a data filter since such a filter cuts down on the amount of information the parties will need to review. Using such as filter also allows the both parties to access documents more quickly since the volume counsel reviews decreases.

There are numerous filter methodologies that are employed to find relevant material and excluded unwanted materials. The Sedona Conference attempted to categorize this ever expanding field of what has become computer logic. Such filters include: (1) Boolean Search Models (use of keywords, proximity, time, stemming and other modifiers); (2) Bayesian Classifiers (ranking based on probability theories); (3) Fuzzy Search Models (algorithms designed to stem words or identify similar meaning concepts, misspellings among search terms); (4) Statistical Clustering (grouping similar documents – often used as an initial assessment of the data); (5)Machine Learning/Semantic Representation (use of computer logic to identify different words with similar meanings); (6) Concept and Categorization Tools (use of thesauri, taxonomies and ontologies to capture group and relational concepts); (7) Visualization Tools (use of shapes, graphs and other viewable information to organize and understand data).[83]

At times, entities employ a search filter and elect to avoid "eyes on" attorney review of each document. More recently, as technology has advanced, e-discovery firms have created "predictive coding" software that uses a computer logic that "learns" how to treat a given document based on sample of documents that have had "eyes-on" attorney review. Using this logic, it extrapolates to the universe and makes categorical determinations as to the disposition of each document in the data set.[84]

Regardless of the type of filter used to cull non-responsive or privileged data from a data set, filters do not necessarily guard against inadvertent disclosure under the attorney client privilege. [85] This is important in healthcare investigations where the company under investigation may have obtained legal analysis of the practices under investigation from in-house counsel or an outside law firm. Accordingly prior to the production of electronic materials, which can be voluminous, parties often agree to a clawback agreement pursuant to Fed. R. Civ. P. 26(b)(5) and FRE 502 (requiring the clawback to be enforceable agreement to be entered as a court order). A clawback agreement is simply any bilateral agreement between the parties that outlines the procedure when an inadvertent disclosure of privileged information occurs. Courts differ as to the applicability and enforceability of clawback agreement, especially those not entered as an order pursuant to FRE 502. Counsel should always be aware of how their respective jurisdiction handles such agreements This is especially true in healthcare fraud and abuse investigations involving the government where the option of having a court enter an agreement may not be available. Nevertheless, even if a clawback is used, it is very difficult to "un-ring" the bell once the government has reviewed privileged information.

One cannot use the filtering process to conceal relevant documents nor can one omit key terms in its filtering. In 2008, Qualcomm was ordered to pay over $8 million in attorney's fees and costs incurred during litigation for "intentionally hiding or recklessly ignoring relevant documents, ignoring or rejecting numerous warnings that Qualcomm's document search was inadequate

---

[83] *See The Sedona Conference Best Practices Commentary on the Use of Search and Information Retrieval Methods in E-Discovery* (Aug. 2007), *available online at* https://thesedonaconference.org/download-pub/76.

[84] *See* Judge Peck Order permitting use of predictive coding in Moore, et al., v. Publicis Groupe and MSL, Group 11 Civ. 1279 (S.D.N.Y. 2011).

[85] *See* Victor Stanley, Inc. v. Creative Pipe, Inc., 250 F.R.D. 251, 257 (D. Md. 2008) holding that a seventy word search term using Boolean filter which failed to segregate privileged materials that were inadvertently produced to plaintiff's counsel was insufficient and that the attorney client and work product status had been waived. *C.f..See* Rhoads Industries, Inc. v. Building Materials Corp. of America, 254 F.R.D. 216, 224 (E.D. Pa. 2008), the court determined that the use of additional search terms could have prevented the inadvertent disclosure of over 800 privileged documents but ultimately held that the attorney-client privileged was not waived.

and blindly accepting Qualcomm's unsupported assurances that its documents search was adequate."[86] Moreover, when dealing with the government, intentional concealment is tantamount to obstruction and could result in prosecution.

## § 9-3(f)   Document Review

Once a vendor has identified the relevant data for production, the vendor typically exports the materials that pass through the filter and creates a load file to import the data to a document review platform. Document review accomplishes two overall goals: (1) identify non-privileged, relevant materials for production and (2) inform counsel about the underlying facts in the investigation. Often times numerous contract attorneys are brought on to assist in the arduous task of review. Establishing a review protocol with step by step guidelines is critical to maintain consistency and at times can be used as evidence that the review, although imperfect, followed a sound and defensible protocol. At minimum such a protocol should include guidelines on what is and what is not responsive material, with examples.

In a healthcare investigation, the document review protocol may need to be trained on key concepts of healthcare law, including Stark, kickbacks law, billing and/or coding guidelines. It should also include a listing of attorneys (in-house and outside counsel) and the firms that the particular entity uses or used in the past to facilitate the identification of privileged materials. Not only are such guidelines helpful to avoid inadvertent disclosure of privileged or non-responsive materials, creating and following sound guidelines can minimize arguments that counsel acted negligently or intentionally attempted to conceal relevant information through an arbitrary review process.

## § 9-3(g)   Production

The final step in discovery is production. Simply stated, production is the process through which relevant non-privileged materials requested by the opposing party are made available. Prior to the electronic age, productions were paper-based and included either originals or photocopies of relevant materials. While at times, and especially in small matters, producing documents in paper form may be acceptable to the opposing party, electronic productions are now considered the norm. Accordingly, paper documents are generally converted to electronic form prior to production.

There are generally two types of electronic productions: (1) imaged based productions and (2) native productions. Imaged productions include

---

[86] Order Granting in Part and Denying in Part Defendant's Motion for Sanction and Sanctioning Qualcomm, Incorporated and Individual Lawyers, Qualcomm, Inc. v. Broadcom, Co., 2008 WL 66932 (S.D. Cal. Jan. 7, 2008).

documents that have either been scanned from paper and converted to an image file, such as tiff, jpeg or pdf or electronic files that have been converted to an image file. Often these paper-based images are made searchable through optical character recognition software (OCR) or in the case of electronic documents made searchable by including the document's extracted text in the production's load file. These types of productions became popular in the late 1990s and early 2000s. They are less commonplace in today's litigation environment, and often reserved for the production of paper based files.

With the widespread use of electronically driven applications in the healthcare industry, native productions are quickly becoming the norm. Indeed, requesting parties in these matters are typically government agencies who have their own productions standards (aka " production specs") that require production in native format for some if not all file types. A native production simply means that the documents are produced in their original format. In other words, rather than convert an e-mail into an imaged based. pdf, or. tiff, a native production simply produces the original form of the e-mail, an. msg file for example. Producing items in native format can assists the recipient, typically the government, in identifying information such as a given document's author, creation date, when it was last modified or accessed or information about where it was saved and help the reviewer interact with the data in its natural state (rather than review a mere image). Native production can also help decrease the cost of production since vendors charge a premium to convert electronic files to images.

At some point prior to production, if an entity believe that the assimilation of requested information is overly burdensome, costly and unreasonable and are prepared to substantiate these claims, they can petition to modify or set aside a request for ESI.[87] Fed.R.Civ.P. 26(b)(2)(B) does not require parties to produce ESI from sources that "are not reasonably accessible because of an undue burden or cost" and Fed.R.Civ.P. 26(b)(2)(C) also allows parties to weigh whether "the burden or expense" of the proposed production outweighs the benefits. It is unclear whether a party to a government investigation can challenge a document request or demand under FRCP. Often, a case has not been formally filed by the government, or if a case has been filed, it remains under seal. Companies in some instances, may not have a court to seek redress under the FRCP. Nonetheless, the particular subpoena or CID issued will often have built in remedies to limit, quash or otherwise seek redress for unduly burdensome requests. The decision to challenge a production request or quash a government subpoena should be viewed in light of the benefits of cooperation in a government investigation and the likelihood that the scope of production can be successfully narrowed through

---

[87] 31 U.S.C. § 3733(j)(3); 18 U.S.C. § 3486(a)(5).

negotiation with the government. Counsel should also consider the collateral consequences as to participation in federal healthcare programs.[88]

Caution must be exercised with respect to materials produce to the government, especially in light of a recent ruling in the Supreme Court, *FCC v. AT&T, Inc.*[89] The FCC initiated an investigation after AT&T notified the agency that the corporation had been overpaid as participants in a federal program. After excessive ESI production to the FCC, AT&T denied liability and paid a fine of $500,000. Shortly after the investigation was closed, the FCC granted a Freedom of Information Act (FOIA) request by an AT&T competitor, allowing access to "private" information gathered during the government investigation. Despite an effort by AT&T to argue that corporations are considered "persons" under the law, the Court determined that they were not persons and, therefore, not guaranteed any personal privacy protection.[90] The Court held that corporations do not have a right of personal privacy for purposes of the FOIA law enforcement exemption 7(c).

Finally, another issue particular to healthcare investigations is that healthcare entities create and maintain protected health information (PHI). PHI is routinely requested by the government during healthcare fraud and abuse investigations since it is contained in claims data, patient records and may even be in company documents regarding internal audits and other compliance program initiatives. Counsel should ensure that the manner in which information is made available to the government is protected consistent with the privacy and security standards of HIPAA and the HITECH Act.

## § 9-4 RELATIONSHIP BETWEEN CRIMINAL AND CIVIL MATTERS

As a practical matter, in healthcare fraud investigations, it has become commonplace for the government to conduct both a civil and criminal investigation on parallel tracks. However, significant procedural distinctions exist between criminal and civil actions. Civil administrative cases are typically brought by the DHHS-OIG and are heard by an Administrative Law Judge (ALJ), who is employed by DHHS, with rules of evidence applied on an *ad hoc* basis. Civil cases brought under the FCA are handled by the Civil Division of the DOJ and are heard by federal judges and juries. In contrast, criminal cases are always tried before a federal judge who is independent of the federal agency bringing the action. Moreover, in criminal cases, the

---

[88] CMS has the authority to suspend Medicare and Medicaid payments pending investigation of "credible allegations of fraud." Although it is unclear whether such action would be exercised by CMS, healthcare entities should be aware of this possibility when considering non-cooperation with a government investigation. *See* § 5-4 Suspension of Payments.
[89] 562 U.S. ____ (2011).
[90] *Id.*

Federal Rules of Evidence and the constitutional right to a trial by jury apply. The burden of proof in civil cases is one of "preponderance of the evidence," whereas the burden of proof in criminal cases is a much higher standard of "beyond a reasonable doubt."

Criminal statutes also generally contain significant intent requirements, such as proof that the activities were conducted "knowingly and willfully." In contrast, civil cases are based on statutes in which the standard may be negligent conduct (e.g., the provider "should know" that the conduct was illegal) or based on a standard of "deliberate ignorance or reckless disregard" for the truth or falsity of the information or "strict liability" in the case of the Stark Law. Standards of proof required in civil monetary penalty (CMP) cases were heightened by the fraud provisions of HIPAA, which defines the phrase "should know" as "(A) acts in deliberate ignorance of the truth or falsity of the information; or (B) acts in reckless disregard of the truth or falsity of the information, and no proof of specific intent to defraud is required."[91]

The existence of criminal proceedings against a healthcare organization may have an effect on the civil remedies available to or against the organization. For instance, during a pending grand jury investigation for healthcare fraud, a court may stay a provider's request for discovery and other civil proceedings that the court perceives as related to the fraud investigation.[92] This may occur even if the Medicare program has suspended payment to a provider or supplier as a result of the investigation.[93] Moreover, private civil suits pending against a provider or supplier may be delayed while the criminal investigation takes precedence. Alternatively, the threat of criminal proceedings (e.g., convening a grand jury) may increase the likelihood that a healthcare organization will be willing to settle civil charges.

### § 9-4(a)  Double Jeopardy

An important issue in the defense of Medicare fraud is whether it is possible to challenge the imposition of both civil and criminal penalties as being duplicative, and thus in violation of the constitutional protection against double jeopardy contained in the Fifth Amendment of the United States Constitution. The Supreme Court spoke to this issue in *United States v. Halper*.[94] Mr. Halper, a clinical laboratory manager, was convicted under 18 U.S.C. § 287 of submitting sixty-five separate false claims. The claims consisted of upcoding laboratory services performed in a skilled nursing facility. Mr. Halper billed under the code appropriate when testing only one patient, which paid $12 per claim, instead of the correct code to be used

---

[91] 42 U.S.C. § 1320a-7a(i)(7).
[92] *See* Integrated Generics, Inc. v. Bowen, 678 F. Supp. 1004, 1009 (E.D.N.Y. 1988).
[93] *Id.* at 1007–09.
[94] United States v. Halper, 490 U.S. 435 (1989).

## Representing Healthcare Organizations in Fraud and Abuse Matters

when additional patients are tested at the same facility, which paid only $3 per claim. The total amount of the false claim was $585. Mr. Halper was sentenced to a two-year jail term and a $5,000 fine.

Subsequent to the criminal proceeding, the federal government brought a civil proceeding against Mr. Halper pursuant to the FCA.[95] In the civil action, the government relied on the facts established in the criminal conviction to establish civil liability, and the district court granted summary judgment to the government on that issue. At the time the *Halper* case was decided, the FCA provided a recovery of a civil penalty of up to $2,000 per claim, as well as an amount equal to two times the amount of the government's damages and costs of the civil action.[96] Calculation under this formula resulted in Mr. Halper being subject to a penalty of more than $130,000. The Supreme Court held that, under the Double Jeopardy Clause, a defendant who already had been punished in a criminal proceeding may not be subject to a second civil sanction "overwhelmingly disproportionate" to the damages caused, such that the second sanction cannot be characterized as remedial, but only as a deterrent or retribution.[97]

The language of the Supreme Court's opinion stated that the holding was "a rule for the rare case," where the defendant has previously sustained a criminal penalty, and the subsequent civil penalty "bears no rational relation to the goal of compensating the government for its loss."[98] Moreover, the Court stated that the government generally "is entitled to rough remedial justice," and may "demand compensation according to somewhat imprecise formulas," including reasonable liquidated damages or, in 1989, a fixed sum plus double damages. According to the Court in *Halper*, it is only when the formula "does not remotely approximate the Government's damages and actual costs, and rough justice becomes clear injustice" that the Double Jeopardy Clause is implicated.[99]

In *Hudson v. United States*,[100] the Supreme Court "disavowed" its *Halper* analysis, and returned to its double-jeopardy rule prior to *Halper*. The Court held that determining whether a particular punishment is criminal or civil is first a question of statutory construction. Therefore, when the statute contemplates a civil penalty, the court must decide "whether the statutory scheme was so punitive either in purpose or effect as to transform what was clearly intended

---

[95] 31 U.S.C. §§ 3729–3731.
[96] In 1986, damages for violations of the FCA were increased to include a civil penalty of not less than $5,000 and not more than $10,000 per claim (which has been further increased to not less than $5,500 and not more than $11,000 per claim), as well as an amount equal to three times the amount of the government's damages. However, recovery may be limited to double damages in certain specific instances (*see* Chapter 4).
[97] *Halper*, 490 U.S. at 448–49.
[98] *Id.* at 449.
[99] *Id.*
[100] Hudson v. United States, 522 U.S. 93 (1997).

as a civil remedy into a criminal penalty."[101] The Court stated that, instead of focusing on whether the sanction was disproportionate to the harm caused (as it did in *Halper*); it should consider a number of factors. Included among the factors that the Court referred to as "useful guideposts" are whether:

(1) the sanction involves an affirmative disability or restraint;

(2) the sanction has historically been regarded as a punishment;

(3) the sanction comes into play only on a finding of scienter;

(4) the sanction's operation will promote the traditional aims of punishment-retribution and deterrence;

(5) the behavior to which the sanction applies is already a crime;

(6) an alternative purpose to which the sanction may rationally be connected is assignable for it; and

(7) the sanction appears excessive in relation to the alternative purpose assigned.

Therefore, although the decision in *Halper* has been expanded to include the factors in *Hudson*, if these factors lean toward effectively causing a second criminal penalty, then the Double Jeopardy Clause will prevent the government from going forward with a second prosecution of the action.

In this regard, the Eleventh Circuit held in *Manocchio v. Kusserow*[102] that a civil exclusion action brought by the OIG following a criminal proceeding does not implicate the Double Jeopardy Clause, given that the primary purpose of the program exclusion was not punitive, but rather remedial in nature (i.e., to protect the program and its beneficiaries from future misconduct). In *Manocchio*, Dr. Manocchio pled guilty and was convicted of a misdemeanor under 18 U.S.C. §1003 for making a fraudulent demand against the United States by submitting a single fraudulent Medicare claim in the amount of $62.40. He was sentenced to three years' probation, a fine of $1,000, and ordered to pay restitution. Dr. Manocchio then was subject to mandatory exclusion from the Medicare program.

Similarly, the Double Jeopardy Clause is not implicated where a defendant is first subject to CMPs for submission of false claims to Medicare and

---

[101] *Id.* at 99.
[102] Manocchio v. Kusserow, 961 F.2d 1539 (11th Cir. 1992); *see also* U.S. v. Rogen, 517 F.3d 449 (7th Cir. 2008); Patel v. Thompson, 319 F.3d 1317 (11th Cir. 2003); U.S. v. Lumanna, 114 F. Supp. 2d 193 (W.D.N.Y. 2000); Erickson v. United States *ex rel.* Dep't Health and Human Servs., 67 F.3d 858 (9th Cir. 1995); Sokol v. New York State Dep't of Health, 636 N.Y.S.2d 450 (N.Y. App. Div. 1996); Crawford v. Sullivan, 1993 U.S. Dist. LEXIS 906 (N.D. Ill. Jan. 27, 1993), adopted by Crawford v. Sullivan, 1993 U.S. Dist. LEXIS 3240 (N.D. Ill. Mar. 11, 1993); *See* U.S. v. Hawley, citing United States v. Ward, 448 U.S. 242, 248 (1980) in a related analysis under the *Ex Post Facto Clause*—holding that the "FCA's statutory scheme is so punitive either in purpose or effect as to negate Congressional intent to deem it civil." No. C 06-4087–MWB at 21 (N.D. Iowa. Aug. 1, 2011).

## Representing Healthcare Organizations in Fraud and Abuse Matters

then subject to criminal prosecution for submission of false claims to private insurers. The Eleventh Circuit held in *United States v. Mayers*[103] that the Double Jeopardy Clause is not implicated under these circumstances, because the same conduct was not involved in both proceedings. Similarly, the Double Jeopardy Clause is not implicated where a defendant is acquitted and then subject to CMPs.

### § 9-4(b) Ex Post Facto Considerations

The U.S. Constitution also protects defendants from the enforcement of *ex post facto* laws—that is, laws adopted *after* the allegedly illegal conduct took place. In addition to the issues raised earlier, the *Manocchio* case addressed whether Dr. Manocchio's five-year mandatory exclusion violated the Constitution's *ex post facto* clause.[104] The *ex post facto* issue arose from the fact that the law governing civil exclusions from the Medicare and Medicaid programs underwent significant modification in 1987. Prior to the 1987 amendments adopted as part of the Medicare and Medicaid Patient and Program Protection Act,[105] conviction of Medicare fraud triggered mandatory exclusion, but the period of the exclusion was discretionary. The 1987 amendment provided a minimum period of program exclusion of five years.[106] Dr. Manocchio argued that imposition of the mandatory five-year exclusion period enacted in 1987 with respect to a fraudulent claim submitted in 1984 violated the constitutional protection against *ex post facto* laws.[107] Relying on the Supreme Court decision in *Flemming v. Nestor*,[108] the Eleventh Circuit held that, like the Double Jeopardy Clause, the *ex post facto* clause is only implicated where the law in question can be characterized as "punitive" in nature, not a remedial law such as one involving program exclusion.[109]

After the Fraud Enforcement Recovery Act (see discussion in Chapter 4) was passed to overrule *Allison Engine*, courts considered whether the amended provisions of the FCA applied to conduct occurring prior to the its effective date of June 7, 2008. In *United States ex rel. Steury v. Cardinal Health, Inc.*,[110]

---

[103] United States v. Mayers, 957 F.2d 858 (11th Cir. 1992), *cert. denied*, 504 U.S. 989 (1992); *see also* Jung Bea Han v. McDonald, 408 Fed. Appx. 289 and U.S. v. Santodedios, 240 F. Supp. 2d 414 (D. Md. 2002).
[104] Manocchio v. Kusserow, 961 F.2d 1541 (11th Cir. 1992).
[105] Medicare and Medicaid Patient and Program Protection Act of 1987, Pub. L. No. 100-93, 101 Stat. 682 (1987).
[106] Social Security Act § 1128(c)(3)(B); 42 U.S.C. § 1320a-7(c)(3)(B).
[107] Manocchio v. Kusserow, 961 F.2d 1542 (11th Cir. 1992).
[108] Flemming v. Nestor, 363 U.S. 603, *reh'g denied*, 364 U.S. 854 (1960).
[109] Manocchio v. Kusserow, 961 F.2d 1542 (11th Cir. 1992); *see* Seide v. Shalala, 31 F. Supp. 2d 466, 469 (D. Pa. 1998); Patel v. Thompson, 319 F.3d 1317 (11th Cir. 2003); *see also* United States *ex rel.* Baker v. Community Health Systems, Inc., 709 F. Supp. 2d 1084, 1112 (D.N.M. 2010).
[110] United States *ex rel.* Steury v. Cardinal Health, Inc., 625 F.3d 262 (5th Cir. 2010).

the court held that the amended FCA applied because plaintiff's case was pending as of June 7, 2008. However, other courts have held that the FERA amendments do not apply when the defendant does not have "a claim or demand for money [from the government] pending on or after June 7, 2008.[111]

## § 9-4(c) Considerations during Civil Settlements with the Federal Government

Settlement negotiations during healthcare fraud investigations or litigation can commence at any time. Most frequently, these negotiations occur after the government has had opportunity to conduct an investigation by reviewing company documents and interviewing witnesses. Healthcare fraud matters have somewhat specialized considerations during settlement. Parties negotiate a number of issues including but not limited to: the amount of damages; whether a multiplier will be used to calculated damages (up to three times for CMP or FCA violations); whether the amounts paid under the settlement will be over a period of time or in a lump sum; the amount of interest, if any, owed; whether individuals will be released from civil and criminal liability along with the company; the scope of conduct and time period covered by the release; whether the company will be required to enter into a Corporate Integrity Agreement (CIA) with the Office of Inspector General of the Department of Health and Human Services to avoid exclusion under the Social Security Act and how long such CIA will be in effect; whether the OIG is reserving the right to exclude individuals later; and what share of the proceeds will be rewarded to the qui tam relator(s) or to the realtor's counsel for attorney fees if applicable.

Unlike private parties, U.S. Attorneys, who frequently direct healthcare fraud cases on behalf of the federal government, follow specific guidelines for offers of compromise. For civil matters, according to Title 4 of the United States Attorneys' Manual, claims can be compromised if the U.S. Attorney believes: (1) the claim is without legal merit; (2) the claim cannot be factually proven in court; (3) a different claim should be selected for purposes of resolving an open issue of law; (4) the full amount of a claim cannot be collected in full due to the financial condition of the debtor because of the debtors ability to pay; (5) the cost of collecting a claim will exceed the amount recoverable; (6) compromising or closing a claim is necessary to prevent injustice; (7) enforcement policy underlying a claim will be adequately served by a compromise; (8) it would be less costly to compromise a claim than to undertake

---

[111] *See* United States v. Hawley, No. C 06-4087–MWB (N.D. Iowa. Aug. 1, 2011). The *Hawley* court held that "the FCA's statutory scheme is so punitive either in purpose or effect as to negate Congressional intent to deem it civil. As a result, "retroactive application of the [FERA] amendments to the FCA violates the Ex Post Facto Clause because retroactive application of the amendments to the FCA would impose punishment for acts that were not punishable prior to enactment of the amendments. Hawley at 21.

further legal action in defense of a claim; (9) compromise of a claim against the United States is substantially more favorable than the verdict or judgment that would probably result from litigation.[112]

While most settlements of government healthcare investigations involve compromise base on the merits of the case and associated ligation risk the government faces in pursuing it settlements based on the financial condition of the company and its ability to pay are increasing. This is likely in response to the increase in fraud enforcement activities and the associated demands made by government attorneys. The Civil Division of the Department of Justice has created a process through which and entity can negotiate a settlement based on its "ability to pay." It should be noted that individuals and entities do not have a right to assert ability to pay as a defense. Rather, whether the government will permit a matter to be resolved on an ability to pay basis is discretionary. The "ability to pay process" begins when the entity or it counsel determines that the government demand (or prospective government demand) and/or legal fees to defend the case against the government exceed what the entity is able to bear and still be a viable going concern. The DOJ requires individuals who attempt to avail themselves of the "ability to pay" process to fill out an application called "Financial Statement of Corporate Debtor" and attach documents such as tax returns, audited financial statements, information pertaining to current and future earnings, ownership information, available credit lines and other information material to determining valuation and the entity's past, current and future finances. Using this process the government has the discretion to defer payments over time and/or compromise the amount of the settlement in order to achieve the mutual goal of preserving the entity and therefore allowing the government to benefit from some, albeit diminished, recovery. Increasingly, the government is including in settlements, contingency payments in the event the company's financial condition changes through a sale or otherwise.

## § 9-4(d) Criminal Settlement—The Use of Deferred Prosecution and Non-Prosecution Agreements

Using either a Deferred Prosecution Agreement (DPA) or a Non-Prosecution Agreement (NPA), federal prosecutors can offer to reward a corporation's cooperation with a federal investigation during a criminal settlement. Under a DPA, the government defers prosecution and eventually dismisses criminal charges in exchange for the defendant-company's compliance with specific obligations and requirements. In a DPA, a charging document is filed with the court, and the Justice Department agrees to defer judicial proceedings with a goal of dismissal of the charges after a definite period of time

---

[112] United States Attorneys' Manual, Title 4-3.00 Compromising and Closing 4-3.200.

(usually one to three years during which the statute of limitations is tolled), provided the company complies with the agreement. NPAs are substantially the same except that generally no charging document is filed although in some instances the government may reserve the right to do so if the company does not adhere to the agreement.

The parties to the DPA/NPA are usually the agency with the authority to prosecute the crime alleged or that could be alleged in a charging document (e.g., the U.S. Attorney) and the organization against whom the criminal information or complaint was filed or could be filed. As part of the DPA/NPA, the organization may be required to waive right to speedy trial; statute of limitations as defense; and the attorney-client privilege, but the specific requirements are usually DPA/NPA specific.

As noted, the DOJ accords a significant amount of weight to a corporation's cooperation with an investigation in determining whether a pre-trial agreement is feasible or appropriate. In a recent case against Johnson & Johnson, the Department recognized J&J's timely voluntary disclosure, thorough self-investigation of the underlying conduct, the extraordinary cooperation provided by the company and the extensive remedial efforts and compliance improvements undertaken.[113] In a settlement on off-label promotional activities that resulted in a DPA, the DOJ also commended Kos Pharmaceutical's extensive internal investigation, the regular reporting of investigational information to the department, its ongoing cooperation and the remedial measures Kos had undertaken.[114]

Federal criminal settlements using DPAs and NPAs come with enormous company obligations, far surpassing those usually found in an OIG CIA. The use of independent Federal Monitors is now a common provision in DPAs and NPAs. In light of the dearth of guidance originally available concerning either the selection process for choosing a Federal Monitor or defining the roles and responsibilities of a monitor, Acting Deputy Attorney General Craig Morford issued a memorandum entitled "Selection and Use of Monitors in Deferred Prosecution Agreements with Corporations," in March of 2008. It sets forth a series of principles pertaining to the selection of the monitor, the scope of the monitor's duties and the duration of the monitor's responsibilities.[115] Then, in 2010, due to some continued criticism of the program, Acting Deputy Attorney General Gary G. Grindler released a memorandum providing "Additional

---

[113] DOJ, Office of Public Affairs, Johnson & Johnson Agrees to Pay $21.4 Million Criminal Penalty to Resolve Foreign Corrupt Practice Act and Oil for Food Investigation, (Apr. 8, 2011).
[114] Ben Vernin, DOJ Announces $41 Million Settlement of Off-Label Qui Tam with Kos Pharmaceuticals (Dec. 9, 2010), http://falseclaimscounsel.com/wordpress/?p=1147.
[115] See http://www.usdoj.gov/dag/morford-useofmonitorsmemo-03072008.pdf.

## Representing Healthcare Organizations in Fraud and Abuse Matters

Guidance on the Use of Monitors in Deferred Prosecution Agreements and Non-Prosecution Agreements with Corporations."[116]

Prior to the selection of the monitor, the corporation and the government are expected to determine the qualifications necessary based on the particular facts and circumstances of the case. Due to some concern that monitors were being chosen on the basis of favoritism, the guidelines establish monitor selection based on qualifications and merits to avoid any potential conflicts of interest and to encourage public confidence in the process.[117]

A monitor's primary role, as an independent third party, is to be fully aware of the scope of the corporation's misconduct and to monitor compliance with the provisions of the pre-trial agreement to reduce any risk of recurrent wrongdoing.[118] The guidance also emphasizes the importance of communication between the monitor, the corporation and the government in facilitating the agreement. Grindler's "Additional Guidance" establishes the role of DOJ when disputes arise between the monitor and the corporation.[119] The duration of the agreement "should be tailored to the problems that have been found to exist and the types of remedial measures needed for the monitor to satisfy his or her mandate."[120]

## § 9-5 UNDERSTANDING THE PRIVILEGES AND OBLIGATIONS AFFORDED TO LAWYERS AND THEIR CLIENTS

A significant consideration in representing clients in fraud and abuse matters is the preservation of the attorney-client privilege and the work product privilege. These privileges come into play both when assisting with a client's response to a government investigation and when advising a client on the fraud and abuse ramifications of general business activities. Moreover, in certain circumstances, counsel's actions must be guided by the applicable state's Rules for the Professional Conduct of Lawyers imposed by state bars and/or reflected in the American Bar Association's (ABA's) Model Rules, in addition to the common-law pronouncements of these privileges. Since the government has more recently announced

---

[116] Memorandum from Gary G. Grindler, Acting Deputy General, to Heads of Department Components and the United States Attorneys (May 25, 2010) (Memorandum) Additional Guidance on the Use of Monitors in Deferred Prosecution Agreements and Non-Prosecution Agreements with Corporations.

[117] Memorandum from Craig S. Morford, Acting Deputy General, to Heads of Department Components and the United States Attorneys (Mar. 7, 2008) (Memorandum) *available online at* United States Attorney's Manual, title 9 Criminal Resource Manual, art. 163.

[118] *Id.*

[119] Grindler, Additional Guidance, *see above.*

[120] Morford memo.

that it intends to seek penalties against not just companies, but also their employees, officers and directors, healthcare fraud defense attorneys must have a fluent understanding of applicable ethical standards and navigate the waters very carefully.

## § 9-5(a)  The Attorney/Client Communications Privilege

Contrary to popular belief, the attorney/client privilege has not been incorporated into either the Federal Rules of Evidence nor has it been formally recognized by Congress in its own investigations. Although some states have adopted statutes formalizing the attorney/client privilege, generally the privilege originates in common law. As a result, the attorney/client privilege has been developed through the common law so as to extend to all communications made in confidence between client and attorney (i.e., attorney-to-client and client-to-attorney) for the purpose of seeking, obtaining, or providing legal assistance for the client. The attorney/client privilege applies broadly to all such communications, regardless of whether the communication is made in anticipation of litigation, but it applies *only* to the communication itself, and not the underlying facts contained within the communication.[121]

The burden of establishing the existence of the attorney/client privilege falls upon the party asserting the privilege.[122] Generally, five elements are required for a client to invoke the privilege:

1. the person or entity asserting the privilege must be a client;
2. the person to whom the communication was made must be an attorney acting in that capacity at the time of the communication;
3. the communication must have been made by the client" (i.e., not by third persons;
4. the communication must have been made in confidence; and
5. the communication must be to obtain either legal advice or assistance in a legal proceeding.[123]

---

[121] Upjohn v. United States, 449 U.S. 383 (1981); *see also* B.C.F. Oil Ref. v. Consol. Edison Co., F.R.D. 161, 165 (S.D.N.Y. 1996) (holding the privilege "does not extend to fact known to a party that are central to that party's claims, even if such facts came to be known through communications with counsel who had obtained knowledge of those facts through an investigation . . ."); *see also* United States v. Edwards, 39 F. Supp. 2d 716 (M.D. La. 1999).

[122] *See* Fisher v. United States, 425 U.S. 391 (1976); United States v. White, 950 F.2d 426 (7th Cir. 1991).

[123] *See* Valihura, Attorney-Client Privilege and Work-Product Doctrine: Corporate Applications Number 22-4th (2012 Bureau of National Affairs); *see also* Matter of Walsh, 623 F.2d 489, 492 (7th Cir. 1980); *see also* United States v. Landorf, 591 F.2d 36 (9th Cir. 1978).

## Representing Healthcare Organizations in Fraud and Abuse Matters

### § 9-5(a)(1)  Legal Advice

In order to assert the attorney/client privilege, "legal advice" of some kind must have been sought. Therefore, communications made with the purpose of seeking business advice, as opposed to legal advice, are not privileged.[124] For example, although the preparation of tax returns by an attorney may require some knowledge of the law, some courts have held that the privilege does not attach to the communications involved, because the work involved is primarily an accounting service instead of legal advice.[125] Similarly, within the context of a fraud investigation, it sometimes becomes difficult to distinguish between legal and business advice. This is especially true with respect to in-house counsel for healthcare organizations. A healthcare organization can assert the attorney/client privilege for communications with in-house counsel and outside counsel. There is a greater risk, however, that a court will view communications with in-house counsel as being made for the purpose of obtaining business advice, and thus that such communications do not qualify for the attorney/client privilege. This is especially so where the attorney wears multiple "hat" within an organization. The determination as to whether a communication between an attorney and a client is subject to the attorney/client privilege is a question of fact for the court.[126]

### § 9-5(a)(2)  The Attorney

Although it is clear that an attorney must be the recipient of a communication in order to raise the attorney/client privilege, not every attorney is considered an "attorney" for purposes of the privilege. Non-attorney consultants who are not retained by attorneys cannot invoke the privilege, even though the advice may at times take a position on healthcare reimbursement regulations and rules. Similarly, the client cannot raise the attorney/client privilege in situations where a lawyer cannot legally or ethically represent a client. For example, a client cannot invoke the privilege when that client's former attorney is suing to recover unpaid fees, because ethical rules prohibit the representation of a party by an attorney who has a conflict of interest. State rules of professional conduct govern whether it is ethically improper for an attorney to represent a client.

Adding to the complexity, professional conduct rules vary by state, although many of the state rules are based upon the ABA Model Rules. It is commonplace for attorneys to serve as national counsel and advise clients

---

[124] See *In re* Grand Jury Subpoena Duces Tecum dated (Sept. 15, 1983), 731 F.2d 1032, 1037 (2d Cir. 1984).
[125] *See* U.S. v. Davis, 636 F.2d 1028 (5th Cir. 1981). However, accounting services performed ancillary to legal advice may be within the attorney/client privilege. *Id.*
[126] *See* Richards v. Lennox Industries, Inc., 574 So.2d 736 (Ala. 1990).

who may be located in jurisdictions in which the attorney is not admitted to practice. Prior to August 2002, ABA Model Rule 5.5 specifically proscribed practicing law in a jurisdiction where an attorney was not licensed. In 2002, the ABA amended Model Rule 5.5 to continue the proscription on practice without a license, yet permit the practice in four specific circumstances. ABA Model Rule 5.5(c) now provides that:

> A lawyer admitted in another United States Jurisdiction, and not disbarred or suspended from the practice in any jurisdiction, may provide legal services on a temporary basis in this jurisdiction that:
>
> (1) are undertaken in association with a lawyer who is admitted to practice in this jurisdiction and who actively participates in the matter;
>
> (2) are in or reasonably related to a pending or potential proceeding before a tribunal in this or another jurisdiction, if the lawyer, or a person the lawyer is assisting, is authorized by law or order to appear in such proceeding or reasonably expects to be so authorized;
>
> (3) are in or reasonably related to a pending or potential arbitration, mediation, or other alternative dispute resolution proceeding in this or another jurisdiction, if the services arise out of or are reasonably related to the lawyer's practice in a jurisdiction in which the lawyer is admitted to practice and are not services for which the forum requires *pro hac vice* admission; or
>
> (4) are not with paragraphs (c)(2) or (c)(3) and arise out of or are reasonably related to the lawyer's practice in a jurisdiction in which the lawyer is admitted to practice.[127]

Comment 5 to the Amended Model Rule 5.5 provides that "the fact that conduct is not so identified [in the four specific circumstances] does not imply that the conduct is or is not authorized."[128] Therefore, in the context of a national legal practice, it remains unclear what constitutes a violation of ABA Model Rule 5.5.

The American Law Institute states that:

> a lawyer conducting activities in the lawyer's home state may advise a client about the law of another state, a proceeding in another state, or a transaction there, including conducting research in the law of the

---

[127] ABA, MODEL RULES OF PROF'L CONDUCT R. 5.5(c) *available online at* http://www.americanbar.org/groups/professional_responsibility/publications/model_rules_of_professional_conduct/rule_5_5_unauthorized_practice_of_law_multijurisdictional_practice_of_law.html (last visited Feb. 9, 2012).

[128] *Id.*

## Representing Healthcare Organizations in Fraud and Abuse Matters

other state, advising the client about the application of the law, and drafting legal documents intended to have legal effect there.[129]

Similarly, for purposes of asserting the attorney/client privilege, an attorney need not be licensed in the state where the communications have taken place.[130]

In addition, the privilege also has been utilized to protect communications between a client and agents of the attorney, such as accountants and investigators.[131] Generally, the privilege includes all persons who act as the attorney's agents, including secretaries, file clerks, telephone operators, messengers, clerks not yet admitted to the bar, aides, and paralegals (when acting as an attorney's agent and adequately supervised).[132] It is, however, very important for the attorney to document that any third party individuals, including consultants and employees, officers and directors who work for their client, are in fact operating at the direction of counsel. Often such individuals are needed throughout the course of an internal or external investigation and a clear paper trail should exist to aid the client in asserting privilege later.

### § 9-5(a)(3)   Communications

The attorney/client privilege applies to "communications" between counsel and client, including communications between corporate employees and in-house counsel. The privilege covers only the communication, however, and not the informational content or the facts. Information that is told to an attorney is not privileged just because it is in the possession of the attorney, or just because the attorney became aware of the information through a privileged communication.[133] Provided that the facts can be revealed without revealing the context or nature of the privileged communication between the attorney and client, the facts are not protected by the attorney/client privilege.[134] However, the privilege will protect documents summarizing factual

---

[129] RESTATEMENT (THIRD) OF THE LAW GOVERNING LAWYERS Vol. 1 § 3 (2000), stating that "there is no per se bar against such a lawyer giving a formal opinion based in whole or in part on the law of another jurisdiction."

[130] *See* Georgia-Pacific Plywood Co. v. U.S. Plywood Corp., *18 F.R.D. 463 (S.D.N.Y. 1956) holding corporate counsel who represented corporation i*; *see also* X Corp. v. Doe, 805 F.Supp. 1298 (D. Va. 1992) (privilege applies to communications by corporate attorney in California who was only licensed in Pennsylvania).

[131] *See* United States v. Kovel, 296 F.2d 918, 921 (2d Cir. 1961).

[132] *See* Auersperg v. Von Bulow, 811 F.2d 136, 146 (2d Cir. 1987). Nevertheless, there are also situations where client communications to paralegals are privileged when the paralegal is acting separate from the role of an attorney's agent.

[133] *See* American Standard, Inc. v. Bendix Corp., 80 F.R.D. 706, 709 (W.D. Mo. 1978); Electronic Data Systems Corp. v. Steingraber, 2003 U.S. Dist. LEXIS 11818 (E.D. Tex. 2003); *In re* Pfohl Bros. Landfill Litig., 175 F.R.D. 13 (W.D.N.Y. 1997); Hardy v. New York News, Inc., 114 F.R.D. 633, 644 (S.D.N.Y. 1987).

[134] *See* Balistrieri v. O'Farrel, 57 F.R.D. 567, 569 (E.D. Wis. 1972).

information if it is "sufficiently clear that the [documents] would not have been created had plaintiff not needed the assistance of counsel."[135] By way of example, forwarding a document to an attorney does itself establish a basis to assert privilege. But, if the attorney marks up the document or provides comments, those additions to the document may be privileged.

Documents or other physical evidence delivered to one's attorney are not privileged, insofar as they do not pertain to or disclose a privileged communication between the attorney and client.[136] Similarly, neither physical characteristics of a client nor the fee arrangement with a client are considered privileged.[137] Consequently, invoices from a lawyer to the client may not be privileged, even though the descriptions of work performed may be subject to the privilege.

### § 9-5(a)(4)  Confidentiality

A communication must be kept confidential in order for the client to invoke the attorney/client privilege. Communications are confidential when a person, at the time and in the circumstances of the communication, reasonably believes that no one will learn the contents of the communication except a privileged person. Naturally, communications made under circumstances that allow third persons, even if such third person is a spouse or a friend,[138] to overhear or intercept it are not confidential, even though a third person does not actually overhear or intercept the conversation.[139]

Maintaining confidentiality for purposes of the attorney/client privilege has become challenging in the electronic age. Attorneys and their clients routinely use e-mail as a source of communication and online data rooms to share documents. And though healthcare entities in particular employ high security standards to protect company ESI, hackers are still capable of intercepting or accessing information. The question of whether a communication is privileged does not necessarily depend on the form of the communication, or whether someone can get to it. Indeed, if the standard for waiver depended on whether a communication contained on a server could be accessed by a third party, conceivably nothing electronic communication could ever be privileged. Therefore, e-mails, mobile phone communications and other digital means can be sufficient methodology used for a privileged communication

---

[135] *In re* Grand Jury Proceedings, 2001 U.S. Dist. LEXIS 15646, at *98 (quoting AFP Imaging Corp. v. Philips Medizin Sys., 1993 U.S. Dist. LEXIS 18234, at *5 (S.D.N.Y. Dec. 28, 1993)).
[136] *See id.*
[137] *See* United States v. Haddad, 527 F.2d 537 (6th Cir. 1975).
[138] *See* Hazard v. Hazard, 833 S.W.2d 911, 914 (Tenn. Ct. App. 1991) (holding spouse third party); *see also* State v. Soto, 933 P.2d 66, 77 (Haw. 1997) (holding friend third party).
[139] *See* Chandler v. Denton, 741 P.2d 855, 865 (Okla. 1987).

## Representing Healthcare Organizations in Fraud and Abuse Matters

if the court believes that the parties acted diligently and reasonably to protect confidentiality.

It would seem obvious, but social media, like Facebook or Twitter should never be used for privileged communication, nor should any other electronic methodology that permits third parties to access information. This extends to online blogs, chat rooms and the like. Parties need to have a reasonable expectation of privacy for a communication to be deemed confidential. These otherwise public online forums, although widely used for communication, offer no protection.[140]

Currently, no uniform standards exists that courts use to examine communications between attorneys and clients through wireless technology. Cases addressing these forms of communication do not address the attorney/client privilege, but instead usually relate to federal wiretap statutes or Fourth Amendment issues. With respect to mobile telephones and the attorney/client privilege, some courts have held that communications over mobile telephones are not considered privileged, because mobile telephone calls can be overheard with the use of a scanner.[141] These opinions were written during a time in which analog cellular phones were in use and should therefore not apply to digital phones, which are very difficult to intercept. Many of these opinions also were written before federal wiretap statutes were amended to make it illegal to intercept a mobile telephone call.[142] Attorneys and their clients would be wise to be cautious in their use of smart phones and portable electronic media.

With respect to electronic mail and facsimiles, most courts and the ABA have found it reasonable to expect that communications made using these technologies are considered confidential.[143] ABA Formal Opinion 99-413 concludes that, despite some risk of interception and disclosure, unencrypted email sent through the Internet is consistent with a lawyer's ethical duties under ABA Model Rule 1.6.[144] However, the ABA opinion only addresses the ethical duty of confidentiality, not the attorney/client privilege; further, the ABA opinion relied on technology as of 1999.

---

[140] *See* Castano v. Am. Tobacco Co., 896 F. Supp. 590, 596 (E.D. La. 1995) (holding documents available on the internet are not privileged).

[141] *See* Tyler v. Berodt, 877 F.2d 705 (8th Cir. 1989); Edwards v. Bardwell, 632 F.Supp. 584, 586 (M.D. La. 1986); State v. Howard, 679 P.2d 197, 206 (Kan. 1984).

[142] Electronic Communications Privacy Act of 1986, 18 U.S.C. § 2511.

[143] *See* State v. Canady, 460 S.E.2d 677, 689 (W.Va. 1995).

[144] ABA Comm. on Ethics and Prof'l Responsibility, Formal Op. 99-413 (Mar. 10, 1999) (citing several analogous state opinions and the Electronic Communications Privacy Act, which makes unauthorized interception or dissemination of information a violation of law).

## § 9-5(a)(5)   The Client

The attorney/client privilege belongs exclusively to the client, and not to the attorney.[145] But if an attorney represents a company, who is the client? It is important to remember that in the corporate context, the represented party or client is not an individual who works at the corporation, but rather the corporation itself. For example: if individual officers or board members, who have made confidential communications in connection with the legal representation of the corporation, leave their position, the attorney/client privilege remains with the corporate entity and the new officers or board members are vested with the authority to exercise the attorney/client privilege as they see fit, including waiving the privilege if they choose.[146] However, at least one court has recognized that the existence of a client as an entity separate from the lawyer is not essential for the lawyer to invoke the privilege where the lawyer is his own client,[147] although a law firm cannot claim the privilege for communications between all attorneys in the firm. [148]

Attorneys that represent entities do not represent individuals; nonetheless, individuals and corporate entities alike are entitled to the protection of the attorney/client privilege.[149] Within the corporate context, the client includes both senior management (the control group) and those corporate employees who communicate with corporate counsel at the direction of corporate superiors in order to secure legal advice. Accordingly, courts recognize that communications between the "control group," and the attorney are privileged. [150] Attorney should, whenever possible, document that certain employees are acting at the direction of counsel to ensure that a contemporaneous record exists memorializing the parties' intent to preserve privilege. Finally, the communications must be within the scope of the employee's duties and must be kept confidential.[151]

Lines can easily become blurred when counsel interacts with employees during the course of a government or internal investigation. This is especially true when attorneys interview the individual who may have hired them as counsel in the first place. Attorneys should, therefore, administer a statement

---

[145] ABA, MODEL RULES OF PROF'L CONDUCT R. 1.6, which states absent an exception, "A lawyer shall not reveal information relating to the representation of a client unless the client gives informed consent. . . ."*available online at* http://www.americanbar.org/groups/professional_responsibility/publications/model_rules_of_professional_conduct/rule_1_6_confidentiality_of_information.html (last visited Feb. 9, 2012).

[146] *See* U.S. v. Chronicle Pub. Co. Hantzis, 732 F. Supp. 270 (D. Mass. 1990); *see also In re* Grand Jury Subpoena Duces Tecum, 391 F. Supp. 1029 (S.D.N.Y. 1975) (holding that, where corporation waived privilege on certain matters concerning former officer's work for corporation, the former officer cannot raise the attorney/client privilege).

[147] *See* United States v. Rowe, 96 F.3d 1294 (9th Cir. 1996).

[148] *In re* Sunrise Securities Litigation, 130 F.R.D. 560, 572 (E.D. Pa. 1989).

[149] *See* Commodity Futures Trading Com'n v. Weintraub, 471 U.S. 343, 348 (1985).

[150] Upjohn Co. v. United States, 449 U.S. 383 (1981).

[151] *See* Upjohn v. United States, 449 U.S. 383 (1981).

in connection with the interview that clarifies who the attorney represents and who owns the privilege. This statement, called the Upjohn warning, named after the Supreme Court Case *Upjohn Co. v. United States*, 449 U.S. 383 (1981) clarifies that the privilege is owned by the company rather than the employee. An example of an Upjohn warning appears below:

> *I am counsel for the company and I do not represent you personally. The communication we are about to have is protected by the attorney client privilege and therefore I ask that it remain confidential. The privilege is the company's privilege not yours. The company can decide to waive this privilege and disclose information learned during this and any subsequent communication to third parties including the government.*

## § 9-5(b) The Work-Product Doctrine

In contrast to the attorney/client privilege, the work-product doctrine applies only to materials prepared in anticipation of litigation.[152] Generally, this does not mean that litigation must be pending; rather, only that the prospect of litigation must be fairly obvious and imminent or probable, not merely a remote possibility.[153] The goal of the work-product doctrine is to "protect against disclosure of the mental impressions, conclusions, opinions or legal theories of an attorney or other representative of a party concerning the litigation."[154] Documents, notes, and files not protected by the attorney/client privilege often may be protected by the work-product doctrine.

Where the attorney/client privilege is an absolute bar to discovery, the work-product doctrine can be overcome, in federal court, by a showing of necessity by the opposing party.[155] The Federal Rules of Civil Procedure expressly permit the discovery of attorney work product if the party has substantial need of the material, and the material (or its substantial equivalent) cannot be obtained without due hardship.[156]

Unlike the attorney/client privilege, in which the presence of an attorney is indispensable to the assertion of the privilege, the work-product doctrine may be asserted without the involvement of an attorney. The absence of a lawyer may make assertion of the privilege more difficult, however.[157]

---

[152] Hickman v. Taylor, 329 U.S. 495 (1947). In the civil context, the privilege is codified in FED. R. CIV. P. 26(b)(3), and within the criminal context the privilege is codified in FED. R. CRIM. P. 16(a)(2)–(b)(2).
[153] Fox v. California Sierra Fin. Servs., 120 F.R.D. 520 (N.D. Cal. 1988).
[154] FED. R. CIV. P. 26(b)(3).
[155] *Id.*
[156] *Id.*
[157] *See, e.g.,* Thomas Organ Co. v. Jadranska Slobodna Plovidba, 54 F.R.D. 367, 372 (N.D. Ill. 1972) (the absence of attorney participation gave rise to a conclusive presumption that the investigation was in the ordinary course of business and not in anticipation of litigation).

In contrast to the attorney/client privilege, both the attorney and client must consent in order to waive the work-product doctrine.[158] Further, courts distinguish between disclosure to adversaries and disclosure to non-adversaries, because the privilege is meant to protect against disclosure to adversaries; the disclosure to a third party does not waive the privilege, while disclosure to an adversary waives the privilege.[159]

Similar to the attorney/client privilege, however, courts apply a five-factor test to determine if there has been a disclosure sufficient to waive the work-product doctrine. The five-factor test includes a consideration of the (1) reasonableness of the precautions taken to prevent inadvertent disclosure, (2) time taken to rectify the error, (3) scope of discovery relative to number of documents disclosed, (4) extent of disclosure, and (5) overriding issues of fairness.[160]

## § 9-5(c) Waiver

In order to invoke the attorney/client privilege or the work product privilege, the privilege must not have been waived. Because the attorney/client privilege belongs to the client, it can be waived only by the client.[161] A waiver can be deliberate. At times clients want to avail themselves of advice of counsel defenses and ask the attorney to testify on the client's behalf, or produced privileged documents prepared by the attorney. A waiver can also be inadvertent. Inadvertent waivers most often occur by some party making a disclosure to a third party.

A majority of courts consider waiver an "all or nothing" proposition. Where a person has voluntarily disclosed communications on a subject matter, the attorney/client privilege is waived with regard to all communications related to that subject matter.[162] For example, public use of counsel's report of an internal investigation may constitute a general waiver of the attorney/client privilege as to that matter.[163] Thus, attorneys attempting to preserve the attorney/client privilege as to particular documents and communications should ensure that their clients are aware that privileged documents and communications cannot be disclosed to third parties.

---

[158] *See In re* Sealed Case, 29 F.3d 715, 718 (D.C. Cir. 1994); *see also In re* Sealed Case, 640 F.2d 49 (7th Cir. 1980).

[159] *See* United States v. AT&T, 642 F.2d 1285, 1299 (D.C. Cir. 1980); Westinghouse Elec. Corp. v. The Republic of the Philippines, 951 F.2d 1414 (3d Cir. 1991).

[160] *See, e.g.,* Zapata v. IBP, Inc., 175 F.R.D. 574, 577 (D. Kan. 1997).

[161] Esposito v. United States, 436 F.2d 603, 606 (9th Cir. 1970).

[162] *See In re* Grand Jury Proceedings, 78 F.3d 251, 255 (6th Cir. 1996); *see also* United States v. Mendelsohn, 896 F.2d 1183, 1189 (9th Cir. 1990); *In re* Sealed Case, 676 F.3d 793, 808-09 (D.C. Cir. 1992); *In re* Martin Marietta Corp., 856 F.2d 619, 623 (4th Cir. 1988).

[163] *See* Harding v. Dana Transport, Inc., 914 F.Supp. 1084 (D.N.J. 1996).

## Representing Healthcare Organizations in Fraud and Abuse Matters

There are, however, two distinct types of *limited* waiver of the attorney/client privilege: selective and partial. Selective disclosure refers to privileged communication revealed to one party and not another. Where recognized, selective waiver permits a client who has disclosed privileged communications to one party to continue asserting the privilege against other parties. Partial disclosure refers to revealing only segments of a privileged communication, and permits a client to continue asserting the privilege as to the remaining portions of the same communication. A discussion of voluntary disclosure and selective waiver in conjunction with government investigations appears *infra* §9-5(e).

The ability to successfully argue either a partial or limited waiver has become more difficult over the years, however. For example, in *In re Columbia/HCA Healthcare Corporation Billing Practices Litigation*, the court held that, despite entering into a confidentiality agreement with the government, Columbia/HCA had waived the attorney/client privilege as to all communications on the subject matter to all parties. As a matter of policy, the court held that the government should not "assist in obfuscating the 'truth-finding process' by entering into such confidentiality agreements at all. The investigatory agencies of the Government should act to bring to light illegal activities, not to assist wrongdoers in concealing the information from the public domain."[164]

The attorney/client privilege can also be waived by the inadvertent disclosure of privileged documents.[165] In September 2008, Congress modified the Federal Rules of Evidence by adding Rule 502,[166] which preserves attorney-client privilege and work-product protection for documents that are inadvertently disclosed during discovery in a federal lawsuit. The primary purposes for the new rule were to create uniformity among the courts surrounding the effect of inadvertent disclosure and to eliminate the costs associated with preventing inadvertent disclosure during electronic discovery of large quantities of documents.[167]

Specifically, Rule 502 limits the waiver of attorney-client privilege or work-product protection. It states "When the disclosure is made in a federal proceeding or to a federal office or agency and waives the attorney-client privilege or work-product protection, the waiver extends to an undisclosed communication or information in a Federal or State proceeding only if" the

---

[164] *In re* Columbia/HCA Healthcare Corporation Billing Practices Litig., 293 F.3d 289, 303 (6th Cir. 2002).
[165] *See* Texaco Puerto Rico, Inc. v. Dep't of Consumer Affairs, 60 F.3d 867, 883 (1st Cir. 1995) (holding that disclosure automatically waives); *but see* Milford Power Ltd. v. New England Power Co., 896 F.Supp. 53 (D. Mass. 1995) (holding no disclosure where client took reasonable precautions against disclosure).
[166] Pub. L. No. 110-322, § 1(a), 122 Stat. 3537, 3537 (2008).
[167] S. Rep. No. 110-264, at 3 (2008).

waiver: (1) is intentional; (2) concerns the same subject matter as undisclosed information; and (3) fairness requires the disclosed and undisclosed information to be considered together.[168] Where the disclosure is inadvertent and made in a federal proceeding or to a federal agency, the privilege and protection survives if the individual with the privilege or protection made reasonable attempts to prevent disclosure and promptly takes reasonable measures to remedy the mistake.[169] Disclosure of privileged or protected information in a state proceeding does not establish waiver in a federal proceeding if the disclosure does not constitute waiver under state law or if the disclosure occurred in a federal proceeding.[170]

Some courts still apply a reasonableness standard, used prior to 502, to help determine an inadvertent disclosure. Traditionally, courts consider five factors: (1) the reasonableness of precautions to prevent disclosure; (2) the number of disclosures; (3) the extent of disclosure; (4) the promptness of measures taken to rectify; and (5) whether the overriding interests of justice would be served by keeping the privilege intact. [171] Shortly after Rule 502 took effect, the court decided in *Rhoads Industries, Inc. v. Building Materials Corp.* that the five factor test should be considered "where the party shows minimal compliance with Rule 502 but there is a dispute over whether its actions are reasonable." [172] Despite evidence that weighed heavily in favor of a waiver, the court in *Rhoads* placed significant emphasis on the "overriding interest of justice," ruling an absence of waiver due to the substantial harm the plaintiff would suffer if the information was waived.[173] However, other courts have interpreted 502 more rigorously. In *ReliOn, Inc. v. Hydra Fuel Cell Corp.*, the magistrate judge simply ruled, without considering any of the above five factors, that ReliOn failed "to take *all* reasonable measures of preserving the confidentiality of the documents produced to Hydra, and therefore the privilege was waived." [174]

In order to safeguard against a ruling of waiver by inadvertent disclosure, an increasing number of entities are entering into "clawback" agreements, or contracts, when engaging in a large production of electronically stored information during an investigation or discovery to minimize the cost and time it would take to conduct a document-by-document review of all ESI produced. The parties often embody clawback agreements into a court order under

---

[168] Fed. R. Evid. 502(a).
[169] *Id.* at 502(b), *see also* Fed. R. Civ.P 26(b)(5)(B).
[170] Fed. R. Evid. 502(c).
[171] Fidelity & Deposit Co. of MD v. McCulloch, 168 F.R.D. 516 (E.D. Pa. 1996).
[172] Rhoads Industries Inc. v. Building Materials Corp., 254 F.R.D 216 (E.D. Pa. 2008).
[173] *Id.* at 227.
[174] ReliOn v. Hydra Fuel Cell Corp., 2008 BL 270238 (D. Or. 2008), at 3 (emphasis added). *See also* Clarke v. J.P. Morgan Chase & Co,. 2009 U.S. Dist. LEXIS 54061 (S.D.N.Y. June 19, 2009) (inadvertent disclosure under FRE 502(b) did not apply to e-mail where counsel "had ample opportunity to discover and assert the claimed privileged status of the e-mail" yet failed to do so.

Rule 502(d), which states a "federal court order incorporating an agreement of the parties regarding inadvertent disclosure will govern the waiver ramifications of such disclosure."[175] While courts generally support clawbacks entered as a court order under 502,[176] parties to a government investigation may not always have access to a court to enter such an order. In these instances, attorneys should tread cautiously and have a clear understanding of jurisdictional nuances with respect to their use and effectiveness.

## § 9-5(d)  Crime-Fraud Exception

Both the attorney/client privilege and the work-product doctrine are subject to a crime-fraud exception. To invoke this exception, the party opposing the attorney/client or work-product privilege must present *prima facie* evidence that the allegation of attorney participation in the crime or fraud has some foundation of fact.[177] The evidence must show that the client was engaged in or planning the criminal or fraudulent conduct when the assistance of counsel was sought, and that the assistance was obtained in furtherance of the conduct or was closely associated with it.[178] Even though the exact "quantum of proof" necessary to meet the *prima facie* standard has not been decided by the Supreme Court, several circuits have attempted to define what the standard requires.[179]

---

[175] FED. R. EVID. 502(d).
[176] *See, e.g.,* Zubulake v. UBS Warburg LLC, 216 F.R.D. 280, 290 (S.D.N.Y 2003), the court upheld the use of clawback arrangements by parties "that allow the parties to forego privilege review altogether in favor of an agreement to return inadvertently disclosed privileged documents."
[177] *In re* Grand Jury Subpoenas, 144 F.3d 653 (10th Cir. 1998), *cert. denied*, Anderson v. United States, 525 U.S. 966 (1998); Motley v. Marathon Oil Co., 71 F.3d 1547, 1551 (10th Cir. 1995).
[178] *In re* Grand Jury Subpoenas, 144 F.3d 653 (10th Cir. 1998), *cert. denied*, Anderson v. United States, 525 U.S. 966 (1998); Motley v. Marathon Oil Co., 71 F.3d 1547, 1551 (10th Cir. 1995); *see In re* Grand Jury Investigation (Schroeder), 842 F.2d 1223, 1226 (11th Cir. 1987).
[179] *In re* Grand Jury Subpoenas, 144 F.3d 653 (10th Cir. 1998), *cert. denied*, Anderson v. United States, 525 U.S. 966 (1998); Motley v. Marathon Oil Co., 71 F.3d 1547, 1551 (10th Cir. 1995); *see, e.g., In re* Richard Roe, Inc., 68 F.3d 38, 40 (2d Cir. 1995) (probable cause to believe a crime or fraud has been committed); *Haines v. Liggett Group, Inc.*, 975 F.2d 81, 95–96 (3rd Cir. 1992) (evidence that if believed by the fact finder would be sufficient to *support a finding that the elements of the crime-fraud exception were met); In re* Int'l Sys. & Controls Corp. Sec. Litig., 693 F.2d 1235, 1242 (5th Cir. 1982) (evidence such as will suffice until contradicted and overcome by other evidence); United States v. Davis, 1 F.3d 606, 609 (7th Cir. 1993) (evidence presented by the party seeking application of the exception is sufficient to require the party asserting the privilege to come forward with its own evidence to support the privilege); *In re* Grand Jury Proceedings (Corporation), 87 F.3d 377, 381 (9th Cir. 1996) (reasonable cause to believe attorney was used in furtherance of ongoing scheme); *In re* Grand Jury Investigation (Schroeder), 842 F.2d 1223, 1226 (11th Cir. 1987) (evidence that if believed by the trier of fact would establish the elements of some violation that was ongoing or about to be committed); *In re* Sealed Case, 107 F.3d 46, 50 (D.C. Cir. 1997) (evidence that if believed by the trier of fact would establish the elements of an ongoing or imminent crime or fraud).

In *In re Grand Jury Investigation*,[180] the Ninth Circuit considered the scope of the attorney/client privilege in the context of a grand-jury investigation of potential Medicare fraud. This case is significant for a number of reasons: (1) its discussion of the showing required for the government to persuade a court to review allegedly privileged documents *in camera*; (2) its lesson regarding the significance of maintaining the privilege; and (3) its suggestion that the government may view attorneys advising clients in the healthcare fraud area as co-conspirators.

In connection with the grand-jury investigation in this case, a laboratory was subpoenaed for certain documents. The laboratory claimed that the documents were protected from disclosure by the attorney/client privilege, and declined to produce eleven documents. The government moved the court to examine the documents *in camera*, and the laboratory opposed the motion. One document in particular was the opinion of legal counsel prepared before the challenged program was initiated. The district court found that the laboratory had established a *prima facie* case of attorney/client privilege, and denied the government's motion. On appeal, the government argued for the application of the crime-fraud exception to the attorney/client privilege.[181] According to the U.S. Attorney, the mere fact that the laboratory solicited and received the advice of counsel before instituting a testing program was sufficient to allow *in camera* review of the documents. The court disagreed and upheld the district court's ruling, reasoning that the government's showing did not support a reasonable belief that *in camera* inspection may reveal evidence to establish the claim that the crime-fraud exception applies.

Moreover, the court ruled that the ability to obtain *in camera* review "to ensure that the documents are truly privileged" was similarly unavailable, as the government would have to make the same showing required to establish the crime-fraud exception—that is, "a factual basis sufficient to support reasonable, good faith belief that *in camera* inspection may reveal evidence that information in the materials is not privileged."[182] However, the "good faith belief" standard required for an *in camera* hearing by the judge is not a substitute for the *prima facie* standard used in determining whether the communication will be revealed, that is, sufficient evidence to sustain a finding that communication was made for the purpose of committing a crime or fraud.[183]

Counsel's unawareness of the client's illegal purposes for soliciting advice does not block the application of the crime-fraud exception. One notable example of this fact is the Kansas City, Kansas, Medicare self-referral fraud

---

[180] *See In re* Grand Jury Investigation, 974 F.2d 1068 (9th Cir. 1992).
[181] *Id.* at 1,073.
[182] *Id.* at 1,074–75.
[183] *See* Clark v. United, 289 U.S. 1, 15 (1933); *see also In re* Sealed Case, 107 F.3d 46, 50 (D.C. Cir. 1997) (holding that defendant must produce evidence "that if believed by the trier of fact" would prove the lawyer's services where utilized in furtherance of crime or fraud).

## Representing Healthcare Organizations in Fraud and Abuse Matters

case, which has become known as the *Anderson* case after it was unsealed.[184] Healthcare attorneys were subpoenaed and later compelled to testify in proceedings against their client. (The attorneys also were later indicted; *see* § 9-6, *infra*, for a discussion of the attorneys as defendants.) In applying the crime-fraud exception, the Tenth Circuit noted that the court "by no means impl[ies] that [the attorneys] are guilty of any crimes or that they were, in fact, culpable in any way."[185]

Increasingly, both in-house counsel, attorneys in private practice and consultants are being viewed by prosecutors as potential participants in the criminal scheme. This is most likely because attorneys often give advice pertaining to reimbursement rules or the structure of a transaction or agreement that falls within the penumbra of the fraud and abuse laws. Rightly or wrongly, the government, at times, can view the attorney as a participant. As more fully discussed below in §9-6, in two matters, one involving an attorney for Tenet and a second involving an attorney from GlaxoSmithKline, the government based their allegations of attorney wrong doing based on information obtained by invoking the crime fraud exception.[186]

### § 9-5(e) Waiver as a Result of Voluntary Disclosure and the Selective-Waiver Doctrine

Voluntary disclosure is often a preferred course of action when a healthcare organization discovers evidence of wrongdoing, because historically federal programs and policies have encouraged voluntary disclosure by mitigating potential penalties. However, voluntary disclosure of protected documents can waive the attorney/client privilege and the work-product doctrine. The selective-waiver doctrine is designed to protect organizations that voluntarily turn over documents to the government in cooperation with government efforts from having to disclose the same documents to any third parties that may bring suit against the organization. Currently, the Eighth Circuit is the only federal jurisdiction to adopt the selective-waiver doctrine. It held that disclosure of material protected by the attorney/client privilege to the Securities and Exchange Commission (SEC) during a formal investigation constituted only a selective waiver of the privilege, and therefore the material could not be discovered in subsequent litigation.[187] The court reasoned that, by not following

---

[184] *In re* Grand Jury Subpoenas, 144 F.3d 653 (10th Cir. 1998), *cert. denied*, Anderson v. United States, 525 U.S. 966 (1998). For further discussion, *see* Stuart M. Gerson & Jennifer E. Gladieux, *Advice of Counsel: Eroding Confidentiality in Federal Healthcare Law*, 51 ALA. L. REV. 183 (1999).
[185] *In re* Grand Jury Subpoenas, 144 F.3d 657 (10th Cir. 1998), *cert. denied*, Anderson v. United States, 525 U.S. 966 (1998).
[186] *See* U.S. v. Lauren Stevens, Case No. 10cr694-RWT (D. Md. 2011) and U.S. v. Sulzbach, Case No. 07-61329 (S.D.F.L 2007).
[187] *See* Diversified Indus., Inc. v. Meredith, 572 F.2d 596 (8th Cir. 1993).

the selected waiver doctrine, the practice of hiring outside counsel to conduct internal reviews would be destroyed.[188]

However, the majority of federal jurisdictions provide no protection to documents that are voluntarily produced to a federal investigator.[189] These jurisdictions generally do not provide protection because they believe that a selective waiver would contradict the purpose of the attorney/client privilege and work-product doctrine. For example, the Third Circuit has found that applying the selected-waiver doctrine would create a new privilege for disclosure to government agencies, thus extending the attorney/client privilege beyond its original purpose.[190] In addition, the Second Circuit has held that voluntary disclosures to the government waived work-product protection where the disclosing party is in an adversarial relationship with the government agency.[191] The Sixth Circuit has held that a client waived the attorney/client privilege when speaking to government agents investigating allegations of improper Medicare billing when the client told the government agents that their attorney had reviewed and approved aspects of the company's marketing plan. In *In re Grand Jury Proceedings*,[192] the president and owner of a laboratory being investigated for improper Medicare billings told a government investigator that their attorney, who specialized in Medicare law, had reviewed and approved aspects of the laboratory's marketing plan. The government subsequently moved to compel the attorney's testimony before a grand jury. Affirming in part a lower court's order compelling the attorney to testify, the Sixth Circuit held that the attorney/client privilege was waived where the lab owner and president divulged the underlying facts and rationale upon which the attorney's conclusion was based.

Concerning partial disclosure, courts may alter the scope of the waiver. For example, the Fourth Circuit has held that settlement negotiations with an Internal Revenue Service tax auditor waived the privilege as to the specific statement.[193] In addition, the Second Circuit found that an extrajudicial disclosure of a privileged communication in a book did not waive the privilege

---

[188] *Id.*
[189] *See* United States v. Mass. Inst. of Tech., 129 F.3d 681 (1st Cir. 1997); Genentech Inc. v. United States Int'l Trade Comm'n, 122 F.3d 1409 (Fed. Cir. 1997); *In re* Steinhardt Partners L.P., 9 F.3d 230 (2d Cir. 1993); Westinghouse Electric Corp. v. Republic of the Philippines, 951 F.2d 1414 (3d Cir. 1991); *In re* Martin Marietta Corp., 856 F.2d 619 (4th Cir. 1988); Permian Corp. v. United States, 665 F.2d 1214 (D.C. Cir. 1981). *In re* Quest Communications Int'l Inc. Sec. Litigation, 450 F.3d 1179 (10th Cir. 2006) rejecting confidentiality agreement between defendant and DOJ/SEC and holding documents turned over to the government waived privilege in subsequent criminal proceedings. *See also* Upjohn v. United States, 449 U.S. 383 (1981), in which the Supreme Court addressed the voluntary disclosure plan created by the SEC in order to reduce enforcement costs associated with implementation of the Foreign Corrupt Practices Act.
[190] Westinghouse Electric Corp. v. Republic of the Philippines, 951 F.2d 1414, 1425 (3rd Cir. 1991).
[191] *In re* Steinhardt Partners, L.P., 9 F.3d 230 (2d Cir. 1993).
[192] *In re* Grand Jury Proceedings, 78 F.3d 251 (6th Cir. 1996).
[193] United States v. Martin, 773 F.2d 579, 584 (4th Cir. 1985).

## Representing Healthcare Organizations in Fraud and Abuse Matters

beyond "matters actually revealed."[194] However, the Fifth Circuit found that a defendant offering testimony as to a part of a conversation in court waived the privilege as to the whole conversation.[195]

As was described in greater detail in Chapter 7, compliance audits can be a mitigating factor in assessing penalties and may allow parties to preempt a government investigation through remedial action. As stated, however, submission of an attorney's investigative report to a court of law or government agency may waive the attorney/client privilege with regard to the entire compliance audit. In January 2003, former Deputy Attorney General Larry Thompson promulgated "a revised set of principles to guide Department [of Justice] prosecutors as they make the decision whether to seek charges against a business organization."[196] The so-called "Thompson Memorandum" noted the importance of the extent and sincerity of a corporation's cooperation to the decision whether to prosecute. The memorandum stated that, when assessing the adequacy of a corporation's cooperation, a prosecutor may consider "the completeness of [the corporation's] disclosure including, if necessary, a waiver of the attorney-client and work product protections."[197] The Thompson Memorandum also discouraged corporations from advancing defense costs to employees in connection with an investigation or related proceeding, retaining employees who may have engaged in misconduct, or entering into a joint defense agreement with an employee, as these acts could be interpreted as a company failing to cooperate with the government. Similarly, the November 1, 2004, amendments to the Federal Sentencing Guidelines (Sentencing Guidelines) effectively required an organization to waive the attorney/client privilege and attorney work-product protection in exchange for leniency in sentencing.

Several legal authorities including the American Bar Association and a prominent group of former senior Justice Department Officials (including former Attorneys General, Deputy Attorneys General, and Solicitors General from both political parties) publicly opposed the Thompson Memorandum and the U.S. Sentencing Commission guidelines. The ABA and the former Justice Department officials submitted letters to the Sentencing Commission stating affirmatively that waiver of attorney-client privilege and work product protections should not be a factor in determining whether an organization has cooperated with the government in an investigation.

---

[194] *In re* von Bulow, 828 F.2d 94, 102-103 (2d Cir. 1987).
[195] United States v. Woodall, 438 F.2d 1317, 1325 (5th Cir. 1970).
[196] Memorandum from Larry D. Thompson, Deputy Attorney General, U.S. Department of Justice, to Heads of Department Components, United States Attorneys, Principles of Federal Prosecution of Business Organizations (Jan. 20, 2003) [hereinafter Thompson Memorandum], *reprinted in* Department of Justice, U.S. ATTORNEYS MANUAL. *See* Chapter 7 of this title.
[197] *Id.*

As a result, and after months of hearing and public comment, the U.S. Sentencing Commission reversed its position, and submitted a proposal to Congress that would remove the sentence from the Sentencing Guidelines that was being "misinterpreted to encourage waivers."[198]

Shortly thereafter, former Deputy Attorney General Paul McNulty promulgated the, "Principles of Federal Prosecution of Business Organizations," in 2006.[199] Compared to the Thompson Memorandum, the McNulty Memorandum made it more difficult for prosecutors to demand attorney-client privilege waiver by requiring prosecutors to obtain high-level Department approval before demanding waivers but still encourages voluntary waiver and rewarded unsolicited waiver as a factor in corporate compliance. Specifically, the McNulty Memorandum stated that in cases where there is a legitimate need for a privilege waiver, prosecutors should seek the "least intrusive waiver necessary" to accomplish their task.[200]

In addition, contrary to the Thompson Memorandum, the McNulty Memorandum generally prohibited prosecutors from considering whether a corporation advanced attorneys' fees to employees or agents under investigation or indictment when making a charging decision. In extremely rare cases, prosecutors could only consider the advancement of fees as a factor when the advancement, combined with many other facts, displayed a corporation's intention to impede an investigation.

Similarly, the courts were not persuaded by the Justice Department polices. In *Regents of the University of California v. Superior Court*, a California court determined that the Justice Department was still coercing corporations when they based cooperation on a waiver of the attorney-client privilege.[201] In *U.S. v. Stein*, the Second Circuit determined that the Justice Department's policy in considering whether or not a corporation provided the attorney's fees for an employee in their "cooperation," evaluation amounted to coercion.[202]

Simultaneously to the *Stein* decision, Deputy Attorney General Mark Filip sent a letter to Senators Leahy and Specter detailing new changes to

---

[198] United States Sentencing Commission, Amendments to the Sentencing Guidelines (2006), *available online at* http://www.ussc.gov/Guidelines/2008_guidelines/Manual/Suppl_to_AppendixC_2008.pdf. *See also* Health Lawyers, Sarbanes-Oxley Act Task Force Executive Summary, "United States Sentencing Commission Proposes to Retreat Guideline Amendment Permitting Consideration of Waivers of the Attorney-Client Privilege and the Attorney-Work Product Protection as a Sentencing Factor for Organizations" (May 2006).
[199] Principles of Federal Prosecution of Business Organizations, U.S. Deputy Attorney General Paul J. McNulty (Dec. 12, 2006), *available online at* http://www.justice.gov/dag/speeches/2006/mcnulty_memo.pdf.
[200] *Id.* at 10.
[201] Regents of the University of California v. Superior Court, 81 Cal Rptr. 3d 186 (Cal. Ct. App. 2008).
[202] U.S. v. Stein, 541 F.3d 130, 142 (2d Cir. 2008).

## Representing Healthcare Organizations in Fraud and Abuse Matters

the Department of Justice's policy on cooperation from corporations.[203] First, cooperation credit would be based on willingness to disclose relevant facts and evidence as opposed to willingness to waive privilege. Second, federal prosecutors would not demand, and corporations need not disclose, "non-factual attorney work product and core attorney-client privileged communications." Finally, federal prosecutors shall not determine cooperation credit based on whether the corporation: a) has paid for or advanced attorney's fees to its employees; b) has established a joint defense agreement; or c) retained or sanctioned its employees.

Filip later clarified the Department's position in a speech delivered at the American Bar Association Securities Fraud Conference and described corporations under investigation as being in the best position to provide the relevant records and information to the government in a timely manner to prevent unnecessary injury to victims of illegal activity.[204] Noting the importance of, and respect for the attorney-client privilege in the American legal system, Filip reiterated the new policy on evaluating corporate cooperation, focusing on the desire to obtain factual rather than privileged information while at the same time highlighting that a corporation does not have an obligation to cooperate or to pursue credit for cooperation.[205]

One underlying factor of the cooperation evaluation noted in both the McNulty and Filip Memorandums concerns a corporation's use of a strong, effective corporate compliance program. Fundamental questions in the review include if the corporation's compliance program is well-designed, if it works, and if the program is being applied earnestly and in good faith.[206] This positive duty of oversight, also established in *In re Caremark*,[207] should encourage organizations to proactively implement corporate compliance programs and evaluate their use and effectiveness to detect wrongdoing by employees and deter misconduct to achieve business objectives.

---

[203] Letter from Mark Filip, Deputy Attorney General, U.S. Dep't Justice, to Senators Patrick J. Leahy & Arlen Specter, U.S. Senate (July 9, 2008).
[204] Mark R. Filip, Deputy Attorney General, U.S. Dep't Justice, Remarks at the American Bar Association Securities Fraud Conference (Oct. 2, 2008), *available online at* http://www.justice.gov/archive/dag/speeches/2008/dag-speech-0810022.html.
[205] *Id.*
[206] The Department of Justice, Principles of Federal Prosecution of Business Organizations. Sec.9-28-800–"Corporate Compliance Programs."
[207] *In re* Caremark, Inc., Derivative Litigation, 698 A.2d 959 (Del. Ch. 1996).

## § 9-5(f)   Allied-Lawyer Doctrine and Joint Defense Agreements

The "allied lawyer doctrine" stems from attorney/client privilege and has been specifically recognized in the Fourth, Seventh, and Ninth Circuits.[208] In contrast to the "joint lawyer doctrine," which applies when two lawyers represent the same client, the allied-lawyer doctrine applies when lawyers of two different clients unite in a "common interest." In addition to the elements of the attorney/client privilege that must be maintained, (1) the communications must be made in the course of a joint defense effort, and (2) the statements must be designed to further the effort.[209] Although a common interest can be either "legal" or "strategic," it must be a legitimate common interest.[210]

A joint defense often will be appropriate in a case with multiple defendants, or where a company and its executives each require counsel during an investigation. In a joint-defense situation, communications made between attorneys for separate defendants will be protected by the attorney/client privilege only as long as the communications are made in furtherance of a common interest.

In 1997, the Eighth Circuit rejected the application of the allied-lawyer doctrine when the then-First Lady, Hillary Clinton, claimed a common interest with the White House to protect communications between herself and members of the Office of Counsel to the President. The court found that the White House did not have a common interest in avoiding the prosecution of the First Lady.[211] However, at least one court has found a common interest between parties intending to merge.[212]

A difference of opinion exists as to whether the parties must formalize their arrangement with a written joint defense agreement. Some attorneys favor oral understandings, on the theory that the particulars of a written joint defense agreement may be subject to challenge if the parties fall short of its particulars. In this regard, the Tenth Circuit rejected a claim of privilege in the *Anderson* case, where the chief executive officer (CEO) of the hospital argued that he had an implicit joint defense agreement with the hospital. The circuit court ruled that the CEO failed to establish that documents were related to

---

[208] *See In re* Grand Jury Subpoenas, 902 F.2d 244, 248-49 (4th Cir. 1990); *see also* United States v. McPartlin, 595 F.2d 1321, 1336-37 (7th Cir. 1979); Hunydee v. United States, 255 F.2d 183 (9th Cir. 1965); Continental Oil Co. v. United States, 330 F.2d 347 (9th Cir. 1964).
[209] *See* Matter of Bevill, Bresler & Schulman Asset Manag. Corp., 805 F.2d 120, 126 (3d Cir. 1986).
[210] *See* RESTATEMENT (THIRD) OF LAW GOVERNING LAWYERS § 76 (2000).
[211] *In re* Grand Jury Subpoena Duces Tecum, 112 F.3d 910, 922 (8th Cir. 1997), *cert. denied*, 521 U.S. 1105 (1997).
[212] *See* Niagara Mohawk Power Corp. v. Stone & Webster Engineering Corp., 125 F.R.D. 578, 587 (N.D.N.Y. 1989).

a joint defense strategy.[213] Accordingly, the release of information without a joint defense agreement may result in the release of privileged information to a third party, thereby waiving the attorney/client privilege.

McKesson succeeded in arguing that a common interest agreement it entered into with the government in response to an investigation allowed for a selective waiver rather than a general waiver. In *Saito v. McKesson HBOC*, in connection with a matter involving potentially materially false financial statements, McKesson entered into a confidentiality agreement with the Securities and Exchange Commission and the DOJ with the aim of allowing work product created during McKesson's internal investigation to be disclosed to the government.[214] In a derivative suit, the plaintiff argued that the documents turned over to the government pursuant to the confidentiality agreement were no longer confidential and that the work product privilege had been waived. In discussing the confidentiality agreement, the court noted that "When person sharing a common interest share work product, the parties reasonably expect the disclosures to be confidential."[215] However, the court held that because the government and McKesson were adversaries in the matter the fact that they shared a common interest to disclose the document did not create a "common interest" sufficient to prevent waiver. Discussing the benefits of having corporations voluntary disclose conduct discovered during internal investigations, the court held that the plaintiff was not entitled to view the work product because the confidentiality agreement effectuated a partial or selective waiver. The court specifically adopted a rule whereby, "[c]onfidential disclosure of work product during law enforcement agency investigations relinquishes the work product privilege only as to that agency, not as to the client's other adversaries." [216]

Healthcare attorneys should be aware of two potential risks when entering a joint defense agreement. If one of the members to a joint defense agreement breaches the agreement by disclosing privileged information acquired during a joint-defense strategy session, then the remaining members could be exposed to the possibility that the divulged information could lose protection under the agreement.[217] If the remaining members are unable to establish that the government's information was acquired through a breach of the joint defense agreement, then the disclosed information will be admissible in court.[218] Additionally, joint defense agreements expose members of the agree-

---

[213] *See In re* Grand Jury Proceedings, Intervenor, 156 F.3d 1041, 1043 (10th Cir. 1998).
[214] No. Civ.A. 18553, (Del. Ch. Nov. 13, 2002) *aff'd* 818 A.2d 970 (Del. 2003).
[215] *Id.* at 11.
[216] *Id.* at 28.
[217] *See* United States v. Melvin, 650 F.2d 641 (5th Cir. 1981).
[218] *Id.*

ment to the possibility that certain information may later become unprotected if problems arise in the relationship between the members of the agreement.[219]

## § 9-5(g)  Hiring Outside Consultants

Another significant issue that legal counsel must consider is whether any specialty services (e.g., accounting, billing, e-discovery, litigation support or consulting services) are required in conjunction with a particular matter. If so, counsel must determine whether these services should be engaged through legal counsel as part of the attorney's work product and/or to ensure that the communications among the client, the lawyer, and the outside consulting firm are within the scope of the attorney/client communication privilege.

This does not mean that any expert employed by an attorney comes within the work-product doctrine and/or the attorney/client privilege. The service for which the expert is employed must be intended to assist the attorney to provide legal services. A federal appeals court in *United States v. Kovel*[220] analogized the expert to an interpreter of materials/communications that are beyond the understanding of the attorney; when the consultant acts as interpreter in this way, communication between the consultant and the attorney or client is privileged.[221]

As more fully discussed in §9.3, attorneys who handle fraud and abuse investigations routinely retain litigation support vendors to perform preservation and electronic discovery services. Since these types of vendors often have full access to company information and participate at meetings and during phone conferences with the client, it is absolutely crucial that they are retained by an attorney and act at the attorney's behest to preserve privileges. Similarly, attorneys also retain statisticians, clinicians to review medical records, accountants and the like. It is critical that any internal investigations be conducted in a manner that will provide maximum protection in the event of a later investigation by the authorities, especially because the results of internal investigations conducted without the assistance of legal counsel may be discoverable later in an action against the entity.

## § 9-5(h)  The Self-Critical Analysis Privilege

Internal corporate investigations and audits may also be protected under the judicially created "self-critical analysis privilege,"[222] which is recog-

---

[219] *See In the Matter of a Grand Jury Subpoena Duces Tecum dated (November 16, 1974)*, 406 F.Supp. 381 (S.D.N.Y. 1975).
[220] United States v. Kovel, 296 F.2d 918 (2d Cir. 1961).
[221] *Id.* at 921.
[222] The "self-critical analysis privilege" was first expressed in Bredice v. Doctor's Hospital, Inc., 50 F.R.D. 249 (D.D.C. 1970), *aff'd*, 479 F.2d 920 (D.C. Cir. 1973), and has been given many

nized by a few courts as protecting internal investigative documents. The purpose of this privilege is to prevent companies from being forced to make a choice between aggressively investigating accidents or regulatory violations to self-correct wrongdoing (thereby creating a group of discoverable documents that could be used against it in litigation) or deliberately avoiding investigation (so as to limit claimants' access to documents that could be used in litigation). Where recognized, this privilege protects documents that reflect subjective opinions and criticisms of a corporation's operations and practices from pre-trial discovery, but does not protect objective data or facts. Although the self-critical analysis privilege has been utilized primarily in the context of employment discrimination, it also has been asserted in the healthcare arena, predominantly in the context of medical malpractice claims.[223] The self-critical analysis privilege finds significant application in healthcare by protecting medical peer review, which essentially is a form of self-critical analysis. Most states have codified a privilege for medical peer review.[224]

Despite the limited use of the self-critical analysis privilege generally, courts who do acknowledge its use have endorsed using a four elements test:

(1) the information must result from a critical self-analysis;

(2) the public must have a strong interest in preserving the free flow of information;

(3) the information must be a type whose flow would be curtailed if discovery were allowed (potential "chilling" effect); and

(4) the information must have been prepared with the expectation that it would be kept confidential.[225]

Additionally, courts have used a "balancing test," weighing the relative benefit and harm that might result from disclosure of the documents, in order to determine when the privilege can be exercised.[226]

Use of the self-critical analysis privilege in the context of healthcare fraud is not widespread, as the privilege is not as widely recognized as the

---

different names. *See, e.g.*, Dowling v. American Hawaii Cruises, Inc., 971 F.2d 423 (9th Cir. 1992) ("privilege of self-critical analysis"); *In re* Burlington N., Inc., 679 F.2d 762 (8th Cir. 1982) ("self-critical subjective analysis privilege"); Pagano v. Oroville Hospital, 145 F.R.D. (E.D. Cal. 1993) ("peer review privilege"); Hoffman v. United Telecommunications, Inc., 117 F.R.D. 440 (D. Kan. 1987) ("self-evaluation privilege"); Westmoreland v. CBS, 97 F.R.D. 703 (S.D.N.Y. 1983) ("privilege for confidential self-evaluative analysis").

[223] Pardo v. Gen. Hosp. Corp., 841 N.E.2d 692 (Mass. 2006); Virmani v. Novant Health, Inc. 259 F.3d 284, 290 (4th Cir. 2001).

[224] *See, e.g.*, N.M. STAT. ANN. § 41-9-5; Mass. Gen. Laws ch. 111, § 2014(a)(2003); OH R.C. §2305.252; Ga. Code Ann. 31-7-130; Fla. Stat. 395.0001; Tex. Health & Safety Code 161.0315; Neb. Rev. Stat. 25-12,123.

[225] Reid v. Lockheed Martin Aeronautics Co., 199 F.R.D. 379 (N.D. Ga. 2001).

[226] Tharp v. Sivyer Steel Corp., 149 F.R.D. 177, 182 (S.D. Iowa 1993); *see also* O'Connor v. Chrysler Corp., 86 F.R.D. 211, 217 (D. Mass. 1980).

attorney/client privilege and the work-product doctrine. Healthcare attorneys can attempt to assert the peer review privilege during discovery, but the ability to make such assertion turns on state law. Since the peer review privilege in particular was designed to prevent self-critical information from disclosure during discovery in malpractice cases, government attorneys are not as likely to accept its use when seeking the cooperation of healthcare organizations under investigation. However, this should not deter organizations from performing voluntary compliance assessments, but rather prompt organizations to conduct these internal audits through counsel. The organization can then rely on the attorney-client privilege and avoid the ad hoc approach to the self-critical analysis privilege.

### § 9-5(i)  Lawyers' Ethical Obligations

Although the highest court of each state regulates lawyers' conduct, with the exception of California, all states in the United States have adopted rules that follow the format of the ABA Model Rules of Professional Conduct.[227] By their adoption, the ABA Model Rules of Professional Conduct govern much of the ethical practice of law, and can be a source of guidance when healthcare attorneys and healthcare organizations are confronted with difficult situations.

### § 9-5(i)(1)  Duty of Confidentiality

ABA Model Rule 1.6 requires an attorney to protect all confidential client information from disclosure by the attorney "relating to the representation," whether the information was learned before, during, or after the representation. Absent a client's consent, an attorney cannot make such as disclosure unless the lawyer reasonably believes that disclosure is necessary:

(1) to prevent reasonably certain death or substantial bodily harm;

(2) to prevent the client from committing a crime or fraud that is reasonably certain to result in substantial injury to the financial interests or property of another and in furtherance of which the client has used or is using the lawyer's services;

(3) to prevent, mitigate or rectify substantial injury to the financial interests or property of another that is reasonably certain to result or has resulted from the client's commission of a crime or fraud in furtherance of which the client has used the lawyer's services;

---

[227] *See* American Bar Association Model Rules of Professional Conduct, State Adoption of Rules *available online at* http://www.americanbar.org/groups/professional_responsibility/publications/model_rules_of_professional_conduct.html, (last visited Feb 10, 2012).

## Representing Healthcare Organizations in Fraud and Abuse Matters

(4) to secure legal advice about the lawyer's compliance with these Rules;

(5) to establish a claim or defense on behalf of the lawyer in a controversy between the lawyer and the client, to establish a defense to a criminal charge or civil claim against the lawyer based upon conduct in which the client was involved, or to respond to allegations in any proceeding concerning the lawyer's representation of the client; or

(6) to comply with other law or a court order.[228]

Also, as technology has advanced and methods of communication between attorneys and clients have increased, there has been question as to what methods of communication constitute taking reasonable steps in the circumstances to protect such information against unauthorized use or disclosure. According to the ABA, reasonable steps include choosing a means of communication in which the lawyer has a reasonable expectation of privacy.[229] In the electronic age, when online data rooms, cloud computing and other quasi public internet platforms are used to conduct legal work, what constitutes a "reasonable step" is constantly changing as technology progresses. Accordingly, attorneys should consult not just the ABA rules, but also the controlling rules in the relevant jurisdiction.

Finally, ABA Model Rule 1.8 prohibits an attorney from using confidential information to the disadvantage of the client without the client's consent. The attorney/client privilege is only an issue in the context of ABA Model Rule 1.8 when an attorney is being compelled to testify. The professional duty of confidentiality does not give an attorney license to avoid revealing his client's confidential information when compelled to do so in a court of law. However, the attorney/client privilege may allow an attorney to avoid disclosing certain privileged information in court.

### § 9-5(i)(2)   Duty to Disclose to Court

ABA Model Rule 3.3 requires an attorney to disclose legal precedent to the court in the controlling jurisdiction that is known to the lawyer to be directly adverse to the position of the client and not disclosed by opposing counsel. Moreover, ABA Model Rule 3.3(a)(2) requires an attorney to supply true material facts, which may include confidential information, to a tribunal when disclosure is necessary to avoid assisting a criminal or fraudulent act by the client. Indeed, ABA Model Rule 3.3(b) establishes an affirmative duty upon an attorney to supply the information that the attorney has a duty to

---

[228] ABA, MODEL RULES OF PROF'L CONDUCT R. 1.6(b).
[229] *See also* RESTATEMENT (THIRD) OF THE LAW GOVERNING LAWYERS § 112 cmt. d (providing that confidential client information must be "acquired, stored, retrieved, and transmitted under systems and controls that are reasonably designed and managed to maintain confidentiality").

disclose even if the tribunal proceedings have completed. Failure to correct a client's false assertions can give rise to court sanctions upon an attorney.[230] However, ABA Model Rule 3.3(a)(2) does not require attorneys to tell the court of their suspicion of a client's wrongdoing. The rule is only invoked when an attorney's report of a client's wrongdoing is based on fact.

### § 9-5(i)(3)  Duty to Inquire

The tension created by ABA Model Rule 1.6 and ABA Model Rule 3.3 can put an attorney in a difficult situation, especially when relying on a client's factual assertions. Generally, courts do not place an affirmative duty on an attorney to investigate the factual assertions of a client. However, a prudent attorney should always exercise caution when depending solely on a client's factual assertions. This tension is highlighted by the Tenth Circuit's ruling in *Intervenor v. United States*.[231] In this case, two healthcare attorneys who structured a healthcare provider's referral arrangement and who allegedly did not investigate many of the nuances of the deal were indicted as conspirators in perpetuating a fraud. The judge in this case ordered an acquittal after the government completed presenting its evidence.[232]

### § 9-5(i)(4)  Application of Rules to Government Attorneys

For years, the DOJ took the position that its lawyers were exempt from state ethics rules that it believed interfered with the DOJ's ability to conduct effective investigations. In 1998, however, Congress effectively overturned this policy through the enactment of the McDade Amendment, which provides that "an attorney for the Government shall be subject to State laws and rules and local Federal court rules, governing attorneys in each State where such attorney engages in the attorney's duties, to the same extent and the same manner as other attorneys in that State."[233]

The McDade Amendment potentially affects a broad range of a prosecutor's practices. For example, ABA Model Rule 4.2 prohibits a lawyer from communicating "about the subject of the representation with a party the lawyer knows to be represented by another lawyer in the matter, unless the lawyer has the consent of the other lawyer or is authorized by law to do so." Therefore, a prosecutor cannot communicate with a party who the prosecutor

---

[230] *See* Plunkett v. State, 883 S.W.2d 349 (Tx. App. 1994); *In re Mack*, 519 N.W.2d 900 (Minn. 1994).
[231] Intervenor v. United States (In re Grand Jury Subpoenas), 144 F.3d 653 (10th Cir. 1998).
[232] United States v. Anderson, 55 F. Supp. 2d 1163 (D. Kan. 1999).
[233] 28 U.S.C. § 530B; *see also* 28 C.F.R. § 77 (2005); United States v. Dwyer, 287 F. Supp. 2d 82 (D. Mass. 2003); United States v. Colorado Supreme Court, 189 F.3d 1281 (10th Cir. 1999); Ida v. United States, 207 F. Supp. 2d 171 (S.D.N.Y. 2002).

## Representing Healthcare Organizations in Fraud and Abuse Matters

knows to be represented by a lawyer in the matter, unless specifically authorized by law:

> In the case of an organization, [Rule 4.2] prohibits communications by a lawyer for another person or entity concerning the matter in representation with persons having a managerial responsibility on behalf of the organization, and with any other person whose act or omission in connection with that matter may be imputed to the organization for purposes of civil or criminal liability or whose statement may constitute an admission on the part of the organization.[234]

Rule 4.2 arguably extends to the communication between a prosecutor and corporate employees without the knowledge or consent of the corporation's counsel.[235] Aside from ABA Model Rule 4.2 limiting the communication between the prosecutor and a party, Model Rule 4.2 most likely extends to those who are agents of the prosecutor.[236] Moreover, at least one state Supreme Court has disciplined an Assistant U.S. Attorney for violating the state's analogous rule to ABA Model Rule 4.2.[237]

## § 9-6 FIFTH-AMENDMENT CONSIDERATIONS

Healthcare organizations and their counsel also must consider the use of the Fifth Amendment privilege against self-incrimination when under investigation or when considering cooperating with the authorities. Although cooperation is both appropriate and necessary in most cases, there may be certain instances of egregious activity when it may be appropriate to consider "taking the Fifth."

Generally, the privilege against self-incrimination is applicable only to individuals, and not to corporations or other collective entities. Therefore, a custodian of corporate documents may not resist a subpoena for corporate documents on Fifth Amendment grounds.[238] Moreover, the privilege against

---

[234] ABA, Model Rules of Prof'l Conduct R. 4.2, cmt. 4.
[235] *See* United States *ex rel.* O'Keefe v. McDonnell Douglas Corp., 132 F.3d 1252 (8th Cir. 1998) (affirming a district court's order prohibiting contact with a defendant's current employees in a civil action under the FCA. The Eighth Circuit cited the United States District Court for the Eastern District of Missouri's adoption of the Missouri Supreme Court Rule 4-4.2, which mirrors comment 4 of ABA Model Rule 4.2).
[236] *See, e.g.*, United States v. Thomas, 474 F.2d 110, 112 (10th Cir. 1973) (finding that a special agent was an agent of the prosecutor, when the special agent obtained a statement from a criminal defendant represented by counsel).
[237] *See generally* Matter of Howes, 940 P.2d 159 (N.M. 1997). Although prior to the McDade amendment, the New Mexico Supreme Court found the Assistant U.S. Attorney in violation the state's analogous rule to ABA Model Rule 4.2, when the Assistant U.S. Attorney permitted a police detective to talk to a represented criminal defendant.
[238] Braswell v. United States, 487 U.S. 99 (1988).

self-incrimination applies only to testimony, and not to the production of documents.[239] However, the Fourth Amendment "search and seizure" law may be applicable to documentary evidence, as may the attorney/client privilege and work-product doctrine described earlier.

In a number of circumstances, healthcare organizations are encouraged—indeed, even required—to furnish potentially incriminating information to the authorities. Therefore, despite an individual's constitutional privilege against self-incrimination, healthcare organizations must consider these countervailing reporting requirements, the duty to furnish the OIG with immediate access, and benefits of voluntary disclosures. The Fifth Amendment guarantees that individuals may not be forced to testify against themselves. This privilege applies not only to persons arrested on criminal charges, but also to situations in which an individual is being investigated for other transgressions that may have criminal consequences. The privilege has been held to override an individual's statutory reporting obligations to the extent such reporting obligations are penal, rather than regulatory, in nature.[240] However, an individual who refuses to cooperate with the government on the basis of the Fifth Amendment privilege may consequently be subject to criminal prosecution, civil penalties, and/or program exclusion.

## § 9-7    VICARIOUS LIABILITY AND THE PARK DOCTRINE

Under the vicarious liability doctrine, actions of officers, directors, employees and agents can create civil as well as criminal liability for companies. To impose such vicarious liability on an entity, most courts have held that the employee (or agent) must have acted with actual or apparent authority. Further, some courts have held that in addition to the actual or apparent authority, the employee (or agent) must have acted in order to benefit the principal (referred to generally as the "corporate benefit rule").[241]

At least one federal district court has denied the imposition of vicarious liability where the Government cannot prove some degree of culpability by the employer. In *United States v. Southern Maryland Home Health Services*,[242] a FCA case was brought against a home healthcare provider after an employee falsely represented her qualifications during the hiring process, and subsequently caused false Medicare claims to be filed. The employee, who during the course of her employment treated Medicare patients with physical therapy

---

[239] Fisher v. United States, 425 U.S. 391 (1976).
[240] Whiteside and Co., Inc. v. SEC, 883 F.2d 7 (5th Cir. 1989).
[241] *See, e.g.*, United States v. O'Connell, 890 F.2d 563 (1st Cir. 1989); Grand Union Co. v. United States, 696 F.2d 888 (11th Cir. 1983). *But see* United States *ex rel.* McCready v. Columbia/HCA Healthcare Corp., 251 F. Supp. 2d 114 (D.D.C. 2000) (holding that a corporation is liable for fraudulent acts of its agents even if it received no benefit from its fraud).
[242] United States v. Southern Maryland Home Health Services, 95 F. Supp. 2d 465 (D. Md. 2000).

## Representing Healthcare Organizations in Fraud and Abuse Matters

services without a license, used the name of a licensed physical therapist and provided false references to get the job. There was no evidence that the provider was negligent in the hiring process or had received any complaints to place them on notice of her lack of qualifications. federal prosecutors argued that the provider was vicariously liable under the FCA and sought damages and penalties up to $1.9 million for actual losses of $59,320.

The U.S. District Court for the District of Maryland did not follow precedent developed in other circuits, but instead relied upon general principles of agency law and the Supreme Court case, *Kolstad v. American Dental Assoc.*[243] It held that "when the recovery sought by the Government is substantially higher than its actual losses, an employer is not vicariously liable under the FCA for wrongful acts undertaken by a non-managerial employee unless the employer had knowledge of her acts, ratified them, or was reckless in its hiring or supervision of the employee."[244]

The flip side to vicarious liability is individual liability because of the actions of the institution, that is, the *Park* Doctrine (or Responsible Corporate Office Doctrine). There has been resurgence in the use of the *Park* Doctrine to find corporate officers guilty of criminal violations of federal statutes, such as the federal Food, Drug, and Cosmetic Act (FDCA). Indeed, one of the major emerging themes of government enforcement is individual liability in healthcare fraud corporate matters.

The first case where individual corporate officers were convicted of wrongdoing was *U.S. v. Dotterweich*.[245] In this case, the president and general manager of a small pharmaceutical repackaging firm was charged, along with his company, for violations of the FDCA for shipping misbranded drugs in interstate commerce.[246] The U.S. Supreme Court held that a corporate officer can be found guilty because "[t]he offense is committed...by all who do have such a responsible share in the furtherance of the transaction which the statute outlaws, namely, to put into the stream of interstate commerce adulterated or misbranded drugs."

The Supreme Court, in *Dotterweich*, did not define what constituted a "responsible share" and that question remained unanswered until the Court

---

[243] Kolstad v. American Dental Assoc., 527 U.S. 526 (1999) (holding that an employer must be culpable in some degree in order to have the employee's knowledge and acts imputed to it for punitive damage liability).

[244] United States v. Southern Maryland Home Health Services, 95 F. Supp. 2d 468–69 (D. Md. 2000). The *Southern Maryland* decision is supported in some ways by a Supreme Court case decided several weeks later. In Vermont Agency of Natural Resources v. United States *ex rel.* Stevens, 529 U.S. 765 (2000), the Supreme Court stated that FCA damages are "essentially punitive in nature." The Supreme Court previously had stated in Kolstad v. American Dental Assoc., 527 U.S. 526, 541, that "the common law has long recognized that agency principles limit vicarious liability for punitive awards... a principle, moreover, that this Court historically has endorsed."

[245] 320 U.S. 277 (1943).

[246] *Id.* at 278.

reviewed the *Park* matter.[247] In *Park*, the defendant was the CEO of Acme Markets, a national retail food store chain that operated, at the time the case was heard, 874 retail food stores and 16 warehouses with approximately 36,000 employees.[248] The FDA had sent a number of letters to the company detailing the violating insanitary conditions found during FDA inspections.[249] Park subsequently discussed the FDA letter with his vice president for legal affairs who assured Park that the issues were being investigated and corrective action was being taken.[250] Park testified that he did not believe he could have done anything further than this to remediate the situation.[251] The Supreme Court was clear in its analysis that neither knowledge nor intent were required to impart liability to those corporate officers who, by reason of their position within the corporation had the responsibility and authority to prevent and correct violations that fall under the purview of statutes such as the FDCA.[252] The Court went further to impose an affirmative duty on such officers to ensure violations of federal law, at those that concern public health and welfare, do not occur.[253] To that effect, the Court concluded that "[t]he requirements of foresight and vigilance imposed on responsible corporate agents are beyond question demanding, and perhaps onerous, but they are no more stringent than the public has a right to expect of those who voluntarily assume positions of authority in business enterprises whose services and products affect the health and well-being of the public that supports them."[254]

The FDA, in particular, has announced its intention to use the Park Doctrine to hold responsible corporate officers liable for FDCA violations.[255] This was readily apparent in the government's prosecution of the Purdue Frederick Company and several of its executives.[256] In this case, the company pled guilty to felony misbranding of a drug[257] and three of its executives pled guilty to strict liability misdemeanor misbranding offenses.[258] The FDA updated their

---

[247] U.S. v. Park, 421 U.S. 658 (U.S. 1975).
[248] *Id.* at 660.
[249] *Id.* at 661-65.
[250] *Id.* at 663.
[251] *Id.* at 677.
[252] *Id.* at 672-73.
[253] *Id.* at 672.
[254] *Id.*
[255] See Letter from Margaret A. Hamburg, Commissioner of Food and Drugs, to Senator Charles A. Grassley (Mar. 4, 2010), *available online at* http://grassley.senate.gov/about/upload/FDA-3-4-10-Hamburg-letter-to-Grassley-re-GAO-report-on-OCI.pdf.
[256] See Criminal Information, U.S. v. Purdue Frederick Co., No. 1:07-cr-00029 (W.D. Va. May 10, 2007).
[257] Plea Agreement at 1, U.S. v. Purdue Frederick Co., No. 1:07-cr-00029 (W.D. Va. May 10, 2007).
[258] Plea Agreement at 1, U.S. v. Friedman, No. 1:07-cr-00029 (W.D. Va. May 10, 2007); Plea Agreement at 1, U.S. v.Udell, No. 1:07-cr-00029 (W.D. Va. May 10, 2007); Plea Agreement at 1, U.S. v. Goldenheim, No. 1:07-cr-00029 (W.D. Va. May 10, 2007).

## Representing Healthcare Organizations in Fraud and Abuse Matters

Regulatory Procedures Manual to include guidance for prosecutions brought under the Park Doctrine.[259] In the Manual, the FDA states:

> When considering whether to recommend a misdemeanor prosecution against a corporate official, consider the individual's position in the company and relationship to the violation, and whether the official had the authority to correct or prevent the violation. Knowledge of and actual participation in the violation are not a prerequisite to a misdemeanor prosecution but are factors that may be relevant when deciding whether to recommend charging a misdemeanor violation.
>
> Other factors to consider include but are not limited to:
>
> 1. whether the violation involves actual or potential harm to the public;
> 2. whether the violation is obvious;
> 3. whether the violation reflects a pattern of illegal behavior and/or failure to heed prior warnings;
> 4. whether the violation is widespread;
> 5. whether the violation is serious;
> 6. the quality of the legal and factual support for the proposed prosecution; and
> 7. whether the proposed prosecution is a prudent use of agency resources.[260]

## § 9-8  THE LAWYER AS WITNESS

Attorneys play varied roles in representing healthcare clients—from giving opinions regarding compliance with applicable laws to assisting in structuring, drafting, and negotiating complex transactions. As a result, they often are intimately involved in the decision-making process of their clients. Given this involvement, attorneys increasingly are called as witnesses in government investigations and third-party litigation.

Both in-house and outside counsel often are called upon to conduct internal investigations into regulatory compliance issues and potential violations of healthcare regulatory laws. When such internal investigations give rise to subsequent government investigations—as the result of a voluntary disclosure, a qui tam suit, or some other means—the attorney often is a witness to the internal-investigation procedures and results. Attorneys also may be called as witnesses in litigation against healthcare organization clients brought by third parties. For example, where issues are brought to a provider's attention by an

---

[259] U.S. Food and Drug Administration, Regulatory Procedures Manual § 6-5, Prosecution, *available online at* http://www.fda.gov/ICECI/ComplianceManuals/RegulatoryProceduresManual/ucm176738.htm.
[260] *Id.* at § 6-5-3.

employee who is a suspected whistleblower, counsel often will be involved in the decision regarding whether to terminate such employee. If the whistleblower is ultimately terminated and then sues under a retaliation claim, then the attorney who conducted the internal investigation and who gave advice regarding the termination, and/or the efficacy of the whistleblower's claims of healthcare fraud, may be the best source of information for evidence that will support the client's case.[261] In addition, attorneys may be called as witnesses to discuss advice given to healthcare clients, as well as actions taken pursuant to such advice.

A number of issues are presented when an attorney is called as a witness in a matter. The most notable of these is the issue of attorney/client privilege and the work-product doctrine. Where an attorney is the best source of evidence to help a client's case, the client may decide to waive the applicable attorney/client and work-product privileges so as to avail itself of the attorney's testimony. In addition, as discussed, a client may waive the available privileges to show cooperation in a voluntary disclosure situation. Where an in-house attorney has served in a business capacity and is a witness in litigation where the privileges have not been waived, the attorney must be careful to avoid disclosing any information that remains privileged.

Similar issues arise where attorneys serve as expert witnesses in a case. Under Rule 26 of the Federal Rules of Civil Procedure, information shared with an expert witness that is considered by the expert in forming an opinion also must be disclosed to the opposing party. Although some courts have interpreted Rule 26 to include an attorney's "mental impressions and opinions," other courts hold that attorney work product is not subject to discovery under Rule 26.[262]

Due to the issues surrounding selective waiver of privilege, attorneys must be mindful when testifying about advice given to a client, or about investigations undertaken on a client's behalf. Even in circumstances in which an attorney intends to protect the privilege when testifying on a client's behalf, the attorney may unwittingly disclose privileged information, or may be asked to partially waive privilege to answer particular questions. In those situations, the attorney/client privilege may be deemed waived as to the *entire* scope of the attorney's representation.

---

[261] *See* United States *ex rel.* Scott v. Metro. Health Corp., 2005 U.S. Dist. LEXIS 35591 (W.D. Mich. 2005) (requiring a whistleblower to pay attorneys' fees in excess of her settlement share for a baseless claim of retaliatory firing against a hospital).

[262] *See* 1993 Committee Notes to Fed. R. Civ. P. 26(a)(2); *see also* Mfr. Admin. and Mgmt Sys., Inc. v. ICT Group, Inc., 212 F.R.D. 110, 114 (E.D.N.Y. 2002). *But see In re* Pioneer Hi-Bred Int'l, Inc., 238 F.3d 1370, 1375 (Fed. Cir. 2001) ("fundamental fairness requires disclosure of all information supplied to a testifying expert in connection with his testimony"); Herman v. Marine Midland Bank, 207 F.R.D. 26,29 (W.D.N.Y. 2002) ("expert disclosure requirement of Rule 26(a)(2)(B) trumps the substantial protection otherwise accorded opinion work product under Rule 26(b)(3)").

**Representing Healthcare Organizations in Fraud and Abuse Matters**

The complexity of these issues often calls for the engagement of separate counsel to advise the attorney being called as a witness. This occurs even when the attorney-witness is an expert in healthcare fraud matters, and especially when the testimony arises in the context of a criminal investigation, as it is often difficult to remain objective and prepare oneself for questioning by prosecutors.

## § 9-9  THE LAWYER AS DEFENDANT

One of the most significant events reflecting the government's campaign against healthcare fraud in the 1990s was *United States v. Anderson,* where two healthcare transactional lawyers were indicted for participating in a conspiracy scheme to violate the Anti-Kickback Statute, and for engaging in criminal aiding and abetting.[263] Although the attorneys eventually were acquitted, this case sent a strong message to members of the healthcare bar to beware of the advice being given to clients on matters that can implicate fraud and abuse laws.

Although a significant history exists of various indictments and settlements associated with the *Anderson* case,[264] at the center of the case involving the attorneys was the government's contention that the CEO and Vice President of Baptist Medical Center participated in a conspiracy to pay kickbacks to two physicians (Ronald and Robert LaHue). The government claimed that the agreements between Baptist Medical Center and the LaHues were constructed to cover up the payment of over $2 million to the LaHues by Baptist Medical Center for illegal patient referrals, and not for legitimate consultation services. The U.S. Attorney's Office alleged that, as the authors of the agreements, the attorneys were part of the referral scheme through facilitation.

Prior to their indictment, both attorneys were subpoenaed to appear before the grand jury in 1997 as part of a different indictment proceeding against the hospital, the hospital executives, and the LaHues. Along with the other parties to the investigation, the attorneys moved to quash the subpoena, citing the attorney/client privilege and work-product doctrine. After several appeals and based upon an interpretation of the crime-fraud exception, the attorneys eventually were compelled to testify. The government was able to pierce these privileges by establishing a *prima facie* case that the hospital and its president committed a crime. Thus, the government invoked the crime-fraud exception to the attorney/client privilege and work-product doctrine, and forced the court to conduct an *in camera* review of the privileged materials. (*See* § 9-5, *supra.*)

---

[263] United States v. Anderson, 55 F. Supp. 2d 1163 (D. Kan. 1999).
[264] For a detailed discussion of the facts, *see* Joan Burgess Kilgore, *Surgery with a Meat Cleaver: The Criminal Indictment of Healthcare Attorneys in United States v. Anderson*, 43 St. Louis L.J. 1215 (1999).

In the subsequent indictment, the government charged not only the LaHues and the hospital executives,[265] but also both attorneys for having helped to facilitate this arrangement. The government's theory was that, in documenting the transactions between the hospital and the physicians, the attorneys had helped to further a conspiracy involving the payment and receipt of kickbacks. In support of its argument, the government's brief included statements supposedly made by one attorney to another that:

- the agreement was a "clean-up deal";
- the Lahues' motive was to sell referrals; and
- the defendants did not know what the other physicians did to justify the payments.

The district court dismissed all charges against the two attorneys, holding that no reasonable jury could find beyond a reasonable doubt that they willfully committed any of the criminal acts charged in the indictment. The judge stated that the record revealed that the two attorneys held a "good faith belief" that it was possible to structure the deal between Baptist Medical Center and the two physicians in a legal way. The judge also stressed that the attorneys had advised their clients that, if they paid fair market value for the legitimate consultation services of the two physicians, then the arrangement would be legal. Similarly, the court observed that the two attorneys relied on their clients for information, and were not engaged to monitor the activities of consultants/medical directors who were engaged by the hospital—in this case, the LaHues. Also, when potential compliance problems were brought to the attention of the two attorneys, they urged their clients to ensure they were paying fair market value for real services. The court observed:

> The state of the law was in flux; the lawyers adapted their advice to it as it changed . . . Even if patient referrals were devoutly hoped for and anticipated; even if the volume of patients could be large; even if the parties might never have come together but for Baptist having embarked on a long range plan that depended on attracting nursing home patients, there is nothing in the evidence or the law that would have a priori precluded a legal relationship from being entered into under these circumstances . . . The problem here is that a very simple concept, "payment for patients is illegal," became far from simple as Congress, the Executive Branch, and the Courts got more deeply involved.[266]

The government continues to bring actions against both in-house attorneys as well as corporate compliance officers. For example, in 2007, the

---

[265] By the time the attorneys were indicted, Baptist Medical Center already had entered into a $17.5 million settlement with the federal government.
[266] *Anderson*, 55 F. Supp. 2d at 1170.

## Representing Healthcare Organizations in Fraud and Abuse Matters

Department of Justice filed a complaint against the former General Counsel and Corporate Integrity Program Director for Tenet Healthcare Corporation (Tenet) alleging that the defendant submitted false certifications about Tenet's compliance with federal requirements. Specifically, the government contended that the defendant submitted declarations in June 1997 and June 1998 to the Department of Health and Human Services as part of Tenet's Corporate Integrity Agreement obligations stating that, to the best of her knowledge and belief, Tenet was in material compliance with all federal program legal requirements. However, before making the certifications, the complaint alleged, the defendant had received an internal memorandum raising concerns about a hospital's employment contracts as well as confirmation from outside counsel that the arrangements were illegal. According to the complaint, these documents established that the defendant knew the declarations were false at the time they were made. These actions, the complaint alleged, allowed Tenet to receive payments it was not entitled to and obstructed the government's efforts to recover past improper payments. Ultimately the U.S. District Court for the Southern District of Florida awarded summary judgment to the defendant finding that the government's case was barred by the statute of limitations.[267]

More recently, the government accused a former associate general counsel of GlaxoSmithKline (GSK), Lauren Stevens, with obstruction of justice, falsification and concealment of documents, and making false statements in response to an FDA investigation regarding the off- label promotion of Wellbutrin SR.[268] The government based their allegations on privileged communications between Stevens and GSK they were able to obtain under the crime fraud exception. Fortunately for Stevens, the Maryland federal district court granted the defense motion for acquittal and held that the statements directed to the FDA were done in good faith and found her actions to fall under a safe harbor provided by 18 U.S.C. § 1515(c), for providing lawful, bona fide, legal representation services in connection with or anticipation of a legal proceeding.[269]

Despite the positive outcome in this case for Stevens, both in-house and outside counsel must be reminded of the government's heightened effort to hold individuals, including attorneys, accountable for the actions of large corporations. Careful consideration must be given when advising clients with respect to healthcare transactions. Attorneys should also avoid making false statements or omitting material information when representing entities in response to government investigations or in connection with their corporate compliance obligations.

---

[267] U.S. v. Sulzbach, Case No. 07-61329 Civ Marra. (S.D.F.L 2007).
[268] U.S. v. Lauren Stevens, Case No. 10cr694-RWT (D. Md. 2011).
[269] *Id.*

# 10
# The Future of Fraud and Abuse

Healthcare fraud and the resulting government investigations have matured over the last fifty years, and in light of the fact that there are instances of actual fraud being perpetrated, it will continue to remain a top enforcement priority for states and the federal government. In addition, given the expected growth in healthcare spending, it is inevitable that healthcare fraud enforcement efforts will continue to increase in vigor and sophistication well into the future.

## § 10-1  FEDERAL LEGISLATIVE ACTIVITIES

With the U.S. Congress having spent much of the 1990s enhancing the government's statutory tools to fight fraud, one might think significant legislative activity would not be part of the government's strategies for greater healthcare fraud protections. To the contrary, promotion of new legislative vehicles for fraud enforcement is always attractive to legislators, as healthcare fraud legislation currently is viewed in much the same manner as "motherhood and apple pie." Congress is frequently asked by federal prosecutors to advance legislation to plug so-called "loopholes" in the law, reverse adverse case law, or codify case law interpretations that are prosecutor-friendly. For example, in 2009 as part of the Fraud Enforcement and Recovery Act, Congress overturned the Supreme Court's decision in *Allison Engine*, which was viewed as an impediment to prosecuting false claims submitted by providers to government intermediaries, such as managed care organizations. In 2010, as part of the Patient Protection and Affordable Care Act (the "Health Reform Law") Congress amended the federal healthcare program anti-kickback statute (Anti-Kickback Statute) to provide that a kickback violation could not constitute a false claim under the False Claims Act (FCA). The Health Reform Law further strengthened fraud and abuse laws pertaining to false claims, civil investigative demands and other tools available to government attorneys.

Moreover, in light of budgetary issues, Congress is always looking for ways to balance the federal budget and control federal spending, and new healthcare fraud initiatives generally are viewed as a mechanism by which the federal deficit can be lowered, and efforts in this regard are often "scored" by the Congressional Budget Office as producing savings that can be spent on other Congressional initiatives. Therefore, certain items that previously had been proposed, but not adopted, in other legislation always can be raised again in future legislative sessions. For example, especially as health reform expands federal subsidies to individuals obtaining healthcare coverage from federal and state operated exchanges, Congress might once again consider expanding the federal healthcare program statute to apply to all payors.

With respect to the physician self-referral law (the "Stark Law"), legislative initiatives to modify the law may continue. At various times over the last two decades, an expansion of the Stark Law seemed probable; at other times, legislative initiatives focused on scaling it back. In the mid-1990s, it was assumed that the list of designated health services would be expanded to all healthcare services and/or to all governmental payors. At other times, discussions have focused on *shortening* the list of designated health services, and have posited that the scope of the self-referral ban should be limited to ownership interests only. Most recently, as part of the Health Reform Law, Congress modified the whole hospital exception, so as to limit the establishment of new physician owned hospitals and restrict the expansion of existing hospitals. Moreover, as healthcare fraud enforcers continue to adopt a hardline approach resulting in large-scale settlements in physician self-referral matters (with technical violations "bootstrapped" into false claims), it is altogether possible that efforts will resume on the part of the provider community to advocate modification of the Stark Law, especially with respect to its "strict liability" standard and rigid damages calculation based on all referrals of designated health services. However, depending on the provider communities' experiences under the self-referral disclosure protocol (discussed below and in Chapter 7) and to the extent settlements are reasonable in amount, it may be less likely that wholesale changes to the Stark Law will be deemed a priority.

## § 10-2   FEDERAL REGULATORY INITIATIVES

Regulatory activity always should be expected from the Office of Inspector General (OIG). Each year, the OIG's Work Plan states the OIG's intent to publish new safe-harbor regulations, new fraud alerts, and additional compliance program guidance. Moreover, the OIG's advisory opinion mechanism ensures the continuation of the dialogue between the OIG and the healthcare community regarding precisely what is and what is not fraudulent activity. Legal advisors are no longer able to rely on the general unavailability of advisory opinions as a rationale for blessing "gray area" conduct. Unlike the safe-harbor process, the advisory opinion process has enabled the OIG to protect a greater scope of activities based on *particular* facts and circumstances, as opposed to speculation over what facts may exist. Indeed, the OIG often has stated that the safe harbors are deliberately narrow to avoid protecting

## The Future of Fraud and Abuse

activities where any potential for abuse exists. As this constraint does not exist in the advisory opinion process, the OIG has used advisory opinions to venture into areas previously not addressed by the safe harbors, as well as to describe generally the criteria used to evaluate particular types of activity. Most useful to the healthcare industry has been the OIG's willingness to grant favorable advisory opinions to conduct that technically violates the statute.

Yet advisory opinions are expensive, and take a considerable amount of time to obtain. Moreover, the advisory opinion process could be made more useful from a compliance perspective. For example, certain controversial areas remain (e.g., joint ventures) in which it is difficult to obtain favorable advisory opinions from the OIG, because of its potential precedential effect, even though individuals at the OIG have commented verbally that they do not believe the arrangement to be problematic. In such circumstances, the OIG should consider mechanisms for granting preliminary clearance for the structural aspects of transactions. This might include ongoing operational guidance, as well as a mechanism for a "look-back" period to determine whether the operational guidance was followed. This has worked for other federal agencies, including the Federal Trade Commission and the Internal Revenue Service, that deal in the analytical areas that have both structural and operational components.

Guidance from the Centers for Medicare & Medicaid Services (CMS) on the application of the Stark Law also promises to continue to be a federal regulatory priority. Although the CMS process of issuing voluminous regulations on the Stark Law may largely be over, there are still numerous issues in Stark Law interpretation that remain to be resolved. Toward this end, it is hoped that CMS will begin to issue more physician self-referral advisory opinions, which, except for opinions on specialty hospitals and other limited occasions, generally have not been issued. As with the Anti-Kickback Statute, much of the physician self-referral interpretation likely will be left to the enforcers, either through government-initiated investigations (see below) or through provider self-disclosures through the new CMS self-referral disclosure protocol. Although many self-referral disclosures have been submitted to CMS under the new protocol, very few have made their way through the process to settlement. In light of the devastating impact a technical violation, such as lack of a signed renewal in a longstanding agreement, can have on *all* of the hospital's revenues from the physician's referrals, the provider community remains hopeful that CMS will take seriously its discretion to reduce these potential government windfalls to reasonable settlement amounts.

## § 10-3 FEDERAL ENFORCEMENT ACTIVITIES AND PROVIDER SELF-DISCLOSURE

Proceeds from healthcare fraud enforcement are being returned to fund additional healthcare fraud enforcement, and substantial appropriations are being made to further fund healthcare fraud enforcement activities. As a result, the question is not *whether* fraud enforcement will continue, but rather *what* the focus of such continued enforcement activities will be. Fraud-enforcement activities are often driven by whistleblowers who bring issues to the attention of government prosecutors by filing qui tam suits under the FCA. Increasingly, data analytics and government contractors are also are playing a role in the government's detection of healthcare fraud. As these systems become more sophisticated, and as electronic health records become more commonplace, data analytics should gain momentum in driving healthcare fraud enforcement.

There also is little doubt that the fraud enforcers will continue their attempts to make healthcare policy through fraud enforcement. It has become increasingly difficult for defense attorneys to convince prosecutors that issues raised in qui tam suits are not worthy of pursuit; quite often, allegations raised by whistleblowers represent interpretations of what prosecutors want the law to be, as opposed to what the law is.

A major concern of the healthcare industry has been that certain business activities would be challenged as violating the Anti-Kickback Statute. The Health Reform Law has made this easier, by codifying that a violation of the Anti-Kickback Statute could constitute a false claim.

In addition to kickbacks and false claims, enforcement actions under the Stark Law are becoming more commonplace. Like the Anti-Kickback Statute, the Stark Law has been bootstrapped to false claims actions filed by whistleblowers. Substantial settlements already have occurred in such cases. Prosecutors enforce the strict liability nature of the Stark Law and extract settlements for arrangements that allegedly simply fall short of the technical criteria of a Stark Law exception, even if they do not rise to the level of the Anti-Kickback Statute's intent threshold. It is expected that more such settlements will occur in the future, especially because a substantial "disconnect" exists between the standards imposed by government enforcers and the standards healthcare organizations believe will be imposed against them.

Healthcare fraud enforcement efforts also can be expected to focus more on fraud perpetuated against all health-benefits plans. DOJ officials have long suggested that federal "criminal enforcement efforts will not be confined to fraud committed against government programs."[1] Moreover, as a result of HIPAA, which enacted the general healthcare fraud offense (as well as other criminal statutes, e.g., theft and embezzlement) applicable to both public and private plans providing medical benefits, and expansions of the Civil Monetary Penalty (CMP) and FCA laws, there may be an increase in the filing of

---

[1] House Committee on Governmental Operations, Subcommittee on Human Resources and Intergovernmental Relations, 102d Cong., 2d Sess. (May 7, 1992) (statement of Laurence A. Urgenson, Acting Deputy Assistant Attorney General, Criminal Division).

## The Future of Fraud and Abuse

causes of action for prosecutions related to fraud against private insurance companies.

Although the OIG's role in healthcare fraud enforcement often has been viewed as "second chair" to the DOJ in false claims cases, the OIG has promised to increase the use of its own CMP authority to seek greater administrative enforcement in both the anti-kickback and self-referral areas. It has been some time since the OIG has had only the draconian penalty of federal healthcare program exclusion, or convincing the DOJ to bring a bootstrapped FCA case to prosecute perceived anti-kickback violations. For a number of years, the OIG has had the authority to bring its own cases and impose fines, and it has, more recently been doing so. The OIG should no longer be considered second chair to the Department of Justice in healthcare fraud enforcement.

A new area of OIG enforcement is now beginning to arise out of the implementation of corporate integrity agreements (CIAs). These agreements generally provide the OIG with specific remedies for failure of a healthcare organization to meet its obligations under the CIA, including stipulated penalties in addition to federal healthcare program exclusion. During the first years in which CIAs were used, the OIG did not actively seek these remedies except in egregious circumstances, thus giving healthcare organizations that may not have fully understood their CIA obligations time to come into compliance with the terms of their CIAs. Now, the OIG has stepped up its monitoring activities with respect to organizations operating under CIAs, including conducting site visits to verify information submitted in connection with annual reports. In a number of cases, the OIG has begun to seek stipulated financial penalties from organizations with CIAs, and even exclusion for failure to comply with CIA obligations.

The proliferation of voluntary (and mandatory) compliance efforts, including voluntary disclosures, also has become a major driver of government healthcare fraud enforcement. Since the OIG adopted the Voluntary Self-Disclosure Protocol (Protocol) in 1998, many entities have availed themselves of the Protocol. Although initial results of the Protocol were largely more favorable than would have been expected had the DOJ pursued a false claims case, many healthcare organizations may become dismayed with both the process and consequences of making a voluntary disclosure. In this regard, the OIG initially encouraged voluntary disclosures through the Protocol by entering into favorable settlements—from a financial standpoint, as well as imposing far less-stringent corporate integrity obligations than would otherwise be expected. Early on, OIG representatives took the position that an organization's voluntary disclosure was, in itself, the best evidence of an effective corporate compliance program. Accordingly, the outcome of a voluntary disclosure through the Protocol often was no CIA at all—or, at most, an obligation to certify compliance for a three-year period. After this early period, voluntary disclosure outcomes became far less favorable, with the OIG expecting to impose not only penalty multipliers approaching what one might expect for a DOJ release, but also full-scale CIAs with review by an independent review organization. Moreover, absent the time pressure imposed by a judge in a qui tam case, self-disclosures were taking a longer period of time to reach resolution than similar false claims actions.

As a result, many healthcare attorneys and healthcare organizations began to consider alternative means of making disclosures and repayments to the government. In this regard, the inclusion of mandatory reporting obligations in CIAs has resulted in a new (and potentially more welcome) avenue for a voluntary disclosure to the OIG, rather than relying on the formal Protocol. Additionally, some healthcare organizations began self-disclosing directly to the DOJ or local U.S. Attorneys Office. In response, it seems the OIG has returned to its original position that self-disclosures through the Protocol generally will not result in a CIA and have made significant efforts to expedite the time it takes to resolve those matters.

## § 10-4 LITIGATION

Few providers can risk either the possibility of exclusion from the Medicare and state healthcare programs or the cloud of legal and financial uncertainty of litigating a healthcare fraud case. As a result, many providers find it imperative that they reach a settlement with the government as quickly as possible. This means that most of the government's healthcare fraud theories advanced in major fraud cases have traditionally rarely been litigated. This virtually ensures large financial settlements for the government whenever it pursues a healthcare fraud case. Nevertheless, as enforcement efforts continue to increase and with the possibility of entities facing possible exclusion and or being placed into bankruptcy as the result of an investigation and settlement, more healthcare entities may be willing to litigate.

Although the DOJ's civil settlement posture once was to demand double damages; now, current settlement demands with larger multipliers (e.g., 2.25, 2.5 or even greater) are becoming more commonplace. However, as the government's monetary demands increase, it seems that more settlements are (and will continue to be) concluded on an "ability to pay" basis rather than pursuant to a negotiation based on the merits of the case.

The government also has promised that settlements will not only be "corporate"—that is, that the government will seek individuals within the company to prosecute criminally and/or exclude from the federal healthcare programs as a part of the settlement. This propensity on the part of the government creates greater complexity in managing the investigation as well as greater defense costs, requiring company counsel to coordinate among individual counsel, who often are paid by the company. This can have a devastating

## The Future of Fraud and Abuse

impact on morale within the company and, more and more, can result in the end of both liberty and livelihood for certain healthcare executives.

Therefore, the government should take into account the less than clear – and incredibly complex—regulatory authorities most healthcare entities attempt to navigate and use its investigatory power responsibly.

The states also promise to be an expanding arena for healthcare fraud enforcement and litigation activities. State MFCUs are heavily involved in healthcare fraud enforcement, and Medicaid's anticipated expansion under health reform can only increase this focus. Many of the enforcement actions in the pharmaceutical area have been brought by state attorneys general in the past and they continue to be active in this area. The states will remain an important focal point for pharmaceutical pricing-enforcement litigation over the next number of years, both against pharmaceutical companies and against pharmacies.

Suits between private parties can be expected to continue as a by-product of major government healthcare fraud settlements. Such legal actions may include shareholder derivative suits charging breach of corporate duty as a result of large healthcare fraud settlements, as well as lawsuits by purchasers against sellers of companies charging breach of the representations and warranties contained in the Stock or Asset Purchase Agreements.

Litigation involving qui tam relators, following settlement with or declination by the government also is becoming more frequent. As the number of qui tam cases increases, government resources may not allow the government to take on all qui tam*s*. Thus, healthcare organizations increasingly may find themselves in FCA litigation directly with the relators. Additionally, in government settlements, relators are at times refusing to settle remaining claims for attorney's fees and/or retaliation claims. The outcome of such collateral litigation continues to be a matter of interest, as the relator's pursuit of further monetary gain can backfire, even resulting in awards of attorney's fees *against* the relator.

The proliferation of healthcare fraud litigation also is resulting in a number of healthcare attorneys serving as witnesses in connection with previous advice given to their healthcare organization clients. This may occur when healthcare attorneys have given fraud and abuse regulatory advice in connection with the structuring of a transaction among healthcare entities. It also may occur when healthcare attorneys give federal healthcare program reimbursement or coverage advice, or self-referral or anti-kickback advice with respect to particular arrangements. It may also occur when attorneys conduct internal investigations on behalf of clients or, as noted, when there is continuing litigation with the relator after the settlement of a qui tam action.

Finally, the possibility of healthcare attorneys being the target of government enforcement continues to grow, not only with respect to structuring arrangements in light of the various fraud and abuse laws, but also with respect to representing clients that are subject to government inquiries.

## § 10-5   THE FUTURE AND THE NEED FOR "BALANCE"

Fraud and abuse presents substantial healthcare policy challenges for the foreseeable future. The debate on these significant healthcare policy issues will undoubtedly involve a delicate balancing act. For example, although the primary goal of the Anti-Kickback Statute and the Stark Law is to control overutilization by restricting the referral incentives inherent in ownership interests and other financial relationships, this goal must be reached without the loss of the potential efficiencies that can be achieved through the cooperation and collaboration by and among various providers in healthcare delivery. Moreover, overly aggressive control of physician investment in healthcare can eliminate a substantial source of capital for financing new and innovative healthcare ventures, stifling both cost-effective delivery modes and cutting-edge technological advancements.

Regarding initiatives to combat false claims, the goal of filtering out false and otherwise fraudulent claims must be balanced against the countervailing consideration of ensuring that legitimate claims are processed and paid both accurately and quickly. Agencies pursuing fraud enforcement must recognize that, even in optimum circumstances, mistakes in billing and/or lack of full documentation will occur, and repayment must be accomplished expeditiously and without overtones of "fraud" allegations. Voluntary self-disclosure is a step in the right direction, but it can remain so only if the government maintains a propensity to grant more favorable treatment for matters voluntarily disclosed, and if it is committed to resolving matters voluntarily disclosed in an expeditious and cost-effective manner.

Moreover, a greater willingness on the part of DOJ and OIG to recognize "mistakes" is warranted, even when those mistakes are not discovered and investigated internally and self-disclosed to the government. The OIG has consistently stated that its Office of Investigations "does not investigate individuals, facilities, or entities that merely commit errors or mistakes on claims submitted to the Medicare or Medicaid program,"[2] as opposed to "patterns of misconduct" that would lead to investigation. Nevertheless, healthcare organizations remain unconvinced in this regard, perceiving an enormous gap between the government view and the industry view of what is an "error" as opposed to a "pattern." In this era of consolidation of healthcare companies (with fewer, larger organizations submitting claims through computer technology), a simple error quickly can replicate itself on a larger scale. The

---

[2] Office of Inspector General, *Work Plan Fiscal Year 2005* 45, *available online at* http://oig.hhs.gov/reading/workplan/2005/2005%20Work%20Plan.pdf.

government must recognize that it is possible for even a large number of erroneous claims to result from a "mere error or mistake" without rising to the level of intent necessary for FCA liability or CMP exposure.

With healthcare delivery increasingly in the hands of large national companies that require certainty in their business operations to obtain financing and to consummate business transactions, the government must take further steps in helping to provide national standards, consistent interpretations, and certainty. Regional variations in interpretation and enforcement of the healthcare fraud laws are both frustrating and counter-productive. Government investigatory efforts (and even generalized pronouncements regarding particular activities) can be devastating to particular companies, as well as to entire segments of the healthcare industry, with the potential to drive down stock prices and investment attractiveness. Given that major government investigations typically involve entire industry segments (e.g., the AWP investigations throughout the pharmaceutical industry), once one organization has settled based on the government's "theory of fraud," substantial pressure exists for others to follow suit.

Already, some indications have developed that the government acknowledges its duty to act responsibly in this area. The DOJ and U.S. Attorney's Offices do not appear to be as "trigger-happy" with their subpoena authority and requests for search warrants as in the past, and many government inquiries are now being conducted through the less formal issuance of letters requesting information and cooperation. In addition, significant issuances from the DOJ have detailed the various factors that will lead to non-prosecution of corporations.

Unfortunately, inconsistencies persist among the various U.S. Attorney's Offices with respect to their willingness to proceed using less formal investigatory tools. There is a greater propensity now in some jurisdictions to consider conduct to be criminal that previously would have been considered civil, with corporate criminal pleas often expected in exchange for settlement of false claims cases. Finally, government enforcement activity continues to include major "sting" operations designed to elicit conduct on the part of unsuspecting healthcare organizations that would not ordinarily have occurred absent the "sting," in addition to the development of "theories of fraud" based on governmental interpretations of the law that were unstated prior to the conduct having occurred.

The foregoing suggests that healthcare fraud policy should *not* continue to be established through prosecutions that develop new theories of fraudulent conduct that had not been expressly prohibited by law. Rather, healthcare fraud policy should be established through a continuing dialogue between the healthcare fraud enforcers and the healthcare industry, with a common goal of developing a reasonable policy on fraud and abuse issues that facilitates enforcement against lawbreakers, yet allows the healthcare industry to engage in legitimate business activities.

# Index

## A

**ADMINISTRATIVE SANCTIONS, FEDERAL,** §5-1 to 5-4(f)
Civil monetary penalties, §5-3
　Amount, §5-3(c)
　Conduct that may result in imposition, §5-3(a), 5-3(a)(5)
　　Excluded individuals and entities, dealing with, §5-3(a)(2)
　　Gainsharing, §5-3(a)(4)
　　Inducements to beneficiaries, §5-3(a)(3)
　　Payments to induce reduction or limitation of services, §5-3(a)(4)
　　Submission of improperly filed claims, §5-3(a)(1)
　Hearings, §5-5 to §5-5(f)
　Managed care industry, intermediate sanctions applicable to, §8-4
　Notice of proposed determination to impose, §5-3(b)
Exclusion from Medicare, Medicaid and other state healthcare programs, §5-2
　Additional activities that can result in violations, Appx C
　Civil monetary penalties, §5-3(a)(2)
　Effects, §5-2(e)
　Hearings, §5-5 to §5-5(f)
　Mandatory exclusion, §5-2(a)
　Notice, §5-2(d), 5-2(d)(2)
　　Intent to exclude, §5-2(d)(1)
　　Proposal to exclude, §5-2(d)(3)
　Permissive exclusion, §5-2(b)
　Persons subject to exclusion, §5-2(c)
　Reinstatement, §5-2(f)
Generally, §5-1
Hearings, §5-5 to §5-5(f)
　Appeals
　　Departmental appeal board, §5-5(e)
　　Judicial review of health and human services secretary's final determination, §5-5(f)
　Burden of proof, §5-5(b)
　Evidentiary standards, §5-5(c)
　Rights of parties, §5-5(a)
　Scope of authority in exclusion cases, §5-5(d)
Managed care industry, intermediate sanctions applicable to, §8-4
Suspension of payments, §5-4
　Medicaid providers, §5-4(b)
　Medicare providers, §5-4(a)

**ADVANCED MEDICAL TECHNOLOGY ASSOCIATION,** §6-10(e)

**AGING, ADMINISTRATION ON**
Enforcement, §1-3(c)

**AMBULANCE COMPANIES**
False claims
　Enforcement against particular segments of the healthcare industry, §4-6(l)
Kickbacks
　Fraud alerts and special advisory bulletins
　　Contractual arrangements with ambulance companies, §2-4(j)

**AMBULATORY SURGERY CENTERS**
Implants, Stark Law exceptions and, §3-4(a)(5)
Safe harbors, anti-kickback laws
Investment interest safe harbors, §2-3(b)(5)

**AMERICAN COLLEGE OF PHYSICIANS,** §6-10(c)

**AMERICAN COLLEGE OF RADIOLOGY,** §6-10(b)

**AMERICAN MEDICAL ASSOCIATION,** §6-10(a)

**ANTI-KICKBACK LAWS,** §2-1 to 2-8, 6-3. *See* **KICKBACKS.**

**ANTI-MARKUP RULE**
Stark law, §3-9(d)

**ATTORNEY AND CLIENT**
Representation of healthcare organizations. *See* **REPRESENTING HEALTHCARE ORGANIZATIONS.**

# B

**BALANCED BUDGET ACT OF 1997**
Kickbacks, development of statute prohibiting, §2-2(e)

**BANKRUPTCY CODE**
False claims actions under, §4-7

**BILLING COMPANIES**
False claims
Enforcement against particular segments of the healthcare industry, §4-6(i)

**BONA FIDE EMPLOYMENT RELATIONSHIPS**
Stark law, §3-4(c)(2)

**BRIBERY, COMMERCIAL**
State laws, §6-5

**BURDEN OF PROOF**
Administrative sanctions, federal
Hearings, §5-5(b)
Self-referral
Stark law
Penalties and enforcement, §3-6(d)

# C

**CAPITATION MISCLASSIFICATION**
False claims, §4-5(c)

**CENTERS FOR MEDICARE AND MEDICAID SERVICES**
Administrative sanctions, federal
Exclusion from Medicare, Medicaid and other state healthcare programs. *See* **ADMINISTRATIVE SANCTIONS, FEDERAL.**
Compliance and self-reporting
Guidance, §7-5(g)
Enforcement, §1-3(b)
Medicare prescription drug integrity contractors (MEDICs), §1-3(f), 1-3(f)(3)
Recovery audit contractors (RACs), §1-3(f)(1)
Zone program integrity contractors (ZPICs), §1-3(f)(2)

**CHAMPUS.** *See* **CIVILIAN HEALTH AND MEDICAL PROGRAM OF THE UNIFORMED SERVICE (CHAMPUS).**

# Index

**CIAs.** *See* **CORPORATE INTEGRITY AGREEMENTS (CIAs).**

**CIVILIAN HEALTH AND MEDICAL PROGRAM OF THE UNIFORMED SERVICE (CHAMPUS)**
Kickbacks, §2-7(c)
Self-referral, §3-9(b)

**CIVIL PENALTIES**
Administrative sanctions available to federal enforcers, §5-3 to 5-4(f). *See* **ADMINISTRATIVE SANCTIONS, FEDERAL.**
Kickbacks
 Inducements to beneficiaries
  Civil money penalty statute, §2-7(a)(2)
  State anti-kickback provisions, §6-3
 Managed care industry, intermediate sanctions applicable to, §8-4
Self-referral
 Stark law, §3-6
 State laws, §6-2(d)

**CLINICAL LABORATORIES**
False claims
 Enforcement against particular segments of the healthcare industry, §4-6(d)
Kickbacks
 Fraud alerts and special advisory bulletins, §2-4(e)

**COINSURANCE WAIVERS**
False claims, §4-5(g), 6-7(b)
Kickbacks
 Safe harbor regulations
  Statutory exceptions with analogous safe harbors, §2-3(g)(5)

**COMPENSATION**
Fee-splitting prescriptions, §6-4
Self-referral. *See* **SELF-REFERRAL.**

**COMPLIANCE AND SELF-REPORTING,**
§7-1 to 7-9
Corporate integrity agreements Comparison, Appx E
Corporate integrity agreements (CIAs), §7-8, 10-3
Effectiveness reviews, §7-7
Elements of an effective compliance program, §7-6
 Background checks, §7-6(c)
 Disciplinary action and corrective action, §7-6(g)
 Documentation, §7-6(h)
 Monitoring, auditing, and evaluating the program, §7-6(e)
 Reporting system, §7-6(f)
 Roles and reporting relationships of personnel, §7-6(b)
  Corporate compliance officer (CCO) and other personnel, §7-6(b)(2)
  Relationship with general counsel, §7-6(b)(3)
  Corporate governance, §7-6(b)(1)
 Standards and procedures, establishment of, §7-6(a)
 Training, §7-6(d)
Federal sentencing guidelines, §7-3
Generally, §7-1
Guidance
 Centers for Medicare and Medicaid services guidance to contractors, §7-5(f)
 General accounting office, §7-5(c)

Health Care Fraud
Prevention and Enforcement
Action Team (HEAT),
§7-5(a)
Inspector general, office of
Compliance program
guidance, §7-5(a)
Inspector general and Health
Lawyers resources, §7-5(e)
Roundtables, §7-5(d)
Sarbanes-Oxley act of 2002,
§7-4
Self-reporting generally, §7-9
Sentencing guidelines, federal,
§7-3
Voluntary disclosure, §7-9
CMS protocol, §7-9(b)
OIG protocol, §7-9(a), 10-3
State disclosure processes,
§7-9(c)

**CONSUMER PROTECTION LAWS,** §6-6

**CORPORATE INTEGRITY AGREEMENTS (CIAs),**
§7-8, 10-3
Comparison, Appx E

**CRIMINAL LAW AND PROCEDURE**
False claims, §4-4
Asset freezes to enjoin
fraudulent conduct,
§4-4(i)
Embezzlement, §4-4(g)
False statements, §4-4(f)
Healthcare fraud, §4-4(e)
Mail and wire fraud, §4-4(b)
Miscellaneous offenses,
§4-4(h)
Money laundering, §4-4(d)
RICO violations, §4-4(c)
Social security act, §4-4(a)
Theft, §4-4(g)

Representing healthcare
organizations
Attorney and client relationship
Attorney-client
communications privilege
Crime-fraud exception,
§9-5(d)
Relationship between criminal
and civil matters, §9-4
Double jeopardy, §9-4(a)
Ex post facto considerations,
§9-4(b)

## D

**DAMAGES, CALCULATION OF**
Federal civil false claims act,
§4-2(c)
Kickbacks, §2-8(i)

**DECEPTIVE TRADE PRACTICES,** §6-6

**DEDUCTIBLE WAIVERS,**
§6-7(b)
False claims, §4-5(g), 6-7(b)
Kickbacks
Safe harbor regulations
Statutory exceptions with
analogous safe harbors,
§2-3(g)(5)

**DENTISTS**
False claims
Enforcement against particular
segments of the healthcare
industry, §4-6(k)

**DIAGNOSIS-RELATED GROUP CREEP**
False claims, §4-5(c)

**DRG CREEP.** *See* **DIAGNOSIS-RELATED GROUP CREEP.**

# Index

**DURABLE MEDICAL EQUIPMENT**
False claims
  Enforcement against particular segments of the healthcare industry, §4-6(e)
  Certificates of medical necessity, §4-6(e)(4)
  Provision of medical supplies to nursing homes, §4-6(e)(1)
  Seat lifts, §4-6(e)(2)
  Telemarketing schemes, §4-6(e)(3)

# E

**ELECTRONIC DISCOVERY,** §9-3
Culling data, §9-3(e)
Document review, §9-3(f)
Limiting data set, §9-3(e)
Litigation hold, §9-3(b)
Litigation support vendors, §9-3(c)
Preservation and collection, §9-3(d)
Production, §9-3(g)
Triggering event, §9-3(a)

**ELECTRONIC HEALTH RECORDS AND COMMUNITY-WIDE INFORMATION SYSTEMS**
Kickbacks
  Safe harbor regulations, §2-3(n)
Stark law
  Exceptions
    Compensation arrangements
      Community-wide information system, §3-4(c)(18)

**ELECTRONIC PRESCRIBING**
Kickbacks
  Safe harbor regulations

Statutory exceptions with analogous safe harbors, §2-3(g)(7)

**ENFORCERS**
Administrative sanctions available to federal enforcers, §5-1 to 5-4(f). *See* **ADMINISTRATIVE SANCTIONS, FEDERAL.**
Congress
  Future legislative activities, §10-1
  Generally, §1-6
Generally, §1-1
Health and human services, department of. *See* **HEALTH AND HUMAN SERVICES, DEPARTMENT OF.**
Justice, department of. *See* **JUSTICE, DEPARTMENT OF.**
Miscellaneous federal agencies, §1-4
Multi-agency federal initiatives, §1-5
Private citizens, §1-9
Private payors, §1-8
States, §1-7
Whistleblowers, §1-9

# F

**FALSE CERTIFICATION**
False claims, §4-5(h)

**FALSE CLAIMS,** §4-1 to 4-6(l)
Bankruptcy code, §4-7
Civil
  Additional civil laws, §4-3 to 4-3(b)
  Federal civil false claims act, §4-2
    Anti-kickback violations, §4-2(b)

Index ◄ 585

Calculating damages, §4-2(c)
Key considerations, §4-2(a)
  Claims, §4-2(a)(3)
    "Causing" claim to be submitted, §4-2(a)(4)
  False or fraudulent defined, §4-2(a)(5)
  Knowingly, §4-2(a)(2)
    Deliberate ignorance, §4-2(a)(2)(i)
    Reckless disregard, §4-2(a)(2)(ii)
  Materiality defined, §4-2(a)(6)
  Overpayments defined, §4-2(a)(5)(i)
  Person, §4-2(a)(1)
  Qui tam relators. *See* **QUI TAM RELATORS.**
  Statute of limitations, §4-2(e)
Program fraud civil remedies act, §4-3(b)
Social security act, §4-3(a)
Criminal, §4-4
  Asset freezes to enjoin fraudulent conduct, §4-4(i)
  Embezzlement, §4-4(g)
  False statements, §4-4(f)
  Healthcare fraud, §4-4(e)
  Mail and wire fraud, §4-4(b)
  Miscellaneous offenses, §4-4(h)
  RICO violations, §4-4(c)
  Social security act, §4-4(a)
  Theft, §4-4(g)
Enforcement against particular segments of the healthcare industry, §4-6
  Ambulance companies, §4-6(l)
  Billing companies, §4-6(i)
  Clinical laboratories, §4-6(d)
  Dentists, §4-6(k)
  Durable medical equipment and home medical suppliers, §4-6(e)
    Certificates of medical necessity, §4-6(e)(4)
    Provision of medical supplies to nursing homes, §4-6(e)(1)
    Seat lifts, §4-6(e)(2)
    Telemarketing schemes, §4-6(e)(3)
  Fiscal intermediaries, §4-6(g)
  HIV infusion clinics, §4-6(n)
  Home health agencies, §4-6(f)
  Hospitals, §4-6(a)
    Diagnosis-related group payment window, §4-6(a)(2)
    Inpatient admissions, overutilization of, §4-6(a)(4)
    One day stays/same day stays, §4-6(a)(4)
    Outlier payments, §4-6(a)(3)
    Payments to teaching hospitals, §4-6(a)(1)
  Investigational devices, §4-6(b)
  Medical clinics, §4-6(n)
  Medical device companies, §4-6(m)
  Medicare contractors, §4-6(g)
  Nursing homes and long-term care facilities, §4-6(c)
  Pharmacies and pharmaceutical manufacturers, §4-6(h)
  Physicians, §4-6(j)
  Third-party consultants, §4-6(i)
Generally, §4-1
Investigative demands, §9-2(c)
Managed care industry, §8-5
State laws, §6-7
  Fraudulent billing practices, §6-7(a)

Waivers of coinsurance and deductible amounts, §6-7(b)
Theories applicable to multiple segments of the healthcare industry, §4-5
  Billing for items or services not actually rendered, §4-5(a), 6-7(a)
  Capitation misclassification, §4-5(c)
  Coinsurance waivers, §4-5(g)
  Deductible waivers, §4-5(g)
  Diagnosis-related group creep, §4-5(c)
  False certification, §4-5(h)
  Filing false cost reports, §4-5(e)
  Fragmentation, §4-5(d)
  Homeless and indigent patients, recruitment of, §4-5(j)
  Medicare secondary payor issues, §4-5(i)
  Providing medically unnecessary services, §4-5(b)
  Quality-of-care-cases, §4-5(f)
  Reverse false claims, §4-5(f)
  Unbundling, §4-5(d)
  Upcoding, §4-5(c)

**FEDERAL BUREAU OF INVESTIGATION**
Enforcement, §1-2(d)

**FEE-SPLITTING**
State laws prohibiting, §6-4

**FINES**
Administrative sanctions available to federal enforcers, §5-3 to 5-4(f). *See* **ADMINISTRATIVE SANCTIONS, FEDERAL.**
Kickbacks
  Inducements to beneficiaries
    Civil money penalty statute, §2-7(a)(2)
    State anti-kickback provisions, §6-3
  Managed care industry, intermediate sanctions applicable to, §8-4
Self-referral
  Stark law, §3-6
  State laws, §6-2(d)

**FISCAL INTERMEDIARIES**
False claims
  Enforcement against particular segments of the healthcare industry, §4-6(g)

**FOOD AND DRUG ADMINISTRATION**
Enforcement, §1-3(e)

**FRAGMENTATION**
False claims, §4-5(d)

**FRAUD**
Attorney and client relationship
  Crime-fraud exception, §9-5(d)
False claims
  Civil
    Federal civil false claims act
      Key considerations
        False or fraudulent defined, §4-2(a)(5)
        Overpayments defined, §4-2(a)(5)(i)
        Reverse false claims, §4-2(a)(5)(i)
    Program fraud civil remedies act, §4-3(b)
  Criminal
    Asset freezes to enjoin fraudulent conduct, §4-4(i)
    Embezzlement, §4-4(g)

Index ◄ 587

False statements, §4-4(f)
Mail and wire fraud, §4-4(b)
Miscellaneous offenses, §4-4(h)
Money laundering, §4-4(d)
RICO violations, §4-4(c)
Theft, §4-4(g)
State laws
Fraudulent billing practices, §6-7(a)
Initiatives to combat fraud, state and private. *See* **INITIATIVES TO COMBAT FRAUD, STATE AND PRIVATE.**
Kickbacks
Development of statute prohibiting
Medicare-Medicaid anti-fraud and abuse amendments of 1977, §2-2(b)
Fraud alerts and special advisory bulletins. *See* **KICKBACKS.**
Managed care industry, issues affecting
Medicare managed care, federal efforts to address fraud in, §8-6
Potential fraud liability, §8-8. *See* **MANAGED CARE INDUSTRY, ISSUES AFFECTING.**
National Health Care Anti-Fraud Association (NHCAA) Enforcement, §1-8
Promoting public initiatives to identify fraud, Appx A

**FUTURE CONSIDERATIONS,** §10-1 to 10-5
Balance, need for, §10-5
Enforcement activities, §10-3
Legislative activities, §10-1
Litigation, §10-4

Provider self-disclosure, federal enforcement activities and, §10-3
Regulatory initiatives, §10-2

# G

**GAINSHARING**
Administrative sanctions, federal
Civil monetary penalties
Conduct that may result in imposition
Payments to induce reduction or limitation of services, §5-3(a)(4)
Stark law exceptions
Compensation arrangements, §3-4(c)(21)

**GOVERNMENT INVESTIGATIONS**
Administrative subpoenas, §9-2(d)
Civil investigative demands, §9-2(c)
Civil settlements, §9-4(c)
Congressional subpoenas, §9-2(f)
Criminal settlements, §9-4(d)
Electronic discovery. *See* **ELECTRONIC DISCOVERY.**
Grand jury investigations, §9-2(b)
Inspector general, office of
Immediate access to documents
Subpoenas of documents and witnesses, §9-2(e)(2)
Search and subpoena authority, §9-2(e)
Subpoenas of documents and witnesses, §9-2(e)(1)
Practical guidelines, Appx F
Search warrants, §9-2(a)
Undercover operations, §9-2(g)
Vicarious liability and the *Park* doctrine, §9-7

# Index

**GRAND JURY INVESTIGATIONS,** §9-2(b)

**GROUP PRACTICE**
Stark law, §3-5. *See* **SELF-REFERRAL.**

**GROUP PURCHASING ORGANIZATIONS**
Safe harbor, anti-kickback laws
Statutory exceptions with analogous safe harbors, §2-3(g)(3)

## H

**HANLESTER NETWORK V. SHALALA,** §2-6(b)
Post-*Hanlester* case law, §2-6(c)
  *Anderson, McClatchey,* and *LaHue,* §2-6(c)(5)
  *Bryan,* §2-6(c)(3)
  *Jain,* §2-6(c)(2)
  *Neufeld,* §2-6(c)(1)
  *Shaw,* §2-6(c)(6)
  *Starks,* §2-6(c)(4)
Pre-*Hanlester* case law, §2-6(a)
  Additional cases, §2-6(a)(5)
  *Bay State Ambulance,* §2-6(a)(3)
  *Greber,* §2-6(a)(1)
  *Katz,* §2-6(a)(2)
  *Polk County v. Peters,* §2-6(a)(4)

**HEALTH AND HUMAN SERVICES, DEPARTMENT OF**
Administrative sanctions available, §5-1 to 5-4(f). *See* **ADMINISTRATIVE SANCTIONS, FEDERAL.**
Enforcement, §1-3
  Aging, administration on, §1-3(c)
  Centers for Medicare and Medicaid services. *See* **CENTERS FOR MEDICARE AND MEDICAID SERVICES.**
  Food & Drug Administration, §1-3(e)
  Health Lawyers resources, §7-5(e)
  Health resources and services administration, §1-3(d)
  Inspector general, office of, §1-3(a)
    Compliance and self-reporting guidance, §7-5(a)
    Resources, health lawyers, §7-5(e)
    Future federal regulatory initiatives, §10-2
    Search and subpoena authority, §9-2(e) to 9-2(e)(2)
    Program integrity contractors. *See* **PROGRAM INTEGRITY CONTRACTORS.**
    Roundtables with inspector general's office and health care compliance association, §7-5(d)

**HEALTH CARE COMPLIANCE ASSOCIATION**
Roundtables, §7-5(d)

**HEALTH INSURANCE PORTABILITY AND ACCOUNTABILITY ACT OF 1996**
Kickbacks, development of statute prohibiting, §2-2(d)

**HEALTH LAWYERS RESOURCES**
Compliance and self-reporting guidance, §7-5(e)

Index ◄ 589

**HEALTH MAINTENANCE ORGANIZATIONS, ISSUES AFFECTING**
Generally, §8-1 to 8-8. See **MANAGED CARE INDUSTRY, ISSUES AFFECTING.**
Kickbacks, §2-3(h), 8-2 to 8-2(c). See **KICKBACKS.**
Self-referral, §8-3 to 8-3(c). See **SELF-REFERRAL.**

**HEALTH RESOURCES AND SERVICES ADMINISTRATION**
Enforcement, §1-3(d)

**HIPAA.** See **HEALTH INSURANCE PORTABILITY AND ACCOUNTABILITY ACT OF 1996.**

**HOME HEALTH AGENCIES**
False claims
  Enforcement against particular segments of the healthcare industry, §4-6(f)
Kickbacks
  Fraud alerts and special advisory bulletins, §2-4(f)

**HOME MEDICAL SUPPLIERS**
False claims
  Enforcement against particular segments of the healthcare industry, §4-6(e)
    Certificates of medical necessity, §4-6(e)(4)
    Provision of medical supplies to nursing homes, §4-6(e)(1)
    Seat lifts, §4-6(e)(2)
    Telemarketing schemes, §4-6(e)(3)

**HOSPICE ARRANGEMENTS**
Kickbacks
  Fraud alerts and special advisory bulletins, §2-4(h)

**I**

**INITIATIVES TO COMBAT FRAUD, STATE AND PRIVATE**
Private initiatives. See **STATE AND PRIVATE INITIATIVES TO COMBAT FRAUD.**
Self-referral laws, §6-2 to 6-2(f). See **SELF-REFERRAL.**
State initiatives. See **STATE AND PRIVATE INITIATIVES TO COMBAT FRAUD.**
Trade associations. See **TRADE ASSOCIATIONS.**

**INSPECTOR GENERAL, OFFICE OF**
Administrative sanctions available to federal enforcers, §5-1 to 5-4(f). See **ADMINISTRATIVE SANCTIONS, FEDERAL.**
Compliance and self-reporting Guidance
  Inspector general and Health Lawyers resources, §7-5(e)
  Roundtables, §7-5(d)
Compliance program guidance, §7-5(a)
Enforcement, §1-3(a)
Future federal regulatory initiatives, §10-2
Hot topics, Appx D
Search and subpoena authority, §9-2(e) to 9-2(e)(2)

# Index

**INVESTIGATIONAL DEVICES**
False claims
Enforcement against particular segments of the healthcare industry, §4-6(b)

**INVESTIGATIONS**
False claims, §4-6(b); §9-2(c)
Government investigations. *See* **GOVERNMENT INVESTIGATIONS.**
Self-critical analysis privilege, §9-5(h)
Summaries of significant anti-kickback investigations and settlements, Appx B

**INVESTMENT INTEREST SAFE HARBORS,** §2-3(b)
Ambulatory surgery centers, §2-3(b)(5)
Group practices, §2-3(b)(4)
Large entities, §2-3(b)(1)
Medically underserved areas (MUAs), entities in, §2-3(b)(3)
Small entities, §2-3(b)(2)

**J**

**JUSTICE, DEPARTMENT OF**
Civil Division, §1-2(c)
Criminal Division, §1-2(b)
Federal Bureau of Investigation, §1-2(d)
United States Attorney's Offices, §1-2(a)

**K**

**KICKBACKS,** §2-1 to 2-8, 6-3
Advisory opinions and additional guidance, §2-5, 2-5(b)
Early guidance from CMS to regional offices and fiscal agents, §2-5(a)
Managed care industry, §8-2(c)
Calculation of damages, §2-8(i)
Carving out, §2-8(e)
Case law, §2-6
*Hanlester Network v. Shalala,* §2-6(b)
Post-*Hanlester* case law, §2-6(c)
*Anderson, McClatchey,* and *LaHue,* §2-6(c)(5)
*Bryan,* §2-6(c)(3)
*Jain,* §2-6(c)(2)
*Neufeld,* §2-6(c)(1)
*Shaw,* §2-6(c)(6)
*Starks,* §2-6(c)(4)
Pre-*Hanlester* case law, §2-6(a)
Additional cases, §2-6(a)(5)
*Bay State Ambulance,* §2-6(a)(3)
*Greber,* §2-6(a)(1)
*Katz,* §2-6(a)(2)
*Polk County v. Peters,* §2-6(a)(4)
Civilian health and medical program of the uniformed service (CHAMPUS), §2-7(c)
Credentialing, §2-8(g)
Development of statute prohibiting, §2-2
Balanced budget act of 1997, §2-2(e)
Health insurance portability and accountability act of 1996 (HIPAA), §2-2(d)
Medicare and Medicaid patient program protection act of 1987, §2-2(c)
Medicare-Medicaid anti-fraud and abuse amendments of 1977, §2-2(b)

Medicare prescription drug, improvement, and modernization act of 2003, §2-2(f)
Patient protection and affordable care act of 2010, §2-2(g)
Social security act of 1972, §2-2(a)
Enforcement and interpretation issues, §2-8
Fair market value and "bona fide" nature of services contracted for, §2-8(j)
Federal civil false claims act, §4-2(b)
Fraud alerts and special advisory bulletins, §2-4
Clinical laboratory services, arrangements for the provision of, §2-4(e)
Home health agencies, §2-4(f)
Hospital incentives to physicians, §2-4(c)
Joint ventures, §2-4(a)
Nursing home
Ambulance companies, contractual arrangements with, §2-4(j)
Hospice arrangements, §2-4(h)
Patient assistance programs for Medicare part D enrollees, §2-4(k)
Rental of office in referring physician's space, §2-4(i)
Suppliers, §2-4(g)
Nursing home suppliers, §2-4(g)
Prescription drug marketing practices, §2-4(d)
Routine waivers of coinsurance and deductibles, §2-4(b)
Free goods to referral sources, §2-8(f)
Generally, §2-1

Inducements to beneficiaries, §2-7(a)
Anti-kickback statute, §2-7(a)(1)
Civil money penalty statute, §2-7(a)(2)
Integrated delivery systems, §2-8(b)
Practice acquisition, §2-8(b)(1)
Practice divestiture, §2-8(b)(2)
Managed care industry, effect of anti-kickback statute
Advisory opinions, §8-2(c)
Safe harbors, §2-3(h), 8-2(a)
Beneficiary incentives, §8-2(a)(1)
Group health plans, price reductions, §8-2(a)(2)
Medicare SELECT, §8-2(a)(3)
Shared-risk statutory exception
Contracts involving substantial financial risk, §8-2(b)(2)
Shared risk statutory exception, §8-2(b)
Price reductions offered to eligible managed care organizations, §8-2(b)(1)
Safe harbor protection for contracts involving substantial financial risk, §8-2(b)(2)
Marketing practices of healthcare providers, regulation of, §2-8(c)
Other authorities, §2-7
Physician payment sunshine act, §2-7(d)
Physician recruitment and relocation arrangements, §2-8(h)
Private actions under the anti-kickback statute, §2-8(a)
Professional courtesy, §2-8(d)
Public contracts anti-kickback act, §2-7(b)

# Index

Safe harbor regulations, §2-3. *See* **SAFE HARBOR, ANTI-KICKBACK LAWS.**
State anti-kickback provisions, §6-3
Summaries of significant anti-kickback investigations and settlements, Appx B
Swapping issues, §2-8(e)
TRICARE, §2-7(c)

## L

**LIMITATION OF ACTIONS**
Federal civil false claims act, §4-2(e)

**LONG-TERM CARE FACILITIES**
False claims
Enforcement against particular segments of the healthcare industry, §4-6(c)

## M

**MANAGED CARE INDUSTRY, ISSUES AFFECTING**
False claims, §8-5
Generally, §8-1
Intermediate sanctions, §8-4
Kickbacks, §2-3(h), 8-2 to 8-2(c). *See* **KICKBACKS.**
Medicare managed care, federal efforts to address fraud in, §8-6
Potential fraud liability, §8-8
Capitation misclassification, §8-8(a)
Contracting misrepresentations, §8-8(f)
Cost-shifting, §8-8(g)
Defective rate or bid submissions, §8-8(b)
Discount skimming, §8-8(h)
Enrollment practices, §8-8(c)
Failure to provide required services, §8-8(e)
Formulary development and implementation, §8-8(j)
Marketing schemes, §8-8(c)
Medical loss ratios, §8-8(l)
Misrepresenting services to qualify for higher payments, §8-8(e)
Patient-assistance programs and Medicare part D benefit, §8-8(k)
Payments to providers, §8-8(d)
Pharmacy benefit managers, §8-8(i)
Quality of care, §8-8(e)
Underutilization, §8-8(e)
Self-referral, §8-3 to 8-3(c). *See* **SELF-REFERRAL.**
State Medicaid programs, §8-7

**MEDICARE AND MEDICAID**
Administrative sanctions, federal
Exclusion from Medicare, Medicaid and other state healthcare programs. *See* **ADMINISTRATIVE SANCTIONS, FEDERAL.**
Compliance and self-reporting Guidance
Centers for Medicare and Medicaid services guidance to contractors, §7-5(f)
Enforcement, §1-3(b)
Medicare prescription drug integrity contractors (MEDICs), §1-3(f), 1-3(f)(3)

Recovery audit contractors (RACs), §1-3(f)(1)
Zone program integrity contractors (ZPICs), §1-3(f)(2)
False claims
  Enforcement against particular segments of the healthcare industry
    Medicare carriers, §4-6(g)
  Theories applicable to multiple segments of the healthcare industry
    Medicare secondary payor issues, §4-5(i)
Kickbacks
  Development of statute prohibiting
    Medicare and Medicaid patient program protection act of 1987, §2-2(c)
    Medicare-Medicaid anti-fraud and abuse amendments of 1977, §2-2(b)
    Medicare prescription drug, improvement, and modernization act of 2003, §2-2(f)
  Fraud alerts and special advisory bulletins
    Nursing home
      Patient assistance programs for Medicare part D enrollees, §2-4(k)
  Managed care industry, effect of anti-kickback statute
    Safe harbors
      Medicare SELECT, §8-2(a)(3)
Managed care industry
  Kickbacks
    Effect of anti-kickback statute
      Safe harbors
        Medicare SELECT, §8-2(a)(3)
    Medicare managed care, federal efforts to address fraud in, §8-6
  Potential fraud liability
    Patient-assistance programs and Medicare part D benefit, §8-8(k)
Secondary payor issues
  False claims, §4-5(i)
Self-referral
  Stark law
    Home health services reimbursed by the Medicare program, §3-9(a)

**MEDICARE AND MEDICAID PATIENT PROGRAM PROTECTION ACT OF 1987**
Kickbacks, development of statute prohibiting, §2-2(c)

**MEDICARE-MEDICAID ANTI-FRAUD AND ABUSE AMENDMENTS OF 1977**
Kickbacks, development of statute prohibiting, §2-2(b)

**MEDICARE PRESCRIPTION DRUG, IMPROVEMENT, AND MODERNIZATION ACT OF 2003**
Kickbacks, development of statute prohibiting, §2-2(f)

**MEDICARE PRESCRIPTION DRUG INTEGRITY CONTRACTORS (MEDICs)**
Enforcement, §1-3(f)

# Index

## N

**NATIONAL HEALTH CARE ANTI-FRAUD ASSOCIATION (NHCAA)**
Enforcement, §1-8

**NURSING HOMES**
False claims
  Enforcement against particular segments of the healthcare industry, §4-6(c)
  Provision of medical supplies to nursing homes, §4-6(e)(1)
Kickbacks
  Fraud alerts and special advisory bulletins
    Ambulance companies, contractual arrangements with, §2-4(j)
    Hospice arrangements, §2-4(h)
    Nursing home suppliers, §2-4(g)
    Patient assistance programs for Medicare part D enrollees, §2-4(k)
    Rental of office in referring physician's space, §2-4(i)
    Suppliers, §2-4(g)

## O

**OBSTETRICAL MALPRACTICE INSURANCE SUBSIDIES**
Kickbacks
  Safe harbor regulations, §2-3(j)

**OUTLIER PAYMENTS**
False claims
  Enforcement against particular segments of the healthcare industry, §4-6(a)(3)

## P

**PATIENT PROTECTION AND AFFORDABLE CARE ACT OF 2010**
Kickbacks, development of statute prohibiting, §2-2(g)

**PENALTIES**
Administrative sanctions available to federal enforcers, §5-3 to 5-4(f). *See* **ADMINISTRATIVE SANCTIONS, FEDERAL.**
Civil penalties generally. *See* **CIVIL PENALTIES.**

**PHARMACEUTICAL AND RESEARCH MANUFACTURERS ASSOCIATION,** §6-10(d)

**PHARMACIES**
False claims
  Enforcement against particular segments of the healthcare industry, §4-6(h)

**PHYSICIAN PAYMENT SUNSHINE ACT,** §2-7(d)

**PHYSICIAN SELF-REFERRAL,** §3-1 to 3-9(f). *See* **SELF-REFERRAL.**

**PRESCRIPTION DRUGS**
Food & Drug Administration, §1-3(e)
Kickbacks
  Development of statute prohibiting
    Medicare prescription drug, improvement, and modernization act of 2003, §2-2(f)

Fraud alerts and special advisory bulletins
Prescription drug marketing practices, §2-4(d)

**PRIVATE INITIATIVES TO COMBAT FRAUD,** §6-1 to 6-11. *See* **STATE AND PRIVATE INITIATIVES TO COMBAT FRAUD.**

**PROGRAM INTEGRITY CONTRACTORS**
Comprehensive error rate testing contractors (CERTs), §1-3(f)(3)
Coordination of benefits contractors (COBs), §1-3(f)(3)
Enforcement, §1-3(f)
Medicare administrative contractors (MACs), §1-3(f)(3)
Medicare prescription drug integrity contractors (MEDICs), §1-3(f), 1-3(f)(3)
National Supplier Clearinghouse Contractor (NSCs), §1-3(f)(3)
Recovery audit contractors (RACs), §1-3(f)(1)
Zone program integrity contractors (ZPICs), §1-3(f)(2)

## Q

**QUALITY-OF-CARE-CASES**
False claims, §4-5(f)

**QUI TAM RELATORS**
Federal civil false claims act, §4-2(d)
Dodd-Frank act protections, §4-2(d)(5)
Government declining to intervene, §4-2(d)(2)
Initiation of action, §4-2(d)(1)
Justice department guidance, §4-2(d)
Original source rule, §4-2(d)(3)(ii)
Pleading requirements, §4-2(d)(4)
Public disclosure bar, §4-2(d)(3)(i)
Qualifications, §4-2(d)(3)
Retaliation, §4-2(d)(5)

## R

**RACKETEERING**
State laws prohibiting, §6-5

**RECOVERY AUDIT CONTRACTORS (RACs)**
Enforcement, §1-3(f)(1)

**REFERRALS**
Kickbacks generally, §2-1 to 2-8. *See* **KICKBACKS.**
Self-referral, §3-1 to 3-9(f), 6-2 to 6-2(f). *See* **SELF-REFERRAL.**

**REPRESENTING HEALTHCARE ORGANIZATIONS**
Attorney and client relationship, §9-5
Allied-lawyer doctrine, §9-5(f)
Attorney-client communications privilege, §9-5(a)
Attorneys, applicability to, §9-5(a)(2)
Clients, privilege belongs to, §9-5(a)(5)
Waiver, §9-5(c)
Communications, §9-5(a)(3)
Confidentiality, §9-5(a)(4), 9-5(i)(1)
Crime-fraud exception, §9-5(d)
Legal advice, §9-5(a)(1)

Defendants, lawyers as, §9-9
Ethical obligations of attorneys, §9-5(i)
  Confidentiality, §9-5(i)(1)
  Disclosure from attorney to court, §9-5(i)(2)
  Duty to inquire, §9-5(i)(3)
  Government attorneys, application of rules to, §9-5(i)(4)
Fifth Amendment considerations, §9-6
Joint defense agreements, §9-5(f)
Outside consultants, §9-5(g)
Selective-waiver doctrine, §9-5(e)
Self-critical analysis privilege, §9-5(h)
Voluntary disclosure, §9-5(e)
Witnesses, lawyers as, §9-8
Work-product doctrine, §9-5(b)
  Crime-fraud exception, §9-5(d)
Generally, §9-1
Government investigations. *See* **GOVERNMENT INVESTIGATIONS.**
Litigation, general considerations, §10-4
Relationship between criminal and civil matters, §9-4
  Double jeopardy, §9-4(a)
  Ex post facto considerations, §9-4(b)

**RETALIATION**
Federal civil false claims act
  Qui tam relators, §4-2(d)(5)
Whistleblowers. *See* **WHISTLEBLOWERS.**

**REVERSE FALSE CLAIMS,** §4-5(f)

**RISK-SHARING**
Kickbacks
  Safe harbor regulations
    Statutory exceptions with analogous safe harbors, §2-3(g)(4)
Self-referral
  Managed care
    Risk-sharing arrangements, regulatory exception for, §8-3(c)
  Stark law
    Exceptions
      Compensation arrangements
        Managed care risk-sharing arrangements, §3-4(c)(13)

## S

**SAFE HARBOR, ANTI-KICKBACK LAWS,** §2-3
Ambulance replenishing, §2-3(m)
Cooperative hospital services organizations, §2-3(k)
Electronic health records and community-wide information systems, §2-3(n)
History of issuances, §2-3(a)
Investment interest safe harbors. *See* **INVESTMENT INTEREST SAFE HARBORS.**
Managed care, §2-3(h), 8-2(a)
  Beneficiary incentives, §8-2(a)(1)
  Group health plans, price reductions to, §8-2(a)(2)
  Medicare SELECT, §8-2(a)(3)
  Shared-risk statutory exception
    Contracts involving substantial financial risk, §8-2(b)(2)

Obstetrical malpractice insurance subsidies, §2-3(j)
Personal services and management contracts, §2-3(c)
Practitioner recruitment, §2-3(i)
Referral arrangements for specialty services, §2-3(l)
Referral services, §2-3(e)
Sale of practice, §2-3(d)
Space and equipment rental, §2-3(c)
Statutory exceptions with analogous safe harbors, §2-3(g)
   Coinsurance and deductible waivers, §2-3(g)(5)
   Discounts, §2-3(g)(2)
   Electronic prescribing, §2-3(g)(7)
   Employees, §2-3(g)(1)
   Federally qualified health centers, §2-3(g)(6)
   Group purchasing organizations, §2-3(g)(3)
   Risk-sharing arrangements, §2-3(g)(4)
Warranties, §2-3(f)

**SARBANES-OXLEY ACT OF 2002, §7-4**

**SEARCH WARRANTS**
Government investigations, §9-2(a)

**SELF-CRITICAL ANALYSIS PRIVILEGE**
Investigations, §9-5(h)

**SELF-REFERRAL**
Managed care, §8-3
   Personal-service arrangements, §8-3(b)
   Prepaid health plans, §8-3(a)
   Risk-sharing arrangements, regulatory exception for, §8-3(c)
Stark law
   Additional restrictions, §3-9
   Advisory opinions, §3-7
   Anti-markup rule, §3-9(d)
   Civilian health and medical program of the uniformed services (CHAMPUS), TRICARE and CHAMPVA, §3-9(b)
   Compensation rules, §3-3(c)
      Conditioning compensation on referrals to a particular provider, §3-3(c)(2)
      Definitions, §3-3(b)(4)
      Exceptions, §3-4(a)
      Methodologies, §3-3(c)(1)
      Modifying or amending agreements, §3-3(c)(3)
      Referrals to a particular provider, conditioning compensation on, §3-3(c)(2)
   Definitions, §3-3, 3-3(b)
      Compensation arrangements, §3-3(b)(4)
      Designated health services, §3-3(b)(2)
      Entity, §3-3(b)(8)
      Fair market value, §3-3(b)(5)
      Immediate family member, §3-3(b)(7)
      Ownership or investment interests, §3-3(b)(3)
      Physician, §3-3(b)(6)
      Referral, §3-3(b)(1)
   Disclosure protocol, §3-8
   Disclosure required of certain hospitals and critical access hospitals, §3-9(c), 10-3
   Exceptions, §3-4
      Compensation arrangements, §3-4(c)

# Index

Accountable Care Organizations (ACOs), §3-4(c)(22)
Anti-kickback statute safe harbors, exceptions relating to, §3-4(c)(20)
Bona fide employment relationships, §3-4(c)(2)
Charitable donations, §3-4(c)(17)
Community-wide information system, §3-4(c)(18)
Compliance training, §3-4(c)(14)
Electronic prescribing and electronic health records, §3-4(c)(19)
Fair market value exception, §3-4(c)(10)
Gainsharing, §3-4(c)(21)
Group-practice arrangements with a hospital, §3-4(c)(8)
Indirect compensation, §3-4(c)(15)
Isolated financial transactions, §3-4(c)(7)
Managed care risk-sharing arrangements, §3-4(c)(13)
Medical-staff incidental benefits, §3-4(c)(12)
Non-monetary compensation up to $300, §3-4(c)(11)
Payments for items and services, §3-4(c)(9)
Personal service arrangements, §3-4(c)(3)
Physician recruitment, §3-4(c)(5)
Physician retention, §3-4(c)(6)
Professional courtesy, §3-4(c)(16)
Rental of office space and equipment, §3-4(c)(1)
Unrelated payments, §3-4(c)(4)
Ownership and compensation, §3-4(a)
Academic medical centers, §3-4(a)(4)
Additional exceptions, §3-4(a)(6)
Implants in ambulatory surgical centers (ASCs), §3-4(a)(5)
In-office ancillary services, §3-4(a)(2)
Physician services, §3-4(a)(1)
Prepaid plans, §3-4(a)(3)
Ownership only, §3-4(b)
Hospitals, §3-4(b)(2)
Publicly traded securities and mutual funds, §3-4(b)(1)
Rural providers, §3-4(b)(3)
Reporting requirements, §3-4(d)
Generally, §3-1
Group practice, §3-5
Distribution of expenses and income, §3-5(e)
Full range of care, §3-5(c)
Physician-patient encounters, §3-5(h)
Productivity bonuses, §3-5(i)
Profit shares, §3-5(i)
Services furnished by members, §3-5(d)
Single legal entity, §3-5(a)

Two or more physicians,
§3-5(b)
Unified business,
§3-5(f)
Volume or value of referrals,
§3-5(g)
History of legislation and
regulation, §3-2
Home health services reimbursed
by the Medicare program,
§3-9(a)
Interpretation issues, §3-10
Corporate affiliates,
§3-10(e)
Hospital/physician
arrangements related to
designated health services,
§3-10(d)
Joint ventures unrelated to
the provision of designated
health services, §3-10(c)
Kickback statute, relationship
with, §3-10(a)
Knowledge element
for indirect financial
relationships, §3-10(b)
Penalties and enforcement,
§3-6
Alternative method of
compliance with signature
requirement, §3-6(b)
Burden of proof, §3-6(d)
Period of disallowance,
§3-6(c)
Temporary noncompliance,
§3-6(a)
Scope, §3-3(a)
Stand in the shoes, §3-3(d)
State self-referral laws, §6-2 to 6-2(f)
Advisory opinions, §6-2(c)
Declaratory statements,
§6-2(c)
Disclosure laws, §6-2(e)
Exceptions to prohibitions,
§6-2(b)

Generally, §6-2
Penalties, §6-2(d)
Scope, §6-2(a)

**SELF-REPORTING, §7-1 to 7-9.**
*See* **COMPLIANCE AND
SELF-REPORTING.**

**SENTENCING GUIDELINES**
Compliance and self-reporting
Federal sentencing
guidelines, §7-3

**SHARED-RISK STATUTORY
EXCEPTION**
Kickbacks
Managed care industry,
effect of anti-kickback
statute, §8-2(b)
Price reductions offered to
eligible managed care
organizations, §8-2(b)(1)
Safe harbor protection
for contracts involving
substantial financial risk,
§8-2(b)(2)

**SOCIAL SECURITY ACT
OF 1972**
Administrative sanctions
available to federal
enforcers, §5-1 to 5-4(f).
*See* **ADMINISTRATIVE
SANCTIONS, FEDERAL.**
False claims
Criminal, §4-4(a)
Inspector general, office of
Access to documents,
§9-2(e)(2)
Kickbacks, development
of statute prohibiting,
§2-2(a)

**STAND IN THE SHOES,**
§3-3(d)

# Index

**STARK LAW,** §3-1 to 3-9(f).
*See* **SELF-REFERRAL.**

**STATE AND PRIVATE INITIATIVES TO COMBAT FRAUD,** §6-1 to 6-11
Anti-kickback prescriptions, §6-3
Consumer protection laws, §6-6
Deceptive trade practices, §6-6
False claims, §6-7
    Fraudulent billing practices, §6-7(a)
    Waivers of coinsurance and deductible amounts, §6-7(b)
Fee-splitting prescriptions, §6-4
Fraud prevention and detection, §6-9
    Medicaid fraud control units, §6-9(a)
    Medicaid program integrity, §6-9(b)
    State inspector generals, §6-9(c)
Generally, §6-1
Self-referral laws, §6-2 to 6-2(f). *See* **SELF-REFERRAL.**
Sunshine acts applicable to pharmaceutical and medical device manufacturers, §6-8

**STATUTE OF LIMITATIONS**
Federal civil false claims act, §4-2(e)

**SUBPOENA**
Administrative subpoenas, §9-2(d)
Congressional subpoenas, §9-2(f)
Health and human services
    Enforcement
        Inspector general, office of
            Search and subpoena authority, §9-2(e) to 9-2(e)(2)
Representing healthcare organizations
    Government investigations, categories and types
        Inspector general, office of
            Immediate access to documents
            Subpoenas of documents and witnesses, §9-2(e)(2)
            Search and subpoena authority, §9-2(e)
            Subpoenas of documents and witnesses, §9-2(e)(1)

**SUNSHINE ACTS**
Physician payment sunshine act, §2-7(d)
State laws, §6-8

# T

**THIRD-PARTY CONSULTANTS**
False claims
    Enforcement against particular segments of the healthcare industry, §4-6(i)

**TRADE ASSOCIATIONS,** §6-10
Advanced medical technology association, §6-10(e)
American college of physicians, §6-10(c)

American college of radiology, §6-10(b)
American medical association, §6-10(a)
Pharmaceutical and research manufacturers association, §6-10(d)

**TRICARE**
Kickbacks, §2-7(c)
Self-referral, §3-9(b)

## U

**UNBUNDLING**
False claims, §4-5(d)

**UNDERCOVER OPERATIONS**
Government investigations, §9-2(g)

**UPCODING**
False claims, §4-5(c)

## V

**VICARIOUS LIABILITY**
Government investigations, §9-7

## W

**WARRANTIES**
Kickbacks
    Safe harbor regulations, §2-3(f)

**WHISTLEBLOWERS**
Dodd-Frank act protections, §4-2(d)(5)
Fraud, §1-9

## Z

**ZONE PROGRAM INTEGRITY CONTRACTORS (ZPICs)**
Enforcement, §1-3(f)(2)

# Legal Issues in Healthcare Fraud and Abuse: *Navigating the Uncertainties*

## 2015 Cumulative Supplement to the Fourth Edition

David E. Matyas

Carrie Valiant

Jason Eric Christ

Anjali N.C. Downs

American Health Lawyers Association

Copyright 2015, 2014, 2013, 2012, 2009, 2008, 2007, 2006, 1997, 1994 by
**AMERICAN HEALTH LAWYERS ASSOCIATION**
1620 Eye Street, NW, 6th Floor
Washington, DC 20006-4010
Web site: www.healthlawyers.org
E-Mail: info@healthlawyers.org

All rights reserved.
No part of this publication may be reproduced, stored in a retrieval system, or transmitted, in any form, or by any means, electronic, mechanical, photocopying, recording, or otherwise, without the express, written permission of the publisher.

Printed in the United States of America
ISBN: 978-0-7698-5464-9 (Non-members)
978-0-7698-5463-2 (Members)

*"This publication is designed to provide accurate and authoritative information with respect to the subject matter covered. It is provided with the understanding that the publisher is not engaged in rendering legal or other professional services. If legal advice or other expert assistance is required, the services of a competent professional person should be sought."*

—from a declaration of the American Bar Association

# About the American Health Lawyers Association

Leading health law to excellence through education, information, and dialogue, the American Health Lawyers Association (Health Lawyers) is the nation's largest nonpartisan 501(c)(3) educational organization devoted to legal issues in the healthcare field. Health Lawyers provides resources to address the issues facing its active members who practice in law firms, government, in-house settings, and academia and who represent the entire spectrum of the health industry: physicians; hospitals and health systems; health maintenance organizations; health insurers; managed care companies; nursing facilities; home care providers; and consumers.

RECENT TITLES FROM AHLA

**Data Breach Notification Laws: A 50 State Survey, Second Edition**
© 2015, perfect bound

**Ancillary Providers in Health Care: A Primer, First Edition**
© 2015, perfect bound

**Health Plan Disputes and Litigation Practice Guide, First Edition**
© 2015, perfect bound

**AHLA's Guide to Healthcare Legal Forms, Agreements, and Policies, Second Edition with 2015 Cumulative Supplement**
© 2015, looseleaf

**The ACO Handbook: A Guide to Accountable Care Organizations, First Edition**
© 2015, perfect bound

**Post-Acute Care Handbook: Regulatory, Risk and Compliance Issues, First Edition**
© 2014, perfect bound

**The Stark Law: Comprehensive Analysis + Practical Guide, Fifth Edition**
© 2014, perfect bound

**Health Care Compliance Legal Issues Manual, 4th Edition**
© 2014, perfect bound

**Corporate Practice of Medicine: A Fifty State Survey**
© 2014, perfect bound

**The Fundamentals of Health Law, Sixth Edition with 2015 Medicaid supplement**
© 2014, perfect bound

**False Claims Act & The Healthcare Industry: Counseling & Litigation, Second Edition with 2014 Cumulative Supplement**
© 2014, hardbound

**The Fundamentals of Life Sciences Law: Drugs, Devices, and Biotech, Second Edition**
© 2014, perfect bound

**HIPAA/HITECH Resource Guide, First Edition**
© 2014, perfect bound

**Fraud & Abuse Investigations Handbook for the Health Care Industry, First Edition**
© 2014, perfect bound

# About the Authors

**David E. Matyas** is a Member of the Firm in the Health Care and Life Sciences practice, in Epstein Becker Green's Washington, D.C., office, where he also serves on the firm's Board of Directors and as the Managing Shareholder for the office. Mr. Matyas represents and defends healthcare entities in connection with government audits and investigations; helps clients develop, implement, and evaluate healthcare corporate compliance programs; counsels clients in planning and structuring transactions and business arrangements to minimize fraud and abuse and understand reimbursement implications in matters related to healthcare transactions; and advises clients on legal and regulatory matters in connection with investment documents, offering memoranda, filings with the SEC, and other transactional documents. Mr. Matyas represents an array of healthcare providers, including hospitals and health systems, pharmaceutical and medical device manufacturers, academic medical centers, retail and specialty pharmacies, ambulatory surgery centers, home health agencies, and physician organizations. He also advises investors and other financial institutions that invest in or support the healthcare industry. From 2005 to 2008, by appointment of the Secretary of the Department of Health and Human Services, Mr. Matyas served on the Advisory Committee on Blood Safety & Availability, which provides advice on broad public health, ethical, and legal issues related to the nation's supply of blood and blood products. From 2002 to 2008, Mr. Matyas served as a member of the Board of Directors for the American Health Lawyers Association. In 2005 and in 2010, he was selected by the editors of *Nightingale's Healthcare News* as one of the "Outstanding Fraud & Compliance Lawyers." Mr. Matyas is also listed in the District of Columbia Healthcare category of *Chambers USA* (2007 to 2015), included in *The Best Lawyers in America©* (2011 to 2016) in the field of Health Care Law, and named to the *Washington D.C. Super Lawyers* list (2007 to 2015) in the area of Health Care.

**Carrie Valiant** is a Member of the Firm in the Health Care and Life Sciences practice, in Epstein Becker Green's Washington, D.C., office, where she serves on the firm's Board of Directors and co-chairs the firm's Healthcare Fraud Group. Ms. Valiant has more than 30 years of experience concentrating in healthcare fraud and abuse and government healthcare program payment matters. She defends clients undergoing civil and criminal investigation for healthcare fraud by the Department of Justice, the Department of Health and Human Services' Office of the Inspector General (OIG), and other state and federal governmental authorities, and negotiates corporate integrity agreements. Ms. Valiant also represents all segments of the healthcare industry in managing government healthcare program compliance risks, including the design and implementation of corporate compliance programs, preparation of OIG advisory opinion requests, and handling of internal investigations and voluntary self-disclosures. She advises clients on a variety of government healthcare program payment and certification matters, including substantial overpayment assessments, EMTALA complaints, privacy and security breaches, and the preparation and negotiation of corrective action plans. Ms. Valiant writes and lectures extensively on health law fraud topics. She has been included on *Nightingale's Healthcare News'* 2004 and 2009 lists of "Outstanding Healthcare Fraud & Compliance Lawyers," selected to *The Best Lawyers in America* (2006 to 2016) in the field of Health Care Law, and ranked by *Chambers USA* as one of America's leading Healthcare lawyers (2007 to 2015). Ms. Valiant is also Founder and President of the Health Care Industry Access Initiative, a nonprofit organization

# *About the Authors*

dedicated to promoting collaborative action across the healthcare industry to improve access to healthcare coverage and services.

**Jason Eric Christ** is a Member of the Firm in the Health Care and Life Sciences practice, in Epstein Becker Green's Washington, D.C., office. His practice focuses on representing clients in the healthcare industry in regulatory matters, with an emphasis on state and federal investigations and litigation pertaining to healthcare fraud and abuse laws. On behalf of his clients, Mr. Christ responds to audits, subpoenas, Civil Investigative Demands, and letter requests from fraud enforcement entities, including government and government contractors, and shepherds all phases of such investigations through final resolution. He also assists clients with voluntary disclosures and communications to government entities. Additionally, Mr. Christ provides health regulatory counseling to a variety of entities, including managed care providers, third-party payors, risk adjustment coding entities, hospitals, urgent care centers, hospices, physician groups, pharmacies, manufacturers, suppliers, insurers, skilled nursing facilities, and medical professional staffing organizations. Mr. Christ received his law degree, with honors, from the Francis King Carey School of Law at the University of Maryland. While in law school, he earned University of Maryland's concentration in healthcare law and served as managing editor of the *Journal of Health Care Law & Policy*. For his undergraduate degree, he attended the Pennsylvania State University and the American University in Cairo and received his B.A. with distinction. Mr. Christ writes, speaks, and publishes on matters involving the healthcare fraud and abuse laws and electronic discovery and currently serves is a member of the adjunct faculty at the American University Washington College of Law's Health Law and Policy Institute. He is admitted to practice in the District of Columbia, Maryland, and the U.S. District Court for the District of Columbia.

**Anjali N.C. Downs** is an Associate in the Health Care and Life Sciences practice, in Epstein Becker Green's Washington, D.C., office. She practices in the firm's Healthcare Fraud Group, which focuses on federal and state fraud issues, including anti-kickback, self-referral, false claims, secondary payor issues, and false billings. Ms. Downs represents a variety of healthcare and life science organizations, including health systems, pharmaceutical and medical device manufacturers, pharmacies, clinical laboratories, academic medical centers, physician group practices, dialysis providers, and medical transportation providers. Ms. Downs' experiences include conducting internal health regulatory investigations; assisting clients in preparing self-disclosures; representing and defending healthcare entities undergoing government investigations, inquiries, and audits; assisting clients in developing, implementing, and evaluating corporate compliance programs; and advising clients on physician contracting arrangements and a variety of healthcare joint ventures. Ms. Downs received her law degree, cum laude, from the Francis King Carey School of Law at the University of Maryland and her Masters of Public Health in Community Health Education and undergraduate degree in Psychology from the University of Maryland. While attending law school, Ms. Downs served as an Articles Editor for the *Journal of Health Care Law & Policy*. She is admitted to practice law in Maryland and the District of Columbia. Prior to law school, Ms. Downs was a member of the adjunct faculties of Georgetown University School of Nursing and Health Studies and Howard Community College in Columbia, Maryland.

# Table of Contents

About the American Health Lawyers Association
About the Authors

| Chapter 1 | The Fraud Enforcers: Who Are They and What Do They Do? |
|---|---|
| § 1-1 | Overview |
| § 1-2 | Department of Justice |
| § 1-2(b) | Criminal Division |
| § 1-3 | Department of Health and Human Services |
| § 1-3(b) | Centers for Medicare & Medicaid Services |
| § 1-3(f) | Program Integrity Contractors |
| § 1-3(f)(1) | Recovery Audit Contractors |
| § 1-9 | Private Citizens |

| Chapter 2 | **Federal Anti-Kickback Laws** |
|---|---|
| § 2-3 | Safe Harbor Regulations |
| § 2-3(a) | History of the Various Safe Harbor Issuances |
| § 2-3(n) | Electronic Health Records and Community-Wide Information Systems |
| § 2-3(o) | Accountable Care Organizations and OIGs Waiver Authority |
| § 2-3(p) | 2014 Proposed Safe Harbors |
| § 2-4 | Fraud Alerts and Special Advisory Bulletins |
| § 2-4(b) | Routine Waivers of Coinsurance and Deductibles |
| § 2-4(k) | Patient Assistance Programs for Medicare Part D Enrollees |
| § 2-4(l) | Physician-Owned Entities/Distributorships (PODs) |
| § 2-4(m) | Laboratory Payments to Referring Physicians |
| § 2-4(n) | Physician Compensation Arrangements May Result in Significant Liability |
| § 2-5 | Additional Guidance and Advisory Opinions |
| § 2-5(c) | Applicability of the Anti-Kickback Statute to Qualified Health Plans (QHPs) |
| § 2-6 | Case Law |
| § 2-6(c) | Significant Post-Hanlester Cases |
| § 2-6(c)(1) | The Anti-Kickback Statute's Intent Requirement |

# Table of Contents

| | | |
|---|---|---|
| § 2-7 | | Other Anti-Kickback Authority |
| § 2-7(a) | | Inducements to Beneficiaries |
| § 2-7(a)(3) | | 2010 Modification to the CMP Provision |
| § 2-7(d) | | Federal "Sunshine Law" |

| | | |
|---|---|---|
| **Chapter 3** | | **Federal Physician Self-Referral Prohibitions** |
| § 3-3 | | The Statutory Prohibition and Definitions of Key Terms |
| § 3-3(b) | | Definitions of Key Terms |
| § 3-3(b)(1) | | Referral |
| § 3-3(b)(5) | | Fair Market Value |
| § 3-3(b)(8) | | Entity |
| § 3-3(c) | | Special Rules on Compensation |
| § 3-3(c)(1) | | Compensation Methodologies |
| § 3-4 | | Stark Law Exceptions |
| § 3-4(c) | | Compensation Arrangement Exceptions |
| § 3-4(c)(2) | | Bona Fide Employment Relationships |
| § 3-4(c)(19) | | Electronic Prescribing and Electronic Health Records |
| § 3-5 | | Definition of Group Practice |
| § 3-5(d) | | Services Furnished by Group Practice Members |
| § 3-8 | | Self-Referral Disclosure Protocol |
| § 3-10 | | Major Issues in Stark Law Interpretation |
| § 3-10(f) | | Applying Stark to Medicaid |

| | | |
|---|---|---|
| **Chapter 4** | | **False Claims: Civil and Criminal Enforcement** |
| § 4-2 | | The Federal Civil False Claims Act |
| § 4-2(a) | | Key FCA Considerations for Healthcare Entities |
| § 4-2(a)(4) | | What Is "Causing" a Claim to Be Submitted? |
| § 4-2(a)(5) | | What Is "False" or "Fraudulent"? |
| § 4-2(a)(5)(i) | | Retention of Overpayments and Reverse False Claims |
| § 4-2(a)(5)(ii) | | Use of Statistical Sampling to Establish False Claims Act Liability |
| § 4-2(a)(6) | | What Is "Material"? |
| § 4-2(b) | | Anti-Kickback Violations as False Claims |
| § 4-2(c) | | FCA Damages |
| § 4-2(d) | | Qui tam Relators |
| § 4-2(d)(1) | | How Is a Qui tam Action Initiated? |

# Table of Contents

| | |
|---|---|
| § 4-4 | Criminal Laws Pertaining to False Claims and Fraudulent Billing Activities |
| § 4-4(c) | RICO Violations |
| § 4-5 | False Claims Theories Applicable to Multiple Segments of the Healthcare Industry |
| § 4-5(b) | Providing Medically Unnecessary Services |
| § 4-5(e) | Filing False Cost Reports |
| § 4-5(f) | Quality of Care |
| § 4-6 | False Claims Enforcement Activities Specific to Particular Segments of the Healthcare Industry |
| § 4-6(a) | Hospitals |
| § 4-6(a)(3) | Outlier Payments |
| § 4-6(a)(4) | Inpatient Admissions, Site of Service and One Days Stays |
| § 4-6(a)(5) | Billing for Provider-Based Services |
| § 4-6(e) | Durable Medical Equipment and Home Medical Suppliers |
| § 4-6(f) | Home Health Agencies |
| § 4-6(g) | Medicare Contractors |
| § 4-6(h) | Pharmacies and Pharmaceutical Manufacturers |
| § 4-6(k) | Dentists |
| § 4-6(l) | Ambulance Companies |
| § 4-6(m) | Medical Device Companies |

| | |
|---|---|
| **Chapter 5** | **Administrative Sanctions Available to Federal Enforcers** |
| § 5-2 | Exclusion from Medicare, Medicaid, and Other State Healthcare Programs |
| § 5-2(b) | Permissive Exclusion |
| § 5-2(e) | Effects of Exclusion |
| § 5-3 | Imposition Of Civil Monetary Penalties |
| § 5-2(a) | Actions that May Result in the Imposition of CMPs |
| § 5-2(a)(1) | Submission of Improperly Filed Claims |
| § 5-2(a)(3) | Inducements to Beneficiaries |
| § 5-2(a)(4) | Payments to Induce Reduction or Limitation of Services (Gainsharing) and Other Cost Sharing Initiatives |
| § 5-2(a)(5) | Other Bases for CMPs |
| § 5-2(c) | Amount of CMPs |

## Table of Contents

| | | |
|---|---|---|
| **Chapter 6** | | **State and Private Initiatives to Combat Fraud** |
| § 6-7 | | State False Claims Activities |
| | § 6-7(a) | State Law Governing Fraudulent Billing Practices |
| § 6-9 | | State Initiatives to Prevent and Detect Fraud |
| | § 6-9(a) | Medicaid Fraud Control Units |
| **Chapter 7** | | **Compliance and Self-Reporting** |
| § 7-5 | | Compliance Related Resources |
| | § 7-5(e) | OIG/Health Lawyers Resources |
| § 7-9 | | Self-Reporting and Voluntary Disclosure |
| | § 7-9(a) | OIG Voluntary Self-Disclosure Protocol |
| **Chapter 8** | | **Fraud and Abuse Issues Affecting the Managed Care Industry** |
| § 8-4 | | Intermediate Sanctions Applicable To Mcos |
| § 8-8 | | Examples of Potential Fraud Liability in the Managed Care Industry |
| | § 8-8(a) | Capitation Misclassification |
| | § 8-8(m) | Health Care Exchanges |
| **Chapter 9** | | **Representing Healthcare Organizations in Fraud and Abuse Matters** |
| § 9-4 | | Relationship Between Criminal and Civil Matters |
| | § 9-4(d) | Criminal Settlement—The Use of Deferred Prosecution and Non-Prosecution Agreements |

# 1

# The Fraud Enforcers: Who Are They and What Do They Do?

## § 1-1 OVERVIEW

Healthcare fraud enforcement actions undertaken by various government agencies continue to result in significant recoveries. In Fiscal Year 2014, such actions resulted in recoveries of approximately $3.3 billion. The Department of Justice initiated 924 criminal and 782 civil investigations in Fiscal Year 2014. HHS-OIG enforcement activities also resulted in 867 criminal actions and 529 civil actions in Fiscal Year 2014. Significantly, HHS-OIG also excluded 4,017 individuals and entities from participating in federal health care programs, the so-called "health care death penalty."[1.1]

In total, the federal government has recovered a staggering $27.8 billion to the Medicare Trust Fund since 1997.

[1.1] Department of Health and Human Services and The Department of Justice Health Care Fraud and Abuse Control Program Annual Report for Fiscal Year 2014, *available at* http://oig.hhs.gov/reports-and-publications/hcfac/index.asp.

## § 1-2 DEPARTMENT OF JUSTICE

### § 1-2(b) Criminal Division

Since its inception in 2007, the Medicare Fraud Strike Force has successfully coordinated criminal enforcement efforts among the Criminal Division of the Department of Justice, the Federal Bureau of Investigation and the HHS Office of Inspector General. The Medicare Fraud Strike Force announced its 6th national Medicare fraud takedown since its inception. The latest national sweep resulted in charges against 89 individuals amounting to an alleged $223 million in false billings.[10.1] All told, the Medicare Fraud Strike Force has been responsible for charging almost 1,700 individuals in connection with health care fraud schemes who collectively have allegedly falsely billed Medicare more than $5.5 billion.[10.2] The Medicare Fraud Strike Force currently operates in nine locations Los Angeles, Detroit, Houston, Brooklyn, Baton Rouge, Dallas, Tampa, Miami and Chicago.[10.3]

[10.1] Department of Justice Press Release, Medicare Fraud Strike Force Charges 89 Individuals for Approximately $223 Million in False Billing, May 14, 2013.

[10.2] Department of Justice Press Release, Medicare Fraud Strike Force Set Record Numbers for Health Care Fraud Prosecutions, January 27, 2014.

**§ 1-3** *Legal Issues in Healthcare Fraud and Abuse*

10.3 *See* http://www.stopmedicarefraud.gov/aboutfraud/heattaskforce/.

## § 1-3 DEPARTMENT OF HEALTH AND HUMAN SERVICES

### § 1-3(b) Centers for Medicare & Medicaid Services

Fraud enforcement has increasingly looked to technology as a tool to combat improper payments. The Centers for Medicare & Medicaid Services (CMS) adopted a technology-based fraud prevention system (FPS) for flagging and stopping potentially fraudulent claims. The FPS system is a state of the art program mandated by Small Business Jobs Act of 2012 that uses predictive model technology and data analytics to filter potentially problematic claims. Since June 30, 2011, the FPS has run predictive algorithms and other sophisticated analytics nationwide against all Medicare fee for service (FFS) claims prior to payment.[15.1] The FPS model is chiefly designed to identify suspect or unusual claim activity and prevent improper payments. According to a CMS report to Congress, in its first year of operation the FPS prevented or identified $115 million in improper payments and generated leads for 536 new fraud investigations and provided additional information for 511 existing investigations.[15.2] Both the FPS program and the RAC program are part of a trend to use data driven fraud identification tools rather than traditional sources to identify improper payments.

CMS has also recently used its power to suspend enrollment of certain providers in high risk geographic locations to prevent fraud. In July 2013, CMS used a temporary moratorium to prevent the issuance of new provider numbers to home health providers in Chicago and Miami. CMS also issued a moratorium on enrollment of ground ambulance providers in Houston. These areas were previously deemed "hot spot" areas for fraud, particularly with regard to there being a disproportionate number of providers and suppliers relative to beneficiaries and extremely high utilization.[15.3] In January 2014, CMS added additional moratoriums for home health enrollment in Fort Lauderdale, Detroit, Dallas and Houston. It also issued a moratorium on ground ambulances in the greater Philadelphia area.[15.4] These moratoriums are probably effective at combating shell providers and suppliers run by fly-by-night fraudsters who enroll, generate fake claims, and then disappear. Unfortunately, these moratoriums also affect legitimate providers by creating barriers to entry. They also can prevent the sale of a home health company or an ambulance company since, depending on the type of transaction, the new controlling entity may need to re-enroll.

In 2013, CMS through its Center for Program Integrity (CPI) issued a request for information (RIF) regarding the creation of a Unified Program Integrity Contractor (UPIC). According to CPI, UPICs will unify program integrity across the Medicare and Medicaid program integrity continuum. The RIF for UPICs states that UPICs will integrate the program integrity functions for audits and investigations and ensure that CPI's national priorities for both Medicare and Medicaid are executed and supported locally. CPI anticipates that UPICs will take on the functions that are currently performed by Zone Program Integrity Contractors (ZPICs), Program Safeguard Contractors (PSCs), and the Medicaid Integrity Contractors (MICs). CPI also noted that UPICs may, in the future, assume the role of Medicare Drug Integrity Contractors (MEDICs) as well as Medicare Part C program integrity tasks. But, for the time being, UPICs will address only Parts A and B.[15.5]

[15.1] *See* Centers for Medicare and Medicaid Services, Report to Congress, Fraud Prevention System 2012 *available at* http://www.stopmedicarefraud.gov/fraud-rtc12142012.pdf.

[15.2] *Id.*

[15.3] Centers for Medicare & Medicaid Services, *Second Wave of CMS' Enrollment Moratoria Extended for Home Health and Ground Ambulance Suppliers; Four New Geographic Areas Added* Jan 30, 2014.

[15.4] *Id.*

[15.5] *See* UPIC RIF and Solicitation Notice *available at* https://www.fbo.gov/?id=6ffab1d71e97d03c75e398c971bc0017.

## § 1-3(f)  Program Integrity Contractors

### § 1-3(f)(1)  Recovery Audit Contractors

RACs are unquestionably becoming a major force in healthcare oversight. RACs also have their fair share of controversy, chiefly arising from detractors in the health care industry. In response to growing negative sentiment from Medicare Suppliers and Providers subject to RAC audits, CMS issued a document in late 2012 designed to dispel a litany of so-called "myths." CMS discussed the belief that RACs deny all claims; that RACs have a 30-50% contingency fee; that RACs are not bound by CMS regulatory authority; that RACs do not use physicians for review and a number of other so-called myths.[32.1] The American Hospital Association in particular has been an outspoken critic of the RAC program and issued publications characterizing RACs as "a drain on hospitals" and stated "RACs are often inaccurate and inflict avoidable legal and administrative costs on hospitals."[32.2] RAC appeals have also created an unprecedented backlog in ALJ proceedings. Citing the 357,000 cases in backlogging ALJs, HHS announced that it would not accept appeals from providers for RAC decisions for up to two years.[32.3] This decision was heavily criticized since it closes the avenue through which providers can seek redress. In response,

§ 1-9                    *Legal Issues in Healthcare Fraud and Abuse*

111 members of Congress signed a letter to Secretary Sebelius which states that the backlog is caused, at least in part, by the fact that "RACs are incentivized to deny claims, even when they are correct." The letter urges HHS to reform its ALJ process and reform the manner in which RACs operate and are compensated.[32.4]

[32.1] CMS, *Medicare Fee-For-Service Recovery Audit Program Myths* (Dec. 17, 2012).

[32.2] *See e.g.*, "The RAC Burden" and other AHA materials found at http://www.aha.org/advocacy-issues/rac/index.shtml.

[32.3] 79 Fed Reg 393 (Jan. 3, 2014).

[32.4] *See* February 10, 2014, Letter from Congress of the United States to Katherine Sebelius.

## § 1-9 PRIVATE CITIZENS

In April 2013, HHS Secretary Kathleen Sebelius announced a proposed rule that would increase rewards for successful tips that lead to recovery of Medicare funds. Specifically, under the proposed rules individuals can receive 15% of the total recovery, with a maximum cap of $9.9 million.[57] This represents a gargantuan increase from the current limit, which is capped at 10%, for a maximum recovery of $1000. HHS notes that the changes are modeled after an IRDS program that has successfully returned $2 billion in fraud since 2003.[58]

[57] *See* CMS Press Release, HHA Would Increase Rewards for Reporting Fraud to Nearly $10 Million *available at* http://www.cms.gov/apps/media/press/release.asp?Counter=4583&intNumPerPage=10&checkDate=&checkKey=&srchType=1&numDays=3500&srchOpt=0&srchData=&keywordType=All&chkNewsType=1%2C+2%2C+3%2C+4%2C+5&intPage=&showAll=&pYear=&year=&desc=&cboOrder=date.

[58] *Id.*

# 2

# Federal Anti-Kickback Laws

## § 2-3 SAFE HARBOR REGULATIONS

### § 2-3(a) History of the Various Safe Harbor Issuances

- October 3, 2014—The OIG proposed several new safe harbor regulations, which addressed Part D cost-sharing waivers by pharmacies, cost-sharing waivers for emergency ambulance services, FQHCs and Medicare Advantage organizations, the Medicare gap discount program, and free or discounted local transportation services.⁵⁷·¹

⁵⁷·¹ 79 Fed. Reg. 59,717 (Oct. 3, 2014).

### § 2-3(n) Electronic Health Records and Community-Wide Information Systems

On April 10, 2013, the OIG issued a proposed rule to amend the safe harbor concerning electronic health records items and services. The proposed amendments include an update to the provision under which electronic health records software is deemed interoperable, removal of the electronic prescribing capability requirement and extension of the sunset provision from December 31, 2013 to either December 31, 2016 (which corresponds to the last year for EHR Medicare incentive payments) or December 31, 2021 (which corresponds to the last year for EHR Medicaid incentive payments). In addition, the OIG requested comments on a number of additional issues as to whether the safe harbor should be revised to: (1) cover only the categories of donors originally included in the statute (hospitals, group practices, PDP sponsors and MA organizations); (2) ensure that the safe harbor is not misused to lock-in referrals and that it actually encourages the free exchange of data; and (3) clarify the types of items and services that can be donated as part of the safe harbor.¹⁷²·¹

On December 27, 2013, the OIG issued final regulations to amend the safe harbor concerning electronic health records items and services ("EHR Final Rule"). Under the EHR Final Rule, the OIG adopted its proposed amendments¹⁷²·² to include an update to the provision under which electronic health records software is deemed interoperable, removal of the electronic prescribing capability requirement and extension of the sunset provision from December 31, 2013 to December 31, 2021 (which corresponds to the last year for EHR Medicaid incentive payments). In addition, the EHR Final Rule specifically excludes laboratory companies from the list of eligible "Protected Donors." The OIG clarified that if a hospital furnishes laboratory services through a laboratory that is a department of the hospital for Medicare purposes and bills for the services through the hospital's provider number, then the hospital would not be considered a "laboratory company." Conversely, if a hospital-affiliated or hospital-owned company with its own supplier number furnishes laboratory services that are billed using a company billing number, as opposed to the hospital's billing number, the company is considered a "laboratory company" and is no longer considered a "Protected Donor." Additionally, to promote the free exchange of information, the EHR Final Rule includes limited clarifications to require that no action be taken to limit or restrict the use, compatibility or interoperability of items or services with other electronic prescribing or EHR systems.¹⁷²·³

§ 2-3    *Legal Issues in Healthcare Fraud and Abuse*

**172.1** 78 Fed. Reg. 21314 (Apr. 10, 2013).

**172.2** 78 Fed. Reg. 21314 (Apr. 10, 2013).

**172.3** 78 Fed. Reg. 79,202 (Dec. 27, 2013).

### § 2-3(o)    Accountable Care Organizations and OIGs Waiver Authority

On October 17, 2014, CMS announced the continuation of the effectiveness of the interim final rule and the extension of the timeline for publication of a Final Rule. The timeline for publishing the Final Rule was extended by one year.[176.1]

On February 12, 2015, CMS and the OIG issued a document setting forth additional guidance related to certain conditions of waivers (Additional Guidance Document).[176.2] Specifically, the document provided guidance concerning three areas: (1) public disclosures required under the ACO Pre-Participation and ACO Participation Waivers, (2) notification of failure to submit a timely application by parties who used the ACO Pre-Participation Waiver, and (3) requests for an extension of the ACO Pre-Participation Waiver period.

**176.1** 79 Fed. Reg. 62,356 (Oct. 17, 2014).

**176.2** Department of Health and Human Services, Centers for Medicare & Medicaid Services and the Office of the Inspector General, Medicare Shared Savings Program Waivers: Additional Guidance (Feb 12, 2015), *available at* http.//www.cms.gov/Medicare/Medicare-Fee-for-Service-Payment/sharedsavingsprogram/Downloads/Additional-MSSP-Waiver-Guidance.pdf.

### § 2-3(p)    2014 Proposed Safe Harbors

On October 3, 2014, the OIG published a proposed rule (Proposed Rule) to add new safe harbors to the federal health care program Anti-Kickback Statute (AKS) as well as new exceptions to the civil monetary penalty (CMP) provisions for inducements being offered to federal health care program beneficiaries and to the CMP related to a hospital paying a physician for reducing or limiting the provision of items or services (referred to generally as the "Gainsharing CMP").[176.3]

This proposed rule is the first time in seven years that the OIG has issued either significant changes to or proposed new safe harbors under the Anti-Kickback Statute. It has been nearly 20 years since the OIG first tried to promulgate regulations addressing the Gainsharing CMP. The Proposed Rule is significant because it wrestles with the ever-changing health care industry. To that end, the Proposed Rule sets forth a number of provisions that codify into the regulations certain exceptions and modifications to the laws that Congress has adopted over the last decade. In addition, the Proposed Rule attempts to address the changes in how health care is being paid for and how to align the financial incentives among healthcare providers. The Proposed Rule further attempts to assist patients in being able to access health care in situations in which these laws have arguably impeded health care providers and suppliers from offering services free of charge or at reduced amounts.

## *Part D Cost-Sharing Waivers by Pharmacies*

When Congress adopted the MMA and the Part D program, Congress amended the Anti-Kickback Statute to permit pharmacies to waive or reduce cost-sharing under Part D for financially needy Medicare beneficiaries, as long as certain criteria are met. In the proposed regulation, OIG has set out a new safe harbor that tracks the statutory exception and states the criteria that must be met:

1. The waiver or reduction is not advertised or part of a solicitation;
2. The pharmacy does not routinely waive the cost-sharing; and
3. Before waiving the cost sharing, the pharmacy either determines that the beneficiary has a financial need or fails to collect the cost-sharing amount after making a reasonable effort.

If, however, the waiver is made on behalf of a "subsidy eligible" meaning a "Medicare Low-Income Subsidy" eligible individual (which is defined as a Part D enrollee who has income below 150 percent of the poverty line and meets certain other statutory requirements set out in 42 U.S.C. 1395w-114), then only the first condition must be met.

The word "routinely" in the second criteria remains ambiguous and may prevent a pharmacy from establishing a protocol for waiving the cost-sharing amount. Moreover, additional clarity is necessary to aid pharmacies in determining "financial need" and also in determining when a "reasonable effort" has been made to collect the cost-sharing amount.

## *Cost-Sharing Waivers for Emergency Ambulance Services*

Over the years, the OIG has issued numerous Advisory Opinions on the issue of the reduction or waiver of coinsurance or deductible amounts owed for emergency ambulance services. Because the Advisory Opinions are only binding on the parties that have requested them, and the OIG continues to receive similar Advisory Opinion requests, the OIG proposes to establish a new safe harbor for cost-sharing waivers as long as the following conditions are met:

1. The ambulance provider or supplier must be owned and operated by a state, a political subdivision of a state, or a federally recognized Indian tribe;

2. The ambulance provider or supplier is the Medicare Part B provider or supplier of the ambulance services;
3. The reduction or waiver of coinsurance or deductible amounts is not considered to be the furnishing of free services paid for directly or indirectly by a government entity;
4. The reduction or waiver is offered on a uniform basis, without regard to patient-specific factors; and
5. The ambulance provider or supplier must not later claim the amount reduced or waived as a bad debt.

The proposed new safe harbor is limited to only those circumstances in which the ambulance provider or supplier is owned and operated by a governmental entity. The safe harbor does not address either for-profit or nonprofit (but not government operated) ambulance providers offering such waivers, even if the other above-referenced conditions were satisfied, and even if they are operated pursuant to a federal, state, or municipal contract.

In addition, the OIG states in the preamble that it intends only to address in the safe harbor "emergency ambulance services" and would not include non-emergency transport services. As such, the OIG solicited public comment on whether the terms "emergency ambulance services" and "ambulance provider or supplier" needed to be expressly defined in the safe harbor, as well as public comment on the applicability of the waiver to Medicare or other federal health care programs.

## *FQHCs and Medicare Advantage Organizations*

As part of the MMA, Congress addressed the ability of a Medicare Advantage enrollee being able to obtain services from a Federal Qualified Health Center (FQHC) and that the Medicare Advantage organization must pay the FQHC no less than the level and amount of payment that the Medicare Advantage plan would pay to another type of entity furnishing such services. The OIG has simply mirrored the statutory exception by proposing a safe harbor that would protect any remuneration between a FQHC and a Medicare Advantage organization pursuant to a written agreement that meets certain requirements in the Social Security Act.

## *Medicare Coverage Gap Discount Program*

The Medicare Coverage Gap Discount Program, established by Health Reform, allows prescription drug manufacturers to enter into an agreement with the Secretary of Health and Human Services to provide discounts at point of sale to certain beneficiaries. Health Reform included an exception to the Anti-Kickback Statute to protect these discounts in the price of an "applicable drug" being furnished to an "applicable beneficiary."

The Proposed Rule codifies not only this exception but also the definitions included in the statute of the terms "applicable beneficiary" and "applicable drug" under the program. Specifically, "applicable beneficiary" is defined as:

an individual who, on the date of dispensing a covered Part D drug—

A. is enrolled in a prescription drug plan or [a Medicare Advantage Prescription Drug (MA-PD)] plan;

B. is not enrolled in a qualified retiree prescription drug plan;

C. is not entitled to an income-related subsidy under section 1860D-14(a); and

D. who—(i) has reached or exceeded the initial coverage limit under section 1860D-2(b)(3) during the year; and (ii) has not incurred costs for covered Part D drugs in the year equal to the annual out-of-pocket threshold specified in section 1860D-2(b)(4)(B).

"Applicable drug" is defined as follows:

with respect to an applicable beneficiary, a covered Part D drug—

A. approved under a new drug application under section 505(b) of the Federal Food, Drug, and Cosmetic Act or, in the case of a biologic product, licensed under section 351 of the Public Health Service Act (other than a product licensed under subsection (k) of such section 351); and

B. (i) if the sponsor of the prescription drug plan or the MA organization offering the MA-PD plan uses a formulary, which is on the formulary of the prescription drug plan or MA-PD plan that the applicable beneficiary is enrolled in; (ii) if the [prescription drug plan (PDP)] sponsor of the prescription drug plan or the MA organization offering the MA-PD plan does not use a formulary, for which benefits are available under the prescription drug plan or MA-PD plan that the applicable beneficiary is enrolled in; or (iii) is provided through an exception or appeal.

## *Local Transportation*

The OIG proposed a new safe harbor to protect free or discounted local transportation services (collectively, transportation services) provided to federal health care program beneficiaries who are *established patients* (and, if needed, a person to assist the patient) to obtain medically necessary items or services. The OIG suggested that *established patients* are patients whom the provider offering the free or discounted transportation has previously serviced. However, to prevent impermissible arrangements, the OIG has imposed a number of requirements on the transportation services.

First, the transportation services, whether free or discounted, must be available only to established patients and be determined in a manner unrelated to the past or anticipated volume or value of federal health care program business. Within this condition, the OIG proposed a number of safeguards and limitations, including, but not limited to:

1. Limiting the transportation services to only be offered by an "Eligible Entity," which would exclude individuals and/or entities acting on their behalf that primarily supply health care items (including, but not limited to, durable medical equipment (DME) suppliers or pharmaceutical companies).

2. Limiting whether certain types of health care providers or suppliers of services should not receive protection when they provide transportation services to other health care providers or suppliers that refer to them; specifically, transportation services provided by home health care providers to physician offices that are actual or potential referral sources. The OIG is proposing that the safe harbor would not protect transportation services that an Eligible Entity makes available only to patients who were referred by a particular health care provider or supplier. Similarly, the OIG is proposing that the safe harbor would not protect transportation services that are contingent on a patient seeing a particular provider or supplier that may be a referral source for the Eligible Entity.

Second, the transportation safe harbor restricts the form of transportation to exclude air, luxury (*e.g.*, limousine), and ambulance-level transportation.

Third, the OIG proposed to exclude the following from safe harbor protection: (1) transportation services that are publicly advertised or marketed to patients or to potential referral sources; (2) Eligible Entities paying drivers or others involved in arranging the transportation on a per-beneficiary transported basis; and (3) the marketing of health care items and services during the course of the transportation.

Fourth, the OIG proposed limiting the safe harbor to only local transportation (anything within 25 miles). The OIG solicited comments on determining what "local" means, the approach and method to determine the service area, whether to permit free or discounted local transportation to the nearest facility capable of providing medically necessary items and services, and whether the Stark Law's prohibition related to compensation arrangements regarding "geographic area served by the hospital" would be useful.

Finally, the OIG proposed requiring the Eligible Entity to bear the cost of the transportation services and not shift the burden of the costs onto Medicare, a state health care program, other payers, or individuals.

[176.3] 79 Fed. Reg. 59,717 (Oct. 3, 2014).

## § 2-4 FRAUD ALERTS AND SPECIAL ADVISORY BULLETINS

### § 2-4(b) Routine Waivers of Coinsurance and Deductibles

In September 2014, the OIG released a study showing that safeguards implemented to prevent Medicare Part D beneficiaries from using pharmaceutical manufacturers' co-pay coupons may not be effective.[195.1] The study analyzed co-pay coupons from 30 pharmaceutical companies, as well as the disclaimers included with the coupons and the claims edits used to identify and disallow Part D enrollees. The study found that the safeguards have limited effectiveness because: (1) a patient may still present a coupon despite the disclaimers and warnings, and (2) although claims edits can prevent discounts from being applied, many manufacturers use inaccurate information to identify Part D beneficiaries. With regard to the claim edits, the OIG found that most manufacturers use payer bank identification numbers (BINs) or the patient's date of birth (*i.e.*, the patient's age) to determine whether the patient is a Part D enrollee. According to the OIG, both of these points of data can be unreliable because the BIN information may be outdated or inaccurate and a patient's birthday may not correctly predict Part D coverage.

Simultaneously with the issuance of the study, the OIG also issued a Special Advisory Bulletin regarding Pharmaceutical Manufacturer Copayment Coupons, that addresses the application of the Anti-Kickback Statute when pharmaceutical manufactures offer copayment coupons to insured patients to reduce or eliminate the cost of their out-of-pocket copayments.[195.2] The Special Advisory Bulletin puts manufacturers on notice that they must consider the deficiencies identified in the study and ensure that their co-pay coupon programs do not induce federal health care beneficiaries to purchase their drugs.

[195.1] Department of Health and Human Services, Office of the Inspector General, Manufacturer Safeguards May Not Prevent Copayment Coupon Use for Part D Drugs (2014), *available at* http://oig.hhs.gov/oei/reports/oei-05-12-00540.pdf.

[195.2] Department of Health and Human Services, Office of the Inspector General, Special Advisory Bulletin: Pharmaceutical Manufacturer Copayment Coupons (2014), *available at* https://oig.hhs.gov/fraud/docs/alertsandbulletins/2014/SAB_Copayment_Coupons.pdf.

### § 2-4(k) Patient Assistance Programs for Medicare Part D Enrollees

On May 21, 2014, the OIG issued a Supplemental Special Advisory

Bulletin (Supplemental Bulletin) addressing the risks that Independent Charity Patient Assistance Programs (PAPs) raise under the Anti-Kickback Statute and beneficiary inducement CMPs. The Supplemental Bulletin adds new limitations to the 2005 Special Advisory Bulletin (2005 Bulletin) that the OIG issued regarding PAPs in advance of the 2006 implementation of the Medicare Part D outpatient prescription drug program (Part D). The limitations reflect certain issues that the OIG has observed in the years since Part D was implemented and focus on three areas: disease funds, eligible recipients, and the conduct of donors.

As indicated in the 2005 Bulletin, the OIG recognizes that some bona fide independent charities may focus on particular disease states and that donors may earmark their contributions for support of patients suffering from these particular diseases. However, the Supplemental Bulletin discusses the OIG's concern related to charities' narrowing of disease funds to include a limited number of drugs within such funds. This raises concerns as to whether donor contributions to limited or narrowed disease funds result in donors simply subsidizing their own products.

The Supplemental Bulletin acknowledges that, in the case of Medicare Part D, there may be rare circumstances wherein there exists only one drug covered for a disease in a particular PAP disease fund. In such a circumstance, the OIG states that "the fact that a disease fund includes only one drug or drugs made by a single manufacturer would not, standing alone, be determinative of an [A]nti-[K]ickback [S]tatute violation."

The Supp Bulletin also addresses the OIG's concern related to PAPs establishing or operating disease funds that limit assistance to a certain subset of available products, such as expensive or specialty drugs. According to the OIG, limiting assistance in such a manner could be viewed as a way of steering patients to particular drugs, thus potentially increasing costs to federal health care programs. Limiting assistance may also be viewed as steering patients away from more beneficial or less costly alternatives.

Next, the OIG addresses the criteria of how recipients are deemed eligible by the PAP. The OIG acknowledges that a fund focused solely on federal health care program beneficiaries is not, in and of itself, suspect, because the safeguards related to disease funds and recipient eligibility described in both the 2005 Bulletin and the Supplemental Bulletin should adequately protect federal health care programs. However, the OIG stresses that eligibility criteria must be determined according to a "reasonable, verifiable, and uniform measure of financial need that is applied in a consistent manner." While the OIG does not proscribe a particular methodology for determining financial need, the Supplemental Bulletin emphasizes that the cost of a particular drug is not an appropriate "stand-alone" factor. In addition, the Supplemental Bulletin notes that financial criteria that is overly generous (*i.e.*, the financial need determination is too lax), especially when the fund is limited to a subset of available drugs or drugs of a major donor, could be evidence of an inducement.

The Supplemental Bulletin seems to suggest that donors are not immune from liability under the law. Specifically, the OIG addresses how Advisory Opinions focus on the actions of the charities-not the donors—that requested the opinions, and as such the certifications made in conjunction with the submission of an Advisory Opinion are based on the actions of the charity. The OIG emphasizes that the procedures described in the certifications (*e.g.*, the types of information that will be distributed to donors) are essential safeguards that the OIG relies upon when issuing favorable opinions. The OIG acknowledges that the favorable Advisory Opinions do not address actions that donors may take to determine how their donations ultimately support their own product use. The OIG states, "Such actions may be indicative of a donor's intent to channel its financial support to copayments of its own products, which would implicate the [A]nti-[K]ickback [S]tatute."

The Supplemental Bulletin states that OIG will work with individuals who have received favorable Advisory Opinions to ensure that approved arrangements are consistent with the Supplemental Bulletin. The OIG expressly states that it anticipates needing to modify some Advisory Opinions. However, the OIG also clarifies that favorable Advisory Opinions will continue to protect the arrangement until a modification or termination is issued to the requestors of those opinions.

### § 2-4(l)  Physician-Owned Entities/Distributorships (PODs)

On March 26, 2013, the OIG issued a Special Fraud Alert regarding Physician-Owned Entities/Distributorships (PODs).[209.1] The Special Fraud Alert focused on PODs that derive revenue from selling or arranging for the sale of implantable medical devices ordered by their physician-owners for use in procedures that the physician-owners conduct. The OIG expressed concerns about arrangements that, "exhibit questionable features with regard to the selection and retention of investors, the solicitation of capital contributions and the distribution of profits."[209.2] In particular, the OIG stated that questionable features may include, but are not limited to: (1) selecting investors because they are in a position to generate substantial business for the entity; (2) requiring investors who cease practicing in the service area to divest their ownership interests; and (3) distributing extraordinary returns on investment compared to the level of risk involved.

However, the OIG included in the Special Fraud Alert a list of eight suspect characteristics:

- The size of the investment offered to each physician varies with the expected or actual volume or value of devices used by the physician.
- Distributions are not made in proportion to ownership interest, or physician-owners pay different prices for their ownership.
- Physician-owners condition their referrals to hospitals or ASCs on their purchase of the POD's devices through coercion or promises, for example, by stating or implying they will perform surgeries or refer patients elsewhere if a hospital or an ASC does not purchase devices from the POD, by promising or implying they will move surgeries to the hospital or ASC if it purchases devices from the POD, or by requiring a hospital or an ASC to enter into an exclusive purchase arrangement with the POD.
- Physician-owners are required, pressured, or actively encouraged to refer, recommend, or arrange for the purchase of the devices sold by the POD or, conversely, are threatened with, or experience, negative repercussions (*e.g.*, decreased distributions required divestiture) for failing to use the POD's devices for their patients.
- The POD retains the right to repurchase a physician-owner's interest for the physician's failure or inability (through relocation, retirement, or otherwise) to refer, recommend, or arrange for the purchase of the POD's devices.
- The POD is a shell entity that does not conduct appropriate product evaluations, maintain or manage sufficient inventory in its own facility, or employ or otherwise contract with personnel necessary for operations.
- The POD does not maintain continuous oversight of all distribution functions.
- When a hospital or an ASC requires physicians to disclose conflicts of interest, the POD's physician-owners fail to inform the hospital or ASC of, or actively conceal through misrepresentations, their ownership interest in the POD.

In addition, the OIG stated that PODs that generate disproportionately high rates of return for physician-owners may prompt heightened scrutiny by the government. The OIG said that their concerns are increased when physician-owners: (1) are few in number, such that the volume or value of a particular physician-owner's recommendations or referrals closely correlates to that physician-owner's return on investment, or (2) alter their medical practice after or shortly before investing in the POD. The OIG concluded that PODs that exhibit any of these features potentially raise four major Anti-Kickback Statute concerns: corruption of medical judgment; overutilization; increased costs to federal healthcare programs and beneficiaries; and, unfair competition. POD arrangements raise these concerns because the financial incentives may entice the physician-owner to perform more procedures than are medically necessary and/or to use the devices sold by the PODs in lieu of other, more clinically appropriate, devices. The OIG stressed, "[w]e are particularly concerned about the presence of such financial incentives in the implantable medical device context because such devices typically are 'physician preference items,' meaning that both the choice of brand and the type of device may be made or strongly influenced by the physician . . ."[209.3]

According to the Special Fraud Alert, disclosure to a patient of the physician's financial interest in a POD does not, by itself, address the specific concerns and risks raised by the OIG. The OIG also emphasized that criminal liability may attach to hospitals and ASCs that enter into arrangements with PODs that violate the Anti-Kickback Statute.

[209.1] OIG, Special Fraud Alert: Physician-Owned Entities, *available at* https://oig.hhs.gov/fraud/docs/alertsandbulletins/2013/POD_Special_Fraud_Alert.pdf (Mar. 26, 2013).

[209.2] *Id.*

[209.3] *Id.*

### § 2-4(m) Laboratory Payments to Referring Physicians

On June 25, 2014, the OIG issued a Special Fraud Alert addressing the compensation paid by laboratories to referring physicians and physician groups for blood specimen collection, processing and packaging, and for submitting patient data to a registry or database.[209.4] The Special Fraud Alert describes two specific trends the OIG has identified involving the transfers of value from laboratories to physicians.

The first trend is related to arrangements where laboratories provide remuneration to physicians to collect, process, and package the patients' specimen (Specimen Processing Arrangements). Under Specimen Processing Arrangements, laboratories pay physicians, typically on a per-specimen or per-patient encounter basis, for certain specified duties, which may include collecting the blood specimens, centrifuging the specimens, maintaining the specimens at a particular temperature, and packaging the specimens so they are not damaged during transport.

In the Special Fraud Alert, the OIG discusses the circumstances under which Medicare will allow a person who collects a specimen to bill for the collection services. According to the OIG, when determining the fair market value of compensation provided to a physician, a laboratory should consider whether the services for which it may compensate the physician have, or may be paid, including through a bundled payment, by Medicare. Further, the OIG states, "the laboratory should consider whether payment is appropriate at all; if the services for which the laboratory intends to compensate the physician are paid for by a third party through other means, such as payments intended to reimburse the physician for overhead expenses . . . ."

The Special Fraud Alert describes characteristics of Specimen Processing Arrangements that may be evidence of an unlawful purpose. These characteristics include, but are not limited to, the following:

- Payment exceeds fair market value for services actually rendered by the party receiving the payment.
- Payment is for services for which payment is also made by a third party, such as Medicare.
- Payment is made directly to the ordering physician rather than to the ordering physician's group practice, which may bear the cost of collecting and processing the specimen.
- Payment is made on a per-specimen basis for more than one specimen collected during a single patient encounter or on a per-test, per-patient, or other basis that takes into account the volume or value of referrals.
- Payment is offered on the condition that the physician order either a specified volume or type of tests or test panel, especially if the panel includes duplicative tests (*e.g.*, two or more tests performed using different methodologies that are intended to provide the same clinical information), or tests that otherwise are not reasonable and necessary or reimbursable.
- Payment is made to the physician or the physician's group practice, despite the fact that the specimen processing is actually being performed by a phlebotomist placed in the physician's office by the laboratory or a third party.

The OIG specifically states that it still has concerns regarding Specimen Processing Arrangements even if the specimens are only collected from non-federal health care patients. According to the OIG, "[a]rrangements that "carve out" federal health care program beneficiaries or business from otherwise questionable arrangements implicate the anti-kickback statute and may violate it by disguising remuneration for federal health care program business through the payment of amounts purportedly related to non-federal health care program business." The OIG takes the position that because physicians typically only refer to a few laboratories, Specimen Processing Arrangements that carve-out federal health care business may still be intended to induce referrals of federal health care business.

The OIG specifically states that both the laboratories and the physicians can be liable under the anti-kickback statute.

The second trend that the OIG has become aware of involves arrangements wherein laboratories are paying physicians for submitting patient data and providing specific services related to registries or observational outcomes databases (Registry Arrangements). Specifically, laboratories are establishing, coordinating, or maintaining databases (either directly or through an agent), to collect data on demographics, presentation, diagnosis, treatment, outcomes, or other attributes of patients who have undergone, or who may undergo, certain tests performed by the offering laboratories. According to the OIG, laboratories who participate in Registry Arrangements contend that they are intended to advance clinical research to promote treatment, however, the OIG is concerned that such arrangements may induce physicians to order medically unnecessary or duplicative tests for the purposes of obtaining comparative data. In addition, the OIG is concerned that the physicians may order these tests from laboratories offering Registry Arrangements instead of other superior laboratories.

Despite the OIG's concerns, the Special Fraud Alert acknowledges that Registry Arrangements may be reasonable in certain limited circumstances. The Special Fraud Alert describes characteristics of Registry Arrangements that may be evidence of an unlawful purpose. These characteristics include, but are not limited to, the following:

- The laboratory requires, encourages, or recommends that physicians who enter into Registry Arrangements perform the tests with a stated frequency to be eligible to receive, or to no receive a reduction, in compensation. The laboratory collects comparative data for the Registry from, and bills for, multiple tests that may be duplicative (*e.g.*, two or more tests performed using different methodologies that are intended to provide the same clinical information) or that otherwise are not reasonable and necessary.
- Compensation paid to physicians pursuant to Registry Arrangements is on a per-patient or other basis that takes into account the value or volume of referrals.

- Compensation paid to physicians pursuant to Registry Arrangements is not fair market value for the physicians' efforts in collecting and reporting patient data.
- Compensation paid to physicians pursuant to Registry Arrangements is not supported by documentation, submitted by the physicians in a timely manner, memorializing the physicians' efforts.
- The laboratory offers Registry Arrangements only for tests (or disease states associated with tests) for which it has obtained patents or that it exclusively performs.
- When a test is performed by multiple laboratories, the laboratory collects data only from the tests it performs.
- The tests associated with the Registry Arrangement are presented on the offering laboratory's requisition in a manner that makes it more difficult for the ordering physician to make an independent medical necessity decision with regard to each test for which the laboratory will bill (*e.g.*, disease-related panels).

The Special Fraud Alert acknowledges that the Anti-Kickback Statute does not prohibit laboratories from engaging in, or paying compensation for, legitimate research activities. However, the OIG states that justifications that rely solely on the claim that Registries are intended to promote and support clinical research and treatment are not sufficient to disprove unlawful intent. The OIG states, "[e]ven legitimate actions taken to substantiate such claims, including for example retaining an independent Institutional Review Board to develop study protocols and participation guidelines, will not protect a Registry Arrangement if one purpose of the arrangement is to induce or reward referrals." Similar to Specimen Processing Arrangements, the OIG's concerns are not alleviated by carving out federal health care program patients. Likewise, both the laboratories and the physicians who enter into Registry Arrangements can be liable under the Anti-Kickback Statute.

[209.4] Department of Health and Human Services, Office of the Inspector General, Special Fraud Alert: Laboratory Payments to Referring Physicians (June 25, 2014), *available at* https://oig.hhs.gov/fraud/docs/alertsandbulletins/2014/OIG_SFA_Laboratory_Payments_06252014.pdf.

### § 2-4(n) Physician Compensation Arrangements May Result in Significant Liability

On June 9, 2015, the OIG issued a Fraud Alert regarding physician anti-kickback liability for entering into compensation arrangements, such as medical directorships, that are not fair market value or for *bona fide* services (Fraud Alert).[209.5] In the Fraud Alert, the OIG encourages physicians to consider the terms and conditions of the compensation arrangements before entering into them. The Fraud Alert discusses recent OIG settlements with 12 individual physicians who entered into arrangements for medical directorships and office staff. In those arrangements, the OIG alleged that the compensation paid to the physicians constitutes improper remuneration because, among other things, the payments took into account the volume or value of referrals and did not reflect fair market value for the services being performed and the physicians did not actually perform the services contracted under the agreement. In addition, the OIG alleged that some of the physicians entered into arrangements where an affiliated health care entity paid the salaries of certain of the physicians' office staff. "The OIG determined that the physicians were an integral part of the scheme and subject to liability under the Civil Monetary Penalties Law."[209.6]

[209.5] Department of Health and Human Services, Office of the Inspector General, Fraud Alert: Physician Compensation Arrangements May Result in Significant Liability (June 9, 2015), *available at* http://oig.hhs.gov/compliance/alerts/guidance/Fraud_Alert_Physician_Compensation_06092015.pdf.

[209.6] *Id.*

## § 2-5 ADDITIONAL GUIDANCE AND ADVISORY OPINIONS

### § 2-5(c) Applicability of the Anti-Kickback Statute to Qualified Health Plans (QHPs)

On October 30, 2013, HHS Secretary Kathleen Sebelius issued a letter (the QHP Letter) responding to Rep. Jim McDermott (D-Wash.) detailing that qualified health plans (QHPs), other programs related to the Federally-facilitated Marketplace, and other programs under Title I of the Health Reform Law are not considered to be federal health care programs under the Anti-Kickback Statute.[226.1] According to the QHP Letter this includes the "State-based and Federally-facilitated Marketplaces; the cost-sharing reductions and advance payments of the premium tax credit; Navigators for the Federally-facilitated Marketplaces and other federally funded consumer assistance programs; consumer-oriented and operated health insurance plans; and the risk adjustment, reinsurance, and risk corridors programs." However, in the QHP Letter, Sebelius details other measures that are available to the government to protect consumers and ensure oversight including (1) compliance standards issued on August 30, 2013;[226.2] (2) the OIG's jurisdiction to audit, investigate, and evaluate the HHS-administered programs in Title I of the Health Reform Law; (3) HHS and OIG's authority under section 1313 of the Health Reform Law to investigate the "affairs of an Exchange;" (4) applicability of the False Claims Act to any payments made by through, or in connection with an Exchange if the payments include

§ 2-6   *Legal Issues in Healthcare Fraud and Abuse*

Federal funds; and (5) potential additional federal and state criminal and civil authorities.

However, in addition to the QHP Letter, on November 4, 2013, the Center for Consumer Information & Insurance Oversight of CMS issued a guidance document (the "Guidance Document") that addresses third party premium payments and cost-sharing obligations with respect to QHPs purchased by patients in the Marketplaces.[226.3] The Guidance Document states, "HHS has significant concerns with this practice because it could skew the insurance risk pool and create an unlevel field in the Marketplaces. HHS discourages this practice and encourages issuers to reject such third party payments." In addition, the Guidance Document states that HHS intends to monitor the practice and take appropriate action. The Center for Consumer Information & Insurance Oversight further clarified their response in a subsequent document issued ("Subsequent Guidance Document") on February 7, 2014.[226.4] Specifically, the Subsequent Guidance Document provides that the statements in the Guidance Document do not apply to QHP enrollees from Indian tribes, tribal organizations, urban Indian organizations, state and federal government programs or grantees (such as the Ryan White HIV/AIDS Program). In addition, the Subsequent Guidance Document provides that the Guidance Document does not apply to QHP enrollees from private, not for profit foundations if they meet certain criteria.

[226.1] Letter from Kathleen Sebelius, Secretary, HHS, to Jim McDermott, U.S. House of Representatives (Oct. 30, 2013), *available online at* http://mcdermott.house.gov/index.php?option=com_content&view=article&id=723:hhs-to-mcdermott-qualified-health-plans-are-not-federal-health-care-programs&catid=25&Itemid=20.

[226.2] 78 Fed. Reg. 54,070 (Aug. 30, 2013).

[226.3] CMS, Center for Consumer Information & Insurance Oversight, Third Party Payments of Premiums for Qualified Health Plans in the Marketplaces, Nov. 3, 2013, *available online at* http://www.cms.gov/CCIIO/Resources/Fact-Sheets-and-FAQs/Downloads/third-party-qa-11-04-2013.pdf.

[226.4] CMS, Center for Consumer Information & Insurance Oversight, Third Party Payments of Premiums for Qualified Health Plans in the Marketplaces, Feb. 7, 2014, *available online at* http://www.cms.gov/CCIIO/Resources/Fact-Sheets-and-FAQs/Downloads/third-party-payments-of-premiums-for-qualified-health-plans-in-the-marketplaces-2-7-14.pdf.

## § 2-6   CASE LAW

### § 2-6(c)   Significant Post-Hanlester Cases

#### § 2-6(c)(1)   The Anti-Kickback Statute's Intent Requirement

On September 28, 2012, in *United States ex rel. Jamison v. McKesson*,[246.1] a Mississippi district court ruled for defendants finding that the government had failed to prove the requisite scienter necessary to violate the

Anti-Kickback Statute. In this *qui tam* lawsuit, the Relator, Jamison, claimed that the defendants defrauded the government by forming improper joint ventures, failing to satisfy DME supplier standards, and submitting fraudulent Medicaid cost reports. Under the joint ventures, medical supply companies created DME suppliers within nursing homes that allowed the nursing homes to seek reimbursement under their own DME supplier numbers. Jamison alleged that the monies derived from these joint ventures were kickbacks, and therefore, all claims submitted by the DME suppliers violated the False Claims Act. The government sought $895 million in damages and penalties.

Asserting an "express false certification" theory of liability, the government claimed that because the defendants had violated the Anti-Kickback Statute, all of the claims submitted also violated the False Claims Act (FCA). However, the court ultimately held that there was no violation of the FCA because there was no underlying violation of the Anti-Kickback Statute.

In its decision, first, the court took the position that the government had the burden of establishing fair market value. Ultimately the court determined that the government failed to prove that the defendants offered its services below fair market value, below actual costs, or at a discount, and therefore failed to prove the inducement required for a violation of the Anti-Kickback Statute.

Second, the court held that the government must prove the Anti-Kickback Statute's knowing and willful standard to meet the scienter requirement. Here, the court determined that although the defendants' employees inserted arbitrary numbers into calculations for costs, this did not rise to a willful wrong intentionally committed against the government.

[246.1] 900 F. Supp. 2d 683, 2:08cv214-SA-JMV (N.D. Miss 2012).

## § 2-7 OTHER ANTI-KICKBACK AUTHORITY

### § 2-7(a) Inducements to Beneficiaries

#### § 2-7(a)(3) 2010 Modification to the CMP Provision

Also as part of the Health Reform Law, Congress added a new exception to the definition of remuneration that relates to retailer rewards. Specifically, retailer rewards do not constitute "remuneration" under the CMP if: (1) the rewards consist of coupons, rebates, or other rewards from a retailer; (2) the rewards are offered or transferred on equal terms available to the general public, regardless of health insurance status; and (3) the offer or transfer of the rewards is not tied to the provision of other items or services reimbursed in whole or in part by the Medicare or Medicaid programs.[263.1]

On October 9, 2012, the OIG issued Advisory Opinion 12-14, opining on whether a rewards program in which consumers would earn gasoline discounts based on the amount they spend on purchases in retail supermarkets would violate the CMP or Anti-Kickback Statutes.[263.2] The Requestor owned and operated 13 supermarkets, most of which had in-store pharmacies. The Requestor offered all customers a free preferred customer card which entitled customers to certain benefits, including special pricing and coupons. One of the benefits included a program that enabled customers to earn discounts on gasoline purchases at select gas stations. In particular, for every $10 that a customer spent in a store, the customer would be entitled to a one cent per gallon discount on a single purchase of gas. Historically, the co-payments and deductibles for prescriptions covered by federal healthcare programs were excluded from the gasoline discount program. Under the Proposed Arrangement, the prescription co-payments and deductibles would now be eligible for the gasoline discount program.

Although the OIG determined that the gasoline discount program would implicate both the CMP prohibition on inducement to beneficiaries as well as the Anti-Kickback Statute, the OIG found that the arrangement was not impermissible remuneration as defined in the CMP. First, the OIG determined that the gasoline rewards program under the Proposed Arrangement would meet all of the criteria for the retailer rewards exception: (1) the rewards consisted of coupons, rebates, or retailer rewards; (2) the store card was offered on equal terms to all customers; and (3) the offer or transfer of rewards was not tied to the provision of other items or services reimbursable in whole or in part by the Medicare or Medicaid programs.

With regard to the Anti-Kickback Statute, the OIG determined: (1) that there was little risk that the Proposed Arrangement would steer beneficiaries to the Requestor's supermarket to purchase federally reimbursable items or services; and (2) the Proposed Arrangement would be unlikely to result in overutilization or otherwise increase costs to federal healthcare programs.

Although the Health Reform Law excepted certain retailer reward programs from the definition of remuneration, there are other gift card and rewards programs that the government has found to be impermissible inducements to beneficiaries. For example, on April 20, 2012, Walgreens agreed to pay $7.9 million to the U.S. Government and states to resolve claims that it had offered illegal inducements to government health program beneficiaries in the form of gift cards, gift checks and other promotions to entice beneficiaries to transfer their prescriptions to Walgreens pharmacies.[263.4] The government alleged that Walgreens had offered government healthcare beneficiaries $25 gift cards when they transferred a prescription. The government further alleged that although the company's advertisements that promoted gift cards and gift checks for transferred prescriptions typically acknowledged that the offer was not valid with Medicaid, Medicare or any other government program, Walgreens employees frequently ignored the stated exemptions and gave the gift cards to federal healthcare program beneficiaries.

The Health Reform Law also amended the definition of remuneration so that remuneration does not include the offer or transfer of items or services for free or less than fair market value by a person, if:

- the items or services are not offered as part of any advertisement or solicitation;
- the items or services are not tied to the provision of other services reimbursed in whole or in part by a federal or state healthcare program;
- there is a reasonable connection between the items or services and the medical care of the individual; and
- the person provides the items or services after determining in good faith that the individual is in financial need.[263.5]

[263.1] The Health Reform Law, § 6402; Social Security Act § 1128A(i)(6)(G); 42 U.S.C. 1320a-7a(i)(6)(G).

[263.2] OIG Advisory Op. No. 12-14. *See also* OIG Advisory Op. No. 12-21 (approving a $20 grocery gift card in exchange for a visit to a capitated federally qualified health center).

[263.4] DOJ, Press Release, "Walgreens Pharmacy Chain Pays $7.9 Million to Resolve False Prescription Billing Case," *available at* http://www.justice.gov/opa/pr/2012/April/12-civ-505.html.

[263.5] The Health Reform Law, § 6402; Social Security Act § 1128A(i)(6)(H); 42 U.S.C. 1320a-7a(i)(6)(H).

## § 2-7(d)  Federal "Sunshine Law"

On February 1, 2013, CMS issued final regulations with a lengthy preamble (collectively referred to herein as "Final Regulations") relevant to the Sunshine Act.[289.1]

In the Final Regulations, CMS provided approximately 180-day preparation period to applicable manufacturers and group purchasing organizations (GPOs) to implement the Final Regulations and begin collecting data. Applicable manufacturers and GPOs began data collection on August 1, 2013, and the first report was due to CMS by March 31, 2014. To that end, applicable manufacturers and GPOs are required to register on a CMS website and submit data using submission file specifications (formerly known as data collection templates). CMS will release the data on a public website by September 30, 2014.

§ 2-7   *Legal Issues in Healthcare Fraud and Abuse*

Based on comments to the Proposed Regulations, CMS limited the definition of "applicable manufacturer" to an entity that "operates" in the United States, which means having a physical location or otherwise conducting activities within the United States, and is "engaged in the production, preparation, propagation, compounding, or conversion of a covered drug, device, biological, or medical supply . . . ." An applicable GPO is defined as an entity that, "operates in the United States and purchases, arranges for or negotiates the purchase of a covered drug, device, biological, or medical supply for a group of individuals or entities, but not solely for use by the entity itself." The Final Regulations made clear that entities based outside the United States with operations inside the United States are subject to the reporting requirements. Also, the Final Regulations clarified that entities that manufacture a covered product are applicable manufacturers, even if they do not hold the FDA approval, licensure, or clearance for the covered produced.

The Final Regulations clarified the definition of "payment or transfer or value" in several ways. For example:

- items that may not have a discernible value to the covered recipient, but have an economic value generally, must be reported, even if the covered recipient did not request the item (*e.g.*, providing the physician with a text book that the physician may already own);
- ancillary costs, such as tax and shipping, should be included in the reported value and requires applicable manufacturers to make a reasonable, good faith effort to determine the value of a payment or other transfer of value;
- payments provided to a group practice should be attributed to the individual physician covered recipient(s) who requested the payment or on whose behalf the payment was made;
- payments provided to another person on behalf of a covered recipient must be reported but will include the name of the individual or entity who received the payment; and
- payments provided to one covered recipient, but directed by the applicable manufacturer to another specific covered recipient (*e.g.*, teaching hospital to physician), should be reported in the name of the recipient who ultimately received the payment.

The Final Regulations generally retained the categories for the nature of payment previously described in the Proposed Rule. However, the Final Regulations added categories for compensation for serving as a faculty or speaker for an unaccredited and non-certified continuing education program and space rental and facility fees. Although CMS removed the "other" category, all non-excluded payments or other transfers of value to a covered recipient must be reported, even if a payment or transfer of value does not fit squarely within an identified category. The Final Regulations provided guidance and clarifications to applicable manufacturers and GPOs regarding the various reporting requirements and on excluded items and transfers of value:

- buffet meals, snacks, or coffee at conferences or other similar large-scale settings where it is impractical to identify whether the participating covered recipients are exempt from the reporting requirement. This exclusion includes small incidental items that are under $10 (*e.g.*, note pads, pens) provided at similar events;
- certain educational materials are exempt from the reporting requirements. This exclusion should be interpreted to apply to written and electronic materials and wall and anatomical models used in patient education. Materials, such as medical textbooks and journal reprints that are provided to covered recipients for their personal education, are *not* excluded from reporting;
- *in-kind* items provided to a charitable organization for patients who are unable to pay, or for whom payment would be a significant hardship are exempt from reporting. The exclusion does not apply if the applicable manufacturer provides either (i) in-kind items to a charitable organization for all of the covered recipient's patients, or (ii) a payment or transfer of value that is not an in-kind item;
- the product sample exclusion extends to coupons and vouchers;
- the provision of up to a 90-day supply of disposable or single-use devices falls within the short-term loan exception;
- a payment that is refused by the covered recipient does not need to be reported. Similarly, a payment made to another individual or entity that is not made at the request of a covered recipient does not need to be reported;
- an applicable manufacturer will not need to report funds if it is unaware of the identity of the covered recipient (*e.g.* double-blind research or unrestricted funds to a medical society that may ultimately be received by a covered recipient). However, if an applicable manufacturer could easily ascertain the identity of the covered recipient, then it must do so and report. Alternatively, if the applicable manufacturer "requires, instructs or directs" the payment

to be provided to a known covered recipient, then it must be reported; and

- indirect CME speaker payments that meet all of the following requirements are excluded from reporting:

[289.1] 78 Fed. Reg. 9458 (Feb. 1, 2013).

- o the program satisfies all of the accreditation or certification requirements of certain specified accrediting and certifying organizations;
- o the applicable manufacturer does not select or provide a distinct set of identifiable individuals to be considered; and
- o the applicable manufacturer does not pay the covered recipient directly.

Finally, the Final Regulations provided clarification regarding certain content required in the report.

With regard to reporting of physician ownership and investments, the ownership or investment interest provisions apply to all "physicians" and not just "covered recipients." CMS has interpreted this to mean that ownership and investment interest must be reported for all physicians regardless of whether a physician is an employee of the applicable manufacturer or GPO. Additionally, the requirement to report payments and other transfers of interests apply to such physicians.

CMS specifically declined to expand the scope of applicable GPOs to covered devices or covered medical supplies that, by law, require premarket approval from, or premarket notification to, the FDA. The Final Regulations clarify that entities that engage in rare and circumstantial resale of products are not likely to fall within the scope of an applicable GPO. In an attempt to limit the broad definition of "ownership or investment interest" the Final Regulations only require applicable manufacturers to report those ownership or investment interests that they know to be owned by a physician or an immediate family member[289.2] of a physician.

Finally, the Final Regulations specify that:

- information related to ownership and investment interest and payment or transfer of interest must be reported separately because of the difference in the reporting requirements;
- reports can be aggregated across all family members who hold interests that are subject to the same ownership and investment terms. If an applicable manufacturer or GPO seeks to aggregate

interest across family members, the value of the interest must be aggregated as well; and

- in addition to reporting the ownership or investment interests, the Final Regulations require applicable manufacturers or GPOs to report all payments or other transfers of interest made to physicians, or to third parties on behalf of physicians, holding ownership or investment interests. Applicable manufacturers with physician owners should include such transfers in the same report used to capture payments and other transfers to covered recipients. An applicable manufacturer will need to indicate on the report that the recipient was a physician owner or investor.

Penalties for failing to report include, a civil money penalty of not less than $1,000, but not more than $10,000, for each payment or other transfer of value or ownership or investment interest not reported. The total amount of civil money penalties will not exceed $150,000. Knowingly failing to submit payment information will result in a civil money penalty of not less than $10,000, but not more than $100,000, for each payment. The penalty will not exceed $1,000,000. Combined, penalties may not exceed $1,150,000.

**289.2** CMS finalized the proposed definition of "immediate family member" to include the following: spouse; natural or adoptive parent; child or sibling; stepparent, stepchild, stepbrother, or stepsister; father, mother, daughter, son, brother, or sister-in-law; grandparent or grandchild; or spouse of a grandparent or grandchild.

# 3
# Federal Physician Self-Referral Prohibitions

## § 3-3 THE STATUTORY PROHIBITION AND DEFINITIONS OF KEY TERMS

### § 3-3(b) Definitions of Key Terms

#### § 3-3(b)(1) Referral

Even though the Stark II Final Regulations state that referrals for DHS that are personally performed by the referring physician are not considered "referrals," the 4th Circuit in a 2012 decision, held that the facility component of a physician's personally performed services, that results in a facility fee being billed by a Hospital, does constitute a referral.[47.1]

[47.1] U.S. ex rel Drakeford v. Tuomey Healthcare System, 675 F.3d 394 (4th Circ. Mar. 2012).

## § 3-3(b)(5)  Fair Market Value

Fair market value was also addressed in *United States v. Tuomey Healthcare System*[82.1] a *qui tam* action filed by Michael Drakeford (the "Relator"), a physician employed by Tuomey Healthcare System, Inc. (Tuomey), a hospital in South Carolina. Tuomey entered into exclusive part-time employment negotiations with 19 of its affiliated specialist physicians (among them surgeons, gastroenterologists, obstetricians/gynecologists and ophthalmologists) to prevent these physicians from moving their outpatient business out of Tuomey's ambulatory surgery center and into lower cost competing locations, some of which would be owned by the physicians themselves.

Under the employment agreements, Tuomey agreed to pay each physician 131% of their net revenues collected (or 31% over the amount that the physicians actually generated in revenues) in return for their services and a non-compete agreement. Tuomey hired an attorney to provide a legal opinion as to whether the proposed part-time exclusive employment agreements violated the Stark Law. The attorney found the proposed employment agreement to be problematic because it had the effect of locking in the orthopedic surgeon's referrals (by way of a non-compete) and provided compensation in excess of fair market value. Tuomey fired the attorney and advised him not to put his opinion in writing.[82.2] Thereafter, Tuomey sought legal review of the proposed employment agreement from another law firm. Tuomey's new counsel, relying on the fair market value opinion of Tuomey's expert (who advised that paying the physicians 131% of their net revenues was fair market value compensation), advised Tuomey that the compensation was unlikely to violate the Stark Law, provided: (i) the employment agreements allowed the physicians to not be restricted in honoring the patient's choice (even though Tuomey was the only hospital in the area); and (ii) the physicians were compensated on the basis of revenue generated rather than procedures performed. After both of these legal opinions, the Relator asserted that the Tuomey employment agreements exceeded fair market value, were commercially unreasonable and took into account the volume or value of referrals all in contravention of the Stark Law.

In 2010, the United States District Court for the District of South Carolina, Columbia Division, heard the initial case, in which the government asserted that the Tuomey physicians presented, or caused to be presented, claims for payments to Medicaid and Medicare for designated health services.[82.3] The Government contended that these claims for payments therefore violated the False Claims Act and the Stark Law. A jury held that the compensation arrangement violated the Stark Law; however, the jury also found that the compensation arrangement did not violate the False Claims Act. The judge granted a new trial on the issue of the False Claims Act violation and issued an order in which he found that Tuomey violated the Stark Law (pursuant to the jury verdict) and found for the United States on the issues of payment by mistake and unjust enrichment. Tuomey appealed the 2010 decision to the United States Court of Appeals for the Fourth Circuit.[82.4] The Fourth Circuit remanded the case to the District Court for further proceedings, noting that if there is a "financial relationship . . . between the physicians and [the designated health service entity]," knowingly submitting a claim for either the facility or professional component of a bill to Medicare after a Stark-prohibited referral violates the FCA. In addition, the Fourth Circuit ruled that anticipating referrals in computing physician compensation violated the "volume or value" standard of Stark. While the court acknowledged this consideration of anticipated referrals may make the agreement economically fair, it nevertheless concluded that the consideration was barred by the Stark Law.

On remand, the District Court found Tuomey violated both the Stark Law and the False Claims Act. The court's finding relied, in part, on internal Tuomey documents and board conversations discussing lost revenue calculations if the physicians referred to a newly formed independent ambulatory surgery center instead of the hospital. In addition, the court discussed allegations that Tuomey paid 131 percent of professional fees to the employed physicians in part-time arrangements to show that the value received by Toumey from the physicians' referral value was considered in their compensation.

[82.1] No. 3:05-2858-MBS, 2013 U.S. Dist. LEXIS 141316 (D.S.C. Sept. 30, 2013).

[82.2] The Court in later proceedings found that Tuomey's dismissal of the attorney's legal opinion eviscerated its defense that it later relied on the advice of counsel who found that the compensation arrangement did not violated the Stark Law.

[82.3] U.S. ex rel Drakeford v. Tuomey, 2010 U.S. Dist. LEXIS 143457 (D.S.C., July 13, 2010).

[82.4] U.S. ex rel Drakeford v. Tuomey Healthcare System, 675 F.3d 394 (4th Circ. Mar. 2012).

### § 3-3(b)(8)  Entity

The Council for Urological Interests challenged CMS' revision to the term "entity" as violating the Administrative Procedures Act.[94.1] The Court held that CMS' interpretations and changes did not violate congressional intent or the APA.

[94.1] Council for Urological Interests v. Sebelius, 946 F. Supp. 2d 91 (D.D.C. May 24, 2013).

### § 3-3(c)  Special Rules on Compensation

### § 3-3(c)(1)  Compensation Methodologies

The Council for Urological Interests challenged CMS prohibition on per-click payments that stem from physician referrals as violating the Administrative Procedure Act.[100.1] The Court held that CMS' has reasonably interpreted the Stark Law to allow restrictions on per-click arrangements.

[100.1] Council for Urological Interests v. Sebelius, 946 F. Supp. 2d 91 (D.D.C. May 24, 2013).

## § 3-4  STARK LAW EXCEPTIONS

### § 3-4(c)  Compensation Arrangement Exceptions

### § 3-4(c)(2)  Bona Fide Employment Relationships

In recent years the Courts have begun to address the productivity bonus compensation related to employed physicians. For example, in *United States v. Halifax Hospital Medical Center*[175.1] the Relator alleged that the incentive compensation paid to oncologists violated the AKS and Stark Law and therefore the claims submitted by Halifax Hospital Medical Center (Halifax Hospital) to Medicare during this period violated the False Claims Act. Halifax Hospital owns Halifax Staffing, Inc. (Halifax Staffing), which employed the individuals who work at Halifax Hospital. Halifax Hospital pays all of the expenses and obligations of Halifax Staffing. Halifax Staffing entered into contracts with six oncologists to treat patients at Halifax Hospital on both an inpatient and outpatient basis.

The six oncologists became eligible for an incentive bonus in which the bonus was paid by Halifax Staffing out of an incentive compensation pool. The incentive compensation pool which was equal to 15% of the operating margin for the oncology program and was divided between the six oncologists based on each individual oncologist's personally performed services. Halifax Staffing paid the incentive bonuses to the oncologists for fiscal years 2005–2008. During this time frame, Halifax Hospital submitted thousands of claims to Medicare in which one or more of the oncologists was identified as an attending physician or an operating physician. The government alleged that during the period that the physicians were eligible for incentive bonuses Halifax Hospital submitted claims that resulted from referrals by the oncologists for designated health services and that the bonus did not satisfy the bona fide employment exception because the bonus varied based on the referrals for designated health services, some of which were not personally performed by the oncologists, including services such as outpatient prescription drugs and certain outpatient services. Halifax Hospital argued that the exception within the bona fide employment exception related to productivity bonuses applies because the incentive bonus pool was divided up based upon the oncologists' personally performed services.

In its decision in November 2013, the court found that the compensation arrangement for the oncologists did not constitute a bona fide employment arrangement. Specifically, the court found that the bonus was not solely based on personally performed services, but rather divided up based on services rendered by the oncologists collectively—including revenue from referrals made by the oncologists for designated health services. The court noted that "the fact that each oncologist could increase his or her share of the bonus pool by personally performing more services cannot alter the fact that the size of the pool (and thus the size of each oncologist's bonus) could be increased by making more referrals."

As a result of the court's decision, the Government sought reimbursement of $27,102,000 in Medicare payments generated as a result of these improper referrals. The court failed to grant summary judgment as to the amount of damages. Pending the court's ruling, the $27 million in damages will be trebled and Halifax Hospital will additionally be subject to fines of $5,500 to $11,000 for each separate billing or claim submitted to Medicare.

In March 2014, Halifax Hospital agreed to pay $85 million to resolve the False Claims Act violations.[175.1]

[175.1] 2013 U.S. Dist. LEXIS 161718 (M.D. Fla. Nov. 13, 2013).

[175.1] Department of Justice, Florida Hospital System Agrees to Pay the Government $85 Million to Settle Allegations of Improper Financial Relationships with Referring Physicians (March 2014), *available at* http://www.justice.gov/opa/pr/florida-hospital-system-agrees-pay-government-85-million-settle-allegations-improper.

### § 3-4(c)(19) Electronic Prescribing and Electronic Health Records

On April 10, 2013, the Centers for Medicare and Medicaid Services issued a proposed rule to amend the exception to the Stark Law involving the donation of electronic health records items and services. The proposed revisions to the exception includes an update to the provision under which electronic health records software is deemed interoperable, removal of the electronic prescribing capability requirement and extension of the sunset provision. In addition, CMS requested that the public provide comments on a number of additional issues as to whether the exception should be modified to: (1) cover only the categories of donors originally included in the statute (hospitals, group practices, PDP sponsors and MA organizations); (2) ensure that the exception is not misused to lock-in referrals and that it actually encourages the free exchange of data; and (3) clarify the types of items and services that can be donated as part of the exception.[227.1]

On December 27, 2013, CMS issued final regulations to (EHR Final Rule) amend the exception concerning electronic health records items and services. Under the EHR Final Rule, CMS adopted its proposed amendments to include an update to the provision under which electronic health records software is deemed interoperable, removal of the electronic prescribing capability requirement and extension of the sunset provision from December 31, 2013 to December 31, 2021 (which corresponds to the last year for EHR Medicaid incentive payments). In addition, the EHR Final Rule specifically excludes laboratory companies from the list of eligible "Protected Donors." CMS clarified that if a hospital furnishes laboratory services through a laboratory that is a department of the hospital for Medicare purposes and bills for the services through the hospital's provider number, then the hospital would not be considered a "laboratory company." Conversely, if a hospital-affiliated or hospital-owned company with its own supplier number furnishes laboratory services that are billed using a company billing number, as opposed to the hospital's billing number, the company is considered a "laboratory company" and is no longer considered a "Protected Donor." Additionally, to promote the free exchange of information, the EHR Final Rule includes limited clarifications to require that no action be taken to limit or restrict the use, compatibility or interoperability of items or services with other electronic prescribing or EHR systems.[227.2]

[227.1] 78 Fed. Reg. 21308 (Apr. 10, 2013).
[227.2] 78 Fed. Reg. 78,751 (Dec. 27, 2013).

### § 3-4(c)(22)  ACOs

On October 17, 2014, CMS announced the continuation of the effectiveness of the Interim Final Rule and the extension of the timeline for publication of a Final Rule. The timeline for publishing the Final Rule was extended by one year.[258.1]

On February 12, 2015, CMS and the OIG issued a document setting forth additional guidance related to certain conditions of waivers (Additional Guidance Document).[258.2] Specifically, the document provided guidance concerning three areas: (1) public disclosures required under the ACO Pre-Participation and ACO Participation Waivers, (2) notification of failure to submit a timely application by parties who used the ACO Pre-Participation Waiver, and (3) requests for an extension of the ACO Pre-Participation Waiver period.

**258.1** 79 Fed. Reg. 62,356 (Oct. 17, 2014).

**258.2** Department of Health and Human Services, Centers for Medicare & Medicaid Services and the Office of the Inspector General, Medicare Shared Savings Program Waivers: Additional Guidance (Feb. 12, 2015), *available at* http://www.cms.gov/Medicare/Medicare-Fee-for-Service-Payment/sharedsavingsprogram/Downloads/Additional-MSSP-Waiver-Guidance.pdf.

## § 3-5  DEFINITION OF GROUP PRACTICE

### § 3-5(d)  Services Furnished by Group Practice Members

The following examples are provided to illustrate how the 75% test is calculated an aggregate basis, taking into account that independent contractors need not be counted for purposes of complying with the "substantially all" test:

**Example 1:** A group practice consists of four physician-partners, three full-time physician employees, two part-time physician employees, and a contractor physician who spends one morning a week at the group practice to deliver specialty services. The four partners and the full-time employees practice only through the group. The two part-time employees devote 50% of their time to the group, and the contractor physician spends 10% of her time with the group.

$$7 \text{ physicians at } 100\% = 700\%$$
$$2 \text{ physicians at } 50\% = 100\%$$
$$800\% \text{ divided by } 9 = 88.90\%$$

**Example 2:** In another group practice, two physician-partners spend 100% of their patient care hours through the group. Three part-time physician employees spend 50% each, and one other part-time employee spends 10% of her time at the group practice. A contractor physician devotes 15%.

$$2 \text{ physicians at } 100\% = 200\%$$
$$3 \text{ physicians at } 50\% = 150\%$$
$$1 \text{ physicians at } 10\% = 10\%$$
$$360\% \text{ divided by } 6 = 60\%$$

Note that in both situations, the time spent by the contractor physician is not added for purposes of satisfying the 75% test.

## § 3-8  SELF-REFERRAL DISCLOSURE PROTOCOL

On March 23, 2012, CMS issued a report to Congress regarding the implementation of the SRDP.[326.1] At that time CMS reported that 148 providers of services and suppliers had submitted a total of 150 disclosures.

§ 3-10  *Legal Issues in Healthcare Fraud and Abuse*

According to the report, six of the disclosures had been resolved through settlement ($783,060 total). Fifty-one of the disclosures were under CMS review and CMS was waiting for additional information from another 61 disclosing providers. According to the report, "the remaining disclosures are no longer in the SRDP or are being held due to circumstances outside of CMS's control." As of May 2015, CMS had posted 69 settlements on its website.[326.2]

[326.1] CMS, Report to Congress: Implementation of the Medicare Self-Referral Disclosure Protocol (Mar. 23, 2012), *available at* http://www.cms.gov/Medicare/Fraud-and-Abuse/PhysicianSelfRefer-ral/Downloads/CMS-SRDP-Report-to-Congress.pdf.

[326.2] *Self-Referral Disclosure Protocol Settlements*, http://www.cms.gov/Medicare/Fraud-and-Abuse/PhysicianSelfReferral/Self-Referral-Disclosure-Protocol-Settlements.html (last visited June 16, 2015).

## § 3-10  MAJOR ISSUES IN STARK LAW INTERPRETATION

### § 3-10(f)  Applying Stark to Medicaid

In recent years, more cases are asserting violations of Stark with respect to Medicaid services as the basis of false claims. For example, in *United States ex rel. Schubert v. All Children's Health Sys.*,[392] the Relator brought allegations that all of the claims submitted by the Defendants under Florida's Medicaid program, that were passed to the United States for determining the federal financial participation, were false claims because the claims resulted from referrals by physicians with financial relationships that violated Stark. The court determined that Stark applies to Medicaid claims and thus can serve as a basis for a false claims action.

[392] 2013 U.S. Dist. LEXIS 164075, *14-18 (M.D. Fla. Nov. 15, 2013).

# 4

# False Claims: Civil and Criminal Enforcement

## § 4-2  THE FEDERAL CIVIL FALSE CLAIMS ACT

### § 4-2(a)  Key FCA Considerations for Healthcare Entities

#### § 4-2(a)(4)  What Is "Causing" a Claim to Be Submitted?

In February 2014, Community Health Systems, Inc. agreed to pay $75 million to settle allegations that from August 1, 2000 through December 31, 2010, it violated the FCA by making illegal donations to county governments which were used to fund the state's share of Medicaid payments to the hospitals.[51.1] The government alleged that, by offering illegal donations to various counties, CHS knowingly caused the state to present false claims to the United States to obtain federal matching payments.

New Mexico's Sole Community Provider (SCP) program provided supplemental Medicaid funds to hospitals in mostly rural communities. The federal government reimbursed New Mexico for approximately 75 percent of its health care expenditures under the SCP program. The government's position was that federal law requires that New Mexico's 25 percent "matching" share of SCP program payments must consist of state or county funds, and not impermissible "donations" from private hospitals.

[51.1] Department of Justice, *Community Health Systems Professional Services Corporation and Three Affiliated New Mexico Hospitals to Pay $75 Million to Settle False Claims Act Allegations*, (Feb. 2, 2015), *available at* http://www.justice.gov/opa/pr/community-health-systems-professional-services-corporation-and-three-affiliated-new-mexico.

### § 4-2(a)(5) What Is "False" or "Fraudulent"?

### § 4-2(a)(5)(i) Retention of Overpayments and Reverse False Claims

On February 16, 2015, CMS announced a delay in publication of a Final Rule on reporting and returning overpayments, despite the general guideline that final rules be issued within three years of a proposed or Interim Final Rule. According to CMS, "[b]ased on both public comments received and internal stakeholder feedback, we have determined that there are significant policy and operational issues that need to be resolved in order to address all of the issues raised by comments to the proposed rule and to ensure appropriate coordination with other government agencies."[63.1] The timeline for publication of the Final Rule was extended to February 16, 2016.

The first reported case to test the reverse false claims theory as applied to a delay in returning overpayments beyond 60 days is *United States ex rel. Kane v. Continuum Health Partners, Inc. et al.*, No. 11-2325 (S.D.N.Y. June 27, 2014). There, the DOJ intervened in an FCA action alleging solely a violation of the 60-day overpayment rule.

The complaint alleges that the defendant hospitals received payments for claims wrongly billed to Medicaid and that the defendants received notice of these overpayments from an employee's internal investigation and a state agency.

An employee's investigation revealed approximately 900 specific overpayments totaling over $1 million due to a computer error, which the defendants eventually repaid in full. Instead of reimbursing the overpay-

§ 4-2                 *Legal Issues in Healthcare Fraud and Abuse*

ments within the required 60-day period, the defendants are alleged to have repaid the claims in "small batches" over the next two-plus years. According to the government's complaint, final repayments were not made until March 2013, and repayments were made for more than 300 of the claims only after the Government issued a Civil Investigative Demand to Continuum concerning these payments in June 2012.

The parties are currently litigating a motion to dismiss.

**63.1** 80 Fed. Reg. 8,247 8,248 (Feb. 17, 2015).

### § 4-2(a)(5)(ii)   Use of Statistical Sampling to Establish False Claims Act Liability

Statistical sampling techniques have been used for some time to establish damages in false claims act cases. Increasingly, statistical sampling also is being used to establish false claims act liability.

In *United States ex rel. Martin v. Life Care Centers of America* (E.D. Tenn. 2014),**63.2** the district court denied the defendant's motion for summary judgment which argued that the government should be precluded from the use of statistical sampling for FCA liability purposes. "According to the government, the Company, which operated skilled nursing facilities, pressured its therapists to target Ultra High RUG levels and longer average length of stay periods for patients, and billed Medicare for services that were "medically unreasonable, unnecessary, and unskilled." To prove its case, the government sought to use a random sample of 400 admissions from 82 of the Company's facilities for a six year period.

The court concluded that statistical sampling "is a legally viable mechanism" for attempting to prove FCA claims "in complex FCA actions where a claim-by-claim review is impracticable." The defendant has "tools at its disposal to attack the weight to be accorded to any extrapolated evidence," since statistical sampling "does not and cannot control the weight that the fact finder may accord to the extrapolated evidence."

**63.2** 2014 U.S. Dist. LEXIS 142660 (E.D. Tenn. Sept. 29, 2014).

### § 4-2(a)(6)   What Is "Material"?

In April 2013, the U.S. Court of Appeals for the Sixth Circuit reversed a District Court's FCA ruling against MedQuest Associates Inc., and in doing so drew a distinction between conditions of participation and conditions of payment. The District Court held that Medquest violated the FCA under both implied and express certification theories when it: (1) failed to meet certain physician supervisory requirements; and, (2) used a predecessor's Medicare provider number to bill claims. In the District Court's ruling, each claim submitted by MedQuest was to be assessed a civil penalty, totaling $11.1

million. The Sixth Circuit disagreed. It held that the FCA is triggered when the conduct violates a condition of payment. Since the court also held that Medicare's supervisory requirements were not conditions of payment, the government's false certification theory did not apply and the FCA was not violated.[65.1] The Sixth Circuit also held that Medquest did not violate the FCA when it used an acquired predecessor's Medicare billing number because the government could not show that Medquest was not entitled to continue using the billing number. The Sixth Circuit suggested that Medquest merely failed to update enrollment information. The Sixth Circuit's distinction between a condition of participation and a condition of payment is significant. Government prosecutors have traditionally taken the view that a provider who fails to satisfy a condition of participation makes a false certification and accordingly violates the FCA. This ruling reinforces the notion that not all Medicare rules are material to payment.

[65.1] United States *ex rel.* Hobbs v. Medquest Associates Inc., No. 11-6520 (Tenn. Apr. 1, 2013).

### § 4-2(b)  Anti-Kickback Violations as False Claims

In March 2013, the U.S. District Court for the Southern District of Florida considered whether False Claims Act violations could result from Anti-Kickback actions against Tenet Healthcare Corporation based on false certifications. The complaint alleges that Tenet's leases with physician tenants were significantly below-market per square foot and contained "non-standard" benefits, including a lack of annual rent increases, parking and utility costs, among others. According to the complaint, these actions were sufficient to allege intent to induce referrals and trigger liability under the False Claims Act.[70.1] Tenet moved to dismiss all claims. Tenet argued that it made no certifications regarding compliance with the Stark and Anti-Kickback Statutes because any certifications or promises made on its provider agreement with Medicare and its annual hospital cost reports were too general to trigger liability under the False Claims Act. The court denied the motion to dismiss and stated that healthcare providers like Tenet who promise compliance on the provider agreement "would be virtually unfettered in [their] ability to receive funds from the government while flouting the law."[70.2] The court also held that certifications of compliance with the Anti-Kickback statute on hospital cost report "can" form the basis for liability under the False Claims Act. The court specifically noted that it was not, however, opining as to the materiality of such claims under the FCA.

[70.1] *See* http://healthlawrc.bna.com/hlrc/4225/split_display.adp?fedfid=30345477&vname=hcenotallissues&wsn=497575000&searchid=22138142&doctypeid=9&type=oadate4news&mode=doc&split=0&scm=4225&pg=0.

§ 4-4            *Legal Issues in Healthcare Fraud and Abuse*

**70.2** United States *ex rel.*, Marc Osheroff v. Tenet Healthcare Corp., No. 09-22253-CIV-PCH, Order Motion to Dismiss, citing United States *ex rel.* Hendow v. University of Phoenix, 461 F.3d 1166, 1176 (9th Cir. 2006).

### § 4-2(c)  FCA Damages

On March 21, 2013, Judge Easterbrook issued an opinion in *United States v. Anchor Mortgage Corporation* regarding damages awarded to the government for FCA violations alleged to have occurred during the application phase of 11 federal loan guarantees. The United States suggested a "gross" treble approach, wherein the amount the United States had paid to lenders under the guarantees was trebled and the amounts that had been realized from selling the properties by the date of trial were subsequently subtracted. Anchor Mortgage Corporation proposed a "net" treble approach wherein the amount realized by the United States would be subtracted from the total prior to trebling. Judge Easterbrook's opinion adopted the "net" trebling approach, stating that the courts routinely determine the value of property that is off the market and that damages should not be calculated dependent upon when or if the property is sold.**75.1**

**75.1** United States v. Anchor Mortgage Corporation, 711 F.3d 745 (7th Cir. 2013).

### § 4-2(d)  Qui tam Relators

### § 4-2(d)(1)  How Is a Qui tam Action Initiated?

Although the FCA is a civil statute, in September 2014, DOJ announced a new procedure whereby all new *qui tam* complaints are shared by the DOJ's Civil Division with the Criminal Division as soon as the cases are filed to determine whether to open a parallel criminal investigation. In connection with the announcement, whistleblower counsel were encouraged "to reach out to criminal authorities in appropriate cases, even when you are discussing the case with civil authorities."**85.1**

**85.1** Remarks, Leslie R. Caldwell (Sept. 17, 2014), http://www.justice.gov/criminal/pr/speeches/2014/crm-speech-140917.html.

### § 4-4  CRIMINAL LAWS PERTAINING TO FALSE CLAIMS AND FRAUDULENT BILLING ACTIVITIES

### § 4-4(c)  RICO Violations

Wesley Medical Center sued Forrest General Hospital and AAA Ambulance Service for violations of RICO and the Sherman Act in connection with an alleged conspiracy to divert patients. Specifically, Wesley alleged that patients that should have been delivered to Wesley were routed to Forrest General. The complaint alleged that patients were essentially "kidnapped" because they requested to be transported to Forrest Glen, but were instead diverted to Wesley.**168.1** The case is still pending in the

Southern District of Mississippi.

**168.1** *See generally* Wesley Health System LLC v. Forrest County Board of Supervisors, S.D. Miss., No. 2:12-CV-59, 2014 U.S. Dist. LEXIS 7764 (S.D. Miss. 2014).

## § 4-5 FALSE CLAIMS THEORIES APPLICABLE TO MULTIPLE SEGMENTS OF THE HEALTHCARE INDUSTRY

### § 4-5(b) Providing Medically Unnecessary Services

In January 2014, St. Joseph Health System in Kentucky paid $16.5 million to settle allegations that it submitted Medicare and Medicaid claims for medically unnecessary cardiac procedures.[213.1] The settlement also resolves allegations that Saint Joseph Hospital violated the federal Stark Law and Anti-Kickback Statute by entering into sham management agreements with the cardiologists who performed the procedures. One of the physicians pleaded guilty to a health care fraud offense in 2013 and is currently serving a 30 month prison sentence.

In May 2014 Kings Daughters Medical Center (KDMC) agreed to pay $40.9 million to resolve allegations that it submitted false claims to the Medicare and Kentucky Medicaid programs for medically unnecessary coronary stents and diagnostic catheterizations, and had prohibited financial relationships with physicians referring patients to the hospital. The government alleged that, between 2006 and 2011, KDMC billed for numerous unnecessary coronary stents and diagnostic catheterizations performed by KDMC physicians on Medicare and Medicaid patients who did not need them. The settlement also resolved allegations that KDMC violated the Stark Law by paying certain cardiologists salaries that were unreasonably high and in excess of fair market value. KDMC entered into a 5-year Corporate Integrity Agreement with the OIG.

**213.1** Department of Justice, *Kentucky Hospital Agrees to Pay Government $16.5 Million to Settle Allegations of Unnecessary Cardiac Procedures*, (Jan. 29, 2014), *available at* http://www.justice.gov/opa/pr/kentucky-hospital-agrees-pay-government-165-million-settle-allegations-unnecessary-cardiac.

### § 4-5(e) Filing False Cost Reports

In October 2014, Extendicare Health Services settled for $38 million for providing materially substandard nursing services that were so deficient that they were effectively worthless.[230.1] This was the largest failure of care settlement with a chain-wide skilled nursing facility. As part of the settlement, Extendicare was required to enter into a five year chain-wide Corporate Integrity Agreement with the OIG. The settlement also resolved allegations that Extendicare provided medically unreasonable and unnecessary rehabilitation therapy services to its Medicare Part A beneficiaries.

In contrast to the Extendicare settlement, the Seventh Circuit U.S. Court

## § 4-5    Legal Issues in Healthcare Fraud and Abuse

of Appeals chipped away at the worthless services theory in *United States ex rel. Absher et al. v. Momence Meadows Nursing Center Inc. et al.*[230.2] There, the relator alleged that the defendant nursing center provided substandard care to its residents while receiving full per diem reimbursement from the federal government. The Seventh Circuit reversed a judgment of over $28 million in FCA fines and treble compensatory damages. The court found it would be "absurd" to contend that the nursing home's services were "truly or effectively 'worthless' "—as one of the relators even admitted that her mother received "good care" at the facility. The court held that "[s]ervices that are 'worth less' are not 'worthless' " and "saved for another day" the issue of whether worthless services is a cognizable basis for alleging FCA liability in the Seventh Circuit.

[230.1] Department of Justice, *Extendicare Health Services Inc. Agrees to Pay $38 Million to Settle False Claims Act Allegations Relating to the Provision of Substandard Nursing Care and Medically Unnecessary Rehabilitation Therapy*, (Oct. 10, 2014), *available at* http://www.justice.gov/opa/pr/extendicare-health-services-inc-agrees-pay-38-million-settle-false-claims-act-allegations.

[230.2] 764 F.3d 699 (7th Cir. 2014).

### § 4-5(f)    Quality of Care

In December 2012, the DOJ intervened in a *qui tam* false claims lawsuit filed in Mississippi against Hyperion Foundation Inc., doing business as Oxford Health & Rehabilitation Center. The lawsuit alleges that the nursing home operator billed Medicare and Medicaid for services that were effectively worthless and grossly substandard. Residents allegedly received such a poor quality of care that it violated the nursing home's statutory and regulatory duties under Medicare, Medicaid, and Mississippi law.[246.1] The complaint alleged that there was "consistent and widespread failure to provide the most basic and essential nursing service [to patients]."[246.2] According to the plaintiff, residents suffered bed sores, falls, malnutrition and dehydration as a result of Oxford's conduct. Among other acts and omissions, the government also charged that Oxford failed to observe infection control procedures and maintain sufficient staffing.[246.3]

[246.1] United States *ex rel.* Academy Health Center Inc. v. Hyperion Foundation Inc. d/b/a Oxford Health & Rehabilitation Center, S.D. Miss., No. 3:10 CV0052, 2012 U.S. Dist. LEXIS 20674 (S.D. Miss. 2012), *intervention announced* (Dec. 10, 2012).

[246.2] *See Complaint* United States *ex rel.* Academy Health Center Inc. v. Hyperion Foundation Inc. d/b/a Oxford Health & Rehabilitation Center, S.D. Miss., No. 3:10 CV0052, 2012 U.S. Dist. LEXIS 20674 (S.D. Miss. 2012).

[246.3] *See also DOJ Intervenes in Qui Tam Lawsuit Alleging Nursing Home Billings for Deficient Care* (BNA Dec. 11, 2012).

## § 4-6 FALSE CLAIMS ENFORCEMENT ACTIVITIES SPECIFIC TO PARTICULAR SEGMENTS OF THE HEALTHCARE INDUSTRY

### § 4-6(a) Hospitals

#### § 4-6(a)(3) Outlier Payments

In 2012, Lenox Hill Hospital paid $12 million to settle allegations that it inflated charges to receive outlier payments from Medicare. According to the settlement agreement, Lenox Hill improperly received outlier payments that resulted from the hospital changing its room and board charges in 2002 and not grounding the charges in actual costs of services provided to patients.[289.1]

[289.1] Settlement Agreement: U.S. v. Lenox Hill Hospital No. 12 Civ. 3451 (S.D.N.Y).

#### § 4-6(a)(4) Inpatient Admissions, Site of Service and One Days Stays

The government has recently stepped up its efforts to investigate and prosecute the overuse of the hospital inpatient admission status. In sum, during these investigations, the government often alleges that patients should have been more appropriately deemed outpatient or placed in observation status instead of being admitted as inpatients. Observation and outpatient designations typically, although not always, reimburse at a lower level than an inpatient admission. Of particular concern to the government are "one day stays," (patients who are admitted and discharged in less than a 24-hour period), and "same day stays or zero day stays" (patients who are admitted and discharged in the same calendar day).

In one of the largest recoveries to date involving inappropriate patient rehabilitation admissions, Tenet Healthcare agreed to pay $42.75 million in April of 2012 to settle allegations that the group violated the FCA by billing Medicare for inpatient rehabilitation treatment between 2005 and 2007. According to allegations, Tenet improperly billed Medicare for treating patients at 25 inpatient rehabilitation facilities even though the patients did not meet the standards to qualify for admission.[295.1]

In September 2012, Wyoming Medical Center paid $2.7 million to settle a whistleblower case accusing the center of submitting fraudulent claims to Medicare by changing the admission status of its patients from outpatient to inpatient status without a physician order. The OIG launched an investigation, discovering that the medical center had: (1) submitted inpatient reimbursement claims to Medicare for procedures that had been performed in an outpatient setting; (2) submitted inpatient reimbursement claims for hospital stays in which there was no record of a physician ordering

§ 4-6    *Legal Issues in Healthcare Fraud and Abuse*

inpatient-level care; and (3) submitted inpatient reimbursement claims for services provided to patients who did not meet requirements for inpatient admission.[295.2]

Morton Plant Mease Health Care Inc., a Florida hospital group paid $10.2 million in a settlement with the DOJ to resolve allegations that Morton billed certain interventional cardiac and vascular procedures as inpatient when the services should have been billed as outpatient or observational status.[295.3]

In December 2012, WakeMed Health and Hospitals was criminally charged with Medicare outpatient upcoding in the Raleigh campus' cardiac department from 2003 to 2010. According to the charges, WakeMed billed Medicare for patient overnight stays in its Heart Center Observation Area when the patients had been treated and released the same day. Although the hospital secured a deferred prosecution agreement[295.4] for the criminal charges, WakeMed paid an $8 million civil settlement to Medicare and agreed to a five year corporate integrity agreement with HHS, including extensive compliance training for employees and board members, as well as the establishment of a compliance committee to certify the effectiveness of WakeMed's efforts.[295.6]

In January 2014, the DOJ intervened in eight false claims lawsuits filed by whistleblowers against Health Management Associates Inc. (HMA). The lawsuits allege that HMA hospitals pressured physicians to admit inpatients who could have received outpatient treatment (or have been placed under observation or released) in order to inflate Medicare and Medicaid charges and reach certain "corporate benchmarks." Physicians were allegedly then paid kickbacks based on these admissions. Furthermore, HMA has been accused of "aggressively utiliz[ing]" the computer software program Pro-Med Complaint Test Mapping. Allegedly, the software program automatically ordered tests based on a patient's primary medical complaint, and emergency room nurses were required to order a minimum number of the automatically generated tests. In addition to these claims, the lawsuits also allege that HMA paid kickbacks to physician groups to induce referrals, including providing free office space and staffing to one group in exchange for referrals in Florida. The false claims lawsuits have been filed in Georgia, Illinois, Pennsylvania, North Carolina, South Carolina, and Florida.[295.7]

In August 2014, Community Health Systems (CHS) agreed to pay $98.15 million to settle allegations that it knowingly and improperly sought reimbursement for inpatient services that should have been billed as outpatient or observation services and increased inpatient admissions of Medicare, Medicaid and TRICARE beneficiaries over the age of 65 who originally presented to the emergency departments at 119 CHS hospitals.[295.8] The settlement also resolved FCA allegations that one of its affiliated hospitals, Laredo Medical Center, improperly billed Medicare for certain inpatient procedures and for services rendered to patients referred in violation of the physician self-referral law. CHS has entered into a 5-year Corporate Integrity Agreement with the OIG.

In October 2014 Dignity Health agreed to pay the federal government $37 million to settle allegations that 13 of its hospitals in California, Nevada and Arizona knowingly submitted false claims to Medicare and TRICARE by admitting patients who could have been treated on a less costly outpatient basis.[295.9] The allegations included billing for inpatient care for elective cardiovascular procedures that should have been billed as outpatient surgeries; billing for kyphoplasty procedures, which the government alleged are minimally-invasive and should have been billed as less costly outpatient procedures; and admitting patients for certain common medical diagnoses where admission as an inpatient was medically unnecessary. The qui tam relator in this case, a former employee of Dignity Health, received $6.25 million as a result of the settlement, and the Hospital entered into a 5-year Corporate Integrity Agreement with the OIG.

[295.1] DOJ, Press Release, *Dallas-based Tenet Healthcare Pays More Than $42 Million to Settle Allegations of Improperly Billing Medicare* (Apr. 10, 2012) *available online at* http://www.justice.gov/opa/pr/2012/April/12-civ-446.html.

[295.2] United States *ex rel.* Bryden v. Wyoming Medical Center, No. 07 CV251 (D. Wyo. 2012).

[295.3] *See* United States *ex rel.* Ferrare v. Morton Plant Mease Health Care Inc., M.D. Fla., No. 08:cv:01689-MSS-MAP.

[295.4] *See also* § 9-4(d) for a discussion of the circumstances surrounding WakeMed's deferred prosecution agreement.

[295.6] *See* United States v. WakeMed d/b/a WakeMed Health and Hospitals, No. 5:12-cr-00398-BO (D. NC. 2013).

[295.7] *See* http://www.justice.gov/opa/pr/2014/January/14-civ-037.html.

[295.8] Department of Justice, *Community Health Systems Inc. to Pay $98.15 Million to Resolve False Claims Act Allegations*, (Aug. 4, 2014), *available at* http://www.justice.gov/opa/pr/community-health-systems-inc-pay-9815-million-resolve-false-claims-act-allegations.

[295.9] Department of Justice, *Dignity Health Agrees to Pay $37 Million to Settle False Claims Act Allegations*, (Oct. 30, 2014), *available at* http://www.justice.gov/opa/pr/dignity-health-agrees-pay-37-million-settle-false-claims-act-allegations.

### § 4-6(a)(5)  Billing for Provider-Based Services

In October 2014, Our Lady of Lourdes Memorial Hospital in Binghamton, NY paid more than $3.37 million to resolve self-disclosed billing improprieties and address potential FCA liability for failure to comply with Medicare

§ 4-6    *Legal Issues in Healthcare Fraud and Abuse*

"provider-based" billing requirements.[295.10] The hospital billed Medicare for hyperbaric oxygen therapy services rendered by a third party in a facility using the rate for "provider-based" services but the facility did not satisfy the "provider-based status" requirements for Medicare billing. Since the hospital incorrectly submitted claims using the "provider-based" amounts, Medicare overpaid on the claims. The DOJ cited the hospital's decision to self-disclose as one factor for not imposing treble damages.

[295.10] Department of Justice, *Our Lady of Lourdes Memorial Hospital Has Paid More Than $3.37 Million To Resolve Self-Disclosed Billing Improprieties*, (Oct. 16, 2014), *available at* http://www.justice.gov/usao-ndny/pr/our-lady-lourdes-memorial-hospital-has-paid-more-337-million-resolve-self-disclosed.

### § 4-6(e)    Durable Medical Equipment and Home Medical Suppliers

In April 2012, AmMed Direct paid $18 million to settle allegations that the company submitted false claims to Medicare. Prosecutors alleged that AmMed violated direct marking rules and the FCA. AmMed allegedly offered a free cookbook through television advertisements in an attempt to sell diabetic testing supplies and then contacted the individuals who responded to the free book, some of whom were covered by Medicare and Medicaid. AmMed subsequently billed Medicare and other government healthcare programs for the supplies. The government alleged that some beneficiaries who received the free cookbook returned the diabetic supplies and AmMed failed to properly refund the government programs for the returned items. AmMed paid approximately $17.6 million to the federal government and $439,003 to the state of Tennessee in the settlement.[311.1]

In September 2012, Pinnacle Medical Solutions LLC settled a lawsuit alleging that the durable medical equipment supplier billed Medicare for insulin pump kits and blood glucose test strips that lacked a certification of medical necessity. The $1.8 million settlement came without government intervention.[311.2]

[311.1] United States *ex rel.* McNeese v. AmMed Direct LLC, M.D. Tenn., No. 3:09 CV275, *case unsealed* (Apr. 12, 2012).

[311.2] United States *ex rel.* Horne v. Pinnacle Medical Solutions LLC, N.D. Ala., No. 2:09 CV01193 KOB, *joint notice of voluntary dismissal* (Sep. 5, 2012).

### § 4-6(f)    Home Health Agencies

In September of 2011, Maxim Healthcare Services Inc. settled with 41 states over allegations that the company submitted fraudulent billings for services not rendered or otherwise not reimbursable to government healthcare programs from 2003 through 2009. The $150 million settlement included $20 million in criminal penalties and $130 million in civil settlements to the Veterans Affairs program, the United States and the 41 states.[326.1]

The following month, New York City paid $70 million to settle claims that its Human Resources Administration overcharged Medicaid for personal care services for patients over a 10 year period. The *qui tam* lawsuit alleged that New York City had not performed the necessary assessments and reviews to determine eligibility for 24 hour personal care services.[326.2]

In the hospice care setting, false claims suits have been filed over improper billing for continuous care services. Continuous care is provided when a patient requires in-home skilled nursing services. Medicare reimburses providers at a higher rate for continuous care hospice service as opposed to routine care. In March of 2012, Odyssey HealthCare Inc. settled a $25 million false claims lawsuit alleging that the hospice care provider billed Medicare for services that were either unnecessary or never performed from January 2006 to January 2009. In addition to the settlement agreement, Odyssey entered into a five-year corporate integrity agreement (CIA) with the OIG.[326.3]

In April 2014, Amedisys paid $150 million to settle allegations that it billed Medicare for nursing and therapy services that were medically unnecessary or provided to patients who were not homebound, and misrepresented patients' conditions, allegedly as a result of management pressure on nurses and therapists. The settlement also resolves allegations that Amedisys maintained improper financial relationships with referring physicians.[326.4]

[326.1] United States *ex rel.* West v. Maxim Healthcare Services Inc., D.N.J., No. 04 CV4906, *settlement* (Sep. 12, 2011). United States v. Maxim Healthcare Services Inc., D.N.J., No. 11 CR6107, *deferred prosecution agreement* (Sep. 12, 2011).

[326.2] United States *ex rel.* Feldman v. City of New York. No. 09 Civ. 8381 (JSR), (S.D.N.Y. 2011).

[326.3] United States *ex rel.* Rouse v. Odyessey Health Care Inc., No. 08-C-0383 (E.D. Wisc. 2009).

[326.4] Department of Justice, *Amedisys Home Health Companies Agree to Pay $150 Million to Resolve False Claims Act Allegations*, (Apr. 23, 2014), *available at* http://www.justice.gov/opa/pr/amedisys-home-health-companies-agree-pay-150-million-resolve-false-claims-act-allegations.

### § 4-6(g) Medicare Contractors

In April 2012, four *qui tam* lawsuits were settled by WellCare Health Plans Inc. According to the lawsuits, the company falsely inflated its medical care expenditures, retained overpayments, falsified documents representing patients' medical conditions and treatments, engaged in marketing abuses, falsely reported "grades of service" at its call centers, and operated a "sham" Special Investigations Unit. The settlement requires WellCare to pay the United States and nine states $137.5 million plus interest over a period of three years.[333.1]

[333.1] DOJ, Press Release, *Florida-Based WellCare Health Plans Agrees to Pay $137.5 Million to Resolve False Claims Allegations* (April 3, 2012), *available online at* http://www.justice.gov/opa/pr/2012/April/12-civ-425.html.

### § 4-6(h) Pharmacies and Pharmaceutical Manufacturers

In March 2013, *qui tam* relator Michael Yarberry filed a complaint claiming that Sears Holding Corporation subsidiary Kmart Corp. gave discounts on prescription drugs to Medicare, Medicaid and Tricare beneficiaries via the use of gift cards and coupons from November 2007 through 2013. The complaint alleges that Kmart did not provide adequate training for its employees and that the employees failed to use a computer system to flag ineligible customers. The defendants' safe harbor argument was dismissed by Judge Michael J. Reagan and the case is currently awaiting a trial date.[339.1]

Similarly, in April 2012, the national chain drugstore Walgreen Co. paid $7.9 million to settle government claims that the company offered kickbacks to government health care program participants who transferred prescriptions to Walgreens pharmacies. The government alleged that Walgreens employees were aware that they were prohibited from providing gift cards or gift checks to government health program beneficiaries but offered the incentives anyway.[339.2]

BioScrip Inc., a specialty pharmacy agreed on January 8, 2014 to pay $15 million to settle charges that it had entered into a marketing arrangement for the drug Exjade with Novartis Pharmaceuticals Corporation (NPC). The charges alleged that, from February 2007 to May 2012, NPC provided kickbacks in the form of rebates to BioScrip to promote refills of Exjade. According to the Department of Justice, Bioscrips coordinated with NPC to implement a program of calling Exjade patients to offer clinical "counseling" or "education." However, the DOJ alleged that the real purpose was to "obtain more refill orders so that Novartis could increase its Exjade sales and meet its national Exjade sales target and BioScrip, in turn, could get more patient referrals and higher rebates."[339.3] While Bioscrips has settled these allegations, NPC released a statement on January 9, 2014 saying that it "stands behind" its programs, including outreach to pharmacies, and intends to defend itself in litigation.[339.4]

In late 2011 and 2012, four large settlements by pharmaceutical manufacturers were announced in connection with improper marketing and promotion of drugs. In November 2011, Merck agreed to pay $950 million to settle a federal investigation of the company's promotion of Vioxx, a discontinued painkiller. The government alleged that Merck engaged in off-label marketing by promoting Vioxx to physicians for treatment of rheumatoid arthritis. In addition, Merck made false statements as to the safety of the drug.[339.5]

In August of 2012, Janssen Pharmaceuticals agreed to pay $181 million to 36 states and the District of Columbia to resolve alleged off-label promotion of its antipsychotic drug Risperdal. According to complaints, Janssen promoted Risperdal for unapproved uses as well as concealed and misrepresented information regarding the drug's side effects.[339.6]

In October 2012, Abbott Laboratories, Inc. was ordered to pay $500 million by a federal judge for unlawful promotion of the prescription drug Depakote. In addition to the fine, the drug company paid a forfeiture of almost $199 million.[339.7]

In December 2012, the biotechnology company Amgen Inc. agreed to pay $762 million to resolve criminal and civil liability from the sale and promotion of three drugs: Aranesp, Enbrel and Neulasta. The criminal settlement required Amgen to pay a criminal fine of $136 million and a criminal forfeiture of $14 million for the promotion of Aranesp for off-label treatments unapproved by the FDA. The civil settlement required Amgen to pay $612 million for false claims submitted to Medicare and Medicaid, as well as other government insurance programs. The government alleged that Amgen engaged in off-label promotion for Aranesp, Engrel and Nuelasta; offered kickbacks to various entities to use the drugs; and reported false prices. In addition to the settlement, Amgen agreed to enter into a Corporate Integrity Agreement with the Department of Health and Human Services Office of the Inspector General.[339.8]

In one of the largest settlements in United States history, Johnson & Johnson (J&J) and its subsidiaries agreed in November 2013 to pay over $2.2 billion to settle civil and criminal allegations involving marketing of off-label, unapproved uses for Risperdal, Invega and Natrecor, as well as payment of kickbacks to physicians. The government charged that Risperdal and Invega, both antipsychotic drugs, were marketed for off-label use in treating elderly dementia patients, as well as children and individuals with mental disabilities. In addition, J&J was charged with paying kickbacks to Omnicare, Inc. to promote the use of Risperdal and other J&J drugs in nursing homes. Finally, the civil settlement also resolves allegations that J&J and another of its subsidiaries, Scios Inc., submitted false claims for the heart failure drug Natrecor. The drug, which the FDA approved for patients

§ 4-6    *Legal Issues in Healthcare Fraud and Abuse*

with acutely decompensated congestive heart failure, was marketed by Scios for outpatient infusions for patients with less severe heart failure. In addition to the criminal and civil resolutions, J&J executed a five-year corporate integrity agreement with the OIG.[339.9]

In the largest healthcare fraud settlement in United States history, pharmaceutical company GlaxoSmithKline (GSK) pled guilty and agreed to pay $3 billion to resolve allegations that the company unlawfully promoted various prescription drugs, among other violations. The suit alleged that GSK promoted the drugs Paxil, Wellbutrin, Lamictal and Zofran for off-label uses, paid kickbacks to physicians to prescribe those drugs (as well as Imitrex, Lotonex, Flovent and Valtrex), made false statements regarding the safety of Avandia, and reported false best prices. In addition to the criminal and civil resolutions, GSK executed a five-year corporate integrity agreement with the OIG.[339.10]

In February 2014, Endo Pharmaceuticals paid $192.7 million to settle criminal and civil allegations of off label promotion of Lidoderm.[339.11] The settlement includes a deferred prosecution agreement, monetary penalties and forfeiture totaling $20.8 million, and civil false claims settlements with the federal government and the states and the District of Columbia totaling $171.9 million. The deferred prosecution agreement includes enhanced compliance measures, including making the results of certain clinical trials publicly available and requiring an annual review and certification of its compliance efforts by the Chief Executive Officer of its parent company. Endo also entered into a corporate integrity agreement with the OIG.

[339.1] See generally U.S. *ex rel.* Yarberry v. Sears Holdings Corporation, et al., No. 09-CV-588-MJR-PMF.

[339.2] *See* Department of Justice Press Release *available at* http://www.justice.gov/opa/pr/2012/April/12-civ-505.html.

[339.3] DOJ Press Release, *Manhattan U.S. Attorney Simultaneously Files Additional Healthcare Fraud Claims Against Novartis Pharmaceuticals Corp. and Settles Lawsuit Against Bioscrip, Inc., in Connection With a Multimillion-Dollar Kickback Scheme Involving a Prescription Drug*, *available at* http://www.justice.gov/usao/nys/pressreleases/January14/NovartsBioScrip.php.

[339.4] *See* Press Release, *Novartis*, *available at* http://www.pharma.us.novartis.com/newsroom/pressreleases/137192.shtml.

[339.5] DOJ, Press Release, *U.S. Pharmaceutical Company Merck Sharp & Dohme to Pay Nearly One Billion Dollars Over Promotion of Vioxx®* (Nov. 22, 2011), *available online at* http://www.justice.gov/opa/pr/2011/November/11-civ-1524.html.

[339.6] Jeffrey S. Chiesa v. Janssen Pharmaceuticals, Inc, No. C-75-12 (S.D. NJ 2012).

[339.7] United States v. Abbott Laboratories, No. 1:12-cr-00026-SGW (W.D. Va. 2012), *sentencing* (Oct. 2, 2012).

48

**339.8** See http://www.justice.gov/opa/pr/2012/December/12-civ-1523.html.

**339.9** See http://www.justice.gov/opa/pr/2013/November/13-ag-1170.html.

**339.10** DOJ, Press Release, *GlaxoSmithKline to Plead Guilty and Pay $3 Billion to Resolve Fraud Allegations and Failure to Report Safety Data* (July 2, 2012) *available online at* http://www.justice.gov/opa/pr/2012/July/12-civ-842.html.

**339.11** Department of Justice, *Endo Pharmaceuticals and Endo Health Solutions to Pay $192.7 Million to Resolve Criminal and Civil Liability Relating to Marketing of Prescription Drug Lidoderm for Unapproved Uses*, (Feb. 21, 2014), *available at* http://www.justice.gov/opa/pr/endo-pharmaceuticals-and-endo-health-solutions-pay-1927-million-resolve-criminal-and-civil.

### § 4-6(k) Dentists

In March 2012, All Smiles Dental Center, Inc. and dentist Richard Malouf agreed to pay the government $1.2 million to resolve allegations that they had submitted false claims to the Texas Medicaid program. The government claimed that the center submitted claims for orthodontic services that were never completed and/or were not properly documented. As part of the settlement, All Smiles Dental Center entered into a five-year corporate integrity agreement with the OIG.[355.1]

**355.1** Northern District of Texas Press Release, *Texas Orthodontic Clinic and Former Owner Resolve Allegations of False Medicaid Claims* (Mar. 21, 2012) *available online at* http://www.justice.gov/usao/txn/PressRelease/2012/MAR2012/mar21Malouf_AllSmiles_Settlement_PR.html.

### § 4-6(l) Ambulance Companies

In October 2012, Okechukwu Ofoegbu, the administrator of Cardiomax EMS, pled guilty to submitting false claims to Medicare. According the plea agreement, Ofoegbu submitted falsified ambulance run sheets and conspired to submit claims that were either knowingly miscoded, not medically necessary, or simply not provided. The indictment was part of a national effort resulting in charges against 107 individuals for their participation false billing schemes.[364.1]

**364.1** DOJ, Press Release, *Houston Ambulance Company Administrator Pleads Guilty to Fraud* (Oct. 15, 2012), *available online at* http://www.justice.gov/opa/pr/2012/October/12-crm-1242.html.

### § 4-6(m) Medical Device Companies

In June 2012, Stryker Corp. agreed to pay the DOJ $33 million to resolve sales and marketing allegations related to its OtisKnee custom fit total knee replacement technology. Stryker said its proposed settlement relates to a DOJ subpoena the company received in connection with the sales and marketing of OtisKnee, which was not cleared by the FDA. The final terms of the solution have not yet been announced.[374.1]

**374.1** *Available online at* http://www.reuters.com/article/2012/06/05/us-stryker-doj-idUSBRE85418K20120605.

# 5
# Administrative Sanctions Available to Federal Enforcers

## § 5-2 EXCLUSION FROM MEDICARE, MEDICAID, AND OTHER STATE HEALTHCARE PROGRAMS

### § 5-2(b) Permissive Exclusion

On May 9, 2014, the OIG published a proposed rule amending the regulations related to the OIG's exclusion authority (Proposed Rule).[44.1] Most significantly, under the Proposed Rule the OIG contends that there is no statute of limitations to exclusions, even when the exclusion is based on violations of another statute that might have a specific limitations period. In addition, among other things, the Proposed Rule would amend various provisions, including 42 C.F.R. §§ 1001.1202, 1001.301 of the OIG's permission exclusion authority regulations to reflect the new or expanded authority provided by Health Reform. Further, in the Proposed Rule the OIG proposed, among other things, to:

- Codify regulations related to making false statements or misrepresenting material facts;
- Increase the financial loss aggravating factor to $15,000 and remove the aggravating factor related to overpayments because it is duplicative;
- Broaden the scope of the permissive exclusion for failing to supply certain payment information to apply not only to individuals or entities that "furnish items or services for which payment may be made" but also to individuals or entities that order, refer or certify the need for such items or services;
- Codify regulations related to the OIG's expanded authority to exclude an individual or entity that has been convicted of an offense in connection with the obstruction of an investigation or audit related to any criminal offense;
- Clarify the circumstances pertaining to the length of exclusion

imposed on individuals with ownership or control interests in sanctioned entities. In particular, the Proposed Rule would amend the regulations to state that the length of the individual's exclusion will be for the same period as that of the sanctioned entity with which the individual has or had the prohibited relationship, even if the individual terminates the relationship with the sanctioned entity after it has been excluded; and

- Amend and clarify the reinstatement rules.

[44.1] 79 Fed. Reg. 26,810 (May 9, 2014).

### § 5-2(e)  Effects of Exclusion

On May 8, 2013, the OIG issued an Updated Special Advisory Bulletin on the effect of exclusion from participation in federal healthcare programs (Exclusion Update) which supersedes the original bulletin issued in 1999.[75.1] In addition to reiterating much of OIG's previous guidance, the Exclusion Update also addresses: (i) whether an excluded person may provide an item or service that a health provider needs but that is not for direct patient care or billing; (ii) the obligation of a provider or entity to screen employees against the List of Excluded Individuals and Entities (LEIE); (iii) the distinctions between the information that appears on the LEIE and the information that appears on the General Services Administration's (GSA) System for Award Management (SAM) and other systems that report sanctions or adverse actions taken with respect to health care practitioners, such as the National Practitioner Data Bank (NPDB); (iv) whether a provider that employs or contracts with an excluded person is subject to CMP liability; and (v) the protocol for an employer to disclose when it employs, or contracts with, an excluded person.

According to the Exclusion Update the prohibitions on federal health care program payments for excluded persons apply even if the excluded person changes from one health care profession to another, while excluded. In addition, the OIG emphasized that the prohibition prevents an excluded person from providing patient care but also from furnishing administration and management services that are payable by federal health care programs. However, an excluded person may refer a patient to a non-excluded provider if the excluded provider does not furnish, order, or prescribe any services for the referred patient, and the non-excluded provider treats the patient and independently bills. In addition, although exclusion does not directly prohibit the excluded person from owning a provider that participates in Federal health care programs, the Exclusion Update states that "any provider owned in part (5 percent or more) by an excluded person is potentially subject to exclusion. Additionally, an excluded individual may be subject to liability if he or she has an ownership or control interest in a provider participating in Medicare or State health care programs, or if he or she is an officer or a managing employee of such an entity. According to the OIG, "this means that an excluded person may own a provider, but may not provide any items or services, including administrative and management services, that are payable by Federal health care programs."

In the Exclusion Update, the OIG reiterated its recommendation that providers screen employees and contractors utilizing the LEIE and suggested that providers use the LEIE as the primary source for screening rather than SAM or the NDPB and the Healthcare Integrity and Protection Data Bank. To determine which individuals and entities to screen, the OIG recommends that the provider review each job category or contractual relationship to determine whether the item or service being provided is directly or indirectly, in whole or in part, payable by a Federal health care program. If the item or service being provided is payable by a Federal health care program, the OIG recommends screening all persons that perform under that contract or that are in that job category.

The Exclusion Update lists limited circumstances in which a provider may employ or contract with an excluded person, including if:

- Federal health care programs do not pay, directly or indirectly, for the items or services being provided by the excluded individual; or
- the excluded person furnishes items or services solely to non-federal health care program beneficiaries.

The OIG also clarified that in these limited circumstances, a provider need not maintain a separate account from which to pay the excluded person, as long as no claims are submitted to or payment is received from Federal health care programs for items or services that the excluded person provides and such items or services relate solely to non-Federal health care program patients. Finally, the OIG recommends the use of the Provider Self-Disclosure Protocol[75.2] for providers that identify potential or actual violations.

[75.1] DHHS, OIG, *Special Advisory Bulletin on the Effect of Exclusion from Participation in Federal Health Care Programs*, May 8, 2013, *available online at* http://oig.hhs.gov/exclusions/files/sab-05092013.pdf.

[75.2] *See* HHS, OIG, *OIG's Provider Self-Disclosure Protocol*, *available online at* http://oig.hhs.gov/compliance/self-disclosure-info/files/Provider-Self-Disclosure-Protocol.pdf; *see also* Chapter 7, § 7-9.

## § 5-3 IMPOSITION OF CIVIL MONETARY PENALTIES

### § 5-3(a) Actions that May Result in the Imposition of CMPs

### § 5-3(a)(1)  Submission of Improperly Filed Claims

On October 3, 2014, the OIG published a proposed rule (Proposed Rule) to add new exceptions to the CMP for inducements being offered to federal health care program beneficiaries and to the CMP related to a hospital paying a physician for reducing or limiting the provision of items or services (referred to generally as the Gainsharing CMP).[82.1]

[82.1] 79 Fed. Reg. 59,717 (Oct. 3, 2014).

### § 5-3(a)(3)  Inducements to Beneficiaries

Under the Proposed Rule, the OIG proposes to codify the various statutory exceptions to the OIG's CMP authority that were included in Health Reform:

*Remuneration That Promotes Access/Low Risk of Harm*

In the Proposed Rule, the OIG proposed to codify Health Reform exception to the definition of "remuneration" that protects "any other remuneration which promotes access to care and poses a low risk of harm to patients and Federal health care programs." For purposes of this exception, the OIG is proposing that the phrase "promotes access to care" means that the "remuneration provided improves a particular beneficiary's ability to obtain medically necessary health care items and services." Recognizing that this is a narrow definition, the OIG sought comments as to whether this phrase should be interpreted more broadly, especially in light of the movement towards coordinated or integrated care arrangements that depend, in part, on patient interaction.

The OIG proposed interpreting the phrase "low risk of harm to Medicare and Medicaid beneficiaries and the Medicare and Medicaid programs" to mean that the remuneration: (1) is unlikely to interfere with, or influence, clinical decision-making; (2) is unlikely to increase costs to federal health care programs or beneficiaries through overutilization or inappropriate utilization; and (3) does not raise patient-safety or quality-of-care concerns.

In addition, in the Proposed Rule, the OIG considered whether to make a special provision for incentives offered by participants to beneficiaries covered by these programs and seeking proposals for regulatory text language, including "specific examples of the types of remuneration to beneficiaries" that would implement the principles described herein.

*Remuneration Offered Through a Retailer Rewards Program*

The OIG proposed to codify the retailer rewards exception from Health Reform in the Social Security Act by protecting the offer or transfer of items or services for free or less than fair market value by a person if:

1. the items or services consist of coupons, rebates, or other rewards from a retailer;
2. the items or services are offered or transferred on equal terms available to the general public, regardless of health insurance status; and
3. the offer or transfer of the items or services is not tied to the provision of other items or services reimbursed, in whole or in part, under Medicare or a state health care program.

The OIG's interpretation in the proposed regulation is largely consistent with its interpretation of the exception in its various Advisory Opinions. Moreover, the OIG proposed interpreting the various terms used in the exception, including the term "coupon," which is broadly defined as "something authorizing a discount," so it need not be an actual coupon; "rebates," which is interpreted as "a return on part of a payment"; "other rewards," which is interpreted as free items or services such as store merchandise, gasoline, or frequent flyer miles; and "retailer," which is interpreted "as having its usual meaning" as "an entity that sells items directly to consumers."

The requirement for offering or transferring items on equal terms available to the general public, regardless of health insurance status, is interpreted as consistent with the OIG's longstanding concern about discrimination against or in favor of certain patients (*i.e.*, lemon dropping and cherry picking). Therefore, rewards offered only to Medicare patients would not qualify under the exception. However, a dollar amount off any purchase in the store, including prescriptions, would qualify if offered to everyone in a zip code without regard to health insurance status.

The language of the tying prohibition provides that the offer or transfer of items not be tied to the provision of **other** federal or state health care program items or services.

The OIG interpreted this as requiring a complete attenuation of any connection between federally payable items and services and a loyalty program's rewards to include the manner in which a reward is both "earned" and "redeemed." At the "earning" end, the OIG stated in the Proposed Rule that the reward should not be conditioned on the purchase of goods or services reimbursed by a federal health care program, and should not treat federally reimbursable items and services in a manner that is different from non-reimbursable items.

At the "redeeming" end, the OIG stated in the Proposed Rule that programs in which the rewards themselves are federally reimbursed items or services do not qualify for the exemption.

***Financial Need Based Exception***

Section 1128A(i)(6) of the Social Security Act defines "remuneration" as transfers of items or services for free or which are not fair market value. However, an exception at 1128(A)(i)(6)(h) exists for such transfers provided that:

1. the items or services are not offered as part of any advertisement or solicitation;
2. the items or services are not tied to the provision of other services reimbursed by certain federal and state programs;
3. there is a reasonable connection between the items or services and the medical care of the individual; and
4. the items or services may be provided only after determining in good faith that the individual is in financial need.

In the Proposed Rule the OIG remained consistent with its position on prior issuances regarding the transfer of cash or cash equivalent items to beneficiaries. The OIG restated that such cash or equivalents (which can be converted to cash) are not protected as items or services under the exemption. However, the OIG did not take the opportunity to further clarify or modify what it considers impermissible cash equivalent instruments.

The OIG restated that protected items or services may not be offered as part of any advertisement or solicitation without further clarification on what conduct is considered an advertisement or solicitation.

Moreover, the OIG reaffirmed the position that it took in the retailers reward section above, namely that "we do not interpret the prohibition on tying the free or below-market items and services to services reimbursable by Medicare or Medicaid as requiring a complete severance of the offer from the medical care of the individual," but it is soliciting comments for this provision.

In the Proposed Rule, the OIG stated its belief that this exception was enacted to enable financially needy individuals to access items or services related to their medical care, and was not intended to cause a patient to seek additional care. The term "medical care" was defined broadly in the Proposed Rule as "treatment and management of illness or injury and the preservation of health through services offered by the medical, dental, pharmacy, nursing, and allied health professions." According to the OIG, what constitutes a "reasonable connection" between the remuneration and the patient's medical care requires consideration of two factors; first, whether a reasonable connection exists from a medical perspective, and second, whether a reasonable connection exists from a financial perspective.

Additionally, the OIG suggested that a reasonable connection exists from a medical perspective when the items or services would benefit or advance identifiable medical care or treatment that the individual patient is receiving. The OIG provided limited examples of items and services that, under certain circumstances, might qualify as medical care. However, the Proposed Rule suggested that all of the examples could run afoul of the exemption if, for example, they were provided but were not medically necessary.

The OIG also suggested that financial need would not be limited to "indigence" and "could include any reasonable measure of financial hardship." The Proposed Rule stated that a good faith determination of financial need may vary depending on a particular patient's circumstances and that the offeror of the items or services has some degree of flexibility to consider "relevant variables." Though the OIG has not previously taken the position that the financial need determination was required to be memorialized, it is considering whether it can necessitate the creation of such documentation. The OIG also suggested that, even if it does not ultimately decide to require a memorial, it would nonetheless be "prudent for those seeking protection under the proposed exception to maintain accurate and contemporaneous documentation of the need assessment and the criteria applied."

Finally, the OIG remained consistent with its prior views on routine copayment waivers and states that it proposes to interpret this provision as requiring a good faith individualized assessment of the patient's financial need on a case-by-case basis. The rule states that such an assessment should use an objective, uniform, and reasonable set of income guidelines that takes into account locality.

## *Waivers of Cost Sharing for the First Fill of a Generic Drug*

The OIG also proposed finalizing the exception to the definition of remuneration found in Section 1128A(i)(6)(I). This exception permits Prescription Drug Plan (PDP) sponsors of Part D plans or Medicare Advantage plans to waive enrollee copayments for the first fill of a covered generic drug. The OIG acknowledged that such a waiver could minimize drug costs by encouraging the use of lower-cost generic drugs. The Proposed Rule suggested that sponsors who offer these waivers will be required to disclose the waiver to the Centers for Medicare & Medicaid Services (CMS) in their benefit plan package. Since CMS already permits these waivers as part of Part D and Medicare Advantage plan benefit designs, the OIG clarified that it will not exercise its enforcement authority against plans complying with CMS requirements for these waivers prior to the finalization of the exception.

### § 5-3(a)(4) Payments to Induce Reduction or Limitation of Services (Gainsharing) and Other Cost Sharing Initiatives

The October 3, 2014, Proposed Rule is the first time since 1994 that the OIG has addressed the adoption of a regulation to further define and describe the scope of the Gainsharing CMP through the regulatory process under the Administrative Procedures Act.[126.1]

In the Proposed Rule, the OIG acknowledged that one of the challenges with the gainsharing statute is that it is not limited to incentive plans that reduce or limit "medically necessary" services but, instead, simply those that reduce "services." The OIG stated in the preamble to the Proposed Rule that "given the changes in the practice of medicine over the years, including collaborative efforts among providers and practitioners and the rise of widely accepted clinical metrics, we are considering a narrower interpretation of the term 'reduce or limit services' than [the OIG has] previously held."

In the Proposed Rule, the OIG proposed language that mirrors the statute and the following additional criteria to assess the magnitude of damages in reduction of services enforcement actions:

- nature of payment,
- extent to which the payment encouraged limiting medical care or premature discharge,
- actual or potential beneficiary harm, and
- financial condition of the hospital or physician.

Nevertheless, the OIG asked the public to provide comment on a number of significant issues, including the following:

1. Should the OIG develop a definition of the phrase "reduce or limit services" and, if so, what should it consist of? Should the regulation include a requirement that the hospital and/or physician participating in a gainsharing program notify potentially affected patients about the program?

2. The OIG states in the preamble that it has interpreted the prohibition on payments to reduce or limit services as including payments to limit items used in providing services. Is this interpretation appropriate or necessary?

3. Should a hospital's decision to standardize certain items (*e.g.*, surgical instruments, medical devices) be deemed to constitute

## § 5-3     Legal Issues in Healthcare Fraud and Abuse

"reducing or limiting care"? Would the answer be different if the physician were simply encouraged to choose from the standardized items but could still use other items if the physician so chose?

4. Should a hospital's decision to rely on protocols based on objective quality metrics for certain procedures be deemed to constitute "reducing or limiting care"? Should hospitals deciding to compensate physicians in connection with the use of such protocols be required to maintain quality monitoring procedures to ensure that these protocols do not, even inadvertently, involve reductions in care? What types of monitoring and documentation should be kept?

5. Should a hospital's decision to standardize items or processes be required to establish certain thresholds based on historical experience or clinical protocols beyond which participating physicians could not share in cost savings?

The Proposed Rule is an important step in the development of a workable gainsharing solution. Currently, parties must go through a lengthy Advisory Opinion process to obtain full protection for their gainsharing activities.

[126.1] 79 Fed. Reg. 59,717 (Oct. 3, 2014).

### § 5-3(a)(5)    Other Bases for CMPs

On May 12, 2014, the OIG published a proposed rule amending the regulations related to the OIG's CMP authority (Proposed Rule) to incorporate CMP authorities contained in Health Reform related to, among other things, (1) failing to grant OIG timely access to records; (2) ordering or prescribing while excluded; (3) making false statements, omissions, or misrepresentations in an enrollment application; (4) failing to report and return an overpayment; and (5) making or using a false record or statement that is material to a false or fraudulent claim.[135.1] In addition to updating the regulations to codify the changes made by Health Reform, the Proposed Rule also includes other updates pursuant to the Medicare Prescription Drug, Improvement, and Modernization act of 2003 and other statutory authorities, as well as technical changes. Specifically, the OIG proposes to reorganize 42 CFR part 1003 to make the "regulations more accessible to the public and to add clarity to the regulatory scheme." The OIG believes that with the additions of new CMP authorities over time, part 1003 has become cumbersome. The OIG anticipates that CMP collections may increase in the future in light of the new CMP authorities and other changes addressed in the Proposed Rule.

[135.1] 79 Fed. Reg. 27,080 (May 12, 2014).

### § 5-3(c) Amount of CMPs

As part of the Proposed Rule that was published on May 12, 2014, the OIG proposed modifying the provisions related to the factors considered in determining the exclusion period and the amount of penalties and assessments for violations to propose a single list of primary factors.[157.1] The primary factors include: (1) the nature and circumstances of the violation; (2) the degree and culpability of the person; (3) the history of prior offenses; (4) other wrongful conduct; and (5) other matters as justice may require. The OIG also proposes to update the claims-mitigating factor by increasing the maximum dollar amount considered as mitigation from $1,000 to $5,000. As such, the OIG would consider conduct resulting in more than $5,000 in federal health care program loss as an indication of more serious conduct. In addition, the OIG proposed specific penalties for certain conduct.

[157.1] 79 Fed. Reg. 27,080 (May 12, 2014).

# 6
# State and Private Initiatives to Combat Fraud

## § 6-7 STATE FALSE CLAIMS ACTIVITIES

### § 6-7(a) State Law Governing Fraudulent Billing Practices

On March 15, 2013, the OIG released the *Updated OIG Guidelines for Evaluating State False Claims Acts* (2013 Guidelines), which replaced the original version released in 2006.[93.1] The 2013 Guidelines provide more specific insight into OIG's review process when evaluating state false claims laws and are based on OIG's experience in reviewing over 28 different state false claims laws. In addition, the 2013 Guidelines incorporate the three amendments to the FCA that have occurred since 2006.

Although the 2013 Guidelines became effective upon publication, the OIG indicated that it would accept both enacted state laws for formal review and draft legislation for informal review and discussion.[93.2] State false claims acts that previously have been approved will be considered compliant until March 31, 2013. After that date, a previously approved state false claims act will no longer qualify for the Section 1909 incentive unless it has been: (1) amended and resubmitted to OIG, and (2) either approved by OIG or pending review by OIG. OIG anticipates granting two-year grace periods

## § 6-9  Legal Issues in Healthcare Fraud and Abuse

for approved state laws if any FCA provision relevant to OIG's review is amended in the future.

**93.1** U.S. Dep't of Health & Human Servs., Office of Inspector General, Updated OIG Guidelines for Evaluating State False Claims Acts, *available at* https://oig.hhs.gov/fraud/docs/falseclaimsact/guidelines-sfca.pdf. The Guidelines are effective on March 15, 2013.

**93.2** *Id.* at 1.

### § 6-9 STATE INITIATIVES TO PREVENT AND DETECT FRAUD

#### § 6-9(a) Medicaid Fraud Control Units

On May 17, 2013, the OIG issued a final rule permitting the use of federal matching funds (federal financial participation or FFPs) by MFCUs, under specified conditions, for identification of potential Medicaid fraud through data mining activities (the Final Rule).[112.1] Prior to the issuance of the Final Rule, MFCUs were prohibited from using federal matching funds to conduct "efforts to identify situations in which a question of fraud may exist, including the screening of claims, analysis of patterns of practice, or routine verification with beneficiaries of whether services billed by providers were actually received." This prohibition has commonly been interpreted as a prohibition on federal matching for the costs of data mining by MFCUs.

Under the Final Rule, MFCUs may use federal funds for data mining under certain conditions including:

- identifying (1) the methods of coordination between the MFCU and the State Medicaid agency and (2) the individuals serving as primary points of contract for data mining, and
- ensuring that MFCU employees engaged in data mining receive specialized training in data mining techniques.

In the Final Rule the OIG added a definition of data mining to "emphasize the wider range of the possible uses of data."[112.2] In addition, the OIG is now requiring that MFCUs approved to receive FFP in costs for data mining must provide specific information on their activities, including information related to costs attributed to data mining activities; the amount of staff time; the number of cases generated from data mining activities; the outcome and status of those cases, including the expected and actual monetary recoveries; and any other relevant indicia of return on investment for such activities, in their annual reports to OIG.

The MFCU and the State Medicaid Agency must enter into agreements regarding data mining that will be approved by the OIG. Approval is for a three-year period. At the end of that period, the MFCU may request renewal of its data mining approval for additional three-year periods by written request to the OIG and the submission of an updated agreement with the

State Medicaid agency.

[112.1] 78 Fed. Reg. 29,055, 29,056 (May 17, 2013).

[112.2] Data mining is defined as the practice of electronically sorting Medicaid or other relevant data, including but not limited to the use of statistical models and intelligent technologies, to uncover patterns and relationships within that data to identify aberrant utilization, billing, or other practices that are potentially fraudulent.

# 7
# Compliance and Self-Reporting

## § 7-5  COMPLIANCE RELATED RESOURCES

### § 7-5(e)  OIG/Health Lawyers Resources

On April 20, 2015, the OIG, in collaboration with the American Health Lawyers Association, the Association of Healthcare Internal Auditors, and the Health Care Compliance Association, published additional guidance related to governance compliance oversight, entitled *Practical Guidance for Health Care Governing Boards on Compliance Oversight*[75.1] (*Practical Guidance*). This document covers issues relating to a Board's oversight and review of compliance program functions, including the: (1) roles of, and relationships between, the organization's audit, compliance, and legal departments; (2) mechanisms and processes for issue-reporting within an organization; (3) approaches to identifying regulatory risk; and (4) methods of encouraging enterprise-wide accountability for achievement of compliance goals and objectives.

[75.1] Department of Health and Human Services, Office of the Inspector General, Association of Healthcare Internal Auditors, American Health Lawyers Association, and Health Care Compliance Association, Practical Guidance for Health Care Governing Boards on Compliance Oversight (April 20, 2014), *available at* http://oig.hhs.gov/compliance/compliance-guidance/docs/Practical-Guidance-for-Health-Care-Boards-on-Compliance-Oversight.pdf.

## § 7-9  SELF-REPORTING AND VOLUNTARY DISCLOSURE

### § 7-9(a)  OIG Voluntary Self-Disclosure Protocol

On April 17, 2013, the OIG unveiled an updated Protocol which includes various new provisions, such as limitations on the Protocol's scope with respect to its applicability to the Stark Law, a new minimum damages multiplier, minimum settlement amounts, and guidelines for the content of submissions by providers.[138.1]

In the updated Protocol, the OIG continued to emphasize the importance and benefits of voluntary disclosure and notes that "good faith disclosure of potential fraud and cooperation with the OIG's review and resolution process are typically indications of a robust and effective compliance program." The OIG states that it "instituted a presumption against requiring [corporate] integrity obligations in exchange for a release of OIG's permissive exclusion authorities in resolving an SDP matter." Additionally, the OIG confirmed that individuals and entities that take advantage of the self-disclosure process should pay a lower multiplier for purposes of calculating damages than would normally be expected in a government investigation. Although the precise multiplier may vary based on case-specific facts, the OIG states that it will generally require a minimum multiplier of 1.5.

The OIG also attempted to streamline the internal process for disclosures "to reduce the average time a case is pending with OIG to less than 12 months from acceptance into the [Protocol]." However, in order to keep within this timeframe, the OIG is now requiring that internal investigations and damages calculations be submitted 90 days from the date of an initial submission.

The updated Protocol also expressly states the time period that the OIG expects the disclosing party to investigate in connection with the disclosed potential violation. Specifically, the OIG states that it "expects disclosing parties to disclose with good faith willingness to resolve all liability within the CMPL's six year statute of limitations . . . ." Accordingly, the OIG must agree, as a "condition precedent" to acceptance into the Protocol, that the disclosing party will waive and not plead the statute of limitations, laches, or any similar defense, except to the extent that such defenses would have been available to the disclosing party had an administrative action been filed on the date of submission.

The updated Protocol confirms that the self-disclosure process may be pursued by all health care providers, suppliers, or other individuals or entities subject to the OIG's CMP authorities found at 42 C.F.R. Part 1003 and is not limited to particular industries, specialties, or types of services. However, the updated Protocol clarifies certain eligibility requirements, both in terms of who may take advantage of the process and what type of conduct falls within the scope. The updated Protocol notes, in particular, that pharmaceutical manufacturers are eligible to submit self-disclosures. Additionally, the updated Protocol confirms that disclosing parties that are already subject to a government inquiry are not necessarily precluded from self-disclosing, but the Protocol cannot be used as a means to avoid such inquiry. The OIG also noted that parties that are already subject to a

Corporate Integrity Agreement, which has its own reporting requirements, are also able to use the self-disclosure process.

With respect to the type of conduct that may be disclosed, the updated Protocol confirms that it can be used for conduct that potentially violates federal criminal, civil, or administrative laws for which CMPs are authorized. The OIG specifically states that, in making a disclosure, the disclosing party "must acknowledge that the conduct is a potential violation" and must identify the specific laws that are implicated. Before making a disclosure, disclosing parties must ensure that the conduct concerning the potential violation has ended or that corrective action will be taken and that the improper arrangement will be terminated within 90 days of submission to the SDP.

Finally, the OIG addresses in the updated Protocol that, in addition to the OIG self-disclosure process, the Centers for Medicare & Medicaid Services (CMS) has its own Self-Referral Disclosure Protocol (SRDP) for those arrangements that involve liability only under the federal physician self-referral law, commonly referred to as the "Stark Law." However, the OIG recognized that a large number of submissions relate to potential violations of the AKS, including conduct that may also violate the Stark Law. According to the updated Protocol, disclosing parties must include a succinct statement of all the details that are directly relevant to the disclosed conduct as well as a specific analysis of why each disclosed arrangement potentially violates the AKS and, if applicable, the Stark Law. Further, the description should include the identities of individuals who participated in the conduct, their relationship to one another to the extent that the relationship affects their potential liability, the payment arrangements, and the dates during which the conduct occurred. The OIG also noted that the disclosure should discuss any relevant background and those features of the arrangement that raise potential liability. In the updated Protocol, the OIG provided five examples of information deemed to be helpful when assessing and resolving the disclosed conduct involving AKS, and possibly Stark Law, violations.

Since the government considers AKS and Stark Law compliance to be conditions of payment by the federal health care programs, the disclosing party must submit an estimate of the amount paid by federal health care programs for the items or services associated with the potential violations. In order to quantify this amount, the disclosing party may use the same methodology proposed for conduct related to fraudulent billing (see below). Alternatively, the disclosing party may use another methodology and explain the methodology in the submission.

§ 8-4        *Legal Issues in Healthcare Fraud and Abuse*

The Protocol includes several requirements that must be met and addressed in a disclosing party's submission for acceptance into the Protocol. Disclosures may be submitted electronically through the OIG's website or via mail. In addition to the general requirements that must be included in all disclosures, the OIG provided additional guidance related to specific information that must be included for certain types of conduct, including conduct involving false billing or conduct involving excluded individuals.

In order to "promote transparency and realistic expectations" in the self-disclosure process, the OIG, requires minimum settlement amounts for participants in the Protocol. For kickback-related disclosures, there is a minimum of $50,000 to resolve the matter. For all other accepted matters, there is a minimum of $10,000 to resolve the matter. These minimums include federal health care program damages and any relevant multiplier. According to the updated Protocol, in the event that a disclosing party is unable to pay an otherwise appropriate settlement amount, the disclosing party should raise this "ability to pay" issue and provide the relevant information at the earliest possible time, preferably in the submission.

[138.1] *See* DHHS, OIG., *Updated OIG's Provider Self- Disclosure Protocol* (Apr. 17, 2013), *available at* https://oig.hhs.gov/compliance/self disclosureinfo/ files/Provider-Self-Disclosure-Protocol.pdf.

# 8
# Fraud and Abuse Issues Affecting the Managed Care Industry

### § 8-4    INTERMEDIATE SANCTIONS APPLICABLE TO MCOS

CMS has stepped up its enforcement activity with respect to the imposition of sanctions on Medicare Part C and D plans. There have been 125 enforcement actions (CMPs or intermediate sanctions) since 2008. In 2014, CMS imposed intermediate sanctions suspending marketing and enrollment of Medicare beneficiaries on two health plans, both of which ultimately were successful in having those sanctions lifted.

### § 8-8    EXAMPLES OF POTENTIAL FRAUD LIABILITY IN THE MANAGED CARE INDUSTRY

## § 8-8(a) Capitation Misclassification and Risk Adjustment

In August 2012, SCAN Health Plan settled with the federal government and State of California for $319.85 million.[98.1] According to the government, the State of California paid SCAN rates for long-term-care-certified (LTC) patients that were over the legal ceiling set by a California statute and regulations. They resulted from two actuarial errors made during the state's rate-setting process. Specifically, Medi-Cal paid for SCAN's LTC patients, who were generally cared for at home, as though they were like Medi-Cal fee-for-service LTC patients, who were generally in nursing homes, where the cost of care is much greater. Medi-Cal also failed to account for the fact that SCAN's Medi-Cal contract authorized SCAN to terminate the memberships of LTC patients after they had spent a maximum of two months in a nursing home. Thus, Medi-Cal kept paying SCAN for certain LTC patients even after SCAN was no longer obligated to provide services to them. This was the largest MediCal recovery from one provider in the state's history ($190 million to CA + $129 million to federal government).

The settlement also involved another $3.82 million paid to the federal government related to SCAN's alleged submission of inflated risk adjustment scores that increased Medicare Part C reimbursement. The relator alleged that SCAN contracted with outside companies to review medical charts for severely ill patients to allegedly find additional diagnosis codes to report. According to the government press release, medical record review by outside company is not illegal. However, in this instance, in order to increase risk adjustment scores, CMS was not told that some of the original diagnosis codes would need to be deleted, not just new diagnosis codes added. According to the settlement agreement, if that information had been provided to CMS, Medicare capitation payments to SCAN would have been lower than they were.

Another case dealing with allegations of inflated risk adjustment scores is *U.S. ex. rel. Valdez v. Aveta, Inc.* The case was filed under seal in 2011 by the former CEO of the health plan. Significantly, the government declined to intervene in the case in January 2014, and in July 2014, the relator filed an amended complaint alleging that defendants knowingly overstated, and/or concealed and failed to correct their unsupported reports of diagnosis codes which caused overstatements of risk adjustment scores used by CMS to calculate monthly government payments made to Aveta's two Medicare Advantage Plans in Puerto Rico. According to the complaint, the diagnosis codes that were submitted were unsubstantiated by medical records or by medical conditions of the Medicare beneficiaries, and internal audit showed that over 2/3 of patient risks scores submitted to CMS were unsupported by medical documentation. Additionally, the plan allegedly actively encouraged providers to inflate diagnosis codes, maintaining profit sharing arrangements with Independent Practice Associations (IPAs) where they received 50–60% of the surplus earned on that IPA's member services.

[98.1] Department of Justice, *Long Beach-Based Health Plan Pays Nearly $320 Million To Settle Allegations That It Received Overpayment For Medi-Cal Patients: SCAN Health Plan Pays Another $3.82 Million to Resolve Claims of Inflated 'Risk Adjustment Scores' that Increased Reimbursements From Medicare Part C*, (Aug. 23, 2012), *available at* http://www.justice.gov/usao/cac/Pressroom/2012/112.html; *United States and State of California ex rel. Swoben v. SCAN Health Plan*, CV 09-5013-JFW-JEM (C.D. Cal. filed July 13, 2009).

### § 8-8(m)  Health Care Exchanges

As the Health Reform Law continues implementation across the United States, health care fraud prevention remains a priority for the federal government. In the case of health insurance exchanges, the False Claims Act (FCA) will undoubtedly play a significant role in fraud enforcement. Specifically, Section 1313(a)(6), codified at 42 U.S.C. 18033(a)(6), makes the FCA applicable to payments made by, through, or in connection with an Exchange if those payments include any Federal funds. Health insurance issuers participating in an exchange must also comply with the Health Reform Law's eligibility requirements as a material condition of an issuer's entitlement to receive payments, including payments of premium tax credits and cost-sharing reductions. These conditions and other certification made by insurers may become the basis of future enforcement.

# 9

# Representing Healthcare Organizations in Fraud and Abuse Matters

### § 9-4  RELATIONSHIP BETWEEN CRIMINAL AND CIVIL MATTERS

#### § 9-4(d)  Criminal Settlement—The Use of Deferred Prosecution and Non-Prosecution Agreements

The appropriateness of the use of DPA's in healthcare fraud matters was challenged by a North Carolina district court in early 2013. On December 19, 2012, WakeMed Health and Hospitals agreed to a DPA in connection with same day/one days stays in the Raleigh campus' cardiac department from 2003 to 2010.[120.1] Prosecutors and WakeMed administrators agreed to a two year DPA in which WakeMed was required to pay an $8 million civil settlement as well as participate in a five year corporate integrity agreement with HHS.[120.2]

In the Statement of Facts section of the DPA, WakeMed admitted that it ignored physician orders for "physician designations of status as 'outpatient' and that "nurses . . . were not instructed to, nor did they consult with the referring physicians prior to admitting patients as 'inpatient' on WakMed's electronic database in contravention of a written order . . ." As a result, these [f]alse status designations flowed through to WakeMed's coding and billing department [and] Medicare paid WakeMed substantially more money on the claims than it would otherwise have paid." In the DPA, WakeMed also admitted to conduct including "Fabricating Inpatient Orders."[120.3] Despite the language in the DPA, during a press interview on December 19, 2012, William Atkinson, CEO of WakeMed appeared to waiver between accepting and rejecting the criminal charges, stating "[w]e do not think [the conduct] was intentional, and that is why nobody was prosecuted for it."[120.4] WakeMed released a subsequent statement that attempted to clarify Atkinson's statements days before appearing before U.S. District Judge Boyle to seek approval of the DPA. On January 24, 2013, Boyle took an unprecedented move and refused to accept the DPA, and questioned whether a DPA was appropriate given the degree of criminal conduct alleged by the government. Boyle also questioned why the government did not prosecute senior management and suggested that DPAs are more appropriate for small drug offenses.[120.6] On Feb 5, 2013 Judge Boyle again rejected the DPA and threatened to write his own order.[120.7] Eventually Judge Boyle approved the DPA after expressing concern over the affect it would have to the community if WakeMed was excluded from Medicare. This case may serve as a reminder that DPAs are not to be treated as routine in criminal healthcare fraud matters.

[120.1] Memorandum in Support of Deferred Prosecution Agreement, United States v. WakeMed d/b/a WakeMed Health and Hospitals, No. 5:12-cr-00398-BO (D.N.C. 2013), 13.

[120.2] Deferred Prosecution Agreement, United States of America v. WakeMed d/b/a/ WakeMed Health and Hospitals No. 5:12-CR-398-1 (D.N.C., Dec. 19, 2012).

[120.3] *Id.*

[120.4] *See* WakeMed to pay $8M to End Medicare Fraud Investigation *available at* http://www.wral.com/wakemed-to-pay-8m-to-end-medicare-fraud-investigation/11897827/.

[120.6] *See* The News & Observer Judge Refuse to Accept WakeMed Settlement with Federal Prosecutors, (Jan. 17, 2013).

[120.7] Judge Raises More Questions about WakeMed Medicare Settlement (Feb. 5, 2012) *available at* http://www.newsobserver.com/2013/02/05/2657502/judge-raises-more-questions-about.html#.

# INDEX

[References are to sections.]

## A

**ADMINISTRATIVE SANCTIONS, FEDERAL** §5-1 to §5-4(f)
Civil monetary penalties . . . §5-3
  Amount . . . §5-3(c)
  Conduct that may result in imposition
    . . . §5-3(a); §5-3(a)(5)
    Excluded individuals and entities, dealing with . . . §5-3(a)(2)
    Gainsharing . . . §5-3(a)(4)
    Inducements to beneficiaries . . . §5-3(a)(3)
    Payments to induce reduction or limitation of services . . . §5-3(a)(4)
    Submission of improperly filed claims . . . §5-3(a)(1)
  Hearings . . . §5-5 to §5-5(f)
  Managed care industry, intermediate sanctions applicable to . . . §8-4
  Notice of proposed determination to impose . . . §5-3(b)
Exclusion from Medicare, Medicaid and other state healthcare programs . . . §5-2
  Additional activities that can result in violations . . . Appx C
  Civil monetary penalties . . . §5-3(a)(2)
  Effects . . . §5-2(e)
  Hearings . . . §5-5 to §5-5(f)
  Mandatory exclusion . . . §5-2(a)
  Notice . . . §5-2(d); §5-2(d)(2)
    Intent to exclude . . . §5-2(d)(1)
    Proposal to exclude . . . §5-2(d)(3)
  Permissive exclusion . . . §5-2(b)
  Persons subject to exclusion . . . §5-2(c)
  Reinstatement . . . §5-2(f)
Generally . . . §5-1
Hearings . . . §5-5 to §5-5(f)
  Appeals
    Departmental appeal board . . . §5-5(e)
    Judicial review of health and human services secretary's final determination . . . §5-5(f)
  Burden of proof . . . §5-5(b)
  Evidentiary standards . . . §5-5(c)
  Rights of parties . . . §5-5(a)
  Scope of authority in exclusion cases . . . §5-5(d)
Managed care industry, intermediate sanctions applicable to . . . §8-4
Suspension of payments . . . §5-4
  Medicaid providers . . . §5-4(b)

**ADMINISTRATIVE SANCTIONS, FEDERAL** —Cont.
Suspension of payments —Cont.
  Medicare providers . . . §5-4(a)

**ADVANCED MEDICAL TECHNOLOGY ASSOCIATION** §6-10(e)

**AGING, ADMINISTRATION ON**
Enforcement . . . §1-3(c)

**AMBULANCE COMPANIES**
False claims
  Enforcement against particular segments of the healthcare industry . . . §4-6(l)
Kickbacks
  Fraud alerts and special advisory bulletins
    Contractual arrangements with ambulance companies . . . §2-4(j)

**AMBULATORY SURGERY CENTERS**
Implants, Stark Law exceptions and . . . §3-4(a)(5)
Safe harbors, anti-kickback laws
  Investment interest safe harbors . . . §2-3(b)(5)

**AMERICAN COLLEGE OF PHYSICIANS** §6-10(c)

**AMERICAN COLLEGE OF RADIOLOGY** §6-10(b)

**AMERICAN MEDICAL ASSOCIATION** §6-10(a)

**ANTI-KICKBACK LAWS** §2-1 to §2-8; §6-3
(See KICKBACKS)

**ANTI-MARKUP RULE**
Stark law . . . §3-9(d)

**ATTORNEY AND CLIENT**
Representation of healthcare organizations (See REPRESENTING HEALTHCARE ORGANIZATIONS)

## B

**BALANCED BUDGET ACT OF 1997**
Kickbacks, development of statute prohibiting . . . §2-2(e)

**BANKRUPTCY CODE**
False claims actions under . . . §4-7

[References are to sections.]

**BILLING COMPANIES**
False claims
  Enforcement against particular segments of the healthcare industry . . . §4-6(i)

**BONA FIDE EMPLOYMENT RELATIONSHIPS**
Stark law
  Compensation arrangements . . . §3-4(c)(2)

**BRIBERY, COMMERCIAL**
State laws . . . §6-5

**BURDEN OF PROOF**
Administrative sanctions, federal
  Hearings . . . §5-5(b)
Self-referral
  Stark law
    Penalties and enforcement . . . §3-6(d)

## C

**CAPITATION MISCLASSIFICATION**
False claims . . . §4-5(c)

**CENTERS FOR MEDICARE AND MEDICAID SERVICES**
Administrative sanctions, federal
  Exclusion from Medicare, Medicaid and other state healthcare programs (See ADMINISTRATIVE SANCTIONS, FEDERAL)
Compliance and self-reporting
  Guidance . . . §7-5(g)
Enforcement
  Medicare Prescription Drug Integrity Contractors (MEDICs) . . . §1-3(f); §1-3(f)(3)
  Recovery Audit Contractors (RACs) . . . §1-3(f)(1)
  Unified Program Integrity Contractors (UPICs) . . . §1-3(b)
  Zone Program Integrity Contractors (ZPICs) . . . §1-3(f)(2)

**CHAMPUS** (See CIVILIAN HEALTH AND MEDICAL PROGRAM OF THE UNIFORMED SERVICE (CHAMPUS))

**CIAs** (See CORPORATE INTEGRITY AGREEMENTS (CIAs))

**CIVILIAN HEALTH AND MEDICAL PROGRAM OF THE UNIFORMED SERVICE (CHAMPUS)**
Kickbacks . . . §2-7(c)
Self-referral . . . §3-9(b)

**CIVIL PENALTIES**
Administrative sanctions available to federal enforcers . . . §5-3 to §5-4(f) (See ADMINISTRATIVE SANCTIONS, FEDERAL)

**CIVIL PENALTIES**—Cont.
Kickbacks
  Inducements to beneficiaries
    Civil money penalty statute . . . §2-7(a)(2)
    2010 modification §2-7(a)(3)
  State anti-kickback provisions . . . §6-3
Managed care industry, intermediate sanctions applicable to . . . §8-4
Physician payment sunshine act violations . . . §2-7(d)
Self-referral
  Stark law . . . §3-6
  State laws . . . §6-2(d)

**CLINICAL LABORATORIES**
False claims
  Enforcement against particular segments of the healthcare industry . . . §4-6(d)
Kickbacks
  Fraud alerts and special advisory bulletins . . . §2-4(e)

**COINSURANCE WAIVERS**
False claims . . . §4-5(g); §6-7(b)
Kickbacks
  Safe harbor regulations
    Statutory exceptions with analogous safe harbors . . . §2-3(g)(5)

**COMPENSATION**
Fee-splitting prescriptions . . . §6-4
Self-referral (See SELF-REFERRAL)

**COMPLIANCE AND SELF-REPORTING**
§7-1 to §7-9
Corporate integrity agreements
  Comparison . . . Appx E
Corporate integrity agreements (CIAs) . . . §7-8; §10-3
Effectiveness reviews . . . §7-7
Elements of an effective compliance program . . . §7-6
  Background checks . . . §7-6(c)
  Disciplinary action and corrective action . . . §7-6(g)
  Documentation . . . §7-6(h)
  Monitoring, auditing, and evaluating the program . . . §7-6(e)
  Reporting system . . . §7-6(f)
  Roles and reporting relationships of personnel . . . §7-6(b)
    Corporate compliance officer (CCO) and other personnel . . . §7-6(b)(2)
    Corporate governance . . . §7-6(b)(1)
  Standards and procedures, establishment of . . . §7-6(a)
  Training . . . §7-6(d)

[References are to sections.]

**COMPLIANCE AND SELF-REPORTING**
—Cont.
Federal sentencing guidelines . . . §7-3
Generally . . . §7-1
Guidance
   Centers for Medicare and Medicaid services guidance to contractors . . . §7-5(f)
   General accounting office . . . §7-5(c)
   Health Care Fraud Prevention and Enforcement Action Team (HEAT) . . . §7-5(a)
   Inspector general, office of
     Compliance program guidance . . . §7-5(a)
   Inspector general and Health Lawyers resources . . . §7-5(e)
   Roundtables . . . §7-5(d)
Sarbanes-Oxley act of 2002 . . . §7-4
Self-reporting generally . . . §7-9
Sentencing guidelines, federal . . . §7-3
Voluntary disclosure . . . §7-9
   CMS protocol . . . §7-9(b)
   OIG protocol . . . §7-9(a); §10-3
   State disclosure processes . . . §7-9(c)

**CONSUMER PROTECTION LAWS** §6-6

**CORPORATE INTEGRITY AGREEMENTS (CIAs)** §7-8; §10-3
Comparison . . . Appx E

**CRIMINAL LAW AND PROCEDURE**
False claims . . . §4-4
   Asset freezes to enjoin fraudulent conduct . . . §4-4(i)
   Embezzlement . . . §4-4(g)
   False statements . . . §4-4(f)
   Healthcare fraud . . . §4-4(e)
   Mail and wire fraud . . . §4-4(b)
   Miscellaneous offenses . . . §4-4(h)
   Money laundering . . . §4-4(d)
   RICO violations . . . §4-4(c)
   Social security act . . . §4-4(a)
   Theft . . . §4-4(g)
Government investigations
   Criminal settlements . . . §9-4(d)
Representing healthcare organizations
   Attorney and client relationship
     Attorney-client communications privilege
       Crime-fraud exception §9-5(d)
   Relationship between criminal and civil matters . . . §9-4
     Double jeopardy . . . §9-4(a)
     Ex post facto considerations . . . §9-4(b)

# D

**DAMAGES, CALCULATION OF**
Federal civil false claims act . . . §4-2(c)

**DAMAGES, CALCULATION OF**—Cont.
Kickbacks . . . §2-8(i)

**DATA MINING**
Medicaid fraud control units . . . §6-9(a)

**DECEPTIVE TRADE PRACTICES** §6-6

**DEDUCTIBLE WAIVERS** §6-7(b)
False claims . . . §4-5(g); §6-7(b)
Kickbacks
   Safe harbor regulations
     Statutory exceptions with analogous safe harbors . . . §2-3(g)(5)

**DENTISTS**
False claims
   Enforcement against particular segments of the healthcare industry . . . §4-6(k)

**DIAGNOSIS-RELATED GROUP CREEP**
False claims . . . §4-5(c)

**DRG CREEP** (See DIAGNOSIS-RELATED GROUP CREEP)

**DURABLE MEDICAL EQUIPMENT**
False claims
   Enforcement against particular segments of the healthcare industry . . . §4-6(e)
     Certificates of medical necessity . . . §4-6(e)(4)
     Provision of medical supplies to nursing homes . . . §4-6(e)(1)
     Seat lifts . . . §4-6(e)(2)
     Telemarketing schemes . . . §4-6(e)(3)

# E

**ELECTRONIC DISCOVERY** §9-3
Culling data . . . §9-3(e)
Document review . . . §9-3(f)
Limiting data set . . . §9-3(e)
Litigation hold . . . §9-3(b)
Litigation support vendors . . . §9-3(c)
Preservation and collection . . . §9-3(d)
Production . . . §9-3(g)
Triggering event . . . §9-3(a)

**ELECTRONIC HEALTH RECORDS AND COMMUNITY-WIDE INFORMATION SYSTEMS**
Kickbacks
   Safe harbor regulations . . . §2-3(n)
Stark law
   Exceptions
     Compensation arrangements
       Community-wide information system §3-4(c)(18)

# INDEX

[References are to sections.]

**ELECTRONIC PRESCRIBING**
Kickbacks
  Safe harbor regulations
    Statutory exceptions with analogous safe harbors . . . §2-3(g)(7)
Stark Law
  Exceptions
    Health record items and services . . . §3-4(c)(19)

**ENFORCERS**
Administrative sanctions available to federal enforcers . . . §5-1 to §5-4(f) (See ADMINISTRATIVE SANCTIONS, FEDERAL)
Congress
  Future legislative activities . . . §10-1
  Generally . . . §1-6
Generally . . . §1-1
Health and human services, department of (See HEALTH AND HUMAN SERVICES, DEPARTMENT OF)
Justice, department of (See JUSTICE, DEPARTMENT OF)
Miscellaneous federal agencies . . . §1-4
Multi-agency federal initiatives . . . §1-5
Private citizens . . . §1-9
Private payors . . . §1-8
States . . . §1-7
Whistleblowers . . . §1-9

## F

**FALSE CERTIFICATION**
False claims . . . §4-5(h)

**FALSE CLAIMS** §4-1 to §4-6(l)
Bankruptcy code . . . §4-7
Civil
  Additional civil laws . . . §4-3 to §4-3(b)
  Federal civil false claims act . . . §4-2
    Anti-kickback violations . . . §4-2(b)
    Calculating damages . . . §4-2(c)
    Key considerations . . . §4-2(a)
      Claims §4-2(a)(3)
      "Causing" claim to be submitted §4-2(a)(4)
      False or fraudulent defined §4-2(a)(5)
      Knowingly §4-2(a)(2)
        Deliberate ignorance §4-2(a)(2)(i)
        Reckless disregard §4-2(a)(2)(ii)
      Materiality defined §4-2(a)(6)
      Overpayments defined §4-2(a)(5)(i)
      Person §4-2(a)(1)
      Statistical sampling to establish false claims act liability §4-2(a)(5)(ii)
    Qui tam relators (See QUI TAM RELATORS)
    Statute of limitations . . . §4-2(e)

**FALSE CLAIMS** —Cont.
Civil—Cont.
  Program fraud civil remedies act . . . §4-3(b)
  Social security act . . . §4-3(a)
Criminal . . . §4-4
  Asset freezes to enjoin fraudulent conduct . . . §4-4(i)
  Embezzlement . . . §4-4(g)
  False statements . . . §4-4(f)
  Healthcare fraud . . . §4-4(e)
  Mail and wire fraud . . . §4-4(b)
  Miscellaneous offenses . . . §4-4(h)
  RICO violations . . . §4-4(c)
  Social security act . . . §4-4(a)
  Theft . . . §4-4(g)
Enforcement against particular segments of the healthcare industry . . . §4-6
  Ambulance companies . . . §4-6(l)
  Billing companies . . . §4-6(i)
  Clinical laboratories . . . §4-6(d)
  Dentists . . . §4-6(k)
  Durable medical equipment and home medical suppliers . . . §4-6(e)
    Certificates of medical necessity . . . §4-6(e)(4)
    Provision of medical supplies to nursing homes . . . §4-6(e)(1)
    Seat lifts . . . §4-6(e)(2)
    Telemarketing schemes . . . §4-6(e)(3)
  Fiscal intermediaries . . . §4-6(g)
  HIV infusion clinics . . . §4-6(n)
  Home health agencies . . . §4-6(f)
  Hospice . . . §4-6(f)
  Hospitals . . . §4-6(a)
    Billing for provider-based services . . . §4-6(a)(5)
    Diagnosis-related group payment window . . . §4-6(a)(2)
    Inpatient admissions, overutilization of . . . §4-6(a)(4)
    One day stays/same day stays . . . §4-6(a)(4)
    Outlier payments . . . §4-6(a)(3)
    Payments to teaching hospitals . . . §4-6(a)(1)
  Investigational devices . . . §4-6(b)
  Medical clinics . . . §4-6(n)
  Medical device companies . . . §4-6(m)
  Medicare contractors . . . §4-6(g)
  Nursing homes and long-term care facilities . . . §4-6(c)
  Pharmacies and pharmaceutical manufacturers . . . §4-6(h)
  Physicians . . . §4-6(j)
  Third-party consultants . . . §4-6(i)
Generally . . . §4-1

[References are to sections.]

**FALSE CLAIMS** —Cont.
Investigative demands . . . §9-2(c)
Managed care industry . . . §8-5
State laws . . . §6-7
   Fraudulent billing practices . . . §6-7(a)
   Waivers of coinsurance and deductible amounts . . . §6-7(b)
Theories applicable to multiple segments of the healthcare industry . . . §4-5
   Billing for items or services not actually rendered . . . §4-5(a); §6-7(a)
   Capitation misclassification . . . §4-5(c)
   Coinsurance waivers . . . §4-5(g)
   Deductible waivers . . . §4-5(g)
   Diagnosis-related group creep . . . §4-5(c)
   False certification . . . §4-5(h)
   Filing false cost reports . . . §4-5(e)
   Fragmentation . . . §4-5(d)
   Homeless and indigent patients, recruitment of . . . §4-5(j)
   Medicare secondary payor issues . . . §4-5(i)
   Providing medically unnecessary services . . . §4-5(b)
   Quality-of-care-cases . . . §4-5(f)
   Reverse false claims . . . §4-5(f)
   Unbundling . . . §4-5(d)
   Upcoding . . . §4-5(c)

**FEDERAL BUREAU OF INVESTIGATION**
Enforcement . . . §1-2(d)

**FEE-SPLITTING**
State laws prohibiting . . . §6-4

**FINES**
Administrative sanctions available to federal enforcers . . . §5-3 to §5-4(f) (See ADMINISTRATIVE SANCTIONS, FEDERAL)
Kickbacks
   Inducements to beneficiaries
      Civil money penalty statute . . . §2-7(a)(2)
      2010 modification §2-7(a)(3)
   State anti-kickback provisions . . . §6-3
Managed care industry, intermediate sanctions applicable to . . . §8-4
Self-referral
   Stark law . . . §3-6
   State laws . . . §6-2(d)

**FISCAL INTERMEDIARIES**
False claims
   Enforcement against particular segments of the healthcare industry . . . §4-6(g)

**FOOD AND DRUG ADMINISTRATION**
Enforcement . . . §1-3(e)

**FRAGMENTATION**
False claims . . . §4-5(d)

**FRAUD**
Attorney and client relationship
   Crime-fraud exception . . . §9-5(d)
False claims
   Civil
      Federal civil false claims act
         Key considerations
            False or fraudulent defined §4-2(a)(5)
            Overpayments defined §4-2(a)(5)(i)
            Reverse false claims §4-2(a)(5)(i)
            Statistical sampling to establish false claims act liability §4-2(a)(5)(ii)
      Program fraud civil remedies act . . . §4-3(b)
   Criminal
      Asset freezes to enjoin fraudulent conduct . . . §4-4(i)
      Embezzlement . . . §4-4(g)
      False statements . . . §4-4(f)
      Mail and wire fraud . . . §4-4(b)
      Miscellaneous offenses . . . §4-4(h)
      Money laundering . . . §4-4(d)
      RICO violations . . . §4-4(c)
      Theft . . . §4-4(g)
   State laws
      Fraudulent billing practices . . . §6-7(a)
Initiatives to combat fraud, state and private (See STATE AND PRIVATE INITIATIVES TO COMBAT FRAUD)
Kickbacks
   Development of statute prohibiting
      Medicare-Medicaid anti-fraud and abuse amendments of 1977 . . . §2-2(b)
   Fraud alerts and special advisory bulletins (See KICKBACKS)
Managed care industry, issues affecting
   Medicare managed care, federal efforts to address fraud in . . . §8-6
   Potential fraud liability . . . §8-8 (See MANAGED CARE INDUSTRY, ISSUES AFFECTING)
National Health Care Anti-Fraud Association (NHCAA)
   Enforcement . . . §1-8
Promoting public initiatives to identify fraud . . . Appx A
Technology to combat . . . §1-3(b)

**FUTURE CONSIDERATIONS** §10-1 to §10-5
Balance, need for . . . §10-5
Enforcement activities . . . §10-3
Legislative activities . . . §10-1
Litigation . . . §10-4

[References are to sections.]

**FUTURE CONSIDERATIONS** —Cont.
Provider self-disclosure, federal enforcement activities and . . . §10-3
Regulatory initiatives . . . §10-2

# G

**GAINSHARING**
Administrative sanctions, federal
  Civil monetary penalties
    Conduct that may result in imposition
      Payments to induce reduction or limitation of services §5-3(a)(4)
Stark law exceptions
  Compensation arrangements . . . §3-4(c)(21)

**GASOLINE DISCOUNT PROGRAMS**
Kickbacks
  Inducements to beneficiaries
    Civil money penalty statute
      2010 modification §2-7(a)(3)

**GOVERNMENT INVESTIGATIONS**
Administrative subpoenas . . . §9-2(d)
Civil investigative demands . . . §9-2(c)
Civil settlements . . . §9-4(c)
Congressional subpoenas . . . §9-2(f)
Criminal settlements . . . §9-4(d)
Electronic discovery (See ELECTRONIC DISCOVERY)
Grand jury investigations . . . §9-2(b)
Inspector general, office of
  Immediate access to documents
    Subpoenas of documents and witnesses . . . §9-2(e)(2)
  Search and subpoena authority . . . §9-2(e)
    Subpoenas of documents and witnesses . . . §9-2(e)(1)
Practical guidelines . . . Appx F
Search warrants . . . §9-2(a)
Undercover operations . . . §9-2(g)
Vicarious liability and the *Park* doctrine . . . §9-7

**GRAND JURY INVESTIGATIONS** §9-2(b)

**GROUP PRACTICE**
Stark law . . . §3-5 (See SELF-REFERRAL)

**GROUP PURCHASING ORGANIZATIONS**
Safe harbor, anti-kickback laws
  Statutory exceptions with analogous safe harbors . . . §2-3(g)(3)

# H

**HANLESTER NETWORK V. SHALALA** §2-6(b)
Post-*Hanlester* case law . . . §2-6(c)
  *Anderson, McClatchey*, and *LaHue* . . . §2-6(c)(5)
  *Bryan* . . . §2-6(c)(3)
  *Jain* . . . §2-6(c)(2)
  *Shaw* . . . §2-6(c)(6)
  *Starks* . . . §2-6(c)(4)
  *US ex rel. Jamison v. McKesson* . . . §2-6(c)(1)
Pre-*Hanlester* case law . . . §2-6(a)
  Additional cases . . . §2-6(a)(5)
  *Bay State Ambulance* . . . §2-6(a)(3)
  *Greber* . . . §2-6(a)(1)
  *Katz* . . . §2-6(a)(2)
  *Polk County v. Peters* . . . §2-6(a)(4)

**HEALTH AND HUMAN SERVICES, DEPARTMENT OF**
Administrative sanctions available . . . §5-1 to §5-4(f) (See ADMINISTRATIVE SANCTIONS, FEDERAL)
Enforcement . . . §1-3
  Aging, administration on . . . §1-3(c)
  Centers for Medicare and Medicaid services (See CENTERS FOR MEDICARE AND MEDICAID SERVICES)
  Food & Drug Administration . . . §1-3(e)
  Health Lawyers resources . . . §7-5(e)
  Health resources and services administration . . . §1-3(d)
  Inspector general, office of . . . §1-3(a)
    Compliance and self-reporting guidance . . . §7-5(a)
    Resources, health lawyers §7-5(e)
    Future federal regulatory initiatives . . . §10-2
    Search and subpoena authority . . . §9-2(e) to §9-2(e)(2)
  Program integrity contractors (See PROGRAM INTEGRITY CONTRACTORS)
  Roundtables with inspector general's office and health care compliance association . . . §7-5(d)

**HEALTH CARE COMPLIANCE ASSOCIATION**
Roundtables . . . §7-5(d)

**HEALTH INSURANCE PORTABILITY AND ACCOUNTABILITY ACT OF 1996**
Kickbacks, development of statute prohibiting . . . §2-2(d)

**HEALTH LAWYERS RESOURCES**
Compliance and self-reporting guidance . . . §7-5(e)

**HEALTH MAINTENANCE ORGANIZATIONS, ISSUES AFFECTING**
Generally . . . §8-1 to §8-8 (See MANAGED CARE INDUSTRY, ISSUES AFFECTING)
Kickbacks . . . §2-3(h); §8-2 to §8-2(c) (See KICKBACKS)
Self-referral . . . §8-3 to §8-3(c) (See SELF-REFERRAL)

**HEALTH RESOURCES AND SERVICES ADMINISTRATION**
Enforcement . . . §1-3(d)

**HIPAA** (See HEALTH INSURANCE PORTABILITY AND ACCOUNTABILITY ACT OF 1996)

**HOME HEALTH AGENCIES**
False claims
  Enforcement against particular segments of the healthcare industry . . . §4-6(f)
Kickbacks
  Fraud alerts and special advisory bulletins . . . §2-4(f)

**HOME MEDICAL SUPPLIERS**
False claims
  Enforcement against particular segments of the healthcare industry . . . §4-6(e)
    Certificates of medical necessity . . . §4-6(e)(4)
    Provision of medical supplies to nursing homes . . . §4-6(e)(1)
    Seat lifts . . . §4-6(e)(2)
    Telemarketing schemes . . . §4-6(e)(3)

**HOSPICE**
False claims
  Enforcement against particular segments of the healthcare industry . . . §4-6(f)

**HOSPICE ARRANGEMENTS**
Kickbacks
  Fraud alerts and special advisory bulletins . . . §2-4(h)

# I

**IMPLANTABLE MEDICAL DEVICES**
Physician-owned entities/distributorships (PODs)
  Kickbacks
    Fraud alerts and special advisory bulletins . . . §2-4(l)

**INITIATIVES TO COMBAT FRAUD, STATE AND PRIVATE**
Private initiatives (See STATE AND PRIVATE INITIATIVES TO COMBAT FRAUD)
Self-referral laws . . . §6-2 to §6-2(f) (See SELF-REFERRAL)
State initiatives (See STATE AND PRIVATE INITIATIVES TO COMBAT FRAUD)
Trade associations (See TRADE ASSOCIATIONS)

**INSPECTOR GENERAL, OFFICE OF**
Administrative sanctions available to federal enforcers . . . §5-1 to §5-4(f) (See ADMINISTRATIVE SANCTIONS, FEDERAL)
Compliance and self-reporting
  Guidance
    Inspector general and Health Lawyers resources . . . §7-5(e)
    Roundtables . . . §7-5(d)
Compliance program guidance . . . §7-5(a)
Enforcement . . . §1-3(a)
Future federal regulatory initiatives . . . §10-2
Hot topics . . . Appx D
Search and subpoena authority . . . §9-2(e) to §9-2(e)(2)

**INVESTIGATIONAL DEVICES**
False claims
  Enforcement against particular segments of the healthcare industry . . . §4-6(b)

**INVESTIGATIONS**
False claims . . . §4-6(b); §9-2(c)
Government investigations (See GOVERNMENT INVESTIGATIONS)
Self-critical analysis privilege . . . §9-5(h)
Summaries of significant anti-kickback investigations and settlements . . . Appx B

**INVESTMENT INTEREST SAFE HARBORS**
§2-3(b)
Ambulatory surgery centers . . . §2-3(b)(5)
Group practices . . . §2-3(b)(4)
Large entities . . . §2-3(b)(1)
Medically underserved areas (MUAs), entities in . . . §2-3(b)(3)
Small entities . . . §2-3(b)(2)

# J

**JUSTICE, DEPARTMENT OF**
Civil Division . . . §1-2(c)
Criminal Division . . . §1-2(b)
Federal Bureau of Investigation . . . §1-2(d)
United States Attorney's Offices . . . §1-2(a)

[References are to sections.]

# K

**KICKBACKS** §2-1 to §2-8; §6-3
Advisory opinions and additional guidance
 . . . §2-5; §2-5(b)
 Early guidance from CMS to regional offices and fiscal agents . . . §2-5(a)
 Managed care industry . . . §8-2(c)
Calculation of damages . . . §2-8(i)
Carving out . . . §2-8(e)
Case law . . . §2-6
 *Hanlester Network v. Shalala* . . . §2-6(b)
 Post-*Hanlester* case law . . . §2-6(c)
  *Anderson*, *McClatchey*, and *LaHue* §2-6(c)(5)
  *Bryan* §2-6(c)(3)
  *Jain* §2-6(c)(2)
  *Shaw* §2-6(c)(6)
  *Starks* §2-6(c)(4)
  *US ex rel. Jamison v. McKesson* §2-6(c)(1)
 Pre-*Hanlester* case law . . . §2-6(a)
  Additional cases §2-6(a)(5)
  *Bay State Ambulance* §2-6(a)(3)
  *Greber* §2-6(a)(1)
  *Katz* §2-6(a)(2)
  *Polk County v. Peters* §2-6(a)(4)
Civilian health and medical program of the uniformed service (CHAMPUS) . . . §2-7(c)
Computer software, tests ordered on basis of . . . §4-6(a)(4)
Corporate benchmarks, admission of patients to achieve . . . §4-6(a)(4)
Credentialing . . . §2-8(g)
Development of statute prohibiting . . . §2-2
 Balanced budget act of 1997 . . . §2-2(e)
 Health insurance portability and accountability act of 1996 (HIPAA) . . . §2-2(d)
 Medicare and Medicaid patient program protection act of 1987 . . . §2-2(c)
 Medicare-Medicaid anti-fraud and abuse amendments of 1977 . . . §2-2(b)
 Medicare prescription drug, improvement, and modernization act of 2003 . . . §2-2(f)
 Patient protection and affordable care act of 2010 . . . §2-2(g)
 Social security act of 1972 . . . §2-2(a)
Enforcement and interpretation issues . . . §2-8
Fair market value and "bona fide" nature of services contracted for . . . §2-8(j)
Federal civil false claims act . . . §4-2(b)
Fraud alerts and special advisory bulletins . . . §2-4
 Clinical laboratory services, arrangements for the provision of . . . §2-4(e)
 Home health agencies . . . §2-4(f)
 Hospital incentives to physicians . . . §2-4(c)

**KICKBACKS** —Cont.
Fraud alerts and special advisory bulletins —Cont.
 Joint ventures . . . §2-4(a)
 Laboratory payments to referring physicians . . . §2-4(m)
 Nursing home
  Ambulance companies, contractual arrangements with . . . §2-4(j)
  Hospice arrangements . . . §2-4(h)
  Patient assistance programs for Medicare part D enrollees . . . §2-4(k)
  Rental of office in referring physician's space . . . §2-4(i)
  Suppliers . . . §2-4(g)
 Nursing home suppliers . . . §2-4(g)
 Physician compensation arrangements resulting in significant liability . . . §2-4(n)
 Physician-owned entities/distributorships (PODs) . . . §2-4(l)
 Prescription drug marketing practices . . . §2-4(d)
 Routine waivers of coinsurance and deductibles . . . §2-4(b)
Free goods to referral sources . . . §2-8(f)
Generally . . . §2-1
Implantable medical devices
 Physician-owned entities/distributorships (PODs) . . . §2-4(l)
Inducements to beneficiaries . . . §2-7(a)
 Anti-Kickback Statute . . . §2-7(a)(1)
 Civil money penalty statute . . . §2-7(a)(2)
 2010 modification . . . §2-7(a)(3)
Integrated delivery systems . . . §2-8(b)
 Practice acquisition . . . §2-8(b)(1)
 Practice divestiture . . . §2-8(b)(2)
Intent requirements of the Anti-Kickback Statute . . . §2-6(c)(1)
Managed care industry, effect of the Anti-Kickback Statute
 Advisory opinions . . . §8-2(c)
 Safe harbors . . . §2-3(h); §8-2(a)
  Beneficiary incentives . . . §8-2(a)(1)
  Group health plans, price reductions . . . §8-2(a)(2)
  Medicare SELECT . . . §8-2(a)(3)
  Shared-risk statutory exception
   Contracts involving substantial financial risk §8-2(b)(2)
 Shared-risk statutory exception . . . §8-2(b)
  Price reductions offered to eligible managed care organizations . . . §8-2(b)(1)
  Safe harbor protection for contracts involving substantial financial risk . . . §8-2(b)(2)
Marketing practices of healthcare providers, regulation of . . . §2-8(c)

I-8

[References are to sections.]

**KICKBACKS** —Cont.
Other authorities . . . §2-7
Pharmacies and pharmaceutical manufacturers
  . . . §4-6(h)
Physician-owned entities/distributorships (PODs)
  . . . §2-4(l)
Physician payment sunshine act . . . §2-7(d)
Physician recruitment and relocation arrangements . . . §2-8(h)
Private actions under the Anti-Kickback Statute
  . . . §2-8(a)
Professional courtesy . . . §2-8(d)
Public contracts and the Anti-Kickback Act
  . . . §2-7(b)
Qualified Health Plans (QHPs), applicability of the Anti-Kickback Statute to . . . §2-5(c)
Safe harbor regulations . . . §2-3 (See SAFE HARBOR, ANTI-KICKBACK LAWS)
State anti-kickback provisions . . . §6-3
Summaries of significant anti-kickback investigations and settlements . . . Appx B
Swapping issues . . . §2-8(e)
TRICARE . . . §2-7(c)

# L

**LIMITATION OF ACTIONS**
Federal civil false claims act . . . §4-2(e)

**LONG-TERM CARE FACILITIES**
False claims
  Enforcement against particular segments of the healthcare industry . . . §4-6(c)

# M

**MANAGED CARE INDUSTRY, ISSUES AFFECTING**
False claims . . . §8-5
Generally . . . §8-1
Intermediate sanctions . . . §8-4
Kickbacks . . . §2-3(h); §8-2 to §8-2(c) (See KICKBACKS)
Medicare managed care, federal efforts to address fraud in . . . §8-6
Potential fraud liability . . . §8-8
  Capitation misclassification . . . §8-8(a)
  Contracting misrepresentations . . . §8-8(f)
  Cost-shifting . . . §8-8(g)
  Defective rate or bid submissions . . . §8-8(b)
  Discount skimming . . . §8-8(h)
  Enrollment practices . . . §8-8(c)
  Failure to provide required services . . . §8-8(e)
  Formulary development and implementation
    . . . §8-8(j)

**MANAGED CARE INDUSTRY, ISSUES AFFECTING**—Cont.
Potential fraud liability —Cont.
  Health care exchanges . . . §8-8(m)
  Marketing schemes . . . §8-8(c)
  Medical loss ratios . . . §8-8(l)
  Misrepresenting services to qualify for higher payments . . . §8-8(e)
  Patient-assistance programs and Medicare part D benefit . . . §8-8(k)
  Payments to providers . . . §8-8(d)
  Pharmacy benefit managers . . . §8-8(i)
  Quality of care . . . §8-8(e)
  Underutilization . . . §8-8(e)
Self-referral . . . §8-3 to §8-3(c) (See SELF-REFERRAL)
State Medicaid programs . . . §8-7

**MEDICAL DEVICE COMPANIES**
False claims
  Enforcement against particular segments of the healthcare industry . . . §4-6(m)

**MEDICAL DEVICES, IMPLANTABLE**
Physician-owned entities/distributorships (PODs)
  Kickbacks
    Fraud alerts and special advisory bulletins
      . . . §2-4(l)

**MEDICARE AND MEDICAID**
Administrative sanctions, federal
  Exclusion from Medicare, Medicaid and other state healthcare programs (See ADMINISTRATIVE SANCTIONS, FEDERAL)
Compliance and self-reporting
  Guidance
    Centers for Medicare and Medicaid services guidance to contractors . . . §7-5(f)
Enforcement
  Medicare Prescription Drug Integrity Contractors (MEDICs) . . . §1-3(f); §1-3(f)(3)
  Recovery Audit Contractors (RACs) . . . §1-3(f)(1)
  Unified Program Integrity Contractors (UPICs) . . . §1-3(b)
  Zone Program Integrity Contractors (ZPICs)
    . . . §1-3(f)(2)
False claims
  Enforcement against particular segments of the healthcare industry
    Medicare carriers . . . §4-6(g)
  Theories applicable to multiple segments of the healthcare industry
    Medicare secondary payor issues . . . §4-5(i)
Fraud prevention and detection . . . §6-9
  Data mining . . . §6-9(a)

I-9

**MEDICARE AND MEDICAID**—Cont.
Fraud prevention and detection —Cont.
  Medicaid fraud control units . . . §6-9(a)
  Medicaid program integrity . . . §6-9(b)
  State inspector generals . . . §6-9(c)
Kickbacks
  Development of statute prohibiting
    Medicare and Medicaid patient program protection act of 1987 . . . §2-2(c)
    Medicare-Medicaid anti-fraud and abuse amendments of 1977 . . . §2-2(b)
    Medicare prescription drug, improvement, and modernization act of 2003 . . . §2-2(f)
  Fraud alerts and special advisory bulletins
    Nursing home
      Patient assistance programs for Medicare part D enrollees §2-4(k)
  Managed care industry, effect of Anti-Kickback Statute
    Safe harbors
      Medicare SELECT §8-2(a)(3)
Managed care industry
  Kickbacks
    Effect of Anti-Kickback Statute
      Safe harbors
        Medicare SELECT §8-2(a)(3)
  Medicare managed care, federal efforts to address fraud in . . . §8-6
  Potential fraud liability
    Patient-assistance programs and Medicare part D benefit . . . §8-8(k)
Secondary payor issues
  False claims . . . §4-5(i)
Self-referral
  Stark law
    Home health services reimbursed by the Medicare program . . . §3-9(a)

**MEDICARE AND MEDICAID PATIENT PROGRAM PROTECTION ACT OF 1987**
Kickbacks, development of statute prohibiting
  . . . §2-2(c)

**MEDICARE-MEDICAID ANTI-FRAUD AND ABUSE AMENDMENTS OF 1977**
Kickbacks, development of statute prohibiting
  . . . §2-2(b)

**MEDICARE PRESCRIPTION DRUG, IMPROVEMENT, AND MODERNIZATION ACT OF 2003**
Kickbacks, development of statute prohibiting
  . . . §2-2(f)

**MEDICARE PRESCRIPTION DRUG INTEGRITY CONTRACTORS (MEDICS)**
Enforcement . . . §1-3(f)

# N

**NATIONAL HEALTH CARE ANTI-FRAUD ASSOCIATION (NHCAA)**
Enforcement . . . §1-8

**NURSING HOMES**
False claims
  Enforcement against particular segments of the healthcare industry . . . §4-6(c)
    Provision of medical supplies to nursing homes . . . §4-6(e)(1)
Kickbacks
  Fraud alerts and special advisory bulletins
    Ambulance companies, contractual arrangements with . . . §2-4(j)
    Hospice arrangements . . . §2-4(h)
    Nursing home suppliers . . . §2-4(g)
    Patient assistance programs for Medicare part D enrollees . . . §2-4(k)
    Rental of office in referring physician's space . . . §2-4(i)
    Suppliers . . . §2-4(g)

# O

**OBSTETRICAL MALPRACTICE INSURANCE SUBSIDIES**
Kickbacks
  Safe harbor regulations . . . §2-3(j)

**OUTLIER PAYMENTS**
False claims
  Enforcement against particular segments of the healthcare industry . . . §4-6(a)(3)

# P

**PATIENT PROTECTION AND AFFORDABLE CARE ACT OF 2010**
Kickbacks, development of statute prohibiting
  . . . §2-2(g)

**PENALTIES**
Administrative sanctions available to federal enforcers . . . §5-3 to §5-4(f) (See ADMINISTRATIVE SANCTIONS, FEDERAL)
Civil penalties generally (See CIVIL PENALTIES)

**PHARMACEUTICAL AND RESEARCH MANUFACTURERS ASSOCIATION** §6-10(d)

**PHARMACIES**
False claims
  Enforcement against particular segments of the healthcare industry . . . §4-6(h)

[References are to sections.]

**PHYSICIAN-OWNED ENTITIES/DISTRIBUTORSHIPS (PODS)**
Kickbacks
   Fraud alerts and special advisory bulletins . . . §2-4(l)

**PHYSICIAN PAYMENT (SUNSHINE ACT)** §2-7(d)

**PHYSICIAN SELF-REFERRAL** §3-1 to §3-9(f) (See SELF-REFERRAL)

**PRESCRIPTION DRUGS**
Food & Drug Administration . . . §1-3(e)
Kickbacks
   Development of statute prohibiting
      Medicare prescription drug, improvement, and modernization act of 2003 . . . §2-2(f)
   Fraud alerts and special advisory bulletins
      Prescription drug marketing practices . . . §2-4(d)

**PRIVATE INITIATIVES TO COMBAT FRAUD** §6-1 to §6-11 (See STATE AND PRIVATE INITIATIVES TO COMBAT FRAUD)

**PROGRAM INTEGRITY CONTRACTORS**
Comprehensive error rate testing contractors (CERTs) . . . §1-3(f)(3)
Coordination of Benefits Contractors (COBs) . . . §1-3(f)(3)
Enforcement . . . §1-3(f)
Medicare Administrative Contractors (MACs) . . . §1-3(f)(3)
Medicare Prescription Drug Integrity Contractors (MEDICs) . . . §1-3(f); §1-3(f)(3)
National Supplier Clearinghouse Contractor (NSCs) . . . §1-3(f)(3)
Recovery Audit Contractors (RACs) . . . §1-3(f)(1)
Unified Program Integrity Contractors (UPICs) . . . §1-3(b)
Zone Program Integrity Contractors (ZPICs) . . . §1-3(f)(2)

## Q

**QUALIFIED HEALTH PLANS (QHPS)**
Applicability of the Anti-Kickback Statute to . . . §2-5(c)

**QUALITY-OF-CARE-CASES**
False claims . . . §4-5(f)

**QUI TAM RELATORS**
Federal civil false claims act . . . §4-2(d)
   Dodd-Frank act protections . . . §4-2(d)(5)

**QUI TAM RELATORS**—Cont.
Federal civil false claims act —Cont.
   Government declining to intervene . . . §4-2(d)(2)
   Initiation of action . . . §4-2(d)(1)
   Justice department guidance . . . §4-2(d)
   Original source rule . . . §4-2(d)(3)(ii)
   Pleading requirements . . . §4-2(d)(4)
   Public disclosure bar . . . §4-2(d)(3)(i)
   Qualifications . . . §4-2(d)(3)
   Retaliation . . . §4-2(d)(5)

## R

**RACKETEERING**
State laws prohibiting . . . §6-5

**RECOVERY AUDIT CONTRACTORS (RACS)**
Enforcement . . . §1-3(f)(1)

**REFERRALS**
Kickbacks generally . . . §2-1 to §2-8 (See KICKBACKS)
Physicians, laboratory payment to referring . . . §2-4(m)
Self-referral . . . §3-1 to §3-9(f); §6-2 to §6-2(f) (See SELF-REFERRAL)

**REPRESENTING HEALTHCARE ORGANIZATIONS**
Attorney and client relationship . . . §9-5
   Allied-lawyer doctrine . . . §9-5(f)
   Attorney-client communications privilege . . . §9-5(a)
      Attorneys, applicability to . . . §9-5(a)(2)
      Clients, privilege belongs to . . . §9-5(a)(5)
         Waiver §9-5(c)
      Communications . . . §9-5(a)(3)
      Confidentiality . . . §9-5(a)(4); §9-5(i)(1)
      Crime-fraud exception . . . §9-5(d)
      Legal advice . . . §9-5(a)(1)
   Defendants, lawyers as . . . §9-9
   Ethical obligations of attorneys . . . §9-5(i)
      Confidentiality . . . §9-5(i)(1)
      Disclosure from attorney to court . . . §9-5(i)(2)
      Duty to inquire . . . §9-5(i)(3)
      Government attorneys, application of rules to . . . §9-5(i)(4)
   Fifth Amendment considerations . . . §9-6
   Joint defense agreements . . . §9-5(f)
   Outside consultants . . . §9-5(g)
   Selective-waiver doctrine . . . §9-5(e)
   Self-critical analysis privilege . . . §9-5(h)
   Voluntary disclosure . . . §9-5(e)
   Witnesses, lawyers as . . . §9-8

**REPRESENTING HEALTHCARE ORGANIZATIONS**—Cont.
Attorney and client relationship —Cont.
    Work-product doctrine . . . §9-5(b)
        Crime-fraud exception . . . §9-5(d)
Generally . . . §9-1
Government investigations (See GOVERNMENT INVESTIGATIONS)
Litigation, general considerations . . . §10-4
Relationship between criminal and civil matters . . . §9-4
    Double jeopardy . . . §9-4(a)
    Ex post facto considerations . . . §9-4(b)

**RETALIATION**
Federal civil false claims act
    Qui tam relators . . . §4-2(d)(5)
Whistleblowers (See WHISTLEBLOWERS)

**REVERSE FALSE CLAIMS** §4-5(f)

**RISK-SHARING**
Kickbacks
    Safe harbor regulations
        Statutory exceptions with analogous safe harbors . . . §2-3(g)(4)
Self-referral
    Managed care
        Risk-sharing arrangements, regulatory exception for . . . §8-3(c)
    Stark law
        Exceptions
            Compensation arrangements
                Managed care risk-sharing arrangements §3-4(c)(13)

## S

**SAFE HARBOR, ANTI-KICKBACK LAWS** §2-3
Ambulance replenishing . . . §2-3(m)
Cooperative hospital services organizations . . . §2-3(k)
Electronic health records and community-wide information systems . . . §2-3(n)
History of issuances . . . §2-3(a)
Investment interest safe harbors (See INVESTMENT INTEREST SAFE HARBORS)
Managed care . . . §2-3(h); §8-2(a)
    Beneficiary incentives . . . §8-2(a)(1)
    Group health plans, price reductions to . . . §8-2(a)(2)
    Medicare SELECT . . . §8-2(a)(3)
    Shared-risk statutory exception
        Contracts involving substantial financial risk . . . §8-2(b)(2)
Obstetrical malpractice insurance subsidies . . . §2-3(j)

**SAFE HARBOR, ANTI-KICKBACK LAWS** —Cont.
Personal services and management contracts . . . §2-3(c)
Practitioner recruitment . . . §2-3(i)
Referral arrangements for specialty services . . . §2-3(l)
Referral services . . . §2-3(e)
Sale of practice . . . §2-3(d)
Space and equipment rental . . . §2-3(c)
Statutory exceptions with analogous safe harbors . . . §2-3(g)
    Coinsurance and deductible waivers . . . §2-3(g)(5)
    Discounts . . . §2-3(g)(2)
    Electronic prescribing . . . §2-3(g)(7)
    Employees . . . §2-3(g)(1)
    Federally qualified health centers . . . §2-3(g)(6)
    Group purchasing organizations . . . §2-3(g)(3)
    Risk-sharing arrangements . . . §2-3(g)(4)
2014 proposed safe harbors . . . §2-3(p)
Waiver authority, accountable care organizations and . . . §2-3(o)
Warranties . . . §2-3(f)

**SARBANES-OXLEY ACT OF 2002** §7-4

**SEARCH WARRANTS**
Government investigations . . . §9-2(a)

**SELF-CRITICAL ANALYSIS PRIVILEGE**
Investigations . . . §9-5(h)

**SELF-REFERRAL**
Managed care . . . §8-3
    Personal-service arrangements . . . §8-3(b)
    Prepaid health plans . . . §8-3(a)
    Risk-sharing arrangements, regulatory exception for . . . §8-3(c)
Stark law
    Additional restrictions . . . §3-9
    Advisory opinions . . . §3-7
    Anti-markup rule . . . §3-9(d)
    Civilian health and medical program of the uniformed services (CHAMPUS), TRICARE and CHAMPVA . . . §3-9(b)
    Compensation rules . . . §3-3(c)
        Conditioning compensation on referrals to a particular provider . . . §3-3(c)(2)
        Definitions . . . §3-3(b)(4)
        Exceptions . . . §3-4(a)
        Methodologies . . . §3-3(c)(1)
        Modifying or amending agreements . . . §3-3(c)(3)
        Referrals to a particular provider, conditioning compensation on . . . §3-3(c)(2)

[References are to sections.]

**SELF-REFERRAL**—Cont.
  Stark law—Cont.
    Definitions . . . §3-3; §3-3(b)
      Compensation arrangements . . . §3-3(b)(4)
      Designated health services . . . §3-3(b)(2)
      Entity . . . §3-3(b)(8)
      Fair market value . . . §3-3(b)(5)
      Immediate family member . . . §3-3(b)(7)
      Ownership or investment interests . . . §3-3(b)(3)
      Physician . . . §3-3(b)(6)
      Referral . . . §3-3(b)(1)
    Disclosure protocol . . . §3-8
    Disclosure required of certain hospitals and critical access hospitals . . . §3-9(c); §10-3
    Exceptions . . . §3-4
      Compensation arrangements . . . §3-4(c)
        Accountable Care Organizations (ACOs) §3-4(c)(22)
        Anti-Kickback Statute safe harbors, exceptions relating to §3-4(c)(20)
        Bona fide employment relationships §3-4(c)(2)
        Charitable donations §3-4(c)(17)
        Community-wide information system §3-4(c)(18)
        Compliance training §3-4(c)(14)
        Electronic prescribing and electronic health records §3-4(c)(19)
        Fair market value exception §3-4(c)(10)
        Gainsharing §3-4(c)(21)
        Group-practice arrangements with a hospital §3-4(c)(8)
        Indirect compensation §3-4(c)(15)
        Isolated financial transactions §3-4(c)(7)
        Managed care risk-sharing arrangements §3-4(c)(13)
        Medical-staff incidental benefits §3-4(c)(12)
        Nonmonetary compensation up to $300 §3-4(c)(11)
        Payments for items and services §3-4(c)(9)
        Personal service arrangements §3-4(c)(3)
        Physician recruitment §3-4(c)(5)
        Physician retention §3-4(c)(6)
        Professional courtesy §3-4(c)(16)
        Rental of office space and equipment §3-4(c)(1)
        Unrelated payments §3-4(c)(4)
      Ownership and compensation . . . §3-4(a)
        Academic medical centers §3-4(a)(4)
        Additional exceptions §3-4(a)(6)

**SELF-REFERRAL**—Cont.
  Stark law—Cont.
    Exceptions —Cont.
      Implants in ambulatory surgical centers (ASCs) §3-4(a)(5)
      In-office ancillary services §3-4(a)(2)
      Physician services §3-4(a)(1)
      Prepaid plans §3-4(a)(3)
      Ownership only . . . §3-4(b)
        Hospitals §3-4(b)(2)
        Publicly traded securities and mutual funds §3-4(b)(1)
        Rural providers §3-4(b)(3)
      Reporting requirements . . . §3-4(d)
    Generally . . . §3-1
    Group practice . . . §3-5
      Distribution of expenses and income . . . §3-5(e)
      Full range of care . . . §3-5(c)
      Physician-patient encounters . . . §3-5(h)
      Productivity bonuses . . . §3-5(i)
      Profit shares . . . §3-5(i)
      Services furnished by members . . . §3-5(d)
      Single legal entity . . . §3-5(a)
      Two or more physicians . . . §3-5(b)
      Unified business . . . §3-5(f)
      Volume or value of referrals . . . §3-5(g)
    History of legislation and regulation . . . §3-2
    Home health services reimbursed by the Medicare program . . . §3-9(a)
    Interpretation issues . . . §3-10
      Application of law to Medicaid . . . §3-10(f)
      Corporate affiliates . . . §3-10(e)
      Hospital/physician arrangements related to designated health services . . . §3-10(d)
      Joint ventures unrelated to the provision of designated health services . . . §3-10(c)
      Kickback statute, relationship with . . . §3-10(a)
      Knowledge element for indirect financial relationships . . . §3-10(b)
    Penalties and enforcement . . . §3-6
      Alternative method of compliance with signature requirement . . . §3-6(b)
      Burden of proof . . . §3-6(d)
      Period of disallowance . . . §3-6(c)
      Temporary noncompliance . . . §3-6(a)
    Scope . . . §3-3(a)
    Stand in the shoes . . . §3-3(d)
  State self-referral laws . . . §6-2 to §6-2(f)
    Advisory opinions . . . §6-2(c)
    Declaratory statements . . . §6-2(c)
    Disclosure laws . . . §6-2(e)
    Exceptions to prohibitions . . . §6-2(b)

[References are to sections.]

**SELF-REFERRAL—Cont.**
State self-referral laws —Cont.
    Generally . . . §6-2
    Penalties . . . §6-2(d)
    Scope . . . §6-2(a)

**SELF-REPORTING** §7-1 to §7-9 (See COMPLIANCE AND SELF-REPORTING)

**SENTENCING GUIDELINES**
Compliance and self-reporting
    Federal sentencing guidelines . . . §7-3

**SHARED-RISK STATUTORY EXCEPTION**
Kickbacks
    Managed care industry, effect of Anti-Kickback Statute . . . §8-2(b)
        Price reductions offered to eligible managed care organizations . . . §8-2(b)(1)
        Safe harbor protection for contracts involving substantial financial risk . . . §8-2(b)(2)

**SOCIAL SECURITY ACT OF 1972**
Administrative sanctions available to federal enforcers . . . §5-1 to §5-4(f) (See ADMINISTRATIVE SANCTIONS, FEDERAL)
False claims
    Criminal . . . §4-4(a)
Inspector general, office of
    Access to documents . . . §9-2(e)(2)
Kickbacks, development of statute prohibiting . . . §2-2(a)

**STAND IN THE SHOES** §3-3(d)

**STARK LAW** §3-1 to §3-9(f) (See SELF-REFERRAL)

**STATE AND PRIVATE INITIATIVES TO COMBAT FRAUD** §6-1 to §6-11
Anti-kickback prescriptions . . . §6-3
Consumer protection laws . . . §6-6
Deceptive trade practices . . . §6-6
False claims . . . §6-7
    Fraudulent billing practices . . . §6-7(a)
    Waivers of coinsurance and deductible amounts . . . §6-7(b)
Fee-splitting prescriptions . . . §6-4
Fraud prevention and detection . . . §6-9
    Data mining . . . §6-9(a)
    Medicaid fraud control units . . . §6-9(a)
    Medicaid program integrity . . . §6-9(b)
    State inspector generals . . . §6-9(c)
Generally . . . §6-1
Self-referral laws . . . §6-2 to §6-2(f) (See SELF-REFERRAL)
Sunshine acts applicable to pharmaceutical and medical device manufacturers . . . §6-8

**STATUTE OF LIMITATIONS**
Federal civil false claims act . . . §4-2(e)

**SUBPOENA**
Administrative subpoenas . . . §9-2(d)
Congressional subpoenas . . . §9-2(f)
Health and human services
    Enforcement
        Inspector general, office of
            Search and subpoena authority §9-2(e) to §9-2(e)(2)
    Representing healthcare organizations
        Government investigations, categories and types
            Inspector general, office of
                Immediate access to documents
                      Subpoenas of documents and witnesses §9-2(e)(2)
                Search and subpoena authority §9-2(e)
                      Subpoenas of documents and witnesses §9-2(e)(1)

**SUNSHINE ACTS**
Physician payment . . . §2-7(d)
State laws . . . §6-8

# T

**THIRD-PARTY CONSULTANTS**
False claims
    Enforcement against particular segments of the healthcare industry . . . §4-6(i)

**TRADE ASSOCIATIONS** §6-10
Advanced medical technology association . . . §6-10(e)
American college of physicians . . . §6-10(c)
American college of radiology . . . §6-10(b)
American medical association . . . §6-10(a)
Pharmaceutical and research manufacturers association . . . §6-10(d)

**TRICARE**
Kickbacks . . . §2-7(c)
Self-referral . . . §3-9(b)

# U

**UNBUNDLING**
False claims . . . §4-5(d)

**UNDERCOVER OPERATIONS**
Government investigations . . . §9-2(g)

**UNIFIED PROGRAM INTEGRITY CONTRACTOR (UPIC)**
Enforcement . . . §1-3(b)

**UPCODING**
False claims . . . §4-5(c)

## V

**VICARIOUS LIABILITY**
Government investigations . . . §9-7

## W

**WARRANTIES**
Kickbacks
    Safe harbor regulations . . . §2-3(f)

**WHISTLEBLOWERS**
Dodd-Frank act protections . . . §4-2(d)(5)
Fraud . . . §1-9

## Z

**ZONE PROGRAM INTEGRITY CONTRACTORS (ZPICS)**
Enforcement . . . §1-3(f)(2)